THE OXFORD HANDBOOK OF

CHAUCER

THE OXFORD HANDBOOK OF

CHAUCER

Edited by

SUZANNE CONKLIN AKBARI

and

JAMES SIMPSON

OXFORD

UNIVERSITY PRESS

OXFORD
UNIVERSITY PRESS

Great Clarendon Street, Oxford, OX2 6DP,
United Kingdom

Oxford University Press is a department of the University of Oxford.
It furthers the University's objective of excellence in research, scholarship,
and education by publishing worldwide. Oxford is a registered trade mark of
Oxford University Press in the UK and in certain other countries

Published in the United States of America by Oxford University Press
198 Madison Avenue, New York, NY 10016, United States of America

British Library Cataloguing in Publication Data

Data available

Library of Congress Control Number: 2020941332

ISBN 978-0-19-958265-5

Printed and bound by
CPI Group (UK) Ltd, Croydon, CR0 4YY

In memory of A.G. Rigg (1937–2019)

Contents

PART II CHAUCER IN THE MEDITERRANEAN FRAME

PART III CHAUCER IN THE EUROPEAN FRAME

PART IV PHILOSOPHY AND SCIENCE IN THE UNIVERSITIES

PART V CHRISTIAN DOCTRINE AND RELIGIOUS HETERODOXY

PART VI THE CHAUCERIAN AFTERLIFE

LIST OF FIGURES

Note on the Text and List of Abbreviations

The place of publication is London unless otherwise stated. All biblical references are to the Authorized Version (AV) unless otherwise stated. All references to Chaucer's works are from *The Riverside Chaucer*, ed. Larry D. Benson, gen. ed. (Oxford: Oxford University Press, 1987) (*RC*), unless otherwise stated. Full references are always given within each individual essay other than for the texts whose abbreviations are listed here.

RC	*The Riverside Chaucer* (publication details above)
CT	*Canterbury Tales*
BD	*The Book of the Duchess*
HF	*The House of Fame*
PF	*The Parliament of Fowls*
Tr	*Troilus and Criseyde*
LGW	*The Legend of Good Women*
RR	*The Romaunt of the Rose*
Bo	*Boece*
Astr	*The Treatise on Astrolabe*
Anel	*Anelida and Arcite*
Retr	Chaucer's *Retraction*
Adam	'Chaucer's Wordes Unto Adam, His Owne Scriveyn'
Truth	Chaucer's 'Truth'
Buk	'Lenvoy de Chaucer a Bukton'
b., d., c.,	Born, died, circa
MED	*Middle English Dictionary*

Notes on Contributors

Suzanne Conklin Akbari is Professor of Medieval Studies at the Institute for Advanced Study and was educated at Johns Hopkins and Columbia. She has written books on optics and allegory (*Seeing Through the Veil*, University of Toronto Press, 2004) and European views of Islam and the Orient (*Idols in the East*, Cornell Universit Press, 2009), and edited collections on travel literature (*Marco Polo*, University of Toronto Press, 2008), Mediterranean Studies (*A Sea of Languages*, University of Toronto Press, 2013), and somatic histories (*The Ends of the Body*, University of Toronto Press, 2013). She is completing a monograph titled *Small Change: Metaphor and Metamorphosis in Chaucer and Christine de Pizan* and working on a project on premodern ideas of periodization as seen in universal histories, maps, and diagrams.

Anthony Bale is Professor of Medieval Studies and Executive Dean of Arts at Birkbeck, University of London. He has published widely on late medieval literature, culture, and religion. He has published translations of Sir John Mandeville's *Book of Marvels and Travels* (Oxford University Press, 2012) and *The Book of Margery Kempe* (Oxford University Press, 2015). Most recently, he has edited *The Cambridge Companion to the Literature of the Crusades* (Cambridge University Press, 2018) and, with Sebastian Sobecki, *Middle English Travel: A Critical Anthology* (Oxford University Press, 2019). He is now writing on Margery Kempe.

Peter Brown, Professor of Medieval English Literature at the University of Kent and Director of its Kent-Paris Research Institute in Montparnasse. He has published widely on medieval literature and culture. He is editor of *A New Companion to Chaucer* (Wiley-Blackwell, forthcoming) and the author of *Geoffrey Chaucer* (Oxford University Press, 2011) in the Oxford World's Classics Authors in Context series. One of his most recent essays concerns writing in and about Canterbury during the late-medieval period, in volume 1 of *Europe: A Literary History 1348–1418*, ed. David Wallace (Oxford University Press, 2016).

Katie Ann-Marie Bugyis is Assistant Professor in the Program of Liberal Studies and a faculty fellow of the Medieval Institute and the Nanovic Institute at the University of Notre Dame, and an alumna of the Radcliffe Institute for Advanced Study at Harvard University. She is the author of The Care of Nuns: The Ministries of Benedictine Women in England during the Central Middle Ages (Oxford University Press, 2019), and the co-editor of two volumes: Medieval Cantors and their Craft: Music, Liturgy and the Shaping of History, 800–1500 (York Medieval Press, 2017), and Women Intellectuals and Leaders in the Middle Ages (D. S. Brewer, 2020). She has also published articles and essays on the liturgical and intellectual histories of communities of religious women in the central and late Middle Ages, and she is currently working on a book project on the materiality of Benedictine nuns' liturgical practices in late medieval England.

Jeffrey Jerome Cohen is Dean of Humanities at Arizona State University and the co-president of the Association for the Study of Literature and the Environment (ASLE). He has published books on monsters, race, postcolonial studies, gender, ecotheory, and medieval literature. His book *Stone: An Ecology of the Inhuman* (University of Minnesota Press, 2015) was awarded the René Wellek Prize in Comparative Literature.

Rita Copeland is Rosenberg Chair in the Humanities and Professor at the University of Pennsylvania. Her fields include medieval literature, the history of rhetoric, and literary theory. She is currently writing on rhetoric and the emotions in the Middle Ages. Her publications include: *Rhetoric, Hermeneutics, and Translation in the Middle Ages* (Cambridge University Press, 1991); *Pedagogy, Intellectuals and Dissent in the Middle Ages* (Cambridge University Press, 2001); *Medieval Grammar and Rhetoric: Language Arts and Literary Theory, AD 300–1475* (with I. Sluiter) (Oxford University Press, 2009); *The Cambridge Companion to Allegory* (with Peter Struck) (Cambridge University Press, 2009); *The Oxford History of Classical Reception in English Literature, 800–1558* (Oxford University Press, 2016); and (with Peter Mack) is General Editor of the forthcoming *Cambridge History of Rhetoric*.

Marilynn Desmond is SUNY Distinguished Professor of English and Comparative Literature at Binghamton University. She has published extensively on the reception of classical texts in medieval literary traditions. She is the author of *Ovid's Art and the Wife of Bath: The Ethics of Erotic Violence* (Cornell University Press, 2006), and *Reading Dido: Gender, Textuality and the Medieval Aeneid* (University of Minnesota Press, 1994). She is the co-author of *Myth, Montage and Visuality in Late Medieval Manuscript Culture: Christine de Pizan's Othea* (University of Michigan Press, 2003), and editor of *Christine de Pizan and the Categories of Difference* (University of Minnesota Press, 1998). She is currently completing a book on the Matter of Troy in the Latin West.

Denise Despres is Professor of English and Humanities at the University of Puget Sound. Her scholarship focuses on medieval subjectivity, contemplative and devotional culture, and Middle English visionary literature. She is co-author with Kathryn Kerby-Fulton of *Iconography and the Professional Reader* (University of Minnesota Press, 1999). Her most recent published work explores the lay reception of late-medieval English religious texts in an age of consumption.

Edith Dudley Sylla is Professor Emerita at North Carolina State University in Raleigh, United States. She is primarily interested in the histories of mathematics and physics and their interactions in the fourteenth and fifteenth centuries. She has translated from Latin to English and published with an introduction *Jacob Bernoulli, The Art of Conjecturing* (Johns Hopkins University Press, 2006). She has recently published a guide included in the new editions of John Buridan's questions on Aristotle's *Physics*, Books I and II (Brill, 2015) and Books III and IV (Brill, 2016) and continues to work on the Oxford Calculators.

Martin Eisner is Associate Professor of Italian at Duke University. He is the author of *Boccaccio and the Invention of Italian Literature* (Cambridge University Press, 2013), which argues that Boccaccio plays a crucial role in the shaping of an Italian literary tradition not only as an author of masterpieces like the *Decameron* but also as the scribe of Dante, Petrarch, and Cavalcanti. His new book, *Dante's New Life of the Book*, explores the material transformations of Dante's *Vita nuova* from the medieval manuscript to the digital age.

Jamie C. Fumo is Professor of English at Florida State University. She is the author of *The Legacy of Apollo: Antiquity, Authority, and Chaucerian Poetics* (University of Toronto Press, 2010) and *Making Chaucer's Book of the Duchess: Textuality and Reception* (University of Wales Press, 2015), and the editor of Chaucer's Book of the Duchess: Contexts and Interpretations (D. S. Brewer, 2018). She has also published articles on Chaucer's literary relationships, medieval Ovidianism, the *Roman de la Rose*, Caxton, and fifteenth-century English and Scottish poetry. Her research centres on literary reception and intertextuality in premodern English vernacular poetry.

Matthew Giancarlo is Associate Professor of English at the University of Kentucky. He is the author of *Parliament and Literature in Late Medieval England* (Cambridge University Press, 2007) as well as numerous articles and chapters on medieval English literature and culture.

Alexandra Gillespie is Professor of English and Medieval Studies at the University of Toronto. She is the author of *Print Culture and the Medieval Author* (Oxford University Press, 2006) and has written essays and co-edited various volumes and digital exhibitions about medieval English books and the Tudor antiquaries who collected them. She recently completed a monograph entitled *Chaucer's Books*.

Warren Ginsberg is Philip H. Knight Professor of Humanities at the University of Oregon. His books include *Tellers, Tales, and Translation in Chaucer's Canterbury Tales* (Oxford University Press, 2015); Chaucer's *Italian Tradition* (University of Michigan Press, 2002); *Dante's Aesthetics of Being* (University of Michigan Press, 1999); and *The Cast of Character: The Representation of Personality in Ancient and Medieval Literature* (University of Toronto Press, 1983). He has also edited *Wynnere and Wastour and The Parlement of the Thre Ages* for the Middle English Text Series (1992). A Guggenheim Fellow (1999), he has published essays on Chaucer, Dante, Boccaccio, Petrarch, and Ovid.

E. Ruth Harvey is a professor (emeritus) at the Centre for Medieval Studies at the University of Toronto. She works on medieval medicine and uroscopy.

Jonathan Hsy is an associate professor of English at George Washington University. Author of *Trading Tongues: Merchants, Multilingualism, and Medieval Literature* (Ohio State University Press, 2013) and co-editor of the *Global Chaucers* issue of *Literature Compass* (2018), he has recently published on Chaucer in *postmedieval* (2018), *Chaucer and the Subversion of Form* (Cambridge University Press, 2018), and *The Open Access Companion to The Canterbury Tales* (2017).

David F. Hult is a professor of Medieval French Language and Literature at the University of California, Berkeley. He has published books and articles on courtly literature, Chrétien de Troyes, the *Romance of the Rose*, Christine de Pizan, and the theory and practice of textual criticism. He has most recently published an edition and modern French translation of the anonymous prose *Mort du Roi Artur* (Livres de Poche, 2009) and an English translation of the *Debate of the Romance of the Rose* (University of Chicago Press, 2010). He is currently working on a book devoted to the conception of authorship in medieval French literary production.

Eleanor Johnson is an Associate Professor of English and Comparative Literature at Columbia University. Her books, *Practicing Literary Theory in the Middle Ages: Ethics and the Mixed Form in Chaucer, Gower, Usk, and Hoccleve* and *Staging Contemplation: Participatory Theology in Middle English Prose, Verse, and Drama,* were published by University of Chicago Press in 2013 and 2018. Her other publications include 'The Poetics of Waste: Medieval English Ecocriticism' (*PMLA*, 2012), 'Feeling Time, Will, and Words: Vernacular Devotion in the *Cloud of Unknowing*' (*JMEMS*, 2011), 'Horrific Visions of the Host' (Exemplaria, 2015), and 'English Law and the Man of Law's "Prose" Tale' (*JEGP*, 2015).

Kathryn Kerby-Fulton, FSA, is the Notre Dame Professor of English *Emerita* at University of Notre Dame. She has published on Middle English literature and medieval intellectual history, including censorship, apocalypticism, visionary writing, and women's mysticism. In addition, she works on medieval manuscript studies in England and Anglo-Ireland, medieval literary theory, text-image relations, and reading practices before print. Her books include *Reformist Apocalypticism and Piers Plowman* (Cambridge University Press, 1990); *Iconography and the Professional Reader: The Politics of Book Production in the Douce Piers Plowman,* with Denise Despres (Minnesota University Press, 1999); *Books Under Suspicion: Censorship and Tolerance of Revelatory Writing in Late Medieval England* (Notre Dame University Press, 2006); and *Opening Medieval English Manuscripts: Literary and Visual Approaches*, with Maidie Hilmo and Linda Olson (Cornell University Press, 2012).

Steven F. Kruger is Professor of English and Medieval Studies at Queens College and The Graduate Center of The City University of New York. He is the author of *Dreaming in the Middle Ages* (Cambridge University Press, 1992); *AIDS Narratives: Gender and Sexuality, Fiction and Science* (Garland, 1996); and *The Spectral Jew: Conversion and Embodiment in Medieval Europe* (University of Minnesota Press, 2006). With Glenn Burger, he edited *Queering the Middle Ages* (University of Minnesota Press, 2001). With Deborah R. Geis, he edited *Approaching the Millennium: Essays on Angels in America* (University of Michigan Press, 1997). His current work focuses on writings by medieval Jewish converts to Christianity, from the late eleventh to the fifteenth century.

Stephen E. Lahey is Chair and Happold Professor of Classics and Religious Studies at the University of Nebraska, Lincoln. He is the author of *Philosophy and Politics in the Thought of John Wyclif* (Cambridge University Press, 2003), *John Wyclif* (Oxford

University Press, 2009), and several articles on Wyclif's thought. He has also translated Wyclif's *Trialogus* (Cambridge University Press, 2013) and selections from Wyclif's moral theology (*Wycliffite Spirituality,* with Patrick Hornbeck and Fiona Somerset, Paulist Press, 2014). He is now studying the reception of Wyclif's philosophy and theology at Charles University.

T. Matthew N. McCabe, MD, PhD, is the author of *Gower's Vulgar Tongue: Ovid, Lay Religion, and English Poetry in the* Confessio Amantis (D.S. Brewer, 2011). He works as a resident in Family Medicine at the University of Alberta.

Iain MacLeod Higgins is Professor of English at the University of Victoria, Canada. He also teaches in the Medieval Studies Program and in the postgraduate concentration in Literatures of the West Coast. His teaching and research interests include later medieval English, Scottish, and French literature, travel writing, utopian/dystopian fiction, and poetry both medieval and modern. His most recent book is a translation of the Anglo-French *Book of John Mandeville* (Hackett, 2011) accompanied by excerpts from related texts mostly never before available in English. Since July 2018 he has been editor of *The Malahat Review.*

Deborah McGrady is Professor of French at the University of Virginia. She has written extensively on late-medieval francophone literature and manuscript culture, and is the author of *The Writer's Gift or the Patron's Pleasure? The Literary Economy in Late Medieval France* (University of Toronto Press, 2019).

Karla Mallette (Professor of Italian and Middle East Studies at the University of Michigan) is a scholar of the literature of the medieval Mediterranean. She is author of *The Kingdom of Sicily, 1100–1250: A Literary History* (University of Pennsylvania Press, 2005) and *European Modernity and the Arab Mediterranean: Toward a New Philology and a Counter-Orientalism* (University of Pennsylvania Press, 2010), and co-editor with Suzanne Akbari of *A Sea of Languages: Rethinking the Arabic Role in Medieval Literary History* (University of Toronto Press, 2013). She is currently at work on a monograph, *Lives of the Great Languages: Lingua Franca in the Mediterranean.*

Ronald L. Martinez is Professor of Italian Studies at Brown University. In addition to some sixty articles on topics from Guido Cavalcanti's lyrics to Ariosto's *Orlando furioso,* he collaborated with Robert M. Durling on a monograph on Dante's lyric poetry, *Time and the Crystal: Studies in Dante's Rime Petrose* (University of California Press, 1990), and on an edition, with translation and commentary, of Dante's *Divine Comedy* (Oxford University Press: *Inferno,* 1996; *Purgatorio,* 2003; *Paradiso,* 2011). Martinez is currently preparing a study on the role of the mechanical arts in shaping Dante's poetics.

Melissa Mayus received her doctorate in English from the University of Notre Dame in 2015. She then held a postdoctoral position in the Medieval Institute at Western Michigan University in 2016 and 2017. She is currently an Assistant Professor of English in the Department of Humanities and Communication at Trine University in Angola, Indiana where she teaches a wide range of composition and literature courses.

Her primary research focuses on conceptions of free will and agency in Old English and Old Norse-Icelandic literature. She has previously published 'A Marian Lyric from Bodleian MS. Add. A. 268', *ANQ* 21 (2008): 4–7.

Fabienne Michelet is Assistant Professor of Medieval Literature in the Department of English and the Centre for Medieval Studies, University of Toronto. Her teaching and research focus especially on Old English poetry; cultural geography and questions of space and place; discourses of heroism and heroic agency. She is the author of *Creation, Migration and Conquest: Imaginary Geography and Sense of Space in Old English Literature* (Oxford University Press, 2006).

Jonathan M. Newman (PhD Toronto 2008) is Assistant Professor of Early English at Missouri State University and former SSHRC Visiting Postdoctoral Fellow at Dartmouth College. His dissertation treated dialogism and satire in medieval Latin and Middle English literature. He has since published articles on Middle English, medieval Latin, Italian, and Old Occitan literature in *Journal of Medieval Latin*, *Tenso*, *Mediaevalia et Humanistica* and *Studies in the Age of Chaucer*. He is currently writing a monograph on clerical masculinity and epistolarity in the long twelfth century.

Ruth Nisse teaches in the Department of English and the Center for Jewish Studies at Wesleyan University. Her book, *Jacob's Shipwreck: Diaspora, Translation, and Jewish-Christian Relations in Medieval England* (Cornell University Press, 2017), is about the recovery and reception of ancient texts in medieval Latin, Hebrew, and vernacular literatures. Her first book, *Defining Acts: Drama and the Politics of Interpretation in Late Medieval England* (Notre Dame University Press, 2005), is a study of Middle English Theater in dialogue with contemporary polemical and devotional texts.

Martin Pickavé is a Professor of Philosophy and Medieval Studies and a Canada Research Chair in Medieval Philosophy at the University of Toronto. Most of his published work deals with issues in metaphysics and the philosophy of mind in later medieval philosophy, but he also has research interests in ancient and early modern philosophy. He is currently working on a monograph on medieval theories of the emotions.

David L. Pike is Professor of Literature at American University. His books include *Passage through Hell: Modernist Descents, Medieval Underworlds* (Cornell University Press, 1997), *Subterranean Cities: The World beneath Paris and London 1800–1945* (Cornell University Press, 2005), and *Metropolis on the Styx: The Underworlds of Modern Urban Culture, 1800–2001* (Cornell University Press, 2007). He is co-author of *Literature: A World of Writing* (Pearson, 2nd ed. 2013) and co-editor of the *Longman Anthology of World Literature* (Pearson, 2nd ed. 2008), and has published widely on undergrounds, underworlds, and urban literature, culture and film. Current projects include a cultural history of the slum.

Kellie Robertson is Professor of English and Comparative Literature at the University of Maryland. Her most recent book is *Nature Speaks: Medieval Literature and Aristotelian Philosophy* (University of Pennsylvania Press, 2017), which examines late medieval poetry in the context of its physics, arguing that both domains struggled over how to represent nature in the wake of Aristotelian science. She is also the author of *The Laborer's Two Bodies: Labor and the 'Work' of the Text in Medieval Britain, 1350–1500* (Palgrave, 2006) and the co-editor of a collection of essays entitled *The Middle Ages at Work: Practicing Labor in Late Medieval England* (Palgrave, 2004).

Martha Rust is an associate professor of English at New York University. She is the author of *Imaginary Worlds in Medieval Books: Exploring the Manuscript Matrix* (Palgrave, 2007) and has published many articles on late-medieval English manuscript culture, most recently '"*Qui bien aime a tarde oblie*": Lemmata and Lists in the *Parliament of Fowls*', in *Chaucer: Visual Approaches*, ed. David Rubin and Susanna Fein (Pennsylvania State University Press, 2016); and 'Of *Piers*, Polltaxes and Parliament: Articulating Status and Occupation in Late Medieval England', co-authored with Lawrence Poos in *Fragments: Interdisciplinary Approaches to the Study of Ancient and Medieval Pasts*, 2017.

James Simpson is Douglas P. and Katherine B. Loker Professor of English at Harvard University and former Professor of Medieval and Renaissance English at the University of Cambridge. He is the author of *Piers Plowman: An Introduction to the B-Text* (Longman, 1990); *Sciences and the Self in Medieval Poetry* (Cambridge University Press, 1995); *Reform and Cultural Revolution, 1350–1547*, Volume 2 of *The Oxford English Literary History* (Oxford University Press, 2002); *Burning to Read: English Fundamentalism and its Reformation Opponents* (Harvard University Press, 2007); and *Under the Hammer: Iconoclasm in the Anglo-American Tradition* (Oxford University Press, 2010). His most recent book is *Permanent Revolution: The Reformation and the Illiberal Roots of Liberalism* (Harvard University Press, 2019).

Suzanne M. Yeager is author of *Jerusalem in Medieval Narrative* (Cambridge University Press, 2008), which opened discussion of the medieval devotional phenomenon of virtual crusading. Her interest in mythologized pasts and places contributed to the collection, *Remembering the Crusades: Myth, Image, and Identity* (co-edited with Nicholas Paul) (Johns Hopkins University Press, 2012). Her articles include studies of medieval religious and racial identity in premodern romance, poetry, and prose, and her work explores European literatures related to pilgrimage, Judaism, and Western Asia. She was educated at the University of Toronto and Oxford University, and is an Associate Professor at Fordham University.

INTRODUCTION

Placing the Past

SUZANNE CONKLIN AKBARI

COLLECTIONS of essays on Chaucer, whether handbooks, introductions, or companions, are numerous. While they vary in terms of what they seek to offer readers, they share some common features: above all, a preoccupation with time. They seek at once to place Chaucer in his own historical moment and, in some sense, to place him in our current moment, or even to use him to frame contemporary social and cultural issues. Chaucer's work is both seen as fundamental to a national, English literary history, and described as universal, almost 'modern' in its attentiveness to human nature, the nuances of social structures, and the interior life of the individual subject.

This history of responses to Chaucer, especially regarding the temporal paradox—where Chaucer is seen as being at once genuinely 'medieval' and strikingly 'modern'—is a useful backdrop to the present volume, which places his works in a significantly different context. We have sought throughout to juxtapose contributions by well-established Middle English scholars with chapters by specialists in other fields—Latin and vernacular literature, philosophy, theology, history of science—in order to produce a view of Chaucer's works that is stereoscopic. We intend to produce a complex view, one that does not so much look from the outside into the works of Chaucer as to inhabit the works of Chaucer looking out. For example, instead of soliciting essays by scholars working in Middle English studies who have an interest in medieval French or Italian literature, we have sought out those who are specialists in Machaut or Boccaccio; or instead of a Chaucerian interested in science or theology, we have sought out specialists in those areas, asking them to give an account of the intellectual history in which Chaucer's writings are embedded. In other cases, we have solicited work from scholars whose work sits clearly at the centre of Chaucer studies. By juxtaposing these perspectives, we are able to compose a handbook that breaks new ground and offers substantial room for growth of the field in fresh directions.

Before turning to an overview of this handbook's contents, it may be useful to offer a brief comparative summary of other introductions, handbooks, and companions to

Chaucer, focusing on how each positions the work relative to their own moment in time. This review is not exhaustive but selective, with the purpose being to draw out some important—yet implicit—assumptions concerning temporality and Chaucer. It is first worth noting the kinds of titles that accrue to these volumes: handbook; companion; introduction. What kind of reader is called into being by these labels, and what kind of relationship? That is, how is the book positioned relative to the reader? If a 'companion', an implicit affective relationship is posited, where the book serves almost as a mentor—a kind of Virgil to the reader's Dante. If a 'handbook', the reader is being positioned as a kind of technician who seeks to get to work, requiring only an instruction manual and the right 'tools' to take apart and reassemble the text before him. If an 'introduction', a naive or developing reader is assumed, who needs to be led by the hand.

Accordingly, this spectrum of perspectives is evident in the history of publication: among those books that are most clearly directed at the student as opposed to the specialist, we find some that almost serve as a textbook, such as (for example) Gail Ashton's *The Canterbury Tales*.[1] Peter Brown's 2011 *Geoffrey Chaucer* addresses a similar readership, and is noteworthy for the ways in which it emphasizes a connection not only to the medieval past but also to the student-reader's own moment in time.[2] The volume concludes with a section titled 'New Contexts', and its last subheading reads 'Tomorrow'. Harold Bloom's edited collections *Geoffrey Chaucer* and *Geoffrey Chaucer's The Canterbury Tales* (in the eponymous series 'Bloom's Literary Criticism'), also explicitly address the novice reader.[3]

Among the volumes addressing more experienced readers, Piero Boitani and Jill Mann's *Cambridge Companion to Chaucer* stands out for its systematic nature.[4] Like Brown's 2011 volume, this one also ends with a future-oriented perspective, with Carolyn Dinshaw's contribution 'New Approaches to Chaucer'. Another fine volume by Brown, *A Companion to Chaucer*, addresses the advanced reader and even problematizes the very undertaking of the volume itself, opening with a self-reflective piece on 'The Idea of a Chaucer Companion'.[5] The alphabetical ordering of the book's twenty-nine chapters is particularly interesting: while not every letter of the alphabet is represented, and some letters have multiple essays, the effect produced is one of comprehensiveness and underlying order. The book literally runs the gamut from A to Z.

Steve Ellis's *Chaucer: An Oxford Guide* similarly sets out a comprehensive scope, with relatively short pieces by a large number of contributors producing a kind of mosaic effect.[6] The volume's penultimate section is titled 'Afterlife', followed by a final section dedicated to 'study resources', separated into 'printed resources' and 'electronic resources'. In its effort to include online resources even within the setting of a print volume, Ellis's *Chaucer* looks forward to the central role of web-based resources in Chaucer studies. These include a wide range of formal and informal online fora, as well as *The Open Access Companion to the Canterbury Tales*, produced by an 'Editorial Collective' made up of Candace Barrington, Brantley Bryant, Richard Godden, Daniel Kline, and Myra Seaman.[7] The editors' self-awareness of the temporality of online resources is signalled in the project's landing page, which identifies the author as 'The Editorial Collective of The Open Access Companion to the Canterbury Tales, Summer 2015–September 2017'.

The specificity of this time frame both reflects the period of the editors' initial work and also signals the ephemeral—or, seen from another perspective, up-to-date—nature of the online 'companion'. This emergence of the Open Access companion signals a new horizon, where ongoing crowd-sourced research and peer review offers new scholarly outlets and different patterns of textual circulation both for academics and lay readers.

This very brief, highly selective, and far from exhaustive overview is relevant to the present work not just in general terms, outlining the kinds of functions that a handbook might be expected to serve, but also in bringing out the assumptions concerning time, space, and order that have underlain these earlier examples of the genre. Just about all of the volumes noted above have a peculiar relationship to time. They tend to open with a section titled something like (for example) 'The Age of Chaucer', or with a series of essays that ground Chaucer in his historical moment; and they tend to conclude not in the present moment of the volume's editor but rather—interestingly—by looking forward into the future.[8] This can be seen, for example, with the closing header 'Tomorrow' in Brown's 2011 volume, the conclusion 'New Approaches' in Boitani and Mann's *Cambridge Companion*, and the forward-looking 'electronic resources' that close Ellis's Oxford guide. It is significant that these closing moves do not consist of an effort to link Chaucer's time with our own time, but rather to link the medieval past with some projected future moment: that is, not the now, but what lies ahead of the now. What is suggested by this move is the notion that Chaucer is relevant not just to our own time, but to some potential future time—or, even, relevant to all times, including a range of moments that both extend back into the past and onward into the future. What's suggested is that the end date, the expiration date of Chaucer's relevance, always lies ahead of where we are.

In some ways, this temporal positioning of Chaucer is similar to what we see in the field of Shakespeare studies, where the work is assumed to have not only an enduring pedagogical value but also a 'universal' human appeal. The field of 'Global Shakespeare' studies, along with its little sibling 'Global Chaucers', builds upon this aspiration to capaciousness and universality, suggesting that the works of a single author can offer a kind of epitome or microcosm of humanity itself. Some formulations of this 'universal' quality are explicitly colonial and normative, projecting outward from an imagined stable cultural centre. Others, however, are explicitly postcolonial and explore how different people and different cultures 'write back' to the imperial centre through their appropriation and adaptation of the canonical work, recreating the work of the 'dead white male' writer so that it emerges as a work of art that is, always and essentially, something different.

Chaucer—again like Shakespeare—plays a peculiar role in the stories we tell ourselves about English literary history. In survey courses, and in departmental hiring patterns, Chaucer is consistently positioned as *the* medieval writer, as Shakespeare is for the Renaissance. This is not the place to go into the long history of how the 'medieval' was invented, and especially the ways in which Chaucer specifically was identified, in Spenser's words, as 'the well of English undefiled';[9] it is impossible to ignore, however, the extent to which the fantasy of a pure ('undefiled') language serves the ends of an emergent sense of national identity, from Spenser's time through the emergence of English as a field of study in the nineteenth century. The national philology underlying this view of Chaucer can also be compared with the role of Dante—and the Florentine vernacular—in the self-fashioning of Italian national identity, especially as it was developed in the nineteenth century. The history of the discipline of English is inseparable from the invention of Chaucer as a figure who can be at once localized to the medieval past and also generalized as a man for all times, whose premodern nature aligns seamlessly with an endlessly renewable 'modern' quality.

The implicit claim of universality that is yoked to the study of Chaucer's works is worth reconsidering, whether it be grounded in the apparent social realism of the General Prologue that was a preoccupation of Chaucer scholarship from the nineteenth century through Jill Mann's seminal study of estates satire, or in the multicultural and multilingual engagement and adaptation that is the focus of 'Global Chaucers'. To what extent can this claim to universality stand? What is the ground on which we justify the continued centrality of Chaucer to our discipline? Instead of taking these difficult questions head on, the chapters contained in this handbook address them obliquely, offering a range of perspectives on what we might call the troublesome side of diversity. Confronting the anti-Judaism or antisemitism of the *Canterbury Tales*, as in Steven Kruger's chapter, or the persistence of Hebrew literature in medieval England, as in Ruth Nisse's contribution, allows us to reflect on what was suppressed or elided in the construction of English literary history on the shoulders of Chaucer. Considering the Arabic sources and analogues of the frame tale tradition, as in Karla Mallette's chapter, allows us to decentre not just English literature but European frame tale models more generally, considering the wider scope of literary dissemination and circulation that lies behind the early modern emergence of national literatures. We expect these interventions to open up new directions in future scholarship. Beyond these, the medical accounts of bodily diversity found in the writings of the fourteenth-century physician Henry Daniel, studied by E. Ruth Harvey, offer new insights into the premodern understandings of racialized identities. Similarly, the conceptions of 'nation' found in the medieval histories of Troy described by Marilynn Desmond and in the Anglo-French chronicle of Nicholas Trevet that is the focus of Suzanne Akbari's chapter, underlie the premodern conceptions of collective identity that emerge in Chaucer's narratives of Thebes and Troy. In other words, this handbook offers a range of perspectives on some of the issues that are now central to the field of Chaucer studies, and to the discipline of English more generally, including national or ethnic identities, religious difference, bodily diversity, and race.

What then, is the role of a Chaucer handbook in the current moment? And what is our temporal attitude toward Chaucer and his work right now? Is this volume simply one more in a long history of volumes—companions, handbooks, introductions, and guides—that seek to situate Chaucer relative to their own historical moment? In other words, is this volume reflective of its historical moment in the same way that they all are? Or is there something distinctive about this historical moment, in terms of how the discipline of English is evolving, and how our own sense of temporality is changing with reference to our object of study? It is impossible to deny that the last two decades have brought about a sea change in medieval studies, in part mediated through the fields of queer theory and history of religion, where affective links to the past enable a sort of temporal transgression, whether expressed in terms of a 'queer touch' (in the words of Carolyn Dinshaw)[10] or a 'desire for the past' (in the words of Nicholas Watson).[11] The field of Chaucer studies does not remain undisturbed by this affective turn, which is particularly felt in current scholarship that addresses race, gender, and sexuality in the context of the writer's works. To what extent is our willingness to import the past into our own historical moment, or to project ourselves back into that historical past, at work in today's Chaucer studies? And will Chaucer studies—and even, more generally, the discipline of English itself—look the same in the wake of this turning point? If there is a way forward, it lies in the very heterogeneity of what Chaucer's works offer, which is in part based in the unfinished nature of so much of the work—above all, the *Canterbury Tales*—that in turn engenders a profound heterogeneity of readerly response.

It is this heterogeneity that we have sought to provoke in the selection of contributors to the present handbook. We invited those who are not primarily Middle English specialists to write the chapters on other literary traditions, not simply following the conventional summary of Chaucer's so-called 'French period' and 'Italian period' but rather engaging seriously with the wider linguistic context of late fourteenth-century Europe. We invited specialists in philosophy, history of science, and theology to write the chapters on these contexts for Chaucer's works, mindful that their contributions would not be the last word on Chaucer's own philosophical, scientific, and theological commitments: instead, the chapters gathered in our handbook would be the spur for precisely these new areas of development within Chaucer studies. In other words, we were determined to get outside of the Middle English bubble, and particularly to get out of the Chaucer bubble, in order to see what new regions we might begin to map out within this *terra incognita*.

Our cover image seeks to make this shift in perspective visible, showing a familiar geographical region—north-western Europe—from a point of view that may be less familiar: the world map of al-Idrisi (Abu Abdallah Muhammad ibn Muhammad ibn Abdallah ibn Idris, ca. 1100–66). On this map, which is south-oriented (south at the top), England appears as a promontory extending downward from the European continent, although England (and Scotland) are depicted in elaborate detail on a separate page of Idrisi's *Nuzhat al-mushtāq fī ikhtirāq al-āfāq* ('Book of pleasant journeys into faraway lands'). Also called the *Tabula Rogeriana*, or 'Book of Roger', due to the patronage of Roger II, Norman King of Sicily (1095–1154), this series of regional maps organized sequentially by latitude or climate drew both on Islamic mapmaking traditions and those available at the royal court at Palermo. Yet, as Karen Pinto reminds us, we cannot simply take this image as representative of twelfth-century geographical perspectives, since the earliest manuscript witnesses of Idrisi's maps date from the fourteenth century; and we cannot take it as representative of Islamic mapping practices, since Idrisi's work is in many ways separate from the mainstream tradition.[12] Moreover, the intricate detail of Idrisi's climate maps are not reflected in the world map that opens the volume; as Marina

Tolmacheva notes, this is 'in the classical Islamic cartographic tradition, unrelated to al-Idrisi's own system and not mentioned in the text. There is no direct evidence that al-Idrisi ever drew one complete world map following his own projection and incorporating all the seventy sections.'[13] We can, however, see this world map as representative of the spatial and hermeneutic perspectives that our handbook seeks to provide: defamiliarizing familiar territories; drawing in twelfth-century textual traditions and their mediation through late medieval reception; and providing a Mediterranean perspective on premodern English literary history that seeks to re-centre the field—however provisionally—and to chart out new courses for future research.

The handbook opens with an introductory section 'Biography and Circumstances of Daily Life', exploring the diplomatic, legal, economic, codicological, and rhetorical contexts for Chaucer's life and works. These chapters historicize the writer and his production, understood both as labour and as material codex. We then turn to a pair of complementary groupings: 'Chaucer in the Mediterranean Frame', and 'Chaucer in the European Frame'. Each of these sections situates the Middle English text within the context of other literary traditions: Arabic and Hebrew, French and Italian, as well as Latin. In both sections, we have been guided by our principle of dual perspectives, with contributions by scholars who are specialists in their various fields juxtaposed with contributions by Middle English specialists. Significantly, we have not sought to place Chaucer's writings within the context of 'World Literature' or 'Global Chaucers', instead opting for a networked approach that highlights regions of connectivity, entanglement, and cultural exchange. The next two sections, 'Philosophy and Science in the Universities' and 'Christian Doctrine and Religious Heterodoxy', turn to the context of intellectual history that informs Chaucer's writings. Again, we have juxtaposed work by Middle English specialists with those working in other fields—philosophy, history of science, and theology—in order to maintain a stereoscopic view of the literature. The volume concludes with 'The Chaucerian Afterlife', considering the strands of continuity that emerge in the writings of Gower, Lydgate, Hoccleve, and Henryson. By embedding Chaucer within a series of conceptual contexts, each of which situates this eclectic and capacious figure within a different framework, our handbook breaks fresh ground and offers opportunities for a new generation of investigations in the field.

Notes

1. Gail Ashton, *The Canterbury Tales* (New York: Continuum, 2007).
2. Peter Brown, *Geoffrey Chaucer* (Oxford: Oxford University Press, 2011).
3. Harold Bloom, *Geoffrey Chaucer* (New York: Bloom's Literary Criticism, 2007); Harold Bloom, *Geoffrey Chaucer's The Canterbury Tales* (New York: Bloom's Literary Criticism, 2008).
4. Piero Boitani and Jill Mann, *Cambridge Companion to Chaucer*, 2nd ed. (Cambridge: Cambridge University Press, 2003).
5. Peter Brown, *A Companion to Chaucer* (Oxford: Blackwell, 2000).
6. Steve Ellis, *Chaucer: An Oxford Guide* (Oxford: Oxford University Press, 2005).

7. Candace Barrington, Brantley Bryant, Richard Godden, Daniel Kline, and Myra Seaman, eds., *The Open Access Companion to the Canterbury Tales*, opencanterburytales.dsl.lsu.edu/

8. Dieter Mehl, 'Introduction: The Age of Chaucer', *English Literature in the Age of Chaucer*, ed. Dieter Mehl (New York: Longman, 2001), 1–8.

9. Edmund Spenser, *The Faerie Queene*, 4.2.32.

10. Carolyn Dinshaw, 'Chaucer's Queer Touches/A Queer Touches Chaucer', *Exemplaria* 7.1 (1995): 75–92.

11. Nicholas Watson, 'Desire for the Past', *Studies in the Age of Chaucer* 21 (1999): 59–97.

12. Karen C. Pinto, *Medieval Islamic Maps: An Exploration* (Chicago, IL: University of Chicago Press, 2016), 24–5.

13. Marina Tolmacheva, 'The Medieval Arabic Geographers and the Beginnings of Modern Orientalism', *International Journal of Middle East Studies* 27 (1995): 141–56, quotation from 147.

PART I

BIOGRAPHY AND CIRCUMSTANCES OF DAILY LIFE

CHAPTER 1

CHAUCER'S TRAVELS FOR THE COURT

PETER BROWN

IF 'the court' is loosely defined as including the various royal households with which Geoffrey Chaucer was associated, then all of his recorded travels were 'travels for the court'. There is not another category of 'travel for other purposes'. That is because the surviving evidence takes the form of documents issued by officials for business to be undertaken by or for Chaucer at the court's behest: typically letters of protection, accounts, warrants, mandates, receipts, records of expenses. The information, collected and edited in *Chaucer Life-Records*, is usually scanty, occasionally rich, and always intriguing. Doubtless there were many more such records containing Chaucer's name that have been lost; some may still await discovery. It is in the nature of what survives to hide as much as it reveals, and to focus on the details of monetary transaction and documentary formulae, rather than more circumstantial matters. For example, the records reveal next to nothing about Chaucer's itineraries.[1] One, a warrant of 1368 for a licence for Chaucer to pass at Dover (i.e. a passport), shows where he embarked, but his route there, his destination, and the purpose of the trip, remain unknown. He was not without resources, and took with him two 'hakeneys', 20 shillings for expenses, and £10 'en eschange' since he was away for over three months.[2] The rest is speculation, although it is worth noting that the dates coincide with the marriage in Milan of Prince Lionel (whom Chaucer served from 1357 to 1360) and Violante Visconti—a ceremony attended by Frances Petrarch.[3]

As the last example suggests, Chaucer's travels encompassed England as well as continental Europe, although the bulk of the evidence relates to foreign journeys. Chaucer's travel in England tends to be forgotten in the search for experiences that might have shaped his writing, influenced as it was by French and Italian models. Yet his domestic journeys were no less adventurous and had a similar potential to inform his imagination. As a page of Elizabeth, Countess of Ulster from 1357 to 1360, Chaucer presumably accompanied the household when it visited various royal residences.[4] Although some were within striking distance of London along the Thames valley

(Windsor, Reading) or to the north (Hatfield), others were further afield in the Midlands (Doncaster, Stratford). Yet others were many hundreds of miles away, such as those in the north-west in Liverpool and on Anglesey, or in the West Country (Bristol). At the time, Chaucer was in his teens, but even when he was in his late fifties he was still travelling extensively across the country. Unfortunately, little is known about the circumstances of a royal protection of 4 May 1398 allowing Chaucer to travel 'on the king's arduous and urgent business to divers parts of England' without attracting legal proceedings.[5]

By the time of his first documented domestic trip in 1373, Chaucer was already a seasoned international traveller who had just returned from Genoa and Florence. In Genoa, he had been involved in negotiations to secure an English port for use by Genoese merchants. That suggests why, on his return, he was given a commission to travel to the port of Dartmouth in Devon and deliver back to its master, a merchant of Genoa called John of Nigris, *La Seinte Marie et Seint George*. The ship was a Genoese tarit (a large cargo ship) that had been placed under arrest, but Nigris was now given a safe conduct to trade with his ship and the goods and merchandise it contained 'wherever he please[d] in England'.[6] *La Seinte Marie* had perhaps fallen victim to the kind of piracy Chaucer alludes to in his pilgrim portrait of the Shipman, 'For aught I woot, he was of Dertemouthe' (I.389), whose ship is called the *Maudeleyne* (Mary Magdalene).

Chaucer's appointment as Clerk of the Works (1389–91) entailed a considerable amount of domestic travel since he had to oversee buildings at Westminster, the Tower of London, St George's Chapel at Windsor and other royal castles, lodges, and manors.[7] He was responsible for purveying building materials, commissioning the workforce, and paying wages. It was probably while he was en route to the royal manor and palace at Eltham (eight miles south-east of the centre of London) with wages for labourers that he became the target for a gang of robbers. They attacked him on three separate occasions within the space of a few days. On 3 September 1390 at Hatcham in Surrey, near the aptly named 'le fowle ok', Chaucer lost to the robbers his horse, other property, and £20 of the king's money; on 6 September, also at Hatcham, £9. 43d; and on the same day, at Westminster, £10.[8] The felons were later apprehended and identified as Richard Brierley, William Huntingfield, Thomas Talbot, and Adam Clerk. Brierley and Clerk were subsequently hanged, though for other crimes.

Long before he set foot on it, the European mainland was a significant feature of Chaucer's geographical and cultural awareness. It is likely that the family name, two generations before, was Malyn—after the French name for the Flemish town of Mechelen.[9] When he was a young boy the family moved from London to Southampton so that his father, John, could discharge his duty as deputy butler to Edward III by overseeing shipments of wine from Bordeaux. While the family was in Southampton, a more sinister cargo arrived from France: the Black Death of 1348–9, probably brought to Europe by merchants trading out of Genoa. On returning to London a few years later, the Chaucers settled in inherited property in a part of the city known as the Vintry, populated by merchants and close to the quays on the north bank of the Thames. Close to where Chaucer grew up, he could hear the languages of France, the Low Countries and the Mediterranean, and see merchants, sailors, and artefacts from many parts of the known world. London itself played host to a number of immigrant communities, notably Italians, generally referred to as Lombards, who were particularly active in the financial and wool markets; and Flemings, famous for their weaving. Some Flemings lived close to one of John Chaucer's properties in the Vintry and were to become a target of the rebels in 1381, when a number of them were massacred in the street. And when Geoffrey entered court life as a young adolescent in the household of Elizabeth, Countess of Ulster, he encountered a world where French was the dominant language of literary composition and of diplomacy.[10]

It would be possible to provide other examples, from later phases of Chaucer's career, to demonstrate the cosmopolitan nature of the London he knew. The point of such remarks is to resist the tendency to make too easy a connection between Chaucer's travels and his literary output. His earliest work is already international by the standards of his day because his environment was open to foreign influence and cultural exchange.[11] Europe came to him: quite literally in the case of the French king, Jean II, captured at Poitiers in 1356. Although a prisoner, Jean enjoyed hospitable treatment and became a nexus of literary activity during his four-year sojourn at the court of Edward III. Jean's chaplain was the poet Gace de la Buigne; the king purchased French literary texts in England; and he championed the work of Guillaume de Machaut, whose *dits amoureux* exerted a powerful influence on Chaucer's early compositions.[12] At the court of Edward III Chaucer encountered the love poet and chronicler Jean Froissart, who served as secretary to Queen Philippa from 1361 to 1369. Froissart was from Valenciennes and so, like Philippa, from the Hainault region in the Low Countries. Philippa and Froissart would have conversed in Picard French, the language of Chaucer's wife Philippa Roet, whose father, Sir Paon de Roet, was also from Valenciennes. Some of Froissart's French writings in the love-vision idiom provided Chaucer with ideas and materials for his early compositions. Thus Froissart's *Paradys d'Amour* is a frame of reference for Chaucer's *Book of the Duchess*, composed for John of Gaunt, Edward's second son who, with his wealth, power and ambition, was an international prince in his own right. Again, the Savoyard knight and poet Oton de Grandson was an habitué, like Chaucer, of Edward's court, Gaunt's household, and the court of Richard II. He and Chaucer developed a creative dialogue: Chaucer refers to Grandson by name in his *Complaint of Venus* and Chaucer's writings, especially the *Book of the Duchess* and *Parliament of Fowls*, are in turn reflected in Grandson's compositions.[13]

Perhaps the most striking example of Europe's coming to Chaucer is that of Bohemia. Chaucer would have known of the reputation of the house of Luxembourg, the rulers of Bohemia, as literary patrons. Jean of Luxembourg, killed at the battle of Crécy (1346), had sponsored Froissart, who returned the compliment with lavish praise. Another of Jean's clients was Guillaume de Machaut, who portrays Jean in his *Jugement dou roy de Navarre*—a text that, along with others by Machaut, had a formative effect on Chaucer's writing. Jean's successor, Charles V, consolidated his family's reputation for cultural largesse by presiding in Prague over a Francophone court that actively encouraged engagement with European writers, intellectuals, and artists. After Petrarch visited Prague he wrote of the experience in adulatory terms. Furthermore, Charles encouraged the writing of myths about his family's origins that embedded them in the history of Troy. So when, in 1381, Richard II brought to London as his bride Charles's daughter, Anne of Bohemia, she came with certain associations of interest to a court writer such as Chaucer then was. Anne did not disappoint: she was praised by contemporaries for her literacy, multilingualism, piety, and conciliatory approach to political conflict. Chaucer found the cultural moment that she inaugurated highly congenial. There are vestiges of Anne's patronage in the F-version of the *Legend of Good Women* and in *Troilus and Criseyde*—the latter containing just that cocktail of courtly internationalism, Trojan myth, and chivalric derring-do that 'Bohemia' promised.

Books travel, no less than a Flemish or French poet, or a Bohemian princess. As the previous example demonstrates, Chaucer's mind was sometimes broadened not by travel—he never went to Bohemia—but by encounters with books and individuals that represented a particular place. The idea of Bohemia was itself potent and productive. Thus it is important to recognize that, before Chaucer embarked on his actual journeys, he was already the recipient—through reading, dealings with other writers, experiences at home and at court—of a wide range of impressions of other cultures and countries. It is also the case that travel per se was not necessarily likely to enhance that knowledge, since many of his journeys were business trips of short duration. On the other hand, he was primed and receptive to anything that might add to his store of creative raw materials. Chaucer's encounters with other cultures involved a complex process of exchange.

Implicit in the discussion thus far—in spite of its emphasis on Chaucer as stationary—is the frequency of travel, often over long distances, within his culture. Travel was not exceptional but a state of being. Even the court itself was peripatetic: that of Richard II, especially in its later years, was notorious for being forever on the move. Extensive and regular travel was the norm in many other spheres as well. The enduring war with France, which lasted through and beyond Chaucer's lifetime, entailed a perpetual rotation of expeditions, armies, and supplies across the Channel and deep into enemy lands. England's acquisition of swathes of French territory, held until the later years of Edward III's reign, increased the traffic of clerks and government officials, while the opportunities for ransom, truce, or peace required much to-ing and fro-ing of diplomats and messengers. Representatives of the Church might sometimes be involved, they themselves belonging to an international organization with its own infrastructure and *lingua franca*, long-established customs of travel, hospitality, and long-range diplomacy and governance. The papal *curia*, whether at Avignon or Rome, was a destination for English scholars and clerics.[14] The Church in turn encouraged pilgrimage, that traditional activity of pious lay people.[15] Chaucer's long-standing associate, the Lollard-leaning knight Sir John Clanvowe, undertook a pilgrimage to Jerusalem to atone for his sins on campaign in France, and died there.[16] Universities across Europe provided a further network by means of which scholars might travel and exchange ideas. Finally, the wealth of merchants, so crucial to upholding the policies and finances of the Crown, depended upon overseas trade.[17]

Between 1359, when he was in late teens, and 1387, when he was in his mid-forties, Chaucer made at least fourteen trips overseas.[18] Within this thirty-year span there was a period of a dozen years when his travels were especially frequent: from 1366 to 1378 he was in Europe on eleven occasions, and probably more. In 1377 alone (the year of Edward III's death) he made at least three separate crossings of the Channel.[19] The duration of his trips might be a few days or a year or more—variations that were to some extent dependent on the destination. Of his fourteen journeys, the great majority (ten) were to France and Flanders.[20] There are records of his presence near Rheims (1359) and at Calais (1360 and 1387). He may also have visited Bruges in 1376 and, a year later, was in Paris and Montreuil. But Chaucer also travelled further south. A journey of three months' duration in 1366 took him to Navarre in northern Spain; another to Genoa and Florence began in 1372 and lasted six months; one trip to Lombardy in 1378 took the best part of four months. Other destinations are more shadowy. Letters of protection issued in 1377 cover 'Divers voyages at divers times to divers parts overseas'.[21] Given that the duration was two months or less, Chaucer was probably travelling once more in northern Europe.

Destination and duration were in turn imbricated with the purpose (and complexity) of the journey. The purpose might simply be communicative, as when Chaucer was sent to Calais from England, sometime between 13 and 31 October 1360, 'cum litteris in Angliam', carrying letters from Lionel, Earl of Ulster, in whose household he then served.[22] Or the purpose might be military: Chaucer's *prest* (advance) recorded by Henry de Wakefield in 1369 was £10 'for reward or wages of war' for five months' service to John of Gaunt, Duke of Lancaster, during his expedition to Artois, Picardy, and Normandy.[23] The purpose could also be political. When Chaucer travelled to Navarre with three unnamed companions his patron, John of Gaunt, was endeavouring to support Pedro the Cruel in a campaign to restore him to the throne of Castile. Again, the purpose could be commercial. The aim of the mission to Genoa was to negotiate the provision of a special seaport for use by Genoese merchants. The associated trip to Florence probably had financial objectives: undertaken for the king's secret needs ('pur acunes noz secrees busoignes'), it may have furthered the ongoing discussions with the Bardi banking house about the provision of a loan to Edward III.[24] In a number of cases, secrecy of purpose has remained effective to the present day. All that we know of the reasons for a number of Chaucer's journeys is that they were undertaken on the king's secret business. Occasionally, the purpose, even though of a sensitive political nature, is made overt. One of the objectives of Chaucer's mission to Lombardy with Sir Edward de Berkeley was to engage in discussions with Barnabó Visconti, Duke of Milan—featured in the Monk's Tale as the tyrannical 'God of delit and scourge of Lumbardye' (VII.2400)—and with the powerful English mercenary, Sir John Hawkwood ('cher et loial') about certain needs touching the propagation of war ('pur ascunes busoignes touchantes lexploit de nostre guerre').[25] Chaucer undertook for the same king, Richard II, diplomatic missions with less bellicose themes. In 1381 he received a gift of £22 from Richard for his role in negotiating a possible marriage alliance, and for his peace missions in the time of Edward III.[26]

When they are recorded, the resources available to Chaucer for a particular journey can indicate its level of importance. Generally speaking, there is a correlation between the significance of the trip and Chaucer's status. On campaign with Lionel in 1359—60 he was given the going rate for a *valettus*, 6d. a day. Nine years later, in 1369, on a military expedition with John of Gaunt, he merited £10 over a period of five months (July to November) as a member of the king's *familia*. The mission to Genoa and Florence in 1372–3 produced a large advance of 100 marks (£66. 13s. 4d.) with a further one mark a day (13s. 4d.) as appropriate to his rank, together with messengers. In Lombardy (1378) his allowance was again one mark a day, and £4 for the 'passage and repassage of the sea' for five men and horses.[27] From the first Italian trip onwards Chaucer is regularly referred to as a king's esquire (*armiger regis* or *scutifer regis*).

Sometimes it is possible to flesh out the bare bones of the official documents with corroborative evidence or contextual material. The stated purposes of Chaucer's trips as king's messenger (*nuncius*) to Montreuil and Paris between 1377 and 1381 are specified in an Issue Roll entry as being to discuss peace (*causa tractatus pacis*) and the possibility of a marriage between prince Richard and a French princess.[28] The information is, as ever, tantalizing. Fortunately, the negotiations were recorded by Froissart in his *Chroniques*:

> Si furent envoyet à Monstruel-sus-mer, du costé des François, li sires de Couci, li sires de la Rivière, messires Nicolas Brake et Nicolas le Mercier, et du costé des Englès, messires Guichars d'Angle, messires Richars Sturi et Jeffrois Cauchiés. Et parlementèrent cil signeur et ces parties grant temps sus le marriage dou jone Richart, fil dou prince, et de mademoiselle Marie, fille dou roy de France, et revin-rent arrière en Engleterre et raportèrent leurs trettiés, et ossi li François en France, et furent les trièwes ralongies un mois.
>
> [The French then sent to Montreuil-sur-mer the Lord de Coucy, the Lord de la Rivière, Sir Nicolas Braque and Nicolas Le Mercier, and the English Sir Guichard d'Angle, Sir Richard Stury and Geoffrey Chaucer. These nobles and envoys had long discussions about a marriage between the young Richard, son of the Prince of Wales, and Princess Marie, the daughter of the King of France. Then the English returned to England and the French to France and the truces were extended for another month.][29]

In 1377 Edward III was in a poor state of health (he was to die later the same year). His heir, Edward of Woodstock (the Black Prince) had died the previous year, which made his own son, Richard, the subject of the Montreuil negotiations, heir to the throne. Froissart's account captures Chaucer as an active participant in a significant episode of international diplomacy. If the vignette is at all representative, his travels were fraught with the intricacies of political transactions between enemies, when peace or war might hang in the balance. He emerges as a trusted if ancillary player in a larger enterprise, dealing with senior representatives of the English court, and with their French counterparts.

Contextual materials can be brought to bear on aspects of Chaucer's travel for the court for which there is little direct evidence, such as his itineraries. Chaucer was in Calais in the second half of October 1360 for the ceremonies to mark the Treaty of Brétigny on the 24th of that month. The treaty ratified England's considerable territorial gains in the first phase of its war with France. Its signing was attended by Chaucer's patron Lionel, Earl of Ulster, as well as the Black Prince and Henry, Duke of Lancaster. A clerk in Lionel's household, Andrew de Budeston, recorded a payment of 9s. to Chaucer for carrying letters to England.[30] It is reasonable to suppose, as Pearsall does, that Chaucer was sent ahead of the main party. Chaucer's return route is not recorded by Andrew, but Lionel's is: Calais, Deal, Sandwich, Wingham, Canterbury, Boughton, Ospringe, Sittingbourne, Rochester, Dartford. Pearsall presumes that Chaucer would have followed the same route and concludes: 'This was not the first time, nor was it to be the last by any means, that Chaucer travelled the route by which he sent his pilgrims to Canterbury some years later.'[31] Two caveats come to mind. First, a route taken by a slow-moving royal household, with its need for periodic hospitality, is not necessarily the same as that taken by a relatively unencumbered messenger who was a low-ranking *valettus*. Second, the desire to create evidence of Chaucer's familiarity with Canterbury because he wrote the *Canterbury Tales* (which ends before the pilgrims arrive) should not be allowed to obscure other possibilities. If Chaucer sailed from Calais to Dover (a port he is known to have used on another occasion) then an equally direct route back to London was through Maidstone, not Canterbury.

One of Chaucer's forays into Europe that is considerably enriched by reference to its historical context is that of the previous year, when he accompanied Lionel on campaign in France as one of his many *valetti* or yeomen. Lionel led a company of seventy men, including a banneret (a knight with vassals, serving under his own banner), five other knights, twenty-three esquires, and forty mounted archers. The company formed part of a division led by Lionel's elder brother, the Black Prince. Edward III had marshalled his forces for an attack on Rheims, intending to be anointed there—the customary place for such ceremonies—as king of France. He carried a gold crown in his luggage for the purpose, and had good reason to be confident: the English had won notable battles at Crécy, Calais, and Poitiers and the French king, Jean II, was in captivity. But the siege of Rheims was repulsed, and among the hostages taken by French forces in the course of the campaign was Geoffrey Chaucer, subsequently ransomed by the king for £16—the going rate for a *valettus* of his standing.[32] Twenty-six years later, at a trial in Westminster Abbey to settle a dispute between Sir Richard Scrope and Sir Robert Grosvenor on the right to bear certain arms, Chaucer recalled how he had seen the arms borne by the Scropes 'en Fraunce devaunt la ville de Retters' [in France before the town of Rethel]. Rethel is north-east of Rheims and was where the Black Prince attempted to cross the river Aisne, only to be prevented from doing so by French attacks. Chaucer's evidence continued with a further statement about the Scropes: 'il lez vist armer par tout le dit viage tanqe le dit Geffrey estoit pris' [he saw them armed for the entire journey in the course of which the said Geoffrey was captured].[33] Whether Chaucer was taken hostage at Rheims itself, or in one of the skirmishes at Rethel, is not clear.

What are the literary implications of Chaucer's travels for the court? In the first place those travels argue—if corroboration were needed—for Chaucer's linguistic competence. French underpins Chaucer's literary career. As Ardis Butterfield has observed, Anglo-French is Chaucer's other vernacular, a language as familiar and natural to him as English.[34] It is possible that his first compositions, in lyric form, were in that language.[35] He translated French works, such as the *Roman de la rose*, into English and became famous for doing so. And he continued to have regular recourse to French literature whether for model, source, or inspiration, from the *Book of the Duchess* to the Reeve's Tale. But fluency in French was also an essential qualification for the various missions on which he was sent, for French was the *lingua franca* of diplomacy—as a number of documents cited in this essay show. It is not known if he also had command of Italian by the time of his journey to Genoa and Florence in 1372. He could have acquired a working knowledge of the language from Italian merchants who traded with his family, or from Italians who held prominent positions at court such as Walter de Bardi, the king's moneyer.[36] Two such Italians, highly ranked in Edward's court, were his travelling companions to Genoa. Jean de Mari (Giovanni del Mare) was styled 'Lumbardo' and Sir James de Provan (Jacopo Provano) was Genoese. Post-Genoa, Chaucer would certainly have encountered Italian merchants in London during his work as controller of the wool custom (1374–86).[37] In addition to technical expertise, Chaucer's endeavours were no doubt helped by rhetorical skills. The ability to manipulate words, frame a persuasive argument, lard it with references to appropriate authorities, and adjust the nature and level of discourse to the recipient's status and expectations—all of these are features of Chaucer's writing with direct application to the world of diplomacy.[38]

A similar congruence emerges when examining the patterns of patronage and association that characterize Chaucer's travels on the one hand and his literary output on the other. John of Gaunt, Duke of Lancaster, was the instigator of a military expedition to northern France in which Chaucer participated between July and November 1369. The previous year, Gaunt's wife had died and Chaucer was commissioned to write a memorial poem, 'the book of Blaunche the duchess', which probably got its first public airing in 1372. Two years later, Chaucer received a life annuity from the duke, but whether for literary or other services is unclear.[39] The lines of political and literary patronage are difficult to disentangle because they operated through identical networks.[40] The patron whom Chaucer served on the battlefield was the same patron for whom he wrote his first substantial poem and who was therefore, as the primary addressee of the *Book of the Duchess*, a key member of his audience.

Of particular interest in the latter respect are some of Chaucer's travelling companions on other missions abroad. Chaucer travelled with his audience, or at least with the kind of people who might be expected to appreciate the subtleties of his writing. They were highly literate, experienced, well-connected, and influential people who shared Chaucer's interest in reading, making, and interpreting texts. In 1376, for a mission 'in secretis negociis domini regis' [on the king's secret affairs],[41] and for which Chaucer received a handsome ten marks (£6. 13s. 4d.), his co-traveller was Sir John de Burley, brother of the

Sir Simon Burley who was a *magister* (master) and royal tutor to Richard II. Simon became Richard's confidant and subsequently rose to the powerful post of vice-chamberlain, thereby controlling access to the king. One book owned by the king's tutor was *De regimine principum* (*On the Rule of Kings*) by Giles of Rome, which Simon may well have used to instruct Richard in the arts of governance.[42] A second royal tutor with whom Chaucer travelled was Sir Guichard d'Angle, one of his associates at the marriage negotiations in Montreuil in 1377. Sir Guichard was a Frenchman who had been captured at Poitiers, thereupon deciding to change sides and serve the Black Prince.

Another of Chaucer's companions at Montreuil, Sir Richard Stury, was a lifelong associate with strong literary interests. Stury, too, had been captured and ransomed at Rheims. A friend also of Froissart, Stury possessed a copy of the *Roman de la rose* (now London, British Library, MS Royal 19 B. xiii) and was familiar with the poetry of Eustache Deschamps.[43] Stury became a chamber knight (i.e. he had special access to the king), like another chamber knight with literary leanings, Sir John Clanvowe, whose own compositions betray the influence of Chaucer's writings. Both Stury and Clanvowe were also members of the group of so-called 'Lollard knights' linked to Richard's court until Lollardy became too closely identified with sedition. Stury was obliged by Richard to abjure heresy on pain of execution. Although not a travelling companion as such (except in the figurative sense) Chaucer's friend, the poet John Gower, helped him in his arrangements for foreign travel. The lawyer addressed as 'moral Gower' in the envoy to *Troilus and Criseyde* was given power of attorney while Chaucer was absent in Lombardy from 28 May to 19 September 1378.[44]

The implication of the foregoing remarks is that Chaucer's life records, among which the documents concerning travel form a significant proportion, should not be regarded as in some way distinct from Chaucer's life as a writer, even though they make no specific reference to his literary activities. Documents from the National Archives Office bearing Chaucer's name and poems that he wrote are all evidence of the same life. At the same time, it is necessary to exercise extreme caution in making correlations between life-record and writings. While it is reasonable to assume that travel broadened Chaucer's experience, the process whereby that experience became literary content is less certain.[45] Chaucer, we may be sure, witnessed war at first hand. His perception of war may indeed have been coloured by the kind of chivalric idealism that permeates Froissart's *Chroniques*, but he must also have seen that the practice of war could be horrific. When, in the Knight's Tale, he describes paintings in the temple of Mars, he appears to do so with an eye to realism. The god's effects are captured in a desolate, sterile, and threatening wasteland, 'With knotty, knarry [gnarled], bareyne trees olde, / Of stubbes [stumps] sharpe and hidouse to biholde' (I.1977–8). The narrator goes on to describe a stable blazing with black smoke, a corpse with his throat cut, a town destroyed, and ships burning as they danced on the sea. What better description could there be of the effects of war in France, which included devastating raids, or *chevauchées*, designed to pillage the countryside and terrify the populace, sieges that left towns and cities looted and in ruins, and sea battles, such as the decisive one at Sluys in 1340 that saw the French fleet destroyed by fire'?

Attention to Chaucer's source material creates a rather different impression. The gnarled trees and barren wood derive from Boccaccio's *Teseida*, which may also have suggested the ships, the murder, and the destruction of a city.[46] Even so, there appears to be a residue of vivid detail that is Chaucer's own, such as the sharp, hideous tree stumps. Could not this be a clear-cut case of Chaucer using his first-hand knowledge of war, as gained during travels in France, to ground his description in experience and to accentuate the horrors of a kind of war he saw for himself? This is treacherous ground, a bog of hypothesis and speculation. The truth is, we do not know what Chaucer saw, what he (as opposed to his persona or narrator) thought of war, nor how he transmuted his experience, if at all, into literature. The matter is further complicated by the presence in Chaucer's description of iconographic motifs traditionally associated with the depiction of Mars, and by the presumptions which a modern reader brings to the literature of travel. Romantic notions of the permeability of experience and art are out of place; and the psycho-geographical novella, generated by the interplay of writer and place, had yet to be invented. The *Travels of Sir John Mandeville* (before 1371), purporting to be an eyewitness report but wholly invented, is a cautionary tale.[47]

The fit between travel record and poetry can be more secure. As already noted, Chaucer journeyed to Navarre in 1366 with three unnamed companions. At that time the Black Prince, as Duke of Aquitaine, was in alliance with the former king of Castile, Pedro the Cruel, who had been ousted by his bastard half-brother, Henry of Trastamara.[48] The Black Prince planned to restore Pedro to the throne and so consolidate his own position as a regional overlord. His plans foundered when Henry betrayed and murdered Pedro in 1369. Two years later the Prince's brother, John of Gaunt, married Pedro's daughter, Constance of Castile. Chaucer's wife, Philippa, was for a time a member of Constance's London household. So the events in Navarre, in which Chaucer participated in some way, were also close to home. When he wrote up Pedro's story in the Monk's Tale (VII.2375–90) as an item in the Monk's catalogue of tragic figures, the style was unusually direct and forceful. Pedro is the 'glorie of Spayne', favoured by Fortune but forced to flee from his land by his own brother. Thereafter Henry betrays him at a siege 'by subtiltee', killing Pedro by his own hand after luring him into his tent. Nor does Chaucer mince his words in describing the role of Bertrand du Guesclin, Henry's ally. Categorically identified by his arms as the instigator of 'this cursednesse and al this synne' (2385), Bertrand is held up as an example of treachery as heinous as Ganelon's betrayal of Roland.

When it came to taking advantage of his travels to meet other writers, the English poet was a victim of circumstance and a master of missed opportunities. Present in Rheims in 1360 at the time of the English siege was the French court poet, Guillaume de Machaut. Machaut was one of the young Chaucer's literary idols, whose works he used to model early compositions in the dream vision idiom. Also present in Rheims was Eustache Deschamps, an early reader and admirer of Chaucer's poetry whose *Miroir de Mariage* in turn influenced the English poet.[49] The hostilities, and Chaucer's own capture, were hardly conducive to literary discussions. Thirteen years later, Chaucer was again in close range of two famous writers who were to exert an even more profound influence on his development. While Chaucer was in Florence, Petrarch was not far away at Padua or Arqua and Giovanni Boccaccio was either in Florence itself or in nearby Certaldo. There is no evidence that Chaucer met either of them.

Imagining Chaucer in Florence, hobnobbing with Petrarch and Boccaccio, has its attractions.[50] While Chaucer was there, in 1373, Boccaccio was being touted as the person with the right cultural credentials to deliver the first in a series of lectures on Dante. The *Lecturae Dantis*—the first of which Boccaccio did indeed deliver—were designed by the citizens of Florence to rehabilitate the exiled author of the *Divina comedia* as one of their own.[51] Did Chaucer also admire in the same city—as Boccaccio had done, and as a modern cultural tourist still does—the naturalistic paintings of Giotto and his followers? If so, was that new aesthetic a spur to Chaucer's own narrative realism? Who knows?[52] But Chaucer's visits to Italy constitute, undoubtedly, a special case.[53] For it is after them that the writings first of Dante, then of Petrarch and Boccaccio, take hold of Chaucer's imagination and become an enduring feature of it, from the *House of Fame* (Dante), through the Knight's Tale and *Troilus* (Boccaccio) to the Clerk's Tale (Petrarch). He also absorbed from Italian literary culture the idea of the poet as a semi-public figure acclaimed and recognized for his achievement. Chaucer's pilgrim Clerk claims to have learned his story of patient Griselde 'at Padowe [Padua] of a worthy clerk' called 'Fraunceys Petrak, the lauriat poete, / . . . whos rethorike sweete / Enlumyned al Ytaille of poetrie' (IV.27–33).

If Chaucer's Italianism does not derive from meeting Petrarch and Boccaccio in person it must have been generated by encounters with books obtained through other intermediaries. Given the date from which Italian literature affects Chaucer's work, and the unlikelihood of finding compositions by Dante or contemporary Italian authors in London, Chaucer probably acquired or consulted his Italian books— Filippo Ceffi's translation of and commentary on Ovid's *Heroïdes*, Dante's *Comedía*, Petrarch's *Liber Griseldis*, Boccaccio's *Filostrato, Teseida*, and *Decameron*—as a direct result of visiting Florence and Milan. Paying attention not just to the texts, but to the kind of book Chaucer is likely to have encountered, has important implications for our own reception of his writings. As K. P. Clarke has recently shown, the *paratexte* (the apparatus of glosses, text divisions, rubrics) alerts us to possibilities of meaning and interpretation that would have been apparent to Chaucer himself.[54] He was certainly in each place long enough to undertake literary pursuits. He left England for Genoa and Florence on 1 December 1372, crossing the Alps in winter and arriving back on 23 May of the following year.[55] Allowing approximately one month to travel there and another month to return, Chaucer was in Italy for almost three months. The subsequent visit to Lombardy (1378) gave him some five or six weeks in Milan. In Italy, in the course of supporting the diplomatic endeavours of the English Crown, Chaucer would have mixed with a wealthy and influential intelligentsia of merchants, diplomats, and members of the nobility who knew, admired, and possessed writings by Dante, Petrarch, and Boccaccio. Some even went so far as to make their own copies of admired literary works. Chaucer may also have had access to the Visconti libraries in

Milan and the nearby Pavia—both of them places where Petrarch had worked for his patrons, the Visconti.[56]

As earlier intimated, the processes of cultural influence and exchange are complex, interactive, and obscure. We should not assume too readily that Chaucer's sedentary activities (reading and writing) and his travelling for the court (undergoing experiences) are two sides of the same coin. There were occasions when the experience acquired while travelling affected the content of what was written; very seldom was it the case that the experience was transmuted directly into literature. Travel enabled Chaucer to enlarge his cultural horizons, but if he capitalized on that enlargement it was not by transcribing experience, or by meeting other writers, but by the acquisition of new books. It seems disappointing to conclude that it was, once more, books that were Chaucer's chief point of access to other cultures. Yet without his travels, especially those to Italy, it is doubtful that he would have been alerted to texts that became the foundation stones of some of his most accomplished works. It is also the case that some of the obscurity surrounding Chaucer's travels for the court might yet be dispelled. There is much to learn about their immediate context in the practices of late medieval English diplomacy.[57] A detailed and extended study of the relevant personnel, the patterns of patronage, the objectives of the various missions, and the itineraries, has yet to be undertaken, but it would considerably enlarge our understanding of Chaucer's specific roles and their literary implications.

BIBLIOGRAPHY

Bertolet, Craig E., 'Chaucer's Envoys and the Poet-Diplomat', *Chaucer Review* 33 (1998), 66–89.

Butterfield, Ardis, 'Chaucerian Vernaculars', *Studies in the Age of Chaucer* 31 (2009), 23–51.

Clarke, K. P., *Chaucer and Italian Textuality*, Oxford English Monographs (Oxford: Oxford University Press, 2011).

Crow, Martin C. and Clair C. Olson, eds., *Chaucer Life-Records* (Oxford: Clarendon Press, 1966).

Friedman, John Block and Figg, Kristen Mossler, eds., *Trade, Travel and Exploration in the Middle Ages: An Encyclopaedia* (New York: Garland, 2000).

Hanly, Michael, 'Courtiers and Poets: An International System of Literary Exchange in Late Fourteenth-Century Italy, France and England', *Viator* 28 (1997), 305–32.

Pearsall, Derek, *The Life of Geoffrey Chaucer: A Critical Biography* (Oxford: Blackwell, 1992).

Wallace, David, 'Chaucer's Italian Inheritance', in *The Cambridge Companion to Chaucer*, eds. Piero Boitani and Jill Mann, 2nd ed. (Cambridge: Cambridge University Press, 1986), 19–37.

Westrem, Scott D. 'Geography and Travel', in *A Companion to Chaucer*, ed. Peter Brown (Oxford: Blackwell, 2000), 195–217.

Wimsatt, James I., *Chaucer and His French Contemporaries: Natural Music in the Fourteenth Century* (Toronto: University of Toronto Press, 1991).

NOTES

1. For a reconstruction of Chaucer's probable route to and from Florence and Genoa in 1372-3, see George B. Parks, 'The Route of Chaucer's First Journey to Italy', *English Language History* 16 (1949), 174-87.
2. Martin C. Crow and Clair C. Olson, eds., *Chaucer Life-Records* (Oxford: Clarendon Press, 1966), 29.
3. Wendy Childs, 'Anglo-Italian Contacts in the Fourteenth Century', in *Chaucer and the Italian Trecento*, ed. Piero Boitani (Cambridge: Cambridge University Press, 1983), 75-6; George B. Parks, *The English Traveler to Italy, Volume 1: The Middle Ages to 1525* (Rome: Edizioni di Storia e Letteratura, 1954), 277-81.
4. Crow and Olson, *Chaucer Life-Records*, 13-18.
5. Ibid., 62-4.
6. Ibid., 40-2; David Wallace, *Premodern Places: Calais to Surinam, Chaucer to Aphra Behn* (Oxford: Blackwell, 2004), 187-8.
7. Crow and Olson, *Chaucer Life-Records*, 402-76.
8. Ibid., 477-89.
9. Derek Pearsall, *The Life of Geoffrey Chaucer: A Critical Biography* (Oxford: Blackwell, 1992), 12; Wallace, *Premodern Places*, 102.
10. Richard Firth Green, *Poets and Princepleasers: Literature and the English Court in the Late Middle Ages* (Toronto: University of Toronto Press, 1980), 77-100; Rossell Hope Robbins, 'Geoffroi Chaucier, Poète Français, Father of English Poetry', *Chaucer Review* 13 (1978), 93-115.
11. See, by way of comparison, Derek Pearsall, 'Chaucer and Englishness', in *Chaucer's Cultural Geography*, ed. Kathryn L. Lynch (New York: Routledge, 2002), 281-301.
12. Michael Hanly, 'France', in *A Companion to Chaucer*, ed. Peter Brown (Oxford: Blackwell, 2000), 151-7; Helen Phillips, 'The French Background', in *Chaucer: An Oxford Guide*, ed. Steve Ellis (Oxford: Oxford University Press, 2005), 292-5; Elizabeth Salter, 'Chaucer and Internationalism', in *English and International: Studies in the Literature, Art and Patronage of Medieval England*, ed. Derek Pearsall and Nicolette Zeeman (Cambridge: Cambridge University Press, 1988), 240-4; Ardis Butterfield, *The Familiar Enemy: Chaucer, Language, and Nation in the Hundred Years War* (Oxford: Oxford University Press, 2010) 176-9.
13. For Chaucer's connections with Machaut, Froissart and Grandson see James I. Wimsatt, *Chaucer and His French Contemporaries: Natural Music in the Fourteenth Century* (Toronto: University of Toronto Press, 1991), chapters 4-7.
14. Childs, 'Anglo-Italian Contacts', 78-9.
15. Scott D. Westrem, 'Geography and Travel', in Brown, *Companion to Chaucer*, 198-203; Diana Webb, 'Pilgrims in a Landscape', in *Pilgrimage in Medieval England* (London and New York: Hambledon and London, 2000), 215-32; and her *Pilgrims and Pilgrimage in the Medieval West* (London and New York: Tauris, 1999), 163-7, 225-7.
16. K. B. McFarlane, *Lancastrian Kings and Lollard Knights* (Oxford: Clarendon Press, 1972), 199-206.
17. John Block Friedman and Kristen Mossler Figg, eds., *Trade, Travel and Exploration in the Middle Ages: An Encyclopedia* (New York: Garland, 2000).
18. Summarized in Westrem, 'Geography and Travel', 196-8; Pearsall, *Life of Chaucer*, 51-5.
19. Crow and Olson, *Chaucer Life-Records*, 44-53.
20. Ibid., 44.

21. Ibid., 52.

22. Ibid., 19–22.

23. Ibid., 31.

24. Ibid., 32–40.

25. Ibid., 54.

26. Ibid., 49.

27. Ibid., 61.

28. Ibid., 52–3. On the range of social groups engaged in diplomacy, see G. P. Cuttino, *English Diplomatic Administration 1259-1339*, 2nd ed. (Oxford: Clarendon Press, 1971), 134. Chaucer belonged to Cuttino's 'large and heterogeneous' third group. For a discussion of the role of *nuncius* as a 'living letter' see Donald E. Queller, 'The Nuncius', in *The Office of the Ambassador in the Middle Ages* (Princeton, NJ: Princeton University Press, 1967), 3–25.

29. Froissart, *Chroniques*, ed. de Lettenhove and cited in Crow and Olson, *Chaucer Life-Records*, 50; ed. and trans. Geoffrey Brereton in Jean Froissart, *Chronicles*, rev. ed. (Harmondsworth: Penguin, 1978), 194.

30. Crow and Olson, *Chaucer Life-Records*, 19–20.

31. Pearsall, *Life of Chaucer*, 42.

32. Crow and Olson, *Chaucer Life-Records*, 23–8.

33. Ibid., 370.

34. Ardis Butterfield, 'Chaucerian Vernaculars', *Studies in the Age of Chaucer* 31 (2009), 23–51; her 'French Culture and the Ricardian Court', in *Essays on Ricardian Literature in Honour of J. A. Burrow*, ed. A. J. Minnis, Charlotte Morse and Thorlac Turville-Petre (Oxford: Clarendon Press, 1997), 82–120; and see now her *Familiar Enemy*; also W. Rothwell, 'The Trilingual England of Geoffrey Chaucer', *Studies in the Age of Chaucer* 16 (1994), 45–67.

35. James I. Wimsatt, *Chaucer and the Poems of 'Ch' in University of Pennsylvania Manuscript French 15*, Chaucer Studies 9 (Cambridge: D. S. Brewer, 1982).

36. Howard H. Schless, *Chaucer and Dante: A Revaluation* (Norman, OK: Pilgrim Books, 1984), 4–8; G. A. Holmes, 'Florentine Merchants in England, 1346-1436', *Economic History Review*, n. s. 13 (1960), 200–4.

37. Childs, 'Anglo-Italian Contacts', 66–75.

38. Queller, *Office of Ambassador*, 7–8.

39. Crow and Olson, *Chaucer Life-Records*, 271–4.

40. V. J. Scattergood, 'Literary Culture at the Court of Richard II', in *English Court Culture in the Later Middle Ages*, ed. V. J. Scattergood and J. W. Sherborne (London: Duckworth, 1983), 29–44.

41. Crow and Olson, *Chaucer Life-Records*, 42–3.

42. Stephen H. Rigby, *Wisdom and Chivalry: Chaucer's* Knight's Tale *and Medieval Political Theory*, Medieval and Renaissance Texts and Authors Vol. 4 (Leiden: Brill, 2009).

43. Salter, 'Chaucer and Internationalism', 243–4.

44. Crow and Olson, *Chaucer Life-Records*, 54.

45. See, by way of comparison Wallace, 'In Flaundres', in *Premodern Places*, 91–138 on the idea of Flanders (as well as its actuality) in Chaucer's writing.

46. Piero Boitani, *Chaucer and Boccaccio*, Medium Aevum Monographs, n.s. 7 (Oxford: Society for the Study of Mediaeval Languages and Literature, 1977), 82–7; *Teseida* in Nick Havely, ed. and trans. *Chaucer's Boccaccio: Sources of* Troilus *and the Knight's and Franklin's Tales*, Chaucer Studies 3 (Cambridge: Brewer, 1980), 125–7.

47. M. C. Seymour, 'Sir John Mandeville', in *Authors of the Middle Ages Volume 3: English Writers of the Late Middle Ages*, ed. M. C. Seymour (Aldershot: Variorum, 1994), 1–64; Stephen Greenblatt, 'From the Dome of the Rock to the Rim of the World', in *Marvelous Possessions: The Wonder of the New World* (Chicago, IL: Chicago University Press, 1991), 26–51.

48. Benjamin F. Taggie, 'Chaucer in Spain: The Historical Context', in *Spain and the Mediterranean*, ed. Benjamin F. Taggie, Richard W. Clement, and James E. Caraway, Mediterranean Studies 3 (Kirksville, MO: Thomas Jefferson University Press, 1992), 35–44.

49. Butterfield, *Familiar Enemy*, 174–5; Wimsatt, *Chaucer and His French Contemporaries*, 78–84 and 242–72.

50. Crow and Olson, *Chaucer Life-Records*, Carol Falvo Heffernan, *Comedy in Chaucer and Boccaccio*, Chaucer Studies 40 (Cambridge: Brewer, 2009), 8–13.

51. David Wallace, 'Chaucer's Italian Inheritance', in *The Cambridge Companion to Chaucer*, ed. Piero Boitani and Jill Mann, 2nd ed. (Cambridge: Cambridge University Press, 1986), 39.

52. John Larner, 'Chaucer's Italy', in Boitani, *Chaucer and the Italian Trecento*, 14–18.

53. For discussion see David Wallace, 'Chaucer in Florence and Lombardy', in *Chaucerian Polity: Absolutist Lineages and Associational Forms in England and Italy*, Figurae: Reading Medieval Culture (Stanford, CA: Stanford University Press, 1997), 9–64; David Wallace, 'Italy', in Brown, *Companion to Chaucer*, 218–20; Nick Havely, 'The Italian Background', in *Chaucer: An Oxford Guide*, ed. Ellis, 313–20; Pearsall, *Life of Chaucer*, 102–9.

54. K. P. Clarke, *Chaucer and Italian Textuality*, Oxford English Monographs (Oxford: Oxford University Press, 2011).

55. On possible itineraries and the speed of travel, see Childs, 'Anglo-Italian Contacts', 66.

56. William E. Coleman, 'Chaucer, the *Teseida*, and the Visconti Library at Pavia: A Hypothesis', *Medium Aevum* 51 (1982), 92–101; Robert A. Pratt, 'Chaucer and the Visconti Libraries', *English Language History* 6 (1939), 191–9.

57. Butterfield, 'Chaucerian Vernaculars', 44; Craig E. Bertolet, 'Chaucer's Envoys and the Poet-Diplomat', *Chaucer Review* 33 (1998), 66–89; Michael Hanly, 'Courtiers and Poets: An International System of Literary Exchange in Late Fourteenth-Century Italy, France and England', *Viator* 28 (1997), 305–32.

CHAPTER 2

CHAUCER AND CONTEMPORARY COURTS OF LAW AND POLITICS

House, Law, Game

MATTHEW GIANCARLO

DREAMS OF COURT

FOR an introduction to Chaucer's representations of courts, a good beginning is to look at one of his own introductions. Like the openings of many of his works, the prologue to the *Legend of Good Women* seems almost needlessly complex. The author-narrator begins philosophically, musing on the limits of human knowledge and the value of books that tell 'olde appreved stories' (F 21). He loves these old books and there is no 'game' (33) or diversion that can tear him away from his study. No game, that is, until 'the month of May' (36) comes, when he declares 'Farewel my bok and my devocioun!' (39). He praises spring and his favourite flowers, the 'daysyes' (43) that are his special object of affection. In his 'cas' (70) or plea of love for the daisy he also calls on 'lovers that kan make of sentement / . . . / Whethir ye ben with the leef or with the flour' (69–72), alluding to May Day games of courtly debate between supporters of the flower (beauty, delicacy, evanescence) or the leaf (constancy, strength, endurance). For the narrator, devotion to his flower is the only path. So he goes out before dawn to be at the 'resureccioun' (110) of the flower with the sunrise. There he stays all day, in company with the birds who 'songen all of oon acord' in praise of the spring, 'oure governour and lord' (F 169–70). When the sun goes down, so too do the flower and its devotee. The narrator returns to his house and bids his servants to make him a couch in his garden where he can sleep *en plein air* strewn with flowers (200–7).

Sleeping in this interior space made to resemble an exterior, he dreams of lying again in the field with his beloved flower. But if before the scene was elegant and joyous, now his dream is strangely threatening, even as it repeats many of the same elements. Now he sees 'the god of Love' (F 213) and his queen, both resplendent, and she is festooned 'lyk a daysie for to sene' (224). They are accompanied by a troop of women who, like the birds before, sing 'with o vois' (296) in praise of the daisy. But the god of Love looks on the narrator 'sternely' (239) and threateningly, and he accuses him of capital trespass. He charges the poet not just with presumption for approaching 'so nygh myn oune floure' but with being Love's enemy or 'foo' for having written 'heresye' against his 'lawe' (316, 322, 330). The poet has defamed love and women, and he must answer for it; the punishments for his error will be both cruel and exemplary (340). The ensuing deliberation focuses on a lengthy exchange between the daisy-queen Alceste and the god of Love. Alceste intercedes on behalf of the accused poet like an attorney pleading for a client. There are liars and envious back-biters in the court, she says, who have defamed him; he wrote his offending works in ignorance or under duress of commission; a true lord should not be like 'tirauntz of Lumbardye' (374) who act without justice or due process; and in other works the poet had praised and 'furthred wel' (413) the 'lawe' of the god of Love. The Queen also remarks that the accused should be given the chance to 'replye' to the charges (343). But when the narrator does presume to speak for himself—and this only indirectly to Love, through an appeal to Alceste (455–74)—she tells him to keep quiet: 'Lat be thyn arguynge, / For Love ne wol nat countrepleted be / In ryght ne wrong; and lerne that at me!' (475–7). Love will suffer no 'counterplea', a term of legal art,[1] as courtly games and jocose elegance have abruptly given way to a trial for the poet's life.

The point, which almost certainly was not lost on Chaucer's audience, is that the distance from the one to the other—from noble court to legal court—was very short indeed. Understanding this proximity helps us to make sense of this precipitous shift as we are brought from philosophical ruminations and courtly games, thence to a nervous scene of legal judgment and sentence, and then back again to the poet's diversions, but this time figured as his penance and punishment. In so doing, as fundamentally artful and humorous as it is, the Prologue to the *Legend of Good Women* neatly captures the complexity and serious vicissitudes of 'the court' in Chaucer's time in its different but related meanings: noble household, field of play, court of law.

These juxtapositions are biographically apt. All through his life, from youth to death, Chaucer was a court man. The earliest extant records situate him in a noble household, that of Elizabeth the Countess of Ulster and Prince Lionel the Earl of Ulster. He was a servant in the royal households of Edward III and Richard II, and he was connected to the House of Lancaster from 1374 onwards, down to the time of his final annuities from Henry IV in the last years of his life.[2] Much of the best modern Chaucer scholarship has illuminated the environment of the English court and royal affinity as a cradle of literary and artistic production, for Chaucer and others.[3] But beyond the princely court—itself remarkably complex—there lie the further associations of courts in both social and juridical contexts that give particular life to the many 'jurisprudential topoi' to be found in Chaucer's works.[4] Such imaginings of courts in these related senses—social, legal, and ludic—can sometimes be opaque to the modern reader, and they stand to be situated in the broader context of medieval European court cultures. My focus here, then, will be on explicating that context, and on some of those Chaucerian moments of trial which, like the opening of the *Legend*, help us to understand how his writings often connected these interrelated ideas of court.

HOUSE AND LAW

From the outset it is worth remembering that until relatively recently, Europe was a court culture. Social and governmental formations revolved around princely courts, and the legal systems characteristic of the West developed with them. Roman and non-Roman antecedents provide only loose sources and analogues for what would become, as the legal historian Harold Berman and others have demonstrated, fundamental court elements in medieval societies: far-reaching household jurisdictions; administrative and social apparatuses centred on noble and ecclesial households, primarily (but not limited to) the great households of regional and national elites; the intermingling of 'folk right' or customary law, canon and civil law, and other sources of law, particularly royal statute law; and related to all this, the expansions and multiplicity of competing jurisdictions, as courts and households also often competed.[5] In this regard it is absolutely central that the development of medieval 'states' was predicated upon the plenitude and multiplicity of courts and jurisdictions, and upon their power as social as well as political centres of authority. The 'sociogenesis of the state' in its western manifestations was a product, by and large, of court growth and development, as a *Rechtsstaat* or 'law state' naturally manifests itself in a multitude of courts.[6]

Thus from the early Middle Ages onward, the various fields and elements of law were tied to courts in their social as much as their legal understanding. The situation was highly developed by Chaucer's time but fundamentally no different. England was precocious in its early and vigorous growth of a far-reaching legal apparatus headed by the king's royal courts, and by the regularized body of common law and procedures of jury that came to distinguish its secular jurisdiction. The fourteenth century in particular has been characterized as the time when English expectations of the law and of law-courts formalized into the sort of field-specific and rationalized understanding of 'law' as we have it today: independent juridical tribunals following well-established procedures of justice with a professionalized personnel, body of writing, and bureaucratic apparatus.[7] At the same time English law also retained its courtly nature in the other sense, as law was everywhere still a matter of households: manorial or borough or seigneurial law; the laws of the courts of merchants or guilds or staples; canon law as enforced by the households of bishops and archbishops; urban law as the laws and mercantile regulations of discrete communities; and the household of the king's court, expressed variously in stable courts such as the King's Bench and Common Pleas, or peripatetically with justices in eyre, courts of trailbaston, or the court of the Verge.[8] The king's other courts (Exchequer and Chancery) were eventually, like the King's Bench and Common Pleas, to be located semi-permanently around the palace of Westminster. But this did not alter their fundamental identity as courts of the royal court, subject to the will of the king as the head of his household.

The details of one episode during Chaucer's lifetime can stand as an explanatory example. When Richard II pushed his conflict with the city of London to the point of crisis in 1392, angry at the city's refusal to lend him money, he removed the royal court to York.[9] The sanction was not just the loss of royal prerogative for the city, but as the Westminster Chronicle explains:

> [I]t was rather upon the king and the people of the kingdom that far greater damage was in consequence inflicted than on London, since through the removal of the courts the poor had to abandon their pleas, not only because they had not the money to travel to a place so far away but also because, owing to the suddenness of the transfer and their inability to be their own advisers about their lawsuits, they were so dismayed and shocked that they that they could be said to be almost out of their minds.[10]

Londoners were dismayed as much or more about restricted access to royal law as they were about access to the king. Richard declared his judgment against the city while he was holding his magnificent court at Westminster. Queen Anne is recorded to have pleaded on her knees, Alcestis-like, on behalf of the Londoners.[11] The royal and legal courts returned to London only after the city's submission and the payment of a heavy fine. When he did return, Richard processed from his palace at Sheen to be received by all the city's guilds and the city government. Among the splendours in his progress he received a gold tablet (*tabulum auream*) at Temple Bar, the westernmost boundary of the city between London and Westminster, as well as a large silver and gilt table (*tabulum mensalem argenteam ac deauratum longitudine novum pedum*) presented at a banquet. The gifts expressed the hope that the king's household 'tables' and 'benches', domestic and judicial, would stay firmly located with the city. The chronicler goes on to note that Richard returned all customary liberties to London except three, each pertaining directly to juridical matters: restriction of endowments to chantries; attaint of jurors for false verdicts; and restriction of villein franchise within the city walls.[12] Thus the return of Richard's royal household court was also punctuated by the imposition of his direct control over the law courts and municipal privileges.[13]

The court of the king is the obvious and extreme example of this conflation of house and law, but it is extreme only in degree, not kind. Great lords and 'princes of the realm' were distinguished by their juridical authority and judicial power as much as anything else. They presided as heads of their own baronial and manorial courts, sat on central court benches, served in inquiries of justice, and deliberated as judicial 'peers of the realm' in the king's high court of parliament. Aristocratic court power was legal power, and vice versa. The number and overlapping nature of such jurisdictions—what Musson and Ormrod have called a 'palimpsest of jurisdictions'[14]—can strike a modern observer as remarkable and oppressive, and predictably the weight of the courts fell heaviest on those at the bottom of the social scale. Church consistory courts, manorial and baronial courts, courts of regional communities of the hundred and the vill, as well as urban and mercantile courts, all could impose extensive restrictions and sanctions upon personal and public behaviour. These ranged from taxes and duties to regulations of living and working conditions, and impositions on peasants such as 'heriot' (death duty payments), 'merchet' (fine for marriage of a daughter), 'leyrwite' (fine for female unchastity), and more.[15] The courts were everywhere a strong tool for forcible class exploitation. Indeed the status of a serf or unfree peasant was defined by exclusion from access to royal justice in the king's courts, which is to say it was a court status. The social identity of the serf was bound to the hegemony of a baronial manor expressed in the jurisdiction of the manorial court.

But even for a system of dependent feudal exploitation as stratified as this, it is important to understand how dialectical and complex the actual operations of courts could be. Manorial courts, for example, were highly participatory, including even dependents and peasants as judges.[16] Courts were competitive, as subjects from one jurisdiction or region could flee—and, after the pestilence of 1348, often did flee—to other less exploitive manors and jurisdictions. Ecclesial jurisdiction often overlapped with secular. And from the twelfth century onward in England, the expansion of royal justice directly competed with local and manorial courts.[17] The multiplicity of court jurisdictions was thus not simply a matter of piling oppression upon oppression. It facilitated the possibility of searching out better (or at least more amenable) judgments in different courts. It also fostered a critical awareness of how justice could be defined differently in different settings, and that one form of justice would find its limit or boundary at the borders of another. Justice was not, nor had it ever been, univocal, even as a strong cultural emphasis was put upon the universality and uniformity of reason and justice, and upon speaking 'in accord' and 'with one voice' in matters of faith and law.

The period's obsession with 'trouthe', both personal and public or political, is an indirect and frequently anxious acknowledgment of this conundrum.[18] Generally, the court mentality of the period expressed the complex and sometimes contradictory interplay of strongly held notions of authority and right. Chaucer's era was deeply litigious, and the explosion of litigation seems to have gone hand-in-hand with disillusionment in the very systems of justice and governance so many people were appealing to so widely. Courts were both desired and derided.[19] The well-studied events of the Revolt of 1381 offer fascinating examples of this dynamic, in which even revolutionary acts were guided by court-law ideology.[20] Even in their most violent and illegal actions, the rebels explicitly mimicked or mocked judicial proceedings, as the Westminster chronicler repeatedly notes. The Archbishop of Canterbury and the Royal Treasurer, Simon Sudbury and Robert Hales, as well as other court officials and a group of Flemish merchants, were all ritually beheaded—decollation being a standard judicial punishment—'sine processu sive judicio...sine judicio et sine causa...sine aliquo judicii processu' [without trial or judgment...without judgment or trial...without any judicial process].[21] Famously the Savoy Palace, the opulent London residence of John of Gaunt the Duke of Lancaster, was destroyed and its household records burnt. But anyone daring to steal goods from the house 'sine processu sive judicio ad mortem rapiebatur decapitandus' [was haled away, without trial or judgment, to death by beheading]—a curious imitation of a criminal sentence, but one imposed by criminals for a criminal act committed during a criminal act.[22] Similarly destroyed was the house of Richard Imworth, the keeper of the Marshalsea prison of the courts of the King's Bench, and he too was beheaded. Other houses and courts were targeted, not randomly, but specifically as houses of law and noble or institutional authority: Clerkenwell Hospital, the London Guildhall, Hales' manor house, and others.[23]

Following the killing of the rebel leaders and the re-establishment of official order, the judicial short-shrift and beheadings went the other way. The friends and wives of the murdered Flemings were even allowed to exact punishments personally. Lest all authority and order be upended in an orgy of illegal retributions, the king then declared that a verdict of three separate juries would be necessary for attaint and capital sentence.[24] All but the most central rebel leaders were pardoned the full rigors of the law. But even accounting for the court-legal posturings of both sides, perhaps the most striking aspect of the Revolt is that, as Nigel Saul notes, 'these men were not down-and-outs. Many were among the most successful proprietors in their village [and] a high proportion of the rebels had held office in the manor as well…Three-quarters of the known rebels from Essex, Suffolk, and Kent are known to have served as reeves, pledges, bailiffs, jurors, aletasters, constables or in other positions of local responsibility.'[25] Not just villeins or the disenfranchised, it was, rather, the courtly servants of law and household who were destroying the legal records and burning down the house. They did so with those same courts in mind as inverted models of legitimacy.

Plainly enough, the very idea of a court was socially charged. For Chaucer, the fundamental complexity of this court mentality can inform our understanding of his biography as well as his writing. Certainly Chaucer was no rebel, and the extensive documentary record of his relations with households and courts gives no hint of any sympathies in that direction. But if he was a lifelong court man, he was also uniquely positioned to reflect upon the problematic and sometimes oppressive nature of court authority. Chaucer was a worker in the court system in all senses, acting as a household official and judicial authority in several capacities. His early positions as valet and diplomat were bureaucratic employments in and by the royal household of Edward III, and they are consonant with his various later appointments under Richard II: as controller in the port of London for 1374–86, Justice of the Peace for Kent in 1385–9, Clerk of the King's Works in 1389–91, and others.

Interspersed among these jobs are records of Chaucer's experience with legal and political courts. His legal record is extensive and, for the period, unremarkable. He was a parliamentary representative as Knight of the Shire for Kent in 1386; a justice *ad inquirendum* (that is, justice on a panel of judicial inquiry) for a case of child abduction in 1387; appointed legal guardian for two Kentish heirs in 1375; he gave testimony in the dispute between Sir Richard Scrope and Sir Robert Grosvenor in 1386; stood as main-prise or legal surety (a kind of bail-bondsman) for others on several occasions; had actions of debt, a charge of trespass and contempt, and most infamously a quitclaim of rape brought against him (in 1388–98, 1379, and 1380 respectively); and more.[26] As much as 'Chaucer was the police' or 'an official of the repressive apparatus of the state', as one critic has described him, the poet was also subject to the procedures, inquiries, and harassments of the courts throughout his life.[27] As late as 1398 in what may have been a special favor from Richard II, Chaucer received a royal writ of protection from plaints and lawsuits.[28] And more broadly, in the years of unrest and baronial revolt in 1386–8, and then during Richard's later retaliation and eventual deposition in 1397–9, parliament and the royal court became the literal court-stage for violent struggles between the king and his baronial adversaries. During these periods, and others, political violence played out with all the trappings of legal procedure. Even workers and functionaries at Chaucer's level might get caught up in the trouble, as household turmoils and political manoeuvring could become serious threats to life and limb.[29] Such a long and complex experience with courts—which was for Chaucer, as for others, both adversarial and cooperative—would have had, we might reasonably expect, a similarly complex reflection in his writing.

GAME

A critical perspective on courts and households, then, would not necessarily have entailed only their outright rejection or, as with the rebels of 1381, a mimetic attempt at their dismantling. Nor must we necessarily conclude that, as a poet so bound up in the systems of household and law, 'the end product of Chaucer's literary labours…was the articulation of hegemony' *tout court*.[30] As the Prologue to *The Legend of Good Women* suggests in its form, a courtly author could be caught between the dreamy evocation of elite cultured ideals and a nightmarish legal subjection to those same courts of judgment. If poetry sublimates these hegemonic elements into a literary game, it does so from the critical perspective of personnel whose liminality makes them, as Bourdieu succinctly put it, the dominated segment of the dominating class.[31] For this perspective Chaucer could hardly have a better avatar than the narrator of the *Legend*, who is threatened with attainder and released on mainprise with the requirement that he provide the court with evidence of his reform, namely, a series of acceptably courtly poems. There is little room for counterpleading here, but the dialectic of the opening scenario itself presents tensions that were the ground and condition of critical artistic practice as much as of social identity and legal subjection.[32]

In this regard Chaucer can easily be situated with his contemporaries. Games were a central part of court life and were themselves frequent images and metaphors for it.[33] Courtly games and diversions are central to several of Chaucer's narratives, such as *Troilus and Criseyde* and the Franklin's Tale. The popularity of literary competitions and diversions crossed class and estates' boundaries, from noble households to merchant courts. The 'verdicts' of such games were playful evocations of the law. And as with Chaucer, much of the best late medieval English literature simply declines to render definitive judgments, even when they are repeatedly promised. For example, *Piers Plowman* cycles through courts and houses with perambulatory steadiness, testing their limits and finding each wanting, as the Dreamer's search for the home of Truth becomes a kind of inverted and frustrated judicial eyre. For a literary journey conflating houses, laws, and games, *Sir Gawain and the Green Knight* is the best narrative one could wish for. Gawain takes up the holiday game and is put to the test in regal, baronial, and confessional courts, in almost every sense. Each court mirrors and competes with the others' authority (or lack thereof), and it is up to Gawain to negotiate this palimpsest of jurisdictions—and to keep his head while doing so. And as Elliot Kendall has convincingly argued, it was the assumptions of a household context, in the form of the 'class habitus' of the great noble household and its exchange rituals (magnificence versus reciprocalism), that gives John Gower's *Confessio amantis* its unique thrust and narrative form.[34] Certainly the shifting dedications of that book from Richard to Henry—whatever their chronology—hint how cagy poets could be in positioning themselves on the courtly game board. Much of Chaucer's audience must have been located in the royal and noble courts, as ideally pictured in the Corpus Christi portrait of the poet reading his work.[35] But from a court perspective it is not surprising that recent research has also located a prominent intersection of Chaucer manuscripts at the London Guildhall, a municipal court of the highest prominence.[36] As service and maintenance relationships were subject to competing jurisdictions and rules, so the negotiation of courtly audiences and dedicatees could be a matter of significant artistic self-definition on several levels.[37] Legal and literary deferrals thus presented similarly useful narrative strategies as well as potential safe-houses for occupancy.

For the reader of Chaucer, this is another angle from which to approach his famous lack of narrative closures and his regular demurral to offer final judgments. He does so even when (as with the *Canterbury Tales* and the *Legend of Good Women*) the desire for a verdict drives the narrative in the first place. As in the juridical realm, the promise of a definitive decision is actually an invitation to further wrangling and games-playing. The very structure of the *Canterbury Tales* recapitulates this dynamic as the narrative of a judicial communal assembly, one founded in a public house for the purposes of a *parlement* and that threatens (or promises) to dilate without end. In fact the goal of the journey, the shrine of St Thomas Becket, was a monument to the patron saint of competing jurisdictions: the Chancellor turned Archbishop who opposed the univocal imposition of royal law over ecclesial law in England. It is thus fitting that the organization of the *Tales* by argumentative give-and-take develops organically from among the pilgrims themselves and not from the strict imposition of an estates order. The quitings of the narrative reflect their own logic of competing social and juridical visions.[38] Understood in this context, the *Tales* as a whole are very much a courtly kind of socio-judicial game, giving plea and rejoinder to everything from the refined romance of the Knight to the confessions of the Wife and Pardoner, to the conclusively inconclusive disquisition of the Parson.

At a less abstract level, the settings of Chaucer's narratives also reveal a pervasive court mentality. Courts and courtly elements are omnipresent. An exhaustive catalogue would be unwieldy, but a partial overview is instructive. Legal and political aristocratic courts play obvious key roles in *Troilus and Criseyde*, the *Parliament of Fowls*, the gossipy 'house' of the *House of Fame*, the Knight's Tale, and in the romance settings of The Man of Law's Tale and the Wife of Bath's Tale. In these stories in particular, the journeys and distances between houses and courts (e.g. the royal court of Troy and the Greek camp; Theseus' court and the Theban cousins' courtly combat in the forest; the various courts of Griselda's journey; the courtly parliament of birds), as well as the journeys in and out of them, explore changing social rules and shifting jurisdictions. In this regard they are not too distant from judicial court narratives such as the Physician's Tale and the Tale of Melibee. Other tales are less overt but have similar settings: the 'halle' or 'court' (V.169, 171) of Cambyuskan in the Squire's Tale; the aristocratic and tyrannical household of Walter in the Clerk's Tale; January and his 'court-man' Placebo (IV.1492) in the claustrophobic household setting of the Merchant's Tale, which is similar to the mercantile setting of the Shipman's Tale; and the searching exploration of courtly love, contractual liability, and personal 'trouthe' that takes place in and around the noble household of Arveragus in the Franklin's Tale. The sad narrative of the Manciple's Tale shows a noble court and its wilful personal law as a kind of bird cage, a common enough metaphor in the Middle Ages.[39] In the Nun's Priest's Tale, Chauntecleer in his yard is pithily described as 'roial, as a prince is in his halle' (VII.3184). Even small details or mentions of courtly context—the Pardoner 'that streight was comen fro the court of Rome' with his bulls (I.671), or the Prioress' desire 'to countrefete cheere / Of court' (139–40)—can suggest complex associations of these legal, social, and ludic aspects of courtly order.

The significance of these settings is sometimes crucial for understanding the implicit humour. For example in the Summoner's Tale, after receiving the smelly and indivisible gift of the fart from Thomas, the friar angrily marches to the court ('A sturdy paas doun to the court he gooth' [III.2162]) for an audience with the lord in his 'large halle', to complain about the abuse he has received 'in youre village' and 'in youre toun' (2188; 2176–80). The lord and lady of the manor listen patiently to the friar's complaint. The lady of the manor dismisses the case with a simple class insult—'a cherl hath doon a cherles dede' (2206)—but the lord ruminates further, absurdly, about the implications of Thomas' gift and the challenge of dividing the fart equally. Indeed, the lord has been presented in his court with a proverbial hard case, and he is baffled by it. In his 'traunce' (2216) and pseudo-Solomonic musing, he is a humorous parody of aristocratic judicial authority, since the enraged friar came to the court specifically for manorial justice. But he gets no redress for his plaint. Instead the lord's verdict is to 'lat the cherl go pleye' (2241), turning the mock-legal challenge into a courtly game. Then his squire Jankyn takes the joke even further with a neat solution to the *insolubilium*. The solution of the cartwheel implicitly insults the friar even further by parodying the communal-courtly identity of the fraternal orders as assemblies supposedly inspired by the divine afflatus, and by mocking the self-aggrandizing 'resoun' of their 'worthy men' (2277, 2279). The squire's clever solution is celebrated by all with courtly accord and the churl Thomas is praised for his 'subtiltee / And heigh wit' (2290–1). With that, the case is closed. Here court mentality contextualizes a near-universal parody of aristocratic, judicial, and ecclesial pretensions, presenting them as little more than the sublimated flatulence of the dominant order.

The silly gamesomeness of the end of the Summoner's fabliau provides an amusing portrait of what it meant to operate in a system of household courts. It also points up another frequent element: namely, the collocation of the institutional religious and aristocratic courtly worlds. As Malcolm Vale points out, mendicant preachers and confessors (like the friar) were symbolically significant participants in the magnificent courts of nobles and kings precisely for the contrast of their clerical austerity to the extravagant displays of the secular court.[40] Chaucer himself perhaps participated in this clerkly-courtly social dialectic with his (lost) translations of such spiritual works as the *De contemptu mundi*. Notably in the catalogue of his own works given in the F and G Prologues to the *Legend of Good Women,* only courtly and devotional works are listed. This church-state overlap was subject to criticism, as it is through Chaucer's self-serving friar. But it could also, as I have emphasized, provide a critical perspective on competing jurisdictions, not just by making one particular court or ecclesial order the object of scorn, but by putting the whole system under scrutiny.

Two tales of the *Canterbury Tales* demonstrate this, ones not frequently classed together: the Friar's Tale and the Second Nun's Tale. Both are told by regular members of ecclesial orders, and on the surface they contrast generically as quasi-fabliau and saint's life, courtly 'game' (III.1275, 1279) and serious devotional fare. But they share this trait as well, that they offer characteristically Chaucerian critiques of courts through the contrast of legal jurisdictions. The Friar's Tale is drawn from sermon exempla that look back to the folkloric motif of the heart-felt curse.[41] In all versions, an official of legal authority—a seneschal, bailiff, or most commonly a lawyer or barrister—comes upon a devil, who joins him in his travels. The official pursues his profit in the county courts (*comitatum, forum judiciale*) by fraud or injustice, or by extracting oppressive rents from a village. The devil also goes along for his own profit, in order to, as he says, get what is rightly his or what is sincerely sworn to him.

While the social position of the principal character is roughly the same in the Friar's Tale, only Chaucer's version begins not with the court-man but with the court itself. The tale starts with 'An erchedeken, a man of heigh degree' (III.1302) and a lengthy summary of his court's legal 'jurisdiccioun' (1319) over everything from witchcraft, defamation, and fornication to contracts and testaments (1303–20). A summoner, the archdeacon's servant, practices extensive tricks and injustices in his exploitive 'jurisdiccioun' among the common people (1330, 1321–74).[42] When this summoner encounters a devil in the guise of a yeoman, he is asked 'Artow thanne a bailly?', that is, a bailiff for a secular estate (1392). The summoner answers yes, ashamed to admit that he is really an agent of the ecclesial court. The devil responds joyfully 'Thou art a bailly, and I am another' and goes on to describe the 'house' of which he is the servant 'fer in the north' (1396, 1413–16). He works for his lord 'by extorcions' (1429):

> For sothe, I take al that men wol me yive.
> Algate, by sleyghte or by violence,
> Fro yeer to yeer I wynne al my dispence.
> I kan no bettre telle, faithfully.   (1430–3)

The summoner agrees with this devilish 'extorcioun' (1439) and indirectly reveals (with a curse on 'thise shrifte-fadres' [1442]) that he is actually an ecclesial and not secular official. At this point the supposed yeoman then reveals that he is really a demon: 'I am a feend; my dwellyng is in helle, / And heere I ryde aboute my purchasyng' (1448–9). He also accounts for the limits of his jurisdiction as it is granted by God to devils (1482–1503). But the summoner says that he would not care even if the yeoman were 'the devel Sathanas' (1526), for he cares only about his winning. The two men elaborately swear allegiance to each other—'For to be trewe brother in this cas; / And bothe we goon abouten oure purchas' (1529–30)—and they proceed to their work.

The explicit parallels are indeed caustic: a summoner from an archdeacon's court is like a bailiff from a lord's court (which they both pretend to be), and both are like demons from the realm of the Devil, hell-bent on injustice, fraud, and exploitation. They manipulate appearances and the colours of the law for extortion and private profit. When they come to the old woman whom the summoner plans to swindle, he deploys all the trappings of courtly authority. He brings 'of somonce heere a bille' from the archdeacon's court where she must appear 'Up peyne of cursyng', or excommunication (1586–89). The woman asks for a copy of the 'libel' (1595) and for the right to answer the charge by way of her legal procurator, since she cannot travel to the court because of her ill health. The summoner will let her do so only for the extortionate sum of twelve pence, which she does not have. She pleads but he refuses, clearly abusing his authority.[43] He then tries to embarrass her into paying the bribe by falsely accusing her of adultery. Enraged she swears and curses the summoner to the devil:

> Ne was I nevere er now, wydwe ne wyf,
> Somoned unto youre court in al my lyf;
> Ne nevere I nas but of my body trewe!   (1619–21)

The sincerity of her oath and subsequent curse are enough to send the hapless summoner off with the demon 'Where as that sumonours han hir heritage' (1641), that is, to 'thilke cursed hous of helle' (1652). As the demon predicted when they met, the summoner now will keep company with him in his 'estat' (1460; 1513–22). The alliance of these two court officials is thus made complete. Where the tale began with the archdeacon's court, it ends, we are to understand, in a different but parallel infernal house.

Only in Chaucer's version of the story are these legal and courtly details so prominent and their function so critical. Even the pitiful cry of the old woman as the summoner tries to extort payment—'"Allas!" quod she, "God woot, I have no gilt"' (1612)—hinges on a sharp double entendre of what the courts should or could correct or extract: *gilt/guilt* as moral failing and sin (the jurisdiction of canon law courts like the Archdeacon's) and *gilt/gild* as wealth and payment (what manor courts and ecclesial courts regularly extracted).[44] She does not have the former and so should not be extorted for the latter. But this minor detail of her 'trouthe' is beside the point, we understand, for both the sacred and secular courts. Thus the grim humour comes not just from the wittiness of

Chaucer's revisions but from the insightfully critical analogy he makes between sacred and secular courts and their oppressive practices.

My last example from the Second Nun's 'Tale' has a similar dynamic but goes in a different direction. Chaucer probably drew his version of the life of St Cecile from two sources representing two distinct abridgments of the *Passio S. Caeciliae*: one from the *Legenda Aurea* and the other a liturgical version regularly used to celebrate St Cecilia's feast day.[45] Chaucer's adaptation of the legend shifts from one source to the other roughly at the point where the Christians are interrogated and martyred by the Roman prefect Almachius. The brothers Tiburce and Valerian are executed, and later also Maximus, and then Cecile is brought before Almachius on suspicion of Christianity for having tended to their burials.

The concluding scene of the tale is a court drama, as young Cecile is forced to answer the prefect's charges and interrogatories. But she does not just answer, she feistily counterpleads. She faults Almachius for his errant prosecution and bad procedure; she questions his power and the power of 'yowre princes' and 'youre nobleye' (the sources of his judicial commission); she accuses him of trumping up charges to 'putte on us a cryme and eek a blame' (VIII.449, 455). And in his demands for pagan sacrifice, Cecile adds, he is forcing her into a judicially illegitimate and contradictory self-accusation that only betrays his own incompetence:

> 'O juge, confus in thy nycetee,
> Woltow that I reneye innocence,
> To make me a wikked wight?' quod shee.
> 'Lo, he dissymuleth heere in audience;
> He stareth, and woodeth in his advertence'!   (463–7)

Like the 'traunce' of the judging lord in the Summoner's Tale (III.2216), Almachius' judicial incompetence, alternately raging and wavering, exposes not just his own failure but the lack of legitimate jurisdiction in his court as a whole.[46] Legally the affair is a sham, as Cecile concludes: 'But thou mayst seyn thy princes han thee maked / Ministre of deeth; for if thou speke of mo / Thou lyest, for thy power is ful naked' (484–6). Chaucer here adds a specifically legal term, 'naked' or *nudus,* which was used to describe legal proceedings that were performed without proper attention to the procedure and documentation that would make them 'clothed' or *vestitum* and hence legitimate.[47] Not just brute force (as we might understand 'naked power' today) but illegitimate force and violence is all Almachius has, and all he can do, since he is 'A lewed officer and a veyn justise' (497). When Cecile is eventually executed by decollation—which Almachius' men botch as well, allowing her to survive for three days—her house becomes a church, as she willed (514; 546). Her household is occupied by Pope Urban and the Christian community, and it becomes a shrine to the saint who was also, we recall, a 'gentil wom-man' (425) of station. Almachius' illegitimate court gives way, in the end, to a legitimate and holy assembly, one hallowed by the community for the service of God and the lady of his household.

This triumphal reading is no doubt a bit dreamy or wishful, as saints' lives are by generic convention. But I want to conclude this investigation of Chaucer's courts by pushing it a little further. For if Chaucer revisited and revised his 'Life of St Cecile' by adding the more vibrant ending from the liturgical version, then, as Sherry Reames has suggested, 'the implication is that Chaucer came back to this part of the tale with a new source and a new sense of purpose.'[48] Perhaps what gave it new purpose was this fantastic element of courtly confrontation that the legend so strongly emphasizes. In this, old poets and girl-saints might have had something in common. We can recall that the 'Lyf of Seynt Cecile' (LGW F 426; G 416) is one of the courtly texts mentioned by Alceste in her inventory of evidence listed on behalf of the offending poet in the *Legend of Good Women*. In this intertextual point we can see a small courtly parallel and reversal. For in one story, we find a subjected figure who stands trial before a terrifying and deadly authority and who is silenced in the court of the god of Love; and in the other—one of the texts cited on the first's behalf—we also find a subjected figure who stands trial before a terrifying and deadly authority, but who nonetheless bravely speaks out in court for the love of God. Subjected and defiant, law-bound and law-breaking, aristocratic and, at times, demotic: courtly texts with these competing visions found room in Chaucer's diverse oeuvre, and they give us a sense of the complex richness of the literary and social culture informing them. These were the worlds of courtly house, law, and game that his poetry both reflected and made.

Notes

1. MED s.v. 'cŏuntre- [~pleden, ~pleten]'; J. H. Baker, ed., *Manual of Law French,* 2nd ed. (Brookfield, VT: Scolar Press, 1990), s.v. *counterpleader.*
2. For Chaucer's biography see Martin M. Crow and Clair C. Olson, eds., *Chaucer Life-Records* (Oxford: Clarendon, 1966); Derek Pearsall, *The Life of Geoffrey Chaucer* (Oxford: Blackwell, 1992); and most recently Marion Turner, *Chaucer: A European Life* (Princeton: Princeton University Press, 2019).
3. See the studies of Richard Green, *Poets and Princepleasers: Literature and the English Court in the Late Middle Ages* (Toronto: University of Toronto Press, 1980); Paul Strohm, *Social Chaucer* (Cambridge, MA: Harvard University Press, 1989); James Wimsatt, *Chaucer and His French Contemporaries: Natural Music in the Fourteenth Century* (Toronto: University of Toronto Press, 1991); Barbara Hanawalt, ed., *Chaucer's England: Literature in Historical Context* (Minneapolis, MN: University of Minnesota Press, 1992); Nigel Saul, *Richard II* (New Haven, CT: Yale University Press, 1997); Lynn Staley, *Languages of Power in the Age of Richard II* (University Park, PA: Penn State University Press, 2007).
4. The term 'jurisprudential topoi' comes from Elizabeth Fowler, 'Chaucer's Hard Cases', in Barbara Hanawalt and David Wallace, eds., *Medieval Crime and Social Control* (Minneapolis, MN: University of Minnesota Press, 1999), 124. The standard scholarly study of Chaucer and the law is Joseph Hornsby, *Chaucer and the Law* (Norman, OK: Pilgrim Books, 1988).
5. Harold J. Berman, *Law and Revolution: The Formation of the Western Legal Tradition* (Cambridge, MA: Harvard University Press, 1983). See also Bryce Lyon, *A Constitutional*

and Legal History of Medieval England, 2nd ed. (New York: W. W. Norton, 1980), and Alan Harding, *Medieval Law and the Foundations of the State* (New York: Oxford, 2002).

6. The phrase 'sociogenesis of the state' to describe the legal-political court developments of the West comes from Norbert Elias, *The Civilizing Process,* trans. Edmund Jephcott (Oxford: Blackwell, 1994); see also Joachim Bumke, *Courtly Culture: Literature and Society in the High Middle Ages,* trans. Thomas Dunlap (New York: Overlook Press, 2000). On *Rechtsstaat* see Berman, *Law and Revolution,* 292.

7. For these developments see especially Anthony Musson and Mark Ormrod, *The Evolution of English Justice: Law, Politics, and Society in the Fourteenth Century* (New York: St Martins Press, 1999); Anthony Musson, *Medieval Law in Context: The Growth of Legal Consciousness from Magna Carta to the Peasants' Revolt* (Manchester: Manchester University Press, 2001); and Gerald Harriss, *Shaping the Nation: England 1360-1461* (Oxford: Oxford University Press, 2005).

8. See Paul Brand, *The Origins of the English Legal Profession* (Oxford: Oxford University Press, 1992), and 'Inside the Courtroom: Lawyers, Litigants, and Justices in England in the Later Middle Ages,' in *The Moral World of the Law,* ed. Peter Coss (Cambridge: Cambridge University Press, 2000), 91–112; W. R. Jones, 'The Court of the Verge: The Jurisdiction of the Steward and Marshal of the Household in Later Medieval England'. *Journal of British Studies* 10 (1970), 1–29.

9. See Saul, *Richard II,* 259, 342–3.

10. L. C. Hector and Barbara F. Harvey, eds., *The Westminster Chronicle 1381-1394* (Oxford: Clarendon Press, 1982), 492–3.

11. Ibid., 502–3.

12. Ibid., 506–9.

13. See Saul, *Richard II,* 258–9; Harriss, *Shaping the Nation,* 475–6.

14. Musson and Ormrod, *Evolution of English Justice,* 8.

15. Berman, *Law and Revolution,* 323; see also E. D. Jones, 'The Medieval Leyrwite: A Historical Note on Female Fornication', *English Historical Review* 107, no. 425 (1992), 945–53.

16. Berman, *Law and Revolution,* 322–8.

17. Musson and Ormrod, *Evolution of English Justice,* 115–60; Harriss, *Shaping the Nation,* 47–58; Harding, *Medieval Law,* 123–9.

18. See Richard Green, *A Crisis of Truth: Literature and Law in Ricardian England* (Philadelphia, PA: University of Pennsylvania Press, 2002).

19. Musson and Ormrod, *Evolution of English Justice,* 10–11, 116–19, 189–93; Harding, *Medieval Law,* 147–90. For critical context see also Michael Clanchy, 'Law and Love in the Middle Ages', in *Disputes and Settlements. Law and Human Relations in the West,* ed. John Bossy (Cambridge: Cambridge University Press, 1983), 47–67.

20. On the Uprising of 1381 and courts, see especially Steven Justice, *Writing and Rebellion: England in 1381* (Berkeley, CA: University of California Press, 1994), 13–66.

21. Hector and Harvey, *Westminster Chronicle,* 6–9.

22. Ibid., *Westminster Chronicle,* 4–5.

23. Saul, *Richard II,* 65, 69. As noted by Claire Valente, *The Theory and Practice of Revolt in Medieval England* (Farnham: Ashgate, 2003), 168, 'law and justice were more prominent [in the Uprising of 1381] than in fourteenth-century baronial revolts, suggesting once again that this was truly a communal issue. The peasants were clearly familiar with legal

processes and records and in many cases had personal legal experience as bailiffs and jurors. Unlike the upper ranks, they tended to view the entire system as corrupt.'

24. Hector and Harvey, *Westminster Chronicle,* 16–19. For analysis of the aftermath, see Saul, *Richard II,* 73–82; R. B. Dobson, ed., *The Peasants' Revolt of 1381,* 2nd ed. (London: MacMillan, 1983), 51–65; and Helen Lacey, *The Royal Pardon: Access to Mercy in Fourteenth-Century England* (York: York Medieval Press, 2009), 127–59.

25. Saul, *Richard II,* 61; Musson and Ormrod, *Evolution of English Justice,* 98.

26. Crow and Olson, *Chaucer Life Records,* 148–493. On Chaucer's quitclaim of the charge of *raptus* see especially Christopher Cannon, '*Raptus* in the Chaumpaigne Release and a Newly Discovered Document Concerning the Life of Geoffrey Chaucer', *Speculum* 68 (1993), 79–94; 'Chaucer and Rape: Uncertainty's Certainties', *Studies in the Age of Chaucer* 22 (2000), 67–92.

27. David Carlson, *Chaucer's Jobs* (New York: Palgrave Macmillan, 2005), 1, 20.

28. Crow and Olson, *Chaucer Life Records,* 62–4.

29. See Matthew Giancarlo, 'Murder, Lies, and Storytelling: The Manipulation of Justice(s) in the Parliaments of 1397 and 1399', *Speculum* 77 (2002), 76–112; Frank Grady, 'The Generation of 1399', in Steiner and Barrington, *The Letter of the Law,* 202–29; Andrew Galloway, 'Making History Legal: *Piers Plowman* and the Rebels in Fourteenth-Century England', in Kathleen Hewett-Smith, ed., *William Langland's Piers Plowman: A Book of Essays* (New York: Routledge, 2010), 7–39.

30. Carlson, *Chaucer's Jobs,* 64.

31. See generally Pierre Bourdieu, *The Field of Cultural Production: Essays on Art and Literature,* ed. Randal Johnson (New York: Columbia University Press, 1993).

32. It also suggests, as Green notes in *Poets and Princepleasers,* 20, that a noble household could be a disciplinary environment 'to which the nearest modern analogy might be that of a boarding school or military regiment'.

33. See Bumke, *Courtly Culture;* Wimsatt, *Chaucer and His French Contemporaries;* Malcolm Vale, *The Princely Court: Medieval Courts and Culture in North-West Europe, 1270–1380* (Oxford: Oxford University Press, 2001); Jenny Adams, *Power Play: The Literature and Politics of Chess in the Late Middle Ages* (Philadelphia, PA: University of Pennsylvania Press, 2006).

34. Elliot Kendall, *Lordship and Literature: John Gower and the Politics of the Great Household* (Oxford: Clarendon, 2008).

35. See Pearsall, *Life of Chaucer,* 292.

36. Linne Mooney, 'Chaucer's Scribe', *Speculum* 81 (2006), 97–138; Simon Horobin, 'Manuscripts and Scribes', in Susanna Fein and David Raybin, eds., *Chaucer: Contemporary Approaches* (University Park, PA: Penn State University Press, 2009), 67–82.

37. See Kathleen E. Kennedy, *Maintenance, Meed, and Marriage in Medieval English Literature* (New York: Palgrave Macmillan, 2008).

38. On this point see David Wallace, *Chaucerian Polity: Absolutist Lineages and Associational Forms in England and Italy* (Stanford, CA: Stanford University Press, 1997), 83–103; Matthew Giancarlo, *Parliament and Literature in Late Medieval England* (Cambridge: Cambridge University Press, 2007), 169–78.

39. Giancarlo, *Parliament and Literature,* 81–4.

40. Vale, *Princely Court,* 168–9.

41. See the analogue versions edited by Peter Nicholson, 'The Friar's Tale', in Robert M. Correale and Mary Hamel, eds., *Sources and Analogues of the Canterbury Tales I* (Rochester, NY: D. S. Brewer, 2002), 87–99.

42. Excellent historical context for archdeaconal courts is provided by Thomas Hahn and Richard Kaeuper, 'Text and Context: Chaucer's *Friar's Tale*', *Studies in the Age of Chaucer* 5 (1983), 67–101.

43. In point of detail, here the summoner apparently violates the *ordo judiciarius* or 'due process' of the supposed canonical summons, as the right to have documentation of an accusation and the right to legal representation through an attorney were widely available at this time. Fittingly this abuse rebounds against the summoner, as the subsequent curse and judgment against him appear to proceed summarily by *denunciatio* and *per notorium,* that is, by denunciation (of the woman's curse) and by the sheer notoriousness of the offender's canonical crime, obviating the need for any *ordo judiciarius* and leading to a swift summary judgment. See Paul Hyams, 'Due Process Versus the Maintenance of Order in European Law: The Contribution of the *ius commune*', in *The Moral World of the Law,* ed. Peter Cox (Cambridge: Cambridge University Press, 2000), 62–90; and James Brundage, *Medieval Canon Law* (New York: Longman, 1995), 120–53. As Hornsby wryly notes in *Chaucer and the Law,* 48, 'This devil proves to be something of a canon lawyer'.

44. See MED svv. 'gilt' (n.1) 'sin, transgression, offense, misdeed, crime', and 'gilt' (n. 3) 'gilding, gilt, gilt plate', from 'gilten' (v. 2) 'To overlay (sth.) with gold, gild; to decorate (sth.) with gold', directly cognate to German *Geld* 'money'. The pun here depends on the common use of the word 'gilt' specifically for 'gilt plate', rich gilded plateware, which contrasts with the only houseware the poor widow has, her homely 'newe panne' (1614) that the summoner resolves to take. So when she says 'Alas, I have no guilt!', he responds, 'You have no gilt (i.e. plateware)? Then I'll take your pan instead!'

45. See the analogues edited by Sherry Reames, 'The Second Nun's Prologue and Tale', in Correale and Hamel, *Sources and Analogues,* 491–527.

46. Chaucer's phrasing translates directly from the liturgical version: *parcit et sevit, dissimulat et advertit* (Reames, 'Second Nun's Prologue', in Correale and Hamel, *Sources and Analogues,* 525).

47. On the legal distinction *nudum-vestitum* see Hornsby, *Chaucer and the Law,* 40–1, 48; Berman, *Law and Revolution,* 246–8; also R. E. Latham, *Revised Medieval Latin Word-List* (London: British Academy, 1965), svv. *pact/um nudum, vestitum; possess/io nuda.*

48. Reames, 'Second Nun's Prologue' in Correale and Hamel, *Sources and Analogues,* 496.

BIBLIOGRAPHY

Alford, John and Dennis Seniff, *Literature and Law in the Middle Ages: A Bibliography of Scholarship* (New York: Garland, 1984).

Berman, Harold J., *Law and Revolution. The Formation of the Western Legal Tradition* (Cambridge, MA: Harvard University Press, 1983).

Bumke, Joachim, trans. Thomas Dunlap, *Courtly Culture: Literature and Society in the High Middle Ages* (Woodstock, NY: Overlook Press, 2000).

Giancarlo, Matthew, *Parliament and Literature in Late Medieval England* (Cambridge: Cambridge University Press, 2007).

Green, Richard Firth, *A Crisis of Truth: Literature and Law in Ricardian England* (Philadelphia, PA: University of Pennsylvania Press, 2002).

Green, Richard Firth, *Poets and Princepleasers: Literature and the English Court in the Late Middle Ages* (Toronto: University of Toronto Press, 1980).

Hornsby, Joseph, *Chaucer and the Law* (Norman, OK: Pilgrim Books, 1988).

Musson, Anthony, *Medieval Law in Context. The Growth of Legal Consciousness from Magna Carta to The Peasant's Revolt* (Manchester and New York: Manchester University Press, 2001).

Musson, Anthony and Mark Ormrod, *The Evolution of English Justice: Law, Politics, and Society in the Fourteenth Century* (New York: St Martins Press, 1999).

Vale, Malcolm, *The Princely Court. Medieval Courts and Culture in North-West Europe* (Oxford: Oxford University Press, 2001).

CHAPTER 3

AT HOME AND IN THE 'COUNTOUR-HOUS'

Chaucer's Polyglot Dwellings

JONATHAN HSY

WHAT did Geoffrey Chaucer's London sound like? The polyglot milieu of Chaucer's home has become an increasingly prominent feature in Chaucerian scholarship, informing explorations of urban conflict and the phenomenology of sound, as well as ongoing discussions in postcolonial studies, historical linguistics, and sociolinguistic approaches to medieval literature.[1] Although the precise location of Chaucer's childhood dwelling is disputed, the property of his wine-merchant father was certainly within the Vintry, in close proximity to (and within earshot of) city dwellers who spoke native tongues other than English: e.g. the Hanseatic Steelyard, neighbouring Italian bankers, and waterfront Genoese traders.[2] In his own recreation of the poet's life, Peter Ackroyd claims Chaucer as a quintessential Londoner, a man who 'came to maturity in a cosmopolitan city [and] would have known intimately [its] clamorous thoroughfares.'[3] Depicting Chaucer as a city dweller who, sponge-like, 'thoroughly absorbed the language of the streets', Ackroyd notes the poet's proximity to non-English neighbours in the Vintry and waterfront, and he culls snippets from French songs and English dialogue from Langland's *Piers Plowman* and Chaucer's *Canterbury Tales*.[4] In addition to these verbal utterances, Ackroyd evokes non-human sounds such as gates, horses and carts, the river, and church bells. In Ackroyd's speculative biography, the desire to recreate sounds of Chaucer's polyglot milieu engenders imaginative—even indulgent—narrative fictions.

Reconstructing the ephemeral sounds of the medieval city is, as enticing as it might be, a fraught enterprise. Rather than seeking to discern exactly how Chaucer might transmit 'authentic' sounds of his medieval surroundings, this chapter investigates how London's polyglot character informs Chaucer's fictive portrayal of urban living. What might Chaucer's writing reveal about the poet's affective relationship to the city, as well as its many languages? Focusing on the *House of Fame* and the Shipman's Tale, this chapter explores two London locations closely associated with Chaucer's adult life: his residence above Aldgate along the city wall, and the customs house on the waterfront (Chaucer's place of work). The *House of Fame* and the Shipman's Tale are rarely read together, perhaps since they are often seen as representing 'early' and 'late' stages in Chaucer's career (respectively) and the literary and linguistic traditions informing these works appear so disparate. The *House of Fame*, a dream vision, confronts weighty Latinate and Italian traditions; the Shipman's Tale, a comic fabliau, flirts with light-hearted French contexts. Despite their apparent differences, both works explore the richness of urban living—from quotidian domestic details to professional accounting practices—and these texts can readily be drawn together within the mixed-language milieu of Chaucer's tenure as a customs official for the Port of London. The ensuing discussion explores how Chaucer's writing—in its 'early' and 'late' stages—negotiated some of the rich polyglot spaces the poet inhabited.

In many respects an autobiographical work, the *House of Fame* was composed sometime during Chaucer's tenure as controller for wool customs (c.1374–86).[5] Throughout the 1370s, Chaucer was dispatched to Italy, France, and Flanders on diplomatic missions, but his duties as customs controller for the Port of London during this same period were not nearly as glamorous. Surviving documents attest to the arduous task of maintaining meticulous records and supervising the collection of taxes on a continual stream of commodities deemed most crucial to the state's economy, among them wool.[6] However, the *House of Fame* invests less in the quotidian details of Chaucer's 'day job' to focus on his more personal endeavours. The poem even provides a few clues regarding its creation. For instance, the first-person narrator is addressed as 'Geffrey' (729), and the date of the text's composition, 10 December, appears twice (63, 111). It is in Book Two of the poem, when an eagle speaks to 'Geffrey', that Chaucer's vocation in the customs house is explicitly linked to his private domestic activities:

> But of thy verray neyghebores,
> That duellen almost at thy dores
> Thou herist neyther that ne this;
> For when thy labour doon al ys,
> And hast mad alle thy rekenynges,
> In stede of reste and newe thynges,
> Thou goost hom to thy hous anoon;
> And, also domb as any stoon,
> Thou sittest at another book
> Tyl fully daswed ys thy look [...]   (649–58)

Acknowledging Chaucer's daily journeys from his work on the waterfront back 'hom to thy hous', this passage suggests that the customs official (by day) and poet (by night) inhabits a loud, crowded city. The 'verray neyghebores' who 'duellen almost at [the] dores' produce a significant amount of noise, but 'Geffrey'—so absorbed in his reading, or possibly his own writing—acts *as if* he hears nothing, sitting 'domb as any stoon' at yet 'another book'. In his description, the eagle characterizes 'Geffrey' as a solitary figure, inhabiting a world of silence despite his apparently noisy urban surroundings.

This transient glimpse into the poet's private life juxtaposes the sounds of neighbours with silent activity inside Geffrey's house. Elsewhere in the *House of Fame*, sound and silence characterize domestic and architectural spaces, but within a figurative dream landscape. Most strikingly, a majestic stillness pervades the interior of Fame's castle. Upon entering the great hall, the narrator views representatives of prestigious cultural and linguistic traditions standing atop high pillars. Among these static figures are Latin poets ('Latyn poete, Virgile' and 'Venus clerk Ovide' [1483–7]), Greek authorities ('gret Omer'...'to Grekes favorable' [1466, 1479]), and a Romano-Jewish historian ('Ebrayk Josephus' holds up the 'fame...of the Jewerye' [1433–6]). Just outside this castle, the narrator navigates a street-level soundscape that is anything but silent or solitary. A crowd of poets and musicians bustles 'al withoute...[t]he castel-yate' (1195–1294). Suggesting Chaucer's interests in ephemeral sounds and linguistic diversity, this fictional assemblage includes performers from wide-ranging points of origin: Celtic ('the Bret Glascurion' and other harpers [1208]), Germanic ('[p]ipers of the Duche tonge' [1234]), and Iberian ('[alle that used clarion / In Cataloigne and Aragon' [1247–8]). Moreover, this poetic excursus imports into Middle English a treasure trove of specialized vocabulary from many vernaculars: Francophone musical terminology ('cornemuse and shalemyes' and 'doucet' [1218, 1221]), Middle Dutch names for ring dances ('sprynges, / Reyes, and these straunge thynges' [1235–6]), and other forms of entertainment from Provence and Gascony ('Colle tregetour' [1277]).[7] The poet even punctuates his descriptions with casual, off-hand references to Italian travels. For instance, the castle's gold-plated roof is '[a]s fyn as ducat in Venyse, / Of whiche to lite al in my pouche is' (1348–9). In this episode outside the 'castel-yate', Chaucer suggests a breezy familiarity with many cultural environments, evoking a city teeming with people from afar. Insofar as this scene evokes a holistic vision of Chaucer's London, it imbues the city with a noisy, cosmopolitan sensibility. The poet incorporates material from diverse cultural and linguistic sources, suggesting a dizzying network of connections between his home and the wider world.[8]

One might perceive Chaucer's poem drifting far beyond London at this point, but this episode nonetheless imbues the text with a distinctly local resonance. Setting this episode 'al withoute [the] castel-yate' unexpectedly links the scene back to the earlier portrayal of 'Geffrey' at home. In a document written in authoritative Latin clauses, the Mayor and Aldermen in 1374 granted 'Galfrido Chaucer' the residence that would remain his home during his tenure as controller. Chaucer gains 'totam mansionem supra portam de Algate' [the entire residence along the top of the gate at Aldgate], 'cum domibus superedificatis et quodam celario subtus eandem portam in parte australi eiusdem porte cum suis pertinenciis...ad totam vitam euisdem Galfridi' [along with the rooms built on top, and a certain cellar underneath the said gate, on the southern side, with all its appurtenances...for the lifetime of this same Geoffrey].[9] In the *House of Fame*, this same 'Geffrey' engages in silent nocturnal activity at home. However, this fictive portrayal obscures the extent to which Chaucer's grand *mansio* (abode, dwelling) above the gate was prominently situated in world of urban sound, by day and by night.

The *porta* (gate) at Aldgate, along the fortified city wall, was key to London's defences, and the structure served as a watchtower and a security checkpoint.[10] The top of the gate would not only provide a unique vantage point visually, but also acoustically. In *Troilus and Criseyde*, also written during his tenure as controller, Chaucer conveys some of the sounds that one could perceive from above a city gate: 'The warden of the yates gan to calle / The folk which that withoute the yates were' (5.1177–8). Moreover, the sound of the 'folk' entering the city at nightfall is compounded by the presence of animals: the warden 'bad hem driven in hire bestes alle, / Or all the nyght they moste bleven there' (5.1179–80).

Chaucer's spacious Aldgate abode is not only prime medieval real estate, inundated with quotidian sounds 'withoute the yate'. This location presumably provided access to more extraordinary sounds one might hear during turbulent times. Chaucer, housed in Aldgate, could very well have witnessed the 'hydous...noyse' and shrill 'shoutes' of the Kentish crowd killing Flemish merchants he so briefly evokes in the Nun's Priest's Tale (VII.3393–96), and other passages in the *House of Fame* include more subtle allusions to the noise of 1381. For instance, the dwelling of 'Fame' (reputation or rumour) '[stands] in so juste a place' that 'every soun mot to hyt pace; / Or what so cometh from any tonge, / Be hyt rouned, red, or songe' (719–22). During the 1381 upheaval, an Aldgate alderman named William Tonge allegedly allowed rebels to pour through this very gate into the city, and when Chaucer describes Fame's dwelling 'in so juste a place' that it absorbs sound that 'cometh from any tonge', he may subtly implicate Tonge's own questionable role as warden. During the night, some say, Tonge opened the strategically positioned gate, allowing the crowd to stream into the city, kill people, and burn houses. Potential links between the *House of Fame* and events of 1381 become even clearer once we recognize that Latin records alleging Tonge's complicity in these events deem the Kentish rebels men of 'ill fame', and even a single narrative can transmit truths as well as rumours. One Latin juror account, dated 4 November 1382, refuses to offer a single, authoritative account of Tonge's motivations on that night.[11]

In addition to subtle allusions to local sound, noise, and murmuring, more overt references to Aldgate appear elsewhere in the *House of Fame*. In one scene, the eagle speaks to Geffrey while transporting him across the sky:

> 'Now', quod he thoo, 'cast up thyn yë.
> Se yonder, loo, the Galaxie,
> Which men clepeth the Milky Wey
> For hit ys whit (and somme, parfey,
> Kallen hyt Watlynge Strete),
> That ones was ybrent with hete,
> Whan the sonnes sone the rede,
> That highte Pheton, wolde lede
> Algate hys fader carte, and gye.
> The carte-hors gonne wel espye
> That he koude no governaunce...'   (935–45)

Stephen Russell reads the eagle's lines as 'thick with allusions to the Peasants' Revolt', replete with references to burning houses and 'Watlyng Strete', a major London thoroughfare, as well as a subtle pun on 'Algate' (943), a common Middle English variant of 'Aldgate'.[12] Drawing Phaeton imagery from Ovid's *Metamorphoses*,[13] Chaucer's rich classical allusions arguably participate in a local flurry of Latinate writings recalling the noise of 1381. One contemporary London poem, for example, oscillates between lines in alliterating English and rhyming Latin: 'Laddus loude thay loghte, / clamantes voce sonora; / The bischop wen they sloghte, / et corpora plura decora' [churls loudly laughed, crying with loud voices, as they slew the Archbishop and many excellent people].[14] John Gower's *Vox clamantis*, written in Latin elegiacs, famously depicts 1381 London as 'new Troy', and the poet's account of the upheaval transmits the cries of allegorical rioter-animals.[15]

Chaucer's potential allusions to events of 1381 in *The House of Fame* are certainly open to debate, as the precise year of the poem's composition is not firmly established.[16] Nonetheless, the complex negotiation of Latinate traditions and urban space in this poem is unmistakable. In an astute reading of the eagle's words, Ardis Butterfield observes that 'Geffrey lives an improbably solitary, silent life' while 'Chaucer represents the aporia of the city: the paradox of aphasia in the midst of gossipy excesses of verbal "murmurynge"'.[17] In his portrayal of 'Geffrey' and his Aldgate dwelling, Chaucer achieves more subtle effects: he troubles any clear distinction between the busy, noisy city during the day and the eerie (anti)social space the city becomes once night falls. Just as an earlier scene bridges Chaucer's day job and Geffrey's nocturnal dwelling, so does this 'Aldgate' reference superimpose night and day. Testifying once again to Chaucer's interests in the juxtaposition of languages ('Galaxie' is the Greek form of the Latin *via lactea*, or 'Milky Way'), the *House of Fame* equates daytime work and nighttime leisure. In other words, the poet conflates the Milky Way—filled with stars in the night sky—with Watlyng Strete, the urban thoroughfare filled with daytime pedestrians.

In its portrayal of daily and nocturnal activity, the *House of Fame* provides much more than a series of discrete autobiographical vignettes or even richly encoded allusions to local events. The poem offers a complex poetic inhabitation of city space and evocation of urban rhythms. As many have noted, the *House of Fame* is often structured around key 'contrastive dichotomies' (including fact/fiction, speech/writing, and reputation/rumor, to name a few), but the nuanced relationship between day/night and sound/silence throughout the text also demands closer examination.[18] In this poem, Chaucer explores the coexistence of apparently contradictory phenomena. Day and night are each rendered as *simultaneously* silent and noisy. Similarly, the soundscapes of fictive otherworldly realms recall those of quotidian urban settings. Indeed, Fame's dwelling—like the city itself—has the remarkable capacity to receive and absorb utterances in any human language ('what so cometh of any tonge'), by any mode of aural transmission. Such vocalizations could be spoken, recited, or sung ('rouned, red, or songe'), and it doesn't matter whether these ephemeral vocalizations are even set to writing or (presumably) musical notation.

This discussion of Chaucer's Aldgate dwelling concludes with a brief consideration of the poem's culminating figure: Fame herself. In Middle English, 'fame' (derived from Latin *fama*) denotes 'reputation' or 'rumour', and Marion Turner observes that Chaucer's description of Fame hews more closely to Ovid than to Virgil.[19] Nonetheless, the *House of Fame* transmits a particularly Virgilian obsession with *how* sound is perceived and transmitted. Virgil's *Fama* is, after all, a distinctly urban phenomenon. She flies at night over great cities, stands watch on rooftops and high towers, and with her many tongues she spreads both fact and fiction[20] Virgil's synecdoche and anaphora suggest how readily rumour spreads: '*Tot*…oculi, / *Tot* linguae, *tot*idem ora sonant, *tot* subrigit auris' [as many eyes, as many tongues and mouths speaking, as many upraised ears].[21] Moreover, alliteration conveys the sonic similarity between fact and fiction: '*facta* atque in*fecta* canebat' [she was singing equally fact and fiction].[22] Both the *Aeneid* and the *House of Fame* readily explore urban vantage points and the circulation of sound, and the *House of Fame* is arguably the most laden with anaphora precisely when it describes acoustics and urban spaces (see 856–9, 899–903, 1203–13). Upon closer examination, the *House of Fame* not only participates in Latinate traditions, fusing Ovidian and Virgilian poetic models, but it also incorporates disparate linguistic material—Francophone, Celtic, Germanic, Iberian, and Italian. Transmuting disparate influences, the poet artfully shapes and stylizes his noisy Aldgate dwelling.

WRITING ON THE WALL: CHAUCERIAN TRACES

In this Aldgate context we discern Chaucer's keen awareness of and sensitivity to local linguistic diversity and his Middle English poetry deeply engages with Latinate writing. Quite appropriately, records of Chaucer's official duties in the customs house survive in the form of lengthy Latin documents. His 1374 appointment as controller (*contrarotulator*) for the Port of London (the same year he was granted his Aldgate residence) requires 'quod idem Galfridus rotulos suos in dicta officia tangentes manu sua propria scribat' [that the said Geoffrey shall write his rolls pertaining to the same office in his own hand] and that he 'continue moretur ibidem et omnia que ad officia illa pertinent in propria persona sua et non per substitutum suum faciat et exequatur' [continue to safeguard these same rolls and execute all things pertaining to this office in his own person and not through a substitute].[23] Apparently held personally responsible for writing and maintaining meticulous records, Chaucer elsewhere in the *Canterbury Tales* laments that 'men been distreyned by taylages, custumes, and cariages, moore than hire duetee or resoun is' (X.751). Indeed, in its artful portrayal of the poet's bureaucratic endeavors, the *House of Fame* suggests how much 'labour' is involved in making 'alle [these] rekenynges' (652–3). One might say that the 'labour' of maintaining customs accounts is, quite literally, *taxing*—not only for those whose imports are taxed but also for civic administrators who supervise the collection and movement of revenue.[24]

In addition to voluminous Latin records, Chaucer's tenure as controller can be traced through any number of legalistic French documents. While the oath Chaucer took upon assuming office does not survive, a 1376 oath for the controller of petty customs requires the controller to swear 'qe vous frez continuele demeure en le port de Loundres' [that you will reside continually in the Port of London], and an additional requirement that the controller perform his duties 'en propre personne' [in person] was intermittently relieved by a deputy when Chaucer was abroad performing royal duties.[25] In May 1378, for example, 'Geffrey Chaucer cont[r]erollour de le wolkeye en le port de Loundris' [Geoffrey Chaucer controller of the wool wharf in the port of London] appointed one Richard Barett 'soun lieutenaunt en loffice avant dite' [his deputy in the aforesaid office].[26] In 1385, Chaucer received a royal license to 'avoir suffisant deputee en loffice comptrolour a le wolkee de Londres' [have a satisfactory deputy for the office of controller at the wool wharf of London].[27]

A curiously hybrid Anglo-French coinage 'wolkee' (wool quay) appears within this 1385 license written out by Adam Pinkhurst, a London scribe whose connections to Chaucer are increasingly acknowledged.[28] Such fluid commingling of English and French readily pervaded civic records in London (and other ports). On the waterfront and texts associated with the 'wolkee', interpenetration of languages was particularly common. Nick Havely observes that a 'mixed form of Latin' was readily 'familiar in accounts and inventories' to London's merchant classes, and a 'kind of "pidgin"' on the waterfront could very well have served as a spoken 'portal to Italian'—aiding Chaucer on his Italian missions or transactions with Genoese merchants.[29] Moreover, historical linguist Laura Wright has examined 'macaronic business writing' along the Thames, revealing just how pervasively Latin or French documents (like Pinkhurst's) engaged in 'lexical borrowing', drawing in words from English, Dutch, and other languages.[30] In sum, London's waterfront provided a venue for a spoken *lingua franca* and other intermediate varieties of speech, and it also enjoyed close proximity to other locations in the city where certain specialized forms of mixed-language writing were produced (see Figure 3.1).

Documentary traces in Latin, French, and mixed-language records provide a tantalizing glimpse into 'the polyglot reality of medieval life', but physical traces of such phenomena survive in present-day London's landscape as well.[31] Throughout the city, a series of signs encourages pedestrians to re-trace the steps of the now-lost medieval wall. At the point in the itinerary where Aldgate once stood (near the junction of present-day Aldgate Street and Duke's Place) stands a plaque, affixed to an ordinary brick wall. This sign commemorates the former abode of Aldgate's 'most famous resident', Geoffrey Chaucer. Accompanying its explanatory text is a partial reproduction of the Ellesmere manuscript bearing the handwriting of Pinkhurst, the aforementioned London scribe. The partial image provides an unexpected trace of the scribe's multilingual acuity. A Latin 'Explicit' precedes a Middle English rubric 'Here begynnyth Chaucer[s tale]', so that the plaque attests to the polyglot milieu Chaucer inhabited. Indeed, Pinkhurst not only wrote down the French license granting Chaucer's 'deputee en loffice comptrolour a le wolkee de Londres' (cited above) but he also wrote the most

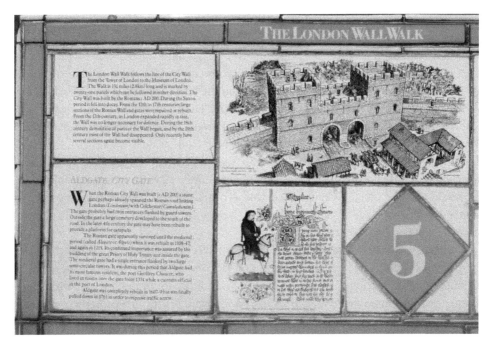

FIGURE 3.1 London Wall Walk, Panel 5 (detail), near the former site of Chaucer's Aldgate residence. Wall outside of Sir John Cass's Foundation Primary School, near the intersection of
Duke's Place and St Botolph Street, London.

Photograph by Jonathan Hsy, 24 May 2010.

famous manuscript containing Chaucer's Middle English texts and its Latin glosses.
Pinkhurst's multilingual output thus conjoins the 'labour' of the daytime Chaucer-
controller and the nocturnal Geffrey-poet. All in all, the *House of Fame* offers a complex
meditation on fame and the endurance of authorial reputation while also transmitting
the most quotidian of details. It is somehow fitting that one testament to Chaucer's
Aldgate dwelling—and the poet's fame—should be preserved as writing on a mundane
city wall.

HOME AND ABROAD: AQUATIC CHAUCER

Chaucer's domestic abode and his workplace at the customs house are explicitly
linked in the *House of Fame,* and the poem suggests some of the intricate connections
between his Aldgate setting and waterfront contexts. This complex interplay between
waterfront settings and overseas trade networks is explored in even greater detail in
another urban poem written later in Chaucer's career: the Shipman's Tale. Necessitating
an imaginative journey across the Channel, this tale transports the reader through a
range of domestic urban spaces and busy polyglot ports beyond London. Departing

from the market town of 'Seint Denis' in France, the merchant-protagonist travels to Bruges where he interacts with Italian bankers. Throughout the tale, Chaucer exhibits a keen sensitivity to the polyglot existence of medieval merchants and sailors and the 'trading of cultures, languages, and goods' that so often characterizes waterfront activity.[32]

A fabliau about a merchant, his wife, and a monk, the text we now call the Shipman's Tale might not initially seem particularly suited to a sailor. Indeed, scholars have long maintained that this lewd fabliau was originally intended for the Wife of Bath, if not some other speaker.[33] Nonetheless, the attribution of this tale to the Shipman in the manuscript tradition (including the Ellesmere manuscript and other early witnesses) foregrounds how readily this fabliau resonates with a maritime milieu. First of all, Anglo-Flemish-French trade networks thoroughly pervade the *Canterbury Tales* as a whole, and both mariners and merchants move within a shared orbit of cross-cultural transactions, rivalries, and exchanges. The Shipman, 'a good felawe' and experienced navigator (I.395, 401–9), potentially steals from merchants whose merchandise he transports: 'Ful many a draughte of wyn had he ydrawe / Fro Burdeux-ward, whil that the chapmen sleep' (I. 396–7). The Merchant, meanwhile, relies upon shipmen to transport his merchandise, concerned that the Anglo-Flemish sea corridor be protected from piracy: 'He wolde the see were kept for any thing / Bitwixe Middelburgh and Orewelle' (I. 276–7). 'Shipmen' (sailors) and 'chapmen' (merchants) relied upon and somewhat distrusted one another, and the Shipman's humorous tale about a merchant suggests some of these vocational animosities.

While the Shipman's Tale arguably exploits professional tensions between the ship-man and merchant, it is the very circulation of language that provides the most salient convergence between these two figures. Elsewhere in the *Canterbury Tales*, the Man of Law praises well-traveled merchants as 'fadres of tidynges / And tales' (II.129–30). Like *Fama*, merchants are adept at spreading stories, and the Man of Law's Tale makes espe-cially clear how maritime networks facilitate both the transport of commodities and the oral transmission of knowledge (II. 171–82). On a much more practical level, mercantile language and sea-terms were highly mobile in the realm of international commerce. In his analysis of medieval shipping terminology, Bertil Sandahl observes that '[m]ore than most other words, sea terms have a tendency to migrate from one country to another', and David A. Trotter further maintains that 'medieval shipwrights and port officials' (the latter category including civil servants like Chaucer) were 'accustomed to encountering (and working with, and on) ships from all over Europe', and employed 'terminology drawn from all over the known world'.[34] In the multilingual nexus of Thames trade extending across the Channel to the Continent, shipmen and merchants transported and exchanged goods just as they imported and exported language.[35]

This fluid movement of language through mercantile networks is an abiding concern of the Shipman's Tale and the most salient feature of its poetic style. While the tale itself is conspicuously devoid of sea terminology (the tale's merchant, albeit a traveller, never actually leaves the Continent), the tale employs an impressive range of merchant vocabulary. In a painstakingly detailed sequence, the 'marchant [of] Seint-Denys' (VII.1) leaves '[to] Flaundres-ward' and comes 'into Brugges murily', where he conducts a series of exchanges through Italian bankers (VII. 300–1). In Bruges, he 'bisily... byeth' merchandise on credit (he 'creaunceth'), spending 'twenty thousand sheeld' in the process (VII. 302–3, 331). At the same time, he enters a pledge to repay the amount: 'he was bounden in a reconyssaunce / To paye twenty thousand sheeld anon' (VII. 330–1). Since the merchandise costs more than he predicted ('that chaffare is so deere' [VII. 328]), he returns to Saint Denis to collect French francs he holds there; he then transports these francs to Paris, where he takes out a loan for the remaining amount he needs to repay to redeem his bond: 'this marchant is to Parys gon / To borwe of certeine freendes that he hadde / A certeyn frankes' (VII. 332–4). To summarize, a chain of transnational exchanges occurs: the merchant spends money in Bruges in the local Flemish currency of credit (shields) but pays back the amount in a different currency (francs) in a different location (Paris).

In the merchant's final transaction, he redeems his bond from a Paris branch of what is apparently an Italian bank run by 'certeyn Lumbardes' who had originally lent him the 'twenty thousand sheeld' in Bruges: 'This marchant, which that was ful war and wys, / Creanced hath, and payd eek in Parys / To certeyn Lumbardes, redy in hir hond, / The somme of gold, and gat of hem his bond' (VII. 365–8). Ultimately, the merchant profits from his (ad)venture: 'hoom he gooth, murie as a papejay, / For wel he knew... / That needes moste he wynne in that viage / A thousand frankes aboven al his costage' (VII. 369–72). Narrated in precise technical language and traversing urban centers, this intricately wrought passage inhabits the perspective of the merchant whose dealings yield a net profit. The proliferation of Francophone business jargon that overtakes the narrative ('creaunce', 'chaffare', 'costage', 'reconyssaunce') mystifies anyone outside the merchant's profession, but such 'murie' and vibrant forays into Francophone lingo befit the tale's fictional setting and intertwined business networks.

Not only does Francophone merchant jargon infuse this narrative, but key puns and multilingual *doubles entendres* also circulate throughout the text, adding another layer of complexity. While the merchant conducts his 'curious bisynesse' (VII. 225) in the 'queynte world'... '[of] chapmanhede' (VII. 236, 238), he is unaware of the 'curious' and 'queynte' liaisons transpiring back home between his wife and his 'fumulier... freend' (VII. 32–3), a monk who frequents the house. In one case of translingual semantic drift, the monk and merchant swear a bond of 'cosynage' or kinship but the connotation of this French-derived term mutates throughout the story. At first 'cosynage' denotes the oath of sworn brotherhood: 'The monk hym [the merchant] claymeth as for cosynage, / And he agayn' (36–7) and '[t]hus been they knyt with eterne alliaunce' (VII. 42). When the monk disavows his bond to the merchant to swear allegiance to the wife instead (VII. 149–55), 'cosynage' shifts into different semantic domain, connoting deception. Underlying the dual valence of 'cosynage' as both kinship and deception is a play on contemporary French usage. Fourteenth-century French readily conveyed the slippage between *coçonage* (connoting 'often shady' commercial transactions) and *cosinage* (kinship).[36]

In a similar instance of translingual slippage, Chaucer famously exploits the auditory correspondence between 'franks' (a French loan word) and 'flanks' (a native English word). The monk says to the wife: 'I wol brynge yow an hundred frankes'—and the narrator adds 'with that word he caughte hire by the flankes' (VII. 202–3). What is at stake in this humorous slippage between native and foreign languages is a simultaneously literal and metaphorical financial transaction: the wife promises to submit to the monk's advances if he gives her one hundred franks, which she needs to pay a debt, and when the monk borrows the money from the merchant and gives it to her, she repays his 'frankes' with her 'flankes'. The most striking instance of wordplay in the text, however, is the manifold deployment of 'taillynge' at the tale's conclusion. When the merchant returns and asks for his payment, the monk says he has given the amount to the wife, and when the merchant asks his wife for the coins, she claims she has already spent them and he can 'score [the debt] upon my taille' in bed (VII. 416). At this point, the narrative resolves: 'Thus endeth my tale, and God us sende / Taillynge ynough unto oure lyves ende!' (434–5). This final convergence between 'taillynge' and tale-telling is a sophisticated pun that would resonate most strongly with multilingual readers, as it nicely parallels 'the play common in French fabliaux on *con/conte* as female genitalia and story' (as Karla Taylor observes); moreover, Chaucer's wordplay must imagine a 'fully competent audience [that] would grasp this as well as other French-inflected puns' within the text.[37]

The above examples demonstrate how readily Chaucer exploits the porous boundaries between vernaculars and the migration of language in mercantile environments. Moreover, these multilingual puns are materially indebted to contemporary mercantile practice and language use. That is, the 'taillynge' pun presumes an audience who has facility with more than one language *and* recognizes how merchant accounts were actually kept. More than just a bilingual pun on 'tale' and 'tail' or a lewd *double entendre* that coins, in English, an equivalent to the French *con/conte*, Chaucer's 'taillynge' effects (if anything) a *triple entendre* that additionally puns on the Middle English equivalent of the modern word 'tally'. Appearing initially as a noun in Latin (*talia/talea*) but later deployed as a verb in both Anglo-Norman (*tallie/taille*) and Middle English (*taille/tayle*), 'taille' refers to the tally stick, one mode of keeping track of debts and payments in the Exchequer or between merchants. A scored tally stick could function as anything from a record of debt, to a receipt, or even an instrument of credit.

The tally stick was just one method of recording debts and payments, as one could also register such transactions in written form, namely, an account book. Silently overlooking merchants' use of tally sticks, John Ganim has posited double-entry book-keeping as the primary accounting practice underlying the flexible merchant jargon in the Shipman's Tale.[38] This bookkeeping system, 'undoubtedly practiced [by] Italian commercial interests' with whom Chaucer would have been acquainted, records how 'debits from one party are credited to another, and vice versa' within the pages of a book, so that 'all profits and losses are simultaneously [and] perpetually in view' to the reader.[39] Transforming 'concrete transactions [into] fluid and manipulable abstractions', double-entry bookkeeping serves as 'a form of rhetoric as well as a technique', and this flexible orientation towards language informs much of the tale.[40]

Ganim's assertion that double-entry bookkeeping assimilates transactions into an 'abstract formal system' certainly informs how the merchant's wife exploits the fluidity of language, abstracting her body ('flankes') and converting it into a form of payment ('frankes'). One could develop Ganim's insights even further, as bookkeeping not only converts transactions into an 'abstract formal system' but it also achieves an important effect: it generates narrative. Like 'taillynge', which implies tallying (use of a tally stick) and tale-telling, the Middle English verb 'rekken' carries multiple valences. To 'rekken' is not only to make a calculation or enumerate something more generally, but it is also to give an account of an event or tell a story. In Middle English usage, both 'taillynge' and 'rekkenynge' refer to the act of rendering an account—whether it gives details of exchanges, the sum of transactions, or a narration of events.

As it turns out, the simplest way for merchants to 'rekken' debts, payments or other transactions in their books was precisely to narrate them. Indeed, the poets Geoffrey Chaucer and John Gower both appear in narrative entries within the French-language account book of the London merchant Gilbert Maghfield, a frequent trader in Flanders whose residence on the Billingsgate wharf stood not far from Chaucer's childhood home.[41] Although this book encompasses forty folios, there is a transitory quality to its entries. Each entry records a debt Maghfield is owed but it is crossed out (scored) once the debt is paid. From July 1392 (later scored): 'Geffray Chauxcer doit dapprest en le xxviij jo[ur] de Juyl a paier le Samedi proschein après – xxvi s. viij d.' [Geoffrey Chaucer owes 26 s. 8 d. from 28 July until the following Saturday].[42] From October 1392 (also scored): 'Memorandum qe Gybon Maufeld ad paye pour Johan Gower esquier a i schippman pour frett dune bras pott mis par lettre de Lynne jesqes a Loundres – xvi d.' [Reminder that Gilbert Maghfield has paid 16 d. 'par lettre' (by bill of exchange) to one shipman, on behalf of John Gower, for the transport of a brass pot sent from Lynn to London].[43]

In addition to recording payments as an 'abstract formal system' (a list of debits and credits), this merchant's account actively narrates its transactions. The merchant pays a 'shippman' a certain amount 'par lettre' for the transport ('frett') of a 'bras pott' shipped to London from Lynn (the port in East Anglia), all on behalf of Gower—who (judging from the scored entry) repaid the amount. Maghfield's account book, then, reverses the operations of the Shipman's Tale. While the poet assimilates the 'taillynge' of merchants in order to generate a narrative, the merchant's own narrative 'taillynge' assimilates poets (i.e. Gower and Chaucer). The mercantile puns on 'score' and 'tally' in the Shipman's Tale suggest just how readily two poets might be drawn into a waterfront merchant's own narrative economy.

Other aspects of Maghfield's account book more transparently conform to accounting practices portrayed in the Shipman's Tale. In Maghfield's book, itemized lists of expenses can run down a folio and then conclude with a 'summa', or tally of the total sum.[44] Other entries suggest an annual December audit of his accounts has occurred: 'Comp[utum] est en le veile de Nowell' [calculated on Christmas Eve].[45] Moreover, Maghfield notes that this extensive list of 'detours' [debtors] has been 'trans[c]riptz' [re-copied] from some other private document into the 'foill[es] apres escriptz' [pages written hereafter] in this book.[46] Like 'Geffrey' in The House of Fame, as well as Maghfield, Chaucer's fictive merchant engages in his own solitary 'rekkenyng' in front of 'another book'. Peter of

Saint Denis ascends to his 'countour-hous'—his private, enclosed *comptoir* (counting house)—to conduct a yearly audit: 'up into his contour-hous' he goes, '[t]o rekene with hymself… [o]f thilke yeer how that it with hym stood' (VII.77–9). Surrounded by 'bookes and his bagges many oon… biforn hym on his countyng-bord' (VII. 82–3), he is interrupted only when his wife knocks: 'How longe tyme wol ye rekene and caste / Youre sommes, and youre bookes, and youre thynges?' (VII. 216–17).

With its puns on 'taillynge' and playful engagement with merchant jargon, the Shipman's Tale not only reflects the material circumstances of merchants (accounting, dwelling) but also, more profoundly, their *linguistic* capacities. For merchants like Maghfield and civil servants like Chaucer, French was not an 'imported or alien tongue [but] a natural language' employed alongside English, as Ardis Butterfield states in a slightly different context.[47] Maintaining a personal account book in French is, for the overseas trader Maghfield, simply good business practice, and Maghfield is quite 'at home' using a variety of French that could serve as a literal *lingua franca* in his dealings with Gascon and Flemish merchants.[48] Maghfield's entries exhibit frequent detours into other languages as well, suggesting a mercantile 'habit of mind' that is more profoundly multilingual than 'French' per se: e.g. 'schippman', 'bras pott' (Middle English), 'frett' (Middle Dutch). Such lexical fluidity can be seen as a rich social consequence of the polyglot world that merchants and shipmen inhabit.

This notion of 'inhabitation' informs the present discussion quite well, since, as Butterfield asserts, French (or any language) is a 'habit of mind'.[49] Multilingual scribes, merchants, and civil servants were all clearly able to move between languages with great ease, infusing even the most workaday writings with complex linguistic textures. Chaucer confines his wordplay within a monolingual poem, but (as Maghfield demonstrates) even monolingual texts exhibit fluid digressions into other languages. Such translingual thinking can also lend creativity to literary representations, allowing poets to artfully convey the fictional setting that their characters inhabit. Take, for example, this instance of 'local colour' when Chaucer's merchant suddenly speaks French. Peter's wife knocks on the door of his 'countour hous', and he responds from within: 'Quy la?' [Who's there?] (VII. 214). This snippet of French encourages the reader to sustain the fiction that the Shipman's Tale—narrated in English—nonetheless transpires on the Continent. Intriguingly, Chaucer's tales set in Italy, Flanders, or other locations abroad make no such attempt to register the 'strangeness' of the setting or characters through such stylized dialogue. The 'foreign' speech of the merchant thus enriches the complexity of this overseas tale, reminding us that characters who speak English and bear 'native' English names (Peter, John) can nonetheless be read, and imagined, as French.

Chaucer's multilingual puns and stylized dialogue suggest a sophisticated target audience who could hold other languages 'on call' and at their disposal, even as they read monolingually.[50] In order for the tale's nuanced dialogue and many puns to 'register', the reader must imaginatively draw upon a multilingual cache of words. Other London poets, writing in French, could similarly invite their readers to activate knowledge of English. In Gower's French *Mirour de l'omme*, 'Marchant Triche' [Merchant Trickery] inhabits London's waterfront. A multilingual traveler who navigates through major ports ('Bourdeaux', 'Civile' [Seville], 'Paris', 'Florence', 'Venise', 'Brugges', and 'Gant'), he enacts illicit transactions upon arrival in the 'noble Cite sur Thamis' [noble city on the Thames].[51] Gower warns that Marchant Triche 'par sa coverte glose / Te dourra craie pour fourmage' [through his sly flattery will give you chalk for cheese].[52] Here, the poet employs a Frenchified rendition of an alliterative Middle English expression ('chalk for cheese') that he uses elsewhere in his work: 'ful ofte chalk for chese / He changeth with ful litel cost'.[53] Gower thus enacts his own inter-vernacular 'inside joke' or unequal linguistic exchange. He invites members of an astute London audience to think in English and recognize a proverbial 'native' expression even as they read—or hear—in French.

Elsewhere in his work, Chaucer suggests that one's subjective sense of 'belonging' to a particular place is tied to one's manner of dwelling: 'This same place that thow clepest exil is contre to hem that enhabiten here'.[54] That is, a location that registers as foreign to a visitor or person in exile might actually feel entirely familiar to a native inhabitant (i.e. someone who resides there). One might metaphorically extend this Chaucerian insight to language as well. Throughout the Shipman's Tale, a language like French might register as 'foreign' to someone who is not fully accustomed to it, yet it may nonetheless feel entirely comfortable to 'hem that enhabiten' the language on a daily basis. The multilingual poet, at home in more than one language, troubles the apparent dichotomy between foreign and native tongues. Texts associated with London's waterfront frequently expose the porous boundaries between languages and suggest a capacity to inhabit different languages at will. Cross-linguistic puns, stylized French/English dialogue, and proverbial English expressions imbedded within French verse all require readers to inhabit more one language simultaneously. Within this setting, a language like French only provisionally registers as alien or familiar, depending on the context in which it is used.

The Shipman's Tale not only suggests the sheer complexity of Chaucer's own multilingualism, but it ultimately offers its own exploration of the relationship between urban space and linguistic difference. The poem's French speech, most pointedly, is uttered at a precise location: the 'countour-hous' door. This architectural structure—where the wife/merchant dialogue is staged—fittingly marks the intersection between domestic life (private dwelling) and professional domains (place of work). The spatial orientation of the characters further enriches the scene, conveying the complex estrangement between the speakers. The merchant, reckoning with himself in his 'contour-hous', speaks French. The wife, standing outside the door, speaks English. Moreover, the poem associates French speech and Francophone business jargon with the merchant to the exclusion of the other characters, conveying the peculiar 'habit of mind' of a person so obsessed his private activities that he is oblivious to affairs transpiring just outside. Evoking 'Geffrey' at home with his books in the *House of Fame*, this urban dweller is a solitary figure curiously isolated from the busy world that surrounds him.

The French setting in the Shipman's Tale not only transports the English reader to a location across the sea but it also evokes, through its fluid language, the polyglot mercantile world that engenders so much narrative. When Chaucer refers to 'eschaunge' (a concern that links the Merchant portrait in the *General Prologue* and the Shipman's Tale) he actually employs a conspicuously Anglo-French, not Continental French, form of the word—and the same could be said about other particularly resonant terms that circulate throughout the Shipman's Tale.[55] Chaucer, in other words, engages in his own linguistic sleight of hand. While his stylized dialogue maintains the 'strangeness' of the story's Continental setting, Chaucer's Middle English poetry is heavily inflected by *local* varieties of Anglo-French and sensitive to the multilingual capacities of his audience. The Shipman's Tale, despite its nominal French setting, evokes most powerfully the features of home: Chaucer's own porous linguistic habitat on London's waterfront.

CONCLUSION: INHABITING LANGUAGES

This chapter has juxtaposed the *House of Fame* and the Shipman's Tale to illustrate the complexity of the shared urban contexts of these works. The intricate representation of bureaucratic accounting practices in these texts evokes Chaucer's own tenure as a customs controller in London. More profoundly, these poems explore the complex relationship between urban space and language use. Chaucer readily inhabits the diverse linguistic and mercantile worlds of Continental France as well as London's own polyglot waterfront, and his fictional portrayals of urban 'rekynynges' and accounting practices exploit the porous boundaries between languages within particular urban settings. At the same time, these works reveal close associations between the civic or bureaucratic space of the 'countour-hous' and other private domestic spaces.

In both of these texts, Chaucer traverses apparently discrete domains of urban activity by virtue of their shared multilingual circumstances. In the *House of Fame*, Geffrey's nocturnal activity in his 'hous' comprise an explicit extension of his seemingly disparate 'day job', his bureaucratic vocation in the 'contour-hous'. Instead of pursuing 'newe things', the poet *replicates* his daytime accounting—which would have, presumably, been recorded in French or Latin—in front of yet 'another book' at home in Aldgate. Textual and numeric forms of 'rekynyng' are effectively elided, and the reckoning of accounts (in Latin or French) parallels, even enables, the generation of written narratives (in English). Likewise, pervasive English/French/Latin puns on 'taillynge' in the Shipman's Tale align vernacular tale-telling with local accounting practices from tally sticks to account books. Chaucer's fictional merchant conducts his annual audit while enclosed in a private 'contour-hous' associated with his own home, and the poet's fictive representation of living and working quarters foregrounds the perceived proximity between two multilingual sites of urban 'rekenyng'.

Placing Chaucer's poetry in conversation with local non-English writing allows us to more fully appreciate the poet's intricate relationship to the city *and* its multiple tongues. Inhabiting a fictional world indebted to Virgilian and Ovidian traditions, the *House of Fame* engages with Latin civic records attesting to Chaucer's urban dwelling. The

Shipman's Tale, an overseas tale laden with Francophone trade jargon, speaks to a waterfront merchant's French account book. As a polyglot inhabitant of, and active participant in, London's bureaucratic and mercantile worlds, Chaucer (and writers like him, literary and non-literary) investigates how one may seek to inhabit a particular space as well as a particular language.

Perhaps we can re-conceive the *House of Fame* and the Shipman's Tale as experiments in what might provisionally be called translingual poetic creation. Such a process is not entirely equivalent to the practice of 'translation' per se (i.e. the unidirectional conversion of something in one language into another), nor can it be adequately characterized as a linguistic phenomenon along the lines of code-switching (i.e. alternating between languages or identifiable registers within one language).[56] Rather, 'translingual' poetics stresses the *simultaneous* activation of languages at any one moment within any given literary text or any similarly stylized textual creation. Indeed, this chapter has illustrated how readily monoglot poets can invite their audiences to entertain cross-linguistic connections and meanings. As Michelle Warren astutely observes in another context, even ' "monolingual" texts [can] become networks of multilingual transactions'.[57]

These readings, above all, have followed the lead of critics like David Trotter and, more recently, Mary Catherine Davidson, who have eloquently challenged Anglophone, monolingualist approaches to medieval linguistics and literary studies.[58] Anglophone medieval literary scholarship, for the most part, still struggles to adopt a mode of critical analysis allows for the possibility of inhabiting multiple languages simultaneously. If we start thinking about language as a dwelling, inhabitation, or habitat (natural or constructed), then we might gain some more flexibility in future approaches to medieval writing. Anglophone and Francophone literary scholars—to cite two capacious vernacular language groupings—have already launched such endeavours, reassessing 'triumph of English' master narratives from both sides of the Channel and beyond. Moreover, medievalists have become increasingly appreciative of the complexity of code switching and translanguaging in polyglot contact zones.[59]

In *Le monolinguisme de l'autre: ou la prothèse d'origine*, Jacques Derrida reflects on his ambivalent relationship to the French language, asking if *any* language—whether it is affectively held as a native tongue or acknowledged as an imposed (colonial) language—can *ever* be properly considered one's own.[60] Language is a faculty that one possesses, but language itself eludes claims to possession. It paradoxically dwells within a subject and constitutes one's dwelling or 'habit of mind'. If we think of language not only as vehicle of speech, sound, and writing but also as a phenomenon that expands and fills space, then any language might be considered a living organism with its own agency. We might even conceive of any polyglot contact zone—like a city—as an ecosystem.[61] Although these readings have focused on discrete locations within one medieval city, this chapter reveals how languages are only provisionally attached to particular communities, speakers, or dwellings. If we appreciate how readily languages coexist and intermingle within a dynamic system, then Chaucer becomes but one participant among many in a polyglot crucible of literary creation.

ACKNOWLEDGEMENTS

I thank Suzanne Akbari, Marion Turner, Ardis Butterfield, Jeffrey Jerome Cohen, and David Wallace for feedback on earlier drafts of this chapter. This chapter also appears in a modified and expanded form in Jonathan Hsy, *Trading Tongues: Merchants, Multilingualism, and Medieval Literature* (Columbus, OH: Ohio State University Press, 2013), 27–57.

NOTES

1. See Ardis Butterfield, 'Chaucer and the Detritus of the City', in *Chaucer and the City*, ed. Ardis Butterfield (Cambridge: D. S. Brewer, 2006), 3–22, and other essays in this collection; Jeffrey Jerome Cohen, 'Postcolonialism', in *Chaucer: An Oxford Guide*, ed. Steve Ellis (Oxford: Oxford University Press, 2004), 448–62; Catherine Mary Davidson, *Medievalism, Multilingualism, and Chaucer* (New York: Palgrave, 2010); Tim William Machan, *English in the Middle Ages* (Oxford: Oxford University Press, 2003); Marion Turner, *Chaucerian Conflict: Languages of Antagonism in Late Fourteenth-Century London* (Oxford: Oxford University Press, 2007); David Wallace, *Chaucerian Polity: Absolutist Lineages and Associational Forms in England and Italy* (Stanford, CA: Stanford University Press, 1997), 156–81.

2. Thomas Bestul, 'Chaucer Life-Records and the Site of Chaucer's London Home', *Chaucer Review* 43, no. 1 (2008): 1–15. On alien (non-citizen) merchant communities in London, see Sylvia Thrupp, *The Merchant Class of Medieval London, 1300–1500* (Chicago, IL: University of Chicago Press, 1948), 220–2.

3. Peter Ackroyd, *Chaucer* (London: Chatto & Windus, 2004), 3–4.

4. Ibid., at 8.

5. On the dating of this poem, see Turner, *Chaucerian Conflict*, 12–13. Helen Cooper ('The Four Last Things in Dante and Chaucer: Ugolino in the House of Rumour', *New Medieval Literatures* 3 [1999]: 39–66) posits 10 December 1384 as a possible date for the poem's composition; see 63–4.

6. For documents pertaining to Chaucer's controllership, see Crow and Olson, *Chaucer Life-Records*, 244–70.

7. Walter Skeat discerns an etymological link between 'tregetour' and the Provençal *transgitar* (juggler); see Walter W. Skeat, ed., *The Complete Works of Geoffrey Chaucer: The House of Fame, The Legend of Good Women, and The Treatise on the Astrolabe*, 2nd ed. (Oxford: Clarendon Press, 1940), 237.

8. For diverse recent perspectives on Chaucer's cosmopolitanism, see Cohen, 'Postcolonialism'; John Ganim, 'Cosmopolitanism and Medievalism', *Exemplaria* 22, no. 1 (2010): 5–27; John Ganim and Shayne Aaron Legassie (eds.), *Cosmopolitanism and the Middle Ages* (New York: Palgrave, 2013).

9. Corporation of London, Letter-Book G, fol. 321. Also transcribed in Crow and Olson, *Chaucer Life Records*, 144–5. All translations are my own.

10. See Crow and Olson, *Chaucer Life-Records*, 146–7.

11. Roll A 24, Membr. 9 [1381]. See A. H. Thomas, ed., *Plea and Memoranda Rolls, Vol. 2: 1364–1381* (Cambridge: Cambridge University Press, 1929).

12. J. Stephen Russell, 'Is London Burning? A Chaucerian Allusion to the Rising of 1381', *Chaucer Review* 30, no. 1 (1995): 107–9.

13. Ovid, *Metamorphoses*, 2.32–328.

14. Cambridge, Corpus Christi College, MS 369, fol. 46v, lines 33–6. See also James M. Dean, ed., *Middle English Political Writings* (Kalamazoo, MI: Medieval Institute Press, 1996).

15. For more on writing about the events of 1381, see Steven Justice, *Writing and Rebellion: England in 1381* (Berkeley, CA: University of California Press, 1994); Christopher Baswell, 'Aeneas in 1381', *New Medieval Literatures* 5 (2002): 7–58.

16. See Cooper, 'The Four Last Things in Dante and Chaucer', 63–4; Turner, *Chaucerian Conflict*, 12–13.

17. Butterfield, 'Chaucer and the Detritus of the City', 11.

18. I draw the phrase 'contrastive dichotomies' from the discussion of *The House of Fame* in Philip Hardie, 'Contrasts', in *Classical Constructions: Papers in Memory of Don Fowler, Classicist and Epicurean*, ed. S. J. Heyworth (Oxford: Oxford University Press, 2007), 141–73, at 157.

19. Turner, *Chaucerian Conflict*, 16–17.

20. Virgil, *The Aeneid*, 4.173–90.

21. Ibid., 4.182–3. Emphases in Virgil quotations are my own.

22. Ibid., 4.190.

23. Kew, The National Archives, C 66/290 (48 Edw. III, m. 13), transcribed in Crow and Olson, *Chaucer Life-Records*, 148.

24. See Jenna Mead, 'Chaucer and the Subject of Bureaucracy', *Exemplaria* 19, no. 1 (2007): 39–66.; David Carlson, *Chaucer's Jobs* (New York: Palgrave, 2007), 5–15.

25. Kew, The National Archives, E 207/5/11, transcribed in Crow and Olson, *Chaucer Life-Records*, 157–8.

26. Ibid., E 207/6/2 (East. I Ric. II), transcribed in Crow and Olson, *Chaucer Life-Records*, 164.

27. Ibid., C 18/1394/87, transcribed in Crow and Olson, *Chaucer Life-Records*, 168. For discussion and image, see Simon Horobin, 'Adam Pinkhurst, Geoffrey Chaucer, and the Ellesmere Manuscript of the Canterbury Tales', *Chaucer Review* 44, no. 4 (2010): 351–67, at 354.

28. See Linne Mooney, 'Chaucer's Scribe', *Speculum* 81 (2006): 97–138; Alexandra Gillespie, 'Reading Chaucer's Words to Adam', *Chaucer Review* 42, no. 3 (2008): 269–83; but note also Lawrence Warner, 'Scribes, Misattributed: Hoccleve and Pinkhurst', *Studies in the Age of Chaucer* 37 (2015): 55–100.

29. Nick Havely, 'The Italian Background', in Ellis, *Chaucer: An Oxford Guide*, 313–31, at 313–14.

30. Laura Wright, *Sources of London English: Medieval Thames Vocabulary* (Oxford: Clarendon Press, 1996).

31. Robert M. Stein, 'Multilingualism', in *Oxford Twenty-First Century Approaches to Literature: Middle English*, ed. Paul Strohm (Oxford: Oxford University Press), 23–37, at 28.

32. Ardis Butterfield. *The Familiar Enemy: Chaucer, Language, and Nation in the Hundred Years War* (Oxford: Oxford University Press, 2010), 223.

33. See Joseph A. Dane, 'The Wife of Bath's Shipman's Tale and the Invention of Chaucerian Fabliaux', *Modern Language Review* 99, no. 2 (2004): 287–300.

34. David A. Trotter, 'Oceano vox: You never know where a ship comes from: On multilingualism and language-mixing in medieval Britain', in *Aspects of Multilingualism in European Language History*, eds. Kurt Braunmuller and Gisella Ferraresi (Philadelphia, PA: John Benjamins, 2003), 15–33; Bertil Sandahl, *Middle English Sea Terms, Vol. 1* (Uppsala: Almqvist & Wiksell, 1951), 28.

35. For a beautiful discussion of the flow of water, people, and currency within medieval urban networks, see Suzanne Conklin Akbari, 'Currents and Currency in Marco Polo's Devisement dou monde and The Book of John Mandeville', in *Marco Polo and the Encounter of East and West*, eds. Suzanne Conklin Akbari and Amilcare A. Iannucci, with John Tulk (Toronto: University of Toronto Press, 2008), 110–30, at 120 and 122.

36. Karla Taylor, 'Social Aesthetics and the Emergence of Discourse from the Shipman's Tale to Melibee', *Chaucer Review* 39, no. 3 (2005): 298–322, at 308.

37. Ibid., 304.

38. John Ganim, 'Double Entry in Chaucer's Shipman's Tale: Chaucer and Bookkeeping before Pacioli', *Chaucer Review* 30 (1996): 294–305.

39. Ibid., 295.

40. Ibid., 294.

41. Kew, The National Archives, E101/509/19. All translations are my own. See also Crow and Olson, *Chaucer Life-Records*, 500–3.

42. Ibid., E101/509/19, fol. 24a.

43. Ibid., E101/509/19, fol. 27a.

44. Ibid., E101/509/19, fol. 38a.

45. Ibid., E101/509/19, fol. 32b.

46. Ibid., E101/509/19, fol. 1a.

47. See Ardis Butterfield, 'Chaucer's French Inheritance', in *Cambridge Companion to Chaucer*, eds. Piero Boitani and Jill Mann, 2nd ed. (Cambridge: Cambridge University Press, 2003), 20–35, at 34.

48. See Wright, *Sources of London English*; Maryanne Kowaleski, 'The French of England: A Maritime lingua franca?' in *Language and Culture in Medieval Britain: The French of England, c. 1100–c. 1500*, eds. Jocelyn Wogan-Browne et al. (York: York Medieval Press, 2009), 103–17.

49. Butterfield, 'Chaucer's French Inheritance', 34.

50. Taylor, 'Social Aesthetics', 302.

51. John Gower, *Mirour de l'omme*, 25,237–9, 25,244–5. Gower citation follows G. C. Macaulay, ed., *The Complete Works of John Gower: The French Works* (Oxford: Clarendon Press, 1899).

52. Ibid., 25,301–2.

53. John Gower, *Confessio amantis*, 2.2346–7. Gower citation follows G. C. Macaulay, ed., *The Complete Works of John Gower: The English Works*, vol. 1 (Oxford: Clarendon Press, 1901). On the proverbial nature of this expression, see Bartlett Jere Whiting and Helen Wescott Whiting, eds., *Proverbs, Sentences and Proverbial Phrases From English Writings Mainly Before 1500* (Cambridge, MA: Belknap Press, 1968), C134.

54. *Boece*, 2. Pro4.107–9.

55. Butterfield, *Familiar Enemy*, 222.

56. On code-switching and medieval poetry about travel, see Jonathan Hsy, 'Translation, Suspended: Literary Code-Switching and Poetry of Sea Travel', in *The Medieval Translator/ Traduire au Moyen Âge, Vol. 12*, eds. Denis Renevey and Christiania Whitehead (Turnhout: Brepols, 2009), 133–45.

57. Michelle R. Warren, 'Translation', in *Oxford Twenty-First Century Approaches to Literature: Middle English*, ed. Paul Strohm (Oxford: Oxford University Press, 2007), 51–67, at 50.

58. David A. Trotter, ed., *Multilingualism in Later Medieval Britain* (Cambridge: D. S. Brewer: 2000), 1–5; Davidson, *Medievalism, Multilingualism, and Chaucer*.

59. See the varied perspectives on multilingualism, code-switching, and translanguaging in the bibliography.
60. Jacques Derrida, *Le monolinguisme de l'autre: ou la prothèse d'origine* (Paris: Editions Galilée, 1996); translation by Patrick Mensah in *The Monolingualism of the Other, or, The Prosthesis of Origin* (Stanford, CA: Stanford University Press, 1998).
61. On the city as ecosystem and networked linguasphere, see Jonathan Hsy, 'City,' in *A Handbook of Middle English Studies*, ed. Marion Turner (Chichester: Wiley, 2013), 315–29. On language ecology, see Machan, *English in the Middle Ages*, 1–20.

BIBLIOGRAPHY

Akbari, Suzanne Conklin, 'Currents and Currency in Marco Polo's *Devisement dou monde* and *The Book of John Mandeville*', in *Marco Polo and the Encounter of East and West,* eds. Suzanne Conklin Akbari and Amilcare A. Iannucci, with John Tulk (Toronto: University of Toronto Press, 2008), 110–30.

Butterfield, Ardis, *The Familiar Enemy: Chaucer, Language, and Nation in the Hundred Years War* (Oxford: Oxford University Press, 2010).

Butterfield, Ardis, 'The Dream of Language: Chaucer 'en son Latin,' Studies in the Age of Chaucer 41 (2019): 3–29.

Ganim, John and Shayne Aaron Legassie, eds., *Cosmopolitanism and the Middle Ages* (New York: Palgrave, 2013).

Holsinger, Bruce, 'Chaucer's Difficult Lives', in *Open Access Companion to* The Canterbury Tales, eds. Candace Barrington, Brantley L. Bryant, Richard H. Godden, Daniel T. Kline, and Myra Seaman (September 2017), https://opencanterburytales.dsl.lsu.edu/refchaucerbio/

Hsy, Jonathan, 'City', in *A Handbook of Middle English Studies*, ed. Marion Turner (Chichester: Wiley, 2013), 315–29.

Hsy, Jonathan, *Trading Tongues: Merchants, Multilingualism, and Medieval Literature* (Columbus, OH: Ohio State University Press, 2013).

Kowaleski, Maryanne, 'The French of England: A Maritime *lingua franca*?', in *Language and Culture in Medieval Britain: The French of England, c.1100–c. 1500*, eds. Jocelyn Wogan-Browne, et al. (York: York Medieval Press, 2009), 103–17.

Nakley, Susan. *Living in the Future: Sovereignty and Internationalism in the* Canterbury Tales (Ann Arbor, MI: University of Michigan Press, 2017).

Taylor, Karla, 'Social Aesthetics and the Emergence of Discourse from the Shipman's Tale to Melibee', *Chaucer Review* 39 (2005), 298–322.

Warren, Michelle R., 'Translation', in *Oxford Twenty-First Century Approaches to Literature: Middle English*, ed. Paul Strohm (Oxford: Oxford University Press, 2007), 51–67.

CHAPTER 4

....

LABOUR AND TIME

....

KELLIE ROBERTSON

CHAUCER'S General Prologue to the *Canterbury Tales* remains perhaps the single most extended poetic meditation in the English language on how work shapes the representation of identity. These representations of work, as well as those found in Chaucer's dream visions, join an on-going medieval conversation about labour, a colloquy made up of many disparate voices: the disembodied voice of Parliament attempting to regulate post-plague labour shortages; the moralist—be he preacher or poet—declaiming the value of work to the common profit; the 1381 rebel affirming the ideological value of 'delving' and 'spinning'; the actor-tormenter of the *York Crucifixion* demonstrating spectacularly bad work; or the urban alderman prescribing when and where 'true labour' should happen.

Whether it is the corn-stealing Miller, the cheating Manciple, or the virtuous Parson weary from crisscrossing his parish, all of Chaucer's portraits conjure a sense of person-hood out of the particulars of profession. Yet these working selves are neither trans-historical nor individual in the modern sense of distinct psychologies. The pioneering work of Jill Mann has shown the extent to which these pilgrim portraits depend on stereotypes of 'bad work' found in preaching manuals and sermon literature that called out segments of society—the various medieval 'estates'—and held them accountable for work done well or badly. While Mann's evidence demonstrates Chaucer's familiarity with this received literary tradition of 'estates satire', his portraits are impressed as well with late fourteenth-century ideas about labour drawn from his own work in adminis-trative and judicial positions where he would have been managing and overseeing the labour of others.[1]

While the value of productive labour was a long-standing theme in medieval reli-gious and political literature, the question of what makes labour 'good' acquired new urgency in the wake of the Black Plague that first reached Britain in 1348. As outbreaks swept across the country, the plague not only decimated the population, reducing it in some areas by as much as a third, but also significantly affected everyday life in country and city alike. One of its most conspicuous consequences was a diminished labour pool that led to rising wages and the prospect of interrupted manorial production as workers travelled to other places looking for higher pay and new opportunities. In the wake of this social upset, the government issued laws that capped wages at pre-plague levels and penalized both employers who paid higher wages and employees who took them. These laws also stipulated that a person could be impressed into the service of a manorial lord during the corn harvest if he could not otherwise prove gainful employment elsewhere; he could also be thrown into stocks if he were caught attempting to travel outside of his usual neighbourhood, moving from town to town in search of better circumstances.[2] Declaimed from parish pulpits, these measures aimed to control the 'malice' and 'idleness' of workers and servants; in doing so, they joined the long-standing estates stereotypes in a broader attempt to define 'true labour'.

New legal definitions of work didn't just affect manual labourers, artisans, and shopkeepers, however. They also affected those whose work was of a more immaterial character, including preachers, priests, and even poets. Laws regulating manual labour that happened in public ended up affecting how literary authors imagined the usually invisible, private work of writing. In the late fourteenth-century poem *Piers Plowman*, for instance, Chaucer's contemporary William Langland imagined his narrator Will being forced to justify his own questionable work habits. The allegorical figure of Reason demands to know why the narrator refuses to participate in the autumn harvest, since Will does not appear to be engaged in other, self-evidently useful employment. Anne Middleton and David Aers have argued that this scene responds to contemporary social pressures inspired by the post-plague labour statutes: in defending himself against the charges of able-bodied begging (now prohibited by the statutes), the poet-narrator is also forced to defend the project of vernacular writing as work. Like Langland, Chaucer shows an awareness of these pressures in his poetry, a knowledge that would have been acquired first-hand during the time he served on a judicial commission in the 1380s whose charge included the enforcement of the very labour statutes to which Langland likely alludes. That Chaucer imagined his own work as subject to similar pressures can be argued from the Prologue to his dream vision, the *Legend of Good Women*, where he is seen responding to accusations of 'bad' literary labour and is forced to make amends for his previous poetic transgressions.[3] While such an *apologia* was a received literary topos, it also resonates with contemporary social practice in suggestive ways.

As a poet, Chaucer frequently took up the question of whether or not an individual's work reflects his or her identity, the same question that he would address, in a different vein, in his career as a bureaucrat and a county justice, positions in which he regularly oversaw and assessed the work of others. From the early dream visions to the *Canterbury Tales*, Chaucer's poetry explicitly engages with a cultural lexicon that seeks to make the labouring body visible. Chaucer's interest in the productive value of labour appears most conspicuously in the General Prologue of the *Canterbury Tales*, a work that melds traditional estates satire with contemporary institutional discourses in order to interrogate how work was potentially related to the bodies that perform it.

In outlining how labour practices reflected social assumptions about time and synchronous understandings of identity, this chapter argues that Chaucer was intent on questioning precisely how 'natural' the relationship between body and labour performance really was. His use of physiognomic description within the conspicuously foregrounded temporal scheme of the General Prologue demonstrates that he was especially interested in whether or not certain bodies were predisposed to labour in particular ways, as well as whether or not inner intentions to labour truly could be 'read off' of bodily exteriors. Productive work and the ways in which it could be reckoned were thus not only ethical issues for Chaucer, but were also aesthetic ones in so far as they demanded a sophisticated theory of bodily representation. Chaucer's narrative technique in the General Prologue, one that has variously been termed 'voice' or the 'subjectivity effect', is created not through psychological or emotional depth but through a polytemporal reckoning of an individual pilgrim's works—past, present and (sometimes) future.[4]

Reckoning labouring bodies in feudal time

When medieval church bells tolled, they not only called monks to prayer or the faithful to worship but also chimed the working hours of peasant and artisans alike. The historian Jacques Le Goff hears in these bells 'an instrument of economic, social, and political domination', a tool jointly wielded by the church and the powerful merchant oligarchs who, in most instances, ran the medieval town.[5] The echo of these bells should also remind a modern audience that medieval labour practices had an embodied, phenomenological context that also needs to be recovered, where possible. Perceptions about the 'naturalness' of labour and production were in part an effect of how labouring bodies were situated in differential temporal regimes, whether those governed by astronomical revolutions, merchants' daily reckonings, or the religious *long durée* of eschatology. This observation is not meant to suggest that urban artisans such as tallow makers, fullers and scriveners experienced time differently from, say, carters, plowmen, or builders (though perhaps they did). Rather, institutional discourses framed working bodies differently in relation to time based on their respective work. This temporal biopolitics required, moreover, a naturalized conception of labouring bodies, one shaped by religious literature, legal statutes, and scientific texts.

Chaucer's labouring pilgrims exist in time's thrall to the extent that the General Prologue freezes the descriptions of their professional accomplishments within the fictional moment of the pilgrimage. The focus is further restricted to the precise moment of the narrator's observation of his fellow pilgrims on a particular spring night, within a particular south London neighbourhood, at a particular hostel. This pointedly specific geo-temporal constriction—the 'tyme and space' of the General Prologue (35)—then suddenly dilates to allow for the improbably wide-ranging temporal signatures found in the pilgrim descriptions. As David Burnley has noted, the events of that specific evening at the Tabard Inn are narrated in the Prologue's 'normal narrative preterite'.[6] The narrator's gaze is focused through his use of the historical past ('A knyght ther was' [43]), and yet the pilgrim labours contain multiple time schemes within them. The shifting time scheme of the General Prologue can be described as 'deictic'—that is, the frames of time and reference found there are all relative to one another: the present of the pilgrimage is described with a simple narrative past, while events previous to it are in the past perfect. And yet this sequence of tenses does not sufficiently account for the temporal dynamics of the pilgrim's professional descriptions, nor does Chaucer always use it consistently. Instead, he refashions the temporal schemes in which his pilgrims exist in order to tell us more not just about their own individual work but also about the social expectations through which such work is habitually judged. The audience must assess the Knight's 'knightliness', for instance, based on the complicated grammatical interplay of his description. The Knight's present state is conveyed by the normal narrative past: he 'wered a gypon / Al bismotered with his habergeon' on the pilgrimage itself (75–6); his previous martial career is rendered in the pluperfect ('In Gernade at the seege eek hadde he be / Of Algezir' [56–7]); but the narrator's statement that the Knight is not disposed to speak badly of others – 'he nevere yet no vileynye ne sayde' (70)—projects us into an implicitly psychologically consistent future with its contingent use of 'yet'. The interchange of verb tenses in this passage, moving as they do from the simple past of the literary 'now' to the martial past perfect to an adverbially implied future, suggests that professional behaviour and psychological persona are knit together in a complicated temporal-syntactic performance.

This elastic temporality is arguably the rhetorical technique most common to all of the descriptions of pilgrim labour in the Prologue. Pilgrim identity is, in part, the effect of the contrapuntal movement between the historical present of the pilgrimage and the pilgrims' polytemporal work lives, a shift from an immediate introspection to labouring retrospection. The intellectual historian Reinhart Koselleck has pointed out the ways in which our expectations of the past may influence our present even more strongly than our expectations of the future.[7] While Koselleck is primarily interested in how post-Enlightenment modernity represents itself to itself, his insight is also useful for understanding a medieval writer such as Chaucer, who had to negotiate his own poetic authority within what we might call the 'long now' of the classical-medieval continuum. Koselleck reminds us that any particular present is but a 'former future' shaped by the specific semantics and concepts that were put in place 'once upon a time'; our desiring relation to such a past is what Koselleck calls an act of 'retroactive expectation'. Chaucer's pilgrim portraits are an example of just such retroactive expectation at work, juxtaposing as they do past work and 'present' pilgrim self, all filtered through a temporally and spatially omniscient narrator. In order to understand the deixis of these pilgrim descriptions, we need to understand the multiple, sometimes competing labour chronologies that were imagined by late medieval society and with which Chaucer's poetry repeatedly engages.

Late medieval life was thought to occur in several differing time signatures, temporalities outlined in the work of twentieth-century historians such as Aaron Gurevich and Jacques Le Goff, as well as the more recent work of literary critics such as Kathleen Davis and Carolyn Dinshaw among others.[8] Le Goff innovatively described the multiple temporalities at work in medieval society. He saw the peasant as dominated by 'meteorological time' subject to 'the cycle of seasons and the unpredictability of storms and natural cataclysms'.⁹ Superimposed on this time, was a 'church time' determined by the daily rhythm of religious offices and tolled from village bell towers. The merchant subsequently refines church time with the development of a 'clock time' measured in precise hours as well as in terms of price and profit. This teleology—meteorological time succeeded by church time followed by merchant time—is founded on and regulated by an ideology of 'natural' peasant time. And yet this natural meteorological time is, of course, a very human construction, one that repeatedly conflates land, labour, and measurable time in a variety of forms.

This triangulation of land, labour, and time finds expression in legal, social, and literary texts that describe agricultural labour, including Chaucer's description of the hardworking Plowman in the General Prologue. The Plowman's seemingly 'timeless' embrace of his role in an explicitly communal, feudal system—to which I'll return later—finds an analogue in received medieval discourses that sought to naturalize seasonal agricultural labour in relation to the bodies that performed it. Such naturalizing tendencies are found in a variety of sources both institutional and popular. The twelfth-century Anglo-Norman writer Philippe de Thaon, for instance, offers several standard etymologies for the Latin 'annum', or year, before departing from his sources to offer his own, alternate history of the word:

> E sacez uncore plus
> Que li bers Romulus
> Primes le contruvad
> E cest nun li dunad
> Quant il out la baillie
> De tute Romanie.
> E achaisun i ad
> Pur quei il le truvad:
> Iceo fud pur sa rente,
> Nent pur altrë entente,
> Quë il aveir volait
> De cels que il mainteneit
> A termë e a ure
> E senz tute demure.

[And know also that the lord Romulus first invented it (i.e. *annum*) and gave it this name when he had possession of all Rome. And there was a reason why he invented it: it was for his rent, and for no other purpose, since he desired to have it from his vassals in timely instalments and without any delay.]¹⁰

Philippe connects the year's inception to Romulus's desire for feudal rents, an equation that effectively elides the labouring body of the peasant into the rents that he or she produces. If the origins of measurable time are founded on a desire to reckon the proceeds of peasant labour, the labour itself must remain invisible. The mythic, eponymous founder of Rome is reframed by Philippe as a medieval manorial lord or bailiff who wants his cash rents on time and with a minimum of fuss. This anecdote queers time for its own ideological purposes by reimagining the classical past in terms of a feudal present.

Philippe's etymology of *annum* participates in the broader cultural logic that sought to present the labour of peasant bodies as both natural and inevitable by situating them within a totalizing astronomical time. The most vivid instantiation of this logic may be that found in the well-known cycle of images constituting the 'labours of the months' in Jean, Duke of Berry's *Très riches heures*, a book of hours that foregrounds noble pursuits such as hunting, hawking, and feasting against a background of seasonally appropriate rural labour. These scenes naturalize the peasant body by making it one with both the distant landscape and the astronomical signs that border the page; visually, the working bodies share the space of the domestic animals in the background, receding from the noble, 'human' foreground. Framed by the astrological signs, these images of peasant labour suggest a series of 'nested' ideological assumptions about peasant bodies and time. The peasant body labours in accord with seasons that are, in turn, regulated by the divisions of the zodiac. The *mise-en-page* reinforces the connection between land, work, and time: the background labouring bodies blend into the astronomical border, providing a foil for the aristocratic pursuits of the foreground.[11] The art historian Michael Camille has noted that similar scenes depicting the 'labours of the months' in the fourteenth-century Luttrell Psalter were designed to be viewed by the lord whose power was based on this cyclical peasant activity. In both manuscripts, the images of the labouring peasant serve to re-enforce the noble reader's sense of the unchanging nature of the manorial work that is arguably the lord's greatest resource.

If the peasant body habitually receded into the distance in visual representations, so too it had a similarly uncanny way of disappearing into the etymological mists surrounding rural production and the codes that governed it. The common term for a day, *journei*, used in both Middle English and Anglo-Norman texts referred not only to the daylight hours between sunrise and sunset but also to the work that could be accomplished during that period. The term derives from the dialect variant 'journal' that denoted the amount of land that could be ploughed in a single day. In this designation, the plowing peasant gets equated with the daylight hours during which he performs his work, together producing the effect of land continuously cultivated, day in and day out.[12] Similarly, the customary laws regulating English manorial labour erased peasant bodies by claiming that the rents derive from the land itself rather than from the peasants who worked it. A tract of land had annual rents associated with it, rents which, in the words of the legal historians Pollock and Maitland, are 'as much a part of it as the trees that grow out of it and the houses built upon it'.[13] Just as in the image from the *Très riches heures*, agricultural labour is naturalized, serving as an unchanging background for the more conspicuous and timely activities of the nobility.

This sense of timeless agricultural labour is conveyed in Chaucer's description of the only journeyman agricultural labourer on the pilgrimage, the Plowman. Brother to the virtuous Parson with whom he travels, the Plowman is described in similarly idealized terms:

> With hym ther was a Plowman, was his brother,
> That hadde ylad of dong ful many a fother;
> A trewe swynkere and a good was he,
> Lyvynge in pees and parfit charitee.
> God loved he best with al his hoole herte
> At alle tymes, thogh him gamed or smerte,
> And thanne his neighebor right as hymselve.
> He wolde thresshe, and therto dyke and delve,
> For Cristes sake, for every povre wight,
> Withouten hire, if it lay in his myght.
> His tithes payde he ful faire and wel,
> Bothe of his proper swynk and his catel.
> In a tabard he rood upon a mere.   (I.529–541)

This description lacks the complicated deixis of the Knight's description, with its seemingly endless sequence of martial pluperfects. Instead, there is only one event of any specificity marked with the plu perfect: the Plowman 'hadde ylad of dong ful many a fother'. But even this plu perfect suggests repetition through time rather than the singular events that comprise the Knight's distinctive (if temporally implausible) *vita*. The Plowman's description achieves a feeling of naturalized, timeless labour, one characteristic of the conflation of past time and feudal labour found in Philippe de Thaon's mythologizing of the origins of *annum*, in the Anglo-Norman etymology of *journei*, and in the images of peasant work found in the pages of the *Très riches heures*. Chaucer achieves a similar effect in the General Prologue by describing the Plowman's work almost solely in the same historic present tense that is used to describe the events simultaneous with the pilgrimage. Similarly, his assertion that the Plowman was a good worker 'lyvinge in pees and partif charitee' uses a past progressive construction to suggest the continuity of this idealized work across time, a feeling reinforced by the subsequent assertion that he loved God 'at alle tymes'. This shallow temporal depth-of-field (to borrow a visual metaphor) suggests that the Plowman's past labour (described almost exclusively in the simple past) blends seamlessly with the 'present' of the pilgrimage; likewise, the particulars of his physiognomy disappear in the powerful professional solvent of his true labour.

The timelessness of Chaucer's description of the Plowman is instructive in relation to the contemporary cultural pressures that would have informed it. This pilgrim portrait is a fantasy of selfless, unpaid labour in contradistinction to the images of 'malicious' and self-interested labourers depicted in the historic estates literature as well as in contemporary labour statutes. Chaucer's portrait of the Plowman evinces a post-plague nostalgia for a manual labourer who likely never existed but who was certainly, by this time, an endangered creature in the increasingly severe portraits of manual labourers found in religious and judicial contexts. The Plowman's portrait thus voices an 'expectation of the past', to return to Koselleck's phrase, in which labourers were more selfless than self-interested, a retroactive anticipation mediated by Chaucer's fiction.

DISPOSITION AND ARTISAN LABOUR

With the rise of urban artisan labour in the later medieval period, the problem of rationalizing why some bodies were predisposed to perform certain types of work became a more pressing question and one lacking ready answers. As opposed to rural agricultural labour, craft or guild labour was difficult to situate in direct relation to the forces governing the natural world. Peasant labour was amenable to naturalization because the body worked in seasonal cycles governed by astrological time. Artisan labour, however, could not be naturalized in the same way. It was largely repetitive and out of synch with natural cycles. As the workforce diversified, more complex strategies were necessary to harness the working body to the traces of institutional time.

Chaucer's description of the five guildsmen in the General Prologue witnesses how this increasing division of labour challenged traditional ways of imagining labour in relation to the body that performed it. Chaucer's guildsmen represent typical specimens of the craft associations that would have been familiar to a late medieval London audience:

> An haberdasshere and a carpenter,
> A webbe, a dyere, and a tapycer –
> And they were clothed alle in o lyveree
> Of a solempne and a greet fraternitee.   (I.361–4)

With the exception of the carpenter, these craftsmen all work in the cloth trades, engaged in the selling, weaving and dying of textiles. They belong not to a single craft guild but to a single 'fraternity', most likely a local parish organization that guaranteed its members mutual aid in legal, social and religious matters or in times of financial need.[14]

The rise of artisan labour created an opposition between labouring bodies governed directly by the seasons and urban labour that was imagined, in some scientific circles, to be mediated by humoural disposition, the fluctuating balance of black bile, phlegm, blood, and yellow bile. These humours were, in turn, understood to be governed by seasonal changes. Where astrology's direct explanatory power faltered, the physiognomy of individual labouring bodies took precedence. Elaborating on a commonplace in Galenic medicine, the influential Arabic polymath Avicenna argued that labour as a form of bodily exercise strengthened the body by expelling excess moisture and thereby restoring its energy: 'labor corpus siccat, validumque reddit' [labour heals the body and returns its vigour].[15] The verb 'siccare' suggests that labour literally 'dries up' the body, by expelling the moist humours that were thought to damage it. Avicenna goes on to suggest that certain professions could influence the body's humoural balance; for instance, the fuller's art (the washing of cloth in order to clean it of impurities) would result in an increase of bodily coldness and moisture, whereas spelting or metalworking would increase heat and dryness. Sailors, such as Chaucer's Shipman, were thought to have cold and wet humours as influenced by their surroundings. By the thirteenth century, medieval medical writers had elaborated this theory into a full-blown typology of humoural dispositions that marked each profession. The Catalan theologian and physician Arnau de Vilanova argued that different labours had distinctive physiognomic repercussions for the body. Arnau dedicates an entire chapter, entitled *De artibus* or 'On crafts' to anatomizing labouring bodies in his influential *Speculum medicine*, wherein he argues that labour affects the body in identifiable and consistent ways.[16] In arguing that profession reliably influences the humoural constitution of the body, Arnau sought to harmonize vocation and anatomy in a way that made such identities appear, once again, natural and transhistorical. Correlatively, he also imagines a mutable body subject not to the zodiac but to the body's own labours. Such attempts to read labour off of the body, however, did not generate a cultural consensus. A late medieval treatise on physiognomy attributed to Aristotle rejects this connection between labour and bodies: 'thus as regards opinions or scientific knowledge, you cannot recognize a doctor or a musician, for the fact of having acquired a piece of knowledge will not have produced any alteration in the bodily signs on which physiognomy relies'.[17] In the absence of a generally accepted understanding as to how urban labour was 'naturally' related to the bodies that performed it, guild ordinances often composed their own narratives emphasizing the constructed nature of the artisan body, a body stabilized through nurture rather than nature.

Chaucer's use of physiognomic detail in portraits such as the Miller's suggests that physiognomy's explanatory power was most useful in relation to manorial labourers. The five guildsmen, on the other hand, are described not physiognomically but rather according to sumptuary and social aspirations: their fine clothing ('o lyveree') and their religious and professional desires. By the 1390s, rationales for craft labour appealed not to the predisposition of astro-biology but to outward manner as well as social genealogies that demonstrated a craft's long-standing history, a history that underwrote the religious probity of its members in the present. The increasing division of labour demanded competing (sometimes conflicting) modes of simultaneous time rather than the largely successive times delineated by Le Goff. Chaucer's rhetorical strategies for portraying his guildsmen's working lives, both actual and aspirational, become clearer when compared with a contemporaneous document that witnesses how guild labour could be legitimated. Written in the 1390s, the anonymous English poem known as the Masons' *Constitutions* is part versified guild ordinance, part foundational myth, and part conduct manual. In its attempts to historicize embodied guild labour in past, present, and future simultaneously, the artisan body surfaces as hyper-visible through a confluence of genealogical time, hagiographical time, and a guild time intent on regulating labour and the body. As a simultaneous attempt to historicize the guild's foundation and to show the epiphenomenal work of contemporary artisan labour within the regime of guild time, the poem enacts a number of competing temporalities. Such a clash lays the groundwork for what Carolyn Dinshaw calls a 'queer history': 'historicism is queer when it grasps that temporality itself raises the question of embodiment and subjectivity'.[18] As a foundational moment of urban guild labour, the *Constitutions* necessarily queer time as they struggle with reconciling a transhistorical body—the *corporatio* of the guild—with the epiphenomenal work performed by individual artisans in the present.

The Masons' *Constitutions* offers a historical origin account purportedly taken from a mythical 'old book' that documented the prehistory of the mason's annual legislative assembly. The poem has three distinct parts. It opens with the English genealogy of mason lore: the founding of geometry by Euclid in Egypt and its subsequent arrival in England under Aethelstan. It then codifies the guild's customs in fifteen articles directed at master masons and a further fifteen points directed at the craftsmen of the guild; while the final section is a generalized conduct manual presumably aimed at improving the behaviour of craft apprentices. These English verse *Constitutions* document the precarious position of fourteenth-century masons, who were organized relatively late into urban craft guilds—when they were organized at all—because of the largely itinerant nature of their work.[19] As Lisa H. Cooper has perceptively argued, the *Constitutions* 'work hard to create an imagined community among artisans whose actual community was frequently dispersed'.[20]

It is with an emphasis on the transhistoric nature of the body, however, that the Masons' guild attempts to create an imagined community of craft knowledge. Regulating the potentially mutable mason body as the site of labours past and present is one of the poem's chief concerns. While the *Constitutions* place special emphasis on the strong and whole mason body, contemporary statutes suggest a more vulnerable one. Among the articles' stipulations, we find that no disabled or maimed men can be apprenticed to the guild; all must be what the articles term 'mighty men'—that is, whole of body, not lame or otherwise 'unparfit'.[21] The idea of 'mighty men' moving from locale to locale in search of work was precisely what the post-plague labour statutes sought to prohibit, making such men liable to punishment in stocks. These statues also urged local authorities to prosecute such 'mighty men', who pretended to physical disability only to gain alms.[22]

To be a journeyman mason in the late fourteenth century was thus to occupy a precarious professional position. Part of the ideological heavy lifting that the *Constitutions* had to perform was to demonstrate that the strong, itinerant mason body was actually amenable to oversight and regulation. In the absence of a dominant cultural discourse that could naturalize guild labour with respect to the body that performed it, the *Constitutions* sought to anchor mason bodies not just in a contemporary guild time that regulated hours of work and leisure but in genealogical and hagiographical time as well. The middle section of the *Constitutions* contains two foundational stories about the guild's origins. The first recounts the martyrdom of four masons who were asked by a pagan emperor to create idols ('mawmetys') intended to lure Christians away from their faith. The good Christian masons, of course, refuse this idolatrous commission and were duly imprisoned and put to death by the evil emperor. In this collective secular *vita*, hagiographical time licenses the coherence of the *corporatio* or guild around the martyred *corpora* of early Christian masons. This saintly legend is followed by an extended description of Euclid, the putative founder of the mason guild, who by the 'grace of Christ' creates not just geometry but the entirety of the *trivium* and *quadrivium*, effectively the basis not just of artisan knowledge but of medieval scholastic knowledge as well. In this description, cultural and religious anachronism renders the pagan past continuous with the Christian present, a continuity that shores up the biopolitically vulnerable body of the mason liable to contemporary impressment and harassment.

These concerns about embodiment are equally visible, if in a slightly different key, in the *Constitutions*' final section, which takes the form of a late medieval conduct manual that directs masons on how to act in church and in everyday life. What looks like a narrative non-sequitur—why move from the guild's origins to a conduct manual?—is actually an important component in the *Constitutions*' attempt to make the mason's body visible to both guild masters and municipal authorities. Moreover, as Claire Sponsler and others have argued, the commodification of conduct was on the rise in the late fourteenth century, and these manuals made visible the labour that goes into the making of the body. So too the *Constitutions*' conduct manual claims that 'good norture will save thy state'.[23] In emphasizing the formative power of nurture over nature, the conduct manual shows us the body in the process of being manufactured rather than presenting us with a pre-determined biological body 'found' out there in nature. The *Constitutions* suggest that the body, just as much as the block of stone waiting to be carved, is a work in progress; a form to be laboured over; ultimately, a built thing. It is at once a transhistorical body, connected through time to the martyred bodies of its forebears but equally one still in a state of becoming, shaped through its own daily labours on the building site as well as in polite society.

While the guildsmen described by Chaucer in the General Prologue (consisting of a carpenter and several textile workers) would have had a more secure social position than the itinerant mason, these urban artisans would also have been governed by guild ordinances and the labours laws that regulated the work of labourers, artificers, and servants.[24] The guildsmen portrait is, like the Masons' *Constitutions*, a snapshot of bodily discipline orchestrated within a complex interplay of time signatures. If the conduct manual at the end of the *Constitutions* sought to discipline and consolidate the bodies of the craftsmen, Chaucer's description of the guildsmen similarly shows them to share a collective bodily exterior, one that, like the masonic guild body, glosses over any potential differences of the actual bodies beneath:

> Ful fressh and newe hir geere apiked was;
> Hir knyves were chaped noght with bras
> But al with silver, wroght ful clene and weel,
> Hire girdles and hir pouches everydeel.   (I.365–8)

The newness and quality of the clothing underlines their shared prosperity as well as their shared social aspirations.[25] The description's ekphrastic specificity directs the audience's gaze first to prosperous outsides and then, implicitly, to aspirational interiors. Rhetorically, this movement is accomplished through antithesis: the guildsmen's clothes are new rather than old, their knives are silver rather than brass, and, moreover, there is a contrast between their current state as members of middling guilds and their possible futures as prominent aldermen.

While the Masons' *Constitutions* attempted to legitimate guild work through the power of 'retroactive expectation' by displaying the martyred body of their forebears, Chaucer's description employs a different temporal sleight-of-hand by inviting his audience to judge present artisan bodies against possible futures. Chaucer's guildsmen do not boast of a prestigious mythical past attributed to their various crafts; rather, it is their shared dress and a collective expectation that underwrites their professional personas:

> Wel semed each of hem a fair burgeys
> To sitten in a yeldehalle on a deys.
> Everich, for the wisdom that he kan,
> Was shaply for to been an alderman,
> For catel hadde they ynogh and rente,
> And eek hir wyves wolde it wel assente;
> And elles certeyn were they to blame.
> It is ful fair to been ycleped 'madame',
> And goon to vigilies al bifore,
> And have a mantel roialliche ybore.   (I.369–78)

Solidarity in social ambition rather than individual craft is what unifies these guild bodies. Unlike the Plowman, who is described almost completely in a simple past connoting timelessness, or the Knight, whose past life is described in the compulsive pluperfect of a lengthy professional *vita*, the guildsmen are proleptically imagined as successful aldermen, a professional fantasy that may have proved difficult to attain in a competitive urban centre like London.

Regulating religious labour and producing ecclesiastical bodies

If artisan labour could be imagined as a stitching together of often competing modes of earthly and spiritual temporalities, so too religious labour was envisioned as a similarly sutured together series of 'nows'. The well-known portrait of Chaucer's Monk shares this narrative affinity with Chaucer's guildsmen. His labour, like theirs, is conjured through the reciprocating movement between present belief and retroactive expectation. The manual and clerical labours formerly valued in monastic orders are contrasted with the Monk's conspicuously embodied present, symbolized by his predilection for hunting, fine horses, and expensive clothing (I.165–207). Like the guildsmen who are proleptically imagined as aldermen, so too the Monk, already a monastic office holder as 'kepere of the celle' (172), is poised on the brink of another possible future: he is 'a manly man, to been an abbot able' (167).

If the temporal asynchrony of Chaucer's guildsman and the Mason's *Constitutions* register unease over the social position of these craftsmen, the Monk's world view (and the narrator's response to it) similarly witnesses a vigorous debate over how spiritual labour should be valued and, when necessary, policed. The quantification and assessment of religious work may seem an unlikely undertaking to a modern audience, but this conversation had both a long medieval history and a new urgency by the time that Chaucer was writing the General Prologue of the *Canterbury Tales*. In mid-thirteenth century Paris, the mendicant orders (represented by Chaucer's wandering Friar in the General Prologue) had argued with secular clerics (represented by Chaucer's Parson) over what kind of spiritual work was most beneficial to the community: was it better to pray continuously for the general welfare of the community? Or was a life spent ministering to the daily spiritual needs of individual parishioners of more benefit? While this argument between seculars and mendicants reflected papal politics as well as the complex tissue of ecclesiastical allegiances at the University of Paris, it was primarily fought on the grounds of what type of religious work was to be most esteemed and who was to regulate it.[26] By the mid-fourteenth century, answering these questions became even more imperative, as plague spread through monastery and town alike, leaving in its wake a shortage of competent clerics of either persuasion. There was not only a dearth of hands to work the fields and build the houses, but also a shortage of parish priests to tend to such workers. This shortage resulted in fewer stipendiary priests available to perform basic 'cure of souls', the day-to-day work of baptizing, marrying, and burying local parishioners. Just as the labour statutes had condemned lazy servants and other greedy workers, priests were likewise condemned by ecclesiastical superiors for 'insatiable avarice' and attempts were made to set their wages at pre-plague rates.[27] These controversies, impelled equally by ideology and demography, bequeathed to Chaucer much of the figurative language used in his religious descriptions of the *Canterbury Tales*.[28] Like their lay travelling companions, the religious pilgrims are judged on their spiritual duties *qua* work, whether in the negative example of the Friar, whose itinerant confession-hearing-for-hire leaves no time to minister to the sick and poor, or the positive one of the Parson, who resists 'sub-letting' his benefice in order to say more lucrative commemorative masses for the souls of the wealthy.

It is against this background of contested spiritual labour that we can read the narrator's surprisingly warm affirmation of the Monk's worldly views on labour, arguably one of the most curious first-person interjections in the poem as a whole. The narrator seemingly approves the Monk's view that past monastic precedent need not necessarily determine present practice:

> And I seyde his opinion was good.
> What sholde he studie and make hymselven wood,
> Upon a book in cloystre alwey to poure,
> Or swynken with his handes, and laboure,
> As Austyn bit? How shal the world be served?
> Lat Austyn have his swynk to hym reserved!   (I.183–8)

It is significant that this confirmation, voiced in *propria persona*, is the narrator's only direct statement about work in the General Prologue, a poem whose central theme is arguably the extent to which labour shapes perceptions of subjectivity. The narrator's rhetorical question 'how shall the world be served?' was precisely the question at the heart of on-going debates over spiritual labour raised by the conflict between seculars and mendicants as well as the post-plague ecclesiastical labour shortages closer to home. The narrator's enthusiasm for the Monk's views is not, however, a useful heuristic either for delving into the ostensibly layered characterization of the narrator as some critics have suggested—this is not an older, wiser narrator looking back on his younger, 'horns-woggled' self[29]—or for figuring out where Chaucer 'stands' on these issues. Instead, the narrator's interjection raises the question: to what extent was such a consensus about monastic work widely held and by whom? In what ways is the present invested in this particular expectation of past religious work (as Koselleck would have it)?

Chaucer's answer to these questions lies in the deictic description of the Monk's person and his work. By framing the monastic outrider's labour in relation to the historic founding moment of his order, the narrator, invoking both the Augustinian and Benedictine rules, interrogates both the 'olde thynges' that the monk would let pass and the 'newe world' he seeks to embrace (I.175–6). Chaucer's contrapuntal narrative technique here is similar to that used elsewhere in the General Prologue, functioning through temporal antithesis and metonymy. Chaucer counterfactually juxtaposes the Monk's extra-clausal labour practices to Augustine's injunction that monks should speed the plow both in the field and, by metaphorical extension, on the page. Unlike the Mason's *Constitutions* that sought to demonstrate continuity between the guild's mythic past and its present labour practices, the rhetorical strategies found in Chaucer's description of the Monk highlights the discontinuity of past and present attitudes towards labour. The Monk's portrait induces a kind of temporal whiplash, as it moves from the Monk's imagined future as abbot to the patristic past of tightly regulated monastic houses, to the continuous sound of the jingling saddle bells that announce the Monk's presence as he rides about the countryside. This description encourages the audience to experience not the depth of the Monk's psychology but rather, in a compressed form, a society's shifting views about religious labour. To the extent that we are encouraged to view the Monk as a character, it is through a triangulation of past, present, and future expectations about what constitutes 'true' monastic practice. The audience is not asked to judge the Monk's penchant for redefining his vocation per se. Rather, we are asked to analyse the competing attitudes toward religious work that make such a redefinition possible at the moment in which Chaucer was writing.

Framing labour and productive value in the General Prologue is a polytemporal undertaking enacted through multiple competing time schemes present in the pilgrim portraits. The narrator's question about the Monk's vocational commitments – 'how shall the world be served?'—is raised to an ethical and aesthetic imperative in the General Prologue of the *Canterbury Tales*. In judging how the world is served, we do not just judge individual pilgrims, clerical or lay. Instead, we judge the wider cultural assumptions about labour that determined Chaucer's present by what it desired of its past. The social and literary models of labour found here suggest that the medieval biopolitics of work, wherein a person's work can be accurately known (or indeed, 'read off' of the body), are treated with suspicion. Chaucer seems to doubt the possibility of transparently legible labouring bodies, whether belonging to gentry, cleric, artisan, or agricultural labourer. His descriptions suggest that, as the cultural consensus about productive work shifted, it became necessary to judge not only an individual's putative labours but also the standards by which the social value of work more generally was to be judged. Chaucer's textualization of labour in the General Prologue suggests that such judgments cannot be made in the abstract. Rather, the 'now' of labour can only be understood materially, in the context of the bodies that perform it, and temporally, in the flux of the past and present expectations that define it.

NOTES

1. See David Carlson, *Chaucer's Jobs* (New York: Palgrave Macmillan, 2004); and Kellie Robertson, *The Laborer's Two Bodies: Labor and the 'Work' of the Text in Medieval Britain, 1350–1500* (New York: Palgrave Macmillan, 2006).
2. See James Bothwell, P. J. P Goldberg, and W. M. Ormrod, eds., *The Problem of Labour in Fourteenth-Century England* (York: York Medieval Press, 2000); Anthony Musson, 'Reconstructing English Labour Laws: A Medieval Perspective', in *The Middle Ages at Work*, eds. Kellie Robertson and Michael Uebel (New York: Palgrave Macmillan, 2004), 113–32; and W. M. Ormrod, 'The English Government and the Black Death of 1348–9', in *England in the Fourteenth Century*, ed. W. M. Ormrod (Woodbridge, Suffolk: Boydell & Brewer, 1986), 178–9.
3. Robertson, *Laborer's Two Bodies*, 51–77.
4. While this chapter deals only with the representation of labour and production in Chaucer, there are several literary studies of medieval labour practices that would usefully supplement it in addition to those on Langland discussed above: Ethan Knapp on Hoccleve in *The Bureaucratic Muse: Thomas Hoccleve and the Literature of Late Medieval England* (College Park, PA: Penn State University Press, 2001); Elliot Kendall on Gower in *Lordship and Literature: John Gower and the Politics of the Great Household* (Oxford: Oxford University Press, 2008); Isabel Davis on gendered labour in *Writing Masculinity in the Later Middle Ages* (Cambridge: Cambridge University Press, 2007); and Lisa H. Cooper on artisan labour across the medieval period in *Artisans and Narrative Craft in Late Medieval England* (Cambridge: Cambridge University Press, 2011).

5. Jacques Le Goff, *Time, Work, and Culture in the Middle Ages*, trans. Arthur Goldhammer (Chicago IL: University of Chicago Press, 1980), 35.

6. David Burnley, *A Guide to Chaucer's Language* (Norman, OK: University of Oklahoma Press, 1983), 47.

7. Reinhart Koselleck, *Futures Past: On the Semantics of Historical Time*, trans. Keith Tribe (New York: Columbia University Press, 1985).

8. Foundational studies include A. J. Gurevich, *Categories of Medieval Culture*, trans. G. L. Campbell (London: Routledge and Kegan Paul, 1985) and Jacques Le Goff, *Time, Work, and Culture in the Middle Ages*, trans. Arthur Goldhammer (Chicago, IL: University of Chicago Press, 1980). Kathleen Davis has explored how modern conceptions of feudal time structure not just historical narratives but also the political systems based upon them; see *Periodization and Sovereignty: How Ideas of Feudalism and Secularization Govern the Politics of Time* (Philadelphia, PA: University of Pennsylvania Press, 2008). More recently, Carolyn Dinshaw has urged us to consider the ways that medieval narratives (such as hagiography and travel literature) reject conventional time schemes and instead embrace asynchrony, an embrace whose reach can extend to the modern critic reading them as well; see *How Soon Is Now? Medieval Texts, Amateur Readers, and Queerness of Time* (Durham, NC: Duke University Press, 2012).

9. Le Goff, *Time, Work, and Culture*, 34–5.

10. Philippe de Thaon, *Comput (MS BL Cotton Nero A.V)*, ed. Ian Short (London: Birkbeck College, 1984), lines 1873–1886. Philippe's *computus* was one of the earliest vernacular scientific texts composed in England; for details of its composition, see Short's introduction. Following Isidore of Seville, Philippe initially notes that some say time is a renewal or *removement*, a starting over as the natural world blossoms each spring; others say the term derives from *anulus* or 'ring' (in Philippe, *l'anels*), since the year always 'wheels back upon itself'.

11. See Camille, *Mirror in Parchment: The Luttrell Psalter and the Making of Medieval England* (Chicago, IL: University of Chicago Press, 1998), 191–2.

12. See MED, s.v. 'journei' (n.) 2a. 'a day's work'. Le Goff also mentions this etymology (*Time, Work, and Culture*, 44). Among many examples of this usage, the MED cites *Piers Plowman* B.14.136 (LdMisc 581): 'Selden deieth he out of dette þat dyneth ar he deserue it, And til he haue done his deuor and his dayes iourne' [Seldom does he die out of debt who dines before he deserves it; and until he had done his obligation and his day's work]. Here the apparent redundancy 'dayes iourne' is apparently necessary in a context where 'iourne' is synonymous with 'labour'.

13. Frederick Pollock and Frederic William Maitland, *The History of English Law*, 2nd ed. (Cambridge: Cambridge University Press, 1895; repr. 1968), 2:144.

14. Mark Addison Amos, 'The Naked and the Dead: The Carpenters' Company and Lay Spirituality in Late Medieval England', in Robertson and Uebel, *Middle Ages at Work*, 91–3.

15. Avicenna, *Liber canonis* (Venice, 1580), I.2.2.12, 'De motu et quiete', f. 169.

16. On Arnau's *Speculum medicine*, see Peter Biller, 'A "Scientific" View of Jews From Paris Around 1300', in *Gli Ebrei e le Scienze/The Jews and Sciences*, ed. Agostino Paravicini Bagliani, *Micrologus* 9 (2002): 147. It is unsurprising that Arnau's medical treatise takes up ethical questions about labouring bodies, since his writings frequently blurred the distinction between medicine and morality; on this tendency, see Joseph Ziegler, *Medicine and Religion, c. 1300: the Case of Arnau de Vilanova* (Oxford: Clarendon Press, 1998), 46–52.

17. Quoted in Simon Swain, ed., *Seeing the Face, Seeing the Soul: Polemon's Physiognomy from Classical Antiquity to Medieval Islam* (Oxford: Oxford University Press, 2007), 641.

18. Carolyn Dinshaw, 'Temporalities', in *Twenty-First Century Approaches to Literature: Middle English*, ed. Paul Strohm (Oxford: Oxford University Press, 2007), 109.

19. Douglas Knoop and G. P. Jones, *The Mediaeval Mason* (Manchester: Manchester University Press, 1967), 152–3.

20. Lisa H. Cooper, 'The "Boke of Oure Charges": Constructing Community in the Masons' Constitutions', *Journal of the Early Book Society* 6 (2003): 1–39, at 4.

21. *Constitutions*, Article 5. These articles are reproduced from the Regius manuscript in Knoop and Jones, *Mediaeval Mason*, 261–69. The text of the two extant versions of the *Constitutions* (found in the Regius MS and the Cooke MS) are in Douglas Knoop, G. P. Jones, and D. Hamer, eds., *The Two Earliest Masonic MSS* (Manchester: Manchester University Press, 1938).

22. Masons were more liable to impressment into building works than other labourers. By the 1350s, the main labour force for royal works was impressed, and the majority of this labour would have been masons. Such impressment would have likely been within Chaucer's oversight as Clerk of the King's Works in the 1390s; see H. M. Colvin, et al., *History of the King's Works* (London: HMSO, 1963), 1:180–7, and Knoop and Jones, *Mediaeval Mason*, 80–5.

23. *Constitutions*, line 722; see Knoop et al., *Two Earliest Masonic MSS*, 236–46.

24. See H. M. Swanson, *Medieval Artisans: An Urban Class in Late Medieval England* (Oxford: Oxford University Press, 1988); Gervase Rosser, 'Crafts, guilds and the negotiation of work in the medieval town', *Past and Present* 154 (1997): 3–31; and Elaine Clark, 'Medieval Labour Law and English Local Courts', *American Journal of Legal History* 27:4 (1983): 330–53.

25. Laura F. Hodges, *Chaucer and Costume* (Cambridge: D. S. Brewer, 2000), 132–6.

26. See D. L. Douie, *The Conflict between the Seculars and the Mendicants at the University of Paris in the Thirteenth Century* (London: Blackfriars, 1954), and Luigi Pellegrini, *L'incontro tra due 'invenzioni' medievali: Università e Ordini Mendicanti*, Scienze Storiche 13 (Naples: Liguori Editore, 2003), 155–80.

27. Bertha Putnam, 'Maximum Wage-Laws for Priests after the Black Death, 1348–1381', *American Historical Review* 21 (1915–6): 12–32.

28. Penn R. Szittya, *The Antifraternal Tradition in Medieval Literature* (Princeton, NJ: Princeton University Press, 1986), 231–46.

29. J. Stephen Russell, *Chaucer and the Trivium* (Gainsville, FL: University Press of Florida, 1998), 77.

BIBLIOGRAPHY

Bothwell, James, P. J. P. Goldberg, and W. M. Ormrod, *The Problem of Labour in Fourteenth-Century England* (York: York Medieval Press, 2000).

Camille, Michael, *Mirror in Parchment: The Luttrell Psalter and the Making of Medieval England* (Chicago, IL: University of Chicago Press, 1998).

Cooper, Lisa H., *Artisans and Narrative Craft in Late Medieval England* (Cambridge: Cambridge University Press, 2011).

Dinshaw, Carolyn, *How Soon Is Now? Medieval Texts, Amateur Readers, and Queerness of Time* (Durham, NC: Duke University Press, 2012).

Gurevich, A. J., *Categories of Medieval Culture,* trans. G. L. Campbell (London: Routledge and Kegan Paul, 1985).

Koselleck, Reinhart, *Futures Past: On the Semantics of Historical Time*, trans. Keith Tribe (New York: Columbia University Press, 1985).

Le Goff, Jacques, *Time, Work, and Culture in the Middle Ages*, trans. Arthur Goldhammer (Chicago, IL: University of Chicago Press, 1980).

Robertson, Kellie, 'Authorial Work', in *21st Century Approaches to Literature: Middle English*, ed. Paul Strohm (Oxford: Oxford University Press, 2007), 441–458.

Robertson, Kellie, *The Laborer's Two Bodies: Labor and the 'Work' of the Text in Medieval Britain, 1350–1500* (New York: Palgrave Macmillan, 2006).

CHAPTER 5

BOOKS AND BOOKLESSNESS IN CHAUCER'S ENGLAND

ALEXANDRA GILLESPIE

WHEN D. S. Brewer says in *The World of Chaucer* that 'one must realize the extreme booklessness of fourteenth-century England', the attentive student of Chaucer might well feel surprised.[1] Chaucer's poems are, after all, full of books. The dream-narrator takes to bed with a book in the *Book of the Duchess*; it contains 'written fables' of 'romaunce', and 'quenes lives', and 'many other thinges smale' (52, 48, 58–9) including a tale from Ovid's *Metamorphoses*. In the *Parliament of Fowls*, the poet nods off over a copy of the *Dream of Scipio*, 'write with lettres olde', its leaves 'totorn', perhaps from over-much sleepy fumbling (19, 110). At the end of a busy day dealing with one manuscript of 'rekenynges', the narrator of the *House of Fame* sits 'daswed' in front of another (653, 658). Chaucer invites the reader of the Miller's Tale to turn over the 'leef' (I.3177) of the book before him if he or she dislikes the tale. He asks the reader of *Troilus* to visualize the physical making of that poem, the pen in the author's hand, the liquid movement of its ink across the page as the personified verses of his poem 'wepen' their tragedy (1.7). In his 'Wordes unto Adam His Owne Scriveyn' a pen-knife replaces the pen, as Chaucer scrapes his parchment free of a scribe's errors. It is one of Chaucer's characteristically 'humble' poses to appear more willing to represent himself as a user and maker of books than as an author of poetry.[2] We are left with the impression that these books are nothing out of the ordinary: they take their place upon medieval shelves with many of their kind.

The central purpose of this discussion is thus to reconcile evidence of Chaucer's 'bookishness' with Brewer's ideas about fourteenth-century 'booklessness'. The chapter begins by describing the conditions in which books were made in England in the Middle Ages. It argues that Chaucer's vivid depictions of medieval manuscript culture were possible not only because he was a member of a privileged, literate minority in England at that time, but because the Middle Ages was more 'bookish' than we moderns sometimes imagine. In Chaucer's time, new technologies and new social circumstances were making it easier, faster, and cheaper to produce and transmit written text. There were professional and amateur makers of books and they employed a variety of techniques to make all sorts of different books, from beautifully illuminated manuscripts to scrappy paper pamphlets. The second part of the chapter is concerned with which of these books Chaucer himself may have encountered at key moments in his career. What were the books in medieval school rooms like? Did household manuscript culture—domestic record-keeping in particular—make a difference to Chaucer-the-page's ideas about books? What sorts of books were involved in Chaucer's travails as a government official at the port of London or among the king's works? And finally, in which of these historical circumstances were manuscripts made out of Chaucer's own writing during his lifetime and soon after it?

THE MATTER OF MEDIEVAL BOOKLESSNESS

Brewer is not the only scholar to stress that books were scarce in medieval England. Christopher de Hamel writes in the recent *Cambridge History of the Book in Britain, Volume II, 1100–1400* that 'most men and women of medieval England probably passed their lives without ever reading or even touching a book'.[3] As far as we know, this is right: the evidence of surviving manuscripts suggests that until about 1200, most books in England were produced by a small number of men and even smaller number of women who lived and worked in religious institutions. Even in later centuries, as more manuscripts were made by lay and urban professionals, the majority of English people were still too busy eking out a living from the land to bother much with reading and writing.

But this history of medieval 'booklessness' does not go very far towards explaining the books that appear throughout Chaucer's texts. The average medieval peasant had little to do with manuscripts; fourteenth-century England lacked processes of mass, mechanized book production and the high literacy rates that characterize modern Western culture. But in the same time and place, Chaucer and other men and women like him—literate inhabitants of England's towns, cities, and larger households—had access to plenty of books. The word 'book' may be partly to blame for obscuring these facts. As the *Oxford English Dictionary* observes, for the modern speaker of English, the word 'book' usually means something printed, or at least something intended for print publication. The medieval word 'book' was not restricted by that logic: printed books were not introduced to England until about sixty years after Chaucer's death in 1400. All books in Chaucer's time were manuscripts, copied by hand. In Middle English, the word 'book' was most often used to describe manuscript 'codices', books compiled from folded parchment or paper leaves, bound between covers. (That is how the word will be mostly used in what follows.) But the word also served more often than it does in modern English as a formal, literary category, used to describe a completed written work or a self-contained section of a work regardless of physical format.[4] This is why Chaucer can call his first major poem 'the book of the Duchesse' in his Retraction to the *Canterbury*

Tales (X.1086). At just 1334 lines, his poem about the death of John of Gaunt's wife Blanche might have been copied in its entirety onto a roll of parchment or a single, unbound pamphlet—a 'quire' or gathering of about twenty leaves. According to Chaucer, it would still be a 'book'. So when we think about medieval books, we should think beyond 'books' in any strict, modern sense of that word, and consider, as context for and aspect of 'book' production, the making of 'lettres olde' on other surfaces—the writing of rolls, quires, single leaf documents, wall and tablet inscriptions, and volumes containing many smaller 'books'. These were a vital part of medieval manuscript culture; they should be a part of our understanding of Chaucer's books.

We also need to be open-minded about the history of medieval book production and distribution. There was no printing in the medieval world, but there was a commercial trade in manuscripts. In the twelfth and thirteenth centuries in Europe, much of this trade was centred upon Paris, where, especially around the university, craftsmen and women offered their services and their wares. They copied, decorated, bound, valued, and sold books. European books from this period are very often in distinctive Parisian styles.[5] From the late 1200s forward, men styled 'stationers'—appraisers and traders of books—also began to set up shop in England, where book production outside of religious institutions had previously been more rare and more scattered than it was in France. The English stationers' business was largely localized to the university town of Oxford and the metropolis of London. But by 1403 there were enough stationers in London to form their own guild.[6] Contemporary descriptions of these medieval stationers' stock suggest that it was most often second-hand, 'begged' or 'borrowed', according to one fifteenth-century French-Flemish text.[7] New manuscripts of texts used commonly in teaching, in the practice of law, or in religious services may have been sold ready-made, but most new manuscripts were made to customers' orders. A stationer could accept and fill a customer's commission for a book himself, or arrange for a manuscript to be copied, decorated, illustrated, and bound by others.[8]

Medieval manuscript production was not the work of stationers alone. A great many other medieval literates—students, bureaucrats, chaplains, friars, men of law—could supplement their income by copying manuscripts. In London in Chaucer's time such men were kept especially busy making accounts, writs, deeds, wills, and other legal documents. In London document writers, the 'writers of the court hand' (the handwriting used for legal texts), formed their own Company of Scriveners in the 1390s. Scriveners and other professional scribes were available to make larger books as well as documents. One member of the Scriveners' Company, Adam Pinkhurst, copied a petition and possibly other records for the Mercers' Company in the 1380s and later became the main scribe of the famous Ellesmere and Hengwrt manuscripts, the earliest copies of *The Canterbury Tales*. The poet Thomas Hoccleve, whose primary employment was as Privy Seal clerk to the king, shared some of the work on the Hengwrt manuscripts. He made some important books of his own poems as well.[9]

Medieval people in need of manuscripts—either documents or books—could also forgo professional scribal services altogether. From 1200, the streets of many English towns included the dwellings of parchment makers, limners, and binders. Local and itinerant merchants sold ink and quills.[10] Anyone who could write and had some pennies to spare could get the materials they needed to make a small manuscript at home, and such a book could be sent out for binding and decorating if it was special enough to deserve such treatment.

Contemporary uses of medieval manuscripts were as various as these ways of making them. While relatively few of the two and a half million people who lived in England in Chaucer's time owned objects that we would think of as books, a great many more of them must have seen and handled manuscript documents. In the *Vision of Piers Plowman* written by Chaucer's contemporary William Langland, the lowly ploughman procures a written letter of confession (a pardon) and he and his kind are also familiar with the rolls and books of manorial bureaucracy.[11] A single medieval book, stored in a church, carried about by an itinerant preacher, or shared between household members or neighbours might become a basis for a broad 'reading' community.[12] Books and Bibles survive from the Middle Ages that were used by the medieval religious—friars and monks, Lollards and nuns, as well as parish priests—to teach literate and illiterate alike.[13] Late medieval texts about good conduct instruct householders and their wives to teach their children and servants from books.[14] And a single medieval book would also connect its readers to hundreds more. It is often observed that the Latin in which the text of most medieval manuscripts was written meant that people's access to books had to be mediated by educated clergymen. But Latinate texts and the books that contained them moved across national boundaries with ease and English manuscript culture subsisted within a wide international network as a result.

In setting out to account for the manuscript culture of Chaucer's moment, this chapter thus seeks to modify preconceived ideas about the scarcity of medieval manuscripts or the isolation of medieval readers. But 'booklessness' must remain a factor in the discussion, because no copy of Chaucer's works made during his lifetime survives, nor any volume that was part of his library, nor even a book that we can be sure he consulted. This should be informative in itself. For every medieval manuscript that survives, dozens, even hundreds, must have been lost. Five large cartloads of books were sold in 1345 by the executors of the famous English bibliophile and bishop of Durham, Richard de Bury. None of these books has ever been identified.[15] A great many medieval English manuscripts were destroyed when monastic institutions were dissolved in the sixteenth century. But even before the ravages of reform and dissolution, books were vulnerable, as Richard de Bury makes clear in a treatise on his 'love of books', the *Philobiblon*. De Bury's text is written in the 'voice' of his books. They complain bitterly of mistreatment by readers whose dirty hands, nose drippings, dinner scraps, spilled candle wax, and decomposing straw bookmarks cause them to 'go to decay', or who simply fail to treasure them enough to protect them from the depredations of fire, water, worms, and rats.[16]

De Bury's account of the casual mistreatment of manuscripts is also a reason to doubt another claim made by scholars that 'the medieval book must always have remained a luxury product'. Some surviving evidence of the cost of manuscript production does suggest great expense. The sheets of parchment for a missal (a large service book) made for Westminster Abbey in 1383–84 cost £4 6s 8d; the scribe was paid £4.[17] If we assume that the average wage labourer was earning about a penny or penny and a half a day in this period, or remember that Chaucer's income was at its highest in the 1380s at about £30, then the meaning of these figures comes clear. Books were worth months or even years of a typical medieval person's income.[18]

However, not all books were gigantic missals made for well-endowed cathedrals. In about 1400, Merton College in Oxford purchased some books for teaching purposes—a copy of Cato (probably the text called Cato's *Distichs*, used for teaching grammar) cost just 2*d*; a grammar by Donatus 3*d*.[19] A peasant-labourer might prefer to use her pennies for bread—she might not be able to read, after all. But such books were not *necessarily* out of reach, even for her.

The cost of manuscript manufacture could be kept down in a number of ways. As noted above, not all book-making required the services of a paid scribe. Italian vernacular manuscripts of the late fourteenth century were often, even usually, made by scribes of middling rank—school teachers and clerks, merchants and their servants—for others of the same rank or for private use.[20] Not much has been written about similar modes of production in late fourteenth- or fifteenth-century England, but we do know that some Middle English scribes copied Chaucer's works for their own and their family's use. For example, a town clerk from Norwich called Geoffrey Spirleng made a copy of the *Canterbury Tales* in the mid-1400s for his own family.[21] The 'rules' under which monks and nuns lived prescribed book-making as a suitably devout daily occupation.[22] A monk calling himself 'Fr. John Pekeryng', for example, copied his own version of Chaucer's *Astrolabe* in the fifteenth century; it survives as Oxford, Bodleian Library, MS Ashmole 360.

Writing materials did not need to be expensive. Larger lay and religious houses might send animal skins from their own flocks to parchmenters. Books and documents from the Middle Ages are sometimes made from irregular 'offcuts' of the sheets that parchmenters supplied. By the mid-1300s, merchants from the Continent were providing even more cost-effective writing support: paper, a Chinese invention, was transmitted to the Islamic world and from there to Europe where its production was commercialized. Reams of paper were arriving on London's wharves with Genoese merchants and English traders by Chaucer's time. Paper was made in water-powered, mechanized mills from used rags and this proved a cheaper process than the production of parchment from animal skins.[23]

Other new, cost-saving manuscript technologies came from abroad. In the fourteenth century, for example, English scribes adopted a habit first seen in French manuscripts of copying longer texts including literary ones in the sort of 'court' handwriting mentioned above: that is, in cursive scripts usually used for the copying of legal documents and records, rather than in the more formal, non-cursive 'gothic' or 'book' scripts that were typical of monastic, ecclesiastical and scholastic book production. English scribes had their own distinctive cursive script called 'Anglicana'. During Chaucer's lifetime, they began to adopt a French script called 'secretary', probably because this was the style of writing preferred in English-controlled Gascony. Both Anglicana and secretary scripts allowed for faster copying, and so more cost-effective use of scribes' time. Most extant Chaucer manuscripts are written in fifteenth-century hybrid Anglicana-secretary hands.[24]

There were other ways to cut costs. Lots of medieval books were kept unbound or were simply stitched onto parchment covers. This saved the cost of clasps, extra thread, decorative endbands, boards and their covers, and all the labour of more elaborate binding processes. Of just four medieval bindings that survive on Chaucer manuscripts, two, Cambridge, St John's College, MS E. 2 and London, Institute of Electrical Engineers, MS 1 (*Astrolabe* manuscripts), have been simply stitched into pieces of parchment.[25] They and many other medieval manuscripts are undecorated—no limner has ever been contracted to make them look more elegant than a scribe could himself by fashioning simple capitals in red and blue paint or ink.

Finally, it is unlikely that even large, decorated manuscripts acquired with trouble and expense always held their value when they passed to the second-hand market for books. 'No dearness of price ought to hinder a man from the buying of books', writes De Bury in his *Philobiblon*, 'if he has the money that is demanded for them, unless it be to withstand the malice of the seller or to await a more favourable opportunity of buying them.'[26] The appearance of five cartloads of books from De Bury's own library in 1345, might be considered precisely such a favourable opportunity—a chance for a bookseller to make a bulk purchase from executors eager to get liquidate the property; a chance, in turn, for someone to snap up some bargains from an overstocked stationer's shelves.

So we should exchange ideas about the 'extreme booklessness' of Chaucer's era for a more positive view of medieval manuscript culture. Relative to the population as whole, there were fewer writers and readers in the Middle Ages than there are now. But those writers and readers were part of communities of others like them in England and abroad. They had access to significant numbers of manuscripts in all kinds of formats—single leaf documents, heavy tomes, rough, homemade books, commercially copied and elegant ones. They were part of an extensive and dynamic international economy for the production and distribution of these manuscripts. This enables us to say *how* Chaucer gained his rather intimate sense of books: how he came to handle, to write, to correct, and even to sleep with them.

CHAUCER'S BOOKS

The second part of this chapter is devoted to the question of *what*. What sort of books might Chaucer have encountered? What does he say about manuscripts in his own texts, and what books were made out of those texts? To answer these questions fully would take more space than is available here, so the discussion focuses on Chaucer's books at three key moments: his first experiences as a reader; his first experiences of manuscript culture as a member of the English 'court'; and the first London-based evidence for the movement of his literary works to a wider group of readers and thereby to posterity.

It is very likely that the first manuscript that Chaucer ever used was not something we would call a book at all, but a tablet of wood. It might have taken the form of a diptych—two boards linked by rope ties that could be folded together—or it might have been a single board covered in a thin piece of translucent, polished horn. It would have carried an alphabet, either written onto the wood, or onto a leaf of paper or parchment nailed to the tablet. The medieval *abecedarium* or 'abece' always began with the sign of the Christian cross and it sometimes had elementary medieval prayers—the Pater Noster and the Ave Maria—at the end.[27] For this reason, the *abecedarium* was sometimes called a 'primer', a word commonly used in the Middle Ages to describe a simple prayer book or book of hours.[28]

Whether they were described as 'primers' or as 'abeces', alphabetic tablets were also called 'books' in Chaucer's time, and they were designed specifically to introduce children to the processes of reading and writing:

> Wan child to skole set be
> A bok him is ibrouth
> Nailed on a brede (board) of tre
> And is icleped an ABC.[29]

Metaphorical play upon the biblical association of Christ's body and the 'Word' of God was a convention of medieval writing. In this lyric from the late fourteenth century, the typically wooden form of a child's first book is used to press this association home. A child will learn letters and words on his 'brede' in order to learn a more fundamental lesson: that Christ is the Word made flesh[30] and he was made to suffer, 'naylyd' to wooden boards, for our sins.

A child had to learn his 'abece' before he could be admitted to a school where formal Latin grammar was taught (as the basis for higher learning); before he entered a religious or noble household; and even, by Chaucer's time, before he took up an apprenticeship with an urban merchant or artisan. He might acquire those skills at an elementary school. The higher song and grammar schools that were attached to cathedrals or monasteries or independently endowed in the Middle Ages sometimes admitted very young children for basic teaching. Often elementary education took place in households with parents or specially hired tutors, or at the lodgings of the local clerks, scribes, friars, and other men who took on a few pupils for cash. Teachers of all kinds must have had collections of basic books as well as wooden alphabets. Families probably kept books of hours partly for teaching purposes: when books do appear in the wills of smaller medieval households—including many urban merchant-class families like Chaucer's—they are almost invariably 'primers' of this kind.[31] If they do not appear often, this may well be because by the time such books had been used by children set 'to scole' they were not worth bequeathing. In the 1430s, for example, John Hardgrave, a grammar school student in Beccles, Kent made a small paper notebook of writing exercises; it includes the sentence—'primarium meum iacet in gremio meo qui scio matutinas Sancte Marie', meaning 'my primer lies in my lap, I that know Our Lady's matins'. The image of a child learning his basic prayers from a book on his knees is confirmed in artistic conventions of the period: small boys in school rooms are often shown with books in their laps, and so are children being taught by their parents, mostly notably in images of St Anne teaching the Virgin to read.[32] Mary might be expected to have kept her book clean, but not so ordinary children: it is the runny noses and food-smeared hands of students that the books in De Bury's *Philobiblon* most fear. A great many children's 'primers' must simply have been read to pieces.

The reading practices of the young are a subject for Chaucer the poet. The 'litel' boy he writes about in the Prioress's Tale overhears and memorizes a song in praise of Mary that the older boys in his grammar school are being taught. He is working on his own more basic lessons from a 'litel book' (VII.516): he knows even less than the 'smal grammeere' that the elder boys have acquired (536). As we have just seen, that little book might have had more than one physical format, and its possible forms add to the figurative strategies of the tale. If the book is imagined as a devotional 'prymer' or book of hours (517) cradled in the boy's lap, then he has already taken words in praise of Mary to himself before he absorbs the words of the song, and before he accepts the 'greyn' (662) from the Virgin herself at the tale's miraculous end. (The grain allows him to sing on even though his throat has been cut by a spiteful Jew.) If we hold onto the other possibility, that the little book is a wooden 'abece', then this too is meaningful. The first lesson learned from such a book is the lesson of the cross, because the sign of the cross appears before the letters, and because the wooden book can itself be a sign of the crucifixion. Because Christ, the Word made flesh, was born of a Virgin and crucified on the cross for humankind, the little boy's salvation is always-already assured. It is inscribed in the wooden form of the 'abece' before him, held by him, even before he can properly understand the complex 'grammeere' of sin and redemption, and even before the texts he sees or hears make sense to him.

Chaucer may have progressed from his first *abecedarium* to a grammar school in the early 1350s, as did the sons of many aspirational London merchants. He may have read more books there. Local London schools had substantial libraries. Two school masters, William Tolleshunt and William Ravenstone, bequeathed some eighty-two texts (in forty-one books) to St Paul's Cathedral almonery school in 1329 and 1358 respectively. St Paul's was very close to Chaucer's residence in Thames Street. At a local school, Chaucer may have learned to copy and compose Latin sentences with chalk on a slate, or using the pens, ink, and small paper or parchment 'quires' for which payments feature in students' and schools' accounts at around this time.[33] However, no record of Chaucer's enrolment at a school survives. Instead, the first extant Chaucer 'life record' appears in a different sort of book: a household account recording the wardrobe expenditure of the Countess of Ulster, Elizabeth de Burgh, for the period June 1356 to April 1359. The account includes payments to Chaucer for clothing suitable for a young man in service at court.[34]

Chaucer's life was based 'at court' from at least the late 1350s until the early 1370s. He was a page to the Countess of Ulster and, when their households merged, a servant to her husband Lionel also. His family placed him in this noble company to secure him patronage and the skills needed for a public life. He learned those skills, becoming a soldier and foreign envoy for Lionel, then for John of Gaunt and the king. He was taken on as a member of Edward III's royal household. He enjoyed royal annuities and gifts from that time forward from Edward, his grandson Richard II, John of Gaunt and finally in 1399–1400 from the new king Henry IV. He became a poet in these early court years. He wrote the *Book of the Duchess* for John of Gaunt in the late 1360s; he may have translated part of the *Romance of the Rose* at this time; in his later works he mentions youthful 'balades, roundeles [and] vyrelayes' (LGW G 411) that are generally ascribed to his years at court. At some point during this period, Chaucer also developed skills as a maker and keeper of manuscripts. This was his job when he was put in charge of official records of the wool custom as comptroller of the port of London (1374–86). It was also a vital part of his business as an overseer of royal building and maintenance work when he was Richard II's Clerk of the Works, from 1389 to 1391.

Writing itself thus serves as a link between the careers of Chaucer the poet and Chaucer the public official. The fragmentary account book in which Chaucer's name first appears is evidence of the fact that by the mid-1300s, running a household of any size involved a great deal of record keeping. Wardrobe books such as London, British Library, MS Additional 18,632 recorded cash outlay for precious items such as clothing, jewellery, and gifts. The Countess of Ulster probably kept several other kinds of accounts. Her famously wealthy grandmother, Elizabeth de Burgh, Lady of Clare (1295–1360) kept accounts for her chamber; wardrobe; the 'diet' (the household's daily consumption); cash, corn and stock; marshalsea; kitchen; and brewing operations. There were indentures between departments, and two kinds of counter-rolls summarizing expenditure. Even the smallest households of the gentry and wealthy merchants tended to have cash, diet, and summary accounts by Chaucer's time.[35]

The process by which written records replaced oral procedures for financial management within lay households, and letters replaced oral messages for dealings within and between households, was gradual. It began about 1150–1250 in the royal courts and offices. Written records were common in lesser households from about 1350 forward.[36] The changes were facilitated by and in turn probably encouraged technological developments in manuscript production. In the twelfth and thirteenth centuries, records were often kept on single sides of membranes and stitched into rolls. In the fourteenth and fifteenth centuries, the overall volume of documentation increased and clerks were increasingly able to procure paper instead of skins for their books. In this context, records really became 'books': the folded and bound format of the codex was better for protecting writing on both sides of a leaf and a much better way to store paper than a roll. The Countess of Ulster's wardrobe accounts are written fragments of just such a parchment book. National and international trends influenced these developments. The earliest small parchment books used in English accounting were made in the royal household c.1300,[37] and they closely resemble parchment-bound books commonly used in the late thirteenth century by Italian traders who did regular business with the English. Some of Chaucer's own trips abroad in the 1370s were taken to deal with such traders on behalf of the royal court.

The rise of documentary culture meant that by Chaucer's time, every household in England had a good stock of writing materials. The relatively modest annual expenditure recorded in the cash accounts of the Shropshire knight Sir Edward Botiller, for example, c.1400, includes payments for supplies of paper and parchment for records and letters and thread and wax for stitching and sealing. Accounts testify to a handy number of skilled writers in each household: men who knew how to shape letters and also where to get materials, how to prepare parchment, how to mix ink, sharpen quills, and stitch leaves into rolls or books. Typically, households employed several clerks, permanently or on an ad hoc basis. Permanent staff—chamberlains and clerks of the works, the kitchen, the household, and so on—ran household departments and were primarily responsible for the visual and aural auditing (checking) of accounts. Lesser clerks who were often casual employees attended to the quotidian business of copying; their labours are attested by payments to them, and also by the sheer number of hands compiling some accounts. The 1340s accounts of John Multon of Lincolnshire's small household, for example, were written by at least nine different scribes.[38]

It is possible that, especially in his early years as a 'page', Chaucer was actually employed copying records—taught how to rule up an account book by the Countess of Ulster's chamberlain, perhaps; or how to correct figures neatly by the king's clerk of the kitchen. As a member of a noble household, he was certainly immersed in a busy and dynamic culture of manuscript-based record keeping. We know that when he travelled abroad to Italy, France, and Spain on royal business, he bore letters of currency exchange and letters of protection;[39] he probably carried diplomatic letters as well. In Genoa, he could have seen paper mills at work and local merchants making use of paper notebooks; in France, his courtly counterparts were already using new secretary scripts.

Chaucer's work as a courtier at home and abroad thus prepared him for his work collecting taxes and managing the king's expenditure in the 1380s and early 1390s. It also gave shape to aspects of his authorial persona. As noted above, Chaucer calls his day-to-day activity his 'rekenynges' in the *House of Fame*. That word, 'rekenyng', was an important part of the vocabulary of language of medieval business management. The Reeve in the *Canterbury Tales* has the 'governynge' and gives the 'rekenynge' of '[h]is lordes sheep, his neet, his dayerye' (I.597–600). The Ordinances of the City of Worcester from 1467 dictate that 'chamberleyns...be swore to make dewe rekenynge' of 'alle maner rentz an other profitez of the cite'. In these instances, the word means 'an act or instance of calculation' and something more besides. It refers also to the responsibility that a reckoner bears for his records, the truth of his account. The Day of Judgment or 'doomsday' was also the 'Day of Reckoning', when one made account of one's good and bad deeds before God.[40] A reckoning could by extension be a narrative account of some true event in one's life, including an account of a dream. 'Whon þat þou comest aȝeyn' King Evelak says to Joseph in *Joseph of Arimathie*, whom he hopes will interpret his dream, 'þou miht haue more redi roume my rikenyng to here'.[41]

Chaucer knew all about due reckoning and even days of reckoning. Reckonings were records of the sort he compiled and checked and in which his own career was documented. It was his job to keep track of goods and taxes at the port of London in such books 'manu sua propria' [in his own hand]; his writing was to be the guarantee of the truth of each account, as Jonathan Hsy notes in his contribution to this volume.[42] At the end of his time as Clerk of the Works Chaucer had to appear at the Exchequer with his 'rekenynges'—indentures for building projects at the Tower, mandates to pay the king's gardeners, and so on—so that these could be audited by his superiors.[43] So when he describes his daily business in this way in the *House of Fame*, and even more when his 'rekenynges' give way in that poem to the dream of literature, Chaucer himself suggests the connection between his work as a bureaucrat and his poetic endeavours. As a clerk and as the narrator of a dream vision or of other pilgrims' tale in the *Canterbury Tales*, Chaucer is not so much an author as a gatherer of information that others will verify and interpret. 'Blameth nat' him if something is amiss (I.3181): so long as he has made an accurate record, his work is done. On the other hand, the author-as-reckoner is one who will himself be held to account, who knows in his Retraction to the *Tales* that any attempt to dodge his responsibilities must nevertheless end in judgment—'that I may been oon of hem at the day of doom that shulle be saved' (X.1091). A man who knows this must be humble and penitent but he must also be more than a bumbling accountant. He must take a risk and be an author, one who makes books 'manu sua propria', one who has the 'gouernynge' of words.

The same Chaucerian mix of humility and ego, of responsibility claimed and disclaimed, and of poetic and clerkly making is evident in 'Chaucers Wordes unto Adam His Owne Scriveyn'. There Chaucer compares the manuscript material before him (perhaps yet more 'rekenynges') with future copies of his masterpieces *Troilus* and *Boece*. He hopes he will not have to 'rubbe and scrape' at errors in his literary works as he does at Adam's present scribal offerings (Adam 6). He emphasizes his manual labour in order to allude to his greatest literary work, as if his most monotonous daily business contains—even as it seems by its ordinariness to undercut—the promise of his literary future.

This is just right. The fame of Chaucer-the-author is intimately connected to the day-to-day manuscript culture of his moment, within and beyond medieval noble household and royal bureaucracies. A better understanding of that manuscript culture can help us to understand how Chaucer's works reached the world at large, how he went from a courtly hanger-on and sometime versifier to 'master' or 'father' Chaucer, the imagined progenitor of English literary tradition.

The *Book of the Duchess* serves as a useful guide to this last topic, because on the one hand it is Chaucer's most occasional, most inward-looking and courtly poem; on the other hand, it survives to the present day because in the late fifteenth century it became stock in England's growing commercial book trade. Chaucer does not make his work as a 'reckoner' of official records a metaphor for his poetic endeavours in the *Book of the Duchess*. Instead, he invokes traditions of song and of memorization and performance. The poem seems to belong to a world in which knights read chronicles and romances aloud after dinner and minstrels entertain kings, a world for which the Black Knight is a noble type as he leans against trees and speaks in lyric.[44] When Chaucer awakes from his dream, he does not think of writing the narrative down; he does not describe pens, ink, or manuscript leaves in need of rubbing and scraping. He simply thinks of putting his thoughts 'in ryme' (1332), as the man in black did.

If we want to imagine a mode of physical circulation for a courtly rhyme such as the *Book of the Duchess*, we might look to Chaucer's contemporary and admirer, the French court poet Eustache Deschamps. Deschamps directed some early 1380s ballades to Chaucer by way of a messenger—'Mais pran en gré les euvres d'escolier / Que par Clifford de moy avoir pourras' [Kindly accept the schoolboy poems that you will have from me via Clifford]. Sir Lewis Clifford was an associate of Chaucer's and a knight of Richard III's chamber. He travelled abroad as an envoy for the king in the 1380s, as Chaucer had; he may have met Deschamps on several occasions, for example when both were in Calais during John of Gaunt's negotiations for peace in 1384. He must have carried Deschamps's poem back to their mutual friend with the other documents he bore from place to place.[45] Medieval authors depended on this mode of 'publication'—the passage of *libelli*, little books, along regular channels of documentary communication and between acquaintances—for the recognition and patronage that was the principal material reward for medieval literary work.[46]

However, this is not the whole story of Chaucer's *Book of the Duchess*. The narrator does not think of taking up a pen when he wakes, but he does think of a book. He cannot help doing so; there is one 'in myn hond ful even'. 'I awook myselve / And fond', he writes, 'the book that I hadde red / Of Alcione and Seys' (1324–7). This book, we recall, is the compilation of works upon which the author fell asleep. Its presence is a promise, just as the passage of the 'bok' of Chaucer's *Troilus* is a promise, when he commands it to 'go' and 'kis the steppes' of great writers who have come before him (5.1786, 1791). Clever 'ryme' and coterie circulation of *libelli* may give the dream of Blanche a place at court, but the 'bok' is the text's way forward in the world.

So what sorts of books were made out of the *Book of the Duchess*? As was noted above, no copy of this or any poem by Chaucer survives from his lifetime, but we do know a great deal about the making of books in England in Chaucer's time. Chaucer's was a world in which an increasing number of clerks and scribes were undertaking an increasing amount of record-keeping activity. Some of this activity took place in wealthy households, and there it provided conditions for the preservation and spread of literary texts such as the *Book of the Duchess*. Dream visions, romances, 'balades, roundeles [and] vyrelayes' made by ambitious young men in service to England's magnates, texts perhaps circulating in and between households as pamphlets or letters, scribbled on the dorse of rolls or on scraps of parchment, might be copied into the sort of books that were also used for household records in the fourteenth century, by the scribes who made those records.

A useful example here is London, British Library, MS Harley 2253. The book is an early (1430s) and rich collection of poetry—romances, lyrics, fabliaux, and complaints in French, Latin, and Middle English. The copyist was a scribe from Ludlow in Shropshire; his hand appears in this book and in a wide variety of legal documents respecting the maintenance and conveyancing of local property as well. He was apparently one of those men whose skills as a writer were vital to management of the households and wealth of the nobility and gentry the later Middle Ages. Evidence from Harley 2253 and these documents suggests that he may have been a parish priest who sold his skills to local gentry, burgesses and barons such as the Ludlows of Stokesay Castle or the noble family of Mortimers of Wigmore. Presumably Harley 2253 was commissioned for or in the proximity of a household of this sort, a gathering place for all sorts of people and therefore all sorts of poems.[47]

So the *Book of the Duchess* could have been copied into a manuscript akin to Harley 2253. In such a book, it would be more likely to survive. It is no coincidence that so much more literature in English survives from the late medieval era and the context of increased documentary production: literary canons are made not only by writers but also by the technologies that sustain textual reproduction. The same technologies and those who promulgated them in the Middle Ages got texts moving in new ways. Medieval household clerks and servants had varied careers. They made legal documents as well as household books; their travels from court to town, across the seas, and in the City facilitated the dissemination of texts. Here, a useful example is the courtly copyist turned London scribe John Shirley. Shirley was a retainer to the earl of Warwick in the early 1400s. He later moved to the metropolis, worked as a scribe for the royal exchequer and on other city-based business. Like the Ludlow scribe, he made some extremely important compilations of Middle English texts: London, British Library, MS Additional 16,165; London, Sion College, MS Arc. L. 40.2/E.4; London British Library, MS Harley 78; and Cambridge, Trinity College, MS R.3.20. As Martha Rust notes in her chapter in this volume, some of these books contain writings by Chaucer: the last has the only surviving copy of the poem 'Chaucers Wordes unto Adam', for example. Shirley came across some of these poems through his noble connections. He is careful to record the courtly circumstances for their composition—a medical recipe in Trinity R.3.20 was, Shirley writes, 'proved by þe nobul duc of lancastre Johan for þe maladye of þe stone'.[48] But his books also attest their circulation to a wider circle of readers. A poem in Additional 16,165 asks that the reader 'sende [th]is booke ageyne / Hoome to Shirley'.[49] Once there were Chaucer manuscripts abroad—gathered up and sent about by Shirley and men like him—and once they were abroad in London in particular, they were in relatively easy reach of England's commercial trade in books.

That trade brings us, finally, to the example of Adam Pinkhurst, the scrivener who copied the earliest versions of the *Canterbury Tales* in the Hengwrt and Ellesmere manuscripts and whom Chaucer may address in his complaint to 'Adam Scriveyn' in 'Chaucers Wordes'. Pinkhurst was never associated with a noble family. Instead, his career was always based in the metropolis, where the business of English and foreign merchants, the vast operations of the royal courts and offices, and the management of several important monasteries, urban residences of lords and bishops, and the City of London itself, created more new work for literate men than anywhere else in England. Pinkhurst may have worked for Chaucer at the port of London or when he was Clerk of the Works. In both positions, Chaucer was required to hire many scribes. Chaucer may also have employed him to make fair copies of his literary works. If so, that might explain how Pinkhurst came to have exemplars of the *Canterbury Tales* soon after the author's death.[50] Perhaps it was not a household copyist such as the Ludlow scribe or Shirley who first made a book out of Chaucer's *Book of the Duchess*. Perhaps it was a scribe like Pinkhurst, one of London's new 'class' of literate businessmen, a 'reckoner' like Chaucer and, like Chaucer, also a maker of poetic manuscripts.

The earliest physical forms of the *Book of the Duchess* will probably always remain unknown, because the oral and small book formats typical of courtly circulation were always ephemeral. But Chaucer's *Duchess* survived for modern readers because at some point the poem passed beyond the coterie, beyond the 'walles white' of the noble castle figured at the end of Chaucer's dream (1318), to a bustling and a book-filled world beyond. Three medieval manuscripts of the poem are extant: Oxford, Bodleian Library, MSS Bodley 638, Tanner 346, and Fairfax 16. All of them were made in the third or final quarter of the fifteenth century; they contain other poems by Chaucer, by Chaucer's friend Sir John Clanvowe, by his follower John Lydgate, and an array of other anonymous authors. The near-identical arrangement of some of their texts suggests that the books must have had a common exemplar. 'Coterie' collections such as Harley 2253 and Trinity R.3.20 suggest both what that exemplar might have looked like and the sort of household scribes who might have been involved in producing it. Surviving manuscripts of the *Book of the Duchess* can also be connected to the commercial trade in books to which Londoners like Adam Pinkhurst belonged: William Abell, a limner and a member of the London Stationers' Company provided the illustrations to Fairfax 16, for example.

At some point, then, the *Book of the Duchess* reached men who made books of poems, some of whom also made their money making such books. From there it could move on, to a wide audience and to renown. In the late fifteenth century, Chaucer's poem found readers beyond the 'walles' of the court. Fairfax 16 was the property of Sir John Stanley, a gentleman from Hooton (d. 1469). Bodley 638 made its way to a London printer's shop in about 1500 where the citizen and printer Wynkyn de Worde used it as copy-text for some editions of Chaucerian poetry. In such editions, poems were printed in dozens, even hundreds of copies.[51] By the end of the Middle Ages, the 'ryme' that Chaucer wrote for his grieving patron John of Gaunt had become the property of London and provincial households and the work of a commercial trade in manuscripts and printed books. It had become a part of several manuscript compilations, the sorts of books of 'thinges smale' that Chaucer fell asleep over at the start of the poem. It had become this in the context of the transformation of European manuscript culture: the arrival of new materials, the development of new technologies, and the training of new makers of books. This context rather than our preconceptions about medieval 'booklessness' should inform our reading of Chaucer's bookish work and the first sustained tradition of English vernacular writing with which he is associated.

NOTES

1. Derek Brewer, *The World of Chaucer* (Woodbridge, UK: D. S. Brewer, 1976; repr. 2000), 59.
2. In *Troilus*, 5.1789–90, Chaucer tells the 'litel book' he has made not to compete but to make itself subject to others' 'poesye'.
3. Christopher de Hamel, 'Books and Society', in *The Cambridge History of the Book in Britain: Volume II, 1100–1400*, eds. Nigel Morgan and Rodney M. Thomson (Cambridge: Cambridge University Press, 2008), 3.
4. *Oxford English Dictionary*, s.v. 'book'; MED, s.v. 'bok'.
5. Richard H. Rouse and Mary A. Rouse, *Manuscripts and Their Makers: Commercial Book Producers in Medieval Paris*, 2 vols. (London: Harvey Miller, 2000).

6. Peter W. M. Blayney, *The Stationers' Company before the Charter: 1403–1557* (London: Worshipful Company of Stationers and Newspapermakers, 2003).

7. Quoted and discussed, Alexandra Gillespie, 'Caxton and the Invention of the Printed Book', in *The Oxford Handbook of Tudor Literature, 1485–1603*, eds. Mike Pincombe and Cathy Shrank (Oxford: Oxford University Press, 2009), 21–3.

8. On commissions for even the most common service and prayer books see Nigel Morgan, 'Books for the Liturgy and Private Prayer', in Morgan and Thompson, *Cambridge History of the Book in Britain*, 291–316. On the economy of commercial urban book production, M. A. Michael, 'Urban Production of Manuscript Books and the Role of University Towns', in Morgan and Thomson, *Cambridge History of the Book in Britain*, 168–94; C. Paul Christianson, 'The Rise of London's Book Trade', in *The Cambridge History of the Book in Britain: Volume III, 1400–1557*, eds. Lotte Hellinga and J. B. Trapp (Cambridge: Cambridge University Press, 1999) (131 for contract).

9. Jean-Pascal Pouzet, 'Book Production outside of Commercial Contexts', in *The Production of Books in England, 1350–1500*, eds. Alexandra Gillespie and Daniel Wakelin (Cambridge: Cambridge University Press, 2011); Linne R. Mooney, 'Vernacular Literary Manuscripts and Their Scribes', in Gillespie and Wakelin, *The Production of Books in England*.

10. A. I. Doyle, 'The English Provincial Book Trade Before Printing', in *Six Centuries of the Provincial Book Trade in Britain*, ed. Peter Isaac (Winchester: St Paul's Bibliographies, 1990), 13–29.

11. See Emily Steiner, *Documentary Culture and the Making of English Literature* (Cambridge: Cambridge University Press, 2003); Gillespie, 'Books', in *Oxford Twenty-First Century Approaches to Literature*, ed. Paul Strohm (Oxford: Oxford University Press, 2007), 86–103.

12. Joyce Coleman, *Public Reading and the Reading Public in Late Medieval England and France* (Cambridge: Cambridge University Press, 1996); Wendy Scase, 'Reginald Pecock, John Carpenter and John Colop's "Common-Profit" Books: Aspects of Book Ownership and Circulation in Fifteenth-Century London', *Medium Ævum* 61 (1992), 261–74.

13. Vincent Gillespie, 'Vernacular Books of Religion', in *Book Production and Publishing in Britain 1375–1475*, eds. Jeremy Griffiths and Derek Pearsall (Cambridge: Cambridge University Press, 1989), 317–44.

14. Nicholas Orme, *Medieval Schools: from Roman Britain to Renaissance England* (New Haven, CT: Yale University Press, 2006).

15. W. J. Courtenay, 'Bury, Richard (1287–1345)', *Oxford Dictionary of National Biography* (Oxford: Oxford University Press, 2004), oxforddnb.com

16. E. C. Thomas, ed. and trans., *The Love of Books: The Philobiblon of Richard de Bury* (London: Chatto and Windus, 1913).

17. H. E. Bell, 'The Price of Books in Medieval England', *Library*, 4th ser., 17 (1936–37), 312–32—the most commonly cited study of the topic; see also Joanne Filippone Overty, 'The Cost of Doing Scribal Business: Prices of Manuscript Books in England, 1300–1483', *Book History* 11 (2008), 1–32; see, by way of comparison, Kwakkel, 'Commercial Organisation and Economic Innovation', in Gillespie and Wakelin, *Production of Books in England*.

18. Derek Pearsall, *The Life of Geoffrey Chaucer: A Critical Biography* (Cambridge: Blackwell, 1992), 210.

19. Orme, *Medieval Schools*, 153.

20. Armando Petrucci, 'Reading and Writing *Volgare* in Medieval Italy', in *Writers and Readers in Medieval Italy: Studies in the History of Written Culture* (New Haven, CT: Yale University

Press, 1995): he considers 213 of 231 scribes of the vernacular that he identifies to be 'non-professional' (199).

21. Richard Beadle, 'Geoffrey Spirleng (c.1426–c.1494): A Scribe of the *Canterbury Tales* in his Time', in *Of the Making of Books: Medieval Manuscripts, their Scribes and Readers: Essays Presented to M. B. Parkes*, eds. Pamela Robinson and Rivkah Zim (Aldershot: Scolar Press, 1997), 116–46.

22. Pouzet, 'Book Production outside of Commercial Contexts', in Gillespie and Wakelin, *Production of Books in England*.

23. Kwakkel, 'Commercial Organisation and Economic Innovation', in Gillespie and Wakelin, *Production of Books in England*; Orietta Da Rold, 'Materials', in Gillespie and Wakelin, *Production of Books in England*.

24. Daniel Wakelin, 'Copying the Words', in Gillespie and Wakelin, *Production of Books in England*.

25. Alexandra Gillespie, 'Bookbinding', in Gillespie and Wakelin, *Production of Books in England*.

26. Thomas, *Philobiblon*, 19.

27. Andrew W. Tuer, *History of the Horn-Book* (London: Leadenhall Press, 1896).

28. *Middle English Dictionary*, s.v., 'abece', 'primer'. The usage survives: elementary readers are still sometimes called primers.

29. This poem was copied by the Franciscan John of Grimestone into Edinburgh, National Library of Scotland, MS Advocates 18.7.21 in 1372, fol. 122v, along with preaching materials: see Edward Wilson, *A Descriptive Index of the English Lyrics in John of Grimestone's Preaching Book* (Oxford: Blackwell for The Society for the Study of Mediaeval Languages and Literature, 1973), no. 198.

30. John 1:14.

31. Susan H. Cavanaugh, 'A Study of Books Privately Owned in England, 1300–1450', 2 vols., unpub. PhD thesis (University of Pennsylvania, 1980).

32. Orme, *Medieval Schools*, 113 (for Hardgrave); 131, 153, 182 (for discussion and images of boys with books in their laps).

33. Ibid., 45, 111–12, 134, 154.

34. Martin M. Crow and Clair C. Olson, eds., *Chaucer Life-Records* (Austin, TX: University of Texas Press, 1996), 16.

35. C. M. Woolgar, ed., *Household Accounts from Medieval Britain* (Oxford: Oxford University Press, 1992), 18.

36. M. T. Clanchy, *From Memory to Written Record 1066–1307*, 2nd ed. (Cambridge: Blackwell, 1993).

37. J. A. Szirmai, *The Archaeology of Medieval Bookbinding* (Aldershot: Scolar Press, 1999), 289–90: the books' Italian origin has been suggested in unpublished papers by Frederick Bearman, whom Szirmai credits with identifying these books.

38. Woolgar, *Household Accounts from Medieval England*; see index entries for various materials; 567–8 for Botiller; 227–9 for Multon.

39. Crow and Olson, *Chaucer Life-Records*, 29–66.

40. MED, s.v., 'rekening(e)', from which sources here, including the 1467 Ordinances of Worcester, are cited.

41. W. W. Skeat, ed., *Joseph of Aramathie*, EETS OS 44 (1871 repr. Woodbridge, UK: Boydell and Brewer, 2000), 443–4.

42. See Chapter 3 of this volume.

43. Crow and Olson, *Chaucer Life-Records*, 445–62.
44. Coleman, *Public Reading and the Reading Public*.
45. Pearsall, *The Life of Geoffrey Chaucer*, 130–1 (with the lines and translation of Deschamps's poem).
46. Alexandra Gillespie, 'Medieval Books, Their Booklets, and Booklet Theory', *English Manuscript Studies* 17 (2011), 1–29.
47. Susanna Fein, *Studies in the Harley Manuscript: The Scribes, Contents, and Social Contexts of British Library MS Harley 2253* (Kalamazoo, MI: Medieval Institute Publications, 2000), especially Carter Revard, 'Scribe and Provenance', 21–109.
48. Cambridge, Trinity College, MS R.3.20, fol. 373.
49. Margaret Connolly, *John Shirley: Book Production and the Noble Household in Fifteenth-Century England* (Aldershot: Ashgate, 1998), 97–8.
50. See Linne R. Mooney, 'Chaucer's Scribe', *Speculum* 81 (2006), 97–138; Alexandra Gillespie, 'Reading Chaucer's Words to Adam', *Chaucer Review* 42 (2008), 269–83.
51. For a summary of scholarship on these books and the further circulation of their contents in the commercial context of early printing, see Alexandra Gillespie, *Print Culture and the Medieval Author: Chaucer, Lydgate, and their Books, 1473–1557* (Oxford: Oxford University Press, 2006), 45–9.

BIBLIOGRAPHY

Clanchy, M. T., *From Memory to Written Record 1066–1307*, 2nd ed. (Cambridge: Blackwell, 1993).

Hellinga, Lotte and J. B. Trapp, *The Cambridge History of the Book in Britain: Volume III, 1400–1557* (Cambridge: Cambridge University Press, 1999).

Gillespie, Alexandra and Daniel Wakelin, eds., *The Production of Books in England, 1350–1500* (Cambridge: Cambridge University Press, 2011).

Gillespie, Alexandra, *Chaucer's Books* (Philadelphia, PA: Penn State University Press, forthcoming).

Hammond, Eleanor Prescott, *Chaucer: A Bibliographical Manual* (New York: Macmillan, 1908).

Hanna, Ralph, *Pursuing History: Middle English Manuscripts and Their Texts* (Stanford, CA: Stanford University Press, 1996).

Lerer, Seth, *Chaucer and His Readers: Imagining the Author in Late Medieval England* (Princeton, NJ: Princeton University Press, 1993).

Mooney, Linne R. and Estelle Stubbs, *Scribes and the City: London Guildhall Clerks and the Dissemination of Middle English Literature, 1375–1425* (Woodbridge, UK: Boydell and Brewer, 2013).

Morgan, Nigel and Rodney M. Thomson, *The Cambridge History of the Book in Britain: Volume II, 1100–1400* (Cambridge: Cambridge University Press, 2008).

CHAPTER 6

....

THE ROLE OF THE SCRIBE
Genius of the Book

....

MARTHA RUST

In his exposition of the four modes of making a book, St Bonaventure (1221–74) provides a succinct description of the role of the scribe: 'someone [who] writes the materials of others, adding or changing nothing'. Emphasizing the lowliness of this part in producing a book, Bonaventure goes on, 'this person is said to be merely the scribe'.[1] Given such a minimal role, the best scribal performance renders itself invisible to an authorial text; by the same token, a scribal act that warrants notice is necessarily amiss. References to the work of scribes from antiquity through to the present day bear out this paradoxical lot of the scribe: that his fame will always tend towards infamy. Authors from Cicero and Jerome to King Ælfric, Roger Bacon, and Petrarch have trumpeted the damages done to texts by scribes, and a full-text search in JSTOR on the adjective 'scribal' reveals contemporary scholars echoing their complaints.[2] The single noun that most frequently follows 'scribal' in scholarly writing of the past several decades is 'error', seconded by the plural, 'errors'. Runners-up situate 'scribal' in an unflattering semantic field that stretches from the deviant to the daft: from 'scribal corruption', 'slips', 'losses', and 'omissions'; to 'scribal interference', 'preference', and 'alteration'; to 'scribal peculiarities' and 'whimsies'. Words and phrases that precede 'scribal' include 'merely', 'more substantive than', and 'simple', as in 'a simple scribal error'. Confronted with such an array of scribes' failures to fulfill their duty to copy texts 'adding or changing nothing', authors and scholars alike might well sympathize with Chaucer when he calls down a dermatological affliction upon the head of his own scribe Adam: 'Under thy long lokkes thou most have the scalle, / But after my makyng thow wryte more trewe' (Adam 3–4).

While 'Chaucers Wordes unto Adam, His Owne Scriveyn' vividly evinces the conventional view of the role of the scribe—that is, from the perspective of an author or scholar—a consideration of the poem's generic antecedents shows that scribes themselves understand their role as multi-faceted, including duties to readers as well as to authors, and responsibilities for books as well as for texts. As Glending Olson has recently pointed out, the malediction Chaucer lays against his scribe is an adaptation of the book curse, a genre that is functionally more invested in the labour of scribes than in the 'makying' of authors.[3] In this way, a curse appended to a Middle English verse paraphrase of the Psalms and written in the voice of a scribe expresses a custodial concern for the book even as it also evinces an awareness of scribes' tarnished reputation as copyists of texts: 'Should anyone steal it, let him be anathema! / Whoever should find fault with the text, let him be accursed.'[4] Another mixes malediction with benediction, for the book-thief and the scribe, respectively:

> May he who wrote this book with his pen
> Ascend to Heaven full well;
> If anyone takes it away again
> May his soul rot in Hell.[5]

Olson notes that this particular book curse protects 'not only the completed codex but also scribal ego' and that as such it is affiliated with that category of finishing note that comments on the life of a copyist.[6]

Along with a wide range of sentiments—from relief with having completed a writing task, to eagerness to be paid, whether with money, a drink, or a pretty girl—these notes often give further expression to scribes' view of themselves as the guardians of books; in addition, they provide glimpses of scribes acting as readers' and book-users' tutors.[7] A colophon written by one Warembert, a ninth-century scribe at the Abbey of Corbie, expresses his care for the book in his directions to readers on how to use it:

> Friend who reads this, hold your fingers in back lest you suddenly blot out the letters; for a man who does not know how to write thinks it isn't work. His latest line is as sweet to a writer as port is to a sailor. Three fingers hold the pen, but the whole body toils. Thanks be to God. I Warembert wrote this in God's name. Thanks be to God.[8]

Mundane as these scribes' specific instructions are, these colophons may strike a modern reader as surprising and bold: first, for the attention each draws to the individual scribe's work; and second, because each portrays that labour in priestly terms. Beyond his proclamation that he has written the text 'in the name of God', Warembert's vividly descriptive 'three fingers hold the pen' works as a subtle representation of the scribe as a mediator between divine and human realms by way of an allusion it makes to a well-known passage from a text on writing by Cassiodorus (*c.* 487–*c.* 580): 'A man multiplies the heavenly words and, if such an allegory is permitted, by three fingers is written what the excellence of the holy Trinity speaks.'[9] In this way, each scribe effectively portrays his role in relation to his physical labour on the one hand and to readers on the other as a kind of mobile and site-specific priesthood, whose liturgy is the scribe's written performance in any given book and whose parishioners include all of the book's readers and viewers.

As far as we know, none of the scribes who laboured to produce Chaucer's work was a priest (though their ranks did include monks and friars), yet there was another priest and scribe whose functions make a useful lens for apprehending the scope of those secular scribes' work: the character of Genius in *De planctu Naturae* (*The Plaint of Nature*) by Alan of Lille (d. 1203), who functions as Nature's priest and secretary.[10] Like that Genius, these are responsible for giving abstract forms—in this case Chaucer's works, or 'makyngs'—material and individualized substance. Like that Genius, Chaucer's scribes also serve custodial and tutelary functions, assuring the continuity of his work with respect both to its written form in books and to its legibility to readers. Also like that Genius, these scribes function at times as a mirror or other self of the author whose work they produce. And finally, like the *genii loci* from which Alan's Genius descends, the scribes of Chaucer's work are associated with specific places, namely, with the books of his oeuvre they worked to bring forth. In this way, these scribes function as the spirit of the locale each book encloses. In this essay I use Alan's Genius as a template for recognizing and understanding this variegated role of the scribe as it is represented in three contexts: in Chaucer's own work, in the manuscripts that preserve his work, and in contemporary scholarship. But first, a brief excursus on the Genius of *De planctu Naturae* is in order.

ALAN'S GENIUS: SCRIBE AND PRIEST AND SCRIBE AS PRIEST

Alan of Lille's *De planctu Naturae* (*c.* 1160 to 1170) has been studied for a range of interests, including its documentation of the stigmatization of homosexuality in the West, its influence on subsequent generations of poets—in particular, Jean de Meun, John Gower, and Chaucer—and its innovative personification of the ancient spirit, *genius*. On this latter topic, Winthrop Wetherbee wrote the truth when he observed of Alan's Genius, '[t]he associations of Genius are complex'.[11] Those associations extend back to two archaic species of *genius*: the *genius loci*, who inhered in a specific place, lending it an individual quality and ensuring its fertility; and the *comes natale*—'companion of birth'—a *genius* born with each individual and accompanying him through life.[12] Alan's Genius's nearest kin, however, are the *genii* of Bernardus Silvestris's *Cosmographia* (1147), who aid and guide the soul's descent from the heavens into embodiment in human form. As Jane Chance Nitzsche and Denise N. Baker have explained, the labours of Bernardus's hierarchy of *genii* are symbolized in *De planctu* by the two functions Alan gives to his personified Genius: the roles of Nature's priest and secretary.[13]

In his first appearance in the poem, Genius is occupied with his role as Nature's secretary, through which Alan renders Bernardus's generative *genii*: as Genius busily writes on parchment with a reed pen, we witness the fleshly becoming of Nature's exemplars, for, 'with the help of his obedient pen, he endowed with the life of their species images of things that kept changing from the shadowy outline of a picture to the realism of their actual being'.[14] As the passage continues, Genius brings to life a procession of famous and infamous personages, from Helen and Ulysses to Cicero and Aristotle—and many more. In this way, Genius's writing activity fittingly allegorizes the descent of the soul into flesh: as Nitzsche explains, his pen 'represents the heavenly source of man's soul'; as pen meets parchment the soul transmigrates 'to the truth of being'.[15] But the generative function of Genius the secretary of Nature may open our eyes as well to the full implications of the work of real, non-allegorical scribes: that is, that in committing authorial works to parchment, they bring them forth as embodied *texts* with 'lives' of their own.

If in the guise of Genius as secretary we may glimpse reflections of real scribes giving being to each text they copy, turning to an examination of Genius in his role as Nature's priest in *De planctu*, we may begin to entertain formulations of the author/text/scribe triangle that are less agonistic than terms like 'scribal interference' connote. Genius is first invoked in this role when Nature writes him a letter asking him to bar men who commit homosexual acts from partaking of the rites of 'our church'.[16] While it has been noted that as a female deity, Nature cannot excommunicate these miscreants herself—as Nitzsche puts it, 'Natura cannot very well be a priestess; she requires a priest'—Genius's priesthood constitutes no mere ad hoc device for a needed excommunication in Alan's plot.[17] Instead, his role as Nature's priest is completely in keeping with the concept of *genius* as a spirit accompanying each indivual as a 'most faithful tutelary and brother', as Martianus Capella put it.[18] In fact, Nature articulates her relationship with Genius in just this way, addressing him at the beginning of her letter as her 'alter-ego' and declaring that she finds her likeness reflected in him 'as in a mirror'.[19] Genius's role as Nature's priest is also in keeping with Bernardus Silvestris's intermediating *genii*: like those *genii*, a priest also serves as intermediary between humans and the divine; just so, Genius acts as the goddess Nature's intermediary in carrying out the rite of banishment she requests in her letter.

While both the tutelary and mediating functions of *genius* are thus represented in Genius's role as priest, we see, as Nature's letter continues, that these duties are inextricably intertwined with his generative functions—that is, with Genius's role as Nature's scribe. As she goes on to confess: 'I am bound to you in a knot of heartfelt love, both succeeding in your success and in like manner failing in your failure.' Nature flourishes as the goddess of procreation, in other words, as long as Genius keeps up with his writing. Moving towards the 'business' of her letter—the excommunication—Nature opines: 'Love...should make our fortunes interchangeable.'[20] Baker captures the interdependency of this pair well: 'Because he participates in Natura's procreative duties, he also shares her responsibilities as moral guide.'[21] Genius's scribal activity incurs a moral liability, in other words; might a real scribe's work seem, by its very nature, to burden him with a similar responsibility? If so, his response to that obligation might take the form of his own composition, though it would draw on the formulas of his training. As such, it might resemble the response of Alan's Genius to Nature's letter: *De planctu* concludes with Genius 'call[ing] forth from the deep recesses of his mind the prearranged formula of excommunication', and delivering his anathema not in writing but in his own voice.[22] Interestingly, many of the scribes who copied *De planctu*—or, in terms of my discussion, brought it into material being—appear to have felt a *genius*-like responsibility towards its Genius, for many reinforced Genius's anathema with one of their own: '*Pereat sodomita*' (Let the sodomite perish).[23]

As we know from his depiction of the goddess Nature in *The Parliament of Fowls*, Chaucer was inspired by Alan's *De planctu Naturae*, which does not mean that scribes of Chaucer's work were inspired by Alan's depiction of Genius. Nevertheless, his linked secretarial and priestly roles make Genius an illuminating model for interpreting scribes' activities and thus for reimagining their roles on a scale more generous than Bernard's narrow 'adding and changing nothing' dictum. With Genius as exemplar, we may envision scribes' duties as running a gamut from the agent and companion of a text's materialization, to intermediary between author and text and text and reader, to an author's 'mirror' or other self. In the following, I consider aspects of each of these roles as they pertain to the scribes of Chaucer's work, to the figure of the scribe within his work, and to contemporary scholars' understanding of the functions of both real and fictional scribes. While I take up these scribal functions one at a time, I also attempt to keep their overlaps and synergistic effects in view. Here too the singular yet multi-faceted character of Genius functions as a guide. In concluding, I evoke yet another personification in Alan's *De planctu*—the fair maiden Truth, daughter of Genius and Nature—and ask where, betwixt the roles of author and scribe, the true object of literary study might be apprehended.

The scribe as agent and companion of a text's birth

Whether mimetic or metaphorical, within the narrative frame or outside it, reflections on matters of textual transmission—its perils, its politics, its frisson—are ubiquitous in Chaucer's oeuvre. We may think, for example, of the letter writing in The Man of Law's Tale, The Merchant's Tale, and *Troilus and Criseyde*; of the Wife of Bath and Jankyn's 'book of wikked wyves' (III.685); of the Knight with the weak oxen in his plough (I.886-87); of the Clerk's Tale's Griselda '[w]han she translated was' (IV.385) and the translating narrator of *Troilus and Criseyde*; and of the monumental texts and whirling rumors of the *House of Fame*.[24] This expansive network of references aside, explicit references to scribes in Chaucer's work number only two: his 'Wordes Unto Adam' and his prayer at the close of *Troilus and Criseyde* that no future scribes 'myswrite' (5.1795) that 'litel bok' (5.1786).[25] Interestingly, both of these references pertain to the transmission of Chaucer's own work—referring to the 'real' world outside the fictional worlds of his poetry—and both also promulgate the familiar view of a scribe's failing at his job of faithfully reproducing an author's work, or, using the terms of Alan's description of Genius as secretary, failing to bring their exemplars into 'the realism of their actual being'. Turning from Chaucer's pessimism about once and future scribes of his own work to portrayals of books and the materials of writing within his work, however, we find that the scribal technologies of writing and page layout—devices that give a work a visual and tactile form—are represented as operating very well. A look at a selection of allusions to page layout and alphabetical characters within Chaucer's work will make way for a study of scribes' labours to substantiate the form of Chaucer's works through which they become the life-long agents and companions of his corpus.

No matter how many artisans eventually plied their craft on any given manuscript page—supplying its decorated initials, lush borders, and illustrations—the scribe was first in line, and thus it fell to him to plan the page's overall design, leaving adequate and appropriate space for elements to be added later.[26] A reference Chaucer makes to one of these features of page design demonstrates just how effectively a text's layout operated to define its constituent parts. Early in *Troilus and Criseyde*, when Pandarus arrives at Criseyde's house to make his first pitch on behalf of the love-lorn Troilus, he finds Criseyde and her companions engaged in reading. In answer to Pandarus's queries about the nature of their reading material—'Is it of love?' he asks—Criseyde tells him that it is a 'romaunce...of Thebes'. Going on, she summarizes the story so far in general terms, as a matter of what they have 'heard'—"we han herd how that kyng Layus deyde / Thorugh Edippus his sone, and al that dede'—and then indicates the point to which they have just arrived by referring to where they are on the page, as a matter of what she sees, 'here we stynten at thise lettres rede – '(2.97–103). These 'lettres rede' would be the letters of a rubric, those titles or chapter headings that have their name from the Latin *ruber*—red—since they were often written in red ink. As Criseyde continues, we read that rubric with her, a brief description of the ensuing chapter: 'How the bisshop.../ Amphiorax, fil thorugh the ground to helle' (2.104–5).[27] In the story logic of this scene—Criseyde's being interrupted in the midst of her leisure reading—it is rather unlikely that she would just happened to have finished a chapter in her book at the moment Pandarus strode in. According to the scene's book—or page layout— logic, though, a rubric would be the *only* place to stop, for as Michelle Brown explains, a rubric 'is not strictly part of the text but...helps to identify its components'; or, borrowing from the language of this scene,—'we stynten at thise lettres reed'—rubrics give a running narrative an episodic form by rendering it on the page in the form of a series of 'stints' of writing.[28]

Chaucer's work includes no summarizing headings like the 'How the bisshop...' rubric in Criseyde's book, but a suggestive line in the *Book of the Duchess* and in its manuscript witnesses hints that both Chaucer and his scribes wrote with this kind of chapter-heading, episode-defining rubric in mind.[29] Chaucer's narrator has just finished describing his abruptly falling to sleep after deciding to pray to Morpheus for relief from his chronic insomnia and has also extolled the wondrousness of his ensuing dream, which, he declares, was such that not even Joseph of Egypt, nor 'skarsly Macrobeus' (284) would be able to interpret it. This lead-up to the dream has tumbled forth in one breathless twenty-line sentence, and the story of the dream itself continues in an equally loquacious way. This stretch of the poem may thus have sounded all of a piece, in the manner of an anecdote—'I had the most amazing dream last night! I dreamed that...'—if it were not for a one-line sentence that effectively divides it into two parts: preface and narrative proper. That line reads, 'Loo, thus hyt was; thys was my sweven' (290). The concision of this line in relation to the verse on either side of it already makes it stand out; considering that along with its initial interjection 'Loo'—'behold, look'— and its demonstrative 'thys'—this here, this, the following—the line has the look and visual rhetorical force of a rubric: a line not properly a part of the text that works not only to identify its components, as Brown asserts, but also to produce them as such. Manuscript evidence suggests that the scribes of the *Book of the Duchess* recognized the rubric-like quality of this line and, in the manner of Alan's Genius, whose job it was to bring souls out of the ether into 'the truth of being', they have brought this poem out with a cleft at just this line. All three surviving witnesses mark the following line— 'Me thoghte thus: that hyt was May' (291)—as the beginning of a new section of the poem, two with large initials, and one with a marginal paraf mark.[30]

Across the manuscripts of Chaucer's work, large decorated initials and rubrics serve most often to signal major narrative divisions in a work: the five books of *Troilus and Criseyde*, for instance, or the four parts of the Knight's Tale. However, scribes also used these devices together with a variety of less ostentatious flagging instruments to bring out the contours of structures and set pieces within those larger narrative frames. As Ardis Butterfield has shown, the scribes of *Troilus and Criseyde* routinely highlight its songs and letters, sometimes with decorated initials and rubrics, thereby visually equating them to book divisions, but more often with paraf marks or marginal annotations.[31] Many scribes of *Troilus and Criseyde* further subdivide the poem by setting each stanza clearly apart from its neighbors and marking each with a one-line decorated initial or paraf mark, in this way grounding the poem's Boethian flights in the 'consolation' of a visually elegant modularity. The versatile paraf allows for the emergence of more idio-syncratic forms as well. As Joel Fredell has shown, a 'dense' pattern of paraf placement in three witnesses to the Miller's Tale functions to draw a parallel between 'Nicholas's beguiling Oswald through *scientia*...and Alison's beguiling Absolon through *affecioun*'; in contrast, a 'sparse' pattern in two other witnesses follows, instead, the histories of Nicholas's and Absolon's efforts to win Alison and also highlights, thereby calling it out as the tale's cynical moral message, the line 'Lo, which a greet thyng is affeccioun!' (I.3611).[32] Scribes employ the low-tech tool of underlining as a means of drawing out still other facets of a text: its embedded lists, in particular. Scribes of two related copies of the *Parliament of Fowls* underline in red ink the individual birds' names in its list of birds— from 'There myghte men the royal egle fynde' to 'The throstil old; the frosty feldefare' (330; 364)—thus calling to mind a *nominale* in which these species names would be linked to their Latin equivalents.[33]

In casting into relief these and other concatenations and centers of gravity through their expert use of the grammar of page design, scribes may be following their exemplars or expressing their own 'genius', reading and responding to the texts as they copy them. In either case, they follow the model of Alan's Genius in giving tangible form and a life in the real world to Chaucer's works, which would otherwise persist as abstractions, like Nature's 'shadowy outlines' before Genius copied them down. These scribes' success at this interpretive labour finds a telling reflection in the language the two scholars I mention above use to discuss page design and its effects. Both refer repeatedly to scribes' decisions with respect to page design as a matter of attending to a work's 'structure', whether that structure be overtly or only latently authorial: so Fredell comments on the 'binary structure' brought out by one pattern of parafs and the 'double-linear plot' brought out by another, and Butterfield concludes that in the hands of its scribes, *Troilus and Criseyde* begins to look like a genre of composition associated with its own kind of physical book, 'a lyric compilation'.[34]

Butterfield's allusion to a codicological structure serves as a felicitous reminder that scribes' formal, form-giving duties pertained not only to the two-dimensional place of the page but also to the three-dimensional place of the book. In building that codicological dimension, a scribe's basic structural unit was the quire. A survey of descriptions of manuscripts containing the works of Chaucer shows a preference for quires of eight leaves: that is, four bifolia folded in half to produce eight leaves and sixteen writing surfaces.[35] Ideally, and often in practice as well, a scribe would copy a work straight through into successive quires of equal numbers of leaves, whose boundaries would be revealed only by the catchwords or quire signatures used to ensure their being bound together in the proper order.[36] But detailed study of their quire structures reveals that medieval manuscripts are to be compared less to orderly monumental edifices constructed from uniform bricks than to rustic garden walls fashioned out of stones of many sizes. As such, a medieval book is a site whose structural units—its quires—allow for all manner of internal adjustments, calling upon and revealing scribes' adept spatial reasoning.

As recent studies have shown, there was a particular need for such adjustments in early manuscripts of Chaucer's *Canterbury Tales*, where scribal interventions at the 'level' of quire structure also provide fascinating glimpses of the 'layers' of a work's composition. Evidence along these lines from Oxford, Corpus Christi College Library MS 198 is, as Estelle Stubbs rightly puts it, 'perhaps the most startling'.[37] Considered in only two dimensions—looking only at its script and page design, that is—the manuscript gives, as Stubbs asserts, 'the impression of seamless continuity and is a masterly example of the professionalism of its scribe'.[38] However, a look at its quire structure afforded by its 1987 rebinding shows that the manuscript's seamlessness is all illusion though that very illusion shows off its scribe's professionalism and ingenuity—or in-*genius*-ness—all the more. By adding whole bifolia in the middle of some quires, tipping in singletons in others, and removing leaves from still more, he has managed to give a smooth face to what would appear to have been an array of exemplars that represented various layers of Chaucer's revising his work.[39] As Stubbs argues, the textual revisions effected by these quire structure adjustments suggest that this scribe was part of a close network of penmen working on the *Tales*, which may have included Chaucer himself.[40] By pursuing the implications of similar quire structure adjustments in Oxford, Christ Church MS 152, Jacob Thaisen has offered a view of another scribe papering over—for in this case the quires in question are made of paper—the discrepancies he finds among the exemplars that came his way.[41] As Thaisen shows, the boundaries of these quire structure revisions correspond to similar 'faultlines' in the texts of Hengwrt and Ellesmere; in this way, this scribe's interventions, like those examined by Stubbs, also yield valuable evidence about the earliest stage of the *Canterbury Tales'* manuscript tradition despite this manuscript's late date (1450–75).[42]

Whether through their labours on the design of the page or on the architecture of the book, the form scribes give to Chaucer's works is hardly a 'form' that could be opposed to 'content'; instead, poetic form—its structure, above and beyond a poem's constituent words—depends for the 'realism of its actual being', borrowing from Alan once more, upon the 'genius' of the scribes who give it bookish form. In the process, in the manner of Alain's Genius and the *genii* of antiquity before him, these scribes also endow each individual manifestation of Chaucer's work with its own unique character, a spirit that accompanies a work's coming into material form and then becomes its life companion. That spirit inhabits the structures of page layout and quire, but it is most ubiquitously yet ineffably present in the part of a book that was the scribe's primary responsibility: the text itself, written in the scribe's 'hand'.

As we have seen, in his role as copyist, a scribe was to add nothing, let alone a spirit, which would properly reside in a text's propositional content and not in its inky letter. This conventional understanding of the separation of letter and spirit notwithstanding, Chaucer suggests at the beginning of his *Troilus and Criseyde* that even the inky physicality of writing is imbued—'literally' saturated—with character: in order to forecast the depth of the sorrowfulness of the story he is about to tell, Chaucer's narrator conjures an emotional responsiveness in the very inscription of its words, which weep as they are written: 'Thise woful vers, that wepen as I write' (1.7). In describing his verses this way, Chaucer follows the opening lines of Boethius's *Consolation of Philosophy*, which portray that work as tearful—*elegi fletibus*—but he does so with a twist: in specifying that the verses weep *as they are written*, he suggests that they are tearful not only themat-ically but physically as well.[43] In this way, Chaucer also elegantly depicts a written text being in-formed with a 'spirit'—manifested here by its emotional sensitivity—at the moment of its physical 'birth', or in-scription. While scribes of Chaucer's *Troilus and Criseyde* do not infuse its written witnesses with quite as empathic a spirit as would enable them to weep, the various decisions scribes have made with respect to which script to use for this work in particular do invest its copies with an equally varying range of dispositions, moods, or 'images', the latter in the sense of a 'public image'—the impres-sion a person creates in the eye of a community, in this case, a reading community.

Three early witnesses to *Troilus and Criseyde* amply demonstrate the variety of visual impressions the poem projects. The earliest, Cambridge, Corpus Christi College MS 61 (ca. 1398) gives a first impression of reserved and stately elegance but reveals upon closer examination a playful touch. It is written in *textura littera quadrata*, a script used primarily for liturgical books. To the steady rhythm of the spur-footed minums that distinguish this script, however, the two scribes who produced this text have added a trill of curling hairline strokes that invite the eye at times to see pictures in the place of letter forms (see Figure 6.1a).[44] For instance, letters T, D, and O at the beginnings of lines suggest harps while Es and Fs sometimes have the look either of gargoyles or

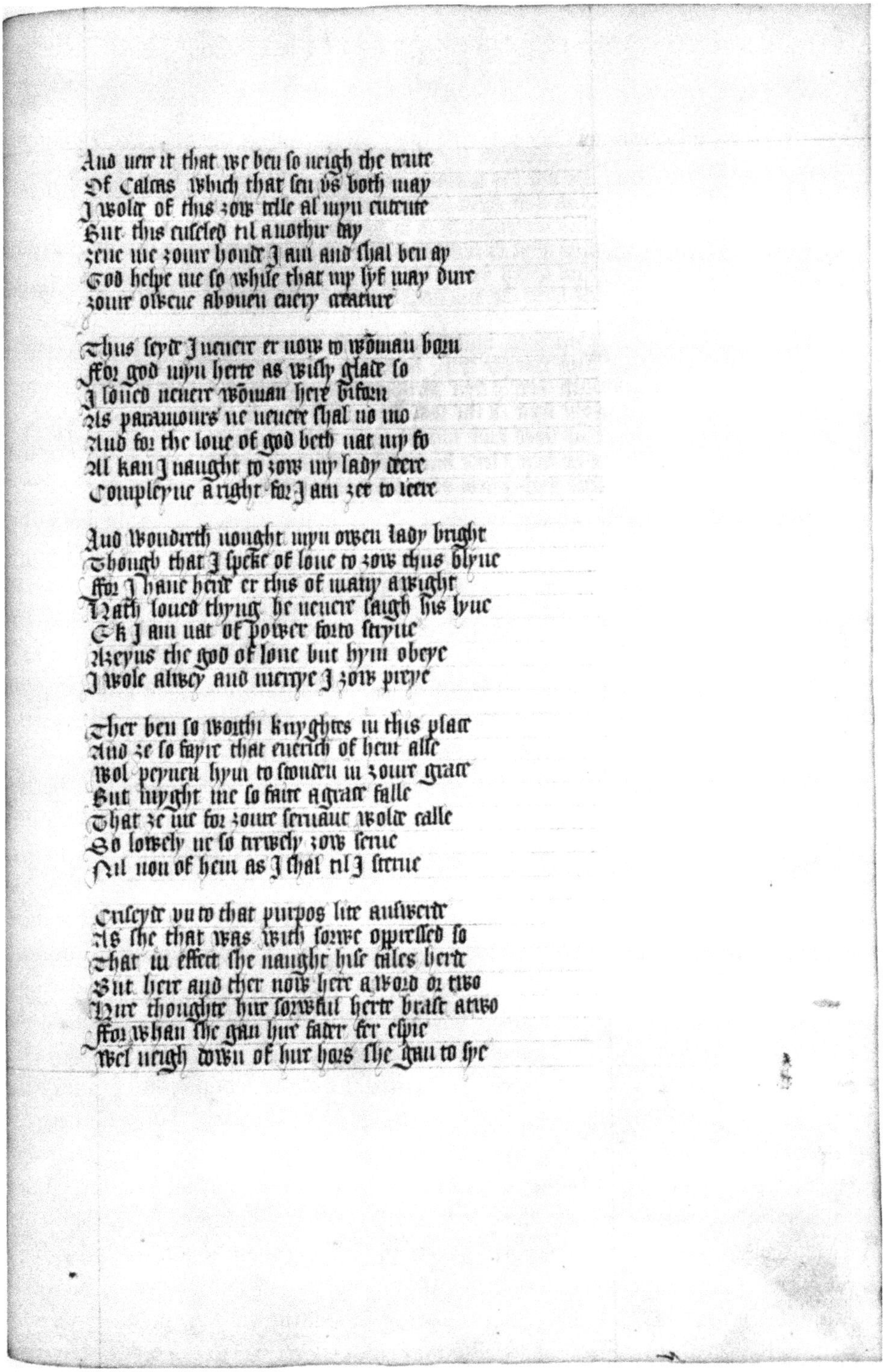
And nere it that we ben so neigh the tente
Of Calcas which that sen vs both may
I wolde of this ȝow telle al myn entente
But this enseled til anothir day
ȝeue me ȝoure honde I am and shal ben ay
God helpe me so whiles that my lyf may dure
ȝoure owene abouen euery creature

Thus seyde I neuere er now to woman born
For god myn herte as wisly glade so
I loued neuere woman here biforn
As paramours ne neuere shal no mo
And for the loue of god beth nat my fo
Al kan I naught to ȝow my lady dere
Compleyne aright for I am ȝet to lere

And wondreth nought myn owen lady bright
Though that I speke of loue to ȝow thus blyue
For I haue herd er this of many a wight
Hath loued thyng he neuere saugh his lyue
Ek I am nat of power for to stryue
Ayeyns the god of loue but hym obeye
I wole alwey and mercye I ȝow preye

Ther ben so worthi knyghtes in this place
And ȝe so fayir that euerich of hem alle
Wol peynen hym to stonden in ȝoure grace
But myght me so faire a grace falle
That ȝe me for ȝoure seruaunt wolde calle
So lowely ne so trewely ȝow serue
Nil non of hem as I shal til I sterue

Criseyde vn to that purpos lite answerde
As she that was with sorwe oppressed so
That in effect she naught his tales herde
But here and ther now here a word or two
Hire thoughte hire sorwful herte brast atwo
For whan she gan hir fader fer espie
Wel neigh down of hir hors she gan to sye

FIGURE 6.1A Cambridge, Corpus Christi College MS 61, f. 122.

Reproduced from *Troilus and Criseyde: A Facsimile of Corpus Christi College Cambridge MS 61* (Cambridge: D.S. Brewer, 1978) with the permission of The Parker Library, Corpus Christi College, Cambridge.

FIGURE 6.1B Detailed view of Cambridge, Corpus Christi College MS 61, f. 122. *Troilus and Criseyde*, V.148–82.

hedgehogs (Figure 6.1b, detail).[45] After Corpus Christi MS 61, the next earliest extant copy of *Troilus and Criseyde* is New York, Pierpont Morgan Library MS M 817 (*c.* 1405), which is written in a *textura*-based secretary.[46] While *textura* offers the eye an orderly verticality and connotes the liturgy, secretary—a cursive script—presents itself in loops and slants and invokes the world of documents, and in fact, Linne R. Mooney and Estelle Stubbs have recently identified this scribe as John Carpenter, common clerk of the London Guildhall from 1417–37.[47] But as Jeanne Krochalis notes, this scribe exhibits a 'textura approach' to secretary, giving his writing an overall 'angular impression'.[48] In addition, by exaggerating ascenders of select letters on top lines, this scribe lends that general angularity an atmosphere of high drama. A third early witness to *Troilus and Criseyde*, Durham, Durham University Library Cosin MS V.ii.13 (s. xv$^{2/4}$), was written by two scribes, one using a 'set secretary', the other 'anglicana formata' with many secretary features, including forward-slanting clubbed ascenders (see Figure 6.2).[49] With the addition of a calligraphic rendering of the first letter of each page together with frequent elaborated ascenders or descenders on top and bottom lines, the text exudes a fashionable flamboyance associated with French court culture.[50]

In the examples I have just cited, a scribe's decision to use a particular script—whether *textura*, secretary, or a combination of the two—affects a text's visual connotation, the way a person's work-day attire may announce a category of employment, whether construction, office, airline, hospital, and so on. At the same time, as M. B. Parkes has argued, a scribe's idiosyncratic habits in executing a script lend it a recognizable individuality apart from its general category, a quality T. A. M. Bishop calls 'inimitable' and 'defying verbal analysis'.[51] Parkes rose to the challenge of analysing this inimitable quality through his development of the terms aspect and *ductus*: aspect, according to Parkes, is the 'first impression' made by a scribe's 'personal *ductus*'; in turn, *ductus* consists of the 'way in which [the scribe] executed the strokes required to produce the configurations which form the basic shapes of the letters'.[52] The use and possible mis-use of these traits for identifying the work of individual scribes has become a matter of intense interest following Mooney's celebrated 2006 essay 'Chaucer's Scribe', which identified the scivener previously dubbed Scribe B as Adam Pinkhurst.[53] While identifying the distinctive features of scribes' hands and linking them to known individuals serves the laudable function aim of filling in the gaps in our knowledge of the world outside the books in which those hands are preserved, the very same idiosyncrasies give us purchase on an 'aspect' of a written text that is original to the scribe, however he or she was known in the world outside the book: born with the written text, in and as a scribe's movements direct the flow of ink onto parchment—or, as Bishop put it, 'in

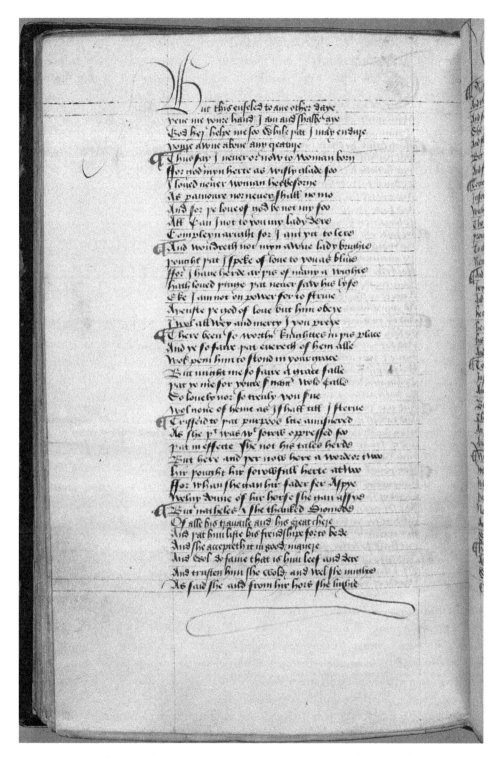

FIGURE 6.2 Durham, Durham University Library Cosin MS V.ii.13, f. 83v. *Troilus and Criseyde*, V.141–89.

the behaviour of the pen as it turns a curve or a corner'—these distinctive features persist in a book as the *genius*, the individual spirit, of the written text—and of the environment that is the book.[54] And even after the historical scribes responsible for them went on to their next commission and eventually out of this life, these 'characters' inscribed by and as their scribes' hands remain active as a kind of 'scribal function'—a complement to the 'author function'—carrying out the traditional duties of the ancient *genii* and of their latter-day attestation Alan of Lille's Genius, though with respect to a written text rather than to a human being or allegorical character. These include the roles of go-between, of guide or tutelary spirit and, at times, even of an author's mirror or other self.

THE SCRIBE AS GO-BETWEEN, GUIDE, AND AUTHOR'S OTHER SELF

In her study of the 'trope of the scribe', Lynn Staley Johnson observes that when an author refers within a work to the scribal production of that same work, the scribe thereby evoked often functions to vouch for the text's authority or for the author's propriety or both. In this way, the proem to Margery Kempe's *Book*, which tells of her second scribe's failing eyesight being cured by his labour over her text, frames her work with evidence of her sanctity; as Johnson puts it, 'the scribe serves to shift attention from her role as a social critic to her status as a holy woman'.[55] Johnson goes on to point out that this scribe could as easily have been Margery's invention as a real person; the work he does as a go-between between Margery and her readers, making her *Book* safe for the eyes of good Christian readers, derives from his presence as a 'trope' in her text. Across his oeuvre, Chaucer employs a range of such intermediary personae; these usually work, as Johnson notes, 'as a means of distancing himself from his writing' rather than of shoring up his authorial stature.[56] In a strict sense, none of Chaucer's distancing personae is a scribe, but one of them does exhibit a scribal sensibility: the 'reporter' of the tale-telling contest documented in the *Canterbury Tales*. In the prologue to the Miller's Tale, this persona professes fidelity to the texts of his 'authors'—the pilgrims—in the manner of a scribe trained by Bonaventure: the possible offensiveness of any given tale notwithstanding, he maintains that he must report 'Hir tales alle, be they bettre or werse, / Or elles falsen som of my mateere' (I.31745). He must tell 'alle' the pilgrims' tales and all of each tale—adding or changing nothing, in other words. In the same passage, however, this scribe-like persona also takes on the *genius*-like role of intermediary between the pilgrims' tales and their readers.

Displaying a diplomatic sensitivity to the potential squeamishness of the genteel members of his audience—'every gentil wight' (3171)—along with an intimate knowledge of the range of alternatives to the Miller's in the collection of tales, this persona is a savvy ambassador from the world of the book, specifically, the book he conjures in referring to its current page, or 'leef':

> And therfore, whoso list it nat yheere,
> Turne over the leef and chese another tale;
> For he shal fynde ynowe, grete and smale,
> Of storial thyng that toucheth gentillesse
> And eek moralitee and hoolynesse.   (3176–80)

Framing a reader's choice of reading material as itself a matter of 'moralitee', our reporter-cum-scribe-cum-*genius* concludes by noting that it is possible to choose wrongly even as he shifts the responsibility for such an error onto the reader: 'Blameth nat me if that ye chese amys. / The Millere is a cherl; ye knowe well this' (3181–2). In thus ensuring the blamelessness of the text he has already brought forth, this persona also provides for its viability and future transmission. Combining the duties of faithful copyist and protective intermediary, he fulfills the secretary and priest functions entailed in the expanded vision of the scribe exemplified in Alan's Genius outlined above. Although they do not always escape blame for doing so, the scribes of Chaucer's work also take after his mediating pseudo-scribe in the *Canterbury Tales* and in the process, in the manner of guardian or custodial spirits, assure its longevity and build the stature of Chaucer-the-author, even if Chaucer's fictive authorial persona would disavow it. John Shirley leads the group by taking up the role of Chaucer's middleman and champion under the sign of his own name; others fulfill this function in the form of explanatory glosses; still others notoriously intervene on Chaucer's behalf as his editors, adjusting his work in large and small ways to assure its presentability to readers on every 'leef'.

The smallest order of scribal mediation involves lexical and syntactic alterations, termed 'variant readings' in the apparatus of modern editions of medieval works. In their analyses of such interventions, scholars see scribes working towards a range of objectives, from simplifying to complicating an authorial text. In their edition of Chaucer's *Legend of Good Women*, for instance, Janet Cowen and George Kane list scribal interventions under five headings—'more explicit readings', 'more emphatic readings', 'easier readings', 'modernization', and 'sophistications'—and attribute them to 'copyists' response to and participation in the meaning of the text'.[57] The text of the *Legend* in Oxford, Magdalene College Library Pepys MS 2006 provides a record of one such copyist: responding to the text as a sentimental reader, he copies into it a group of variants we might include under yet another heading, 'sentimentalizations'. A small selection of these variants drawn from the Legends of Cleopatra and Dido follows (preceded by readings from Cowen and Kane's edition; variants italicized):[58]

TANNER: Al for the loue of Cleopataras
pepys: For the loue of *his lady dame* Cleopatrace   (600)

tanner: Mi worship in this day thus haue I lorn
pepys: My wurshyp *for euer* this day haue I loren   (659)
tanner: But herkeneth, ye that speken of kindenesse
pepys: But herken ye *now* that speken of kyndenes   (665)
tanner: And wol for loue his deth so frelye take
pepys: That wull for love *of his lady* his deth so frely take   (704)
tanner: But al this thing auayleth hir ryght nought
pepys: But al this *pitows complaynt* availleth ryght noght   (1325)
tanner: And stal away [vnto] hys companye
pepys: And *fro hir falsely* stole a wey to his companye   (1327)

Between multiple additions of 'his lady' and intensifiers such as 'for euer', 'falsely', and 'pitows', the Pepys scribe heightens of the overall piteousness of these ladies' plights.

While this scribe's lexical additions and alterations thus evince his 'participation' in the stories of Chaucer's good women, one addition cited above goes further. In changing the line 'But herkeneth, ye that speken of kindenesse' to 'But herken ye *now* that speken of kyndenes', the Pepys scribe has gone beyond amplifying the tale's theme: here he also raises the pitch of the narrator's voice. In doing so, he exemplifies a phenomenon that Bernard Cerquiglini argues is peculiar to vernacular works of the Middle Ages: when a scribe is set to copy a text written in his own spoken tongue, Cerquiglini asserts, 'something is at work to restore life to inert inscription; the language lures the copyist, whom it catches in its snare and sets up as subject'.[59] In the terms of Cerquiglini's analysis, the Pepys scribe has been caught up in the text to the point of rendering its 'speaker' more urgent, more present, more, we might say, alive than it is at this point in Tanner. In the terms of my discussion of scribal activities in the light of the *genius* figure, the Pepys scribe's addition of the single word 'now' is another example of a scribe as the companion of a written text's 'birth', endowing it with a unique and enduring character in the 'now' of its inscription even as he also works, in the manner of a mediator, to usher the tale into the 'now' of any present reading or listening audience: 'ye *now* that speken of kyndenes'.

Beyond making a wide range of such local modifications 'inside' a text—that is, on the level of single lines—scribes also concerned themselves with the structural framework and outer boundaries of Chaucer's works. The textual history of the *Canterbury Tales* provides a wealth of examples of scribes' efforts in this regard, a preponderance of which suggest that their top priority was to present the work as complete, no easy task since Chaucer died leaving his planned *magnum opus* a miscellany of tales in no apparent authorial order—a 'scribe's nightmare', as Helen Cooper has put it.[60] Faced with this state of affairs, scribes' first recourse would naturally have been the narrative links joining tales to each other, which would, in theory, unite all the tales into a well-wrought whole. Here too, however, Chaucer's literary remains offered no certain guide, for it would seem that he wrote more than one version of several of the links, a matter that only intensified the 'nightmare' the *Canterbury Tales* presented to scribes since the adoption of any given version of a link could require re-ordering a whole chain of tales. Despite the proliferating uncertainties these links could create for scribes regarding the order of tale tellers, a sense of their instrumentality to the integrity of Chaucer's *Tales*—to its being a whole work—is evident, paradoxically, in the Hengwrt scribe's willingness to leave several whole-page blank spaces for links that he did not have—leaving the *Tales* visibly *un*-whole—in hopes of acquiring the exemplars that would allow him to make the work truly and properly whole.[61]

It was likely the same concern for the *Tales'* integrity that guided the Hengwrt scribe to leave a generous space for a hoped-for remainder of the *Cook's Tale*; when it was not forthcoming, he left the famous marginal note 'of this Cook's tale maked Chaucer no more'—as if to place blame for the textual lacuna at the tip of Chaucer's pen rather than his own. Indeed, we might hear in the note a hint of pique, for as J. S. P. Tatlock once observed, '[w]hat a scribe most desired, perhaps, was not quite so much to find everything as to avoid glaring gaps'.[62] While it is well known that many scribes avoided the Hengwrt scribe's dire straits by having the Cook tell the Tale of Gamelyn, scholars have begun to suspect the Parson's Tale of constituting a similar scribal interest in providing material for any and all pilgrims who were evidently meant to tell a tale. Having unambiguous evidence in the form of the Parson's Prologue that Chaucer had included this pilgrim among the tale-telling contestants, the scribes may have fabricated one for him from a piece Chaucer never intended to be part of the *Tales*, a piece encompassing both the tale given to the Parson and the 'Retraction', which Charles A. Owen has dubbed a *Treatise on Penitence*.[63] Thus the closure the Parson's Tale and 'Retraction' provide to the *Canterbury Tales* as we know them may also mark, as Míceál F. Vaughan puts it, 'the end point' of 'a process teleologically determined by the scribe's desire to minimize the [*Tales'*] incompleteness'.[64] Going along with this agenda under mild protest, the scribe of Cambridge, Cambridge University Library MS Ii.3.26 includes the Parson's Tale but gives it a concluding rubric that at once points out its generic awkwardness as a tale and suggests an ad hoc decision behind its use as such: '*Explicit Tractatus Galfridi Chaucer de septem peccatis mortalibus ut dicitur pro fabula Rectoris*' [Here ends the treatise on the seven deadly sins, as it is called, by Geoffrey Chaucer for the tale of the Parson].[65] Following the Hengwrt scribe, we might paraphrase this scribe's note as follows: 'Of the tale of the Parson Chaucer maked nothing; therefore this treatise will do for his tale.'

Comments like the ones on the truncated Cook's Tale and the possibly ad hoc Parson's Tale have their origins in specific instances of scribes' efforts to endow given copies of the *Canterbury Tales* with the appearance of wholeness—that is, to fulfill their *genius*-like function as custodian spirits of a work's physical form—but to the extent that they explicate a part of the text that would not be obvious to an ordinary reader, these comments are also specimens of another facet of scribes' work: that of providing texts with explanatory glosses—or, put another way, that of acting as guides and tutelary spirits for readers, thereby assuring the viability of a text and the good reputation of its author. Over their long history in western manuscript culture, glosses have taken a variety of forms—from interlinear synonyms for or translations of difficult words to extensive marginal commentaries running the gamut from explanatory or source notes, to complementary extracts from *auctores*, to allegorical and tropological interpretations.[66] Even before a marginal apparatus was read, its very appearance on the page lent the commented-upon text an aura of authority, and Chaucer or an early 'glossator' shows his canny understanding of this salutary function of a gloss in the extensive marginal commentaries accompanying the Wife of Bath's Prologue even as that text itself is an irreverent send-up of the by-then well-known use of glossing to manipulate or obscure a text's meaning rather than to guide a reader to a fuller understanding of it.[67] 'Standardized' *glossae ordinariae* like those associated with the study of civil law, canon law, the Bible, and even Chaucer's Wife of Bath's Prologue would have been copied by scribes but not composed by them.[68]

Such authoritative, institutionalized glosses aside, scribes of Chaucer's work were not shy about composing their own, original glosses. Of all Chaucer's works, his *Troilus and Criseyde* garnered the most glosses; among its sixteen surviving manuscript witnesses, London, British Library MS Harley 2392 has been endowed in this way more abundantly than any other—all in the hand of its scribe 'Style'.[69] In the manner of a tutelary guide or spirit, this manuscript's interlinear glosses assist a reader's comprehension of the text by supplying synonyms for difficult words and referents for pronouns when they may be unclear, as in the following stanza:

> id est destine
> But O Fortune, executrice of wyerdes,
> O influences of thise heuenes hye,
> id est gouernours
> Soth is, that vnder God ye ben oure hierdes,
> id est couered
> Though to vs bestes ben the causes wrie
> Cres
> This mene I now, for she gan homward hye,
>
> But execut was al bisyde hire leue
> The goddes wil, for which she moste bleue.   (3.617-23)

Beyond these interlinear glosses, Style has provided numerous marginal annotations, some of which function partly as explanatory notes and partly as finding aids, primarily for mythological characters; for instance, next to the lines 'Or elles were hym levere, soule and bones, / With Pluto kyng as depe been in helle / As Tantalus' (3.591-3)—spoken by Pandarus while trying to convince Criseyde of Troilus's earnestness—Style has written '*Pluto / deus inferni*' and '*tantalus*'.

But the largest portion of Style's marginal notes has a moral valence and thus fulfills the specifically moral aspect of the *genius* figure's tutelary role. In this category of annotation, which takes the form of a simple 'nota' written in the margin, Style focuses on the poem's proverbial wisdom, especially that which pertains to the perils of romantic love. Book One, for instance, features nine 'nota' marks, including one that highlights an apostrophe to Fortune, 'O blynde world, O blynde entencioun!' (1.211); another pointing out an explanation of Troilus's rationale for keeping his love a secret, 'Remembryng hym that love to wide yblowe / Yelt bittre fruyt, though swete seed be sowe' (384–5); another next to the last line of Pandarus's famous comparison of himself to a whetstone, 'By his contrarie is every thyng declared' (637); and one next to the line 'Unknowe, unkist, and lost that is unsought' (809), which is from Pandarus's speech urging Troilus to pluck up his courage but whose wisdom easily stands alone. Given Style's appropriation by way of his 'nota' marks of the role of moral mediator between text and reader, it is interesting to observe that six of his 'nota' marks in Book One call attention to the words of Pandarus, the advice-giver and go-between *extraordinaire* in the poem.

For a scribe that might look a lot like Pandarus in one light but who resembles Alan's Genius and his forerunner *genii* in another, one could do no better than London scribe and bibliophile John Shirley (1360s–1456). Like Pandarus, who 'packages' Troilus for Criseyde in hyperbolic praise and a modicum of invented gossip, Shirley prefaces his texts with head-notes that sing their authors' fame along with concrete details about their lives. Shirley saves his highest praise for Chaucer and his work, to the extent that, as Seth Lerer has put it, '[m]aintaining Chaucer's reputation as the laureate and aureate poet seems almost an obsession with him'.[70] Beyond these shared traits as salespeople, it would appear that Shirley himself saw Pandarus-the-facilitator as a model for his role as scribe, for beneath a bookplate poem in his second major anthology, Cambridge Trinity College MS R.3.20, he penned Pandarus's 'whetstone stanza':

> A whetston is no kervyng instrument,
> And yet it maketh sharppe kervyng tolis;
> And there thow woost that I have aught mys-went,
> Eschuw thow that, for swich thing to the scole is;
> Thus ofte wise men ben war by foolys.
> If thow do so, thi wit is wel bewared;
> By his contrarie is every thyng declared.   (1.631–7)

Shirley gives this stanza the heading 'Pandarus to Troilus', but given the self-referential quality of the bookplate poem that appears above it, which concludes with the plea 'Whane yee þis boke haue over redde and seyne / To Johan Shirley restore yee it agayne', a reader is invited to view the 'I' of the whetstone stanza as a reference to Shirley as well as to Pandarus and in doing so to catch that he is declaring himself a 'fool' who may nevertheless teach 'wise men'.[71] Of course Pandarus was no fool and neither was Shirley; on the contrary, Shirley epitomizes the role of scribe as kindred spirit as it was exemplified by both Alan's Genius and the traditional *genius* figure, for he functions as *genius* of the place that is the book, as *genius* the moral guide, and as Alan's Genius as a generative 'other self', in this case, Chaucer's.

If the *Canterbury Tales* narrator briefly steps out of his role as a pilgrim telling the story of a journey in order to speak as a denizen of the very book in a reader's hand— suggesting that he or she might want to 'Turne over the leef and chese another tale'— then Shirley performs the trick in reverse and takes it further, figuring the process of reading a book as a journey and identifying himself both as the author of its itinerary and as the constant and trustworthy guide for the reading 'traveler'. Shirley writes himself into these roles in two versified tables of contents, both composed for volumes he produced containing works by Chaucer.[72] In both poems, Shirley begins by detailing his efforts in acquiring exemplars, copying them, and having them bound into books. While such inventories of scribal labour are unusual in themselves, Shirley goes on to note that he has also ordered the texts. Given that the order of a book's texts is the essence of a table of contents and given that a table of contents is a specifically bookish form, the ensuing versified lists of contents effectively establish their author Shirley as the guiding intelligence of each book—the *genius* of these two places. In the earlier of the two poems, the subsequent list of contents reads like an advertisement for a day's sight-seeing written by a local expert, pulling the customer/reader in by addressing him in the second person and framing each text in future-tense phrases: either as an attraction you—the reader—'shall' find or see or know, or as a sight (or site) that will follow 'next'— as long as you keep turning the pages, as long as 'ye wol þe writing suwe'.[73] Having once entered upon the territory defined by the bindings of any one of Shirley's productions, a reader would find herself addressed at every turn by that same local expert, now in the form of the garrulous head-notes Shirley supplies for his texts.

It is in these head-notes that Shirley most closely fulfills the intertwined roles of priest and secretary exemplified by Alan's Genius, for here he not only enacts but also gives verbal expression to a sense of the moral obligation to a text that goes along with bringing it into material form; like Alan's Genius, he fulfills his duty using a formula of his training, for a head-note is essentially an expanded rubric. Also like Alan's Genius, whom Nature dubbed her 'alter-ego', Shirley serves as a mirror or other self to Chaucer, thereby making their 'fortunes interchangeable'.[74] A look at Shirley's head-note to Chaucer's *Anelida and Arcite* in Trinity College MS R.3.20 will illustrate these extraordinary dimensions of his scribal practice:

> Takeþe heed sirs I prey yowe of þis compleynt of Anelyda Qweene of Cartage. Roote of trouthe and stedfastnesse þat pytously compleyneþe vpon þe varyance of Daun Arcyte lord borne of þe blood Royal of Thebes englisshed by Geffrey Chaucier in þe best wyse and moost Rettoricyous þe moost vnkouþe metre coloures and Rymes þat euer was sayde tofore þis day – redeþe and preveþe þe sooþe.[75]

Beginning with a direct address to readers indicating the points of moral interest they should take heed of in the text that follows—the steadfastness of Anelida and the 'varyance' of Arcite—Shirley goes on to praise Chaucer in all superlatives (to which I return shortly) and to conclude by admonishing readers to read the work and see for themselves if what he announces is true. In his directions to readers in this head-note, Shirley at once protects the text—by working to assure readers' appreciation of it—and performs the role of priestly intermediary between Chaucer and his readers, reminding the latter of their own responsibility to recognize 'þe sooþe' in anything they read.

In its praise of Chaucer, this head-note is one of many that functions, as Lerer has argued, to create the Chaucer we know today, for they invent 'the controlling idea of a lyric, public Chaucer', as he puts it.[76] In this particular head-note, as Lerer explains, Shirley's 'moost vnkouþe metre' refers to Chaucer's use in *Anelida and Arcite* of the unusual decasyllabic line while his 'moost Rettoricyous...coloures and Rymes' refers to his figurative language and elaborate stanzaic structure: the superlatives all tout, in other words, Chaucer's '[v]irtuosity in metrical and stanzaic form'.[77] Beyond setting terms for the aesthetic value of Chaucer's poetry, however, this head-note is also one of many that performs the more basic task of naming Chaucer as a poem's author, and thus it is that it is Shirley we have to thank for much of the canon of Chaucer's short poems, including the unique witness to Chaucer's 'Wordes Unto Adam, His Owne Scriveyn', also preserved in Trinity College R.3.20, right below Pandarus's 'whetstone stanza'. In this way, both by attributing poems to Chaucer and by defining and then championing their aesthetic value, Shirley's Chaucer is our Chaucer; put another way, Shirley functions as Chaucer's mirror and as an alter ego to the Chaucerian persona who, as we have seen, would prefer to distance himself from his work. Moreover, Shirley's head-notes promulgated his own fame as well as Chaucer's; indeed, both author and scribe could boast a network of 'heirs' in the fifteenth century.[78] Lerer has observed that by inscribing 'Chaucer's Wordes Unto Adam' where he does, Shirley 'presents himself as this labouring Adam to Chaucer's near-divine authority'.[79] As I have shown, Shirley's actual performance of his scribal labours was more in the manner of partner to a near-divine authority than servant, in the manner of the partnership between Alan's Genius and the goddess Nature.

AUTHOR, SCRIBE, AND THE TRUE OBJECT OF LITERARY STUDY

Given the various and sundry roles of the scribe I have touched upon in this essay, the question arises, what do we study—and what might we study—when we study the work of scribes? With respect to John Shirley, one answer to this question is that we study the processes of canonization, appreciating the ways Chaucer was packaged and represented by the hand of Shirley and his descendants. With respect to scribes' work as glossators, scholars may find information, as B. A. Windeatt has put it, about 'the points of difficulty for the contemporary reader of Chaucer's diction'.[80] In relation to their work as editors, Lee Patterson would have it that in the form of scribal productions, we find a text that has been 'preread' by scribes and altered according to their interpretations, which we study in order to 'reverse this process, to return the text to a readable, but as yet unread, condition'—the condition of the text as Chaucer, before interacting with the scribe, intended it.[81] Yet another answer to this question I have already noted above in concluding my discussion of scribal hands: a study of scribal labour yields valuable insight into the circumstances of production and routes of transmission of the works of Chaucer. Returning now to Linne Mooney's essay on Adam Pinkhurst, a ground-breaking example of that use of scribal evidence, we may find that her vision of Chaucer's and Pinkhurst's relationship bears some resemblance to the relationship I have been describing between Chaucer and his work on the one hand and his scribes as Geniuses and *genii* on the other—and to the ties between Nature and Genius and individual humans and their *genii* before that. Mooney's assertions that Pinkhurst 'offers a model of a scribe who specialized in copying the work of a single author' and, further, that the connection between Chaucer and Pinkhurst might have begun as early as the 1380s and have been 'sufficiently close for the poet to write a jesting poem to him' all suggest the kind of loyal, durable, and mutually beneficial companionship that marks the bond between an individual and his *genius*.[82]

All of these answers to the question of what we study when we study the work of scribes focus on matters outside the literary work that scribes actually bring into being, however. In concluding my exploration of the role of the scribe, I return to Alan of Lille's *De planctu Naturae*, to its description of Truth, or *Veritas*—the daughter of Nature and Genius—in order to discover a conception of the object of literary study that partakes of the work of scribes. In a passage that is strikingly evocative of the traditional notion of the literary 'work' (as an entity independent of its material forms), Alan notes, 'On her face could be read [*legebatur*] the divinity of heavenly beauty which disdains our mortal nature', after which he goes on to explain that her garments, 'proclaiming the work of the right hand of a heavenly craftsman', were impervious to age and were joined to her body in such a way as to be inseparable.[83] Truth, it would seem, is the offspring of a loving communion between matter and form and exists in and as a combination of the two. Revisiting the question of what we *might* study when we study the work of scribes with this allegory in mind, we could answer that it would be possible to study the product of a relationship, looking neither solely at the material labour of scribes nor solely beyond that for the intellectual work of authors. The product of such a relationship could be figured, in fact, in an allegorical reading of Chaucer's 'Wordes Unto Adam'. Following Mooney's sense of the work as a 'jesting poem', we may recognize that it is in the context of an affectionate relationship that the speaker asks his scribe to 'write more trew'. Envisioning a kindly union between an author's 'makyng' and a scribe's writing might lead us to an object of literary study that is 'more trew' for Chaucer's work than the traditional object that recognizes value in the author's 'makyng' alone.

NOTES

1. St Bonaventure, '*Aliquis enim scribit aliena, nihil addendo vel mutando; et iste mere dicitur scriptor*'. Latin text and English translation quoted from Alexandra Gillespie, *Print Culture and the Medieval Author: Chaucer, Lydgate, and Their Books, 1473–1557* (Oxford: Oxford University Press, 2007), 11.

2. For complaints about scribes beginning with Cicero, see John Scattergood, 'The Jongleur, the Copyist, and the Printer: The Tradition of Chaucer's Wordes unto Adam, His Own Scriveyn', in *Courtly Literature: Culture and Context: Selected Papers from the 5th Triennial Congress of the International Courtly Literature Society*, ed. Keith Busby and Erik Kooper (Amsterdam: J. Benjamins, 1990), 499–508, at 503–4. For Ælfric's criticisms, see Orietta Da Rold, 'Textual Copying and Transmission', in *The Oxford Handbook of Medieval Literature in English*, ed. Elaine Treharne and Greg Walker with the assistance of William Green (Oxford: Oxford University Press, 2010), 33–56 at 36–42.

3. Glending Olson, 'Author, Scribe, and Curse: The Genre of Adam Scriveyn', *Chaucer Review* 42 (2008), 284–97. Chaucer distinguishes authorial 'makyng' from scribal writing in the fourth line of his poem to Adam: 'But after my makyng thow wryte more trewe'. For the varied senses of 'makyng' in reference to medieval textual production as well as the distinction between it and writing, See Glending Olson, 'Making and Poetry in the Age of Chaucer', *Comparative Literature* 31 (1979), 272–90. For an excellent survey of book curses from antiquity into the early modern period, see Marc Drogin, *Anathema! Medieval Scribes and the History of Book Curses* (Montclair, NJ: Allanheld and Schram, 1983). See also Lynn Thorndike, 'Copyists' Final Jingles in Mediaeval Manuscripts', *Speculum* 12 (1937), 268; and 'More Copyists' Final Jingles', *Speculum* 31 (1956), 321–8. In addition to the book curses collected here, word searches on 'anathema' or 'maledictus' in online library catalogues (e.g. the British Library) yield many more.

4. '*Quicunque alienaverit anathema sit. / Qui culpat carmen sit maledictus. Amen*' (Drogin, *Anathema!*, 69); translation based on Drogin's.

5. *Libri contractor calamis celi potiatur; Si quis subtractor, in Avernis sic moriatur* (Drogin, *Anathema!*, 83).

6. Olson, 'Author, Scribe, and Curse', 288.

7. For examples of colophons alluding to material rewards, see Thorndike, 'Final Jingles' and 'More Final Jingles'. Taking the pretty girl reference a step further, one scribe claims that it was one of these who taught him to use his pen: '*Scribere cum penna docuit me pulcra puella*' ('More Final Jingles', 323).

8. '*Amice qui legis, retro digitis teneas, ne subito litteras deleas, quia ille homo qui nescit scribere nullum se putat habere laborem; quia sicut navigantibus dulcis est portus, ita scriptori novissimus versus. Calamus tribus digitis continetur. Totum corpus laborat. Deo gratias. Ego, in Dei nomine, Vuarembertus scripsi. Deo gratias*' (Paris, Bibliothèque nationale, MS Lat. 12,296). Latin text from Leslie Webber Jones, 'The Scriptorium at Corbie: I. The Library', *Speculum* 22 (1947), 191–204, at 200. English translation by David F. Harvey in Drogin, *Anathema!*, 24.

9. '*verba caelestia multiplicat homo, et quadam significatione contropabili, si fas est dicere, tribus digitis scribitur quod virtus sanctae Trinitatis effatur*'. Cassiodorus, *Institutiones divinarum et humanarum lectionum*, in ed. R. A. B. Mynors, *Cassiodori Senatoris Institutiones Edited from the MSS* (Oxford: Clarendon Press, 1937), bk. I, ch. 30.1, lines 21–3 (75); trans. J. W. Halporn, *Institutions of Divine and Secular Learning and On the Soul* (Liverpool: Liverpool University Press, 2003), 163.

10. On manuscripts of Chaucer's works associated with houses of monks, friars, and nuns, see Linda Olson's ' "Swete Cordyall" of "Lytterature": Some Middle English Manuscripts from the Cloister', in *Opening Up Middle English Manuscripts: Literary and Visual Approaches*, eds. Kathryn Kerby-Fulton, Maidie Hilmo, and Linda Olson (Ithaca, NY: Cornell University Press, 2012), 291–371, at 303–14.

11. Winthrop Wetherbee, 'The Theme of Imagination in Medieval Poetry and the Allegorical Figure of "Genius" ', *Medievalia et Humanistica* n.s. 7 (1976), 45–64, at 57.

12. On these early *genii*, see Jane Chance Nitzsche, *The Genius Figure in Antiquity and the Middle Ages* (New York: Columbia University Press, 1975), 7–20.

13. Denise Baker, 'The Priesthood of Genius: A Study of the Medieval Tradition', in *Gower's Confessio Amantis: A Critical Anthology*, ed. Peter Nicholson (Cambridge: D. S. Brewer, 1991), 143–57; Nitzsche, *Figure of Genius*, 88–107. On Bernardus's system of *genii* see the same, 65–87.

14. Alan of Lille, *De planctu Naturae*, '*A Genii templo tales anathema merentur / Qui Genio decimas et sua iura negant*', ed. Nikolaus M. Häring, in *Alan of Lille, De planctu naturae*

(Spoleto: Centro Italiano di Studi sull'Alto Medioevo), 876, lines 71–672; trans. James. J. Sheridan, *The Plaint of Nature* (Toronto: Pontifical Institute of Mediaeval Studies, 1980), 216. All quotations from and translations of the *De planctu* are from these editions.

15. Nitzsche, *Figure of Genius*, 92–3.

16. Alan of Lille, *De planctu Naturae*, '*abhominationis filios a sacramentali ecclesie nostre communione seiungens, cum debita officii sollempnitate, seuera excommunicationis uirga percutias*', ed. Häring, 872, ll. 211–14; trans. Sheridan, 207–8.

17. Nitzsche, *Figure of Genius*, 89.

18. Martianus Capella, quoted from Nitzsche, 15–16.

19. Alan of Lille, *De planctu Naturae*, '*…uelut in speculo Nature resultante similitudine inueniendo me alteram*' ed. Häring, 871, ll. 190–1; trans. Sheridan, 207.

20. Ibid., '*nodo dilectionis precordialis astringor aut tecum in tuo profectu proficiens aut in tuo defectu equa lance deficiens. Quare circularis debet esse dilectio, ut tu, talione dilectionis respondens*', ed. Häring, 871, ll. 190–3; trans. Sheridan, 207.

21. Baker, 'The Priesthood of Genius', 149.

22. Alan of Lille, *De planctu Naturae*, '*Genius…pretaxatam excommunicationis seriem a penetralibus mentis forinsecus euocauit*', ed. Häring, 878, l. 138; trans. Sheridan, 220.

23. For a discussion of this phenomenon, see Elizabeth Pittenger, 'Explicit Ink', in *Premodern Sexualities*, eds. Louise Fradenburg and Carla Freccero (New York: Routledge, 1996), 223–41.

24. On Chaucer's use of the plough as pen metaphor in the Knight's and the Miller's tales, see Lynn Staley Johnson, 'The Trope of the Scribe and the Question of Literary Authority in the Works of Julian of Norwich and Margery Kempe', *Speculum* 66 (1991), 820–38, at 825.

25. An argument has been made that this number of references to scribes should be halved; for provocative discussions of the authorship of 'Chaucer's Wordes Unto Adam', see Seth Lerer, *Chaucer and His Readers: Imagining the Author in Late-Medieval England* (Princeton, NJ: Princeton University Press, 1993), 121; Julia Boffey and A. S. G. Edwards, 'Chaucer's "Chronicle," John Shirley, and the Canon of Chaucer's Shorter Poems', *Studies in the Age of Chaucer* 20 (1998), 201–18, at 207–8; Alexandra Gillespie, 'Reading Chaucer's Words to Adam', *Chaucer Review* 42 (2008), 269–83, at 275; and A. S. G. Edwards, 'Chaucer and "Adam Scriveyne"', *Medium Ævum* 81 (2012), 135–8.

26. For descriptions of each of the steps in the production of a manuscript page, see Raymond Clemens and Timothy Graham, *Introduction to Manuscript Studies* (Ithaca, NY: Cornell University Press, 2007), 18–34. For overviews of the use of page design elements in books produced in late-medieval England, see Kathleen L. Scott, 'Design, decoration and illustration', in *Book Production and Publishing in Britain 1375–1475*, eds. Jeremy Griffiths and Derek Pearsall (Cambridge: Cambridge University Press, 1989), 31–64; and Stephen Partridge, 'Designing the Page,' in *The Production of Books in England 1350–1500*, ed. Alexandra Gillespie and Daniel Wakelin (Cambridge: Cambridge University Press, 2011), 79–103.

27. In his note on this line, Stephen A. Barney explains that summarizing chapter headings often began with 'How…'. ('Explanatory Notes', *Riverside Chaucer*, 1032).

28. Michelle P. Brown, *Understanding Illuminated Manuscripts: A Guide to Technical Terms*. (Malibu: J. Paul Getty Museum, 1994), 111. Brown's *Guide* is now also available at the British Library Website: bl.uk/catalogues/illuminatedmanuscripts/glossary.asp. On rubrics, see also Clemens and Graham, *Introduction to Manuscript Studies*, 24–5.

29. For further reflections on the possibility of Chaucer thinking like a scribe, see Partridge, 'Designing the Page', 102.

30. In Oxford, Bodleian Library MS Fairfax 16, the line is marked with a three-line blue initial with red flourishing (f. 133v); Bodleian Library MS Bodley 638 marks it with a two-line red initial with decorative in-filling also in red ink (f. 115v); Bodleian Library MS Tanner marks it with a small paraf mark (f. 105r).

31. Ardis Butterfield, 'Mise-en-page in the Troilus Manuscripts: Chaucer and French Manuscript Culture', Huntington Library Quarterly 58 (1995), 49–80.

32. Joel Fredell, 'The Lowly Paraf: Transmitting Manuscript Design in The Canterbury Tales', Studies in the Age of Chaucer 22 (2000), 213–80, at 238–40.

33. The witnesses are Oxford, Bodleian Library MSS Bodley 638 (ff. 101v–102v) and Fairfax 16 (ff. 124v–125r). On nominales, see Werner Hüllen, English Dictionaries 800–1700 (Oxford: Oxford University Press, 2006), 67–9. For their relation to the underlining in these two manuscripts, see my essay "Qui bien ayme a tarde oblie: Lemmata and Lists in the Parliament of Fowls', in Visual Approaches to Chaucer, ed Susanna Fein and David Raybin (College Park, PA: Pennsylvania State University Press, 2016), 195–217.

34. Fredell, 'The Lowly Paraf', 238 and 239; Butterfield, 'Mise-en-page in the Troilus Manuscripts', 63.

35. My survey is based is based on M. C. Seymour's A Catalogue of Chaucer Manuscripts, 2 vols. (Aldershot: Scolar Press, 1995).

36. On quires and systems for ordering them, see Brown, Guide, s.v. 'quire', 'bifolium', and 'catchword'. See also Clemens and Graham, Introduction to Manuscript Studies, 49–50.

37. Estelle Stubbs, '"Here's one I prepared earlier": The Work of Scribe D on Oxford, Corpus Christi College, MS 198', Review of English Studies 58 (2007), 133–53, at 143.

38. Ibid., 144.

39. For a full narration of these activities and their relations to the Hengwrt Manuscript and London, British Library Harley MS 7334, see Stubbs, 'The Work of Scribe D', 144–8.

40. Stubbs, 'The Work of Scribe D', 151–3.

41. Jacob Thaisen, 'The Merchant, the Squire, and Gamelyn in the Christ Church Chaucer Manuscript', Notes and Queries 253 (2008), 265–9.

42. Ibid., 268. Date as given by Seymour in Catalogue of Chaucer Manuscripts, vol. 2, 201. A possible layer of authorial revision is evinced by quire revisions in some Troilus and Criseyde manuscripts as well—affecting Troilus's Boethian soliloquy (4.983–1085)— on which see Barry Windeatt, 'The Text of the Troilus', Essays on Troilus and Criseyde, ed. Mary Salu (Cambridge: D. S. Brewer, 1979), 1–22, at 3–11. For yet another exemplary analysis of a scribe's interventions in quire structure, see Orietta Da Rold, 'The Quiring System in Cambridge University Library MS Dd.4.24 of Chaucer's Canterbury Tales', The Library 4 (2003), 107–28.

43. Boethius writes that the words dictated to him by the muses cause him to weep: 'they now dampen my face with lachrymose elegy's [elegi fletibus] truth'. Boethius, Consolatio Philosophiae, ed. James J. O'Donnell (Bryn Mawr: Bryn Mawr College, 1990), line 4; trans. Joel C. Relihan, The Consolation of Philosophy (Indianapolis, IN: Hackett, 2001).

44. Script identification from M. C. Seymour, A Catalogue of Chaucer Manuscripts: Volume I. Works Before the Canterbury Tales (Aldershot: Scolar Press, 1995), 56. As M. B. Parkes explains in Their Hands Before Our Eyes: A Closer Look at Scribes (Aldershot: Ashgate, 2008), in textura quadrata (of which littera quadrata is a specimen), scribes applied a short diagonal stroke to the base of minims using the full width of the pen's nib 'often forming a spur where the pen changed direction'; this 'prototype movement' lent the script a 'rhythmic and unified effect' (104). On the script in Corpus Christi MS 61, see M. B. Parkes, 'Palaeographical Description and Commentary', in Troilus and Criseyde:

A Facsimile of Corpus Christi College Cambridge MS 61 (Cambridge: D. S. Brewer, 1978), 1–13, at 5–6. See also Linne R. Mooney et al, *Late Medieval English Scribes* (York: University of York, 2011), which includes an example of a letter E from this manuscript that the editors liken to a hedgehog (www.medievalscribes.com). See this site for further examples of the hands of all the scribes mentioned in this essay.

45. Parkes sees gargoyles ('Palaeographical Description', 6); the editors of *Late Medieval English Scribes* see hedgehogs (s.v. Cambridge, Corpus Christi College 61).

46. Seymour, *Chaucer Manuscripts*, 2:60.

47. Linne R. Mooney and Estelle Stubbs, *Scribes and the City: London Guildhall Clerks and the Dissemination of Middle English Literature 1375–1425* (York: York Medieval Press, 2013), 86–106.

48. Jeanne Krochalis, 'Introduction', in *The Pierpont Morgan Library Manuscript M.817: A Facsimile* (Norman: Pilgrim Books, 1986), xvii-xxix, at p. xix. Find additional analysis of Carpenter's hand along with a sample page from M.817 at Linne Mooney, Simon Horobin, and Estelle Stubbs, *Late Medieval English Scribes* (https://www.medievalscribes.com, accessed 15 July 2019).

49. Script identifications from 'Medieval Manuscripts in the University Library' (Durham University, 2015), s.v. DUL MS Cosin V.II.13 (https://www.dur.ac.uk/library/asc/theme/medmss/apvii13/ accessed 1 September 2015).

50. Parkes discusses the influence of 'the aesthetics of an international culture' on 'all art forms, including handwriting' in *Their Hands Before Our Eyes*, 108–9.

51. T. A. M. Bishop, *Scriptores Regis: Facsimiles to Identify and Illustrate the Hands of Royal Scribes in Original Charters of Henry I, Stephen, and Henry II* (Oxford: Clarendon, 1961), 9.

52. M. B. Parkes, 'Richard Frampton: A Commercial Scribe', in *The Medieval Book and a Modern Collector: Essays in Honour of Toshiyuki Takamiya*, eds. Takami Matsuda, Richard A. Linenthal, and John Scahill (Cambridge: D. S. Brewer, 2004), 113–24, at 115. Parke's definitions of aspect and *ductus* first appeared in *English Cursive Book Hands, 1250–1500* (Berkeley, CA: University of California Press, 1969), xxvi. See also Parks, *Their Hands before Our Eyes*, 59–63.

53. Mooney's identification of Pinkhurst was published in her 'Chaucer's Scribe', *Speculum* 81 (2006), 96–138. For a recent history of 'The Pynkhurst Phenomenon', see the so-titled introduction to Lawrence Warner's *Chaucer's Scribes: London Textual Production 1384–1432* (Cambridge: Cambridge University Press, 2018), 1–12. This scribe was given the moniker Scribe B in A. I. Doyle and M. B. Parkes, 'The Production of Copies of the *Canterbury Tales* and the *Confessio Amantis* in the Early Fifteenth Century', in *Medieval Scribes, Manuscripts, and Libraries: Essays Presented to N. R. Ker*, eds. M. B. Parkes and Andrew G. Watson (London: Scolar, 1978), 163–210, at 170.

54. Bishop, *Scriptores Regis*, 9.

55. Johnson, 'The Trope of the Scribe', 837.

56. Ibid., 822.

57. Janet Cowen and George Kane, eds., *Geoffrey Chaucer: The Legend of Good Women* (East Lansing, MI: Colleagues Press, 1995), 84–100.

58. Cowen's and Kane's copy text is Oxford, Bodleian Library Tanner MS 346. Readings from Pepys are my transcriptions from the manuscript facsimile, *Manuscript Pepys 2006: A Facsimile*, Intro by A. S. G. Edwards (Norman, OH: Pilgrim Books, 1985). For a discussion of scribal 'editing' that touches on a tendency to sentimentalize along with several of the types of intervention Cowen and Kane list, see B. A. Windeatt, 'The Scribes as Chaucer's Early Critics', *Studies in the Age of Chaucer* 1 (1979), 119–41.

59. '…*quelque chose est en jeu qui redonne vie à l'inscription inerte; la langue miroite et prend dans son piège le copiste, qu'elle institue en suget'*. Bernard Cerquiglini, *Eloge de la Variante: Histoire Critique de la Philologie* (Paris: Éditions du Seuil, 1989), 19; trans. Betsy Wang, *In Praise of the Variant: A Critical History of Philology* (Baltimore, MA: Johns Hopkins University Press, 1999), 2–3.

60. Helen Cooper, 'Averting Chaucer's Prophecies: Miswriting, Mismetering, and Misunderstanding', in *A Guide to Editing Middle English*, eds. Vincent P. McCarren and Douglas Moffat (Ann Arbor, MI: University of Michigan Press, 1998), 79–93, at 80.

61. For a full explanation of this and other problematic links, see Norman Blake, 'The Links in the *Canterbury Tales*', in *New Perspectives on Middle English Texts: A Festschrift for R. A. Waldron*, eds. Susan Powell and Jeremy J. Smith (Woodbridge: D. S. Brewer, 2000), 107–18. For a more recent analysis, see Simon Horobin, 'Adam Pinkhurst, Geoffrey Chaucer, and the Hengwrt Manuscript of the *Canterbury Tales*', *Chaucer Review* 44 (2000): 351–67.

62. J. S. P. Tatlock, 'The *Canterbury Tales* in 1400', *PMLA* 50 (1935), 100–39, at 119.

63. Charles A. Owen, 'What the Manuscripts Tell us About the Parson's Tale', *Medium Ævum* 63 (1994), 239–49, at 239. For a detailed analysis of scribal responses to the unfinished Cook's Tale, see A. S. G. Edwards, 'The *Canterbury Tales* and *Gamelyn*', in *Medieval Latin and Middle English Literature: Essays in Honor of Jill Mann*, ed. Maura Nolan (Woodbridge: D. S. Brewer, 2011), 76–90.

64. Mícheál F. Vaughan, 'Creating Comfortable Boundaries: Scribes, Editors, and the Invention of the Parson's Tale', in *Rewriting Chaucer: Culture, Authority, and the Idea of the Authentic Text, 1400–1602*, eds. Thomas A. Prendergast and Barbara Kline (Columbus, OH: Ohio State University Press, 1999), 45–90, at 55.

65. Quoted in Owen, 'What the Manuscripts Tell Us', 240.

66. For a historical overview of the practice of glossing together with a look at Chaucer's exploration of its use and abuse, see Robert W. Hanning, ' "I Shal Finde It in a Maner Glose": Versions of Textual Harassment in Medieval Literature', in *Medieval Texts and Contemporary Readers,* eds. Laurie A. Finke and Martin B. Shichtman (Ithaca, NY: Cornell University Press, 1987), 27–50.

67. On this aspect of the Wife of Bath's Prologue, see Hanning, 'I Shal Finde It in a Maner Glose', 44–50. On the authorship of the commentary, see Graham D. Caie, 'The Significance of the Early Chaucer Manuscript Glosses (With Special Reference to the *Wife of Bath's Prologue*)', *Chaucer Review* 10 (1976), 350–60, at 357–8.

68. Beryl Smalley provides a succinct history of the development of *glossae ordinariae* in *The Study of the Bible in the Middle Ages* (Oxford: Blackwell, 1952), 46–66.

69. In the following discussion I draw from Tamara Pérez Fdez and Ana Sáez Hidalgo, ' "A Man Textueel": Scribal Readings and Interpretations of *Troilus and Criseyde* through the Glosses in Manuscript British Library Harley 2392', *Journal of the Spanish Society for Mediaeval English Language and Literature* 14 (2007), 197–220; and C. David Benson and Barry A. Windeatt, 'The Manuscript Glosses to Chaucer's *Troilus and Criseyde*', *Chaucer Review* 25 (1990), 33–53.

70. Lerer, *Chaucer and His Readers*, 46.

71. The bookplate poem and whetstone stanza appear on page 361 of one of Shirley's anthologies, Cambridge, Trinity College Library MS R.3.20. For the text of the former together with a discussion of the juxtaposition of the two, see Lerer, *Chaucer and His Readers*, 133.

72. The poems are *IMEV* 1426 and 2598, which appear in London, British Library Additional MSS 16165 and 29,729, respectively. Both poems have been edited by Margaret Connolly, in *John Shirley: Book Production and the Noble Household in Fifteenth-Century England* (Aldershot: Ashgate: 1998), 206–11.

73. *IMEV* 1426, line 72, ed. Connolly, in *John Shirley*, 208.

74. Alan of Lille, *De planctu Naturae*, trans. Sheridan, 206, 207.

75. Quoted in Lerer, *Chaucer and His Readers*, 102.

76. Ibid., 119.

77. Ibid., 102.

78. I quote from the title of Linne Mooney's recent article 'John Shirley's Heirs', *Yearbook of English Studies* 33 (2003), 182–98.

79. Lerer, *Chaucer's Readers*, 121.

80. Windeatt, 'The Scribes as Chaucer's Early Critics', 127.

81. Lee Patterson, 'The Logic of Textual Criticism and the Way of Genius: The Kane-Donaldson *Piers Plowman* in Historical Perspective', in *Textual Criticism and Literary Interpretation*, ed. Jerome J. McGann (Chicago, IL: Chicago University Press, 1985), 55–91, at 72.

82. Mooney, 'Chaucer's Scribe', 121 and 119. Simon Horobin presents documentary evidence of a connection between Chaucer and Pinkhurst in 1385 in his 'Adam Pinkhurst, Geoffrey Chaucer, and the Hengwrt Manuscript of the *Canterbury Tales*'. See also Mooney and Stubbs, *Scribes and the City*, 67–85.

83. Alan of Lille, *De planctu Naturae*, 'Huius in facie diuinae pulcritudinis deitas legebatur, nostre mortalitatis aspernata naturam. Vestes uero celestis artificis dexteram eloquentes, indefesse rutilationis splenditatibus inflammate, nullis poterant uetustatis tineis cancellari. Que uirgineo corpori tanta fuerant conexione iugate, ut nulla exuitionis dieresis eas aliquando a virginali corpore faceret phariseas'. Ed. Häring, 877, ll. 98–102; trans. Sheridan, 218.

BIBLIOGRAPHY

Alan of Lille, *The Plaint of Nature*. Trans. James. J. Sheridan (Toronto: Pontifical Institute of Mediaeval Studies, 1980).

Butterfield, Ardis, '*Mise-en-page* in the *Troilus* Manuscripts: Chaucer and French Manuscript Culture', *Huntington Library Quarterly* 58 (1995), 49–80.

Da Rold, Orietta, 'The Quiring System in Cambridge University Library MS Dd.4.24 of Chaucer's *Canterbury Tales*', *The Library* 4 (2003), 107–28.

Doyle, A. I. and M. B. Parkes, 'The production of copies of the *Canterbury Tales* and the *Confessio Amantis* in the early fifteenth century', in *Medieval Scribes, Manuscripts, and Libraries: Essays presented to N. R. Ker*, eds. M. B. Parkes and Andrew G. Watson (London: Scolar, 1978), 163–210.

Drogin, Marc, *Anathema! Medieval Scribes and the History of Book Curses* (Montclair, NJ: Allanheld and Schram, 1983).

Fdez, Tamara Pérez and Ana Sáez Hidalgo, '"A Man Textueel": Scribal Readings and Interpretations of *Troilus and Criseyde* through the Glosses in Manuscript British Library Harley 2392', *Journal of the Spanish Society for Mediaeval English Language and Literature* 14 (2007), 197–220.

Fredell, Joel, 'The Lowly Paraf: Transmitting Manuscript Design in *The Canterbury Tales*', *Studies in the Age of Chaucer* 22 (2000), 213–80.

Johnson, Lynn Staley, 'The Trope of the Scribe and the Question of Literary Authority in the Works of Julian of Norwich and Margery Kempe,' *Speculum* 66 (1991), 820–38.

Mooney, Linne, 'Chaucer's Scribe,' *Speculum* 81 (2006), 96–138.

Mooney, Linne R. and Estelle Stubbs. *Scribes and the City: London Guildhall Clerks and the Dissemination of Middle English Literature 1375–1425*. York: York Medieval Press, 2013.

Olson, Glending, 'Author, Scribe, and Curse: The Genre of Adam Scriveyn,' *Chaucer Review* 42 (2008), 284–97.

Nitzsche, Jane Chance, *The Genius Figure in Antiquity and the Middle Ages* (New York: Columbia University Press, 1975).

Vaughan, Míceál F., 'Creating Comfortable Boundaries: Scribes, Editors, and the Invention of the Parson's Tale', in *Rewriting Chaucer: Culture, Authority, and the Idea of the Authentic Text, 1400–1602*, eds. Thomas A. Prendergast and Barbara Kline (Columbus, OH: Ohio State University Press, 1999), 45–90.

CHAPTER 7

'GAUFRED, DEERE MAISTER SOVERAIN'

Chaucer and Rhetoric

JAMES SIMPSON

OUR purchase on Chaucer (1340–1400) lacks crucial traction: we do not know how he was educated. Many poets from the beginning of the sixteenth-century were, verifiably, university educated. For those poets we can look to demonstrable curricula, and track literary filiations of both content and style within the terms of those curricula. For Chaucer, by contrast, we know that he was not university educated; we also know that he was in court or royal service between at least 1356 and 1374, when he became Controller of Customs.[1] Our resources for understanding his early education and rhetorical training, then, are as follows: his own, largely literary, texts; and assumptions about the need for rhetorical skill in court. That is, our understanding of Chaucer's rhetorical education depends on inference.

Chaucer's own texts supply plentiful evidence of his knowledge of standard school texts designed to train boys in basic Latin comprehension; basic production of Latin poetry and prose; and translation skills.[2] Chaucer's literary texts also supply plentiful evidence of his rhetorical understanding, training, and skill. Our knowledge of the institutions through which Chaucer received that training will remain forever clouded in uncertainty; our knowledge of the intellectual traditions and books through which Chaucer received a rhetorical culture is, however, much more certain. Despite the possibility of this certainty, for most of the twentieth century professional Chaucerian scholarship was extremely cautious about claiming it. That scholarship was instead either dismissive of rhetoric, blinkered in its understanding of rhetorical practice, or exactingly sceptical and cautious about the means by which Chaucer absorbed a rhetorical culture. That situation persisted and survived until the 1980s, when literary theory liberated a much fuller, richer, and more relaxed account of Chaucer and rhetoric.

The present chapter, then, will focus on rhetoric. My target audience is the student rather than the professional scholar. My broadest aim is to persuade the student of the richness and literary fertility of Chaucer's rhetorical culture. I briefly survey and characterize twentieth-century scholarship on Chaucer and rhetoric. I then argue that Chaucer's understanding of rhetoric is directly derived from late twelfth-century Neoplatonic sources. Rhetoric in that culture is embedded in a disciplinary scheme whose outer layer is the speculative science of cosmology, and whose proximate, practical sciences are ethics, economics, and politics.[3] I offer the student embarking on study of Chaucer's reception of rhetorical culture examples that demonstrate Chaucer's flexible familiarity with each branch of twelfth-century Neoplatonic rhetoric and poetics. I end by suggesting that Chaucer profoundly modified the Neoplatonic rhetoric he received. The late twelfth-, early thirteenth-century rhetorician Geoffrey of Vinsauf might be Chaucer's 'dere mayster soverayn,' but among the many skills taught by rhetoric is that of only ostensibly following one's master.[4]

RHETORIC AND ITS RECEPTION
IN CHAUCER STUDIES

Rhetoric is the art of persuasion. Because persuasion as an art stands in uncertain relation to truth, rhetoric has, and has always had, enemies in literate Western cultures. In those cultures, rhetoric's powerful enemies customarily fall into one of three categories: claimants to philosophical truth; claimants to theological truth; and (especially from the late eighteenth century) claimants to personal truth, whose ideals are Nature and sincerity, originality and creativity. These last enemies of rhetoric claim that rhetoric obscures true character, without realizing that the very category of 'character' is itself a product of rhetorical culture. Each of these anti-rhetorical positions has long and enduring traditions, beginning with Socrates.[5] Each gives primacy to a vertical relation of truth and expressivity. Each measures the expressive quality of utterance by its capacity to approximate a non-situated, ahistorical, higher truth, whether that truth is philosophical, theological or ethical.

In a truly rhetorical culture, by contrast, expressive quality is measured by horizontal, situated relations. A text's expressivity is produced and measured not, primarily, by its responsibilities to a higher, absolute truth. On the contrary, the expressive quality of an utterance is both produced and measured by the interrelations of the following categories: author, source text and subject, and audience. The situated author calibrates the style of his or her text with interactive reference to his or her own source and its subject; and, perhaps above all, with interactive reference to the author's target audience. One shapes a structure and a style, that is, by the fit (what rhetoricians would call 'convenience', or appropriateness) of utterance with both its subject and audience.[6] Speaking to learned adults about a given subject produces, for example, a different structure and style from talk to unlearned children about the same matter. Truth, or what Chaucer calls 'sentence', will be in there somewhere, but 'Whereas a man may have noon audience, / Noght helpeth it to tellen his sentence' (Tales VII.2801–2). The rhetorician somehow always knows the potentially dangerous truth that the medium is the message.

For Chaucer's earliest readers, his rhetorical achievement was his greatest achievement. To look no further than the judgment of Thomas Hoccleve (c.1367–1426), Chaucer was the 'firste fyndere of our fair language,'[7] by which he does not mean, as was once absurdly thought, that Chaucer somehow invented the language;[8] instead, Hoccleve draws on and anglicizes a rhetorical term, *inventio*, to describe Chaucer. Hoccleve is declaring that Chaucer, as the first 'inventor' in (not of) English, was the first to generate matter for poetry from within the standard resources of rhetorical training.

By and large, rhetoric held its place as a grand art until the late eighteenth century. Then Romantic claims for the absoluteness of the self, in its citadel of the imagination, and the need for original expression from the deepest sources of that unfettered self, displaced and despised rhetoric. For most of the twentieth century, and particularly in the 1960s and their aftermath, rhetoric continued to have a bad name, less because rhetorical persuasion occluded philosophical or theological truth, and more because the rhetorical continued to be considered a hurdle to the true self. The very word 'rhetorical' denoted the merely verbal, and the inflated verbal, as distinct from the ideal of the pure, untutored voicing of a pure self. Scholarship devoted to Chaucer and rhetoric moved with extreme unease, since to suggest that Chaucer was rhetorical was, at best, to suggest that Chaucer was a bore.

Twentieth-century scholarship devoted to Chaucer's own rhetorical culture arrived in broadly three stages.[9] The posture of extreme unease characterizes the first and, in part, the second of these waves. The scholarly stages can be characterized as follows. The first stage started in 1926, with an article by J. M. Manly, 'Chaucer and the Rhetoricians'.[10] In this relatively early, empirical phase of the discipline of English Studies, Manly's article called a small phalanx of figure-counting studies into being.[11] But the posture underlying this scholarship consigned it to the margins. For Manly, in Robert Payne's words, Chaucer's poetic greatness consisted of 'setting down in words the exact likenesses of men and women he knew'; so far from being a source of poetic strength, rhetorical training was an obstacle, one of the 'constant distracting pressures of literary tradition toward generalization, stylization, conventionalization'.[12] Manly's self-imposed, self-dismissive intellectual stricture also delimited his and his followers' evidential purview: such scholars mostly looked, that is, for evidence of 'rhetoric' only at the relatively superficial level of specific, nameable figures of speech and thought (schemes and tropes).

The second stage of scholarship on Chaucer's rhetorical culture—dating from between 1960 and 1980 or so—is more variegated.[13] To be sure, two major studies, in 1963 and 1967 respectively, set Chaucer's rhetorical practice within a much more ambitious range of rhetorical challenges. For Robert Payne in 1963, Chaucer derived an ethical posture from rhetorical culture: rhetoric served as a way of preserving the 'key of remembrance' in a fallen and labile world; language was subject to misprision as it traverses historical time, different languages, and, not least, the space between the poet and his own audience.[14] So Payne's task was much less a detailed empirical account of what technical skills and techniques Chaucer derived from rhetorical manuals, than an account of a Chaucerian poetics as a way of managing communication across and within history.

In 1967 Robert M. Jordan also understood Chaucer's rhetorical practice in a frame much wider than the extremely narrow frame of figures that dominated the first stage. Jordan heralded, well *avant la lettre*, the postmodern rhetorical turn of the 1980s: he was struck by the inorganic, delimited, constructed quality of Chaucer's poetry. Jordan noticed that Chaucer, instead of trying to hide the maker's hand, drew our attention to that hand as it made; instead of trying to produce the illusion of a style sincerely expressive of inner 'character', Chaucerian style was cleanly divisible into contrastive segments. Jordan tried to go further, by arguing, with reference to Platonic cosmology, that in this cosmological tradition (a tradition available to Chaucer via Plato's *Timaeus*), the made surface was irreducible to its maker. By the terms of that Platonic culture, we should not seek for a single voice or mind behind the broken stylistic surface; Chaucer's poetry is, by Jordan's account, 'less a unified presentation than a composite of several narrating attitudes and positions, often mutually contradictory'.[15]

Two major studies in the 1960s, then, opened up rhetoric for a much wider set of investigative possibilities. Another influential essay, however, tried to close the operation down again. James J. Murphy was the key rhetorical scholar of his generation in the Anglo-American world. In 1964, however, Murphy invested his authority to deny that Chaucer had any serious rhetorical culture at all.[16] The lengths to which Murphy had to go to make this denial produced a frankly strange essay. In the following sentences, I summarize the heads of Murphy's arguments before setting a brief riposte in square brackets after each. Knowledge of nameable rhetorical treatises in Chaucer's England is not demonstrable. [This is incorrect].[17] Such trivial knowledge of rhetorical figures as Chaucer evinces could have been gleaned from grammatical, not rhetorical treatises. [This distinction is not at all solid].[18] The passages in Chaucer's poetry that deploy technical rhetorical terms are very few, 'a total of forty-three relevant lines of verse from a total of more than 22,000'.[19] [This is a questionable measure of 'knowledge': if Chaucer knew something, he knew it, regardless of how many times he says he knew it]. When Chaucer used the word '*rethor*' he 'probably relied upon other written material, not upon his own personal background'.[20] [To what could this distinction possibly amount?]

Murphy's treatment of Chaucer's knowledge of Geoffrey of Vinsauf's *Poetria nova* (c.1201) is the most strained of a set of strained arguments: in the first sequence of the essay, Murphy argues that Chaucer knew not rhetorical texts, but grammatical texts, among which he includes Geoffrey's *Poetria nova*.[21] After having denied that this text is a rhetorical text, Murphy then expends considerable energy across four later pages to question Chaucer's knowledge of the *Poetria nova*. He concludes that the case that Chaucer studied 'Vinsauf is less than convincing'.[22] These pages would be otiose if the original argument that the *Poetria nova* is a grammatical text had weight, but the energetic four pages rightly, if implicitly, deny the weight of that earlier argument. Murphy knows that Chaucer's apparent knowledge of the *Poetria nova* is the largest obstacle to his broad argument. He must therefore reach for the omni-applicable but nearly weightless argument that we cannot be absolutely sure that exact, repeated, intelligent, named quotation amounts to certain quotation. Murphy must enlist all his energies and overlook some deep contradictions in his own essay to deny that Chaucer had serious knowledge of the *Poetria nova*. The essay continued to have a baleful influence on studies of Chaucerian rhetoric,[23] and I shall return to its manifest weaknesses in the next section of this chapter.

The third stage of Chaucer and rhetoric studies is rhetoric's renaissance after two centuries of cultural caution and almost one century of scholarly caution. In the 1980s postmodernism reversed the standard relation between speaker and text, and asked readers to confront the irreducibly rhetorical nature of texts. That theoretical move gave license to scholars of rhetoric. High theory aside, however, the 1980s and subsequent decades also saw much more sustained medieval scholarship in the following areas: the history of literary theory;[24] the precise workings of rhetorical culture in the production of texts;[25] the intimate relations of rhetoric, translation and interpretation;[26] the powerful and wide extent of 'grammatical' culture;[27] the nature and effect of rhetorical exercises in education;[28] and, by no means least, the transmission of rhetorical texts.[29]

RHETORICAL TREATISES AND THEIR PARTS

Rhetoric, as has been said, is the art of persuasion. Ancient Roman rhetoric falls into three principal categories: judicial (or forensic); deliberative; and demonstrative. None of these is concerned with the writing of poetry: judicial rhetoric informs the legal advocate as he shapes a case in a law court;[30] deliberative rhetoric trains the speaker in the political assemblies of the powerful; and demonstrative (or epideictic) rhetoric trains the speaker in the court of the ruler and his army, where speeches of praise or of blame are required. Ancient Rome did produce rhetorical treatises devoted to the writing of poetry, but these were, as rhetoric always is, dependent on separate, primarily legal, forms of training.[31]

Rhetoric, then, derives from the verbal protocols of different institutions within certain kinds of society. As classical Rome's power retracted, so too did its rhetorical practices retract: demonstrative, rather than deliberative or forensic, rhetoric dominated in late imperial culture of the third and fourth centuries. As classical rhetorical culture retracted, new institutions and their attendant rhetorical cultures took their place. Thus classical rhetorical norms came under attack in the early Christian centuries (particularly the fourth to the sixth centuries). Then Christian apologists needed to attack the pagan canon and curricula of their own training. They also needed to shape a Christian rhetoric designed more, in the silence of the monastic cell, for hermeneutic analysis of Biblical rhetoric than for public performance. The career of Augustine of Hippo (354–430) exemplifies this transformative historical moment most fully.[32]

By the twelfth century in Europe a demonstrable culture of verbal education consisting of the three arts (the so-called Trivium) of Grammar, Rhetoric, and Logic, grounded in the cathedral schools of France, is fully in place.[33] This culture certainly drew on classical forensic rhetorical treatises, just as it registered the rhetorical needs of new institutions: the rhetoric of sermons (*artes praedicandi*),[34] and the rhetoric of letter writing for bureaucratic and diplomatic business (*ars dictaminis*).[35]

This grammatico-rhetorical culture, whose deepest roots were in legal rhetoric,[36] also produced a poetics. The most remarkable and influential poetic treatise was the *Poetria nova* (c.1201) of Geoffrey of Vinsauf.[37] This early thirteenth-century text translates various branches of rhetoric (especially forensic and epideictic rhetoric) into a poetics of high ambition. Geoffrey of Vinsauf wrote his prescriptive rhetoric in a mannered Latin verse; like Robert Hollander's delightful *Rhyme's Reason*,[38] Geoffrey exemplifies rhetorical models by putting them, no less delightfully than Hollander, into action. The resulting work, a runaway success for the next few centuries (more than 200 manuscripts survive from the first three centuries of its life), is great fun to read once one has the taste for it.

Although Chaucer demonstrably knew Horace's *Ars poetica*,[39] Geoffrey's was the poetics that most profoundly and directly influenced him, just as it influenced early fifteenth-century poets.[40] Precisely because logic overthrew rhetoric as the principal trivial art in thirteenth-century universities,[41] rhetorical-poetics of the kind derived from twelfth-century French cathedral schools was *not* taught in late medieval universities.[42] It remained the preserve of late medieval poets, of whom Chaucer is the most signal English example. The remainder of this section is devoted to exemplifying Chaucer's familiarity with this rhetorical culture, and especially with Geoffrey of Vinsauf's *Poetria nova*.

Twelfth-century poetic treatises are, as we have seen, ultimately derived from literature's closest cousin, the law. Legal advocates and poets both need to shape narratives with persuasive intent, so it is no accident that the lessons of legal rhetoric were regarded by those interested in poetic training as a transferable skill.

What were the divisions of a prescriptive poetic treatise? The *Poetria nova* is divided thus:

1. Invention: poetic conception
2. Ordering poetic material
3. Shaping poetic material (amplification and abbreviation of material)
4. Ornaments of style (tropes and schemes)
5. Memory and delivery

In what follows, I connect Chaucerian poetic practice to Vinsalvian poetic prescription. The fit of practice and prescription is, as we shall see, very close.

1. Invention: poetic conception

Geoffrey prescribes deep inner thought before the material act of poetic composition:

> If a man has a house to build, his impetuous hand does not rush into action. The measuring line of his mind first lays out the work, and he mentally outlines the

successive steps in a definite order. The mind's hand shapes the entire house before the body's hand builds it. Its mode of being is archetypal before it is actual.[43]

I said in my introduction that twelfth-century poetics were Neoplatonic; and that they were embedded in a broader scheme of sciences, whose outer limit was the speculative science of cosmology. I substantiate that claim briefly here, by pointing to the intimate relation between Geoffrey's account of poetic making and twelfth-century Neoplatonic accounts of divine making.

In his gloss (c.1130) on the one Platonic text that did survive in good part throughout the medieval period, Plato's cosmological dialogue the *Timaeus*, William of Conches defines God's wisdom as the formal cause of the world, since God formed the world according to the pattern of his wisdom. William immediately goes on to make a comparison between God as maker and the human maker:

> As, indeed, an artisan, if he wishes to make something, first disposes it in his mind; afterwards, having sought the material, he works according to his mental pattern. So too the creator, before he should create anything, first had it in his mind, and then fulfilled it in act. It is this which is called by Plato the world archetype: 'world' because it contains everything that is in the world; 'archetype' because it is the principal form (or model).[44]

I need not belabour the closeness of Geoffrey's conception of poetic making to the Neoplatonic conception of divine making. If I were to belabour that connection, I would do so via the intensely Neoplatonic account of poetic making and divine making in Alan of Lille's *Anticlaudianus* (c.1180).[45]

Did Chaucer know Geoffrey of Vinsauf's account of poetic invention? Quite certainly yes. Chaucer was familiar with the Neoplatonic idea of God as the artistic maker of the world, the 'yevere [giver] of the formes, that hast wrought / Thjs fayre world and bar it in thy thought / Eternally er thow thy werk began' (LGW F. 2228–30) He also knew Geoffrey of Vinsauf's advice to poets to act on the analogy of that divine 'yevere of the formes'. The narrator of *Troilus and Criseyde* (c.1385) makes many connections between Pandarus and different kinds of artistic maker. Above all, he presents Pandarus as architect. Pandarus begins his artisanal plans thus:

> For everi wight that hath an hous to founde
> Ne renneth naught the werk for to begynne
> With rakel hond, but he wol bide a stounde,
> And send his hertes line out fro withinne
> Aldirfirst his purpos for to wynne.
> Al this Pandare in his herte thoughte,
> And caste his werk ful wisely or he wroghte.[46]   (Tr 1.1065–71)

Murphy dismisses this passage about the need for a plan in house building as 'a commonplace *sententia* found in Scripture (Luke 14.28–30)'.[47] He also asserts a 'general absence of verbal resemblance'. This must be the weakest point among many other weak points. This is evidently not a bland *sententia*, or maxim, but a detailed, subtle translation and quotation. As with any number of Chaucer's quotations, reference back to the original text reveals a generative difference in the source and its Chaucerian reception.

2. Ordering poetic material

In this section Geoffrey outlines the fundamental difference of two ways of ordering poetic narrative: the natural order and the artificial order. Geoffrey also instructs the would-be poet in how to begin, depending on whether the choice is for natural or artificial order. In a natural order, the poet narrates events in the order in which they happened; an artificial order mixes those events in various ways, beginning, for example, *in medias res*. Modern narratology defines what is effectively the same distinction, between *histoire* (French for 'story') for the natural order that readers mentally reconstruct, and *discours* (here denoting 'narration') for the narrative as presented. Geoffrey, who consistently prefers the verbose and complex to the plain and simple (no puritan rhetorician he), declares the artificial order to be much superior. One of the ways of beginning a poem in the artificial order is to begin with a proverb; another is to begin at the end: 'Let the end, as a worthy precursor, be first to enter and take up its place in advance, as a guest of more honourable rank, or even as master.'[48]

Do Chaucerian orderings and openings conform to Galfridian advice? Answering that question would require an essay to itself. I take only two examples that indicate Chaucer's familiarity with these different possibilities. *The Parliament of Fowls* (c.1378), a poem profoundly informed by late twelfth-century Neoplatonism, begins with a proverb. This proverb is itself in origin rhetorical, though here applied to the 'craft' of love: 'The lyf so short, the craft so long to lerne' (PF 1). My second example is drawn again from Pandarus as expert in the craft of love, who plans his love-making by the art of making poems. As Pandarus decides how to tell Criseyde in Book Two of *Troilus and Criseyde* that she has an admirer in Troilus, he deliberates as a rhetorician:

> How so it be that som men hem delite
> With subtyl art hire tales for to endite,
> Yet for al that, in hire entencioun
> Hire tale is al for som conclusioun.
> 'And sith th'ende is every tales strengthe,
> And this matere is so bihovely,
> What shold I peynte or drawen it on lengthe
> To yow, that ben my frend so feythfully'? (Tr 2.256–63)

Pandarus works as a rhetorician, judging the level of his style ('subtyl art', 'peynte'), and its narrative order in terms both of the intent ('entencioun') of the poet and the poet's relation with his target audience. Needless to say, Pandarus does not observe the rhetorical protocol that he explicates; in fact, the stated protocol is part of a larger strategy, according to which Pandarus uses much verbal 'painting' and much subtle narrative art before he comes to his 'end'. Chaucer reveals himself here as both a dutiful student of prescriptive rhetoric (he knows the rules of ordering and beginning), and an adept student (he has Pandarus break the rules).

3. Shaping poetic material (amplification and abbreviation of material)

Now that Geoffrey has dealt with invention and narrative plan, he turns to the shaping of the narrative itself:

> The way continues along two routes: there will be either a wide path or a narrow, either a river or a brook. You may advance at a leisurely pace or leap swiftly ahead. You may report the matter with brevity or draw it out in a lengthy discourse.[49]

The very way in which Geoffrey articulates his advice points to his preferences. Geoffrey writes for poets who write for patrons with time on their hands. All rhetorical practice is underwritten by economic practice; Geoffrey has no interest in a bourgeois ethics of thrift or a bourgeois ethic of work. On the contrary, his preference in this section as in others is for the longer, more repetitive route. He prefers the rhetoric of conspicuous display. Therefore, just as he repeats different formulations in different metaphors for the different ways of moulding the material, so too does he spend a good deal more time instructing the poetic novice in how to repeat and expand material than he does in how to abbreviate it. He offers no fewer than eight ways of expanding material: repetition, periphrasis, comparison, apostrophe, personification, digression, description and opposition.

Once again, proper treatment of how Chaucer shapes poetic material, either by expansion or abbreviation, would require a separate essay. One would consider the summary treatments of classical texts (e.g. Virgil's *Aeneid* in the *House of Fame*; the *Somnium Scipionis* in the *Parliament of Fowls*) as rhetorical exercises of the kind required of schoolboys, reproduced by the mature poet Chaucer as exercises in *inventio*. One would contrast Chaucer's simultaneous and contrasting treatment of Boccaccian source texts: *The Knight's Tale*'s abbreviation of the *Teseida*, and *Troilus and Criseyde*'s expansion of *Il Filostrato*. In both treatments, Chaucer's narrator meditates explicitly on the processes involved: the Knight repeatedly draws attention to the need for brevity, just as the narrator of *Troilus* meditates subtly on the scale of his narrative. In Book Three, for example, he promises 'shortly of this proces for to pace' (470), before pausing to address a possible objection from his audience:

> But now, paraunter, som man wayten wolde
> That every word, or soonde, or look, or cheere
> Of Troilus that I rehercen sholde,
> In al this while unto his lady deere –
> I trowe it were a long thyng for to here –

> Or of what wight that stant in swich disjoynte,
> His wordes alle, or every look, to poynte.   (Tr 3.491–7)

The account of Chaucer's practice of abbreviation and expansion of poetic matter could be much expanded. We are, however, already in a position to see that he is explicitly conscious of the prescriptions of poetics, even as he divagates from those prescriptions. Let us conclude this brief demonstration with a bravura display as if drawn directly from Galfridian models. In the previous sub-section I pointed to the opening of the *Parliament of Fowls* as exemplary of an artificial beginning. The whole first stanza exemplifies many Galfridian ways of expanding matter:

> The lyf so short, the craft so long to lerne,
> Th'assay so hard, so sharp the conquerynge,
> The dredful joy alwey that slit so yerne:
> Al this mene I by Love, that my felynge
> Astonyeth with his wonderful werkyng
> So sore, iwis, that whan I on hym thynke
> Nat wot I wel wher that I flete or synke.   (PF 1–7)

Recall that Geoffrey recommends eight ways of expanding material: repetition, periphrasis, comparison, apostrophe, personification, digression, description and opposition. The first stanza of *The Parliament of Fowls* exemplifies repetition (the same idea repeated); periphrasis (Love is referred to in various circumlocutions); comparison (the comparisons embedded in the opening metaphors); and personification (i.e. Love). Just as Chaucer expands poetic matter over the long haul of narrative, so too does he expand on a micro-scale.

4. Ornaments of style (tropes and schemes)

As the Platonic divine maker produces the cosmos as a whole from a beautiful form, so too does he embellish it with surface adornment (our modern word 'cosmetic' preserves the ancient connection between the beauty of whole and of surface). The word used in Latin translations of Platonic cosmology for this surface adornment is *ornatus*. As for the making of the cosmos by God, so too for the making of poems by poets: not only must they have an archetypal idea, but they must also have a surface adornment in keeping with that idea. Adornment of this kind amounts to what classical and medieval rhetoricians called tropes and schemes. Figures of thought, or 'tropes' (from Greek *tropein*, to twist) are licensed twistings of proper language use, perceptible only by the mind. When we deploy metaphor, for example, in the sentence 'John is a lion', we twist the word 'is' from its proper usage. 'Conceit' (from 'concept') is a synonym for trope, as in the phrase 'metaphysical conceit'. Schemes, or figures of speech, are, by contrast, patternings of language perceptible to the eye and ear, as in rhyme or alliteration, for example. Geoffrey calls tropes 'difficult' ornament, and schemes 'easy' ornament. He reserves the phrase 'rhetorical colours' (*colores rhetorici*) for schemes.[50]

I argued earlier in this chapter that the first stage of twentieth-century scholarship on Chaucer and rhetoric confined itself to the single, delimited and relatively superficial category of tropes and schemes. Such work produced counts of perceptible figures. I do not propose to replicate that puerile practice in this chapter, but restrict myself to the more conceptual aspect of figure-use by poets.

The fundamental unifying precept, whether by observance or breach, of all rhetorical practice is variously called *convenientia*: decorum, propriety, or fitness. Choice of style must necessarily be made with respect to the needs of both audience and subject matter. When Geoffrey treats *ornatus* more conceptually, he stresses this principle above all:

> When you are teaching the arts, let your speech be native to each art; each delights in its own idiom. But see that its idiom is kept within its own borders; when you come out into the common market-place it is desirable to use the common idiom. In a common matter, let the style be common; in specialized matters let the style be proper to each. Let the distinctive quality of each subject be respected: in the use of words this is a very commendable practice.[51]

Is Chaucer aware of this concept? Once again, most certainly, yes. His young, trainee speakers are especially conscious of this precept. Take for example the Squire, who balks at the thought of providing a *descriptio*, or verbal portrait, of Canacee the princess:

> But for to telle yow al hir beautee,
> It lyth nat in my tonge n'yn my konniyng;
> I dar nat undertake so heigh a thyng;
> Myn Englissh eek is insufficient.
> It moste been a rethor excellent
> That koude hise colours longynge for that art,
> If he sholde hire discryven every part.
> I am noon swich,e I moot speke as I kan.   (V.34–41)

The other young male among the Canterbury pilgrims who will need to master rhetorical skills is the Clerk. When the Host asks a tale from the Clerk, he speaks as a prescriptive rhetorician. The Host warns the Clerk in exactly the way Geoffrey warns his pupils against using terms fit for specialized environments in more common spaces:

> Telle us som murie thing of aventures.
> Youre termes, youre colours, and youre figures,
> Keepe hem in stoor til so be ye endite
> Heigh style, as whan that men to kynges write.
> Speketh so pleyn at this tyme, we yow preye,
> That we may understonde what ye seye.   (IV.15–20)

The Clerk agrees to obey the Host, though he does so adroitly: he agrees that his source, Petrarch's tale of Griselda, begins with a high style topographia of Piedmont, which he judges irrelevant to his story. Instead of beginning with that 'heigh stile.../ Er he the body of his tale writeth' (41–2), the Clerk begins instead with another rhetorical exercise—a summary of the topographia—in which he compresses Petrarch's prologue into a single stanza. Already, then, the Clerk obeys both his source and his Host, though by negotiating with both (a strategy directly pertinent to the tale of obedience he is about to tell).

Chaucer as poet is consistently sensitive to the stylistic level of his poems. His career as a whole can be described as an effort to extend the range of that style by extending the social reach of his poetry. This effort is not wholly a private, authorial matter, but rather derives from interactions between author and audience. Thus in *Troilus and Criseyde* the narrator freely invites his audience to raise or lower the style as appropriate:

> For myne wordes, heere and every part,
> I speke hem alle under correccioun
> Of yow that felyng han in loves art,
> And putte it al in youre discrecioun
> To encresse or maken dymynucioun
> Of my langage, and that I yow biseche.   (Tr 3.1331–6)

5. Memory and delivery

At this point in vernacular poetic treatises that derive ultimately from the genre of the *Poetria nova*, we might expect a sequence on meter. Geoffrey does not supply such a section. Instead, he reverts to the legal sources of his poetic treatise, and offers brief sections devoted respectively to memory and delivery. The lawyer must memorize his speech, and deliver it in a style so persuasive that the speech transmits the lawyer's own upright character or *ethos*. So too, in a society where poetry remains a fundamentally public and performative art, must the poet master the techniques of memorizing poems and delivering them effectively.

One could argue that Chaucer makes little explicit mileage from these categories. To be sure, there are references to memorization of poetry that surprise us in the *Canterbury Tales*: after the Knight's Tale, we learn that all the pilgrim audience enjoyed it, especially the well born, who considered it 'worthy for to drawen to memorie' (I.3112). On reflection, however, rather than being too small to see well, the topic is rather too large to see well: the entire *Canterbury Tales* is imagined as an act of public, performed poetry, in which each pilgrim is imagined to have learned long poems by heart, and in which each is imagined to deliver those poems to a live audience. The same fictional conditions are true of *Troilus and Criseyde*. Not only that, but the very quality we most admire in the tales, the creation of 'character', is itself a product of this rhetorical culture.[52]

CONCLUSION

Chaucer's rhetorical sources are broader than the rhetorico-poetic culture he derives from late twelfth-century sources: the art of letter writing (*ars dictaminis*) informs fictional letters within his texts;[53] the *ars praedicandi*, or art of delivering sermons, informs his *Pardoner's Tale*. But from this admittedly brief survey of only some striking points of connection, we can say with certainty that Chaucer's own rhetorical practice fits very neatly with the prescriptive poetics of the kind Geoffrey of Vinsauf produced. In conclusion, however, we might also notice that in almost each of the examples cited above, Chaucer enjoys adapting a prescriptive rhetoric to his own, specific ends. Let us end by citing Chaucer's most explicit reference to Geoffrey, a reference whose exuberance, not to say comic joyfulness, acknowledges Geoffrey even as it mocks a prescriptive rhetoric.

The Nun's Priest's Tale adapts the school material of animal fable to shape a sophisticated, joyful meditation on rhetoric. The simple tale is a source of elaborate rhetorical invention. As the fox takes Chauntecleer's throat in his jaws and runs, Chaucer apostrophizes the potential tragedy in such a way as to transform tragedy into stylistic comedy. He makes fun of different tragedies (Chauntecleer's capture, and the death of King Richard I), just as he makes fun of his own rhetorical master, 'Gaufred, deere maister soverayn':

> O destinee, that mayst nat been eschewed!
> Allas, that Chauntecleer fleigh fro the bemes!
> Allas, his wif ne roughte nat of dremes!
> And on a Friday fil al this meschaunce.
>   O Venus, that art goddesse of plesaunce,
> Syn that thy servant was this Chauntecleer,
> And in thy servyce dide al his power,
> Moore for delit than world to multiplye,
> Why woldestow suffre hym on thy day to dye?
>   O Gaufred, deere maister soverayn,
> That whan thy worthy kyng Richard was slayn
> With shot, compleynedest his deeth so soore,
> Why hadde I now thy sentence and thy loore,
> The Friday for to chide, as diden ye?
> For on a Friday, soothly, slayn was he.[54]   (VII.3338–52)

On the one hand, this is tragic, and the potential tragedy is not that of a cock eaten by a fox. It is instead the tragedy of the pure, expressive, animal voice (Chaunte-cleer) being silenced and strangled. All we hear in its place is the insistent voice of the belated, over-learned rhetorician, lamenting his *in*ability to speak. On the other, this is deeply refreshing, since Chaucer transforms the tragedy of a world in which there is nothing but belated rhetoric into a candid celebration of our irreducibly rhetorical condition. He salutes his 'deere maister soverayn' even as he pretends inability to do so.

Notes

1. For Chaucer's early career and likely education, see Derek Pearsall, *The Life of Chaucer: A Critical Biography* (Oxford: Blackwell, 1992), 29–46.
2. For the curriculum of basic education, see Jill Mann, '"He Knew Nat Catoun": Medieval School-Texts and Middle English Literature', in *The Text in the Community: Essays on Medieval Works, Manuscripts, Authors and Readers*, ed. Jill Mann and Maura Nolan (Notre Dame, IN: University of Notre Dame Press, 2006), 41–74; for the skills imparted, see Christopher Cannon, 'The Middle English Writer's Schoolroom: Fourteenth-Century English Schoolbooks and the Contexts', *New Medieval Literatures* 11 (2009): 19–38.
3. For a full exposition of this declaration (much fuller than is possible in the present article), see James Simpson, *Sciences and the Self in Medieval Poetry: Alan of Lille's* Anticlaudianus *and John Gower's* Confessio amantis (Cambridge: Cambridge University Press, 1995).
4. For the place of Geoffrey of Vinsauf in thirteenth-century rhetorical culture, see Chapter 21 of this volume.
5. For the hostility of Plato to rhetoric, see especially the *Gorgias*.
6. For Chaucer's understanding of what I describe in this chapter as a 'truly rhetorical culture', see Robert Payne, 'Rhetoric in Chaucer: Chaucer's Realization of Himself as Rhetor', in *Medieval Eloquence: Studies in the Theory and Practice of Medieval Rhetoric*, ed. James J. Murphy (Berkeley, CA: University of California Press, 1978), 270–83.
7. Thomas Hoccleve, *The Regiment of Princes*, ed. Charles R. Blyth (Kalamazoo, MI: Western Michigan University, 1999), 4978. For discussion, see James Simpson, 'Chaucer's Presence and Absence, 1400–1550', *A Chaucer Companion*, ed. Jill Mann and Piero Boitani, 2nd ed. (Cambridge: Cambridge University Press, 2003), 251–69.
8. See Christopher Cannon, *The Making of Chaucer's English: A Study of Words* (Cambridge: Cambridge University Press, 1998), 12–13.
9. For an excellent, earlier stock-taking of studies on Chaucer and rhetoric, see Robert Payne, 'Chaucer and the Art of Rhetoric', in *A Companion to Chaucer Studies*, ed. Beryl Rowland (Toronto: Oxford University Press, 1968; repr. New York, Oxford University Press, 1979), 42–64; I am indebted to, though not bound by, Payne's own discussion.
10. John Matthews Manly, 'Chaucer and the Rhetoricians', *Publications of the British Academy* 12 (1926): 3–21.
11. See James J. Murphy, 'New Look at Chaucer', *The Review of English Studies* n.s. 15 (1964): 1–20, especially p. 1, note 1, for a generous sampling.
12. Payne, 'Chaucer and the Art of Rhetoric', 50.
13. For a convenient listing of relevant studies, see Payne, 'Rhetoric in Chaucer', 271, note 5.
14. Robert O. Payne, *The Key of Remembrance: A Study of Chaucer's Poetics* (Westport, CT: Greenwood Press, 1963; repr. 1978).
15. Robert M. Jordan, *Chaucer and the Shape of Creation: The Aesthetic Possibilities of Inorganic Structure* (Cambridge, MA: Harvard University Press, 1967), 150. Jordan's stylistic observations remain very powerful; for a direct rebuttal of his understanding of the cosmological grounds of his argument, see James Simpson, '"Ut Pictura Poesis": A Critique of Robert Jordan's *Chaucer and the Shape of Creation*', in *Interpretation Medieval and Modern*:

J. A. W. Bennett Memorial Lectures, eighth series, eds. Piero Boitani and Anna Torti (Cambridge: D. S. Brewer, 1993), 167–87.

16. Murphy, 'New Look at Chaucer'.
17. According to Marjorie Curry Woods, Cicero's *De inventione* was, for example, 'a basic textbook in medieval schools and was one of the most widely known books of the Middle Ages…It has survived in as many as 600 manuscripts copied before 1500…There can be no doubt that Chaucer knew the *De inventione*.' See Marjorie Curry Woods, 'Chaucer the Rhetorician: Criseyde and her Family', *Chaucer Review* 20 (1985): 28–39 (at 29). Figures for the survival of manuscripts of Geoffrey of Vinsauf's *Poetria nova* are also remarkable both for the number (more than 200 between 1200 and 1500), and for their Europe-wide dispersal, for which see Marjorie Curry Woods, *Classroom Commentaries: Teaching the Poetria nova Across Medieval and Renaissance Europe* (Columbus, OH: University of Ohio Press, 2010). It is true that attestation of the *Poetria nova* is not as strong in England as on the Continent, but see pp. 227–33 for manuscript and other indirect evidence of knowledge of the text in England. For more targeted analysis of the reception of the *Poetria Nova*, and of reworkings of the rhetorical culture of that text in England, see both Martin Camargo, 'Chaucer and the Oxford Renaissance of Anglo-Latin Rhetoric', *Studies in the Age of Chaucer* 34 (2012), 173–207, and Rita Copeland, 'Chaucer and Rhetoric', in *The Yale Companion to Chaucer*, ed. Seth Lerer (New Haven, CT: Yale University Press, 1991), 122–46. Camargo's argument, which Copeland supports, is that the *Poetria Nova*, along with other thirteenth-century rhetorical texts, enjoyed a renaissance in English Benedictine circles in the last decades of the fourteenth century. Chaucer's knowledge of Geoffrey of Vinsauf is either direct or mediated, but can be dated to the second half of Chaucer's career. I warmly thank Rita Copeland for guidance on this scholarship, which was published well after the original composition of my chapter.
18. For the extensiveness of 'grammatical' culture, see Martin Irvine and David Thompson, '*Grammatica* and Literary Theory', in *The Cambridge History of Literary Criticism*: *Volume 2, The Middle Ages*, ed. Alastair Minnis and Ian Johnson (Cambridge: Cambridge University Press, 2005), 15–41, and further references. See also J. J. Murphy, 'The Arts of Poetry and Prose', in *The Cambridge History of Literary Criticism: Volume 2*, ed. Minnis and Johnson, 42–67, at 44.
19. Murphy, 'New Look at Chaucer', 7.
20. Ibid., 9.
21. Ibid., 3–4.
22. Ibid., 12–15 inclusive.
23. See, for example, the otherwise useful essay by J. D. Burnley, 'Chaucer, Usk and Geoffrey of Vinsauf', *Neophilologus* 69 (1985): 284–93. See also Amanda Holton, *The Sources of Chaucer's Poetics* (Aldershot: Ashgate, 2008), 70, for uncritical acceptance of Murphy's argument.
24. For which see A. J. Minnis, *Medieval Theory of Authorship: Scholastic Literary Attitudes in the Later Middle Ages* (London: Scolar Press, 1984).
25. See Rita Copeland, 'Rhetoric and Vernacular Translation in the Middle Ages', *Studies in the Age of Chaucer* 9 (1987): 41–75.
26. See Rita Copeland, *Rhetoric, Hermeneutics, and Translation in the Middle Ages: Academic Traditions and Vernacular Texts* (Cambridge: Cambridge University Press, 1991).
27. See Irvine, '*Grammatica* and Literary Theory'.

28. See Suzanne Reynolds, *Medieval Reading: Grammar, Rhetoric, and the Classical Text* (Cambridge: Cambridge University Press, 1996), and Marjorie Curry Woods and Rita Copeland, 'Classroom and Confession', in *The Cambridge History of Medieval English Literature*, ed. David Wallace (Cambridge: Cambridge University Press, 1999), 376–84.

29. See especially Woods, *Teaching the* Poetria nova *Across Medieval and Renaissance Europe*. See also now the magnificent handbook *Medieval Grammar and Rhetoric: Language Arts and Literary Theory, AD 300–1475*, ed. Rita Copeland and Ineke Sluiter (Oxford: Oxford University Press, 2009).

30. The most influential prescriptive treatises on how a lawyer should speak in court through out the medieval period and beyond are: Cicero's *De inventione* (84 BCE), *De oratore* (55 BCE) and the pseudo-Ciceronian *Rhetorica ad Herennium* (early first century BCE).

31. See especially Horace, *Ars poetica*, in *Satires, Epistles, Ars poetica*, ed. and trans. H. Rushton Fairclough (Cambridge, MA: Harvard University Press, 1926). See also Jeffrey Walker, *Rhetoric and Poetics in Antiquity* (Oxford: Oxford University Press, 2000).

32. See especially Augustine's *Confessions* (397–8 CE), the autobiography of Augustine's conversion, a good part of which consists of his rejection of his training and career as *rhetor*; and his *De Doctrina Christiana* (397–426 CE), a rhetorical and hermeneutic guide to Biblical writings.

33. The most illuminating primary text is John of Salisbury, *Metalogicon: A Twelfth-Century Defense of the Verbal and Logical Arts of the Trivium*, trans. Daniel McGarry (Berkeley, CA: University of California Press, 1962). For scholarship, see Winthrop Wetherbee, 'The Study of Classical Authors: From Late Antiquity to the Twelfth Century', in Minnis and Johnson, *The Cambridge History of Literary Criticism: Volume 2*, 99–144, and Vincent Gillespie, 'The Study of Classical Authors: from the Twelfth Century to c. 1450', in Minnis and Johnson, *The Cambridge History of Literary Criticism: Volume 2*, 160–78.

34. For examples see T. M. Charland, *Artes praedicandi: Contribution à l'histoire de la rhétorique au moyen âge* (Paris: Vrin, 1936), and Marianne Briscoe, *Artes Praedicandi*, Typologie des sources du moyen âge occidental 61 (Turnhout: Brepols, 1992).

35. See Ronald G. Witt, 'The Arts of Letter Letter-Writing', in Minnis and Johnson, *The Cambridge History of Literary Criticism: Volume 2*, 68–83. See also Martin Camargo, *Ars Dictaminis, Ars Dictandi*. Typologie des sources du moyen âge occidental 60 (Turnhout: Brepols, 1991).

36. See Karin M. Fredborg, 'Ciceronian Rhetoric in the Schools', in *Learning Institutionalized: Teaching in the Medieval University*, ed. John van Engen (Notre Dame, IN: University of Notre Dame Press, 2000), 21–41.

37. For the Latin text of the *Poetria nova*, see *Les Arts Poétiques du xiie et du xiiie siècle*, ed. Edmond Faral (Paris: Champion, 1924; repr. 1958). This text is available in a heroic translation: *Poetria Nova of Geoffrey of Vinsauf*, trans. Margaret F. Nims (Toronto: Pontifical Institute of Mediaeval Studies, 1967). All further citations of the *Poetria nova* will be made from the Nims's translation, by page number. See also Douglas Kelly, *The Arts of Poetry and Prose*, Typologie des sources du moyen âge occidental 59 (Turnhout: Brepols, 1991).

38. Robert Hollander, *Rhyme's Reason: A Guide to English Verse*, enlarged edition (New Haven, CT: Yale University Press, 1989).

39. See James Simpson, 'Dante's "*Astripetam Aquilam*" and the Theme of Poetic Discretion in the *House of Fame*', *Essays and Studies*, n.s. 39 (1986), 1–18. To the Horatian passage about poetic discretion discussed there, one should also add Pandarus' detailed stylistic advice

to Troilus in composing a letter to Criseyde, urging him to vary his formulae, and not to mix different registers, 'Ne jompre ek no discordant thyng yfeere', which produces an effect of absurdity (Tr 2.1030–43). This derives from the opening of Horace's *Ars poetica*, 1–13.

40. I have mentioned Hoccleve's translation above. See also Osbern Bokenham, *Legendys of Hooly Wummen*, ed. Mary S. Serjeantson, EETS 206 (London: Oxford University Press, 1938), Prologue, lines 84–96, in which Bokenham very explicitly gives pride of rhetorical place to 'Galfridus anglicus, in hys newe poetrye' (line 88).

41. For an amusing poem about the deadly disciplinary fight between rhetoric and logic, see Henry d'Andely, *The Battle of the Seven Arts*, ed. and trans. Louis Paetow, *Memoirs of the University of California*, 4.1, History, 1.1 (Berkeley, CA: University of California Press, 1914). See also Osmund Lewry, 'Grammar, Logic and Rhetoric 1220-1320', in *The Early Oxford Schools*, ed. Jeremy Catto (Oxford: Oxford University Press, 1984), 401–34.

42. Even if thirteenth-century universities also produced flexible descriptive stylistic and structural schemes for all manner of texts, including the more literary texts of the Bible. For which see Minnis, *Medieval Theory of Authorship* (see Index under *forma tractatus*; *forma tractandi*), and James Simpson, 'From Reason to Affective Knowledge: Modes of Thought and Poetic Form in *Piers Plowman*', *Medium Aevum* 55 (1986): 1–23.

43. *Poetria Nova of Geoffrey of Vinsauf*, trans. Nims, 17.

44. William of Conches, *Glosae super Platonem*, ed. E. Jeauneau (Paris: Vrin, 1965), 27d, cap. 32, p. 99. The translation is mine.

45. For the detailed elaboration of this argument, see Simpson, '"Ut Pictura Poesis"'.

46. Thomas Hoccleve independently translated the same passage, though as part of specifically poetic advice. See Thomas Hoccleve, 'Dialogue', in *'My Compleinte' and Other Poems*, ed. Roger Ellis (Exeter: University of Exeter Press, 2001), ll. 638–42.

47. Murphy, 'A New Look at Chaucer and the Rhetoricians', 15. On the same page he cites another citation of this passage so as to suggest that Chaucer might have known the passage through an intermediary. Chaucer's citation and translation is much more extensive than the intermediary passage cited by Murphy. The differences must point to an independent source.

48. *Poetria Nova of Geoffrey of Vinsauf*, trans. Nims, 19.

49. Ibid., 23.

50. Ibid., 56.

51. Ibid., 55.

52. For ethos and character, see Marjorie Curry Woods, 'Chaucer the Rhetorician: Criseyde and her Family', *Chaucer Review* 20 (1985): 28–39; for delivery and ethos, see Martin Camargo, 'Medieval Rhetoric Delivers; Or, Where Chaucer Learned How to Act', *New Medieval Literatures* 9 (2007): 41–62.

53. Martin Camargo, *Middle English Verse Epistle* (Tübingen: Niemayer, 1991).

54. See, by way of comparison, *Poetria Nova of Geoffrey of Vinsauf*, trans. Nims, 29.

BIBLIOGRAPHY

Camargo, Martin, 'Chaucer and the Oxford Renaissance of Anglo-Latin Rhetoric', *Studies in the Age of Chaucer* 34 (2012), 173–207.

Cannon, Christopher, 'The Middle English Writer's Schoolroom: Fourteenth-Century English Schoolbooks and the Contexts', *New Medieval Literatures* 11 (2009), 19–38.

Copeland, Rita, *Rhetoric, Hermeneutics, and Translation in the Middle Ages: Academic Traditions and Vernacular Texts* (Cambridge: Cambridge University Press, 1991).

Copeland, Rita, 'Chaucer and Rhetoric', in *The Yale Companion to Chaucer*, ed., Seth Lerer (New Haven, CT: Yale University Press, 1991), 122–46.

Gillespie, Vincent, 'The Study of Classical Authors: from the Twelfth Century to c.1450', in A. J. Minnis and Ian Johnson, *The Cambridge History of Literary Criticism: Volume 2, The Middle Ages* (Cambridge: Cambridge University Press, 2005), 160–78.

Manly, John Matthews, 'Chaucer and the Rhetoricians', *Publications of the British Academy* 12 (1926), 3–21.

Mann, Jill, '"He Knew Nat Catoun": Medieval School-Texts and Middle English Literature', in *The Text in the Community: Essays on Medieval Works, Manuscripts, Authors and Readers*, eds. Jill Mann and Maura Nolan (Notre Dame, IN: University of Notre Dame Press, 2006), 41–74.

Minnis, A. J. and Ian Johnson, eds., *The Cambridge History of Literary Criticism: Volume 2, The Middle Ages* (Cambridge: Cambridge University Press, 2005).

Minnis, A. J., *Medieval Theory of Authorship: Scholastic Literary Attitudes in the Later Middle Ages* (London: Scolar Press, 1984).

Murphy, James J., 'A New Look at Chaucer and the Rhetoricians', *The Review of English Studies* n.s. 15 (1964), 1–20.

Payne, Robert O., The Key of Remembrance: *A Study of Chaucer's Poetics* (Westport, CT: Greenwood Press, 1963; repr. 1978).

Wetherbee, Winthrop, 'The Study of Classical Authors: From Late Antiquity to the Twelfth Century', in A. J. Minnis and Ian Johnson, *The Cambridge History of Literary Criticism: Volume 2, The Middle Ages* (Cambridge: Cambridge University Press, 2005), 99–144.

Woods, Marjorie Curry, *Classroom Commentaries: Teaching the Poetria nova Across Medieval and Renaissance Europe* (Columbus, OH: University of Ohio Press, 2010).

PART II

CHAUCER IN THE MEDITERRANEAN FRAME

CHAPTER 8

ANTI-JUDAISM/ ANTI-SEMITISM AND THE STRUCTURES OF CHAUCERIAN THOUGHT

STEVEN F. KRUGER

'THE FAME OF THE JEWERYE': CHAUCER'S JEWISH MATTER

FROM its inception, Christianity has defined itself against Judaism, the religion out of which it largely arose. Scholars distinguish between anti-Judaism, which operates mainly by identifying Jewish doctrinal, devotional, and theological positions that from a Christian perspective are erroneous, and anti-Semitism, a more virulent, irrational, and violent hatred of Jews that especially associates them with animality, monstrosity, and the demonic.[1] Generally, historians see the earlier Christian Middle Ages, until the twelfth century (or so), as characterized mainly by anti-Judaism, with anti-Semitism properly speaking arising later.[2] One significant pivot point in this history is the First Crusade (1096), when some groups of crusaders attacked Jewish communities in Western Europe.[3] Later medieval anti-Semitism comes to be characterized especially by accusations that impute to Jews violent, conspiratorial, anti-Christian actions: well-poisonings, ritual murders of Christian children, desecration of the consecrated Eucharist, and the blood libel (the idea that Jews kill Christian children at Passover in order to use their blood in making ritual foods).[4]

England saw its fair share of anti-Semitic accusation and action: Jews were massacred at York, Norwich, London, and elsewhere in 1189–90, at the time of the Third Crusade (which corresponded, as well, with Richard I's coronation). The first ritual murder accusation in medieval Europe was made against the Jewish community of Norwich in 1144, when Jews were charged with the killing of a twelve-year-old English boy, William.

In 1181, the Jews of Bury St Edmunds were similarly accused of murdering a Christian boy named Robert, and in 1255, the death of Hugh of Lincoln was blamed on the local Jewish community. Similar accusations arose at Gloucester (1168), Bristol (1183), Winchester (1191), and London (1244, 1276).[5]

Direct confrontations in England between Christians and Jews ended in 1290, when King Edward I expelled Jews from the country. The expulsion resulted from a complicated set of factors, including both religious animosity and economic calculation. Popular anti-Semitism, as reflected in the anti-Semitic accusations noted above, was one contributing factor, but the expulsion also brought economic advantages, including the confiscation of Jewish property and cancellation of debts owed to Jews.[6] While some Jews may have remained in, or clandestinely (re)entered, England, and while the Domus Conversorum in London, which housed Jewish converts to Christianity, continued to operate after 1290, there were no visible Jewish communities in England during Geoffrey Chaucer's life (or until the seventeenth century).[7] Jews appear relatively rarely in Chaucer's writing, and we might take this as a logical consequence of the absence of Jews from the contemporary English scene. It would be erroneous, however, to see English Christianity as unconcerned with Judaism after 1290; Christian identity remained dependent upon a relationship to its Jewish 'ancestor', and, as I hope to show, anti-Jewish/anti-Semitic thinking remained significant for Chaucer, as for many fourteenth- and fifteenth-century English writers.

Such thinking appears in Chaucer most prominently and extensively in the Prioress's Tale, the only one of his poems to place Jewish characters at its centre. Taking up a popular medieval anti-Semitic genre, a 'Miracle of the Virgin' involving the Jewish murder of a Christian innocent, it puts this narrative into the mouth of one of the few female narrators of the *Canterbury Tales*.[8] Readings of the tale have ranged from those that see it as fully expressive of a normative medieval anti-Semitism to those that regard it as, more or less gently or harshly, satirizing its narrator, the 'plesaunt', 'charitable' Prioress (I.138, 143), and as thus potentially positioning Chaucer as a (subtle, indirect) critic of the anti-Jewish attitudes of his time.[9] Beyond the Prioress's Tale, explicit mentions of Jews and Judaism in the *Canterbury Tales* are relatively rare. We find:

- A reference to the 'peple Ebrayk' (II.489) in the Man of Law's Tale, within an allusion to the exodus from Egypt. Beyond this, the tale includes a good deal of 'Old Testament' material—references, for instance, to Daniel (II.473), Samson (201), Jonah (486), David and Goliath (934–5), and Judith and Holofernes (939–40).
- A moment in the Merchant's Tale, in which the pagan goddess Proserpyna, rejecting the 'auctoritees' of the Biblical 'Salomon', refers to him as 'this Jew' (IV.2276–7).
- Several references in the Pardoner's Tale, clustered around the description of the Pardoner's relics in the prologue (VI.350–1, 364), and the three rioters' swearing of oaths in the tale, which is compared to the Jews' 'tearing' of Christ's body at the Crucifixion (472–5).[10]
- A glancing reference, in the Tale of Sir Thopas, to Thopas's 'hawberk' as 'al ywroght of Jewes werk' (VII.863–4).[11]

- A focus in the Monk's Tale on Anthiochus's 'hate' for the 'Jewes' (VII.2591–8). Other of the Monk's 'tragedies'—of Adam, Samson, Nabugodonosor, Balthasar, Holofernes—take up stories from the Hebrew Bible and apocrypha, but without explicit reference to 'Jews'; the Samson, Nabugodonosor, and Balthasar narratives, however, do mention Israel (2060, 2152) and Jerusalem (2147, 2196).[12]
- A number of references in the Parson's Tale: on swearing as dismemberment of Christ's body, as in the Pardoner's Tale (X.591, 599); on the role of Jews in attacks on Jesus (662–3); and on the difference between Jewish and Christian law (889).[13]

Outside the Canterbury frame, Chaucer refers to Judaism as a religion or the Jews as a discrete people only in the *House of Fame* and the *Treatise on the Astrolabe*. In the former, the narrator describes a series of pillars that commemorate diverse literary traditions, including that represented by the ancient Jewish historian Josephus Flavius, 'Hym of secte saturnyn, / The Ebrayk Josephus the olde, / That of Jewes gestes tolde; / And he bar on hys shuldres hye / The fame up of the Jewerye' (HF 1432–6).[14] In framing the *Treatise on the Astrolabe*, Chaucer defends his translation of the text into English: 'But natheles suffise to the these trewe conclusions in Englissh as wel as sufficith to these noble clerkes Grekes these same conclusions in Grek; and to Arabiens in Arabik, and to Jewes in Ebrew, and to Latyn folk in Latyn' (28–33).[15]

We might expand this list by considering less direct references to Jews and Judaism—for instance, allusions in the Wife of Bath's portrait and prologue to her three pilgrimages to Jerusalem (I.463, III.495), and the Parson's evocation of 'the righte wey of Jerusalem celestial' (X.80, and see 51). Chaucer's work contains references to many 'Old Testament' figures or narratives in addition to those noted above (but without an explicit fore-grounding of their Jewishness): Absolom and Esther in the Prologue to *The Legend of Good Women* (F 249, 250, 539), and Absolon (the character) in the Miller's Tale; Moses's and Solomon's legendary rings in the Squire's Tale (V.247–51);[16] Song of Songs in the Merchant's Tale; Solomon (and his wisdom) in a large number of the *Canterbury Tales* (especially a sententious tale like the Melibee). Nevertheless, the thematizing of Jews and Judaism in Chaucer's work remains at best a minor consideration. As we would expect, given the canonical position of the Hebrew Biblical text within medieval Christianity, the 'Old Testament' references in Chaucer are largely positive, presenting exemplary figures and instructive material; they would not necessarily have evoked, for Chaucer and his original audiences, contemporary, European Jews. Of the explicit refer-ences to post-Biblical Jews noted above, a couple seem neutral or positive, suggesting a certain acknowledgment of Jewish expertise, as in the Tale of Sir Thopas (Jews as expert metal workers) and *Treatise on the Astrolabe* (Jews, alongside Arabs, 'clerkly' Greeks, and Latin 'folk', as expert astronomers). The remainder—and especially of course the more extended representation of a Jewish community in the Prioress's Tale—participate more or less strongly in medieval anti-Jewish/anti-Semitic discourses.

In this chapter, while attending to such direct representations of Judaism, I pose a broader question: to what extent might late medieval Christian intellectual and historical engagements with Judaism be productive for readings of Chaucerian texts not only when Jews are directly represented but also in the absence of such explicit reference? As Sylvia Tomasch recognizes, in examining the absence of Jewish figures in Dante's *Commedia*, Christian ideas about Judaism nonetheless crucially shape Dante's work.[17] And as Lisa Lampert suggests—invoking Toni Morrison's argument in *Playing in the Dark* that, even or especially in American literary works that do not foreground histories of slavery, racial division, and discrimination, an 'Africanist presence' remains of central importance—for the medieval English context, 'Despite this lack of a Jewish population,… the figure of the Jew also had a type of presence in that it was a fundamental component of Christian ideologies in England and was a shaping component of representations of Christians and Christianity.'[18] Too often students of the Middle Ages conceive of Christianity as standing alone, triumphant, dictating the terms of a dominant thought settled once and for all. Medieval Christian thought was, however, dynamic and changing, and it grappled consistently and insistently with its inheritances from and relationship to Judaism. In a very different context, Eve Kosofsky Sedgwick argues that 'many of the major modes of thought and knowledge in twentieth-century Western culture as a whole are structured—indeed, fractured—by a chronic, now endemic crisis of homo/heterosexual definition, indicatively male, dating from the end of the nineteenth century', and she shows persuasively how 'an understanding of virtually any aspect of modern Western culture must be, not merely incomplete, but damaged in its central substance to the degree that it does not incorporate a critical analysis of modern homo/heterosexual definition.'[19] My contention here is similar: to adapt Sedgwick's words, an understanding of virtually any aspect of medieval culture (and of Chaucer's poetry) must be not merely incomplete, but damaged in its central substance, to the degree that it does not incorporate a critical analysis of medieval Jewish-Christian definition.

Keeping especially the Prioress's Tale in view, given its extensive engagement with a late-medieval set of anti-Jewish/anti-Semitic ideas, but considering also other Chaucerian texts in which Jewish material is less obviously present, I argue here that the encounter with Judaism shapes several of the major modes of late-medieval Christian (and hence also Chaucerian) thought: conceptions of (1) temporality and history—both world history and the history of the individual self—dependent as these are on ideas of supersession, of the 'new' replacing the 'old', (2) metaphysics, where what transcends the material world (the Idea, or Mind, or God) is understood as the Being from which all other, partial and imperfect, beings derive, and (3) spatiality, topography, and geography, especially ideas of enclosure or inclusion and exclusion, closeness and distance, wholeness and fragmentation.

TEMPORALITY

Christianity defines its historical relationship to Judaism as one of temporal supersession.[20] In this construction, the Incarnation of Christ is a definitive historical break that changes everything that follows. All preceding history must also, retroactively, be redefined, and pre-incarnational Judaism comes to be understood as always directed toward the telos of the Incarnation. Within Christian practice, this understanding expresses itself especially strongly in the treatment of the Hebrew Bible, now rigorously reread to highlight a new teleology, its pointing toward the Incarnation and the consequent instantiation of Christianity.

This rereading of the Hebrew Bible involves three related, mutually reinforcing moves. First, direct, historical connections between the Hebrew Bible and the New Testament are emphasized. We see this, for instance, in the genealogical material in the gospels of Matthew and Luke, which shows Hebrew Biblical histories leading directly to Jesus's nativity. Similarly, a claim like the one that Jesus makes in Matthew 5:17—'Do not think that I am come to destroy the law, or the prophets. I am not come to destroy, but to fulfill'—insists on a continuity between Jewish law and prophecy and Christ's 'fulfilment' of these. Second, however, despite the claim that Jesus comes not to destroy but to fulfil, Christianity moves definitively to declare that certain Biblical Jewish laws and practices (e.g. circumcision and kosher food restrictions) are obviated under Christ's new dispensation. Third, certain allegorizing protocols, especially typology, operate to reconceive figures and events from the Hebrew text, even those not historically connected to Jesus, as prefiguring the life of Christ. Thus, for instance, the sacrifice of Isaac is read as a 'type' (hence, 'typology') of the Crucifixion. Such readings consistently construct the Hebrew Bible as taking its full, true meaning only when connected to the new, Christian scriptures, and it is this strategy of rereading that constructs an 'Old Testament' that must be understood in light of a 'New'.

The basis for each of these supersessionary movements is found in the New Testament gospels and (especially the Pauline) epistles, and by the Middle Ages, such an understanding of the temporal relationship between Christianity and its Jewish ancestor would have been felt as 'natural' within Christian culture, even among those who were not intellectuals, or even literate, given the ways in which, for instance, typology is inscribed in public, widely available works of art (stained-glass windows and church sculpture) and in sermons. Furthermore, what is, on the one hand, a conception of history also comes to be deeply implicated in Christian thinking about the course of an individual life, about the ways in which each human being, tainted by the original sin of Adam, might gain access to the renewal provided through Christ's sacrifice. In the Pauline formulation: 'put off... the old man, who is corrupted according to the desire of error... And put on the new man, who according to God is created in justice and holiness of truth.'[21] Paul's own status as a convert from Judaism to Christianity solidifies the sense that this movement from 'old' to 'new' also entails the supersession of the Jewish by the Christian. In this individualizing form, the opposition of the old (Jewish) and new (Christian) made itself an intimate part of Christian moral, spiritual life.

Such supersessionist modes of thinking left surviving Jews in difficult straits within Christendom: they belonged, from the point of view of the majority, to a superseded past, and their very existence thus posed a problem. Saint Augustine had early on, and influentially, confronted that problem by articulating the 'doctrine of witness', suggesting that surviving Jewish communities provided Christianity with the important service of standing witness to the emergence of Christianity by preserving Hebrew Biblical texts and understanding. Jews were thus to be protected precisely because they (paradoxically) bore witness to their own outmoded status. As Jeremy Cohen has shown, however, this protective doctrine had begun to weaken by the later Middle Ages, as a stronger anti-Semitism developed.[22] An old question now came to be re-posed in new, newly powerful ways. If Judaism had been superseded, why continue to allow it to thrive? Beginning in the thirteenth century, the missionizing activity of the new fraternal orders, intended to convert Jews to Christianity, provided one relatively gentle answer.[23] Political solutions like expulsion or violent attack answered the question more injuriously.

A number of explicit deployments of Christian supersessionist thinking appear in Chaucer's works. The Parson's 'Jerusalem celestial', as the proper goal of the pilgrimage of the life of the Christian (X.51, 80), stands opposed to the earthly Jerusalem inhabited, once upon a time, by Jews. The Biblical exempla of the Man of Law's Tale—in, for example, the passage that surveys the miraculous preservation of Daniel in the lion's den, Jonah in 'the fisshes mawe' (II.486), and the 'peple Ebrayk' (489) crossing the Red Sea—function as miraculous predecessors to the unlikely survival, in the tale, of the Christian Constance. Elsewhere, in non-religious, and at least largely comic, contexts, typological thinking is deployed parodically, as in the profane re-enactment of the Noah story in the Miller's Tale and the echoes of Song of Songs in the Merchant's.

The Prioress's Tale, too, depends upon this mode of temporal thought. In the prologue, it employs a conventional typological figure, comparing Mary as (paradoxical) 'mooder Mayde' and 'mayde Mooder' (VII.467) to the (similarly paradoxical) 'brennynge', 'unbrent' bush of Exodus (468). The tale itself is set in the past, 'Ther was in Asye…' (488), but in concluding it emphasizes its significance for the present: 'Preye eek for us, we synful folk unstable' (687). Most emphatically, the tale foregrounds the youth of its Christian hero, the 'litel clergeon, seven yeer of age' (503), referring to him repeatedly as 'yong(e)' (515, 524, 644), 'tendre…of age' (524), and (especially) 'litel' (503, 509, 516, 552, 587, 596, 667, 682). It makes his youth synonymous with an innocence (538, 566, 635, and see 608) in explicit contrast to the 'cursednesse' (631) of the Jewish community presented as responsible for his murder. That community is, moreover, explicitly associated with ancient sin and its originating agent, 'Oure firste foo, the serpent Sathanas, / That hath in Jues herte his waspes nest' (558–9). A few lines later, the Jews' status as 'cursed' (574, and see 570, 578, 599, 685) is reemphasized through a parody of the renewal that the Christian dispensation is understood to effect. The tale's narrator apostrophizes them as a 'newe' people, but here a 'folk' whose newness, instead of renovating sin, violence, and death, reiterates these: 'O cursed folk of Herodes al newe' (574). Through their murder of the 'litel clergeon', the Jews renew the death-dealing of the (problematically) Jewish Herod by replaying the New Testament massacre of the innocents for which he is responsible.[24] The false 'newness' of these Jewish 'Herodes' is emphasized in contrast not only to the youthful innocence of the clergeon but also to his mother, described, while mourning her son, as 'this newe Rachel' (627).[25] This Christian 'Rachel' explicitly echoes a typological moment in Matthew's account of the massacre of the innocents: 'Then was fulfilled that which was spoken by Jeremias the prophet, saying: A voice in Rama was heard, lamentation and great mourning; Rachel bewailing her children, and would not be comforted, because they are not'.[26] (The passage takes up Jeremiah 31:15, itself an allegorization in which the Rachel of Genesis is made to stand for Israel.)

Figures of age and youth, the old and the new, recur frequently in Chaucer, and not all of these resonate equally with the typological, supersessionist thinking that characterizes Christianity's distinction of itself from Judaism. Still, an awareness of such thinking elucidates many such figures. Most obviously, given that the Pardoner explicitly associates his relics and the swearing of the three rioters in his tale with Jews, when he presents in that tale 'An oold man' (VI.713) who cannot die, we are justified in thinking of the superseded, yet still living, dispensation of Judaism. As critics have noted, this figure may be related to the legendary Wandering Jew,[27] and his proximity to death and pestilence, and to a treasure itself allied with death, evokes the unregeneracy of the Jews understood to have rejected Christ's life-giving Incarnation.

Elsewhere, when Chaucer poses old characters against younger ones—January against May in the Merchant's Tale; or the Wife of Bath against her three older husbands, on the one hand, and her two younger ones, on the other—we might also hear echoes, comic in some instances, more seriously moralizing in others, of the traditional distinction between an old, outmoded Judaism and a new, vital Christianity. The traditional figuration of this distinction through a contrast between two female personifications—a faltering, blind *Synagoga* and a triumphant *Ecclesia*—especially resonates with Chaucer's depictions of female health and debility. Relatedly, Christine Rose, in reading the Man of Law's Tale, argues persuasively that the Muslim and pagan mothers-in-law of the tale evoke the figure of 'Synagoga' as 'the mother-in-law of the Christian Church'.[28]

When the corrupt summoner in the Friar's Tale proposes to his sworn 'brother', a demon, that they defraud an old woman described as an 'old rebekke' (III.1573),[29] where 'rebekke' is identical to the name of the Jewish matriarch Rebecca as it is used in the Merchant's Tale (IV.1363, 1704; also see VII.1098), we might think of him as imputing to her something like an unregenerate Jewishness in contrast (say) to the newness of the Prioress's 'newe Rachel'. (Rebecca was, after all, Rachel's mother-in-law.) If so, the imputation is ironic, given that the 'old rebekke' escapes the damnation the summoner wishes upon her and it is the crooked summoner instead whom the tale shows stubbornly refusing to 'repente' (III.1629) and therefore given over to the 'foule feend' (1639).

In a very different register, we should also consider to what extent Chaucer's reflections on the relationship between 'olde bokes' and 'newe science' in the *Parliament of Fowls* (24-5); his consideration of 'olde appreved stories' (LGW F 21) and 'olde bokes' (F 25, 98) in relation to his own, new writing in the prologue to *The Legend of Good Women*; and his evocation of longstanding literary traditions (including the tradition of 'The Ebrayk Josephus' [HF 1433], noted above) in relation to a search for 'newe thynges' (654, 1887) and 'newe tydynges' (1886, 2045) in the *House of Fame* recall the religious distinction between Old and New Testaments. The idea that the New Testament preserves but also supersedes the Old might, that is, significantly shape how a late-medieval poet like Chaucer conceives the relation of his own work to authoritative predecessors that he honours and emulates but nonetheless also strives to surpass.

METAPHYSICS

One dominant mode of thinking in the West, originating in large part in ancient Greek thought, emphasizes a certain counterintuitive way of thinking about the 'real' and the 'true'. As in Plato's allegory of the cave, this transcendental metaphysics tends to treat the phenomenal world of everyday perception and experience as only a dim reflection of a Truth located elsewhere, identified with the Good, the One, and God. While this line of thought is not essentially or necessarily Christian, it strongly influenced early Christian, patristic and medieval, philosophy and theology, especially via late-antique Neo-Platonism. The anti-material emphasis of this tradition, however, also stands in tension with a Christianity that defines divinity not simply as a transcendent, ethereal One, but marries that transcendence to an insistent corporeality, in the figure of a Son of God who takes on flesh, is borne by Mary and born into the world in which he lives, suffers, and experiences death.

This complex Western Christian metaphysics expresses itself in an equally complex set of anti-Jewish constructions concerned with ideas of presence and absence, the material and the spiritual. On the one hand, medieval Christian thinkers show themselves concerned to defend incarnational thought against a deeply sceptical Judaism. Indeed, medieval Jewish writers did sometimes attack what they saw as an untenable Christian association of the infinite, ineffable Godhead with perishable human flesh.[30] On the other hand, Christianity also allies itself with a spiritual rejection of the material world, and it casts Judaism as deeply enmeshed in that world's corporeality. Reflecting this complexity, while Jews are often depicted as more, and more grossly, bodily than Christians, there is also a strong medieval tendency to cast the Jew as 'virtual' or 'spectral'—to emphasize his/her absence from the order of the real—and hence (wishfully) to neutralize any threat s/he might pose.[31]

The view of Judaism as a corporeal religion meshed with the temporal thinking by which a death introduced through the fleshly sin of Adam and Eve is compensated for—bodily, but also in a transcendence of body and death—by Christ's sacrifice and the consequent institution of a new human order. And medieval anti-Semitism often relies upon a set of visceral, anti-corporeal tropes. Jews come to be grouped, for instance, with prostitutes and with lepers, that is, with certain kinds of unclean fleshliness; they are associated, too, with stench and decay, with excrement, and with the materiality of money. Permitted Jewish occupations in the Middle Ages most often involved commerce, and frequently, money lending; Jewish communities closely connected to and protected by royal families took on unpopular duties like tax collection. Jews consequently came to be strongly associated with mercantilism and with 'usury', thought of as involving the 'unnatural' reproduction of money (and thus affiliated with the 'unnatural' sexual acts grouped, in the Middle Ages, under the catch-all category of 'sodomy'). In the intellectual realm, Jewish corporeality was conceived of as conditioning an inability to read spiritually, a literalism accounting for Jews' failure, or 'stubborn' refusal, to see the truth in their own Scriptures. This lack of a proper spirituality was thought, that is, to account for Jews' inability to recognize the truth of the Christian reading practices discussed above that see the 'Old Testament' as referring typologically to the coming of a future Christian dispensation. Such failures of Jewish understanding are consistently figured as blindness, as, that is, intellectual flaws evoking, too, the sense of an essentially damaged Jewish embodiment.

In the Prioress's Tale, as befits the complex status of corporeality in Christian thought, the corporeal is not simply rejected or transcended. Indeed, the body of the tale's 'litel clergeon' becomes the centre of Christian devotion, despite the violent Jewish attack on it, and that Christian body maintains, long enough to sing God's and Mary's praise, a miraculous life after death. Appropriately, it is Mary, as the vessel of the Incarnation, who makes this miraculous bodily survival possible, and she does so through the materiality of the 'greyn' she places on the clergeon's 'tonge' (VII.662). Standing clearly opposed to the holy body of the tale's martyr, however, is the corporeality of the 'Jewerye' (489), associated, in the tale's opening stanza, with 'foule usure and lucre of vileynye' (491). Later, of course, the Jews are also explicitly tied to excrement: the 'homycide' (567) they hire casts his victim, throat cut, 'in a pit' (571), 'a wardrobe...Where as thise Jewes purgen hire entraille' (572–3). The Jews' superior physical strength, however, is ultimately defeated by the clergeon's miraculous body, which becomes the crystal around which the Christian community coalesces even as it destroys the Jewish body politic.[32]

The Prioress's Tale also reflects Christian notions of the difference between (literal) Jewish and (spiritual) Christian reading practices. Here, Jewish interpretation (as prompted by Satan) appears in the community's construal of the clergeon's song of praise to the Virgin Mary as an attack on their 'lawes reverence' (VII.564). This reading is literally accurate: the *Alma redemptoris mater* is an attack on Judaism insofar as it celebrates what is (or should be) the end of the religion out of which Mary herself arises. But, properly understood (that is, heard with Christian ears), the song praises the necessary rearrangement of reality that the miracle of the Virgin Birth accomplishes, and the Jews 'should' hear here not an attack on their 'lawes reverence' but that law's necessary fulfilment and supersession. Here, the 'litel clergeon's' own understanding— despite (or because of) his failure to understand literally the Latin words of the song—is far superior to the Jews'. All he needs to know is that the song praises Mary. Here, Christian spirituality is reflected not in allegorizing reading practices but in a rote learning that nonetheless suggests a 'real', spiritual penetration of the text's essence, a naïve, miraculous understanding of truth that is emphasized, too, in the Prioress's Prologue: 'For noght oonly thy laude precious / Parfourned is by men of dignitee, / But by the mouth of children thy bountee / Parfourned is, for on the brest soukynge / Somtyme shewen they thyn heriynge' (455–9).

Distinctions of presence and absence, and corporeality and spirituality, abound in Chaucer's writing, and given the complex intellectual pedigree of such ideas, these do not reflect in any uniform way the Christian-Jewish encounter. Still, given that the Pardoner's false relics (which should embody holiness but instead seem empty of real spiritual capacity) are directly associated with Jewishness, one might reasonably see reflections of the anti-corporeal tropes of medieval anti-Semitism in other of the tale's corporeal signs: the material treasure that comes to be identified with (literal and spiritual) death; the 'olde breech', stained 'with thy fundement' that the angry Host claims the Pardoner would pass off as the 'relyk of a seint' (VI.948–50); the Pardoner's (missing?) testicles performatively 'shryned in an hogges toord' (955) by the Host.

Less obviously, figures like the Wife of Bath and January, both growing old and both nonetheless undeterred from the pursuit of sexual pleasure, are wrapped up in a sensual corporeality in part coded as Jewish. The Wife, after all, cites the 'bigamye' (III.33, 54, 86, 96) of Old Testament figures like Solomon (35), Lamech (54), Abraham (55), and Jacob (56)—part of a Jewish history and law that Christianity supersedes—to justify her own multiple marriages. January, too, relies on Old Testament authority in justifying his decision to marry (IV.1362–74), and later he quotes Song of Songs, the most erotic book of Hebrew scripture but one consistently denied its eroticism by medieval Christian commentators, as he attempts to seduce May into his pleasure garden. January here is of course blind, literalizing the blindness of Jews thought unable to read their own scriptures with true, spiritual insight.

Elsewhere, when Chaucer highlights the differences between distinct types of reading practice, we also hear echoes of Jewish-Christian distinction. In the dream debate of the Nun's Priest's Tale, Pertelote's somatising reading of Chauntecleer's dream might be seen as 'Jewish' and Chauntecleer's allegorizing, prophetic reading as 'Christian'. Of course, the distinction here is comic, part of an erudite dream debate put into the mouths of a hen and cock. Earlier in Fragment VII (also the fragment that contains the Prioress's Tale), part of the implicit critique of the 'failed' Monk's Tale may be that it immerses itself too fully in literal history, without paying adequate attention to spiritual or moral meaning. And, that other failed tale of Fragment VII, the 'drasty rymyng…nat worth a toord' (VII.930, and see 923) of the Tale of Sir Thopas evokes the qualities of a Judaism understood through an excremental lens.

SPATIALITY

The medieval relationship between Christianity and Judaism also has significant spatial dimensions, expressed in formulations about the 'proper' placement of Jewish and Christian communities and individual bodies in space.[33] From the pre-Christian Roman Empire on, Jews had settled in Europe, first largely along trade routes in the Mediterranean, then increasingly in Northern and Western Europe. Jews in significant numbers probably arrived in England after the Norman Conquest, along with the Norman noble families that came to rule and settle in the new realm.[34] Many locations in Western Europe during the early, high, and late Middle Ages housed Jewish communities; while these were often small, they could also be large and socially influential, as in some parts of both Muslim and Christian Iberia.[35] Geopolitically then, Judaism posed a different problem for European Christian society than did Islam, which, even as it occupied the margins of Europe in Iberia and in the East, presented itself as 'native' to a largely distinct geopolitical space.[36] Jews, on the other hand, lived within Europe itself, often in separate quarters (though ghettos, strictly speaking, were not instituted until the sixteenth century), but nonetheless in close proximity to Christians.

The Christian majority responded to this ambivalent situation with a variety of measures intended to solidify religious segregation: rules that prohibited Jews and Christians from living or eating together; laws ensuring that Christians did not work for Jews in intimate situations (e.g. as nursemaids); an insistence on distinct dress for Jews, and ultimately legislation that Jews wear the badge in order to mark their difference. Still, there is much evidence that medieval Jews and Christians lived side-by-side, and largely cooperatively, sharing business, civic, and cultural interests.[37] Indeed, the very need for (repeatedly renewed) legislation to ensure separateness suggests that day-to-day Christian-Jewish interaction was a significant part of life in much of medieval Europe.

The geopolitical reality of medieval European Christian-Jewish relations thus plays out a certain dialectic of inclusion and exclusion, which is also often expressed through the terms of distance and proximity. One way of grappling with the nearness of Jewish communities is fantasmatically to project essential Jewishness elsewhere. Thus, for instance, the idea of a large community of Jews (sometimes identified with the ten lost tribes of Israel, sometimes with Gog and Magog) that has been confined in a mountainous area somewhere in the East (often the Caucasus), and thus closed away from contact with Europe, is current in a number of medieval texts.[38] Here, ideas of distance and expulsion are brought together in such a way as more firmly to ensure the (imagined) spatial segregation of Jews from Christian Europe. What might be thought of as a certain flipside of this fantasy, one that acknowledges, in phobic fashion, the reality of Jewish presence in Europe, is the idea that scattered, small European Jewish communities are able, conspiratorially, to communicate with each other, and to organize anti-Christian actions (like well-poisoning). Here, the discomfort of a Christianity housing a minority population is expressed through the fantasy that that largely powerless group might reverse the terms of geopolitical dominance to establish a Jewish power Christianity cannot resist.

As we see in the legislation noted above, however, Christian grappling with the Jewish presence in Europe was not only fantasmatic. In the most striking cases, Christian communities or realms acted to destroy or expel their Jewish populations. The riots and massacres associated with the crusades participated in such a movement: Jews were in a number of cases given a choice between conversion to Christianity and death, either of which would result in a 'purified' Christian community. Outbreaks of plague in the fourteenth century were sometimes explained as the effect of Jewish conspiratorial action, and violent attacks on Jewish communities followed. We see wholesale expulsions of Jews like that from England in 1290 occurring also in France in 1182, 1306, and 1394 (the first two instances were followed by readmissions), various parts of Germany in the twelfth, thirteenth, and fourteenth centuries, and Iberia in 1492.

In thus trying to enact the fantasy of a 'pure' Christian society, European communities and realms participated in another common kind of spatialized thinking, in which the integrity of the body politic is assured by its homogeneity. The religious 'other' within is here viewed as a contaminant to be expelled. Such geopolitical thinking resonates strongly with a more strictly religious way of conceiving holiness, as wholeness or purity of body, over against a corporeality that is permeable, subject to fragmentation and decay. As the work of Caroline Bynum shows, such thinking is at the centre of medieval Christian devotion; even when that devotion embraces illness, fragmentation, and the abject, it does so in the service of notions of wholeness and impermeability, a paradoxical completeness that reflects, especially, the ways in which Christ's human body on the cross might be attacked and injured and yet remain the inexhaustible source of life-giving flesh and blood.[39]

Related, then, to attempts to keep Christians and Jews separate are distinctions that make Christian bodies whole and pure and Jewish bodies fragmented and contaminated. Thus, in one widespread myth, Jewish men are depicted as bleeding monthly.[40] Such ideas powerfully overlap both with the idea of Jewishness as old and superseded and with the notion that Jews are excessively dedicated to the material and corporeal; here, Jewish bodies in their debility and fragmentation come to be seen as essentially different from Christian bodies.

The Prioress's Tale clearly foregrounds the geopolitics of Jewish distance and proximity. The story is set 'in Asye' (VII.488), at the opposite end of the world, on an East-West axis, from the reader's England.[41] But the comfort of this distance is not simply asserted and maintained: the culture the tale depicts—in its Latin, Christian devotion to the Virgin, in its emphasis on a sentimentalized mother-child bond, in its representation of Church hierarchy—is more familiar than exotic. If the narrative nonetheless remains at a certain distance, the tale's last lines more insistently bring it home, with a direct address to the English boy martyr Hugh of Lincoln, and the claim that the kind of story told here is not foreign to England: 'O yonge Hugh of Lyncoln, slayn also / With cursed Jewes, as it is notable, / For it is but a litel while ago, / Preye eek for us, we synful folk unstable' (684–7).

The geography of the 'greet citee' (VII.488) in the Prioress's Tale also reflects anxieties about the space of religious distinction in medieval European cities. The 'Jewerye' stands at the centre of the city and is yet separate from it; open to Christians, including, fatally, the 'litel clergeon', it also serves, incompletely, to contain the Jewish community in its own space. Within the city, conceived as a body, the open but enclosed 'Jewerye' recalls the structure of the human alimentary canal, and following the boy's murder, as his mother searches desperately for him, the whole of the 'Jewerye' comes to be strongly associated with the 'pit' or 'wardrobe' where Jews void their entrails and where they attempt to conceal the clergeon. Their space comes, that is, to be reduced to the hidden and secret places of their conspiratorial action, and particularly the excremental space where they dispose of their victim. Contrarily, after the boy's discovery, the tale moves into Christian spaces that are open—the 'greet processioun' (623) through the city—or enclosed not to contain dirt, but instead to enshrine holiness—the 'abbay' that houses the boy's 'beere' (624, 627), where the miracle of his survival is revealed, and the 'tombe of marbul stones cleere' in which 'his litel body sweete' is finally enclosed (681–2).

This firm distinction between the civic and religious spaces of Jews and Christians is clearly echoed within the tale in the fates of human bodies. Subject to attack, 'throte' 'kut unto' the 'nekke boon' (VII.649), the holy Christian body of the clergeon nonetheless survives intact, its deep wound only emphasizing its miraculous wholeness. In contrast, the Jewish conspirators, all 'That of this mordre wiste' (630), have their own bodies taken apart, 'torment[ed]' and dedicated to a 'shameful deeth' (628): 'with wilde hors he dide hem drawe, / And after that he heng hem by the lawe' (633–4). The 'Jewerye' is decimated, while the Christian community comes together as one before the body of the singing child (675–83).

The largest geopolitical questions raised in the Prioress's Tale—its simultaneous setting in Asia and evocation of England—participate in a broader consideration of geopolitics in the *Canterbury Tales*. We hear echoes of the Prioress's Tale in all those tales where distance and proximity are foregrounded, particularly the Man of Law's Tale, with its navigation between and among Syria, Rome, and England. Here, too, the geopolitical and the temporal intersect: the England depicted in the Man of Law's Tale is (unlike that evoked at the end of the Prioress's Tale) ancient and pagan rather than contemporary and Christian. Chaucer's other 'Oriental' tales—the Squire's Tale; in part, the Monk's—and classicizing poems like the Knight's Tale and *Troilus and Criseyde* that depict pre-Christian European and Asian locales, also 'map' religious difference in simultaneously spatial and temporal terms. Chaucer's representation of a world scene that includes departures from and returns to Europe and England recognizes how geopolitical distance intersects complexly with religious difference and how historical change (including Christianity's own emergence and distanciation from Judaism) intersects with the geopolitical.

The spatial dynamics of inclusion and exclusion are also played out in a variety of Chaucerian texts. Think, for instance, of the intimate enemy, Damian, in the Merchant's Tale, or of that daughter of a traitor, Criseyde. Both participate in actions where dwelling places are made strange and potentially dangerous to those who should feel most at home within them. Would the affective responses circulating around such foreign yet intimate presences echo medieval Christian emotions regarding Jewish presence within European cities? Elsewhere in Chaucer, such foreign presences are, as in the Prioress's Tale, given a more explicitly religious valence—in the Second Nun's Tale, for example, where the Christians are an oppressed minority, the pope lives underground (VIII.186), and Cecelia and those she converts are perceived as impure social presences that must be violently eliminated.

In the Second Nun's Tale, however, the depiction of a primitive Christianity in Rome reverses the dynamics of medieval Christian-Jewish interaction, in which Christianity now stands in the powerful place of the Roman state and Judaism in the place of the small, persecuted community of original Christians. In Chaucer's tale, the dissonances of these parallels are muted or denied, however, by the ways in which the Christians of the Second Nun's Tale also resemble the Christians of the Prioress's Tale; after all, as in the depiction of the 'litel clergeon', the besieged body of the Christian Cecelia remains miraculously intact and alive. Likewise, the Roman body politic, like the Prioress's 'Jewerye', comes under effective Christian attack, losing integrity through the conversions Cecelia's preaching effects. In any case, considering the Second Nun's Tale with anti-Semitic constructions in mind suggests that the tale's depiction of a now long-past Christian minority's survival and growth is enmeshed with the (inter)religious thinking of the present. The picture is complicated even further when we consider that the Second Nun's Tale is paired with the Canon's Yeoman's. Here, another subgroup of characters (the tale's Christian alchemists) is shown living in the margins of the city, 'Lurkynge in hernes and in lanes blynde' (VIII.658), like the Jews in their 'Jewerye', but also like the Christian pope in the Second Nun's Tale. Their actions, however, unlike Cecelia's or the pope's, but in some ways like those of the Prioress's violent Jews, corrupt or destroy bodies rather than purify them. Fragment VIII of the *Canterbury Tales* thus provides a rich site for thinking about the embodied, religious but also secular, geopolitics of life in cities that might present themselves as unified, 'pure' spaces but which a more complex 'sociological' view will show always to be riven by divisions, whether or not these are strictly speaking religious.

CONCLUSION

As the complex spatial relationships just sketched begin to suggest, Jewish-Christian differentiations interact dynamically with other sorts of religious distinction—the geopolitics of Muslim-Christian and pagan-Christian conflict in the Man of Law's Tale, the recognition of a Mongol other in the Squire's Tale, the changes within Christianity itself suggested by the depiction of a primitive Church in the Second Nun's Tale, deviations from 'true' Christianity in the Canon's Yeoman's Tale, and in fact in all the tales that thematize clerical corruption (the Friar's and Summoner's, the Pardoner's). I hope to have shown that, in analysing Chaucerian structures of thought, it is useful, as a first move, to isolate certain crucial anti-Semitic/anti-Jewish ideas and to consider how these might have shaped even texts where Jews are not explicitly represented. Our analysis, however, need not stop here: we might push forward also to note how medieval anti-Judaism and anti-Semitism are themselves wrapped up with other significant medieval structures of thought. These need not be, as in the cases I have just cited, religious in nature. Thus, Tomasch has suggested that Chaucer's ongoing project of defining Englishness is intimately connected to his representations of Jews.[42] We might notice, too, that in many of the cases where Chaucer puts into play an old/new dichotomy, including tales as different as the Prioress's and Wife of Bath's, gender, particularly as expressed in women's roles (mother, wife, ruler, narrator), is significantly in play. As Judith Butler has suggested, 'though there are clearly good historical reasons for keeping "race" and "sexuality" and "sexual difference" [we might add here, "religion"] as separate analytic spheres, there are also quite pressing and significant historical reasons for asking how and where we might read not only their convergence, but the sites at which one cannot be constituted save through the other'.[43] That is, as we think about the ways in which Jewish-Christian differentiations shape the Chaucerian text, we should ask too what other sorts of difference—other religious distinctions, but also class, nation, ethnicity, and race, gender and sexuality—are simultaneously and constitutively at work.[44]

ACKNOWLEDGEMENTS

I thank the members of my writing group—Valerie Allen, Jennifer Brown, Glenn Burger, Matthew Goldie, Michael Sargent, and Sylvia Tomasch—for their careful reading of an earlier version of this chapter.

NOTES

1. On the associations with monstrosity and the demonic, see Joshua Trachtenberg, *The Devil and the Jews: The Medieval Conception of the Jew and Its Relation to Modern Anti-Semitism* (Philadelphia, PA: Jewish Publication Society of America, 1983 [1943]), and Debra Higgs Strickland, *Saracens, Demons, and Jews: Making Monsters in Medieval Art* (Princeton, NJ: Princeton University Press, 2003). On animality, see Kenneth Stow, *Jewish Dogs: An Image and Its Interpreters* (Stanford, CA: Stanford University Press, 2006).
2. See, for influential (and sometimes conflicting) formulations of this history, Amos Funkenstein, 'Basic Types of Christian Anti-Jewish Polemics in the Later Middle Ages', *Viator* 2 (1971), 373–82; Jeremy Cohen, *The Friars and the Jews: The Evolution of Medieval Anti-Judaism* (Ithaca, NY: Cornell University Press, 1982); R. I. Moore, *The Formation of a Persecuting Society: Power and Deviance in Western Europe, 950–1250* (Oxford: Basil Blackwell, 1987; 2nd ed. 2007); Robert Chazan, *Daggers of Faith: Thirteenth-Century Christian Missionizing and Jewish Response* (Berkeley, CA: University of California Press, 1989), 169–81; Gavin I. Langmuir, *History, Religion, and Antisemitism* (Berkeley, CA: University of California Press, 1990), 275–305; and Jeremy Cohen, *Living Letters of the Law: Ideas of the Jew in Medieval Christianity* (Berkeley, CA: University of California Press, 1999).
3. On the events of 1096, see Robert Chazan, *European Jewry and the First Crusade* (Berkeley, CA: University of California Press, 1987), and Jeremy Cohen, *Sanctifying the Name of God: Jewish Martyrs and Jewish Memories of the First Crusade* (Philadelphia, PA: University of Pennsylvania Press, 2004).
4. For a broad overview of anti-Semitism, see Gavin I. Langmuir, *Toward a Definition of Antisemitism* (Berkeley, CA: University of California Press, 1990). For a fine treatment of some of the accusations lodged against medieval Jews, see Miri Rubin, *Gentile Tales: The Narrative Assault on Late Medieval Jews* (New Haven, CT: Yale University Press, 1999).
5. For an overview of earlier English material, see Anthony Bale, 'Fictions of Judaism in England before 1290', in *Jews in Medieval Britain: Historical, Literary and Archaeological Perspectives*, ed. Patricia Skinner (Woodbridge, VA: Boydell Press, 2003), 129–44. For a treatment of later 'English Antisemitisms', see Anthony Bale, *The Jew in the Medieval Book: English Antisemitisms, 1350–1500* (Cambridge: Cambridge University Press, 2006).

6. On the multiple factors involved in the expulsion, see Robin R. Mundill, *England's Jewish Solution: Experiment and Expulsion, 1262-1290* (Cambridge: Cambridge University Press, 1998).

7. On evidence for the presence of Jews (and 'Saracens') in Chaucer's England, see Henry Ansgar Kelly, 'Jews and Saracens in Chaucer's England: A Review of the Evidence', *Studies in the Age of Chaucer* 27 (2005), 129-69. On the Domus Conversorum, see Robert C. Stacey, 'The Conversion of Jews to Christianity in Thirteenth-Century England', *Speculum* 67 (1992), 263-83.

8. On the genre of Miracles of the Virgin, to which the Prioress's Tale belongs, and on the anti-Semitic versions of such Miracles, see Carleton Brown, 'The Prioress's Tale', in *Sources and Analogues of Chaucer's Canterbury Tales*, eds. W. F. Bryan and Germaine Dempster (Chicago: University of Chicago Press, 1941), 447-85; Robert Worth Frank, Jr, 'Miracles of the Virgin, Medieval Anti-Semitism, and the "Prioress's Tale"', in *The Wisdom of Poetry: Essays in Early English Literature in Honor of Morton W. Bloomfield*, eds. Larry D. Benson and Siegfried Wenzel (Kalamazoo: Medieval Institute Publications, 1982), 177-88; Carole Stone, 'Anti-Semitism in the Miracle Tales of the Virgin', *Medieval Encounters* 5 (1999), 364-74; Laurel Broughton, 'The Prioress's Prologue and Tale', in *Sources and Analogues of the Canterbury Tales*, 2 vols., eds. Robert M. Correale and Mary Hamel (Cambridge: D.S. Brewer, 2002-5), 2:583-647; Bale, *Jew in the Medieval Book*, 55-103; and Roger Dahood, 'English Historical Narratives of Jewish Child-Murder, Chaucer's *Prioress's Tale*, and the Date of Chaucer's Unknown Source', *Studies in the Age of Chaucer* 31 (2009), 125-40.

9. On earlier critical views of Chaucer's tale, see Florence Ridley, *The Prioress and the Critics* (Berkeley, CA: University of California Press, 1965), and Carolyn Collette, 'Critical Approaches to the *Prioress's Tale* and the *Second Nun's Tale*', in *Chaucer's Religious Tales*, eds. C. David Benson and Elizabeth Robertson (Cambridge: Boydell and Brewer, 1990), 95-107. Consideration of the tale's anti-Semitism is voluminous; for a few of the more recent, influential treatments, see Louise O. Fradenburg, 'Criticism, Anti-Semitism, and the *Prioress's Tale*', *Exemplaria* 1 (1989), 69-115; Emily Stark Zitter, 'Anti-Semitism in Chaucer's *Prioress's Tale*', *Chaucer Review* 25 (1991), 277-84; Denise L. Despres, 'Cultic Anti-Judaism and Chaucer's Litel Clergeon', *Modern Philology* 91 (1994), 413-27; and Lee Patterson, '"The Living Witnesses of Our Redemption": Martyrdom and Imitation in Chaucer's *Prioress's Tale*', *Journal of Medieval and Early Modern Studies* 31 (2001), 507-60.

10. On the Jewish thematics of the *Pardoner's Tale*, see Leo J. Henkin, 'Jacob and the Hooly Jew', *Modern Language Notes* 55 (1940), 254-9; William Chester Jordan, 'The Pardoner's "Holy Jew"', in *Chaucer and the Jews: Sources, Contexts, Meanings*, ed. Sheila Delany (New York: Routledge, 2002), 25-42; Catherine S. Cox, 'Water of Bitterness: The Pardoner and/as the Sotah', *Exemplaria* 16 (2004), 131-64; and Catherine S. Cox, 'The Jewish Pardoner and Chaucer's *Canterbury Tales*', in *The Judaic Other in Dante, the Gawain Poet, and Chaucer* (Gainesville, FL: University Press of Florida, 2005), 111-44. On the widespread Christian belief in the Jews' central role in the Crucifixion, see Jeremy Cohen, 'The Jews as the Killers of Christ in the Latin Tradition, from Augustine to the Friars', *Traditio* 39 (1983), 1-27.

11. See H.S. Ficke, 'Iewes Werk', *Philological Quarterly* 7 (1928), 82-5; and Jerome Mandel, '"Jewes Werk" in *Sir Thopas*', in Delany, *Chaucer and the Jews*, 59-68.

12. The explicit references to Jews in the Tale of Sir Thopas and the Monk's Tale, along with the Prioress's Tale, make Fragment VII by far the richest locus for the thematization of Judaism in the *Canterbury Tales*. One might argue, too, that even those tales of Fragment

VII that do not explicitly depict Jews echo those that do: the questionable mercantile practices of the Shipman's Tale evoke the 'usure' (VII.491) referred to at the opening of the Prioress's Tale; the Tale of Melibee makes extensive use of sententious 'Old Testament' material; the Nun's Priest's Tale engages with the dream thematics of the Biblical Joseph and Daniel narratives. For readings of Jewish themes in Fragment VII (which also make connections to other tales and fragments), see Lisa Lampert, 'Reprioritizing the Prioress's Tale,' in her *Gender and Jewish Difference from Paul to Shakespeare* (Philadelphia, PA: University of Pennsylvania Press, 2004), 58–99; Miriamne Ara Krummel, 'Globalizing Jewish Communities: Mapping a Jewish Geography in Fragment VII of the *Canterbury Tales*', *Texas Studies in Literature and Language* 50 (2008), 121–42; and Miriamne Ara Krummel, 'The Pardoner, the Prioress, Sir Thopas, and the Monk: Semitic Discourse and the Jew(s)', in *The Canterbury Tales Revisited: 21st Century Interpretations*, ed. Kathleen A. Bishop (Newcastle: Cambridge Scholars Publishing, 2008), 88–109.

13. For an overview of Chaucer's explicit references to Jews in the *Canterbury Tales*, see Sylvia Tomasch, 'Postcolonial Chaucer and the Virtual Jew', in *The Postcolonial Middle Ages*, ed. Jeffrey J. Cohen (New York: St Martin's Press, 2000), 243–60, reprinted in Delany, *Chaucer and the Jews*, 69–85.

14. On the Jews as 'secte saturnyn', see Amanda H. Miller, 'Chaucer's "Secte Saturnyn"', *Modern Language Notes* 47 (1932), 99–102.

15. For a reading of the *Treatise on the Astrolabe* that emphasizes its 'markers of ethnicity and race' (357), see Jenna Mead, 'Reading by Said's Lantern: Orientalism and Chaucer's *Treatise on the Astrolabe*', *Medieval Encounters* 5 (1999), 350–7.

16. On the traditions invoked here, see Vincent DiMarco, 'A Note on Canacee's Magic Ring', *Anglia* 99 (1981), 399–405.

17. Sylvia Tomasch, 'Judecca, Dante's Satan, and the *Dis*-placed Jew', in *Text and Territory: Geographical Imagination in the European Middle Ages*, eds. Sylvia Tomasch and Sealy Gilles (Philadelphia, PA: University of Pennsylvania Press, 1998), 247–67.

18. Lampert, *Gender and Jewish Difference*, 169; Toni Morrison, *Playing in the Dark: Whiteness and the Literary Imagination* (New York: Random House, 1993).

19. Eve Kosofsky Sedgwick, *Epistemology of the Closet* (Berkeley, CA: University of California Press, 1990), 1.

20. See Kathleen Biddick, *The Typological Imaginary: Circumcision, Technology, History* (Philadelphia, PA: University of Pennsylvania Press, 2003), and Steven F. Kruger, *The Spectral Jew: Conversion and Embodiment in Medieval Europe* (Minneapolis, MN: University of Minnesota Press, 2006).

21. Ephesians 4:22–4. See also Romans 6:6, Ephesians 2:15, and Colossians 3:9–11.

22. Cohen, *Living Letters of the Law*.

23. Cohen, *Friars and the Jews*, connects the foundation of the Dominican and Franciscan orders to the rise of anti-Semitism in Europe.

24. Matthew 2:16–18.

25. See Robert Adams, 'Chaucer's "New Rachel" and the Theological Roots of Medieval Anti-Semitism', *Bulletin of the John Rylands University Library* 77 (1995), 9–18.

26. Matthew 2:17–18.

27. Nelson Sherwin Bushnell, 'The Wandering Jew and *The Pardoner's Tale*', *Studies in Philology* 28 (1931), 450–60. More generally on the legend of the Wandering Jew, see Galit Hasan-Rokem and Alan Dundes, eds., *The Wandering Jew: Essays in the Interpretation of a Christian Legend* (Bloomington, IN: Indiana University Press, 1986).

28. Christine M. Rose, 'The Jewish Mother-in-Law: Synagoga and the *Man of Law's Tale*', in *Hildegard of Bingen: A Book of Essays*, ed. Maud Burnett McInerney (New York: Garland, 1998), 191–226; reprinted in Delany, *Chaucer and the Jews*, 3–23, citation at 3.

29. 'Rebekke' may mean 'fiddle' and refer, like its synonym 'ribibe' (III.1377), to an old woman, but it is also identical to a Middle English form of the Hebrew Biblical name 'Rebecca'. The MED suggests that the etymology of 'rebekke n. (2)', 'A disparaging term for an old woman, a crone', may be from the Latin 'Rebecca', but notes as well the word's similarity to 'rebekke n. (1)', fiddle.

30. See, for instance, Joseph Kimhi, *The Book of the Covenant*, trans. Frank Talmage (Toronto: Pontifical Institute of Mediaeval Studies, 1972), 36–7.

31. See Tomasch, 'Postcolonial Chaucer', and Kruger, *Spectral Jew*.

32. For a more extended reading along these lines, see Steven F. Kruger, 'The Bodies of Jews in the Late Middle Ages', in *The Idea of Medieval Literature: Essays on Chaucer and Medieval Culture in Honor of Donald R. Howard*, eds. James Dean and Christian Zacher (Newark, DE: University of Delaware Press; London and Toronto: Associated University Presses, 1992), 301–23.

33. For recent discussion of the place of Jews in medieval Europe, see Suzanne Conklin Akbari, 'Placing the Jews in Late Medieval English Literature', in *Orientalism and the Jews*, eds. Ivan Davidson Kalmar and Derek J. Pensler (Waltham, MA: Brandeis University Press, 2005), 32–50, and Akbari, 'The Place of the Jews' in her *Idols in the East: European Representations of Islam and the Orient, 1100–1450* (Ithaca, NY: Cornell University Press, 2009), 112–54.

34. Nevertheless, as Andrew Scheil has argued, Judaism is significant to the culture of pre-Conquest England; *The Footsteps of Israel: Understanding Jews in Anglo-Saxon England* (Ann Arbor, MI: University of Michigan Press, 2004).

35. For what remains the fullest account of the social life of Jews in medieval Europe, see Salo Wittmayer Baron, *A Social and Religious History of the Jews*, 2nd ed., 18 vols. (New York: Columbia University Press, 1952–83).

36. Any absolute geopolitical distinction between Christian Europe and a Muslim Middle East and North Africa does not hold up, given that the Roman Empire had unified some of these spaces and that Christianity was present and influential in North Africa and the Middle East before the emergence of Islam. For a consideration of how one Christian writer, Guibert of Nogent, negotiated Jewish and Muslim difference simultaneously and differentially in his writing, see Steven F. Kruger, 'Medieval Christian (Dis)identifications: Muslims and Jews in Guibert of Nogent', *New Literary History* 28 (1997), 185–203, and Kruger, 'Body Effects: Individual and Community Identity in the Long Twelfth Century', in his *Spectral Jew*, 23–66. For readings of Chaucer that recognize the overlap between representations of 'Saracens' and Jews, see Rose, 'Jewish Mother-in-Law', and Sheila Delany, 'Chaucer's Prioress, the Jews, and the Muslims', in Delany, *Chaucer and the Jews*, 43–57.

37. For one case study of Jews and their supportive Christian neighbors, see Joseph Shatzmiller, *Shylock Reconsidered: Jews, Moneylending, and Medieval Society* (Berkeley, CA: University of California Press, 1990). On shared Jewish-Christian culture, see Ivan G. Marcus, *Rituals of Childhood: Jewish Acculturation in Medieval Europe* (New Haven, CT: Yale University Press, 1996). On the complex nature—communal and nonetheless conflictual—of the living together of Jews and Christians (in this specific case, in Iberia and Southern France), see David Nirenberg, *Communities of Violence: Persecution of Minorities in the Middle Ages* (Princeton, NJ: Princeton University Press, 1996).

38. See Andrew Colin Gow, *The Red Jews: Antisemitism in an Apocalyptic Age, 1200–1600* (Leiden: E. J. Brill, 1995).

39. See, for instance, Caroline Walker Bynum, *Holy Feast and Holy Fast: The Religious Significance of Food to Medieval Women* (Berkeley, CA: University of California Press, 1987), and *Fragmentation and Redemption: Essays on Gender and the Human Body in Medieval Religion* (New York: Zone Books; Cambridge: MIT Press, 1992).

40. See Willis Johnson, 'The Myth of Jewish Male Menses', *Journal of Medieval History* 24 (1998), 273–95, and Irven M. Resnick, 'Medieval Roots of the Myth of Jewish Male Menses', *Harvard Theological Review* 93 (2000), 241–63.

41. For a fuller consideration of the place of England in medieval geographical thought, see Kathy Lavezzo, *Angels on the Edge of the World: Geography, Literature, and English Community, 1100–1534* (Ithaca, NY: Cornell University Press, 2006).

42. Tomasch, 'Postcolonial Chaucer'.

43. Judith Butler, *Bodies That Matter: On the Discursive Limits of 'Sex'* (New York: Routledge, 1993), 168.

44. For work that performs this kind of analysis, see, for instance, Sharon Farmer and Carol Braun Pasternack, eds., *Gender and Difference in the Middle Ages* (Minneapolis, MN: University of Minnesota Press, 2003), and Cordelia Beattie and Kirsten A. Fenton, eds., *Intersections of Gender, Religion and Ethnicity in the Middle Ages* (Houndmills: Palgrave Macmillan, 2011).

BIBLIOGRAPHY

Akbari, Suzanne Conklin, 'Placing the Jews in Late Medieval English Literature', in *Orientalism and the Jews*, eds. Ivan Davidson Kalmar and Derek J. Pensler (Waltham, MA: Brandeis University Press, 2005), 32–50.

Bale, Anthony, *The Jew in the Medieval Book: English Antisemitisms, 1350–1500* (Cambridge: Cambridge University Press, 2006).

Cohen, Jeremy, *Living Letters of the Law: Ideas of the Jew in Medieval Christianity* (Berkeley, CA: University of California Press, 1999).

Cox, Catherine S., *The Judaic Other in Dante, the Gawain Poet, and Chaucer* (Gainesville, FL: University Press of Florida, 2005).

Delany, Sheila, *Chaucer and the Jews: Sources, Contexts, Meanings* (New York: Routledge, 2002).

Fradenburg, Louise O., 'Criticism, Anti-Semitism, and the *Prioress's Tale*', *Exemplaria* 1 (1989), 69–115.

Kruger, Steven F., 'The Bodies of Jews in the Late Middle Ages', in *The Idea of Medieval Literature: Essays on Chaucer and Medieval Culture in Honor of Donald R. Howard*, eds. James Dean and Christian Zacher (Newark, DE: University of Delaware Press; London and Toronto: Associated University Presses, 1992), 301–23.

Kruger, Steven F., *The Spectral Jew: Conversion and Embodiment in Medieval Europe* (Minneapolis, MN: University of Minnesota Press, 2006).

Krummel, Miriamne Ara, *Crafting Jewishness in Medieval England: Legally Absent, Virtually Present* (New York: Palgrave Macmillan, 2011).

Lampert, Lisa, *Gender and Jewish Difference from Paul to Shakespeare* (Philadelphia, PA: University of Pennsylvania Press, 2004).

CHAPTER 9

'O HEBRAIC PEOPLE!'

English Jews and the Twelfth-Century Literary Scene

RUTH NISSE

By the time Chaucer sat down to write a condemnation of the 'Hebrayk Peple', in the Prioress's Tale, there were no Jews left in England, as they had been expelled en masse by Edward I in 1290. Scholars frequently celebrate the polyglot and multicultural English society that informed Chaucer's works, most of which are translations in some form; yet they overlook the Anglo-Hebrew authors and the body of their writing lost in the expulsion. This is perhaps reasonable since most of the twelfth and thirteenth-century Christian authors who preceded Chaucer paid little attention to the Hebrew language except to find the authentic 'literal' sense of the Old Testament, often with the assistance of Jewish teachers, and to decry the perfidy of the rabbis and their 'modern' unbiblical Talmud. Revealed in detail by the Jewish convert Peter Alfonsi in the early twelfth century in his *Dialogus contra Judaeos*, rabbinic writing increasingly became the focus of anti-Jewish polemics in England as well as France, where the Talmud was publicly burned in 1242. In Peter's *Dialogus* and the works it influenced by Bartholomew of Exeter and Peter of Blois, the Talmud is a destabilizing force both to Christian exegesis of the bible and Jewish conversion.[1] The extraordinary set of interlinear psalters written in Hebrew and Latin with the help of Jewish scribes in the 1230s and 1240s is an exception to this negative dynamic. Prepared for a circle of scholars associated with the theologian and scientist Robert Grosseteste, these manuscripts showcase a rare example of Christian collaboration with Jews and an attempt at bilingualism, however ambivalent on both sides.[2] By the late fourteenth century, there were barely any Hebrew manuscripts, except for these pedagogical texts, left in England; either the Jews had managed to take them to the continent or monks had repurposed them. The absolute loss of Hebrew writing for Chaucer is, nevertheless, a productive memory for his current readers.

By comparison to the golden age of the Northern French and German Tosafists, the Talmud commentators and religious poets who succeeded Rashi (1040–1105), the Insular Jews' cultural and intellectual contributions were slight.[3] Nevertheless, as Cecil

Roth most notably has shown, the English community, while closely related to the French, also produced some eminent scholars and writers, particularly in the mid-to-late thirteenth century.[4] The most remarkable of these figures is the thirteenth-century Tosafist Elijah of London, author of commentaries on several tractates of the Mishnah and the Passover Haggadah, as well as a number of important Halakhic, or legal decisions.[5] The most complete work of Halakhah is Jacob ben Judah's *Etz Ḥayim*, produced just before the expulsion: a huge compendium modelled on and often citing Maimonides's legal code, the *Mishneh Torah*, the text preserves various uniquely English customs. Jacob ben Judah also includes a few of his original poems in the *Etz Ḥayyim*, signed with acrostics and all apparently intended for the ten penitential days between Rosh Ha-Shanah and Yom Kippur; although composed in conventional biblical terms, they also refer to the worsening persecution of the Jews.[6] A more accomplished poet, Meir of Norwich, composed stylistically versatile works that range from a liturgical lament decrying the abuse of English Jews at the hands of Christians, to a long and deeply erudite poem for the seventh day of Passover interpreting the events of Genesis and Exodus, to a series of sixteen short secular poems penned for a friend.[7] Both poets express a hope for the speedy arrival of what Israel Yuval has pointedly called the 'vengeful messiah'—a figure who will destroy 'Edom' (Rome and by extension Christian Europe) and give over its empire to the Jews.

England was also known for its grammarians, especially Moses ben Isaac ha-Nessiah, the author of the *Sefer ha-Shoham (The Onyx Book)*, a comprehensive guide to the Hebrew language that reflects the influence of the 'modern' Spanish and Southern French philologists, of whom the best known is Abraham Ibn Ezra. Moses also cites his English predecessor, Berekhiah ha-Nakdan, the subject of the rest of this chapter. His profession, 'ha-Nakdan' [the pointer], literally means a scribe who inserts vowels and other diacritical marks into a Hebrew manuscript. This twelfth-century Anglo-Norman man of Hebrew letters, however, was much more. He was an eminent rabbinic authority, but most of his works have been lost. As a result of this accident of literary history, Berekhiah is best known for two translations from Latin to Hebrew: the *Fox Fables* (*Mishle Shu'alim*), a book of Aesopian tales, and *Uncle and Nephew* (*Dodi ve-Nekhdi*), a dialogue on natural science freely adapted from Adelard of Bath's *Quaestiones naturales*. Both works are related to Chaucer's own sources: one speaks to the beast fable as an ideal genre for subversive play, as the Nun's Priest's Tale demonstrates to full effect; the other emerges from twelfth-century English scientific thought that at least indirectly informs the *Treatise on the Astrolabe*.

The literary flowering during the reign of Henry II and Eleanor of Aquitaine was marked in England by, among other things, the popularity of Aesopic fable collections. The most famous of these is justifiably Marie de France's *Fables*; in addition, the theologian and scientist Alexander Nequam wrote both a *Novus Aesopus* and *Novus Avianus* in elegiac verse as rhetorical exercises, and an otherwise unknown 'Walter the Englishman' composed by far the most popular metric fable collection, which became a standard Latin school text.[8] In this multilingual cultural milieu Berekhiah ha-Nakdan produced his own collection, the *Fox Fables*.[9] Berekhiah, like the others, for the most part translated and adapted his tales from the medieval prose translations of the first-century Latin poet Phaedrus known in various forms as *Romulus*.[10] He also drew on fables by the early fifth-century poet Avianus, and on three occasions he used extra sources from the Hebrew version of the eighth-century Arabic frame-narrative *Kalila wa-Dimna*, Peter Alfonsi's *Disciplina clericalis*, and, to great dramatic effect, the Babylonian Talmud.[11] It is possible, given his Anglo-Norman literary milieu, that he was acquainted with Marie's Old French Fables as well.[12] Berekhiah ha-Nakdan was, then, the very unusual Northern European Jewish author who engaged with the contemporary Latin and French literary world. Besides his collection of beast fables and the *Quaestiones naturales*, he translated an Anglo-Norman Lapidary, another text that shows his interest in the philosophical and scientific ideas of the so-called 'Twelfth-Century Renaissance'.[13] He also wrote two treatises, the *Book of Instruction* and the *Book of the Crucible* based on the ethical thought of Saadia Gaon and other sages, and also several lost works of biblical exegesis.[14] As a 'nakdan' or 'pointer', he was in a larger sense a grammarian and rhetorician who knows all the intricacies of the Hebrew language; his immense learning is evident in the puns based on the roots of Hebrew words that structure almost every rhymed-prose line of the *Fox Fables*. Berekhiah's work is a *tour de force* of translation from a dominant Latin cultural model into a diasporic Hebrew idiom, yet he preserves a dialogue between the two throughout a work that deals harshly with both the Jews and Christians of England, 'ii ha-yam' [the island of the sea].[15]

There are, unfortunately, only three documents outside of his literary and scientific works that mention Berekhiah and can be firmly attached to him. A codex written in Rouen by his son Elijah in 1233 celebrates Berekhiah as a biblical commentator and Talmud scholar as well as a collector of proverbs; a badly damaged second codex appears to expand on the first, mentioning Berekhiah's commentaries on all of the bible and his rabbinic responsa, calling him a 'prophet' and comparing him to Solomon in his wisdom and abundant proverbs.[16] The third, which locates him in Oxford under the French equivalent of his name, Benedict le Puinteur, records his contribution of £1 6s 8d to the 1194 *Northhampton donum*—the heavy tallage levied when Richard I returned from captivity in Germany. The most intriguing piece of evidence is that Berekhiah at some point resided in Oxford, a centre of Jewish learning and almost certainly the easiest place in England for a Jewish scholar to obtain Latin books like the *Romulus* collections, *Avianus*, or Adelard's *Quaestiones*, most likely through Christian university friends or possibly from the considerable number of books pawned to Jews.[17] There is even a good chance that Berekhiah was acquainted in some way with his fellow fabulist and exact contemporary in Oxford: Alexander Nequam, a lecturer in theology; both after all wrote poetry in the Latin fable tradition as well as works indebted to Adelard of Bath's scientific ideas.[18] Nequam, moreover, is highly unusual for his time in including a Talmudic fable about resurrection in one of his Oxford sermons (also cited by Berekhiah in his *Compendium*) and citing 'Gamaliel', a term used by Christians for rabbinic texts, several times in his writings along with telling references to his cordial scholarly conversations with Jews.[19]

Berekhiah most likely wrote the *Fox Fables* during the reign of Richard I or John, precisely at the beginning of a century's decline for English Jews. Before 1189, a number of Jews in London and elsewhere in the country had become fabulously wealthy through dealing in precious metals, pawnbroking, and moneylending.[20] In one notable case, the abbot of Peterborough pawned his church's relics, 'including…the arm of St. Oswald'.[21] Through money-lending to the gentry, Jews frequently acquired the land of their debtors, which they would usually sublet or sell at a profit.[22] The Jews' legal status defined them and their possessions as the crown's property, and therefore their great fortunes were always available to the Angevin kings. Henry II in particular exploited the Jews' wealth for short-term credit and then later increased Jewish taxes.[23] The kings' enemies, in turn, often borrowing from Jewish lenders to pay the crown, viewed these quasi-foreigners as royal agents.[24] These Jews, nevertheless, lived in relatively secure luxury within Christian England. Despite notorious anti-Jewish incidents like the Norwich blood-libel accusation of 1144, they were spared the large-scale violence that finally erupted at Richard I's coronation. The dangerous conditions were the gentry's combination of zeal for the Third Crusade and widespread resentment of the Jews' acquisition of their land through money-lending. Chaotic attacks on the delegation of prominent Jews who tried to attend the coronation ceremony in London quickly spread to further murderous riots in Bury, King's Lynn, Norwich and other towns. The crusader-led fury culminated in the 1190 massacre at York on *Shabbat ha-Gadol* where around 150 Jews sacrificed themselves or were murdered, their houses were burned, and Jewish bonds were destroyed by erstwhile debtors.[25]

Even though no local Anglo-Hebrew literature has survived in direct response to the events of 1189–90, Susan Einbinder has argued that the prevalent Jewish literary ideal in England was deeply connected to the martyrological verse and chronicles written by the Tosafist poets of France and Germany in the wake of the pogroms of First and Second Crusades.[26] These texts glorify their subjects' Sanctification of the Name (*Qiddush ha-Shem*), a heroic act that revivifies previous sacrificial ideas. This martyrdom takes as its models, from intimate to epic: Abraham's sacrifice of Isaac (the *Aqedah*) to account for parents killing their children; various accounts of the 'Ten Martyrs', Talmudic sages killed by the Romans—in some versions to atone for the selling of Joseph by his brothers—and the *Sefer Yosippon*, on the fall of the Second Temple and the mass suicide at Masada.[27] After Count Thibaut of Blois sentenced thirty-two Jews to burn at the stake in 1171, a new generation of poets' martyrological texts influenced the vocabulary of Jewish resistance to Christian persecution. These poems, which Einbinder interprets in detail, all stress an absolute refusal to convert.[28]

The English events were commemorated by Ephraim of Bonn's chronicle *Sefer Zekhirah* and two *piyutim* by continental poets, Joseph of Chartres and Menachem ben Jacob. All of these works exalt those who sacrificed themselves and their children in sanctification of the Name and call for revenge against the English or 'Romans'; Joseph of Chartres curses Richard in particular—'the king of the Isles under whose robe is the blood of innocent souls'—and traces that blood back to the day he was crowned.[29]

These texts, together with many other French and German examples, express a common medieval literary voice in the face of Christian violence: an absolute defiance through the cultivation of memory and lamentation in liturgical texts, a glorification of martyrs past and present who have atoned for their community's sins, and a call for divine salvation and the destruction of the Christians. Against this ideological background to the era of King Richard the Lionheart, Berekhiah ha-Nakdan's voice in his introduction to the *Fox Fables* is shocking. Far from offering any kind of praise or immediate comfort to his fellow English Jews, he excoriates them in the manner of the biblical prophets for their 'radical corruption'.[30] The inherently strange aspect of his text is not so much that Berekhiah chooses to apply the prophets' responses to the imminent fall of the First Temple to the crisis of the 1190s, but rather that he does so in a work mostly translated from Latin that also links him to the larger intellectual trends of the Anglo-Norman twelfth century. These dichotomies in the *Fox Fables* make Berekhiah's text generically unstable and culturally transformative. It is a translation of Latin prose into Hebrew rhyme that necessarily questions contemporary ideas of the renewal of ancient texts or *translatio studii*; at the same time, it is a work meant to be read only by Jews that never quite abandons a love for the culture of Edom, the Roman and Christian oppressors who destroyed the Second Temple and the York Jewry alike.

Ancient and medieval European fable collections crucially define translation itself as their project, since their origins are always with a distant and mythical author 'Aesop' who serves the works' ideological claims. The most influential *Romulus* collections begin with a prologue by the fictional Roman emperor 'Romulus' explaining to his son 'Tiberinus' that he has translated Aesop's fables from Greek to Latin for his edification in all moral matters.[31] Berekhiah's contemporary Marie de France, in her opening dedication to 'a flower of chivalry', traces her fables to Aesop, who in this version translated them from Greek to Latin for his master Romulus; in an epilogue she then reveals her patron as 'Count William' and inscribes her own name 'Marie' and her translation of the text into 'Romanz' from the English of King Alfred who translated it from Aesop's Latin.[32] Marie's elaborate *translatio imperii et studii*, from a Roman empire rooted in Greek culture to a unified polyglot Angevin empire exemplifies how the popular fables support a linear model of transmission that, in Rita Copeland's terms, underlines historical difference.[33] Marie's fiction of the displacement of the Latin text by two subsequent vernacular versions—English and French—in different historical eras, emphasizes the long-established imperial authority of an insular culture.

Berekhiah's *Fox Fables*, while influenced like Marie's or Nequam's projects by twelfth-century Renaissance concerns with textual recovery, Latinity, and transmission, turns to a different model of language and history. His introductory poem creates one of the text's many dualities between Hebrew and Latin: the genre, he explains, is a collection of instructive 'fables of foxes and beasts'.[34] With the term 'fox fable' itself, he invokes a specific type of Talmudic parable, many of which were in turn derived from or modelled on Aesopic fables and associated with figures of great erudition, notably Rabbi Meir, who was said to know 300. The rabbinic genre, almost entirely lost, also alludes to the loss of the great sages' wisdom and culture after the fall of the Second Temple.[35] Berekhiah makes it clear, nonetheless, that if his work recovers the Jewish past it is intercultural as well, and that he is actually translating texts from other traditions, written down by 'people of every language'. Since his 'faith is different from their faith', he has added much material and versified the fables so that they are now 'adorned with sapphires';[36] that is, they are endowed with a value possible only in the Hebrew language.[37] In a sense this is a Jewish inversion of *translatio studii*; the common medieval language—the unspoken 'imperial' Latin of the 'Romulus' texts and Avianus's fables—is made holy through a translation into a prior language that infuses it with biblical meaning and metaphor. Berekhiah's dialectic of rejection of and desire for Latinity is an expression of the multi-faceted Jewish response to the Roman conquest of Jerusalem. In the central rabbinic text devoted to this theme, *Midrash Lamentations Rabbah*, the Jews and their Roman rulers alike bear responsibility for the *ḥurban*, the destruction of the Temple. In *Sefer Yosippon*, the influential medieval Hebrew version of Josephus' *Jewish War*, the Jewish rebels, as in the original, are to blame along with Vespasian and Titus. In the subsequent European diaspora, the Jewish and Roman cultures become necessarily intermeshed more than ever.

The locale of Berekhiah's work, like the other fable collections, is Angevin England but its Hebrew is an exilic idiom. In this diasporic rather than linear model, the fables come from 'various tongues' rather than the distant Greek 'Aesop' whose name is never mentioned, and Latin becomes one of many languages to convert into a different religion, transfer to a true rather than illusory eternity, and ideally erase. As Berekhiah explains in his translation of Adelard's *Quaestiones*: 'I purified [the text] from the hand of strangers and wrote it out in the Holy Language, which is the best language.'[38] Even a Neoplatonic work in the Latin tradition like Adelard's can be recuperated and improved with Hebrew. By this account, *translatio* or *targum* (the Hebrew equivalent, as it were) geographically follows the scattered communities of Jews rather than the intellectual centres of a new European empire. A. M. Haberman, the most recent editor of the *Fox Fables*, suggests that 'Rabbi Berekhiah ben Natronai ha-Nakdan' saw himself as a peripatetic translator, deliberately following in the footsteps of the Talmudic sage Bar Kappara, who in a famous midrash recounted hundreds of Fox Fables both for entertainment and criticism of his peers. His son's exaggerated claim that he wrote 3000 proverbs at least supports an identification with Bar Kappara.[39]

Berekhiah's initial meditation on literary practice gives no warning about the scathing polemics that immediately follow. In his prologue, he confronts the plight of late twelfth-century Jews not as a result of oppression from their external enemies but as a communal internal catastrophe. His view of his fellow-Jews is low indeed: 'the congregation of England is bereft of intelligence/and crowned with shame...'[40] He draws inspiration from the Hebrew prophets, whom he quotes throughout the text, and his message is theirs: the injustice, pride and idolatry of the Jews will lead to utter ruin unless they heed his warning. He begins by characterizing his text as divine, a 'scroll of remembrance' that references Malachi 3.16: 'A scroll of remembrance has been written at

His behest concerning those who revere the Lord and remember his name.' The authority he claims for his 'pen', however, is not only for his Hebrew prophetic message but also for the translated fables that follow.

The governing image of Berekhiah's prologue is a malevolent wheel of fortune that 'turns in England, for the one to die and the other to live'.[41] The same 'ofan' [wheel] has also upended the community's own moral status, overturning truth for falsehood, righteousness for abomination, honesty for treachery, prayer for vanity, sacrifice for iniquity, discretion for whoredom.[42] The rich 'covet silver and love gold', but hoard their wealth and 'will not bend their necks to worship their Creator'.[43] Berekhiah saves a special disgust for those who have profited the most from financing the king: 'I direct my pen to a parable against falsehood'. He couches much of his invective in biblical quotations: 'They have become fat and sleek[44] from all their guile, profit from fraudulent dealings, and hypocritical flattery'.[45] As for their delusions about their London mansions and their place in English society, he characterizes them with one of the gloomiest psalms: 'They call lands by their own names, they who are like cattle'.[46] Worst of all, 'there is rejoicing in the community of hypocrites…[47]/but in the camp of the upright a voice is heard wailing'.[48] His message is clear enough if disturbing: the recent misfortunes of the English Jews have been brought on by their own relentless acquisition of money from Christians and Jews alike without regard for righteousness; as any of the biblical prophets would say, they deserve punishment for their terrible injustices to their own congregation. The passage from Jeremiah above, for example, continues: ' "Shall I not punish for these things?" says the Lord; "shall my soul not be avenged on a nation such as this?" '.[49] More specifically, Henry II and now Richard have kept the Jews as their subjects for mutual benefit; but however much property they have, the king's boot is always on their necks. An incident, furthermore, like the London coronation massacre, in which great rabbinic scholars were killed, happened because of the London magnates' own arrogance, insincere flattery, and impiety. In his own prophetic terms, 'Berekhiah curses and abjures the times'.[50]

Berekhiah concludes of his community's fall from good to evil: 'the wheel that joins all this together constantly runs over us'.[51] The wheel of change is of course a common ancient image, and versions even appear in a few rabbinic texts.[52] Given his project, however, Berekhiah here clearly evokes the Boethian wheel of *Fortuna* ubiquitous among Christian scholars in an opening display of Latinity. His central frame of reference, however, is ultimately not to a wheel that represents the changeable nature of the world within a Neoplatonic frame; rather, he refers to the wheels in the Book of Ezekiel, the great post-exilic prophet. In his prologue, Berekhiah describes his metaphoric wheel as part of a 'merkava' [chariot], choosing a term that immediately evokes the celestial chariot in Ezekiel's visions of the throne of the Divine Presence.[53] Rashi explicates Ezekiel 1.4, 'A tempest was coming from the north': 'That is the chariot [merkava] of the throne of the glory of the God's presence [shechinah]. Since it came with fury to destroy Israel, it is therefore likened to a tempest and a cloud'.[54] In the prophet's elaborately detailed visions, the spinning wheels, their rims lined with eyes, support the fiery heavenly beings—or cherubs—who attend first to God's call to Ezekiel[55] and then to the doom of the Temple and Jerusalem.[56] These wheels are the opposite of the wheel of fortune destroying the English Jews from a human perspective; they represent a divine perspective that now foresees the destruction of a diaspora city rather than Jerusalem. The imagery becomes clear with Berekhiah's even more explicit and bizarre reference to Ezekiel. He describes himself as filled with a kind of prophetic 'secret' discourse' and then tells his reader—as God tells Ezekiel—to 'eat this scroll, for out of the eater shall come forth meat, and sense shall issue from the sensible'.[57] This 'scroll', however, is not Ezekiel's message of lamentation but rather the collection of translated Aesopic beast fables, which Berekhiah explains are intended 'to strengthen hands that are weak'.[58] Berekhiah's learned readers would have been steeped in the prophets from Shabbat *haftarot* readings and liturgical poetry both ancient and recent, yet the prophetic language with which Berekhiah blasts his immediate community is destabilized and reinvigorated by its new context. Berekhiah interprets the prophets beyond the realm of traditional rabbinic commentary and poetry, in a work that is *hizoni*, outside any kind of Hebrew canon, and almost entirely translated from other languages.

Berekhiah shows his identification with Ezekiel in another particularly clever pun in Fable Sixty-Six that is well worth mentioning because of its relation to another sometime 'Anglo-Norman' author. He borrows a short parable from the Jewish convert Peter Alfonsi's *Disciplina clericalis* about a mule who, when asked by a curious fox about his parents, responds with shame over his ass father by talking instead about his uncle, a powerful horse. In Peter's frame-narrative, the occasion for this fable is an Arab poet insulting another poet with a 'noble mother' and a 'lowborn father' who glories in his eminent poet uncle instead.[59] Berekhiah, with some subtlety but not too much, savages the author with his own Latin text. For Berekhiah, Peter, who had converted in name and faith from Moses to one of the most vehement Christian opponents of his own former religion in his *Dialogi contra Judaeos*, deserves a special kind of translation from literary Latin into his 'original language' of Hebrew. Not only is Berekhiah's fable unusually heavily laden with biblical and Talmudic phrases, but it also attacks the very idea of conversion. Peter Alfonsi, revered by the Christians, is an ugly mule, an ignorant poet, and worse. In his second short epimythium he declares: 'I Berekhiah said rashly, "woe to the one who will be called from the family of shame [Buzi] /All who fall from their father's merits [i.e. Peter] would be better off as stillborn foetuses." ' The punning wordplay here is on 'Ezekiel son of Buzi': the name literally refers to the Hebrew word for the disgraceful essence of the convert's actions.

If the collections of 'Romulus', Marie de France and 'Walter the Englishman' intend to impart wisdom to the reader, so too does the *Fox Fables*. Berekhiah elevates this pedagogical function, however, to the potential salvation for his corrupt community, and he carries over his prophetic voice into the unit of the fable. As in the other collections, each fable has an epimythium or 'mashal' explaining its meaning; frequently, Berekhiah, writing in first person and sometimes inscribing his name, adds a second epimythium in verse, gesturing toward a very cranky frame-narrative. Berekhiah's authentic work consists of around 110 fables from various sources but predominantly the familiar Latin texts.[60] Although there is not enough space in this chapter to consider the bulk of

Berekhiah's text, four further fables from different sources will demonstrate his theory of translation, ambivalence towards his source material, and adaptation of the genre into his style of fiery social criticism. For Berekhiah, the *Fox Fables'* palimpsest of Hebrew texts produced mostly from Latin is a means of presenting a polyvocal account of a fragile thirteenth-century England. Just as Marie de France's *Fables* occasionally offer an overt critique of the Angevin courts that she evidently knew first-hand, Berekhiah's prophetic scroll unravels the rest of the woes of a Jewry that eventually would be ruined by the very same powers.[61]

Berekhiah's Fable Seven, 'Dog, Ewe, Lion and Wolf', is a classic Aesopic tale of harsh injustice and pathos that appears in both the *Romulus Nilanti* and Marie's *Fables*: A Dog accuses a Ewe of stealing bread and has two false witnesses—a Wolf and an Eagle—back him up.[62] The judges are duly bribed and sentence the Ewe to pay back the weight of the bread she had stolen. The Ewe has nothing other than her fleece, which she has shorn off and uses to pay the false debt. Without her fleece, she is subject to the torments of summer and winter, and she sorrows for her children as well. When she finally dies, the Wolf and the Eagle reappear and devour her carcass. Berekhiah's epimythium explains that the fable is for a generation that commits violence and deceit, and 'the ruler listens to falsehood'.[63] While this 'mashal' likely sums up the opinion of most English Jews following the persecutions of Blois, London, and York, Berekhiah's larger innovations to the text are of an exegetical nature. The meaning of his fable hinges on a pun based on the word for 'ewe' [rechelah] and the matriarch Rachel: the ewe [Rachel] weeps for her children,[64] and then in the snow the ewe [Rachel] 'die[s] by the way'.[65] These intertexts, besides underlining Berekhiah's cleverness and addition of lambs to the fable, demonstrate how translation from Latin to the holy language of Hebrew—from 'ovis' to 'rechelah'—reveals the text as an allegory of Jewish identity and exile.

Much of the Jewish medieval exegetical tradition on these texts derives from *Midrash Genesis Rabbah*. One of the glosses of *Genesis Rabbah* to 'And Rachel died and was buried...' reads 'Rabbi Simeon ben Gamaliel taught...We find Israel [the nation] named after Rachel as it says: Rachel weeping for her children...' A further gloss explains: 'What was Jacob's reason for burying Rachel in the way to Ephrath? Jacob foresaw that the exiles would pass on from thence, therefore he buried her there so that she might pray for mercy for them. Thus it is written, "A voice is heard in Ramah...Rachel weeping for her children...Thus says the Lord: refrain your voice from weeping...and there is hope for your future..."'[66] The Ewe of the fable may be the victim of a predatory Christian society that is a condition of exile, but the focus of Berekhiah's text shifts to the figure if Rachel as both the Israelite nation and intercessor for the nation's sins. With this, the allegory returns to the prophetic idea of the prologue in which the drama of Jewish diaspora and return has little to do with the Romans and their successors.

Given that the fable does consider the oppression of Jews by Christians, however, the well-known Christian interpretations of the same biblical passages also clearly underlie Berekhiah's text. Jerome reads Jeremiah 31.14 as a major point of controversy between Jewish and Christian exegesis, citing the 'literal' Jewish exegesis in order to discredit it.[67] The Christian tradition derives from Matthew 2.16–18: for the apostle, the passage refers to Herod's futile attempt to murder Jesus in the 'massacre of the innocents' after Mary and Joseph flee to Egypt: 'Then was fulfilled what had been spoken through the prophet Jeremiah.' Berekhiah incidentally refutes the Christian interpretation through his linguistic certainty about the meaning produced by Hebrew itself, as opposed to a Latin translation of Hebrew and Greek like the Vulgate; his view of the gospel, however, seems to be the same as his view of Jewish scripture: its leading believers have become deeply corrupt, violent, Herod-like rulers and have abandoned its message.

Berekhiah leaves the one tale taken from *Kalila Wa-Dimna* virtually unchanged in plot, perhaps because it already suited his grim view of human existence: in Fable Sixty-eight, a man is trapped in a pit between a lion above and a serpent below, and he stands on two spikes while a black and a white mouse gnaw them away; he finds honey in the side of the pit, which makes him happy until the spikes break and he falls into the serpent's lair.[68] More or less as in the Arabic original, the pit represents the world, the lion death, the serpent the evil inclination that is the open mouth of hell, the mice the day and night of passing time, and the honey the pleasures of the world that make him oblivious to the dangers. Berekhiah's rewriting is not only to add numerous biblical passages but to make the Persian physician Borzouyeh's universal tale into a particularizing reminder of the Jews' corruption, this time applying Deuteronomy 32.15 from the song of Moses to Israel, to the fable's honey of pleasure. Since in the previous line a generous God feeds his people honey and oil, Berekhiah adds: 'but Jeshurun grew fat and kicked', a line that begins a long account of how the people have become 'fat and gross and coarse' and above all, idolators. Their pleasure has become a rejection of the Creator.[69]

In Fable Six, Berekhiah is at his most subversive, reinventing the most famous 'Fox Fable' of the Talmud, 'Fox and Fishes'. In B. Berekhot 61b, Rabbi Akiva tells this parable to Pappas ben Judah in order to explain his own willingness to die for the Torah by publicly teaching against the edict of the Roman government. The text as a whole addresses the nature of martyrdom itself, and as such is vital to Berekhiah's polemics against his contemporaries. In the fable, a fox sees swarms of fish swimming around frantically and asks them what they're fleeing; they reply that they're trying to escape from fishermen's nets. The fox tries to trick them into coming up onto land by offering them the memory of a distant peace that they used to have with his ancestors. The fish, however, answer that since they live badly enough in their own element of water, it would be much worse on land where they would die. The 'epimythium' that Rabbi Akiva provides is: 'So it is with us. If such is our condition when we sit and study the Torah, of which it is written, "for that is thy life and the length of thy days",[70] if we go and neglect it how much worse off we shall be!' Rabbi Akiva, having affirmed his own element as Torah, is martyred in the exemplary fashion of suffering his body to be raked with iron combs while reciting the Shema. After his death, 'a *bat kol* went forth and proclaimed, happy are you, Rabbi Akiva, that you are destined for the life of the world to come'.[71]

In Berekhiah's essentially parodic version of the fable, the Fox observes in the water that the fish are ruining each other with dissension, the big chasing and attacking the small. The Fox gives a political speech much lengthier than the original in his effort to rule over them: he first asks them whether the law of their community is that they destroy each other: 'Each fights his brother every man his neighbour.'[72] He then rather persuasively cites a number of messianic passages from the bible as part of his vision for his kingship, including: 'Nation shall not lift sword against nation'[73] and 'Nothing evil or vile shall be done'.[74] One of the fish finally replies more or less exactly like Rabbi Akiva's fish: their situation is precarious because, even when they are living in peaceful waters, external forces like fishermen and hunters assail them. He then warns the fox that even if he were king he could never be secure, and finally offers as a kind of excuse for the vicious fish-hierarchy: the ironic comment that 'even humans quarrel with each other out of jealousy / But one high official is protected by a higher one, and both of them by still higher ones'.[75]

Having twisted Rabbi Akiva's fox fable from a parable of martyrdom into a tale of hypocrisy, Berekhiah proceeds to deliver a damning epimythium or mashal followed by a second, in which he repeats the same sentence from Mishnah Sotah: 'The face of this generation is the face of a dog':[76] that is, shameless. In the context of the *Fox Fables*, this expression is a dire pronouncement about the state of things after the fall of the Second Temple, but before the advent of the messiah. In this era, when the Roman Empire has become Christian, the Jews will abandon all values of scholarship and family: 'insolence will increase and honour dwindle'. Berekhiah's further biblical curses include: 'When there is rebellion in the land, hypocrites multiply';[77] and, in the second epimythium, 'they are spies but there is no Joshua or Caleb among them'.[78] In this dizzying display of creative commentary on rabbinic exegesis, Berekhiah's point is nonetheless focused: he absolutely denies his own English community's claim to Rabbi Akiva's and other martyrs' exemplarity to define their current situation, despite the literary precedents of the Crusade Chronicles and liturgical laments written in France and Germany. Against the grain as it is, Berekhiah's acid tone actually leaves open the possibility that he rejects twelfth-century martyrological writing. His epimythium, with its multiplying hypo-crites, is in particular an attack on the contemporary celebration of well-known rabbinic legends like the *Midrash of the Ten Martyrs*, which describes the Romans' grisly executions of ten of the great sages, including Rabbi Akiva, Rabbi Ishmael, and Rabbi Haninah ben Teradion.[79] As with the Talmudic 'fox fable', the possibility of the Jews' finding a pure source of imitation in such texts is foreclosed by their rampant hypocrisy: Berekhiah's fish destroy *each other*, but then deploy the idiom of martyrdom. His era, Berekhiah finally declares, is like that of the disobedient spies whom God punishes in Numbers 13–14; just as there are no righteous men like Joshua and Caleb, there are also none like the rabbinic sages. Jews may die at the hands of oppressive rulers, but they rarely have the merit to be martyrs.

Finally, Fable Ninety-Five, 'Statue and Man', is the most self-reflexive and therefore most tricky of Berekhiah's parables, features a talkative idol as both protagonist and antagonist. The fable is one of several that Berekhiah takes from the Late Latin poet Avianus, a source used by Nequam but neither by the 'Romulus' collections nor Marie de France. In the original text, a craftsman puts a marble statue of Bacchus up for sale, and the potential buyers are a man who wants to put it on his future tomb and a man who wants to put the god in his temple. The statue pipes up and attempts to persuade the craftsman that consigning him to his 'death sentence' on the tomb will reflect badly on his work. The outcome is unresolved, and Avianus simply concludes that it applies to those who have the power to do good or bad.[80] The idol (as Haim Schwarzbaum notes, assessing the previous literature), is a satirical powerless figure, reduced to begging for his life.[81]

The first thing that is striking about Berekhiah's version is that the idol—by definition the worst possible object in Judaism—retains some of his charming if pathetic character. Berekhiah immediately establishes that the statue is absolutely an idol, a 'no-god' in the ubiquitous term of the prophets. A rich man nonetheless wants to make it his god because of its beauty (it is 'drawn and painted in vermilion', another derogatory description of idols by the prophets),[82] and, as in Avianus, a second man wants it to adorn a tomb. At this, the idol starts to cry and begs the craftsman to sell him to the man who will 'fear' and 'worship' him, and perversely he uses phrases to seduce the craftsman that in the bible apply to God: '[I am] the clay, and you are the potter'[83]; 'Do not subject me to the will of my foes'.[84] His final plea is that if his maker sells him to the worshipper, 'everyone in the Isles ('iim) will agree and bow down to the work of your hands'.[85] After this, the craftsman gives in and sells him to the Englishman who will turn him from a no-god into a god.

The fable appears to be yet another condemnation of the English (everyone in the Isles) for their idolatry, Christians and Jews alike. Possibly Berekhiah even literally means to suggest idols common to Christians and Jews like the aforementioned arm of St. Osbert and other religious articles pawned to Jews, or Christian religious items produced by Jewish metalworkers.[86] The epimythium, however, vindicates the idol's obsequious personality by approving of flattering the powerful. Quoting passages from the Talmud, Berekhiah affirms that a 'great sage' said, discussing Jacob's flattery of Esau, that 'it is permissible to flatter the evil in this world'. Another sage, referring to Joseph's brothers bowing to him, recommended the 'popular saying': 'bow down to the fox in his day of power!'[87]

In this extraordinary ending, Berekhiah refers to the unvoiced underlying theme of the precarious relations between Jacob, metaphor for the Jews, and his brother Esau, metaphor for the Romans and then the Christians. In doing so, however, he projects an ambiguous Jewish identity back onto the abject weeping idol who flatters his powerful seller. Although it lacks a certain coherence as a Jewish 'fox fable', the tale operates on an allegorical level that shows Berekhiah's consideration of his own relationship to the work of 'Esau', his Latin sources, and by extension the suppressed, even if absurd, idol of Bacchus from Avianus. For Berekhiah, this is the moment to assess his practice of translating the words of the Roman 'idolators' into the 'Holy language'. While the transformation from the Latin works to the full Hebrew text is in a sense thoroughgoing, filled with biblical and rabbinic material and characterized as a prophetic message, the genre of the fables and even the epimythia in many cases remain much the same. Berekhiah's Bacchus is then, in addition to the no-god of the prophets, the allegorized no-god or *integumentum* of the Latin medieval mythographers, a symbol of drunkenness and transgression distantly derived from Ovid's havoc-wreaking trickster. Berekhiah's English contemporary, the so-called 'Third Vatican Mythographer', attributes a wide range of meanings to Bacchus, most having to do with wine; he also, however, draws a connection between Bacchus/Liber and poetry, both because 'poems merit eternity' like the ivy consecrated to Bacchus and because 'like the Bacchae, poets are insane'.[88] Bacchus' trace in this fable is the sign of Berekhiah's own transgressive literary practices: while he has recuperated for Jacob the multiplicity of lost Talmudic 'fox fables' recited by Bar Kappara or Rabbi Meir he has also flattered Esau in the form of Romulus, Avianus and even Boethius for his Latin poetic art.

Berekhiah ha-Nakdan is a singular Jewish author both in his fury toward his peers and in his attraction to and transformative rejection of Latin in his Hebrew adaptations and free translations. He was, despite his situation within a marginalized community, truly a writer of the Angevin historical moment. Berekhiah's choice of genres, including Adelard of Bath's scientific-philosophical dialogue and the lapidary, were those on the cutting edge of Anglo-Latin and Anglo-French literature revived from ancient sources. Berekhiah's voices resound from his masterpiece of reinvention, the *Fox Fables*, as the 'prophet' that his son Elijah called him but also a fox of cultural adaptation; Berekhiah was enraged by everything around him yet determined to write a 'scroll' of instruction for Jews out of the Latin Aesop. In his range of concerns with the social injustices of 'the Isle of the Sea' and his many literary, scientific and philosophical interests, Berekhiah is like Chaucer, a quintessentially English author.

NOTES

1. On Peter Alfonsi's direct influence on twelfth- and thirteenth-century English anti-Jewish polemics, see R. W. Hunt, 'The Disputation of Peter of Cornwall against Simon the Jew' in *Studies in Medieval History Presented to Frederick Maurice Powicke*, ed. R. W. Hunt et al. (Oxford: Clarendon Press, 1948), 143–56.

2. Raphael Loewe, 'The Medieval Christian Hebraists of England: The Superscriptio Lincolniensis', *Hebrew Union College Annual* 28 (1957), 205–52; Beryl Smalley, *Hebrew Scholarship among Christians in XIIIth Century England as Illustrated by some Hebrew-Latin Psalters* (London: Shapiro, Valentine, 1939).

3. The standard work on the Tosafists—twelfth-century commentators on the Talmud and Rashi's commentary on the Talmud and biblical exegetes—is E. E. Urbach, *The Tosafists: Their History, Writings and Methods* 5th ed., 2 vols. (Jerusalem: Bialik Institute, 1986), 493–520 [Hebrew]; his chapter on the English Tosafists is in vol. 2, 493–520. On the commentaries, see also Israel Moses Ta-Shma, 'Tosafot'. *Encyclopaedia Judaica*. Ed. Michael Berenbaum and Fred Skolnik. 2nd ed., vol. 20 (Detroit, MI: Macmillan Reference, 2007), 67–70.

4. Cecil Roth, *The Intellectual Activities of Medieval English Jewry* (Oxford: Oxford University Press, 1948).

5. On this figure, see the important recent study by Pinchas Roth and Ethan Zadoff, 'The Talmudic Community of Thirteenth-Century England, in *Christians and Jews in Medieval England: The York Massacre of 1190, Narratives and Contexts*. Ed. Sarah Rees Jones and Sethina Watson (York: York Medieval Press, 2013), 184–203.

6. Jacob ben Yehuda Hazan of London, *Etz Hayyim*, ed. Israel Brodie, vol. 1 (Jerusalem: Institute HaRav Kook, 1962), 127–31. For a comprehensive account of the text see the two articles by David Kaufmann, 'The Etz Chayim of Jacob B. Jehudah of London, and the History of His Manuscript', *Jewish Quarterly Review* 5 (1893), 353–74, and 'The Prayer-Book According to the Ritual of England before 1290', *Jewish Quarterly Review* 4 (1891), 20–63.

7. A new edition and translation of all Meir's poems is *Into the Light: The Medieval Hebrew Poetry of Meir of Norwich*, trans. Ellam Crasnow and Bente Elsworth (Norwich: East Publishing, 2013). See also Susan Einbinder, 'Meir ben Elijah of Norwich: Persecution and Poetry among Medieval English Jews', *Journal of Medieval History* 26 (2000), 145–62.

8. For an overview, see Jill Mann, *From Aesop to Reynard: Beast Literature in Medieval Britain* (Oxford: Oxford University Press, 2009), 1–52. Marie de France's *Fables* have been edited and translated by Harriet Spiegel (Toronto: University of Toronto Press 1987). On Nequam's fables, see R. W. Hunt. *The Schools and the Cloister: The Life and Writings of Alexander Nequam (1157–217)*, ed. Margaret Gibson (Oxford: Oxford University Press, 1987). See also A. Neubauer and Joseph Jacobs, 'Berechiah Naqdan', *Jewish Quarterly Review* 2 (1890), 520–6. Nequam's six fables from Avianus are in *Novus Avianus*, ed. Thomas Klein in *Favolisti Latini Medievali e Umanistici* 7 (Genoa: Università di Genova, 1998); his forty-two fables from the 'Romulus' collections are in *Novus Aesopus*, ed. Giovanni Garbugino, *Favolisti Latini Medievali e Umanistici* 2 (Genoa: Università di Genova, 1987). For the unidentified 'Walter the Englishman', see *The Fables of 'Walter of England'*, ed. Aaron E. Wright (Toronto: Pontifical Institute of Medieval Studies, 1997).

9. Berekhiah ha-Nakdan, *Mishle Shu'alim (Fox Fables)*, ed. A. M. Haberman (Jerusalem: Shocken, 1946), in Hebrew. A. Neubauer and Joseph Jacobs, 'Berechiah Naqdan', *Jewish Quarterly Review* 2 (1890), 520–6.

10. Of the texts most relevant to this study: the 'Romulus Nilanti' is collected in the five-volume Léopold Hervieux, ed., *Les fabulistes Latins depuis le siècle d'Auguste jusqu'à la fin du Moyen Âge*, vol. 2 (Paris:Firmin-Didot, 1894), 512–63. The *Romulus Vulgaris* is in Georg Thiele, ed., *Der Laeinische Äsop des Romulus und die Prosa-Fassungen des Phädrus* (Heidelberg: C. Winter, 1910), and Hervieux, *Les fabulistes Latin*, 197–264. The original *Phaedrus* is edited and translated by Ben Edwin Perry in *Babrius and Phaedrus* (Cambridge, MA: Harvard University Press, 1965), 191–417.

11. The fables of Avianus are edited and translated by J. W. Duff and Arnold Duff in *Minor Latin Poets* vol. 2 (Cambridge, MA: Harvard University Press, 1935), 669–749; The *Kalila wa-Dimna* of Ibn al Muqaffa' has been translated into French by André Miquel as *Le Livre de Kalila et Dimna* (Paris: Klincksieck, 1957; repr. 2012). Berechiah would have used the twelfth-century Hebrew translation attributed to a certain 'Rabbi Joel': *Deux versions Hébraique du Livre de Kalilah et Dimnah*, ed. Joseph Derenbourg (Paris: F. Vieweg, 1881), 1–309. I quote Petrus's *Disciplina clericalis* from the translation by Joseph Jones and John Keller as *The Scholar's Guide* (Toronto: Pontifical Institute of Medieval Studies, 1969).

12. Tovi Bibring, ' "Would that my words were Inscribed": Berechiah ha-Naqdan's *Mishlei Shu'alim* and European Fable Traditions', in *Latin-into-Hebrew: Texts and Studies*, ed. Resianne Fontaine and Gad Freudenthal (Leiden: Brill, 2013), 1:309–29. Bibring makes a convincing argument for Berechiah's borrowing of details from some of Marie's fables in his own versions.

13. Berakhyah ben Natronai Ha-Nakdan, *Sefer Ko'aḥ Ha-Avanim (On the Virtue of the Stones)*, ed. and trans. Gerrit Bos and Julia Zwink (Leiden: Brill, 2010).

14. Roth, *Intellectual Activities*, 48–51; Norman Golb, *The Jews of Medieval Normandy* (Cambridge: Cambridge University Press 1998), 324–47.

15. This term ('ii ha-yam), taken from Isaiah 11.11 was used as a name for England in the twelth and thirteenth centuries. See Ephraim of Bonn, *Sefer Zechirah*, ed, A. M. Haberman (Jerusalem: Bialik Institute, 1970), 34; and Joseph of Chartres, 'A Hebrew Elegy on the York Martyrs of 1190', ed. Cecil Roth, *Transactions of the Jewish Historical Society of England* 16 (1945/51), 212–20.

16. Both documents are edited and deciphered by Golb, *Jews of Medieval Normandy*, 324–33.

17. Cecil Roth, *The Jews of Medieval Oxford* (Oxford: Clarendon Press, 1951), 118–19. Several scholars believe that Berechiah spent time in Angevin Normandy as well as in England. Based on his son Elijah's testimony, Golb argues that Berechiah was born in Rouen and educated and based in Normandy, despite the clearly English *Fox Fables*. While this is certainly possible, there appears to be no solid evidence of the account. It is also no surprise that Berechiah's son would have moved to Normandy in the thirteenth century, as did many English Jews as the situation in England worsened under Henry III.

18. See Hunt, *Schools*, 73 on Adelard's influence on Nequam's *De naturis rerum*.

19. Hunt, *Schools*, 108–10; Raphael Loewe and R. W. Hunt, 'Alexander Neckam's Knowledge of Hebrew', *Medieval and Renaissance Studies* 4 (1958), 17–34. The most striking of Neckham's rabbinic references is a Gematria about the names of Sarah and Abraham.

20. Robert Stacey, 'Jewish Lending and the Medieval English Economy' in *A Commercialising Economy: England 1086-c.1300*, ed. R. H. Britnell and Bruce Campbell (Manchester: Manchester University Press, 1995), 78–101; Joe Hillaby, 'The London Jewry: William I to John', *Jewish Historical Studies* 33 (1992–94), 1–44.

21. Hillaby, 'London Jewry', 9.

22. H. G. Richardson, *English Jewry under Angevin Kings* (London: Methuen, 1960), 83–92.

23. Richardson, *English Jewry*, 121.

24. Robin Mundill, *England's Jewish Solution, Experiment and Expulsion, 1262–1290* (Cambridge: Cambridge University Press, 1998), 17–18; see also M. T. Clanchy, *From Memory to Written Record, England 1066-1307*, 2nd ed. (London: Wiley-Blackwell, 1993), on Jews as foreigners within England.

25. The best accounts of these events are R. B Dobson's *The Jews of York and the Massacre of March 1190*, 2nd ed. (York: Borthwick Institute, 1996) and Robert Stacey's 'Crusades, Martyrdoms, and the Jews of Norman England, 1096–1190', in *Juden und Christen zur Zeit der Kreuzzüge*, ed. Alfred Haverkamp (Sigmaringen: Jan Thorbecke Verlag, 1999).

26. Susan Einbinder, *Beautiful Death: Jewish Poetry and Martyrdom in Medieval France* (Philadelpia, PA: University of Pennsylvania Press, 2002), 17–44.

27. For the most comprehensive treatment of these constructs, see Jeremy Cohen, *Sanctifying the Name of God: Jewish Martyrs and Jewish Memories of the First Crusade* (Philadelphia, PA: University of Pennsylvania Press, 2004); on the uses of the Aqedah narrative, see the classic work by Shalom Spiegel, *The Last Trial*, trans. Judah Goldin (New York: Jewish Lights, 1967).

28. Einbinder, *Beautiful Death*, 45–69.

29. Joseph of Chartres, 'York Martyrs', 217.

30. Walther Zimmerli, *Ezekiel 1: A Commentary*, trans. Ronald Clements (Philadelphia, PA: Fortress, 1979), 58.

31. 'Romulus Nilanti', in Hervieux, *Les fabulistes Latin*, 513–14; Thiele, *Der Lateinische Äsop*, 2–6.

32. See R. Howard Bloch, *The Anonymous Marie de France* (Chicago, IL: University of Chicago Press, 2003), 114–15.

33. Rita Copeland, *Rhetoric, Hermeneutics and Translation in the Middle Ages* (Cambridge: Cambridge University Press, 1995), 106–7.

34. Berekhiah ha-Nakdan, *Fox Fables,* 1. There is a full English translation of *Fox Fables* by Moses Hadas, *Fables of a Jewish Aesop* (New York: Columbia University Press, 1967); however, this work (a draft published after his death) has some errors and omissions and is rendered in an archaic English. It also includes no references to Berehiah's biblical and rabbinic citations. I follow Hadas's translations when appropriate or emend them. I include page references to them regardless alongside Haberman's edition. For Berekhiah's quotations from the bible, I use the translations in the Jewish Publication Society's Hebrew-English Tanakh, second edition (Philadelphia, PA: Jewish Publication Society, 1999). Haim Schwarzbaum's exhaustive work examines each fable separately: *The Mishle Shu'alim (Fox Fables) of Rabbi Berechiah Ha-Nakdan: A Study in Comparative Folklore and Fable Lore* (Kiron, Israel: Institute for Jewish and Arab Folklore Research, 1979).

35. As in the famous catalogue of sages who have died as an index of decline in Mishnah Sotah 9.15: 'When Rabbi Meir died there were no more makers of parables.' Rabbi Meir also appears in BT Sanhedrin 38b: 'Even as R. Johanan said: When R. Meir used to deliver his public discourses, a third was Halacha, a third Haggadah, and a third consisted of parables. R Johanan also said: R. Meir had three hundred *parables of foxes,* and we have only three left' (emphasis added).

36. Song of Songs 5.14.

37. Berekhiah, *Fox Fables,* 1; Hadas, *Fables* 1.

38. Berekhiah ha-Nakdan, *Uncle and Nephew (Dodi ve-Nekhdi),* ed. and. trans. Hermann Gollancz (Oxford: Oxford University Press, 1920), English, 16 (translation slightly emended); Hebrew, 10.

39. *Midrash Qohelet Rabbah,* 1.3; see A. Cohen, trans., *Midrash Ecclesiates Rabbah,* (London: Soncino Press, 1983), 9–10; Berekhiah, *Fox Fables,* vi-vii. In his interpretation of the *Fox Fables,* Marc Michael Epstein begins by asking why 'the possibility that medieval Jews, the inheritors of biblical and talmudic literature, might have continued the tradition of political and theological uses of fables not merely in emulation of the surrounding culture, but as a very pointed and effective means of expression and critique is seldom considered'; ' "The Ways of Truth are Curtailed and Hidden": A Medieval Hebrew Fable as a Vehicle for Covert Polemic', *Prooftexts* 14 (1994), 205–31, at 206.

40. Berekhiah, *Fox Fables,* 5; Hadas, *Fables,* 4. Epstein reads Berekhiah's assessment of England as largely an attack on Christians that is similar in tone to other Jewish polemics: 'A Medieval Hebrew Fable', 217–21. He focuses on Fable 107, 'Elephant and Hunter' as an allegory of Christian intellectual persecution of the Jews.

41. Berekhiah, *Fox Fables,* 3. I follow the translation of Neubauer and Jacobs, 'Berekhiah Naqdan', 522.

42. Berekhiah, *Fox Fables,* 4. Hadas, *Fables,* 3. All of these oppositions involve elaborate plays on words that exemplify Berekhiah's linguistic pyrotechnics: the most obvious is the play on *mashal* (fable) and the differently pointed verb *mashal* (it rules).

43. Berekhiah, *Fox Fables,* 4. Hadas, *Fables,* 2–3.

44. Jeremiah 5.28.

45. Berekhiah, *Fox Fables,* 4 Hadas, 3.

46. Psalms 49.12.

47. Job 15.34.

48. Berekhiah, *Fox Fables,* 5; Hadas, *Fables,* 4.

49. Jeremiah 5.29.

50. Berekhiah, *Fox Fables*, 4–5; Hadas, *Fables*, 4. Although excessive, Berekhiah's warnings reflect a side of the English Jews that is occasionally revealed in official government records: their lawsuits (including a duel between two Jews), the rivalries among the king's financiers, and their conspicuous consumption. See Richardson, *English Jewry*, 113; Hillaby, 'London Jewry', 19–21; Roth, *Intellectual Activities*, 42–4. Needless to say, Berekhiah's disgust likely derives just as much from issues that arose in rabbinic courts or from rabbinic judges themselves.

51. Berekhiah, *Fox Fables*, 4; Hadas, *Fables*, 3.

52. A wheel of change (not a *rota fortunae*) appears in a famous passage on poverty and wealth in B. Shabbat 151.

53. 'The wheel of the chariot (Exodus. 14.25) turns around in its stratagems (Job 37.12), over the good to subjugate them and over the evil to deliver them'. Berekhiah, *Fox Fables*, 3; Hadas, 2.

54. Menachem Cohen, ed., *Mikra'ot Gedolot 'Ha-Keter': Ezekiel*, (Ramat-Gan, Israel, 2000), 3–4; A. J. Rosenberg, trans., *The Book of Ezekiel*, vol. 1 (New York: Judaica Press, 2000), 5.

55. Ezekiel 1.

56. Ezekiel 10.

57. Berekhiah, *Fox Fables*, 5; Hadas, *Fables*, 4. See also Epstein, 'A Medieval Hebrew Fable', 215–16 for an insightful approach to Berekhiah's authorial relationship to a Jewish version of Umberto Eco's 'ideal reader'—here the ideal eater.

58. Berekhiah, *Fox Fables*, 5; Hadas, *Fables*, 5.

59. Alfonsi, *Scholar's Guide*, 47. For a discussion of Peter Alfonsi as a culturally 'Norman' author in terms of the *Disciplina clericalis*'s popularity and literary influence, see Suzanne Conklin Akbari, 'Between Diaspora and Conquest: Norman Assimilation in Petrus Alfonsi's *Disciplina clericalis* and Marie de France's *Fables*', in *Cultural Diversity in the British Middle Ages: Archipelago, Island, England*, ed. Jeffrey Jerome Cohen (New York: Palgrave Macmillan, 2008), 17–37.

60. In his edited volume of Berekhiah's *Fox Fables*, Haberman discusses the manuscripts of the *Fox Fables* and the various inauthentic fables added in later versions, vii.

61. See Bloch, *The Anonymous Marie de France*, 175–205. It should be said that Berekhiah is not the sole medieval Jewish writer to transmit parables ultimately from the Greek and Latin traditions. In one misogynistic example from the Talmud, an enigmatic reference in B. Kiddushin 80b to 'A certain woman: It once happened that she took him out' prompts a retelling, in the Tosafot, of the bawdy tale of 'The woman who hangs her dead husband's body on a tree to save her lover' or 'The Widow of Ephesus', which appears in Petronius' *Satyricon*, all of the *Romulus* collections, Marie de France's *Fables* (as 'De la femme ki fist pendre sun mari', in which she somewhat tones down the misogyny) and of course Berekhiah's text, Fable eighty. See Schwarzbaum, *The Mishle Shu'alim*, 399.

62. The original in *Phaedrus* is very different in its punishment of a wrongdoer: there, after the 'trial', the sheep finds the wolf, the false witness, dead in a pit a few days later. Perry, *Phaedrus*, 213. Berekhiah's version is closest to the 'Romulus Nilanti' (Hervieux, *Les fabulists Latin*, 515); Marie interestingly treats it in her epimythium as a fable about social injustices perpetrated by the rich (Spiegel, *Fables*, 40–3).

63. Berekhiah, *Fox Fables*, 15; Hadas, *Fables* 19.

64. Jeremiah 31.14.

65. Genesis 35.19.

66. H. Freedman, trans., *Midrash Rabbah, Genesis II* (New York: Soncino, 1983), 759–61.

67. Jerome, *In Hieremiam prophetam libri VI*, ed. S. Reiter (Turnhout: Brepols, 1960), 306–8.

68. Miquel, *Le Livre de Kalila et Dimna*, 47–8.
69. Berekhiah, *Fox Fables*, 75–6; Hadas, *Fables*, 122–3.
70. Deuteronomy 30.20.
71. B. Berakhot 61b, Soncino Talmud, trans. Maurice Cohen (London: Soncino, 1990).
72. Berekhiah, *Fox Fables*, 13; Hadas, *Fables*, 16.
73. Isaiah 2.40.
74. Isaiah 65.25.
75. Ecclesiates 5.7. Berekhiah, *Fox Fables*, 14; Hadas, *Fables*, 17.
76. M Sotah 9, Soncino Talmud, trans. A. Cohen (London: Soncino, 1994).
77. Proverbs 28.12, with 'kings' replaced by 'hypocrites'.
78. Berekhiah, *Fox Fables*, 14; Hadas, *Fables*, 18.
79. For an English translation by David Stern of this text, also known as *Midrash Eleh Ezkerah*, see David Stern and Mark Jay Mirsky, *Rabbinic Fantasies: Imaginative Narratives from Classic Hebrew Literature* (Philadelphia, PA: Jewish Publication Society, 1990), 143–63.
80. Avianus, *Minor Latin Poets*, 716–19.
81. Schwarzbaum, *Mishle Shu'alim*, 468–73.
82. Jeremiah. 22.14; Ezekiel. 23.14. Berekhiah, *Fox Fables*, 103; Hadas, *Fables*, 171.
83. '[I am] the clay, and you are the potter / We are all the work of your hands' (Isaiah 64.7).
84. Psalms 27.12.
85. Berekhiah, *Fox Fables*, 103; Hadas, *Fables*, 172.
86. The involvement of Jews with Christian religious items seems to have been fairly common, despite laws against it: see Richardson, *English Jewry*, 113.
87. B. Sotah 41b; B. Megillah 16b. Berekhiah, *Fox Fables*, 103; Hadas, *Fables*, 102.
88. The work of the so-called 'Third Vatican Mythographer', is attributed in several mss. to Alberic of London; a few scholars believe that the prolific Alexander Nequam himself was the author. The *Vatican Mythographers*, ed. Ronald E. Pepin (Fordham University Press: New York, 2008), 7–9; on Bacchus, 318–22.

BIBLIOGRAPHY

Berechiah ha-Naqdan, *Mishle Shu'alim (Fox Fables)*, ed. A. M. Haberman (Jerusalem: Shocken, 1946).

Einbinder, Susan, *Beautiful Death: Jewish Poetry and Martyrdom in Medieval France* (Philadelphia, PA: University of Pennsylvania Press, 2002).

Hadas, Moses, ed., *Fables of A Jewish Aesop* (New York: Columbia University Press, 1967).

Hillaby, Joe, 'The London Jewry: William I to John', *Jewish Historical Studies* 33 (1992–4), 1–44.

Jones, Sarah Rees and Sethina Watson, eds., *Christians and Jews in Medieval England: The York Massacre of 1190, Narratives and Contexts* (York: York Medieval Press, 2013).

Mann, Jill, *From Aesop to Reynard: Beast Literature in Medieval Britain* (Oxford: Oxford University Press, 2009).

Neubauer, A. and Joseph Jacobs, 'Berechiah Naqdan', *Jewish Quarterly Review* 2 (1890), 520–6.

Richardson, H. G., *English Jewry under Angevin Kings* (London: Methuen, 1960).

Roth, Cecil, *The Intellectual Activities of Medieval English Jewry* (Oxford: Oxford University Press, 1948).

CHAPTER 10

THE HAZARDS OF NARRATION

Frame-Tale Technologies and the 'Oriental Tale'

KARLA MALLETTE

'FRAME' TALES

WE call them *frame tales*, a term that designates not precisely a genre but rather a shared formal characteristic. Petrus Alfonsi's *Disciplina clericalis*, Don Juan Manuel's *Conde Lucanor*, Boccaccio's *Decameron*, Sercambi's *Novelle*, Bosone da Gubbio's *Avventuroso Siciliano*, Ser Giovanni's *Pecorone*, and Chaucer's *Canterbury Tales*, as well as anonymous texts like the *Thousand and One Nights*, *Kalila and Dimna*, *Barlaam and Josaphat*, *Secundus the Silent Philosopher*, and the *Book of Sindbād* (known as the *Seven Sages of Rome* in the West): in these works, characters within a story take over the narrative reins and tell stories themselves, creating a nested tale within a tale. Most of the works in this list were enormously popular during the late Middle Ages. Yet the name we use to designate them—*frame tales*—is of nineteenth-century vintage. Premodern witnesses did not have a technical name to describe the formal characteristics these works shared. They did not seem to understand them to belong to a distinct generic or formal category. And they did not share our fascination with the formal elegance of framing: its recursive structure, its plasticity, its self-reflexivity.

The words used in the European languages to describe the literary frame—English *frame*, French *cadre*, Italian *cornice*—first appear during the second decade of the nineteenth century. The French *cadre* has a broad lexical range; in a literary context, it may refer to a tale's setting, the tableau created by an author as backdrop for a fictional narrative. It seems to take on the technical meaning it has for us thanks to one work in particular. In *De la littérature du Midi de l'Europe* (1813), Jean Charles Léonard Simonde de Sismondi used the word regularly to refer to the structure of Boccaccio's *Decameron*. And following the translation of this book into Italian (1820), the Italians came to use *cornice* to describe the framing mechanism of the *Decameron* as well as other early Italian narratives.[1] In English, as in French, one may 'frame a tale' in a general sense, without creating a *frame tale* in the formal sense. An English work which appeared one year after Simonde's—*The History of Fiction* by John Colin Dunlop (1814)—used the word *frame* as Simonde did: in a technical sense, to describe the narrative structure of Boccaccio's *Decameron* but also of other works, including *Kalila and Dimna*, the *Seven Sages of Rome*, and Chaucer's *Canterbury Tales*. And as the nineteenth century progressed, these words and the formal structure they described came to represent the quality that increasingly attracted readers' attention to these works: the fact that they stitched together brief narratives by allowing fictional characters to narrate tales themselves.

Certainly this formal aspect of the narratives did not attract the attention of the man who was (to my knowledge) the first to discuss the works recognized by us to be the classics of the 'genre'—the oldest, most widely translated, most formally remarkable, most beautiful framed narratives in world literature: the *Thousand and One Nights, Kalila and Dimna*, the *Book of Sindbād, Barlaam and Josaphat*. Ibn al-Nadīm—a book-dealer in tenth-century Baghdad who compiled a catalogue of all the books he had encountered in his professional life—lists a great number of works and summarizes the plots of some of them. He does not mention the device of framing. Neither does he describe any of the embedded tales in the narratives; what details he gives have to do with the framing narrative itself. And none of the vocabulary he uses to designate these tales refers to the formal characteristic which moderns would consider to be their salient quality. Rather, Ibn al-Nadīm is concerned with other dimensions of the works: their linguistic origin (whether they were written first in Sanskrit or Pahlavi) and movement through languages; the fact that they made no claim to historical accuracy but were avowedly invented narratives; that the ancestors of these works were gathered for the purpose of amusing kings, and they function as mirrors for princes—albeit, in some cases, distorted fun-house mirrors; that some of these works are risqué, even morally corrupt, as if intended to parody the more upright exemplars of the genre. As even a cursory survey of Ibn al-Nadīm's catalogue of narratives proves, the category 'frame tales' held no interest for him. He grouped frame tales, alongside narrative collections without a framing device, under headings that had nothing to do with the formal structure of the narratives: 'evening stories and fables'; 'the names of the books which the Persians composed about biography, and the evening stories about their kings which were true'; 'the books of the Indians about fables, evening stories, and anecdotes'; 'the books of the Byzantines about evening stories, histories, fables, and proverbs'; and so on.[2] The linguistic and cultural provenance of the narratives and their veracity mattered to Ibn al-Nadīm rather more than the formal quality so important to us.

We think of the framed narrative as a way to call attention to the storyteller's craft, and to the storyteller's investment in the tale that he or she tells in particular. But that is a modern perspective on the genre. In the frame tales which tradition holds to be the oldest and which were demonstrably the most widely circulated—*Kalila and Dimna, Barlaam and Josaphat*—embedded tales are essentially parables and the frame serves a primarily hermeneutic function. Tales are told for the purpose of instruction or suasion, and the narrators might themselves call out the moral for the benefit of their (fictional and real) audience. Other framed narratives, however, are more equivocal, and the interpretations offered by their narrators are at times questionable and even suspect. This helps to explain Ibn al-Nadīm's distaste for the *Thousand and One Nights*, so often discussed in the scholarship, and presumably inspired at least in part by the subversion of the moral function in that collection. Shahrazād is meant to be telling tales for one reason (to pass the time while she waits for dawn, when she will be executed) but in truth has another motive (to compel the king to keep her alive in order to finish her tale); and the stories she tells the king seem to deliver even darker, encoded messages (the men you trust the most have the most power to betray you; you can be destroyed by words alone).

This long preamble—think of it as a frame tale of sorts—clears away some of the obstructions that block our view of the literary landscape of the late medieval Mediterranean. During the Middle Ages framing might serve a simple pragmatic function: it allowed the author or compiler to string together shorter narratives in order to create a book-length collection. But Ibn al-Nadīm's historical account (and the silence of premodern European observers on the topic) demonstrates that framing as a formal device held scant interest for medieval observers. In this chapter, I will follow Ibn al-Nadīm's lead and survey the progress of a short list of framed narratives—those with the most robust transmission history—between languages. I will then focus on a sub-category of framed narratives: those (like the *Thousand and One Nights*) which present narration as a high-stakes wager that may save a populace in peril.

My discussion will pose late medieval Italy as telos for three reasons. First and foremost, as the brief list of framed narratives at the beginning of this chapter suggests, Italian authors made important contributions to the development of framed narratives during the late Middle Ages. Secondly, the Italian frame tales reproduce a short list of narrative dynamics emphasizing the stakes of narration: the movement of character-narrators through space in order to flee danger; the measuring out of story-telling through a determined number of days (or years); storytelling as a strategy to save a populace at risk. And finally, the Italian narrative tradition held particular importance for Chaucer himself. Although he may not have embraced the innovations introduced in these works, the circumstances of his life made it likely that he was exposed to them. This narrative environment was one which Chaucer's Italian travels made available to him, and hence provides a context in which his own literary decisions may be better understood and appreciated.

FRAMED NARRATIVES IN MOTION

Though they traced prodigiously complex paths between languages, the major framed narratives shared in common two stages in their long and eventful transmission histories: all were attested in the Abbasid East and in late medieval Europe.[3] In some cases, these works—*Kalila and Dimna*; *The Book of Sindbād*; *Barlaam and Josaphat*; the *Thousand and One Nights*—survive in premodern Arabic, Pahlavi, Sanskrit, Greek or Turkic versions, and Ibn al-Nadīm's detailed discussion of the literary scene in tenth-century Baghdad indicates that provenance was already a question of consuming interest for *litterateurs* of his age. He records conflicting versions of the origin of the narratives, weighing divergent accounts that traced them to Pahlavi or Sanskrit originals. And the surviving literary record complicates our understanding of an already ambiguous trans-mission history. Some works that Ibn al-Nadīm describes have vanished (of the Abbasid-era Arabic versions of these works, only *Kalila and Dimna* survives). The pre-vious Pahlavi or Sanskrit versions from which, according to Ibn al-Nadīm, the Arabic translations were made do not survive (again, with the exception of *Kalila and Dimna*, of which an early Sanskrit text has been found, though not the Pahlavi version from which Ibn al-Muqaffa' [d. ca. 756] made his Arabic translation). And in some cases we have fragmentary texts attesting to the existence of versions which Ibn al-Nadīm does not mention: Syriac versions of *Kalila and Dimna* and the *Book of Sindbād al-Ḥakīm*, for instance, and a Turkic version of *Barlaam and Josaphat*. Whatever the origins of these works—whether they were translated from pre-existing works in Sanskrit, Pahlavi, or some other East or Central Asian language, or were first composed in Arabic—Ibn al-Nadīm's testimony makes two facts apparent. The works moved slowly from east to west, and in the process passed through an abundance of languages in an abundance of variant versions. And the challenge of unravelling their movement through time, space, and languages has provided a trans-historical topic of speculation for literary professionals: from the literary salons of tenth-century Baghdad to the philologists of nineteenth-century Europe.

As they spilled toward the Mediterranean, these works continued to generate new redactions within languages and to spread to new audiences through translation. *Kalila and Dimna* would enter the European languages via a Greek translation from the Arabic made in Sicily during the eleventh century. A Castilian translation from the Arabic was commissioned by Alfonso el Sabio and executed in 1251; this version would be retranslated into Latin by Raymond de Béziers. And John of Capua made a Latin translation of a Hebrew version, known as the *Directorium vitae humanae*, in Rome between 1263 and 1278. The *Book of Sindbād* vanished beneath the waters of the Mediterranean, to resurface as the *Seven Sages of Rome* in the European languages. The means of its transmission are not known, but it existed (and manuscripts survive) in a dizzying number of versions in virtually all the European languages. Curiously, while the framing narrative remained the same on both sides of the Mediterranean, all but one of the embedded narratives have been replaced with new tales. *Barlaam and Josaphat* seems to have travelled both via the Mediterranean trade routes and via the Fur Route: north from Baghdad, across the Black Sea (or through the Caucasus and Georgia to the east of the Black Sea), and into Eastern Europe. It survives in early versions in Georgian (from which the oldest Greek translation was made), German and Norwegian, as well as the languages of Mediterranean Europe. *The Thousand and One Nights*, of course, is not thought to have reached the European languages until Antoine Galland's French translation, published in the opening decades of the eighteenth century. We will see evidence, however, that parts of it at least were known in Western Europe during the late Middle Ages.

STORIES THAT SAVE LIVES

From their diverse origins, following distinct paths, the framed narratives converged on Western Europe between roughly the eleventh and thirteenth centuries, to provide a source of narrative material first for Latin composition and then for the burgeoning new vernacular traditions. What did these narratives bring to European writers which they did not already possess in their own, long-familiar narrative traditions? One could argue that a remedial form of framing was present in the European traditions—in sermon literature, for instance, or in Aesop's *Fables*: serial collections of stories knitted together by a sense of hermeneutic purpose. Indeed, the more avowedly didactic collections— *Barlaam and Josaphat* and *Kalila and Dimna* in particular—do seem similar in narrative construction to the countless versions of the *Fables* of Aesop in the European languages made during the Middle Ages.[4] The frame itself is relatively anodyne. The audience is in need of instruction and these tales will teach: this, in essence, summarizes the centrifugal force generated by the framing narrative in these collections. In other works, however, the frame provides a diffracted hermeneutic lens, allowing for a number of competing interpretations, in particular when embedded tales convey a message which seems to skew the narrator's stated moral. This rather more robust conception of framing—a device which calls our attention to the situation and the stakes of narration—was not (to my knowledge) available to Western European readers before the arrival of two framed narratives in particular: the *Book of Sindbād/Seven Sages of Rome* and the *Thousand and One Nights* (in whatever form that work may have been known).

In both of these collections, narrators pit their storytelling skills against an auditor who has power over themselves or over another character within the frame. And the stories they tell may or may not affect the outcome of the frame narrative. The *Thousand and One Nights*—this tale, at least, is familiar to a general audience today—puts a well-educated girl (Shahrazād in Arabic, Scheherazade in English) in the bed of a king whose murderous misogynist rage has emptied the city of virgins, all the marriageable maidens having been wedded to him for a single night then executed. She tells tales that aim to beguile the king; if he is so intrigued that he must keep her alive until the next night to hear the tale's continuation, she wins a stay of execution. In the *Seven Sages of Rome*, it is a prince who is threatened by a woman's ravenous sexual appetite. She is his father's second wife (in the western versions, his stepmother). She invites him to work with her to overthrow the father and seize power. When he refuses to join her coup, she accuses him of attempted rape. Because the son—in another plot twist—is obliged to keep perfect silence for a week (if he speaks, according to an astrological reading, his death is certain), others must speak on his behalf. The eponymous seven sages, the boy's tutors, tell stories in his defence; the stepmother tells stories to illustrate his guilt and the necessity of putting him to death. His father, the king, listens to the stories and condemns or exonerates him, following the storyteller's aim; the father lacks moral gravitas to an astonishing degree. When the seven days have passed, the prince tells the final tale of the collection in his own defence. The stepmother's guilt is revealed and (in most versions) she is executed at the end of the book.

Clearly, these frames create a contingent and fraught environment for the tales they contain. Today, Shahrazād is often read as a resistance heroine. Her knowledge of Arab cultural and intellectual traditions is celebrated in the frame tale. And, when the story-telling begins, she uses her familiarity with Arab narrative traditions not only to whet the king's appetite to hear more, but also to unsettle his psyche: the tales she tells seem intended to convince him that his position is unstable and risky, that danger may come from any direction. The *Seven Sages of Rome* frames tales from two diametrically opposed positions, the one perspective aiming explicitly to undermine the other. The feckless, addled king swings in the breeze, unduly influenced time and again by the tales (no matter how flimsy) told by the two camps. Within a robust frame like this, the value of a tale must be measured differently, in terms of its proximate moral purpose as well as its independent value as narrative entertainment.

This is not Aesop's *Fables*! Rather, these frames are tooled to focus our attention on the stakes of narration. And to a striking degree, the original framed narratives written in Italian during the late Middle Ages follow similar framing strategies. Rather than simply combine tales told for didactic purpose, they create a frame which may by turns celebrate or undermine the fictional narrators' stated aims. Often lives are at stake, and storytelling may have a direct or indirect capacity to save or to threaten, to imprison or to liberate the characters within the frame. In all cases, the frame serves to heighten the sense that narration matters—and, in a more subtle way, to condition our interpretation of the tales told. And the Italian framed collections also adopt specific narrative ingredients plausibly derived from the story collections translated only recently from the languages of the eastern Mediterranean: the measuring out of narration through a numbered ser-ies of days (or years); movement through space, typically in order to seek refuge from danger; a backdrop of psychological or civil malaise which may be symbolically healed through narrative therapy. These elements are present in embryonic form in the eastern models (if indeed the *Book of Sindbād* and the *Thousand and One Nights* provided inspiration for the Italian narratives). The theme of movement is central to the framing narratives of both works. Characters first set out from the city: in the *Thousand and One Nights*, two brothers travel to escape the evils of women; in the *Book of Sindbād*, the prince and the sages travel to the secluded place where the prince is to be educated. And when these characters return they bring disorder to the city, and the scene of action is drastically narrowed. The palace provides the stage for the narration that will constitute the bulk of both collections—the sultan's bedchamber in particular in the *Thousand and One Nights*. Both tales, it seems, are drawn to the households torn apart by the psycho-sexual troubles that set their narrative machines in motion. Both works also mete out the action of narration by counting days (or nights), although the *Book of Sindbād* con-stricts the duration significantly, from a thousand and one iterations (a number meant to signify a near-limitless or uncountable quantity) to seven. Both, finally, represent narration as a means to evade civic catastrophe. The late medieval Italian framed narratives will produce a number of variations on this short list of formal elements, and their authors will fill the belly of their books with a dazzling variety of invented or reinvented tales.

FRAMED NARRATIVES IN ITALY

The first framed narrative written in Italian as an original work of literature (rather than a translation), Bosone da Gubbio's *Avventuroso Siciliano* (1311), is anomalous in a number of ways. It survives in a single manuscript. And it is not precisely a framed narrative, but rather a pseudo-historical work—it describes the heroic deeds of five (fictional) Sicilian barons—that is framed by the briefest of prefaces and studded with the occasional interpolated tale, some told by characters in the narrative and others in the author's own voice. Yet it makes a significant contribution to the early history of the framed narrative in Europe for two reasons in particular. First, it includes a cognate to the tale of the poisoned book which is used as a murder weapon in the narrative of King Yunan and the Sage Duban from the *Thousand and One Nights*,[5] and so it provides a shred of evidence that the *Nights* was known in Europe in some form before Galland's translation at the beginning of the eighteenth century. And second, in his introduction to the work, Bosone explains why he embeds tales within the framework of the larger narrative:

> Ispesse fiate aviene che, volendo trattare d'alcune materie, non si puote appieno solo parlare di quelle sanza alcuno argomento d'altri diri, donde per li predetti argomenti s'intende quello di che l'uomo vole parlare e trattare.
>
> Ma conviene che la materia di che parlare si vole dipenda da quella con che s'argomenta o per dirivamento o per essempro. E questi argomenti fare si conviene per lo presente trattato, di che noi intendiamo parlare nel presente libro.[6]
>
> [Often it happens that, wishing to speak of certain matters, one can't speak only of those without touching on other matters; since by means of the aforesaid arguments, that which the man wishes to say and speak about is understood.
>
> But it is fitting that the matter of which one wants to speak should depend upon that which one describes along with it, either as explanation or illustration. And it befits this treatise to make such arguments, concerning the matters we intend to speak about in this book.]

This could work equally as a rationale for interrupting a narrative with exempla or, indeed, any kind of digression. Yet the material that Bosone integrates into his tale typically consists of brief, clearly fantastic tales, lifted from various sources and repurposed to fit his own narrative—like the tale of a poisoned book sent to assassinate the King of England (which, in this case, misfires and kills a lowly attendant).

Bosone's *Avventuroso Siciliano* followed in the venerable tradition of some of the most ancient framed narratives in another sense as well: it is cousin to the 'mirror for princes' genre. The genre of the work has posed a problem for literary historians (as has, frankly, its literary quality). It seems possible that Bosone chose a particularly heroic epoch as backdrop for his narrative—the period that inspired the valour of Gianni da Procida, who drove the haughty French out of Sicily—but modelled his narrative not (or not only) on the historians, but also on the narrative collections that used a fictionalized courtly setting to frame tales of ethics and princely valour. Literary scholars more typically categorize the work as 'compilation', 'romance', or 'florilegium'.[7] But in the contemporary context—given the presence of recent translations of *Kalila and Dimna* and the *Seven Sages of Rome* in northern Italy—it makes sense to see the work as, in part, a response to this new literary stimulus.

The impetus that drives the characters in *Avventuroso Siciliano* is distilled from the themes of civic malaise, movement, and (more subtly) narration spanning a measured period of time. Bosone's tale begins, like the *Thousand and One Nights* and the *Book of Sindbād*, in a land beset by troubles: Sicily under the yoke of French rule. And like the *Thousand and One Nights* and the *Book of Sindbād*, his narrative marks time toward a goal (albeit in this case only vaguely specified). His barons leave Sicily at the beginning of the book for a period of ten years, because 'in their land they can't live well, because of the adversities that have come into their land',[8] and their peregrinations and their adventures while they are on the move provide the narrative material for the book. Bosone does not tick off the years (as in the *Nights* the passing of each night is noted; as in the *Seven Sages* each day is filled out with two tales and two swings of the king's verdict). Movement, however, is crucial to his narrative formula. The adjective *avventuroso* which he attaches to the Sicilian knight of his title signifies 'fortunate' or 'risky', but also 'one who travels in search of circumstances to test (and, potentially, reward) his bravery and strength'.[9]

The formula that Boccaccio uses to frame the *Decameron*—the next contribution to the genre in the Italian context, and a decisive contribution—makes clear sense when viewed in the context of the contemporary literary landscape. Physical displacement does not take up a great deal of space in the *Decameron*. Yet movement from Florence to the countryside allows Boccaccio's storytellers to escape the miasma of the city, giving them room, in a literal and figurative sense, for narrative expansion. But Boccaccio adopts and elaborates the motif of civil disorder. The plague serves as the stimulus that sets his great narrative engine in motion, the dark tapestry against which his storytellers' inventions show in dazzling relief. In the *Avventuroso Siciliano*, a land besieged by an invading army and a backdrop of militia on the move—the French, the Aragonese, and the Sicilian rebels converging on the coveted island in the middle of the Mediterranean—creates a sense of urgency, a drumbeat which provides dramatic counterpoint to the exploits of his individual barons. But the *Decameron* (like the *Thousand and One Nights* and the *Seven Sages of Rome*) brings the sense of impending menace home: to the sitting-rooms of the ladies of Florence, the merchants' wives to whom he famously dedicates his work. And Boccaccio makes more effective use than Bosone of the chronological motif found in earlier framed narratives. The ten days of storytelling which gave the work its title—*Decameron* is an Italianization of the pseudo-Greek *deka hemeron*—acquire, in the course of Boccaccio's book, an almost magical therapeutic power, somehow neutralizing the peril of the plague which had driven the ten young aristocrats out of Florence. Boccaccio, famously, is responsible for the codicological paraphernalia of the *Decameron*. He himself wrote the rubrics that introduce each day. And he provided the title for the work as well, one that underscores its chronological dynamic and ensures that the reader will not forget its chronological limits. He gives us no rationale for his use of a chronological device to measure out the length of his work. The ten days of narration serve to delimit a course of treatment, a therapeutic dynamic underscored by the rhythm of the daily themes. As we cycle through those themes— good fortune; bad fortune followed by good; the terrible fourth day, when we are required to wallow in our misery (or, more accurately, to wallow in Filostrato's misery); the wonderful release of the fifth day, when we celebrate happy love (or, more accurately, happy hook-ups), and so on—we move toward a temporal goal dictated but never explained by the book's title. Boccaccio grants us ten days—not an hour more or less—of escape from the plague. It may seem a miserly gift. Shahrayar gave Shahrazād close to three years; Bosone gave his barons ten years. Only the Seven Sages of Rome are granted less time: just seven days. But in this case, of course, ten days prove to be just enough. In part because Boccaccio is a literary genius and the reader is always safe in his hands, in part because of established genre practice and genre expectations, the device of measuring the duration of narration by ticking off days (or years) satisfies us; for the chronological distribution of tales constituted part of the tradition which Boccaccio received. A community menaced by a grim, overpowering, irrational danger and a steady movement toward liberation and redemption, parcelled out into a series of precisely delineated chronological units: this is the formula which achieved its apotheosis in the *Decameron*.

The *Decameron* proved both inimitable and an irresistible model for imitation. Vittore Branca has discussed the tradition of copying the *Decameron* with new narrative material, replacing Boccaccio's tales with others from the late medieval inventory.[10] The men of letters for whom Boccaccio wrote—mercantile men of vernacular letters— delighted in spinning tales, and were willing and able to produce their own versions of works they loved and wanted to keep close to hand. Giovanni Sercambi (1348–1424), who wrote a collection known as the *Novelliere*—one of the most ambitious early tributes to the *Decameron*—fits this demographic with precision. Sercambi was politically active in his native city, Lucca; he wrote a history of Lucca, the *Croniche*; and he earned his living as *speziale* (roughly, a pharmacist). In northern Italy at this time, the *speziale* also served as merchant of paper and of books, and so Sercambi (like Ibn al-Nadīm) had a professional's appreciation of the contemporary literary market. We know that Sercambi owned *volgarizzamenti* (or vernacular translations) of Latin and French narratives as well as a copy of the *Decameron* because we have an inventory of the books in his library at the time of his death. The sources from which he derives the 155 tales in his *Novelliere* demonstrate his access to a variety of narrative traditions: the fabliaux; the *cantari*, popular Italian narratives; Dante's *Commedia*; the *Seven Sages of*

Rome; volgarizzamenti of Valerius Maximus, Lucan, Ovid's *Metamorphoses*, the *Ludus scacchorum* by Jacob of Cessolis, and Petrus Alfonsi's *Disciplina clericalis*; the *Travels* of Marco Polo; Fazio degli Uberti's *Dittamondo*; and of course the *Decameron*—more than once named as source in Sercambi's own introductions to his tales.[11] Sercambi's access to works not included in this list is demonstrated by the presence among his tales of a cognate to the frame story of the *Thousand and One Nights*.[12]

Sercambi creates a frame for the *Novelliere* by selecting and replicating elements from Boccaccio's frame. The plague threatens Lucca, and a group of citizens sets forth to escape it. They wander restlessly from city to city throughout the Italian peninsula. As they travel, musicians and dancers entertain the party. Religious attend to their spiritual needs. And a storyteller—identified in an acrostic poem in the introduction as Giovanni Sercambi himself—tells them tales to pass the time. Here, the theme of travel as flight from the plague displaces all the other elements of Boccaccio's frame. In the *Decameron*, movement from Florence to the countryside sets the narrative in motion. Sercambi's exilic band, however, moves ceaselessly, the names of cities and towns flickering by in the brief introductions to the tales. Neither the geographical backdrop of the *Novelliere* nor the character of Sercambi's pilgrims is developed. The frame serves a narrowly defined function: a scaffolding to hold together the tales it contains.

Sercambi's collection was left unfinished at the time of his death—by a bitter irony, caused by the plague—and is preserved in only two copies, neither of which apparently circulated outside the family. The work is of value chiefly as a record of tales that were known and told in northern Italy at the end of the fourteenth century and the beginning of the fifteenth. Another framed narrative of the era had greater fortune in Italy and in England during the late Middle Ages and the Renaissance. A sonnet appended to the end of the work gives its title (somewhat mysteriously) as the *Pecorone* (the augmentative form of *pecora*, sheep; also used as a pejorative term for people of scant intelligence). The same sonnet names the author as 'ser Giovanni', or Sir Giovanni; modern scholars typically refer to him as 'ser Giovanni fiorentino'. And it gives the date of composition, 1378. Scholarship has not linked the Florentine Giovanni identified in the sonnet with any historical figure.

The *Pecorone* is, by any standard, a curious work of literature. In the framing narrative—sketched with minimal strokes—a young man falls in love with a nun, and takes his vows himself in order to serve as chaplain at her convent. The two make regular assignations to meet in a private place, and there they tell each other stories in order to quell the flames of their desire. Enzo Esposito, editor of the modern edition of the work, suggests that it is disgust for the two lovers' tepid ardour—Boccaccio's heroes and heroines certainly would have found better use for their time together—that inspired the title by which the work became known; *pecorone*, he suggests, may imply one who 'is induced to wait, or is inclined to those deferments, repeated without outlet, which characterize the sentimental experience' of ser Giovanni's lovers.[13] The two lovers meet on twenty five occasions. Each day that they meet two tales are told, each lover telling a tale to the other. The tales in the first third of the work are drawn from a variety of sources. At a certain point, however, ser Giovanni turns to Giovanni Villani's history of Florence, the

Nuova cronica, as narrative source. The two tales of the eighth day, the second of the tenth day, and every tale thereafter come from Villani (adorned with the occasional grace note added from other sources). Once it reached England, the *Pecorone* provided source material for both Shakespeare's *The Merry Wives of Windsor*[14] and, more famously, *The Merchant of Venice*.[15]

The *Pecorone* brings us to the cusp of modernity, and marks the eclipse of the framed narrative that uses a short list of ingredients to invest narration with the power to sustain human life. The lover of the *Pecorone* travels from Florence to his beloved's convent in Forlí. But the journey appears to have little significance to ser Giovanni, other than to separate the lover from his previous life and unite him with his beloved. The tales that make up the bulk of the collection are rationed out, two per day. But the pacing of narrative through time has no discernible therapeutic effect; at the end the lovers are no different than they were when the storytelling began. Forbidden romance adds a *frisson* to ser Giovanni's book, as the amorous pair tell tales to each other in order to bank the flames of desire. But heaving bosoms and abbey assignations are scarcely a match for the horrors of the plague, described in unforgettable detail in the Introduction to the *Decameron*. If Boccaccio displaced the sexual energies explicit in the framing narratives of the *Seven Sages* and the *Thousand and One Nights* into the tales themselves—his *brigata* is chaste; the characters in the stories they narrate are not—the *Pecorone* uses buzzing sexual energy as a framing mechanism. In part for this reason, it is not nearly as successful as the *Decameron*. Boccaccio would have known at least to throw his lovers into each other's arms at some crucial juncture: at the midpoint of the collection, say, or at the end. The Author's Epilogue to the *Decameron* is famously self-mocking. Boccaccio lets loose a string of double *entendres* that push the verbal energy of the tales themselves to the boundary between invention and reality, creating a portrait of the author as a randy old man able to keep up with any of his invented characters. The sonnet that closes out the *Pecorone*, which names the author and his work and gives the year of its composition, perhaps pays tribute to this conclusion as self-parody. It may have been written by the author, or by a reader who has compared the *Pecorone* to the *Decameron* and finds that it does not measure up to Boccaccio's standards.

Of the framed narratives I have discussed in this chapter, only the *Decameron* and the Italian versions of the *Seven Sages of Rome* were likely to be introduced to Chaucer during his Italian travels. Bosone's *Avventuroso Siciliano* is preserved in a single manuscript, and Sercambi's *Novelliere* in only two; the *Pecorone* appears to have been written too late for Chaucer's notice. Yet these narratives provide the useful service of sketching the literary landscape: showing us what a contemporary Italian audience thought worthy of note and of imitation. And it seems evident that Chaucer—if he did indeed learn from the Italians—chose very selectively from the narrative elements present. Like Sercambi's refugees, Chaucer's pilgrims make a long journey toward a distant goal the pretext for embedded narratives. By trimming the other elements present in the Italian framed narratives—the city under threat; physical danger and sexual tensions defrayed by narration; the finite, numbered sequence of days into which tales are slotted—Chaucer's framed narrative, it seems, loses the very qualities that gave the Italian frame tales (and their predecessors) a sense of urgency. Yet if the Italian narratives drew much of their power from their manipulation of pre-existing models, Chaucer's formula seems to have had imitators in modern letters in a way that the medieval texts I have described in this chapter did not. One could point to later narratives in which a journey with only a notional sense of destination provides the occasion for narration (and adventure) as avatars of the *Canterbury Tales*: Mark Twain's *Adventures of Huckleberry Finn*, for instance, or Jerome K. Jerome's *Three Men in a Boat*, or the Coen Brothers' *O Brother Where Art Thou?* Of course, these works draw as much on Homer's *Odyssey*—a work unknown to Chaucer—as they do on the *Canterbury Tales*: yet another indication of the complex paths that narratives travel through time, space and language. But that (it scarcely needs saying) is another story.

Notes

1. Simonde uses the word *cadre* often in *De la littérature du Midi de l'Europe*, generally in a non-technical sense, to mean 'setting'. The Italian translator (who is not identified in the published edition) translates the French *cadre* with the Italian *cornice* only when Simonde uses it to refer to the frame narrative of the Decameron (see e.g. chapter 3, part 5, entitled '*Cornice* altamente seria in cui l'autore colloca un disegno scherzevole' [An extremely serious frame in which the author embeds a humorous sketch]).

2. Ibn al-Nadīm, *The Fihrist*, trans. Bayard Dodge, 2 vols. (New York: Columbia University Press, 1970), 712–24; *Al Fihrist*, ed. Yusuf Ali Tawil (Beirut: Dar al-Kutb al-'Ilmiya, 1996), 475–81.

3. For the most accessible overviews of the transmission history of these works, see: *Kalīlah and Dimnah, or the Fables of Bidpai: Being an Account of their Literary History, with an English Translation of the Later Syriac Version of the Same*, ed. and trans. I. G. N. Keith-Falconer (Cambridge: Cambridge University Press, 1885); Carl Brockelmann, 'Kalīla Wa-Dimna', in *Encyclopaedia of Islam*, 2nd ed., through brillonline.com; the *Sindbād/Seven Sages* tradition, J. P. Guillaume, 'Sindbād al-Ḥakīm', in *Encyclopaedia of Islam*, 2nd ed., through brillonline.com; Killis Campbell, 'A Study of the Romance of the Seven Sages with Special Reference to the Middle English Versions', *PMLA* 14 (1899), 4–15; St. John Damascene (John of Damascus), *Barlaam and Ioasaph*, ed. and trans. G. R. Woodward and Harold Mattingly (London: MacMillan, 1914); David Marshall Lang, 'Bilawhar Wa-Yūdāsaf', *Encyclopaedia of Islam*, 2nd ed., at brillonline.com; Dwight Reynolds, 'A *Thousand and One Nights*: A History of the Text and Its Reception', in *Cambridge History of Arabic Literature: Arabic Literature in the Post-Classical Period*, eds. Roger Allen and D. S. Richards (Cambridge: Cambridge University Press, 2006), 270–91.

4. The Spanish framed narratives (*Disciplina clericalis*, *El Conde Lucanor*) follow this framing philosophy, using a simple didactic frame to bind together embedded narratives.

5. Bosone da Gubbio, *L'avventuroso Siciliano*, ed. Roberto Gigliucci (Rome: Bulzoni, 1989), 120–1.

6. Ibid., 36.

7. Ibid., 20.

8. Ibid., 53.

9. 'avventuroso, *agg*.', *Tesoro della lingua Italiana delle Origini*, tlio.ovi.cnr.it/TLIO.

10. Vittore Branca, *Boccaccio medievale e nuovi studi sul Decameron* (Florence: Sansoni, 1986), 9.
11. Giovanni Sercambi, *Il novelliere*, ed. Luciano Rossi, 3 vols. (Rome: Salerno, 1974), xiv.
12. Sercambi, *Il novelliere* 2:324–33 (Novella 119).
13. Giovanni Fiorentino, *Il Pecorone*, ed. Enzo Esposito (Ravenna: Longo, 1974), xv–xvi.
14. Compare with William Shakespeare, *The Merry Wives of Windsor*, I.ii.
15. Shakespeare, *The Merchant of Venice*, IV.i. The 1558 editio princeps edited by Lodovico Domenichi—which gave the fourteenth century original a Renaissance touch-up—has been reprinted most widely and is best known both in Italian and in translation. The work has recently been published in an edition based on the three complete early manuscripts.

BIBLIOGRAPHY

Campbell, Killis, *The Seven Sages of Rome* (Boston, MA: Ginn, 1907).
Falconer, I. and G. N. Keith, ed. and trans., *Kalīlah and Dimnah, or the Fables of Bidpai: Being an Account of their Literary History, with an English Translation of the Later Syriac Version of the Same* (Cambridge: Cambridge University Press, 1885).
Fiorentino, Giovanni, *The Pecorone of Ser Giovanni*, trans. W. G. Waters, 3 vols. (London: Society of Bibliophiles, 1898).
Haddawy, Husain, trans., *The Arabian Nights* (New York: Norton, 1990).
Irwin, Robert, *The Arabian Nights: A Companion* (London: Allen Lane, 1994).
[John of Damascus] St John Damascene, *Barlaam and Ioasaph*, eds. and trans. G. R. Woodward and Harold Mattingly (London: Heinemann and New York: MacMillan, 1914).
Keller, John Esten, trans., *The Book of the Wiles of Women* (Chapel Hill, NC: University of North Carolina Press, 1956).
Kinoshita, Sharon, 'Translation, Empire, and the Worlding of Medieval Literature: The Travels of Kalila wa-Dimna', *Postcolonial Studies* 11 (2008), 371–85.
Knatchbull, Wyndham, trans., *Kalila and Dimna, or the Fables of Bidpai, Translated from the Arabic* (Oxford: Baxter, 1819).

CHAPTER 11

FICTIONS OF ESPIONAGE

Performing Pilgrim and Crusader Identities in the Age of Chaucer

SUZANNE M. YEAGER

From shipmen and pilgrims 'with scrippes bret-ful of lesinges [lies]' (2123) in *The House of Fame*, to the portrayal of the Wife of Bath as wandering to satisfy her 'coltes tooth' (III. 602), Geoffrey Chaucer's travellers are shown as both unreliable and morally questionable. Even Chaucer's Knight, who tends to be regarded as an idealized figure in *The Canterbury Tales*, is condemned in some studies depending on the perception of his past travels, as critics speculate on the sincerity of his pilgrimage, his multiple campaigns, and even his 'bismotered' coat of mail (I.76). Chaucer's depictions of fictitious travellers aptly reflect contemporary uneasiness about the practice of pilgrimage and the ways such travel could be abused. Surely not all medieval pilgrims took up their journeys with dutiful attention to the sacred, but it may be noted that those who created written records of their travels portray themselves as quite serious about the enterprise. To examine this particular brand of self-fashioning, this chapter is part of a larger study which explores the social and political work that pilgrim narratives performed on behalf of their narrators. This study examines the little-discussed function of the late medieval pilgrimage account as a productive place for constructing a perception of personal authority and reputation, whether purely political, religious, or otherwise. By approaching the topic of pilgrimage in this way, I hope to explore how certain writers used crusading topoi both to negotiate the omnipresent cultural critique of pilgrimage, and also to create an authorial persona whose exploits may have enjoyed some social utility at home.

Chaucer's portrayal of potentially fallible travellers represents a complex view of pilgrimage in the fourteenth century to creative and sometimes amusing effect. By placing Chaucer's depictions alongside contemporary, late medieval travel accounts, one observes a broader scene where ostensibly religious journeys to distant places could function as bids for such prizes as elevated social status within a community, and could even earn tangible rewards. In these cases, premodern pilgrims who memorialized their travels treated their writings seriously, situating their texts as devices for consolidating the writers' identities as devout pilgrims and reliable authors. In particular, medieval travellers contended with a popular view which held their writing suspect, as seen in Chaucer's satire of the pilgrim's tendency to *curiositas* as the prevailing failure and motivation of medieval travel.

In this study, I hope to show that some premodern travel writers successfully negotiated the pitfalls of *curiositas* and even used its topoi to their advantage. These negotiations are exemplified in significant ways in the fourteenth-century pilgrim accounts composed separately by Simon Simeonis and Thomas Brygg. These texts illustrate the broad range of pilgrim genres in circulation during the premodern period; in them, one observes how easily the experiences and displacement of travel opened new venues for the pro-duction of authorial identity. Moreover, further study of Simon Simeonis and Thomas Brygg's texts allows new interpretations of Chaucer's characters to emerge, suggesting that Chaucer used travel as an important feature of character development deployed variously to modulate the perception of a figure's virtue, piety, and even social position within the fictitious bounds of his carefully composed pilgrim group.

There are a multitude of reasons why some fourteenth-century travellers recorded their experiences. Some works were written simply for personal use instead of wider circulation; yet, of those pieces which seem to have been composed for sharing, many of the later accounts written by Chaucer's contemporaries could serve several ends, including that of souvenir, instrument for affectively reliving the experience at home or animating it for others, proof of penance fulfilled, bragging rights to an adventure, entertainment, and many other purposes. The two texts of interest here describe the Jerusalem pilgrimage experienced by narrators roughly contemporary with Chaucer, and depict the complexities behind constructed pilgrim personas. The work of Simon Simeonis, a Franciscan friar traveling from southern Ireland, is a highly personalized account, while that by Englishman Thomas Brygg, chaplain or squire to Lord Thomas de Swinburne, is a more standardized production. It is unknown whether or not Chaucer encountered either of these narratives, but they can tell us a great deal about the range of pilgrim-narrator personas circulating during his day. There is no doubt that Chaucer came across other current travel texts from English and Continental sources, and that, in all probability, he had read the account attributed to Sir John Mandeville. But here I focus on two generically different texts whose English authors achieve shared ends: they negotiate the pitfalls of *curiositas*, invent new identities, earn some reward, and situate their traveling subjects as anything but liars, lusty wanderers, or tale-spinners.

PILGRIMAGE'S DETRACTORS AND
THE CRIMES OF *CURIOSITAS*

In critiquing pilgrims and their predilection for tall tales, Chaucer was far from alone. Historical evidence shows that there was a medieval concern about the pilgrim's motivations; this included the worry that pilgrims might use their experience to gratify a taste for novelty or to satisfy their vanity by fabricating stories designed to gather attention. Pilgrimage was being critiqued even before Jerome, and it had its share of detractors throughout the medieval period. According to Jacques de Vitry in 1220, 'light-minded and inquisitive persons' would 'go on pilgrimage not out of devotion but out of mere curiosity and love of novelty. All they want to do is travel through unknown lands to investigate the absurd, exaggerated stories they have heard about the east'.[1] For the same reasons, William Langland's fictitious travellers fail to pass muster, for, once his pilgrims return from their journeys, they 'hadden leve to lyen al hir lif after'.[2] Less-orthodox thinkers also questioned pilgrims, including Chaucer's contemporary, the Lollard William Thorpe, who noted, 'if [they] be a month out in their pilgrimage, many of them shall be, a half year after, great janglers, tale-tellers, and liars'.[3]

Pilgrims were not only accused of exaggeration, but also of neglecting to notice things of spiritual import; this was a habit linked in premodern texts to the sin of *curiositas*, which was seen as a failing related to pride and sloth. As Christian Zacher puts it, 'the temptation of *curiositas* referred to any morally excessive and suspect interest in observing the world, seeking novel experience, or acquiring knowledge for its own sake'.[4] In England, as early as Bede's treatises and as late as the fourteenth-century sermons of Bishop Brinton of Rochester, moralists were cautioning against the vice.[5] Though many early theologians such as Cassian, Gregory the Great, and Aquinas commented on this perceived shortcoming, Augustine expanded upon it at length in his *Confessions*, observing that the sin of *curiositas* utilized the senses, sight in particular, to affect one's moral decisions and worldview. Augustine couched this way of perception as a temptation, or, 'a certain vain desire and curiosity... cloaked under the name of learning and knowledge'. He cautioned against seeking useless knowledge, averring that 'God is tempted when signs and wonders are demanded, not for any purpose of salvation, but solely for the experience of seeing them'.[6] Curiosity about the world, from this standpoint, would distract humanity from the contemplation of God and the self-reflection necessary to attain salvation. For all of the novel experiences that were part of travel, *curiositas* came to be seen as a vice particular to pilgrims.

Pilgrims Simon Simeonis and Thomas Brygg show that, in spite of the temptations of *curiositas*, some writers were fully capable of interpreting their new experiences through scriptural lenses. It is this interpretive capability, I would posit, that counteracts the 'useless knowledge' that Augustine feared would distract Christians from the divine. As seen in the texts discussed here, interaction with foreign cultures, like contact with the sacred, is a positive experience: it expands the borders of the self, establishes connections abroad both imaginary and real, and provides a type of knowledge meant to be rewarded. To mitigate the pressures of novelty, some Christian pilgrim writers appealed to *auctoritas*, authenticating their interpretations of new experiences by means of previously-written sources, relying on the textual authority of the past, including, predictably, the Bible and early crusading sources, and, perhaps less predictably, the Qur'an and recent accounts by little-known Christian pilgrims. Both Simon Simeonis and Thomas Brygg, although dissimilar in approach, demonstrate a shared interest in proving that something of immense personal import did, in fact, happen to the pilgrim while he was abroad. To this end, both writers show concern with how the pilgrim protagonist would be perceived upon his return, and both texts represent a claim on the pilgrim's renewed role within his own community.

COMPARING THE FOURTEENTH-CENTURY
PILGRIM SOURCES

Simon Simeonis's account, wherein colourful details and opinions about life abroad spill out at every seam, makes a sharp contrast with Thomas Brygg's work, which is comparatively plain and conventional. Recent research into pilgrimage studies has shown that uniformity could be expected around many medieval pilgrim texts, specifically with regard to the particular sites of interest mentioned and the order in which they were recorded. Though most late medieval accounts of visits to the Holy Land can hardly be called identical, they do demonstrate certain likenesses which suggest that pilgrims were often preparing their works with reference to pre-existing texts. Through the similarities she has noted among the post-1300 accounts of the Jerusalem pilgrimage, Josephie Brefeld has shown that there may have been an original work, now lost, from which pilgrims faithfully copied.[7] This text would have been made available to pilgrims by the Franciscan friars in Jerusalem, for an anonymous Franciscan work of 1427 tells of the frequency with which the brothers were asked to provide written material for the pilgrims. The similarities of pilgrim accounts from different time periods, ranging, for example, from 1336 to 1546, and across nationalities and languages, show striking resemblances: the holy places are described in a set order, many contain the same unusual turns of phrase, there are identical prayers written out verbatim, and there are repeated references to a 'book (or books) of pilgrimage'.[8] These written descriptions were in the care of Jerusalem's Franciscan Order which owned a monastery on Mt. Sion from c. 1335–1524.[9] Though the later dispersal of the Franciscan library means that a specific source text or texts have yet to be found, the comparative evidence of international accounts which share uncanny similarities, alongside those writings which even claim to have been composed in conjunction with 'a book' at Mt. Sion, show the important influence of this order on the formation of pilgrim accounts from the early fourteenth- to the mid-sixteenth centuries.[10]

In all of the standard, exemplary texts, one finds detailed attention to the major pilgrim sites as if they were events numbered in a task list. Variety, in the main, tends to be expressed in the 'extra' sites which may be added to the traditional stations; yet even these more extensive accounts tend to follow the same patterns and include similar information. This chapter discusses one text that adheres to this pattern and one that does not. Yet both of the works I explore here illustrate that pilgrims were very aware of their audiences at home and strove to create models of their own religious, political, or social aspirations through association with the Holy Land. In Simon's case, extensive personalized commentary emerges around his perilous experiences, crusading enthusiasm, and perceptions of Islam. With the exception of the Jerusalem-based material, Simon's account represents a unique, personal experience of much of his pilgrimage. As I point out below, it is significant that he presents his experiences as mediated through various authorities, such as the Bible, the Qur'an, and other pilgrim writings. He also anchors this experience and persona in accepted images of crusading. These approaches work to justify Simon's travel, for the novel and exotic always has a purpose, thereby avoiding the tint of *curiositas*. There are many examples of personalized pilgrim narrative in the fourteenth century, but I have selected Simon's work for the unique contrast it offers the account of Thomas Brygg.

SIMON SIMEONIS (1323)

One of the most compelling fourteenth-century presentations of the author-self appears in the writing of Simon Simeonis, thought to have been an Anglo-Irishman who set off 'from Hibernia' for the Holy Land on March 15, 1323, in the company of Hugh, both of whom were Franciscan friars.[11] The single surviving manuscript of Simon's account is written in Latin in an English fourteenth-century hand;[12] the manuscript is incomplete, and some consider it a copy of a now lost original.[13] The text includes Simon's pilgrimage from Ireland to Egypt, and finally to Jerusalem. While much of the text offers personal detail, the Jerusalem material is very similar to the standard descriptions of its day, complete with the usual depictions of the Church of the Holy Sepulchre and other important sites, such as Mount Calvary and the Tower of David; after the description of Jerusalem, the manuscript breaks off abruptly.[14]

Currently neglected by modern scholarship, Simon's text is more of a personal account, as seen by his use of first-person singular and plural pronouns throughout. He also makes many additions to the traditional pilgrim genres, for instance, by including extensive information about the defences of the cities he visits, or his emotional state at the loss of his companion, Brother Hugh. Another remarkable characteristic is that Simon depicts himself as taking part in a continued scriptural narrative of the Holy Land, contextualizing his efforts through the language of biblical exegesis. This method is not unique to Simon; indeed, examples of it are seen as early as Egeria's fourth-century account, and it continues to be present in works like Saewulf's twelfth-century *Itinerarium* and some later texts of the fourteenth and fifteenth centuries. However, this use of exegesis was not the practice in the Franciscan exemplars, and Simon's interpretive method frames most of the events he records. For example, to begin his journey Simon does not simply offer a date, time, and departure point as most contemporary travel writers did; instead, he also provides an exegetical frame: he leaves his land and paternal home 'as did of old, Abraham' to 'wander religiously', 'like Asella', a female disciple of Jerome, thereby placing his experience as a linear development from the time of the Patriarchs, to the Church Fathers, extending through to his present day.[15]

In his use of exegesis, Simon shows substantial knowledge of Christian scripture; yet his account also demonstrates more than passing familiarity with Islamic scripture and customs. His work includes a lengthy section, beginning 'And this the Saracens do...;'[16] this portion shares some points of contact with writers not covered in this study, such as the (later) Anonymous English pilgrim and the writer of *The Travels of Sir John Mandeville*, both of whom seem to have been influenced by William of Tripoli. Simon includes the section in case it is of interest to his readers at home, and it prefaces his description of Alexandria. He mentions curiosities like hygienic practices and chicken hatcheries he claims to have observed, but he seems most interested to record the patterns of religious observance and Muslim views of Christ and Paradise.[17]

What is unique to Simon is his knowledge of the Qur'an, and the way he uses it in his descriptions. One would hardly call Simon an Islamophile—his references to mosques as 'synagogues of Satan' and his accusations of Muslim drunkenness during Ramadan preclude this[18]—but his appeal to the Qur'an is remarkable for this time period and genre. His depictions of Egypt require broad descriptions of its inhabitants, and he turns to the Qur'an as an authoritative matrix for his observations. This practice occurs almost a dozen times throughout the first half of the text concerning Egypt and its environs. He uses the Qur'an as a work of serious information as he cites Muslim teaching on such topics as the Christian Trinity, Christ's nature and his crucifixion, Muslim prayer, the import of Islamic purification rituals, women's modesty customs, and other concepts.[19] He quotes loosely from the Qur'an, as editor Girolamo Golubovich says, 'a senso, e non sempre alla lettera' [loosely, and not always literally], drawing from identifiable books and suras.[20] In all cases, Simon's quotations of scripture treat the Qur'an as a source of veracity, authenticating (or providing contrast to) some of the behaviours he says he has observed.

While Simon shows an interest in understanding the Islamic Egyptians on their own terms, and seems to acknowledge the Qur'an as an important text, he also works to counter any impression of admiration of Islam by adding a derogatory sentence of his own design after each Qur'anic quotation. Thus after referencing a scriptural passage explaining moral conduct,[21] Simon adds 'Hec, porcus Mochometus mulierum amator' [These things (say) the swine, M..., lover of women];[22] or, after loosely quoting a passage from the Qur'an on marriage,[23] Simon adds, 'Hec porcus Machometus, pudicitie et castitatis suffocator' [These things (say) the swine, M..., extinguisher of honour and chastity].[24] The remarks are puzzling in their vehemence; they are ad hominem attacks, often inconsistent with the content of the scriptural passage. In the latter instance, mentioned above, the scripture quoted relates what would seem to be useful advice, safe-guarding the status of the marriageable women involved. And yet, as Simon inter-weaves material from Islamic scripture throughout much of his work, after each loosely rendered quotation, he rarely misses an opportunity to insult. In another instance, Simon loosely translates the Qur'an to provide an exhortation to courage and valour,[25] which he follows with another polemical comment, 'Hic primogenitus Sathane Machometus humanigeneris inimicus' [This (says) M..., first-born of Satan, enemy of humankind].[26] It is obvious that these passages reflect a deep hostility in fourteenth-century Christian attitudes toward Islam, Muhammed, and the Qur'an. The comments are so repellent that mid-twentieth-century editor Eugene Hoade did not offer them in his English translation of the work. Simon's reflections—if they are indeed his, and not the work of a later, premodern reviser—are important to acknowledge in order to understand the very conflicting views about Islamic culture which some medieval clerical writers and their audiences held. Clearly, Islamic scripture is important to Simon—he uses it to underpin his own authority and to authenticate his experience—but he nevertheless repudiates the source on which he relies. Likewise, he would not have quoted the scriptures if they did not hold some clout with his audiences. It is impossible to say whether or not Simon's portrayal of his simultaneous interest and aversion is in earnest or a topos meant to provide cover for his interest in Islamic texts, but the depiction is congruent with attitudes surrounding Christian scholarly and religious study of the Qur'an in premodern England.

Simon may have been knowledgeable of the Qur'an through Englishman Robert of Ketton's Latin translation, produced as part of Peter the Venerable's project *c.* 1143. Other translations of the Qur'an would have been available in the fourteenth century, but it was Robert's paraphrasing of Islamic scripture, translated 'sensibiliter' [by sense],[27] that was the most widely read of medieval translations in northern Europe. In his preface to the work, Robert refers to Muhammed as 'pseudopropheta' [pseudo-prophet] and the Qur'an as 'lex…letifera' [deadly law],[28] but this negative language is not his sole view of Islam. Tracing western European reading habits of the Qur'an, Thomas Burman and David Howlett have shown that, while western Christian translators like Robert of Ketton were in no way Islamophiles, they prepared the Qur'an in Latin prose of the type that rhetorical manuals suggested should be used for important documents; moreover, the Latin translations of the Qur'an were made in consultation with other Islamic texts and exegesis.[29] Audiences, many of them clerical, would have encountered Robert of Ketton's translation with its high style and decorative pages as a book of intellectual import, representing the Qur'an as 'less the propaganda of a polemicist than the coherently purposeful project of a man demanding that his fellow Christians take the [Qur'an] seriously'.[30] In contrast to this even-handedness, crusading rhetoric appears in Robert's *Prefatio* to the Qur'an which he addressed to the abbot. Peter the Venerable commissioned the work between the First and Second Crusades; accordingly, Robert selects language suitable for the conflict between Christianity and Islam, equating his role of translator with that of a 'peditis' [foot soldier][31] whose duty it is to 'vias et aditus…patefeci; propugnaculaque…diruere' [(lay) open…the ways and approaches] in order to 'pull down…the bulwarks (of Islam)'.[32] It is tempting to speculate that Robert of Ketton's complex approach to the Qur'an influenced Simon's representation of Muslim peoples, for Simon offers a similar mix of aggression and occasional, respectful interest. In particular, as if mirroring Robert the translator-crusader, Simon represents crusading concerns through his reconnaissance in Egypt; here, it is possible that Simon enacts this crusading posture as a narrative topos employed to temper his praise of faithful Muslim adherence to scripture.

This second unusual aspect of Simon's account—his inclusion of detailed military intelligence regarding the localities through which he passes—offers insight into the ways that crusading was influencing late medieval pilgrimage and how pilgrims envisioned themselves. It also shows Simon gathering knowledge as if for a higher purpose, rather than love of novelty. As he sets out, Simon makes plain that non-Christian regions and their rulers will be contrasted to England under Edward II, who 'has a number of ships greater than all the kings of the whole of Christendom, and so on the high seas he rules alone and dominates all'.[33] Simon is full of praise for the English, and in addition to describing the riches and relics of London and surrounding English towns, he also adds a militant crusading flavour, praising Edward I, buried in Westminster, as 'the most Maccabean King of the English, who with St. Louis, the most Christian king of the Franks, with warlike hand, crossed to the land of the Saracens'.[34] Clearly, it is important to him that Edward joined St Louis during the Eighth Crusade in 1267, and that he went on crusade to Acre in 1270. Though there was certainly an upsurge in fourteenth-century titles urging the reclamation of the Holy Land, the typical pilgrim text did not tend to focus on these matters to the extent that Simon does. Even the late-medieval Mandeville writer, for all of his encouragement of crusade, does not include the scope of would-be military intelligence seen here.

It is clear that Simon seems to have an acquisitive fixation on Egypt, and that his interest in things militant increases in Alexandria. Even his pilgrim route, atypical of others of his day, begins there. By comparison, the majority of extant accounts by fourteenth-century European pilgrims trace a route through Italy, taking ship at Venice or Genoa and passing from island to island eastward across the Mediterranean until landing at Jaffa. From there, a short tour would include the major sites of Syria and Judaea; an extended tour would then bring the pilgrim from Jerusalem to St Catherine's monastery in Egypt, and then back again to Jaffa for the return trip home. Simon follows a reverse route: beginning in Egypt, he writes that the Port of Alexandria is well-guarded and overseen meticulously by Muslim administrators. Alexandria's defences are equally imposing: as Simon reports, 'the...city has a double wall, with towers and moats on one side'. It is 'well fortified with machines and other warlike apparatus; within which are two sandy hills'; tellingly, Simon speaks of the good vantage point of the sea that these hills offer. The city gates 'are guarded with great vigilance and especially those facing the port, together with that by which you ascend towards [Cairo]'.[35] Perhaps it is not surprising that, when Simon and Hugh are examined by the local consuls, they are accused of being spies, an accusation which they deny.[36]

This type of intelligence-gathering continues as Simon makes his journey from Alexandria to Cairo. Even the farmers' homes come under his scrutiny: 'They are fortified with moats and nothing of other fortifications, but they are unarmed and unsuitable for piercing the ranks of the enemy...as are also the Saracen people'.[37] From Simon's point of view, the greatest strategic strengths of the Egyptians rest both in their army and in the situation of their landscape; he speaks of the trust that the Egyptians put in these defences:

> there are things in which they...believe themselves to be protected and from the attacks of the enemy to be defended and liberated: first in the Sultan's army, which almost always is stationed in the city of [Cairo], and which has 30,000 horsemen; the

second is the oft-mentioned river…and the third is the sandy desert, which also is their tower of strength, by which the whole country is surrounded as far as the Mediterranean Sea. And hence it is that to enter the land of Egypt is impossible except by sea or by desert, or by descending from India.[38]

Here, it is worth observing that later in his travels, as Simon crosses from Cairo to Jerusalem, he takes note of the comprehensive guardianship of what he identifies as the entry point between 'India' and Egypt.[39] It is this persistence which suggests that some sort of invasion of Egypt is continually on Simon's mind. Once he reaches Cairo, he continues appraising militaristic strengths. Alongside the usual accounts of the city's beauty and riches, he comments on its liabilities; it is 'defended neither by moats or other war apparatus, unless weakly enough around the centre; where it has most excellent gates covered with iron plates, and somewhat of a wall, which extends from the fort, herein described, to the north one mile'.[40] The Citadel of Cairo, however, 'in which are continually stationed 10,000 of the most excellent paid horsemen', is much more formidable, but, Simon notes, still vulnerable: 'although it may be well furnished with the apparatus of war, yet has it within it no water and its walls, as we understood, are easy enough to breach'.[41]

Crusading sources show that Egypt was seen by European leaders as a strategic node for securing Jerusalem once and for all. Moreover, speculation about the position of Egypt was thick on the ground; just over a year before Simon began his pilgrimage, Christian author Marino Sanudo in his later, expanded version of the *Secreta fidelium crucis* of 1321 again proposed a blockade of the region in a narrative aimed at Jerusalem's recovery.[42] However, so little historical information is known of Simon and Brother Hugh that further speculation on their potential involvement—more particularly, their alleged roles as spies—becomes difficult. On the one hand, pilgrims who also served as spies were not unknown. Christopher Tyerman mentions hybridized pilgrim-crusader activity occurring throughout the fourteenth century, and refers to the spying activities in 1330s of pilgrim James of Verona. He notes an attitude of surveillance by pilgrims in many late medieval itineraries; this is certainly present in Simon's account.[43] Other models existed in popular Middle English romance, such as *Richard Coer de Lion* (sic), in which the protagonist, the future King Richard I, and his men visit the Holy Land disguised as pilgrims in order to plot out their subsequent crusading strategies.[44] On the other hand, it is possible that Simon was writing without practical plans in mind, but was reacting to the unrest he perceived in Egypt, for the region was known to be unstable at this time. Simon endures most of his hardships there, and this may have influenced his interest in subjugating it. He reports that there, 'For the name of Jesus we were spat upon, struck with stones, and saturated with other insults and reproaches'; and there, upon being examined by the local consuls, 'when the examiners saw images of the crucifix, the Blessed Virgin Mary and John the Evangelist, which we had taken devoutly and reverently with us from Ireland, immediately blaspheming and spitting on them, they in clamorous voices began to insult'.[45] Chief among their sufferings, Brother Hugh dies of dysentery in Egypt, and Simon portrays this loss as he would a comrade fallen in battle. This crusading persona would have allowed Simon to take up a devotional practice

I have identified elsewhere: that of the virtual crusade.[46] In this case, embodying the role of vigilant crusader embellishes Simon's experience of the Holy Land, overlaying it with added challenge and spiritual reward.

THOMAS BRYGG (1392)

Simon's text is full of new experiences which he works to contextualize as useful knowledge. In contrast, Brygg's work[47] generally avoids the new, instead offering simple lists of places with few descriptive modifiers. Moreover, while Simon probably composed his own account, it was not uncommon to hire someone else to do so. Such is the case with the English knight, Lord Thomas Swinburne, for whom Thomas Brygg wrote. Very little is known of Brygg aside from the fact that he is thought to have been either Swinburne's squire or chaplain. More is known of Swinburne, whom Richard II had made Lord of the Castle of Guines in 1390, less than two years before Lord Thomas's pilgrimage; therefore, at the time of his travels, Swinburne was a noble positioned for further promotion. He would later become the Mayor of Bordeaux, and, in 1408, Lord of Fronsac.[48] Swinburne and his company, along with Brygg, departed for the Holy Land from the fort of Guines on 6 August 1392, returning less than one year later. Of the two works mentioned in this study, Brygg's is the shorter, filling roughly three folio pages of Latin text, compared to Simon's (incomplete) thirty-six folio pages. The piece contains very little personal information either about Brygg or Swinburne, and uses first-person pronouns only when mentioning travel from place to place, describing, for instance, 'on Monday, September second, we boarded a galley belonging to Venetian merchants [bound for] Alexandria'.[49]

Brygg's work is of interest here precisely because it lacks many of those personal touches discussed thus far. It contains no subtext of exegesis, pays no particular attention to Islamic or crusading issues, and mentions nothing of personal suffering. According to Brefeld, Brygg's text is close to what would have been produced by someone working closely with the written materials of Mt Sion. Because of this, it shares much in common with other, more standardized pilgrim accounts of the fourteenth and fifteenth centuries, and with authors of different provenance from all over Western Europe.[50] What sets Swinburne's pilgrimage apart from those covered in Brefeld's case study is that he approaches the Holy Land from the west, calling first at Alexandria, just as Simon had done half a century earlier. Apart from this likeness, important details differentiate this piece from Simon's text. For instance, Swinburne is described as a 'soldier of England' and he travels with other soldiers; by the time he reaches Venice, his party includes the Lords Hans Van Hoske, Snutt Van Fetau, soldiers and 'shield bearers' from Bohemia and Germany, with their servants.[51] Also, only the broadest contours of the journey are known, and, apart from the calendar dates assigned to specific sacred sites, there is a lot of time left unaccounted for.

Brygg describes no events after departure from Guines until the men reach Venice, where they then take ship for Alexandria. In Alexandria, Brygg describes certain traditional holy places, including the site of Catherine's martyrdom, and provides brief anecdotes of local custom. Shortly thereafter the group leaves for Cairo and, along with mentioning a few sacred sites, he includes the first of only a handful of personalized details: on the Nile they see 'in several places those aquatic monsters called crocodiles, larger and also longer than men'.[52] Alongside this material, however, they see many of the traditional Egyptian sites as are found in Brefeld's Franciscan exemplar. Unlike Simon who had followed the same route, Brygg records no information about the fortifications and military assets of the region.

Once in proximity to Jerusalem, the account loses any hint of narrative and becomes a ledger of one-sentence entries as Brygg introduces the material as part of the 'sanctum circulum' [holy circuit] for Jerusalem and its environs.[53] From this point he simply offers a list of sites; a typical entry reads 'Also, where the blessed Virgin met Jesus carrying the cross', followed by, 'Also the school where the blessed Virgin learned her letters', and 'Also the house of Pilate, where Christ was whipped'.[54] These three subsequent entries, like the rest that follow, provide no orienting apparatus, nor do they account for the pilgrim's experience with the sites; first-person usage disappears almost entirely. Exceptions to this rule include reference to the most significant locations, for 'we entered' the Church of the Holy Sepulchre on 11 December and 'we left it' on 13 December.[55] The text also includes crosses in the margins to indicate certain amounts of indulgences; these markings would have constituted a record of the spiritual merit of Swinburne's pilgrimage.

It is difficult to imagine that that the group was able to visit all of the places recorded in the account, for Swinburne and his party reach Jerusalem on 10 December, spending the eleventh to the morning of the thirteenth inside the Church of the Holy Sepulchre, making excursions to the Jordan area, Jericho, and Mt. Quarantine between the thirteenth and seventeenth, and claiming to have seen the rest of Jerusalem's many sites amongst this flurry of activity. Having left Jerusalem for good, they visit Nazareth and the region of the Galilean Sea. The list form gradually falls away toward the very end of the piece once the group reaches the city of Damascus on 25 December; here they stay for seven days, though no activities there are described. Their last recorded stop is Beirut on 3 January 1392, 'a city once called Tyre', where they remain for twelve days, waiting for passage to Rhodes. In his last site-related entry, Brygg tells us that they 'made an end to [their] pilgrimages to the Holy Land' outside Beirut, at a chapel where St George slew the dragon.[56] Such a record certainly would work to Swinburne's benefit as proof of indulgences earned. As if to insure that the reader perceive Swinburne's spiritual accomplishments, Brygg's concluding paragraphs review all of the indulgences according to value, and, after this spiritual accounting, provide an expenses sheet where some of the costs incurred on the pilgrimage are entered.[57] The fee schedule cannot be complete, but includes figures for such things as sea passage, hire of an interpreter, payment to the hospices, guards, camel rental, tribute to the Sultan, admission to certain sites, and wine and victuals. The list form of the receipt, with its short, grammatically simple entries and repetition of the word 'item,' make an uncanny mirror of the account of Jerusalem's sites.

There are many possible reasons that Swinburne thought his pilgrimage important enough to hire Brygg to accompany him on his journey in order to document it. When one considers his knightly status, alongside his choice to travel in company of other soldiers during a time when crusade was being planned, it is impossible not to entertain the possibility that he was doing reconnaissance work. Swinburne travelled nearly thirty years after the disastrous invasion of Alexandria by Peter I of Cyprus in 1365, and the memory of that very bloody campaign remained culturally present in Western Europe. Crusading was a live issue in the late fourteenth century, and Aziz Atiya points to the years 1344 to 1396 as times of concentrated activity.[58] J. J. N. Palmer notes that traffic to Jerusalem was particularly heavy during the last decade of the fourteenth century, describing the number of English knights, including Swinburne, who took up pilgrimage to the Levant at this time. Significantly, Palmer suggests that these pilgrimages may have been 'exploratory missions' for those who financed the expeditions.[59] Together with the powers of Venice and Hungary, some of the most influential figures of England and France—among them, the Dukes of Burgundy, Orleans, and Lancaster—were organizing a campaign in the last decade of the fourteenth century, and by 1393 plans had begun in earnest to launch a crusade in 1395.[60] Brygg's account, then, would provide an excuse for sanctioned travel, should Swinburne be apprehended.

Along with the timeframe of Swinburne's pilgrimage, Brygg's text suggests a potentially active crusader identity for his master by describing him twice as 'soldier', traveling armed in the company of other knights and soldiers. Also, Swinburne's party approaches Jerusalem atypically; they begin in Alexandria, which was still considered strategically important in order to seize the holy city. Swinburne then makes his way east to Palestine and Syria, traveling north along the Mediterranean, and eventually taking ship for Rhodes, a longstanding crusader stronghold and staging point. But these details are not enough to classify Swinburne as a crusader. As Tyerman has shown, by the fourteenth century crusades and pilgrimages were 'intimately associated but separable', especially as one is able to differentiate between licenses and safe-conducts given for each.[61] However, the possibility of a pilgrimage inadvertently turning into crusade during this century was not unheard of. There was a great deal of pilgrim travel through Rhodes, and Tyerman speaks of the ever-present 'opportunity to fight alongside the Hospitallers' which some pilgrims entertained. At least one fourteenth-century English knight, Sir Hugh of Hastings, is known to have done so after ostensibly beginning his journey as a pilgrim. Because Swinburne's name is missing from the Patent Rolls, it is impossible to know by the length of his term whether he viewed his tour as pilgrimage or crusade, or both.[62]

There were many theoretical connections between pilgrimage and crusade, both in form and merit, making it probable that Swinburne could have been positioning himself for armed involvement all the while performing pilgrimage to the betterment of his soul. The spiritual merit earned on crusade was so valued even in the late medieval era that some knights were known to substitute peaceful pilgrimage for campaigning during periods when crusading was unavailable. The popularity of crusading in the Mediterranean and Baltic among English nobles in the fourteenth century is shown in the numbers who participated in and supported it, some of whom Chaucer would have known at court, including families of Beauchamps, Uffords, Bohuns, Percies, Despensers,

FitzWalters, Beaumonts, Scropes, Courtenays, Montagues, Cliffords, and Ferrers of Groby.[63] It is significant that these crusading families were also known to have several family members participate in pilgrimage; indeed, there was a high coincidence of social and family groupings who had been pilgrims and had also taken up arms as crusaders.[64] Such a family tradition may be seen in Henry Grosmont who fought against the Moors in Spain and against the Slavs in the Baltic; in like manner, Grosmont's grandson, Henry Bolingbroke, sought active involvement in crusading. His arrangements for fighting with the French in Tunis fell through, however, leading him to seek new opportunities in Prussia. These plans, too, were foiled, leading some historians speculate that because Bolingbroke was unable to take part in these crusading activities, he substituted another experience: he went to the Holy Land as a pilgrim in 1392.[65]

It is probable that for the nobility, and especially for the aspiring nobility, the activity of inhabiting the image of pilgrim, like that of the crusader, brought with it certain merit. This may have been true for Swinburne: having made his visit, he received civic promotions shortly thereafter. Many pilgrims had connections with the royal court, thereby easing any potential crusade planning; it is therefore tempting to speculate that it may have been no coincidence that Swinburne and Bolingbroke missed each other in Jerusalem by a little over a month. Both men received substantial career promotions after their respective pilgrimages; most notably, Bolingbroke would later become King Henry IV. Though the latter's pilgrimage was not the cause of this promotion, the perception of Bolingbroke as a Christian leader would have been bolstered with his visit to the Holy Land. It is in this regard that we may view Brygg's account as Swinburne's 'receipt' of having visited the region. Though no causal relationship between experience and reward can be proven here, the context of these travels provides a new way to view pilgrim writing. Not only would Swinburne have earned the political interest owing to such experience abroad, but the spiritual capital—that is, the amount of indulgences earned—is carefully noted and itemized as is the record of expenses at the end of his work. In this sense, it is important that Brygg's is a 'bare-bones' account, for, in being as close as possible to the Franciscan exemplar, it is yoked to a narrative form then recognized as authoritative throughout Europe. The Franciscan-based pilgrimage account, then, represented transferrable currency of many types, including political authority.

I would like to suggest that there were many tangible as well as spiritual rewards available to Swinburne for his efforts. Brygg portrays Swinburne as deserving of these rewards not through any personal information about his master, but by documenting the fact that Swinburne successfully performed and completed the Holy Land pilgrimage almost to the letter. Such a formal style also would have kept Swinburne clear of accusations of vain *curiositas*. Moreover, what these patterns tell us about the pilgrim genre is that, depending on the situation, the plainer, more standardized account could have granted its pilgrim-protagonist just as much social and spiritual reward as its more embellished contemporaries did. It would seem that, depending on the pilgrim's aims and social status, suitable modes of pilgrim writing had already developed to establish specific kinds of merit, whether at court, in the cloister, or among one's friends. If this is so, then the varied modes of describing Holy Land experience indicate that there were different textual receptions based on factors such as the pilgrim's social status, or what that pilgrim stood to gain by producing evidence of the experience.

THE REWARDS OF PILGRIMAGE
AND CRUSADE

The works of Simon Simeonis and Thomas Brygg offer a vantage point from which to consider the framing of fourteenth-century pilgrim travel. The varied presentation of new experience sanctioned by textual *auctoritas*, and by the pilgrim-protagonist who adopts long-established roles (as crusader, biblical figure, etc.), shows little to suggest authorship by liars or tale-spinners. In fact, both works demonstrate attention to narrative authority and to specific performances designed to authenticate pilgrim identity. In Simon's account can be observed deftly produced approaches to religious others, crusading, and personal trial, all of which took on much greater emphasis in the context of pilgrimage. At the same time, Brygg's text applies a received, carefully executed form to its pilgrim protagonist, providing evidence of several kinds that the tour had been made, that the required places had been visited, that a certain number of indulgences had been earned, and even that a substantial outlay of funds had been spent.

Both accounts establish the authenticity of the pilgrimage and the accomplishment of the pilgrim, albeit in different ways. Both can be viewed as different kinds of proof of experience, and also considered as strategies for the mitigation of *curiositas*. In assessing texts as different as Simon Simeonis's and Thomas Brygg's are from one another, it is fair to say that the content of their writing would have conveyed a complex network of cultural messages to their audiences, reflecting the pilgrim protagonists' religious, political, and social aspirations. In this chapter, I hope to have expressed how the rather plain, exemplar-based pilgrimage accounts flourished alongside those more colourful, personalized ones, and that both of these could have performed important social, political, and spiritual work for the pilgrim. Brefeld's evidence shows that the shorter, plainer, more 'standardized' accounts like Brygg's were popular and had some sort of utility. While it is true that an increasing amount of fantastic material was making its way into late medieval pilgrim writing, Simon's text demonstrates that there were ways to manage such marvel-laden content and make it meaningful in then-orthodox Christian terms. Likewise, this chapter offers further layers of complexity for present-day discussion about which travel texts would have been considered curiosity collections and which were not. As seen in this chapter, in Simon and Brygg's accounts, 'curiosities' are balanced with the other materials which do not point toward the fabulizing use of *curiositas* alone, but to other, then-laudable pursuits to be performed by the premodern proto-crusader.

This study therefore adds to continued discussion of Chaucer's characters, especially that of the Knight. Several years ago, scholarly criticism of the Knight suggested that he would have represented for medieval audiences an outmoded form of chivalry expressed in crusading. Simon and Brygg's texts, however, exemplify a very active crusading culture in the fourteenth century, and thereby add to the many scholarly voices who posit a positive medieval reception of the Knight as a man of his time.[66] Other scholarly detractors have suggested that Chaucer's audience would have perceived the Knight's many campaigns as evidence that he was nothing more than a mercenary soldier; indeed, those who hold this point of view may even find some support in Brygg's example.[67] On the one hand, it is easy to see how Swinburne's promotions seem to indicate a causal relationship between crusade, pilgrimage, and worldly advancement; in this regard, Swinburne would have been the image of Chaucer's Knight as viewed by his present-day detractors. On the other hand, it is notable that both Simon and Swinburne show interest in Alexandria—the town mentioned first among the Knight's conquests, and, incidentally, the campaign most loudly condemned by the Knight's present-day critics.[68] In light of such critique, it is perhaps significant that Simon, the non-combatant friar pilgrim, enthusiastically borrows crusading identity especially when he is in Alexandria, shamelessly adopting an attitude of surveillance as a positive attribute of his persona.

There were many ways to construct cultural identity in the fourteenth century, and travel writing was only one of them. Over the past century, Chaucer's work has presented and continues to present rich questions surrounding the uses of and production of authority in its medieval textual and socio-political contexts. As is evident, the premodern receptions of travellers' tales were variable. Yet it is telling that Chaucer, even as he condemned shipmen and pilgrims, crafted a pilgrimage to frame his *Canterbury Tales*. Certainly this is an invitation to view Chaucer's pilgrim-characters as unreliable narrators, but it is also, as I have shown here, a move which would have imbued their figurative voices with a singular kind of authority, or reliability, based in the experience attributed to the medieval voyager. The historical Chaucer was, among other things, also a traveller who is known to have ventured abroad on diplomatic missions, encountering new cultures, knowledge and texts along the way. Chaucer the narrator, likewise, often appears in his longer poems as a character spirited away on an other-worldly voyage (usually in a dream) to gain insight; his other interests in the act of traveling may be inferred from his work on the *Treatise on the Astrolabe*, the instrument, itself, a voyager's tool. Chaucer may have presented an outward face of suspicion toward pilgrims as guilty of vices like *curiositas*, but he also provides some of his characters with their most redeeming qualities as travellers. It is significant that at the outset of the *Canterbury Tales* the crusader Knight models a would-be pilgrim role and receives honour for it; perhaps in this context his rust-stained tunic offered just as much evidence of merit as any written text.

NOTES

1. Jacques de Vitry, *Historia orientalis*, ed. Jean Donnadieu (Turnhout: Brepols, 2008), ch. 83, 333.
2. William Langland, *Piers Plowman* (B), ed. A. V. C. Schmidt (London: J.M. Dent, repr. 1995), Prol. 3–4; see 46–52, esp. 49.
3. 'Examination of Master William Thorpe, Priest, of Heresy', in *Fifteenth-Century Prose and Verse*, ed. A.W. Pollard (London: Archibald Constable, 1903), 97–174; see 141.

4. Christian K. Zacher, *Curiosity and Pilgrimage: The Literature of Discovery in Fourteenth-Century England* (Baltimore, MD: Johns Hopkins University Press, 1976), 18–41; see 4.

5. See Bede, *In Primam Epistolam S. Joannis*, Patrologia Latina 93:92; and Thomas Brinton, *The Sermons of Thomas Brinton, Bishop of Rochester (1373–1389)*, ed. Mary Aquinas Devlin, Camden Third Series, vols. 85 and 86 (London: Offices of the Royal Historical Society, 1954), 300.

6. Augustine, *Confessiones*, PL 32, col. 802, s. 54; Bk. 10.35: 'experiendi per carnem vana et curiosa cupiditas, nomine cognitionis et scientia palliata'; in translation, see Augustine, *Confessions*, trans. F. J. Sheed (Indianapolis: Hackett, 1942), 200. See also col. 802, s. 55: 'Deus tentatur, cum signa et prodigia flagitantur, non ad aliquam salutem, sed ad solam experientiam desiderata'.

7. Josephie Brefeld, *A Guidebook for the Jerusalem Pilgrimage in the Late Middle Ages* (Amsterdam: Hilversum, 1994), 29, 179. Brefeld substantiates the hypothesis of an original text first suggested by Reinhold Röhricht and Heinrich Meisner in *Deutsche Pilgerreisen nach dem Heiligen Lande* (Berlin: Weidmannsche Buchhandlung, 1880), 8–9.

8. Brefeld, *Guidebook*, 38–42.

9. Ibid., 29–30.

10. For more on a common source, see Brefeld, *Guidebook*, 33–61. Little is known of the late-medieval contents of the Franciscan della Vigna monastery in Venice and the Mount Sion monastery in Jerusalem since they were either dispersed or lost in the Second World War.

11. Cambridge, Cambridge University, Corpus Christi College MS 2.2.2 407, fols. 1–36; Simon Simeonis, *Itinerarium fratrum Symonis Semeonis et Hugonis illuminatoris, ordinis fratrum Minorum professorum ad Terram Sanctam, A.D. 1322*; for the original Latin, see Girolamo Golubovich, ed., *Biblioteca Bio-Bibliografica della Terra Santa*, vol. 3 (Florence: Quracchi Press, 1919), 237–82. For a modern English translation, see *Western Pilgrims*, ed. Eugene Hoade (Jerusalem: Franciscan Printing Press, 1952; repr. 1970), 2–46.

12. Simon, *Itinerarium* in Golubovich, *Biblioteca*, 246; trans. Hoade, *Western Pilgrims*, 1.

13. Golubovich, *Biblioteca*, 245.

14. Simon, *Itinerarium* in Golubovich, *Biblioteca*, 281–2; trans. Hoade, *Western Pilgrims*, 44–6.

15. Simon, *Itinerarium* in Golubovich, *Biblioteca*, 246; trans. Hoade, *Western Pilgrims*, 2.

16. Simon, *Itinerarium* in Golubovich, *Biblioteca*, 257–79; trans. Hoade, *Western Pilgrims*, 13–16.

17. Simon, *Itinerarium* in Golubovich, *Biblioteca*, 259–60; trans. Hoade, *Western Pilgrims*, 16–17.

18. Simon, *Itinerarium* in Golubovich, *Biblioteca*, 257; trans. Hoade, *Western Pilgrims*, 14.

19. Simon, *Itinerarium* in Golubovich, *Biblioteca*, 257–8, 261–2; trans. Hoade, *Western Pilgrims*, 14–15, 19–20.

20. Simon, *Itinerarium* in Golubovich, *Biblioteca*, 259.

21. Qur'an 24:31; cf. Golubovich, *Biblioteca*, 262, n.1.

22. Simon, *Itinerarium* in Golubovich, *Biblioteca*, 262. My translation.

23. Qur'an 4:3; Golubovich notes the rather loose rendering of the passage, suggesting that Simon may have been working from a commentary, see Golubovich, *Biblioteca*, 268, n.1.

24. Simon, *Itinerarium* in Golubovich, *Biblioteca*, 267–8. My translation.

25. The passage seems to be loosely based on Qur'an 8:16. Golubovich's edition features Simon's attribution of the passage to Sura 17, but the lack of consistency to the chapter suggests a mistaken transcription of the numerals, perhaps by a medieval copyist.

26. Simon, *Itinerarium* in Golubovich, *Biblioteca*, 274–5. My translation.

27. See Robert of Ketton's preface to his translation of the Qur'an, *Prefatio Roberti Tractoris ad Dominum Petrum Cluniacensem Abbatem in libro legis Sarracenorum quem Alchoran vocant*

[*Preface of Robert the Translator the the Lord Peter Abbot of Cluny on the Book of Law of the Saracens Which They Call the Qur'an*], in *Insular Inscriptions,* ed. David Howlett (Dublin: Four Courts Press, 2005), 168–71; see l.30, 170.

28. Robert, *Prefatio,* l.48, in Howlett, *Insular Inscriptions,* 170.

29. Howlett, *Insular Inscriptions,* 175; see also Robert's *Prefatio* to the *Lex Machomet pseudo-prophete* in Howlett, *Insular Inscriptions,* 169–71; and Thomas E. Burman, *Reading the Qur'an in Latin Christendom, 1140–1560* (Philadelphia, PA: University of Pennsylvania Press, 2007), 2, 5, 15, 32–5, 122.

30. Howlett, *Insular Inscriptions,* 175.

31. Robert, *Prefatio,* 'pseudopropheta', l.4 of Robert's working title; 'peditis', l.5, in Howlett, *Insular Inscriptions,* 169.

32. Robert, *Prefatio,* 'vias et aditus', l.5; 'propugnaculaque, etc.', l.4 in Howlett, *Insular Inscriptions,* 169.

33. Simon, *Itinerarium* in Golubovich, *Biblioteca,* 247; trans. Hoade, *Western Pilgrims,* 2.

34. Simon, *Itinerarium* in Golubovich, *Biblioteca,* 247; trans. Hoade, *Western Pilgrims,* 3.

35. Simon, *Itinerarium* in Golubovich, *Biblioteca,* 260; trans. Hoade, *Western Pilgrims,* 18.

36. Simon, *Itinerarium* in Golubovich, *Biblioteca,* 256; trans. Hoade, *Western Pilgrims,* 13.

37. Simon, *Itinerarium* in Golubovich, *Biblioteca,* 266; trans. Hoade, *Western Pilgrims,* 26.

38. Simon, *Itinerarium* in Golubovich, *Biblioteca,* 266; trans. Hoade, *Western Pilgrims,* 26.

39. Simon, *Itinerarium* in Golubovich, *Biblioteca,* 279; trans. Hoade, *Western Pilgrims,* 42.

40. Simon, *Itinerarium* in Golubovich, *Biblioteca,* 266; trans. Hoade, *Western Pilgrims,* 26.

41. Simon, *Itinerarium* in Golubovich, *Biblioteca,* 269; trans. Hoade, *Western Pilgrims,* 29–30.

42. Aziz Atiya notes the prevalence of recovery narratives between 1292 and 1344, citing Sanudo's first edition of 1309 and its iteration in 1321, including the trade bans on Egypt enforced by pain of excommunication. See his *Crusade, Commerce, and Culture* (Bloomington, IN: Indiana University Press, 1962), 95–9.

43. James of Verona, *Liber Peregrinationis,* Revue de l'Orient Latin 3 (1895); and Christopher Tyerman, *England and the Crusades, 1095–1588* (Chicago, IL: Chicago University Press, 1988), 296.

44. *Richard, Coer de Lion,* ed. Karl Brunner, in *Weiner Beiträge zur Englischen Philologie* 42 (Vienna: Wilhelm Braumüller, 1913), ll. 595–650.

45. Simon Simeonis, *Itinerarium* in Golubovich, *Biblioteca,* 256; trans. Hoade, *Western Pilgrims,* 12.

46. Suzanne M. Yeager, *Jerusalem in Medieval Narrative* (Cambridge: Cambridge University Press, 2008), 78–134.

47. Cambridge, Cambridge University, Gonville and Caius College MS 449, 167 r–169 r. Thomas Brygg, *Itinerarium in terram sanctam domini Thomae de Swynburne, castellani Ghisnensis et postea Burdigalensis majoris,* ed. Paul Riant in *Archives de l'Orient Latin,* vol. 2 (Paris, 1884), 380–8. See an English translation in *Western Pilgrims,* ed. Eugene Hoade (Jerusalem: Franciscan Printing Press, 1952; repr. 1970), 77–86. English translations given are my own; page numbers to the Riant and Hoade editions, respectively, are provided.

48. Paul Riant, 'Voyage en Terre-Sainte d'un Marie de Bordeaux au XIVe siècle', in *Archives de l'Orient Latin,* vol. 2 (Paris, 1884), 378–9.

49. Brygg, *Itinerarium,* in Riant, *Archives,* 380; trans. Hoade, *Western Pilgrims,* 78.

50. Brefeld, *Guidebook,* 193–213.

51. Brygg, *Itinerarium,* in Riant, *Archives,* 380; trans. Hoade, *Western Pilgrims,* 78.

52. Brygg, *Itinerarium,* in Riant, *Archives,* 381; trans. Hoade, *Western Pilgrims,* 78.

53. Brygg, *Itinerarium*, in Riant, *Archives*, 383; trans. Hoade, *Western Pilgrims*, 80.
54. Brygg, *Itinerarium*, in Riant, *Archives*, 383; trans. Hoade, *Western Pilgrims*, 81.
55. Brygg, *Itinerarium*, in Riant, *Archives*, 385; trans. Hoade, *Western Pilgrims*, 82.
56. Brygg, *Itinerarium*, in Riant, *Archives*, 386; trans. Hoade, *Western Pilgrims*, 84.
57. Brygg, *Itinerarium*, in Riant, *Archives*, 387–8; trans. Hoade, *Western Pilgrims*, 84–6.
58. Atiya, *Crusade, Commerce*, 93; and J. J. N. Palmer, *England, France, and Christendom, 1377–99* (Chapel Hill, NC: University of North Carolina Press, 1972), 206.
59. Palmer, *England, France, and Christendom*, 198.
60. With Hungary's delay, however, these plans deteriorated, leaving only the reduced force which ventured out in 1396 to take up the ill-fated campaign at Nicopolis. See Palmer, *England, France, and Christendom*, 198–9.
61. Tyerman, *England and the Crusades*, 282.
62. Ibid., 286–7.
63. Maurice Keen, 'Chaucer's Knight, the English Aristocracy and the Crusade', in *English Court Culture in the Later Middle Ages*, eds. V. J. Scattergood and J. W. Sherborne (New York: St Martin's Press, 1983), 51–6; and Tyerman, *England and the Crusades*, 268.
64. Tyerman, *England and the Crusades*, 287.
65. Ibid., 266.
66. For examples of positive scholarly views, see J. M. Manly, 'A Knight Ther Was', *Transactions and Proceedings of the American Philological Association* 38 (1907), 89–107; Muriel Bowden, *Commentary on the General Prologue to the Canterbury Tales* (New York: Macmillan, 1948), 44–73; E. T. Donaldson, *Chaucer's Poetry: An Anthology for the Modern Reader* (New York: Ronald Press, 1958), 881–2; and Jill Mann, *Chaucer and Medieval Estates Satire: The Literature of Social Classes and the General Prologue to the Canterbury Tales* (Cambridge: Cambridge University Press, 1973), 113.
67. Negative interpretations include Charles Mitchell, 'The Worthiness of Chaucer's Knight', *Modern Language Quarterly* 25 (1964), 66–75; and Terry Jones, *Chaucer's Knight: The Portrait of a Medieval Mercenary* (London: Weidenfeld and Nicolson, 1980; repr. Methuen, 1984); Terry Jones, 'The Monk's Tale', *Studies in the Age of Chaucer* 22 (2000), 387–97; see 388–93.
68. For a positive revision of Alexandria, see Celia Lewis, 'History, Mission, and Crusade in the *Canterbury Tales*', *Chaucer Review* 42, no. 4 (2008), 353–82.

BIBLIOGRAPHY

Brefeld, Josephie, *A Guidebook for the Jerusalem Pilgrimage in the Late Middle Ages* (Amsterdam: Hilversum, 1994).

Brygg, Thomas, *Itinerarium in terram sanctam domini Thomae de Swynburne, castellani Ghisnensis et postea Burdigalensis majoris*, ed. Paul Riant in *Archives de l'Orient Latin*, vol. 2 (Paris, 1884), 380–8.

Burman, Thomas E., *Reading the Qur'an in Latin Christendom, 1140–1560* (Philadelphia, PA: University of Pennsylvania Press, 2007).

Howlett, David, *Insular Inscriptions* (Dublin: Four Courts Press, 2005).

Lewis, Celia, 'History, Mission, and Crusade in the *Canterbury Tales*', *Chaucer Review* 42 (2008), 353–82.

Palmer, J. J. N., *England, France, and Christendom, 1377–99* (Chapel Hill, NC: University of North Carolina Press, 1972).

Simeonis, Simon, *Itinerarium fratrum Symonis Semeonis et Hugonis illuminatoris, ordinis fratrum Minorum professorum ad Terram Sanctam, A.D. 1322*, ed. Girolamo Golubovich, in *Biblioteca Bio-Bibliografica della Terra Santa*, vol. 3 (Florence: Quracchi Press, 1919), 237–82.

Tyerman, Christopher, *England and the Crusades, 1095–1588* (Chicago, IL: Chicago University Press, 1988).

Yeager, Suzanne M., *Jerusalem in Medieval Narrative* (Cambridge: Cambridge University Press, 2008).

Zacher, Christian K., *Curiosity and Pilgrimage: The Literature of Discovery in Fourteenth-Century England* (Baltimore, MD: Johns Hopkins University Press, 1976).

PART III

CHAUCER IN THE EUROPEAN FRAME

CHAPTER 12

....

OVID

Artistic Identity and Intertextuality

....

JAMIE C. FUMO

Prisca iuvent alios: ego me nunc denique natum
Gratulor: haec aetas moribus apta meis.
[Let ancient times delight other folk: I congratulate myself that I
was not born till now; this age fits my nature well.]

Ovid, *Ars amatoria* 3.121–2

TEMPORALITIES

....

OVID, revelling archly in his 'modernity' as a champion of Roman *cultus* in 2 CE, is nothing short of prescient. After intermittent periods of critical exile, the ancient poet has enjoyed the warmest of welcomes in both academic and popular spheres in the late-twentieth and early twenty-first centuries, stimulating an impressively vibrant industry of scholarly commentary, theoretical inquiry, fictional adaptation, poetic conversation, even Broadway performance. This cosmopolitan poet so concerned, especially in his exile writings, with the currency of his name in a hostile and unstable world has achieved a modern apotheosis, felicitously, not just on the lips of the people ('ore...populi')[1] but on their laptops. It is only too easy to imagine Ovid's delight in the communicative infinities of cyberspace.[2]

Chaucer's articulation of his own artistic moment fourteen centuries after Ovid's brazen pronouncement of modernity could not be more different, despite the two poets' common urbanity. Chaucer regarded Ovid as a figure of the past: part of the power structure of (pagan) *auctoritas* epitomized by 'olde bookes' and, as such, morally incomplete and subject to ethical correction. At the same time, at least early in his career, Chaucer associated Ovid's poetry with the incorruption of the valorized 'former age', when 'men loved the lawe of kinde' (BD 56)—a bygone *rusticitas* which Ovid, of course, lampoons in *Ars amatoria* 3.[3] For Chaucer, modernity was a liability, one largely incompatible with a stance of authorship. As Lee Patterson has argued: '[Chaucer's] poetry everywhere records the attraction of modernity but is finally unwilling to annul its own historicity.'[4] The closest word in Chaucer's vocabulary to the sense of emphatic contemporaneity expressed by Ovid's 'nunc' is not so much the adverb 'nou' (used relatively infrequently) but the adjective 'newe'. Lexical consideration of the 'newe'/'olde' binary is this chapter's first step in situating Chaucer's stance on poetic temporality and the status of antiquity, after which it proceeds to survey recent critical understandings of Chaucer's multifaceted Ovidianism, and to propose some new points of entry into Chaucer's intertextual appropriations of Ovidian poetry in a European context.

The *Parliament of Fowls* offers what seems to be a straightforwardly affirmative model of literary transmission from past to present: 'newe science' issues from 'olde bokes' (24–5) in a process of regeneration analogous to that occurring in the natural world. This textual metamorphosis can easily be stunted, however, as it is at the end of the poem when the narrator, frustrated in his search for raw materials (90–1) and lacking any clear resolution of his dream, settles for continued reading in *more* old books, deferring the oneiric creation of something new and current, something 'for to fare/The bet', to a vague 'som day' in the future (698–9, 697). Indeed, in his tongue-in-cheek *apologia* at the end of the General Prologue, such novelty is precisely what the Chaucer-narrator professes to fear. To 'fynde wordes newe' is to 'feyne', to tell a 'tale untrewe' (I.735–6); instead, he will transmit the already-said words of his 'authorities'. Elsewhere, when not used in the typological sense (as in 'This newe Rachel brynge fro his beere' [VII.627]), 'newe' often carries in Chaucer's poetry the derisive connotation of 'faddish' or 'superficial', or even an association with deceit and fickleness. The Pardoner's dubious fashion sense is figured as whoring (unconvincingly) after 'the newe jet' (I.682). The faithless Arcite has a heart that is 'newe and grene', lusting after a 'newe lady' (Anel 180, 183); Walter pretends to reject Griselda for 'a newe lady of [the] toun' (IV.1005); and Pandarus, transmitting vintage Ovidian wisdom, offers Troilus a remedy that paradoxically will heal Criseyde instead: 'The newe love out chaceth ofte the olde' (Tr 4.415).

Pandarus may think himself cutting-edge (in fact, his Ovidian tag is so old, in ancient Troy, that it's 'new'—Ovid's words lie in the textual future), but the Chaucerian perspective closest to that of Ovid's self-congratulation in *Ars amatoria* 3 is that of the Monk in the General Prologue. By medieval standards, Chaucer's Monk is positively avant-garde: shrugging off 'old and somdel streit' monastic rules, 'This ilke Monk leet olde thynges pace,/And heeld after the newe world the space'—and the narrator even congratulates him for his modernity (I.174, 175–6, 183). In rejecting 'olde thynges', including the scrutiny of books (184–5), the Monk distances himself from his benighted colleagues who are occupied not only with prayer and manual labor but, presumably, the study and preservation of the works of classical authors such as Ovid, an activity newly flourishing in certain English monasteries in the late fourteenth century.[5] Instead of reading Ovid, however, the Monk *lives* Ovid: his enthusiastic commitment to 'venerie', his robust 'prikyng', and his 'love-knotte' all distinguish him as a card-carrying student of Ovidian *artes*, to which the popular medieval notion of consanguinity between *eros* and the hunt can be traced (I.166, 191, 197).[6] The Monk's Ovidian identity may even wryly attest to the paradoxical entwinement of the medieval Ovid in the web of ascetic self-definition, supporting Warren Ginsberg's contention that '[t]he ascetic textuality of the commentary tradition', by participating exegetically in Ovidian strategies of ironic subversion, 'is not alien to Ovid's erotics but its fraternal twin'.[7] For all the incongruity of the plodding Monk's Tale with the sketch of a libertine given in the General Prologue, it is not insignificant that the Monk's near-endless series of tragedies, which begins by invoking the precedent of 'olde bookes' (VII.1974) and the form of hexameter verse (1979), approximates more than any other narrative in the *Canterbury Tales* an Ovidian *carmen perpetuum*: a story collection structured on the radical changes suffered by individuals (utterly formulaic here, of course, in contrast with Ovid's use of the device), and narrated—if one follows the Ellesmere MS ordering of the Modern Instances—more or less 'ab origine mundi' down to the Monk's own 'tempora'.[8] As such, it provides not only a (failed) counter-model of a story collection within the larger *Canterbury Tales*,[9] but an alternative vision of Ovidian storytelling against which Chaucer, it will later be suggested, positions himself as a neo-Ovidian author.

Ovid stakes a claim not just for modernity but, at the end of the *Metamorphoses*, eternity. Appropriately then, he has been regarded not only as an honorary 'postmodern' but as the first 'medieval' author *avant la lettre*.[10] Condemned on account of an unspecified *carmen et error*[11] to live out his days as an exile in Tomis, Ovid positioned his late poetry as belated and marginal, a restive postscript to his earlier attempts to master time artistically in the *Metamorphoses* and, especially, in the poetic calendar *Fasti* (also known as 'Tempora', after its opening word)—both works having been arrested in various stages of development upon their author's banishment. Ovid's exile poetry consists self-consciously of the efforts of a 'modern' poet forced into posterity and submerged in solitude—a time warp of sorts—that prefigured that of the monks who one day would pore over his writings like so many 'forpyned' ghosts (I.205).[12] If Ovid's geographic removal to the fringes of the Roman empire was experienced as a temporal dislocation to a time *after* the golden age of Augustan Rome, it was also, for Ovid, a reversion to a 'backwards' *rusticitas* in the form of illiteracy, barbarism, and cultural distance.[13] Rome, the eternal city, is absent in both scenarios, as Ovid finds himself nightmarishly either in the state of chaos that preceded it[14] or the 'darkness' of the era that would succeed it. Geographic and temporal deracination, furthermore, engenders a process of textual displacement in Ovid's exile poetry, which both nostalgically rereads and, more strikingly, critically glosses the poet's own earlier works, especially the *Metamorphoses*. Strategies of interpolation,[15] critical commentary, and ethical reflection shape the exiled Ovid's melancholic re-visitation of his previous writings.[16] Such strategies established an auto-referential precedent for medieval exegetical confrontations with Ovid's works, which notably foregrounded Ovid's exile as an interpretive and ethical framework for his corpus.[17]

Chaucer, at least according to the literary histories which from an early period positioned him as a nationalistic point of origin, occupied a comparable time warp: *ahead* of his time, publicly invested in trends of Italian humanism and poetic succession rather than native minstrelsy, endowing the legitimizing interests of a political line that achieved power only one year before his death. Until quite recently, a defining paradox of Chaucer's reception has been that this preeminent medieval English poet has (for varying reasons) been valued for what is not 'medieval' about him.[18] John Dryden, influentially comparing Ovid and Chaucer in his Preface to *Fables Ancient and Modern* (1700), regarded their ideological convergence as one of an epochal, even reciprocal, nature. 'With Ovid', wrote Dryden, 'ended the golden age of the Roman tongue; from Chaucer the purity of the English tongue began.'[19] If Ovid, whose 'resemblances' to Chaucer Dryden catalogues at length, had one toe in the Black Sea, by implication he had the other in the Thames. Such temporal positionings, of course, serve subsequent interests and lineages more than historical fact, jarring as they do against these poets' own chronographic claims (fidelity to the 'new' and the 'old', respectively). Still, these wrinkles of temporality—the *tempora* Chaucer and Ovid envision for themselves, as well as those against which they chafe, and toward which they peer—are productive for an understanding of the textual collisions, ethical calibrations, and reciprocal metamorphoses that characterize the intertextual relationship between these two poets, which at every point is more fraught than that between master and student, agent and delegate.[20] Ovid offered Chaucer more than a repository of myths or a toolkit of poetic techniques: he facilitated ways of thinking about poetic identity, the nature of storytelling, and the permeability of texts, which profoundly shaped Chaucer's output as well as his posture of influence as an English vernacular author. Indeed, to understand Chaucer's self-fashioning and importance as a writer in a European framework, we must attend closely to his complementary status as a reader, which his poetry emphasizes in equal if not greater measure. No source of reading exerted a steadier and more encompassing influence on Chaucer's literary imagination from the beginning to the end of his career than did the works of Ovid.

Chaucer mentions Ovid by name a stunning twenty times (thrice as 'Naso')—compared with eight citations of Virgil's name, six of Dante's, and five of Boethius's—and adapts material substantively from several of his major works (*Metamorphoses, Heroides, Fasti*, etc.) while also showing, according to some critics (more on the varieties of opinion later), active acquaintance with his arts of love and exile poetry. Chaucer's explicit references to Ovid surface in the expected contexts of erotic experience and metamorphosis, as well as in the more surprising territories of homely wisdom and moral *sententiae* (e.g. in the Tale of Melibee, where his amatory works are invoked by Prudence). His appropriations of Ovidian source material span his entire career, from his earliest major poem, the *Book of the Duchess*, to the prominently placed final poetic tale in the *Canterbury Tales*, that of the Manciple. Chaucer assimilated Ovid on a number of levels, confronting his texts through the varied lenses of scholastic commentary and allegorization, mediating translation (at least in the case of the *Heroides*),[21] vernacular adaptation and neo-Ovidian invention, and direct poetic conversation. Moreover, medieval biographies of Ovid offered a master ethical narrative in which the output of medieval love poets could itself be situated. To elucidate these forms of appropriation, the next section of this chapter offers a sketch of the current state of critical understanding of the forms in which Chaucer read Ovid, the paradoxical value Ovid provided as a master of artistic *eros* and as a moral authority, and the striking variety of 'Ovidianisms' located in Chaucer's poetic procedures by major scholars of the past three decades. This broad critical context frames the final section of this investigation, which suggests that Ovid's creative attractiveness to Chaucer is centred—saliently if not exclusively—on two artistic axes: the idea of 'the book' and the myth of poetic production.

Methodologically, my procedure is to situate Chaucer's appropriation of Ovidian material and uncanny absorption of Ovidian personality—a much-noted phenomenon observed first by Eustache Deschamps and, later, John Dryden—in light of recent developments in the 'hermeneutics of reception'[22] and theories of intertextuality as practiced especially by the current generation of classicists. The field of classics is newly attuned to a wide range of creative receptions of and by ancient poets such as Ovid, emphasizing the fluid intercalations of the past in various 'presents'—a phenomenon that has been anticipated in our consideration of the cross-hatching of Ovid's and Chaucer's respective poetic temporalities. Rapid advancements in critical understanding of Ovid's own allusive techniques and poetic self-consciousness[23] have stimulated renewed interest in his creative reinvention by later artists, particularly those of the Renaissance and modern periods. However, despite several excellent historicist examinations of Chaucer's Ovid (to be discussed shortly), medieval studies have been slow to acknowledge the dynamic temporalities and allusive constructions uncovered in contiguous fields.[24] I aim here to make a case for Chaucer as a dynamic partner in and active contributor to Ovidian intertextuality. Approached in this light, Chaucer emerges not simply as a conveyor of or apprentice to Ovid, but as a *collaborator* in an Ovidian poetic, one who necessarily and wilfully transforms Ovid's 'book' into his own.

OVIDIANISMS

The bibliography on Chaucer and Ovid, not surprisingly, is vast. A survey of trends in criticism over the past century must limit itself here to book-length studies dealing substantially with the two poets' relationship, although briefer entries in the ongoing critical conversation will be acknowledged in light of recurring threads of discussion. All modern students of the relationship between Chaucer and Ovid owe a significant debt to Edgar Finley Shannon, whose influential 1929 book *Chaucer and the Roman Poets* devoted more space to Ovidian allusions in Chaucer's corpus than to the influence of any other ancient poet. Renewed interest in Chaucer's Ovidianism after the heyday of New Criticism in the 1960s and 1970s engendered supplementation and nuancing of Shannon's source study, notably in Richard L. Hoffman's illumination[25] of a range of Ovidian allusions in the *Canterbury Tales*—a work undervalued by Shannon, who held that Chaucer outgrew his bookish classicism as he matured into an English poet—as well as in studies of shared narrative and thematic interests apart from textual overlap. John Fyler's *Chaucer and Ovid*[26] is a key contribution in this latter area, focusing on Ovid's amatory works rather than the *Metamorphoses* to demonstrate Chaucer's affinity with Ovid as a love poet and a master of sceptical irony. Chaucer's Ovidianism was updated for the 1990s by Michael Calabrese in *Chaucer's Ovidian Arts of Love* (1994), which maps the coordinates of Ovid's life, as understood by medieval readers, at its points of imaginative contact with the identities of characters in *Troilus and Criseyde* and the *Canterbury Tales* as they apply Ovidian *ars* to their own narrative conditions. Ovid functions ethically for Calabrese, who regards Ovidian *ars* as frequently in tension with Boethian or Christian remedy; in this respect, his approach recalls other interpretations of Ovid—from widely varying critical perspectives—as an ethical influence on Chaucer's poetry (e.g. Hoffman, adopting a Robertsonian perspective on the 'two loves', and Allen and Moritz, on the *Canterbury Tales* as possessing an ethical structure derived from medieval commentary on the *Metamorphoses*).[27] Most recently, Ovidian gender politics, particularly as articulated in the amatory poetry, has attracted the interest of Chaucerians (for example, Hagedorn and Desmond)[28] committed to bringing current theoretical concerns of feminist and queer studies to bear on the venerable insight that Chaucer and Ovid share a deep, often subversive fascination with female psychology and perspective (first remarked upon by Shannon).[29]

For all their differences of approach, these studies as well as other more focused or differently oriented treatments of Ovid's influence[30] generally agree on the validity of the following points, which surface repeatedly: (1) Ovid modelled for Chaucer the viability of love as a subject of poetry, and by extension the poet's artistic condition in relation to desire; (2) Chaucer and Ovid share a repertoire of poetic strategies that tend to operate sceptically and meta-poetically, particularly at the expense of valorized loci of masculine, epic authority; (3) both poets deploy highly developed narrative personae, internal narrators, and artistic surrogates, displaying an acute interest in storytelling as a theme, especially in relation to structures of power and culpability;[31] and (4) Ovid characteristically figures in Chaucer's poetry in conjunction with multiple, often starkly different creative influences and outlooks, facilitating a literary relationship that is both diachronic (transmission from classical past to medieval present) and synchronic (the mediation of proximate artistic materials).

This last observation in particular demands unpacking, for it has been the most generative in recent years in sustaining an integrated vision of Chaucer's 'classicism' in relation both to his vernacular European context and his self-fashioning as an author. Chaucer, it has increasingly been recognized, does not merely *allude* to Ovid or share his poetic temperament: he assimilates and actively rethinks Ovidian poetry—often as mediated by medieval poets, such as Jean de Meun, who have already appropriated Ovid toward their own ends—to develop a stance, an optic, for 'articulating his relationship to the multiple literary traditions in which he wrote: vernacular and Latin, courtly and learned'.[32] The centripetal force of Ovid's poetry, already textually overdetermined in its own right (i.e. in its internal constitution as a body of texts in heated dialogue with other ancient texts), drew tumultuously into its wake, while supplying an alternative vision of, rival forms of *auctoritas* including the Bible, Dante, and the French love poets.[33] This insight is developed most fully and provocatively in James Simpson's recent essay on 'Chaucer as a European Writer' (2006), the title of which conceals its structuring focus on Ovid's influence. Yet this concealment is precisely Simpson's point: his thesis is that Ovid in fact functions as a key—even *the* key—ingredient of Chaucer's 'European tradition' insofar as Ovid was a 'perfect enabling poet' who offered a 'model of "subsidiary" writing' through which Chaucer, an English outsider to Continental literary fashion, accessed the sphere of European invention and the authority it increasingly allowed vernacular poets.[34] Here again we find Ovid, in his position of belatedness and marginality as well as in his pervasive scepticism, functioning as a model for a medieval poetic encounter not only with the receding shoreline of the ancient patrimony but, in Simpson's account, with the shifting sands of contemporary poetic ambition. 'Ovid', in other words, is not only an object of reading but a *way* of reading.

Sophisticated investigations such as these into the ways in which Chaucer 'thinks' Ovid may create the impression that there is basic agreement regarding the material dimensions of Chaucer's knowledge of the ancient poet, but that is far from the case. Scholars remain divided over the number of Ovid's works known to Chaucer (or 'used' by him, which may not be the same thing). Widely diverging viewpoints also exist concerning the relevance to Chaucer of the many varieties of medieval scholastic apparatus that prefaced and surrounded Ovid's works in the fourteenth century, as well as the significance of moralizing translations and compendia such as the anonymous *Ovide moralisé* and Pierre Bersuire's *Ovidius moralizatus*. It is not difficult to concur, as critics have generally done, that where Chaucer does appear to draw on such 'medieval Ovids'— for an extended example, see Twycross[35]—he dwells on their narrative detail and eschews both their allegories and their focus on metamorphosis (which Chaucer famously omits in almost all cases). Disagreement persists, however, regarding the extent to which Chaucer shares the ethical and ascetic interests that provided a rationale for such commentaries and moral anatomies.[36]

Chaucer's demonstrable appropriations of Ovid's works, both in the form of narratives borrowed overtly and in more oblique allusions, have been scrupulously catalogued elsewhere and will not be reiterated here.[37] None deny that Chaucer knew the *Heroides*, *Metamorphoses*, and *Fasti* (which supplies the Legend of Lucrece), but opinions vary widely on his knowledge of the *Amores*, *Ars amatoria*, *Remedia amoris* and, most controversially, the *Tristia* and *Ex Ponto*. Helen Cooper and Douglas Gray hold to the conservative view that 'there is little evidence that Chaucer knew the love poems at first hand',[38] but other scholars credit Chaucer with direct imaginative contact at least with the *Ars* and the *Remedia*—which as cornerstones of the medieval school curriculum were widely known—even if mediating texts such as the *Roman de la Rose* often (if not in every case) coloured his reading.[39] Indeed, scholarly dogmatism about whether Chaucer had in mind the 'pure' Ovid or one of the medieval texts that enlarged and updated his *artes*, or some heterogeneous mixture of these, would likely have puzzled Chaucer, for whom such stark divisions between ancient texts and their medieval 'translations' were hardly conceivable.

Ovid's exile poetry has proven to be a more difficult case. Hoffman admits the likelihood that Chaucer 'was both widely and deeply read in Ovid' and that he 'knew all of Ovid's works', though perhaps not all in equally 'intimate' measure.[40] Fyler, following Shannon, finds only the scantest of verbal reminiscences of *Tristia* and *Ex Ponto* in a small handful of Chaucerian lines.[41] Calabrese, adopting a radically different perspective, argues that

Chaucer 'could not have seen Ovid as the poet of love without seeing him as the poet of exile'.[42] This claim is strengthened by the fact that although Ovid's exile poems circulated widely in the Middle Ages, close textual borrowings from the elegies themselves were less common than general references to 'the fact of exile', by which medieval readers were fascinated.[43] Calabrese's assumption of Chaucer's knowledge of Ovid's entire *oeuvre*, including the pivotal status of the exile poetry within it, is based on the circulation of medieval biographies of Ovid, prominent in virtually all manuscripts of Ovid's poetry in the fourteenth century, which, in their various permutations, emphasized Ovid's exile as a consequence of his teachings on love and positioned his range of works—often in unorthodox chronologies—in strategic relation to his exile (e.g. as attempts at moral renovation). In these *vitae*, exile emerges as a creative epicentre for Ovid—and a cautionary model for his successors—as a poet subject to ethical discipline. Exploring a number of suggestive resemblances between moments in Chaucer's poetry and Ovid's exile writings, Calabrese interprets Ovidian exile as a reflex of the mutability that inevitably overwhelms all attempts to artistically regulate reality (as the amatory works had done). Consequently, Chaucer's *Troilus and Criseyde* becomes a kind of *summa* of Ovidianism collated with Ovid's medieval *vita*: as the protagonist's tragedy unfolds, 'the world of the *Troilus* evolves from the *Ars amatoria* and the *Remedia amoris* into the *Metamophoses* and the *Tristia*', prompting Chaucer's Christian conclusion (love of Christ as the only true *remedium* and escape from exile).[44] Similarly, argues Calabrese, the life of Ovid merges with Chaucer's own identity as 'a love poet confronting his work and his own death' at the end of the *Canterbury Tales*, in which the turn to a Christian anti-poetics of salvation in Parson's Tale and Retraction affords Chaucer the poet a way out of his 'exile' as an Ovidian artist.[45]

Another layer of Ovid's relevance to Chaucer as a model of self-reading in the final fragment may be found, we might add, in the Manciple's Tale, which is the most strictly Ovidian narrative in the *Canterbury Tales*, directly preceding the Parson's Tale and Retraction in all important MSS.[46] Whatever its date of composition, the Manciple's Tale amounts, in the crucial position it occupies near the end of the *Tales*, to a radical intervention in Ovidian patterns of transmission[47] and a nihilistic salvo against the generative possibilities of Ovidian poetry—a pre-emption, in fact, much like that effected by Augustus.[48] Uniquely in the Manciple's retelling of Ovid's narrative of Apollo and Coronis, the transgressive crow is a poet-figure who is quite specifically *exiled* ('slong' out of the house [IX.306]) for two profoundly Ovidian offenses: a *carmen* (emphatically identified as such by Phebus: 'Allas, what song is this?' [IX.247]) and an *error* (having seen a sexual act that he should not have witnessed, also emphasized [261]).[49] As is the case with Ovid in exile (at least according to his own self-pitying account), the crow is condemned to lose his powers of *carmen* (300, 304), and even to 'crie agayn tempest and rayn' (a major preoccupation of Ovid's in frigid Tomis).[50] The Manciple's Tale, then, quite strategically resurrects the spectre of Ovid and his association with the ethical consequences of tale-telling, precisely at the moment that the *Canterbury Tales* is metamorphosed irrevocably and its author exposed as culpable, like Ovid in the medieval biographies, for his own creation.

TEXTUALITIES

These lines of critical inquiry encourage the observation that Chaucer's Ovid is not simply a static icon of ancient authority shouldering his reputation as 'Venus clerk' on a pillar in Fame's house (HF 1487) or suspended in eternal procession on the 'steppes' of 'poesye' at the end of *Troilus and Criseyde* (5.1790–2). As a way of reading and a model of self-reading, this chapter has argued, Ovid configures for Chaucer the radical permeability of texts—texts which, as the dreamer discovers in the *House of Fame* with Ovid's help (i.e. in his revisionist encounter with the *Aeneid* in the Temple of Venus), may or may not reflect the whole truth. Chaucer is quick to acknowledge that he can neither match the forbidding 'art poetical' of the ancient poets nor rival Dante's Christian boldness in a similar venture (issues that accumulate around Ovidian allusion in the invocation of Apollo in *House of Fame*, Book Three),[51] but he does share with the denizens of Fame's house one key trait: fallibility. The qualification 'yif I kan', after all, applies as much to the dreamer recounting Virgil's *Aeneid* ('Non other auctour alegge I') as it does to 'Virgil' himself in the primary act of epic narration (HF 143, 314). For his part, Ovid predicated his claim to immortal *fama* upon a question that is left at least partly open: 'si quid habent ueri uatum praesagia' [if there is any truth in the predictions of bards].[52] Chaucer, as it were, answers this question in his dramatization of the dwelling of Ovidian *Fama* with an emphatic 'of course there isn't—or at least not much' (see the amalgamation of 'soth' and 'lesynge' at HF 2089).[53] Fissures in the edifice of classical authority such as those Chaucer highlights—both with Ovid's help and at his expense—are precisely what scholars of intertextuality discern in the dynamic nature of literary influence: the notion that 'source' texts are not static or fixed, but part of a two-way negotiation of meaning that necessitates 'the interpretation not of one text but of two'. According to Alessandro Barchiesi, 'Both these interpretations are ever on trial, in process, and continually influencing one another. The new text rereads its model, while the model in turn influences the reading of the new text.'[54] For Chaucer, the fallibility that opens ancient texts to reinvention, and his own to future correction, is an empowering by-product of artistic creation, one that enables him to capitalize upon (by strategically exposing) deficits in his sources that require amelioration. In so doing, Chaucer necessarily changes our reading of those sources, and hence our understanding of the very texts they influence—including his own.

The wielding of this creative ellipsis is a supremely Ovidian tactic, and Chaucer employs it to great effect in *Troilus and Criseyde* and the *Legend of Good Women* in particular, where he takes advantage of the ancient setting of these narratives to explore issues of poetic temporality and the interventionist capacity of the author as reader. In *Troilus*, Chaucer performs a sea-change upon Boccaccio's *Filostrato* by importing a range of allusions that endow the poem with a profoundly tragic shape, while developing the character of the narrator as a writer at odds with his own material. In the process, Chaucer compels the literate reader to confront the dizzying potential of his story to take place differently than it does, to record events (such as Criseyde's change of heart) that might 'mean' differently depending on how they are represented, to gesture toward a 'future' which is, to the medieval reader, part of the textual past. One among many examples of this strategy is Chaucer's invention of the dinner party at Deiphebus's house, in which the less-than-innocent familiarity between the host and his sister-in-law Helen not only advances growing concerns about familial deception and destructive passion, but 'reminds' us of the future conjugal union of Helen and Deiphebus represented (by means of flashback) in *Aeneid* Book Six, culminating in Helen's treacherous facilitation of her lover's slaughter.[55] The hyper-textuality of Chaucer's Troy contributes to its acute historical position as a city encased on the one side by Theban history—which haunts the books and dreams of Chaucer's Trojans—and on the other by Virgilian epic, in which Trojan history is conveyed (essentially) from the point at which Chaucer's *Troilus* leaves off, through to the establishment of a new *patria* in Italy. Many critics have struggled with the implications of Chaucer's creative interpolation of his Trojan poem within a body of known texts, which it foreshadows and revises in an odd mixture of prolepsis and retrospection. Winthrop Wetherbee, always attuned to Chaucer's shifting conversations with the ancient poets, suspects that the 'burden of knowledge' that we carry from, for example, Virgil's *Aeneid* is something we must 'resist' if we are to appreciate Chaucer's unique narrative emphases.[56] The source text, in this view, is fixed; it is a potential impediment that exists in an uneven power relationship with Chaucer's poem as the latter attempts to forge its own narrative structures (Holton makes a comparable point about Chaucer's rejection of the intertextual dynamics of Ovid's *Metamorphoses*).[57] And yet it is difficult to accept that source texts *are* truly fixed. In the case of Chaucer's fictive world in the *Troilus*, the *Aeneid* does not even yet exist, much less have the capacity to bind; it is still, as it were, in a state of formation—a twinkle in its author's eye—and Chaucer's poem, in a brilliant subversion of poetic chronology, is itself *part* of that formation. It is a writer's fantasy: *Chaucer's* poem supplies the precedent, the backstory, in which Virgil (who records only the death of Troilus) will, so to speak, find his ideas anticipated. If we must be 'Virgilian reader[s] of Chaucer' to recognize his allusions to the *Aeneid*, we also perforce become Chaucerian readers of Virgil.[58] We were encouraged to do precisely this (again, with Ovid's help) in the *House of Fame*, in which the priority of the *Aeneid* is occluded by the authorial powers animated in Chaucer's dream, which 'sees' the events of the *Aeneid* as if in unmediated form, and in turn 'tells' its story (HF 149–50).[59]

In *Troilus*, Ovid's works likewise possess a future status in relation to ancient Troy, where they circulate in the form of raw materials and as-yet-uncodified erotic instincts: Oenone's pirated letter to Paris has not yet been immortalized as *Heroides* 5; Pandarus's love-advice is still the homely profusion of a windbag rather than an elegant compendium of elegiac couplets. Ovid, who frequently performs these sorts of tricks on Virgil,[60] is not the only author to supply a precedent for Chaucer's intertextual play: Dante is if anything more aggressive in rewriting Virgil and other ancient poets by 'correcting' their poetic testimonies with his own.[61] Dante's self-legitimization, however, rests on a bold appropriation of Scriptural authority that positions him as 'the author of the Spirit's present text',[62] whereas Chaucer claims no such privileged perspective on the imperfect, proliferating networks of communication among past and present texts. Even in *Troilus*'s momentous final stanzas, the presence of 'other bokes' (5.1776)—books Chaucer did not write, books Chaucer would rather have written, books that might not be understood, books Chaucer will write one day—unsettles the certainty of *this* book in a way that recalls Ovid's playful emphasis on the endless intersections among his own acts of writing and his texts' susceptibility to change through abridgment, redirection, misreading, and so on.

In the *Legend of Good Women*, a collection based on Ovid's *Heroides* and its medieval exegetical apparatus, Chaucer adopts an even more fully Ovidian poetic framework to develop an extended practical example of the troubling power of perspective to shape narrative meaning, a concern, we have seen, raised on a theoretical level in the *Troilus*. The events occurring in the Prologue of the *Legend*, as many have recognized, resonate strongly with the punishment of Ovid as depicted in his medieval biographies and as used to ethically structure his works. Like Ovid in the medieval *accessus ad auctores*, 'Chaucer' is taken to task for the objectionable emphases of his love poetry and condemned by an authoritarian God of Love, atoning for his offense by virtuously publishing his way out of exile.[63] In the legends themselves, Chaucer steps cleverly into Ovid's intertextual funhouse. Where Ovid had subversively rewritten masculine epic tradition by focusing selectively and sympathetically on the women it marginalized, Chaucer subversively rewrites Ovid—whom he cites prominently throughout—by adopting an even more selective perspective that shiftily undermines the ostensible project of the collection by casting the heroines in a less than advantageous light. With this strategy, Chaucer highlights (as does the God of Love's selective reading of Chaucer's poetry) the flawed, even porous nature of textuality itself.[64]

Chaucer's conjurings of Ovid, whether through allusion or perspectival maneuvers like the ones we have been considering, frequently coincide with meditations on the physical status of his own creations as *books*. Ovid has been characterized as 'the most daring of ancient poets in personifying texts and animating books'—books whose obligations include 'communicating *with other texts*'.[65] It seems wholly appropriate that the Ovidian collision course on which Chaucer finds his 'bokes' in the *Legend* represents the aftermath of a textual journey on which the 'book of Troilus' (X.1085) was launched at the end of Chaucer's Trojan epic, in the pivotal 'Go, litel bok' stanza (Tr 5.1786), which itself derives from a trope in Ovid's exile poetry.[66] These mid-career Chaucerian works are particularly attuned to Ovidian ways of thinking about textual relations and poetic identity, as well as to the independent potency of 'bokes' to supplant (LGW F 1-28), distort (Tr 5.1060), or circumvent (LGW G 342) lived experience. 'Bokes' in *Troilus* and the *Legend* exist in fraught power relationships with their creators; frequently animated with independent life or volition, books are presented as erroneous, mobile, abusive, or reparatory. If we look to the early and later stages of Chaucer's career, we find an attention to books—read and written—as a thematic preoccupation in its own right that develops in tandem with Chaucer's appropriation of Ovidian subject matter. We might even say that Chaucer's poetic *oeuvre* is bookended, rather literally, by Ovid. Chaucer opened the book of Ovid (the story of Ceyx and Alcyone) in the *Book of the Duchess* and shut it emphatically, as we have seen, in the final poetic narrative of the *Canterbury Tales* (which contains the last reference to 'olde bookes' in the *Tales* [IX.106]). Books come to sustain an almost mythic sense of agency for Chaucer, as they did even more frequently for Ovid, who represented the metamorphosis of human bodies (such as Daphne's and Hyacinthus's) into textual objects and who equated his own books with the parricides Oedipus and Telegonus.[67] The myth of poetic production and the identity of the poet are equally implicated in the Ovidian associations with 'the book' embedded in Chaucer's works.

The eagle in the *House of Fame* memorably identifies Ovid's *Metamorphoses* as Chaucer's 'oune bok' (712). Crucially, in the *Book of the Duchess*, Chaucer's 'oune bok'—source of the story of Ceyx and Alcyone—is translated oneirically into a new medium to become *Chaucer's* own book, the poem whose final lines testify to its own status as a material object (BD 1330–4). This process is anticipated earlier in the *Book of the Duchess*, when for a passing moment the acts of making 'this book' (the poem we are reading) and reading Ovid's book are collapsed into a single imaginative activity:

> Such sorowe this lady to her tok
> That trewly *I, that made this book,*
> Had such pittee and such rowthe
> To *rede* hir sorwe that, by my trowthe,
> I ferde the worse al the morwe
> Aftir to thenken on hir sorwe.
>
> (BD 95–100; emphases added)

More than an innocent digression, these lines temporarily derail the narration of Alcyone's story in a way that gives Chaucer—'I, that made this book'—creative precedence over Ovid, whose narrative (or, possibly, a medieval redaction of it such as the *Ovide moralisé*) had shortly before been referred to as 'this bok' (BD 52). Something similar occurs, as we have seen, in Chaucer's Ovidian intervention into Virgil's *Aeneid* as oneirically repossessed by the dreamer in the *House of Fame*. It is tempting to suggest that Chaucer's provocative tendency to represent Ovidian encounters in relation to the contact between books in a state of formation or contestation responds to Ovid's own contemplation of himself *as* a book at the end of the *Metamorphoses*, in the famous closing passage in which the poet imagines a day when his body, his 'corpus', returns to dust but his 'parte…meliore' [better part] is dispersed immortally beyond the stars everywhere that Rome's power extends.[68] In a final metamorphosis, Ovid's corpse becomes his corpus, and it lives on: the last word of his epic is 'uiuam', I shall live. In the *Retraction*, Chaucer also meditates on the relation between his corpse and his corpus; there, however, the sheer proliferation of 'bokes' (a label attached to almost all of his 'worldly vanitees', and extended *ad infinitum* in the reference to 'many another book, if they were in my remembrance') comes to *threaten* eternal life (X.1084, 1086). This renunciation, too, has an Ovidian precedent: in the exile poetry, the poetic triumph forecasted at the end of the *Metamorphoses* is invalidated by Ovid's removal to a 'barbarian' land, under Rome's power, in which neither the Latin language nor his own poetry thrives. In Ovid's exile poetry, remembering engenders a process of poetic dismemberment in which his own books turn fatally against their author and break away in a state of traumatic rupture. Ovid's books, with their powers of circulation, have a mobility that their author lacks in his place of exile, where he wishes, in a poignant twist on the end of the *Metamorphoses*, to be transformed into his own book: 'di facerent, possem nunc meus esse liber!' [Would that the gods might grant me now to be my book!].[69]

Ovid's exile poetry forms the final chapter in his ongoing exploration of the etiology of poetic creation and its relation to the poet's fragile authority as human artist. Like Ovid, Chaucer experiments with the myth of the poet, perhaps most intricately in the Introduction to the Man of Law's Tale, which playfully turns to Ovid as an alter-ego for Chaucer's own poetic profile as a master of stories of 'loveris up and doun' (II.53). This second Chaucerian self-catalogue occurring in an acutely Ovidian context (the Prologue of the *Legend of Good Women* is the first) again collocates the dimensions of Chaucer's canon with the precedent of Ovid and the materiality of books. All the stories of lovers have been told already, complains the Man of Law, because if Chaucer 'have noght seyd hem.../In o book, he hath seyd hem in another' (compare the proliferation of books in the *Retraction*)—outdoing even Ovid, who is credited here with only *one* book (the 'Episteles') (II.51–5). The Russian doll structure of this passage has the Man of Law playing the part of the 'modern' poet, griping about his own creator's interference with his material, a creator who in turn is in competition with a still more ancient precursor identified with a related body of material—all of which results in a list of stories that raises more questions than it answers about Chaucer's canon. The design of this Introduction recalls Ovid's much-noted habit of embedding artistic surrogates within the *Metamorphoses* to highlight his own concerns and procedures as an artist in the age of Augustus. The Man of Law himself appears to footnote this parallel in his jumbled allusion to the contest between the Muses and the Pierides—a classic example of artistic punishment—and his prominent citation of the title of Ovid's 'Methamorphosios' (II.92–93).[70] Moments like this one intensify the possibility that Chaucer had the *Metamorphoses* more than casually in mind when designing the narrative framework of his story collection, a notion that has been treated with caution[71] but which is afforded new relevance by recent insights into the *Metamorphoses'* complex narratological structures, its embodiment of a highly developed Ovidian persona, and its deployment of internal narrators pointing with varying degrees of obliquity to the author.[72] Indeed, one recent critic's view of the *Metamorphoses* as an embodiment of the 'artistic condition' as shaped by performative motivations and audience reactions, and localized in the inset narratives of individual artist-figures, summons a range of associations with the *Canterbury Tales* as a continuous story collection fascinated by the social implications of storytelling and their pertinence to the poet's vocation.[73]

The Introduction to the Man of Law's Tale supplies a fitting conclusion to this exploration of Chaucer's Ovidianism for another reason as well. Folding his own sense of belatedness into the orbit of Chaucer's poetic *vita*, at the gravitational centre of which is 'Ovide', the Man of Law (and through him, Chaucer) manipulates poetic temporality with a canniness that Ovid himself, prophet of 'nunc', would have applauded. I am referring to the Man of Law's assertion that Chaucer '[h]ath seyd hem [i.e. stories of lovers] in swich Englissh as he kan/Of *olde tyme*, as knoweth many a man' (II.49–50; emphasis added). By 'olde tyme', the Man of Law of course means 'long ago', a reading corroborated by his attribution of particular works to Chaucer 'in youthe' (57). But 'olde tyme' is a terrifically loaded phrase in the immediate context. It aligns Chaucer the poet, first of all, squarely with 'Ovide', whose 'Episteles' are, according to the speaker, '*ful olde*' (55; emphasis added). Second, it strategically summons associations with two very similar phrases occurring in pregnant moments in Chaucer's earlier works: (1) the account of the rock of ice in the *House of Fame*, displaying the names of 'folkes that hadden grete fames/Of *olde tyme*' (1154–5; emphasis added), and (2) the 'bok' read by the narrator in the *Book of the Duchess*, in which 'were written fables/That clerkes had in *olde tyme*/And other poetes, put in rime' (52–4; emphasis added). The net effect of these cross-references is to create the impression that 'Chaucer', from the Man of Law's belated perspective, is akin in essential ways to an ancient poet. More than just a successor to Ovid here, Chaucer actually inhabits an Ovidian temporality, the 'olde tyme' of his youth standing as an analogue to Ovid's ancient condition—and perhaps even to his (vexed) authority.

It is for this reason, I suggest, that the Man of Law's claim at the beginning of his cata-logue that 'in youthe he [i.e. Chaucer] made of Ceys and Alcione' startles the reader as it does (II.57). The content of the entire *Book of the Duchess* is reduced here to the *Ovidian* story of Ceyx and Alcyone that the dreamer begins by reading, the one that 'I, that made this book' risks—but steps back from—appropriating as his own creation (96). Yet this, according to the Man of Law, is what Chaucer 'made of'; in fact, it is the wellspring of his entire *oeuvre* as a love poet in the catalogue presented. It is uncannily appropriate that this catalogue unsettles Chaucer's canon even as it attempts to fix it, by proceeding to list narratives that defy the constitution of the *Legend of Good Women* (the 'large volume' cited at II.60) as it has come down to us but which—crucially—match the contents of Ovid's collection of heroines in every instance that they fail to line up with Chaucer's. In this moment, Chaucer represents himself as an author by imagining himself *as Ovid*; stepping into Ovid's shoes enables him to stand tall in his own. The Man of Law must gain a foothold on *his* shoulders. Here then, in Fragment II of the *Canterbury Tales*, the elision of Ovid (proceeding from allusion *to* Ovid) reaches its apex: Chaucer stands firmly in the Roman poet's place, twisting the arm of his own creation (the Man of Law) to adopt, if only for a moment, the mantle of a poet of 'olde tyme'—to read his own name in the rock of ice, and to see his own reflection among those 'clerkes' and 'poetes' who put in rhyme fables to dream by.

ACKNOWLEDGEMENTS

I wish to thank Maggie Kilgour for her helpful comments on this chapter and for sharing work on Ovid and Milton in advance of publication that enriched my understanding of Ovid's concern with time.

NOTES

1. Ovid, *Metamorphoses* 15.878.
2. On the 'postmodern Ovid' see Theodore Ziolkowski, 'Ovid in the Twentieth Century', in *A Companion to Ovid,* ed. Peter E. Knox (Chichester: Wiley-Blackwell, 2009), 465–7.
3. John M. Fyler, *Chaucer and Ovid* (New Haven, CT: Yale University Press, 1979), 71; and *Language and the Declining World in Chaucer, Dante, and Jean de Meun* (Cambridge: Cambridge University Press, 2007), 64–5.
4. Lee Patterson, *Chaucer and the Subject of History* (Madison, WI: University of Wisconsin Press, 1991), 21.
5. On which see James Clark, *A Monastic Renaissance at St Albans: Thomas Walsingham and his Circle c.1350–1440* (Oxford: Clarendon, 2004), 209–38.
6. Richard L. Hoffman, *Ovid and the Canterbury Tales* (Philadelphia, PA: University of Pennsylvania Press, 1966), 28–34.
7. Warren Ginsberg, '*Ovidius ethicus?* Ovid and the Medieval Commentary Tradition', in *Desiring Discourse: The Literature of Love, Ovid through Chaucer* (Selinsgrove, PA: Susquehanna University Press; London: Associated University Presses, 1998), 68–9.
8. Ovid, *Metamorphoses* 1.3–4. The Monk's apology in his Prologue for arranging his tragedies out of order, 'som bifore and som bihynde,/As it now comth unto my remembraunce' (VII. 1988-9) is suspicious in its echo of the Chaucer-narrator's admission in General Prologue that he has 'nat set folk in hir degree/Heere in this tale, as that they sholde stonde' (744–5). In neither case is the *ordinatio* as jumbled as the narrators suggest. On Chaucer's deviation from standard estates models in his ordering of the General Prologue portraits, see Jill Mann, *Chaucer and Medieval Estates Satire: The Literature of Social Classes and the* General Prologue *to the* Canterbury Tales (Cambridge: Cambridge University Press, 1973), 5–7. On Ovid's own (by no means watertight) chronological arrangement of the legendary narratives constituting *Metamorphoses,* see Denis Feeney, '*Mea Tempora*: Patterning of Time in the *Metamorphoses*', in *Ovidian Transformations: Essays on the Metamorphoses and Its Reception,* eds. Philip Hardie et al. (Cambridge: Cambridge Philological Society, 1999), 13–30.
9. Helen Cooper, *The Structure of the Canterbury Tales* (London: Duckworth, 1983), 48.
10. See John V. Fleming, 'The Best Line in Ovid and the Worst', in *New Readings of Chaucer's Poetry*, eds. Robert G. Benson and Susan J. Ridyard (Cambridge: D.S. Brewer, 2003), 51.
11. Ovid, *Tristia* 2.207.
12. Ralph J. Hexter, *Ovid and Medieval Schooling: Studies in Medieval School Commentaries on Ovid's* Ars Amatoria, Epistulae ex Ponto, *and* Epistulae Heroidum (Munich: Arbeo-Gesellschaft, 1986), 83–99; 'Ovid in the Middle Ages: Exile, Mythographer, and Lover', in *Brill's Companion to Ovid*, ed. Barbara Weiden Boyd (Leiden: Brill, 2002), 416–24; Jeremy Dimmick, 'Ovid in the Middle Ages: Authority and Poetry', in *The Cambridge Companion to Ovid*, ed. Hardie (Cambridge: Cambridge University Press, 2002), 286. See, by way of comparison, Stephen Hinds, 'After Exile: Time and Teleology from *Metamorphoses* to *Ibis*', in Hardie et al., *Ovidian Transformations*, 48–67, on Ovid's own narrative confrontation with the 'corruption' of time in exile.
13. See, by way of comparison, Alessandro Schiesaro, 'L'intertestualità e i suoi disagi', in *Memoria, arte allusiva, intertestualità/Memory, Allusion, Intertextuality*, eds. Stephen Hinds and Don Fowler, *Materiali e Discussioni* 39 (1997), 99–100, cited in Hinds, 'After Exile', 52.
14. Hinds, 'After Exile', 58–9.
15. See esp. Ovid, *Tristia* 1.7.33–40.

16. Hinds, 'After Exile'; Hinds, 'Booking the Return Trip: Ovid and *Tristia* 1', in Knox, *Oxford Readings in Ovid*, 415–40; Alessandro Barchiesi, *Speaking Volumes: Narrative and Intertext in Ovid and Other Latin Poets*, eds. and trans. Matt Fox and Simone Marchesi (London: Duckworth, 2001), 27–8.

17. On this medieval emphasis, see Michael A. Calabrese, *Chaucer's Ovidian Arts of Love* (Gainesville, FL: University Press of Florida, 1994), 11-32; and Dimmick, 'Ovid in the Middle Ages', 273–6.

18. For early examples, see A. C. Spearing, *Medieval to Renaissance in English Poetry* (Cambridge: Cambridge University Press, 1985), 16–18. John M. Bowers, *Chaucer and Langland: The Antagonistic Tradition* (Notre Dame, IN: University of Notre Dame Press, 2007), argues that Chaucer quite intentionally participated in his own construction as an author linked to a chain of succession extending into the future, obsessed (Bowers's formulation) with 'constructing a literary genealogy in which he figured as heir to prior achievements' (17). In Bowers's political reading, this genealogy was a strictly European (and classicizing) one that ignored—even suppressed—native English poetic tradition.

19. John Dryden, *John Dryden: A Critical Edition of the Major Works*, ed. Keith Walker (Oxford and New York: Oxford University Press, 1987), 557.

20. On Chaucer's negotiation of the pressures of antiquity and modernity, see also Robert R. Edwards, *Chaucer and Boccaccio: Antiquity and Modernity* (Basingstoke: Palgrave, 2002), who traces these issues to Boccaccio's influence but also observes, in terms that invite application to Ovidian discourse, that 'the most important feature of modernity in Chaucer's poetry...is not just contemporaneity but *the experience of change*' (6; emphasis added).

21. Sanford Brown Meech, 'Chaucer and an Italian Translation of the *Heroides*', *PMLA* 45 (1930), 110–38.

22. Subtitle of Charles Martindale, *Redeeming the Text: Latin Poetry and the Hermeneutics of Reception* (Cambridge: Cambridge University Press, 1993).

23. For example, Alden Smith, *Poetic Allusion and Poetic Embrace in Ovid and Virgil* (Ann Arbor, MI: University of Michigan Press, 1997); Stephen Hinds, *Allusion and Intertext: Dynamics of Appropriation in Roman Poetry* (Cambridge: Cambridge University Press, 1998); Heather Van Tress, *Poetic Memory: Allusion in the Poetry of Callimachus and the Metamorphoses of Ovid* (Leiden; Boston: Brill, 2004).

24. Major voices in classical reception studies such as Philip Hardie, Charles Martindale, and Stephen Hinds all extend their insights into the Italian or English Renaissances but leave the English Middle Ages untouched. A rare example of a medievalist contributing to this classics-centred field is Hexter, 'Literary History as a Provocation to Reception Studies', in *Classics and the Uses of Reception*, eds. Charles Martindale and Richard F. Thomas (Oxford: Blackwell, 2006), 23–31.

25. Hoffman, *Ovid and the Canterbury Tales*.

26. See now also John M. Fyler, 'The Medieval Ovid', in Knox, *A Companion to Ovid*, 416–22.

27. Hoffmann, *Ovid and the Canterbury Tales*; Judson Boyce Allen and Theresa Anne Moritz, *A Distinction of Stories: The Medieval Unity of Chaucer's Fair Chain of Narratives for Canterbury* (Columbus, OH: Ohio State University Press, 1981).

28. Suzanne Hagedorn, *Abandoned Women: Rewriting the Classics in Dante, Boccaccio, and Chaucer* (Ann Arbor, MI: University of Michigan Press, 2004); Marilynn Desmond, *Ovid's Art and the Wife of Bath: The Ethics of Erotic Violence* (Ithaca, NY: Cornell University Press, 2006).

29. Edgar Finley Shannon, *Chaucer and the Roman Poets* (Cambridge, MA: Harvard University Press, 1929), 373.

30. See: Robert W. Hanning, 'Chaucer's First Ovid: Metamorphosis and Poetic Tradition in *The Book of the Duchess* and *The House of Fame*', in *Chaucer and the Craft of Fiction*, ed. Leigh A. Arrathoon (Rochester: Solaris Press, 1986), 121-63; Helen Cooper, 'Chaucer and Ovid: A Question of Authority', in *Ovid Renewed: Ovidian Influences on Literature and Art from the Middle Ages to the Twentieth Century*, ed. Charles Martindale (Cambridge: Cambridge University Press, 1988), 71-81; Cooper, 'The Classical Background', in *Chaucer: An Oxford Guide*, ed. Steve Ellis (Oxford and New York: Oxford University Press, 2005), 255-71; Douglas Gray, 'Ovide', in *The Oxford Companion to Chaucer*, ed. Douglas Gray (Oxford: Oxford University Press, 2003), 358-59; James Simpson, 'Chaucer as a European Writer', in *The Yale Companion to Chaucer*, ed. Seth Lerer (New Haven, CT: Yale University Press, 2006), 55-86; Jamie C. Fumo, 'Argus' Eyes, Midas' Ears, and the Wife of Bath as Storyteller', in *Metamorphosis: The Changing Face of Ovid in Medieval and Early Modern Europe*, eds. Alison Keith and Stephen Rupp (Toronto: Centre for Reformation and Renaissance Studies, 2007), 129–50.

31. On these phenomena in Ovid, see Barchiesi, *Speaking Volumes*, 49–78; Niklas Holzberg, 'Playing with His Life: Ovid's "Autobiographical" References', in Knox, *Oxford Readings in Ovid*, 51–68; Patricia J. Johnson, *Ovid Before Exile: Art and Punishment in the* Metamorphoses (Madison, WI: University of Wisconsin Press, 2008); Barbara Pavlock, *The Image of the Poet in Ovid's* Metamorphoses (Madison, WI: University of Wisconsin Press, 2009).

32. Hanning, 'Chaucer's First Ovid', 121.

33. For the Bible: Fleming, 'The Best Line in Ovid and the Worst'; For Dante: Fyler, *Chaucer and Ovid,* 21-2, 162-63, and Winthrop Wetherbee, *Chaucer and the Poets: An Essay on Troilus and Criseyde* (Ithaca, NY: Cornell University Press, 1984), 110; for the French love poets, Hanning, 'Chaucer's First Ovid'.

34. Simpson, 'Chaucer as European Writer', 62.

35. Meg Twycross, *The Medieval Anadyomene: A Study in Chaucer's Mythography*, Medium Ævum Monographs n.s. 1 (Oxford: Blackwell for the Society for the Study of Mediaeval Languages and Literature, 1972).

36. For arguments that he did, see: Hoffman, *Ovid and the Canterbury Tales*, 11–19, 207; Allen and Moritz, *A Distinction of Stories*; Calabrese, *Chaucer's Ovidian Arts of Love*; Fleming, 'The Best Line in Ovid and the Worst'.

37. See Shannon, *Chaucer and the Roman Poets*; John Leyerle and Anne Quick, *Chaucer: A Bibliographical Introduction* (Toronto: University of Toronto Press, 1986), 85-7; and especially Fyler, 'The Medieval Ovid', 416-22.

38. Quoted from Cooper, 'Chaucer and Ovid', 71; see also Gray, 'Ovide', 358-9 and Cooper, 'The Classical Background', 258.

39. Fyler, *Chaucer and Ovid,* 17-20; John V. Fleming, *Classical Imitation and Interpretation in Chaucer's* Troilus (Lincoln, NE: University of Nebraska Press, 1990), 26-7; Calabrese, *Chaucer's Ovidian Arts*, 33-80; Desmond, *Ovid's Art and the Wife of Bath*, 116-43; Fyler, 'The Medieval Ovid', 418-19.

40. Hoffman, *Ovid and the Canterbury Tales*, 207.

41. Fyler, 'The Medieval Ovid', 422.

42. Calabrese, *Chaucer's Ovidian Arts*, 15.

43. See Hexter, *Ovid and Medieval Schooling*, 93.

44. Hoffman, *Chaucer's Ovidian Arts*, 79.

45. Hoffman, *Chaucer's Ovidian Arts*, 115.

46. See Stephen D. Powell, 'Game Over: Defragmenting the End of the *Canterbury Tales*', *Chaucer Review* 37, no. 1 (2002), 40-58.

47. Jamie C. Fumo, 'Thinking upon the Crow: The *Manciple's Tale* and Ovidian Mythography', *Chaucer Review* 38, no. 4 (2004), 355–75.

48. Jamie C. Fumo, *The Legacy of Apollo: Antiquity, Authority, and Chaucerian Poetics* (Toronto: University of Toronto Press, 2010), 226–7.

49. It has widely been speculated that Ovid's own *error* was similar in form, perhaps involving the sexual escapades of Augustus's granddaughter Julia.

50. For example, in Ovid, *Tristia* 1.1.42, 1.2, etc.

51. See Jamie C. Fumo, 'Chaucer as *Vates*?: Reading Ovid through Dante in the *House of Fame*, Book 3', in *Writers Reading Writers: Intertextual Studies in Medieval and Early Modern Literature in Honor of Robert Hollander*, ed. Janet Levarie Smarr (Newark, DE: University of Delaware Press, 2007), 89–108.

52. Ovid, *Metamorphoses* 15.878–9.

53. See, by way of comparison, Hanning 'Chaucer's First Ovid', 141–58.

54. Barchiesi, *Speaking Volumes*, 142.

55. Fleming, *Classical Imitation*, 249–50 and, more fully, John V. Fleming, 'Criseyde's Poem: The Anxieties of the Classical Tradition', in *New Perspectives on Criseyde*, ed. Cindy L. Vitto and Marcia Smith Marzec (Asheville, NC: Pegasus Press, 2004), 277–98.

56. Wetherbee, *Chaucer and the Poets*, 91–2.

57. Amanda Holton, *The Sources of Chaucer's Poetics* (Aldershot: Ashgate, 2008), 10, 147.

58. Fleming, *Classical Imitation*, 250.

59. See, by way of comparison, Lisa J. Kiser, *Truth and Textuality in Chaucer's Poetry* (Hanover: University Press of New England, 1991), 28.

60. See Hinds, *Allusion and Intertext*, 104–22.

61. On the artistic and spiritual progress of Chaucer's narrator as Dantean, see Wetherbee's *Chaucer and the Poets*.

62. Peter S. Hawkins, *Dante's Testaments: Essays in Scriptural Imagination* (Stanford, CA: Stanford University Press), 81.

63. Rita Copeland, *Rhetoric, Hermeneutics, and Translation in the Middle Ages: Academic Traditions and Vernacular Texts* (Cambridge: Cambridge University Press, 1991), 193-5; Calabrese, *Chaucer's Ovidian Arts*, 18; Florence Percival, *Chaucer's Legendary Good Women* (Cambridge: Cambridge University Press, 1998), 141-2; Dimmick, 'Ovid in the Middle Ages', 284; Simpson, 'Chaucer as a European Writer', 77.

64. Fyler, *Chaucer and Ovid*, 109; Sarah Annes Brown, *The Metamorphosis of Ovid: From Chaucer to Ted Hughes* (London: Duckworth, 1999), 26.

65. Barchiesi, *Speaking Volumes*, 26. Emphasis in original.

66. John S. P. Tatlock, 'The Epilog of Chaucer's *Troilus*', *Modern Philology* 18 (1921), 115–18, citing Ovid's *Tristia* 1.1.1–3, 15, 57, 3.7.1-2ff., and *Ex Ponto* 4.5.1–2ff.

67. Ovid, *Tristia* 1.1.113–14.

68. Ovid, *Metamorphoses* 15. 873, 875. Joseph Farrell contends that the immateriality of vocal performance rather than the materiality of text is vindicated in this passage and elsewhere in *Metamorphoses* ('The Ovidian *Corpus*: Poetic Body and Poetic Text', in Hardie et al., *Ovidian Transformations*, 127–41). However, as Wheeler observes of the performative character of Ovid's epic, 'the narrator's own fiction of speech is ironic, for the implied writer of the *Metamorphoses* must be aware of the paradox that writing is ultimately the means by which his voice will be preserved' (*A Discourse of Wonders: Audience and Performance in Ovid's* Metamorphoses [Philadelphia, PA: University of Pennsylvania Press, 1999], 58). On this point, see also Johnson, *Ovid Before Exile*, 123–4.

69. Ovid, *Tristia* 1.1.58.

70. On the Pierides as punished artists in Ovid, see Johnson, *Ovid Before Exile,* 41-73; on the implications of the Man of Law's allusion, see especially Cooper, 'Chaucer and Ovid', 81, and Simpson, 'Chaucer as a European Writer', 79.

71. For example, in Cooper, 'The Frame', in *Sources and Analogues of the Canterbury Tales,* eds. Robert M. Correale and Mary Hamel, vol. 1 (Cambridge: D. S. Brewer, 2002), 7, despite its defense in Hoffman, *Ovid and the Canterbury Tales,* 3–11, and Allen and Moritz, *A Distinction of Stories.*

72. Gianpiero Rosati, 'Narrative Techniques and Narrative Structures in the *Metamorphoses*', in *Brill's Companion to Ovid,* 271–304; Barchiesi, *Speaking Volumes,* 49–78; Alessandro Barchiesi, 'Narrative Technique and Narratology in the *Metamorphoses*', in Hardie, *The Cambridge Companion to Ovid,* 180–99.

73. On Ovid: Johnson, *Ovid Before Exile,* 26–9; On Chaucer: Patterson, *Chaucer and the Subject of History.*

BIBLIOGRAPHY

Akbari, Suzanne Conklin, 'Ovid and Ovidianism', in *The Oxford History of Classical Reception in English Literature, Volume 1 (800–1558),* ed. Rita Copeland (Oxford: Oxford University Press, 2016), 187–208.

Calabrese, Michael A., *Chaucer's Ovidian Arts of Love* (Gainesville, FL: University Press of Florida, 1994).

Cooper, Helen, 'Chaucer and Ovid: A Question of Authority', in *Ovid Renewed: Ovidian Influences on Literature and Art from the Middle Ages to the Twentieth Century,* ed. Charles Martindale (Cambridge: Cambridge University Press, 1988), 71–81.

Dimmick, Jeremy, 'Ovid in the Middle Ages: Authority and Poetry', in *The Cambridge Companion to Ovid,* ed. Philip Hardie (Cambridge: Cambridge University Press, 2002), 264–87.

Fyler, John M., *Chaucer and Ovid* (New Haven, CT: Yale University Press, 1979).

Hardie, Philip et al., eds., *Ovidian Transformations: Essays on the* Metamorphoses *and Its Reception* (Cambridge: Cambridge Philological Society, 1999).

Hexter, Ralph J., *Ovid and Medieval Schooling: Studies in Medieval School Commentaries on Ovid's* Ars Amatoria, Epistulae ex Ponto, *and* Epistulae Heroidum (Munich: Arbeo-Gesellschaft, 1986).

Hinds, Stephen, *Allusion and Intertext: Dynamics of Appropriation in Roman Poetry* (Cambridge: Cambridge University Press, 1998).

Hoffman, Richard L., *Ovid and the Canterbury Tales* (Philadelphia, PA: University of Pennsylvania Press, 1966).

Shannon, Edgar Finley, *Chaucer and the Roman Poets* (Cambridge, MA: Harvard University Press, 1929).

Simpson, James, 'Chaucer as a European Writer', in *The Yale Companion to Chaucer,* ed. Seth Lerer (New Haven, CT: Yale University Press, 2006), 55–86.

CHAPTER 13

CHAUCER AND THE TEXTUALITIES OF TROY

MARILYNN DESMOND

TOWARDS the end of *Troilus and Criseyde,* Chaucer's narrator—in imitation of Dante's narrator in *Inferno* 4—places himself and his poem in the shadow of the *auctores*: 'But litel book, no makyng thow n'envie,/But subgit be to alle poesye;/And kis the steppes where as thow seest pace/Virgile, Ovide, Omer, Lucan, and Stace' (5.1789–92). Virgil and Ovid were two Latin poets whose canonical texts were used in the schools and who consequently shaped the classical traditions of the medieval West. Not only had elaborate commentary traditions developed around these Latin texts, but these texts were also assimilated into vernacular literary traditions through translation, adaptation and imitation. The Latin texts of Lucan and Statius likewise circulated widely. The names Virgil, Ovid, Lucan and Statius consequently referred to clearly identified textual traditions. Homer, the single Greek poet included in this list, represented a more refracted form of authority in the Latin West, since the Greek texts of the Homeric epics did not circulate in Western Europe, and literacy in Greek was extremely limited. For Chaucer and his readers, Homer was an *auctor* whose textual corpus was limited to a schematic, thousand-line Latin summary of the *Iliad,* known as the *Ilias Latina.*[1] As a school text, the *Ilias Latina* circulated widely—frequently under the signature of 'Homer'—thereby acting as a placeholder for the Homeric epics in the Latin curriculum. While the *Ilias Latina* enabled Chaucer to include Homer in the list of *auctores* at the end of the *Troilus,* it influenced neither his vision of Troy nor the narrative of the Trojan War found in *Troilus and Criseyde.* In that respect, Chaucer's *Troilus* is emblematic of the non-Homeric traditions of Troy in the Latin West.

The narrator's invocation of classical authority at the end of the *Troilus* may imitate Dante, but it also cites another Chaucerian text, the *House of Fame.* The allegorical vision of the *House of Fame* stages the dreamer/narrator's mnemonic encounter with a series of statues of famous authors. These figures, perched on pillars, represent the pinnacle of textual fame. The five authors named by the *Troilus*-narrator—Statius, Homer, Virgil, Ovid and Lucan—are all present in Fame's house, and each *auctor* is characterized by the fame of his texts. Statius holds up the fame of Thebes and Achilles, while Virgil bears 'The fame of Pius Eneas' (1485), and so forth. While each of the Latin poets is situated singly, Homer does not stand alone, and his fame is highly contested:

> And by him stood, withouten les,
> Ful wonder hy on a piler
> Of yren, he, the gret Omer;
> And with him Dares and Tytus
> Before, and eke he Lollius,
> And Guydo eke de Columpnis,
> And Englyssh Gaufride eke, ywis;
> And ech of these, as have I joye,
> Was besy for to bere up Troye.
> So hevy therof was the fame
> That for to bere hyt was no game.   (HF 1464–74)

As a Greek poet, Homer is flanked by several Latin prose historians who must assist in any effort to 'bere up Troye': 'Dares' (Dares the Phrygian), 'Tytus' (Dictys Cretensis), 'Guydo … de Columpnis' (Guido delle Colonne). Having identified the historical authorities on Troy, the narrator proceeds to describe the traditions on the Trojan War:

> But yet I gan ful wel espie,
> Betwex hem was a litil envye.
> Oon seyde that Omer made lyes,
> Feynynge in hys poetries,
> And was to Grekes favorable;
> Therfor held he hyt but fable.   (HF 1475–80)

This passage encapsulates the textualities of Troy in the medieval West, particularly the traditional critique that Homer was not truthful ('Oon seyde that Omer made lyes'), a charge that animates both Latin and vernacular accounts of Troy in the Middle Ages. Despite his controversial stature, however, Homer is not only resident in the House of Fame but remains the primary figure responsible 'for to bere up Troy'.

The *House of Fame* stages the historiographical paradox that Homer presented to the literary cultures of the Latin West: although his texts were inaccessible beyond the Latin summary available in the *Ilias Latina*, Homer nonetheless embodies a poetic authority that classifies him with Latin *auctores* such as Virgil and Ovid and thereby excuses any apparent historical inaccuracies. As the *House of Fame* illustrates, the story of the siege and sack of Troy permeated the textual cultures of Western Europe, both Latin and vernacular, so that the matter of Troy emerges as one of the most prominent textual traditions found in non-religious literary cultures. Though Chaucer only occasionally cites Homer as an *auctor*, he repeatedly draws on the non-Homeric narratives of the Trojan War in his depiction of siege warfare in *Troilus and Criseyde* as well as his construction of the historical framework of the Trojan War evoked in the *House of Fame*. The legacy of these non-Homeric traditions is also evident in the allusions to Troy and the Trojan War scattered throughout the *Canterbury Tales.*

The traditions of the Trojan War in antiquity extend well beyond the Homeric epics. As a fortified city situated above the plain of Scamander, Troy reputedly defended itself against a Greek onslaught for ten years before its walls were breached, its inhabitants slaughtered or captured, and its urban foundations reduced to ruins. The *Iliad,* however, narrates only a small fraction of the war, since it depicts fifty days in the tenth year of the conflict, including only four days of battles and duels. The *Odyssey* recounts the *nostoi,* or homecoming, of the victorious Greeks—although in the case of Odysseus, the home-ward journey becomes quite prolonged and arduous. Jonathan Burgess has suggested that we see the *Iliad* and the *Odyssey* as part of the vast mythological tradition known as the 'Epic Cycle,' an interlocking network of narratives recounting the origins, conduct, and aftermath of the Trojan War.[2] Known only from later references, the 'Epic Cycle' became fixed in the archaic age, and the Homeric epics became canonical in the classical period; however, as Burgess argues: 'it is enough to think of the texts within the Homeric and Cyclic traditions as generally resulting from the mythical tradition of the Trojan War as it was known in the Archaic Age.'[3] The Troy matter that circulates in the Latin West thus represents a survival of this vast mythical tradition rather than a transmission of the Homeric epics.

According to ancient traditions, the Trojans who survived the sack of this city in Asia Minor set out on the sea to settle elsewhere. While the most famous Trojan to flee the burning city was Aeneas, whose settlement in Italy provided a foundation legend for Rome and its imperial project according to Virgil's *Aeneid,* the legends of this Trojan diaspora predate Virgil's *Aeneid* by several centuries.[4] Virgil's text, however, seamlessly grafts the founding of Rome onto the fall of Troy, thereby assuring that the fall of Troy would be foundational to the historical vision of the Roman empire, and by extension, western Christendom. The full account of the siege and sack of Troy as it circulated in the medieval West went well beyond the Virgilian account, however, since Virgil's *Aeneid*—in imitation of the *Iliad*—covered only a fraction of the war and its aftermath. The depiction of the fall of Troy in the second book of Virgil's *Aeneid* offers Latin readers only a glimpse of the final paroxysms of the defeated city; the rest of the story was avail-able to western European readers through Latin epitomes of Greek texts on the Trojan War. *De excidio Troiae historia,* attributed to Dares Phrygius (or Dares the Phrygian) takes a Trojan point of view, while the *Ephemeris belli Troiani,* attributed to Dictys Cretensis (or Dictys of Crete), is told from the perspective of the Greeks. Both texts pre-sent themselves as eyewitness accounts that have been translated from Greek into Latin. Modern scholars confirmed Dictys's claim to have worked from a Greek original when the first of several papyrus fragments of a Greek version of the *Ephemeris* was discovered in 1900. The existence of a Greek source text for the *Ephemeris* suggests that the transla-tor's claim to be working from a Greek version of *De excidio Troiae* is likewise accurate.[5] These two texts facilitate the Latin reception of the textual traditions that had developed from the 'Epic Cycle' which had emerged more than a millennium earlier in the Archaic Age. Although the texts assigned to Dares and Dictys are very late developments from this tradition, they act as a conduit—not for the Homeric epics as such—but for the wider traditions of the Trojan War, of which the Homeric epics formed only one component.

Dares's *De excidio Troiae historia* forms the *locus classicus* of the anti-Homeric rhetoric found throughout the textual traditions on Troy. Dares's prologue to *De excidio* explicates the author-function of the narrative as well as the materiality of its transmission; in the process, the Dares-narrator presents his text as a purposeful correction to the Homeric tradition. In order to claim *auctoritas* for the Latin text, the translator delineates each step in the transmission of the Greek 'source-text' attributed to Dares:

> Inveni historiam Daretis Phrygii ipsius manu scriptam, ut titulus indicat, quam de Graecis et Troianis memoriae mandavit. quam ego summo amore conplexus continuo transtuli. cui nihil adiciendum vel diminuendum rei reformandae causa putavi, alioquin mea posset videri. optimum ergo duxi ita ut fuit vere et simpliciter perscripta, sic eam ad verbum in latinitatem transvertere, ut legentes cognoscere possent, quomodo res gestae essent: utrum verum magis esse existiment, quod Dares Phrygius memoriae commendavit, qui per id ipsum tempus vixit et militavit, cum Graeci Troianos obpugnarent, anne Homero credendum, qui post multos annos natus est, quam bellum hoc gestum est.
>
> [I found the history which Dares the Phrygian wrote about the Greeks and the Trojans. As its title indicates, this history was written in Dares's own hand. I was very delighted to obtain it and immediately made an exact translation into Latin, neither adding nor omitting anything, nor giving any personal touch. Following the straightforward and simple style of the Greek original, I translated word for word. Thus my readers can know exactly what happened according to this account and judge for themselves whether Dares the Phrygian or Homer wrote the more truthfully—Dares, who lived and fought at the time the Greeks stormed Troy, or Homer, who was born long after the war was over.][6]

This prologue to a fifth-century Latin rendition of an ostensibly second-century Greek text attempts to erase the temporal distance between itself and the Trojan War by emphasizing the presence of the text itself: the translator claims to have discovered this text in Athens, written in Dares's own hand. The journalistic texture of *De excidio* as an eyewitness account of the war is later clarified just before the catalogue of ships: 'Dares Phrygius, qui hanc historiam scripsit, ait se militasse usque dum Troia capta est, hos se vidisse, cum indutiae essent, partim proelio interfuisse' [Dares the Phrygian, who wrote this history, says that he did military service until the capture of Troy and saw the people listed below either during times of truce or while he was fighting].[7] In presenting himself as a Trojan combatant who fought in the battles and observed the troops during periods of truce, 'Dares the Phrygian' presents authorship as eyewitness testimony. For his part, the Latin translator emphasizes his efforts to find Latin equivalents for each word of the Greek. The lines of transmission evoked here are all equally critical: the translator claims to work from an autograph manuscript of an eyewitness participant and to seek lexical equivalencies ('sic eam ad verbum in latinitatem transvertere'), so that the implied reader might come as close as possible to the Trojan War itself. Thus he argues that the Latin text not only preserves the texture of the Greek 'source-text', but the translator enjoys the same authority as Dares, the eyewitness-author who supposedly lived through the war and fought against the Greeks. The fidelity claimed for the *translatio* parallels the ostensible veracity of the supposedly eyewitness, autograph text. The book stands in for the author.

This praise of Dares's authenticity is juxtaposed to the credibility gap found in the Homeric tradition: 'de qua re Athenis iudicium fuit, cum pro insano haberetur, quod deos cum hominibus belligerasse scripserit' [When the Athenians judged this matter, they found Homer insane for describing gods battling with mortals].[8] According to Dares, Homer not only lived too late to witness the events of the war, but what he did depict violated the canons of verisimilitude when he depicted the gods waging war on humans. This rhetorical emphasis on the primacy of Dares's account brackets the Homeric poems as fiction by contrast to Dares's supposedly accurate report. The gods consequently do not appear as characters in the *De excidio*, though the narrative includes references to temples and cults of the ancient deities. While the name of Homer was attached to the limited account of the Trojan War contained in the *Ilias Latina*, the names of Dares and Dictys were attached to a globalizing narrative that—with some variations—gave western Europe a non-biblical story of origins. The text of *De excidio*— along with Dictys's *Ephemeris*—engendered the medieval narratives on the fall of Troy, including texts such as Benoît de Saint-Maure's *Roman de Troie*, Boccaccio's *Filostrato*, as well as the Trojan segment in texts of universal history, both in Latin and the vernacular. Chaucer's engagement with the textualities of Troy—his Trojan allusions, his citations of the matter of Troy, and his own version of the Troy narrative in *Troilus and Criseyde*— participates directly in this proliferation of textual traditions derived from Dares. Unlike the presence of Virgilian or Ovidian material in the Chaucerian corpus, the matter of Troy was drawn from a highly diffuse textual tradition that essentially lacked an *auctor* at its center.

Benoît de St. Maure's *Roman de Troie* (c.1160–5) initiates the vernacular traditions on the Trojan War. While the other *romans antiques*, including the anonymous *Roman d'Eneas* and the *Roman de Thebes*, were adaptations of Roman epics by the *auctores* Virgil and Statius, Benoît's *Roman de Troie* grounded its narrative on the prose texts attributed to Dares and Dictys rather than the inaccessible Homeric epics or the *Ilias Latina*, which stood in for the Homeric epics in the schools. In order to establish the *auctoritas* of his text, Benoît imitates *De excidio* in emphasizing the materiality of *translatio studii*. Benoît reiterates Dares's credentials as outlined in the prologue to the Latin text: he states that Homer lived more than a hundred years after the siege of Troy, so that the Homeric account of the war is fictional. Benoît fleshes out the details of textual transmission provided in *De excidio* by describing Dares's book as an artefact, supposedly found at Athens and translated from Greek into Latin by Cornelius, whom Benoît identifies as the nephew of Sallust through a misreading of the proper name Nepos as a noun. He suggests that Cornelius found the text of *De excidio* by serendipity: 'Un jor quereit en un aumaire/Por traire livres de gramaire:/Tant i a quis e reversé/Qu'entre les autres a trové/L'estoire que Daire ot escrite,/En greque langue faite e dite' [One day he searched in a book cupboard to take out books of grammar; when he had searched and turned it over, among the others he found the history that Dares had written, composed and recounted in the Greek language].[9] Following Dares's prologue, Benoît first argues for the truth-value of Dares's original Greek account as an accurate record of the Trojan War, a truth-value preserved through the fidelity of his own ostensibly word-for-word translation of *De excidio*: 'Ci vueil l'estoire comencier:/Le latin sivrai e la letre,/ Nule autre rien n'i voudrai metre,/S'ensi non com jol truis escrit./Ne di mie qu'aucun bon dit/N'i mete, se faire le sai,/Mais la matire en ensivrai' [Here I want to begin the story; I will follow the Latin and the letter; I do not want to put anything else into it except what I find written. I do not say that I might not put any good saying in, if I know how, but I will follow the matter of it].[10] Benoît presents his vernacular narrative of the siege and fall of Troy as a faithful translation of a Latin rendition of an eyewitness account in a Greek source-text. Instead of evoking the authority of the *auctor* of his Latin source-text, Benoît emphasizes his efforts as translator in the preservation of the *auctoritas* represented by the book itself as material witness to the war. Authorship and translation become interchangeable.

The *Roman de Troie,* however, does not follow the Latin texts of Dares and Dictys; instead, Benoît greatly expands Dares's and Dictys's schematic account of the Trojan War into a dramatic narrative depicting a medieval city under siege. In the process, the matter of Troy acquires the ethos of a medieval romance, and the military campaign against Troy takes on the trappings of medieval warfare. In 30,000 lines of octosyllabic verse, the *Roman de Troie* depicts twenty-two separate battles fought before the walls of Troy. The accounts of these battles are punctuated by truces, council scenes and embassies between the Greeks and Trojans, as well as descriptions of court life and love affairs— most notably, the affair between Troilus and Briseida, which Benoît invented. Towards the end of the romance, Benoît follows Dictys's *Ephemeris de Historia belli Troiani* in order to relate the conclusion of the war, finally brought about through the treachery of two Trojans, Antenor and Eneas, whose pact with the Greeks enables the construction of a marvellous wooden horse on wheels. When Eneas and Antenor convince Priam to bring the horse into Troy, the Trojans have to tear down the walls so that the horse can be dragged in, thereby allowing the Greeks access to the previously impermeable city. Once the walls are breached, the Greeks mercilessly slaughter the Trojans. The romance concludes with an account of the Greek homecoming.

From England to Sicily, the *Roman de Troie* was one of the most widely read texts of the high Middle Ages; the *Roman de Troie* consequently engendered other Troy narratives, often overshadowing its Latin source-texts in the process. In all these texts, the romance of Troilus and Briseida forms the iconic amatory plot that drives the narrative and displaces the love affair of Paris and Helen. Though originally produced in the court of Henry II and Eleanor of Aquitaine, the *Roman de Troie* had a particular currency in thirteenth-century Italy where it was frequently copied.[11] Most significantly, the *Roman de Troie* was transformed into French prose as a 'de-rhymed' text.[12] Five distinct versions of the *Roman de Troie en prose* survive, one of which perhaps served as the source-text for Guido delle Colonne's *Historia destructionis Troiae*.[13] The *Historia destructionis*

Troiae, a Latin prose translation of a French prose rendition of Benoît's romance, was produced in Sicily between 1272 and 1287. While Guido repeats the traditional view that Homer 'turned the pure and simple truth of his story into deceiving paths' ('ystorie puram et simplicem ueritatem in uersuta uestigia uariauit')[14] and he praises the 'fidelissimi relatores' [most faithful reporters] Dares and Dictys, he does not appear to have worked directly from the Latin texts attributed to Dares and Dictys but to have relied instead on the vernacular citations of these texts in Benoît's text and its prose imitations. Guido's characterizations of the Homeric epics, however, are based on the *Ilias Latina*.[15] The *Historia destructionis Troiae* circulated throughout Europe, and was in turn translated into several vernaculars, including French, Italian and English.[16] 'Translations' of the Troy matter thus moved from Latin (Dares and Dictys) into French (Benoît's *Roman de Troie* and its redactions), which were then translated back into Latin without direct reference to the initial Latin source-texts attributed to Dares and Dictys, followed by *volgarizzamento* back into Italian and translation into French. Alison Cornish notes the 'notion of multiple authorship that accompanies the story of Troy' in medieval Italy.[17] Boccaccio's *Filostrato* (c.1335), an Italian verse romance, emerges from this multi-lingual, multi-textual tradition.[18] As the primary source for Chaucer's *Troilus and Criseyde*, the *Filostrato* transmits the textual richness of the Troy material from the Italian peninsula to late fourteenth-century England. If the 'matter of Troy' lacks an *auctor* in the Latin West, the vernacular traditions of Troy nonetheless achieved tremendous authority. Given the enormous proliferation of texts on Troy, no one text alone authoritatively summarizes the Troy narrative; instead, multiple textualities and intertexts on the Trojan War remained operative from the twelfth century onwards. To a fourteenth-century English author such as Chaucer, the narratives of the Trojan War were available in any number of sources, including the Latin texts of Dares and Dictys, Benoît's *Roman de Troie*, and its prose versions, Guido delle Colonne's *Historia destructionis Troiae*, and Boccaccio's *Filostrato*, as well as the vernacular prose text of the *Histoire ancienne jusqu'à César*.[19]

Troilus and Criseyde, Chaucer's contribution to the textual traditions of the Trojan War, is closely modelled on Boccaccio's *Filostrato*. The *Troilus* not only follows the plot of Boccaccio's romance, but as Barry Windeatt notes, 'the distribution of narrative and dialogue into stanzas is identical in the two poems for substantial stretches: over and over again, the first line of each English stanza is very closely rendered from the parallel Italian line, stanza by stanza.'[20] Chaucer, however, never names Boccaccio as his *auctor*, preferring instead to represent the *Troilus* as a translation of a Latin text that the *Troilus*-narrator attributes to a historian named Lollius. Chaucer also included Lollius in his list of Latin historians in the *House of Fame*, where Lollius takes his place alongside Dares, Dictys, Guido delle Colonne and Geoffrey of Monmouth (HF 1468), the historians who 'bere up Troy'. While no ancient or medieval author by the name of Lollius survives, Horace's *Epistle* 1.2, addressed to Lollius Maximus, may have led Chaucer to assume that Lollius was the name of an ancient Roman historian who had composed a history of the Trojan War.[21] In constructing the textual fiction that the *Troilus* is a vernacular rendition of a Latin text, Chaucer's narrator claims a truth-value for his account. The fictional Lollius confers the same sort of authority on the *Troilus* that Dares confers on the *Roman de Troie*, since a vernacular text such as Boccaccio's *Filostrato* clearly lacked the *auctoritas* attributed to a Latin historical narrative. The *Troilus*-narrator thus locates his vernacular narrative in a textual tradition with its own *auctor*, a tradition comparable to the 'Troian gestes' that he implies were available to the learned members of his audience: 'In Omer, or in Dares, or in Dite,/Whoso that kan may rede hem as they write' (1.146–7). This list suggests an equivalency between Dares and Dictys and an author named 'Omer', which, as we have seen, was the name frequently attached to the *Ilias Latina*. While the *Troilus*-narrator only names Lollius once in the first book and once in the last book of the *Troilus*, he refers throughout to 'myn auctour' ('Myn auctour shal I folwen, if I konne' [2.49]), and he explicitly characterizes his translation as an act of vernacularization ('But out of Latyn in my tonge it write' [14]), as though the *Troilus* were a *translatio* of a Latin source-text rather than an English rendition of a vernacular romance. In translating Boccaccio under the cover of Lollius, Chaucer invents a Latin *auctor* for the amorous adventures of Troilus and Criseyde, a story that actually originates in a medieval vernacular romance (the *Roman de Troie*) rather than an ancient Latin text. In addition to the imaginary *auctoritas* of Lollius, Chaucer notes the survival of Troy narratives in other 'old bokes', and he also nods to Dares and Dictys, whom he may have known only by name from the *Roman de Troie*. Chaucer's invocation of a fictional *auctor* paradoxically points to the multiplicity of the textual traditions on the Trojan War even as he purports to follow his imaginary Latin *auctor* Lollius.

The *Troilus*-narrator's deferential tone in reference to his *auctor* imparts a sense of historicity to his depiction of the Trojan War.[22] At the start of the poem, the narrator—in a passage that closely translates the *Filostrato*—invokes the siege Troy as a well-known historical fact:

> Yt is wel wist how that the Grekes stronge
> In armes with a thousand shippes wente
> To Troiewardes, and the cite longe
> Assegeden, neigh ten yer er they stente,
> And in diverse wise and oon entente,
> The ravysshyng to wreken of Eleyne,
> By Paris don, they wroughten al hir peyne.   (1.57–63)

This passage treats the ten-year assault on Troy as a consequence of the Trojan abduction of Helen. While Chaucer's text, like Boccaccio's, excludes the battle-scenes that animate so much of the *Roman de Troie*, the *Troilus* nonetheless dwells on the experience of a city under siege. Through the figure of Criseyde, Chaucer explores the perspective of the female non-combatant, a perspective that addresses the impact of war rather than the intricacies of military strategy. As Troilus's courtship and seduction of Criseyde proceeds, the experience of siege warfare contextualizes Criseyde's lack of agency. The narrator introduces Criseyde by emphasizing her vulnerability as a widow whose father has defected to the enemy: she suffers from 'Hire fadres shame, his falsnesse and tresoun' (1.107). Her father's betrayal of Troy not only causes her sorrow but also makes her fear for her safety: 'For of hire lif she was ful sore in drede' (95). When Hector intervenes to offer her protection, he expressly addresses her physical vulnerability in his promise that 'youre body shal men save' (122). Criseyde's predicament at the start of the narrative dramatizes how the exigencies of warfare render the gender-relations of the city more starkly than in peacetime: Criseyde needs a male protector to assure not only her honor but also her life.

When Pandarus approaches Criseyde in Book Two with news that should please her, she asks hopefully: 'is than th'assege aweye?/I am of Grekes so fered that I deye' (123–4). Her acute awareness of life within the walls of a city under attack colours her response to being wooed by a king's son known for his prowess in battle, and her accommodation of Troilus's desires occurs within this framework. When the constraints of war lead the Trojans to accept the Greek proposal that Criseyde be traded for Antenor, she literally becomes the equivalent of a Greek prisoner of war. Despite Hector's public declaration that 'she nys no prisonere' (4.179), the citizens of Troy betray Criseyde by transferring her to her father in the Greek camp, since her status as daughter of a traitor overrides her status as a Trojan woman and widow.

The truce and the exchange of prisoners only forestalls the downfall of the city which Calkas continues to foretell ('And thus shal Troie torne to asshen dede' [4.119]). The narrator concurs with this prediction when he reminds his audience that it is Antenor who will betray the city once he has been freed by the prisoner-of-war exchange: 'For he was after traitour to the town/Of Troye' (204–5). The narrator assumes that the implied audience of the *Troilus* always already knows of Antenor's betrayal and the outcome of the war. The Trojan women, by contrast, see the exchange of Criseyde for Antenor as a harbinger of peace rather than destruction. When a group of women call on Criseyde after the parliament has agreed to the trade, one woman explicitly expresses this view: 'I hope, ywis, that she/Shal bryngen us the pees on every syde' (691–2). The narrator, however, classifies such talk of peace as 'wommanysshe thynges' (694). In a later scene, when Criseyde and Troilus face their impending separation, she holds out hope for a peaceful settlement between the Trojans and the Greeks since such a settlement would remove the obstacles to their affair. Criseyde refers to the terms that a peaceful settlement might take:

> Ye sen that every day ek, more and more,
> Men trete of pees, and it supposid is
> That men the queene Eleyne shal restore,
> And Grekis us restoren that is mys.   (4.1345–8)

Criseyde proceeds to anticipate the peaceful co-existence of the Greeks and the Trojans:

> For if that it be pees, myn herte deere,
> The nature of the pees moot nedes dryve
> That men moost entrecomunen yfeere,
> And to and fro ek ride and gon as blyve.   (4.1352–5)

In his response, Troilus expresses scepticism ('I not if pees shal evere mo bitide' [4.1464]) and suggests that they steal away out of Troy. In countering this proposal,

Criseyde returns to the possibility of a peaceful settlement, and she cites the dishonour they would face as Trojan exiles after the cessation of hostilities: 'the sorwe and wo ye wolden make,/That ye ne dorste come ayeyn for shame!' (1564–5). Only Criseyde and the Trojan women invoke the category of peace as a potential outcome of war: the notion of a peaceful settlement becomes a feminine gloss on the masculine conduct of war.

Once Criseyde has been transferred to the Greek camp in Book Five, the narrative more persistently addresses her isolation and her vulnerability. Although she has promised Troilus that she would return to Troy within ten days, she worries about the enormous risk entailed by crossing enemy lines:

> And if that I me putte in jupartie
> To stele awey by nyght, and it bifalle
> That I be kaught, I shal be holde a spie;
> Or elles—lo, this dred I moost of alle—
> If in the hondes of som wrecche I falle,
> I nam but lost, al be myn herte trewe. (5.701–6)

As a Trojan woman in the Greek camp, Criseyde has no agency: she has become completely defined by the war. In wooing her, Diomede emphasizes that Troy is doomed when he tells her 'For Troie is brought in swich a jupartie/That it to save is now no remedie' (5.916–7). When Criseyde considers Diomede's offer of love, she weighs his status against her predicament:

> Retornyng in hire soule ay up and down
> The wordes of this sodeyn Diomede,
> His grete estat, and perel of the town,
> And that she was allone and hadde nede
> Of frendes help. (5.1023–7)

Although the *Troilus*-narrator professes at the start of Book Four that the *matere* of his text is 'how Criseyde Troilus forsook' (15), the narrative in Book Four dwells increasingly on the experiences of a female non-combatant in the context of siege warfare whose decisions are shaped by the contingencies of military conflict more than love. When the *Troilus*-narrator nears the conclusion of his text, he acknowledges that other textual traditions record Troilus's military exploits: 'In many cruel bataille, out of drede,/ Of Troilus, this ilke noble knyght,/As men may in thise olde bokes rede' (5.1751–3). The narrator then specifically sends his readers to Dares:

> And if I hadde ytaken for to write
> The armes of this ilke worthi man,
> Than wolde ich of his batailles endite;
> But for that I to writen first bigan
> Of his love, I have seyd as I kan—
> His worthi dedes, whoso list him heere,
> Rede Dares, he kan telle hem alle ifeere. (5.1765–71)

In claiming that his narrative has focussed on love to the exclusion of war because it has not depicted Troilus in battle performing 'worthi dedes', the *Troilus*-narrator ironically refuses to credit the war for the course of the love affair he has charted. The reference to Dares's in these lines probably refers to the *Frigii Daretis Ilias* (*c.* 1185) a verse rendition of Dares's *de excidio* composed by Joseph of Exeter.[23] In pretending that his narrator has to forge an authorial identity by privileging 'Lollius' over other Latin *auctores* when he is actually generally relying on texts in Italian and French, Chaucer claims the same authority that Benoît claims in the prologue to the *Roman de Troie*. As we have seen, Benoît locates his supposedly literal *translatio* of Dares's *De excidio* in a textual genealogy linked to an original eyewitness account in Greek. Chaucer's Lollius performs the same authenticating role for the *Troilus*.

The Fall of Troy frequently sets the historiographical horizon for the Canterbury pilgrims. The more learned among the Canterbury pilgrims locate Troy in a specific place and assign the events of the Trojan War to a precise time. Thus the Man of Law cites Hector's fate as part of universal destiny: 'In sterres, many a wynter therbiforn,/Was writen the deeth of Ector, Achilles,/Of Pompei, Julius, er they were born' (II.197–9). The brevity with which he mentions the fall of Troy places those events in a verifiable moment in the past: 'I trowe at Troye, whan Pirrus brak the wal/Or Ilion brende' (288–90). The Knight likewise appeals to the historicity of the Trojan War as a way to establish the historical facts of Theban history. When Arcite has been killed, the lamentation of the Athenians is compared to the Trojan mourning after the death of Hector: 'So greet wepyng was ther noon, certayn,/Whan Ector was ybrought, al fresh yslayn,/To Troye' (I.2831–3). The comparison of Arcite to Hector—a comparison found in Boccaccio's *Teseida*, the source-text for the 'Knight's Tale'—connects Theban history to the Fall of Troy. Since the Theban matter and the Trojan War were often compiled together in sequence in vernacular traditions of universal history, this simile grafts *Troilus* onto the 'Knight's Tale'.[24] The Squire, by contrast, betrays his fetish-like interest in marvellous and enchanted artefacts when he invokes the Trojan horse purely as an object of wonder: 'Swich wondryng was ther on this hors of bras/That syn the grete sege of Troie was,/Theras men wondreden on an hors also' (V.305–7). Given the extensive network of Troy narratives, the Trojan War provided a stock of brief allusions that Chaucer could deploy to suggest the knowledge and intellectual predilections of his pilgrims.

Chaucer's composition of the *Book of the Duchess* early in his career dramatizes how the Troy narrative constructs the dreamer-poet. When the insomniac narrator of the *Book of the Duchess* takes up a 'romance', he encounters the Ovidian narrative of Ceyx and Alcyone. Upon learning about Morpheus, the god of sleep, the narrator himself falls asleep and dreams that he has awakened in a luxurious chamber encased with stained glass windows. This architectural detail allows the narrator-dreamer to provide a brief ekphrasis:

> For hooly al the story of Troye
> Was in the glasynge ywroght thus,
> Of Ector and of kyng Priamus,
> Of Achilles and of kyng Lamedon,

> And eke of Medea and of Jason,
> Of Paris, Eleyne, and of Lavyne.   (BD 326–31)

As a complement to the Troy matter on the windows, 'And alle the walles with colours fyne/Were peynted, both text and glose,/Of al the Romaunce of the Rose' (BD 332–4). Unlike the narrative of Ceyx and Alcyone, or the text and gloss of the *Romance of the Rose*, this 'story of Troye' exists not in texts, but in a visual program. The dreamer experiences the luminosity of the Troy matter as the sun shines through the stained glass windows: 'And throgh the glas the soone shon/Upon my bed with bryghte bemes,/With many glade gilde stremes' (336–8). The reflected yet legible figures impart the traditions on the fall of Troy without reference to any one *auctor* or text. The dreamer-narrator in the *Book of the Duchess* is thus constructed as a viewer, and the matter of Troy appears to be transparently accessible. Though Chaucer later engaged the complexity of the textualities of Troy by creating reader-narrators in the *House of Fame* and *Troilus and Criseyde* who had to negotiate texts identified with specific *auctores*, this ekphrasis in the *Book of the Duchess* is nonetheless an apt vision for a medieval poet's encounter with the textualities of Troy.

NOTES

1. Marco Scaffai, *Baebii Italici, Ilias Latina: Introduzione, Edizione critica, Traduzione Italiana e Commento* (Bologna: Pàtron, 1982); 'Tradizione manoscritta dell'*Ilias Latina*' in '*In Verbis Verum Amare*': *Miscellanea dell'istituto di filologia latina e medioevale dell'università di Bologna* 5 (1980): 205–77. For translation, see Kathryn L. McKinley, 'The Medieval Homer: The *Ilias Latina*', *Allegorica* 19 (1998): 3–61.
2. Jonathan S. Burgess, *The Tradition of the Trojan War in Homer and the Epic Cycle* (Baltimore, MD: John Hopkins University Press, 2001).
3. Burgess, *Tradition of the Trojan War*, 5.
4. Andrew Erskine, *Troy between Greece and Rome: Local Tradition and Imperial Power* (Oxford: Oxford University Press, 2001), 131–56.
5. Stefan Merkle, 'The Truth and Nothing but the Truth: Dictys and Dares', *The Novel in the Ancient World*. Ed. Gareth Schmeling (Leiden: Brill, 1996), 563–80.
6. Ferdinand Meister, ed., *Daretis Phrygii de Excidio Troiae historia* (Leipzig: B. G. Teubner, 1873) 1; translation: R. M. Frazer, Jr *The Trojan War: The Chronicles of Dictys of Crete and Dares the Phrygian* (Bloomington, IN: Indiana University Press, 1966), 133.
7. Meister, *Daretis Phyrgii*, 14; Frazer, trans. *Trojan War*, 142.
8. Meister, *Daretis Phyrgii*, 1; Frazer, trans., *Trojan War*, 133.
9. Léopold Constans, ed. *Le Roman de Troie par Benoît de Sainte-Maure*. 6 vols. (Paris: Firmin Didot, 1904–1912), lines 87–92.
10. Constans, *Le Roman de Troie*, 138–44.
11. On the manuscript tradition of the *Roman de Troie*, see Marc-René Jung, *La Légende de Troie en France au moyen âge*, Romanica Helvetica, vol. 114. (Tübingen: Francke, 1996), lines 16–330.
12. Jung, *La Légende de Troie en France au moyen âge*, 440–562; see also, Luca Barbieri, *Le 'epistole delle dame di Grecia' nel Roman de Troie in prosa*. Romanica Helvetica vol. 123. (Tübingen: Francke, 2005).

13. Jung, *La Légende de Troie en France au moyen âge*, 563–67.
14. Guido de Columnis, *Historia Destructionis Troiae,* ed. Nathaniel Edward Griffin (Cambridge, MA: Cambridge University Press, 1936), 4; translation: Guido delle Colonne, *Historia Destructionis Troiae*, trans. Mary Elizabeth Meek. (Bloomington, IN: Indiana University Press, 1974), 1.
15. For instance, at the end of the ninth book of the *Historia destructionis Troiae*, Guido cites Homer's catalogue of the ships: 'Homer in his time said there were one thousand one hundred and eighty-six', 88 a number that tallies exactly with the ships enumerated in the *Ilias Latina*: 'His ducibus Graiae Troiana ad litora puppes/bis septem venere minus quam mille ducentae' [These leaders approached the Trojan shores/with their Greek ships, fourteen less than twelve hundred (220–1).
16. See Alison Cornish, *Vernacular Translation in Dante's Italy: Illiterate Literature* (Cambridge: Cambridge University Press, 2010), 89–99.
17. Cornish, *Vernacular Translation in Dante's Italy*, 98.
18. For the text of the *Filostrato,* see *Tutte le Opere di Giovanni Boccaccio,* vol. 2, ed. Vittore Branca (Milan: Mondadori, 1964); for a translation, see N. R. Havely, *Chaucer's Boccaccio: Sources of Troilus and the Knight's and Franklin's Tales* (Woodbridge: Boydell & Brewer, 1980).
19. See Jung, *La Légende de Troie en France au moyen âge*, 334–430; Barbieri, *Le 'epistole delle dame di Grecia'*, 3–10. On the English tradition, see C. David Benson, *The History of Troy in Middle English Literature* (Cambridge: D. S. Brewer, 1980).
20. Barry Windeatt, *Troilus and Criseyde* (Oxford: Clarendon Press, 1992), 50–1. For an edition of the Italian and English texts side by side, see Geoffrey Chaucer, *Troilus and Criseyde: A New Edition of the 'Book of Troilus'*, ed. Barry A. Windeatt (London: Longman, 1984). Although scholars have occasionally proposed that Chaucer worked from a French translation of the *Filostrato,* the recent editors of that translation argue that the French version is too late to have been available to Chaucer. See Gabriel Bianciotto, *Le Roman de Troyle,* 2 vols. (Rouen: Publications de l'Université de Rouen, 1994), 44–93.
21. John V. Fleming, *Classical Imitation and Interpretation in Chaucer's* Troilus (Lincoln, NE: University of Nebraska Press, 1990), 179–200; G. L. Kittredge, 'Chaucer's Lollius', *Harvard Studies in Classical Philology* 28 (1917), 47–133; Robert A. Pratt, 'A Note on Chaucer's Lollius', *Modern Language Notes* 65 (1950), 183–7.
22. For a reading of the *Troilus* in relation to contemporary English culture rather than the continental traditions on Troy, see Sylvia Federico, *New Troy: Fantasies of Empire in the Late Middle Ages* (Minneapolis, MN: University of Minnesota Press, 2003), 65–98.
23. For a summary of the evidence for Chaucer's use of Joseph of Exeter, see Windeatt, *Oxford Guides,* 75–7; on Chaucer's reliance on the *Roman de Troie,* see Barbara Nolan, *Chaucer and the Tradition of the Roman antique* (Cambridge: Cambridge University Press, 1992), 198–246.
24. See Jung, *La Légende de Troie en France au moyen âge*, 334–40.

BIBLIOGRAPHY

Barbieri, Luca, *Le 'epistole delle dame di Grecia' nel Roman de Troie in prosa* (Tübingen: Francke, 2005).
Beaune, Colette, *The Birth of an Ideology: Myths and Symbols of Nation in Late-Medieval France,* trans. Susan Ross Huston (Berkeley, CA: University of California Press, 1991).

Buchthal, Hugo, *Historia Troiana: Studies in the History of Mediaeval Secular Illustration* (London: Warburg Institute, 1971).

Burgess, Jonathan S., *The Tradition of the Trojan War in Homer and the Epic Cycle* (Baltimore, MD: Johns Hopkins University Press, 2001).

Desmond, Marilynn, 'Trojan Itineraries and the Matter of Troy', *The Oxford History of Classical Reception in English Literature: Vol. I: 800–1588*, ed. Rita Copeland (Oxford: Oxford University Press, 2016), 251–268.

Desmond, Marilynn. 'The *Translatio* of Memory and Desire in the *Legend of Good Women:* Chaucer and the Vernacular *Heroides*', *Studies in the Age of Chaucer* 35 (2013), 179–207.

Erskine, Andrew, *Troy between Greece and Rome: Local Tradition and Imperial Power* (Oxford: Oxford University Press, 2001).

Jung, Marc-René, *La Légende de Troie en France au moyen âge* (Tübingen: Francke, 1996).

Nolan, Barbara, *Chaucer and the Tradition of the Roman Antique* (Cambridge: Cambridge University Press, 1992).

Windeatt, Barry, *Troilus and Criseyde* (Oxford: Clarendon Press, 1992).

CHAPTER 14

THE *ROMANCE OF THE ROSE*

Allegory and Lyric Voice

DAVID F. HULT

As any literary history informs us, the *Romance of the Rose* (hereafter, the *Rose*) is a thirteenth-century narrative poem attributed to two authors, who worked not in collaboration but in succession: the first, Guillaume de Lorris, composed sometime around 1230 a dream narrative that, through the allegorical terms of a quest for the eponymous rose, object of amorous desire, figures the narrator's expressed desire for the lady to whom he addresses the poem. Left manifestly unfinished—the narrator neither wakes from his dream nor arrives at an expected fictional conclusion, such as the attainment of the rose—the initial fragment of some 4000 lines of rhyming octosyllabic couplets was completed several decades later, probably in the early 1270s, by a continuator named Jean de Meun, who appended more than 17,500 lines that thoroughly dwarfed the work of his predecessor. The *Rose*, thus brought to a conclusion in the last quarter of the thirteenth century, soon thereafter became a runaway best-seller and without any doubt the most widely known and acclaimed work in French in the fourteenth and fifteenth centuries, copied in astonishing numbers of manuscripts of which hundreds have survived; it only faded from sight after the middle of the sixteenth century, following upon a new wave of circulation thanks to a succession of printed editions published during the early Renaissance. Its impact on fictions of love and on allegorical narrative of all varieties was enormous, both in France and in neighbouring countries. The time-honoured characterization of the two authors, while nowadays considered old-fashioned, superficial, or plainly wrong, can still serve a useful heuristic function, if only by lending itself to subversion or unpacking by modern critical paradigms: Guillaume de Lorris sketched a vision of love that was idealistic, courtly, sentimental, aristocratic, and, for these reasons, narrow in its ideological purview; Jean de Meun, for his part, distinguished by his clerical learning, his bourgeois outlook, his eclecticism, and his taste for obscenity and misogyny, mangled the delicate allegorical framework of Guillaume, burying it under heaps of digressive material adapted from his extensive readings of the Latin classics as well as of works by noteworthy contemporaries.

A professor of mine in graduate school, one of the leading Middle English scholars of his generation, used to call the *Rose* a 'huge ragbag' by which he meant, in a positive light, a useful repository of just about every medieval cliché drawn from the fields of moral reflection, philosophy, science, theology, and, most pertinently, love lore. But of course he also meant by this expression that it was a disorganized mess or, as the *OED* defines it, 'a miscellaneous or muddled collection of things'. This view of the romance was imposed most notably by the massively influential *Allegory of Love* of C. S. Lewis, who, while praising the allegorical effectiveness and poetic nuances of Guillaume de Lorris's opening to the *Rose*, totally disparaged the vast continuation, referring to its 'chaos' and its 'vice of diffuseness', while declaring flatly that Jean was not 'an allegorist'.[1] In spite of Alan Gunn's vigorous and highly detailed defence of the unity of the romance taken as a whole, the stigma of incoherence or unreadability hung over the poem for decades, especially with regard to Jean de Meun. Even the scholar whose edition brought new attention to the work in the late 1960s, Félix Lecoy, refers to it, on the surface at least, as a 'chaotic heap that defies analysis'.[2] The *Rose's* subsequent rehabilitation was undoubtedly due to the wide availability of this edition as well as to the intervention in the early 1970s of the French scholar Daniel Poirion, who performed a convincing re-evaluation of the work in literary, and not primarily moral or theological, terms. Since that time, and particularly as of the late 1980s, the books and articles devoted to the *Rose* have multiplied, evincing an appreciation of the work that it has not known for centuries— perhaps not since the Middle Ages. One could rightly say that during the past three decades, not only has the *Rose's* reputation been rehabilitated, but it has experienced a renaissance among medievalists who have, in much of their recent critical work, stressed its provocative indeterminacy and its beguiling ambiguity. Although I do not take issue with the latter assessments, I do think that if we stand back a bit to consider them in their critical context(s), one could say that the 'chaos' and 'digressiveness' of early critics are simply one side of the same coin occupied by indeterminacy on its other side— indeterminacy which, in the wake of poststructuralism, has become a mark of distinction and an index of intellectual value. Thus Sarah Kay would refer in the closing lines of her excellent 1995 introduction to the *Rose*, to the work's 'elusive and ironic manner': 'its preoccupations', she writes, 'are those of many writers widely admired today, such as Freud, Lacan, or Foucault; I think there are considerable similarities between [Jean de Meun] and Derrida'.[3] One person's chaos is another's opportunity to deconstruct.

One of the major challenges to the reader stems from the multiplicity of discourses encased in Jean de Meun's continuation and that same reader's natural desire to locate and articulate the author's intention, while that intention remains for many readers difficult to locate. This interpretive challenge entails approaching the *Rose* as the vast, suggestive, frustrating and unique monument that it certainly was in the Middle Ages, and remains in its current scholarly treatment. Much recent work on the allegorical poem has wisely avoided overarching interpretations and instead focused upon isolated thematic or interpretive issues: questions of sexuality and love, moral instruction, cultural and social satire, the philosophical relation between nature and art, between contingency and predestination, between sincerity and deceit. Rather than simply add another voice attempting to articulate the work's meaning or meanings, this chapter will situate the *Rose* in a lineage of narrative fiction going back to the twelfth-century predecessors of the two authors and attempt to describe their respective innovations, which would forever change the shape of narrative fiction.

It would not be much of an exaggeration to claim that narrative fiction and history composed in the twelfth and thirteenth centuries in the language spoken in continental France and the British Isles, a number of regional dialects collectively referred to as Old French, served as a primary model and source for vernacular traditions of narrative composition in the other major languages of western Europe—English, Italian, German, Spanish, Old Norse, and Dutch. In the opening years of the fourteenth century, Dante famously characterized the accomplishments of Old French language, which he referred to as the 'language of *oïl*' (for the word used to say 'yes'), in the following manner:

> [It] could maintain on its part that, because it is the vernacular language read with the most facility and most pleasure, whatever is translated or invented in vernacular prose is its alone, such things as the Bible or the histories of the Trojans or Romans, or the most attractive wandering adventures of King Arthur, or any number of other historical and doctrinal works.[4]

Even though Dante refers specifically to the prose form, which would undoubtedly have been the means by which he had access to the Arthurian material (the *Prose Lancelot* is referred to explicitly in the *Divine Comedy*) and to historical narrative (either works such as the *Faits des Romains* [*Deeds of the Romans*] or the *Histoire ancienne jusqu'à César* [*History of the ancients up to Caesar*]), or perhaps one of the prose renderings of Benoît de Sainte-Maure's highly influential verse *Roman de Troie* (*Romance of Troy*), he is with the same gesture referring obliquely to a long tradition of verse narrative composition without which the later prose tradition would not have been possible, namely, works such as the antique romances of the mid-twelfth century, the *Tristan* romances of Thomas and Béroul, the Arthurian romances of Chrétien de Troyes, the Breton lais and fables of Marie de France, and novel creations of numerous other narrative poets.

Among the remarkable innovations of the generation of writers in France and England in the period 1160–90 was the development of the persona known widely nowadays as the 'clerkly narrator'. Unlike the narrator of epic poetry, typically figured as a singer and performer from a fairly humble class, writers of erudite fiction, starting with hagiography and extending to the stories of the ancient world before branching out to encompass the fictions of Celtic myth, depicted themselves as learned translators or transmitters of a rich body of Latin literature heretofore available only to literate clerks who could read and write. Even transmission of oral works becomes a factor of erudition: Marie de France declares, for instance, in the prologue to her collection of *lais* that she had considered translating something from Latin into French but that this project would have gained her little distinction, inasmuch as so many others were doing the same thing; she would therefore translate the tales she had heard sung and commit them to writing in order to assure their preservation. Moreover, as Michel Zink has described a phenomenon that he calls a 'metamorphosis in literary consciousness', the self-effacing narrator transmitting events of historical import becomes increasingly involved in the 'very nature of the literary text'.[5] Not only does the issue of artistry and design begin to trump that of referential truth, but the fundamental importance accorded to the theme of romantic love in fictions of the time leads to complex descriptions of love psychology and an increasing assimilation of narrator and lover. In a number of romances written around the turn of the century, such as the anonymous *Partonopeu de Blois* or Renaut de Bâgé's *Le Bel Inconnu*, the narrator's personal situation provides a liminal, parallel narrative to the experience of the protagonist, typically a knight seeking adventure and experiencing amorous encounters.

In a general sense, much experimentation in the early thirteenth century revolved around what Zink calls the 'redistribution of lyric and narrative forms'.[6] The lyric tradition in Old French imitated the poetry of the troubadours, poets from the South of France who composed their works in the Occitan language, starting as early as the first quarter of the twelfth century. The lyric genre known in the North as the *chanson* was the primary expression of poetic subjectivity, the poet singing of his desire for his lady in a first-person voice mixing joy and pain, hope and despair. In the twelfth century, romance writers were also on occasion lyric poets, as was Chrétien de Troyes, but the genre conventions typically remained distinct. The redistribution mentioned by Zink included the insertion of lyric poems into romances, the narrativization of lyric poets' putative real-life experience, and so on, as Sylvia Huot has abundantly documented.[7]

Guillaume de Lorris's intervention in this context of innovation and rethinking of genres ultimately altered in a radical fashion the possibilities of authors for generations to come, for his apparently simple, straightforward allegorical poem constitutes in fact a complex interweaving of hitherto disparate fictional modes. As H. R. Jauss in particular has shown,[8] the taste for allegorical narrative in the vernacular goes back to the twelfth century, but these works remain anchored in a didactic, religious context. From vernacular paraphrases of the Bible incorporating traditional moralizing exegesis, to dream tales recounting fantastic voyages providing moral lessons frequently spiked with pointed satires of contemporary behaviour, these writers sought to instruct a readership consisting of both lay and clerical readers. Armand Strubel considers Raoul de Houdenc's *Songe d'Enfer* (*Dream of Hell*), c.1210, to be the 'first great allegorical poem'.[9] In it, Raoul recounts a dream he had in which he follows a path to Hell, along which he meets a succession of personifications (e.g. Covetousness, Avarice, Drunkenness) who question him about their acolytes on earth; this provides Raoul the opportunity to confirm, with obvious satirical intent, that the followers of these vices are thriving in his society and indeed winning the battle against their adversaries, the corresponding virtues. Among a host of elements that Guillaume takes from this allegorical tradition are the dream framework and the large-scale use of personified qualities. However, in a crucial innovation, Guillaume draws his personifications not predominantly from the moral categories of Christian homiletics, but from the array of psychological qualities found in the secular courtly love tradition (e.g. Beauty, Youth, Courtliness, Largesse). Whereas no developed allegories of the sort Guillaume undertook were to be found in previous courtly narrative, writers such as Chrétien de Troyes and Gautier d'Arras took pleasure in punctuating their chivalric romance adventures with vignettes featuring personified abstractions. The lyric tradition, for its part, had shown an increasing tendency to turn its principal abstract nouns into forces that act upon the poet's psyche, thus moving in the direction of psychological allegory. The other important strand from which Guillaume draws is the extensive body of love-debate literature, featuring most notably elaborate descriptions of the God of Love, a corpus that certainly predates him by at least a generation.

But what is perhaps Guillaume's single most significant innovation, and the marker of a new dimension of courtly narrative, is his transfer of the first-person speaking voice from its episodic use in lyric poetry to its implementation as a frame for an entire narrative, turning it into a type of autobiographical fiction. To be sure, works such as Raoul's *Songe d'Enfer* had likewise told a dream narrative from a first person perspective, but previous to Guillaume these narrators tended to be observers or commentators (satirical, moralizing, ironic) with little or no personal connection to the experience being recounted. As Charles Muscatine remarked many years ago, 'An "I", a protagonist, is rhetorically present, but the allegory tells us nothing about him as an individual personality'.[10] And whereas the 'truth' of didactic allegory, especially that based upon Biblical interpretation, resided in the historicity of the literal level, once the literal level became that of an individual's dream, the question of the narrative's truth value was left open. As the anonymous author of the thirteenth-century *Fablel dou Dieu d'Amors* (*Tale of the God of Love*), puts it: 'Conter vos voel le moie avision,/Ne sai a dire se chou est voirs u non'[11] [I want to recount my dream vision to you, (but) I can't say whether it is true or not]. Raoul's statement at the opening of the *Songe d'Enfer* is slightly more ambiguous: 'En songes doit fables avoir,/Se songes puet devenir voir:/Dont sai-ge bien que il m'avint/ Qu'en sonjant un songe, me vint/Talent que pélerins seroie'[12] [Dreams must contain falsehoods, even if a dream can come true: Thus I know indeed that it happened, while dreaming a dream, that I conceived the desire to be a pilgrim]. Raoul affirms what it is that he dreamed, suggesting that it, like all other dreams, contained some measure of falsehood, but he does not claim that his dream has any truth value other than what would apply to his own psyche. As though a direct rejoinder to these remarks, Guillaume, in his justly famous prologue, goes to great lengths to stress the prophetic value of his dream as based upon his later experiences while awake:

> Aucunes genz dient qu'en songes
> n'a se fables non et mençonges;
> mes l'en puet tex songes songier
> qui ne sont mie mençongier,
> ainz sont aprés bien aparant,
> si en puis bien traire a garant

un auctor qui ot non Macrobes,
qui ne tint pas songes a lobes,
ançois escrit l'avision
qui avint au roi Scypion.
Qui c'onques cuit ne qui que die
qu'il est folor et musardie
de croire que songes aviegne,
qui se voudra, por fol m'en tiegne,
quar endroit moi ai ge fiance
que songes est senefiance
des biens as genz et des anuiz,
que li plusor songent de nuiz
maintes choses covertement
que l'en voit puis apertement.
El vintieme an de mon aage,
el point qu'Amors prent le paage
des jones genz, couchier m'aloie
une nuit, si con je souloie,
et me dormoie mout forment,
et vi un songe en mon dormant
qui mout fu biaus et mout me plot;
mes en ce songe onques riens n'ot
qui tretot avenu ne soit
si con li songes recensoit.

[Some say that there is nothing in dreams but lies and fables; however, one may have dreams which are not in the least deceitful, but which later become clear. In support of this fact, I can cite an author named Macrobius, who did not consider that dreams deceived, but wrote of the vision that came to King Scipio. Whoever thinks or says that it is foolish or stupid to believe that a dream may come true, let him think me mad if he likes; for my part I am confident that a dream may signify the good and ill that may befall people, for many people dream many things secretly, at night, which are later seen openly. In my twentieth year, at the time when Love claims his tribute from young men, I lay down one night, as usual, and fell fast asleep. As I slept, I had a most beautiful and pleasing dream, but there was nothing in the dream that has not come true, exactly as the dream told it.][13]

Contained in this passage is a subtle but very carefully delineated frame for the narrative to follow: as in the didactic allegorical tradition, Guillaume sets up two corresponding levels of meaning, the literal level of the allegorical dream, which signifies in an obscure or hidden manner (*covertement*) and the corresponding real events that will afterward be seen clearly or openly (*apertement*). By subsequently addressing the poem to his beloved, who is left unnamed but who 'tant a de pris/et tant est digne d'estre amee/qu'el doit estre Rose clamee' [is so precious and so worthy of being loved that she ought to be called Rose],[14] he provides one single but crucial key to our deciphering of the poem: the rose, object of his pursuit in the dream, is a figure for the Lady he loves and for whom he is putting into rhyme his cryptic dream. The 'coming true' of the dream is guaranteed by the narrator's affirmation that all the events of the dream actually took place just as the dream told it, albeit under an allegorical cover. Furthermore, the narrator's careful delineation of his personal chronology—he had the dream at the age of twenty, which was five years prior to his present moment—provides an additional mark of the dream's 'autobiographical' truth. The elaborate timeline thus constructed, all revolving around the narrator's putative lived experience, has the prophetic allegorical dream narrative followed later by the events' taking place and ending with the narrator's decision to rhyme the dream events as a poetic offering to his beloved—in this, he is parallel to the lyric poet, who sends his poems as sentimental entreaties to his lady, hoping that she will be swayed by his sincerity and his poetic skill.

But there is more, for the narrator's lady is not the only addressee. He goes on to claim that the God of Love both 'begs and commands' him to write this poem, following it with the most famous couplet of the poem among medieval readers: 'ce est li *Romanz de la Rose,*/ou l'art d'Amors est tote enclose' [it is the *Romance of the Rose*, in which the whole art of love is contained].[15] Critics have often noted the oblique reference to Ovid's well-known *Art of Love*, but what is more important is that to categorize the *Rose* as an art of love is to make its message or underlying meaning not only personal but open to a general public as a form of instruction. So, reverting to the didactic allegorical tradition, the narrator leaves the reader in a conundrum: how indeed are we supposed to read the 'events' of the narrative, as disguised events understood as foreshadowing an individual, personal experience, or as a guideline or form of instruction for would-be lovers? Or both?

As the narrative unfolds, the dream protagonist (whom I will call 'the Lover') comes to a walled garden which was constructed by Delight (*Deduit*) and enters, encountering a large group of personified qualities participating in a dance, including the God of Love with his arrows. Curious to explore the rest of the garden, the Lover goes off and comes upon the fountain of Narcissus, which is also the fountain of Love. Gazing into the fountain, the Lover spies in its reflection the rose bush laden with rosebuds and succumbs to his desire for one of them. On the protagonist's way toward the rose bush, the God of Love, who had been tracking him, shoots him with his allegorical arrows designating the five steps leading to infatuation (Beauty, Candor, Courtesy, Companionship, and Favorable Appearance) and makes the Lover swear homage to him before going into a lengthy enumeration of his commandments and a rehearsal of the pains that lovers must endure. The God of Love disappears and the balance of the narrative relates the Lover's encounter with the personifications that will become the protagonists of what follows, several of which figure the conflicting dispositions or emotions of the beloved: Fair Welcoming (*Bel Acueil*), Resistance (*Dangier*), Noble Spirit (*Franchise*), Pity (*Pitié*), Shame (*Honte*) and Fear (*Poor*). Other personifications get involved who are less easily attributed to the psychological state of either lover or beloved, most notably Jealousy (*Jalousie*) and Bad Mouth (*Male Bouche*) (a figure culled from the lyric tradition, typically referring to the lover's rivals, slanderers or gossips in the social context of the court). Ultimately outraged by the Lover's transgressive kiss of the rose, Jealousy builds a castle in which the rose and Fair Welcoming are imprisoned, with Resistance, Bad Mouth,

Shame and Fear stationed as guardians at the gates. The text breaks off in the midst of the Lover's lament, addressed to the male personification of the lady's good wishes, Fair Welcoming, expressing hope that they will at some time be reunited.

The text's lack of an overt conclusion prevents the reader from figuring out the relationship between the personal thread of the narrative and the nature of the art of love presented in the romance, an interpretive uncertainty that is all the more frustrating in that the account is periodically punctuated with promises to reveal the underlying signification of the dream at the end, as in the following address from narrator to reader:

> Li diex d'Amors lors m'encharja,
> tot issi com vos oroiz ja,
> mot a mot ses comandemenz.
> Bien les devise cist romanz;
> qui amer veut, or i entende,
> que li romanz des or amende.
> Des or le fet bon escouter,
> s'il est qui le sache conter,
> car la fin dou songe est mout bele
> et la matire en est novele.
> Qui dou songe la fin ora,
> je vos di bien que il porra
> des jeus d'Amors assez aprendre,
> puis que il veille tant atendre
> que je die et que j'encomance
> dou songe la senefiance.
> La verité, qui est coverte,
> vos sera lores toute overte
> quant espondre m'oroiz le songe,
> car il n'i a mot de mençonge.

[Then the God of Love gave me his commandments, word for word as you shall hear them now. They are well expounded in this romance, and anyone who aspires to love should pay attention, for the romance now improves. From now on it will be well worth listening to, if there is anyone to recite it, for the end of the dream is very beautiful, and the matter of it is new. I can assure you that whoever hears the end of the dream will be able to learn a great deal about the games of Love, provided that he is willing to wait until I have begun to expound the significance of the dream. The truth, which is hidden, will be completely plain when you have heard me explain the dream, for it contains no lies.][16]

One can readily detect in this passage the tantalizing pivotal role of the first-person voice, serving to articulate the adventure(s) of the past self in the dream and at the same time to communicate information from the exterior dreamer-become-poet about his composition of the romance itself. In fact, the first-person presence (or absence) inhabits the entire narrative space, as it encompasses the adventures of the dream protagonist and the current efforts and concerns of the narrator who, we must remember, is writing the poem in order to procure the good will of his lady. Here, the recall of words from the prologue quoted above is patent: the strategic use of the *songe/mensonge* (dream/lie) and *coverte/overte* (hidden/open) rhymes as well as reference to the work's novelty: 'La matire est et bone et nueve' [The matter is fair and new].[17] But what is especially striking is the repeated reference, here and elsewhere, to the poem's end, which will contain the explanation of the truth behind this obscure narrative—an end that, for whatever reason, is absent. Precisely because of the repeated promises, the lack of an ending containing the explanatory gloss consequently serves to frustrate the expectations of the reader, who is led to wonder whether this fragmentation is due to an unfortunate accident in the poet's life (death, whether literal or metaphorical) or in the text's transmission (the early mutilation of a holograph manuscript). Or perhaps, as I have suggested elsewhere, the lack of a conventional conclusion underscores the fundamental problem of desire and fulfillment in the courtly love tradition and simultaneously begs the hermeneutic question of text and gloss through its highlighting of the very urge to interpret.

We have no certain idea how or under what conditions Jean de Meun would have come upon this fragment, nor do we know what would have induced him to append to his predecessor's poem such a massive continuation and conclusion. What we do know is that all the information we have about the poem's two parts and the dual authorship is provided by the continuator in a much-discussed passage in the middle of his text that raises as many issues as it settles, for at the same time that it appears to provide biographical information about both himself and the first author, it creates an enormous paradox in terms of the relations among the dream narrative, its translation into lived events, and the positionality of the author/narrator.

It is important to note that modern editions of medieval texts and many manuscripts (which are themselves 'editions' of the texts they transmit) provide a mediated, occasionally misleading, vision of those texts. Medieval romance writers do not routinely divulge their identity but when they do, it is usually found in an extradiegetic remark, either in the prologue or epilogue—common features dating from the beginning of the romance tradition—or within the work when the narrator speaks in his own voice about his or her storytelling, as do, for instance, both Thomas and Béroul in their Tristan romances. The first author of the *Rose* does not name himself in his prologue nor does he reveal his identity in his self-conscious references to the writing of his work, such discretion being perhaps a function of the obscure nature of his allegorical work or an adaptation of the kind of anonymity characteristic of the lyric *chanson*. And of course there is no epilogue, so, strictly speaking, what we have been calling Guillaume de Lorris's fragmentary poem is actually an anonymous work. A second factor which is pertinent in Jean de Meun's discussion of the work's dual authorship is related to the formal nature of his continuation. Far from calling attention to his intervention in any overt manner, Jean continues the narrative thread seamlessly, grammatically fusing his addition by completing a sentence left open-ended and developing the narrator's ending lament in the same first-person voice. It is only some 6500 lines later that Jean divulges the precious authorial information but not in the narrator's voice: it is contained in a speech delivered by the God of Love to his barons in order to rally their support for the attack of the castle guarding the rose. In other words, the text itself, contrary to the above-mentioned editions and manuscripts, does not signal the break in the first-person narrative flow, the passage from one authorial figure to another, at the moment it occurs.

In one of the most astonishingly destabilizing moments in medieval literature, the God of Love points to the lover/narrator in the dream (who, having just renewed his vows of homage, is standing by his side) and identifies him as 'Guillaume de Lorris', a love poet who, in the lineage of Tibullus, Gallus, Catullus and Ovid, will go on to serve him by beginning the 'romance that will', he says, 'contain all my commandments'[18]— the very romance we are in the process of reading! The God of Love then quotes the final lines Guillaume will write and 'here' (referring either to the physical space in the dream or to the textual space he has just located verbally) he will repose in his tomb. The quotation refers back to lines 4023–28 of the Lecoy edition, some 6500 lines prior to this moment in the text: the reader can only ask who is responsible for these intervening lines if Guillaume died before they were written. Furthermore, with Guillaume dead, who could continue to write using the same first-person voice? The wait for an answer will not be long, however, for immediately the God of Love affirms, continuing his prophetic mode, that a certain 'Jean Chopinel . . . who will be born in Meung-sur-Loire'[19] will so value the romance that he will want to bring it to a close: 'where Guillaume stops, Jean will continue, more than forty years after his death'.[20] Jean fully exploits the chronological contortions by having his future birth be prophesied by a fictional character in a romance that hasn't even been begun within the fictional dream, at the same time that we have already read the dead poet's fragment and over 6000 lines of his future continuator's addition.

For generations, critics mined this passage for its biographical data, as outlined in the first paragraph of this chapter, without asking any questions about the highly paradoxical nature of its revelation or the unaccustomed insertion of authorial naming *within* the fiction, not to mention the sheer audacity of Jean's gesture. If Jean's surreptitious continuation of his predecessor's poem suggests that he wanted to conceal his agency, why would he suddenly reveal it in this stunning passage, strategically situated at the mid-point of the two-part romance? Does it make a difference whether the information is communicated by the fictional God of Love or by the narrator in his own voice? How are we to understand Jean de Meun's purported absence during these revelations (the God of Love follows his statement that Jean has not yet been born by insisting that 'he is not present here')[21] even when we are told in no uncertain terms that he is responsible for penning these lines? What, moreover, does it mean to say that the first-person narrator we have been following for thousands of lines does not necessarily refer deictically to the same authorial voice that began the narrative? What is the nature of such a gesture of displacement? No one has attacked the positivistic biographical illusion more vigorously than Roger Dragonetti, who argued not only that to take these indications at face value creates a fundamental incoherence (how, for instance, could Jean de Meun have known what happened in the dream if Guillaume died before finishing his account and Jean would only begin his continuation forty years later?) but suggested that the biographical interlude is a fictional 'effect of the writing of the work' and, more precisely, that it proposes 'two fictions inserted into the work of a single, unique author, the writer of the entire *Roman*.[22] While Dragonetti's assertion of a single author having composed the entire work is doubtful when confronted with the givens of the manuscript tradition and of literary history (there is scant, but convincing, codicological evidence that the fragment attributed to Guillaume de Lorris circulated separately from Jean's continuation; Gui de Mori, who produced a revised version of the *Rose* around 1290, tells us that he first came across Guillaume's work and only later discovered a manuscript containing the continuation of Jean), it is, more importantly, theoretically inconsistent, for to posit a single author is just as problematic as to insist upon two. Perhaps the real question to be asked is not 'who authored the work?' or 'one author or two?', but rather 'what does it matter?'.

Before attempting something of an answer to these questions, it is necessary to speak briefly about the construction of Jean's continuation and its questionable unity, including scholars' numerous accusations of discursive incoherence mentioned earlier. Whereas the part of the romance attributed to Guillaume de Lorris is predominantly composed of descriptive passages and allegorical action, there are a couple of digressions that interrupt the narrative flow: the tale of Narcissus (lines 1437–1508), the God of Love's commandments and instructions (lines 2074a–2748); and Reason's attempt to convince the Lover to abandon his quest for the rose (lines 2982–3079). The most distinctive characteristic of the massive continuation is the inflation of digressive episodes consisting primarily of lengthy monologues or dialogues in which the personified qualities hold forth on some aspect of love, which explains why, in the midst of the authorial discussion, the God of Love says that the book, as completed by Jean de Meun, should be renamed *The Mirror for Lovers*, for all who read it will find in this encyclopedic work profitable information (the Latin word *speculum*, meaning 'mirror', was commonly used at this time to refer to encyclopedic compendia of scientific, moral and historical knowledge). Speakers range from the supernal goddesses, Reason and Nature (the latter joined by her confessor Genius), to the cynical Ovidian spokespersons, Friend and the Old Woman, to the personification of religious hypocrisy, False Seeming. The words of these six characters alone occupy nearly 13,000 of the continuation's roughly 17,500 lines, according to Poirion's count,[23] overflowing with passages translated from a large number of classical and medieval Latin authors, including Ovid, Virgil, Cicero, Horace, Juvenal, Boethius, Alan of Lille, and John of Salisbury. Indeed, one likely explanation for the great success of the combined *Rose* is the access it provided a French-speaking audience to ideas gleaned from the Latin philosophical and literary tradition, at a time (the late thirteenth century) when the production of translations for the aristocracy and even for members of the clergy, who found it easier to read their mother tongue than Latin, was in its early stages. The array of discourses thus assembled touches upon a wide cross-section of amorous and sexual behaviours: friendship, parental affection, marriage, prostitution, adultery, rape, homosexuality, castration, procreation. The persistent misogyny of the text comes to a head in the notorious conclusion, the narrator/Lover's grotesque and blasphemous penetration of the castle and taking of the rose, in the guise of a devout pilgrim, the allegorical details of which read like an anatomically correct description of the sexual act. Perennial questions critics have asked include the most essential one, what was Jean's intention in this vast enterprise? Does he champion one or another of the speakers' stances or does he simply, as some critics suggest, present the personifications without commentary, leaving it to the reader to decide? What is his attitude toward the Lover-figure by the time we reach the bawdy end of the work: approval, ridicule, ironic detachment?

In order to obtain historically informed purchase on the nature of Jean's textual manipulations—his curious revelation of the text's authorship, his ambiguous relation to the various love authorities—not to mention his intention, it is useful to come back to the first sustained medieval discussion of the *Rose*, the documents known collectively as the 'Debate of the Romance of the Rose', in particular the letters of Christine de Pizan and the allegorical treatise against the *Rose* composed by Jean Gerson, dating to the opening years of the fifteenth century.[24] As is well known, and oft-repeated, the two critics of the allegorical poem were motivated by the work's obscenity, irreverence, and licentiousness, as well as by the misogyny that punctuates the text throughout, though most notably in the speech of the Jealous Husband, a lengthy rant of 1000 lines, itself encased as a long quotation in the midst of Friend's intervention. But the formal gesture of embedding one fictional character in the discourse of still another personification created a problem, for one can always claim along with the author, as does Pierre Col, his principal defender in the debate, that to portray a misogynous character does not mean that the author is in agreement with the sentiments expressed by that character. Which means that Gerson and Christine feel obliged, each in his or her own way, to comment upon the nature of the allegorical construct as much as, if not more than, on its objectionable content. For Gerson (in the words of his main protagonist, Theological Eloquence), anyone who would claim that it is not the author but other characters who speak is making an inadequate argument, for 'C'est trop petite deffence pour si grant crime' [This is too slight a defense for such a great crime].[25] Then Gerson's personified character, advocate of the Court of Christianity, asks the following question:

> lequel est pis: ou d'ung crestien clerc preschier en la persone d'ung Sarrasin contre la foy, ou qu'il amenast le Sarrazin qui parlast ou escripst? Toutefois jamais ne seroit souffert le segond oultraige; si est toutefois pis le premier (c'est a dire le fait du Crestien), de tant que l'ennemy couvert est plus nuisable que l'appert.
>
> [What is worse: for a Christian cleric to preach counter to the faith, having adopted the persona of a Saracen, or to bring forward the Saracen himself to speak or write? In any event, the latter outrage would never be allowed; yet the first, that is, the deed of the Christian, is nonetheless worse, so much more harmful is the hidden enemy than the overt one.][26]

In other words, she goes on to say, it would be tantamount to concealing poison in honey or striking someone while one is hugging him. Christine is slightly less precise, but she insists upon the fact that the personifications, especially Reason, do not represent the abstractions that correspond to their name. This unreasonable Reason is for Christine an affront to God, her father.

What seems to frustrate both of these critics more than everything else is a textual effect that can be considered a form of contamination, which, for these readers at least, makes the text seem everywhere penetrated by Jean de Meun's malicious spirit. Gerson does not use the author's name, preferring to designate him in his clever allegory as the Foolish Lover, but makes it clear that the latter, in addition to being the licentious figure in the dream, is also the author responsible for assembling his objectionable materials in the form of a book. With regard to this textual effect, here is once again Theological Eloquence:

> Tout semble estre dit en sa persone; tout semble estre vray come Euvangille, en espe-cial aux nices folz amoureulx auxquelz il parle; et, de quoy je me dueil plus—tout enflamme a luxure, meismement quant il la samble reprouver: neis les bien chastes, s'ilz le daingnoient estudier, lire ou escouter, en vaurroient pis.

> [Everything seems to be said in his person; everything seems as true as the Gospel, especially to the naïve, foolish lovers he is addressing. What distresses me most is that everything feeds the flames of lust, especially when he seems to be reproaching it. Even the very chaste, were they to deign to study, read, or listen to the work, would end up the worse for it.][27]

As for Christine, she compares the *Rose* to the books of the alchemists, because 'les uns les lisent et les entendent d'une maniere, les autres qui les lisent les entendent tout au rebours' [some people read them and understand them in one way, while others who read them understand them in the opposite way].[28] While Christine's primary intent is to disparage Jean by dismissing him as a fraud, thinking as do the alchemists that he can turn excrement into gold, she nonetheless thereby accords Jean de Meun an enormous power inasmuch as his almost magical transformative actions on the level of words have no uncertain effects on those who read his text. The repetition of forms of the verb *arguer*, including *argument*, echoes Christine's word for alchemist, *arguemiste* or *arquemiste* (depending upon the manuscript), revealing her underlying association of verbal sophistry and uncanny persuasive ability with the figurative notion of transub-stantiation attributable to the protoscientific discipline. It is thus not surprising that these remarks lead directly to a rant on the issue of deceit, seemingly personified by Jean de Meun, and considered by Christine the worst of all vices: 'Dieux! comme tout noble couraige se doit bien garder d'avoir en soy si villain vice, qui passe tous autres en mauvais effait!' [God! How every noble heart must be on its guard against the appearance within it of such a reprehensible vice, which surpasses all others in its pernicious effects!].[29]

Without specifically mentioning False Seeming, the personification of religious hypocrisy in the *Rose*, Christine forges a connection between him and the elusive author, reaffirming what is already an association by contiguity in the *Rose*, in view of the fact that False Seeming's discourse on deceitful behaviour follows immediately upon the authorial discussion at the centre of the work that reveals Jean's surreptitious interven-tion in the writing of the work. Moreover, this discourse is noteworthy for its being the only one of the major digressions in the *Rose* that says almost nothing about the topics of love or sexuality, while it develops the motif of disguise and trickery and, at the same time, the paradox of the liar who speaks truthfully about his mendacity. The performative doubling of this character, the quintessential hypocrite divulging a portrait of himself with absolute frankness, resonates with the figurative doubling of the author figure. It is true that, as in Dragonetti's analysis, the dual authorship denotes figuratively the two 'poles of a dialogic structure in counterpoint,'[30] but it is also the case that the way it is specifically introduced highlights what I would call a problem of voicing, in this case the relation between the words an author speaks or writes and the intention lying behind those words. The interlocking themes of voicing and intention are omnipresent in the *Rose*, beginning with the very structure of the succession of speeches voiced by the personified authorities. If these discourses provide a complex interweave of quotations taken from Latin *auctores*, who is responsible for what they say? This is precisely the issue raised by the participants in the *Rose* debate, but it is also very much in evidence at various points in the work itself. As Eric Hicks stated pithily many years ago, 'If the *Roman* fits itself so well into the debate, it is that the debate existed already in the romance.'[31] Among the passages Hicks undoubtedly had in mind is the famous first-person apology the narrator supplies later in the *Rose*, in which he anticipates eventual reproaches of his most daring social critiques, those of women (in the mouth of the jealous husband) and of the hypocrisy of the mendicant orders (False Seeming's major theme). Saying in both cases that one of his motivations in recording these speeches was to provide knowledge, 'car il fet bon de tout savoir' [for it is good to know everything], he goes on to say, regarding the misogynous passages:

> D'autre part, dames honorables,
> s'il vos samble que je di fables,
> por manteür ne m'an tenez,
> mes aus aucteurs vos an prenez
> qui an leur livres ont escrites
> les paroles que g'en ai dites,
> et ceus avec que g'en dirai;
> ne ja de riens n'an mentirai,
> se li preudome n'en mentirent
> qui les anciens livres firent.
> …
> je n'i faz riens fors reciter…

[Moreover, honourable ladies, if it seems to you that I am making things up, do not call me a liar, but blame those authors who have written in their books what I have said, as well as those things that I will say; I shall tell no lie, unless the worthy men who wrote the ancient books also lied…I do nothing but quote…][32]

I do nothing but quote…As Alastair Minnis has reminded us, such a deferral of responsibility for what one says is a time-honoured way of protecting oneself against hypothetical future blame.[33] But in this case the situation is more complicated, as Jean de Meun has already made use of the verb *reciter* in order to talk about what one can and cannot licitly say. In the comic yet serious linguistic discussion between Reason and the

Lover, a true dialogue if not a debate, the latter reproaches the goddess who created human language at God's instance for having pronounced a dirty word, an obscenity that should never be voiced. Yet he (and we recall that this first-person speech is actually penned by Jean de Meun, though it is attributed to the Lover in the dream) states a rule that is quite pertinent for the question of quotation:

> Si m'a mes mestres deffendu,
> car je l'ai mout bien entendu,
> que ja mot n'isse de ma boiche
> qui de ribaudie s'aproiche.
> Mes des que je n'en sui fesierres,
> j'en puis bien estre recitierres;
> si nomeré le mot tout outre.

[My master, as I have clearly understood, has forbidden me to allow any word which is in the least indecent to fall from my lips. But since I am not the perpetrator, I may certainly repeat the word, so I shall say it straight out.][34]

The point is that once one has heard an objectionable word said by an *other*, one can oneself use the word blamelessly, especially if it is in a meta-discourse about the very use of that word. This reflexion is at the heart of Jean's self-exculpation: I am simply quoting something said by another and therefore I incur no blame.

This leads us back to the importance of the authorial discussion, for it first introduces the biographical notion of authorial intention, external to the fiction itself, by placing the two medieval authors in the lineage of famous Latin poets only to undermine that notion by making their identification contingent upon the speech of the fictional God of Love. But more radically, it reminds us that the first-person pronoun is no longer the guarantor of sincerity or of signifying intention, because it does not point to a single authorial instance. Moreover, to have the God of Love speak authoritatively about the external conditions of the book's creation while designating the putative future author, 'Guillaume de Lorris', from the outside has the effect of objectifying the latter, who we thought was the subjective guarantor of the entire work. The 'reality effect' of the romance is thereby turned inside out. Jean is asking us to consider, seven centuries before Foucault, 'What is an author?'.

Jean de Meun's extraordinary manipulation of narrative can usefully be understood against the backdrop of Bakhtin's concept of dialogism, which refers to the polemical tension or cognitive space between 'ordinary speech' common to a linguistic or literary community and the opposing or questioning nuance of an individualized speaker. The inherently dialogic nature of discourse constitutes Jean's profound contribution at this turning point in the development of narrative fiction and he flaunts this untouchable linguistic power by directing it toward satire and outrageous blasphemy of the most effective kind. Furthermore, the concomitant institutionalization and fictionalizing of the author figure, placing him both within and outside the poem, itself a dream world, will open the path to poets such as Machaut and Froissart, whose *dits* play with the oneiric rapport between historical and fictional poetic persona. But finally, the most striking aspect of Jean's poetics, one that is abundantly revealed by the Debate participants, is that, no matter how much he attributes authority to his quoted authors, no matter how much he foists responsibility for interpretation on the reader, no matter how much he seems to be affirming his absence from the text he is writing, his fundamental poetic perspective, betokening a form of ventriloquism, gives us the uncanny sense that he is, like his *alter ego*, Faus Semblant, everywhere present and nowhere recognizable,[35] due to his powers of disguise and his inscrutable design:

> Parjurs sui; mes ce que j'afin,
> set l'en enviz devant la fin [...]
> Trop sé bien mes habiz changier,
> prendre l'un et l'autre estrangier.
> Or sui chevaliers, or sui moines, [...]
> briefment je sui de touz mestiers. [...]
> Autre eure vest robe de fame,
> or sui damoisele, or sui dame; [...]
> Que vos diroie? En tele guise
> con il me plest je me desguise.
> Mout est en moi muez li vers,
> mout sunt li fet au diz divers.

[I am a perjurer, but when I pull something off, it is hard for people to know about it before it is over...I am very good at changing my clothes, at donning one outfit and discarding another. At one moment I am a knight, at another a monk....in short, I am of every calling.... Sometimes I don women's clothes: I may be a maiden or a lady;...What can I say? I assume whatever disguise I like. I am not at all what I seem, and my deeds are very different from my words.][36]

NOTES

1. C. S. Lewis, *The Allegory of Love* (London, Oxford, New York: Clarendon Press, 1936), 141, 145, and 137, respectively.
2. Guillaume de Lorris and Jean de Meun, *Le Roman de la Rose*, 3 vols., ed. Felix Lecoy, Les Classiques français du moyen âge 92, 95, 98 (Paris: Champion, 1965–70), 1:xix. All quotations from the *Rose* are taken from this edition and identified by line numbers. English translations are taken from Frances Horgen, trans., *The Romance of the Rose* (Oxford: Oxford University Press, 1994) and identified by page number.
3. Sarah Kay, *The Romance of the Rose* Critical Guides to French Texts 110 (London: Grant & Cutler, 1995), 116.
4. Robert S. Haller, ed. and trans., *Literary Criticism of Dante Alighieri*, Regents Critics Series (Lincoln, NE: University of Nebraska Press, 1973), 15 (translation altered).
5. Michel Zink, 'Une Mutation de la conscience littéraire', *Cahiers de Civilisation Médiévale* 24, no. 1 (1981), 3–27; Zink, *La Subjectivité Littéraire* (Paris: Presses universitaires de France, 1985), 42.
6. Zink, *La Subjectivité*, 43.

7. Sylvia Huot, *From Song to Book: The Poetics of Writing in Old French Lyric and Lyrical Narrative Poetry* (Ithaca, NY: Cornell University Press, 1987).

8. Hans Robert Jauss, 'La Transformation de la forme allégorique entre 1180 et 1240: d'Alain de Lille à Guillaume de Lorris,' in *L'Humanisme médiéval dans les littératures romanes du XIIe au XIVe siècle*, ed. Anthime Fourrier (Paris: Klincksieck, 1964), 107–44.

9. Armand Strubel, 'La Littérature Allégorique,' in *Précis de littérature française du Moyen Age*, ed. Daniel Poirion (Paris: Presses universitaires de France, 1983), 255.

10. Charles Muscatine, 'The Emergence of Psychological Allegory in Old French Romance,' *PMLA* 68, no. 5 (1953), 1163.

11. I. C. Lecompte, 'Le Fablel dou Dieu d'Amors,' *Modern Philology* 8 (1910), 71.

12. Raoul de Houdenc, *Songe D'enfer*, in *Trouvères Belges, Chansons d'Amour, Jeux-Partis, Pastourelles, Satires, Dits et Fabliaux*, ed. Scheler (Louvain: P. and J. Lefever, 1879), 176 (ll. 1–5).

13. de Lorris and de Meun, *Le Roman de la Rose*, ll. 1–30; Horgen, trans., *Romance of the Rose*, 3.

14. de Lorris and de Meun, *Le Roman de la Rose*, ll. 42-4; Horgen, trans., *Romance of the Rose*, 3.

15. de Lorris and de Meun, *Le Roman de la Rose*, ll. 37-8; Horgen, trans., *Romance of the Rose*, 3.

16. de Lorris and de Meun, *Le Roman de la Rose*, ll. 2055–74; Horgen, trans., *Romance of the Rose*, 32.

17. de Lorris and de Meun, *Le Roman de la Rose*, ll. 39; Horgen, trans., *Romance of the Rose*, 3.

18. de Lorris and de Meun, *Le Roman de la Rose*, ll. 10,519–20; Horgen, trans., *Romance of the Rose*, 162.

19. de Lorris and de Meun, *Le Roman de la Rose*, ll. 10,535–37; Horgen, trans., *Romance of the Rose*, 162.

20. de Lorris and de Meun, *Le Roman de la Rose*, ll. 10,557–60; Horgen, trans., *Romance of the Rose*, 162.

21. de Lorris and de Meun, *Le Roman de la Rose*, ll. 10,579; Horgen, trans., *Romance of the Rose*, 163.

22. Roger Dragonetti, *Le Mirage des sources: L'Art du faux dans le roman médiéval* (Paris: Seuil, 1987), 90.

23. Daniel Poirion, *Le Roman de la Rose*, Coll. Connaissance des Lettres (Paris: Hatier, 1973), 121.

24. Quotations of the original text are taken from Eric Hicks, ed., *Le Débat sur le Roman de la Rose*, Bibliothèque du XVᵉ siècle 43 (Paris: Champion, 1977), while English translations come from David F Hult, ed. and trans., *Debate of the* Romance of the Rose (Chicago, IL: The University of Chicago Press, 2010), both identified by page number.

25. Hicks, *Le Débat sur le Roman de la Rose*, 72; Hult, trans., *Debate of the* Romance of the Rose, 117.

26. Hicks, *Le Débat sur le Roman de la Rose*, 73; Hult, trans., *Debate of the* Romance of the Rose, 118.

27. Hicks, *Le Débat sur le Roman de la Rose*, 74; Hult, trans., *Debate of the* Romance of the Rose, 118–19.

28. Hicks, *Le Débat sur le Roman de la Rose*, 126; Hult, trans., *Debate of the* Romance of the Rose.

29. Hicks, *Le Débat sur le Roman de la Rose*, 128; Hult, trans., *Debate of the* Romance of the Rose.

30. Dragonetti, *Le Mirage des sources*, 206.

31. Hicks, *Le Débat sur le Roman de la Rose*, xix.

32. de Lorris and de Meun, *Le Roman de la Rose*, ll. 15,185–94, 15,204; Horgen, trans., *Romance of the Rose*, 235 (emended).

33. Alastair Minnis, *Magister Amoris: The* Roman de la Rose *and Vernacular Hermeneutics* (Oxford: Oxford University Press, 2001), 94–9.
34. de Lorris and de Meun, *Le Roman de la Rose,* ll. 5683–5689; Horgen, trans., *Romance of the Rose,* 87–8.
35. Noah Guynn is one of the few recent critics to recognize in Jean's overtly deconstructive gestures such an intangible yet undeniable presence, a move that is ideologically coercive rather than indeterminate and liberating: 'if Jean is on one level unlocatable within the poem…he could also be understood to be everywhere within it' (*Allegory and Sexual Ethics in the High Middle Ages* [New York: Palgrave Macmillan, 2007], 154). In this, he follows Minnis, who claims that Jean de Meun's use of the satirical mode is a sign of his 'utterly mainstream' (193) view of cultural values.
36. de Lorris and de Meun, *Le Roman de la Rose,* ll. 11,141–2, 11,157–9, 11,164, 11,177–8, 11,189–92; Horgen, trans., *Romance of the Rose,* 171–2 (emended).

BIBLIOGRAPHY

Guynn, Noah, 'Authorship and Sexual/Allegorical Violence in Jean de Meun's *Roman de la Rose*', *Speculum* 79(3) (2004), 628–59.

Hult, David F., *Self-Fulfilling Prophecies: Readership and Authority in the First Roman de la Rose* (Cambridge: Cambridge University Press, 1986).

Hult, David F., 'Words and Deeds: Jean de Meun's *Romance of the Rose* and the Hermeneutics of Censorship', *New Literary History* 28(2) (1997), 345–66.

Huot, Sylvia, *From Song to Book: The Poetics of Writing in Old French Lyric and Lyrical Narrative Poetry* (Ithaca, NY: Cornell University Press, 1987).

Huot, Sylvia, *The Romance of the Rose and its Medieval Readers: Interpretation, Reception, Manuscript Transmission* (Cambridge: Cambridge University Press, 1993).

Jauss, Hans Robert, 'La Transformation de la forme allégorique entre 1180 et 1240: d'Alain de Lille à Guillaume de Lorris', in *L'Humanisme médiéval dans les littératures romanes du XIIe au XIVe siècle,* ed. Anthime Fourrier (Paris: Klincksieck, 1964), 107–44.

Kay, Sarah, *The Romance of the Rose,* Critical Guides to French Texts 110 (London: Grant & Cutler, 1995).

Lewis, C. S., *The Allegory of Love* (London: Clarendon Press, 1936).

Minnis, Alastair, *Magister Amoris: The* Roman de la Rose *and Vernacular Hermeneutics* (Oxford: Oxford University Press, 2001).

Muscatine, Charles, 'The Emergence of Psychological Allegory in Old French Romance', *PMLA* 68(5) (1953), 1160–82.

Poirion, Daniel, *Le Roman de la Rose,* Coll. Connaissance des Lettres (Paris: Hatier, 1973).

CHAPTER 15

CHALLENGING THE PATRONAGE PARADIGM

*Late-Medieval Francophone Writers and
the Poet-Prince Relationship*

DEBORAH MCGRADY

THE fourteenth-century francophone poet Jean Froissart removed all evidence of conventional patronage when composing the presumed last redaction of the prologue to Book One of his *Chroniques*. Dating from between 1395–1404, thus approximately twenty years after the first redaction of Book One, this final iteration eschewed references to Robert de Namur and Gui de Blois, alleged early sponsors of the work, as well as to the various noblemen named in intervening versions of this introduction.[1] Froissart instead identified his work as a product of a diverse literary network that included the men who provided the tales, the knights who accomplished the inscribed deeds, and the young readers who would be inspired to achieve similar feats. This literary circuit was presented as a variation on the feudal model of the three orders, albeit with critical recalibrations intended to spotlight the writer's magisterial role:

> Premierement, li vaillant honme travellent lors corps en armes pour conquerir la glore et renonmee de che monde; li peuples parole recorde, et devise de lors estas; auquns clers escripsent et registrent lors œuvres et baceleries, par quoi elles soient mises et couchies en memores perpetueles. Car par les escriptures puet on avoir la congnissance de toutes coses, et sont registré li bien et li mal, les prosperités et les fortunes des anciiens.[2]

> [First, courageous men work their bodies in arms to achieve glory and fame in this world; the common people recount and tell tales about their accomplishments; certain clerics write and record their works and heroic deeds so that they are placed and shall remain in perpetual memory. For through writing, one can acquire knowledge of all things, and therein are recorded the good and the bad, the successes and failures of the ancients.]

Although identifying writers as servants to the courageous, Froissart asserted in this passage that heroic men were dependent on writers to assure their sustained presence and influence on future generations.

This recasting of the prologue to the *Chroniques* documents important adjustments in Froissart's conception of audience. Moreover, the reader relations sketched out here differ not only from his past iterations but also from modern descriptions of medieval francophone literary dynamics, where the poet-prince relationship frequently dominates discussion. From Daniel Poirion's now institutionalized yoking of the two figures in his *Poète et le prince* to David Wallace's description of Froissart's contemporary, Eustache Deschamps, as practicing 'land-locked poetics, fixated on nobility',[3] francophone writers are presumed to have rarely wandered far outside castle walls, much less to have challenged their masters' authority. As a result, while Froissart and his most illustrious francophone contemporaries, Deschamps and Guillaume de Machaut, are frequently acknowledged as cosmopolitan writers whose works influenced late-medieval literature on both sides of the Channel, scant attention is given to their critical treatment of poet-prince dynamics and the influence they had on promoting dynamic literary communities that extended beyond this hierarchical relationship.[4]

Cross-Channel studies must be wary of binaries that might pit Chaucer the 'social poet' against the francophone 'court writer' who, in the words of Douglas Kelly, is one who 'makes of his or her mind a scribe to the thoughts and sentiments of the prince'.[5] Even Poirion recognized that francophone 'court writers' often openly challenged their lords. In fact he acknowledged in Machaut's case that given his conflicting treatment of his patrons, the poet was best defined as a 'poète pour la cour, donc, mais non pas tout à fait poète de cour' [a poet for the court, therefore, but not entirely a poet of the court].[6] This assessment could easily be extended to Machaut's fellow writers whose texts also often conflict with the modern tendency to privilege patronage relations in discussions of late-medieval francophone writers. For instance, while true that the Hundred Years War period witnessed an increased dependence on writers to articulate, disseminate, or defend the practices of nobility in the form of official letters, commissioned histories, and blatant propaganda pieces, few if any of the writers celebrated today would have been defined as sycophants by their contemporaries.

Consider the three authors already mentioned. Longstanding ties with the royal family did not keep Machaut from challenging King John's imprisonment of King Charles of Navarre in 1357 in his *Confort d'amy* addressed to the prisoner-king. Nor did Deschamps stifle criticism of King Charles VI or Duke Louis of Orleans in whose households he held important administrative positions. He accused the king of being 'lasches et desconfis' [cowardly and without hope][7] and when the duchess of Orleans was banished from Paris, he came to her defence, giving little heed to the risks that he might face at court.[8] Froissart's penchant for praising nobility in highly nostalgic terms is well known and yet he took umbrage at the notion that Guy de Blois's financial support would taint his accounts and asserted in an early version of Book One that his lord held no sway over his writing.[9]

Late-medieval francophone literature provides abundant evidence of writers critically engaging with the poet-prince paradigm and introducing new audience relations. Literary examples as diverse as Machaut's fictional account of a poetic exchange between poet and prince in the *Fonteinne amoureuse*, Deschamps's treatment of patron relations in his supplication poetry, and Froissart's recollections in the *Chroniques* of literary dealings with various lords invite reconsideration of these self-conscious literary moments as potential sites of contestation. These unconventional portrayals of the poet-prince relationship shared space with lengthy reflections on a larger and diverse audience that competed for the author's attention. In this vein, Ardis Butterfield has studied the vituperative exchanges between anglo- and francophone poets during the Hundred Years War as sites of unexpected cross-Channel collaboration that engaged fellow poets in linguistic exploration.[10]

In a similar vein, work on late-medieval francophone debate culture has exposed a vibrant literary network in which literary continuations as much as the production of anthologies promoted poetic exchange and creative collaboration.[11] Similar to the intimate circle of fellow civil servants and littérateurs that Paul Strohm associated with Chaucer, francophone writers populated their texts with clerks, secretaries, lawyers, and fellow courtiers performing as active readers.[12] A case in point is the *Voir dit*, where Machaut incorporated into an account of poetic exchange between the aged poet and an aspiring female pupil multiple exchanges between intellectuals, including Thomas Paien, a fellow canon at Reims.[13] As is well known, Deschamps engaged in lyric correspondence with fellow writers, from Chaucer to Christine de Pizan.[14] As regards Froissart, the knights and esquires who provided him with the material for his *Chroniques*, progressively emerged as collaborators in Books Three and Four, where men like Espan de Lion became fellow storytellers.

Extant manuscripts testify to the success of these three writers to attract an audience outside the expected poet-prince paradigm; in fact, their survival owes much to a new literary class of learned civil servants and parliamentary figures who owned many of the now extant manuscripts of their works.[15] This chapter will explore the interdependence of these two communities with particular attention given to the use of poet-prince accounts by late-medieval writers to reassess the relationship between authors and audience and to reflect on the status of poetry in late-medieval society.

Scholars often identify Machaut's *Fonteinne amoureuse* as the quintessential model of poet-prince creative relations,[16] but to read the work in this manner is to ignore the highly problematic framing of the story. Scholars describe this hybrid *dit* as a composition written on behalf of Duke John of Berry on the eve of his departure for England in 1360 as one of several princely hostages sent to replace King John the Good per the treaty of Brétigny. According to Ernst Hoepffner, the closing anagram confirmed the duke's identity. Even though Hoepffner's solution to this literary puzzle has since been challenged, thus opening the anagram up to possible alternative named recipients,[17] this claim has bolstered arguments for situating the *dit* within a patronage transaction. The prologue, however, subverts the notion that patronage dictated production. The poet provocatively privileged his own pursuit of pleasure over the needs or desires of a patron when beginning his tale by declaring that he wrote for himself: 'Pour moy deduire et soulacier' [To amuse and comfort myself].[18] He subsequently offered the work in honour of his unnamed lady, only to then embrace a literate mass as his audience—'ceuls qui le liront' [those who will read it].[19] These paratextual obfuscations that resist privileging the princely reader produce a destabilizing account of the actual patronage dynamics that might have shaped this work.[20] Reference to multiple readers in verse as well as the elusive anagram signal the possibility that Machaut purposefully invited multiple readers to see themselves (both figuratively and literally) in place of a patron. In this respect the allusions to different privileged readers in the prologue might be read as the poet's savvy designation of a potentially unlimited audience, ranging from any woman of high standing to any reader who could find a trace of his (or her) name in the anagram.

Only after locating the *Fonteinne amoureuse* within a crowded literary network did Machaut finally turn attention to the prince. The tale begins with the poet-narrator situating himself within the proverbial castle walls, but he confesses his unfamiliarity with both castle and prince. Far from home, the poet is unable to sleep. To make matters worse, as he tosses and turns, he hears the haunting moans of an unknown creature ('...une creature/oÿ...').[21] Initially filled with fright, he burrows beneath his covers only to realize that the moans issue from a grieving lover. The narrator will thereafter leave his bed to transcribe the lover's lament. William Calin identified this scene as one of many self-deprecating comic turns in Machaut's literature that underscored his inferior status to the princely lover.[22] Yet, although this scene certainly invites laughter at the thought of the trembling poet unable to distinguish moans from poetry, it also presents a startling portrait of the prince. Our first mediated reaction to the prince is one of horror: '...j'en os horreur et frëour' [I experienced horror and fear].[23] Far from figuring as a comic buffoon or, at best, as a docile scribe in this opening scene, the narrator Guillaume claims for himself a commanding role as creator of a language pulled from inchoate gibberish; for, this unintelligible creature owes its metamorphosis into a worldly prince to the diligent poet who finally distinguished speech: 'Finablement tant atendi/ En ce meschief que j'entendi/La creature qui parla' [In the end, I lingered long enough in this dangerous state that I finally heard the creature begin to speak].[24] As the story progresses the poet's masterful role becomes apparent. From the prince's pre-emptive promise of a hefty reward for the desired poem of 2000 silver marcs[25] to the ensuing friendship that establishes the two men as equals, the tale radically overturns notions of the poet's subservience.[26]

But it is especially the unprecedented conclusion to this narrative that heralds a new understanding of the vernacular writer's relationship to nobility. When the two men must part ways, the poet escorts the prince to an awaiting ship that receives him as a prisoner of war. The prince seals their friendship with a parting reward intended as recompense for the poet-narrator's helpful guidance and his poetic gift. The prince's gift surpasses his earlier promise of 2000 silver marcs for a poem when he bequeaths to the poet all of his possessions: 'Tout son païs m'abandonna/Et de ses joiaus me donna/ Liberalment et largement' [All of his land, he handed over to me and his riches, he gave to me].[27] Such extreme generosity transfers to the poet all of the prince's social markers of authority.[28] Whereas the prince ends up an impecunious and landless prisoner, our previously trembling poet emerges in control of both intellectual capital and the material wealth typically reserved for nobility. This power reversal assigns all forms of authority to the poet while casting the lord out to sea. Possibly in an effort to downplay the extravagance of the scene, Machaut turned, in the final line, to his readers to gauge their reception of his fantasy: 'Dites moy, fu ce bien songié?' [Tell me, was this well dreamt/ thought up?].[29] This allusion to the fictionality of his tale, however, cannot overwrite the fantasy played out in a narrative where the poet asserted not only his pleasure in writing poetry but of his imaginary professional rise to the status of a prince. This irreverent role reversal generated an unconventional closing illustration to this text in what is often labelled an author-supervised copy of Machaut's collected works, Bibliothèque Nationale de France, MS fr. 1584.[30] Here the poet remains on the shoreline—on horseback rather than bended knee—whereas the prince drifts out to sea, rapidly fading from a narrative that details the poet's pleasure rather than the prince's.

No less than Machaut, Deschamps treated poet-prince relations extensively in his impressive corpus of nearly 1500 lyric pieces ranging from *formes fixes* to *dits*, such as the *Fiction du Lyon* and the *Miroir de mariage*. But far more than the topic of literary patronage, it was his administrative service that figured prominently in his writings. The frequent references in his poetry to his multifaceted professional ties to the royal family surely influenced Poirion's identification of him as a court poet, but even he later conceded that Deschamps's corpus progressively registered a striking *dénigrement* of this world.[31] Many of these critical portraits appear in works directly addressed to members of nobility, although they were far more likely to have pleased fellow courtiers. Deschamps registered numerous discontents certainly shared by a wide range of royal servants, including complaints about soldiering in inhospitable climates, court corruption, preposterous court cases in the countryside that he was obliged to oversee, and personal financial and material harm caused by the failure of royalty to achieve peace.[32] Yet other poems directly addressed fellow servants to complain about court life and the general corruption of the ruling class as well as his regular grousing about the failure of nobility to recognize the advantage of surrounding oneself with wise men and the tendency of knights to disdain knowledge.[33] In fact, there is good reason to forego discussion of conventional patronage relationships when speaking of Deschamps's literary output to favor instead the cultivation of an intimate circle of equals as his privileged audience. Manuscript evidence supports this recalibration of his intended audience given that civil servants owned most of his extant manuscripts.[34]

Even when lords do figure as Deschamps's primary interlocutors, they are often the subject of strong criticism. In the over two dozen supplication poems in which Deschamps exposed the failure of several lords to fulfill their financial and material obligations to him, humor and satire only slightly soften the poet's repeated accusations that lords regularly shirked their responsibilities.[35] Recurring appeals included requests for funds to repair Deschamps's residence after an English campaign as well as outstanding reimbursements or defaulted stipends promised to him by the royal family.[36] Vestiary needs also regularly appeared, whether to request a *houppelande* to keep the poet-soldier warm during military campaigns, new clothing to replace worn out garments, or the right to wear a hat at all times at court to fight the cold.[37] It turns out that Deschamps's lyric voice wielded political might. As James Laidlaw has detailed, Deschamps's poetic pleas for financial assistance sometimes ended up recorded nearly verbatim in court communiqués as justification of payments to Deschamps and ensuing court mandates submitted to the treasury office confirm that these poetic demands for aid were satisfied.[38] This evidence provocatively points to the social and political power of poetry first, to charge lords with their ethical responsibilities toward servants and second, to affect change in behaviour and practices through lyric supplication. Deschamps's poetry, as in the *Fonteinne amoureuse*, functions less to please the princely reader or to articulate a patron's desires and more to expose moral failings and to demand justice—a strategy that assigns authority, both symbolically and materially, to the poet.

Although Deschamps typically refrained from including his poetic activity among his unrewarded services, two supplication poems (B788 and B1125) stand out for their uncommon reference to Deschamps's poetic activities. In Ballade 788 the poet recalls 200 francs promised to him by the king four years prior and the refrain repeats a direct request to the king that his treasurer Montagu be ordered to pay his debt. If not the first time that the poet evoked the king's debt, this ballade holds the distinction of recording a poetic threat, a form of poetic justice, if you will. The poem opens with the facts concerning the king's promise of a reimbursement for a visit to his home, most likely in 1384. The first two stanzas focus on these past events, but the third stanza turns to the future when the poet announces that if the owed sum is not soon received, he will be reduced to shepherding to survive and as a result, he will no longer write— 'Plus ne fera chançons, livre ne chans' [No longer will I compose songs, books or poems].[39] But he quickly adds that his poetic talents will be put to use in his new state: 'Ainsois joura de la turelurette/Et s'en yra dire, comme uns truans,/A Montagu qu'il ly paye sa debte' [Thus I will play the turelurette and will go about demanding, like a beggar, from Montagu that he pay the king's debt].[40] Donning the minstrel's instrument and the beggar's tactics, he threatens to speak publically of the debt owed him. What first appears as a comic turn that transforms the sergeant-at-arms into a street performer takes the shape of a warning. Deschamps threatens to forego books and poems, presumably composed in honour of the king, and to use hereafter his talents not simply to beg, but to proclaim publicly the king's failure to pay his debt. The royal court would have easily understood such loosely veiled threats. In fact, wandering minstrels were sometimes subject to statutes that declared certain topics off limits in their performances, such as a 1395 Paris statute forbidding songs that criticized either pope or king.[41] Court records registering a payment of 200 francs to Deschamps on 3 November 1388, however, suggest that this poem, which dates itself to around October 1388, wielded particular influence at court.[42] The court's rapid response to the poet's demands offers tantalizing evidence that royalty indeed prized and even feared the power of the literary word.

Yet another supplication poem, Ballade 1125, encourages this interpretation of lyric beggary as a menacing reminder of the power of poetry.[43] This second ballade conjoins a request for poetic justice with the threat of poetic retaliation. Deschamps alludes to a previous royal commission to chronicle the achievements of the royal family that he now threatens to abandon after thirty-two years. The poem opens with a threat masked as a wish: 'je vueil cesser mon livre de memoire' [I want to end my book of memory].[44] Deschamps describes the now lost work, the 'livre de memoire', in the first stanza as a record of the feats of the past generation of leaders. As the lyric unfolds, he identifies his subjects' indifference to his work as triggering his desire to abandon the project, but he provides a stark account of the risk Charles VI and Louis of Orleans face should the poet follow through with his threat. Ballade 1125 opens with fulsome praise for the reign of Charles V and the heroic life of his knight Bertrand de Guesclin, but by the close of stanza one, those past glory days have ended with the death of both men. The second stanza recalls the people's lament and then memorializing of these heroes. Stanza three leaves behind 'ceste vie en gloire' [this life of glory][45] to turn to the troubling years surrounding the rise of the poet's current lords, Charles VI and the king's brother Louis of Orleans. Recent rebellions and the general instability marking the rise of power of these two men dominate the closing stanza. Deschamps offers only faint praise for the king's reign since his 1380 coronation: 'la chose fut assez bien gouvernée' [things were fairly well governed].[46] The use of the past tense shuts down further discussion of the king's activities as well as any prophecy for his future reign. The poet reinforces this silence in his concluding remarks when explaining that since the coronation, he has been kept from his lords and thus has nothing to report:

> Puis son sacre me fut paine donnée
> Estans o eulx, d'encerchier et enquerre
> Et d'escripre leurs faiz par la contrée.[47]

[Since his coronation, it has been difficult for me to be with them, to seek out and inquire, and to write of their feats throughout the lands].

The return to the refrain—'Noble chose est de bon renom acquerre' [it is a noble thing to acquire fame]—provides a stark contrast to the poet's lack of news to report while also underscoring the causal link between writers spreading news of accomplishments throughout the realm and the acquisition of fame. As was the case with Ballade 788, Deschamps registers here the immediate impact of his unique form of poetic justice. The two brothers find their story anchored in the present poem to uncertain chaotic times rather than to an account of their successes. Whereas no court document has been located that might register a direct response to this threat, the accumulation of posts and stipends offered by both royal princes and his sustained poetic dialogue with them until the poet's death suggest that Deschamps continued to enjoy their favour. Yet, Deschamps placed his writings outside prescribed patronage dynamics that are said to hinge on the poet's willingness to submit to the thoughts and desires of the master in exchange for compensation. Poetry functioned instead for Deschamps as a gift that could assure a deserving leader's fame or as the ultimate curse when it exposed the moral failings of leadership or when it remained silent about achievements.

In many regards Froissart bridged his elders' views on the power and value of poetry, but he seems to have reconciled himself over his long career to the increasing indifference that men of power expressed for poetry. And yet, the author attributed the beginning of his literary career to Philippa of Hainault, queen of England, who, around 1361, accepted the first fruits of his lyric endeavours, a verse account of the events of Poitiers. His literary career subsequently veered in a different direction, ostensibly to cater to the queen's interests, as he shifted from historical events to more courtly topics.[48] Following the queen's death in 1369, Froissart eventually returned to his first subject of interest to write a prose history of contemporary wartime events. The resulting four-volume *Chroniques* would keep the writer occupied until his final days in 1404. But Froissart never abandoned poetry; he continued to write, to disseminate, and to reflect on his poetic corpus throughout the composition of the *Chroniques*.[49] So important was his poetry that not only did he remain committed to sharing his past writings with new acquaintances, but he further inserted his poetic adventures into his account of contemporary history.

Books Three and Four of the *Chroniques* record two scenes in which the author presented his poetry to actual princes. Book Three registers the 1389 experience of reading his Arthurian romance, *Méliador*, to Gaston Phoebus, the count of Foix. Froissart prefaces this account with a synopsis of the romance's history, a complicated narrative in itself since the romance underwent at least two redactions that transformed a single-author tale into a collaborative endeavour between Froissart and Wenceslas of Brabant who had died six years earlier. Later in Book Four the author would recount his 1395 experience of offering a collection of his lyric writings to Richard II. As with the *Méliador*, this experience of recycling past poetic texts written in large part for Queen Philippa, Richard's grandmother, and her extended family and friends inspired a strongly nostalgic belief that this lyric recycling would reinvigorate the poet in his old age. Each account proved bittersweet; for both poetic offerings failed to reproduce in their new readers the commitment to lyric that the author associated with his past patrons, Wenceslas and the queen. Even though he was often described as a writer who mythologized his contemporaries and sought to restore past models,[50] in these two accounts, Froissart sharply contrasted past patrons who supported poetry with his contemporary noble readers who failed to recognize its value.

Froissart's account of a public reading of his imposing, more than 30,000-line Arthurian romance *Méliador* at the court of Gaston Phoebus opens with background information concerning his previous patron's earlier contributions to the work:

> L'accointance de li a moy pour ce temps fu telle, que je avoie avecques moy aporté un livre, lequel je avoie fait a la requeste et contemplacion de monseigneur Wincelaus de Boesme, duc de Lucembourc et de Braibant, et sont contenus ou dit livre, qui s'appelle de *Meliader*, toutes les chançons, balades, rondeaulx, virelaiz que le gentil

duc fist en son temps, lesquelles choses parmi l'ymaginacion que je avoie en dicter et ordonner le livre, le conte de Fois vit moult volentiers; et toutes les nuis aprés son soupper je lui en lisoie, mais en lisant, nul n'osoit parler ne mot dire, car il vouloit que je feusse bien entendu, et aussi il prenoit grant solas au bien entendre. Et quant il cheoit aucune chose ou il vouloit mettre debat ou agruement, trop volentiers en parloit a moy...[51]

[The acquaintance between [Gaston Phoebus] and me was such at this time that I had brought with me a book produced upon the request and in accordance with the thinking of my lord Wencelas of Bohemia, duke of Luxembourg and Brabant; and in this book, which is entitled *Méliador*, are contained all of the songs, ballades, rondeaux, virelais that the kind lord had composed during his lifetime (based on these writings, with the aid of imagination, I narrated and ordered the book), the count of Foix was happy to see it and every night, after his dinner, I would read to him from it. When reading it, no one dared pronounce a single word because he desired that I be well heard and because he took great joy in listening attentively. And when he found something that he wanted to debate or discuss, he very willingly spoke of it to me.]

This vivid and informative account of the 'biography' of *Méliador* fails, however, to provide the full story. Only by reading Froissart's alternative account of this event in the *Dit du Florin* (c.1389) do we learn that Wenceslas died before the romance was completed and thus never enjoyed the fruits of their collaborative enterprise. Moreover, it is only in the *dit* that Froissart discloses that he did not offer his copy of the *Méliador* to Gaston Phoebus but did accept a monetary reward from the count for his public reading of the text.[52] The discrepancies between the prose and verse accounts of this event call attention to the loss, trauma, and abandonment associated with the making of the *Méliador*. The desire to find a worthy substitute for the work's original patron drives both narrative accounts of the public reading before Gaston Phoebus. In the *Chroniques* account, Gaston Phoebus stands in as a viable surrogate for the poet's former literary partner. In this version, the count fills in for the duke's absence and his conversation matches the duke's previous contribution of the seventy-nine poems inserted into Froissart's composition. Through these two interlocking gifting patterns, Froissart constructs a seamless passage from one prince to the next that intimates the passing of the *Méliador* to a new patron. By suspending discussion of the actual outcome of their meeting, Froissart maintains focus on the nostalgic portrait of poet and prince communing. In contrast, Froissart disclosed in the *Florin* that, in fact, he maintained possession of the codex. Froissart reports in this version that he was paid for his performance of the text, thereby replacing intimacy with an economic transaction. He further speculates that the count was displeased with this final outcome. Perhaps Gaston truly desired a copy of the romance, but what is even more likely is that the prince would have interpreted the poet's visit and presentation of his work as an offering. Instead, this version of events details that the poet withheld the gift and left the prince empty-handed and with no claim to the title of patron.

A similar subterfuge informs Froissart's two-part *Chroniques* account of presenting his lyric corpus to Richard II in 1395. In Book Four Froissart first recalled his decision to oversee the production of a luxury manuscript of his poetry that he planned to offer the king during an upcoming visit to England. As a storehouse of works written for Richard's grandmother, the material product grandly repackaged poetry as a gift worthy of a king.[53] Froissart displayed for all its luxuriousness, describing it as 'enluminé, escript et historié et couvert de vermeil velours à dix clous attachiés d'argent dorés ... et richement ouvrés ou milieu de roses d'or' [illuminated, written, and decorated, and covered with red velour attached with ten nails of silver painted gold and richly worked with gold roses in the middle].[54] He then recounted offering his book to the king, an inaugural gesture evoking the formalized ritual of gift exchange in practice in late medieval European courts. As Brigitte Buettner has remarked, these events served increasingly as 'metaspectacles' performed before a court public.[55] In this case, however, the king interrupted the metaspectacle to inquire into the contents of the work: 'Adont me demanda le roy de quoy il traittoit' [Then the king asked me what it was about].[56] To the author's response that it treated the subject of love, the king unfastened the golden clasp to peruse the book's contents. Whether the king's actions were motivated by mock interest in a poet who so extravagantly repackaged poetry written for a time long past or in sincere fascination with a linguistic and artistic heritage that linked him to Queen Philippa is anyone's guess.[57] What happened next in the narrative helps little to clarify.

Ceremonial convention would have dictated that the book pass from the king's hand to be registered and moved into storage. The king instead removed the gift-book from this ritual when he redirected it to his *chambre de retraite*. While common to interpret this gesture as a sign of the king's particular appreciation of this book, we can also liken it to the public reading of Froissart's work at the court of Gaston Phoébus. As such the king's gesture might be interpreted as dismissive and the book's removal from the usual circuit as an indicator that it was not deemed worthy of inclusion in the king's library. That Froissart would never see his book again during his many weeks at court, never discuss its contents with the king, never enjoy a follow-up commission, and apart from being allowed to remain in the king's retinue, never receive a monetary reward worth mentioning either by Froissart or by the king's treasury may lend some credence to pursuing a less positive interpretation of the gesture.[58] Rather than address these issues, the king fades from the *Chroniques* after the book presentation to be replaced with his men who seek out Froissart to share their wartime stories. Rather than discuss his poetry, these men celebrate Froissart as a chronicler and desire to share with him their version of past events.[59]

Froissart's recollections of the circulation and reception of his poetic corpus might first appear to reinforce Machaut's fictional account of the incalculable value of poetry, but upon closer consideration, we begin to understand that much like Deschamps, Froissart inscribed disturbing evidence that nobility undervalued poetry. Deschamps's threats to stop writing for his lords find no comparable vow in Froissart's writings, but the chronicler's actions later in life, especially when revising Book One bespeak a similar sentiment. As noted at the outset of this chapter, Froissart appeared to have later in life turned to cultivating an audience consisting of men of lesser rank rather than the noblemen and women to whom he presented his poetry. In both of these troubled book scenes, this shift is already perceptible. Although Froissart tells of princes engaging with his poetry, these accounts are framed by knights and lesser lords, whether Espan de Lion, Sir Thomas Percy and Sir Richard Sury, who favour his history writings. Their interest and admiration stand in stark contrast to the unrecorded or sparse words attributed to the illustrious recipients of his poetry. It is their familiarity with and enthusiasm for his prose work that he increasingly spotlighted in the *Chroniques*. Ultimately these readers would supplant the ruling class as Froissart's privileged audience, as confirmed by the revised prologue to Book One.

Drawing from these examples that represent three distinctive genres—the narrative *dit*, lyric poetry, and historical narrative—this chapter has argued for a more critical and nuanced reading of tales of poet-prince relations in late-medieval francophone literature. Rather than reflecting reality, poet-prince narratives by Machaut, Deschamps and Froissart register a critical engagement with the contemporary status of vernacular poetry as well as the poets who created them. Their writings document a strong nostalgia for an intimacy that 'never was',[60] but each in his own way pointed to the failure of the privileged class to value poetry: Machaut pushed to the limit the notion that poetry was an invaluable gift that made of writers princes' equals, Deschamps provocatively explored poetry's ability to serve as either a gift or a curse, and Froissart waxed nostalgic on past collaborations that romanticized poet-prince relations while implying that contemporary nobility fell short of the poet's expectations. Far from serving as mouthpieces to their princely superiors, these writers often used the patronage paradigm to assert the inestimable worth of poetry and the invaluable wisdom and authority of writers, while also recognizing the all too frequent habit of the nobility to underrate the poetic gift.

ACKNOWLEDGEMENTS

I am grateful to my colleague Anthony C. Spearing for his crucial input on an early version of this chapter and Katherine Zeimann for several rounds of conversation regarding this study. This chapter was completed during fellowship at the National Humanities Center and was supported by the Florence Gould Foundation.

NOTES

1. For details on the making of the *Chroniques* and the various redactions undertaken by the author, see J. J. N. Palmer, 'Book I (1325–1378) and Its Sources', in *Froissart: Historian*, ed. J. J. N. Palmer (Suffolk: Boydell Press, 1981), 7–25, and G. T. Diller, 'Froissart: Patrons and Texts', in Palmer, *Froissart: Historian*, 148. Debate surrounds the chronology of the extant versions of Book One, but the two early versions are distinguished by their prologues in which the possibly earliest version reproduced in the Amiens manuscript names several illustrious princes without identifying them as benefactors whereas the subsequent versions, known as A and B and edited by Siméon Luce, announce that the work is pursued upon the request of Robert de Namur. For these early versions, see M le baron Kervyn de Lettenhove, ed., *Oeuvres de Froissart. Publiées avec les variantes des divers manuscrits*, vol. 1

(1867–1877); *Chroniques*, ed. Siméon Luce, vol. 1 (Paris: Société de l'histoire de France, 1869–1888); *Chroniques. Livre I, Le manuscrit d'Amiens, Bibliothèque municipale, n. 486*, ed. George T. Diller (Geneva: Droz, 1992), 2.

2. Jean Froissart, *Chroniques. Dernière redaction du premier livre. Édition du manuscrit de Rome Reg. Lat. 869*, ed. George T. Diller (Geneva: Droz, 1972), 37. All translations of primary citations are the author's.

3. David Wallace, *Premodern Places: Calais to Surinam, Chaucer to Aphra Behn* (Malden, MA: Blackwell Publishing, 2004), 60.

4. The key work on the francophone literary influence on Chaucer is, of course, James I. Wimsatt, *Chaucer and his French Contemporaries: Natural Music in the Fourteenth Century* (Toronto: University of Toronto Press, 1991).

5. Paul Strohm, *Social Chaucer* (Cambridge, MA: Harvard University Press, 1989) and Douglas Kelly, 'The Genius of the Patron: The Prince, the Poet, and Fourteenth-Century Inventions', *Studies in the Literary Imagination* 20 (1987), 77–97, esp. 77.

6. Daniel Poirion, *Le Poète et le prince: l'évolution du lyrisme courtois de Guillaume de Machaut à Charles d'Orléans* (Geneva: Slatkine Reprints, 1978), 196.

7. 3:388, line 21. All references to Deschamps's poetry are from *Oeuvres completes d'Eustache Deschamps*, ed. le marquis de Queux de Saint-Hilaire, 10 vols. (Paris: Firmin Didot, Société des anciens textes français, 1878–1903). Translations are my own.

8. Saint-Hilaire, ed. *Oeuvres completes d'Eustache Deschamps*, 4:771.

9. Jean Froissart, *Chroniques*. Cited and discussed by Michael Jones, 'The Breton Civil War', in Palmer, *Froissart: Historian*, 69.

10. Ardis Butterfield, *The Familiar Enemy: Chaucer, Language and Nation in the Hundred Years War* (Oxford: Oxford University Press, 2010), see especially 111–268.

11. See: Jane Taylor, *The Poetry of François Villon: Text and Context* (Cambridge: Cambridge University Press, 2001); Jane Taylor, *The Making of Poetry: Late-Medieval French Poetic Anthologies* (Turnhout: Brepol Publishers, 2007); Emma Cayley, *Debate and Dialogue: Alain Chartier in His Cultural Context* (Oxford: Oxford University Press, 2006); Adrian Armstrong, *The Virtuoso Circle: Competition, Collaboration and Complexity in Late Medieval French Poetry* (Phoenix, AZ: ACMRS Publications, 2012).

12. Strohm, *Social Chaucer*.

13. See Elizabeth Eva Leach, 'Machaut's Peer, Thomas Paien', *Plainsong and Medieval Music*, 18 (2008), 91–112. More generally on inscribed readers in the *Voir dit*, see Deborah McGrady, *Controlling Readers: Guillaume de Machaut and His Late Medieval Audience* (Toronto: University of Toronto Press, 2006), 55–75.

14. Butterfield has proposed that Deschamps's address to Chaucer was far from collaborative in nature. Rather she argues that Deschamps 'wants to keep him [Chaucer] firmly on the other side of a linguistic boundary' (*The Familiar Enemy*, 151). Such a reading, while shedding light on the linguistic complexity of the ballade that allows for multiple readings, glosses over many allusions to a collaborative vision of the literary community that Deschamps associated with Chaucer's efforts. After all, he likened Chaucer to a gardener intent on cultivating a community of writers by bringing into his garden works of those worthy of being regarded as authorities. Moreover, Deschamps insisted in the closing envoi on the similarities between the two writers when he addressed Chaucer as both squire and poet, a dual identity similar to the one Deschamps adopted when identifying himself as a poet as well as a seneschal.

15. As a case in point, consider the library of Arnauld de Corbie, a prominent member of the emerging parliamentary class in the fifteenth century, where we find copies of the works of Machaut, Froissart, and Deschamps, all produced by his favored copyist, Raoul de Tainguy. Marie-Hélène Tesnière, 'Les manuscrits copies par Raoul Tainguy: un aspect de la culture des grands officiers royaux au début du XVe siècle', *Romania* 107 (1986), 282–368.

16. See Poirion, *Le Poète et le prince*, 194, 197; Douglas Kelly, 'The Genius of the Patron'. An important nuanced reading of Machaut's use of poet-prince dynamics to valorize his status as a 'professional court poet' is noted by Kevin Brownlee in *Poetic Identity in Guillaume de Machaut* (Madison, WI: University of Wisconsin Press, 1984), 195.

17. See Laurence de Looze's insightful discussion of Machaut's enigmatic naming of recipients and Hoepffner's acknowledged manipulation of the text to arrive at his reading in 'The Anagrams of Guillaume de Machaut', *Romanic Review* 79, no. 4 (1988), 537–57, esp. 545. On the infinite possibilities associated with another insolvable anagram in Machaut's *Voir dit*, see Jacqueline Cerquiglini-Toulet, *'Un Engin si soutil': Guillaume de Machaut et l'écriture au XIVe siècle* (Paris: Champion, 1985), 235.

18. Guillaume de Machaut, *Fonteinne amoureuse*, l. 1. All line references are from Jacqueline Cerquiglini-Toulet, *Guillaume de Machaut. La Fontaine amoureuse* (Paris: Stock, 1993).

19. Machaut, *Fonteinne amoureuse*, l. 8; ed. Cerquiglini-Toulet, 13.

20. For Sylvia Huot, the passage from the lady to the larger audience is one of inspiration and transmission rather than a question of different audiences. See 'Reading the Lies of Poets: The Literal and the Allegorical in Machaut's *Fonteinne amoureuse*', *Philological Quarterly* 85(1–2) (Winter 2006), 25–48; 29–30.

21. Machaut, *Fonteinne amoureuse*, ll. 70–1.

22. William Calin, *A Poet at the Fountain: Essays on the Narrative Verse of Guillaume de Machaut* (Lexington, KY: University Press of Kentucky, 1974), 149–51.

23. Machaut, *Fonteinne amoureuse*, ll. 75.

24. Ibid., ll. 193–5.

25. Ibid., ll. 1290.

26. For discussion of the literary development of the poet-patron bond developed through the account of their shared dream experience, see Deborah McGrady, '"Tout son païs m'abandonna": Reinventing Patronage in Machaut's *Fonteinne amoureuse*', *Yale French Studies* 110 (December 2007), 19–31, and on the visual depiction of this friendship in select manuscripts where their identities are blurred, see Deborah McGrady, 'Machaut and His Material Legacy', *A Companion to Guillaume de Machaut*, eds. Deborah McGrady and Jennifer Bain (Leiden: Brill, 2012), 361–86.

27. Machaut, *Fonteinne amoureuse*, ll.2835–37.

28. For further development of this scene, see Deborah McGrady, 'Tous son païs', 29–30.

29. Machaut, *Fonteinne amoureuse*, ll. 2848.

30. On the debate surrounding Machaut's supervision and ownership of this codex, see McGrady, *Controlling Readers*, 81–3. The image is discussed and reproduced in McGrady, 'Machaut's Material Legacy'.

31. Poirion, 'Eustache Deschamps et la société de cour', in *Littérature et société au Moyen Âge: Actes du colloque des 5 et 6 mai 1978*, ed. Danielle Buschinger (Paris: Honoré Champion, 1978), 89–109, esp. 90. For Ian S. Laurie, after 1380, Deschamps 'can no longer be described exclusively as an establishment poet': 'Eustache Deschamps: 1340(?)–1404', in *Eustache*

Deschamps, French Courtier-Poet: His Work and His World, ed. Deborah M. Sinnreich-Levi (New York: AMS Press, 1998), 1–72; 12.

32. Saint-Hilaire, ed. *Oeuvres completes d'Eustache Deschamps*, 4:801, 1:63, 5:1036, 5:864.

33. Ibid., e.g. 3:356, 3:401, 6:1244, 2:300, 3:324.

34. Thierry Lassabatère, 'Diffusion et postérité de l'œuvre politique d'Eustache Deschamps, le témoignage des manuscrits', in *Les 'Dictez vertueulx' d'Eustache Deschamps: Forme poétique et discours engagé à la fin du Moyen Âge*, eds. Miren Lacassagne and Thierry Lassabatère (Paris: Presses de l'Université de Paris-Sorbonne, 2005), 107–20, esp. 118, 120.

35. See Susanna Bliggenstorfer, 'Les Poèmes de supplication d'Eustache Deschamps', in *Les Niveaux de vie au Moyen âge: measures, perceptions et representations*, Actes du Colloque international de Spa (21–5 octobre 1998), eds. J.-P. Soson et al. (Louvain-la-Neuve, 1999), 49–75, and James Laidlaw, 'Les Supplications de Deschamps: Le Pouvoir de persuasion', *Les 'Dictez vertueulz' d'Eustache Deschamps: Forme poétique et discours engagé à la fin du Moyen Âge*, eds. Miren Lacassagne et Thierry Lassabatère (Paris: Presses de l'Université de Paris, Sorbonne, 2005), 73–84.

36. e.g. Saint-Hilaire, *Oeuvres completes*, 2:247, 6:1190, 7:1375.

37. e.g. Ibid., 4:801, 4:679, 7:1378.

38. See especially Laidlaw, 'Les Supplications de Deschamps', 75.

39. Deschamps, Ballade 788, 21.

40. Ibid., 23–4.

41. See Le Roux de Lincy et Tisserand, *Paris et ses historiens aux XIVe et XVe siècles* (Paris 1867), 431.

42. Laidlaw associates this payment with Deschamps's numerous supplication poems ('Les Supplications de Deschamps', 83).

43. On the gift as curse, see Jacques Derrida, *Given Time: I. Counterfeit Money*, trans. Peggy Kamuf (Chicago, IL: University of Chicago Press, 1992), 12–13.

44. Deschamps, Ballade 1125, 1.

45. Ibid., 25.

46. Ibid., 32.

47. Ibid., 33–5.

48. On Froissart's activities during his early years especially and possible patronage after Philippa, see Nigel Wilkins, 'A Pattern of Patronage: Machaut, Froissart and the Houses of Luxembourg and Bohemia in the Fourteenth Century', *French Studies* 37 (1983), 257–82; and Godfried Croenen, 'Froissart et ses mécènes: Quelques problème biographiques', in *Froissart dans sa forge: Colloque réuni à Paris, du 4 au 6 novembre 2004*, ed. Michel Zink (Paris: Academie des Inscriptions et Belles-Lettres, 2006), 9–32.

49. Key verse works produced during the time of writing the *Chroniques* include the *Joli Buisson de Jeunesse* (1373), a second redaction of *Méliador* (c.1383), and the *Dit de Florin* (c.1389). As will be discussed, he refers to the continued dissemination of his poetry in later works.

50. Godfried Croenen, for example, describes the *Chroniques* as a 'réécriture profonde d'un passé récent, qui, sous la plume de Froissart, devient presque mythique', 'Froissart et ses mécènes', 14. Peter Dembowski refers to *Méliador* as a 'derivative' work in *Jean Froissart and His 'Méliador': Context, Craft, and Sense* (Lexington, KY: French Forum, 1983), 21.

51. Froissart, *Chroniques: Le Manuscrit Saint-Vincent de Besançon*, Book III, vol. 1, ed. Peter F. Ainsworth (Geneva: Droz, 2007), 188–9.

52. 'Le Dit dou florin', in *Jean Froissart, 'Dits' et 'débats'*, ed. Anthime Fourrier (Geneva: Droz, 1979), 175–90, see esp. lines 293–312, 345–89.

53. Susan H. Cavanaugh notes the similarities between Froissart's binding of his book and rebinding of works commissioned by the king in 1385. See 'Royal Books: King John to Richard II', The Library Series 6, 10, no. 4 (Dec. 1988), 304–16, esp. 315.

54. Lettenhove, *Oeuvres de Froissart*, 20:167.

55. Brigitte Buettner 'Past Presents: New Year's Gifts at the Valois Courts, ca. 1400', *Art Bulletin* 83(4) (2001), 598–625, 609a.

56. Lettenhove, *Oeuvres de Froissart*, 20:167.

57. Scholars have generally interpreted this scene as a favorable reception of Froissart's work. Arguing that BnF, MS fr. 831 might possibly be the copy offered to the king, scholars have plumbed the material artifact to understand what might have been specifically attractive to the king. The assumption here, of course, is that it is certainly not the poetry in and of itself that interested Richard. See: Godfried Croenen, Kristen M. Figg, and Andrew Taylor, 'Authorship, Patronage, and Literary Gifts: The Books Froissart Brought to England in 1395', *Journal of the Early Book Society for the Study of Manuscripts and Printing History* 2 (2008), 1–43; and Andrew Taylor, ' "Moult bien parloit et lisoit le franchois" or Did Richard II Read with a Picard Accent?' in *The Vulgar Tongue: Medieval and Postmedieval Vernacularity*, eds. Fiona Somerset and Nicholas Watson (University Park, PA: Pennsylvania State University Press, 2003), 132–44.

58. Of course, Richard II does not have a reputation for active or generous patronage. See V. J. Scattergood, 'Literary Culture at the Court of Richard II', in *English Court Culture in the Late Middle Ages*, eds. V. J. Scattergood and J. W. Sherborne (London: Gerald Duckworth, 1983), 29-44; 41. That said, it is noteworthy that there is no reference to the book in the king's inventory.

59. Lettenhove, *Oeuvres de Froissart*, 20:168.

60. Svetlana Boym, *The Future of Nostalgia* (New York: Basic Books, 2001).

BIBLIOGRAPHY

Armstrong, Adrian, *The Virtuoso Circle: Competition, Collaboration and Complexity in Late Medieval French Poetry* (Phoenix, AZ: ACMRS Publications, 2012).

Croenen, Godfried, 'Froissart et ses mécènes: Quelques problème biographiques', in *Froissart dans sa forge: Colloque réuni à Paris, du 4 au 6 novembre 2004*, ed. Michel Zink (Paris: Académie des Inscriptions et Belles-Lettres, 2006), 9–32.

Lacassagne, Miren and Thierry Lassabatère, eds., *Les 'Dictez vertueulx' d'Eustache Deschamps: Forme poétique et discours engagé à la fin du Moyen Âge*. Paris: presses de l'Université Paris-Sorbonne, 2005.

McGrady, Deborah, *The Writer's Gift or the Patron's Pleasure? The Literary Economy in Late Medieval France* (Toronto: Toronto University Press, 2018).

McGrady, Deborah, 'What is a Patron? Benefactors and Authorship in MS Harley 4431, Christine de Pizan's Collected Works.' In *Christine de Pizan and the Categories of Difference*, edited by Marilynn Desmond (Minneapolis, MN: Minnesota University Press, 1998), 195–214.

Mahoney, Dhira B., 'Courtly Presentation and Authorial Self-Fashioning: Frontispiece Miniatures in Late Medieval French and English Manuscripts', *Mediaevalia* 21 (1996), 97–160.

Medeiros, Marie-Thérèse de, 'Le pacte encomiastique: Froissart, ses *Chroniques* et ses mécènes', *Le moyen âge. Revue d'histoire et de philology* 94 (1988), 237–55.

Paviot, Jacques, 'Le mécénat des princes Valois vers 1400.' In *Création artistique en France autour de 1400*, edited by Elisabeth Taburet-Delahaye (Paris: La documentation française, 2006), 19–24.

Poirion, Daniel, *Le Poète et le prince: l'évolution du lyrisme courtois de Guillaume de Machaut à Charles d'Orléans* (Geneva: Slatkine Reprints, 1978).

Swift, Helen, 'Circuits of Power: A Model for Rereading Poet-Patron Relations in Late-Medieval Defences of Women.' Special issue, *Digital Philology: A Journal of Medieval Cultures* 2(2) (2013), 222–42.

Taylor, Jane, *The Making of Poetry: Late-Medieval French Poetic Anthologies* (Turnhout: Brepol Publishers, 2007).

Tyson, Diana B., 'French Vernacular History Writers and Their Patrons in the 14th Century', *Medievalia et Humanistica* 14 (1986), 103–24.

Vale, Malcolm, *The Princely Court: Medieval Courts and Culture in North-West Europe, 1280–1380* (Oxford: Oxford University Press, 2001).

Wilkens, Nigel, 'A Pattern of Patronage: Machaut, Froissart and the Houses of Luxembourg and Bohemia in the Fourteenth Century', *French Studies* 37 (1983), 257–82.

Wimsatt, James I., *Chaucer and his French Contemporaries: Natural Music in the Fourteenth Century* (Toronto: University of Toronto Press, 1991).

....

CHAPTER 16

DANTE AND THE AUTHOR OF THE *DECAMERON*

Love, Literature, and Authority in Boccaccio

....

MARTIN EISNER

Boccaccio begins the *Decameron* by declaring the work's connection to Dante's *Commedia*: 'Comincia il libro chiamato *Decameron*, cognominato prencipe Galeotto, nel quale si contengono cento novelle in dieci dí dette da sette donne e da tre giovani uomini' [Here begins the book called the *Decameron*, surnamed Prince Galeotto, which contains a hundred *novelle* told in ten days by seven women and three young men].[1] By quoting the name that Francesca uses in *Inferno* 5 to condemn both the book that she was reading and its author—'Galeotto fu 'l libro e chi lo scrisse' [Galeotto was the book and the one who wrote it]—Boccaccio uses Dante to introduce the problem of the relationship between love, literature, and authority that will be one of the *Decameron*'s major topics. Whether Boccaccio intends this surname to be descriptive ('this book will help you find love and satisfy your desires') or prescriptive ('be careful how you read, because reading a Galeotto can lead you to hell'), it clearly inscribes the work in a Dantean context and suggests how Boccaccio uses Dante to frame the meaning of his work and construct his own figure as an author.[2]

Boccaccio's extensive use of Dante in the *Decameron* has been evident to readers since its earliest circulation, from Benvenuto da Imola's fourteenth-century commentary on Dante's *Commedia*, which uses several *Decameron* stories to gloss Dantean episodes, to the Florentine Deputati who note in their *Annotazioni* (1573) that Boccaccio 'always had Dante so fixed in his soul and just as familiar in his mouth that he very often expressed his ideas with the words of the poet'.[3] Modern critics have charted Boccaccio's various debts to Dante, which include his appropriation of Dantean figures (Guiglielmo Borsiere, Filippo Argenti, Guido Cavalcanti), his redeployment of narrative motifs, like the infernal hunt, and more general analogies, such as the shared macrotextual feature of containing a hundred parts.[4] While some, like Francesco De Sanctis, take these Dantean references as parodic inversions characteristic of the contrast between Boccaccio's human comedy and Dante's divine one, others, like Vittore Branca, have understood Boccaccio's work as following an ethical ascent that complements Dante's.[5] Another group of critics, meanwhile, has increasingly noted the systematic nature of Boccaccio's invocations of Dante which they have interpreted as confrontations engineered by Boccaccio. Whereas Erich Auerbach, for example, contends that Boccaccio's Ghismonda is merely sentimental in contrast to the tragic quality of Dante's Francesca, critics have increasingly argued that the difference between Boccaccio and Dante should be interpreted not as Boccaccio's failure to understand Dante but instead Boccaccio's attempt to challenge him.[6]

In this chapter, I argue that far from being occasional, accidental, or haphazard, Boccaccio's engagement with Dante structures the authorial interventions in the frame of the *Decameron*, following the trajectory of Dante's own poem and its three major reflections on love, literature, and authorship. While the importance of Dante to Boccaccio's work has been widely noted, Boccaccio's meticulous engagement with Dante in the frame has been overlooked, partly because of a critical tendency to treat the work as a collection of individual tales, instead of examining it as an artistic whole. Boccaccio not only borrows Galeotto from *Inferno* 5 in the Proemio, but also takes elements from the terrace of lust (*Purgatorio* 26) in the Introduction to the Fourth Day, and recombines several ideas from the Heaven of Venus (*Paradiso* 8–10) in the Author's Conclusion.[7] Transforming these moments that are crucial to Dante's self-authorization, Boccaccio constructs his own distinct authorial persona in the *Decameron*, imagines a different kind of literary community, and defends literature as part of the diversity of human society.[8] Through these allusions to Dante, Boccaccio not only explores his favourite themes of desire, love, and language but also crafts a new space for literature, defending it not on the basis of a transcendent truth, but through an appeal to the diversity of human experience.[9]

Boccaccio's interest in the variety of human experience is among the several connections that critics have noted between Boccaccio's *Decameron* and Chaucer's *Canterbury Tales*. Although scholars have increasingly acknowledged the likelihood that Chaucer knew the *Decameron*, since nearly a quarter of the *Canterbury Tales* have analogues in Boccaccio's work, this chapter does not aim to address this relationship directly.[10] Instead, it explores the complexity of Boccaccio's engagement with Dante as he attempts to craft a new literary community.[11] By investigating the multiple ways Boccaccio uses Dante to explore the relationship of love, literature, and authorship in the frame of the *Decameron*, this study illuminates analogous strategies that Chaucer deploys in dealing with Boccaccio and the earlier Italian tradition.

THE LUSTFUL (*INFERNO* 5) IN THE PREFACE AND INTRODUCTION TO THE FIRST DAY

The uncertain meaning of Boccaccio's appropriation of Galeotto in the context of the *Decameron* is linked to the equally complex problem of the word's significance in Dante's poem. Many commentators have seen Dante as condemning a certain kind of courtly literature. For the fourteenth-century commentator Jacopo della Lana 'one should spurn those readings, which upset people's souls and leads them to vice'.[12] In her late twentieth-century commentary Anna Maria Chiavacci Leonardi similarly comments, 'it seems indubitable that Dante wants here, at the conclusion of the tale, to make responsible, as he had at the beginning, the whole literary culture that had celebrated that love'.[13] In his commentary, Dante's son Pietro Alighieri connects this idea to a broader discourse about the value of literature: 'So our author shows that men should avoid reading such books for the above reason. Thus, Isidore, in his *Book of Sentences*, says: "The Christian is forbidden to read the figments of the poets and other writers, and similar books, because by the allure they offer they incite the mind to too much lust." '[14] Boccaccio's commentary offers no similar condemnation of literature. For Boccaccio, Galeotto means 'that that book, which she and Paolo were reading, performed the same task for the two of them that Gallehault fulfilled for Lancelot and Queen Guinevere'.[15] Indeed, Boccaccio dedicates considerable space to disputing positions like that of Isidore quoted by Pietro in his defence of poetry in the *Genealogie deorum genitlium* (*Genealogies of the Gentile Gods*).[16] For Boccaccio, the allurements of literature have no force without the reader's consent.

Francesca's condemnation of 'il libro e chi lo scrisse' [the book and the one who wrote it], moreover, should not be confused with Dante's view. Francesca personifies the book and its author to justify her actions by giving them an agency that would exculpate her. Francesca refuses to consider her own role as reader and take responsibility for her actions.[17] When Boccaccio writes in the Author's Conclusion that his stories 'will not come running after you' demanding to be read, he picks up on Francesca's personification of the book as Galeotto to reveal the absurdity of attributing agency to the work, instead of assuming responsibility as reader.[18] In other words, the literary condemnation that critics have noted in the episode is complicated by the identity of the speaker whose whole discourse is dedicated to defending herself from blame.

If closer scrutiny of the term Galeotto shows that neither Dante nor Boccaccio condemn literature, what of 'chi lo scrisse' (the one who wrote it)? Many have seen Dante's faint at the conclusion of the encounter as a sign that he feels implicated in Francesca's condemnation, but it is probably best to analyse that moment in terms of a contrast between the poet and the pilgrim. The pilgrim may be moved by Francesca's confession but the poet creates the ethical structure in which Francesca appears. Dante's decision to have Francesca call the author 'chi lo scrisse' significantly avoids the word *autore* which Dante uses only for Virgil and, with the significant variant 'verace autore', for God.[19] This problem of the relationship between love and authorship was a major issue in the cultural legitimation of vernacular literature. How can one be an author in love? As Alastair Minnis neatly summaries the problem: 'how could a poet who wrote about love, and/or expressed his own (limiting and probably demeaning) emotional experiences, be trusted as a fount of wisdom, accepted as a figure worthy of belief? An *auctor amans* was an utter paradox, almost a contradiction in terms'.[20] In the *Vita nuova*, Dante offers a first response to this problem, insisting on the reasonableness of his love for Beatrice, as he does in the *Commedia*.

In the Proemio, Boccaccio confronts this problem of the relationship between love and reason, encoded in the surname Galeotto, by emphasizing that he is no longer in love. Although he had once been among those whose reason was subjected to desire, now he is 'free of love' [ora che libero dir mi posso]. Newly liberated, Boccaccio wants to repay those who comforted him, but, since they do not need help, he chooses to assist those who do, namely women in love. Boccaccio emphasizes the difference between the sexes, noting that while women are confined, men are free and therefore able to distract themselves from love in ways that ladies cannot. At the same time, the author violates this gender differentiation since he is more similar to those ladies who suffer from love than the men who were able to free themselves from it by doing things.[21] Boccaccio's love did not end because of rational argument or shame but because of the immutable law of mutability (God 'gave as an immutable law that all earthly things must come to an end' [diede per legge incommutabile a tutte le cose mondane aver fine]). Boccaccio returns to this theme in the Author's Conclusion, where he observes that 'le cose di questo mondo non avere stabilità alcuna ma sempre essere in mutamento' [the things of this world do not have any stability, but are always changing].[22] Despite these allusions to a cosmic, Boethian perspective, Boccaccio will not pursue this question philosophically, but instead through a variety of narrative forms. He writes:

> intendo di raccontare cento novelle, o favole o parabole o istorie che dire le vogliamo, raccontate in diece giorni da una onesta brigata di sette donne e di tre giovani nel pistelenzioso tempo della passata mortalità fatta, e alcune canzonette dalle predette donne cantate al lor diletto.
>
> [I plan to tell a hundred novelle or fables or parables or histories or whatever we want to call them, recounted in ten days by an honest *brigata* of seven ladies and three young men, in the time of the plague that recently caused so many deaths, and some songs that these seven ladies sang for their delight.]

In other words, he will use stories instead of normative philosophical arguments.[23]

Boccaccio continues to call on the model of *Inferno* 5 in the Introduction to the First Day. Francesca concludes her story saying 'quel giorno non vi legemmo avante' [that day we read no further], by which 'she quite cleverly lets the readers know, even without saying it, what followed after she was kissed by Paolo', according to Boccaccio in his commentary.[24] Boccaccio, by contrast, asks his readers to continue to 'leggere avante' [read ahead], despite the difficult beginning of the plague. At the same time, Boccaccio does not proclaim himself to the be the author, attributing his knowledge to an informer: 'sí come io poi da persona degna di fede sentii' [as I heard later from a person worthy of faith].[25] Boccaccio's phrase 'degna di fede' echoes the conventional definition of an 'author'.[26] Boccaccio may be liberated from love, but does not take responsibility as author.

THE TERRACE OF LUST (*PURGATORIO* 26 TO 30) IN THE INTRODUCTION TO THE FOURTH DAY: THE MONTANARO AND THE MAKING OF A LITERARY COMMUNITY

In the Introduction to the Fourth Day, the author figure reappears to complain that envy has found him even though he composed novelle which were 'non solamente in fiorentin volgare e in prosa scritte per me sono e senza titolo, ma ancora in istilo umilissimo e rimesso quanto il piú si possono' [not only written by me in the Florentine vernacular and in prose and without a title but even more in a style as very humble and low as possible]. Some have interpreted the phrase 'senza titolo' [without a title] as a reference to Ovid, whose *Amores* was also known as the *Sine titulo*, as Boccaccio himself notes in his *Esposizioni*. Others, however, such as the Deputati, who were responsible for the expurgated edition of 1573, note that the idea that the work would be without a title does not fit with a work that not only has a name, *Decameron*, but also a surname, *Galeotto*.[27] The Deputati thus interpret *senza titolo* to mean 'without the author's name'. This interpretation corresponds to what we find in Boccaccio's autograph of the *Decameron* in Hamilton MS 90,[28] which does not contain his signature or name, although paleographical evidence confirms that it is in Boccaccio's hand. For an author who flagrantly inscribes his name in other works, like the *Amorosa visione*, where he encodes his name in that poem's elaborate acrostic, this absence of a signature is notable, particularly in light of the personal nature of the defence that follows.

In this defence, Boccaccio confronts five criticisms: he loves ladies too much; he is too old to desire ladies; he should write about higher subject matters; he should pursue a lucrative profession instead of poetry; and, finally, the stories he tells are lies. These issues can be divided into two broader categories: the first two deal with love while the last three concern literature. Boccaccio replies to the first charge (that he loves ladies too much) by telling what he describes as 'non una novella intera' [an incomplete novella] so that it will not be 'mescola[to]' [mixed] with those of the *brigata*.[29] The story recounts how after the death of his wife Filippo Balducci takes his son live with him in a small monastic cell in the mountains outside Florence, removed from the world of desires where what one loves can be lost. Filippo makes occasional trips to Florence to obtain supplies but one day, weary from his labours, he accepts his eighteen-year-old son's offer of assistance. Arriving in Florence, the son is amazed by the palaces, houses, churches that he sees and he asks his father numerous questions about the various sights which his father is happy to answer. The appearance of a group of women, however, changes the tenor of their exchange. Boccaccio writes:

E cosí domandando il figliuolo e il padre rispondendo, per avventura si scontrarono in una brigata di belle giovani donne e ornate, che da un paio di nozze veniono; le quali come il giovane vide, cosí domandò il padre che cosa quelle fossero.

A cui il padre disse: 'Figliuol mio, bassa gli occhi in terra, non le guatare, ch'elle son mala cosa'.

Disse allora il figliuolo: 'O come si chiamano'?

Il padre, per non destare nel concupiscibile appetito del giovane alcuno inchinevole disiderio men che utile, non le volle nominare per lo proprio nome, cioè femine, ma disse: 'Elle si chiamano papere'.

Maravigliosa cosa a udire! Colui che mai piú alcuna veduta non avea, non curatosi de' palagi, non del bue, non del cavallo, non dell'asino, non de' danari né d'altra cosa che veduta avesse, subitamente disse: 'Padre mio, io vi priego che voi facciate che io abbia una di quelle papere'.

'Oimè, figliuol mio', disse il padre 'taci: elle son mala cosa'.

A cui il giovane domandando disse: 'O son cosí fatte le male cose'?

'Sí', disse il padre.

E egli allora disse: 'Io non so che voi vi dite, né perché queste sieno mala cosa: quanto è, a me non è ancora paruta vedere alcuna cosí bella né cosí piacevole come queste sono. Elle son piú belle che gli agnoli dipinti che voi m'avete piú volte mostrati. Deh! se vi cal di me, fate che noi ce ne meniamo una colà sú di queste papere, e io le darò beccare'.

Disse il padre: 'Io non voglio; tu non sai donde elle s'imbeccano'! e sentí incontanente piú aver di forza la natura che il suo ingegno; e pentessi d'averlo menato a Firenze.

[And so they continued, the son asking questions and the father answering, until they encountered upon a group of beautiful and elegantly dressed young ladies, who were coming from a wedding. As soon as the the young man saw them, he asked his father what they were.

To which the father replied, 'My son keep your eyes on the ground and don't look at them, for they are evil'.

The son then asked, 'But what are they called, father?'

The father, so as not to awaken any less than useful desire in the young man's carnal appetite, did not want to call them by their name, that is, women, but said, 'They are called goslings'.

What an amazing thing to hear! He who had never before seen a woman no longer cared about the palaces, the oxen, the horses, the asses, the money or any of the other things he had seen and immediately said, 'My father, I beg you to arrange it that I can have one of those goslings'.

'Oh no, my son', said the father 'be quiet: they are evil'.

To which the young man asked, 'Are evil things made like this'?

'Yes', said the father.

And he then said, 'I do not know what you are saying, nor why these are evil. As far I am concerned, it does not seem to me that I have ever seen anything as beautiful and pleasing as these are. They are more beautiful than the painted angels that you have shown me many times. Come on! If you care about me, arrange it so that we can bring one of these goslings up there and I will feed it'.

The father said: 'I do not want to; you don't know where they feed'! And he immediately perceived that nature was stronger than his wit, and he regretted having brought his son to Florence.]

Filippo's effort 'not to awaken any less than useful desire in the young man's carnal appetite' by avoiding their proper name does not deter his son's desires, which the father aligns with nature. Boccaccio applies the lesson of the story to his own situation: if 'someone who was nurtured, reared, and matured on a solitary and savage (*salvatico*) mountain in the confines of a small cell, without any companion but his father' could not resist women, how could the author? Note, too, the literary dimension of the episode. The father worries that the proper word might excite his son's desires, so he chooses the more innocuous goslings. Far from allaying his son's desires, however, the new image allows the son to express his desires more fully: he wants to feed them.

In his fourteenth-century commentary on Dante's *Commedia*, Benvenuto da Imola tells a version of Boccaccio's story of Filippo Balducci and his son to gloss the simile that Dante uses to describe the reaction of the lustful to his appearance in *Purgatorio* 26:[30]

> Non altrimenti stupido si turba
> lo montanaro, e rimirando ammuta,
> quando rozzo e salvatico s'inurba,
> che ciascun' ombra fece in sua paruta;[31]

[Not otherwise is the mountain peasant struck with awe and troubled, falling silent as he gazes, when, crude and rustic, he enters the city, than each soul then appeared.][32]

Benvenuto's allusion highlights the intersection of these two scenes not only for their similar narrative situations, but also because Boccaccio uses Dante's *salvatico* to describe the 'savage' upbringing of Filippo's son. Robert Hollander argues that Boccaccio's episode 'reverses the Dantean priorities. In the *Commedia* reformed heterosexual lovers behave like bumpkins upon seeing a living soul who betokens God's grace and the possibility of undoing the sin of lust; here a country bumpkin discovers his sexual appetite with a similar amazement.'[33] Strictly speaking, what excites the amazement of Filippo's son is not his own desires, but 'una brigata di belle giovani donne e ornate, che da un paio di nozze venieno' [a party of elegantly dressed and beautiful young ladies, who were coming away from a wedding].[34] Whereas the scene in *Purgatorio* is about Dante's privileged status as a living man who casts his shadow among the dead, in the Introduction to the Fourth Day (as in the Proem), Boccaccio emphasizes women as a group.

Dante's treatment of the lustful in *Purgatorio* 26 constitutes the climax of a genealogy of Romance lyric that Dante develops throughout *Purgatorio*. On the terrace of lust,

Dante has Guido Guinizelli, 'il padre/mio e de li altri miei miglior che mai/rime d'amor usar dolci e leggiadre' [the father of me and of the others, my better, who ever used sweet and graceful rhymes],[35] introduce Arnaut Daniel as 'miglior fabbro del parlar materno' [the best craftsman of the vernacular tongue].[36] Guinizelli emphasizes that Arnaut's supremacy is not uncontested. Others celebrate the Provençal Giraut de Bornelh, as Dante himself does in the *De vulgari eloquentia* (2.2.9), and Italian Guittone d'Arezzo, as Dante did not, but the true genealogy is the one that embraces the Provençal Arnaut Daniel and the Italian Guido Guinizelli instead.[37] Just as Dante claims to have always loved Beatrice with 'lo fedele consiglio della Ragione' [the faithful counsel of reason] in the *Vita nuova*, in the *Commedia* he constructs a tradition that joins love and virtue.[38]

Boccaccio evokes this scene in the Introduction to the Fourth Day not only in the tale of Filippo Balducci's son but also in the poetic genealogy he uses to defend himself. Arguing that he is not the only person who has continued to love ladies as an older man, Boccaccio invokes the examples of three vernacular poets, Cavalcanti, Dante, and Cino da Pistoia, to support his case. He writes:

> io mai a me vergogna non reputerò infino nello stremo della mia vita di dover compiacere a quelle cose alle quali Guido Cavalcanti e Dante Alighieri già vecchi e messer Cino da Pistoia vecchissimo onor si tennero, e fu lor caro il piacer loro. E se non fosse che uscir sarebbe del modo usato del ragionare, io producerei le istorie in mezzo, e quelle tutte piene mostrerei d'antichi uomini e valorosi, ne' loro più maturi anni sommamente avere studiato di compiacere alle donne.[39]

> [Until the end of my life I will never be ashamed to have to please those whom Guido Cavalcanti and Dante Alighieri, already old, and Cino da Pistoia, very old, held in honor and whose pleasure was dear to them. And if it were not a departure from the customary mode of discourse, I would produce stories here, and show how they are filled with worthy men from antiquity who in their more mature years tried greatly to please ladies.]

Although some critics connect this passage to Dante's encounter with the classical poets in *Inferno* 4, Boccaccio's construction of a vernacular, instead of classical, tradition follows *Purgatorio* 26.[40] It is significant in this respect that although Boccaccio claims that he could tell tales of ancient worthies who loved ladies, he only names three vernacular poets.[41] Boccaccio also transforms Dante's account. Whereas Dante celebrates a poetic genealogy that joins love and truth, Boccaccio emphasizes desire alone.

Boccaccio's vernacular community may be characterized by a shared fallibility with respect to desire, but Boccaccio aims to legitimize that community. He makes this goal clear when immediately after the list of poets in the Introduction to the Fourth Day, he claims that he has not strayed from Parnassus in composing these stories: 'queste cose tessendo, né dal monte Parnaso né dalle Muse non mi allontano quanto molti per avventura s'avisano' [in composing these stories, I am not going as far from Mount Parnassus or from the Muses as many people may perhaps think]. Whereas Dante has Guinizelli elucidate a tradition that Dante will pointedly surpass both when he is crowned and mitered by Virgil at the end of *Purgatorio* 27, Boccaccio makes no suggestion of being superior to the group of Dante, Cino, and Cavalcanti. Instead, he constructs a community of vernacular poets who both persist in their desires and approach Parnassus.

The Heaven of Venus in the Author's Conclusion

As Dante ascends from the Heaven of Venus (love) to the Heaven of the Sun (wisdom), he presents himself as God's scribe in an important address to the reader:

> Or ti riman, lettor, sovra 'l tuo banco,
> dietro pensando a ciò che si preliba,
> s'esser vuoi lieto assai prima che stanco.
> Messo t' ho innanzi: omai per te ti ciba;
> ché a sé torce tutta la mia cura
> quella materia ond'io son fatto scriba.[42]

[Now stay there, reader, on your bench, thinking back on your foretaste here, if you wish to rejoice long before you tire; I have set the meal before you: now feed yourself, for all my care is claimed by that matter of which I have become the scribe.][43]

At the moment he turns to the reader in *Paradiso* 10, Dante has finally journeyed beyond the shadow of earth and can assume the role of prophet.[44]

Boccaccio transforms this idea of the author as scribe in the Author's Conclusion to the *Decameron* where Boccaccio also claims to be a scribe, not to assert any divine authority, but to argue that he cannot be held responsible for the quality of stories. Boccaccio explains.

> Saranno similmente di quelle che diranno qui esserne alcune che, non essendoci, sarebbe stato assai meglio. Concedasi: ma io non pote' né doveva scrivere se non le raccontate, e per ciò esse che le dissero le dovevan dir belle, e io l'avrei scritte belle. Ma se pur presuppor si volesse che io fossi stato di quelle e lo 'nventore e lo scrittore, che non fui, dico che io non mi vergognerei che tutte belle non fossero per ciò che maestro alcun non si truova, da Dio in fuori, che ogni cosa faccia bene e compiutamente.[45]
>
> [Similarly, there will be some of you who will say that it would have been better if some of the stories included here were omitted. I concede the point, but I neither could nor should have written them except as they were told, so those that told them should have told better and I would have written them better. But even if one wants to suppose that I was both the inventor and writer—which I was not—I reply that I would not have been ashamed that they were not all beautiful since one does not find any master, besides God who has made everything well and completely.]

Whereas Dante is God's scribe and therefore a prophet in the tradition of Moses, Boccaccio evokes a cosmic perspective to emphasize the fallibility of the human crafts-man and to assert that he is only transcribing from other storytellers, in keeping with his claim in the Introduction to be reporting a story he heard from 'una persona degna di fede' ['someone worthy of faith'].[46]

In the next paragraph of the Author's Conclusion, Boccaccio expresses this same idea in terms of human diversity.

> Conviene nella moltitudine delle cose diverse qualità di cose trovarsi. Niun campo fu mai sí ben coltivato, che in esso o ortica o triboli o alcun pruno non si trovasse mescolato tra l'erbe migliori. Senza che, a avere a favellare a semplici giovinette come voi il piú siete, sciocchezza sarebbe stata l'andar cercando e faticandosi in trovar cose molto esquisite, e gran cura porre di molto misuratamente parlare. Tuttavia che va tra queste leggendo, lasci star quelle che pungono, e quelle che dilettano legga: elle, per non ingannare alcuna persona tutte nella fronte portan segnato quello che esse dentro dal loro seno nascoso tengono.[47]

> [In a multitude of things one necessarily finds different qualities. No field was ever so well cultivated that nettles or brambles or other thorny shrubs were not found mixed among the better plants. Moreover, for speaking to simple young women, as most of you are, it would have been silly to go searching and exhaust myself to find very refined things, and to take great care to speak in a very measured style. Nonetheless, whoever goes reading among these tales, leave aside those that prick and read those that delight. In order not to deceive anyone, all the stories bear sign on their brows that which they have hidden within their breast.]

Boccaccio's self-presentation as scribe is more than a rhetorical pose not only because he literally transcribes the *Decameron* in the Hamilton 90 manuscript, but also because he uses scribal means as part of his self-defence. Boccaccio claims that the brief summaries of the stories' plots in the rubrics that preface the *novelle* should help readers choose those that may delight them and ignore those that might do them harm.[48] Whereas Francesca claims that her reading 'for delight' [per diletto] was responsible for her damnation, Boccaccio urges a mode of reading for delight that emphasizes the reader's agency: 'leave aside those that prick and read [legga] those that delight,' where Boccaccio draws on the etymology of the verb 'leggere,' which means not only 'to read' but also 'to choose' and 'to gather'.[49] To read, then, is to make a choice to read. The text is blameless.

Boccaccio's appeal to diversity in his defence recalls Dante's concerns with human diversity in the Heaven of Venus, where Carlo Martello explains how divine providence creates human diversity:

> "Dunque esser diverse
> convien di vostri effetti le radici:
> per ch'un nasce Solone e altro Serse,
> altro Melchisedèch e altro quello
> che, volando per l'aere, il figlio perse."[50]

["Therefore your different effects must have different roots: hence one is born Solon, another Xerxes, another Melchisedech, and another the one who, flying through the air, lost his son."]

Boccaccio quotes this last terzina in the third (and final) redaction of his *Vita di Dante* (*Life of Dante*) to describe the variety of human dispositions.[51] The emphasis on nature echoes Boccaccio's exploration of natural desire in the story of Filippo Balducci's son in the Introduction to the Fourth Day, but here it is poetry that is naturalized.[52] Boccaccio transforms Dante's discussion of social diversity into a defence of the pursuit of poetry as an institution.

These arguments about being a scribe and the appeal to diversity support Boccaccio's earlier claim in the Author's Conclusion that the significance of the work relies on the reader.

> Niuna corrotta mente intese mai sanamente parola: e cosí come le oneste a quella non giovano, cosí quelle che tanto oneste non sono la ben disposta non posson contaminare, se non come il loto i solari raggi o le terrene brutture le bellezze del cielo. Quali libri, quali parole, quali lettere son piú sante, piú degne, piú reverende, che quelle della divina Scrittura? E sí sono egli stati assai che, quelle perversamente intendendo, sé e altrui a perdizione hanno tratto.
>
> [No corrupt mind has ever understood a word sanely. And just as worthy words do not help the corrupt mind, so those that are not so worthy cannot contaminate the well-disposed mind, except insofar as the mud contaminates the sun's rays or the terrestrial ugliness the heaven's beauties. What books, what works, what letters are more sacred, more worthy, more revered than those of Sacred Scripture? And there have been very many, who by interpreting them in perverse ways, have brought themselves and others to perdition.]

Boccaccio picks upon the idea of the work that might lead one to hell but identifies an example not in the romances Francesca read but in Scripture itself. Reiterating his claim that the reader, not the text, is responsible, Boccaccio establishes a significant parallel between his collection and Scripture. Dante's claim to be God's scribe has been examined at length, but Boccaccio's comparison of his work to Scripture is rarely discussed, probably because Boccaccio advances this bold claim in what appears to be a concession. His point is not only that, like scared texts, profane ones, like his, are not responsible for readers' interpretations, but also that the *Decameron*, like Scripture, has more than a literal or surface meaning. Whereas Dante constructs his own authority by establishing a link between the truth of his account and the truth of Scripture, Boccaccio invokes Scripture not to emphasize the variety of interpretations a text may elicit, which cannot be the responsibility of the author.

Boccaccio claims to be a scribe in what his autograph rubric calls the 'Conclusione dell'autore' (Author's Conclusion)—a clash of terms that underlines his desire to explore these categories. Boccaccio's play with his own role as author was perceived by Petrarch, who calls attention to Boccaccio's authorial interventions in the letter that prefaces his Latin translation of Boccaccio's Griselda story.[53] I have argued elsewhere that Petrarch's translation of Griselda is a sign of Boccaccio's success in convincing Petrarch about the value of the vernacular, which is underlined by Petrarch's placement of the translation at the end of the *Seniles* (*Letters of Old Age*).[54] The triumph comes, however, at a significant cost, since Petrarch transforms Boccaccio's story into an allegory of the relationship between the soul and God. When Chaucer translates Petrarch's Griselda in *The Clerk's Tale*, he reframes the story once again. The clerk may initially appear in the guise of Griselda ('as coy and stille as doth a mayde / Were new espoused, sittinge at the bord') who obeys ('obeisaunce') the Host's commands, but he shows himself to be even bolder than Gualtieri. He kills off Petrarch ('deed and nayled in his cheste'), claims to omit Petrarch's 'proheme', even as he retains much of it, and alters Petrarch's moralizing conclusion. Burying Petrarch, as the Envoy of the tale will later bury both Griselda and her patience, Chaucer brings back to life Boccaccio's ironic conclusion where Dioneo suggests that Griselda should have abandoned Gualtieri instead of enduring his abuse. The ambiguities of the tale's ironic envoy and the complex attribution of its voice (is the Clerk or Chaucer speaking?) bring us back to Boccaccio's authorial strategies in the *Decameron*, where he engages the earlier tradition to craft a new literary space just as Chaucer will do in *The Canterbury Tales*.

NOTES

1. All quotations from the *Decameron* are from Giovanni Boccaccio, *Decameron*, ed. Vittore Branca, 2 vols. (Turin: Einaudi, 1992), Unless otherwise noted, all translations are my own.

2. For different interpretations of Dante's use of the term *Galeotto*, see Robert Hollander, *Boccaccio's Two Venuses* (New York: Columbia University Press, 1977), 102–6; Daniela Delcorno Branca, '"Cognominato prencipe Galeotto". Il sottotitolo illustrato del Parigino it. 482', *Studi sul Boccaccio* 23 (1995): 78–88; and Thomas C. Stillinger, 'The Place of the Title (*Decameron*, Day One, Introduction)', in *The 'Decameron' First Day in Perspective*, ed. Elissa B. Weaver (Toronto: University of Toronto Press, 2004), 29–56.

3. For a discussion of several of the Boccaccio stories that Benvenuto alludes to in his Commentary, see Franco Quartieri, *Benvenuto da Imola: Un moderno antico commentatore di Dante* (Ravenna: Longo, 2001), 130–46. Giuseppe Chiecchi, ed. *Le annotazioni e i discorsi sul Decameron del 1573 dei deputati fiorentini* (Padova: Antenore, 2001), 31.

4. For these characters, see Boccaccio, *Decameron*, 1.8, 9.8, and 6.9 respectively. For studies of Dante and Boccaccio, see Cesare Segre, 'La novella di Nastagio degli Onesti (*Dec* V, 8): I due tempi della visione', in *Semiotica filologica* (Turin: Einaudi, 1971), 87–96; Franco Fido, 'Dante personaggio mancato nel *Decameron*', in *Boccaccio: Secoli di vita (Atti del Congresso Internazionale, 17–19 Ottobre 1975)*, ed. Marga Cottino-Jones and Edward F. Tuttle (Ravenna: Longo, 1977), 177–89; Attilio Bettinzoli, 'Per una definizione delle presenze dantesche nel *Decameron*. I: I registri 'ideologici', lirici, drammatici', *Studi sul Boccaccio* 13 (1981–2), 267–32; Attilio Bettinzoli, 'Per una definizione delle presenze dantesche nel Decameron. II: Ironizzazione e espressivismo antifrastico-deformatorio', *Studi sul Boccaccio* 14 (1983–4), 209–24; Franco Fido, 'Dante personaggio mancato nel *Decameron*', in *Boccaccio: Secoli di vita (Atti del Congresso Internazionale, 17–19 Ottobre 1975)*, ed. Marga Cottino-Jones and Edward F. Tuttle (Ravenna: Longo, 1977), 177–8; Robert Hollander, *Boccaccio's Dante and the Shaping Force of Satire* (Ann Arbor, MI: University of Michigan Press, 1997); Victoria

Kirkham, 'The Tale of Guigliemo Borsiere (I.8)', in *The Decameron: First Day in Perspective*, ed. Elissa Weaver (Toronto: University of Toronto Press, 2004), 179–206; Jonathan Usher, 'A "ser" Cepparello Constructed from Dante fragments (*Decameron* I, 1)', *The Italianist* 23 (2003): 181–93; Much earlier scholarship tacitly agrees with the claim that Boccaccio read the *Comedy* 'as if one were dealing with a large collection of stories' and without an understanding of its moral dimension; see, for example, Giorgio Padoan, 'Mondo aristocratico e mondo comunale nell'ideologia e nell'arte di Giovanni Boccaccio', in *Il Boccaccio, le Muse, il Parnaso e l'Arno* (Florence: Olschki, 1978; 1964), 1–91; 30. Boccaccio also transcribes Dante's works in three manuscripts that are now four: Toledo 104.6, Riccardiano 1023, and the original configuration of what are now Chigi L V 176 and Chigi VI 213, both in the Vatican Library.

5. For the contrast between Boccaccio's 'commedia umana' and Dante's *Divina commedia*, see Francesco De Sanctis, *Storia della letteratura italiana*, ed. Gianfranco Contini (Turin: Tea, 1989). On the *Decameron* as an ascent, see Vittore Branca, *Boccaccio medievale e nuovi studi sul Decameron*, ed. Saggi Sansoni, 2nd ed. (Milan: Sansoni, 1956; repr., 1996, 1998, 2010), 38–41.

6. Erich Auerbach, *Mimesis: The Representation of Reality in Western Literature*, trans. Willard R. Trask (Princeton, NJ: Princeton University Press, 1953; repr., 2003), 203–31. For a critique of Auerbach, see Albert Russell Ascoli, 'Boccaccio's Auerbach: Holding the Mirror Up to Mimesis', *Studi sul Boccaccio* 20 (1991–1992): 377–97. For a discussion of Boccaccio's conscious and purposeful challenge to Dante in the context of Day 3 and the story of Ferondo (*Decameron* 3.8) in particular, see Martin Eisner, 'The Tale of Ferondo's Purgatory (*Decameron* III.8)', in *The Decameron: Third Day in Perspective*, eds. Pier Massimo Forni and Francesco Ciabattoni (Toronto: University of Toronto Press, 2014), 150–69.

7. That Dante would associate Venus with moments of authorial self-presentation reflects his association of Venus with rhetoric in the *Convivio* (2.13.13–14). Boccaccio similarly mentions Venus as patron of poetry and writing in the *Genealogie deorum genitlium*.

8. For Dante's construction of his authoritative position in the *Commedia*, see Teodolinda Barolini, *Dante's Poets: Textuality and Truth in the Comedy* (Princeton, NJ: Princeton University Press, 1984). For an examination of this problem in Dante's other works, as well, see Albert Russell Ascoli, *Dante and the Making of a Modern Author* (Cambridge: Cambridge University Press, 2008).

9. Dante is not only the figure that Boccaccio uses to construct this authorial identity. For discussion of Ovid's similarly strong presence, see Robert Hollander, 'The *Decameron* Proem', in *The 'Decameron' First Day in Perspective*, ed. Elissa Weaver (Toronto: University of Toronto Press, 2004), 12–28 on the Proem; Janet Levarie Smarr, 'Ovid and Boccaccio: A Note on Self-Defense', *Mediaevalia* 13 (1987): 247–55 on the Author's Conclusion, with mention of the Intro to Day; and, most recently, on all three moments, see Alessandro Barchiesi and Philip Hardie, 'The Ovidian Career Model: Ovid, Gallus, Apuleius, Boccaccio', in *Classical Literary Careers and their Reception*, ed. Philip Hardie (Cambridge: Cambridge University Press, 2010), 59–88; 79–88.

10. On this shared concern with diversity in both Boccaccio and Chaucer, see Nicholas S. Thompson, *Chaucer, Boccaccio and the Debate of Love: A Comparative Study of the Decameron and the Canterbury Tales* (Oxford: Oxford University Press, 1996), 8–42. A sign of the shift in the evaluation of Boccaccio's potential presence in Chaucer can be seen in Helen Cooper, 'Sources and Analogues of Chaucer's *Canterbury Tales*: Reviewing the Work', *Studies in the Age of Chaucer* 19 (1997): 183–210. For a collection of essays examining

this question, see Leonard Michael Koff and Brenda Deen Schildgen, eds., *The 'Decameron' and the 'Canterbury Tales': New Essays on an Old Question* (Madison, WI: Fairleigh Dickinson University Press, 2000). For the argument that Chaucer knows Boccaccio's work but strategically circumvents him by drawing on Boccaccio's own sources, see Robert Hanning, 'The *Decameron* and the *Canterbury Tales*', in *Approaches to Teaching Boccaccio's Decameron*, ed. James H. McGregor (New York: MLA, 2000), 103–18. For a positive view that Chaucer must have known Boccaccio's collection, see David Wallace, 'Chaucer's Italian Inheritance', in *The Cambridge Companion to Chaucer*, ed. Piero Boitani and Jill Mann (Cambridge: Cambridge University Press, 2004), 35–57. For a recent reading of the two works together see Frederick M. Biggs, *Chaucer's Decameron and the Origin of the Canterbury Tales* (Cambridge: D. S. Brewer, 2017).

11. For Boccaccio's efforts to create an Italian literary community, see Martin Eisner, *Boccaccio and the Invention of Italian Literature: Dante, Petrarch, Cavalcanti and the Authority of the Vernacular* (Cambridge: Cambridge University Press, 2013).

12. Cited from commentary to *Inferno* 5.130–8 by Jacopo della Lana (1324–8): 'Si dee schifare quelle lezioni, le quali disordinano li animi delle persone e perducenli a vizio', as found in the Dartmouth Dante Project, http://dante.dartmouth.edu.

13. Commentary to *Inferno* 5.137 by Anna Maria Chiavacci Leonardi (1991–7), Dartmouth Dante Project: 'Sembra indubbio che Dante voglia qui, a conclusione della storia, coinvolgere nella responsabilità, come ha fatto all'inizio, tutta la cultura letteraria che quell'amore aveva celebrato'. One could debate whether this literature really celebrate this kind of love, since it also occurs in a very particular political moment (the War with Galehaut) and leads to anything but positive consequences for the kingdom—as well as the repentence of the lovers themselves, as Dante well knew from his reference to Lancelot's conversion in the *Convivio*.

14. Commentary by Pietro Alighieri (1359–64) as found in A. J. Minnis, A. B. Scott, and David Wallace, eds., *Medieval Literary Theory and Criticism c.1100–c.1375: The Commentary Tradition*, Rev. ed. (Oxford: Clarendon, 1991), 489.

15. Giovanni Boccaccio, *Boccaccio's Expositions on Dante's 'Comedy'*, trans. Michael Papio (Toronto: University of Toronto Press, 2009), 286.

16. For Boccaccio's arguments against the claim that classical literature should not be read by Christians, see *Genealogie* (14.9). Even as Boccaccio would oppose Isidore's views on the suitability of classical poetry quoted by Pietro, he also uses him as one of his sources for his positive defense of poetry and literature, following his etymology of poet in *Genealogie* (14.7).

17. For a discussion of Francesca's complex self-representation here, see Teodolinda Barolini, 'Dante and Francesca da Rimini: Realpolitik, Romance, Gender', in *Dante and the Origins of Italian Literary Culture* (New York: Fordham University Press, 2006; Originally published as 'Dante and Francesca da Rimini: Realpolitik, Romance, Gender" *Speculum* 75 (2000), 1–28.), 304–32. For the separation of author, work, and reader, see Ovid, *Tristia* 2.

18. In the *Genealogie* (14.16), Boccaccio makes a similar point when he argues that those who accuse poets of being seducers are themselves at fault since 'they have followed uninvited and of their own free will'. The translation is from Charles G. Osgood, ed. *Boccaccio on Poetry: Being the Preface and the Fourteenth and Fifteenth Books of Boccaccio's 'Genealogia Deorum Gentilium'* (Princeton, NJ: Princeton University Press, 1930; repr. 1956), 77.

19. Francesca's reference to Virgil as 'il tuo dottore' (*Inferno* 5.123) immediately preceding her tale of reading shows that this issue of names is very much at stake in this episode. Dante only uses *autore* twice in the *Commedia*, once for Virgil and once for God, who is,

significantly, the 'verace autore'. For interpretations of Dante's strategic uses of the word *autore*, see Barolini, *Dante's Poets*, 268–9 and Ascoli, *Dante and the Making of a Modern Author*. Dante provides his own definition of *autore* in *Convivio* 4.6.3–5.

20. A. J. Minnis, *Fallible Authors: Chaucer's Pardoner and Wife of Bath*, The Middle Ages series (Philadelphia, PA: University of Pennsylvania Press, 2008), 7. Also see his extensive treatment of the issue in Alastair J. Minnis, *Magister amoris: The 'Roman de la Rose' and Vernacular Hermeneutics* (New York: Oxford University Press, 2001).

21. For more on Boccaccio's distinctions between men and women, see Barolini, 'Le parole son femmine'. For a discussion of the implications of the author figure's association with the ladies, see Carla Freccero, *Queer/Early/Modern* (Durham, NC: Duke University Press, 2006), 46–7.

22. Boccaccio, *Decameron*, 1. Conclu.27.

23. For a similar strategy that avoids persuasion through access to a transcendent truth, and pursues it instead through storytelling, see the discussion of the so-called medical philosophy in the Hellenistic age in Martha Craven Nussbaum, *The Therapy of Desire: Theory and Practice in Hellenistic Ethics* (Princeton, NJ: Princeton University Press, 1994), 35.

24. Boccaccio, *Expositions* Inf. 5.litt.184 (Papio trans., p. 286).

25. Boccaccio, *Decameron*, 1. Intro.49.

26. Stillinger, 'The Place of the Title (*Decameron*, Day One, Introduction)', 31.

27. Chiecchi, *Le annotazioni e i discorsi sul Decameron del 1573 dei deputati fiorentini*, 53. Following Boccaccio's use of 'without a title' in his *Esposizioni sopra la Comedia* (4.litt.119), the phrase could refer either to Ovid's *Amores*, which was known as the *Sine titulo* in this period or to the work's variety of topics. For a summary of views, see Giovanni Boccaccio, *Decameron*, ed. Vittore Branca, 2 vols. (Turin: Einaudi, 1992), 1: 468. For a reading of 'senza titolo' as meaning that the *Decameron* 'was purposely constructed to be anonymous', see Victoria Kirkham, *Fabulous Vernacular* (Ann Arbor, MI: University of Michigan Press, 2001), 87. For comprehensive studies of the early circulation of the *Decameron*, see Vittore Branca, *Tradizione delle opere di Giovanni Boccaccio*, vol. 2 (Rome: Edizioni di Storia e Letteratura, 1991), 71–303 and Marco Cursi, *Il Decameron: Scritture, scriventi, lettori (Storia di un testo)* (Rome: Viella, 2007).

28. Berlin, Staatsbibliothek Preußischer Kulturbesitz, MS Hamilton 90.

29. Boccaccio uses the same verb *mescolare* to describe the accusation against him that he loves women too much: 'Altri, più maturamente mostrando di voler dire, hanno detto che alla mia età non sta bene l'andare omai dietro a queste cose, cioè a ragionar di donne o a compiacer loro. E molti, molto teneri della mia fama mostrandosi, dicono che io farei più saviamente a starmi con le Muse in Parnaso che con queste ciance mescolarmi tra voi'.

30. For Benvenuto da Imola's use of *Decameron* 4. Introduction to gloss *Purgatorio* 26, see Michelangelo Picone, 'Le papere di Fra Filippo (Intr. IV)', in *Boccaccio e la codificazione della novella: Letture del 'Decameron'* (Ravenna: Longo; 2002), 171–83. For another mention of the relationship between the two moments that does not mention Benvenuto, see Hollander, *Boccaccio's Dante*, 75.

31. Dante, *Purgatorio* 26.68–71.

32. Robert M. Durling, ed. and trans. *Dante Alighieri: Purgatorio* (New York: Oxford University Press, 2003).

33. Hollander, *Boccaccio's Dante*, 75.

34. Boccaccio, *Decameron*, 4. Intro.20.

35. Dante, *Purgatorio* 26.97–9.

36. Ibid. 26.117.

37. See Barolini, *Dante's Poets*, 84–153. For another interpretation of what is at stake in the canto that sees them in relation to the petrose recalled in the encounter with Forese Donati, see Gianfranco Contini, 'Dante come personaggio-poeta della *Commedia*', in *Un'idea di Dante: Saggi danteschi* (Turin: Einaudi, 1976; 1958), 33–62; 56–60.

38. Dante, *La vita nuova*, 2.9.

39. Boccaccio, *Decameron*, 4. Intro.33–4.

40. For the proposed connection to *Inferno* 4, see Luigi Surdich, *Boccaccio* (Bologna: Il mulino), 108.

41. Boccaccio also distinguishes himself from Dante by not including any extra-Italian poets, in contrast also to Petrarch who includes Arnaut Daniel in his quite poetic genealogy in *Lasso me* (*Rerum vulgarium fragmenta*, 70).

42. Dante, *Paradiso* 10.22–7.

43. Durling, *Dante Alighieri: Purgatorio*.

44. See Teodolinda Barolini, *The Undivine Comedy: Detheologizing Dante* (Princeton, NJ: Princeton University Press, 1992), 3–20 and 194–217 and Ascoli, *Dante and the Making of a Modern Author*, 108–29.

45. Boccaccio, *Decameron*, 4. Intro.7.

46. Minnis writes that this scribal pose reveals 'Boccaccio's impulse to discard the convention and come out in the open as the unashamed inventor of his stories, the self-confessed craftsman whose creativity parallels (in so far as is humanly possible) the perfect creation of God'. Alastair J. Minnis, *Medieval Theory of Authorship: Scholastic Literary Attitudes in the Later Middle Ages* (London: Scolar Press, 1984), 204.

47. Dioneo uses a similar of the rose to describe the act of interpretation in *Decameron* 5.10, but neither the word *leggere* nor *diletto*—those key markers of Francesca's discourse—appear. For a discussion of Dioneo's complex phrase, see Martin Eisner and Marc Schachter, '*Libido Sciendi*: Apuleius, Boccaccio, and the Study of the History of Sexuality', *PMLA* 124 (2009): 817–37.

48. This claim is, however, easily unmasked since the rubrics rarely reveal any lascivious content unless the sexual metaphor itself is already known. For careful examinations of the rubrics, see Antonio D'Andrea, 'Le rubriche del *Decameron*', in *Il nome della storia* (Naples: Liguori, 1982), 98–119 and A Milanese, 'Affinità e contraddizioni tra rubriche e novelle del *Decameron*', *Studi sul Boccaccio* 23 (1995): 89–111.

49. Boccaccio also uses the verb *ingannare* is his commentary on *Inferno* 5, Francesca 'vedendosi ingannata'. If Francesca was tricked, his readers won't be.

50. Dante, *Paradiso*, 8.124–6.

51. See Boccaccio, *Vita di Dante*, third redaction, par. 145 (Giovanni Boccaccio, *Vite di Dante*, ed. Pier Giorgio Ricci [Milan: Mondadori, 1974; repr. 2002]). Boccaccio also refers to *Paradiso* 8 in the *Esposizioni* on *Inferno* 7 for its discussion of Fortune. These appeals to the Heaven of Venus in both texts suggests how much it informs Boccaccio's thinking about cosmic influence.

52. For discussions of Boccaccio's naturalism, see Aldo D. Scaglione, *Nature and Love in the Late Middle Ages: An Essay on the Cultural Context of the Decameron* (Berkeley, CA: University of California Press, 1963), 101–25 and Gregory B. Stone, *The Ethics of Nature in the Middle Ages: On Boccaccio's poetaphysics* (New York: St Martin's Press, 1998).

53. See Boccaccio, *Decameron,* 10.10 and Petrarch, *Seniles,* 17.3. For an English translation, see Petrarch, *Letters of Old Age = Rerum Senilium Libri I-XVIII*, trans. Aldo S. Bernardo, Reta A. Bernardo, and Saul Levin, 2 vols. (Baltimore, MD: Johns Hopkins University Press, 1992), 2: 643–71.
54. Eisner, *Boccaccio and the Invention of Italian Literature*, 113–15.

BIBLIOGRAPHY

Ascoli, Albert Russell, 'Boccaccio's Auerbach: Holding the Mirror Up to Mimesis', *Studi sul Boccaccio* 20 (1991–92), 377–97.

Barolini, Teodolinda, 'Le parole son femmine e i fatti sono maschi: Toward a Sexual Poetics of the Decameron', in *Dante and the Origins of Italian Literary Culture* (New York: Fordham University Press, 2006; originally published, 1993), 281–303.

Branca, Vittore, *Boccaccio medievale e nuovi studi sul Decameron,* 2nd ed. (Milan: Sansoni, 1956; repr. 2010).

Eisner, Martin, 'The Tale of Ferondo's Purgatory (*Decameron* III.8)', in *The Decameron: Third Day in Perspective*, eds. Pier Massimo Forni and Francesco Ciabattoni (Toronto: University of Toronto Press, 2014), 150–69.

Fido, Franco, 'Dante personaggio mancato nel *Decameron*', in *Boccaccio: Secoli di vita (Atti del Congresso Internazionale, 17-19 Ottobre 1975)*, eds. Marga Cottino-Jones and Edward F. Tuttle (Ravenna: Longo, 1977), 177–89; repr. *Il regime delle simmetrie imperfette* (Milan: Angelia, 1988), 111–23.

Minnis, Alastair J., *Medieval Theory of Authorship: Scholastic Literary Attitudes in the Later Middle Ages* (London: Scolar Press, 1984).

Osgood, Charles G., ed., *Boccaccio on Poetry: Being the Preface and the Fourteenth and Fifteenth Books of Boccaccio's 'Genealogia Deorum Gentilium'* (Princeton, NJ: Princeton University Press, 1930; repr. 1956).

Stillinger, Thomas C., 'The Place of the Title (*Decameron*, Day One, Introduction)', in *The 'Decameron' First Day in Perspective*, ed. Elissa B. Weaver (Toronto: University of Toronto Press, 2004), 29–56.

CHAPTER 17

BOCCACCIO'S EARLY ROMANCES

WARREN GINSBERG

IN many ways, Boccaccio's early romances, *Il Filocolo*, *Il Filostrato*, and *Teseida delle nozze d'Emilia*, are meditations on love and history.[1] The *Filocolo* (c.1336–9?), a long work in prose set in late antiquity, chronicles the travails of Florio and Biancifiore. Separated by Florio's father, the king of Spain, the lovers, after numerous adventures, are finally reunited in Alexandria. When the Egyptian *ammiraglio*, as Boccaccio calls him, discovers they have married in secret, he condemns them to death. Venus, however, makes both invulnerable. After Florio, who has long since called himself Filocolo (afflicted by love), battles his host's troops, the admiral discovers that the youth is his nephew and allows the couple to return to Spain. On their way, they convert to Christianity in Rome, then journey on to Marmorina, where Florio succeeds his father and proselytizes the new religion. In the *Filostrato* (c.1335–7?), Boccaccio recounts the joys and sorrows of Troiolo, who loved and lost Criseida during the Trojan War. In the *Teseida* (c.1339–41), we hear first how Teseo conquered the Amazons and wed their queen Ipolita, then how Palemone and Arcita, two high-born Thebans defeated by Teseo, fought to win Ipolita's sister, Emilia.

For many readers, Boccaccio's lovers pursue their destinies against the backdrop of the providential movement of events toward salvation. Before Christianity made possible a more perfect union of love and peace, earthly happiness, these romances seem to suggest, was doomed to end in grief. When love took root in war, even the most harmonious marriage harboured seeds of the discord from which it sprang.

As chronicles of the past, then, the *Filocolo* explicitly, the *Filostrato* and *Teseida* implicitly, supported the critique of classical culture that St Augustine had made the hallmark of medieval Christian historiography. On this reading, the works have two plots. One tracks the wanderings of the central characters; the other measures their triumphs and setbacks against the march of time toward revelation. These plots are arranged hierarchically, so that the first points to and ultimately is absorbed by the second; they are coordinated by the same interpretive protocols that allowed theologians to read Hebrew scriptures and classical texts as prefigurations of the New Testament. Steven Grossvogel, for instance, has argued that Boccaccio expected the audience of the *Filocolo* to understand its events typologically. For Victoria Kirkham, the *Filocolo* everywhere reflects the canon law Boccaccio was studying when he wrote it; its storyline, however, follows the liturgy of Pentecost. James McGregor (1991) shows that Boccaccio rewrote scenes from Vergil's *Aeneid* in all three romances to stress the ephemerality of the rewards their heroes win by dint of their merits. David Anderson has similarly shown how much Statius's *Thebaid* undergirds the *Teseida*. Robert Hollander has argued that two Venuses, one lecherous, the other licit, preside over all Boccaccio's *opere minori in volgare*; the first is an emblem of pagan, carnal love, the second, who personifies Christian charity, channels sexual passion into lawful wedlock.

At the same time, however, Boccaccio counters whatever teleological impetus the tales may have by radically personalizing them. Each work contains a prefatory dedication in which the author expresses his love for his lady and tells her that the story he has composed re-enacts incidents in their own lives. In the *Filocolo*, the narrator includes his account of how he fell in love with Fiammetta in the narrative. One Saturday morning, he says, about ten o'clock, in the Franciscan church of St Lawrence, he saw the illegitimate daughter of Robert of Anjou, king of Naples, who had named her Maria. In epiphanic language that recalls Dante's rapture when he first saw Beatrice, the narrator describes how Maria's beauty inflamed him; he then recounts a second meeting with Maria, now christened Fiammetta, at which she commissions him, for the love he bears her, to write the story of Florio and Biancifiore.[2]

The *Filostrato* opens with a letter that the narrator has written to Filomena, who has left Naples for the inland city of Sannio. He explains to her that he had always thought thinking about one's beloved gives greater delight than seeing or speaking to her. But the bitter experience of her departure has taught him how wrong he was. In order to let Filomena understand his suffering, he sought a story that he could use 'as a cloak for the secret grief of his love'. So in the poem he now sends her, she will find herself reflected in descriptions of Criseida's beauty, just as Troiolo speaks for him when he expresses the joy he felt loving her and his anguish when she left him.

The *Teseida* also begins with a letter; this time, however, the narrator's correspondent once again is Fiammetta. Even though his memories of the past happiness they shared cause him pain and sorrow, he continues to picture her perfect loveliness in his mind. Indeed, his love for her persists despite the fact that she now spurns him. He still remembers her longstanding desire to hear and read stories about love; to remind her of the passion she had once felt, he is sending her a very ancient tale that he has put into their own tongue. In it she will recognize herself in the heroine and himself in the person of one of the two noblemen who court her.

These invented *mise-en-scènes*, which comprise chapters in Boccaccio's amorous autobiography, invert the way we read the fictions they frame. If, inside the tales, we are encouraged to refer Filocolo's adventures to those 'huge cloudy symbols of high romance', which Christians thought the heavens had unfurled like a scroll even before Christ's advent, outside their stories Troiolo, Palemone, and Arcita become surrogates or projections of the poet's psyche. From this point of view, their experiences restage episodes from the book of love in which he and his lady play the leading roles.

By regarding the romance not as a palimpsest of Christian revelation but as a veiled version of personal history, Boccaccio's prefaces quickly bring about a collision of discursive expectations. Because each narrator always has his own purposes in mind when he addresses his beloved, we continually find ourselves called on to reconcile the universalizing, osmotic tendencies of Christian allegory, which we become aware of as the tale progresses, with a backward-looking, rhetorical interrogation of particular intentions and private understandings. Whenever we come across an incident that advances the protagonists toward their happy or sad end, we feel encouraged to refer it to the happy or sad ending of all stories and to think of it as a reimagined episode from the author's affair. But when we do look through this end of the telescope, more often than not we find our attention focused less on the anagogic aptness of a connection—its likeness to end times—and more on the possible motives for which it has been made. Are the knights and ladies, we again and again will ask, really emblems of the ideal that the narrator would have us take them to be, or masks for his self-interest? By placing his authorial stand-ins at the centre and the circumference of these works, Boccaccio asks us to discern their figural dimensions and to wonder if the very forms of figuration that give his fictions the moral structure of providential history have also been deployed to screen selfish investments.

Another way to put this is to say that the prefaces, by realigning in advance, as it were, the reader's interpretive perspective, translate the mode of meaning of the romances. 'Mode of meaning' is a phrase I have adopted from Walter Benjamin's essay 'The Task of the Translator'; I am using it, *grosso modo*, to indicate those linguistic, literary, and cultural traditions that shape the events a text records and make them understandable to its audience.[3] According to Benjamin, the translator's task is to express 'the central reciprocal relationship between languages'. This relationship is revealed through the disclosure of the intention that underlies each language as a whole. The differences in sound and letter that distinguish 'bread', for example, from the French equivalent *pain*, underwrite discrete chains of associations; when the words are substituted for one another, the morphological and cultural logic that connects the English word with, say, a rhyme like 'bled' on one hand and 'wine' on the other (a loaf of bread, a jug of wine), disarticulates and is disarticulated by the logic that connects *pain et vin* (either in phonic terms or as the fare one once received in bistros for the cover charge). Since all such philological and social incompatibilities ultimately arise from different combinations of vowels and consonants prior to their having assumed a meaning in any language, Benjamin called the aggregation of these divergences 'pure speech'. The orientation of any individual language to this collective 'pure speech' determines its intentional mode, and it is a language's mode of intention that Benjamin says translations should seek to translate. When a corresponding manner is found, the original and the translation will second and undo the other's claim that it is the first or final word.

Translators have not found Benjamin's ideas particularly helpful, in part because they are difficult to realize, but mostly, I think, because the public they actually address is not simply bilingual but bifocal as well. The only people who will discern how manners of meaning in source and translation correspond to and disarticulate one another are those who see each text as a whole and both simultaneously. For Chaucerians reading Boccaccio's romances, however, Benjamin's theory is invaluable; it offers the opportunity to read each work on its own terms, and both reciprocally, without subordinating one to the other. In this chapter, I will therefore approach Boccaccio's early romances as if they were intralingual translations; I will examine, that is to say, some of the ways in which their prologues simultaneously collude with and controvert the intentional orientation of tales they introduce. I will also suggest some of the ways in which Chaucer, who seems either not to have known or to have ignored these prefaces, nevertheless produced poems that are Benjamin-like translations of them.

Before I begin, however, I must offer a prefatory word of my own. In the following pages I will not analyse the *Filocolo* as a discrete work but only in relation to the *Filostrato* and *Teseida*. My justification in giving such short shrift to this long and important predecessor of the *Decameron* is that its influence on Chaucer, if he knew it at all, was insignificant compared to that of the two other poems.[4]

IL FILOSTRATO/THE TROILUS

In the *Filostrato*, the mode of meaning that gives character and event their coherence is the 'the orality of writing'.[5] To a great extent, everything in Boccaccio's poem depends on the ways in which writing tries to voice itself. Behind his decision to cast his work as a form of 'visible speech' (a phrase Dante invented to characterize God's art in the *Purgatorio*[6]), a particular version of Italian literary, social, and cultural history pre-conditioned the meanings writing itself had, which Boccaccio engaged when he assigned it particular values as an element in verbal mediation. In *Troilus and Criseyde*, the corresponding mode is recitation as such. Instead of writing that tries to script its own utterance, English conventions and ideologies have prompted Chaucer to present a narrator and characters who speak the texts they write or read. It is precisely in this difference, the difference, that is, between the company which the textual and the oral keep with each other, that Chaucer's and Boccaccio's works translate each other.

In the widest sense, Troiolo, Criseida, and especially Pandaro, who plays so central a role in their affair, are direct responses to the idea of means and mediation in those late medieval philosophies of mind and action that formed the intellectual backdrop of the *dolce stil novo*. The northern Italian poets who composed in this 'sweet new style' in the last half of the thirteenth century transformed love poetry by drawing on the scholastic sciences of pneumatology and faculty psychology.[7] To describe the inner constitution of their passion, they turned to Aristotle, who taught that when we see or hear something, we do not know it as it materially exists but by means of an 'intention', an image of the object that its form produces in the eye or the ear. When these images were acted on by the inner senses—common sense, the imagination or phantasy, the estimative or cogita-tive sense, and memory—they underwent a second grade of abstraction; now called phantasms, they could be generated and retained even when the things they image were no longer present. Together with the vital and animal spirits (the subtlest form of matter, imperceptible to the senses, which mediated between flesh and soul by circulating throughout the body), these inner faculties, located in various areas of the brain, produced sensitive knowledge. By dividing and combining phantasms, the *vis cogitativa*, for instance, granted humans spontaneous insight into the nature of objects, which triggers the opinions and emotional responses we have about them.

Poets like Guido Guinizelli and Guido Cavalcante thought that love was born and held sway in this domain. Dante went further; because Beatrice was, he insisted, as much a supernal ideal as a mortal woman, his love for her had to be informed by reason and will, the intellectual operations that made human beings little less than angels. Dante drew on two epistemological traditions to describe these operations. One pivoted about the Augustinian 'word of the heart', the unvoiced, inner utterance that says 'this is true', which God speaks in us. Dante praised Beatrice by taking this word as his model; when he looked at her, the beauty that transported him was not corporeal but transcendental, the beauty that embellishes each thing according to its goodness. His lady's *onestà*, her *gentilezza*, her *umiltà*, the qualities that complement this beauty, were likewise intellective; by celebrating them in figures and tropes, Dante gave his songs a matching cognitive sweetness, which his readers experience when they see through the enigmatic ornamentation and understand that in Beatrice personal attributes are metaphysical categories as well.

The other noetic tradition was Thomistic; for Aquinas, reason began its work when the active intellect illuminates the imagination's phantasms and abstracts from one image of Fido and another of Spot that which makes Fido and Spot dogs. The resulting universal likeness, called the 'intelligible species', is then impressed on the passive intellect, which in response forms its own likeness of the essential form. This was the '*verbum mentis*', the universal concept, expressed by a single word; it allows us to comprehend the object with respect to its own nature. Understanding the 'dogness' of Fido, however, doesn't account for how he actually exists, individuated by his matter; the mind therefore returns to the phantasms, armed with the abstracted concept, and judges it true or false by producing a proposition: 'Fido is a dog.' Once reason has fully defined an object, the will inclines toward it insofar as the soul judges it desirable in relation to the good in general. In contrast to sensitive appetite, whose irascible and concupiscible powers move a person toward or away from a physical thing, the will is rational; it prompts us to reach for the apple not because it tastes good but because we know that eating it will make us healthy.

In the *Comedy*, Dante wanted his words to serve as verbal signs of fully comprehended material objects, but he also wanted them to stand as a testament to and performance of his faith, which Paul had defined as the substance of things hoped for, the evidence of things not seen ('fides sperandorum substantia argumentum non parentum').[8] To the extent that he recounts what he saw and heard in Hell, Purgatory, and Heaven, Dante therefore presents himself not as author but as scribe of the *poema sacro*, as he calls it. But to the extent that his tercets make palpable to others the height, the depth, and the breadth of his belief, so that others will believe by seeing him believe, he maintains he is the author of the *Commedia*.

Dante lays claim to both identities—reporter and maker—in a famous moment of self-identification in Purgatory. On the sixth terrace, Bonagiunta of Lucca asks if he sees before him the man who brought forth 'the new rhymes'. Dante initially responds by pronouncing himself Love's amanuensis: 'I am one who, when Amor breathes in me', I note (it)' ('Io mi son un che quando / Amor mi spira, noto'). Love's breath, that is, like God's in Genesis, creates him, one might say, poet *in se*, an *Io* who is *mi*, 'myself', not reflexively, by means of an action Dante performs on himself, but by being the object of Love's action, which makes him the subject he is. The *mi* of the man who says 'I' mi son un che' is the reflection of the *mi* Amor breathes forth ('Amor mi spira'); as such, the speaker's *mi* takes on nominative force, becomes a predication of Dante as first person pronoun. 'I' mi son un che'; not 'ego sum qui sum'. Dante is himself to the extent that his *mi* copies the one Love breathes into being.[9]

In 'noting' Amor's procreative inspiration, however, the secretarial I becomes authorial when Dante translates the translation Love brings about in him by finding a mode that matches the mode in which Amor's suspiration turns into words in his mind. He 'goes signifying', he says, not Love's inner hail, which no human tongue is equipped to express, but 'in the mode which he dictates within' ('a quel modo / ch'e' ditta dentro, vo significando').[10] Whether realized as quillstroke, or as the music of his lines, or as the form that gathers them into stanzas, Dante's 'inscriptional' noting—the poem he makes—by replicating the mode in which Love's breath has become internal speech, makes Dante the particular poet he is. As he moves through the world, the *mi* in 'I' mi son un che' exhibits Dante writing and being in accordance with the way 'Amor mi spira e…ditta dentro'.[11]

In the *Filostrato*, Boccaccio in essence replied that such a translation of inspiration into utterance can never be so transparent, nor can a poet's realization of himself through or as his work ever be so uninflected by personal motives. For Boccaccio, authorship is not an ontological state—a self that one assumes by walking the earth as an embodied analogy of the creating Word—but a position one occupies, the stance a writer takes with regard to the ethical potential of fiction. Instead of faith, the subject that interests Boccaccio is fidelity, and the language he moulds to represent it follows the ebb and flow of desire, not the rhythms of belief. Script or speech, he will show, does not simply derive its value from the end it is used for; it gives value to its end as well.

The prologue of the *Filostrato*, which purports to account for its origin, establishes its intratextual and intertextual dynamics. Besides locating the narrator's entire experience within the confines of a rhetorical love-debate, the particular question he contemplates invites us to read the *Filostrato* in conjunction with the *Filocolo*, where the question also appears.[12] In the latter work, a lady named Graziosa asks whether seeing the person one loves or thinking amorously about her provides greater delight. Fiammetta, the debate's judge, holds that thinking gives more joy; the learned terminology she uses is very much in the style of the *stil novo*.

The narrator of the *Filostrato* acknowledges that he once thought as Fiammetta did. But the 'bitter experience' of his lady Filomena's relocation to Sannio has, he says, taught him, as Criseida's removal to the Greek camp taught Troiolo, that thought's ability to 'make a loved one kind and responsive according to one's desires'[13] dissolves into nothing in the face of not being able to see her.

The differing responses to the repeated question invite us to invent a history of Boccaccio's literary development. No longer can recourse to the airy dialectics of love disputations offer consolation; only the temporal distance of sad historical events can stand as an adequate analogue to the despair that the spatial distance of Filomena's absence has caused him.[14]

Yet how distant, one finally must ask, is the *Filocolo's* analytical psychology from the fervid professions of the *Filostrato*? To admit that he was on the wrong side in a debate seems, at the least, a strangely dispassionate way for the narrator to express the overwhelming grief in his heart. Because he no longer could see Filomena, he tells her, among other things, he once was forced to cry out in Jeremiah's anguished words: 'how solitary sits the city, which was once full of people and mistress among nations'. This lamentation from *Lamentations* is shocking, not merely because it is second-hand, a borrowed articulation of the narrator's personal sorrow, but because it is two-faced. Readers of the *Vita nuova*, of whom Boccaccio was one, would immediately recall that Dante had used these same words to herald Beatrice's death. To equate her passing with Filomena's having gone a few days ride away is both outrageous and calculating. The allusion is meant, of course, to express the magnitude of Filostrato's misery. But there is an insidious side to his quotation. In light of the story he is about to tell, Filomena's forsaking Naples makes it not only Jeremiah's widowed city but a latter-day Troy. If we remember how Troy was left desolate, we remember a series of betrayals and desertions. By granting himself the historian's privilege of future-perfect retrospection, the narrator can conceal within his appeal to his lady—see, these are the dimensions of the suffering you have caused me, so great is the love I bear you—a warning that he will have his vengeance if she, like the widowed Criseida, turns out to have betrayed him. Filostrato desperately wants to persuade Filomena to return to Naples, yet he also seems ready to condemn her if she does not. Indeed, he says his life depends on his poem's ability to induce her to return, but his resentment peeps through his supplication, and anger has no desire at all to persuade. Rather we begin to suspect that under the guise of persuasion, Filostrato also wants to upbraid Filomena, not only for not having returned, but for having left in the first place.

The narrator accordingly frames his experience as a love debate precisely because he is not yet able to judge the truth or falseness of his lady. It may turn out that Filomena remains faithful, just as events proved Criseida was disloyal. But Filostrato is motivated neither by fairness nor by equity to hold his hopes and doubts in balanced abeyance; his seeming even-handedness actually masks his hijacking of the protocols of argumentation to accuse Filomena of perfidy at the same time that he swears he believes in her fidelity. Rather than determining the veracity of her love by arguing both sides of the case, as students were trained to do in school, Filostrato prosecutes the divided urgings of his soul. For him truth is the 'manner of meaning' he fashions to determine it, to say to Filomena '*odi et amo*', which he would translate as 'I love, I hate, it depends on you'.

For all his idealization of Filomena, therefore, his own identification of himself with Troiolo makes the reader suspect that her return is not his ultimate goal, but only a means to it; he wants to sleep with her, just as Troiolo slept with Criseida. The persuasiveness of the story he will tell, from which Filomena can infer her goodness by the extent of his ardor for her, at the same time is a blind for his own exercise in salacious wish-fulfillment.

Moreover, any conventionally moral reading of the story, which would teach that false women like Criseida must be avoided, or that her faithlessness epitomizes the flaws of love in the pre-Christian past, becomes similarly self-serving. Boccaccio's audience knew that Criseida was untrue because her duplicity had become part of the story of the Trojan war. But in Filostrato's hands, history is neither an impartial recitation of what was nor a primer on the ultimate failing of human endeavours; it is an excuse for him to tell the story backwards. By positing Criseida's guilt from the start, the narrator can, *sotto voce*, threaten to blacken Filomena's name for leaving or hector her into rejoining him.

Boccaccio, however, did not merely make the preface's opportunistic translation of his story's didactic possibilities the theme of the *Filostrato*, he lent it flesh and gave it a name: Pandaro. If we compare the *quistione* in the *Filostrato* with its counterpart in the *Filocolo*, we notice that the former proposes a third possibility, speaking to the lady, in addition to sight and thought, as the greatest delight in love. This option, unconsidered by Graziosa and now rejected by Filostrato, is exactly the function he gives the poem that bears his name as its title: he hopes its words will prove as effective with Filomena as Pandaro's did with Criseida. In Troy, though, Pandaro pandered by speaking to his cousin face to face. Because his mistress has left Naples, the *Filostrato* will be able to act as go-between only by addressing her indirectly, not as the narrator's speech but as his writing, as the pleadings of an absent suitor. In the end, however, there is no difference between Pandaro's persuasion and the poem's because Pandaro is the performance of the *Filostrato's* mode of meaning: he is the *orality* of its writing. Within the poem, he is the figure through whom Filostrato gives voice to his absence and presence in the text he has made, so that Filomena might gauge the loss of staying away against the gain of returning; beyond the poem, he is the figure through whom Boccaccio co-opts the impartiality of means and ends in rhetorical disputation to explore the possibilities and the limits of coaxing, directing, indeed, pre-scripting his absent readers' responses. Pandaro is an idea of fiction; through his comings and goings, Boccaccio writes the conversation disinterestedness has with personal motive whenever anyone seeks to learn and tell the truth.

In Italian cities, where aristocratic families commonly participated in commerce that required records of transactions, where a notary's signature could replace those of parties to a contract and validate it as a 'public instrument', the proposition that speaking writing could be a mode of meaning may have less surprised readers of the *Filostrato* than the meaning and character Boccaccio ascribed to it. After all, by the mid-fourteenth century, Troy's fall had long since been baptized as a moment in salvation history. A Christian audience that knew it was about to hear Troiolo's story would likely assume that it, no less than the events St. Paul had said 'happened to [the Israelites] in figure', had been 'written for our correction…'.[15] What the Florentine merchant or Neapolitan nobleman would not have anticipated, or perhaps liked, was Boccaccio's narrator's demonstration that the same means of figuration could be used to pen a history that was not intent on everyone's profit but on his own.

Chaucer quotes Paul's injunction twice in *The Canterbury Tales* at moments that underline its importance to his poetics of storytelling; in the *Troilus*, the final stanzas suggest that Paul's view of historiography also directly influenced his response to Boccaccio's insinuation of personal motives into it.[16] From my perspective, however, it is not the presence of the saint's ideas that makes Chaucer's tragedy a translation of the *Filostrato*; it is the absence of writing as a mode of meaning. I do not mean that the English work is less textual than its Italian counterpart; writing is everywhere, from Troilus's and Criseyde's letters, to the naming of the narrator's sources and the attention he calls to his translation of them, to the poem itself, which the poet worries scribes will mis-meter. But in each instance, writing is folded into recitation. In the *Filostrato*, the narrator composes an epistle-poem that speaks to Filomena through Troiolo, Criseida, and Pandaro, who are made ventriloquists of the double-edged message he wants his lady to hear. By contrast, Chaucer's narrator announces that he will read aloud the poem he has composed about Troilus's sorrows to a general audience for everyone's benefit:

> The double sorwe of Troilus to tellen,
> That was the kyng Priamus sone of Troye,
> In lovynge how his aventures fellen
> Fro wo to wele, and after out of joie,
> My purpos is, er that I parte fro ye.   (1.1–5)

Of course, as he recites what he has written, the narrator reads himself into all the characters and the events that they take part in; even as he is making his introductions, he foresees leaving us, just as Criseida will leave Troy and Troilus. But instead of providing louche lessons in the art of self-gratification, the narrator's Trojan entanglements, which are as personal and urgent as Filostrato's, become a model of ecumenical compassion. Rather than sending a letter to a lady he loves, he addresses all who hear him; rather than calling on her to read the work he has composed, he asks us to pray, not only for those he has written about—'for hem that ben despeired / In love', as Troilus was, and 'for hem that falsly ben apeired, / Thorough wikked tonges, be it he or she', as, perhaps, one might hope Pandarus and Criseida have been—but for himself, as someone who does not dare to love, due to his 'unliklynesse'(1.16), and 'for hem that ben at ese', as we all hope we will be (1.43). Prayer, which gains wings with its saying, even when said silently, rescues mediation from the parochial ends to which Boccaccio's narrator had put writing. The men and women of Troy no longer are scrims, behind which Filomena can see herself and her lover, to her delight or at her peril; by begging us to beg for mercy for everyone, Chaucer detaches our self-interestedness from the imaginative investment in the characters that his narrator both models and encourages. Unlike Filostrato's entreaties to a distant Filomena in Sannio, the woman to whom Chaucer asks his audience to direct their appeals is Mary, in heaven as far above the children of Eve as she is close to them on earth. It is she, he trusts, who will pass his hope on to her son, that Troilus, that Criseida, that all of us might reach the point where all desire has ended. In Chaucer, prayer becomes a mode of meaning that translates Filostrato's self-absorption into ethical concern for others.

Il Teseida/The Knight's Tale

In a sense, the preface to the *Filostrato* marks the work as an extended gloss on Francesca's indictment of books and their makers, whom she blames for fueling her adultery with Paolo: 'galeotto fu 'l libro e chi lo scrisse'[17]:'the book was a pander, and he who wrote it'. The charge so shocked Dante that when he heard it, he 'fell as a dead body falls'. Boccaccio's narrator, on the contrary, fervently hopes her words will come true, that the *Filostrato* will be a Gallehaut for its author. The preface of the *Teseida* also pivots around something Francesca says; this time the narrator inverts the implications of her famous lament, drawn from Boethius, with which she prefaces her account of her affair: 'nessun maggior dolore / che ricordarsi del tempo felice / ne la miseria' [No greater sorrow than to recall a happy time in misery].[18] The unnamed speaker begins his dedicatory letter by echoing her grief; unlike Francesca, however, he tells Fiammetta that he often and willingly renews the pain by remembering her beauty:

> Come che a memoria tornandomi le felicità trapassate, nella miseria vedendomi dov' io sono, mi sieno di grave dolore manifesta cagione, non m'è per tanto discaro il reducere spesso nella faticata mente, o crudel donna, la piacevole imagine della vostra intera bellezza.[19]
>
> [Although recollecting past joys in my present state of misery clearly causes me to suffer grievously, it is not, however, disagreeable to me to summon frequently to my wearied mind, o cruel lady, the pleasing image of your perfect beauty.]

Even now, amid the sorrows that her ending their liaison has caused, the joy he feels when he recalls her comeliness is the joy he felt the first time he saw her. Indeed, were it not for the harassing cares of a hostile Fortune that assail him on all sides ('le pronte sollecitudini delle quali la nemica fortuna m'ha circondato'), he believes he would die from the almost ineffable blessedness he embraces by contemplating her form ('io credo che così contemplando, quasi gli ultimi termini della mia beatitudine abracciando, morre'mi').[20]

Twice within these opening lines the narrator claims that two contrary states coexist in him. Although he knows that Fiammetta no longer loves him, he still is in love with her. Although he obeys her command not to see or approach her, he continually ushers her image into the chambers of his mind. Remembering her increases his pain; remembering her also produces a pleasure he gladly replicates. His life, he says, is at risk, but the danger that menaces him comes not from too much suffering but from too much bliss. Like Boethius's bad fortune, his adversities bring benefits; without them, he would have expired in a rapture of delight.

Naturally the narrator paints this image of his divided soul in the hope that Fiammetta will contemplate it the way he contemplates her in his mind. But he has not pictured himself a man both in love and past its loss, heartsick to the point of death, thought-happy beyond mortal endurance, simply to excite her sympathy or reignite her affection. By simultaneously insisting that he knows his love endures and that she has expunged him from her heart, the narrator subtly rigs the rules that govern how Fiammetta, and through her all readers, will read the book he has written for her.

The poem, in fact, he tells her, is proof of his unaltered devotion. Like the servant who anticipates his mistress's pleasure, he has laboured to put into verse a very ancient but little known tale because he remembers she has always loved stories about love. She will be sure, he continues, that he has composed the work for her when she sees she is figured in Emilia and that he shares the fate of one of the knights who court her:

> che ciò che sotto il nome dell'uno de' due amanti e della giovane amata si conta essere stato, ricordandovi bene, e io a voi di me e voi a me di voi, se non mentiste, potreste conoscere essere stato detto e fatto in parte.[21]
>
> [that in what is said to have happened under the name of one of the two lovers and under the name of the young beloved, remembering truly, you shall be able to recognize, if you didn't lie, something of what I have said and have done for you, and something of what you have said and have done for me.]

Which lover is his surrogate the narrator does not say, for he knows Fiammetta will discern it ('ché so che ve ne avvedrete'). And, he adds, if she finds that he has exaggerated certain things, he has done so only to conceal what no one but they should know.

This gambit, which cleverly unites the narrator with Fiammetta and sets them against other readers, is hard to resist. Older critics could not; they had to pierce the veil. But for every Hulbert who argued that Boccaccio identified himself with Arcita, there was a Whitfield who said he stood with Palemone. Later, after Branca showed that the prefaces are fabrications, 'neither' has seemed a better answer. Were we able, though, to ask Fiammetta what she thought of those earlier efforts to see with her eyes, I can imagine she would say she found them amusing, even as I can see her telling those who would bracket the narrator's allegory that they've missed the point. For the moment she read the plot of the *Teseida*, which her lover includes in his letter, and learned that Arcita wins Emilia, but dies in gaining her, and that Palemone, who never stopped loving her, subsequently marries her, Fiammetta would have understood that her once and future admirer has cast himself as both knights. To the extent that he acknowledges her affection for him has died, the narrator is Arcita; to the extent that he remains as devoted to her as ever he was, he is Palemone. No matter which cousin she recognized as his proxy, he is the other one as well.

Neither we nor Fiammetta, then, should be surprised to discover that from the start the knights act more in concert than as individuals; every admirable action undertaken by Arcita seems balanced by an equally magnanimous gesture on Palemone's part, every misfortune Palemone suffers seems to find its match in Arcita. Through Books Three and Four, as prisoners of Teseo, they comfort each other's sorrow and encourage each other in love. Once they gain their liberty, they become sworn enemies, but they continue to complement each other's thoughts and actions. Whether friends or foes, they move in tandem.

Why does Boccaccio choreograph the cousins' exploits to stress their mutuality rather than their distinctiveness? One reason, the major one, I think, appears in the most extensive of the glosses he wrote to elucidate the poem's mythological allusions. The evening before each knight and his hundred champions do battle to decide which of them will marry Emilia, all three offer sacrifices to their patron deities. Arcita prays to Mars for victory; Palemone begs Venus for help to win not the battle but Emilia; Emilia prays to Diana for peace between the lovers or, if she must wed, that she be joined with the knight who loves her most.

These prayers seem to invite us, like Ascalione's *questione* in the *Filocolo*,[22] to judge which of the two noble suitors loves a beautiful and virtuous maiden with greater courtesy. But in his commentary on the gods' temples, to which the prayers, now personified, fly, Boccaccio makes it clear that Palemone's passion and Arcita's exertions are two aspects of a single act of desire:

> ...in ciascuno uomo sono due principali appetiti, de' quali l'uno si chiama appetito concupiscibile, per lo quale l'uomo disidera e si rallegra d'avere le cose che, secondo il suo giudicio, o ragionevole o corrotto ch'egli sia, sono dilettevoli e piacevoli; l'altro si chiama appetito irascibile, per lo quale l'uomo si turba o che gli sieno tolte o impedite le cose dilettevoli, o perché quelle avere non si possano.[23]

> [In each man there are two principal appetites, one of which is called the concupiscible appetite, through which man desires and rejoices in having things which, according to his judgment, whether it is rational or corrupt, are delightful and pleasing. The other is called the irascible appetite, through which man becomes upset either if delightful things are taken away from him or his access to them is impeded, or because those things cannot be had.]

Boccaccio's analysis could have come from the *Summa Theologica;* Aquinas also says that although sensitive appetition is one generic power, it operates in two modes. The concupiscible appetite inclines a creature to acquire the suitable and to avoid the harmful; the irascible prompts it to resist anything that would hinder acquiring the suitable or flee from something that would do it harm. Both appetites obey reason, but they counteract each other: as Aquinas puts it, 'concupiscence, being roused, diminishes anger, and anger, being roused, very often diminishes concupiscence'. Moreover, 'the passions of the irascible appetite rise from the passions of the concupiscible appetite and terminate in them'.[24]

By having Palemone pray to Venus, Boccaccio clearly aligns him with the concupiscible side of sensation; by praying to Mars, Arcita clearly stands under the banner of the irascible. The nature and function of each appetite regulates the character of each knight and the manner in which he conducts himself. Palemone prays to have Emilia because he is disposed to do all he can to acquire her; Arcita asks for victory because that will thwart anyone but him winning her. They differ the way a desire for something differs from the means that achieve it, but each inheres in and presupposes the other. The relation between the appetites accordingly shapes the events they both experience, from Palemone's falling in love with Emilia before Arcita to Arcita's dying wish that Palemone marry her.

In his letter, the narrator unites in himself the appetites he had individuated in his tale. The resignation he now professes marks the end of the anger he likely felt when Fiammetta prevented him from coming to her; his continuing passion shows that his irascible appetite, which arose out of the concupiscible, has now terminated in it. By identifying both Palemone and Arcita as versions of himself, he gives Fiammetta a complete account of his sensuality.

The narrator, however, is not content simply to turn the knights and their appetites into extended metaphors of his qualities as a lover. By having their story double for his, he signals that they are metaphors of his poetic achievement as well. He makes the relation between the knights a correlative of the *Teseida* itself, the first work in the vernacular to marry epic with romance.

Boccaccio identifies arms and the woman as his subjects at the outset by invoking Mars and Venus:

> Siate presenti, o Marte rubicondo,
> nelle tue armi rigido e feroce,
> e tu, madre d'Amor, col tuo giocondo
> e lieto aspetto, e 'l tuo figliuol veloce
> co' dardi suoi possenti in ogni mondo:
> e sostenete e la mano e la voce
> di me che 'ntendo i vostri effetti dire
> con poco bene e pien d'assai martire.[25]

[Be present, o rubicund Mars, fierce and severe in your arms, and you, o mother of Amor, with your gay and cheerful looks, and your swift son, with his darts powerful in every realm, and sustain my hand and my voice, for I intend to speak of your effects with much anguish and very little benefit to myself.]

The poem certainly begins in martial strain. In the first two books, Teseo battles the Amazons in Scythia and Creon at Thebes; at this point, a reader might reasonably suppose that the rest of the poem will rehearse the other ten feats of the king of Athens, as Boccaccio would later list them in the *Genealogia Deorum*.[26] Thereafter, however, Teseo withdraws from the action; he reappears only to determine the direction of Palemone's and Arcita's fate. In retrospect, though, we realize that his combat with Ipolita and the marriage that concludes it is as much a story of the concupiscible and irascible appetites

as the Theban knights' pursuit of and wedding to Emilia. With Teseo, in whom the irascible dominates and gives birth to the concupiscible, Boccaccio presents as epic what
Palemone and Arcite play out as romance. The union of the two genres finds perfect
expression in the work's title: *Teseida di nozze d'Emilia.*

Boccaccio in fact, explicitly equates his poem with the dispositions of his heroes when
he introduces Palamone and Arcita. He prays that Cupid

> Ponga ne' versi miei la sua potenza
> quale e' la pose ne' cuor de' Tebani
> imprigionati, sì che differenza
> non sia da essi alli loro atti insani…[27]

[put his power in my verses as he put it into the hearts of the Theban prisoners, so that there
be no difference between them and their mad deeds.]

Then, at the end of the tale, the narrator boasts of his book's achievement by highlighting
once again the temperaments it has married:

> Poi che le Muse nude cominciaro
> nel cospetto degli uomini ad andare,
> già fur di quelli i quai l'esercitaro
> con bello stilo in onesto parlare,
> e altri in amoroso l'operaro;
> ma tu, o libro, primo a lor cantare
> di Marte fai gli affanni sostenuti,
> nel volgar lazio più mai non veduti.[28]

[Since the Muses began to go unclothed in men's sight, there have indeed been those who
exerted themselves on their behalf with refined style in virtuous speech, and others used
them to speak of love; but you, o book, are first to have them sing the labours of Mars, never
before seen in the vernacular of Latium.]

This stanza, as editors always note, speaks to Dante, who had said in the *De vulgari
eloquentia* that there are three subjects a vernacular poet might treat: 'armorum probitas,
amoris accensio, directio voluntatis' (uprightness in battle, the kindling of love, the
governing of will).[29] Cino da Pistoia is an example of the second kind of poet, Dante
himself of the third, but no one, he remarks, has yet written about arms in the *vulgare
illustre.* Boccaccio obviously thinks that the *Teseida* remedies the want, but his ambition
goes beyond a desire to be recognized as the Italian Statius. His poem is not simply a
narrative of 'prowess of arms'; it also is a tale about 'the sparking of passion' and 'the
bending of will (toward virtue)'. Boccaccio implicitly crowns and miters himself master
of all three forms of poetry.[30]

The *Teseida* thus fittingly concludes with two sixteen line sonnets. In the first, the
narrator addresses the Muses, who in Boccaccio's day were invoked only by the epic poet
seeking inspiration. He prays that they act as intermediaries both between him and
Fiammetta and between him and poetic fame. Together they should decide on a name
for the poem, and its place, and its course.[31]

In the second 'sonnetto', the Muses respond that they delivered the book to Fiammetta, who read it alone and sighed to herself: 'Ahi, quante d'amor forze in costor foro' [Alas, how great were the forces of love in them].[32] Then, completely set ablaze by the flame of love ('Poi di fiamma d'amor tututta accensa'), Fiammetta begged the Muses that these well-written acts of chivalry ('le ben scritte prodezze') and the beauty ('la biltate') not go 'mute', that is, without a title. It pleased her to name the poem *Teseida di nozze d'Emilia*, and the Muses proclaim that it will bring them vast fame in every age. Echoing each of Dante's genres, Boccaccio one final time joins Mars and Venus, and translates them into his two loves: Fiammetta and the epic Muses. The poet in love has created the poem of love and war, which makes the lady he worships in contemplation one with the goddesses of poetic inspiration, even as they make him worthy to wear their '*grazioso alloro*'.

CHAUCER'S USE OF THE *TESEIDA*

In his prologue, Filostrato, uncertain whether Filomena has betrayed him, tells her that the story of Criseida is a verbal mirror, in which she will be able to see or not see herself, depending on whether or not she stays in Sannio. He makes his letter-poem his pander, coordinating the presence and the absence of its writing with his expressed and hidden desires, so that as Filomena reads his lament she can hear his sighs and their whispered words of warning. In Filostrato's hands, history is not a record of the past but an instrument to engineer possible futures; all that Troiolo and Criseida did, all that he and Filomena have done, has been transformed into shadow-bearing prefaces of his joy if she returns to him and the soiling of her reputation if she does not.

In the *Teseida*, the narrator again says he has rehearsed an old tale to tell his own; because he accepts he has no future with Fiammetta, however, history has ostensibly reclaimed its charter as the uninflected report of former events. Remembering and contemplation, along with the felt but unsensed pleasure and pain they generate, replace Filostrato's hopeful, fearful anticipation. Images only the mind's eyes can see stand in for bodies that are no longer visible because they have ridden away. Rather than trying to achieve the immediacy of speech, writing in the *Teseida* therefore capitalizes its textuality, its literariness. The *hic et nunc* of ink on parchment, the there and not-thereness of the objects those quill-strokes represent, become modal correlates of both the narrator's present condition (in concert with the way that Arcita mirrors who he was but no longer is, Palemone who he was and continues to be), and his aspiration to be Italy's first epic love poet.

The manner in which writing means in the *Teseida* thus translates the manner in which it means in the *Filostrato*. Their shared form (they alone contain an introductory prose epistle followed by a poem in *ottava rima* stanzas), the classical subjects from Greek heroic tradition they uniquely treat, suggest that Boccaccio wanted his readers to consider these works together as well as separately. Chaucer engaged both deeply; he may not have realized, though, that the narrator of the *Filostrato* and the narrator of the *Teseida* were supposed to be the same man.[33] Even if he did, unless he also was familiar with the *Filocolo's* description of his miraculous experience in the church of St Lawrence, he might not have been struck either by Filostrato's apparent infidelity or by its sly propriety. One can, of course, imagine that the narrator's intrigue with Filomena preceded his sighting of Fiammetta; the explanation I think Chaucer would have preferred, however, is that Boccaccio used his prefaces to fit his authorial surrogate's actions to those of the story he would tell. Before we see Criseida abandon Troiolo for Diomede, we discover a Filostrato who has forsaken his first love and has taken another in her place. Boccaccio does something similar in the *Teseida*. Here, the narrator noticeably lacks a name; dead in Fiammetta's regard, he will show in Arcita's death the death of the appetite that most strives to gain a man a name in the world. Only Fiammetta can make him the man he used to be by speaking again his name in her heart, which he hopes she will do by naming the poem he has written for her, also mute and titleless until she christens it.

Nevertheless, we know that Chaucer did think about both poems at once.[34] When Arcita returns to Athens in The Knight's Tale, he says his name is Philostrate (I.1427); in the *Teseida*, he says he is called Penteo. Troilus's soul's flight to the eighth sphere comes from the *Teseida*, where Arcita also looks down on the earth and laughs.[35] But it is, I think, the Knight himself who allows us to see Chaucer reading Boccaccio's romances as translations of each other.

Although he incorporated passages from the *Teseida* in *The Parliament of Fowles, The Legend of Good Women, The Franklin's Tale,* and, perhaps, *The House of Fame,* Chaucer engaged the poem most extensively in the *Anelida and Arcita* and The Knight's Tale.[36] For me, the *Anelida,* if in fact Chaucer composed both parts of it, is most interesting as a translation of Boccaccio's experiments in mixed forms and genres; instead of intertwining prose preface and verse tale, epic and romance, Chaucer attempted to make narrative and lyric companionable.[37] The wholesale changes he introduced—Palemone has disappeared; Arcita has become a faithless lover who has not abandoned Emilia but a distraught Anelida—show that Chaucer was ready to challenge Boccaccio even as he followed him. His biggest intervention, though, may have been to invent a story to go with Anelida's complaint. Like *The Legend of Good Women,* in which the ballade in praise of Alceste also brings the action of a dream-preface to a halt, Chaucer left the *Anelida* unfinished; in this instance, the incompleteness and the awkward suturing of elements may indicate he thought this effort to combine French conventions and Italian matter was not successful.

The Knight's Tale is a far more radical reworking of Boccaccio's premises. In it Chaucer translated the mode of meaning of the *Teseida* by turning its merged forms and genres into ethopoesis. He joined epic and romance, that is to say, to create the character of the Knight. His many campaigns ally him with Mars, Theseus, Arcita, and through them the irascible appetite; the courtly refinements that make him 'wys' as well as 'worthy' (I.68)—his maiden-like comportment, the respectful manner in which he speaks to everyone—align him with Venus, Palamon, and the concupiscent appetite. Both aspects coexist in him in perfect balance.

When Chaucer replaced the narrator's prefatory epistle to the *Teseida* with the portrait of the Knight in the General Prologue, which is what I am suggesting he effectively did, even if his manuscript lacked Boccaccio's letter, he also uncoupled time and history from faculty psychology and personal allegory.[38] In contrast to his approach in the *Troilus*, Chaucer now depersonalized Boccaccio. He discarded the conceit that would have the events in the Knight's tale correspond to events in his life. In its place he developed the idea that the Knight would be not so much an extension of the tale he tells and the way he tells it as a translation of its content and style. Unlike the narrator of the *Teseida*, who urges Fiammetta to collapse the divide that separates pagan from Christian times, the Knight, who has fought many battles at Christendom's borders, fashions a story that emphasizes it. In Theseus's age, one could do no more, as he says, than make a virtue of necessity. In the Knight's, choice no longer is limited by predestined outcomes. Chaucer made this difference make all the difference in their worlds. Within The Knight's Tale, the superimposition of perspectives forces readers to register the imperfection in the 'parfit joye', compounded out of 'sorwes two', that Theseus says will attend Palamon's and Emilye's wedding; it causes us to realize how unrealizable his fond blessing of their joy, which he declares will last 'everemo', really is (I.3071–72). Outside the tale, and serving as prologue to it, Chaucer enacts a small drama in which free will and fate are also in play; on the road to Canterbury, however, the Knight introduces a crucial note of 'game' into the 'ernest' chance that obligates him to tell the first tale:

> And shortly for to tellen as it was,
> Were it by aventure, or sort, or cas,
> The sothe is this: the cut fil to the Knyght,
> Of which ful blithe and glad was every wyght,
> And telle he moste his tale, as was resoun,
> By foreward and by composicioun,
> As ye han herd; what nedeth wordes mo?
> And whan this goode man saugh that it was so,
> As he that wys was and obedient
> To kepe his foreward by his free assent,
> He seyde, 'Syn I shal bigynne the game,
> What, welcome be the cut, a Goddes name!
> Now lat us ryde, and herkneth what I seye'.   (I.843–55)

Glossing in advance everything the Knight will say, this scene, which inaugurates the story-telling pilgrimage, creates an imagined community of auditors whose beliefs will re-weave the fabric of his tale into a happier design, which turns a marriage that begins and ends in death into a comedy brought about by a death in Jerusalem, a death the pilgrims believe made life that lasts 'evermo'.

The debt that Chaucer owed the *Filostrato* and *Teseida* was enormous. These romances significantly recast the complex relation between preface and story that he already knew from the *Romance of the Rose*, Machaut, Froissart. Boccaccio's innovations, not the least of which was his formal separation of letter from poem, helped Chaucer move from a singular framing 'I', more or less aware of his own emotional investment in the men and women he spoke of, to the gathering of a diverse group of 'I's who are also 'he's and 'she's, framers of the tales they tell, framed by their pilgrimage to Becket's shrine. In the *Tales*, the portraits in the General Prologue, the individual introductions and prologues, the endlinks, all stand as translations of each other and the story they are attached to. They all express—each in a different form—a distinct orientation, a coordinating idea or set of concerns. For the Knight, those concerns are providence, history, obsolescence and, behind them all, the crisis in chivalry in fourteenth-century England. For the Miller the idea is repetition, for the Clerk, transit and transition, for the Wife it is substitution, for the Franklin it is projection and assimilation, for the Pardoner it is subversion. The translations are all Chaucer's own, but the spirit that animates them is a spirit Boccaccio would have recognized and welcomed and called kindred.

NOTES

1. All citations from Boccaccio's works are from *Tutte le opere di Giovanni Boccaccio,* ed. Vittore Branca, 12 vols. (Milan: Mondadori, 1964–). All translations are my own. Readers may consult the following English translations of the *Filocolo, Filostrato,* and *Teseida: Il Filocolo,* trans. Donald Cheney with the collaboration of Thomas G. Bergin (New York: Garland, 1985); *Il Filostrato,* Italian text ed. Vincenzo Pernicone, trans. Robert P. Roberts and Anna Bruni Seldis (New York: Garland, 1986); *Teseida; The Book of Theseus,* trans. Bernadette Marie McCoy (New York: Medieval Text Association, 1974).

2. Dante tells readers of the *Vita Nuova* that his first sighting of Beatrice opened a new chapter in the book of his memory, the transcription of which is the little volume they now have before their eyes. Boccaccio's first view of Maria deliberately recalls the astronomical elevation and sacramental grandeur of Dante's description; his second meeting with Maria, where she commissions the work we will now read, works an elegant variation on Dante's conceit.

3. For a more detailed discussion of Benjamin's theory of translation, which I read partly under the influence of Paul de Man's response, see my *Chaucer's Italian Tradition* (Ann Arbor, MI: University of Michigan Press, 2002), 8–10, 148–89.

4. A few similarities between Florio's and Troilus's bedroom scenes and the concluding envoys are suggestive; most Chaucerians, however, do not believe he knew the *Filocolo*. On the *Filocolo,* in addition to Steven Grossvogel, *Ambiguity and Allusion in Boccaccio's* Filocolo (Firenze: L.S. Olschki, 1992) and Victoria Kirkham, *Fabulous Vernacular: Boccaccio's Fiction and the Art of Medieval Fiction* (Ann Arbor, MI: University of Michigan Press, 2001), see Roberta Morosini, *'Per difetto rintegrare': Una lettura del Filocolo di Giovanni Boccaccia* (Ravenna: Longo, 2004) and Tobias Foster Gittes, *Boccaccio's Naked Muse: Eros, Culture and the Mythopoeic Imagination* (Toronto: University of Toronto Press, 2008). Menedon's question of love in the fourth book is an analogue to the Franklin's Tale; for recent discussions see Dominique Battles, 'Chaucer's *Franklin's Tale* and Boccaccio's *Filocolo* Reconsidered', *Chaucer Review* 34 (1999), 38–59, Michael Calabrese, 'Chaucer's Dorigen and Boccaccio's Female Voices', *Studies in the Age of Chaucer* 29 (2007), 259–92, Robert R. Edwards, 'Source, Context, and Cultural Translation in the *Franklin's Tale*', *Modern Philology* 94 (1996), 141–62 and *Chaucer and Boccaccio: Antiquity and Modernity* (New York: Palgrave, 2002), John Finlayson, 'Invention and Disjunction: Chaucer's Rewriting of Boccaccio in the *Franklin's Tale*', *English Studies* 89 (2008), 385–402, Warren Ginsberg, '"Gli scogli neri e il niente

che c'è": Dorigen's Black Rocks and Chaucer's Translation of Italy', in *Reading Medieval Culture*, eds. Robert Stein and S. Prior (Notre Dame, IN: University of Notre Dame Press, 2005), 387–408, Gerald Morgan, 'Boccaccio's *Filocolo* and the Moral Argument of the *Franklin's Tale*', in *Chaucer*, eds. Valerie Allen and Ares Axiotis (New York: St Martin's Press, 1997), 63–76.

5. I have analysed the *Filostrato* in greater detail in two works (*Chaucer's Italian Tradition*, and '*Troilus and Criseyde* and the Continental Tradition', in *Approaches to Teaching Troilus and Criseyde and The Shorter Poems*, eds. Tison Pugh and Angela Weisl, Modern Language Association [New York: MLA, 2007], 38 42). This chapter expands my earlier discussions. For other important readings of the poem, see Fabian Alfie, 'Love and Poetry: Reading Boccaccio's *Filostrato* as a Medieval Parody', *Forum Italicum* 32 (1998), 347–74; Robert Hanning, 'Come in Out of the Code: Interpreting the Discourse of Desire in Boccaccio's *Filostrato*', in *Chaucer's Troilus and Criseyde: 'Subgit to alle poesie'*, ed. R. A. Shoaf (Binghamton, NY: Medieval and Renaissance Texts and Studies, 1992), 120–37; Robert Hollander, *Boccaccio's Two Venuses* (New York: Columbia University Press, 1977); Janet Smarr, *Boccaccio and Fiammetta* (Urbana and Chicago, IL: University of Illinois Press, 1986); Thomas C. Stillinger, *The Song of Troilus: Lyric Authority in the Medieval Book* (Philadelphia, PA: University of Pennsylvania Press, 1992); David Wallace, *Chaucer and the Early Writings of Boccaccio*, Cambridge Studies 12 (Cambridge: Cambridge University Press, 1985); David Wallace, 'Love-Struck in Naples (*Filostrato*)', in *Boccaccio. A Critical Guide to the Complete Works*, eds. Victoria Kirkham, Michael Sherberg, and Janet Levarie Smarr (Chicago, IL: University of Chicago Press, 2013), 77–86.

6. Dante Alighieri, *Purgatorio* 10.95.

7. In this discussion, I am following chiefly Norman Kretzmann, Norman, A. Kenney, and J. Pinborg's *The Cambridge History of Later Medieval Philosophy: From the Rediscovery of Aristotle to the Disintegration of Scholasticism, 1100–1600* (Cambridge: Cambridge University Press, 1982), 602–22. See also Nicholas Steneck, 'Albert on the Psychology of Sense Perception', in *Albertus Magnus and the Sciences: Commemorative Essays, 1980*, ed. James Weisheipl (Pontifical Institute of Medieval Studies, Toronto: University of Toronto Press, 1980), 263–90.

8. Hebrews 11.1.

9. The idea of Love's breath invoked here looks forward both to *Purgatorio* 25.71, where God breathes the rational soul into a human embryo ('*e spira / spirito novo*' [and He breaths (into it) a new spirit], and, ultimately, to *Paradiso* 10.1–2: '*Guardando nel suo Figlio con l'Amore/che l'uno e l'altro etternalmente spira*' (gazing in His Son with the Love that the one and the other eternally breathe).

10. Dante, *Purgatorio.* 24.52–4.

11. For a more detailed discussion of this passage, see Warren Ginsberg, *Tellers, Tales, and Translation in Chaucer's Canterbury Tales* (Oxford: Oxford University Press, 2015), 45–7.

12. Boccaccio, *Filocolo* 4.59–62.

13. Boccaccio, *Filostrato*, Proemio, 5.

14. We cannot, in fact, say which work was composed first. Early critics naturally dated the *Filocolo*, which contains the scene of the narrator's enamourment within the narrative, before the *Filostrato*, which for many years was mistakenly thought addressed to Fiammetta, not Filomena. Vittore Branca, among others, showed that Boccaccio's prefaces are as fictive as the tales they introduce ('Profilo biografico', in *Tutte Le Opere di Giovanni Boccaccio*, vol. 1., [1967], 3–203, 39 ff.); since then, most Boccaccisti have agreed with him

that the *Filostrato* (c. 1335-7?) predates the *Filocolo* (c. 1336-9?). The grounds on which these arguments are based are speculative; they rely primarily on stylistic impressions of the relative maturity of the prose in each work (e.g. Pier Giorgio, 'Per la dedica e la datazione del *Filostrato*'. *Studi sul Boccaccio* 1 [1963], 333-47). The *Filostrato* has been dated as early as 1335; more recently, however, other scholars, who base their arguments on the presence of Petrarch's lyrics in the poem, have dated it as late as 1340. For a recent review of the dating, see William Rossiter, *Chaucer and Petrarch* (Cambridge: D. S. Brewer, 2010), 82-4. By considering the works as Benjamin-like translations, the question of the priority of one or the other of the works can be bracketed.

15. 1 Corinthians 10:11.

16. The most detailed comparison of Chaucer's *Troilus* and the *Filostrato* remains Sanford Meech, *Design in Chaucer's Troilus* (Syracuse, NY: Syracuse University Press, 1959). Other studies include: Edwards, 'Source, Context, and Cultural Translation in the *Franklin's Tale*; Robert Hanning, 'The Crisis of Mediation in Chaucer's *Troilus and Criseyde*', in *The Performance of Middle English Culture: Essays in Honor of Martin Stevens*, eds. James Paxson et al. (Cambridge: D. S. Brewer, 1998), 143-59; Laura D. Kellogg, *Boccaccio's and Chaucer's Cressida* (New York: Peter Lang, 1995); C. S. Lewis, What Chaucer really did to *Il Filostrato*', in Selected Literary Essays (Cambridge: Cambridge University Press, 1969), 27-44; James H. McGregor, 'Troilus's Hymn to Venus and His Choice of Loves in Boccaccio's *Filostrato*', *Romance Philology* 41 (1987), 48-57; and Stillinger, *The Song of Troilus*. For side by side editions of the two poems, see Barry Windeatt, *Troilus and Criseyde* (Oxford: Clarendon Press, 1992).

17. Dante, *Inferno* 5.137.

18. Ibid. 5.121-3. On the *Teseida*, see: Piero Boitani, *Chaucer and Boccaccio*, Medium Aevum Monographs, New Series VIII (Oxford: Society for the Study of Medieval Languages and Literature, 1977); Eren Branch, 'Rhetorical Structures and Strategies in Boccaccio's *Teseida*', in *The Craft of Fiction*, ed. Leigh A. Arrathoon (Rochester, MI: Solaris Press, 1984), 143-60; William C. Maisch, 'Boccaccio's *Teseida*: The Breakdown of Difference and Ritual Sacrifice', *Annali d'italianistica* 15 (1997), 85-98; Ronald L. Martinez, 'Before the *Teseida*: Statius and Dante in Boccaccio's Epic', in *Boccaccio 1990: The Poet and His Renaissance Reception,* eds.; Kevin Brownlee and Victoria Kirkham, 'Premessa' by Vittore Branca, Special section of *Studi sul Boccaccio* 20 (1992), 205-19; Michael Sherberg, 'The Girl outside the Window (*Teseida delle Nozze d'Emilia*)', in eds. Kirkham et al, *Boccaccio. A Critical Guide to the Complete Works*, 95-106; Janet Smarr, *Boccaccio and Fiammetta*; and Winthrop Wetherbee, 'History and Romance in Boccaccio's *Teseida*', in *Boccaccio 1990: The Poet and His Renaissance Reception, Studi sul Boccaccio* 20 (1992), 173-84.

19. Boccaccio, Preface to *Teseida*, 1.

20. Ibid., 5.

21. Ibid., 14.

22. Boccaccio, *Filocolo* 4.55-8.

23. Boccaccio, *Teseida*, Book 7; gloss to stanza 30.

24. Thomas Aquinas, *Summa Theologica* I, q. 81, a. 2, 3.

25. Boccaccio, *Teseida*, 1.3.

26. Boccaccio, *Genealogia Deorum*, Book 10, ch. 49.

27. Boccaccio, *Teseida*, 3.2.

28. Ibid., 12.84.

29. Ibid., 2.8.

30. Boccaccio more than hints that, like Theseus returning to Athens crowned with laurels in Statius's *Thebaid*, his *Teseida* is a poetic victory that makes him worthy to wear the conqueror's bays: 'Iamque domos patrias Scithice post aspera gentis / Proelia laurigero... curro' [And now he returns in the laurel-bearing chariot to his native land after harsh battles with the Scythian people (*Thebaid*, 12, 519–20)].) On this stanza, see also Boitani, *Chaucer and Boccaccio*, 11. At the same time, as Vittore Branca has noted, Boccaccio also drew on the *cantari*, poems in *ottava rima* performed by street singers, that were popular during the fourteenth and fifteenth century: 'Il Boccaccio del *Filostrato* e del *Teseida* e la tradizione cantarina', in *Il Cantare Trecentesco e il Boccaccio del* Filostrato *e del* Teseida (Florence: G. C. Santoni, 1936).

31. The word I've translated as 'place' is '*canto*'. Boccaccio, I think, is alluding to the mixed matter of his song, which is as much a poem about love as a poem about war.

32. This line echoes Dante's response to Francesca's lament about how Love led her and Paolo to one death: 'Oh, lasso, / quanti dolci pensier, quanto disio, / menò costoro al doloroso passo!' [O how many sweet thoughts, what great desire have brought them to this woeful pass! (*Inferno* 5. 113)].

33. As William Coleman has pointed out (with Edvige Agostinelli, 'The Knight's Tale', in *Sources and Analogues of The Canterbury Tales*, vol. II, eds. Robert M. Correale and Mary Hamel *Chaucer Studies* 35 [Cambridge: D. S. Brewer, 2005], 98), in the inventory of the Visconti library, all manuscripts of Boccaccio's works were attributed to him except the one copy of the *Filostrato* and the two copies of the *Teseida*. Chaucer most likely acquired his version of the *Teseida* when he was in Milan in 1378.

34. On Chaucer's reworking of the *Teseida*, the most extensive analysis is Boitani, *Chaucer and Boccaccio*. For an edition and translation of Chaucer's manuscript, with essential information about it, including whether it contained Boccaccio's glosses, and an analysis of Chaucer's use of it in The Knight's Tale, see William Coleman, 'The Knight's Tale', 87–247.

35. Boccaccio, *Teseida*, 11.1–3.

36. On Chaucer's repeated use of the *Teseida*, see Robert K. Pratt, 'Chaucer's Use of the *Teseida*', *PMLA* 62 (1947), 598–621.

37. Based on his study of the manuscripts, A. S. G. Edwards has raised the possibility that Anelida's complaint, which precedes the story in some early manuscripts, was composed independently from the story, which was awkwardly attached to it by scribes in the fifteenth century. Edwards has also called into question Chaucer's authorship of the narrative part of the poem. 'The Unity and Authenticity of "Anelida and Arcite": The Evidence of the Manuscripts' *Studies in Bibliography* 41 (1988), 177–188.

38. As seems almost certain. See again William Coleman's magisterial chapter on The Knight's Tale in *Sources and Analogues of The Canterbury Tales-II*, 87–247.

BIBLIOGRAPHY

Anderson, David, *Before The Knight's Tale: Imitation of Classical Epic in Boccaccio's* Teseida (Philadelphia, PA: University of Pennsylvania Press, 1988).

Boitani, Piero, *Chaucer and Boccaccio*, Medium Aevum Monographs, New Series VIII (Oxford: Society for the Study of Medieval Languages and Literature, 1977).

Coleman, William and Edvige Agostinelli, 'The Knight's Tale', in *Sources and Analogues of The Canterbury Tales*, eds. Robert M. Correale and Mary Hamel, vol. 2, *Chaucer Studies* 35 (Cambridge: D. S. Brewer, 2005), 87–247.

Edwards, Robert R., *Chaucer and Boccaccio: Antiquity and Modernity* (New York: Palgrave, 2002).

Ginsberg, Warren, *Chaucer's Italian Tradition* (Ann Arbor, MI: University of Michigan Press, 2002).

Ginsberg, Warren, *Tellers, Tales, and Translation in Chaucer's Canterbury Tales* (Oxford: Oxford University Press, 2015).

Grossvogel, Steven, *Ambiguity and Allusion in Boccaccio's Filocolo* (Firenze: L. S. Olschki, 1992).

Heliotropia, www.heliotropia.org (accessed 3 October 2019).

Hollander, Robert, *Boccaccio's Two Venuses* (New York: Columbia University Press, 1977).

Kirkham, Victoria, *Fabulous Vernacular: Boccaccio's Fiction and the Art of Medieval Fiction* (Ann Arbor, MI: University of Michigan Press, 2001).

Kirkham, Victoria, Michael Sherberg, and Janet Levarie Smarr, eds., *Boccaccio. A Critical Guide to the Complete Works* (Chicago, IL: University of Chicago Press, 2013).

McGregor, James H., *The Image of Antiquity in Boccaccio's Filocolo, Filostrato, and Teseida* (New York: P. Lang, 1990).

Smarr, Janet, *Boccaccio and Fiammetta* (Urbana and Chicago, IL: University of Illinois Press, 1986).

Wallace, David, *Chaucer and the Early Writings of Boccaccio*, Cambridge Studies 12 (Cambridge: Cambridge University Press, 1985).

CHAPTER 18

CHAUCER'S PETRARCH

'enlumyned ben they'

RONALD L. MARTINEZ

WHEN Geoffrey Chaucer, charged with commercial and diplomatic missions, travelled to Genoa and Florence in 1372–3 and to Lombardy in 1378, he likely enjoyed access to works by Francis Petrarch.[1] Perhaps equally significant was his undoubted contact with Petrarch's reputation—his *fama*. At his death in 1374, Petrarch was one of the most famous persons in Europe: surely the only minor cleric whose notoriety was comparable to that of Pope Urban IV or the Holy Roman Emperor Charles IV, both recipients of letters from Petrarch.[2] Indeed Petrarch had been famous for almost half a century, even before he orchestrated his own laureation on the Roman Campidoglio in April of 1341. The exchange between Francis of Florence and Rinaldo da Villafranca of Verona makes it clear that as early as 1336 Petrarch's political, patriotic *Epystole* 1.2 and 3 (which circulated independently of the collection of *Epystole*, completed in 1357) were read publicly in Verona: Rinaldo's verse letter touts how he and the Veronese burnish Petrarch's fame.[3] The grand Roman occasion confirmed his reputation by recognizing him as 'magnus poeta et historicus' and as a master teacher, and put him on speaking terms with King Robert of Anjou—his examiner for the honour—and on a similar footing with Cicero, the ancient Roman orator whose writings nourished Petrarch's coronation oration.[4] The honorific *poeta laureatus* accompanied Petrarch for the rest of his life, appearing boldly in the *tituli* of manuscripts containing his works,[5] so that for Chaucer Petrarch was inevitably, in the Clerk's terms, the 'lauriat poete' (CT IV.31). Petrarch's was the most prominent name among a group that included Albertino Mussato (awarded the laurel in 1315 in Padua) and Zanobi da Strada (crowned by the Emperor in Pisa, 15 May 1355); neither of Petrarch's closest competitors for poetic fame, Dante Alighieri (1265–1321) and Giovanni Boccaccio (1313–75), obtained the honour of the laurel.[6]

Fame was not only Petrarch's signal acquisition, it was his principal theme; to him fell the 'great labor...of safekeeping great fame'.[7] His collection of vernacular lyrics, *Rerum vulgarium fragmenta*, made Laura famous, though her historical identity remains obscure.[8] Numerous Latin works—the unfinished *Africa*, various editions of the *De viris illustribus*—set out to preserve the fame of Scipio Africanus the Elder 'perque ultima secula mundi' [down to the last centuries of the world].[9] and Petrarch throughout his work trumpets the achievements of Rome, most illustrious of cities.[10] In words Pietro Aretino would use of himself, but that are better applied to the laureate of 1341, in the fourteenth century it was largely because of Petrarch that fame was famous.

At the same time—and this is something Chaucer, author of the *House of Fame*, with its keen sense of the capriciousness of reputation, could well appreciate—Petrarch's greatest claim to fame was edified on shaky ground, for the principal work for which he received the laurel crown, his epic *Africa*, remained unfinished at his death: rarely has so much prestige been granted on the basis of things unseen.[11] Yet through Petrarch's *Secretum* and through Boccaccio we know that the promise of the *Africa*, the 'magnum opus et egregium' [great and outstanding work][12] that would rival the ancients, hovered for decades as a persisting mirage within Petrarch's circle. One fragment of thirty-seven lines, released without Petrarch's authorization by his friend Barbato da Sulmona, did circulate:[13] according to Petrarch, it could be found inscribed everywhere on the library portals of the learned.[14]

Just as Virgil, Lucan, Ovid, and Claudian bear up the fame of their respective subjects in the *House of Fame*, Petrarch, as chief contemporary giver and taker of fame, was one of the masters who fired Chaucer's desire to be more than a mere courtly maker.[15] In that same early work Chaucer makes Dante responsible for the fame of Hell along with the poet Claudian, and the *envoi* of *Troilus and Criseyde* commends the poem to 'be subgit to alle poesye' (5.1790) and to 'kis the steppes' of 'Stace' (1791–2) and the other great poets, echoing Dante's 'bella scola' in Limbo[16] and the account of Virgil lighting the way for Statius in *Purgatorio*.[17] The allusions are important, for although it might be just possible to discuss Chaucer's Dante and Chaucer's Boccaccio without reference to the other 'Tuscan crowns', Chaucer's Petrarch can scarcely be treated without bringing in the other two.[18]

At first glance Chaucer's reception of Petrarch appears minuscule in terms of direct textual impact: one sonnet translated in *Troilus and Criseyde* (5.400–20); a reference to him as a source for the life of Zenobia in the Monk's Tale (VII.2325–6), and in the Clerk's Tale, the acknowledged use of Petrarch's Latin version of Boccaccio's *Decameron* 10.10, the story of Valterius and Griselda. Petrarch nevertheless looms large in Chaucer's purview. Chaucer stages his references to Petrarch through fictional personae whose roles augment the textual connections: the character of Troilus, who sings the translated sonnet, revoices not only the author of lyrics in Italian *volgare*, but is also a well-programmed heroic imitator of the idolatrous lover of Laura. Chaucer's Monk, an aspiring compiler of versified tragedies, recalls Petrarch the poet-historian and *maister* of studies. The Clerk, arguably least distant from both Petrarch and Chaucer as 'worthy clerk'—Petrarch benefited from several canonries—who would 'gladly teche' (I.308), lavishly praises the Italian laureate poet.[19] It is probably coincidental that the set of roles just enumerated reiterates the honorifics *poeta*, *historicus*, and *magister* assigned to Petrarch at his crowning,[20] but it does suggest how Petrarch's fame shaped his reception.

Petrarch thus claims a limited but privileged place in Chaucer's consideration of the poets who formed him as a writer. But given the delayed appearance of both the *Africa* and the *De viris illustribus*, the chief works on which Petrarch's reputation was founded, his place is much less clearly defined than that of Dante.[21] Each of Chaucer's known Petrarchan borrowings is similarly surrounded by a penumbra of uncertainties that make it hard to know the precise contours of Chaucer's cognizance of Petrarch's texts, and even the precise shape of the texts he did know—for Petrarch often revised his works after sending them to their dedicatees. Doubt still exists, for example, whether Chaucer thought the *De casibus virorum illustrium* a work of Petrarch rather than Boccaccio.[22] Is Chaucer's version of Petrarch's poem 132 from the *Rerum vulgarium fragmenta* one he might have known, as long supposed, as an isolated poem or part of a small set of excerpts, or as included in one of the versions of the collection that circulated after about 1360? Since he drew the Clerk's story of Grisilde in the *Canterbury Tales* from Petrarch's *Seniles* 17.3, did he know *Seniles* 17.2 and 4 as well? Did he know Boccaccio's 'original', *Decameron* 10.10? To complicate matters further, several of Petrarch's best-known texts are explicitly presented as collections of fragments, so that the determination of a given Petrarchan 'text' is problematized from the start.[23] The tendency of reputation or disgrace to exceed the actuality of its origin is of course intrinsic to fame itself, as in Virgil's description of *fama*,[24] or in passages from Boethius that Chaucer knew well ('For thilke folk that ben preysed falsly, they mote nedes han schame of hire presynges' [Bo 3. pr6.10–12]). In certain respects, Chaucer's reception of Petrarch appears conditioned by the elastic relation between fame and tangible achievement that the English poet rendered as Lady Fame's arbitrary distribution of notoriety (HF 1629–30).[25]

The Monk's Tale displays the entanglement of Chaucer's Italian authors.[26] Petrarch and Dante are named and praised (VII.2325, 3652), but despite the probable indirect acknowledgement of Boccaccio represented by the *De casibus virorum illustrium* subtitle found in some manuscripts of the *Tale*, his real name goes unmentioned, as always in Chaucer's work.[27] The subtitle is suggestive: Boccaccio's *De casibus* as well as his *De mulieribus claris* represent a Petrarchan intellectual agenda insofar as they are works of Latin humanist scholarship that preserve the fame, for good or ill, of ancients and moderns. For both works, Dante and Petrarch are Boccaccio's preceptors and guiding lights:[28] Dante (dead since 1321) appears in *De casibus* as a victim of ill fortune, exiled but unbowed;[29] Petrarch, still living, appears girt with the laurel to Boccaccio-author in the preface to Book Eight of the same work in order to re-energize his disciple's scholarly vocation, which alone brings 'glory' and the 'second life' that is fame at its best. If Dante instructs Boccaccio regarding subject-matter, Petrarch's cameo marks him as the chief inspiration for the project, just as Boccaccio's reference to Petrarch's *De viris illustribus* in beginning *De mulieribus claris* yields precedence to the laureate as a preserver of the fame of illustrious men (Petrarch excluded women from his collection).

Boccaccio's list of Fortune's victims and the Monk's share names in common, but Chaucer follows Boccaccio closely only in the life of Zenobia, the third-century CE queen of Palmyra who dared rise against Rome,[30] which draws from Chapter 100 of *De mulieribus claris*, but concludes with an excerpt drawn from Boccaccio's conclusion to her biography in *De casibus*.[31] The sixteen stanzas dedicated to Zenobia make hers the longest and most elaborate of the Monk's seventeen exemplary stories. The stanza concluding her *vita* marks the halfway point of the *Tale*, reflecting the queen's position as the last antique example in Boccaccio's *De mulieribus claris*, after which Boccaccio skips eight centuries and turns to names familiar to him from … Dante's poem; a similar strategy governs *De casibus*.[32] Given that Petrarch himself is described by Boccaccio as one of the 'viri illustri' of antiquity, Zenobia's placement is likely to be in recognition of Petrarch's humanist purism.[33]

Dante for his part supplies the source for the Monk's tale of Hugelyn (2407–62). The death of Dante's Count Ugolino della Gherardesca occurred in 1289, only a decade prior to the ideal date of the poet's journey to the afterlife (1300). Chaucer's special indebtedness to Dante—the Hugelyn stanzas are Chaucer's sole rewriting of an episode of the *Commedia*[34]—probably results from Dante's appearance in *De casibus* to insist that Giovanni write about Walter of Brienne, Duke of Athens, the tyrant expelled from Florence in 1343, a nearly contemporary event for both Boccaccio *and* Chaucer. Boccaccio's use in both *De mulieribus claris* and *De casibus* of names out of Dante to mark chronological jumps to the contemporaneous is thus the germ for the Monk's inclusion of modern instances.[35] Such inclusion also sharply distinguishes Boccaccio's compilation from that of Petrarch, who refused to place any moderns in *De viris illustribus*, even against the suggestion of admirers.[36] Thus Boccaccio stages the debate about ancients and moderns through his two guides, Dante and Petrarch.

The Monk's inclusion of modern instances thus involves all three Italian writers.[37] The life of Zenobia that the Monk attributes to Petrarch's learning marks the locus for insertion of the modern instances in the majority of Chaucer manuscripts, when they are not placed last: both positions are of course emphatic.[38] The majority order, with the modern instances directly following Zenobia's life, suggests a face-off or *paragone* between Petrarch and Dante. In the minority, Ellesmere manuscript order, the 'Petrarchan' Zenobia still occupies the mid-point, but Chaucer's account of Hugelyn becomes the final episode,[39] so that the Monk's Tale ends by affirming Dante's mastery as the infallible *auctor*[40] who can fill in Hugelyn's story in exhaustive detail, 'fro point to point' (VII.2462).[41] Such seamlessness contrasts with the Monk's report on Petrarch's knowledge: 'How that she was biseged and ytake – / Lat hym unto my maister Petrak go, / that writ ynough of this, I undertake' (2324–6). The lines reflect Boccaccio's frequent naming of Petrarch as *praeceptor*, and refer to Petrarch's ability, invoked at the end of *De casibus*, to supply what is lacking ('ut suppleatur quod omissum sit').[42] In the Monk's 'ynough' lurks Boccaccio's concession that Petrarch's *De viris illustribus* is more copious than his own works ('latiori … volumine'),[43] but the word might also hint that despite Petrarch's ample authority, its contours remain blurred.

The assembled influences of the Tuscan crowns in a tale where the genre is tragedy also thrusts the Monk into the midst of some daunting potential comparisons.[44] The Monk interprets the genre in the Boethian terms of a happy beginning and terrible end ('Of hym that stood in greet prosperitee, / And is yfallen out of heigh degree / Into myserie, and endeth wrecchedly' [1975–7]),[45] but the fact that he mentions tragedies in heroic verse (*exametron*) invokes classical epics in hexameters, such as Virgil's *Aeneid* (viewed by Dante as an 'alta ... tragedía')[46] and Statius's *Thebaid*, the fount for Boccaccio's *Teseida* and Chaucer's Knight's Tale.[47] Even parts of the book of Job, echoed in the Monk's episode of Hugelyn, were in medieval exegesis thought of as heroic poetry in hexameters;[48] while the Monk's branding of his account of Hugelyn as a 'tragedye'[49]—the only episode thus distinguished—reflects Chaucer's understanding of Dante's *Inferno* as a series of tragic episodes.[50]

In combining pretensions both poetic and historical, the Monk distantly honours the humanist criteria of Petrarchism: the Romans Lucan, a historical poet, and Suetonius, a historian, are invoked as authorities for the ruin of Caesar and Pompey (2719–23).[51] But the Monk's 'tragedyes' begin with Lucifer and Adam and do not adopt the artificial order Horatian literary theory prescribes for narrative epic:[52] the attempt at reinventing classical epic that was Petrarch's *Africa* remains outside his ken. On the other hand, in his role as tragedian the Monk (and his creator, Chaucer), while 'bewailling' the deceitfulness of Fortuna, surely recalls how Boethius' 'tragedian',[53] decries the effects of glory and fame.[54] This is especially evident when the Monk remarks the 'laude and heigh renoun' (2096) of Hercules and the 'glorie and ... delit' Nebuchadnezzar enjoys before his fall (2150),[55] putting a different slant on *fama* than the one Petrarch commends when stimulating Boccaccio in *De casibus*.[56]

Chaucer's other excursion into 'tragedye' is his ambitious narrative poem *Troilus and Criseyde*, an adaptation and magnification of Boccaccio's *Filostrato*. Troilus's arduously pursued affair with Criseyde begins in love-madness, and despondency comes of it in the end; at a critical juncture in the narrative Troilus himself must 'biwaill' his condition. An argument can be made that Chaucer expressed Troilus both ensnared by love and beset by disillusion with texts adapted from lyrics of Petrarch, making the Trojan prince the first heroic 'Petrarchan' lover in European literature.

The first adaptation is marked in some *Troilus* manuscripts as the first *Cantus* or *Canticus Troili*, an unattributed translation of Petrarch's *Rerum vulgarium fragmenta* 132, set in the narrative just after Troilus has been smitten by Criseyde (Tr 1.400–20). Once thought a misconstruction, Chaucer's decision to have the first line signify 'If no such thing as love exists', rather than identifying Love as the cause of what the lover feels—as Petrarch's line is usually read—is now taken to be a canny adaptation.[57] As a statement about the existence of love itself, Troilus's first line, 'If no love is, O God, what fele I so?' (1.400) evokes a topos that originates in the opening definitions of Andreas Capellanus' preface to his treatise on courtly love, *De amore*: 'Amor quid sit?' [What is love?].[58] The question is later taken up as a topic of debate in Italian vernacular lyrics.[59] In light of these traditions, Troilus's first lyric outburst synthesizes French theory and Italian practice.

Troilus's preparation for his *canticus* is elaborate, concluding a meditation over the five preceding stanzas, and the narrator affirms that the lyric is a word-for-word translation that amplifies the mere 'sentence', the unadorned meaning, found in his source, Lollius (that is, Boccaccio, again obscured). Chaucer even inserts a deictic gesture ('Loo, next this vers he may it fynden here', [1.399]), as if a *manicula* alerting copyists to the place where the lyric begins: testimony to Chaucer's high valuation of the sonnet he is moving into English, and perhaps of the boldness of his forgery in replacing Boccaccio's source text with one by Petrarch, without acknowledging its author.

Different procedures govern each stanza of Chaucer's expansion.[60] The first four lines of the first stanza follow Petrarch's first quatrain closely, but thereafter Chaucer adds lines, not found in Petrarch, which frame Troilus's desire in terms at once sensual (Love's adversities are 'savory') and suggestive of a spiritual thirst ('For ay thurst I, the more that ich it drynke' [1.406]).[61] These lines gloss that amatory idolatry defined by Andreas Capellanus, richly documented in Petrarch's poems to Laura, into which Troilus has just entered.[62] In the third stanza the English poet follows Petrarch, but by end-stopping the overrunning topic in the middle of the rhyme royal stanza's second line, and inserting the logical connective 'Thus'—with no counterpart in Petrarch—Chaucer sharpens the syllogistic and narrative force of the sonnet: most important, he emphasizes the turn to the nautical metaphor, and Troilus's conflicted state 'Amydde the see, bitwixen wyndes two'—a line that sums up the previous stanzas' debate:[63]

> And if that I consente, I wrongfully
> Compleyne, iwis. Thus possed to and fro,
> Al stereless withinne a boot am I
> Amydde the see, bitwixen wyndes two,
> That in contrarie stonden evere mo.   (Tr 1.414–18)

This turn is further framed by the insertion of a medical diagnosis non-existent in Petrarch ('what is this wondre maladie?' [419]) to open the final couplet, thus providing a rationale for the 'Petrarchan' antitheses of heat and cold, to which Troilus attributes lethal power ('For hote of cold...I dye' [420]). The reprise of the first stanza's interrogative mood ties the three stanzas together, explaining the thirsting and drinking of the first stanza and Troilus's languor ('that I feynte' [410]) in the second: all recognizable as medical symptoms of love-melancholy, *amor hereos*.[64] The nautical metaphor, and the account of Troilus's love as a malady, prepare for later developments.

Admired as well as criticized, Chaucer's translation of *Rerum vulgarium fragmenta* 132 has also been held by most Chaucer scholars as an isolated incident: the sole textual trace of Petrarch's vernacular lyrics in Chaucer's work, and the sole translation into English of Petrarch until the Tudor versions of Wyatt and Surrey.[65] But at least one student of Chaucer, Tom Stillinger, makes the argument that the third of Troilus's lyric passages (marked *canticus Troili* in some manuscripts), which renders Troilus's meditation on Criseyde's absence in the fifth book, should be seen as inspired by a Petrarchan sonnet, *Rerum vulgarium fragmenta* 189, 'Passa la nave mia colma d'oblio', later translated by Wyatt as 'My galley charged with forgetfulness'. Stillinger's analysis of this third *canticus* associates the scarcely coherent sequence of topics in Troilus's song, and its scrambled representation of Petrarch's presumed original, with Troilus's psychic disintegration and with the emphasis in *Troilus* on instability as a theme.[66]

The fertile premise of Stillinger's argument is the probability that Chaucer knew not an isolated sonnet of Petrarch, but a 'complete' version of *Rerum vulgarium fragmenta* (which will henceforth be referred to in this chapter as '*Rvf*'). This was perhaps a manuscript of the Chigi (1357–63?) or the Malatesta (1373), or a final version (Vat. lat. 3195), since Chaucer's text of sonnet 132 had the reading consistent with these of the seventh line ('O quike deth' [1.411]), translates 'O viva morte', which is 'o vita o morte' in other versions).[67] That *Rvf* 189 concludes the first part of the Chigi collection, and in that version caps a series including the motif of travel,[68] might have made the sonnet stand out for Chaucer, who in Book Five treats of Troilus suffering Criseyde's removal from Troy. Just as important, *Rvf* 132 and 189 are themselves closely related: although the nautical metaphor is frequent in Petrarch's collection,[69] in the case of *Rvf* 132 and 189 the parallels are tightly coordinated:[70]

> O sterre, of which I lost have al the light,
> With herte soor wel oughte I to biwaille,
> That evere derk in torment, nyght by nyght,
> Toward my deth with wynd in steere I saille;
> For which the tenthe nyght, if that I faille
> The gydyng of thi bemes bright an houre,
> My ship and me Caribdis will devoure.   (5.638–644)

Charged with forgetfulness in one case and with error in the other, the speaker-lover's 'single state of man' risks destruction because of winter, winds, error, high seas, and most critically, the misdirection or lack of its steering oar, its *governo*. *Rvf* 132 has no mention of the lady's eyes as guiding stars, but 'i duo miei dolci usati segni' are mentioned in *Rvf* 189: and the latter sonnet also has the reference to *Caribdi*, in Latinate spelling, retained in the *canticus* as the agent of Troilus's destruction.[71]

The third *canticus Troili* has a much briefer preparation than the first (just one stanza) and is explicitly brief ('of wordes but a fewe' [633]); yet it is equally 'Petrarchan', perhaps even more so, for if the first sonnet comes to occupy three stanzas through *amplificatio*, *abbreviatio* diminishes the second to a quatrain and a tercet syntactically linked, thus a half-sonnet (the tangled logic of the fragment results in part from this).[72] Both procedures have mimetic force: his heart swelling with love, Troilus augments his source; when his spirit contracts in despair, the shrunken third *canticus* mirrors his crumbling confidence in his beloved: the word is 'cosyn to the dede' (1.742). Formal mimesis is also at work, for Chaucer has composed a sonnet *fragment*, as if taking Petrarch at his word when he entitled his first published collection *Fragmentorum liber*.[73]

If the first *canticus* displays a Chaucerian innovation in its first line, the second *canticus* contains in its last line a bold departure from *Rvf* 189. The poem ends with 'devour', a word absent from Petrarch's lyrics: for a precedent we must go to Dante, whose Hell-bottom swallows the damned ('il fondo che le mal anime *divora*').[74] Both the idolatrous apostrophe to Criseyde as a guiding star, and the fear of destruction body and soul, reflect Chaucer's intensification of Petrarch's tempered lyric diction to render Troilus's peril: as Criseyde's lover sings his *canticus*, he risks a narrative future like that of Dante's Ulysses, devoured by the sea, finally by Hell.[75]

The plurality of lyric borrowings is itself significant. Petrarch's lyrics in *Rvf* are explicitly described as an anthology of scattered lyric fragments ('rime sparse'), and Chaucer's poem translates a work by Boccaccio, *Filostrato*, that is itself textured with lyric insets, so that it has appeared to readers as a hybrid of lyrics and narrative.[76] Significantly, additional 'lyric' segments in *Troilus* are abundant in the same regions of the poem as the Petrarchan borrowings, though only in Chaucer's poem are *both* moments marked with a *canticus*, for there is none after the first scene in *Filostrato*.[77] Troilus's first *canticus* is followed by his submission to the god of Love, three stanzas that seem like another song, and which in some manuscripts excerpting the *canticus* were joined to the Petrarchan material.[78]

The context of the third *Canticus Troili* is even richer in lyric patches: *Troilus* 5.561–81, recalls, in a series of clauses beginning with or using *yonder*, Troilus's meetings with Criseyde, including his first sight of her ('And in that temple . . . Me kaughte first my righte lady dere' [566–7]), the occasion of the first *canticus*, as well as his winning of her ('in that yonder place / My lady first me took unto hire grace' [580–1]). The equivalent passage in Boccaccio's *Filostrato* has five iterations of *quivi* [here], four of *colà* [there], and one of *là*, and has been rightly placed in relation to *Rvf* 112, recalling Laura with ten iterations of *qui*: '*qui* tutta umile, et *qui* la vidi altera' [*here* I saw her all humble, and *there* haughty]. If Chaucer handled a copy of Petrarch's songbook, he might well have noted the resemblances; it is striking that although both Petrarch and Troilus recall their ladies singing ('Qui cantò dolcemente'; 'with vois melodious / Syngen so wel' [577–8]) Boccaccio's Troilo does not remember his lady in this way.[79] Troilus's systematic recollection of Criseyde's image is an exercise that echoes Petrarch's dwelling on Laura 'dolce ne la memoria' in such cardinal texts as *Rvf* 126.41 (which has verbal parallels with *Rvf* 112).

In addition to the multiple lyric occasions leading up to Troilus's last *canticus*,[80] the immediate framing of the lyric insert displays a rich sampling of Petrarchan topics and phrasing: just before beginning his song Troilus 'swich lif right gan he lede / As he that stood bitwixen hope and drede' (5.629–30). Echoing 'bitwixen wyndes two' in the first *canticus*, these lines find no close counterpart in *Filostrato*; but *Rvf* 134.2 and 14, following hard on 132, offers: 'e temo e spero; et ardo, et son un ghiaccio / . . . / in questo stato son, donna, per voi' [and I fear and hope, and burn and am of ice. . . In this state am I, Lady, on account of you]. Troilus would by singing 'his woful herte for to lighte' (5.634), but where Boccaccio's Troilo sings 'alcuna sosta al dolor dando' [giving pause to the pain] Petrarch claims in *Rvf* 293.10 that his intent was 'pur di disfogare il doloroso core' [only to give vent to my sorrowing heart]. After the *canticus*, Troilus's comment on the breeze from the Greek camp, 'this eyr, that is so soote / That in my soule I fele it doth me boote' (5.671–72) might evoke *Rvf* 109.7–9: 'The gentle breeze [l'aura soave] that moves from her bright face. . . always in that air [quell'aere] seems to comfort me'. Boccaccio mentions wind, but not air: '. . . that which he felt blowing [soffiarsi] on his face, he believed to be the sighs Criseida sent [mandati sospiri]'.[81] That Petrarch's text might be implicit in the 'eyr' wafting from the Greek camp is suggestive, since the *aura/Laura* pun, entwined with reference to Petrarch's distinctive laurel (*lauro*), constellates the *Rvf*.[82] As Chaucer's eagle contends in the *House of Fame*, 'eyr' is the very substance of *fama*.[83]

No doubt verbal and narrative parallels to the preceding examples can be found, if not in the same passages of Boccaccio's *Filostrato*, then elsewhere in that work, and they are in any case topoi of courtly poetry. Such objections are especially valid in light of the fact that Petrarch may have read *Filostrato*, composed as early as 1336, during his first visit to Naples, making Boccaccio's narrative an early influence on Petrarch, rather than vice-versa.[84] But if Chaucer adapted both *Rvf* 132 and 189, the hypothesis of direct Petrarchan influence becomes more attractive. Where do we draw the boundary between Boccaccian and Petrarchan influences in *Troilus*?[85] It may be, again, that for Chaucer Petrarch's greater fame tips the scales.[86] David Wallace takes the winds tugging at Troilus in his first *canticus* to be Chaucer's Italian masters Boccaccio and Petrarch: this makes Troilus's stanzas the earliest contested ground of the attributional debate itself.[87]

Petrarch's lyrics serve Chaucer's narrative of Criseyde's inconstancy; in The Clerk's Tale, a verse translation of Petrarch's Latin prose translation of Boccaccio's Italian prose *novella* (*Decameron* 10.10), Chaucer offers an extensive and complex treatment of a work by Petrarch where constancy (and perhaps obstinacy) reign supreme.[88] All three forms of the story are difficult for readers and challenging to the interpreter, in part because the humbly-born Griselda's patience before her noble husband's repeated testing of her is itself so extreme.[89] The unrealistic excesses may derive from the story's origin in the late antique Cupid and Psyche story,[90] and from allusive relations to other narratives of extremity: one is the biblical story of Job, with its powerful interrogation of theodicy, and another is Dante's account of Ugolino—one of the Monk's 'tragedyes'—that all but concludes *Inferno* with a glimpse of inhuman cruelty.[91]

In taking up *Seniles* 17.3, containing the story of Valterius and Grisildis, which circulated independently of Petrarch's last collection of letters,[92] Chaucer read an extreme work in the chronological sense, for Petrarch died upon finishing *Seniles* 17.4. Chaucer also knew from Petrarch's prefatory remarks to the translation that Boccaccio had written the original vernacular *novella*, the last (the extreme) part of a much larger book.[93] Although Chaucer's direct knowledge of *Decameron* 10.10, the novella of Gualtieri and Griselda narrated by Dioneo, the most subversive of the *Decameron*'s ten fictional storytellers, has not been conclusively shown,[94] Chaucer's possible use of it will be entertained in these remarks in order to assess the entanglement of Chaucer's Italian authors in what has been called 'the Griselda intertext'.[95]

The *novella*, the epistle and the tale all present Griselda as an unapproachable example: for Dioneo she is a divine spirit descended to earth, unique in her heroism;[96] for Petrarch, her lofty example is not directed to wives, but a stimulus for men to bear God's testing patiently;[97] for the Clerk, who repeats Petrarch's *moralitee*, Grisilde's virtue exceeds the reach of present-day wives. Her humility and obedience recall the Annunciate Virgin, and the Clerk has her dwelling in 'an oxes stalle' like the manger of Christ's Nativity (IV.207, 397–99).[98] That all the versions also bear an allegorical charge is assured by the persisting allusion to Job 1:21 ('Naked came I out of mother's womb, and naked shall I return thither: the Lord gave, and the Lord hath taken away') which Chaucer could observe emerging with increasing clarity from *novella* (*Decameron* 10.10.45) to epistle (*Seniles*. 17.3.30): the Clerk perfects the citation, adds one of his own (Job 3:3) and then mentions Job explicitly (IV.871–3, 901–3, 931–2), a reference 'clerkes' like him would make.[99] To clerks and their readers, Job was exemplary of the human soul seeking to justify God's way to man, and of everyman facing death; in his patient suffering, he was a figure of Christ.[100]

The kernel of the story is a test of faith, a *probatio fidei* (James 1:3). Mazzotta writes that 'Petrarch makes of the ordeal of Griselda and the cruel arbitrariness of [Boccaccio's] Gualtieri the allegory of the soul tested by God'.[101] The Job allusion is central to all versions because the soul's nudity at birth and death and before God's absolute power ('The Lord giveth, the Lord taketh away') informs the crucial scenes of Griselda re-vested at her new spouse's command.[102] Stripped of her rough garb and clothed as a noblewoman, only to be again stripped—after the removal of her two children under false pretences— and sent back to her father's house clad only in a shift (*camisia*), Griselda's ordeal confronts the reader with a dilemma: if the tale represents God's testing of the human soul, then it seems God rewards human merit with callous cruelty; but if we accept Dioneo's view that Gualtieri (and Valterius and Walter) is monstrous, then the harmony of Walter's aristocratic world with the designs of Providence is nullified, and the allegory breaks down.[103]

Griselda's second stripping, and her re-expedition to her father to resume what Boccaccio calls her 'Romagnole motley'[104] is also at the core of Petrarch's metanarrative because it articulates the no less asymmetrical relationship of Petrarch and Boccaccio that Chaucer could observe in the preface to *Seniles* 17.3. Petrarch's offer to let Boccaccio judge whether he has disfigured or adorned the story ('an mutata veste deformaverim an fortassis ornaverim, tu iudica')[105] means he thinks of the story as Griselda herself. In translating the story, as in Walter's translation of Grisilde, Petrarch clothes it in the literary Latin that had made him celebrated among his contemporaries.[106] His claim that in sending the translation he 'returns' the Griselda story to Boccaccio, henceforth to be responsible for her fortunes, is therefore deeply disingenuous.[107] Significantly, Petrarch does not transmit Dioneo's insistence that Griselda's virtue shines even through her ragged *pannicelli*,[108] and since Griselda's father's name can be read as a diminutive of Giovanni, Boccaccio's first name, for Petrarch going to her father's house could in metanarrative terms only mean that the tale returns to the poverty of Boccaccio's vernacular original.[109] Although Chaucer likely did not know directly the vernacular Tuscan lyric convention by which poets sent texts to each other for completion (either by adding music, or offering an interpretation), as in the text described as a 'pulzelletta nuda' [naked virgin] that Dante sends to an unknown interlocutor, the minor lyric genre neatly parallels how Griselda is 'textualized' as the Italian *novella* passes into Petrarch's Latin epistle and, through the Clerk's translation, into a humble English vernacular.[110] The Clerk's sense of what is at stake in the story's linguistic dress is evident in his restoration of Boccaccio's emphasis—absent in Petrarch—on Griselda's intrinsic virtue despite her external trappings (IV.918–31),[111] and in the Clerk's ambivalence about the 'heigh stile' that he identifies as the mark of Petrarch's Latin ('in heigh stile he enditeth' [IV.41]).[112] The ambivalence is especially pointed regarding the resonant period beginning Petrarch's tale, which describes in Virgil-saturated Latin how the noble and majestic Po, king of rivers, spreads out as it descends with violent impetus to the Adriatic: in metanarrative terms, the period is designed to drown out Italian vernacular eloquence with Latin, even as the regality of the river warrants the feudal nobility of the Marquess of Saluzzo.[113] Suspicious of this aristocratic exordial display and its hegemonic claims, the Clerk deems the period 'impertinent'.

Most of all, Chaucer could have seen—and this has been the other central preoccupation of criticism—how the interactions of his Italian authors in the Griselda intertext not only offer opportunities for interpretation, but imply a series of debates.[114] Dioneo's treatment of Gualtieri—who is the tale's undoubted protagonist according to Boccaccio's rubric—not as a *magnifico*, but as a *bestia*, means that the *novella* is in polemical non-conformity with *Decameron* Day 10, on which Panfilo, the king for the day, requires the narration of magnificent gestures. At day's end, the ladies of the storytelling *brigata* are divided in their estimations of Gualtieri's cruel experiment, an idea Petrarch adapts in *Seniles* 17.4 by setting up two readers, one overcome by Griselda's patience, one sceptical of its credibility.[115] More generally, Petrarch uses his version to blunt Dioneo's criticism of Gualtieri, and validate Valterius's claim of ultimately benign intentions:[116] all of which is then undermined in Chaucer's Tale by the Clerk's critiques of Walter's behaviour (IV.78–80, 456–62, 619–23).

Petrarch's imposition of Latin and the ripostes within and between the versions of the Griselda intertext may also be viewed in the context of the apportionment of *fama*. Boccaccio's introduction to the Ninth Day[117] celebrates the tale-telling *brigata* itself; Petrarch, in accord with his humanist program, enrols Griselda among renowned classical female martyrs to marital fidelity.[118] In Petrarch's version, Griselda's *fama* spreads beyond the marquisate: admirers are drawn from afar in terms that recall Laura's fame as proclaimed in *Rvf* 248, an emphasis that is maintained in Chaucer's translation (IV.418–20, 428–41)[119] Even Job is famous, because 'Men speke of Job' (IV.932).[120] But Chaucer's Clerk underlines Gualtieri's infamy: what for Dioneo is a poor *reputazione*[121] that brings down blame on him ('biasimo') as a cruel man ('crudele uomo'), is for Petrarch's Valterius the 'decolor fama' [stained reputation] that renders him 'infamous and hateful',[122] and is then magnified by the Clerk as the 'sclaundre of Walter…wyde yspradde' and the 'sclaundre of his diffame' (IV.722, 730), an estimation that the Clerk privately shares ('yvele it sit'[IV.460]). Heaping praise on Grisilde and blame on Walter, Chaucer adapts to new circumstances the opposition of 'Clere Laude' and 'Sklaundre' capriciously assigned by the Queen of Fame (HF 1575, 80).[123]

In the authorial metanarrative, *fama* is also at stake: since a Latin vesture will open the work to non-Italian readers ('nostri etiam sermonis ignaros'),[124] Petrarch offers his translation to Boccaccio as likely to increase its fame; it is also notorious, Petrarch insists, that Griselda's proper home is with Boccaccio ('Nota domus, notum iter').[125] But after belittling the book as an unserious, juvenile work which he has hardly read, except for the beginning and the end, it becomes clear that the translation of Griselda's story—the one part of the *Decameron* Petrarch considers worth preserving—is designed rather to aggrandize his own reputation. Although Petrarch's Latin version did paradoxically function as a kind of vulgarization, disseminating the story as he claimed it would,[126] his celebrity ensured that the story began to circulate in European humanist circles not as Boccaccio's work, but as Petrarch's.[127] Petrarch's selection of a single tale fragments Boccaccio's beautifully finished book: even this procedure, congenial to the author of scattered lyrics ('rime sparse'),[128] accrued fame to Petrarch, as it fostered the Renaissance fashion for the single *novella* detached from a framing narrative.[129]

Chaucer's additions to Petrarch's version, especially the Clerk's qualification that Griseldas are no more to be found, and the virtuosic added stanzas for the 'archewyves' (IV.1195), significantly referred to as a *canticum* or *cantus* in numerous manuscripts,[130] waggishly encouraging seizure of the *governaille*, appear to resume Dioneo's contentious voice, and suggest a 'dialogic' framing of the tale's possibilities more consistent with the *novella* than with Petrarch's translation.[131] The Clerk's answer to the Wyf of Bath ('for the Wyves love of Bathe' [IV.1170]) extends the dialogic principle to the exchanges between pilgrims. Chaucer's rendering of Petrarch's Latin prose narrative into English rhyme royal stanzas also endows the story with a formal dignity Petrarch left it without, while robing it in a *sermo humilis* suited to the poverty Boccaccio praises in Griselda rather than the high estate, and 'heigh stile' to which Valterius translates her.[132] Still, although the Clerk, in asserting that he 'lerned' the tale directly from Petrarch the 'worthy clerk' (IV.27), assimilates Petrarch's claim to have memorized Boccaccio's tale and related it to his friends,[133] he also deletes Boccaccio from the chain of transmission: thus Chaucer completes Petrarch's strategy for diminishing Boccaccio's authorship.[134]

Indeed, Chaucer so greatly bears up the fame of Petrarch that he makes him the sole modern secular author named (and twice!) as a source or model for one of the *Canterbury Tales*.[135] Though sometimes dismissed as merely conventional, the Clerk's praise of Petrarch, as Boitani observed,[136] is the most fervent tribute to another poet in Chaucer's oeuvre: 'Fraunceys Petrak, the lauriat poete,/Highte this clerk, whos rethorike sweete/ Enlumyned al Ytaille of poetrie (IV.31–3).[137] The registration of the poet's name, followed by mention of the laurel, echoes the *tituli* of Petrarch's manuscripts, and is an implicit claim that Chaucer had seen some of them. It can also be thought of as a writerly supplement to the Clerk's assertion that the story was transmitted orally by Petrarch himself. The emphasis on all Italy, and the designation of Italy—not Saluces, or 'West Lumbardye' (IV.46)—as Grisilde's place of burial may also imply that the Clerk's praise is of a sort that Chaucer, a poet with his own national ambitions, would have wished, *mutatis mutandis*, to be made of himself. This wish the poet John Lydgate fulfilled in dubbing Chaucer the virtual laureate of England ('worthy was the laurer for to have/of poetrye'). With 'Chaucer is deed', Lydgate also echoed Chaucer's obituaries for both Petrarch ('...deed and nayled in his cheste' [IV.29]) and Griselda ('Grisilde is deed and...buryed in Ytaille' [IV.1177–8]).[138] Although the Clerk consigns the crowned Italian poet firmly to the past, the confinement does not diminish him: from Lydgate's perspective, the reputations of Petrarch, Griselda, and Chaucer are closely linked, and all enjoy the fame that in Petrarch's formulation draws the dead from their graves[139] and provides a 'quasi vita alia' [second life].[140] Indeed, the Clerk's use of the blink of an eye to define the brevity of life in the same passage caps the tale's meditation on mutability (IV.29–38, 115–26) by pointing to the Pauline text on the dead changed 'in ictu oculi' [in the blink of an eye] and clothed with the glorious bodies of the Resurrection.[141] Earthly fame may be 'translated' into glory.

The encomiastic force of the passage may be still stronger, for there is a possible echo in these lines of Petrarch's first bucolic eclogue, *Parthenias*, regarding the epic poets whom Silvius, Petrarch's pastoral alter ego in this poem, wishes to emulate: 'tum silvas et rura canunt atque arma virosque / Et totum altisonis illustrant versibus orbem' [they sing forest and field and arms and men, and embellish the whole world with high resounding verses].[142] The transfusion into the line of the woods, fields, and weaponry of the medieval canon of Virgil's works (*Eclogues, Georgics,* and *Aeneid*) along with part of the celebrated opening of the *Aeneid* ('Arma virumque...') clearly points to Virgil as the chief exemplar. If Chaucer knew these lines—and he could have, as the *Bucolicum Carmen* circulated after 1359[143]—then Petrarch is the more magnified in being implicitly included alongside Virgil among poets who light the world with their verses.

Still, by praising Petrarch in terms borrowed from Dante, 'the grete poete of Ytaille', Chaucer hedges his bets on who is the more famous and authoritative poet. Well informed about painters' colours thanks to his commercial experience, Chaucer was likely sensitive to Dante's use of the Italian word corresponding to *enlumyne*, and of the same implicit codicological metaphor,[144] when discussing the relative fame of poets and painters in *Purgatorio.* There, on the terrace for correcting pride, Dante has Oderisi da Gubbio speak of manuscript illumination as 'quell'arte *ch'alluminar* si chiama in Parigi'.[145] For Dante, renown is both noise *and* light: it resounds for Giotto but darkens for Cimabue ('la fama di colui è scura').[146] Chaucer was, we saw, also keenly aware of Dante's account of how Virgil enlightened Statius and precipitated his conversion with the words of the Fourth Eclogue,[147] which includes Dante's only other use of the verb: 'prima appresso dio *m'alluminasti*':[148] here too, a continuity between fame and glory is implied. That the passage in *Purgatorio* 11 treats nevertheless of the perishability of artistic fame and the perils of artistic pride makes it a suitable allusive context for the solemn and complex moment when one poet endows another with lasting fame.

NOTES

1. On Chaucer's travels and contacts with Italy and Italians, see R. A. Pratt, 'Chaucer and the Visconti Libraries', *English Literary History* 6 (1939), 191–9; Wendy Childs, 'Anglo-Italian Contact in the Fourteenth Century', in *Chaucer and the Italian Trecento,* ed. Piero Boitani (Cambridge: Cambridge University Press, 1983), 65–87; Derek Pearsall, *Life of Chaucer* (London: Blackwell, 1992), 103–9; David Wallace, *Chaucerian Polity: Absolutist Lineages and Associational forms in England and Italy* (Stanford, CA: Stanford University Press, 1997), 1–28; Warren Ginsberg, *Chaucer's Italian Tradition* (Ann Arbor, MI: University of Michigan Press, 2002), 144–7; Nick Havely, 'The Italian Background', in *Chaucer: An Oxford Guide,* ed. Steve Ellis (New York: Oxford University Press, 2005), 315–17; William T. Rossiter, *Chaucer and Petrarch* (Cambridge: D.S. Brewer, 2010), 38–44.

2. See for example Petrarch's *Epystole* 1.3, 2.5; *Familiares* 10.1; *Seniles*.7.1; Petrarch was indeed one who 'to kynges write' (Clerk's Tale IV.18; see Rossiter, *Chaucer and Petrarch,* 50).

3. Michele Feo, 'La prima corrispondenza poetica fra Rinaldo da Villafranca e Francesco Petrarca', *Quaderni Petrarcheschi* 4 (1987), see 25: '...iam fama per urbem / est vaga, censeris iamque poeta novus'. In his answer to Rinaldo (lines 21–2), Petrarch held him worthy of the laurel (Feo, 'La prima corrispondenza poetica', 21). Boccaccio refers to Petrarch's *Epystole* 1.2 in his life of Petrarch; see *De vita et moribus Domini Francisci Petracchi de Florentia secundum Iohenem Bochacci de Certaldo* in *Epistole e lettere* ed. and trans. Ginetta Auzzas, in eds. Vittore Branca et al., *Tutte le opere di Giovanni Boccaccio,* 10 vols. (Milan: Mondadori, 1992),

5.1:898–911, 900–1, and see note 11, 950. Petrarch recalls his own widespread fame in *Epystole* 1.70-2 (in Francesco Petrarca, *Poesie latine*, eds. Guido Martellotti and Enrico Bianchi [Milan: Einaudi, 1976], 86).

4. The titles were conferred with the *privilegium lauree* granted to Petrarch along with the laurel crown. On the laureation ceremony, see E. H. Wilkins, *The Making of the Canzoniere and other Petrarchan Studies* (Rome: Edizioni di storia e letteratura, 1951), 9–69; Sara Sturm-Maddox, 'Dante, Petrarch, and the Laurel Crown', in *Petrarch and Dante: Anti-Dantism, Metaphysics, Tradition*, eds. Zygmunt G Barański and Theodore J. Cachey, Jr (Notre Dame, IN: University of Notre Dame Press, 2009), 290-319; Ronald G. Musto, *Apocalypse in Rome* (Berkeley, CA: University of California Press, 2003), 54-6. On the oration, see Dennis Looney, 'The Beginnings of Humanistic Oratory: Petrarch's *Coronation Oration*', in *Petrarch: A Critical Guide to the Complete Works*, eds. Victoria Kirkham and Armando Maggi (Chicago, IL: University of Chicago Press, 2009), 131-40. Petrarch describes his laureation in *Familiares* 3.2-8; *Bucolicum carmen* 3; *Epystole* 2.1; *Africa*, 9.398-402, *Posteritati* (*Seniles* 18.1.26-30), and *Rerum vulgarium fragmenta* 119.102-105; he also recalls it at *Familiares* 17.2.26-27, sent to Boccaccio. King Robert granted Petrarch a ceremonial cloak that Boccaccio sees on Petrarch ('regio amictum pallio') in *De casibus* 8.1.5. Warren Ginsberg notes that Petrarch is there addressed in terms of Dante's Cato in *Chaucer's Italian Tradition* (Ann Arbor, MI: University of Michigan Press, 2002), 204-5.

5. See for example the Chigi manuscript of the *Canzoniere*, 'Viri illustris atque poete celeberrimi francisci petrarce de florentia rome nuper laureati fragmentorum liber incipit feliciter' and the *Compendium* of the *De viris illustribus* finished by Lombardo della Seta and released in 1379, 'Francisci petrarce poete laureati quorumdam clarissimum heroum...epithoma' (illustrated in Michele Feo, ed., *Petrarca nel tempo. Tradizione lettori e immagini delle opere* Catalogo della mostra in Arezzo, 22 novembre 2003-27 gennaio 2004, [Pontedera: Bandecchi e Vivaldi, 2003], 46, 365, respectively). Petrarch acknowledged the value to him of the laurel in his pastoral poem, *Bucolicum carmen*, 10, 376-77: 'Laurea cognomen tribuit michi, laurea famam, / laurea divitias' [The laurel gave me my name, the laurel my fame, the laurel my riches].

6. Dante's hopes are expressed in his verse epistle to Giovanni del Virgilio (1.43-4); Boccaccio aspires to the laurel for the *Teseida* (1.1.4-6), his vernacular epic deriving from Statius's epic *Thebaid*.

7. Petrarch: 'magnus enim labor est magne custodia fame' (*Africa* 7.292); quoted in Boccaccio's *Epystole* 2.14, 273 and *Familiares*. 7.7. 5-6 (see *Secretum* 392 n.271). For other references in *Africa*, see Pierre Laurens, ed. and trans., *L'Afrique/Affrica* [I-V] (Paris: Les belles lettres, 2006), LXXXV-XCIV.

8. Petrarch noted in his Ambrosian Virgil how Laura was 'famous through [his] verses', quoted in Rossiter, *Chaucer and Petrarch*, 92 n.74. Her fame is set next to Achilles' at *Rerum vulgarium fragmenta* 185-7, a typical Petrarchan topos (e.g. *Africa* 9.54; see Laurens, *L'Afrique/Affrica*, LXXVI-LXXVII).

9. Petrarch, *Africa* 9.44.

10. Piero Boitani, *Chaucer and the Imaginary World of Fame* (Cambridge: D. S. Brewer, 1984), 105. On the many forms of the *De viris* in Petrarch's lifetime, see Feo, *Petrarca nel tempo*, 363-67; Rossiter, *Chaucer and Petrarch*, 163; Petrarch also wrote a *Vita caesaris*; for Scipio and Rome in *Africa*, see Laurens's introduction in Laurens, *L'Afrique/Affrica* (esp. LXXIV-V), Rome and Scipio are paired at 3.208 ('Roma caput rerum: Scipio dux summus in illa est'); Rome's great fame is the principal subject of *Africa* 2.482-580; in Petrarch's

Contra eum qui maledixit Italie history is but praise of Rome, *Romana laus* (para. 15; ed. Crevatin, p. 94) and in *Familiares* 11.16.4 the world with one voice acknowledges Rome's supremacy.

11. For the fate of *Africa*, which Petrarch intended to burn (see Petrarca, *Secretum/Il mio segreto*, ed. Enrico Fenzi [Milan: Mursia, 1992], 400–1 n. 333–6), and its publication in 1394, after Petrarch's death, see Laurens, *L'Afrique/Affrica*, XIII–XLVIII. The promise of the *De viris illustribus*, also unfinished, was a factor in earning the laurel. Ginsberg (*Chaucer's Italian Tradition*, [262]) notes that for Chaucer, Petrarch was 'more heard of than read'.

12. Fenzi, *Secretum*, 262.

13. See Petrarch, *Africa* 6.885–918, the final voyage and death of the Carthaginian general Mago, Hannibal's brother (see Feo, *Petrarca nel Tempo*, 255, 269–71). A section on the pagan gods (3.136–262) was sent to Pierre Bersuire; the first verses of the poem, 'Et mihi conspicuum meritis belloque tremendum / Musa, virum referes' were also disseminated; see Feo, *Petrarca nel Tempo,* 255.

14. Petrarch, *Seniles* 1.1.13.

15. On the distinction of 'maker' and 'poet', see Winthrop Wetherbee, *Chaucer and the Poets: An Essay on 'Troilus and Criseyde'* (Ithaca, NY: Cornell University Press, 1984), 20–2, 226; Karla Taylor, 'Chaucer's Uncommon Voice: Some Contexts for Influence', in *The Decameron and the Canterbury Tales: New Essays on an Old Question*, eds. L. M. Koff and Brenda Deen Schildgen (Madison, WI: University of Wisconsin Press, 2000), 50–2; Havely, 'The Italian Background', 324–5; for a contestation, see Seth Lerer, *Chaucer and his Readers: Imagining the Author in Late Medieval Europe* (Princeton, NJ: Princeton University Press, 1993), 25–56, for whom Chaucer remained the 'maker' in this respect.

16. Dante Alighieri, *Inferno* 4.84–96.

17. See Dante, *Purgatorio* 22.64–9, and Wetherbee, *Chaucer and the Poets*, 20–22, esp. notes 2–3; 226; 242–43.

18. Boccaccio tirelessly spread Petrarch's fame as a laureate; see Boccaccio, *Epistole* 2.9 ('Mavortis milex'); the early *Notamentum* in the Zibaldone Laurenziano; *Epistole* 7.1; *Epistole* 11.1; and especially the biography, *De vita et moribus Domini Francisci Petracchi de Florentia secundum Iohannem Bochacci de Certaldo* in *Vite de Petrarca, Pier Damiani e Livio*, ed. Renata Fabbri, in Branca, *Tutte le opere*, 5.1:881–955: all works with little circulation, however. See E. H Wilkins, 'Boccaccio's Early Tributes to Petrarch', *Speculum* 38 (1963), 79–87 and Giuseppe Velli, "Il *De vita et moribus domini Francisci Petrarchi de Florentia* del Boccaccio e la biografia del Petrarca, *Modern Language Notes* 102 (1987): 32–9. Petrarch admits to his thirst for glory in Fenzi, *Secretum*, 256–58, 262, 264.

19. A series of ratios connect Chaucer, the Clerk, Griselda, and Petrarch: the Clerk is like Griselda, poor and like 'a mayde' (IV.2); he is like Petrarch insofar as he is a clerk who loves books, study and teaching; he is like Chaucer (not a clerk) for some of the same reasons (his story follows one of Chaucer's); Petrarch is like Griselda in that both are dead and buried in Italy. Carolyn Dinshaw (*Chaucer's Sexual Poetics* [Madison, WI: University of Wisconsin Press, 1989], 135–7) speaks of 'transference'.

20. Petrarch's oration did not circulate, but the *privilegium* obtained a certain diffusion; see Wilkins, *The Making of the Canzoniere*, 53–61; J. B. Trapp, 'The Owl's Ivy and the Poet's Bays: An Enquiry into Poetic Garlands', *Journal of the Warburg and Courtauld Institutes* 21 (1958), 238–41; Feo, *Petrarca nel Tempo*, 17.

21. Chaucer is unlikely to have known any form of *De viris illustribus*; an *Epithoma* of the work edited by Lombardo della Seta only emerged in 1379 (Par. lat. 6069F); but Chaucer

might have heard about the series of medallions of famous men, based on information supplied by Petrarch, painted between 1367 and 1379 in the Sala dei Giganti of Padua; see Theodor E. Mommsen, 'Petrarch and the Decoration of the *Sala virorum illustrium* in Padua', *Art Bulletin* 34 (1952), 95–116, Giovanni Cipriani, 'Petrarca e i ritratti degli uomini illustri', *Quaderni petrarcheschi* IX–X (1992–93) (*Il Petrarca latino e le origini dell'umanesimo.* Atti del Convegno internazionale, Firenze 19–20 maggio 1991), 489–511, and Wallace, *Chaucerian Polity,* 299–301.

22. In *Chaucer and the Imaginary World of Fame*, Boitani proposes that Chaucer mistakenly attributed *De casibus* to Petrarch; see Rossiter, *Chaucer and Petrarch*, 59.

23. This is the case with the *Rerum vulgarium fragmenta* (an early title was *fragmentorum liber*), the *Epystole*, and the *Familiares*, all of which Petrarch characterizes as collections of scattered verse or prose. See Feo, *Petrarca nel tempo,* 41–367, Rossiter, *Chaucer and Petrarch*, 163–5.

24. Virgil, *The Aeneid* 4.173–195. For fame as a topic in work of the 'three crowns' see Boitani, *Chaucer and the Imaginary World of Fame*, 73–90 (Dante), 90–102 (Boccaccio) and 103–24 (Petrarch). Vergil's account of *fama* is adapted in Boccaccio's *Filostrato* (4.78) and *Teseida* (1.21) and in Chaucer's *Troilus* (5.659–65); see also *House of Fame*, 345–52. Boccaccio depicts worldly glory in the *Amorosa visione* (4.49–72); poets, especially, seek 'glory and high fame' in Boccaccio's *Genealogie deorum gentilium* 15.13.

25. For assessments of fame attaching to the 'three crowns', see Boitani, *Chaucer and the Imaginary World of Fame*, 5; Rossiter, *Chaucer and Petrarch*, 135.

26. For accounts of the *Monk's Tale*, see Piero Boitani, *The Tragic and Sublime in Medieval Literature* (Cambridge: Cambridge University Press, 1989), 40–55; Henry Ansgar Kelly, *Chaucerian Tragedy* (Cambridge: Cambridge University Press, 1997), 65–79, Wallace, *Chaucerian Polity,* 299–328, Richard Neuse, 'The Monk's De Casibus: the Boccaccio Case Reopened', in Koff and Schildgen, *Decameron and the Canterbury Tales*, 247–77; Rossiter, *Chaucer and Petrarch,* 55–68. Ginsberg's study (*Chaucer's Italian Tradition*, 197–239) includes a study of *De casibus*.

27. The name Lollius, of uncertain origin, replaces it; see *The New Riverside Chaucer*, 241; 930. For the rivalry of the three authors, see Jonathan Usher,' "Sesto tra cotanto senno" and *appetentia primi loci*: Boccacio, Petrarch, and Dante's Poetic Hierarchy', *Studi sul Boccaccio* 35 (2007), 157–98.

28. Petrarch calls Boccaccio's Dante *prima studiorum fax* in *Fam.* 21.15.2; Petrarch is a *iubar* [splendor] in Boccaccio's *De casibus* 9.27.6 ('...iubar vividum est, Franciscus Petrarca laureatus, insignis preceptor meus'). See Rossiter, *Chaucer and Petrarch*, 78, on Chaucer's literary fathers.

29. Boccaccio, *De casibus*, 9.23.6–7.

30. Boccaccio's debt is recorded in the proem to *De mulieribus claris*, where Petrarch's *De viris* is mentioned, and in the conclusion to *De casibus*, where Petrarch is again called upon (9.27.6); and from other passages of *De casibus* (3.14.6; 8.1.6–23).

31. Boccaccio, *De casibus*, 8.6.

32. In Boccaccio's *De mulieribus claris*, Zenobia appears in chapter 100; Dantean names surface in 103 with Gualdrada daughter of Bellincione Berti (*Paradiso* 15.112) and in 104 with Constance of Hauteville (*Paradiso* 3.118); chapters 105 and 106 are Boccaccio's contemporaries the Sienese Camiola (1339), and Joanna of Sicily (1346). In *De casibus*, Dante appears at 9.23: although that book begins with Brunichildis Queen of the Franks (9.1, AD 700) and Desiderius (9.5, AD 797), it enters Dantean territory with William III of Sicily (14.0;

Paradiso 20.61–3); virtually all subsequent chapters before Dante's appearance include characters and citations out of his text (e.g. ch. 18, on Frederick II and Manfred, the reference to Charles of Anjou's victory achieved by 'old Alardo' in 9.19, Ugolino and Boniface VIII in 9.20, and the suffering under torture of Jacques de Molay and the Templars [9.21–2; *Purgatorio* 20.91–3] compared to Mucius Scaevola and St. Lawrence, Dante's examples of constancy [*Paradiso* 5.83–4]).

33. Both in the *De casibus* 8.1.23 and the *Genealogia deorum gentilium* (15.6.11) Boccaccio describes Petrarch as worth listing among the famous men of antiquity ('inter veteres illustres viros numerandarum potius quam inter modernos induco'). See also the Chigi manuscript of the vernacular collection for Laura, '*Viri illustris* atque poete…francisci petrarce de florentia…' Wallace (*Chaucerian Polity*, 300–5) critiques the ideology behind the celebration of *viri illustres*.

34. For Chaucer's modifications of the Ugolino episode, see Boitani, *Tragic and Sublime*, 47–54; note that Ugolino's purpose in relating his cruel death to the pilgrim is the propagation of Ruggieri's infamy (Dante, *Inferno* 33.7–9).

35. Some of the modern instances, not discussed here, derive from the *Roman de la Rose*.

36. Petrarch in *De viris illustribus*, ed. Guido Martellotti (Florence: Sansoni, 1964), 218–24; see Wallace, *Chaucerian Polity*, 302; Rossiter, *Chaucer and Petrarch*, 56. Accounts of *De viris* are found in Feo, *Petrarca nel tempo*, 363–7, Ronald G. Witt, 'Literary Debut, Latin Humanism, and Orations. The Rebirth of the Romans as Models of Character (*De viris illustribus*)', in Kirkham and Maggi, *Petrarch: A Critical Guide*, 103–112, Rossiter, *Chaucer and Petrarch*, 55–8.

37. The two placements probably represent an author's variant; the Ellesmere order, with the modern instances last, might be Chaucer's last thoughts on the matter. See Donald K. Fry, 'The End of the Monk's Tale', *Journal of English and Germanic Philology* 71 (1972), 362, Wallace, *Chaucerian Polity*, 319.

38. The other modern instances are also Dantesque: the Visconti fratricide anticipates Ugolino's capture at Ruggieri's behest. I have not seen it observed that the anaphora on the interjective 'O' in these instances echoes four examples of fallen pride in *Purgatorio* (12.37–46, compare with 'O Saúl', etc.). On Petrarch's and Chaucer's special interest in the Visconti, see Wallace, *Chaucerian Polity*, 313–29.

39. In either case, the work ends with a stanza with a rhyme on 'faylle', one of the Monk's trademarks (the related 'falle' is found in rhyme six times, illustrating VII.1975).

40. Echoing Dante's praise of his own memory in *Inferno* 2.6, and of Livy, 'che non erra' (*Inferno* 28.12).

41. The Monk's terms imply not only rhetorical points (as in *Inferno*. 5.132), but also the integrity of the *Commedia*: the pilgrim loses the straight way at a *punto* (*Inferno* 1.11); Hell is a *punto* at 34.108; God too is the *punto* from which all nature hangs (*Paradiso* 28.16, 33.94): the poem extends 'fro point to point'.

42. Boccaccio, *De casibus* 9.27.6. Petrarch's lines on Zenobia in the *Triumphus fame* (2.107–17), may have led Chaucer, if he knew that work, to think of Petrarch as a source. Rossiter, in *Chaucer and Petrarch* (58), discounts the possibility, but Petrarch's list, including Helen, Semiramis, and Cleopatra, is a variant of Dante's in *Inferno* 5, with the addition of the 'virtuous' Zenobia marking Petrarch's difference, thus gaining in significance despite its brevity.

43. Boccaccio, *De mulieribus claris*, prologue: 'Scripsere iam dudum non nulli veterum sub compendio de viris illustribus libros; et nostro evo, latiori tamen volumine et accuriatiori stilo, vir insignis et poeta egregius Franciscus Petrarca, preceptor noster, scribit; et digne.'

On the semantic range of 'ynough', see Jill Mann, 'Satisfaction and Payment in Middle English Literature', *Studies in the Age of Chaucer* 5 (1983), 17–48.

44. All Chaucer's uses of *tragedye* in *Canterbury Tales* are in the Monk's Tale and its links: from the Monk's first proposal and explanation of *hexametron* in verse and prose ('Tragedie is to seyn a certeyn storie...' [1973:]; 'I wol biwaille in manere of tragedie' [1990]; 'Of this tragedie it oghte ynough suffise' [2457]; 'Tragedies noon oother maner thyng /...biwaille' [2760:]; Nun's Priest's Tale: 'and als of a tragedie / Right now ye herde.../ biwaille' [2783]). The Monk's narrative failure frees the *Canterbury Tales* to be, in the main, 'some comedye' (Tr 5.1788).

45. Discussion of the Monk's 'tragedyes' focuses on the Boethian model: see Paul G. Ruggiers, 'Notes Toward a Theory of Chaucerian Tragedy', *Chaucer Review* 8 (1973), 89–9; Kelly, *Chaucerian Tragedy*, 65; Donald L. Lepley, 'The Monk's Boethian Tale', *Chaucer Review* 12 (1978), 162–70; and Neuse in 'The Monk's De Casibus'. For proposed Senecan analogues, see Renate Haas, 'Chaucer's *Monk's Tale*: An Ingenious Criticism of Early Humanist Conceptions of Tragedy', *Humanistica Lovaniensia* 36 (1987), 44–70.

46. Dante, *Inferno*, 20.113.

47. See David Anderson, *Before the Knight's Tale: Imitation of Classical Epic in Boccaccio's Teseida* (Philadelphia, PA: University of Pennsylvania Press, 1988) on the 'epic' *Teseida*, and on *metrum heroycum* (146–54). The Monk's tale thus opens an implicit debate on the forms of tragic and epic narrative in Chaucer's context. For a view diverging from Kelly's tight scheme for Chaucerian tragedy (Kelly, *Chaucerian Tragedy*, 65, 77); see also Haas, who suggests in 'Chaucer's *Monk's Tale*' that the Tale is Chaucer's stalking-horse for sceptically experimenting with Senecan tragic models.

48. Beginning with Job 3:1, Job's curse on his birth. For the heroic Job, see Ann W. Astell, *Job, Boethius, and Epic Truth* (Ithaca, NY: Cornell University Press, 1994) and Astell, 'Translating Job as Female', in *Translation Theory and Practice in the Middle Ages*, ed. Jeanette Beer (Kalamazoo, 1997), 59–69. For Job and Dante, see Boitani, *The Tragic and Sublime*, 50–51, and Ronald L. Martinez, 'Dante's Forese, the Book of Job, and the Office of the Dead: A Note on *Purgatorio* 23', *Dante Studies* 120 (2002), 1–16.

49. The Monk's boast of a 'hundred' tales in his 'celle' (VII. 1972), suggests his exemplar is Dante's century of cantos in the *Commedia*. His 'celle', his monastic chamber, is also his memory; see, by way of comparison, Chaucer's 'celle phantastik' in the Knight's Tale (I.1376), Petrarch's 'albergo' in *Rerum vulgarium fragmenta* 72.76–8, and G. de Vinsauf, *Poetria nova* 1972 (*cellula*).

50. Pier della Vigna's downfall ('...i lieti onor tornaro in tristi lutti' [Dante, *Inferno*, 13.69]) recalls the reversals described by the Monk. Troy's fall is a tragedy of pride brought low by fortune: '...quando la fortuna volse in basso/l'altezza dei Troian, che tutto ardiva' [*Inferno* 30.13–14]). Fourteenth-century commentators thought of Dante's poem as tragic, comic, and satirical; see Martinez, 'The Book without a Name: Petrarch's Open Secret (*Sine nomine liber*)', in Kirkham and Maggi, *Petrarch: A Critical Guide*, 461 n. 57.

51. Petrarch's criteria for epic required attention to the historical record; thus work on *Africa* and on *De viris illustribus* was closely paired in his mind, see Fenzi, *Secretum*, 274–75 and 412–13, notes 404–5. See also Laurens, *L'Afrique/Affrica*, LVII–LXXII and Feo, *Petrarca nel Tempo*, 255–71.

52. 'I by ordre telle nat thise thynges' [VII.1985]). Neuse (in 'The Monk's De Casibus') links the Knight's interruption of the Monk to his own 'epic' narrative (the following Nun's Priest's Tale is mock-epic); see Rossiter, *Chaucer and Petrarch*, 66–7. Horace's *Ars Poetica* (147–52)

recommends beginning *in medias res*, but the Monk begins with Lucifer and Adam, as if (in Horace's terms) telling the Troy story beginning with Leda's eggs; Boccaccio, beginning *De casibus*, is explicitly selective: 'absit tamen ut omnes dixerim!' For Haas (Chaucer's *Monk's Tale*, 67) and Wallace (*Chaucerian Polity*, 312) the Monk's overambitious narrative marks him as a failed humanist.

53. Boethius, *The Consolation of Philosophy*, 3.pr 6.1–6.

54. Boethius cites two lines from Euripides's *Andromache*, 319–20.

55. See also of Balthasar, in the *Monk's Tale*, lines 2710, 'glory and honor', etc.

56. Petrarch of course also presents the Boethian and Ciceronian case for the vanity of glory and fame in his *Secretum* (ed. Fenzi, 260–76), and in *Africa* 2.279–402.

57. See E. H. Wilkins, 'Cantus Troili', *English Language History* 16 (1949), 167–73, Patricia Thompson, '"The "Canticus Troili": Chaucer and Petrarch', *Comparative Literature* 11 (1959), 313–16; for the relation of Petrarch's to Dante's *Vita nuova* sonnet, see Boitani, *The Tragic and Sublime*, 59–61, Rossiter, *Chaucer and Petrarch*, 111–12, 119–20 ('S'amor non è').

58. See *Andreas Capellanus on Love* 32. Andreas's synthesis of the course of love in the same passage is virtually the plot of *Troilus*.

59. See comments by Marco Santagata, ed. in Petrarca, *Canzoniere*, 2nd ed. (Milan: Mondadori, 1997), 642–45, and Bettarini, ed. in Petrarca, *Canzoniere: Rerum vulgarium fragmenta*, 2 vols. (Turin: Einaudi, 2005), 1: 641–3.

60. Rossiter, *Chaucer and Petrarch*, 123.

61. Dante's 'dolce ber che mai non m'avria sazio' (*Purgatorio* 33.138): or the purgatorial thirst of Guinizelli, 'in sete e 'n foco ardo' (*Purgatorio* 26.18) spring to mind here.

62. For Petrarch's idolatry of Laura, see Robert M. Durling, 'Petrarch's Giovene donna sotto un verde lauro', *Modern Language Notes* 86 (1971), 1–20, and John Freccero, 'The Fig Tree and the Laurel: Petrarch's Poetics', *Diacritics* 5 (1975), 34–40.

63. Rossiter, *Chaucer and Petrarch*, 127–8.

64. For Troilus's love-melancholy see: Boitani, *Tragic and Sublime*, 67–8, 72; Barry Windeatt, *Oxford Guides to Chaucer: Troilus and Criseyde* (Oxford: Clarendon Press, 1992), 234–5, Rossiter, *Chaucer and Petrarch*, 125–6.

65. Tom Stillinger, *The Song of Troilus: Lyric Authority in the Medieval Book* (Philadelphia, PA: University of Pennsylvania Press, 1992), 172–3, Rossiter, *Chaucer and Petrarch*, 127–9.

66. Stillinger, *Song of Troilus*, 165–189, esp. 188.

67. Wilkins, *The Making of the Canzoniere*, 199–203; Stillinger, *Song of Troilus*, 172–4; Rossiter, *Chaucer and Petrarch*, 117 (who is unaware of Stillinger); see also John V. Fleming, *Classical Imitation and Interpretation in Chaucer's* Troilus (Lincoln, NE: University of Nebraska Press, 1990), 119–21, who assumes Chaucer's knowledge of the *Rerum vulgarium fragmenta*. For the versions of Petrarch's lyric collection, see Santagata, *Canzoniere*, CLXXXVI–CXC; and Feo, *Petrarca nel tempo*, 41–9.

68. Petrarch, *Rerum vulgarium fragmenta*, 176–7; this last including an instance of the ship topos. For the sequence, see Theodore Cachey, Jr, 'From Shipwreck to Port: *Rerum vulgarium fragmenta* 189 and the Making of the *Canzoniere*', *Modern Language Notes* 120 (2005), 40–1.

69. See, by way of comparison, Petrarch, *Rerum vulgarium fragmenta* 29.42, 73.46–8, 80, 132.10–12, 177.7–8, 189, 235.5–14; 264.121, 277.6–7, 292.11, 323.13–21 (a partial list).

70. Dominique Diani, 'Pétrarque: *Canzoniere* 132', *Révue des études italiennes* 18 (1972), 157; Michelangelo Picone, 'Il sonetto CLXXXIX', *Lectura petrarce* 9 (1989), 158–9; Stillinger, *The Song of Troilus*, 176–7. The *Troilus* narrator's exordium to Book Two (1–7) also adopts

the nautical trope, fusing allusion to Dante, *Purgatorio* 1.1–3 with, one might argue, Petrarch's language for the steerless ship.

71. See Picone, 'Il sonetto CLXXXIX', 151–77; see *Africa* 3.436. Compare with *Roman de la Rose* 4303 (*Caripdis*) and *Romaunt* 4713 ('Karibdous').

72. See *Troilus* 3.1335, on 'encresse or maken dymynucioun'. Chaucer's augmentation is perhaps related to the early Tuscan lyric practice of inserting short lines between hendecasyllables (*sonetto rinterzato*, etc.): no examples in Petrarch, however. Rossiter (*Chaucer and Petrarch*, 124) offers ideas about Chaucer's expansions.

73. Rossiter (*Chaucer and Petrarch*, 117) suggests Chaucer might have seen a manuscript of Petrarch's lyrics in which the sonnets were written in seven-line blocks (two verses per line): this was not the format of sonnets in the Chigi, though later editions adopt it.

74. Dante, *Inferno*, 31.142. Virgil, *Aeneid* 3.422 has *sorbet* ('sucks') for Charybdis's devouring force. Dante's text also helps articulate Troilus's meditation at V.578–80 ('Syngen so wel, so goodly, and so cleere, / That in my soule yet me thynketh ich here / The blisful sown...') which echoes the effect of Casella's song on the pilgrim ('Cominciò elli allor sí dolcemente, / che la dolcezza ancor dentro mi suona' [*Purgatorio* 2.113–14]). Not in Howard Schless, *Chaucer and Dante: A Revaluation* (Norman, OK: Pilgrim Books, 1984).

75. Dante, *Inferno* 26.139–42; for Picone ('Il sonetto CLXXXIX', 163–8), Ulysses is an implied protagonist of *Rerum vulgarium fragmenta* 189; see Cachey, 'From Shipwreck to Port', 37–8.

76. The two modes both alternating (as in the cases here), on other occasions fitting seamlessly. Stillinger, *Song of Troilus*, (181–7) finds the first Petrarchan *canticus* clearly framed, the second placed in a frame that fails.

77. The song in Boccaccio's *Filostrato* is a *canzone* by Cino da Pistoia, whose first line is included by Petrarch in *Rerum vulgarium fragmenta* 70.40. *Troilus* also includes a variety of further lyrics, e.g. the narrator's hymn at 3.1–49, and 3.1744–71, Troilus's second *canticus*; see Stillinger, *Song of Troilus*, 165–6, 179–83, and appendices in James I. Wimsatt, 'The French Lyric Element in *Troilus and Criseyde*', *Yearbook of English Studies* 15 (1985), 31–2, proposing a very large number of lyric insets.

78. Stillinger, *Song of Troilus*, 251 n.3, 254 n.49; Rossiter, *Chaucer and Petrarch*, 121.

79. Rossiter, *Chaucer and Petrarch*, 100–1, also 95–108; for the 'lyrical book' see Giulia Natali, 'A Lyrical Version: Boccaccio's Filostrato', in *The European Tragedy of Troilus*, ed. Piero Boitani (Oxford: Clarendon Press, 1989), 49–73 and Stillinger, *Song of Troilus*, 179–89.

80. I leave to the side 'O paleys desolat', Troilus's address of the empty house of Criseyde, a *canzone di lontananza*; see *New Riverside Chaucer* 1051 for the genre of *paraclausithyron*.

81. Boccaccio, *Filostrato*, 5.70.4–5. Barry Windeatt, ed., in *Troilus and Criseyde: A New Edition of 'The Book of Troilus'* (London: Longmans, 1984) adduces *Filostrato*, prologue: 'Quindi ogni aura o soave vento che viene, così nel viso ricevo quasi come il vostro sanza niuna fallo abbia tocco'. This is suggestive, but the idea of comfort ('boote') is absent.

82. Petrarch, *Rerum vulgarium fragmenta*, 246 1–2: 'L'aura che'l verde lauro et l'aureo crine/ soavemente sospirando move'. *Rerum vulgarium fragmenta* 194.1, 196.1–98.1 are a series on *l'aura*; see also 109.9. *L'aura* is the counterpart to Petrarch's self-inscription via adaptations of Arnaut Daniel's *senhal* of heaping up the air ('ieu amas l'aura'), *Rerum vulgarium fragmenta* 212.2 ('abbracciar l'ombre et seguir l'aura estiva') and especially 239.36–7 ('...andrem cacciando l'aura/In rete accolgo l'aura...').

83. *House of Fame* 765–86, esp. 768 ('speche is eyr ybroken') and 766–7 ('every speche that ys spoken...In his substaunce ys but air'). Petrarch, too, could dismiss fame as smoke and wind; see *Africa* 2.348–50.

84. The narrative placements of Troilus's *cantici* are also easy to see as Petrarchan: the first *canticus* comes after Troilus is surprised by love in a 'temple', the narrative situation that Petrarch arranges in poems 2–3 of his collections; one wonders about the preface to *Filostrato*: 'E voi, amanti, priego ch'ascoltiate...' in relation to the first line of *Rerum vulgarium fragmenta*: 'Voi ch'ascoltate in rime sparse'. See Rossiter, *Chaucer and Petrarch*, 104–5. The opening is standard for *cantari*, but there may also be a common learned source; see Ronald L. Martinez, 'Mourning Laura in the *Canzoniere*: Lessons from Lamentations', *Modern Language Notes* 118 (2003), 1–4.

85. On the direction of influence, see: Armando Balduino, 'Reminiscenze petrarchesche nel *Filostrato* (e sua datazione)', in *Boccaccio, Petrarca e altri poeti del Trecento* (Florence: Olschki, 1984), 231–47; Giuseppe Velli, 'La poesia volgare di Boccaccio e i "Rerum vulgarium fragmenta": primi appunti', *Giornale storico di letteratura italiana* 169 (1992), 183–99; Vittore Branca, *Boccaccio Medievale e nuovi studi sul Decameron* (Florence: Sansoni, 1996), 323–25; Marco Santagata, *Per moderne carte: la biblioteca volgare di Petrarca* (Bologna: Mulino, 1990), 246–70; Petrarca, *Canzoniere*, ed. Santagata, 520–1; Natascia Tonelli, 'Petrarca (*Rerum vulgarium fragmenta* 2–3), Boccaccio, e l'innamoramento nel tempio', *Studi sul Boccaccio* 28 (2000), 206–19.

86. See Ginsberg, *Chaucer's Italian Tradition*, 111; Rossiter, *Chaucer and Petrarch*, 127.

87. Wallace, *Chaucerian Polity*, 63. See also R. A. Shoaf, *Chaucer's Body: The Anxiety of Circulation in the* Canterbury Tales (Gainesville, FL: University of Florida Press, 2001), 116; and Rossiter, *Chaucer and Petrarch*, 126–9.

88. Branca (Giovanni Boccaccio, *Decameron*, ed. Vittore Branca [Milan: Mondadori, 1976], 1556) points out that the names Criseyde and Griselda are phonetically similar.

89. On the appealing difficulty of the tale, see Dinshaw, *Chaucer's Sexual Politics*, 133; Anne Middleton, 'The Clerk and His Tale: Some Literary Contexts', *Studies in the Age of Chaucer* 2 (1980), 121; Robert Edwards, 'The Sclaundre of Walter', in *Medievalitas: Reading the Middle Ages*, eds. Piero Boitani and Anna Torti (Cambridge: D. S. Brewer, 1996), 20–4.

90. On the tale's folk-tale origins, see Rossiter, *Chaucer and Petrarch*, 144–45, 151. Study of the notes on Apuleius's Cupid and Psyche in the *Zibaldone Laurenziano* shows that Boccaccio conceived Griselda's shift ('camiscia') in allegorical terms (as her 'sapientia'); see Igor Candido, 'Amore e Psiche dalle chiose del *Laur*. 29.2 alle due redazioni delle *Genealogie* e ancora in *Dec.* X.10', *Studi sul Boccaccio* 38 (2009), 192–6. Boccaccio added mention of the *camiscia* to the rubric of the *novella* in his 1372 holograph of the *Decameron* (Candido, 'Amore e Psiche', 193–4). Petrarch alluded to Apuleius's Cupid and Psyche in the satirical epistle, *Sine nomine* 18; see Ronald L. Martinez, 'The Book without a Name' in Kirkham and Maggi, *Petrarch: A Critical Guide*, 299–300.

91. Compare Ugolino's impassibility ('sanza far motto' [Dante, *Inferno* 33.48]) with Griselda's ('senza mutar viso' [Boccaccio, *Decameron* 10.10.28]) when confronted with the prospect of the death of their children. Dante also has Ugolino's children recall Job 1:21 ('tu ne vestisti / queste misere carni, e tu le spoglia' [*Inferno* 33.62–3]).

92. On Chaucer's Petrarchan ms. sources, see: J. Burke Severs, *The Literary Relationships of Chaucer's* Clerkes Tale (New Haven, CT: Yale University Press, 1942); Germaine Dempster, 'Chaucer's Manuscript of Petrarch's Version of the Griselda Story', *Modern Philology* 41 (1943), 6–16; and Thomas J. Farrell, 'The 'Envoi de Chaucer' and the *Clerk's Tale*', *Chaucer Review* 24 (1990), 329–36. *Seniles* 17.3 ('Librum tuum') appeared about 1400 in an 'edition' (ms. Ricc. 991) with illustrated frontispiece showing both Petrarch and Boccaccio; see Gabrielle Albanese, 'Fortuna umanistica della *Griselda*', in *Quaderni Petrarcheschi* 9–10

(1992–3), 598–9, and Giovanna Lazzi, 'Per il facsimile della 'Griselda' (Ms. Ricc. 991)', in *Favole Parabole Istorie: Le forme della scrittura novellistica dal medioevo al rinascimento (Atti del Convegno di pisa 26–28 ottobre 1998)*, eds. Gabriella Albanese, Lucia Battaglia Ricci e Rossella Bessi (Rome: Salerno: 2000), 309–16. Charlotte C. Morse ('What to Call Petrarch's Griselda', in *The Uses of Manuscripts in Literary Studies: Essays in Memory of Judson Boyce Allen*, eds. Charlotte C. Morse, Penelope Reed Doob and Marjorie Curry Woods [Kalamazoo, Michigan, 1992], 263–303) discusses the many titles under which the tale traveled after leaving Chaucer's pen: a good default setting is *Historia Griseldis*.

93. Some readers suppose Chaucer's knowledge of *Seniles* 17.4, even 17.2, as well. See Middleton, 'The Clerk and his Tale', 131–5 and Rossiter, *Chaucer and Petrarch*, 171–2; Morse ('What to Call Petrarch's Griselda', 265) observes that it was very rarely copied with 17.3.

94. Helen Cooper. 'Sources and Analogues of Chaucer's Canterbury Tales: Reviewing the Work' *Studies in the Age of Chaucer* 19 (1997): 183–210 (at 184, 193–9). See: Koff and Schildgen, *Decameron and the Canterbury Tales*, esp. Taylor, 'Chaucer's Uncommon Voice', 62–76; Thomas J. Farrell, 'Source or Hard Analogue? *Decameron* X, 10 and the *Clerk's Tale*', *Chaucer Review* 37 (2003), 346–64; Rossiter, *Chaucer and Petrarch*, 166. The problem awaits further study.

95. Rossiter, *Chaucer and Petrarch*, 149. On Chaucer and Dioneo's *Decameron* 10.10, see John Finlayson, 'Petrarch, Boccaccio, and Chaucer's *Clerk's Tale*', *Studies in Philology* 97 (2000), 57–72, Glending Olson, 'Petrarch's View of the *Decameron*', *Modern Language Notes* 91 (1976), 69–79, Edwards, 'The Sclaundre of Walter', 24–30, Amy W. Goodwin, 'The Griselda Game', *Chaucer Review* 39 (2004), 46–9.

96. Boccaccio, *Decameron* 10.10.68. Griselda's divinity is opposed to Gualtieri's *matta bestialità* in terms familiar from Aristotelian political analysis; both are extremes, in fact 'monsters'; see Giuseppe Mazzotta, *The World at Play in Boccaccio's* Decameron (Princeton, NJ: Princeton University Press, 1986), 122–30; Edwards, 'The Sclaundre of Walter', 24–6; Goodwin, 'The Griselda Game', 47–8.

97. Petrarch, *Seniles* 17.3.38.

98. Ibid. 17.3.22, 'quicquid tu vis, ego etiam volo'; the Virgin answers Gabriel with 'fiat mihi secundum verbum tuum'; see Clerk's Tale 351–64, 505–11 for the 'oxes stalle'. Dolores Warwick Frese ('Chaucer's *Clerk's Tale*: The Monsters and the Critics Reconsidered', *Chaucer Review* 8 [1973], 133–46) points out Chaucer's borrowings from monastic language and the phraseology of prayer.

99. On the allegory, see: Charlotte C. Morse, 'The Exemplary Griselda', *Studies in the Age of Chaucer* 7 (1985), 51–86; Morse, 'Critical Approaches to the *Clerk's Tale*', in *Chaucer's Religious Tales*, eds. C. David Benson and Elizabeth Robertson (Cambridge 1990), 71–83; Marga Cottino-Jones, 'Fabula vs. Figura: Another Interpretation of the Griselda Story', *Italica* 50 (1973), 38–52; Mazzotta, *World at Play in Boccaccio's* Decameron, 122–30; and Rossiter, *Chaucer and Petrarch*, 133–7, 143, 150–3. For Griselda's 'translation' as Job, see Astell, 'Translating Job as Female'. K. P. Clarke ('Reading/Writing Griselda: A Fourteenth-Century Response [Florence, Biblioteca Medicea Laurenziana, Ms. Plut. 42, 1]' in *On Allegory: Some Medieval Aspects and Approaches*, eds. Mary Carr, K. P. Clarke, and Marco Niedergeist [Newcastle: Cambridge Scholars, 2008]), gives late Trecento evidence regarding reception of Boccaccio's *novella*.

100. There are nine readings from Job in the liturgical Office of the Dead, widely available in Books of Hours; four of the Job references by Chaucer's Parson come from these. Job in the Middle Ages is discussed in Lawrence L. Besserman, *The Legend of Job in the Middle*

Ages (Cambridge, MA: Harvard University Press, 1979); see also Astell, *Job, Boethius, and Epic Truth*. The *mulier fortis* of Proverbs 31:10–28 is also invoked; see the *Riverside Chaucer* 880; Rossiter, *Chaucer and Petrarch*, 154–6.

101. Mazzotta, *The World at Play in Boccaccio's* Decameron, 123.

102. John P. McCall ('The *Clerk's Tale* and the Theme of Obedience', *Modern Language Quarterly* 27 [1966], 260–9) sees the story as signifying the soul's preparation for death; the Job references (see note 84) support his thesis. On God's absolute power in the context of Nominalist philosophy, sometimes identified as the 'logyk' that absorbs the Clerk, see the studies cited in Kathryn L. Lynch, 'Despoiling Griselda', *Studies in the Age of Chaucer* 10 (1988), 42–3, 58–9.

103. By citing James 1:13, distinguishing God's testing from temptation, Petrarch attempts to circumvent the problem. Abraham and Job are mentioned later in James's epistle (2:21–3 and 5:11) as examples of patience before testing. John McNamara ('Chaucer's Use of the Epistle of St. James in the *Clerk's Tale*', *Chaucer Review* 7 [1972–3], 184–93) argues that Walter's testing of Griselda marks his own failure to resist temptation, as spelled out in James 1:14 (see IV.456–62). For Giulio Savelli ('Struttura e valori nella novella di Griselda', *Studi sul Boccaccio* 14 [1983–4], 299–301), the interpretive dilemma is itself an early crisis of modernity, requiring truth and value to be determined empirically.

104. 'pannicelli romagnoli' (Boaccaccio, *Decameron*. 10.10.52); see also 'abito villesco' (10.10.25); '*pannicelli...stracci*' (10.10.65). For the significance of stripping, see Dinshaw, *Chaucer's Sexual Politics*, 133–5, 142–5, Wallace, *Chaucerian Polity*, 283–5.

105. Petrarch, *Seniles* 17.3.5.

106. For the linguistic issue, see Dinshaw, *Chaucer's Sexual Politics*, 148–50; Ginsberg, *Chaucer's Italian Tradition*, 121–5; and esp. Wallace, *Chaucerian Polity*, 283–9, Shoaf, *Chaucer's Body*, 116–21, Dolores Warwick Frese, 'The "Buried Bodies" of Dante, Boccaccio, and Petrarch: Chaucerian "Sources" for the Critical Fiction of Obedient Wives', *Studies in the Age of Chaucer* 28 (2006), who are right to assert that Petrarch despoils Boccaccio of his text. Rossiter (*Chaucer and Petrarch*, 11–15) seems deaf to Petrarch's condescending tone; Olson explains it away by claiming its conventionality, which enables Petrarch's scorn by masking it. See also Middleton, 'The Clerk and his Tale', 125–7, Taylor, 'Chaucer's Uncommon Voice', 57, Ginsberg, *Chaucer's Italian Tradition*, 248–52.

107. In *Familiares* 22.2.26 Petrarch uses the same idea of 'returning' Ovid's words to him unpilfered by altering his imitation so that it is less apparent to the eye. Boccaccio in fact never saw Petrarch's version, as he did not receive any of the letters that make up *Seniles* 17.1–4 before his death; see Boccaccio's *Epistola* 24.41 (in Boccaccio, *Epistole e lettere* ed. and trans. Ginetta Auzzas in Branca, *Tutte le opere*, 5.1:735).

108. Boccaccio, *Decameron*, 10.10.65. That she is a *donna* despite her *stracci* (tatters) echoes Dante's canzone of exile, 'Tre donne intorno al cor mi son venuto', where Justice, despite torn clothes and low status as an exile, is a lady by virtue of herself alone ('sol di sé par donna'; the phrase can also mean 'lady *of* herself alone').

109. Griselda's father, Giannucole in the *novella*, is Ianicula for Petrarch: this is one of numerous diminutives in Petrarch's text, including *virguncula* (17.3.10), *puellula* (3.20), and especially, from the last words, 'quod pro suo mortali coniuge rusticana hec muliercula passa est' (3.38). In Dante's terms, vernacular is the language 'remissus...et humilis' (modest and lowly) in which even simple women converse ('in qua et muliercule communicant'), see the Letter to Can Grande, *Epistole* 13.32: Petrarch's echo of the letter is intended dismissively. See Albanese, 'Fortuna umanistica della *Griselda*', 579; Frese, 'The "Buried

Bodies" of Dante, Boccaccio, and Petrarch', 253–6; and Alison Cornish, *Vernacular Translation in Dante's Italy: Illiterate Literature* (Cambridge: Cambridge University Press, 2011), 159–63.

110. Dante Alighieri, *Rime*, ed. Gianfranco Contini (Turin: Einaudi, 1970), 20–3, 145–8. In a letter to Boccaccio (*Familiares* 22.2.12), Petrarch compares his own style to a comfortable cloak ('toga habilis') when discussing his imitative practice.

111. Where Job is mentioned, in fact (IV.932).

112. On Petrarch's use of *stilo alio*, which Chaucer will render as 'heigh style', possibly due to a scribal error, see Ginsberg in the *Riverside Chaucer*, 880; Rossiter, *Chaucer and Petrarch*, 147. But in writing to Boccaccio about Dante, Petrarch refers to Latin both as *alius stilus* and *altior eloquium* (*Familiares* 21.15.21, 24); see also *Seniles* 5.2.23, where the phrase *altior stilus* designates Latin.

113. For the opening period, see Emilie P. Kadish, 'The Proem of Petrarch's Griselda', *Mediaevalia* 2 (1976), 189–206; Ginsberg, *Chaucer's Italian Tradition*, 259–61; Frese, '"Buried Bodies" of Dante, Boccaccio, and Petrarch"', 251–3; and Rossiter, *Chaucer and Petrarch*, 146–9. Petrarch uses terms related to nobility four times in his opening paragraph, twice for the river landscape and twice for Walter's bloodline. *Pace* the eirenic Rossiter (*Chaucer and Petrarch*, 11–15, 133–5), Petrarch's belittling of Boccaccio's vernacular work, and stimulus of his Latin, was programmatic; see Ginsberg, *Chaucer's Italian Tradition*, 121–25; and Usher, ' "Sesto tra cotanto senno" ', 167–71.

114. Critical debates not least among them: for Ginsberg's nuanced replies to Wallace, who argues Petrarch's sympathy with Walter's tyranny, and 'Lombard' tyranny in general (*Chaucerian Polity*, 299–302, 282–3) see Ginsberg, *Chaucer's Italian Tradition*, 244–6; and see also on Walter's 'tyranny', Rossiter, *Chaucer and Petrarch*, 179, 184–5; 193–5.

115. Space prevents discussions of contributions regarding Griselda's resistance to Walter; see *inter alia* Linda Georgianna, 'The Clerk's Tale and the Grammar of Assent', *Speculum* 70 (1995), 793–821; Gail Ashton, 'Patient Mimesis: Griselda and the *Clerk's Tale*', *Modern Language Review* 101 (2006), 232–8; and, in a quite different sense, Laura Ashe, 'Reading like a Clerk in the Clerk's Tale', *Chaucer Review* 32 (1998), 935–44. Also see Rossiter, *Chaucer and Petrarch*, 178–80.

116. Petrarch, *Seniles*, 17.3.36.

117. Boccaccio, *Decameron* 9. Intro.4.

118. Petrarch, *Seniles*, 17.4.5.

119. Ibid., 17.3.15: 'Iamque non solum intra patrios fines sed per finitimas quasque provincias suum nomen celebri preconio fama vulgabat, ita ut multi ad illam visendam viri ac matrone studio fervente concurrerent'. Compare *Rerum vulgarium fragmenta* 248.1–2, of Laura: 'Chi vuol veder . . . venga a mirar costei.'

120. Echoing James 5:11: 'Sufferentiam Job audistis' [You have heard of the patience of Job].

121. Petrarch, *Seniles*, 10.10.39.

122. Ibid., 17.3.26.

123. The *diffame* is the opinion of the mob, so it is of course in part undercut (see 995–1001, on the 'stormy peple'); and see Rossiter, *Chaucer and Petrarch*, 187.

124. Petrarch, *Seniles*, 17.3.4.

125. Ibid., 17.3.5.

126. Boccaccio's book, with the title the *Centonovelle*, was held a 'popular' vernacular work of lesser prestige until Lorenzo de' Medici's cultural policy and Bembo's canonization of its prose enhanced its value; see Albanese, 'Fortuna umanistica della *Griselda*', 599–625.

127. Albanese, 'Fortuna umanistica della *Griselda*', 584, 590–1; see Rossiter, *Chaucer and Petrarch*, 133–5. I have had to slight the French reception of Petrarch's Latin version; but see Middleton, 'The Clerk and His Tale', 124–5, 146–9, and Havely, 'The Italian Background', 310–23.

128. Petrarch's translation of the *novella* springs from his restlessness of mind ('...die quodam, inter varios cogitatus animum more solito discerpentes' [my mind torn between various thoughts]). See Shoaf, *Chaucer's Body*, 120–1.

129. Albanese, 'Fortuna umanistica della *Griselda*', 607–610: for example, the mid-fifteenth century *Historia de duobus amantibus* of Aeneas Sylvius Piccolomini (Pope Pius II) and the *Novella del grasso legnaiuolo*, the most celebrated version of which was written by Antonio di Tuccio Manetti.

130. For the designations of the *Envoi*, and its attribution to the Clerk or Chaucer, see Howell Chickering, 'Form and Interpretation in the "Envoy" to the *Clerk's Tale*', *Chaucer Review* 29 (1995), 356.

131. Rossiter, *Chaucer and Petrarch*, 162–3, 166.

132. Taylor, 'Chaucer's Uncommon Voice', 57.

133. Petrarch, *Seniles*, 17.3.3.

134. In *Familiares* 21.15.14 Petrarch protests to Boccaccio that he has no wish to usurp Dante's fame.

135. Jacobus da Varagine, source for the Nun's Priest's Tale, is the nearest contemporary author; Livy is credited, but not followed, for the Physician's Tale of Virginia; and an unnamed merchant provides the Merchant's Tale, probably imitating how the Clerk sources his tale, which precedes the Merchant's. Dante furnishes only a portion of the Monk's Tale.

136. Boitani, *Chaucer and the Imaginary World of Fame*, 157.

137. 'Rethorike sweete' evokes Boccaccio's praise of Petrarch's sweet eloquence ('*dulcedinis in loquendo*', echoing ancient topoi); see *De vita et moribus* 22 (ed. Velli 908) in Boccaccio, *Rime—Carmina—Epistole e lettere—Vite—De Canaria.*, eds. Vittore Branca, Giorgio Padoan, Giuseppe Velli, Ginetta Auzzas, Renata Fabbri and Manlio Pastore Stocchi (Milan: Mondadori, 1992); and see Lerer, *Chaucer and his Readers*, 29–30.

138. See Rossiter, *Chaucer and Petrarch*, 191–92; Lerer (*Chaucer and his Readers*, 22–56) gives a detailed account of the construction of a 'laureate/aureate' Chaucer after his death, departing from the tribute to Petrarch in the Clerk's Tale.

139. Petrarch, *Triumphus fame*, I.i.9.

140. Boccaccio, *De casibus*, 8.1.11.

141. 1 Corinthians 15:52.

142. Petrarch, *Bucolicum Carmen* 1.89–90.

143. See Nicholas Mann, 'The Making of Petrarch's *Bucolicum carmen*: A Contribution to the History of the Text', *Italia medioevale et umanistica* 20 (1977): 127–86.

144. Chaucer used *enlumyne* three other times: of Criseyde's radiance ('O paleis, whilom crowne of houses alle, / *Enlumyned* with sonne of alle blisse!' [V.548]), of the heart in the Parson's Tale ('*enlumyne* and lightne the herte of the synful man' [X.245]); and in Chaucer's lyric 'An ABC' in reference to an illuminated manuscript of a liturgical calendar ('Kalenderes *enlumyned* ben thei' [73]), as a metaphor for souls 'lighted' by Mary's grace (see Chaucer, *The Complete Works of Geoffrey Chaucer* [*Romaunt of the Rose; Minor Poems*], ed. Walter W. Skeat [Oxford: Clarendon Press, 1894], 265 and 434). Not listed as a Dantism in Schless, *Chaucer and Dante*.

145. Dante, *Purgatorio*, 11.81.

146. Dante, *Purgatorio,* 11.96.
147. Dante, *Purgatorio,* 22.64–6.
148. Chaucer consulted the passage for LGW F 924–6: 'Glorye and honour, Virgil Mantoan / Be to thy name! and I shal, as I can / Folwe thy lanterne, as thow gost byforn, / How Eneas to Dido was forsworn' and recalled related passages in the envoi to *Troilus.* This passage is recorded as a Dantism in Schless, *Chaucer and Dante,* 159.

BIBLIOGRAPHY

Albanese, Gabriella, 'Fortuna umanistica della *Griselda*,' *Quaderni Petrarcheschi* 9–10 (1992–93), 571–627.
Boitani, Piero, *Chaucer and the Imaginary World of Fame* (Cambridge: D. S. Brewer, 1984).
Durling, Robert M., ed. and trans., *Petrarch's Lyric Poems: The* Rime sparse *and Other Lyrics* (Cambridge, MA: Harvard University Press, 1976).
Feo, Michele, ed., *Petrarca nel tempo. Tradizione lettori e immagini delle opere (Catalogo della mostra in Arezzo, 22 novembre 2003–27 gennaio 2004)* (Pontedera: Bandecchi e Vivaldi, 2003).
Ginsberg, Warren, *Chaucer's Italian Tradition* (Ann Arbor, MI: University of Michigan Press, 2002).
Havely, Nick, 'The Italian Background,' in *Chaucer: An Oxford Guide,* ed. Steve Ellis (New York and Oxford: Oxford University Press, 2005), 313–31.
Kirkham, Victoria and Armando Maggi, eds., *Petrarch: A Critical Guide to the Complete Works* (Chicago, IL: University of Chicago Press, 2009).
Rossiter, William T., *Chaucer and Petrarch* (Cambridge: D. S. Brewer, 2010).
Stillinger, Tom, *The Song of Troilus: Lyric Authority in the Medieval Book* (Philadelphia, PA: University of Pennsylvania Press, 1992).
Wallace, David, *Chaucerian Polity: Absolutist Lineages and Associational Forms in England and Italy* (Stanford, CA: Stanford University Press, 1997).

CHAPTER 19

DANTE AND THE MEDIEVAL CITY

How the Dead Live

DAVID L. PIKE

DANTE'S *Commedia* is arguably the most sustained vision of the city in medieval literature; however, this vision has the determinant peculiarity that all of its inhabitants are dead. The city provided the model for Dante's Hell, his Paradise, and even, arguably, his Purgatory, but it was the underworld that most reflected his conception of everyday life in contemporary Florence, and that has had the strongest influence on subsequent urban representations. This power of Dante's poem begins in the novel combination of a mimesis of everyday urban life with an eschatological framework: not just how life is in the city or what it might be like to be dead, but how the dead live. While unquestionably an underworld of pain and suffering, Dante's inferno is also teeming in an often profoundly nostalgic way with the sights, smells, and choice words to be encountered on any given day in the home town from which he had been exiled for over a decade. This chapter examines the infernal mode of representation of urban experience, a mode that holds that the only way to grasp the essence of the city is to descend into and pass through its accursed depths. I begin with a survey of the vertical city, urban variation on the vertical cosmos of the Last Judgment, with the souls divided between heaven above and hell below. Dante's vision reproduces this cosmos within the microcosm of the city. I then look at the place of hell within this city, the types of urban experience represented within it, and the relationship of the infernal city to the heavenly city as which Dante figures paradise. The final section of the chapter surveys the dissemination of this urban model into the diverse cityscapes of Dante's successors, including Boccaccio, Chaucer, François Villon, and Christine de Pizan. The consequences of the most influential medieval city text being located underground and in hell are neither as simple as the established Christian model nor as negotiable as the secular one that was then taking form. When Dante's poetics of the underground is translated into the surface model of the lived city, it brings its prior spatial meanings along with it. Attention to the spatial

dynamics of medieval urban representation provides an overview of the representational framework from which the ostensibly surface-dwelling narratives of Chaucer and
other later writers emerged.

Thinking Vertically

> ...for as, on its round wall, Montereggioni
> is crowned with towers, so there towered here,
> above the bank that runs around the pit,
> with half their bulk, the terrifying giants.
>   (Dante, *Inferno*   31.40–3)

Journey narratives can be viewed as essentially horizontal in structure, progressing from
point A to point B in space and in time (and sometimes, although less often, back again).
But that narrative movement is frequently complicated by the more equivocal spatio-
temporal structure of verticality, which renders the journey as a descent (followed
sometimes, although not always, by a return). In classical epic, this structure takes the
form of a descent to the underworld, finding its pre-Dantean paradigm in the hero's
journey to the Elysian Fields for a reunion with his father Anchises in Virgil's *Aeneid*.[1] In
medieval romance, it more frequently takes the form of a wandering in the other world
of a magical wood. In both genres, there is tension between the essentially linear and
pragmatic teleology of the protagonist's quest and the allegorical, often hieratic, and
essentially static quality of verticality. There are several components to this stasis. The
first is its diversionary character: the underworld distracts, tempting the protagonist
from the end goal of his descent: Odysseus must ignore the lure of the soul of his mother
until he has accomplished his task of speaking with the seer Teiresias; Aeneas may chat
only briefly or not at all with the many lost friends, family, and comrades-in-arms he
meets on the way to join his father, and must accept the unwanted return to the surface
world; Dante is constantly reminded by his guide Virgil that their allotted time is short
and that he must not tarry overly long with any of the souls he meets. The second component is the introspective character of verticality: in both personal and social terms,
the descent is at least as much temporal as it is spatial, and the physical movement downward generally functions primarily to signify temporal movement—always backwards
into the past but often also forwards into prophetic time. Its meanings are figural and
syntactic, tightly compacted, rather than diachronic and paratactic, accumulating sense
as they go along. As such, verticality tends to privilege the ideological conceptions of its
spatial representation rather than the discrete moments of the horizontal trajectory.

   This ideological conception becomes especially weighted in medieval narratives, as
the dominant representation of space in medieval Europe was the overwhelmingly
vertical conception of the Christian cosmos, which divided its afterlife between a subterranean hell and a heaven among the stars above. The powerfully vertical hierarchy of
medieval feudalism insinuated this cosmos further into everyday social structures,
ordering society from God through divinely authorized rulers and downward through
the entire feudal system, not to mention the equally elaborate celestial and infernal

hierarchies. This verticalized space was highly amenable to visual expression, in particular in the cathedral, whose architectural spaces neatly reproduced the cosmos from the heavens-aspiring towers (nearly always the highest point on the horizon) to the earth-embedded crypts, and in the last judgments of paintings (often themselves inside churches and cathedrals) and illuminated manuscripts, which graphically depicted the division between the damned souls being devoured by a monstrous hellmouth and the blessed souls rising toward God. Nevertheless, as Henri Lefebvre makes clear, the dominant spatial conception of a particular place and time is never its only one, although it tends to be the most clearly and consistently represented of an 'intertwinement of social spaces'.[2] Church doctrine is the historical document of ongoing struggle to define and maintain orthodoxy, while popular faith has always far more readily incorporated fragments of pagan, folk, and heterodox beliefs into its own practices and spatial representations. Devil- and hell-lore are foremost among these representations, visible in the margins of artworks and the nooks and crannies of the grandest cathedrals; for they were the most amenable locations for assimilating heterodox creeds and alternate deities.

Medieval cities and towns, which arose all over Europe during what David Nicholas terms the first urban revolution that occupied much of latter part of the Middle Ages and extended through the early modern period,[3] were a key site of alternative spatial practices. Indeed, the spatial conception that emerged from this revolution—the city as an autonomous and centralized economic, political, and cultural force—would become the dominant spatial organization of early modern Europe. The medieval town had a paradoxical relationship to feudalism: on the one hand, with its free citizens, law courts, and existence outside of feudal law and custom, it formed an exception to the feudal order, yet feudal lords were instrumental in creating these towns and their institutions, as a source of income and power and as a way of containing the forces and ideas that inspired them.[4] This fraught relationship was a powerful force in urban development, for example, in the way Norman rulers introduced urban laws that would 'water down' the populations of 'troublesome centres of English resistance'.[5] Spatially, the medieval city was as flat and horizontally oriented as the surrounding landscape; moreover, with the exception of the handful of surviving grids from the Roman empire, its streets tended to follow the haphazard patterns of everyday use rather than the *ex nihilo* geometries of imperial planners.[6] The only buildings that rose above the fairly uniform low height—churches for the clergy and towers for the nobility—were also the buildings that embodied medieval verticality.

These buildings presented the symbolic means whereby the medieval city could be incorporated positively within the vertical conception of the cosmos, for according to the influential formulation of Augustine's *City of God*, the earthly city was by definition a deceptive and sinful lure rather than a viable stopping point, a community doomed 'to suffer eternal punishment with the devil' rather than 'to reign eternally with God'.[7] For Augustine, the only proper mode in which to inhabit the earthly city was as if one were on a journey, a pilgrim only passing through on the way to the true, celestial city of God in the next life; for this reason, only Cain, and not his blessed brother Abel, built a physical city on this earth.[8] Augustine's image of the city—and, indeed, of life itself, since he explicitly cast his image in allegorical terms—was fairly consonant with the tenuous and isolated early medieval life of feudal courts and rural monasteries. This pessimistic account of the fall of Rome as the most recent in the inevitable fall of every earthly city, imperial and decadent, provided a neatly apocalyptic tenor to that life. However, the more that medieval cities became established as viable and permanent communities and the more that a merchant class established modes of association based on earthly bonds such as profession and individual rights, the more the eschatological representation of medieval space proved inadequate as an account of everyday life. In cultural terms, as Walter Benjamin argued, this conflict was expressed as a battle between pagan myth and Christian allegory.[9] The multiplicity of the classical myths suggested a more variegated range of meaning-making than the rigid framework of the Christian cosmos; moreover, Roman poetry offered models of urban representation unknown to the abstractions of medieval writing. Some Romans, including Ovid and Catullus, had to be surreptitiously read for their suspiciously celebratory depiction of the everyday life of a big city; however, satirists such as Juvenal could be more easily recuperated for their critical (and less obscene or libertine) stance, and Statius offered a tragic vision of his city as the failed society of Thebes, while Virgil offered a full-fledged counter-vision to Augustine's decadent capital—a benevolent imperial centre easily assimilated to a heavenly city in a far more concrete way than Augustine's concession that hidden within the 'obvious presence' of the earthly city was the 'symbolic presence of the heavenly city'.[10]

This should not suggest that the emerging and essentially horizontal urban spatiality of late medieval Europe in any way eliminated the vertical cosmos of medieval Christianity. Rather, we could say that the former developed against the framework of the latter. Moreover, because it was a framework that could scarcely be questioned, much less dispensed with, urban writers found ways of working in the margins and gaps of this framework rather than outside or in direct opposition to it. In a poet such as Dante, as in many other medieval writers, there is no reason to question the sincerity of his faith or his poetry's expression of that faith. Indeed, a poem such as the *Commedia* is meaningless unless we take its faith seriously at least in a hermeneutic sense, as 'truth claims'.[11] However, it is equally meaningless if we ignore the deep investment in the secular life of the city that dictates so much of its individual content and so much of its emotional power.[12] Italian city-states such as Dante's Florence were an early and persuasive model for a social organization based on the principles of secular government and political autonomy. Because their territories encompassed surrounding farmland and, often, adjoining villages and small towns, these city-states were in many ways closer to proto-nations in organization than to today's conceptions of urban agglomeration. Nevertheless, the city was at the centre of their identity and of their spatial practice, and produced particular cultural forms able to negotiate the contradictions of sociality arising from an urban space in which the traditional identities of medieval Christianity no longer sufficed.[13] How do you negotiate a space in which the timeworn authority structures of feudalism and Christianity continued to dominate its contours even as so much of what occurred within those contours no longer fit the conceptions of those structures?

Hell Is Where the Heart Is

> Be joyous, Florence, you are great indeed,
> for over sea and land you beat your wings;
> through every part of Hell your name extends!
> (Dante, *Inferno*   26.1–3)

Dante's infernal city is a hodgepodge composed of lived experience, the exile's nostalgia, Augustinian abstraction, literary convention, Virgilian myth, and bitter polemic. It could be said that any urban representation is a similar hodgepodge, but Dante's blend can be particularly confusing. It is quite different from the spatial representation characteristic of the modern industrial city, even as that representation is itself composed in large part of the darker elements of Dante's hell—as a glance, for example, at the urban iconography of Gustave Doré's illustrations to the *Inferno* (1857) and the infernal iconography of his illustrations to *London: A Pilgrimage* (1872) quickly demonstrates. To grasp the lineaments of Dante's representation, we need to dissociate it from our later expectations. Marion Turner has persuasively argued in a similar context that the expectation of a cohesive conception of urban space somewhat skews David Wallace's admirable account of London (or its absence) in Chaucer.[14] Because Dante adapted Augustine's vision of the two cities to his conception of the afterlife, an abstract conception of the city is seldom absent from the *Commedia* even in the depths of Hell. The first two uses of the word in the poem are by Virgil to refer to the heavenly 'city' from which he is forever excluded.[15] Beatrice, Dante's beloved and his guide through Paradise, defines her state of blessedness as being 'sanza fine cive / di quella Roma onde Cristo è romano' [without end a citizen of that Rome whereof Christ is a Roman].[16] The doctrine comes directly from Augustine, although, as Peter Hawkins observes, its identification of Rome with the heavenly city is a travesty of the doctrine's spirit.[17] In contrast, the language comes from the *Aeneid*, when Jupiter promises a worried Venus *imperium sine fine* for her son Aeneas and his exiled Trojan people. Dante's programmatic syncretism is first and foremost textual—the *Commedia* is a tissue woven of biblical language, patristic commentary, classical literature, pagan myth, and contemporary lyric and romance, among other sources—but that syncretism equally informs other aspects of the poem, including its representation of urban space. That representation is most apparent in *Inferno*, with the cityscape of Dis as its defining feature and its manifest modelling after the dysfunctional civil society of Dante's Florence, but it is present in the other two canticles as well, even in *Purgatorio*, which is set on a mountain thousands of miles distant from any human habitation, and in *Paradiso*, which is set in an outer space bereft of urban outposts in any conventional sense.[18]

We would be mistaken, however, to consider even Dante's hell to be anything like the precise reproduction of an earthly city. To be sure, the entirety of hell is implicitly walled and explicitly gated, and lower hell—the sixth through ninth circles—is enclosed by the walls and towers of the 'city' of Dis, and the ninth circle is further fortified by the circle of giants the poet compares to the towers of Montereggioni.[19] And Dante uses its spaces as a 'testing-ground of curiality and ethical values' and as an imaginary space for representing 'the possibility of human political order'.[20] But this cohesive spatial conception tends to obscure the equally strong presence of the lived urban experience of Dante's Florence and of the other cities he knew nearly as well from his travels both before and after he was exiled. In all three canticles, we experience the city as such primarily through traces of spatial practice rather than as a cohesive representation of space. As traces, these practices function simultaneously to maintain a sense of everyday familiarity in the potentially alien space of an otherworld and also to maintain a sense of distance from the city as it currently exists.

The canticle to canticle movement of the poem's landscape progressively farther from any physical resemblance to the space of a city reflects the way Dante severs himself and his readers from their accustomed attachment to the material world and their received idea of what a city could be. Hell, with its towers and walls, bridges and moats, and variety of characters and types such as is met with only in a great metropolis, certainly provides the most directly mimetic of the three canticles. The realism of this mimesis is heightened by the fact that it is not as solely negative as we might expect an infernal city to be. The great tension of *Inferno* is that its walls enclose not only those figures whom Dante eagerly and proleptically consigned there in his role as scourging prophet and urban satirist, such as the Florentine nobles who had sown civil strife for many decades or the Roman pope Boniface VIII. They also contain beloved friends and respected figures from his own life in the city such as his mentor Brunetto Latini and the father of his friend and fellow poet Guido Cavalcanti. The canticle is replete with the everyday associations that define urban life for good as well as for ill. Countless times, the poet is stopped because a soul recognizes his local idiom or hears him mention his native city. Local gossip occupies a great deal of the conversation. Cities are called out for their idiosyncrasies and specific vices—the alchemists of Siena, the flatterers and barraters of Lucca, the panders of Bologna, the usurers and thieves (among other sinners) of Florence—but also remembered for their specific sights and monuments, especially in similes such as those which inform us that a tower resembles one in Pisa, or that the giant Nimrod's face is the shape of a famous iron pine cone at St. Peter's basilica in Rome. That these forms of association persist in hell is a sign that the sins and iniquities of the earthly city are unable to quench the human spirit and also a figure of the heavenly city to come, already visible in the infernal one. In eschatological terms, hell is cut off from that other city, but in Dante's figural terms it can also be read as a distorted reflection of and aspiration toward it.

At the same time, as Mikhail Bakhtin observed, the material realism of Dante's hell is so powerful as to aspire to exist on its own terms, regardless of the condemnation of heaven.[21] This effect is especially evident in several cantos of Malebolge, the eighth circle, where the sin of fraud is punished. Dante renders these cantos in the popular form of an urban *fabliau* or novella featuring a complicated three-way struggle between demon guardians, condemned shades, and the two travellers.[22] It is hard not to admire the dexterous ingenuity with which a hooked Navarrese barrater saves his skin by promising to sell out his fellows, who are hiding more successfully than he had done from the demons' forks beneath boiling pitch. Or, rather, it *would* be easy to admire his ingenuity if we were in the secular context of Boccaccio's *Decameron* or Chaucer's *Canterbury Tales* where one is prompted to read situationally rather than holistically, in terms of the specific events rather than their theological significance. There is verve in Dante's similes—from the scene-setting description, a profligate three tercets long, of the ship-yards of Venice,[23] through the off-colour comparison of a sacred relic of Lucca with the exposed backside of a local barrater and the images of urban low-life (a cook 'who has his urchins force the meat with hooks / deep down into the pot, that it not float'; a beggar beset by dogs),[24] to the deftly sketched portrait of an underworld association of criminals beneath the boiling pitch, complete with its own argot and secret signs, an urban community that could exist only in the unique space of the fifth pouch of the eighth circle of Dante's Hell. In its dedication to imagining a specific social milieu regardless of its place within the broader ideological framework, Dante's poem in such moments declares its allegiance to a new conception of the city—and of the world—as a material site irreducible to anything else, autonomous and free. For Bakhtin (the 'realist and historical' chronotope appears to trump the 'extra-temporal chronotope'[25]) or Erich Auerbach ('In the very heart of the other world, [Dante] created a world of earthly beings and passions so powerful that it breaks bounds and proclaims its independence'[26]) horizontality supercedes verticality.

Read on something closer to its own terms, one could say rather that the framework of Dante's poem repudiates the very allegiance to horizontality that puts pressure on the verticality of its cosmic order. Much of the poem's power comes from the way that it incorporates this tension within its very structure, with the reader always caught at the threshold between two incompatible spatial conceptions. For example, the central argument of *Purgatorio* is not so much, as it was for Augustine's *Confessions*, that nothing in earthly life is capable of satisfying us or making us happy, as that we must learn to identify and to separate what makes us happy about that earthly life from what does not. The more enthralling, the more temptingly real those people and things and experiences that we must condemn become, the more likely we are to be able to recognize what is worth saving about them. Paradise in Dante's conception does not so much leave the earthly city behind as sublate it into something simultaneously recognizable and utterly transformed: 'that Rome whereof Christ is a Roman'. The fulcrum of the process occurs in Purgatory, where Dante heightens the affect of what must be left behind in order to stress its enduring value. The 'city' of Purgatory is the opposite of a static space: the members of this community are defined as pilgrims from the outset, a city of god leaving the stable moorings of the earthly city behind them. Nevertheless, while there is constant movement on its slopes, the mountain of Purgatory is also something like a hilltop town, if on a massive scale.[27] As Keen notes, it retains 'physical features that recall a city' despite its far-flung setting: 'a well-guarded gate in a set of protective walls, inside which the mountain is divided into separate sections as street-like as the circles of Malebolge and linked by rocky flights of steps'.[28] Similarly, the familiar urban associations remain intact; indeed, Dante stresses their importance, as when the thirteenth-century Mantuan poet Sordello embraces Virgil warmly on the strength only of a shared native city, no matter the temporal gap of well over a millennium.[29] At the same time, the city enters the poem through invective aimed to dissociate the negative, earthly qualities from those able to survive the process of purgation. Whereas the city of god is eternal, the city of Florence is unreliable and unstable: 'How often, in the time you can remember,/ have you changed laws and coinage, offices/and customs, and revised your citizens!'[30] Even though the climax of the poem finds the poet reunited with his beloved Beatrice, of whom as an individual he knew nothing beyond their brief encounters on the streets of Florence in a now distant youth, it takes place in the earthly paradise, as far removed physically from a cityscape as it is possible to be. In Dante's vision, the heavenly city is dissociated from material spatial practice to the same degree that the shades are dissociated from their bodies. By the same token, however, they remain invested in what we came to know in the first canticle as the infernal city in the degree that drinking of the river Eunoe has restored 'good memory' to them. Moreover, reunion with their bodies after the Last Judgment will restore the bodily memory of spatial practice engrained by years of city life, the memory that leads Dante near the end of the poem to compare his sight of the celestial Rose of the blessed souls to the 'stupefaction' of the barbarians in their capacity as tourists from the sticks, seeing 'Roma e l'ardüa sua opra' [Rome and all her vast works],[31] and, by extension, the perfect ease of the heavenly 'multitude'[32] to the practiced confidence of the eternal urbanite.

We should not be surprised in a poem written by a man who had lived most of his life in one of the largest and most important cities of medieval Europe, who had been a guild member, who had held one of the highest political posts his city had to offer, and who had spent his last years wandering in painful exile from that same city, that this city appears not only in recognizably physical ways, but that its spatial practice also imbues each of the poem's three canticles in less self-evident but even more prevalent ways.[33] Throughout the poem, Dante and his guides encounter crowds of individuals such as would be encountered only in a major urban setting. The very structure of the poem around a series of encounters between a pair of motile individuals and one or several others who separate themselves from larger crowds in order to converse closely reproduces the typical situation of urban citizens strolling through the streets of their city. Thus Farinata interpellates Dante among the heretics as both a stranger *and* a citizen of Florence:

> O Tuscan, you who pass alive across
> the fiery city with such seemly words,
> be kind enough to stay your journey here.
> Your accent makes it clear that you belong
> among the natives of the noble city
> I may have dealt with too vindictively.[34]

Furthermore, the landscape itself at times closely maps the contours of the city street (that is, streets rendered circular by the hand of God); in particular, there are the various pockets of Malebolge where crowds of damned souls circulate endlessly the path through the centre of their particular ditch, and the terraces of Purgatory, similarly flat and narrow circular pathways this time defined by the narrow space between cliff and cliff-face, where the blessed souls similarly circulate. The shades condemned for pandering and seduction, for example, are compared in an extended simile to 'the great crowds' at the year 1300 Jubilee in Rome, so numerous that authorities divided them into two-way traffic lanes to pass over a busy bridge.[35] On the mountain of Purgatory, we find a 'turba magna' [mighty throng] speeding around the terrace of the slothful, just as one could see 'of old … crowds and clamour / whenever Thebans had to summon Bacchus'.[36] As they would in a comprehensive city-walk, Dante and Virgil encounter individuals of a wide range of situation and degree, from noble spirits such as Farinata and Ulysses, to baser shades such as Ciacco, the anonymous Florentine suicide, or Master Adam the counterfeiter in Hell; and poets, statesmen, artists, family and friends in Purgatory. At times, Dante even reproduces in exaggerated form the material circumstances of the city, including the cemetery in which he encounters the heretics near the walls of Dis and the filthy excrement in which the flatterers are immersed in Malebolge.[37] Urban similes are especially frequent in *Inferno*, but they persist even into *Paradiso*, as we saw above. They are especially common as a way of stressing the resemblance of crowds and specific populations of souls to particular cities or to particular urban activities, as when he compares the racing sodomites of the seventh circle to the participants in a competition in Verona,[38] or the tombs of the heretics to the famous necropolises of Arles and Pola.[39]

In addition to these physical recollections, the ways in which individuals in Dante's afterlife respond to and interact with one another are based on associations indelibly rooted in urban space. They self-identify as inhabitants of individual cities, members of specific guilds or practitioners of specific trades. Their conversation deals with topics of art and politics just as if they were meeting in a central plaza or square. And while there are certainly strong traces of feudal structures in the poem (particularly in the hierarchical and segregated divisions that constitute each realm), and Christian structures (particularly in the vertical organization of the afterlife and its eschatological framework), both structures are poised in a tense relationship with the inclusive context of the city as a place of equal differences—in particular, the conception of Rome. Consequently, it is more the attitude taken toward the spatial practice of the city than the degree of its presence that changes from canticle to canticle. In *Inferno*, the dominant image is of mass death—the kind of vision only possible in the metropolitan experience of disease and disaster either from natural causes or through the siege and sack of cities. The chaos and destruction expressed through these viscerally physical images are reinforced by the intimate depiction of the breakdown of sociality equally strongly expressed through the essentially urban crimes of fraud documented in painstaking detail in the cantos of Malebolge. In *Purgatorio*, we find predominantly Dante's Augustine-tinged version of the *Aeneid*'s city in exile, Aeneas carrying his household gods with him as he travels from the failed city of Troy to the promised city of Rome to come, a community surviving through mutual support and united by a common goal. Throughout *Purgatorio*, Dante aims to define the 'household gods' of his Florence, the essence of his heretofore infernal natal city that is worth preserving in the city of God toward which all the pilgrims on the mountain are journeying, a task as hard and huge as founding the Roman empire.

Given this set-up, we should perhaps not be overly surprised to find the most extended mimesis of an actual city in the ethereal tracts of the planets of *Paradiso* rather than within the bleak walls of Hell: the three-canto-long speech of Dante's ancestor Cacciaguida, with at its centre his utopian recollection of Florence as it once was.[40] Like Aeneas's journey up the Tiber to visit King Evander in the Arcadian backwater that already somehow contains the *genius loci* of the city of Rome to come,[41] Cacciaguida's Florence strives to combine rustic local virtues with cosmopolitanism in its urban vision. In both instances, the space of the city incorporates rather than excludes or dominates nature. And like Virgil's simultaneously backwards- and forwards-looking utopia, Cacciaguida's Florentine utopia draws its power from the experience of the infernal journey that preceded it. This is a smaller, purer, and simpler place, 'so tranquil and so lovely'. Nevertheless, its 'ancient Baptistery' of San Giovanni where Dante was christened and where his ancestor 'at once became Christian and Cacciaguida'[42] suggests the continuity between past and present, even as the prior allusion to the same location in *Inferno* 19 had focused on the disturbing image of the author's shattering of one of those very fonts.[43] Similarly, the misty-eyed nostalgia of this speech is mitigated by the overt way in which Cacciaguida uses the vision as a club with which to hammer the present, and the degree to which he stresses the ties that bind one Florence with the other. These ties redound both to the cityscape itself and to the family names he details one by one. If for Augustine, the earthly city offered a model of social dysfunction that needs must be rejected wholeheartedly in favour of a 'city of god' which was urban only in terms of its assemblage of a great population, for Dante, the medieval city-state is also the spatial model that preserves the autonomy and individuality of 'diversi porti / per lo gran mar de l'essere' [different ports across the great sea of being][44] through which he defines the blessed. The city—local associations, political engagement, art and culture, family and friends—embodies everything that the greater organization of the empire and the afterlife threatens, but is finally unable, to eliminate. The city for Dante is the paradoxical survival of all the earthly bonds that a Christian needs must sever, stubbornly persisting even into the heart of the empyrean realm.

The Afterlife of Dante's Infernal and Celestial Cities
> Through me the way into the suffering city.
> (Dante, *Inferno*   3.1)

Dante's *Commedia* brought together as an authoritative summation the medieval conception of the heavenly city, rooting its abstract Augustinian metaphorics in the spatial practices of the medieval city. At the same time, the poem provided an important early articulation of the materially grounded representation of urban space that would be central to later representations of the city as a space of everyday experience and secular authority. Both representational modes are strongly evident in late medieval literature, although never with the knife-edged balance achieved in the *Commedia*. The fading spatial metaphor of the heavenly city received its most sustained expression in Christine de Pizan's *The Book of the City of Ladies* (1405), while urban spatial practice figures prominently in later medieval literature from the post-Dantean Florence of Boccaccio's *Decameron* (1350–3) to the low-life mid-fifteenth-century Paris of François Villon's strongly autobiographical verse to the fragmented London that refracts throughout Chaucer's writings. The degree to which the verticality of the medieval cosmos remains present in the spatial conception of these city writings determines the degree to which they manifest a sense of cohesive representation. The relative lack of this conception in *The Canterbury Tales* in relation to the strong structural cohesion of the *Commedia* and the *Decameron* is partly responsible for Wallace's influential formulation of the absence of London in the former versus the dominant presence of Florence in the latter.

The *Book of the City of Ladies* provides an excellent example of the vertical model in the absence of any horizontal narrative impulse. Indeed, we can regard the physical stasis of the poem's structure as an implicit response of a Paris-based writer to the local urban university discourse that she viewed not only as strongly misogynist but as fundamentally impious and sinful in its rejection of order and decorum. Although plausibly urban in premise—a writer beset on all sides in her library by defamatory volumes is visited by three allegorical ladies with whom she will build and inhabit a new city cleansed of these volumes' calumnies—the poem's allegory is explicitly fictional and the spatial dynamics of its frame are resolutely interiorized. The narrator journeys in her mind and through the world of letters. Now, this is not to say that the author's experience as an inhabitant of Paris and a widow supporting her family as a professional writer does not enter into the text; after all, Christine ended the dream vision of her most explicitly Dantean work, the *Livre du chemin de longue estude* (*Book of the Path of Long Study*), with the author rudely awakened by her mother telling her she has overslept. Moreover, the text is full of concrete details of women's work and women's subversive undertaking of 'men's work'. In fact, the tactile details of her many rewritings of foundation myths—from Nicostrata/Carmentis's invention of the Latin alphabet and her identity as a 'school-mistress' to the story of Dido's founding of Carthage and the 'brick-by-brick' construction of the allegory of the city—stress the need to examine individual examples rather than make sweeping generalizations. Nevertheless, Christine's is a highly idealized city, a revision of the idealized cities of the past tradition (in particular Augustine's City of God and the Rome of Virgil and Dante), as well as a recuperation of the damned cities of that same tradition—the Carthage of Dido and the Babylon of Semiramis, among others—that has little to do with early fifteenth-century Paris. The degree to which this idealization redounds to her birth in Venice and the influence of her father, court astrologer in the Republic of Venice before he was appointed in a similar capacity to the court of Charles V of France, is a matter for speculation. But there is no question that Christine counterposed an Italian-based tradition of authority running from Virgil through Augustine to Dante to a tradition embodied for her by the Paris-based Jean de Meun, whose clerkly continuation (c.1268–85) of Guillaume de Lorris's courtly allegory *Le roman de la rose* (c.1230), was in many ways a secular and worldly counterpart to Dante's eschatological summa of medieval knowledge.[45]

Like Dante, Christine proposes an allegorical city built on virtue, in which qualified women from the station of queen down to commoner were 'convocquees a estres souveraines citoyennes'.[46]

Where Christine differs from Dante, and where we can glimpse the influence of the secularizing urban space in which she lived and laboured, is in the tacit refusal of his eschatological framework. Notwithstanding that her city is built of past examples of virtuous ladies and that its towers are constituted by the deeds of Christian martyrs, its aims are explicitly based in the current world. Rather than existing as 'real' souls in the afterlife, Christine's exempla are patently textual, derived as they are from the shelves of their author's study. Christine devoted *Le tresor de la cité des dames*, a sequel to the *Livre de la cité des dames*, to the education of its new citizens, in order of degree from royalty down to the common woman. While there is no more reason to doubt the sincerity of Christine's faith than that of Dante, her city puts that faith to work in the present life far more explicitly. This impetus was always present in the *Commedia*—the 'moral' level of its allegory would apply the lessons of the afterlife to the present state of the Christian reader in this life—but subordinated to the hierarchical framework and prophetic authority of the vertically structured afterlife. While Christine availed herself of this structure of authority, she did it mediated through Dante's example and with the implicit and ironically articulated caveat that she, as a woman writer, had no direct access to its prophetic claim to truth. It is a paradoxical manoeuvre, for Christine wants the openness to difference and autonomy of the new urban spaces but without the materiality of the experience, and she wants the authority and weight of the heavenly city but without the hierarchical baggage that relegated her as woman to a subordinate position. And, just as her city is simultaneously radically utopian in its feminism and profoundly conservative in its rejection of physical experience and material culture, her writing is forwards and backwards looking in equal measure.

While it is difficult to mount a persuasive argument disputing the faith of Dante or Christine, it is equally difficult to demonstrate with any certainty that the protestations of faith that dot the thirteenth-century writing of Jean de Meun or the later works of Boccaccio, Chaucer, or Villon are anything other than formal lip service to the discourse of medieval piety. The irony that hovers irresolutely around the virtuous framings of the multiplicity of urban experience leaves us always in doubt as to where we should stand in relation to the world around us. The libertine Parisian setting of Jean and of Villon leaves less doubt than either Boccaccio's band of Florentine youths, whose one hundred stories gleefully and non-judgmentally detail the gamut of human experience even as its personal conduct remains unimpeachable, or Chaucer's pilgrims, whose order is (mostly) maintained by their host and whose behaviour may be less decorous than that of Boccaccio's youthful elite but nevertheless remains far this side of criminal or illicit. But we are nevertheless a long way from modernist writers from Charles Baudelaire through Djuna Barnes to Ralph Ellison that would take Dante's *Inferno* as their practical guide to the urban underworld around them while overtly repudiating the ideological framework surrounding that underworld.

Boccaccio does radically secularize Dante's vision of hell, drawing out and amplifying any trace of everyday Florentine life in the *Inferno* and transforming it into a series of object lessons of survival in a city in which the divine hierarchy no longer even pretends to govern daily interactions. In the realpolitik of Boccaccio's Florence, the quick wits and sharp tongues inherited from Dante's innovative vernacular representation of damned souls are the only tools merchants and other less powerful citizens have with which to protect themselves from the enduring authority of the elite. As Wallace demonstrates in his careful reading of the story of Cisti the baker, Boccaccio demonstrates how a complex set of verbal interactions and interpretations was able to use the language of feudalism to negotiate very modern social relationships.[47] Wallace persuasively claims that, 'Through this transfer of tokens and messages, which owes as much to the devices of courtly love as to the protocols of Florentine politics, Boccaccio suggests an ideal unity of the Florentine body politic in the face of external treachery.'[48] But it is equally possible to read the utopianism of the author's vision of Florence in context of the threat of disaster that the telling of these stories is striving to avert. As Dante contrasted the dysfunctionality of Florence with its potential as the terrestrial emblem of the heavenly city, so Boccaccio frames his storytellers' catalogue of survival strategies with the devastating opening portrait of a city laid waste both physically and socially by the ravages of plague. Boccaccio's opening gambit also serves to ground Dante's eschatology of infernal dysfunction in a historical disaster. In this sense, he asserts a measure of epistemological unity absent, for instance, from the solipsistic cities of Jean de Meun and Villon—all the latter provides with which to frame his exuberant exploration of the city's criminal and sexual underworld is the poet's execution at the end of his poem. That Villon's *Testament* is composed primarily of a bawdy and irreverent catalogue of legacies tells us worlds about the speaker's attitude but provides very little from which to glean broader significance. There is, in other words, no sustained moral allegory to be drawn from this city any more than from Jean's. It comes very close to the modern situation of existing in and for itself.

If the 'urban ideology' of Florence that Wallace would see in Dante and Boccaccio is able to posit 'a momentary but decisive meeting, on level terms, of a powerful merchant-politician and a lowly baker,'[49] the spatial practice of late-medieval Paris would appear to reject the need for such a meeting altogether, finding meaning in an embrace of physical experience, or what Bakhtin termed the 'bodily lower stratum'. Wallace finds Chaucer's London more equivocal, arguing that the brief glimpses of the city demonstrate that, 'any discourse beginning with aspirations to inclusiveness soon comes to discover special allegiances and unbridgeable hostilities.'[50] While this distinction seems persuasive on the level of local discourse, it is less evident to me that it denotes a material difference in spatial practice rather than a different response to a fairly consistent set of practices. That is, while there exist specific material differences in the histories of medieval Florence, London, and Paris that are partially responsible for determining the different discourses and urban representations we have observed, there are also shared circumstances that suggest an underlying commonality. In particular, in all of the writers discussed here, we can glimpse, whether positively or negatively, the dominant presence of the medieval conception of the city and the Christian cosmos given its most enduring form in Dante's *Commedia*. Local circumstances may have strongly influenced the mode of response that led Dante and Boccaccio to frame the new urban experience in terms of the old vertical cosmos, Villon to explode that frame completely, and Chaucer neither to repudiate nor to represent it, and perhaps we could argue that one of the characteristics of the new spatial conception of the city was its insistence on representational difference and local autonomy. As Turner puts it, Chaucer's 'poetry opens up fourteenth-century urban life to us in all its disreputable diversity'.[51] But one reason that these texts continue to be periodized as medieval is that, despite their growing allegiance to a new horizontality, we never fail to glimpse the black pit of verticality opening up at their feet.

NOTES

1. On katabatic narrative, see Rachel Falconer, *Hell in Contemporary Literature: Western Descent Narratives since 1945* (Edinburgh: Edinburgh University Press, 2005), 42–62.
2. Henri Lefebvre, *The Production of Space*, trans. Donald Nicholson-Smith (Oxford: Blackwell, 1991), 86. Michael Camille makes a similar distinction between 'lived social place' and 'disembodied abstract space', although his analysis privileges the former over the latter, which he views, at least in its terminology, as anachronistic ('Signs of the City: Space, Power, and Public Fantasy in Medieval Paris', *Medieval Practices of Space*, ed. Barbara Hanawalt and Michal Kobialka (Minneapolis: University of Minnesota Press, 2000), 1–36, at 9.
3. David Nicholas, *Urban Europe, 1100–1700* (New York: Palgrave Macmillan, 2003), viii. For other recent historical overviews of the medieval city, see Norman John Grenville Pounds, *The Medieval City* (Westport: Greenwood, 2005), and Keith D. Lilley, *Urban Life in the Middle Ages: 1000–1450* (New York: Palgrave Macmillan, 2002).
4. Pounds, *Medieval City*, 9.
5. Lilley, *City and Cosmos: The Medieval World in Urban Form* (London: Reaktion Books, 2009), 147.
6. Lilley in *City and Cosmos* well captures the symbolic function of geometric form in plotting theological and feudal structures in terms of cosmic order through urban planning and what I would term an ordered horizontality of bodies in space. My focus here is on the interplay between this ordered horizontality, the less intentional and more disordered horizontality of everyday life, and the different symbolism of the vertical cosmos.
7. Augustine, *City of God*, 15.1. Otto of Friesing, the twelfth-century abbot, bishop, and advisor to Frederick I, took this image as the ruling metaphor of his universal history, *The Two Cities*; historian Malcolm Barber has adapted it as the 'overall model' for his synthesis of medieval European history in terms of the 'tension' between 'the pressures and the temptations of the material world' and 'the deeply held belief in the need to aspire towards a higher, spiritual life' in *The Two Cities: Medieval Europe 1050–1320* (1992, 2nd ed. New York: Routledge, 2006), 1–2.
8. Augustine, *City of God* 15.2. For a concise and lucid summary of Augustine's doctrine, see Peter Hawkins, 'Divide and Conquer: Augustine in the *Divine Comedy*', *PMLA* 106, no. 3 (May 1991), 471–82.

9. Walter Benjamin, *The Origin of German Tragic Drama*, trans. John Osborne (London: Verso, 1985), 220–26.

10. Augustine, *City of God* 15.2.

11. Teodolinda Barolini, *Dante and the Origins of Italian Literary Culture* (New York: Fordham University Press, 2006), 2–3; see also *The Undivine Comedy: Detheologizing Dante* (Princeton, NJ: Princeton University Press, 1992), 3–20.

12. For an innovative attempt to recover the 'social place' of vernacular texts such as Dante's lyrics and the *Commedia* in the context of Dante's historical readership particularly in Florence and Bologna, see Justin Steinberg, *Accounting for Dante: Urban Readers and Writers in Late Medieval Italy* (Notre Dame, IN: University of Notre Dame Press, 2007).

13. David Wallace, *Chaucerian Polity: Absolutist Lineages and Associational Polity in England and Italy* (Stanford: Stanford University Press, 1997), 156–81.

14. Marion Turner, 'Greater London', in *Chaucer and the City*, ed. Ardis Butterfield (Cambridge: D. S. Brewer, 2006), 25–40, at 27–8. For an even-handed look at Wallace's influential argument and recent work in general on Chaucer and London, see David Raybin, 'Chaucer as a London Poet: A Review Essay', *Essays in Medieval Studies* 24 (2007): 21–9.

15. Dante, *Inferno* 1.126–8. As Nick Havely observes, this opening usage introduces the theme of the city on a note of exclusion that is counterbalanced by Beatrice's identification of herself as a citizen (*Dante* [Oxford: Blackwell, 2007], 134).

16. Dante, *Purgatorio* 32.101–2.

17. Hawkins, 'Divide and Conquer', 472.

18. On Florence as model for the society of hell, see Joan Ferrante, *The Political Vision of the Divine Comedy* (Princeton: Princeton University Press, 1984), and John Najemy, 'Dante and Florence', in *The Cambridge Companion to Dante*, ed. Rachel Jacoff (Cambridge: Cambridge University Press, 2007), 236–56, at 239. As Catherine Keen rightly observes, Dante's representation of the city has generally been approached in terms of this political vision; hers is the first book-length study to focus on the centrality of an 'urban imaginary' to the poetics of the *Commedia* (*Dante and the City* [Stroud, Gloucestershire: Tempus Publishing, 2003], 12–15s).

19. Dante, *Inferno* 31.40–43.

20. Keen, *Dante and the City*, 239.

21. Mikhail Bakhtin, 'Forms of Time and of the Chronotope', in *The Dialogic Imagination*, ed. Michael Holquist, trans. Caryl Emerson (Austin: University of Texas Press, 1981); see also Falconer's discussion (*Hell in Contemporary Literature*, 47–50).

22. Dante, *Inferno* 21–3.

23. Dante, *Inferno* 21.7–15.

24. Dante, *Inferno* 21.56–7; 21.67–9.

25. Falconer, *Hell in Contemporary Literature*, 47.

26. Erich Auerbach, *Mimesis: The Representation of Reality in Western Literature*, trans. Willard Trask (Princeton: Princeton University Press, 1968), 200.

27. Jeffrey Schnapp, 'Introduction to *Purgatorio*', in Jacoff, *Cambridge Companion to Dante*, 192–207, at 193.

28. Keen, *Dante and the City*, 158.

29. Dante, *Purgatorio* 6.70–5.

30. Dante, *Purgatorio* 6.145–8.

31. Dante *Paradiso* 31.34.

32. Dante *Paradiso* 31.20.

33. Similar arguments have been made of the even more oblique presence of London in Chaucer's writings. Turner maintains that Chaucer's 'sense of London is often most evocatively and suggestively expressed through atmosphere and tone rather than through explicit references' ('Greater London', 36), while Ruth Evans concludes that, 'in Chaucer's poetry the medieval city is a powerful *virtual* presence' ('The Production of Space in Chaucer's London' in Butterfield, *Chaucer and the City*, 41–56, at 56).

34. Dante, *Inferno* 10.22–7.

35. Dante, *Inferno* 18.25–32.

36. Dante, *Purgatorio* 18.91–5.

37. For a discussion of excrement and other waste in the context of urban discourse, the body politic, and Chaucer's London, see Susan Signe Morrison, *Excrement and Filth in the Late Middle Ages: Sacred Filth and Chaucer's Fecopoetics* (New York: Palgrave Macmillan, 2008), 57–72.

38. Dante, *Inferno* 15.121–4.

39. Dante, *Inferno* 9.112–16.

40. Dante, *Paradiso* 15–17.

41. Virgil, *Aeneid* 10.

42. Dante, *Paradiso* 15.130, 134–5.

43. Dante, *Inferno* 19.16–21.

44. Dante, *Paradiso* 1.112–13.

45. David L. Pike, *Passage through Hell: Modernist Descents, Medieval Underworlds* (Ithaca: Cornell University Press, 1997), 153–67.

46. Christine de Pizan, *Le tresor de la cité des dames de degré en degré et de tous estatz*, prologue (Project Gutenberg ebook, 2008).

47. Wallace, *Chaucerian Polity*, 166.

48. Wallace, *Chaucerian Polity*, 166.

49. Wallace, *Chaucerian Polity*, 179.

50. Wallace, *Chaucerian Polity*, 180.

51. Marion Turner, 'Politics and London Life', *A Concise Companion to Chaucer*, ed. Corinne Saunders (Malden: Blackwell, 2006), 13–33, at 32. For an overview of recent work on Chaucer and the city, see Raybin, 'Chaucer as a London Poet', and the essays in Butterfield, *Chaucer and the City*. For additional specific essays, see, among others, Craig E. Bertolet, ' "My wit is sharp; I love no taryinge": Urban poetry and the Parlement of Foules', *Studies in Philology* 93, no. 4 (1999): 365–89; John Micheal Crafton, 'Chaucer and the City: Troilus as Urban Poetry', *Medieval Perspectives* 17, no. 2 (2002): 51–65; Jean E. Jost, 'Urban and Liminal Space in Chaucer's *Knight's Tale*: Perilous_or_Protective?', *Urban Space in the Middle Ages and the Early Modern Age*, ed. Albrecht Classen (Berlin: De Gruyter, 2009), 373–94; Robert Sturges, 'The Pardoner in Canterbury: Class, Gender, and Urban Space in the "Prologue to the Tale of Beryn"', *College Literature* 33, no. 3 (2006): 52–76.

BIBLIOGRAPHY

Benson, C. David, 'London', in *Chaucer: An Oxford Guide*, ed. Steve Ellis (Oxford: Oxford University Press, 2005), 66–80.

Butterfield, Ardis, ed., *Chaucer and the City*. (Cambridge: D. S. Brewer, 2006).

Classen, Albrecht, ed., *Urban Space in the Middle Ages and the Early Modern Age* (Berlin: De Gruyter, 2009).

Essays in Medieval Studies 24, special issue on *The Medieval City* (2007), 21–9.

Ferrante, Joan, *The Political Vision of the Divine Comedy* (Princeton, NJ: Princeton University Press, 1984).

Jacoff, Rachel, *The Cambridge Companion to Dante* (Cambridge: Cambridge University Press, 2007).

Keen, Catherine, *Dante and the City* (Stroud: Tempus Publishing, 2003).

Lefebvre, Henri, *The Production of Space*, trans. Donald Nicholson-Smith (Oxford: Blackwell, 1991).

Lilley, Keith D., *City and Cosmos: The Medieval World in Urban Form* (London: Reaktion Books, 2009).

Lilley, Keith D., *Urban Life in the Middle Ages: 1000–1450* (New York: Palgrave Macmillan, 2002).

Nicholas, David, *Urban Europe, 1100–1700* (New York: Palgrave Macmillan, 2003).

Pounds, Norman John Grenville, *The Medieval City* (Westport, CT: Greenwood, 2005).

Steinberg, Justin, *Accounting for Dante: Urban Readers and Writers in Late Medieval Italy* (Notre Dame, IN: University of Notre Dame Press, 2007).

Wallace, David, *Chaucerian Polity: Absolutist Lineages and Associational Polity in England and Italy* (Stanford, CA: Stanford University Press, 1997).

CHAPTER 20

HISTORIOGRAPHY

Nicholas Trevet's Transnational History

SUZANNE CONKLIN AKBARI

THIS chapter addresses Chaucer's chief model for the writing of universal history: the early fourteenth-century Anglo-Norman chronicle of Nicholas Trevet.[1] While many readers have some familiarity with Trevet's work, that knowledge most likely comes through the so-called 'tale of Constance', adapted by Chaucer as the Man of Law's Tale and by Gower (as an exemplary narrative about the sin of envy) in his contemporary *Confessio amantis*. Typically, studies of Trevet's *Chronicle* focus very narrowly on this part of the work as a source text.[2] Much more can be learned, however, through an examination of the ways in which Trevet's larger vision of history is reflected in Chaucer's writings.

To start with, even though it is often assumed that Chaucer used the work of Geoffrey of Monmouth directly, it is clear that Trevet's *Chronicle* was an important mediator through which Chaucer knew the *History of the Kings of Britain*: all the correspondences between Geoffrey's British history and Chaucer's writings also appear in Trevet's work, which makes abundant use of Geoffrey.[3] Trevet digests Geoffrey's British history, however, in some significant ways, especially with regard to national identity. This, in turn, provides a useful context for the reading of Chaucer—but not in the usual sense, where Chaucer's works are classified (in ways that Kathryn Lynch has cogently called into question) as being part of his 'French period' or 'Italian period', before moving into the confidently 'English' literary monumentality of the *Canterbury Tales*.[4] On the contrary, considering Chaucer's engagement with Trevet allows us to approach the question of national identity from another angle, that of medieval historiography, asking the question 'How were notions of national identity articulated in the history-writing of fourteenth-century England'?[5] In Chaucer's case, we are fortunate in being able to look at a universal history that he clearly knew (because it is the primary source of the Man of Law's Tale, including details from Trevet that do not appear in the analogue found in Gower's *Confessio amantis*),[6] and then to consider the ways in which Trevet places the history of England in the transnational frame, before turning to an examination of how national identity—especially with regard to language—is expressed in Chaucer's work.

The first section of this chapter sketches out the overall nature of Trevet's world history, indicating its scope and considering what view it presents of English national identity, especially in terms of genealogical descent and territorial claims ('The River of Time'). It then turns to the Constance narrative that provided a model for the Man of Law's Tale, illustrating how Trevet's version highlights the role of language in the establishment of national identity, and in the mediating of fundamental changes to that national identity. Selected other passages in Trevet's work also illustrate the role of language in articulating the boundaries that separate nations and, sometimes, bring them together ('Language and Nation'). The chapter closes by identifying what it is that Trevet's historical vision offers readers of Chaucer's histories, such as *Troilus and Criseyde* or the Knight's Tale: namely, a capacious temporal scope that makes room for a plural vision of multiple historical contexts—biblical, apostolic, Trojan, Roman, Theban, British, Saxon, and English.

THE RIVER OF TIME

Chaucer's sense of history has been studied at length, through a wide range of methodological approaches: New Historicist, psychoanalytic, postcolonial, and so on. These studies most often focus on the ancient histories that lie in the distant past, especially the narratives of Troy and Thebes.[7] Less work has been done on the alternative historiographical models that lie behind his work, including the histories of Geoffrey of Monmouth, Ranulf Higden, and Paulus Orosius. The history of Geoffrey of Monmouth lies behind the evocations of the Chaucer's two 'Britains', the insular Briton land of the Wife of Bath's Tale and the continental Briton lands of the Franklin's Tale.[8] The national history of the English people, couched not only in terms of territorial claims and genealogical descent but also of the English language, is the focus of Higden's *Polychronicon*, especially as it is presented in the Middle English translation of John Trevisa.[9] Finally, in the universal history of Orosius, biblical and imperial histories are intricately intertwined, forming a basic model or template for many later writers of chronicles.[10]

We might think of universal chronicles and national histories as being two fundamentally different kinds of writing, because we do sometimes see national histories that do not aspire to provide an international scope, and we also find universal histories—such as that of Orosius—that carefully avoid privileging any national group in their account of the past. More commonly, however, we find the most powerful articulations of national identity—even a sense of national destiny or purpose—articulated within the framework of the universal history. Examples include the thirteenth-century *Histoire ancienne jusqu'à César*, which celebrates not only the French aspirations to lead a Christian empire, but also the special role of Flanders as a nation;[11] or the fourteenth-century *Polychronicon*, which situates its history of England within the context of universal history, creating a kind of teleological vision of the past that gradually comes to fruition with the emergence of the English nation.[12] A similar convergence of the national and the universal appears in Trevet's *Chronicle*. Here, however, the nation does not simply emerge out of the framework of the universal history, as it does in the *Histoire ancienne* or the *Polychronicon*. Instead, for Trevet, sixth-century England is a point of origin—not just for his own 'modern', fourteenth-century England, but for Christian Rome itself.

Trevet had a model for this kind of history-writing, in which the nation he celebrates does not simply emerge from the international framework but also profoundly influences that universal setting, in Geoffrey of Monmouth. For Geoffrey, however, the intersection of his chosen nation—Britain—with the mighty empire of Rome is generally combative. There are some successful intermarriages that bring peace, such as the marriage of the Briton Arveragus with the daughter of the Roman emperor Claudius, but usually the encounter of Britain and Rome is a repeated series of conflicts and competition.[13] For Geoffrey, the enhanced status of Britain comes from the nation's willingness to defy and even conquer Rome (if only temporarily). Trevet, by contrast, presents a nation that is able to contribute to the ongoing, vital circulation of goods, knowledge, and—above all—religious law between the metropolitan centre of Rome and its surrounding nations.

The shape of Trevet's *Chronicle* is unusual in its refusal to compartmentalize history into the neat, scholastic building blocks we ordinarily find in universal histories such as Vincent of Beauvais' *Speculum historiale* or Higden's *Polychronicon*.[14] Instead, Trevet's *Chronicle* is a prose romance—romance not just in the sense of being in the romance vernacular (that is, 'en romans'), but also in its narrative form. Although we do encounter dividing lines in the narrative (in the form of the six ages, or the sequence of the books of the Bible, or significant turning points in salvation history) what we fundamentally experience is a slow but steady flow of narrative, one that mimics the flow of the stream of time. Trevet uses the standard ordering structure of the six ages popularized by Orosius in the early fifth century and repeated throughout the Middle Ages. The first age extends from Adam to Noah and the Flood; the second ends with the birth of Abraham; the third with the end of King David's reign in Jerusalem; the fourth with the Babylonian Captivity; and the fifth age ends with the birth of Christ. All history from that time onward is the sixth age, a long history of waiting for the great punctuation of the Apocalypse that will herald the arrival of the seventh age.

Trevet carefully identifies each of these transitional moments in his text. In addition, he makes explicit the biblical framework of his undertaking by structuring the first ten parts of his *Chronicle* according to books of scripture, both canonical and apocryphal, following the pattern of Peter Comestor's *Historia scholastica*.[15] Significantly, Trevet includes the biblical and apocryphal books that allow him to interpolate non-scriptural history most freely: Genesis and Exodus; Joshua, Judges, Kings, Esdras and Machabees; the Gospels and the Acts of the Apostles. Just before the Gospels, however, Trevet inserts a non-biblical source, but one which was invaluable in the medieval historian's effort to integrate biblical history with all the other strands of ancient history: that is, Josephus. In his account of the fall of Jerusalem at the hands of the Roman rulers Titus and Vespasian, Josephus provided a narrative of the intersection of Roman might and

Christian potential, mediated by the dispersal of the Jews from Jerusalem in a parodic inversion of the waves of pilgrims and crusaders that, in the later Middle Ages, would wind their way to the Holy City.

The biblical books (plus Josephus) form less than a third of Trevet's text, just over thirty-three out of roughly 114 folios in the Paris manuscript.[16] What follows is a history of what Trevet invariably refers to as 'Britain, which is now called England' [Brutaigne, qe est ore apelé Engleterre (115; f.55 vb)]. At a superficial glance, a reader might be forgiven for thinking that what we have in the *Chronicle* is a prose vernacular rendition of the Bible, followed by a history of England. This is not exactly correct. Trevet's *Chronicle* does not simply provide an integrated chronology, in which dates in different parts of the world are matched up with one other to provide fixed points of reference. More than an integrated chronology, Trevet offers an integrated narrative, one that is braided or twisted to combine different group identities into an intricately woven narrative pattern.

Continuously throughout the *Chronicle*, rulers from widely different parts of the world are juxtaposed. Early in biblical history—while we are still in Genesis—we encounter the history of the Britons for the first time. Following Geoffrey of Monmouth, but embedding British history within a biblical matrix, Trevet goes on to explain how the settlement of Britain takes place, and the ways in which the territory is divided:

> And then the realm of Britain was divided among five kings, that is to say, of Albania, which is Scotland, Stateryk was made the king; and of Northumbria, Yonan; and of Logres, which is England, Pynece; and of Wales, Rudauk; and of Cornwall, Clotoun. . . . In the time of this Joas, king of Jerusalem, Zacharie the son of Joiada, was made high priest [lit. 'bishop'] of the law, and after him Azarié.

> [Et donqe estoit le roialme de Brutaigne departi entre cink rois, c'est assavoir qe de Albanie, q'est Escoce, fu fait roy Stateryk; et de Northumbre, Yonan; et de Loegrie, [q'est] Engleterre, Pynece; et de Wales, Rudauk; et de Cornewaille, Clotoun. . . . En le temps cist Joas, roi de Jerusalem, estoient fait evesqe de la ley Zacharie, le fitz Joiada, et aprés lui Azarié   (f.19 b).]

This is typical of Trevet's habit of juxtaposing or intertwining different historical strands: all elements of the past—biblical, apostolic, Trojan, Roman, British, Saxon, and so on—are merged in the romance of the *Chronicle*. In the midst of a history of Judges, we are reminded of the fall of Troy; in an account of Kings, we hear about Romulus and Remus.

What is perhaps most striking in Trevet's history of the nation, embedded within the universal framework, is its heterogeneity. Repeatedly throughout the *Chronicle*, Trevet lays out the complexity that lies within the apparent singularity of the nation. For example, in his account of the early conversion missions on the island and the establishment of bishoprics, Trevet emphasizes the ways in which episcopal jurisdiction corresponds to territorial boundaries internal to the nation:

> To these three [cities, that is, 'Loundres, Ewerwyk, et la cité de Legiouns', or Caerleon] were subject twenty-seven bishops, for to the archbishop of Everwyk was subject Deira (that is, Northumberland) and Albania (that is, Scotland), divided into dioceses

beyond the Humber, which separated them from Loegres, which now is called England. To the archbishop of London, Loegres and Cornwall were subject.

[A ceux trois estoient subgetz vint et sept evesqes, qar a l'ercevesqe de Everwyk estoit subget Deira, c'est Northumberlond, et Albania, c'est Escoce, divisez par diocises outre Humbre, qe les departe de Loegres, q'ore est apellé Engleterre. A l'ercevesqe de Loundres estoient subgetz Loegre et Cor[ne]waille   (f.44vb).]

Here, we are given not only the territorial boundaries upon which the bishoprics were established, but their 'modern'—that is, fourteenth-century—equivalents. A similar inclination to emphasize the heterogeneity within the nation appears in Trevet's account of how the various Germanic populations were diffused among the different British populations:

And then he granted to the three aforesaid types of people to dwell in diverse counties with the Britons—that is to say, the Jutes in Kent and the Isle of Wight, and in Sussex, and in the Isle of Selsey; and the Saxons in Hampshire, Wiltshire, Berkshire, Dorset, Somerset, and Devonshire; and the English in all the other counties in the land as far as Scotland. And because the English occupied, among the Britons, the greater part of the land, forever afterward the whole island was called 'England'.

[Et puis granta a lez avauntditz trois maners dez gentz pur habiter en diverses countés ove lez Brutouns—c'est assavoir lez Jutes en Kent et en l'isle de Wiht, et en Southsex, et en l'isle de Selseie; et les Sessouns en Hampteshire, Wilteshire, Barcshire, Dorsete, Somercete, et Deveneshire; et les Engleis en totez les autres counteez de la terre jesqe Escoce. Et pur ceo qe lez Engleis occuperent entre lé Brutouns la greindre partie de la terre par touz jours aprés estoit tut le isle apelé Engleterre   (115; f.56a).]

He then goes on to give a detailed breakdown of each of these Germanic 'regnes' or petty kingdoms, starting with 'le regne de Kent'" (117), going on to 'Southsex' (121), 'Westsexe' (135), 'Northumbre' (137), and so on.

A similar emphasis on intra-national heterogeneity appears in Trevet's account of Uther Pendragon, the father of Arthur. Trevet describes how in the time of Uther and his brother, Aurelius Ambrosius, an alliance was formed with 'three types of peoples who came from Germany to Britain, which is now called England...that is to say, Saxons, English, and Jutes' ['trois maneres dez genz qe venerent de Germane en Brutaigne, qe est ore apelé Engleterre...c'est asavoir Sessouns, Engleis et Jutes' (114; f.55 vb)]. So far, this intra-national heterogeneity is familiar. Trevet goes on, however, to couple this emphasis on difference and division with a move to integrate the various strands of his intricately braided history: he gives a genealogy for the Germanic Hengist, tracing his lineage back to Wetta, the son of Woden, who—Trevet declares—was the son of Shem, the son of Noah (115; f.55 vb). While the part of the passage about Aurelius Ambrosius and Uther Pendragon comes from Geoffrey of Monmouth, the discussion of the various Germanic tribes is new in Trevet, as is the descent of Woden from Noah, via Shem. Geoffrey does mention Woden: Hengist states that his people worship Mercury under the name of Woden (157). Trevet euhemerizes the Germanic god, making him into a real man, the father of Wetta and the son of Shem, and—therefore—a grandson of Noah.[17] The union of biblical and Germanic history is ever more tightly woven.

While Trevet follows Geoffrey of Monmouth in many respects, there are some disjunctions between the two, the most significant of which concerns the distinction between 'Britain' and 'England'. For Geoffrey, British identity is the stable point upon which he can fix the identity of an emergent nation; for Trevet, by contrast, British identity is invariably subordinated to English identity. Perhaps this is at its most striking in Trevet's very first reference to Geoffrey, in which he makes Geoffrey into a celebrant of English national identity: 'Here begins the History of the British Kings of Great Britain, which now is called "England"' [Ci comence l'estoire des Brutouns rois del Greindre Bretaigne, q'est ore 'Engleterre' apellé (69; f.12b)]. There is a passage in the *House of Fame* in which the great poets of antiquity appear as statues on pillars, including the statue of 'Englyssh Gaufride' (line 1470). Some critics have hesitated to identify this figure as Geoffrey of Monmouth, in spite of the fact that Geoffrey was indeed 'besy for to bere up' the fame of 'Troye' (line 1672).[18] If we find, however, that Chaucer's Geoffrey is the same Geoffrey of Trevet's *Chronicle*, it would be almost impossible to think of him as anything other than 'English Geoffrey'.

As noted above, British identity is consistently subsumed within English identity in Trevet's *Chronicle*, through the continuous reference to Britain in this way. Even when quoting Geoffrey of Monmouth, Trevet refers to 'Brutaigne, q'ore est dit Engleterre' or, more simply, 'Brutaigne, q'est dit Engleterre' (e.g. 111–13; ff.55b–va). The effect is to assimilate the British past to the expected, inevitable English future. Not just Geoffrey of Monmouth, and not just Britain in general, but King Arthur himself is assimilated to this all-encompassing English identity. Trevet recounts how 'Arthur, who was . . . full of beautiful virtues and of generosity, and so gracious in every trait and good quality that all people loved him, was crowned King of England after his father, Uther Pendragon' [Arthur, qi fu . . . plein de beles vertues et de largesse, et si gracious de tut nature et de bounté qe totes gentz l'amoient, fu coroné roi d'Engleterre aprés son pere Uter Pendragoun (141; f.60a)]. This is clearly not a one-time mistake, because Trevet goes on to relate how Arthur 'conquered Scotland and all the lands around England, Ireland, and France' [conquist Escoce et totes les terres entour Engleterre, Yrlande, et Fraunce (141; f.60a–b)], and there are several more references to England (without mention of Britain) throughout the passage.

A second striking feature of Trevet's historiography is directly relevant to the role of the Constance story within the *Chronicle*: that is, the presence of highly focused moments of intensification. These are of two types: first, the symbolic space, which can be comprised simply of enclosed space itself or of a physical object, often a monumental structure; and, second, the condensed short narrative. Two representative examples of this symbolic space appear relatively early in the *Chronicle*, both of which are defined in terms of the cardinal directions of North, South, East, and West. Trevet describes how various nations were united under the yoke of Alexander the Great—'Persia and Macedonia and Syria and Greece and Egypt' [Perse et Macedoyne et Surie et Grece et Egipte" (f.26b)]—but with Alexander's death, they were dispersed among his heirs: 'that is to say, Philip, King of Macedonia; Antigonus, King of Asia; Seleuk [Seleucus], King of Syria; and Ptolemy… King of Egypt' [c'est assavoir, Phelipe, roi de Macedoine; Antigonus, roy de Asye; Seleuk, roy de Sury; et Ptholomeu… roi de Egipte (f.26va)]. Here, the convergence of cardinal directions and disparate lands marks a turning point in history, one of the great shifts in the history of *translatio imperii* as formulated by Orosius in the early Middle Ages.[19] A comparable example appears in Trevet's account of the division of the tribes of Israel upon their arrival in the Promised Land. They too are arranged according to the cardinal directions, in a long descriptive passage that ends by describing how:

> In the midst of these dwelling places ['habitations'] to the East and the West, the South and the North, Joshua placed the habitation of the tabernacle. And about the tabernacle to the East he placed twelve cities for the habitations of the priests who came of Aaron; to the West he placed the thirteen cities for those who came of Gersan; to the South he placed ten cities for those who came of Caath; to the North he placed twelve cities for those who came of Merari.
>
> [En myliu ceste[s] habitaciouns de l'orient et occident, meridien et septentrion, mist Josué l'abitacioun del tabernacle. Et entour le tabernacle a l'orient mist il douze citez pur les habitacions des prestres qe vindrent de Aaron; al occident mist il trezze citez a ceux qe vindrent de Gersan; al meridien mist il dis citez a ceux qe vindrent de Caath; al septentrion mist il duzze cités a ceux qe vindrent de Merari   (59; f.10va).]

Here, the convergence of the cardinal directions around a fixed point heightens the symbolic power of that focal centre: that is, the ark of the covenant containing the tablets of the Law.

This scene is mirrored later on when Jeremiah, aware of the destruction soon to befall Jerusalem, decides to conceal the precious items contained in the ark of the covenant: these include the tablets of the Law, the staff of Aaron, and a golden vessel filled with manna. He hides these away within a stone, seals it with an iron seal inscribed with the name of God (76; f. 21a) and hides the stone away in the desert between two mountains, near the site of the graves of Moses and Aaron. Jeremiah declares, however, that the day will come when these hidden items will reappear:

> And Jeremiah said that no one will show forth the ark except for Aaron, and the tablets will not be handled by priest or prophet except for Moses, the elect of God, who will raise them up in his first resurrection; and at that time the ark will issue forth from the stone, and be placed on Mount Sinai, and before the ark will assemble all the saints awaiting the coming of Our Lord.
>
> [Et dit Jeremié qe nul purra moustrer l'arche fors Aaron, et les tables ne purra overer prestre ne prophete [forpris] Moises, le eslist Dieux, qi relevera en sa primer resurection, et dont s'en istra l'arche de la pere, et serra mise en le Mont de Synay, et s'asembleront devant l'arche touz les seintz entendaunt la venue Nostre Seignur
> (f.21b).]

Here, the objects formerly contained in the ark form a new sacred centre, this time not providing a centre of gravity for the new inhabitants of the Promised Land, as in the scene discussed previously, but rather for those who will be gathered together on the Day of Judgement, in a typological fulfilment of the literal Promised Land.[20]

Another manifestation of such moments of intensification can be seen in the condensed short narrative. Within the narrative flow of Trevet's romance/history, the Constance episode stands out as being by far the longest of the short narratives included in the *Chronicle*. The use of extended narratives is not unprecedented: Geoffrey of Monmouth, for example, has a few of these, most famously the story of Arthur and his father, Uther Pendragon, but also the extended story of King Leir.[21] It is perhaps not too much to say that the Constance story serves an anchoring role not entirely dissimilar from the Arthur narrative in Geoffrey's text: both represent a kind of fixed point, simultaneously a crucial moment of transition and a promise of hope for the future. These stories serve as a microcosm of larger currents in the text, where the didactic function of the work is intensified: for Geoffrey, that didactic function is expressed through prophecy, while for Trevet, it is expressed through the power of conversion.[22]

Before turning to the Constance story in more detail, examining the relation of Trevet's version to that of Chaucer in the light of Trevet's larger aims and practices, I would like to make it clear that I am not arguing that the 'real' historical template for Chaucer's vision of history is to be found in Trevet's *Chronicle*. On the contrary, what I want to suggest is that there are multiple templates, and that their multiplicity is exactly the point. When Chaucer writes about history, he often writes through the medium of Boccaccio, as in the Knight's Tale, the Monk's Tale, and—above all—*Troilus and Criseyde*. This is a vision of history that comes from Latin epic—the *Thebaid* of Statius and the *Aeneid* of Virgil—by way of romance: not just Italian romance, in the form of Boccaccio's works, but also French romance, in the form of the *Roman de Troie* and the *Roman de Thebes*. It is, accordingly, crucial to emphasize that what we find in Trevet is not Chaucer's singular model of history-writing, but rather one in a series of historiographical options, various overlapping templates with which to structure the shape of time. These include the universal, explicitly non-national perspective of Orosius; the English nationalism of Higden; the Trojan ancestry of Britain found in Geoffrey of Monmouth (whether by way of Trevet or directly); the tragic history of Troy, the triumphal history of Rome, and the abjected history of Thebes.

LANGUAGE AND NATION

Having outlined the historiographical framework found in Trevet's *Chronicle*, let us turn to the Constance narrative, illustrating how it highlights the role of language in the establishment of national identity, and in the mediating of fundamental changes in that national identity. This can best be accomplished by placing Chaucer's Man of Law's Tale in two different contexts that can highlight some of the crucial issues pertaining to national identity as constituted in premodern literature: first, the transnational, cross-cultural framework that has become increasingly important in the field of medieval Mediterranean studies; and, second, the national framework that is a central preoccupation of the tale's source—that is, Trevet's *Chronicle*. In considering the competing claims of these two frameworks, and particularly in thinking about the role of vernacular languages in mediating between cultures or—sometimes—erecting insurmountable barriers between cultures, we see almost immediately that the transnational and the national are always intricately intertwined. The national narrative always conveys, I would suggest, an implicit claim about the nature of the wider world.

For Chaucer, very much unlike Trevet, the subject of the Constance story is circulation itself: circulation of the 'tidynges / And tales' (II.129–30) that merchants carry with them from port to port, along with their cargo of goods and currency; circulation of the word—that is, the Word of God—as Christianity is transmitted throughout the world; and, finally, the figure of Custance herself, who travels from port to port, both a desirable object and an agent of change. Her ability to impact the cultures she encounters is mediated not so much through language as through her ineffable ability to make change happen: as the Tale puts it, 'alle hir loven that looken in hir face' (II.532). Analogues to Chaucer's tale of Custance, of which there are a considerable number, sometimes highlight the extent to which the woman functions as a passive commodity, and sometimes the extent to which she functions as an active subject. This distinction can be most succinctly summarized by a comparison with two tales in Boccaccio's *Decameron*, the story of Gostanza (Day 5, Story 2) and the story of Alatiel (Day 2, Story 7). Like Chaucer's Custance in Northumbria, Boccaccio's Gostanza is washed up on the shore of an unfamiliar land. For Gostanza, however, language proves to be both an index of familiarity and unfamiliarity, an initial barrier that turns out to be a means of local assimilation. The woman who finds Gostanza on the shore near Tunis addresses her in Italian: Boccaccio writes, 'hearing herself addressed in Italian, the girl wondered whether she had been driven back to Lipari by a change of wind'.[23] Gostanza is soon taken in by a Muslim (or 'Saracen') lady who has a household full of women, into which Gostanza is soon assimilated: 'Her benefactress and the other ladies were remarkably kind and affectionate towards her, and before very long they had taught her to speak their language.'[24]

Gostanza's experience of assimilation, language acquisition, and the generous company of women contrasts sharply with the story of Alatiel, recounted earlier in the *Decameron*. Unlike Gostanza, who is able to make her way in foreign places through the acquisition of languages, Alatiel remains cut off by the barrier of language as she is traded, bartered, and stolen by a sequence of men all around the Mediterranean. Her inability to communicate is repeatedly emphasized by Boccaccio, who relates how Alatiel tries to 'explain' her situation 'by means of gestures' and notes that 'she was unable to make herself understood [except] by way of her gestures'.[25] When Alatiel is seated between two men, Boccaccio states, 'the pleasure of conversing with her was denied them because she understood little or nothing of their language'.[26] When at last her old associate, Antioco, encounters Alatiel and she is finally able to communicate, the end of the language barrier serves to punctuate the repeated cycle of circulation that Alatiel has undergone and to introduce the resolution: '[Antioco] was familiar with her language, and this pleased her immensely because for several years she had been more or less forced to lead the life of a deaf-mute as she could neither understand what anybody was saying nor make herself understood.'[27]

Turning back to the Man of Law's Tale, we can see that Custance inhabits a linguistic space comparable to that of Alatiel. She is not, like Alatiel, 'Fortune's plaything'; she is, however, the 'sonde' of God, the thing that God has sent. Both Alatiel and Custance are objectified: they are things that are significant for what they are rather than subjects who are significant for what they say or think. The Mediterranean framework of trade and exchange provides one very useful way of contextualizing Chaucer's tale and, in particular, of explicating how Custance's limited language ability can be seen in connection with the Mediterranean language of trade. The 'maner Latyn corrupt' (II.519) that she speaks when washed up on the shores of Northumberland marks her out as the product of the trade and exchange routes of the late fourteenth century, an object that reflects the vernacular of the shipboard rather than a speaker who belongs to any one native land.

The nature of Custance's language ability and its implications for both her individual identity, and for the group identities whose transformation she mediates, is illuminated through a closer look at the source passages in Trevet's *Chronicle*. Here, as in the analogous passage in Gower's *Confessio amantis*, Custance's linguistic ability is highlighted: she is the only child of an indulgent father, who has her taught [enseigner] the Christian faith and educated [endoctriner] in the seven Liberal Arts and 'various languages' [diverses langages] (151, f.63a). This education is what underlies her ability to effect conversions in Northumberland, not just through her knowledge of the Articles of the Faith (which she expounds word for word in the course of her preaching) but through her linguistic range. Trevet's description of Constance's arrival in Northumberland can be seen as an inversion of the scene of linguistic recognition and misrecognition experienced by Boccaccio's Gostanza: shipwrecked near Tunis, Gostanza at first supposes that she is in a foreign land, then hears Italian spoken and thinks she may be back home, then realizes that she has simply encountered a foreigner who speaks her own tongue. In Trevet's scene, Constance is shipwrecked and encountered by a friendly passer-by, Olda (the constable in Chaucer's Man of Law's Tale):

> And this Olda came down to the girl in her ship and asked her who she was. And she responded in Saxon, which was the language of Olda, because she had been taught to speak various languages, as has been said before, and she told him that she was of the Christian faith.... And as soon as Olda had heard her speak his language so well, and discovered her with so much treasure, he hoped that she was the daughter of some king of the Saxons over the sea, either of Germany, or of Saxony, or of Sweden, or of Denmark.
>
> [Et cist Olda descendi a la pucele en sa nef, et lui demaunda de son estre. Et [ele] lui respoundi en Sessoneis, qe fu langage Olda, come cele q'estoit aprise en diverses langages, come avant est dit, et lui disoit qe quant a sa creance ele estoit de Cristiene foi.... Et puis qe Olda l'avoit oy si renablement parler sa lange, et trova ove lui si grant tresour, esperoit qe ele estoit fille de ascun roi des Sessouns outre mere, come d'Alemay[n]e, oue de Sessoine, ou de Suece, oue de Denemarche   (159, f. 64b).]

Here, Constance's speech at first marks her as the same—not a local inhabitant, to be sure, but a 'Saxon' nonetheless. Remembering what we have observed earlier of Trevet's habit of emphasizing the heterogeneity located within national groups, we will be especially attuned to the way that, in this passage, Trevet highlights the range of local inhabitants in the British Isles—not just the Britons and the Germanic pagans, but the subgroups within each of these larger categories. In particular, he divides the non-British inhabitants of the Isles as the Jutes, the Saxons, and the English, each having their own language. These three subgroups are, for Trevet, minorities within the larger category of the English; as he puts it, all three subgroups are said to be gathered together within 'Engleterre' because out of the three groups, 'the English occupied, among the Britons, the greater part of the land' [lez Engleis occuperent entre lé Brutouns la greindre partie de la terre" (115; f.56a)]. At the same time, these subgroups of the Jutes, Saxons, and English are affiliated with larger groups resident outside the British Isles. This is why Olda recognizes—or thinks he recognizes—Constance as a 'Saxon'; not a local 'English' Saxon, but perhaps a Saxon from Germany, or from Saxony, or from Sweden, and so on.

This ambiguous way of characterizing ethno-linguistic groups as both subtypes within a larger group and part of a larger, transnational group is reflected, in Chaucer's work, through his transnational depiction of Britain. The local inhabitants of Northumberland, in the Man of Law's Tale, include both the 'pagan' English and the Christian Britons; at the same time, in the Franklin's Tale, we learn that the Continent has its own 'Britons'. The first line of the Franklin's Tale sets us 'In Armorik, that called is Britayne' (V.729), and the tale's domestic crisis is precipitated when Arveragus goes to 'dwelle a yeer or tweyne / In Engelond, that cleped was eek Briteyne' (809–10). The tale wobbles back and forth between 'Armorik Briteyne' (1061) and the fourteenth-century reader's own 'Briteyne', in a way similar to the familiar yet strange British setting of the Wife of Bath's Tale. Both time and place sever the reader from the unproblematic sense of familiarity, the reassurance of a securely locatable place of origins.

This quality in Chaucer's *Canterbury Tales* is foreshadowed in the apparently—but deceptively—simple nationalism of Trevet's universal chronicle. It is not necessary to look to the Mediterranean context to discover the transnational framework of Chaucer's writings, because an acute awareness of the polyglot, transnational nature of 'England' was already vividly present, as we see here and as we have already seen elsewhere in Trevet's *Chronicle*. Other moments in the text lend emphasis to this transnational quality of Trevet's 'England'. For Trevet, the story of Constance serves as a nexus to draw together the history of Christian Rome and the history of England: he inserts it as a kind of long, digressive back-story to the rule of Moris (Maurice), Emperor of Rome. In keeping with this story's integrative function, it draws together local vernacular languages with the divine, transnational voice of God, as in the scene where Hermengild effects the conversion of the blind Briton who appeals to her for help:

A poor blind Christian Briton... who was entirely unknown to them, but taught by the Holy Spirit, began to cry out before them all: 'Hermengild, wife of Olda and disciple of Constance, I beg you in the name of Jesus Christ, in whom you believe, that you make the sign of the cross upon my blind eyes'. At this word, Hermengild, very afraid, was abashed; but Constance, hearing the power of God in the words of the blind man, comforted Hermengild, and said to her, 'Do not hide, lady, the power that God has given you'. And Hermengild, before Olda and the retinue of men that was with him, with good and firm faith, made the sign of the cross upon the eyes of the blind one, and said to him in her Saxon language: 'Bisne man [in] Jhesu name in [rode] yslawe, have thi siht [Blind man, in the name of Jesus who was slain upon the cross, have your sight]'. And he was now illuminated and could see well and clearly.

[[U]n povre Cristien Bruton enveuglés...q'estoit dc touz cstrange mes apris del Seint Esperit, comensa a crier devant touz: 'Hermegild, la femme Olda et la disciple Constance, te pri en le noun Jhesu Crist, en qi tu creiz, qe tu me facet le signe de la crois sur mes eux enveuglés'. A ceste parole, Hermegild, trop affraié, estut abaié, mes Constaunce, entendant la vertue Dieux [en] la parole l'eveugle, conforta Hermegild, et lui dist: 'Ne muscez pas, dame, la vertue qe Dieux te ad doné'. Et Hermegild, devaunt Olda et sa meine qe lui sui, de bone foi et ferme fist sus les euz de lui enveugle la seinte croiz et lui dit en sa langage Sessoine: 'Bisne man [in] Jhesu name in [rode] yslawe, have thi siht'. Et sil [meintenaunte] fu aluminé et regardoit bien / et clerement   (163, f.64vb–65a).]

The blind Briton appeals to Hermengild in direct speech, just as Constance encourages Hermengild in direct speech; Hermengild's words, however, come not just in direct speech but in their 'original' language. As performative speech, the speech that serves as the medium of the miracle, her words must be preserved just as they were uttered. It is useful to contrast the other moment in this tale when performative language appears, again unaltered from its original iteration:

He had hardly finished his speech when a closed hand like the fist of a man appeared...and struck such a blow on the criminal's neck that both of his eyes flew out of his head and his teeth out of his mouth, and the criminal fell defeated upon the ground. And at that moment a voice said, in the hearing of all, 'You raised up a scandal against the daughter of Mother Church; you did this, and I have not kept silent'.

[A peine avoit parfini la parole qe un main enclose come [poyn] de homme apparut... et feri tiel coup en le haterel le feloun, que ambedeux les eux lui envolerent de la teste et les dentz hors de la bouche, et le feloun chei abatu a la terre. Et a ceo dit un voiz en l'oy de / touz: 'Adversus filiam matris ecclesie ponebas scandalum; hoc fecisti et non tacui'   (167, f. 65va–vb).]

In this passage, which reworks Psalm 50:21, the performative language is not a kind of transnational vernacular language (Saxon), but rather the transnational language of God—Latin, the administrative language of the Church and of the Vulgate Bible. Trevet's use of Latin here is not naive: elsewhere, he describes at length the production of the Septuagint and repeatedly discusses the evolution of various liturgical formats and prayers within the Church. The Latin that Trevet's God speaks is an administrative language, a language of institutions: it is therefore appropriate that it is spoken in the

enclosed, formal space of a royal audience hall, in contrast with the sandy beach where
Hermengild effects her miracle. For Trevet, the vernacular is complex and polyvalent,
the place where boundaries are drawn between peoples and, more rarely, where those
boundaries fall away. It is therefore appropriate that Hermengild's Saxon speech is
uttered at the wild edge of the seashore.

There are a number of other moments in Trevet's *Chronicle* that also illustrate the role
of language in articulating the boundaries that separate nations and, sometimes, bring
them together—although none is quite as striking as these moments we have just noted
in the tale of Constance. The simultaneous separation and joining of Briton and Saxon
identity can also be seen in the account of a law established by Marcia, a female ruler of
the realm in the time of Darius of Persia and Alexander the Great. Marcia is, in some
ways, a prefiguration of Constance herself, exemplifying similar virtues: she is 'very
wise and well educated in all the arts' [trop sages et bien aprisé en touz artz (f.26a)].
She institutes a law that binds both the Britons and the Saxons, unifying them under
the law, but the law exists under two different names, reiterating the difference that
separates the two communities: 'She established the law that the Britons call "the
law Marcian", and the Saxons, "Marchenlaw"' [ele controva la lei qe les Brutouns apellent
'leis Marcianes', et les Sessons, 'merchenlawe' (f.26a)]. A similar moment of linguistic
convergence appears in the story of how the Briton Vortigern married the English
daughter of Hengist, adapted by Trevet from Geoffrey of Monmouth. To cement the
union of their two peoples, Vortigern is careful to reply to her toast 'Wesheil' with the
correct response 'Drinkheil'; he does this 'just as he had been instructed by the English
well before she was joined to him in marriage' [sicom il estoit enfourmé par lez Engleis
bien devant q'ele estoit a li espose (115; f.55vb)].

In those two passages, language brings together two disparate groups, while still preserving their difference, whether under the rule of the law or in the union of marriage.
In another passage, however, the difference of language divides—or, we might even say,
cuts apart the potential union of two peoples in peace. In an episode adapted from
Geoffrey of Monmouth, Trevet tells the story of the treason of Hengist. At a feast to celebrate the 'peace between the Britons and the Saxons' [pees entre les Brutons et les
Sessouns], a 'false sign of peace' [faux signe de pees] is used to divide Britons from
Saxons: 'When the feasting was at its most joyous for the Britons, such that they sus-
pected no treason, suddenly a cry was made by the Saxons in their language—which was
unknown to the Britons—saying "Draweth your sexes!", which means "Take out your
knives!"' [[Q]uant la mangerie fut plus lee a les Brutons, qe nul treison penserent,
sudeinement fu un crie faite par Sessouns en lour langage, qe fu desconu a les Brutouns,
en disaunt/'Draweth youre sexes!' qe fait a dire 'Treietz vez cotels!' " (125; f.57b–va]. A
bloody battle follows, and the peace is broken. Language unites, but it also splits.

What can a broader sense of Trevet's historical vision offer us in reading Chaucer's
historical romance? I would suggest that he offers a remarkably capacious framework
that makes room for a plural vision comprised of multiple historical contexts—biblical,
apostolic, Trojan, Roman, Theban, British, Saxon, and English. Differences are not simply
elided; they are pulled tightly together, an act that exposes the difference that inevitably

remains. Even in the repeated phrase, 'Britain, which now is England', Britain is always there: we are constantly reminded of the movement of nation from one state of being to another, reminded of the gap that separates disparate moments in time. For Trevet, the episodes that I have identified as moments of intensification—whether depictions of symbolic space or tightly compressed narratives, like the story of Constance—provide a kind of microcosm in which the separation of those discrete moments is collapsed into a geometric form. In this way, Trevet models an historiographical poetics that emphasizes the cyclical nature of time, a departure from the linear and typological modes of other medieval chronicles.[28]

This cyclical quality is evident both in the cosmological points of reference in Trevet's history, and in its integrated chronologies—above all, in the great temporal hinge of the Incarnation. Trevet explains how those who lived in the first generations after Adam lived to a great age, because 'God gave them a longer life in order to seek out and discover the noble sciences of astronomy and geometry, which cannot be acquired in any less than five hundred years' [Dieux lour dona plus longe vie pour enserchir et controver les nobles sciences de astronomie et geometrie, les qels ne poent conquere en meins q'en cynk centz aunz]. Only by achieving that great age can they hope to comprehend the celestial cycle of the 'great year, which is accomplished by the course of the planets, which in so large a period of time return to their initial places' [grant an, qu'est acompli par cours des planetes, qe en tant de temps retornent a lour primer lieu (7; f. 2vb)]. As a counterpoint to the celestial cycles of the planets, we find the 'primer lieu' par excellence in the Incarnation, which Trevet identifies with a whole series of other date markers, forming an intricately integrated time stamp: 'Here ends the fifth age of the world. . . . Here begins the sixth age of the world. The year after God made Adam, four thousand eight hundred and two, Our Lord Jesus Christ was born' [Ci termine le quint age du siecle . . . Ci commence le sisme age du siècle. L'an après qe Dieu fist Adam quatre mil et cent oytant-isme second, nasceoyt Nostre Seigneur Jhesu Crist]. Trevet provides the day of the week and the date of Christ's birth, as well as the dominical letter; he states that this was the forty-second year in the reign of Augustus Caesar, and the thirtieth year in the reign of Herod; he gives the number of years since the prophecies of Daniel, and the number of years since the founding of Rome. In this way, Trevet signals the coming together of all timelines to mark this very special moment when all lineages are braided together, marking the transition from the Old Covenant to the New.

Taking stock of the cyclical vision of history in Trevet's *Chronicle* provides a useful final insight into the presentation of historical time in Chaucer's works. It is often the case that Chaucer's historical poetry, especially the Knight's Tale and *Troilus and Criseyde*, is seen as fundamentally based on earlier poetic models of history, especially Virgil, Statius, and Boccaccio. The cyclical quality that is so evident in the temporality of both the Knight's Tale and *Troilus and Criseyde* is attributed to a Boethian overlay, as Chaucer integrates what he had learned through his engagement with (and translation of) the *Consolation of Philosophy*. Without taking away from Chaucer's evident interest in and commitment to Boethian philosophy, it may be the case that Trevet's cyclical vision of history also played a part. We may need to rethink the common wisdom that the Knight's Tale and *Troilus and Criseyde* have a Boethianism that is overlaid on—is even at odds with—the historical vision of the poem. On the contrary, Trevet's commentary on Boethius was the interpretive filter through which Chaucer knew the rich interpretive tradition of the prosimetrum. It is not far-fetched to consider that Chaucer may have found Trevet's vision of history, as presented in the *Chronicle*, to be fully compatible with the Boethian temporality of Trevet's commentary.

How might this intersection—this temporality that is at once historiographical and philosophical—be reflected in Chaucer? I would suggest that it can be found in the moments of intensification in Chaucer that correspond to the moments of intensification that we have already seen in Trevet, such as the elaborate ekphrases of the Knight's Tale; the cycles of siege in *Troilus and Criseyde*, marked by epistles that track the decline in the fortunes of the city and the despair of Troilus; and the reiterative patterns of descent found in the Monk's Tale and the *Legend of Good Women*.[29] For Trevet—and, at least sometimes, for Chaucer—history is recursive, repetitive, and ultimately circular.

NOTES

1. Earlier versions of this material were presented at the University of Pennsylvania (17 March 2011) and at the 15th Biennial Romance in Medieval Britain Conference hosted by the University of British Columbia (16 August 2016). I would like to thank Jonathan Brent for his assistance with transcriptions and translations from Trevet's *Chronicle*.

2. The Constance narrative from Trevet's *Chronicle*, together with an excellent introduction by Robert Correale, appears in *Sources and Analogues of the Canterbury Tales*, volume 2, eds. Robert M. Correale and Mary Hamel (Cambridge: D.S. Brewer, 2005), 277–350 (introduction at pp. 277–94; Trevet excerpt, in Anglo-French and Modern English translation, at 297–329; analogue by Gower at 330–50). See also the foundational studies by Correale, 'Chaucer's Manuscript of Nicholas Trevet's Cronicles', *Chaucer Review* 25 (1991), 238–65, and Robert A. Pratt, 'Chaucer and *Les Cronicles* of Nicholas Trevet', in *Studies in Language, Literature, and Culture in Honor of Rudolph Willard*, ed. E.B. Atwood and A.A. Hill (Austin, TX: University of Texas Press, 1969), 303–11.

3. Delany argues that Chaucer draws on Geoffrey of Monmouth directly for the description of the dying Piramus beating his heels on the ground in the Legend of Thisbe (LGW 863); Sheila Delany, 'Geoffrey of Monmouth and Chaucer's *Legend of Good Women*', *Chaucer Review* 22 (1987), 170–4.

4. Kathryn L. Lynch, 'Dating Chaucer', *Chaucer Review* 42 (2007), 1–22.

5. On premodern articulations of national identity specifically in Chaucer's work, see Suzanne Conklin Akbari, 'Orientation and Nation in the *Canterbury Tales*', in *Chaucer's Cultural Geography*, ed. Kathryn L. Lynch (Basic Readings in Chaucer and his Time. London: Routledge, 2002), 102–34. On the wider context of premodern articulations of English national identity, see Suzanne Conklin Akbari, 'The Hunger for National Identity in *Richard Coer de Lion*', in *Reading Medieval Culture: Essays in Honor of Robert W. Hanning*, ed. Robert M. Stein and Sandra Pierson Prior (Notre Dame, IN: University of Notre Dame Press, 2005), 198–227.

6. Robert M. Correale, 'Gower's Source Manuscript of Nicholas Trevet's *Les Cronicles*', in *John Gower: Recent Readings: Papers Presented at the Meetings of the John Gower Society at the International Congress on Medieval Studies, Western Michigan University, 1983–88*, ed. R. F. Yeager (Studies in Medieval Culture 26. Kalamazoo, MI: Western Michigan University, 1989), 133–57. For a systematic overview of the distribution of place names, proper names, and other linguistic features in all three texts of the Constance story, including tables, see Hélène Dauby, 'From Trevet to Gower and Chaucer', *Caliban: French Journal of English Studies* 29 (2011), 79–88.

7. On the productive tension of the histories of Troy and Thebes in Chaucer's work, see Lee Patterson, *Chaucer and the Subject of History* (Madison, WI: University of Wisconsin Press, 1991). A detailed account of the various strands of Theban history behind this tension, including universal histories, the *Roman de Thebes*, and Statius's *Thebaid*, can be found in David Anderson, 'Theban History in Chaucer's *Troilus*', *Studies in the Age of Chaucer* 4 (1982), 109–33.

8. See Chapter 29.

9. On the composition and circulation of the *Polychronicon*, see John Taylor, *The Universal Chronicle of Ranulf Higden* (Oxford: Clarendon Press, 1966), esp. 36 ff. On the English reception of the work and its broader impact on vernacular culture, see Emily Steiner, 'Radical Historiography: Langland, Trevisa, and the *Polychronicon*', *Studies in the Age of Chaucer* 27 (2005), 171–211, esp. 174–8.

10. On Orosius's views of Greek history as a context for reading Chaucer, see Patterson's *Chaucer and the Subject of History*, 99–100, and Anderson's 'Theban History' (referring to the *Histoire ancienne jusqu'à César* as the 'French *Orose*'), 117–18. On the textual connections between the second redaction of the *Histoire ancienne* and Chaucer's *Legend of Good Women*, see Suzanne Conklin Akbari, 'Ovid and Ovidianism', in *The Oxford History of Classical Reception in English Literature, Vol. 1: The Middle Ages*, ed. Rita Copeland (Oxford: Oxford University Press, 2015), 187–208, esp. 199–204.

11. On the teleological drive toward Flanders within the *Histoire ancienne*, see Suzanne Conklin Akbari, 'Embodying the Historical Moment: Tombs and Idols in the *Histoire ancienne jusqu'à César*', *Journal of Medieval and Early Modern Studies* 44 (2014), 617–43, esp. 628–31.

12. 'Unlike Orosius's history, however, the *Polychronicon* is not universal because it is polemical or apocalyptic, but rather because it claims totality within a specifically English context. It synthesizes all histories, periods, and genres, and drives them resolutely toward the English present, toward English localities, conquests, and lineages, and even to the deeds of the Chester nobility' (Steiner, 'Radical Historiography', 174).

13. On Geoffrey of Monmouth in the context of Insular historiography, see the still-classic study by Robert W. Hanning, *The Vision of History in Early Britain: From Gildas to Geoffrey of Monmouth* (New York: Columbia University Press, 1966); also Monika Otter, *Inventiones: Fiction and Referentiality in Twelfth-Century English Historical Writing* (Chapel Hill, NC: University of North Carolina Press, 1996), esp. chapter 2, '"Gaainable Tere": Foundations, Conquests, and Symbolic Appropriations of Space and Time.'

14. On the structure of Vincent of Beauvais's encyclopaedia, see Mary Franklin-Brown, *Reading the World: Encyclopaedic Writing in the Scholastic Age* (Chicago, IL: University of Chicago Press, 2012), esp. chapter 2, 'Narrative and Natural History: Vincent of Beauvais's *Ordo juxta Scripturam*'. On the structure of Higden's universal history, see Emily Steiner,

'Compendious Genres: Higden, Trevisa, and the Medieval Encyclopedia', *Exemplaria* 27 (2015), 73–92, esp. 76–80.

15. On the structure of the *Historia Scholastica*, see James H. Morey, 'Peter Comestor, Biblical Paraphrase, and the Medieval Popular Bible', *Speculum* 68 (1993), 6–35, esp. 14–16. See also the provocative account of the text's development in Mark J. Clark, *The Making of the Historia Scholastica, 1150–1200* (Studies and Texts 198. Toronto: Pontifical Institute of Mediaeval Studies, 2015).

16. Paris, Bibliothèque nationale de France, MS français 9687 (P). The biblical section runs from the top of f.2a to the bottom of f.35ra. P is the most elaborately decorated of the manuscripts, and one of the earliest. Correale identified it, moreover, as the closest to that used by Chaucer and John Gower ('Chaucer's Manuscript' and 'Gower's Source Manuscript'). Quotations from Trevet are cited in the text by folio number in P and by page number in the forthcoming edition with facing-page translation currently in preparation by Jonathan Brent and myself, based in part on the largely uncorrected transcript of Correale. Note that page numbers are provided only for the passages that will appear in the edition and translation; others are cited by folio number only.

17. On the integration of Noachid genealogy and Germanic descent in the *Anglo-Saxon Chronicle*, see Daniel Anlezark, 'Sceaf, Japheth, and the Origins of the Anglo-Saxons', *Anglo-Saxon England* 31 (2002), 13–46, esp. 17–18. Thanks to Jonathan Brent for pointing out this source.

18. 'And by him stood, withouten les, / Ful wonder hy on a piler / Of yren, he, the gret Omer; / And with him Dares and Tytus / Before, and eke he Lollius, / And Guydo eke de Columpnis, / And Englyssh Gaufride eke, ywis; / And ech of these, as have I joye, / Was besy for to bere up Troye' (HF 1464–72).

19. On cardinal directions in Orosius, see Suzanne Conklin Akbari, 'Alexander in the Orient: Bodies and Boundaries in the *Roman de toute chevalerie*', in *Postcolonial Approaches to the European Middle Ages: Translating Cultures*, ed. Ananya Jahanara Kabir and Deanne Williams (Cambridge: Cambridge University Press, 2005), 105–26, esp. 106–08.

20. For a comparative reading of the Ark of the Covenant in the Ethiopian *Kebra Nagast* and the depiction of Custance as a 'habitacioun' in Chaucer's Man of Law's Tale, see Suzanne Conklin Akbari, 'Modeling Medieval World Literature', *Middle Eastern Literatures* 20 (2017), 2–17, esp. 8–14.

21. Tolhurst suggests that Geoffrey of Monmouth includes the story of Leir, along with other embedded stories involving women's actual or potential rule, 'to interrupt and critique his epic narrative' (78). Fiona Tolhurst, 'The Britons as Hebrews, Romans, and Normans: Geoffrey of Monmouth's British Epic and Reflections of Empress Matilda', *Arthuriana* 8 (1998), 69–87.

22. On prophecy in Geoffrey, see Paul Dalton, 'The Topical Concerns of Geoffrey of Monmouth's *Historia Regum Britannie*: History, Prophecy, Peacemaking, and English Identity in the Twelfth Century', *Journal of British Studies* 44 (2005), 688–712, esp. 692–701.

23. Boccaccio, *Decameron*, 5.2; Giovanni Boccaccio, *Decameron*, ed. Vittore Branca (Florence: Presso l'Accademia della Crusca, 1976) 344; *Decameron*, trans. G.H. McWilliam (London: Penguin, 2003), 380–81.

24. Boccaccio, *Decameron*, 5.2; ed. Branca 345, McWilliam 382.

25. Boccaccio, *Decameron*, 2.7; ed. Branca 124 ['con atti'], 125 ['co' fatti']; trans. McWilliam 128, 130.

26. Boccaccio, *Decameron*, 2.7; ed. Branca 128, trans. McWilliam 134.

27. Boccaccio, *Decameron*, 2.7; ed. Branca 133, trans. McWilliam 140.

28. For example, on secular typologies in the *Histoire ancienne jusqu'à César*, see Akbari, 'Embodying the Historical Moment', 631–36.

29. On letters in the cycles of siege in *Troilus and Criseyde*, see Akbari, 'Ovid and Ovidianism', 199–204.

BIBLIOGRAPHY

Akbari, Suzanne Conklin, 'Orientation and Nation in the *Canterbury Tales*', in *Chaucer's Cultural Geography*, ed. Kathryn L. Lynch (Basic Readings in Chaucer and his Time. London: Routledge, 2002), 102–34.

Anderson, David, 'Theban History in Chaucer's *Troilus*', *Studies in the Age of Chaucer* 4 (1982), 109–33.

Correale, Robert M. 'Chaucer's Manuscript of Nicholas Trevet's *Cronicles*', Chaucer Review 25 (1991), 238–65.

Correale, Robert M. 'Gower's Source Manuscript of Nicholas Trevet's *Les Cronicles*', in *John Gower: Recent Readings: Papers Presented at the Meetings of the John Gower Society at the International Congress on Medieval Studies, Western Michigan University, 1983–88*, ed. R. F. Yeager (Studies in Medieval Culture 26. Kalamazoo, MI: Western Michigan University, 1989), 133–57.

Dauby, Hélène, 'From Trevet to Gower and Chaucer', *Caliban: French Journal of English Studies* 29 (2011), 79–88.

Hanning, Robert W., *The Vision of History in Early Britain: From Gildas to Geoffrey of Monmouth* (New York: Columbia University Press, 1966).

Otter, Monika, *Inventiones: Fiction and Referentiality in Twelfth-Century English Historical Writing* (Chapel Hill, NC: University of North Carolina Press, 1996).

Patterson, Lee, *Chaucer and the Subject of History* (Madison, WI: University of Wisconsin Press, 1991).

Steiner, Emily, 'Radical Historiography: Langland, Trevisa, and the *Polychronicon*', *Studies in the Age of Chaucer* 27 (2005), 171–211.

PART IV

PHILOSOPHY AND SCIENCE IN THE UNIVERSITIES

CHAPTER 21

···

GRAMMAR AND RHETORIC C.1100–C.1400

···

RITA COPELAND

FOR the study of grammar and rhetoric, the distance between the twelfth century and the fourteenth century seems almost as great as that between the fourth and the twelfth centuries. So significant were the breakthroughs and innovations in these sciences during the course of the twelfth century, and so successful did the standardized forms of these become, that a student or scholar of the fourteenth century would not always have recognized the teaching of 200 years earlier. An English student of Chaucer's era would likely not appreciate what was owed to the pedagogical and disciplinary revisions of the twelfth century, and would have accepted as givens the technologies at his (and, rarely, her) disposal. But historians cannot treat the educational outlook of the later Middle Ages in isolation from what went before. To understand what fourteenth-century students, schoolmen, and readers could take for granted in the trivium arts of grammar and rhetoric, we need to consider how the ground was laid in the fertile environment of twelfth-century scholarship and teaching. As in many other fields, so in the history of the trivium arts: the twelfth century is the western European watershed. How grammar and rhetoric were studied in the fourteenth century can be traced back to what was discovered, developed, and changed 200 years earlier, and to what was discarded as a result.

GRAMMATICAL STUDY IN THE TWELFTH CENTURY

··

The last decade of the eleventh century and the first decades of the twelfth already saw the expansion of grammatical study into the theoretical terrain of linguistic thought. The increasing intellectual advancement of grammatical study provided the milieu for developments in the most elementary grammatical teaching, and it is to the elementary level of Latin learning that we should turn first.

In northern Europe, a schoolboy acquiring basic Latin literacy, whether in the older monastic settings or the newer urban cathedral schools, or in some form of private tutelage (as in Guibert de Nogent's description of his private lessons at the hands of an inept and irritable tutor) would be introduced to grammar through the catechetical format of Donatus's *Ars minor* (written in the fourth century CE). From Donatus the young student would learn the alphabet as well as the parts of speech, and from there would be given some basic exercises in reading, construing, memorizing, and reciting or chanting, typically using the Psalter or liturgical prayers as texts. Pupils might also memorize and learn to chant prayers such as the Pater Noster, thus instilling the feel of the Latin language.[1] In this we see a traditional teaching structure based on oral repetition. The famous description by John of Salisbury of the grammatical recitations conducted by Bernard of Chartres in the early years of the twelfth century may illuminate elementary as well as more advanced levels of teaching.[2]

Once the pupil had grasped the basics of Latin literacy, he would be given readings from late classical or early medieval works that were considered appropriate for that stage. These might include the *Disticha Catonis*, a work of the third century CE containing moral precepts, the *Fabulae* of Avianus, a Latinized version of the Greek Aesopic fables, and the *Ecloga* of Theodulus (a tenth-century work). The origins of the basic reader of 'six authors' that came much later to be known as the *Liber catonianus* seem to lie here. Conrad of Hirsau, writing his *Dialogus super auctores* in the first half of the twelfth century, already recognizes a preliminary form of the grouping of Cato, Avianus, and Theodulus.[3] The grouping that came later to be known as *Liber catonianus* usually consisted of *Disticha Catonis,* the *Ecloga* of Theodulus, the *Fabulae* of Avianus, the *Elegiae* of Maximianus, *De raptu Proserpinae* of Claudian, and the *Achilleid* of Statius. Later it expanded to include or substitute some Christian works, and often went under the name *Octo auctores*. The standardization of this grouping would manifest itself in the thirteenth century (whence derive the earliest manuscripts of this collection), although the ground is laid for it in the classical literary and grammatical teachings of the twelfth century and earlier.[4]

Alongside such basic readings we would likely find some form of vocabulary building. The evidence for this includes lexicographical glosses on the simpler school readings, such as the Latin glosses (from a slightly earlier period) on the late-classical bible epics by Arator and Prudentius studied and edited by Wieland. We would also find word lists and guides to word origins, some of which might be older texts (such as the *Elementarium* by the eleventh-century lexicographer Papias), and some newer additions to the genre, such as the rather esoteric *De utensilibus* by Adam of Balsham (Adam du Petit Pont or Parvipontanus, from his career in the Paris schools), written in the middle of the century[5] or Osbern of Gloucester's *Derivationes*.[6] Alexander Neckam produced a number of word lists, including one from the last decades of the twelfth century, *De nominibus utensilium*, which, like that by Adam of Balsham (and probably inspired by it), is a vocabulary of everyday objects that one would encounter in a house or other quotidian environment.[7] Neckam may have composed this vocabulary while he was master of the school at St Albans, adding a practical edge to the pupils' Latin training.[8]

The entry into literary study and appreciation would come at a slightly more advanced level. Older sets of glosses, such as the Pseudo-Acronian scholia on Horace, might supply a useful direction for the schoolmaster; and in fact these Horace scholia seem to have been very popular in twelfth-century teaching, as the large number of manuscripts copied suggests.[9] The glosses by the school of the Carolingian master Remigius of Auxerre on various classical works, especially the *Disticha Catonis,* seem also to have been valued among twelfth-century readers.[10] But more importantly, twelfth-century masters produced their own pedagogical glosses on the *auctores,* explaining words and phrases, figures and tropes, mythological references, and metrical details, and above all driving home the grammatical lessons contained in the text. Reynolds illustrates this range of grammatical-literary teaching through a twelfth-century marginal gloss on Horace's *Satires*; Hexter shows the same range of concerns at work in a lemmatic (free-standing) school commentary on Ovid's *Ars amatoria.*[11] What has long been recognized as an Ovidian renaissance in twelfth-century literary culture at large had its counterpart in the twelfth-century classroom, as indicated by the profusion of school commentaries and textual copying.[12] In those centers of learning where Ovidian poetry attracted sophisticated philosophical attention, there was also a perceived demand for simpler pedagogical glossing. For example, Arnulf of Orléans, well-known to modern scholars for his allegorization of the *Metamorphoses,* produced at the same time a grammatical and mythographical gloss on the work which was designed to be read alongside his allegorical commentary (both produced around 1180).[13]

It is into this category of grammatical introductions to the classical *auctores* that we can place the *Liber Tytan* of the grammarian Ralph of Beauvais, who studied at Paris with Abelard in the 1130s and lived into the 1180s. Although Ralph studied in the orbit of the theologians, theoretical grammarians, and logicians of Paris, he maintained an affiliation for teaching the pagan classics and positive grammar. The *Liber Tytan* uses lines from Ovid and Lucan as *exempla* for observations about often elementary grammatical points.[14] Along with grammatical glosses, guides to literary content provide some sense of the function the curricular authors were thought to serve. Conrad of Hirsau's *Dialogus super auctores* progresses through a curriculum, starting with the easy Bible epics of late antiquity and culminating in a tribute to the majestic poetry of Virgil.[15] This is a monastic production, having much in common with the well-known collection of *accessus ad auctores* (introductions to the authors) which were also composed in a Benedictine house in Germany around the middle of the century.[16] In such introductions to the literary curriculum, as in many other individual *accessus* from the twelfth century, we see a stress on moral lessons to be drawn from pagan authors; where the content is explicitly erotic (as in *Ars amatoria* or *Heroides*), the moral to be drawn is avoidance of the kind of love that drives characters to desperate acts. Conrad reserves his stylistic praise for the advanced authors of the curriculum, Lucan, Juvenal, and especially Virgil, suggesting that style itself commands a higher level and quality of readerly preparation.[17]

The classical orientation of the grammar curriculum finds its fullest expression in the classicism of twelfth-century literary culture: in the great philosophical allegories on Boethius (William of Conches), Virgil (attributed to Bernardus Silvestris), and Ovid

(Arnulf of Orléans); in the imitations of classical epic (notably Walter of Châtillon's *Alexandreis* and Matthew of Vendôme's *Tobias*); and in the range and ease of classical reference among the great prose and verse writers, such as William of Malmsbury, Heloise, John of Salisbury, Walter Map, Alan of Lille, and even Peter of Blois, who reveal a veritable saturation in the pagan *auctores*. In one of his later works from the early thirteenth century, Alexander Neckam looks back to the world of his own twelfth-century education and provides an idealized vision of a classical literary curriculum which would represent the entry into the fullness of literary knowledge: Virgil and Statius, Juvenal, Horace, and Ovid, Sallust and Cicero, Martial and Petronius, a large comple-ment of historians including Suetonius and Livy, and Seneca.[18] Whether or not any advanced course could have covered such a reading list, Neckam's model illuminates the principles that guided grammatical education in the pagan classics.

The study of grammar for itself, that is, the study of language as a subject (not simply learning the language as a tool for reading and writing) represented a highly advanced scientific endeavor. Here especially twelfth-century scholarship made its mark, with historical consequences that none of the greatest exponents of the science could have predicted. The key text for grammatical science had long been the *Ars maior* of Donatus, which gives thorough explanations of the principles outlined in the skeletal *Ars minor*. Donatus's *Ars maior* was to remain an essential reference. But grammar as a scientific inquiry came into its own, at the very end of the eleventh century and the beginning of the twelfth, with a new and almost unprecedented interest in Priscian's *Institutiones grammaticae* (written in the early sixth century). This was a revolution that started among a small group of scholars in the cathedral schools of northern France and the Rhineland, with a possible extension to Durham Cathedral in England. For the beginnings of what proved to be a momentous shift we have only the most fragmentary evidence, a series of free-standing commentaries on Priscian's *Institutiones* known as the *Glosulae* (so named by R. W. Hunt, who first identified the commentaries). These glosses present a sustained philosophical and critical analysis of the semantic questions in Priscian's voluminous text, reporting the opinions of various masters who disagree with Priscian and with each other over the *causa inventionis* (the reason for the invention) of grammar and the sig-nificative differences of the various parts of speech. The discussions represented in these free-standing glosses were the channels through which twelfth-century theologians such as Abelard and Gilbert of Poitier turned to grammatical analysis as their starting points. The *Glosulae* inaugurated the philosophical grammatical turn of the twelfth century, and heralded two of the greatest achievements of twelfth-century grammar, William of Conches's commentary on Priscian (c.1125–35), which drew directly on the *Glosulae*, and Petrus Helias's innovative and influential *Summa super Priscianum* (c.1140–50), which was inspired by William of Conches's earlier effort.[19] At the highest levels of grammatical study across the twelfth century, we see a turn to semantics, a development that was to have a tremendous impact on the role that grammar played in university arts faculties during the following centuries.

But we should also remember that twelfth-century grammatical thinkers, notably William of Conches, Petrus Helias, and his student Ralph of Beauvais, did not abandon the literary dimension of grammar. For William of Conches in particular, grammar—even in its most theoretical avatar—opened a route back to deeper understanding of literary, philosophical, and sacred discourse. The separation of semantics from literary application was to manifest itself later.

RHETORICAL STUDY IN
THE TWELFTH CENTURY

Rhetorical study can denote the teaching of Latin composition, or it can denote the study of classical rhetorical texts, that is, commentaries on the Ciceronian rhetorics. The first of these is how most students would have encountered some kind of rhetorical instruction, in the sense of techniques for constructing one's own composition in verse or prose. But this kind of instruction would be part of the grammatical curriculum, as it had been since antiquity. From exercises in imitation and paraphrase to recognizing and deploying structural and stylistic devices, the compositional teaching would be linked with increasing linguistic competence in Latin. The teaching of prose might be aided by the relatively new genre of the *ars dictaminis* (art of letter writing and prose composition), which emerged in northern Italian cities and was taken up at certain centres in France (Tours and Orléans) by the mid century.[20] Much more generally, Horace's *Ars poetica*, with its advice about unity and stylistic decorum, remained an authoritative reference, copied over two hundred times in the eleventh and twelfth centuries.[21] But schoolmasters were also creating their own glosses and commentaries on the *Ars poetica* to augment the late antique scholia that were often copied with the text. One commentary from the middle of the century, found in multiple copies, takes a new approach to the *Ars poetica* as a composition manual. The 'Materia' commentary, so named from its incipit by Friis-Jensen who identified and studied it,[22] reinterprets the Horatian doctrine of unity and decorum in the light of the stylistic teaching of the pseudo-Ciceronian *Rhetorica ad Herennium* (first century BCE), which was becoming widely read after many centuries of neglect. The 'Materia' commentary rationalizes, simplifies, and updates the teaching of Horace's *Ars poetica*, which can be so archly obscure in its meaning that it is a wonder it could ever have served for elementary teaching. Friis-Jensen has proposed that the 'Materia' commentary is the 'missing link' between the 'old poetics' of Horace and the new arts of poetry that emerged during the second half of the twelfth century and reached their heyday in the first decades of the thirteenth.

Where do we see the study of the Ciceronian rhetorics themselves, that is, the *De inventione* (a work of Cicero's youth which had claimed the greatest attention among late antique commentators on rhetoric and thereby vastly overshadowed Cicero's later, mature writings) and the *Rhetorica ad Herennium*, a work contemporary with the *De inventione* and long believed to be by Cicero? We find a great deal of commentary activity on the two Ciceronian rhetorics in the twelfth century: fifteen different commentaries from northern France, the Rhineland, and Italy have been identified. But this represented a relatively advanced subject, pursued in the higher reaches of scholarship and teaching in the cathedral schools. The newly popular *Rhetorica ad Herennium* exerted some impact on the more elementary teaching, as noted above; the treatise on style in Book Four of the *Ad Herennium* not only helped to reshape composition teaching in general, but also gradually began to rival the traditional grammatical source for teaching the figures and tropes, Book Three of Donatus's *Ars maior* (the *Barbarismus*).[23] However, sustained attention to the heart of classical rhetorical theory, that is, the doctrine of invention with its subsidiary fields of status theory and topics, was never an elementary subject; it had its counterpart in advanced dialectical studies. The great expositors of Ciceronian rhetoric, those whose names we know, were the most distinguished masters of their day and were also recognized for their scholarship on logic, theology, and the theoretical aspects of grammar and the quadrivium: these include the Rhineland master Manegaldus, the Parisian master William of Champeaux (known as one of Abelard's early teachers), Abelard himself, Thierry of Chartres, Thierry's younger Parisian colleague Petrus Helias, and a 'Master Alanus' who commented on the *Ad Herennium* late in the twelfth century (thus inviting a possible identification with Alan of Lille, who also deals at length with rhetoric in his *Anticlaudianus*).[24] Twelfth-century scholarly interest in rhetoric is part of a larger intellectual picture of scientific encyclopedism and in the structures of knowledge represented by received systems of disciplinary classification. Thus Ciceronian rhetoric found a privileged place in the advanced studies of the cathedral schools, appreciated for teaching how to lend eloquence to hard-edged argumentative skills.

Transitional developments

The twelfth century was almost too successful for itself. The plethora of innovative approaches, the revival of older traditions, and the new syntheses and standardizations of those older approaches, laid the ground for some revolutionary departures that would make twelfth-century practices seem antiquated and slow-moving by comparison. The leisurely, deliberate immersion in logic and grammar that John of Salisbury fought a rear-guard action to defend in his *Metalogicon* would have seemed, to an intellectual of the fourteenth century, a rather quaint outlook. In other words, the successes of the twelfth century had built in their own obsolescence.

Grammar after the twelfth century

At the end of the twelfth century, the pressure to respond to a rapid expansion of students seeking Latin literacy and to provide grammatical instruction that truly addressed the needs of modern vernacular speakers occasioned one of the greatest breaks from the past: two new grammatical textbooks written with modern European students in mind. With the *Doctrinale* by Alexander of Villa Dei from 1199[25] and the *Graecismus* by Eberhard (Évrard) of Béthune from 1212,[26] the possibilities for a comprehensive grammatical course expanded to unprecedented horizons. Both of these texts distill the teachings in Priscian's *Institutiones,* but add the dimension of the figures and tropes as taught in Book Three of Donatus's *Ars maior.* Both are in verse, making the teaching especially easy to retain. Both texts assume that the student will have mastered Donatus's *Ars minor* (which remained the basic text for rank beginners), and provide streamlined access to the sophisticated teaching of Priscian's work which covers not only parts of speech but also etymologies, syntax, and prosody. Both works aim towards the goal of literary understanding. Alexander's *Doctrinale* explicitly recognizes that teachers will convey the information contained in his grammar in the vernacular. Eberhard's *Graecismus* puts the figures and tropes at the beginning of the treatise, making them immediately accessible. Almost from their first appearance the verse grammars attracted commentary and glossing. Some of this glossing appears to be teachers' aids, but some of it is quite advanced, indicating that these texts were used at the highest reaches of grammatical scholarship at the early universities and apparently also imported from the universities back to secondary schools.[27]

With these verse grammars, the products of the practical and literary orientation of grammatical study in the twelfth century, the rift between positive grammar (the descriptive treatment of words and their constructions, that is, usage) and speculative or theoretical grammar grew even more marked. The division between these realms was cemented with the emergence of the universities in Paris and Oxford. The curricula of the university arts faculties give grammar a privileged place, but it is a grammar oriented to uncovering the underlying principles by which concepts in the mind are expressed in language.[28] The texts which students read or heard read numerous times during their studies were Priscian's *Institutiones,* with the *Barbarismus* (Book Three of Donatus's *Ars maior*) mentioned as an auxiliary text at Paris, while it was required for determination in arts at Oxford.[29] Figures and tropes might play a role in theoretical explorations of language, not for their literary value but for the way that they test the limits of the rules of semantics.[30] Modistic grammar was an outgrowth of speculative grammar from late in the thirteenth century; technically, modistic grammar studied words and expressions in terms of their *modi significandi* which derive from conceptual understanding (*modi intellegendi*) which, in turn, derives from the *modi essendi,* that is, the modes of being of the thing understood and expressed. The *modistae* (especially the Parisian masters Martin of Dacia and Boethius of Dacia from the 1270s, and culminating with Thomas of Erfurt's *De modis significandi* from about 1310), like the speculative grammarians before them, sought to determine the scientific status of grammar by projecting certain universal, unchanging properties onto it.[31] This is far removed from a *grammatica usualis,* which codifies and teaches usage.

Even beyond the apogee of the *modistae* in the early fourteenth century, grammar remained linked with dialectical study: that is, positing and interpreting the semantics of propositions. After the speculative grammarians and the *modistae,* grammar might be subsumed under dialectic for the general principles which assured its elevated status as a science. This was the model of grammatical study entrenched in universities. Its exponents, whatever their positions on mental and verbal propositions, show little concern for the integration of grammar with literary studies, an interest that, in stark contrast, had been central to the great twelfth-century grammatical thinkers. *Grammatica usualis*, grammar that aimed to teach language and enable literary appreciation, was to follow its own course quite distinct from anything that engaged the attention of university masters. This division is vividly captured in Henri d'Andeli's *Bataille des VII Ars* from about 1230, which imagines a war between the new centre of logical studies, Paris, and the traditional centre of *belles lettres*, Orléans, which was quickly losing its ground to Paris. In this brilliant academic satire, the literary and grammatical authors educated at Orléans are ranged against the logical and philosophical authors studied at Paris. Towards the end of the poem, Dame Logic, commanding the Parisian forces, sends a messenger to Dame Grammar to offer terms for a truce; but the messenger, a young Parisian arts student, is so inept in *grammatica usualis* that he is incapable of communicating the message and returns to Dame Logic in shame.[32] About 1280, Hugh of Trimberg, a German grammar master, writing a curricular guide for his students, ruefully (perhaps ironically) complains of the mind-boggling difficulties of dialectic. As a satisfying compensation for those who will not become dialecticians, Hugh offers his survey of the *auctores*, who at least provide ethical knowledge.[33]

Rhetoric after the twelfth century

The innovative teaching of the twelfth century also had a decisive impact on the future course of rhetorical study. We have already noted how Horatian doctrine about composition was streamlined by the author of the 'Materia' commentary (from the middle of the century), and how this commentary seems to have informed what became the new genre of the *artes poetriae*. Matthew of Vendôme produced the earliest of these in the second half of the century, the *Ars versificatoria*, a prose work in which Matthew inserts classical verse and his own verse compositions as student models for techniques of description and style. Over the last decades of the twelfth century and through the first decade of the thirteenth, Geoffrey of Vinsauf, an English grammar master, produced several compositional textbooks in prose, leading to his most famous work, the *Poetria nova,* written in hexameter verses and composed in the years around 1210.[34] The *Poetria nova* offered an astute combination of Ciceronian and Horatian doctrine in memorable verse form. The extraordinary success of the *Poetria nova* overshadowed all earlier and later compositional manuals: it survives in over 200 manuscripts from across Europe, a good many of them containing glosses and commentaries on the text, and it was used into the early modern period.[35] Its success can be measured all the more acutely when we compare its vast circulation to the limited transmission of the next of the arts of poetry, Gervase of Melkley's *Ars versificaria* (about 1215, surviving in four manuscripts), which situates itself in what Gervase recognized as a tradition inaugurated by Matthew of Vendôme and Geoffrey of Vinsauf. John of Garland's *Parisiana poetria*, a prose work of about 1229, was the most ambitious and comprehensive of these arts, combining theoretical reflections on poetic style with advice on composition in both verse and prose (for the latter, drawing on the *ars dictandi* tradition). One later compositional handbook, of limited influence (although of inherent interest), closes out the tradition of the *ars poetriae*: Eberhard the German's *Laborintus*, most likely from the second half of the thirteenth century.[36] These works, products of the innovative teaching of twelfth-century masters, revolutionized writing instruction, superseding Horace's *Ars poetria* as a teaching text and providing dynamic, streamlined, and practical approaches to composition and stylistic embellishment. It is important to stress that such compositional teaching would typically be the province of a grammar master, and that the writing skills that these texts promised were aimed at enhancing students' Latinity.

The outcome of this pedagogical revolution in rhetoric can be compared to what we see in grammatical study, although the effects in rhetorical teaching were even more dramatic. In northern Europe, the success of the *artes poetriae* drove apart the practical teaching of rhetoric and the advanced theoretical study of the art to the point where the latter had no further role. In the cathedral schools of the twelfth century, the same master engaged in grammatical scholarship could also teach the classical rhetorical tradition. Petrus Helias, most famous for his *Summa super Priscianum*, also commented on Ciceronian rhetoric and, according to John of Salisbury's reminiscences,[37] taught it effectively.[38] But the great northern universities (which superseded the cathedral schools as the metropolitan centres of higher learning) had no official place for rhetoric in their curricula. As we have seen, the focus of the powerful arts faculties at Paris and Oxford was logic and grammar as subtended by logic, and these were the disciplines that under-graduates had to absorb in some depth. Rhetoric was recognized as an allied science of the trivium, and at Paris lectures on rhetoric were permitted on feast days. Here the key text mentioned was Book Four of Boethius's *De topicis differentiis*, which com-pares dialectical *topoi* (topics of invention) with those of rhetoric.[39] While the twelfth century could boast as many as fifteen different commentaries on the Ciceronian rheto-rics, the university milieux of France and England produced virtually none during the thirteenth century.[40]

This does not mean that the universities were devoid of rhetoric. For example, John of Garland brought his combined interests in grammar and rhetoric to the University of Toulouse, where he was Master of Grammar during the dispersion of the University of Paris in 1229–31, and he was a figure at the University of Paris until his death in 1272. University statutes did acknowledge that there would be interest in rhetoric and allowed 'extraordinary' (i.e. extra-curricular) lectures on the subject.[41] Moreover, interest in com-prehensive classification of the sciences would entail some knowledge about the elem-ents of rhetoric and how it comprises one part of the trivium; a group of 'student guides' to the sciences, of Parisian origin and now in Barcelona Arxiu de la Corona d'Aragó MS Ripoll 109, has been used as important evidence of this.[42] But in-depth studies of rhet-oric at the university level would be evidenced by a proliferation of commentaries on the Ciceronian sources, and as noted, the universities did not produce these. Even the entry of Aristotle's *Rhetoric* onto the academic scene around 1269 (in William of Moerbeke's Latin translation) seems to have had little effect on the pursuit of technical rhetoric per se. The long commentary on Aristotle's *Rhetoric* by Giles of Rome (c.1270–2) shows enormous interest in Aristotelian thought and in the disciplinary links between rhetoric, ethics, and politics, but makes virtually no reference to the Ciceronian rhetorical tradition.[43]

Thus while grammar might be encountered at the extreme ends of the school culture and in two very different forms, *grammatica usualis* in the elementary and intermediate schools and speculative grammar at the university, for the most part rhetorical study was a truncated version of itself. The higher end of rhetorical study had no official place in advanced study at northern European universities, while its 'lower' pedagogy, in the form of the popular composition manuals, spread rapidly to serve the needs of a growing literate class. It is possible to say that rhetoric became part of a broader remit of the grammar classroom.

Only in the Italian cities would rhetoric have been consistently part of the higher educational culture. This was because the study of law (in particular at the University of Bologna) went hand in hand with training in the *ars dictaminis* or rhetorical prose composition. In thirteenth-century Bologna, dictaminal masters such as Guido Faba and Boncompagno da Signa claimed the kind of prestige that most grammar masters of northern Europe could only imagine. It was in Italian milieux that the study of Ciceronian rhetoric achieved some of its key advances, the earliest vernacular treatments of technical rhetorics.[44] Brunetto Latini produced a partial translation and commentary on Cicero's *De inventione* in Italian around 1260, although this was little known outside of Italy. But his *Trésor*, written in French during the same period, was transmitted widely not only in French but in an Italian version and in other languages. Book Three of the *Trésor* gives what is in effect an advanced course on Ciceronian rhetoric, paraphrasing the *De inventione* and augmenting it with new examples and applications to contemporary rhetorical situations (for example, embedding a treatment of letter-writing or *ars dictaminis*).[45]

GRAMMAR AND RHETORIC IN FOURTEENTH-CENTURY ENGLAND

The first curricular statutes for Oxford's faculty of arts were set out in 1268 and specified that students would hear two courses of lectures on Priscian's syntax and one course on the *Barbarismus* of Donatus. Book Four of Boethius's *De topicis differentiis* (dealing with rhetoric) was explicitly not required.[46] While emphases might change over the following generations and individual colleges might supplement the required teaching, Oxford did not officially restate curricular requirements until 1409, when the requirements for grammar changed only slightly, and rhetoric still played no role.[47] There is no evidence that the interests of the arts faculty and its masters shifted away from logic and semantics during the fourteenth century. Rather, the major change would be that modistic grammar fell out of fashion, to be replaced by the new and more precise semantic thought of the Parisian John Buridan and his Oxford counterpart William of Ockham. The arts faculties of Oxford and Cambridge did oversee elementary grammar teaching for those entering students who required it and also for the production of licensed grammar masters,[48] and inevitably grammar schools operated on the peripheries of both universities.

Outside the formal university curriculum, grammatical teaching would have continued to develop from the lines established in the thirteenth century: the use of Donatus's *Ars minor* along with the *Doctrinale* and the *Graecismus* as the now-standard grammatical references. These later works brought with them a streamlined version of the 'Priscianic turn' of the twelfth century, giving them (as noted above) a usefulness at all levels of study. English schoolmasters of the fourteenth century also produced their own particular grammatical treatises or sets of notes based on digests of authorities. Some of these reflect an interesting change, a use of English rather than French as the language of teaching or comparison. John of Cornwall, whose *Speculum grammaticale* dates from 1346, is mentioned by John Trevisa for inaugurating this change, although we know that English was used (along with and sometimes instead of French) even earlier as a language for glossing Latin vocabulary.[49]

The literary culture of the fourteenth-century grammar classroom could trace itself back to developments of the twelfth century and the standardized forms these assumed in the thirteenth. The common grouping that comprised the *Liber catonianus* or *Sex auctores* had already expanded and changed by the late thirteenth century, losing much of the classical character of its earlier incarnations and incorporating newer Christian materials.[50] But at the same time we can trace strong interest in classical texts. The ideal classical reading list as envisaged by Alexander Neckam may not have been a practical ambition. But the desire to maintain the standards set earlier shows itself in thirteenth- and fourteenth-century copying, circulation, and glossing of favourite classical authors such as Persius, Juvenal, Horace, and—as McKinley shows for the fourteenth century— especially Ovid.[51] Not all the authors seem to be well represented in surviving manuscripts from the fourteenth century, for example, Claudian[52] and also, interestingly, Virgil. Baswell's census of thirty-seven Virgil manuscripts written or owned in England in the Middle Ages lists only two produced during the fourteenth century, both of them with contemporary glosses: one of these, Oxford Bodleian MS Auct. F.1.17, is an omnibus volume of 301 folios, containing not only the works of Virgil but Alan of Lille's *Liber parabolarum* (often included with the expanded *Liber catonianus*), the *Tobias* of Matthew of Vendôme, epigrams by Marbod of Rennes, the *Poetria nova*, works of Ovid, and the Bible epics of Sedulius and Prudentiua.[53]

But as a whole, the resources for classical learning were ample. The expansion of classical holdings in English monastic houses from the fourteenth century onward has been well documented. Such new holdings would include many books copied earlier that would continue to be of use.[54] The major secular schools, such as St Paul's, benefited from large bequests of collections that would include older copies of classical texts; and grammar masters themselves could equip their smaller schools with their own collections.[55] And of course there is the English phenomenon, identified and studied by Smalley, of the 'classicizing friars' (products of thirteenth-century schooling) who applied their enthusiasm for classical antiquity to the exigencies of preaching and sacred commentary (although this 'movement' proved eccentric to dominant fourteenth-century clerical interests).[56] As such varied examples show, students in the fourteenth century had good access to classical poetry and prose. But their reading was probably more typically organized by the classical samples presented in grammars, in *florilegia*, and sometimes in the *artes poetriae*, or by poems specially written for medieval student audiences such as Neckam's revisions of the fables of Avianus; or they read selections from the more modern literary authors, including Walter of Châtillon, Matthew of Vendôme, Peter Riga, Alan of Lille, and others.

The depth and richness of classical reference that we associate with Chaucer and Gower were inspired by their early education, but it is important to remember that they were also the achievement of their own courses of intellectual and literary maturation. Chaucer's classicism, whatever his school training, would have been enhanced by his continental travels and especially contacts with Italian intellectual milieux. Similarly, Gower's broad classicism developed through his close association with the highest echelons of the English royal court and its international exchanges.

Rhetorical education in fourteenth-century England presents different questions of textual access and doctrinal transmission. We will not find our answers in the formal teaching of the Universities of Oxford and Cambridge.[57] How was rhetorical knowledge conveyed? The manuscript traditions of the *artes poetriae* tell a complex story. We would expect that the *artes poetriae* would have continued through the fourteenth century as popular teaching texts in England, just as they did on the Continent. But the manuscript evidence for England is surprising. In an important article, Camargo throws new light on this evidence and on the knowledge and teaching of rhetoric in the late fourteenth-century.[58] In England the manuscript copying of Geoffrey of Vinsauf's *Poetria nova* and his earlier *Documentum de modo et arte dictandi et versificandi*, as well as of the arts by Matthew of Vendôme, Gervase of Melkely, and John of Garland, fall into two main periods, early thirteenth-century copies (close to the periods when they were written) and a resurgence of copying in the late fourteenth century and the years after that. This means that during the period of Chaucer's youth in the 1340s, these texts were apparently not being regularly copied for schoolroom use.

Some aspects of 'rhetorical' knowledge, that is, teaching on style and the figures and tropes, would have remained continuously available through the teaching of grammar. The main grammatical texts, *Doctrinale* and *Graecismus*, included sections devoted to the figures and tropes as part of their syntheses of Donatan and Priscianic doctrine. Lists of figures and tropes, sometimes also called *colores*, might also have supplemented these main texts along with sample poems illustrating the *colores*. Since the teaching on stylistic embellishment had long been shared between grammatical and rhetorical texts, this element of rhetorical teaching would have remained fully accessible in any curricular setting.

But the 'renaissance' of rhetoric had to wait for the later fourteenth century when the Benedictines at Oxford began a program of copying the old rhetorics and synthesizing old and new rhetorical knowledge.[59] Benedictine numbers at Oxford had been swelling since the late 1330s, and the Benedictine colleges sought to devise their own shortened and practical version of an arts course in order to speed the progress of their students into the higher faculty of theology. The revival of rhetoric in Benedictine houses began with recognizing the pragmatic value for members of the order of advanced instruction in Latin composition, especially for the purpose of writing official letters. It led to a full-scale revival of rhetorical teaching, encompassing the *Poetria nova* and John of Garland's *Parisiana poetria*, as well as the classical Ciceronian texts. The main interests were in letter writing, the *ars dictandi*, but the new treatises that emerged from Benedictine houses were eclectic and synthetic. The most important of these is the *Tria sunt*.[60] Along with their new interests in medieval and classical rhetorics, the Benedictines also seem to have followed the model of thirteenth-century collections by copying literary texts in the same volume with rhetorical manuals.

Thus it is only in the last decades of the fourteenth century that we see in England a comprehensive engagement with the art of rhetoric, and a new availability of medieval and classical rhetorical texts. Chaucer's own knowledge of rhetoric during his literary career seems to follow the arc of this development, his later works exhibiting a stronger and more complete sense of the art than his earlier ones.[61] It is also possible that Chaucer encountered rhetorical lore during his early travels to Italy, where classical and medieval rhetoric never lost its vital presence; but it is also likely that it was his more immediate milieu of the rhetorical scholarship in Oxford that activated his interest in the art. Chaucer and Gower are the only English vernacular poets of the fourteenth century to demonstrate a solid grasp of rhetorical theory (that is, a knowledge that goes beyond the art of stylistic embellishment and that recognizes the core features of inventional theory). If Chaucer's and perhaps Gower's knowledge can be linked to the resurgence and new professional prestige of rhetoric among the Benedictines at Oxford, what other sources were available to them? It is clear that Gower knew something of Ciceronian rhetoric, but was his source the *De inventione* or *Rhetorica ad Herennium*? There is another source that presents itself more directly: Brunetto Latini's *Trésor*, which stands clearly behind his extended treatment of rhetoric in Book Seven of *Confessio amantis*.[62] The *Trésor* had a wide European circulation, and as a book in French offered a convenient exposition of classical doctrine. Other candidates for Chaucer's and Gower's knowledge of rhetoric are the *De nuptiis Philologiae et Mercurii* by Martianus Capella, and Alan of Lille's *Anticlaudianus*, which provides a solid survey of ancient rhetorical matter drawn partly from Martianus Capella.[63] But most important, and whatever their immediate sources, what seems to have prompted such mature literary interest in the theory of rhetoric was not what they learned at school in the first half of the century, but what was recovered and generated anew in the later years of the century.

CONCLUSION

The transition from the twelfth-century schools to the learning of the fourteenth century is not transparent. The innovative approaches and technologies of the early schools were absorbed, regularized, assimilated, and often thus taken for granted and their original *raisons d'être* forgotten by the later beneficiaries. Without the Priscianic turn of the early twelfth century, the comprehensive and streamlined grammars of the thirteenth and fourteenth centuries would have been impossible. Without the decisive classicism of twelfth-century teaching, the 'digested' and anthologized classicism of the later periods would have been unlikely. The course for the divergence between higher and lower orders of subject matter, of teaching in universities and in schools, was set at the end of the twelfth century. And the relative indifference of formal university curricula to the art of rhetoric created a space for the regeneration of rhetorical knowledge in a new pragmatic guise, and gave new scope to late fourteenth-century literary apprehensions of rhetoric.

Notes

1. Katherine Zieman, 'Ex Ore Infantium: Literacy and Elementary Educational Practices in Late Medieval England', in *Singing the New Song: Literacy and Liturgy in Late Medieval England* (Philadelphia, PA: University of Pennsylvania Press, 2008), 1–39.
2. John of Salisbury, *Metalogicon* 1. 24.
3. Marcus Boas, 'De librorum Catonianorum historia atque compositione', *Mnemosyne* n.s. 42 (1914), 25–7, 46.
4. See handlist of *artes and auctores* up to c.1100 in Martin Irvine, *The Making of Textual Culture: 'Grammatica' and Literary Theory, 350–1100* (Cambridge: Cambridge University Press, 1994), 395–404.
5. Tony Hunt, ed., *Teaching and Learning Latin in Thirteenth-Century England*, vol. 1 (Cambridge: D. S. Brewer, 1991), 165–76.
6. Osbern of Gloucester, *Derivationes*, ed. P. Busdraghi et al. (Spoleto: Centro italiano di studi sull'Alto Medioevo, 1996).
7. Hunt, *Teaching and Learning Latin*, 1:177–89.
8. R. W. Hunt, *The Schools and the Cloister: The Life and Writings of Alexander Nequam (1157–1217)*, ed. and rev. Margaret Gibson (Oxford: Clarendon Press, 1984), 4–7, 19–20, 125; Rita Copeland, 'Naming, Knowing, and the Object of Language in Alexander Neckam's Grammar Curriculum', *The Journal of Medieval Latin* 20 (2010), 38–57.
9. Otto Keller, ed., *Pseudoacronis scholia in Horatium vetustiora*, 2 vols. (Leipzig: Teubner, 1902–4).
10. Birger Munk Olsen, *L'Étude des auteurs classiques latins aux XIe et XIIe siècles*, vol. 4 (Paris: CNRS, 1982–2009), 54–6, 97, 122.
11. Suzanne Reynolds, *Medieval Reading: Grammar, Rhetoric, and the Classical Text* (Cambridge: Cambridge University Press, 1996), 32–41; Ralph J. Hexter, *Ovid and Medieval Schooling: Studies in Medieval School Commentaries on Ovid's Ars amatoria, Epistulae ex Ponto, and Epistulae Heroidum* (Munich: Arbeo-Gesellschaft, 1986), 42–77.
12. Günter Glauche, *Schullektüre im Mittelalter: Entstehung und Wandlungen des Lektürekanons bis 1200 nach den Quellen dargestellt* (Munich: Arbeo-Gesellschaft, 1970), 105.
13. Frank T. Coulson, 'Ovid's *Metamorphoses* in the School Tradition of France, 1180–1400: Texts, Manuscript Traditions, Manuscript Settings', in *Ovid in the Middle Ages*, eds. Frank T. Coulson, James G. Clark, and Kathryn L. McKinley (Cambridge: Cambridge University Press, 2011), 50–5.

14. Ralph of Beauvais, *Liber Tytan*, ed. C. H. Kneepkens, Artistarium 8 (Nijmegen: Ingenium, 1991), xiv–xvi.

15. R. B. C. Huygens, ed., *Accessus ad auctores, Bernard d'Utrecht, Conrad d'Hirsau* (Leiden: Brill, 1970).

16. Huygens, *Accessus ad auctores*.

17. Winthrop Wetherbee, 'From Late Antiquity to the Twelfth Century', in *The Cambridge History of Literary Criticism* 2, eds. Alastair Minnis and Ian Johnson (Cambridge: Cambridge University Press, 2005), 125–6; Rita Copeland, 'Producing the *Lector*', in *Medieval and Early Modern Authorship,* eds. Lukas Erne and Guillemette Boulens (Tübingen: Guntar Narr, 2011).

18. Alexander Neckam, *Sacerdos ad altare*, ed. C. McDonough, *Corpus christianorum continuatio medievalis* 227 (Turnhout: Brepols, 2010), 174–5; translation in Rita Copeland and Ineke Sluiter, eds., *Medieval Grammar and Rhetoric: The Language Arts and Literary Theory, AD 300 to 1475* (Oxford: Oxford University Press, 2009), 531–4; Copeland, 'Producing the Lector'.

19. R. W. Hunt, 'Studies on Priscian in the Eleventh and Twelfth Centuries, I: Petrus Helias and his Predecessors', in *The History of Grammar…Collected Papers,* ed. R. W. Hunt (orig. publ. 1941–3), 1–38; Margaret Gibson, 'The Early Scholastic *Glosule* to Priscian, *Institutiones grammaticae*: The Text and its Influence', *Studi medievali* 3rd ser. 20 (1979), 235–54; Margaret Gibson, 'Milestones in the Study of Priscian, circa 800–circa 1200', *Viator* 23 (1992), 17–33; Anne Grondeux and Irène Rosier-Catach, 'Les *Glosulae super Priscianum* et leur tradition', in *Arts du langage et théologie aux confins des XI e et XII e siècles. Textes, maîtres, débats, Turnhout, 2011,* ed. Rosier-Catach (Turnhout: Brepols, 2011), 107–79; Karin Margareta Fredborg, 'Petrus Helias on Rhetoric', *Cahiers de l'institut du moyen âge grec et latin* 13 (1974), 31–41; partial translations in Copeland and Sluiter, *Medieval Grammar and Rhetoric,* 376–89, 444–60.

20. Martin Camargo, *Ars dictaminis, Ars dictandi*, Typologie des sources du moyen âge occidental 60 (Turnhout: Brepols, 1991), 31–7.

21. Munk Olsen, *L'Étude des auteurs classiques*, 1, 426.

22. Karsten Friis-Jensen, ed., 'The *Ars Poetica* in Twelfth-Century France: The Horace of Matthew of Vendôme, Geoffrey of Vinsauf, and John of Garland', *Cahiers de l'institut du moyen âge grec et latin* 60 (1990), 319–88.

23. Martin Camargo, 'Latin Composition Textbooks and *Ad Herennium* Glossing: The Missing Link'? in *The Rhetoric of Cicero*, eds. Virginia Cox and John O. Ward (Leiden: Brill, 2006), 267–88; Grondeux, Anne, 'Teaching and Learning Lists of Figures in the Middle Ages', *New Medieval Literatures* 11 (2009), 133–58.

24. J. O Ward, *Ciceronian Rhetoric in Treatise, Scholion, and Commentary* (Turnhout: Brepols, 1995), 105–67; J. O. Ward, 'The Medieval and Early Renaissance Study of Cicero's *De inventione* and the *Rhetorica ad Herennium*: Commentaries and Contexts', in *The Rhetoric of Cicero*, eds. Cox and Ward, 23–50; Karin Margareta Fredborg, 'Abelard on Rhetoric', in *Rhetoric and Renewal in the Latin West 1100–1540: Essays in Honour of John O. Ward*, eds. Constant Mews, Cary J. Nederman, and Rodney M. Thomson (Turnhout: Brepols, 2003), 55–80.

25. Alexander of Villa Dei, *Das Doctrinale des Alexander de Villa-Dei: kritisch.-exegetische. Ausgabe,* ed. Dietrich Reichling. 1845 (New York: Burt Franklin Reprint, 1974); partial translation in Copeland and Sluiter, *Medieval Grammar and Rhetoric*, 573–83.

26. Eberhard of Béthune, *Graecismus*, ed. Johann Wrobel, Corpus grammaticorum medii aevi I. (Breslau: G. Koebner, 1887); partial translation in Copeland and Sluiter, *Medieval Grammar and Rhetoric*, 584–93.

27. *Admirantes* gloss on the *Doctrinale* in *Notices et extraits de divers manuscrits latins pour servir à l'histoire des doctrines grammaticales au moyen âge,* ed. C. Thurot (Frankfurt: Minerva repr. 1964 [orig. publ. 1869]); Irène Rosier, 'Le traitement spéculatif des constructions figurées au treizème siècle', in *L'héritage des grammairiens latins de l'Antiquité aux Lumières. Actes du colloque de Chantilly,* ed. Irène Rosier (Louvain: Diffusion-Peeters, 1988), 181–204. Anne Grondeux, *Le Graecismus d'Évrard de Béthune à travers ses gloses. Entre grammaire positive et grammaire spéculative du XIIIe au XVe siècle* (Turnhout: Brepols, 2000), 45–122, 297–399; Anne, Grondeux, ed., *Glosa super Graecismum Eberhardi Bethuniensis, capitula I-III, de figuris coloribusque rhetoricis,* Corpus christianorum continuatio mediaevalis 225 (Turnhout: Brepols, 2010), vii–xxiii; Anne Grondeux, 'La tradition manuscrite des commentaires au *Graecismus* d'Évrard de Béthune', in *Manuscripts and Tradition of Grammatical Texts from Antiquity to the Renaissance,* vol. 2, eds. Mario de Nonno, Paolo de Paolis, and Louis Holtz (Cassino: Università degli Studi di Cassino, 2000), 499–531.

28. Irène Rosier-Catach, 'La tradition de la grammaire universiatire médiévale', in Nonno et al, *Manuscripts and Tradition of Grammatical Texts,* vol. 2, 458.

29. Osmund P. Lewry, 'Grammar, Logic and Rhetoric, 1220–1320', in *The History of the University of Oxford* 1: *The Early Oxford Schools,* ed. J. I. Catto (Oxford: Clarendon Press, 1984), 401–33; Copeland and Sluiter, eds., *Medieval Grammar and Rhetoric,* 687–8.

30. Irène Rosier, 'Le traitement spéculatif des constructions figurées au treizième siècle'; Robert Kilwardby (Pseudo), *In Donati Artem Maiorem III* [on *Barbarismus*], ed. L. Schmuecker (Brixen: Weger 1984).

31. Jan Pinborg, 'Speculative Grammar', in *The Cambridge History of Later Medieval Philosophy: From the Rediscovery of Aristotle to the Disintegration of Scholasticism, 1100–1600,* eds. Norman Kretzmann, Anthony Kenny, Jan Pinborg, and Eleanore Stump (Cambridge: Cambridge University Press, 1982), 254–69.

32. Henri d'Andeli, *Bataille des VII ars,* ed. and trans. L. J. Paetow, *The Battle of the Seven Arts. A French Poem by Henri d'Andeli, Trouvère of the Thirteenth Century* (Berkeley, CA: University of California Press, 1914), lines 372–97; text in Copeland and Sluiter, *Medieval Grammar and Rhetoric,* 721–2.

33. Hugh of Trimberg, *Das 'Registrum multorum auctorum' des Hugo von Trimberg,* ed. K. Langosch. Germanische Studien 235 (Berlin: Emil Ebering, 1942), lines 1–65; trans. in Copeland and Sluiter, *Medieval Grammar and Rhetoric,* 658–9.

34. Martin Camargo, 'From *Liber versuum* to *Poetria nova*: The Evolution of Geoffrey of Vinsauf's Masterpiece', *Journal of Medieval Latin* 21 (2011), 1–16.

35. Marjorie Curry Woods, *Classroom Commentaries: Teaching the Poetria nova across Medieval and Renaissance Europe* (Columbus, OH: Ohio State University Press, 2010). See also Chapter 7 in this volume by James Simpson.

36. For references, editions, and selections from these texts see Copeland and Sluiter, *Medieval Grammar and Rhetoric,* 544–656. The *Poetria* by the Swedish scholar Matthias of Linkoping, written in the first half of the fourteenth century and preserved in only one manuscript, is less an art of poetry than a treatise on poetics reflecting the impact of the Latinized Averroistic-Aristotelian *Poetics.* See edition by Birger Bergh, *Magister Mathias Lincopensis Testa nucis and Poetria* (Arlöv: Berlings, 1996).

37. John of Salisbury, *Metalogicon* 2.10.

38. Fredborg, 'Petrus Helias on Rhetoric', 31–41; Ward, 'The Medieval and Early Renaissance Study', Appendix, 70–5.

39. Heinrich Denifle and Émile Chatelain, eds., *Chartularium Universitatis Parisiensis,* vol. 1 (Brussels: Culture et civilisation, 1964 [orig. publ. Paris, 1889–1897]), 78, 278.

40. J. O. Ward, 'From Antiquity to the Renaissance: Glosses and Commentaries on Cicero's *Rhetorica*', in *Medieval Eloquence*, ed. J. J. Murphy (Berkeley, CA: University of California Press, 1978), 37–8; Fredborg, 'Ciceronian Rhetoric and the Schools', in *Learning Institutionalized: Teaching in the Medieval University*, ed. John van Engen (Notre Dame, IN: University of Notre Dame Press, 2000), 21.

41. J. O. Ward, 'Rhetoric in the Faculty of Arts at the Universities of Paris and Oxford in the Middle Ages: A Summary of the Evidence', *Archivum latinitatis medii aevii (Bulletin du Cange)* 54 (1996), 159–231.

42. Essays and texts in Claude Lafleur and Joanne Carrier, eds. *L'enseignement de la philosophie au XIIIe siècle. Autour du 'Guide de l'étudiant' du ms. Ripoll 109* (Turnhout: Brepols, 1997).

43. Overview and partial translation in Copeland and Sluiter, *Medieval Grammar and Rhetoric*, 792–811.

44. Cox, 'Ciceronian Rhetoric in Late Medieval Italy', in Cox and Ward, *The Rhetoric of Cicero*, 109–43.

45. Brunetto Latini, *Trésor*, eds. and trans. Pietro G. Beltrami, Paolo Squillacioti, Plinio Torri, and Sergio Vatteroni (Turin: Einaudi, 2007).

46. Strickland Gibson, ed., *Statuta antiqua universitatis Oxoniensis* (Oxford: Clarendon Press, 1931), lxxxix–xc, 25–6.

47. J. M. Fletcher, 'Developments in the Faculty of Arts 1370–1520', in *The History of the University of Oxford* 2, eds. J. I Catto and T. H. R. Evans (Oxford: Clarendon Press, 1992), 317–23.

48. R. W. Hunt, 'Oxford Grammar Masters in the Middle Ages', in *The History of Grammar. Collected Papers*, ed. R. W. Hunt (Amsterdam: J. Benjamins B. V., 1980) [orig. publ. 1964]), lxxxv–lxxxvi; Strickland Gibson, ed., *Statuta antiqua*; Damian Leader, *A History of the University of Cambridge* 1, *The University to 1546* (Cambridge: Cambridge University Press, 1988), 114–16.

49. Christopher Cannon, 'The Middle English Writer's Schoolroom: Fourteenth-Century English Schoolbooks and their Contents', *New Medieval Literatures* 11 (2009), 19–38; David Thomson, *A Descriptive Catalogue of Middle English Grammatical Texts* (New York: Garland, 1979); David Thomson, ed., *An Edition of the Middle English Grammatical Texts* (New York: Garland, 1984); English glosses listed in Tony Hunt, *Teaching and Learning Latin*, vol. 3, 189–94.

50. Vincent Gillespie, 'From the Twelfth Century to c. 1450', in Minnis and Johnson, *Cambridge History of Literary Criticism* 2, 145–235; M. C. Woods and Rita Copeland, 'Classroom and Confession', in *The Cambridge History of Medieval English Literature*, ed. D. Wallace (Cambridge: Cambridge University Press, 1999), 380–5; Hunt, *Teaching and Learning Latin* vol. 1, 70–9; compare with Richard Hazelton, 'The Christianization of "Cato": The *Disticha Catonis* in the Light of Late Mediaeval Commentaries', *Mediaeval Studies* 19 (1957), 157–73.

51. Hunt, *Teaching and Learning Latin* vol. 1, 53–66; E. J. Kenney, 'The Manuscript Tradition of Ovid's *Amores, Ars amatoria,* and *Remedia amoris*', *The Classical Quarterly* n.s. 12 (1962), 1–31; Kathryn L. McKinley, 'Manuscripts of Ovid in England, 1100–1500', in *English Manuscript Studies 1100–1700* 7, eds. Peter Beal and Jeremy Griffiths (London: The British Library, 1998), 41–85.

52. Claudian, *De raptu Proserpinae*, ed. J. B. Hall (Cambridge: Cambridge University Press, 1969), 3–32.

53. Christopher Baswell, *Virgil in Medieval England: Figuring the* Aeneid *from the Twelfth Century to Chaucer* (Cambridge: Cambridge University Press, 1995), Appendix 1, 301–3; on MS Auct. F.1.17 as a possible model for Chaucer at school, see Bruce Harbert, 'Chaucer and the Latin Classics', in *Writers and their Background: Geoffrey Chaucer*, ed. Derek Brewer (Athens, OH: Ohio University Press, 1975), 138–41.

54. James T. Clark, 'Ovid in the Monasteries, the Evidence from Late Medieval England', in Clark et al., *Ovid in the Middle Ages*), 181–2.
55. Nicholas Orme, *English Schools in the Middle Ages* (London: Methuen, 1973), 124–7.
56. Beryl Smalley, *English Friars and Antiquity in the Early Fourteenth Century* (Oxford: Blackwell, 1960), 299–307.
57. The revised statutes of Oxford University issued in 1431 prescribe readings in both Ciceronian and Aristotelian rhetoric; but the import of these has been treated with great suspicion because there are no Oxford-produced commentaries on rhetoric to complement such readings. Such a humanistic syllabus may have been created to impress a university patron such as Duke Humfrey. See Fletcher, 'Developments in the Faculty of Arts, 1370–1520', in Cato and Evans, *The History of the University of Oxford* 2, 324.
58. Martin Camargo, 'Chaucer and the Oxford Renaissance of Anglo-Latin Rhetoric', *Studies in the Age of Chaucer* 34 (2012), 173–207.
59. Camargo, 'Chaucer and the Oxford Renaissance'.
60. Overview and partial translation by Camargo in Copeland and Sluiter, eds., *Medieval Grammar and Rhetoric*, 670–81.
61. Camargo, 'Chaucer and the Oxford Renaissance'.
62. Rita Copeland, *Rhetoric, Hermeneutics, and Translation in the Middle Ages: Academic Traditions and Vernacular Texts* (Cambridge: Cambridge University Press, 1991), 208–11.
63. James Simpson, *Sciences and the Self in Medieval Poetry: Alan of Lille's* Anticlaudianus *and John Gower's* Confessio amantis (Cambridge: Cambridge University Press, 1995), 19–21.

BIBLIOGRAPHY

Camargo, Martin, 'Chaucer and the Oxford Renaissance of Anglo-Latin Rhetoric', *Studies in the Age of Chaucer* 34 (2012), 173–207.

Cannon, Christopher, *From Literacy to Literature: England, 1300–1400* (Oxford: Oxford University Press, 2016).

Copeland, Rita, *Rhetoric, Hermeneutics, and Translation in the Middle Ages: Academic Traditions and Vernacular Texts* (Cambridge: Cambridge University Press, 1991).

Copeland, Rita and Ineke Sluiter, eds., *Medieval Grammar and Rhetoric: The Language Arts and Literary Theory, AD 300 to 1475* (Oxford: Oxford University Press, 2009).

Donavin, Georgiana, *Scribit Mater: Mary and the Language Arts in the Literature of Medieval England* (Washington, D.C.: Catholic University of America Press, 2012).

Gillespie, Vincent, 'From the Twelfth Century to c.1450', in *The Cambridge History of Literary Criticism* 2, eds. Alastair Minnis and Ian Johnson (Cambridge: Cambridge University Press, 2005), 145–235.

Hunt, R. W., *The Schools and the Cloister: The Life and Writings of Alexander Nequam (1157–1217)*, ed. and rev. Margaret Gibson (Oxford: Clarendon Press, 1984).

Hunt, Tony, ed., *Teaching and Learning Latin in Thirteenth-Century England*, vol. 1 (Cambridge: D. S. Brewer, 1991).

Reynolds, Suzanne, *Medieval Reading: Grammar, Rhetoric, and the Classical Text* (Cambridge: Cambridge University Press, 1996).

Woods, Marjorie Curry, *Classroom Commentaries: Teaching the Poetria nova across Medieval and Renaissance Europe* (Columbus, OH: Ohio State University Press, 2010).

Zeeman, Nicolette, 'In the Schoolroom with the "Vulgate" Commentary on Metamorphoses I', *New Medieval Literatures* 13 (2009), 1–18.

CHAPTER 22

PHILOSOPHY, LOGIC, AND NOMINALISM

FABIENNE MICHELET AND MARTIN PICKAVÉ

GEOFFREY Chaucer is undeniably an erudite poet. Eustache Deschamps addresses Chaucer not only as a (medieval) Seneca and an Ovid, but first of all as a 'Socrates plains de philosophie'.[1] And it is beyond doubt that Chaucer is interested in philosophy. After all he rendered a popular work of late Antique Latin philosophy, Boethius' *Consolation of Philosophy*, into Middle English and frequently alluded to it in his writings. Moreover, by medieval standards, every enthusiast about astronomy is also an enthusiast about philosophy, as the Middle Ages considered sciences like astronomy as belonging to natural philosophy, then an important branch of philosophy.[2] Nevertheless an inquiry into the exact nature of Chaucer's relationship to philosophical currents of his time remains legitimate. Was he familiar with fourteenth-century philosophers and philosophy? If so, what philosophers or philosophical debates would he have known? And more point-edly, what does this tell us about the philosophical character of his writings? These are the questions that we shall pursue in this short chapter. We will first sketch the philosophical landscape of late fourteenth-century England, including some of the figures commonly linked to Chaucer. The second and third parts will address two recurring topics in discussions of Chaucer's philosophical leanings: the protracted issue of whether or not Chaucer endorsed nominalism and Chaucer's views about human action, and especially his concerns about free will and determinism.

ENGLISH PHILOSOPHY IN THE FOURTEENTH CENTURY

To speak of 'philosophy' and 'philosophers' in the Middle Ages may seem anachronistic. For starters, many of the best-known figures in medieval philosophy were members of religious orders (often Dominicans or Franciscans) and were masters of theology. However, this does not mean that philosophy was identical with theology. In fact, the thinkers of the later Middle Ages distinguished two forms of rational inquiry, one based on revelation, and one based only on what is accessible to us through our natural cognitive capacities. The first form of inquiry characterizes theology while the second delineates the scope of philosophy. Obviously, there are many intellectual issues medieval thinkers pursued from a purely natural, i.e. philosophical, point of view: logic is maybe the clearest example. But to the extent that theological texts do address some topics from the point of view of natural reason, theologians also engage in a philosophical enterprise.

Philosophy, whether pursued for its own sake or for the sake of supporting theological insights, is closely tied to a particular medieval institution: the university, and above all its arts faculty. Though there were certainly figures investigating philosophical issues outside of a university setting (for instance, at royal or local courts),[3] there can be no doubt that the universities were the driving force behind philosophical inquiry in the thirteenth- and fourteenth centuries. It is thus primarily to the universities that we should turn for a picture of fourteenth-century philosophical currents.

It is often said that the fourteenth century saw the development of a specifically English style in medieval philosophy and theology. During the 1310s, the number of English scholars teaching at the University of Paris was in steady decline, and by 1320 hardly any English masters were left in what was still the pre-eminent center of learning in the Christian world. Concomitantly, the number of Englishmen studying in Paris shrunk and the lively exchanges and circulation of texts that had existed between Paris and Oxford for so long plummeted, although the extent to which the flow of ideas actually diminished remains disputed. In any case, the fact is that more scholars and students stayed at home and this probably contributed to the strength of philosophy and theology in Oxford in the first half of the fourteenth century.[4] Among the figures linked to this 'golden age' are Walter Burley (c.1274/5–c.1344), Richard of Campshall (c.1280–c.1350), William of Ockham (c.1285–1347), Walter Chatton (1285–1343), Thomas Bradwardine (c.1290–1349), Robert Holcot (c.1290–1349), Adam Wodeham (c.1295–1358), Richard Halifax (c.1300–after 1350), Richard Fitzralph (c.1300–60), as well as Richard Kilvington (c.1302/5–61) and other so-called 'Oxford Calculators'. This extraordinary period prompted Richard of Bury to boast that Minerva had 'passed by Paris, and now has happily come to Britain'.[5] We have some reason to believe that Oxford philosophy and theology declined during the second half of the fourteenth century, but the scarcity of research devoted to the period following the first wave of the Black Death in 1348–9 still cautions one against any definitive judgment. With the exception of John Wyclif (c.1320–84), we know relatively little about the leading thinkers active in that period, such as Richard Brinkley (active 1350–73), Ralph Strode (active 1360–87), William Heytesbury (before 1313–72/3), and John Sharpe (c.1360–after 1415).[6]

Generalizations about intellectual currents are always a contentious matter. But with respect to fourteenth-century Oxford theology and philosophy modern interpreters have identified a series of trends concerning both the issues discussed and the forms in which they were discussed. Since the middle of the thirteenth century and as a formal requirement for promotion to master of theology, every bachelor of theology had to comment on Peter Lombard's *Sentences*. Unlike their Parisian counterparts, fourteenth-century English *Sentences* commentaries tend to limit themselves to issues especially popular at the time: the Trinity, beatitude and fruition, divine will and human freedom, future contingents, and the nature of grace. In discussing these, theologians not only used ever more sophisticated logical and mathematical tools, they also explored problems of natural philosophy such as the nature of motion, change, and speed.[7] With regard to logic and epistemology, fourteenth-century authors were particularly interested in semantic paradoxes, epistemic logic, the semantics of propositions, supposition theory, and so-called 'proofs of propositions'—a method of analyzing propositions in terms of the more basic proposition from which they can be derived.[8] Yet, behind many of the period's theological and philosophical innovations lie popular forms of logical genre: *sophismata*, *insolubilia*, and *obligationes*. A *sophisma* is usually nothing more than a discussion of a puzzling sentence and it was so closely associated with university teaching that it is not surprising to find Chaucer's Host telling the Clerk in the *Canterbury Tales* that he must have studied 'som sophyme' (IV.5). *Insolubilia*, on the other hand, deal with semantic paradoxes such as the liar paradox (i.e. statements like 'Everything I say is false'). Treatises about *obligationes* examine how rules of logical consequences and inferences are applied in a dispute between two discussants. Many of the authors mentioned above left us works dealing with *sophismata*, *insolubilia*, and *obligationes*. We may get a better picture of later fourteenth-century philosophy and theology by looking at two scholars in particular: Richard Brinkley and Ralph Strode.[9]

Richard Brinkley was a Franciscan at Oxford and must have been active between 1350 and 1373. Not much is known about his life, and he is best known today for his *Summa logicae*. Although a complete edition of this work is still lacking and the *Summa* in its entirety is now preserved in only two manuscripts, we know that the work had a huge impact on medieval logicians. In his day, Brinkley was also a famous theologian. Until recently his theological works were known only from quotations in his contemporaries' writings, but thanks to recent discoveries, some of these works have now come to light.[10] They testify to Brinkley's interest in epistemological discussions, in debates about divine foreknowledge and future contingents, and in the question of divine causality and the origin of contingency. His theological views were widely known and discussed by scholars in Paris in the decades following 1360.

In the *Summa logicae*, which Brinkley allegedly composed at the request of his Franciscan superiors to replace William of Ockham's *Summa*, he adopts a moderate realist stance. Common natures (such as the nature *human being*) exist in reality, although they do not exist apart from individuals. This attitude is not uncommon for a fourteenth-century Oxford logician. Despite the nominalist arguments that Ockham brought forward earlier in the century, Oxford philosophy and theology were predominantly realist.[11] Brinkley's realist perspective can also be seen in his treatment of the semantics of propositions. Unlike nominalist philosophers, he denies that that which is signified by a proposition (*significatum propositionis*), can simply be reduced to the 'significates' (*significata*) of a proposition's constitutive parts (e.g. subject and predicate).

Although Brinkley was a Franciscan, he should not be considered to belong to a distinct 'school'. He is definitely no Scotist, for as far as his extent writings indicate, he more often than not disagrees with John Duns Scotus, and in particular with his teaching on the origin of contingency. Moreover as William Courtenay has convincingly argued, Oxford's intellectual climate and institutional setting led to a disappearance of distinct schools of thought.[12] For these reasons, it is again somewhat anachronistic to talk about Thomists, Ockhamists, or Scotists in late fourteenth-century England.

Among Chaucer scholars, 'philosophical Strode' (Tr 5.1857) is a household name, since it is to him and to the poet John Gower that Chaucer dedicated his *Troilus and Criseyde*. Ralph Strode was a fellow of Merton College in the late 1350s and it is presumably in Oxford—maybe even at Merton College—that he first met John Wyclif, someone with whom he remained connected throughout his life. Like Brinkley, Strode wrote an introductory handbook of logic. His *Logica* was rarely transmitted as a whole, but its six parts were quickly read as separate treatises and were used in this form as textbooks in Italian universities. Other English logicians (such as Richard Heytesbury or Richard Billingham) experienced a similar popularity south of the Alps and the Italian success of Strode's *Logica* is not really indicative of his philosophical stature at Oxford or abroad.[13] Indeed, the reception of English logic in Italy owes much to Paul of Venice, a member of the Augustinian order who studied in Oxford in 1390 and then introduced many of the English textbooks to Italy when he returned to teach at Padua a couple of years later. In the 1370s Strode reappears in the records, this time as a lawyer. In 1373 he is elected common sergeant or pleader of the city of London (basically a public prosecutor), a position he held until 1382. Strode died in London in 1387.[14]

The identification of Strode the scholar with Strode the lawyer has been disputed, but the lawyer's strong connections to former *socii* of Merton College—on a couple of occasions he served as surety for members of the college—tips the balance in favor of this hypothesis. Moreover, as William Courtenay has pointed out, other later fourteenth-century academics moved from the arts faculty to a career in law.[15] In earlier years, the typical career of a philosopher would have meant either staying in the arts faculty or moving to a higher degree in theology; but by the middle of the fourteenth century the law faculty had begun to outrank the theology faculty, if not in official status then at least in terms of its appeal to students.

Chaucer and Strode were friends and remote neighbors in London from 1374 to 1386, and in 1381 they were involved in a legal issue on behalf of John Hende, a London merchant and future mayor of London. Their relationship has prompted much speculation among modern scholars about their philosophical exchanges and has led some to claim that it 'could have meant for Chaucer a virtual ten- to fifteen-year tutorial' on philosophical issues.[16] Nothing forces us to assume that Chaucer and Strode actually had exchanges on philosophical issues. But if Strode had tutored Chaucer in philosophy, then it would certainly not have been about the difference between nominalism and realism, as some Chaucer scholars seem to believe. As a former arts master, Strode would probably have organized such philosophical 'tutorials' along the lines of the Oxford arts curriculum.[17] He would have instructed Chaucer in the basic notions of Aristotelian philosophy and logic, maybe even using his own handbook. Discussions of semantics of terms and propositions would have included a treatment of universals—presumably Strode would have taught Chaucer some highly technical arguments for why universals have to be considered as existing in extra-mental reality. Yet there is no reason to believe that Strode would have highlighted disagreements about the ontological status of universals more than disputes about any other philosophical issue. Moreover, as Edith Sylla has pointed out in her contribution to this volume, it is much more likely that Strode and Chaucer would have discussed theological issues because we know from Wyclif's writings that Strode and his former Oxford colleague were debating theological matters during Strode's London period.[18]

NOMINALISM AND REALISM

'Nominalism' and 'realism' are two labels that have now gained widespread currency in Chaucer scholarship. Some commentators argue that Chaucer's poetry shows him leaning towards nominalism, while others contend that Chaucer betrays realist sympathies. A shared premise of these conflicting views is that Chaucer engages either with nominalism or with realism.[19] To the historian of philosophy, this outlook is surprising, since the two labels usually characterize two approaches to ontology. And why should abstract issues about the fundamental structure of reality matter to a poet and his audience?

A late medieval nominalist is someone who does not believe in a strict isomorphism between language and reality. Singular terms like 'Socrates' or 'Plato' name individuals, but general terms such as 'tree' or 'human being' do not name separate things (such as the natures of 'treeness' or 'humanity') as distinct from individual trees or human beings. For a nominalist, singular and general terms all signify individuals, but they do so differently. There is no such thing as a common nature in which individuals participate and which a general term names. Whereas the realist maintains that common natures ('treeness', 'humanity') exist as real things (res) outside the mind—hence the label 'realist'—the nominalist holds that common or universal entities exist only in the mind. Note that nominalists do not necessarily deny the existence of natural kinds (or classes)—i.e., the idea that natural objects (such as trees) fall into natural groupings (such as the species 'elm', 'birch', etc.) that are not merely artificial, human constructs. It is no contradiction to maintain on the one hand that only individual human beings exist and on the other that they make up the class of human beings insofar as all human beings are significantly similar. What the nominalist denies is that it is in virtue of participating in a common nature—'humanity' (humanitas)—that we resemble each other and all belong to that class.

'One should not multiply entities without necessity' (entia non sunt multiplicanda sine necessitate/praeter necessitatem): this motto, also known as 'Ockham's razor', is often considered the battle cry of nominalism. This is only partially correct, since realists too want to be ontologically parsimonious. But they differ from nominalists in that they do not believe that we can account for important features of reality without common natures. The motto does however advertise a reductionist approach to ontology, and nominalists are indeed arch-reductionists. This can, for instance, be seen in their understanding of Aristotle's famous ten categories (e.g., substance, quantity, quality, relation, place, time, position, possession, action, and passion). For a nominalist, the categories are not a classification of ten kinds of being, but of ten kinds of predicates. According to Ockham, undoubtedly the most famous fourteenth-century nominalist, there are only two fundamental kinds of beings: substances and qualities. Yet this does not mean that we speak nonsense when we talk about quantity or relations. For the nominalist, statements such as 'The stone has a volume of three cubic inches' or 'Socrates's whiteness resembles Plato's whiteness' are not wrong; the extension of the stone (quantity) exists and so does the similarity (relation) between Socrates's and Plato's whitenesses. The nominalist's point is that quantities and relations do not exist as distinct entities (*res*) apart from substances and qualities, and as real things added to them. Needless to say, not all nominalist philosophers and theologians follow Ockham's radical reduction of the categories to only two real kinds of being. But there is a strong enough similarity in how thinkers such as Ockham, John Buridan (c.1295–1360), Albert of Saxony (c.1316–90), Nicole Oresme (c.1320–82), Marsilius of Inghem (c.1340–96), and Peter of Ailly (1350–1420) approach questions of ontology for them to be labelled nominalists.

   Are there real-life consequences of being a nominalist vs being a realist? In fact there are not that many, despite what the two opposing sides may want us to believe. For a realist, nominalism leads, among other things, to the denial of scientific knowledge. Scientific knowledge, for the realist, is about universals. The botanist studying, say, elm trees, is not primarily concerned with each individual elm tree, but with the nature of elm trees. And if the nature of elm trees is not something real, this branch of botany is not a real science anymore. This is what the realist says about the nominalist. But the nominalists themselves do not deny that there can be scientific knowledge of elm trees. What they deny is merely that scientific knowledge presupposes the extra-mental existence of common natures. For them, sciences are primarily about propositions, and since the general terms in scientific propositions stand for individual real things, scientific knowledge is possible.[20] On the other hand, a nominalist deems realism not only philosophically naïve, but also a road to heresy. If universals exist in individuals, then the realist ought to explain how the universal (or 'common nature') is distinct from the individual 'in' which it is. For the realist, this distinction is not simply a product of human reason but is somewhat grounded in the object itself—or 'a parte rei', to use medieval terminology. But this causes complications. I can, for instance, affirm many truths about the individual Socrates—that he is a human being, that he is an animal, that he is a substance, and so on—so there must be many distinct common natures in him. The main reason for assuming such a multiplicity of common natures and distinctions in an individual seems to be the need to ground the truth of essential predications. However, I can say many true things about God as well: that God is good, that God is omnipotent, etc. Therefore, realists seem to be forced to make—with respect to divine nature— distinctions similar to those they admitted in the creatures (that is, a multiplicity of common natures), an idea that potentially jeopardizes divine simplicity. Realists, naturally, reject these allegations as malicious misinterpretations.

All this is to say that despite what realists and nominalists contend, everyday practices and language do not become problematic because one is a nominalist or one is a realist. To be sure, nominalists and realists disagree about why exactly, and in virtue of what, propositions such as 'Socrates is a human being' are true. For the former, the statement is true because both subject and predicate terms stand for the same thing; for the latter, it is true because the predicate term names a nature 'in' Socrates. But apart from this and some disagreement about properly ontological assertions, life does not change.[21] This is important, because it follows that it is extremely difficult to infer from an author's statements whether he has nominalist or realist leanings, unless of course these statements either articulate or allude to nominalist or realist arguments, are flatly incompatible with either nominalist or realist views, or the context removes any doubt that particular utterances refer to nominalist or realist views.

To the extent that nominalists and realists disagree about semantics, they also disagree about the nature of language. However, these disagreements certainly do not concern the question of whether or not language is arbitrary. It is wrong to insinuate that nominalism entails anything like the loosening of the natural relationship between words and objects, whereby all signification becomes merely arbitrary or otherwise unstable.[22] Nominalists as well as realists hold that words signify things in the world: our 'mental words' (i.e. concepts) are natural signs of objects in the world, whereas our written and spoken words are conventional signs. The main difference between the nominalist and the realist is about *what* general terms signify, not *that* they signify. For the nominalist, general terms signify individuals, but not in the same way that proper names signify individuals, whereas the realist argues that general terms signify common natures.[23]

The characterization of nominalism employed here might seem rather narrow, but it is in line with the historical records. Not all late medieval nominalists call themselves 'nominalists' (*nominales*), although the term did exist, since it first occurs in the early twelfth century. More importantly, when these late medieval *nominales* (or followers of the so-called *via moderna*) express their differences from realists (or followers of the *via antiqua*) they do so primarily with respect to universals, the categories, and their commitment to ontological reductionism.[24]

We insist on this narrow understanding of nominalism, because the label 'nominalism' is often—wrongly—used to cover a wide variety of other views. Literary scholars sometimes use the phrase 'nominalist epistemology' or associate nominalism with skepticism.[25] This is unfortunate. As we have seen, nominalism is indeed linked to a distinct understanding of the nature of scientific knowledge, one that can do without positing common natures and extra-mental universals. And since nominalists maintain that universals only exist in the mind, they have to explain how we get from the experience of singular material objects to universal concepts. But realist philosophers too have to explain how our concepts arise from sensory experience. Realists do not claim that we sense universals nor do they hold that human cognition consists in a direct grasp of common natures. They too are bound to the view, common among medieval philosophers, that human cognition arises from sensory experience. In other words, nominalists and realists disagree about what is ontologically first and fundamental, but they agree that all human cognition starts with the sensory cognition of singular objects. Since medieval philosophers distinguish between different cognitive faculties—the senses (interior and exterior) and the intellect—a debate developed, especially after Aquinas, as to the division of labor between those faculties. The point of contention was whether our intellect itself can (and must) have cognition of singulars, or whether this is the preserve of our senses. Yet, this debate cuts across the nominalist/realist divide, and there was no obvious 'party line'![26]

Given the importance they attach to sensory experience, medieval philosophers and theologians need to explain how sensory experience can ever lead to knowledge of the essence of things. For the senses primarily acquaint us with an object's accidental properties (such as shape, size, color, etc.) but not directly with what the object essentially is. The proposed solutions this question has received could be arranged along a scale ranging from empiricism at one extreme to innatism and theories of divine illumination at the other. But again none of these solutions stands out as decidedly nominalist or realist.

Furthermore, it is not clear why nominalism, any more than realism, should lead to skepticism. Generally speaking, medieval philosophers make modest claims regarding what we can know about the world, and about the natural world in particular. In his darker moments, even Thomas Aquinas, traditionally considered a realist, goes so far as to say that 'our cognition is so weak that no philosopher was ever able to inquire perfectly into the nature of a single fly'.[27] But this does not mean that knowledge—even knowledge of essences—is impossible! Be this as it may, it is hard to see why nominalists more than realists should be prone to skepticism. Ockham, to use a prominent example, thinks that our cognitive capacities are generally reliable and lead to truth; and it is well known that John Buridan, an important fourteenth-century nominalist active in Paris, explicitly rejected skeptical arguments.[28]

Admittedly, the term 'nominalism' is now often used in a much wider sense, and in some circles it even has a decidedly pejorative meaning. According to one such understanding, 'nominalism' stands for a late medieval intellectual movement that combines ontological views with a general skeptical attitude and an emphasis on the contingency of the creation and on God's absolute power (*potentia dei absoluta*). As William Courtenay and others have shown, this view—which remains popular—is very much a child of the scholarship of the 1920s and is now considered obsolete among historians of philosophy and theology.[29] And even if it turned out that there existed some such 'nominalist' movement in the fourteenth and fifteenth centuries, it would not include the better-known figures associated with nominalism: Ockham, for instance, is not a nominalist in this sense.

Firmly placing Chaucer in either the nominalist or the realist camp, as many literary scholars have tried to do, is extremely problematic. In what precedes, we have implicitly touched upon some of the arguments usually put forward to brand Chaucer a nominalist. Although Chaucer scholars agree that he never explored the ontological aspects of universals, it should by now have become clear that even establishing that Chaucer was interested in 'nominalist questions' (to use Russell Peck's phrase) is difficult, simply because many of these allegedly 'nominalist questions' are not actually genuine to the nominalist enterprise. Take for instance the notion that Chaucer emphasizes the role of experience as 'the most direct approach to knowledge'.[30] In this context, critics often point to the prologue of his *Legend of Good Women*, where Chaucer has his narrator-alter ego toss his books aside to enjoy spring time with all its pleasant experiences: singing birds, blooming flowers, etc. (F 29–39). But if Chaucer really advocates experience over bookishness in these lines, is it not curious that his narrator should choose to abandon his books and turn his gaze on such a common literary topos: the ideal landscape which, in Ernst Robert Curtius's words, 'forms the principal motif of all nature description' from classical literature to the end of the Middle Ages? Such passages may more profitably be read in the context of the figure—recurrent in Chaucer's poetry—of the bookish narrator who falls asleep and dreams, rather than as a statement of some abstract philosophical theory.[31] Nor is Chaucer's interesting use of the Aristotelian image of the mind as a blank slate (*tabula rasa*) in the *Book of the Duchess* (779–84) evidence of a commitment to nominalism.[32] The image is ubiquitous in medieval philosophical literature and may at most indicate that Chaucer subscribed to an empiricist epistemology. And, as stated previously, one should not confuse empiricism with nominalism. Yet using this appearance of the Aristotelian image of the blank slate to shed light on Chaucer's philosophical views raises other questions. How legitimate is it to equate a given author's ideas with what one of his characters says? How indicative of their author's philosophical ideas may isolated passages be? Yes, the image of the mind as a blank slate is popular among empiricist-minded philosophers, but let us not overlook the traces of innatism (i.e. the view that our knowledge is—at least partly—innate and that the soul is not a blank slate) present in Chaucer's work. In fact, Boethius's *Consolation of Philosophy* famously advocates innatism.[33] Should we then conclude that Chaucer is an innatist because he translated this work and obviously appreciated it, since he uses it so extensively in his writings? Surely that would be equally rash.

Another popular argument in support of Chaucer's nominalism is more indirect. Chaucer, so the argument goes, shows himself to be a nominalist in his refusal of allegory, at least in his mature works.[34] Whatever Chaucer's attitude towards allegory may be, this reasoning presupposes a straightforward connection between allegory and realism about universals. But why should such a straightforward connection exist? What does an abstract ontological question have to do with what is, in the end, a question of literary style? Or put differently: why could Ockham not have written allegorical poems in his spare time?

That the evidence for Chaucer's nominalism looks at best inconclusive does not entail that an interpretation of Chaucer as a realist about universals would fare any better. It would be equally difficult—some might say: equally hopeless—to make a conclusive argument for that case. For instance the idea that, in Chaucer's portrayal of the *Canterbury Tales* pilgrims, the 'representation of type as it exists in individuals'[35] is an argument for philosophical realism is valid only if such a stylistic device were strictly tied to a particular philosophical view and if it could be shown by other means that this mode of representation is a literary analog of the philosophical claim that individual substances instantiate a common nature. And this connection between a literary device and a philosophical view is difficult to establish without using circular reasoning.

HUMAN FREEDOM AND ACTION

The problem of human freedom, and in particular of how human free will and divine foreknowledge may be compatible, is the clearest instance of a philosophical question appearing in Chaucer's poetry. That Chaucer should be intrigued by the problem of human freedom is hardly surprising. Earlier in the fourteenth century, Thomas Bradwardine called precisely this issue of whether everything that happens happens of necessity the 'most famous question (*quaestio famosissima*) of his time.[36] Chaucer knew Bradwardine at least by name since he mentions him alongside Augustine and Boethius in the Nun's Priest's Tale in a passage addressing the very issue of divine knowledge. Chaucer writes:

> O Chauntecleer, acursed be that morwe
> That thou into that yerd flaugh fro the bemes!
> Thou were ful wel ywarned by thy dremes
> That thilke day was perilous to thee;
> But what that God forwoot moot nedes bee,
> After the opinioun of certein clerkis.
> Witnesse on hym that any parfit clerk is,
> That in scole is greet altercacioun
> In this mateere, and greet disputisoun,
> And hath been of an hundred thousand men.
> But I ne kan nat bulte it to the bren
> As kan the hooly doctour Augustyn,
> Or Boece, or the Bisshop Bradwardyn,
> Wheither that Goddes worthy forwityng
> Streyneth me nedely for to doon a thing –
> 'Nedely' clepe I symple necessitee –
> Or elles, if free choys be graunted me
> To do that same thyng, or do it noght,
> Though God forwoot it er that I was wroght;
> Or if his wityng streyneth never a deel
> But by necessitee condicioneel.
> I wol nat han to do of swich mateere;
> My tale is of a cok, as ye may heere,
> That tok his conseil of his wyf, with sorwe,
> To walken in the yerd upon that morwe
> That he hadde met that dreem that I yow tolde.   (VII.3230–55)

The rhyming 'altercacioun' and 'disputisoun' as well as the repetition of the adjective *greet* draw attention to the magnitude of the debate concerning the compatibility of free will and divine foreknowledge and seem to echo Bradwardine's remark regarding the notoriety of this issue. Obviously however, the tone of the passage is ironic, and the voice of the one 'parfit clerk' whom the narrator invokes as his authority on this question dissolves into the comically inflated number of a hundred thousand discussants.

In his *De causa Dei*, no doubt the work for which Chaucer grants him a place next to Augustine and Boethius, Bradwardine defends divine causality against what he considers a revival of Pelagianism (i.e. of the heresy that maintains that human nature and human free will are sufficient for virtuous action). William of Ockham has often been pointed out as one of Bradwardine's likely targets. Indeed, some of Ockham's contemporaries considered his writings to hold Pelagian views. John Lutterell, the Oxford Chancellor who instigated the papal process against Ockham and prepared a list of problematic statements taken from Ockham's commentary on the *Sentences*, refers to five theses involving the 'error of Pelagius'. Even the list prepared by the papal commission in Avignon in 1326 reiterates the accusation of Pelagianism.[37] Obviously, Ockham himself denied having Pelagian leanings.[38] All this is to say that by referring to Bradwardine, Chaucer seems to point to a contemporary, or at least recent, debate.

Moreover, Chaucer alludes to a technical detail in the lines mentioned above: namely, the distinction between conditional and absolute (or simple) necessity. Boethius uses this distinction prominently in the solution he offers to the question regarding divine foreknowledge in Book Five, Prose Six of the *Consolation*. According to him, God's immutable knowledge indeed renders future contingent events necessary, but future human actions are so only with a conditional necessity. Because God knows them, future human actions will come about in the way they have been foreseen by him. But this does not mean that God's foreknowledge is the cause of human actions. There is a difference between human beings, who act freely, and non-free agents such as animals that lack free will and thus do what they do by (absolute) necessity. Divine foreknowledge does not affect a thing's proper nature and thus, in the case of human beings, does not impose absolute necessity on our actions.

Note however that the distinction between the two kinds of necessities on its own does not yet amount to a real solution to the question of how divine foreknowledge can be compatible with human freedom,[39] for it remains to be seen how God's foreknowledge does indeed impose only conditional, and not absolute, necessity on human actions. This is the central crux, and a philosophical problem to which Chaucer offers no answer anywhere in his works. Here in the Nun's Priest's Tale, the narrator prefaces his exposition of the two kinds of necessity by saying that he cannot go to the heart of the matter, as Augustine, Boethius or Bradwardine could; he instead emphatically turns his back on the problem: 'I wol not han to do of swich mateere' (VII.3251). And why should the Nun's Priest actually offer a solution to the problem of the compatibility of divine foreknowledge and human action when, as he points out in the following line, 'My tale is of a cok [...] That tok his conseil of his wyf, with sorwe' (3252–3)? This abrupt return to the world of the beast-fable and of marital trials is a bathetic moment that further undercuts the Nun's Priest's evocation of this philosophical question. For how relevant can the question of human freedom be to Chauntecleer and Russell, a cock and a fox in a barnyard? These lines are part of the playful multiplication of genres and registers (philosophical, medical, rhetorical, courtly, Biblical, classical, etc.) that constitutes the very fabric of this tale and its comic trigger. The contrast between Bradwardine— who goes on to examine thirty-three rival views on the compatibility between divine foreknowledge and human free will before stating his own position in *De causa Dei*— and Chaucer's light-footed allusion to the scholastic debate, could not be starker.

In a well-known passage of Book Four of *Troilus and Criseyde*, Chaucer paraphrases a long passage from the *Consolation of Philosophy*[40]—a passage that is a key part of Boethius's treatment of precisely this question of divine foreknowledge and human free will. Chaucer frequently uses material from the *Consolation*, but these 120 lines (4.958–1078), content of a long monologue by Troilus, constitute the most extended borrowing from Boethius's work and are an instance of the overlaps between Chaucer's philosophical interests and his poetry. There is nothing in the literary sources of the Troilus story that would correspond to this extensive appropriation. As in the Nun's Priest's Tale, this long Boethian passage falls short of a full engagement with the philosophical conundrum in question. For it is an elaborate yet partial adaptation of Boethius's discussion that only includes the parts describing the problem that divine foreknowledge seems to pose to our free will. What Chaucer leaves out in Troilus's long monologue are Lady Philosophy's replies in support of the compatibility of divine foreknowledge and human free will from Book Five, proses Four and Five of the *Consolation*. Chaucer has obviously no interest in explaining how divine foreknowledge might in fact not undermine our freedom. Rather, incorporating the philosophical puzzle that Boethius raises in *Consolation* Book Five, Prose Three into Troilus's monologue allows him to create a series of artistic effects. First of all, the philosophical material underlines how Troilus, tormented by sorrow and his fear of displeasing his beloved, conceives of his situation as hopeless. Troilus's inaction and passivity are emphasized by the high-flying speculation with which he convinces himself that nothing can be done.[41] Yet, the use of the material from the *Consolation* also creates a comical effect. The philosophical character of his monologue makes Troilus look impractical. That he is capable of putting the problem in such a sophisticated way but at the same time is unable to see how it might be solved portrays him as somewhat half-educated. And what sense does it make for him to ask Jove for an early death if Troilus actually believes in what he just said, namely in the necessity of all events? No wonder Pandarus, who is clearly not impressed by his friend's behavior, rebukes him with these words: 'Who say evere a wis man faren so?' (4.1087).

These findings are somewhat at odds with the opinion—not uncommon among Chaucer scholars—that Chaucer's works display a 'strong investment in major philosophical problems such as the conflict between free will and determinism'.[42] Some modern interpreters, however, go even further. They contend that Chaucer is more ambitious in that he actually deals, in a very subtle way, with the philosophical issues raised by divine foreknowledge. Accordingly, *Troilus and Criseyde* could actually be read as an enactment of Boethius's 'most difficult philosophical concept' insofar as the work actualizes the question of whether the reader's knowledge of the story of Troy necessitates the occurrence of an event or a character's fate in the poem.[43] After all, an educated reader is familiar with both the tale of Troy's fall and the love story embedded in it: these events are well-known and thus to some extent foreknown. But this reading is hardly convincing. First, every retelling of familiar literary material would, in the last instance, become a similar re-enactment of Boethius's views on divine foreknowledge and free will. Second, and more importantly, the point of Boethius's discussion in Book Five of the *Consolation of Philosophy* is to explain *how* human freedom and divine fore-knowledge can be compatible. It is, however, not clear how *Troilus and Criseyde* can be an enactment of that point, for the poem leaves out crucial elements of the solution, such as for instance the nature of divine eternity.[44]

Naturally, much more could be said about Chaucer's view of human agency. Let us mention here his alleged 'voluntarism'. In medieval philosophy of action, voluntarism is the view that human agents owe their role as agents, and as free agents in particular, to their faculty of will and that the will is the highest faculty of the human soul. According to voluntarists, the will is not determined by our cognitive capacities, but is the prime mover in action. Intellectualism, the opposite view, gives primacy to the intellect and sees free human agency primarily rooted in our capacity of thought and reflection. Voluntarism was a prominent view in later medieval philosophy and so it is no wonder that Chaucer has been linked to it. Kathryn Lynch, for instance, has argued that the *Parliament of Fowls* is best understood as a text engaging with voluntarism. This may be so, but one has to be careful with the evidence for such an interpretation. That Chaucer emphasizes choice, decision, and a power for opposite courses of action is not enough to tip the balance towards a voluntarist background.[45] Both intellectualists and voluntar-ists hold that human agents have free will, free choice, and can make decisions and have genuine alternatives open to them. What they disagree about is whether we owe our free will (freedom of choice, decision-making, etc.) to our intellect or to our will.

Chaucer's texts do not give us any clue as to which of the two options he prefers. One passage from the *Parliament of Fowls* is especially interesting in this context, a passage which has been described as a 'Buridan's ass' scenario (141–54).[46] Early in the dream vision, Africanus brings the narrator to a gate that has two inscriptions, one in gold, and the other in black, promising either bliss or misery. These contradictory inscriptions trouble the narrator so much that he cannot choose, since both options—to go or not to go through the gate—have equal force on him. Though the image that Chaucer uses here is in fact that of a piece of iron posed between two lodestones, this scene has been read in conjunction with the famous ass that contemplates two identical and equidistant heaps of straw and, since there is nothing to lead him to prefer one heap over the other, ends up starving to death. Buridan's ass is often used to argue that human choices cannot entirely be explained in terms of reason and intellect. It is at least theoretically imaginable that two options appear equally appealing to us, yet this doesn't prevent human beings from choosing the one over the other. We can do so—and avoid starving—because there is something in human beings that would break the tie, namely the faculty of will. Note however that if the *Parliament* scene is really meant to allude to a Buridan's ass scenario, then it ends up making the wrong point. For the tie is not broken by the narrator's will, but by Africanus pushing him through the gate.

To infer from Chaucer's texts certain underlying psychological views is problematic not only with respect to the will, but also with respect to other aspects of his alleged philosophical psychology. We are thus skeptical of a more recent trend that detects elements of high scholastic psychology in Chaucer.[47] But whether or not Chaucer was absolutely *au fait* with contemporary philosophical psychology, he still remains a fine observer of the human psyche, including the philosophical problems posed by it. This can be seen for instance in his discussions of the nature of love, a recurring motif in many of his works. He seems particularly interested in the agency of lovers. There can be little doubt that part of his motivation for including Petrarch's Sonnet 88 in Book One of *Troilus and Criseyde* (1.400–20) comes from the paradoxical description of Troilus's condition it provides. On the one hand, Troilus realizes that love is always something we consent to voluntarily—we cannot love against our will—on the other hand, love seems to put us at the mercy of external factors and thus takes away from our will. Or take the passage from the *Book of the Duchess* where the Black Knight reflects on his Lady and his obligation to love her:

> 'Nede'? Nay, trewly, I gabbe now;
> Noght 'nede', and I wol tellen how:
> For of good wille myn herte hyt wolde,
> And eke to love hir I was holde
> As for the fairest and the beste.   (BD 1075–79)

The knight realizes that his love is free, because (a) he wills it (1077) and (b) it accords with his judgment of his beloved's moral excellence (1078–9). Had he loved someone one lesser value, he presumably would have considered himself as being 'unfree'. This raises the question of whether true love is not in some sense always determined—namely by a judgment of what is best. If the true lover can only love what he judges the best, in what sense is he still free? This question actually finds echoes in many medieval philosophers.

CONCLUSION

In a chapter published twenty years ago, William Watts and Richard Utz concluded that 'there is no consensus about how Chaucer's poetry should be understood in relationship to fourteenth-century nominalism', a conclusion which is still valid and could be broadened to include fourteenth-century philosophy in general.[48] There is no denying the fact that Chaucer often uses philosophical expressions and alludes to philosophical ideas;

what remains controversial however is how these allusions should be understood, to what extent they are evidence of their author's real mastery of philosophical knowledge, and whether all the sophisms and *insolubilia* that interpreters have been keen to find in Chaucer's works actually are instances of these forms of scholastic debate. In this contribution we have limited ourselves to some iconic passages. More could be said about other examples frequently discussed in Chaucer scholarship: for instance the description of sound in the *House of Fame*, the account of dreams in the Nun's Priest's Tale, or the division of the fart in the Summoner's Tale. Most uncontroversial are Chaucer's allusions to Boethius, an author who was not part of the philosophy curriculum in the fourteenth-century university and yet enjoyed great popularity in literary circles. As to Bradwardine, the only fourteenth-century philosopher Chaucer ever mentions apart from Strode, it is not clear whether Chaucer ever read a line of his work. A definitive assessment of Chaucer's relationship to the philosophical trends of his time is therefore bound to remain elusive.[49]

Chaucer's poetry undoubtedly deals with fundamental philosophical questions, such as the nature of love and human agency. To appreciate this dimension of his writings, it is not absolutely necessary to know Chaucer's exact place in fourteenth-century philosophy, although a more precise knowledge of his intellectual background would be an invaluable complement to our picture of him as a poet. Yet despite our mostly pessimistic assessment of previous efforts to do precisely this, we do not think that research that endeavours to obtain a better understanding of Chaucer's relationship to the philosophical trends of his time is futile. Two things would help in the search for more definite results. First, it would be useful if more historians of ideas and historians of philosophy were interested in the impact philosophy had on literary works. With the exception of scholarship on Dante, historians of philosophy and ideas have not betrayed much curiosity for what one could call 'popular philosophy'. And Dante scholarship provides a successful model for a fruitful interaction between the history of philosophy and of ideas and literary criticism.[50] Second, we simply need to know more about late fourteenth-century philosophy. Except for some major figures early in that century, we possess only the faintest knowledge of the philosophical scene in Chaucer's time. Only when this background becomes clearer can one really know what to look for in contemporary Middle English texts, be they by Chaucer or by other writers.[51]

NOTES

1. Le Marquis de Queux de Saint-Hilaire, ed., *Œuvres complètes d'Eustache Deschamps*, vol. 2 (Paris: Didot, 1880), 138. For more testimonies of Chaucer's reputation as a philosopher, see Kathryn L. Lynch, *Chaucer's Philosophical Visions* (Cambridge: D. S. Brewer, 2000), 7–9.
2. It is not surprising that Chaucer's use of the term *philosophye* also covers magic, alchemy, astrology, and learning in general. See Larry D. Benson, 'Glossary', in *The Riverside Chaucer*, ed. Larry D. Benson, 3rd ed. (Boston, MA: Houghton Mifflin, 1987), s. v. *philosophye* and *philosophre*.

3. Many English philosophers and theologians from the first half of the fourteenth century belonged, for instance, to the circle of Richard of Bury, the erudite archbishop of Durham.

4. Chris Schabel, 'Paris and Oxford between Aurioli and Rimini', in *The Routledge History of Philosophy: Medieval Philosophy*, ed. John Marenbon, vol. 3 (London: Routledge, 2000), 386–401; William J. Courtenay, 'The Role of English Thought in the Transformation of University Education in the Late Middle Ages', in *Rebirth, Reform and Resilience: Universities in Transition 1300–1700*, eds. James M. Kittelson and Pamela J. Transue (Columbus, OH: Ohio State University Press, 1984), 103–62.

5. Richard of Bury, *Philobiblon*, c. 9, ed. and trans. E. C. Thomas (London: Kegan Paul, 1888), 212.

6. See William J. Courtenay, *Schools and Scholars in Fourteenth-Century England* (Princeton, NJ: Princeton University Press, 1990). For the Oxford Calculators, see Edith Sylla's contribution to the present volume.

7. For a concise overview, see William J. Courtenay, 'Theology and Theologians from Ockham to Wyclif', in *The History of the University of Oxford. Vol. II: Late Medieval Oxford*, eds. J. I. Catto and Ralph Evans (Oxford: Clarendon Press, 1995), 1–34.

8. E. Jennifer Ashworth and Paul Vincent Spade, 'Logic in Late Medieval Oxford', in Catto and Evans, *History of the University of Oxford*, 35–64.

9. For John Wyclif, see the contribution by Stephen Lahey in the present volume; Strode is also discussed in Edith Sylla's contribution.

10. For Brinkley's biography, see Laurent Cesalli, *Le réalisme propositionnel. Sémantique et ontologie des propositions chez Jean Duns Scot, Gauthier Burley, Richard Brinkley et Jean Wyclif* (Paris: Vrin, 2007), 241–7. See also Zenon Kaluza, 'L'œuvre théologique de Richard Brinkley', *Archives d'histoire doctrinale et littéraire du moyen âge* 56 (1989), 169–273.

11. Courtenay, *Schools and Scholars*, 378–9.

12. Ibid., 171–92.

13. According to two manuscripts of *Troilus and Criseyde*, Chaucer's dedication is to a 'sophistical Strode'. See Karl Reichl, 'Chaucer's Troilus: Philosophy and Language', in *The European Tragedy of Troilus*, ed. Piero Boitani (Oxford: Oxford University Press, 1989), 133–52, at 134. This variant attests to Strode's work as a logician, but gives us no clue about his reputation as a philosopher.

14. For detailed information about Strode's life, see A. B. Emden, *Biographical Register of the University of Oxford to A.D. 1500*, vol. 3 (Oxford: Clarendon Press, 1959), 1807–8.

15. Courtenay, *Schools and Scholars*, 366.

16. Rodney Delasanta, 'Chaucer and Strode', *Chaucer Review* 26 (1991), 205–18, at 205.

17. For what this amounted to, see James A. Weisheipl, 'Curriculum of the Faculty of Arts at Oxford in the early Fourteenth Century', *Mediaeval Studies* 26 (1964), 143–85.

18. See Chapter 25 of this volume. For some more recent speculations regarding how Strode might have influenced Chaucer see Glending Olson, 'Snub and White: Chaucer, Logic, and Strode', *Journal of English and Germanic Philology* 117 (2018), 185–211.

19. A recent article begins: 'That the philosophical tenets of scholastic nominalism underwrite Chaucer's poetry has been firmly established in Chaucer studies, yet whether Chaucer's allegiance on the question of universals lies with realists or nominalist epistemology—or with neither—still remains a point of critical contention' (Jelena Marelj, 'The Philosophical *Entente* of Particulars: Criseyde as Nominalist in Chaucer's *Troilus and Criseyde*', *Chaucer Review* 47 [2012], 206–21, at 206). See also William H. Watts and Richard J. Utz, 'Nominalist Perspectives on Chaucer's Poetry: A Bibliographical Essay', *Medievalia et Humanistica* n.s. 20 (1993), 147–73.

20. See for instance William of Ockham, *Expositio in libros Physicorum Aristotelis*, prol. § 4 (*Opera philosophica* 3, ed. V. Richter and G. Leibold [St. Bonaventure: Franciscan Institute, 1985], 11–12).

21. Of course, for a nominalist propositions such as 'Common natures exist', etc. are obviously false. But we doubt that such statements play a big role in everyday communication. We thus disagree with Chaucer interpreters such as Russell Peck, who claim: 'One beauty of nominalism is that it helps people to live as individuals wherever they are, even in contingent and in-between circumstances' (see his 'Chaucer and the Nominalist Questions', *Speculum* 53 [1981], 745–60, at 755).

22. For an example of this—unfortunately—widespread misconception, see Holly Wallace Boucher, 'Nominalism: The Difference for Chaucer and Boccaccio', *Chaucer Review* 20 (1986), 213–20, at 215: 'The firm bonds between signifier and signified (*vox* and *conceptus*) had unraveled: so had the necessary tie between sign and reality (*res* or referent)'.

23. The idea that there is a special natural relationship between a linguistic sign and a thing is sometimes called 'Cratylic realism' (from Plato's *Cratylus*). That 'Cratylic realism' is not a very helpful understanding of fourteenth-century realism has also been emphasized by Robert Myles, *Chaucerian Realism* (Cambridge: D. S. Brewer, 1994), 1–22.

24. See for instance the famous 'Defense of Nominalism' with which Parisian nominalists responded to Louis XI's prohibition of nominalist teaching in Paris in the 1470s. The text is printed in Franz Ehrle, *Der Sentenzenkommentar des Peters von Candia* (Münster: Aschendorff, 1925), 322–6; for an English translation of this document, see Lynn Thorndike, *University Records and Life in the Middle Ages* (New York: Norton, 1975), 355–60. For an excellent and concise description of nominalism (medieval and modern), see the introduction in Claude Panaccio, *Le nominalisme: ontologie, langage et connaissance* (Paris: Vrin, 2012).

25. For the talk of 'nominalist epistemology', see for instance Peck, 'Chaucer and the Nominalist Questions', 747ff. and Lynch, *Chaucer's Philosophical Visions*, 44ff.; for skepticism, see Peck, 'Chaucer and the Nominalist Questions', 757.

26. Moreover, some literary scholars (e.g. Peck and Lynch) consider the distinction between intuitive and abstractive cognition as a sign of a nominalist or 'Ockhamist' epistemology. However, it would be hard to find any fourteenth-century philosopher who does not discuss human cognition in these terms.

27. Thomas Aquinas, *Expositio in Symbolum Apostolorum*, proem, in *Opuscula theologica*, vol. 2, ed. R. M. Spiazzi (Turin: Marietti, 1953), 192.

28. Claude Panaccio and David Piché, 'Ockham's Reliabilism and the Intuition of Non-Existents', in *Rethinking the History of Skepticism: The Missing Medieval Background*, ed. Henrik Lagerlund (Leiden: Brill, 2010), 97–118; Jack Zupko, 'Buridan and Skepticism', *Journal of the History of Philosophy* 31 (1993), 191–221.

29. William J. Courtenay, 'In Search of Nominalism: Two Centuries of Historical Debate', in *Ockham and Ockhamism: Studies in the Dissemination and Impact of His Thought*, ed. William J. Courtenay (Leiden: Brill, 2008), 1–19.

30. For this and the following comments on the *Legend of Good Women* and the *Book of the Duchess*, see Peck, 'Chaucer and the Nominalist Questions', 748–51.

31. Ernst Robert Curtius, *European Literature and the Latin Middle Ages*, trans. Willard R. Trask (New York: Harper & Row, 1963), 195. For other instances of the bookish narrator dreaming, see the beginning of the *House of Fame* and of the *Parliament of Fowls*; see also Marshall W. Stearns, 'Chaucer Mentions a Book', *Modern Language Notes* 57 (1942), 28–31. For another invocation of 'experience', see *House of Fame* lines 737–46 and 787–803. The

allusion to 'experience' in these lines leads Laurence Eldredge to conclude that the Eagle has nominalist leanings. See Laurence Eldredge, 'Chaucer's *Hous of Fame* and the *Via Moderna*', *Neuphilologische Mitteilungen* 71 (1970), 105–19, at 114.

32. 'Paraunter I was therto most able, / As a whit wal or a table, / For hit ys redy to cacche and take / Al that men wil theryn make, / Whethir so men wil portreye or peynte, / Be the werkes never so queynte'; see Aristotle, *On the Soul* III.3 (429b31–430a2).

33. Boethius, *The Consolation of Philosophy*, 3.m11; 5.m3–4; 5.pr5.

34. See for instance Rodney Delasanta, 'Nominalism and Typology in Chaucer', in *Typology and English Medieval Literature*, ed. Hugh T. Keenan (New York: AMS Press, 1992), 121–39, at 126; or more recently Richard Utz, 'Philosophy', in *Chaucer: an Oxford Guide*, ed. Steve Ellis (Oxford: Oxford University Press, 2005), 158–73, at 170.

35. James I. Wimsatt, 'John Duns Scotus, Charles Sanders Peirce, and Chaucer's Portrayal of the Canterbury Pilgrims', *Speculum* 71 (1996), 633–45, at 642. That Chaucer might be a realist in a broader sense of the term has been argued for in Myles, *Chaucerian Realism*.

36. Thomas Bradwardine, *De causa Dei*, lib. 3, cap. 12 (London, 1618; repr. Frankfurt: Minerva, 1964), 688.

37. For Lutterell's list, see Fritz Hoffmann, *Die Schriften des Oxforder Kanzlers Johannes Lutterell* (Leipzig: St. Benno Verlag, 1959), 3–7; for the list of the papal commission, see Auguste Pelzer, 'Les 51 articles de Guillaume d'Occam censurés, en Avignon, 1326', *Revue d'histoire ecclésiastique* 18 (1922), 240–70, at 251.

38. William of Ockham, *Quodlibet* VI, q. 1 (*Opera theologica* 9, ed. Joseph Wey, St Bonaventure: Franciscan Institute, 1980, 588–9).

39. We thus disagree with F. Anne Payne ('Foreknowledge and Free Will: Three Theories in the "Nun's Priest's Tale"', *Chaucer Review* 10 [1978], 201–19) who thinks that Chaucer presents three solutions in the lines quoted above, solutions which he then refutes in a poetic way.

40. Boethius, *Consolation of Philosophy*, 5.pr3.

41. A similar reading was put forward already a century ago. See Howard Rollin Patch, 'Troilus on Predestination', *Journal of English and Germanic Philology* 17 (1918), 399–422, at 420. See also John Huber, 'Troilus's Predestination Soliloquy', *Neuphilologische Mitteilungen* 66 (1965), 120–5.

42. Mark Miller, *Philosophical Chaucer: Love, Sex, and Agency in the Canterbury Tales* (Cambridge: Cambridge University Press, 2004), 27.

43. For this interpretation see, for instance, Frank Grady, 'The Boethian Reader of *Troilus and Criseyde*', *Chaucer Review* 33 (1999), 230–51, at 230; Barry Windeatt, *Oxford Guides to Chaucer: Troilus and Criseyde* (Oxford: Oxford University Press, 1992), 264.

44. Another example of an extensive borrowing from Boethius's *Consolation of Philosophy* is Theseus's 'First Mover' speech in the Knight's Tale (lines 2987–3016 and 3035–40; see Boethius, *Consolation of Philosophy*, 2.m8; 3.m9; 3.pr9–10; 4.pr6; 4.m6.). For a short commentary on these borrowings, see Helen Cooper, *The Canterbury Tales*, 2nd ed. (Oxford: Oxford University Press, 1996), 70–1. For a more thorough commentary focusing on the philosophical background, see Stephen H. Rigby, *Wisdom and Chivalry: Chaucer's* Knight's Tale *and Medieval Political Thought* (Leiden: Brill, 2009), 231–72. Throughout Chaucer's works there are of course innumerable minor allusions to the *Consolation*.

45. See however Lynch, 'Choice without Preference, Preference Without Choice in the Parliament of Fowls', in *Chaucer's Philosophical Visions*, 83–110. See also Elizabeth Robertson, 'Apprehending the Divine and Choosing To Believe: Voluntarist Free Will in Chaucer's Second Nun's Tale', *Chaucer Review* 46 (2011), 111–30.

46. For Lynch's discussion of this passage, see *Chaucer's Philosophical Visions*, 89–97.
47. For a radical example of this trend, see Lois Roney, *Chaucer's Knight's Tale and Theories of Scholastic Psychology* (Tampa, FL: University of South Florida Press, 1990).
48. Watts and Utz, 'Nominalist Perspectives', 161.
49. See also William H. Watts, 'Chaucer's Clerks and the Value of Philosophy', in *Nominalism and Literary Discourse: New Perspectives*, eds. Hugo Keiper, Christoph Bode, and Richard J. Utz (Amsterdam: Rodopi, 1997), 145–55. Watts also reminds us not to overlook the satirical context of many of Chaucer's references to philosophical issues and language.
50. See Rigby, *Wisdom and Chivalry*, which offers an interpretation of the Knight's Tale on the background of medieval philosophical thought, for a good recent example of how this sort of approach can work.
51. For some very sensible thoughts on this issue, see William J. Courtenay, 'The Dialectic of Divine Omnipotence in the Age of Chaucer: A Reconsideration', in Keiper et al., *Nominalism and Literary Discourse*, 111–21, at 120. Courtenay, however, limits himself to the topic of God's ordained and absolute power.

Bibliography

Courtenay, William J., 'In Search of Nominalism: Two Centuries of Historical Debate', in *Ockham and Ockhamism: Studies in the Dissemination and Impact of His Thought*, ed. William J. Courtenay (Leiden: Brill, 2008), 1–19.

Courtenay, William J., 'The Dialectic of Divine Omnipotence in the Age of Chaucer: A Reconsideration', in Keiper et al, *Nominalism in Literary Discourse: New Perspectives* (Amsterdam: Rodopi, 1997), 111–21.

Courtenay, William J., *Schools and Scholars in Fourteenth-Century England* (Princeton, NJ: Princeton University Press, 1990).

Emden, A. B., *A Biographical Register of the University of Oxford to A.D. 1500*, 3 vols. (Oxford: Clarendon Press, 1957–9).

Keiper, Hugo, Cristoph Bode, and Richard J. Utz, eds., *Nominalism in Literary Discourse: New Perspectives* (Amsterdam: Rodopi, 1997).

Lynch, Kathryn L., *Chaucer's Philosophical Visions* (Cambridge: D. S. Brewer, 2000).

Panaccio, Claude, *Le nominalisme: ontologie, langage et connaissance* (Paris: Vrin, 2012).

Peck, Russell, 'Chaucer and the Nominalist Questions', *Speculum* 53 (1981), 745–60.

Rigby, Stephen H., *Wisdom and Chivalry: Chaucer's Knight's Tale and Medieval Political Thought* (Leiden: Brill, 2009).

Watts, William H., 'Chaucer's Clerks and the Value of Philosophy', in Keiper et al., *Nominalism and Literary Discourse: New Perspectives* (Amsterdam: Rodopi, 1997), 145–55.

Watts, William H. and Richard J. Utz, 'Nominalist Perspectives on Chaucer's Poetry: A Bibliographical Essay', *Medievalia et Humanistica* n.s. 20 (1993), 147–73.

CHAPTER 23

....

THE POETICS OF
TRESPASS AND DURESS
Chaucer and the Fifth Inn of Court

....

ELEANOR JOHNSON

THOUGH the importance of Oxford and Cambridge to philosophy and science in medieval England cannot be overstated, it is crucial to remember a cluster of educational institutions whose contribution to philosophy and science—particularly to the philosophy and science of law—is of equal importance: the Inns of Court.[1] Though Oxford and Cambridge were the centres for the study of civil and canon law, the Inns of Court were the de facto universities and centres of study for the English Common Law.[2] In the Inns of Court, new and often complex procedural shifts in property law, criminal law, and tort law are examined and worked through by legal professionals throughout the late English Middle Ages. Perhaps the most significant single shift in the Common Law during the thirteenth and fourteenth centuries is the rise and coalescence of trespass law, both as a theory of legal relationality and as a practice of litigation. In this chapter, I will explore how the shifts in the law of trespass impact on the evolution of English law. From there, I will suggest how these legal shifts inform experiments in other discourses, notably poetry.

As literary critics have increasingly recognized, legal forms and logics suffuse Middle English literature, so much so that it makes sense to think of legal evolution and poetic as convergent—each discursive mode informing, challenging, and shaping the other.[3] Many short medieval poems, particularly debate poems, centre on trial scenes, making their ideational and procedural relationship to the law explicit from the outset.[4] Many larger-scale fictions, including *Piers Plowman* and *The Canterbury Tales*, weave episodic trial scenes into their intricate plots, creating juridical sub-genres within their larger narrative frameworks.[5] Rather than focusing on overt courtroom scenes, this chapter will focus on how the coevolution of trespassory logic and of the courts of equity provides Chaucer with a sturdy but flexible scaffold on which to build complex fictive explorations of human intention in his poem *Troilus and Criseyde*.

Trespass law uniquely offers an arena of legal thought and practice in which human intention plays a decisive role in the verdict of the judge and punishment of the accused. Trespass law comes into being in the thirteenth century as a juridical mode intended to try non-felonious crimes or 'wrongs', done by one party to another. Theft, assault, pound-breach, damaging property, stealing animals, breaking down structures, and rape become actionable in trespass. But trespass is defined not simply by the *kinds* of cases that can be brought, but also by the *manner* in which those cases could be litigated. Trespass law, more than perhaps any other branch of the elaborate legal system in medieval England, carries with it a distinctive logic and set of procedures. In the early days of trespassory litigation, a crime has to be committed literally 'against the King's peace' and 'with force and arms' in order to be actionable in trespass. That is, in order for a writ of trespass to be successfully prosecuted, it must include the formulae *contra pacem regis* and *vi et armis*. In the thirteenth century, if violence against the King's peace could not be demonstrated, the trespass suit would fail; if it could be proven, the suit would succeed.

By Chaucer's time, however, the formulaic strictures that constitute a trespass case begin to loosen. Although 'by force and arms' and 'against the King's peace' continue to be used in many trespass trials, the courts gradually admit that what determines trespass is not physical violence, nor necessarily any physical breaking of the King's peace.[6] Eventually, to accommodate this shift in legal theory and practice, new formulae come into the courtroom as the verbal signs of trespass. These new formulae do not imply physical violence, or any kind of physical action at all. Instead, they denote the interior state of a person at the time of committing a crime: the new terms are *maliciose* and *scienter*.[7] By the end of the fourteenth century, then, what makes a deed trespassory is not its level of physical violence, or its breaking of the royal peace, but its origin in bad intention.[8]

This change in legal practice and theory has enormous consequences for Chaucer's poetic experimentation as well. Trespass has become a legal framework in which to assess action in the context of intention. Because of its focus on intention as the *sine qua non* of criminality or innocence, trespass law affords Chaucer a systematic method with which to explore a problem that he finds limitlessly fascinating in his poetry: how we are to understand social relationships, obligations, intentions, and their intersection with environment and circumstance. To set out how Chaucer integrates and experiments with the forms and procedures of trespass law in his poetry, I will first review not just what words a plaintiff has to use to make his accusation, but also exactly what defendants could say in response to an accusation of trespass. After all, at law, the move to recognize inten-tion as the primary element in adjudicating trespass emerges not only in the plaintiff's presentation of the case, but also in the types of counterpleas available to defendants.

If accused of any trespass, a defendant has multiple new courses of action available to him as counterpleas. First, as in modern trials, a defendant can plead guilty. For instance, if Farmer B is accused of killing Farmer A's dog, Farmer B can plead guilty, saying, 'I did kill A's dog', and hope for the best. Second, he can plead not guilty 'on the general issue', which is to say, he can plead not guilty of the crime of which he stands accused, as in 'I did not kill A's dog'. Both of these modes of pleading are available in other types of common law suits as well; as in contemporary law, one can plead guilty or not guilty to any kind of legal accusation. Third, however, the defendant can attempt a 'special traverse', which is not available in any other type of legal proceeding in late medieval England.[9] In a special traverse, one admits guilt of the act in question, but claims exemption from criminal prosecution for one of two reasons. First, Farmer B can say, 'I killed a dog, but it did not belong to A'. This kind of special traverse relies upon a misstatement of fact or evidence on the part of the plaintiff, or upon some other procedural error in the presentment of facts. The other kind of special traverse, by contrast, relies on extenuating circumstances in the commission of the deed under examination. In this kind of special traverse, a defendant might claim, 'I killed A's dog, but I was within my legal rights to do so because the dog was attacking my sheep'. The problem here is not with A's suit, but with the circumstances under which B did the act of which he is accused. Thus, special traverses show that trespassory litigation has opened up a conceptual space at law wherein a person can be guilty of the *act* for which he is charged, but can simultaneously be innocent of *crime*. Special traverse pleas body forth the defendant side of the changes we see in plaintiff's writs: if a defendant can demonstrate that he committed an act, but did not mean to commit that act as a crime against the plaintiff—that is, if he can demonstrate a lack of *intention to commit a crime*—he can be exonerated. He may have committed the act, but he did not commit it *scienter*, nor *maliciose*; rather, extenuating circumstances were what produced the trespassory deed. Because of his lack of knowing malice, Farmer B should not be prosecuted further for killing A's dog.

For legal history, one of the most important consequences of this new legal emphasis on intention and extenuation, in both the plaintiff's formulae and the defendant's available responses, is discernible in the coalescence of the common law of contract. Prior to the middle of the fourteenth century, matters of contract are sued in ecclesiastical courts, rather than in common law courts of trespass. But, by the time Chaucer, Langland, and Gower are writing, contract has become actionable in the King's court, under the rules of trespass.[10] Although this introduction of contract to the King's court brings certain advantages, both to lawmen and to litigants, the new common law of contract is a highly contentious issue throughout Richard II's rule.[11] Part of the reason for this contentiousness has to do with the blurriness of the procedural and conceptual boundaries of contract litigation in trespass; throughout the period, it remains somewhat unclear when a contract is legally binding, and when a person can, by counterpleading in special traverse, insist that, although the contract has been breached, no crime has knowingly or intentionally been committed. That is, it remains unclear when lack of malicious, knowing intention to invalidate a contract could be an 'out' for the accused party.

Between about 1350 and 1450, another major innovation occurs in the English legal system, which partially clarifies the blurry boundaries of trespass litigation at common law. It does so by clarifying the relationship between intention and contractual obligation. The Court of Chancery, which eventually evolves into the Court of Equity, comes into being as a fully-fledged office of the law during these years.[12] The idea that underpins this legal office is that the Chancery should act as a representative of the King's 'grace', offering a remedy to the unjust application of law at lower or more local courts of common law.[13] Chancery is thus designed to address matters of legal fairness or 'equity', what medieval lawmen often call 'grace', 'conscience', or 'good faith'.[14] In practice, the job of the Chancery court is to hear cases in which the plaintiff, who has often formerly been a *defendant* at a lower court, feels she has not received justice at those lower courts.[15] A plaintiff at Chancery might complain that another party is so powerful, so manipulative, or so wealthy, that the plaintiff has been unable to attain justice at a lower court.[16] For instance, the Court of Chancery might retry a failed special traverse action on a trespassory suit of contract breach: the party, accused of breaking a contract, who has claimed that she has not received adequate justice on her claim that, yes, although she did break the contract, she should not be prosecuted as a criminal, might take her case to a higher authority for redress.

The Chancery court makes specific the situations in which such retrials of trespassory contract breach could be brought. The first such circumstance is when the ultimate intentions of one party had been kept secret from the other; in this case, the Chancery court can absolve the deceived party of any and all legal obligation to the person who had sued as plaintiff in the initial trespassory suit.[17] Second, when the contract itself stands in violation of the law, the court of Chancery can rule the contract is not legally binding to begin with: no contract between two parties has validity if it abrogates the King's laws. Third, when the contract is impossible to fulfil, Chancery can judge the party who failed to fulfil its terms not guilty. Fourth, Chancery can annul a contract entered into under duress.[18] Finally, Chancery can overrule contracts if they are either abrogated because of 'unavoidable accidents' or are created through 'surprise'.[19] Thus, if a person fails to convince a justice in a lower court trespass suit that she did not break a contract *maliciose* and *scienter*, she can pursue exoneration in Chancery, claiming that the contract was enacted under false pretenses, or that extenuating circumstances make the contract unenforceable. The new trespassory modes of pleading, and the rise of Chancery jurisdiction, have tremendous consequences throughout the English legal landscape, creating far more flexibility in how a lawyer or defendant would formulate a narrative about why a contract was breached.[20]

Not just in the legal landscape, these new modes and jurisdictions have consequences throughout the poetic landscape, though often because poets seek to restage these new legal forms as strategies for literary representation, and to interrogate the fictions at work in the law. Chaucer, being well-versed in contemporary legal practice and theory, through his exposure to the Inns of Court, is well aware of this shift in legal thought and the actionability of contract, and, moreover, well aware of the ideological revolution taking place in the coalescence of the positive law of equity, conscience, or the King's 'grace'.[21]

As I now move into my primary case study, I will suggest two things. First, I propose that Chaucer interprets Boccaccio's *Filostrato* as, in effect, a literary conviction of Criseyde as a breaker of contract; in his own poem, he seeks to re-examine her culpability.[22] Second, and this will take up the lion's share of my expository energy, I will suggest that the strategies Chaucer uses to re-examine Criseyde's culpability are distinctively English and distinctively legal: inspired by the evolutions in the Common

Law, he re-imagines *Troilus and Criseyde* as a test case of the procedures of trespass and of the logics of equity. In his poem the audience is asked to play the role of Chancellor, examining Criseyde not simply by the strict letter of the law, but always with an eye toward extenuating circumstances, and with an openness to the possibility that the contract she entered into was, *prima facie*, non-binding.[23] If this poetic equity trial were to carry, Criseyde's misdeed, though 'wrong', would not be criminal.

In devising this poetic retrial, Chaucer's poem never undercuts the basic assumption of his received narrative: Criseyde breaks her vow of amatory fidelity to Troilus every bit as clearly in Chaucer's poem as in the *Filostrato*.[24] Moreover, he takes pains to depict the relationship between Troilus and Criseyde as specifically contractual, based upon a mutual exchange of consent, solemnized by the exchange of tokens, and articulated as an explicit verbal agreement to be faithful to each other.[25] Later, when Criseyde's 'slydynge corage' (5.825) leads her to realign herself with Diomede, the poem makes quite clear that she breaks that verbal contract to Troilus.[26] Interestingly, however, the narrator of the *Troilus* has a famously hard time condemning her to any particular punishment for her uncontested faithlessness. This delicately balanced moral tension in the poem manifests a particular facet of Chaucer's literary craft, namely his ability to mobilize and explore the logics and forms of the law in his poetic projects, but to do so in a way that ultimately sheds light on poetry itself as a means of exploring and critiquing the law itself.[27]

Though it is clear that Criseyde wrongs Troilus, the poem evokes three of the primary grounds for dismissing a contract-breach conviction in a court of equity: legality, impossibility, and duress. Indeed, much of the 'new' material Chaucer adds to his Boccaccian source unsettles the notion that Criseyde can be seen as technically 'criminal' along precisely these lines. The 'legality' claim may be the least intuitive, so I will start there. There are two reasons to consider the legality clause when assessing Criseyde's culpability. First, clandestine marriages, although not uncommon, were technically illegal, unless eventually solemnized in public.[28] Since that never happens in the poem, their sexual contract remains, for all legal purposes, illicit. Second, and far more important to the overarching thematic commitments of the poem, Criseyde was ordered, in a scene that Chaucer invents for his telling of this tale, to abandon Troy by an act of Parliament.[29] Although she and Troilus entertain the possibility that she might flout this edict and elope with Troilus, the poem makes clear that, in the charged political environment of Troy, doing so would constitute a breach of royal law. Troilus calls attention to their legal entrapment, by lamenting their fates using a pointedly legal lexicon, 'O verrey lord! . . . Syn ye Criseyde and me han fully brought / Into youre grace, and bothe oure hertes seled, / How may ye suffre, allas, it be repeled'? (4.288, 292–4). By noting that their hearts are 'sealed' into love's grace, Troilus again evokes the conflicting systems of legal obligation in which he and Criseyde find themselves. By then acknowledging that Parliament's edict specifically 'repeals' that 'seal', he registers that his former contract with Criseyde has been rendered non-legal by its conflict with royal law. Already, then, Criseyde's contract with Troilus is imperilled, since it is legally incumbent upon her to leave Troy. She recognizes this herself, in markedly legalistic discourse, saying of her imminent departure, 'Ther is non other remedie in this cas' (5.60). Caught between Parliamentary mandate and personal contract, there is no legal recourse, no 'remedy'.

But of course, the partial invalidation of her contract does not necessarily invalidate the whole of it; that she must go over to the Greeks does not mean she is contractually allowed to fall in love with Diomede. But the poem's case is not yet fully made. When we eventually see Criseyde in the Greek camp, we are made perhaps painfully aware of her sense that she has no options. We are made aware, that is, that she views her contract as impossible to uphold: as hard as Criseyde may try to remain loyal to Troilus, there are physical realities to bear in mind, chiefly, the reality of her physical vulnerability among the Greeks and of the protection that Diomede represents. In a passage Chaucer adds to his less equitably inclined Boccaccian source, we read of Diomede,

> This Diomede, as bokes us declare
> Was in his nedes prest and corageous,
> With sterne vois and myghty lymes square,
> Hardy, testif, strong and chivalrous
> Of dedes, lik his fader Tideus… (5.799–804)

Immediately following this aria on masculine power, we read of Criseyde a truly pathetic counterpoint: 'Criseyde mene was of hire stature; / Therto of shap, of face, and ek of cheere…' (5.806–7). Diomede is strong of voice and body; Criseyde is small, demure, and shy. Criseyde can clearly profit from making friends with this strong-voiced, strong-armed man, and she does so. Once Diomede has befriended her, however, it becomes clear that he has ulterior motives, and he quickly specifies that he wants to be Criseyde's lover. Criseyde begs time to consider, and, in a wonderful passage of introspective rumination, Criseyde:

> Retorn[es] in hire soule ay up and down
> The wordes of this sodeyn Diomede,
> His grete estat, and perel of the town,
> And that she was allone and hadde nede
> Of frendes help; and thus bygan to brede
> The cause whi, the sothe for to telle,
> That she took fully purpos forto dwelle. (5.1023–9)

Criseyde is alone and has 'nede of frendes help'. She needs an ally; Diomede offers himself to her, however disingenuously, as precisely that. Thus, in a practical, self-preservationist sense, it is impossible for her to keep her contract with Troilus, because she perceives that her safety hinges on her alliance with Diomede. Amplifying the sense that Criseyde has no choice in this initial betrayal, the *Troilus*-narrator adds in a large new passage in which we witness Criseyde's regret about 'falsing' Troilus (5.1054–5). Evidently, she regrets her choice, and she means Troilus no harm, saying, 'I wolde sory be / For to seen yow in adversitee' (1082–3). She does not mean him harm; she does not intend injury. So, by the logic of trespass, Criseyde's lack of malice would partially exonerate her; by the procedures of equity, her lack of choices would.

But we do not have to go to the fifth book to witness the *Troilus*-narrator's exploration of the reasons why Criseyde might not, technically, deserve legal censure. The poem begins its appeal earlier, when it makes plain that Criseyde is coerced into her contract with Troilus in the first place. The poem's poetic staging of this legal coercion comes in four parts: first, the murkiness of the agreement she enters into; second, the power imbalance between Criseyde and Troilus; third, that Criseyde is manipulated by her friend, Pandarus, into entering into the contract; fourth, that Criseyde is physically entrapped— more than once and by more than one cause—when she agrees to terms of the contract.

When Pandarus initially brings Troilus's suit of love, the poem makes clear that Pandarus's true intentions are not clear to Criseyde: twice, she explicitly registers the difficulty of discerning Pandarus's 'meaning' or intention.[30] Pandarus's sphinx-like demeanor constitutes the equivalent of a sealed document, because it prevents Criseyde from fully understanding to what she commits herself. He promises Criseyde that he does not seek to 'bynde' her to Troilus 'thorugh no byheste' (2.359), though, of course, that is precisely what he seeks to do. He keeps his intentions secret—indeed, he actively lies about them—sealing them off from Criseyde's full knowledge. Criseyde sees that contractual binding of some sort is precisely at issue, and she seems to see that Pandarus's true intentions are being kept from her: she laments that she is being manipulated in 'this dredful cas', by a secret, or 'paynted process', to follow Pandarus's 'byheeste' and grant her love to Troilus (426, 424, 423). Criseyde's redeployment and augmentation of legal terminology, which do not appear in Boccaccio's poem, alerts the reader to her initial perception of the situation: she is being coerced into a binding obligation by secret and manipulative actions. Though she eventually yields, she makes clear that she does so only under pressure: 'I shal myn herte ayeins my lust constreyne' (476).[31]

Building on this initial 'constraint', the poem reveals that Criseyde has another kind of constraint to contend with. As she considers her situation, in a passage absent in the *Filostrato*, Criseyde realizes that her freedom in the situation is further compromised by Troilus's high social standing—'Ek wel woot I my kynges sone is he' (2.708)—and that, if she holds aloof from him, he may respond by holding her in 'dispit, / Thorugh whicch I myghte stonde in worse plit' (711–12). In this recognition, the poem makes clear that Criseyde feels keenly her lack of power, relative to the party with whom she is meant to make a covenant. The poem makes clear, then, that another major ground for dismissing a suit of contract breach is in effect: the power disparity between the two parties is so great that the alleged unfaithful party has no realistic legal recourse.

The constraint under which Pandarus and Troilus have put Criseyde becomes more ineluctable and more ironically 'legal' when Pandarus contrives, in another Chaucerian invention, to invent a fictitious legal proceeding against her, supposedly initiated by Poliphete, a Trojan knight who 'wolden don oppressioun; / and wrongfully han hire possessioun' (2.1418–19). Pandarus's fictitious threat to her holdings and possessions agitates and amplifies her already present awareness of her legal dependency on her uncle, whom she earlier called her 'beste frend', who should 'defende' her (412, 413). But of course, Pandarus's friendship with Criseyde is far from friendly: when Criseyde arrives at court, 'al innocent of this' intricate legal scheme that Pandarus has dreamed up (1562), she allies herself with Troilus, who, as she herself has already noted, is the 'kynges sone' and can protect her through his 'grace' from the legal loss.[32] After a great deal of pressure from Pandarus, and in exchange for Troilus's legal protection, she accedes to Troilus's request to be her servant, but with a crucial caveat: 'Myn honour sauf, I wol wel trewely / And in swich forme as he gan now devyse/ Receyven hym fully to my servyse' (3.159–61). In this scene, Criseyde's awareness of the disparity in social power between her and Troilus is mobilized coercively, to get her to grant amatory favour to Troilus, despite her own wish to keep her own 'sovereignete' (171). More crucially, her fears are mobilized by Pandarus, notionally her friend and ally, on whom she should be able to rely for her defence. By the logics and procedures of equity, Criseyde should not be held to this contract.

The coercion becomes particularly apparent later in book three, when, significantly, the contract between Troilus and Criseyde is consummated, both verbally and sexually. What is crucial to note about Chaucer's adaptation of the poem is his addition of the particular kind of pressure that is brought to bear on Criseyde before she chooses to consummate. In the night-time scene at Pandarus's house, Criseyde is effectively imprisoned: she is shut into a tiny room, with no possibility of egress, due both to the fact that it is night, and to the fact that it is raining. Entering into a contract during imprisonment was, in the fourteenth century, a paradigmatic instance in which the contract was non-binding, and could be annulled at any future point by the coerced party. Once again, the narrative is designed to stage the legal reality that Criseyde is not technically accountable for her 'slydyng corage'.

Through the *Troilus*-narrator's careful and programmatic representation of the constraint under which Criseyde entered into her union with Troilus, Chaucer's poem becomes a Middle English thought experiment that reconsiders the accusations that have been made in literary history, and explores how the new rules of the English Common Law could engineer new readings of the poem. The *Troilus*-narrator does not deny that Criseyde broke faith with Troilus; instead, he questions whether that breaking of faith should be seen as criminal, since the relationship was entered into under a number of technical modes of constraint. The suggestion is that, yes, C did 'falsen' T, but C had perfectly good reasons for doing so and, besides, the contract was legally unenforceable to begin with.

The narrator's incantatory insistence that Criseyde 'did al for goode' (924) is further critical to his push for clemency: Criseyde acts without malice, not 'maliciose', when she betrays her contract with Troilus. When the narrator reveals that Criseyde 'did al for goode', he is not being casual, but instead is making a technical legal claim about the nature of her intention; by framing this claim generally—she did 'al' for good—he makes a correlative claim not just about this particular scene, but about how we are to see Criseyde's actions throughout the story. She may do wrong, but she does not *mean* wrong. She may err, but she does not commit a crime, because her intentions are good. The special traverse against the action of contract-breach that the narrator has been making throughout the poem is securely and programmatically grounded in cutting-edge medieval legal practice and theory, in which intention trumps action.

In case his readers are still eager to condemn Criseyde, the narrator himself models and urges an equitable judgment of her. When we encounter, in the final book of the *Troilus*, the narrator's many efforts to curry sympathy for Criseyde, we should read them as manifestations of his equity, conscience, grace, and pity, as well as appeals to our own. When the narrator confesses that he does not wish to 'chyde' Criseyde, 'Forther than the storye wol devyse', he explains that her bad reputation should be punishment enough for her infraction, and that he, the narrator himself, 'wolde excuse hire yet for routhe' (5.1093–5, 1099). The narrator creates himself, then, as an advocate for equitable read-ings of Criseyde, though he still acknowledges in full the wrong that is done to Troilus. This, indeed, is the elegance of late medieval trespassory litigation, in relation to equity: it allows negative event (crime), positive intention (non-malice), and nuanced judg-ment (equity) to coexist within the logic of a single narrative. This is also the elegance of Chaucer's legal and poetic project in *Troilus and Criseyde*: he composes his poem as a meditation on a series of interrelated contemporary legal problems about contractual relationality. The poem does not offer a definite answer as to whether Criseyde ultimately deserves the shame and slander of literary history, but it certainly raises a series of jurid-ical reasons why an audience might think twice about condemning her too forcefully in a court of law.

Not only does the narrator model equity, he has Criseyde model it as well when she is given the chance to judge her lover. In the third book, when Troilus appears before her in the tiny room in Pandarus's house, and admits that he has coerced her into seeing him, he throws himself on her 'grace' for his 'trespace': 'And if that in tho wordes that I seyde / Be any wrong, I wol no more trespace. / Doth what yow list; I am al in youre grace' (3.1174–6). In a move of exemplary grace and equity, which Chaucer adds to his literary sources, Criseyde forgives Troilus, modelling exactly the ideal workings of a court of conscience, or 'grace', 'This accident so pitous was to here / And ek so like a sooth at prime face.../ That though that she did hym as thanne a grace / Considered alle thynges as they stoode / No wonder is, syn she did al for goode' (918–24). Criseyde does Troilus the 'grace' of equitable judgment. She recognizes that his error is borne more of 'accident' than malice, and that it deserves 'pity' rather than censure. In this markedly equitable scene, the *Troilus*-narrator pre-forms in his readership a tendency toward equitable judgment of Criseyde through Criseyde herself. Chaucer's 'litel tragedy' is thus designed to stage prob-lems of trespass and to contemplate the nature of equity. Chaucer is invested in exploring these legal procedures and logics because they provide dramatic, psychological resources for English poetics, available conventions through which fiction writers can explore com-plex ideas about morality, intention, and forgiveness, both on an interpersonal and a social scale. Indeed, Chaucer seems to recognize that the laws of trespass and equity share an interest in how and whether intention and motive can be systematically assessed: both legal and poetic discourse are interested in diagnosing behaviour not only as a function of character, but also, and increasingly, as a function of circumstance. The logics and pro-cedures of equity and trespass provide him with a scaffold on which to build complex investigations of intention and action in his poem.

But Chaucer's 'litel tragedy' is not designed just as an equitable trespass trial of Criseyde. It is also designed as a poetic exploration of trespass and equity themselves: the poem is a test of the limits and boundaries of new modes of assessing intention and its social ramifications. Indeed, rather than suggesting that the *Troilus* be read as a trial of Criseyde where the goal is to exonerate her, I am inclined to read it more as a poetic version of a particular legal sub-genre: a moot or reading from the Inns of Court. At the four major Inns—Lincoln, Middle Temple, Inner Temple, and Gray's—the most revolutionary statutory changes and procedural shifts in what the Common Law could do and, more importantly, how it worked were explored and ironed out. In the Inns, lawmen would hear lectures on, discuss, and try out the boundaries of new legislation and new writs and procedures, taking notes and debating the particular significances of legal innovations. In their studies, scholars of the law would not only take notes on actual cases, but would also engage in imaginative exercises in which they explored and examined the limits of the Common Law. These imaginative exercises and interactive lectures were called moots and readings, and it was through them that lawyers received their upper-level training as practitioners of the Common Law.[33] Chaucer's sustained engagement with trespass and equity in *Troilus and Criseyde* can be read as a poetic moot or poetic reading on the Common Law, a scholarly exercise taken out of its standard context in the Inns of Court and reworked into vernacular literature. In his poetic 'moot' or 'reading' of trespass and equity, Chaucer explores whether certain kinds of obligation might not be legally binding because of extenuating circumstances. He designs his poem to test the limits of the law's emerging theory of intention, its practice of trespass, and its courts of equity.

Though there are legions of other discourses and sources that deal with the rules and obligations of amatory contract, ranging from Boccaccio's Italian *Filostrato* to the archive of the debate poetry of the courtly tradition to the Canon Law, Chaucer deploys and tests the new conceptual and procedural armatures of the English Common Law. But he does so not so much to lionize or praise the new law, as to critique it and expose its particular weaknesses. Indeed, though the *Troilus*-narrator shows how Criseyde, legally, is not guilty of 'trespace', we must remember that, even in the *Troilus*-narrator's own imagination, Criseyde does not get off the hook. Literary history, as the narrator reminds us time and again, has always already mercilessly convicted her for her infidelity. And it likely always shall: if we look to the next instantiation of the Troilus and Criseyde narrative in English, Robert Henryson's *Testament of Cresseid*, it should be abundantly clear that, for the purposes of literary history, the *Troilus*-narrator's plea for equity does not hit its mark—not by a long shot. Instead of showing mercy to Cresseid, Henryson, famously, makes her a leper, too lowly and sullied for the Trojans even to recognize in the aftermath of the Trojan War.[34] And we do not even need to go so far as Henryson to find Criseyde under censure, since the *Troilus*-narrator himself, in his incessant lamentations for Criseyde, is well aware that his plea for grace on her behalf is destined to fail. But this staged failure of equitable judgment even after the case for it has been so strongly made is precisely Chaucer's point: no matter how carefully designed and executed the procedures of the common law may be, there will always be failures and shortfalls in the near-impossible task of assessing intention justly.

As invested as it is in this exploration of intention, then, Chaucer's poem remains agnostic about the efficacy of any regularized, regimented, or formalized mode of assessing intention as a guarantor of moral judgment or equitable reading of character. In effect, while the *Troilus*-narrator seems keen to avail himself of the resources of equity and trespass in literature, Chaucer's poem is always already aware that these new legal logics and procedures are overly optimistic, and based on a two-tiered fantasy: the first, that anyone would ever truly be able to 'felen what [another person] meneth'; the second, that any system of justice, be it poetic or legal, would be able to make adequate use of intention, even if it were fully representable in narration. In the end, it seems that Chaucer designs his deeply legal poem both to register the bold optimism of the law's new procedures, and to acknowledge that the equitable assessment of intention is, more often than not, the stuff of legal fantasy, rather than legal reality.

NOTES

1. John Baker, *The Legal Profession and the Common Law: Historical Essays* (London: Hambledon, 1986).
2. On the medieval origins and studies of civil and canon law in the universities, see James A. Brundage, *The Medieval Origins of the Legal Profession: Canonists, Civilians, and Courts* (Chicago, IL: University of Chicago Press, 2008); William J. Courtenay, Jürgen Miethke, and David B. Priest, eds., *Universities and Schooling in Medieval Society* (Boston, MA: Brill, 2000), 1–32; Dorothy M. Owen, *The Medieval Canon Law: Teaching, Literature and Transmission* (Cambridge: Cambridge University Press, 1990); Alan B. Cobban, *The Mediaeval English Universities: Oxford and Cambridge to c. 1500* (Berkeley, CA: University of California Press, 1988); J. A. Clarence Smith, *Mediaeval Law Teachers and Writers, Civilian and Canonist* (Ottawa: University of Ottawa Press, 1975); Hastings Rashdall, *The Universities of Europe in the Middle Ages*, vols. 1–3, eds. F. M. Powicke and A. B. Emden (Oxford: Clarendon Press, 1936).
3. As Maura Nolan puts it: 'For a vernacular poet such as Chaucer, seeking to establish not only his own authority but also the authority of poetic and secular discourse itself, the language of the law could provide an essential vocabulary of legitimacy.' See Maura Nolan, 'Acquiteth Yow Now', in *The Letter of the Law: Legal Practice and Literary Production in Medieval England*, eds. Emily Steiner and Candace Barrington (Ithaca, NY: Cornell University Press, 2002), 152. Bruce Holsinger calls attention to 'an emerging...area of investigation, the effort among scholars in the field to delineate literature and law as "parallel forms of discourse"'. See Bruce Holsinger, 'The English Jurisdiction of *The Owl and the Nightingale*', in Steiner and Barrington, *Letter of the Law*, 155.
4. Examples of medieval English debate poems that use the formal logics of the law both to stage and destabilize legal ideas and paradigms are *The Owl and the Nightingale*, which Holsinger examines, *Wynnere and Wastoure*, *The Parlement of the Thre Ages*, *Mum and the Sothsegger*, *Richard the Redeless*, and Chaucer's *Parlement of Fowles*.
5. Anne Middleton has analysed the role, for instance, of the Statute of Labourers in structuring Langland's revision of the poem from version B to version C. See Anne Middleton, 'Acts of Vagrancy: The C-Version Autobiography and the Statute of 1388', in *Written Work: Langland, Labor, and Authorship*, eds. Steven Justice and Kathryn Kerby-Fulton

(Philadelphia, PA: University of Pennsylvania Press, 1997), 208–310. See also Matthew Giancarlo's brilliant argument about the third passus of *Piers* in 'Piers Plowman, Parliament, and Public Voice', *Yearbook of Langland Studies* 17 (2004), 135–74.

6. For a fuller treatment not only of why the trespass law evolved this way, but how that evolution happened in practice, see S. F. C. Milsom, *A Natural History of the Common Law* (New York: Columbia University Press, 2003), 25–50.

7. For an excellent introduction to the nature of trespass trials, their evolution, and the special modes of pleading they introduced into the English *imaginaire,* see the introduction to Morris S. Arnold, ed., *Select Cases of Trespass from the King's Courts: 1307–1399* (London: Selden Society, 1985).

8. S. F. C. Milsom demonstrates that, by the end of the fourteenth century, the acceptable procedural boundaries within which the trespass writ could be sued were under *scienter* and *maliciose*. See Milsom, *Studies in the History of the Common Law* (London: Hambledon Press, 1985).

9. A description of how to sue on special traverses can be found in Morris S. Arnold, ed., *Select Cases of Trespass from the King's Courts 1307–1399* (London: Selden, 1985), xxvi–xxix.

10. The development of a theory of contract in the Common Law courts is slow and gradual. Prior to the end of the fourteenth century, 'non-doing', or not fulfilling one's contractual obligation, is not 'malfeasance', and hence, is not held to be trespassory. See S. F. C. Milsom, 'Not Doing is No Trespass; A View of the Boundaries of Case', *Cambridge Law Journal* 12(1) (1954), 105–17; see also Milsom, 'Trespass from Henry III to Edward III', *Law Quarterly Review* 74 (1958).

11. Richard Firth Green, *A Crisis of Truth: Literature and Law in Ricardian England* (Philadelphia, PA: University of Pennsylvania Press, 1999).

12. See 'Introduction', in William Pailey Baildon, ed., *Select Cases in Chancery* (1364–1471) (London: Bernard Quaritch, 1896): 'The English procedures and doctrines that are called equity evolved during the period of roughly 1350–1450. It was a process of evolution that occurred as the royal chancery became a court of law' (xix).

13. Baildon, *Select Cases in Chancery,* xviii.

14. Ibid., xxix–xxx.

15. Ibid., xvi.

16. Ibid., xxii.

17. The classic situation is one in which the contractee is not allowed to see the specific stipulations of a contract, which remain under seal during the fixing of the contract. See W. H. Bryson, ed., 'Introduction', in *Cases Concerning Equity,* vol. 1 (London: Selden Society, 2001), xxii.

18. For a further anatomization and analysis of the history of the law of contract, see A. W. B. Simpson, *A History of the Common Law of Contract* (Oxford: Oxford University Press, 1975), 506–38. On the non-actionability of contracts entered into under duress, see also David Ibbotson, *A Historical Introduction to the Law of Obligations* (London: Oxford University Press, 1999), 4–5, 71–2.

19. Bryson, 'Introduction', xxx.

20. Indeed, when explaining the effect of trespassory modes of pleading on the Common Law, Milsom cites these modes' productive tendency to generate legal 'fictions': 'The common law had been pushed into greatness because its practitioners could not quite stop talking about what had actually happened' (Milsom, *Studies in the History of Common Law,* 189).

21. See D. S. Bland, 'Chaucer and the Inns of Court', *English Studies* 33 (1952), 145–55; John Gardner, *Life and Times of Chaucer* (New York: Barnes and Noble, 1999), 133. For a treatment

of the history and evolution of the Inns of Court, see J. H. Baker, *The Legal Profession and the Common Law: Historical Essays* (London: Hambledon, 1986).

22. Assessing and condemning amatory infidelity, or trying to do so, was by no means new: see William Calin, 'A Reading of Guillaume de Machaut's *Jugement du Roy de Navarre*', *Modern Language Review* 66 (1971), 294–7; see also Kevin Brownlee, 'Machaut's Motet 15 and the *Roman de la Rose*', *Early Music History* 10 (1991), 1–14. For work in the love-debate poetry of Christine de Pizan, see also Barbara K. Altmann, *The Love Debate Poems of Christine de Pizan: Le Livre du debat de deux amans, Le Livre des trois jugemens, Le Livre du dit de Poissy* (Gainesville, FL: University Press of Florida, 1998).

23. Anne M. Taylor also notes a trial-like aspect to Criseyde's depiction in the poem, but focuses her analysis on the exchange of Antenor for Criseyde, and on how the poem alludes to Christ's trial before Pilate, whereas Chaucer's source does not make this allusion. See Taylor, 'A Scriptural Echo in the Trojan Parliament of *Troilus and Criseyde*', *Nottingham Medieval Studies* 24 (1980), 51–6.

24. Scholarship has long debated the precise nature of Criseyde's infidelity, and the debates have centred on the question of whether Criseyde and Troilus enact a 'clandestine marriage' in the third book of the *Troilus*. See H. A. Kelly, *Love and Marriage in the Age of Chaucer* (Ithaca, NY: Cornell University Press, 1975); Zacharias P. Thundy, 'Clandestine Marriages in the Late Middle Ages', in *New Images of Women*, ed. Edelgard E. DuBruck (Lewiston, ID: Edwin Mellen Press, 1989), 303–20; Frederik Pedersen, 'Did the Medieval Laity Know the Canon Law Rules on Marriage? Some Evidence from Fourteenth-Century York', *Mediaeval Studies* 56 (1994), 111–52; Myra Stokes, 'The Contract of Love-Service: Lancelot and Troilus', *Litteraria Pragensia* 18 (1999), 62–83. I would suggest that the 'marriage' question is not where Chaucer innovates. Where he innovates is in his depiction of how the 'contract', whatever its precise nature, is entered into.

25. They exchange their 'entente' (3.1239), and Criseyde gives Troilus 'a broche, gold and asure, / In which a ruby set was lik an herte' (1370–1). Chaucer tells us 'syn they were oon' (1405).

26. The *Troilus*-narrator calls her 'slydynge of corage' (5.825).

27. Cannon has read Criseyde's letter in book five of the *Troilus* as a manifestation of Chaucer's awareness that women had relatively little access to legal representation in the late English Middle Ages. See Christopher Cannon, 'The Rights of Medieval Women: Crime and the Issue of Representation', in *Medieval Crime and Social Control*, eds. Barbara A. Hanawalt and David Wallace (Minneapolis, MN: University of Minnesota Press, 1999), 156–85.

28. See Karl P. Wentersdorf, 'Some Observations on the Concept of Clandestine Marriage in *Troilus and Criseyde*', *Chaucer Review* 15 (1980), 101–26.

29. 'For which delivered was by parlement / For Antenor to yelden out Criseyde, / And it pronounced by the president, / Altheigh that Ector "nay" ful ofte preyde. / And fynaly, what wight that it withseyde, / It was for nought; it moste ben and sholde. / For substaunce of the parlement it wolde' (4.211–7).

30. She asks Pandarus directly, 'Shal I nat witen what ye meene of this?' (2.226), and, shortly thereafter, having become no clearer on exactly what he wants from her, she internally muses on his meaning, resolving to suss out his actual designs: 'I shal felen what he meneth, ywis' (387). Later, Criseyde's inability to understand Pandarus's 'meaning' recurs in book three, when she exclaims, 'Yet wist I nevere wel what that he mente' (3.126).

31. Later, when she does eventually respond to Pandarus's pressure by deciding to write a letter to Troilus, she emphasizes constraint again: 'I nevere dide thing with more peyne / Than writen this, to which ye me constreyne...' (2.1232).

32. The poem also uses the word 'innocent' to describe Criseyde when she is unable to see Pandarus's underlying motivations: 'Al innocent of Pandarus entente' (2.1723).

33. See Robert Richard Pearce, *A History of the Inns of Court and Chancery, With Notices of Their Ancient Discipline, Rules, Orders, and Customs, Readings, Moots, Masques, Revels, and Entertainments* (London: R. Bentley, 1848), 65–72. See also John Fraser Macqueen, *A Lecture on the Early History and Academic Discipline of the Inns of Court and Chancery* (London: S. Sweet, 1851), 14–18.

34. See Robert Henryson, *The Poems of Robert Henryson*, ed. Robert L. Kindrick (Kalamazoo, MI: Medieval Institute Publications, 1997), lines 334–43, 495–7.

BIBLIOGRAPHY

Arnold, Morris S., ed., *Select Cases of Trespass from the King's Courts: 1307–1399* (London: Selden Society, 1985).

Baildon, William Pailey, ed., *Select Cases in Chancery (1364–1471)* (London: Bernard Quaritch, 1896).

Baker, John, *The Legal Profession and the Common Law: Historical Essays* (London: Hambledon, 1986).

Green, Richard Firth, *A Crisis of Truth: Literature and Law in Ricardian England* (Philadelphia, PA: University of Pennsylvania Press, 1999).

Holsinger, Bruce, 'The English Jurisdiction of *The Owl and the Nightingale* in Steiner, Emily and Candace Barrington, eds., *The Letter of the Law: Legal Practice and Literary Production in Medieval England* (Ithaca, NY: Cornell University Press, 2002), 154–84.

Milsom, S. F. C., *A Natural History of the Common Law* (New York: Columbia University Press, 2003).

Milsom, S. F. C., *Studies in the History of the Common Law* (London: Hambledon Press, 1985).

Nolan, Maura, 'Acquiteth Yow Now: Textual Contradiction and Legal Discourse in the Man of Law's Introduction', in Steiner, Emily and Candace Barrington, eds., *The Letter of the Law: Legal Practice and Literary Production in Medieval England* (Ithaca, NY: Cornell University Press, 2002), 136–53.

Pearce, Robert Richard, *A History of the Inns of Court and Chancery, With Notices of Their Ancient Discipline, Rules, Orders, and Customs, Readings, Moots, Masques, Revels, and Entertainments* (London: R. Bentley, 1848).

Simpson, A. W. B., *A History of the Common Law of Contract* (Oxford: Oxford University Press, 1975).

Steiner, Emily and Candace Barrington, eds., *The Letter of the Law: Legal Practice and Literary Production in Medieval England* (Ithaca, NY: Cornell University Press, 2002).

CHAPTER 24

MEDICINE AND SCIENCE IN CHAUCER'S DAY

E. RUTH HARVEY

WHILE Chaucer was writing his poetry in his London lodgings over Aldgate and earning his living at the nearby custom-house, another scholar, formerly of London, was diligently creating the foundation of the medical sciences in English. A great deal of medical theory and other scientific works existed in Latin textbooks, but almost none of this had found its way into the vernacular. The first task of medieval English scientists was to appropriate into their own language the scientific learning available in Latin, and to lay the foundations for future development. The contemporary of Chaucer who started the process was a Dominican friar named Henry Daniel.[1] He is little known today, but he deserves greater fame: he played a major part in creating an English to serve the purpose of establishing medical science. Daniel's surviving works, two big books, share a teasing resemblance to some aspects of Chaucer's work: a searching interest in the potential of vernacular English, a wide-ranging grasp of secular scientific learning, an audience of 'burel clerks'—a literate, but not necessarily Latinate society. In his books London appears with its gardens, apothecaries (hand-in-glove with physicians),[2] butchers, libraries, queen, and noble ladies, even elegant young men who 'cherish their long flaxen locks';[3] outside London Daniel mentions lodging-house experiences, sick-beds, stretches of wild country,[4] cities such as Bristol and Lincoln, and technical discussions between various groups of professional healers, from the 'King's physician' to a village herb woman.[5] It is recognizably Chaucer's world from a different viewpoint. An exhaustive study of Daniel's writings would be a huge enterprise, so here I should like to focus on two main aspects: his ambition to present medical science in the English language, and the interlocking, organic nature of the learning that he presents.

To take the second point first: all learning in Daniel's day was unified by its dependence on the writings of Aristotle and his foundational idea of a First Mover, generally accepted as identical to the God of Christianity. Most medical texts begin, like Aristotle's *Physics*, by explaining the fundamental idea that all earthly matter was made up of the four elements, earth, water, air, and fire. This conception of material things underlay not just medicine, but all medieval science.[6] In medicine a description of the four elements and their properties led directly to an explanation of the four humours or liquids within the human body: blood, phlegm, bile, and melancholy. The humours echoed the combinations of the elements in fluid form inside man: thus blood was hot and moist, and was linked in this way to air, which had the same qualities; melancholy was cold and dry, and hence played much the same role as earth in the exterior world; phlegm was paralleled to water, choler to fire. Health and sickness depended upon the proper balance of the humours. Since man's body was part of the world, made of the same ingredients, it was intricately connected to its whole environment, and a good physician had to understand the nature of matter at large. This in turn meant that medical learning, by its very nature, also instructed the novice in the theories which explained the properties of matter and the physical composition of the whole universe.

As its beginning in the *Physics* suggests, medieval science did not separate its 'chemistry' from its 'physics'. The forces that cause movement, that characteristic of life on earth, were inseparable from the nature of matter itself. The elements had their own characteristic motions: air and fire tended to move upwards, earth and water downwards, and all their fruitful interactions and exchanges were themselves caused by the movements of the heavenly spheres. The planets and stars, in their celestial circlings around the central earth, poured down their influence and generated all movement within it. In this way astronomy and cosmology became part and parcel of the intellectual conception of the material and physical structure of the earth and all life upon it.

The movements of the heavens were themselves held to be the result of the movement of the outermost shell of the universe, the 'First Moved' or *Primum mobile*. To provide a logical end to an infinite progression, Aristotle had therefore posited his hypothetical Unmoved First Mover, the ultimate unchanged and unstirring source of all motion and forces. Christians never doubted that the Unmoved Mover was God himself, the Christian deity whose interactions with humanity were detailed in the Bible. So world history, biblical geography, and Christian theology join the medieval unified theory of knowledge. There were awkwardnesses and stress points in thus overlaying the Christian moral and religious system on ancient Greek science, but, by and large, the strains get elided in medieval science, especially in its more practical forms. The model worked so well that it remained stable for centuries, and was relinquished only with considerable mental pain; the discoveries of Columbus, Vesalius, Copernicus, Harvey, and Galileo all contributed to its ultimate destruction.

The career and work of Henry Daniel provides an unparalleled example of scientific knowledge in the England of Chaucer's day. There are no external records of his life: all we know of him is gleaned from his books.[7] His first known work is a fairly conventional treatise in Latin on the foundational skill of medieval medicine: uroscopy, or the art of diagnosis by examination of the urine. In itself a sizable treatise (a transcription runs to about ninety pages), this Latin prose book is constructed upon the framework of Giles of Corbeil's famous twelfth-century Latin poem, *De urinis*, supplemented by the comprehensive prose treatise of the same name by Isaac Judaeus (tenth century) and, to a lesser degree, by other Latin writers.[8] The uroscopical tradition was a long one, and its roots go back through Galen to the Hippocratic writings. Daniel must have written his Latin book before 1377, because in that year he produced the first version of an English translation of his own work, now called *Uricrisis* or *Liber uricrisiarum*, to which he helpfully added a preface (in Latin) explaining his rationale and purpose. The preface was addressed to a friend and colleague, Walter Turner of Keten (most probably Ketton, a village some five miles from Stamford, Lincolnshire), because Walter had urged Daniel to throw open his book to those who could read but had no Latin. Daniel claims that he was a bit hesitant about this idea since there was no precedent for it, and expresses some (conventional?) doubts about his own skill in languages. The notion must have grown on him, however, because in subsequent years he made a series of revisions and expansions of his English uroscopical work, and then followed it up with a very large herbal-cum-medical encyclopaedia. Within these books he promises to make English versions of an ever-expanding series of related texts. As far as we know, only the uroscopy and the herbal survive: the uroscopy in its various versions in more than twenty manuscripts and an abridged printed edition, the herbal in two manuscripts. It is apparent from reading them that Daniel became more and more fired up with the desire to make English versions of other primary medical texts available to his new audience.

From passing remarks in these two books, Daniel seems to have been already quite old at the time of writing. He seems definitely to have been still alive in 1382 (when he wrote the last version of his preface), and probably lived some years after that, working on his herbal, but we have no other dates to go on. The herbal volume survives only in two incomplete versions, so perhaps Daniel did not live to finish it to his satisfaction. Most of the standard biographical notes on Daniel around today contain two erroneous statements: that the *Uricrisis* is a translation of Isaac Judaeus, and that Daniel was murdered in 1379.[9] Neither is true. The *Uricrisis* uses Isaac Judaeus, and is a translation, but a translation of Daniel's own original Latin work. The idea that he was murdered in 1379 is derived from a misreading of *ferour* as 'friar', rather than 'farrier': the murderee in the record cited was a smith of the same name, not the author.[10]

The first thing we should consider is the whole question of translation. All scientific learning generally available to scholars in the medieval West was in Latin. Insofar as science was studied at all in the universities, it would have required many years of training in Latin to access it. By the end of the fourteenth century it is clear that there was an increasing need to reproduce some of this learning in the European vernaculars, languages which had not hitherto been thought to have the vocabulary or sophistication to convey the arcane technicalities of science. Daniel responded to this need, and he tells us his reasons in his preface to the *Uricrisis*. His motive for putting Latin learning into English seems to have been fundamentally utilitarian: he was acquainted with a variety of medical colleagues who seem not to have been either university trained or fluent in Latin, and who needed a learned handbook which would cover the essentials of the art of diagnosis by urine. Uroscopy, a 'faire and wonderful' science,[11] was the first step in medical diagnosis. It had gradually become a highly elaborate craft in formal medicine: the urine had to be collected and examined according to a strict protocol, its twenty possible colours and approximately eighteen different 'contents' distinguished, and many minute discriminations among the variables carefully discerned. An impressive list of maladies could be diagnosed this way, and the whole craft was couched in resoundingly-learned terminology, much of it derived from Greek. Moreover, to understand the rationale behind the science, the practitioner must also grasp the fundamentals of human internal anatomy and physiology, and understand the impact of the whole external world upon the human organism. Here there was a need for even more technical terms, many of them Greek, some of them Arabic, most of them Latin. The English language had to be made capable of transmitting this lore.

Daniel, like many early translators, was very exercised in the problems of translation in contemporary English. He is conscious that he is doing something new: 'I have noght mynde that I have redde, ne harde neyther, this science giffen in English.'[12] He doubts, conventionally enough, his own capabilities, but he is also daunted by the task, 'for the langage is unsufficiant in itselfe', and he is 'nouther witty ne wise of this tonge', which is not his favourite, even though he was born to it.[13] But, urged on by the confusion, uncertainty, and ignorance of his non-Latinate audience, he girds himself for the task. It requires covering, he says, not only the technicalities of uroscopy, but the 'diffinicions and exposicions of termes of sekenes or infirmites, and of membres withoutforth and withinforthe, and with meny other thinges notable in this crafte'. It will require words new to English: 'Do not be surprised, reader, if you find me putting forward at times Latin terms, at times almost-Latin ones: I do it for the sake of brevity.'[14] He is not snobbish about existing English words: he employs such ancient terms as *thonewongs, paxfax, hame, haterel, paunch* and *schar*, or *the sneke, the pose, the daze, the itch* and *hert-quale*, but he is the first recorded user of such words as *dissenterie, diabet, cerebre, coagulacion, inflammacion, infeccion, helcosy, incisors*, and *fetus*. His choice of technical words is not restricted to the Latin of his sources: he introduces a colourful array of rare words of native or Scandinavian origin, like *gubbe, mosselen, orksum, pobyl, quibbish, rove* and *squob*. To enlarge the language and to educate his readers he adopts a series of devices: the glossing definition ('definition or description of a thing is the describing what a thing is'; 'demonstracion, a shewing'), or the doublet (*fumositas* is translated 'smokihedes and smotherheedes'; *coagulari* as 'clammeth and clatteth and clumpreth togeder'), and above all, the cross-reference. In an early version of his preface he writes, 'when I have explained a term once, whenever it occurs afterwards I don't explain it again'; instead, he gives a detailed cross-reference to the place he first mentioned it.[15] A good example of Daniel's careful method for alerting his English readers to the precision of technical terminology is his explanation for the proper name for kidney disease, *nefresis*:

> *Nefresis* and *nefresia*, and *nefretica passio*, al on: quan on hath the ston, or siknesse in the reynes, in the lendis; *nefreticus*, he that hath nefresi; *calculus* is quan on hath the ston in the vesie, in the bleddere; and *lapis* is generally for every maner maledy of the ston, and *lapidosus* is he that hat it. *Nefresis* or *nefretica* is seyd of this woord in Grek *nefresin*, i.e. ren; ren is the nere [kidney] of man and beste. Ren is also takyn for that place ther the neres lyn, i.e. for the place betwen the bak and the ars; and that place we callyn the lendes in Englysch, *reynes* in Frensch. Bocheres callyn it the loyne and the nere pece.[16]

A typical cross reference to this passage would be '*nefresis* in the 2 bok, 4 capitle, *De albo colore*, lef 38'. It is characteristic of Daniel that he matches equivalent terms, not just in Latin, Greek, and French, but also adds the word used by contemporary butchers.

Daniel is highly important as a creator of technical vocabulary, and he was similarly thorough in the formal qualities of an explanatory textbook. His uroscopy text was not merely put into English words: he set out to transpose bodily the whole concept of a learned Latin treatise into English. His *Uricrisis* is carefully subdivided into books and chapters, and equipped with a Latin (later English) preface which explains the general layout. It was provided with such helpful devices as a volvelle (a paper wheel attached to the page by a central thread to match two series of numbers), various tables, and diagrams; it was usually written out with shoulder-notes and running heads. Mnemonic verse tags in Latin are included and rendered into English:

> *Versus: Qui bene digerit, ingerit, egerit, est bene sanus.*
> Yif thou wel etyst, defyest and schitest,
> Thou art heyl quer thou go or sittyst.[17]

It concluded with a set of verses in Latin, in which he noted the dates of the years when it was written. And Daniel worried constantly about clarity: in his major revision of the text, as well as including more material and altering wording, he redid all of the chaptering to make the chapters much more numerous, but each one a good deal shorter (this would have made the cross-references much easier to find). By its final version it was a very elaborate treatise indeed.

Daniel's thoroughness extends even to the problem of dialect and spelling. We know practically nothing about his background, but he seemed to be confident that he spoke and wrote an English central enough to be standard: he asks his scribes to be very careful in copying his text because 'as for the langage of Englissh tong as anentz a discrete man and him that hath the gift of tunge, trewe and parfite craft of ortographie is taught in this bok'.[18] He frequently fusses about the etymological meaning of words, and his obsessional care for accuracy extends from notes on correct spelling to the pronunciation of both English and Latin: 'understond that it sulde be wretyn and seyd *ambulla* with -b- and not with -p-, for it is seyd and conpounyd of this word *am*, i.e. *circum*, and *bulla* that hath many significacions'; '*Isope, isop*; it is a noble erbe ... it schuld be seid *esopus* ... *Esope* is a proper name of a poet'; '*Vicia*, a tare or veche, and it schuld not be seid fech'.[19] This suggests that he considered himself to be initiating formal professional learning in the English language, correcting English usage to accord with an ideal standard, and thereby laying the foundations for its future development.

His statement that he used eleven different authorities in his *Uricrisis* does not mean it is a slavish rendering of passages from Latin authors. He is, indeed, punctilious about acknowledging passages he does translate—he always adds a 'thus he' or 'woord for woord' after an actual translated quotation—but the whole book is much more than a translation. Daniel not only precedes the most famous translator of the period, John Trevisa (fl.1385–1402), but can also claim credit for a much more adventurous enterprise:

an intelligent combination and assessment of a number of authorities, and increasingly, in his different revisions, notes from his own experiences and ideas. To the authoritative descriptions in the textbooks he adds some brief case-histories of patients he has himself known: a dropsical woman, a young man given up for dead who surprised everyone by recovering, a woman with a *mola* or false pregnancy.[20] He comments on his own health from time to time, complaining of kidney disease, preoccupation with other affairs, and the difficulty of getting hold of the right books. He has his own voice: his English is colourful, with a register ranging from the formal and academic to the colloquial and earthy. Some folk, he says, engage overmuch in lechery, to the detriment of their health, 'and thei foles the more', or miscontrue language, 'Latyn hath many unstedefast knokkeris at his gate'.[21] His characteristic quirks of style are a love of doublets, especially alliterating ones, a devotion to the suffixes *-ish* and *-head*, and a brisk dismissal of 'smatterers', 'dogleeches', and 'bunglers'.[22] And, once he has got started in his enterprise, he begins to voice his hopes of making more and more texts available in translation.

Daniel felt from the beginning that a book on diagnosis required a companion volume on cures. He wrote in his preface to the *Uricrisis*: 'do not be surprised that although I have dealt with diseases and sicknesses in this book, I do not mention the medicines that are appropriate for them'. Remedies were a different subject, and he needed more books and better health in order to deal with it, 'but, God willing, if I live and my order allows it, I promise that I will make a book on that'.[23] The 'herbal', which he sometimes calls 'The Book of Remedies' must be the fulfilment of this promise. It takes the place of a modern pharmacopoeia.

Daniel's 'herbal' is trickier to describe because it is more than a herbal, and it exists in two very different versions: again, his perfectionism and revisionist urges led him to rework his text completely in the interests of clarity. One of the surviving manuscripts, British Library Additional 27,329, offers a lengthy text divided into two sections: the first is an encyclopaedic list of herbs with their medicinal uses, arranged from A to Z; the second is a similar list of trees, but includes as well fungi, oils, minerals, and technical medical terms, also arranged from A to Z. The whole is entitled 'Aaron' (the name of the first herb) after the fashion of herbals. The other manuscript, British Library Arundel 42, offers an untitled text where the two alphabetical series have been merged into one; the individual entries are expanded beyond herbs and simples (single ingredients) and made more detailed, but the work ends at G. Most of the terms that are not simples are technical medical words derived from the *Alphita*,[24] a kind of medical glossary which existed in various forms, the earliest dating from the twelfth century. Daniel took the opportunity, in translating the *Alphita*'s terminology, to disambiguate some Latin words for his English audience: '*glis* is *lappa*, a burr... but than it is *glis, glissis*; and *glis, gliris* is argilla, cley, and *glis, glitis* is a feld mous'.

Much of the text of Daniel's large 'Book of Remedies' is in the form of quotations from a variety of Latin authorities: the *Alphita*, Platearius, Bartholomaeus Anglicus, John Mesue, Macer and Henry of Huntingdon, all carefully translated into English, and properly ascribed (Daniel is rather vexed that he does not know the proper name of one of his sources). But again, it would be a mistake to think that this big book is mere translation. Daniel not only added a number of his own comments and descriptions, but the whole compilation must have required a huge amount of editorial labour: medieval herbals are beset by enormous problems of identification and nomenclature, and it clearly took Daniel more than one try to organize a satisfactory system for presenting his material. In the later version he must have decided on an elaborate index (now no longer extant) comprising all the plant names that were used, which would direct the reader to the one he had chosen for the main entry. Then each individual entry was properly alphabetized, and all the possible alternate names were listed at the beginning. A few entries still have cross references at the end, but, by and large, Daniel seems to have decided on a single main-entry system, and an 'abc' as he calls it, at the end.

In the 'Book of Remedies', when Daniel explains the technical medical terms that he found in the *Alphita*, he often references 'our *Uricrisis*', sometimes even giving the chapter number (all such references are to the revised version with many more, and shorter, chapters (see, for example, Arundel, 'butalmon', Aaron 'calamenta' and 'coloquintida'). This family of references makes plain how one book grew out of the other, and that they were intended to be used together. Even using both together, however, left certain subjects uncovered. So foundational was uroscopy that it constantly pointed in all directions to other areas of medicine which needed to be understood as well. Daniel often found himself tugged off course ('for to speke fully of cretyk days it nedith a book be the self'; S 38v); or, for instance, when he mentions the pulse:

> For to spekyn of powses, it askith a book be the self, and al a doyng be the self. For on [one] craft of lechecraft ther is be demyng of seyghte in a mannys face, another doyng be spatle of mowth, another be powsis, and the ferthe be the egestioun [excrement] of man; and alle I wolde undon in comoun speche, that alle men myghtyn understonden and knowe, if ony man wolde fynde me myn sustenance.[25]

This note suggests that the translation of a treatise on pulses and diagnostic signs never got beyond the planning stage, but throughout his two books Daniel makes a series of references to other works he seems both to have planned and executed. He seems to have written a medical *practica*, a handbook on all the different diseases. The first reference is just a promise: 'of this forsaide maladyes and of al other maladyes that ar toched in thise three bokes, if God gif me lif, and myn ordre me suffre, I shal teche by themself'.[26] In a later revision he writes 'of these soris and siknesse, and of alle that arn towchid in these three bookes, and in alle the siknessis in mannys body that I may fyndyn in phisik, see in owre praptyk'.[27] No trace remains of it now, nor of the work he calls 'our Operarie'; nor is anything now known of his translation of a commentary on the *Antidotary* of Nicholas. The *Antidotary* was a Salernitan text, a primitive pharmacopoeia dating from early in the twelfth century. There were numerous commentaries upon it: Daniel refers to one divided into a prologue and at least eight books containing tracts on medical weights and measures, of tastes and odors, and the making of syrups; the implication is that he translated it himself.[28] At another point he directs his readers to 'the book of medicines laxatives', but we know no more of this, apparently English work, either.[29]

One way Daniel did manage to save himself some labour was to incorporate other short English texts within his larger works. In the herbal, he includes most of his own, probably previously existing, translation of a little tract on the herb rosemary,[30] and an English translation of something called *Borith, or the book of the Sixteen Herbs* (identified by Keiser as the *Book of Secrets* falsely attributed to Albertus Magnus).[31] That translation does not sound like Daniel's own work: perhaps he found it circulating independently. Similarly, the long astrological passage on the fates of men incorporated into the later versions of the *Uricrisis* is not written in Daniel's characteristic style. He must have found it and incorporated it as an appendix to his own digression on astronomical medicine—some of which might too have an extraneous source.

Daniel's herbal fills out our knowledge of his life a little more. In the *Uricrisis* he admitted that he never formally studied uroscopy, but the herbal reveals that he had been deeply interested in herbs all his life. He says when he was younger he had a garden in Stepney (east of London) in which he grew 'twelve score and twelve' (i.e. 252) different kinds of herb.[32] The anecdotes he tells show that he had a variety of experience in the healing arts, mainly in the centre of England: he mentions East Anglia, Stamford, and Lincoln, with forays into Kent and the Bristol region. While in the *Uricrisis* he noted that he had learned uroscopy only from books, in the herbal he mentions a revered teacher and a number of colleagues. He spent seven years learning about herbs, but says nothing at all about his formal schooling; but the quotations from Aristotle's *Metaphysics* and the remark that Latin is the language dearest to him (in the preface to the *Uricrisis*) seem to indicate that he had attended a university. A phrase he uses in reference to the herb-garden he had 'while I might yet maintain me'[33] suggests that he had not always been a friar. The picture that tentatively emerges is of an educated man with decent Latin, bookish, with a genuinely scholarly mind, a little older than Chaucer, who had been an herbalist and healer as a layman, and later in life became a member of the Dominican order. He was well read in formal Latin medicine, but also had long practical experience as a healer, and was wholly dedicated to making his contribution to medicine as clear and comprehensive as he possibly could.

The other main aspect of Daniel that I want to focus on here is the incidental picture of fourteenth-century scientific learning that he offers. The beginning with uroscopy was fortuitous: it was the first diagnostic skill a physician learned, but what shows up in the urine flask was crucial because it provided a picture, perhaps the only picture the medieval practitioner had, of what was going on inside the body of the patient. Uroscopy defined how this was to be interpreted. But since a central tenet of medieval belief was that man was a microcosm of the whole universe, to interpret the 'little world' of man the physician had to understand mankind's place in the entire cosmos.[34] Because man was made out of the same stuff as the rest of the physical universe, almost everything in the universe could be used to heal him; hence a good doctor must understand the nature and behaviour of matter. By studying the urine, the practitioner could theoretically divine the nature and location of the imbalance within the body, and suggest a remedy to counteract it. Since each individual was affected by all the interactions of the elements in his surroundings, these, too, had to be taken into account in diagnosis. Hence the diligent uroscopist would study and inquire about the patient's customary constitution and habits, age, sex, occupation, diet, and dwelling-place; the weather, climate, and season must also be considered. The first part of Daniel's *Uricrisis* explains all of these conditions in great detail, providing the reader with charts of the interlocking combinations of elements in the four seasons of the year, in the ages of man, and in the four main winds and their subsidiary winds—all this as part of the explanation of how the temperament of the patient, the particular combination of the four vital fluids within the body, would be affected by the world around him. This was all standard medical lore, and Daniel clearly felt that one could not practice uroscopy properly without understanding it.

Proper uroscopy then required a detailed knowledge of the processes of digestion, which in turn entailed some understanding of human anatomy. Daniel's knowledge of anatomy was entirely bookish—the dissection of humans did not take place in England until the sixteenth century—but he included what he knew by his characteristic method of structured digression, cross-referenced from other parts of his work. His section on anatomy was heavily derivative on a standard brief Latin text on the four main physical systems in the body: the brain and nerves, the heart and arteries, the liver and veins, and the genitals.[35] Similar digressions dealt with such things as the pulse, the crisis of a sickness, and the various kinds of sputum. The physiology of digestion was covered in Book One with an elaborate account of the functions of the liver, heart and bladder.

Medicine's focus on the matter which composed the human body was supplemented by medieval physics, the theory of movement and life. This necessarily led the physician to turn his attention to the skies, from whence all movement derived. Life is characterized by movement, and maintaining life meant understanding the chain of causation through the physical universe. Particularly relevant to medicine was the idea that the heat of the sun was the source of warmth and life: heat by itself could breed primitive kinds of life in the warm mud of the Nile delta, or, in the inner world of man, generate worms in the guts. The movements of the planets affected all life on earth, and could be co-opted in the cause of healing. We are familiar with Chaucer's superlative Physician, 'grounded in astronomye' who 'kepte his pacient...in houres by his magyk natureel' (I.414–16). Daniel tells his audience how it is done, and his digressive method, like Chaucer's, nicely illustrates the problem of interconnected learning.

Halfway through the *Uricrisis* in his discussion of milky urine, Daniel has occasion to use the term 'erratic' or 'planetary' fever, and explains, with characteristic etymological fervour, why planets are so named: they are 'errant and uncertain', that is, they appear to wander across the sky against the movement of the firmament. They do not really wander, of course: they simply fulfil their natural course, which happens to be contrary to the natural movement of the sky. Daniel continues, 'And for as mikel as I touched of planets, and every wise leech must know somewhat of the planets, understand that there be seven planets...'. and this becomes an enormous, and ever-expanding, digression. In the earlier version he names the seven planets: Moon, Mercury, Venus, Sun, Mars,

Jupiter, and Saturn, and describes the two kinds of movement they show: one eastwards, against the fixed stars, the other westwards, as they are swept along together with everything under the circle of the stars. Then he describes the planets one by one, explaining their qualities, the length of each one's course, the zodiac, when different religions start the day and why, and the way physicians divide the day into four quarters, each dominated by a different humour. He then explains how time is divided up into hours, and ever-smaller fractions called 'points', 'moments', 'uncia' and 'thomos', and how the Sun determines the calendar, the regular course of our year, and how to calculate leap years by dividing the number of the year by four. This is very handy because he includes an example ('*verbi gratia*, we are now in the 1378 year of Christ...') which dates some of his various revisions very precisely, even in manuscripts which have lost their colophon. Here are various mnemonics and charts to enable the reader to understand all these things. After this he moves on to the disposition of the spheres of the four elements— earth at the bottom, then water, air, and fire, and gives Ptolemy's measurements of the distances between all the spheres and the sizes of the planets, working upwards from the Moon to the fixed stars. He concludes with a note on the zodiac, the relationship between the signs and the planets, lists which part of the body each sign controls, and adds an injunction to the physician not to treat any member when the Moon is in that sign. At the end there is a Moon table and a diagram to show which hour of each day is governed by which planet.[36] At the end of all of this astronomy, which has been carefully referenced to Ptolemy's *Almagest*, Daniel acknowledges the digression: 'thogh I have gone out of my waie (i.e. a litil fro my purpos) I thonk God I have not erryd'.[37] Then he plunges back into milk-coloured urine.

The pull of the contiguous subjects grew stronger with the various revisions. The astronomical passage, in particular, received a great deal of attention. Daniel next adds a demurral, 'I spek noght as an astronomer', but goes on to supply brief references to the noise made by the spheres as they rotate, and gives more sources: 'Alphagram, Algazel, and Richard of Seynt Albon'.[38] A scriptural reinforcement of the Christian view that the day begins at midnight is added. There is a lengthy piece on eclipses, the course of the Moon, and two descriptions of the seven 'climes' or regions of the habitable earth, one reckoning by length of day, the other by the domination of the governing planet. The paragraph interpreting the 'wheel of heaven' diagram is greatly expanded. And, at the end of the digression, another very lengthy insertion appears. A couple of manuscripts add some short paragraphs stating the effects of the planets on the physique and personality of people born under their influence: 'Luna disposys man to round face, mene statur, and vile servage' is an example.[39] The manuscripts containing the fullest text,[40] however, add a whole new chapter: 'thes ben the faces and fortunes of hem that ben born uppoun the cours of the Son by all the 12 signes',[41] or, in Latin, 'Here begins the judgement of the nativities of men according to the astrologers'. This material is frankly astrological, and exists independently of Daniel.[42] Since the chapter is included in his revised numerical scheme which is cross-referenced from the herbal, one can only assume that Daniel found this material already in English and decided to copy it into his book as yet more useful material for an aspiring physician. At the end of the digression, Daniel's comment is altered: 'This faculte myn herte desirith for to techin in Englysch, as bookes of Astronomye techith in Latyne; but go we ageyn to our purpos and owre matere'.[43] The manuscript evidence does not make it clear whether 'this faculte' applies to the newly added astrology of this Chapter Thirty-Six, or to the astronomy that preceded it. Perhaps the distinction is meaningless in the fourteenth century (although there is really no medical relevance to the astrological material, and no medical conclusions are drawn). Nonetheless, Daniel, like Chaucer's Physician, felt that the urine flask would not give up its secrets in full to anyone who did not understand the motions of the planets and their relations with one another as well as their rule over the earth.

Not exactly a digression, because signs in the urine by which one could diagnose pregnancy had already appeared in Giles of Corbeil's poem, but still slightly surprising is an elaborate discussion on sex and gender which runs through the *Uricrisis*. The strange behavior of the uterus and the effects on its possessor are discussed early in Book Two; the diagnosis of pregnancy and indications of the sex of the foetus are in Book Three. These fill out the 'theory of life' sketched out in the description of the Sun. Fundamentally, warmth generates life, and the better the warmth, the higher the form of life: babies turn into boys because the conjoined seed of conception lodges itself into the warmer side of the mother's body; the ones on the cooler side turn into girls.[44] Daniel goes into considerable and rather startling detail about the whole process. On a deeper level, it connects with his discussion of 'vital' or 'natural' heat and the causes of death. Warmth and life, movement and change, are all bound up with the heavenly bodies, and in man, the microcosm faithfully mirrors the activity of the macrocosm.

Daniel's closing remark on his biggest digression suggests the seamless nature of the learned medieval world. It was hard to know where to stop: to understand the urine one had to understand the elements and humours; to appreciate how they were affected by the world around them meant grasping the structure of the medieval universe; to treat the maladies diagnosed it was necessary to catalogue all of the physical substances that might be used as remedies. To use the remedies one needed to know a proper system of weights and measures for dosage, and recipes for concocting the various medicines, flavoured wines, and syrups to deliver them. Daniel tried to tackle all these subjects, forging an appropriate language as he went. The uroscopy treatise and the herbal are massive achievements, and they make us regret that we do not have the other works he promised or completed. What we do have is evidence of an achievement unparalleled in England in the medieval period.

It is important to remember that this whole 'scientific' universe was ultimately embedded inside a theological framework. Daniel sounds so modern in his medical scepticism, inquiring mind, careful analysis of terms, and meticulous sourcing of quotations that it comes as a slight shock to find him making casual reference to the 'fact' that the world was created in April, locating the site of Hell and the place of Heaven, using a biblical verse to explain why the day should properly begin at midnight, or employing St Augustine's arcane piece of religious numerology to account for the development of the human embryo.[45] Not only are his physics, chemistry, astronomy, and medicine intimately linked, but they are fitted comfortably into biblical history and theology.[46] Medicine, he tells us, is necessary because of the Fall of Man, which made us all, except for Jesus, physically and morally imperfect. Medicine will not be needed in the future life, but it can help one to live well in the present one. The only aspects of medicine which do not fit with any great neatness into the ideas of medieval Christianity are those which go back, beyond Christianity itself, into the world of Hippocrates and Galen. The Greek idea of harmony and balance, both physical and mental, could not be made to sit easily with Christian asceticism and fervour for all kinds of abstinence. Daniel reveals an almost-Chaucerian tolerance for the demands the frail human body puts upon the soul. Fasting, he notes, is not good for you,[47] nor is 'watching', or doing without sleep. Pregnant women need to be cosseted. Everybody needs sex, especially widows and young girls after puberty.[48] Desire is natural: the warmth of men and the cool of women are naturally drawn to each other;[49] love can be an illness, and is usually sinful, but it can be 'with-outen vice'.[50] Like the Wife of Bath, people are born with pre-existing temperaments and tendencies, and imperfection is wholly inevitable. A healthy environment and sensible diet are necessities of life. True, excess is a menace to health as well as morals, but the answer is temperance, not penance.[51] Although habited as the Friar and learned as the Clerk, Daniel would understand the earthly needs of the other pilgrims far more for-givingly than the Parson.

We know extraordinarily little about Daniel's circle or audience. His books mention various noble ladies and well-born persons he met or knew: he describes how they used various treatments or composed special medicines. He talks about making inquiries of both the learned of the day and the local 'apothecaries and druggers' about the proper meaning of the terms 'diuretic' and 'stiptic'.[52] The learned here are an interesting cat-egory: 'summe that I have had colacion with, and were ryght connyng in many divers sciences, and ek in this faculte haddyn ryght mechil of the speculatyf and ryght mekyl of the praptyk, more than summe that werin letyn and knowyn gret maystres and couthe lechys'. This suggests a group of practitioners who knew medical theory and practice much better than various unnamed famous contemporary academic doctors. He cites the experience of practitioners who were illiterate,[53] learned from converted Jews,[54] and discovered much from one 'who was once my pupil and is now my master'.[55] He knew and helped a lady who made ointments for burns out of camomile,[56] mentions 'lady Sowche' (lady Zouche), a 'gret lady, of wommen the best leche in this lond' and her recipe for nerval,[57] and a 'man of gret gre [rank]' who used plantain for his gout.[58] Some priests reported to him a tale about how an earl's servant used centonica juice to kill a spider.[59] He had met a young man who knew a great deal of medicine but did not practice it for money because he was rich, but would sometimes oblige for charity's sake. At Lincoln he was present at a consultation of 'diverse leches', one of them the king's physician, who happened to be passing though the town, and was called upon to help. He translated his book for a *socius*, a 'felawe', perhaps a fellow physician, who did not read Latin, but must have been literate in English. Some remarks imply that he knew a considerable number of people who fell into this category, such as those he had in mind when he wrote his digression on the planets: 'evory wyse leche must know sumwhat of the planettes'. He sees himself as raising the level of general medical knowledge; when expounding the subtleties of urine that shows the presence of choler, he notes the distinction in levels of learning:

> And that ny every leche can telle, suche lechys as we han in these dayes. But to farun craftily therwith and for to proporsion thys general significacion, that is *dominium coloris* that the body stondyth by, and to alle hys spicys [kinds] and particulers is a ful nobul knowyng and a ful nedful, and that longyth only to [a] wyse leche.[60]

Daniel recognizes 'wise leeches' who cannot read Latin. He is not looking at the learned, clerical world; all his remarks suggest a bustling thoroughfare full of many kinds and conditions of people. He seems to belong with Gower's 'burel clerkes' or Chaucer's knowledgeable citizens, not with the austere doctors and theologians of the Dominican order or the clever men of Oxford. He is the very opposite of the stereotypical pompous medieval academic cleric who despised the herbwife and guarded his subject jealously from the lay and unlearned.

APPENDIX

A NOTE ON THE MANUSCRIPTS
OF HENRY DANIEL

- There is only one manuscript of the Latin text of the *Uricrisis*: Glasgow, MS Hunter 362, fols 1–83v.
- For a list of the English manuscripts, see the article by Hanna. The manuscripts differ greatly in completeness, and the text varies considerably in the different manuscripts. For the purpose of this article I use several to illustrate various points, and employ the following sigla for citations:
- R = London, British Library, MS Royal 17 D i (shorter text; contains the English version of the prologue).
- M = Oxford Bodleian MS e Musaeo 116 (Latin prologue). The text in this manuscript is an early version until about halfway through, then the scribe switched to a different copytext, containing the enlarged, many-chaptered version.
- S = London, British Library, MS Sloane 1101 (enlarged version of the text); supplemented by E = London, British Library, MS Egerton 1624; W = London, Wellcome Historical Medical Library MS 225; and A = Oxford, Bodleian Library MS Ashmole 1404.
- The earliest date given in any manuscript of the English *Uricrisis* is 1377 (M, first half of text); Daniel updated this to 1378 in another (expanded) revision (represented by London, British Library, MS Sloane 1100 and Sloane 1721, among others); two manuscripts of this revision have the Latin prologue translated into English (as R). A more elaborate revision, with different chapter numbering, is contained in the manuscripts A, S, E, and W (among others).
- The last reference for the purpose of dating is to the great earthquake in 1382 (in the Latin verses at the end of M).

NOTES

1. See the appendix to this chapter for information on the manuscripts of Henry Daniel. Unless otherwise noted, all references below are to Henry Daniel's works.

2. Arundel, 49v, 'bisara': 'every gode apothecarye scholde ben gode leche, and no perfit leche nedyth other apothecarye than hymsilve, but eyther of hem is to other servaunt, and under hem bothen to mykyl folk arn deceyuant'.

3. *Uricrisis*, II 38 (S 100v): 'Betwen qwyght and yelwz, as we sen in yonge men that nurschith here longe lokkes, qwiche colour we callin in Latin *flauus*.'

4. Arundel 19r, 'Altea': a kind of mallow found in 'the forest of Rokyngham bytwene Stanford and Cleve'; 23v, 'Amyamia': a low-growing juniper in a heath near Shaftesbury, and another kind in Kent, near Chatham.

5. See *Uricrisis*, II 16 (S 70r–70v) for a dropsical woman attended by a group of physicians; II 38 (E 129v) for the consultation over the sick man at Stamford; see I 18 (S 28v) for the discussion on terminology.

6. Daniel starts his explanation of elements and humours at I 10 (S 15v). Bartholomaeus Anglicus organized his encyclopaedia, *De proprietatibus rerum*, on the principle of the four elements.

7. An account of Daniel and a short excerpt from the *Uricrisis* may be found in Ralph Hanna III, 'Henry Daniel's *Liber uricrisiarum* (excerpt)', in *Popular and Practical Science of Medieval England*, ed. Lister M. Matheson (East Lansing, MI: Colleagues Press, 1994), 185–218; see also Paul Acker, 'Scientific and Medical Writing', in *The Oxford History of Literary Translation in English*, vol. 1 to 1550, ed. Roger Ellis (Oxford: Oxford University Press, 2008), 407–20; George R Keiser, 'Through a Fourteenth-Century Gardener's Eyes: Henry Daniel's Herbal', *Chaucer Review* 31 (1996), 58–75; and the entry by John Harvey in the *Oxford Dictionary of National Biography*. Joanne Jasin's edition of the *Liber uricrisiarum* is an unpublished dissertation; see bibliography.

8. The only known copy of it is in the Hunterian Library at Glasgow, MS Hunter 362, 1–83v.

9. Rossell Hope Robbins, 'Medieval Manuscripts in Middle English', *Speculum* 45 (1970), 399, remarks that Daniel's work 'is actually a translation of the *De Urinis* of Isaac Judaeus', repeated by C. H. Talbot, *The Medical Practitioners of Medieval England: A Biographical Register*, NS vol. 8 (London: Publications of the Wellcome Historical Medical Library, 1965), 79 and others as recently as 2009 (e.g. the article by Acker cited above). The 1379 date of death was proposed by Hanna (see above), and is also repeated by Acker.

10. For the surname 'ferour' see Gustav Fransson, *Middle English Surnames of Occupation*, 1000–1350, Lund Studies in English III (Lund: Gleerup, 1935); this error was also noted by Keiser, 'Henry Daniel's Herbal'.

11. Preface: R 4r; *Pulcra sit scientia et mirabilis*, A 3v.

12. R 4r; A 3r: *quia nec hanc scientiam in anglico traditam memini me legisse sed neque audisse*.

13. A 3r: *Tum quia huius lingue, licet in ea natus, neque gnarus neque disertus*; A 4r (variants from Huntington 505): *Collegi nuper…pro hiis qui capere sciunt [in latino] tractatum breuem huius facultatis medullam plenius continentem [et scripsi in] lingua utique mihi cara*.

14. M 65v: *Nec mireris, o lector, si invenires me ponere terminos quandoque latinas et quandoque prope latinum, quod facio magis brevitatis causa* (this sentence does not appear in the English version).

15. M 65v: *Quapropter etiam exposito uno termino pro quanto michi occurrerit non iterum expono eundem* (this sentence does not appear in the English version).

16. S 72r.

17. S 42r.

18. R 5r; A 4r: *nam pro omni ydeomate anglice lingue apud donum linguarum habentem vere atque perfecte ars orthografie in hoc libro docetur.*

19. S 138r; Aaron, 103r, 'isopus', 84v, 'erbus'; see the long discussion on the etymology and proper meaning of the terms 'diuretic' and 'stiptic' in *Uricrisis* I 14 (S 28v).

20. The dropsical woman is *Uricrisis* II 16 (S70r–70v). The man of Stamford is II 38 (E 129v). The *mola matricis*, to which Daniel gives the English names 'the wunder gubbe or gobet, the wunderlumpe', 'the elvysch kechil' or 'the elvysch cake' is II 14 (S 64v–65r, 67r).

21. *Uricrisis*, II 19 (S 73v); *Uricrisis*, II 12 (S 56r–56v).

22. Arundel, 34r, 'Argentilla': 'bongelers and smaterers in erberye callen it water betoyne, but it is in no poynt lik water betoyne'.

23. R 4v, 'Ne wonder noght eny man if I sewe noght medicynes perteynyng to the sekenes and the infirmites tochede in this boke, ffor God helping and the obedience of myn ordre noght agaynstanding, I bihete me forto make a werk by itself therto'.

24. The textual tradition of this work is very confused. An early version is printed in Salvatore de Renzi, *Collectio Salernitana* (Napoli: Tipografia del Filiatre-Sebezio, 1852–59), 3.272–322; and a fifteenth-century one by J. I. G. Mowat, *Alphita: A Medico-Botanical Glossary* (Oxford: Clarendon Press, 1887). Neither of these texts is close to the one Daniel is using.

25. S 41v.

26. *Uricrisis* II 13 (R 82v); I 8 (S 11r): promises a work of medicines, 'if God gif lif'.

27. *Uricrisis*, I 5 (S 8v).

28. Arundel, 50v', bistorta'; Aaron, 32r, 'bistorta'; 33r, 'borage'; Arundel, 52r, 'brasica'; Aaron, 67r, 'coloquintida', Aaron, 171r, 'castorium', 183v, 'diagridium', 189v, 'exagium'.

29. Aaron, 163v, 'boletus'. In Aaron, 5r, 'absinthium' he says 'se in our table'; in 7r, 'acus muscata', and 8v, 'agresta lactuca', 'se in our herbarie'.

30. Aaron, 16v, 'Anthus'; he says the queen's mother sent her the Latin copy of this booklet. In Arundel, 91v, he says he acquired one of his herbs from Queen Philippa's garden.

31. Aaron, 47r, 'caniculata'. In Arundel this section is moved to the end of the main text, 99r.

32. References to his garden are in Arundel, 28r', anemicon'; 80v, 'erbus', 81v, 'esula', 91v, 'garofilus'.

33. Arundel, 28r, 'anemicon'.

34. Daniel speaks of the correspondence of macrocosm and microcosm in *Uricrisis*, I 10 (A 18v).

35. He calls this text 'Galen's Book of Anatomies' (S 33r); see Joanne Jasin, 'The Transmission of Learned Medical Literature in the Middle English "*Liber uricrisiarum*"', *Medical History* 37 (July, 1993), 322.

36. In the shorter version, this is *Uricrisis* II 6 (R 44v–51v).

37. R 51v.

38. A 76v.

39. *Uricrisis* II 34 (A 87r).

40. These would be Sloane 1101, Ashmole 1404, Egerton 1624, Wellcome 225, and Gonville & Caius 376 [596]; but Sloane has a large number of pages missing; Ashmole is lacking a couple of leaves, and Wellcome breaks off just before the astrological chapter.

41. A88v.

42. It is *Uricrisis*, II 36 (A 88v); partly present in S, which has some preceding pages missing (S 85r–99r); a version of the same material is also in Sloane 3124 and Sloane 3285.

43. A 99r.
44. *Uricrisis*, II 14 (Sl 62r–62v).
45. For the location of Hell, see *Uricrisis*, A 85v, of Heaven, A 86v; Augustine, S 63r.
46. Daniel contrasts the differing views of 'divinite' and 'phisyck' on minor matters, such as the ages of man: *Uricrisis*, I 10 (A 8r–18v).
47. *Uricrisis*, I 14 (S 26r–26v): 'The fastyng and abstinence of Cristene folk schul be fastyng and abstinence fro vicis of wikke levyng, and in goode dedis doyng, and susteynyng the [lyf] to the honour of owre Creatour'.
48. *Uricrisis* II 14 (S 65v–66r).
49. *Uricrisis*, I 10 (S 16r–16v).
50. *Uricrisis* I 14 (S 25v): the passage is a little confused.
51. *Uricrisis*, I 12 (S 21v): 'for in al maner thing and doyng kynde lovith mene and hatyth exces'; repeated at I 14 (S 27r).
52. S 28v.
53. Notably Master Giles of Stafford, S 20v, 'that never knew lettre, yit he dede many grete dedis. Among Sarzinis he seyde he lerid'; perhaps the same as the 'Cristene man that longe haved woned amonge Saracenus and Juys' in Arundel 26v' 'anagalla' and 37r, 'athanasia'.
54. Arundel, 18v, 'allogallica', Aaron, 95v, 'genciana', 108v, 'lunaria'.
55. Arundel, 31v, 'apiaria' mentions a wise master who taught him about borage; 10v, 'adactis' a 'worthy leche' he once assisted; 11r 'adarasta' the one 'that was my disciple and now is my mayster' who was a rare expert on hellebore.
56. Arundel, 21r, 'amaruscus', Aaron, 55v, 'celifolia'; described more fully in Arundel, 66r, 'cerfolius' as a 'gode womman, a deynte lyvere' whom Daniel witnessed curing inflammations with a dressing of chervil and egg.
57. Aaron, 81v' 'epatica', Arundel, 22r, 'ambrosia'.
58. Aaron, 20v' 'arnoglossa'.
59. Aaron, 57r, 'centonica'.
60. *Uricrisis*, II 41, quoted here from M, 110v.

BIBLIOGRAPHY

Conrad, Lawrence I., Michael Neve, et al., eds., *The Western Medical Tradition 800 BC to AD 1800* (Cambridge: Cambridge University Press, 1995).

Daniel, Henry, *Liber Uricrisiarum*, edited by E. Ruth Harvey, M. Teresa Tavormina, Sarah Star, Jessica Henderson, and C. E. M. Henderson (Toronto: University of Toronto Press, forthcoming).

Harvey, John, *Medieval Gardens* (London: Batsford, 1990).

Jacquart, Danielle and Claude Thomasset, *Sexuality and Medicine in the Middle Ages*, trans. Matthew Adamson (Princeton, NJ: Princeton University Press, 1988).

Jones, Peter Murray, *Medieval Medicine in Illuminated Manuscripts* (London: The British Library, 1984).

Matheson, Lister M., ed., *Popular and Practical Science of Medieval England* (East Lansing, MI: Colleagues Press, 1994).

Rawcliffe, Carole, *Medicine and Society in Later Medieval England* (Stroud: Alan Sutton, 1995).

Siraisi, Nancy G., *Medieval and Early Renaissance Medicine* (London and Chicago, IL: University of Chicago Press, 1990).

Wallis, Faith and Paul Dutton, *Medieval Medicine: A Reader* (Toronto: University of Toronto Press, 2010).

CHAPTER 25

LOGIC AND MATHEMATICS

The Oxford Calculators

EDITH DUDLEY SYLLA

CHAUCER has long had the reputation of being a philosophical poet. His translation of Boethius's *On the Consolation of Philosophy* provides as much evidence as anyone might want of his philosophical predilections. Other scholars have studied the relation of Chaucer to Oxford and Cambridge universities in general.[1] The topic for this contribution is, however, not his engagement with philosophy in general, but the possible appearance in his work of ideas coming from the 'Oxford Calculators'—a group of logicians, mathematicians, and natural philosophers who were active at Oxford primarily in the period 1320–50.[2] The most typical Oxford Calculator was William Heytesbury, who, among other works, composed *Rules for Solving Sophismata* (*Regule solvendi sophismata*, 1335) and *Sophismata*. Heytesbury's 'rules' primarily derived from the *logica moderna*, but also included tools coming from mathematics, in particular from Thomas Bradwardine's *On the proportions of velocities in motions* (*De proportionibus velocitatum in motibus*, 1328).[3] In addition to Heytesbury and Bradwardine, the name 'Oxford Calculators' refers primarily to Walter Burley, Richard Kilvington, Roger Swineshead, Richard Swineshead, and John Dumbleton. I have chosen the name 'Oxford Calculators' over the name 'Merton school' used elsewhere for the group surrounding Heytesbury and Bradwardine because the main individuals involved were not all affiliated with Merton College, but all were affiliated with Oxford University.

Several recent publications have linked Chaucer to one or the other of the Oxford Calculators or to a more amorphous group called 'nominalists'.[4] If nominalism is taken to be primarily ontological minimalism, namely the view that many nouns correspond to mental concepts and not to something existing in the external world, then William Heytesbury was a nominalist, and probably so too were John Dumbleton and Richard Swineshead. As nominalists, these core Oxford Calculators fall into a natural group including also contemporary philosophers active at the University of Paris including

John Buridan, Albert of Saxony, Nicole Oresme, and Marsilius of Inghen. At the source of this fourteenth-century resurgence of nominalism was William of Ockham, famous for the maxim that one should not multiply entities beyond necessity.

In the fourteenth century, there was no single label applied to this collection of Oxford and Paris philosophers. In the fifteenth and sixteenth centuries, when a clash developed between the heirs of these thinkers and the heirs of the leading thirteenth-century philosophers such as Albertus Magnus, Thomas Aquinas, and Aegidius Romanus, the thirteenth-century thinkers were called '*antiqui*' and the fourteenth-century thinkers were called '*moderni*'.[5] I have chosen here to call the fourteenth-century thinkers at issue *moderni*, rather than by any other label that has been applied to them (e.g. 'nominalists', 'Ockhamists'), because *moderni* has fewer problems than the other choices and because this is a natural grouping for which one wants to have some label. Richard Utz calls them 'nominalists', but the characteristics of 'nominalists' that he lists, quoting Armand Mauer, go far beyond the meaning of 'nominalism' as opposed to 'realism' in logic.[6] Against the label 'Ockhamist', William Courtenay has argued that there was no Ockhamist school at Oxford or Paris in the fourteenth century.[7] The *moderni* were not skeptics.[8] And so forth for other possible labels or characterizations. A more accurate label would be 'progressive', while the fifteenth- and sixteenth-century thinkers who returned to the approaches of the thirteenth century were 'conservative', but previous historians have not used these words.

In proposing to describe the characteristics of the Oxford Calculators insofar as Chaucer might have picked up some of their ideas, then, I will describe their work both in itself and insofar as they were *moderni* in the sense just described, sharing the approaches of William of Ockham and of the Parisians John Buridan, Albert of Saxony, Nicole Oresme, et al.[9] I will also mention theological issues, partly because in the work of John Wyclif, the most important successor to the Calculators at Oxford, theological issues become dominant. Among the *moderni*, many were voluntarists rather than intellectualists. They argued that God freely creates the world. God could, by his absolute power (*de potentia Dei absoluta*) break the laws of the natural world that he has established by his ordained power (*de potentia Dei ordinata*). They were also concerned to explain how God's omniscience and providence are compatible with human free will. Even if some *moderni*, like Ockham, were both nominalists and voluntarists, the doctrines of nominalism and voluntarism are distinct.[10]

THE IDEAS AND METHODS OF THE OXFORD CALCULATORS, NARROWLY AND BROADLY CONSTRUED

The heart of the work of the Oxford Calculators involved preparing undergraduate students in the Faculty of Arts to participate in disputations, particularly disputations on what were called 'sophismata' or sophisms. A good introduction to sophismata is the modern edition, translation, and commentary on the *Sophismata* of Richard Kilvington.[11] *Sophismata* could concern all the disciplines of the university. A 'sophism sentence' was an apparently puzzling proposition, such as 'All the apostles are twelve', 'Infinite are the finite' (*Infinita sunt finita*), or 'Socrates is whiter than Plato begins to be white' (the last is the first sophism in Kilvington's collection). For each sophism sentence, there was a 'case' set out in terms of which the truth or falsity of the sophism sentence could be argued. The tools for solving sophismata (Heytesbury's 'rules' or what John Murdoch has called 'analytical languages'[12]) were logical more than anything else, but to these logical tools were added methods of measure, of ratios and proportions, and discussions of continuity and infinity, as found in the work of Thomas Bradwardine and later in the *Book of Calculations* (*Liber calculationum*) of Richard Swineshead, later called 'the Calculator'.

In the mid-fourteenth century, Oxford University became famous all over Europe for the rigour of its undergraduate studies starting with the discipline of logic. A key feature of the *logica anglicana* (basically, the *logica moderna*) was the analysis of the truth or falsity of propositions by paying attention to the supposition (*suppositio*) of their categorematic terms (terms referring to things in one of Aristotle's categories) as influenced by so-called 'syncategorematic' terms (terms such as 'all' or 'some' not falling into a category) and word order. Curtis Wilson provides an excellent summary of this approach in his study of Heytesbury's *Rules*.[13] If necessary, propositions of ordinary speech (in Latin, of course), were 'expounded' into propositions spelling out the meaning of the original proposition in formal syntax. In a proposition such as 'Socrates begins (*incipit*) to be white' the word 'begins' was said to require exposition because it refers, implicitly, to two times, the time before Socrates is white and the time when he is white. To determine its truth, the original proposition was therefore expounded, saying that it is equivalent to the compound proposition 'Socrates is now white and immediately before this Socrates was not white'.[14] In the propositions produced by the expositions, the supposition of categorematic terms depended on their place in the proposition. If a syncategorematic term like 'infinite' appeared at the beginning of a proposition it led to one kind of supposition (called 'merely confused') for terms that followed, but if it appeared later in the proposition, it led to a different supposition (called 'determinate'). From this perspective, the proposition 'Infinitely divisible is a continuum' is true, and means that no matter how many times a continuum has been divided, it can be divided still further, whereas the proposition 'A continuum is infinitely divisible' is false, because it means that a continuum can be divided an actually infinite number of times (resulting in an actual infinite).[15] The decision to adopt a technically correct interpretation of a proposition based on its syntax even though this meant that one had to concede that some propositions, for instance those in the Bible, are false by virtue of their form (*de virtute sermonis*), although true as their authors intended them, led many later scholars, including John Wyclif, to reject this approach.

In preparing for and participating in disputations on sophismata, students would learn the rules for dealing not only with such terms as 'begins', 'ceases' and 'infinite', but also with such words as 'to know', 'to doubt', and with 'measure languages' by which one measured velocities of local motion, alteration (*intensionem et remissionem*), or augmentation and diminution, or determined the *maxima* and *minima* of force and resistance or the intensity of light, and so forth. In such contexts, the technical term 'latitude' (*latitudo*) was widely employed to mean an extension, interval, or distance not in space, but in a qualitative form such as love or heat.[16]

When, after rigorous training in logic and in solving sophismata using such analytical languages, students went on to study theology and to comment on Peter Lombard's *Book of Sentences*, they often applied these logical and calculatory tools to theological subjects. For example, in Christian theology God's decision that Mary should be without sin was thought to take effect immediately after her conception, so the question was debated whether there was a first instant of Mary's existence in which she might have sinned before God's action to preserve her sinlessness: how could this be so if all actions take time?[17] There was practically no theological topic to which logical and calculatory methods were not applied—including questions of the place and motion of angels, although as far as anyone has discovered they did not dispute how many angels can dance on the head of a pin.[18]

Oxford logic and the work of the Oxford Calculators was widely emulated on the Continent in the later fourteenth century, first in Paris, and later in Italy, Spain, and the new universities of Eastern Europe.[19] At Paris, Albert of Saxony and Nicole Oresme wrote works *De proportionibus* patterned on Bradwardine's work, and Oresme extended discussions of the latitudes of forms in significant ways. British students went to Paris to study theology, and Continental students later studied in England. The analytical languages and other methods applied in resolving sophismata became popular all over Europe.[20]

As *moderni* the Oxford Calculators like the fourteenth-century Parisians tended to hold the following views, traces of which may be found in Chaucer's writings:

1. There are separate scientific disciplines, each having its own principles from which it demonstrates conclusions. In some disciplines some principles are known a priori in themselves, such as the principle of the excluded middle in logic or the principle that equals added to equals produce equals in mathematics. In other disciplines, however, the principles are learned by experience, such as the principle in astronomy that the stars are contained in an aether sphere which rotates east to west in approximately a day. Or the principle that the moon is eclipsed when it is on the ecliptic (the apparent path of the sun through the stars) a hundred and eighty degrees away from the sun. From experience, one may learn reliably *that* (*quia*) the moon is eclipsed. Once one has a complete discipline of astronomy with principles and conclusions proved on their basis, one can show *why* (*propter quid*) an eclipse occurs. In other words one can show theoretically the cause of the effect known by experience. Because scientific disciplines are organized structures of propositions connected by deduction, it is important to understand clearly the rules of logical and mathematical deduction. Scientific disciplines exist as habits in the minds of experts in those sciences. To develop scientific expertise, repeated practice is important. One can establish new scientific habits by sense, memory, and experience, and by learning to make demonstrations linking principles to conclusions. Once a science has been established, one can learn it from a teacher

or a book. This complex of ideas comes to mind when the word 'demonstracioun' appears in Chaucer.[21]

2. Humans have gone a long way to establishing sciences and there is much to be proud of, but many sciences are still works in progress. For instance, it is known that the stars move slowly in relation to the celestial equator and ecliptic (i.e. there is precession of the equinoxes), but this motion is so slow (and may accelerate or decelerate over time) that it will take centuries more of observation and record keeping to judge its speed precisely. It is worth reading old books to build upon what has already been accomplished. This value of old books is found, for instance, in the *Parliament of Fowls* ('out of olde bokes, in good feyth, Cometh al this newe science that men lere' [24–25]).

3. God has established the order of the cosmos according to his ordained power (*de potentia Dei ordinata*) and the sciences concern this order, but God has absolute freedom. God could have established the cosmos differently and God could, even now by his absolute power (*de potentia Dei absoluta*), violate the laws of nature that have been observed and confirmed. God can do anything that is not a logical contradiction. So God could annihilate everything inside the sphere of the moon even though naturally there are no vacua in the universe. One may consider *secundum imaginationem* that God has done such a thing and then consider what follows. The use of 'ymaginacioun' in Chaucer may sometimes reflect this connection.

In light of views such as these, it emerges why the *moderni* in general and the Oxford Calculators in particular thought that training students in disputation was important. They were not being trained to use rhetorical methods of persuasion, but rather rational, logical, and mathematical methods of demonstration.[22] In connection with the Oxford disputations on what were called obligations (*obligationes*), sophismata, insolubles (*insolubilia*), and so forth, students were taught valid and invalid forms of demonstration or proof, read the work of earlier masters and students on the same problems, and practiced argument until critical habits of thought became ingrained. In many of these disputations, one started from a 'case' or with something posited as the case, and disputed while keeping the case in mind. The cases could be imaginary, fictitious, or based on supposing that such and such is the case. Quantification or 'the near frenzy to measure' has often been connected with the Oxford Calculators.[23] I suggest that reasoning about cases supposed for the sake of investigation is also typical.

The relation of Chaucer to the Oxford Calculators

In what follows I will discuss some cases in the works of Chaucer in which I (or previous scholars) detect ideas or approaches typical of the Oxford Calculators or of the larger group of fourteenth-century *moderni*. Of course, a similarity or resonance between

Chaucer and the Calculators does not mean that Chaucer picked up what he wrote from the Calculators. Some features of the Aristotelian cosmos had, by the late fourteenth century, been taught to so many generations of students and been incorporated into so many books, such as Boethius's *On the Consolation of Philosophy*, one might suppose that Chaucer would have learned about them as a school boy if not before. Some of the cases I will discuss have been explained differently by previous scholars, and I do not claim to be able to prove that my analysis is the only right one. John North compares the situation of trying to find connections within Chaucer's works to something outside to the problem of induction. One can propose different possible causes of a given effect (in this case, why Chaucer included particular themes or ideas in his writing), without being able to determine which of the causes is the real or most important one.[24] For example, where North uses astronomy to explicate the Franklin's Tale, I see a role for the nominalist argument that from the impossible anything follows. Dorigen believes that it is impossible for Aurelius to remove the rocks, so she believes that she will never have to fulfil her promise.[25]

There is no compelling evidence that Chaucer ever studied at Oxford, although his son became a student about 1390.[26] What is known about Chaucer's education suggests that, from around 1350 when he was seven years old, he likely studied at the Almonry School of St. Paul's Cathedral, where he may have been taught by William Ravenstone. Ravenstone later left a fairly considerable collection of books to the school.[27] What is notable about Ravenstone's books is that, while he had many books on grammar, language, and literature, he seems not to have been interested in the discipline of logic.[28] Later in life, Chaucer may have studied at the Inns of Court, where one of the central methods of study involved consideration of 'cases' and what ought to be decided about them.[29] If this is so, Chaucer's familiarity with methods and ideas to be found at Oxford or other universities might be explained by his education at St. Paul's and at the Inns of Court, or it might be explained by wide reading, the hearing of sermons, and conversation with university graduates as an adult.

The single individual most frequently cited as possibly linking Chaucer, assuming he had not been a university student himself, to known activity at Oxford is Ralph Strode, whose writings on logic are extant and to whom Chaucer dedicated, together with Gower, his *Troilus and Criseyde*.[30] A. B. Emden reports that after his move to London, Strode maintained his connection to Merton College.[31] In 1374, Strode appeared with John Wyclif as surety for the appearance at trial of a former Merton contemporary. The evidence linking Chaucer and Strode dates from after 1373, when both Chaucer and Strode lived and worked in London, Chaucer as Controller of Customs, and Strode as common pleader of the City of London.

Scholars have labelled Strode a Thomist and moderate realist, but this is apparently a hold-over from the now-rejected view that he was a Dominican.[32] Recent scholarly work on Strode's logic tends to group him with earlier Oxford logicians adopting the approach of the *logica moderna*.[33] There is an extant work by John Wyclif entitled *Responsiones ad argumenta Radulphi Strodi*, in which Wyclif says he is someone that Strode knew at school, and another work by Wyclif entitled *Responsio ad decem questiones magistri Ricardi Strode*. Strode's arguments and questions to which John Wyclif responded are not extant except for their quotation in Wyclif's work, but their topics are theological not logical. If Chaucer and Strode spoke in London about matters academic, it seems much more likely that—supported by the evidence coming from Wyclif—they would have spoken about theology, rather than logic.

For example, in the *Responsiones ad argumenta Radulfi Strode*, Strode's first argument is that 'If the Catholic church were the whole number of the predestined, and continually through the process of time that number were renewed, it follows that the Church would be continually renewed and thus in the articles of faith certitude would perish on account of the incertitude of the believed truth'.[34] Here Wyclif is making the kind of argument that would be expected of someone who had studied the *logica moderna* or the analytical languages of the Calculators, but Johann Loserth, the editor of this work, thinks it must date to later in Wyclif's career (after 1378) when he was more clearly challenging the institutional church.

Although the current state of knowledge about Ralph Strode is not sufficient to make his work an independent source of evidence about the relations of Chaucer to what went on in Oxford University, the case is different for John Wyclif, who was quite influential at Oxford in the 1370s. In logic and natural philosophy, Wyclif was a realist and an atomist.[35] In theology, Wyclif questioned transubstantiation of the Eucharist and the dominion and wealth of the Church. If Chaucer was cognizant of activities going on at Oxford after 1370, then one might expect to find traces of controversies started by Wyclif and his followers—who, as a matter of fact, made a conscious effort to spread their views to the laity outside of academic circles.[36] The evidence available so far indicates that Wyclif was much more influential because of his views of the church and of theology, than he was influential because of his realism or atomism.

So there may well be traces of Wyclif's ideas in Chaucer, as well as traces of the Oxford Calculators. Ironically, there is less extant evidence to link what happened at Oxford between 1350 and 1400 to the trends started by the Oxford Calculators before 1350 than there is evidence to link the Oxford Calculators to what went on at Continental universities in the later period.[37] Can we discover how long the methods of the Oxford Calculators were influential at Oxford, and when they might have been modified or replaced by Wycliffite methods and ideas? Of all the Oxford logicians and calculators, William Heytesbury seems to have worked longest at Oxford. A.B. Emden reports that Heytesbury was Chancellor of the University before 1363 and again in 1371, and that he died in December. 1372 or early 1373.[38] It is well known that Heytesbury's works were frequently, printed, read, and commented upon in Italy in the fifteenth century, but what of the continuing influence of Heytesbury's work in England in the late fourteenth century? A potential source of information is the work of Paul of Venice, a member of the Augustinian order, who, after having studied at Padua, studied at Oxford for three years beginning in 1390.[39] In his many publications one can see that he knew the logical work of Heytesbury, but followed the realism of John Wyclif rather than the nominalism of Heytesbury. It would appear that in Paul's mind, accepting some of the ideas of Wyclif did not mean rejecting the approaches of the Oxford Calculators.

Although the Oxford Calculators were famous within their academic context for their frenzy to measure, they were not the only advocates of quantification in their time.[40] All quantification to be found in Chaucer's writings need not be a reflection of the Oxford Calculators. In the Shipman's Tale, for instance, the time the merchant spends in his counting house reckoning his profit and loss is emphasized (VII.74–88). In his employment Chaucer had a great deal to do with quantification, reckoning, or calculation—in the *House of Fame* it is said of him as a character, 'And hast mad alle thy rekenynges' (653)—and this was not mathematics that came from university learning but from commercial arithmetic and reckoning books.

There is only one place in which Chaucer names any one of the Oxford Calculators, and that is Thomas Bradwardine. In the Nun's Priest's Tale, Chaucer refers to issues of predestination and free will:

> But what that God forwoot moot nedes bee,
> After the opinioun of certein clerkis.
> Witnesse on hym that any parfit clerk is,
> That in scole is greet altercacioun
> In this mateere, and greet disputisoun,
> And hath been of an hundred thousand men.
> But I ne kan nat bulte it to the bren
> As kan the hooly doctour Augustyn,
> Or Boece, or the Bisshop Bradwardyn,
> Wheither that Goddes worthy forwityng
> Streyneth me nedely for to doon a thyng –
> 'Nedely' clepe I symple necessitee –
> Or elles, if free choys be graunted me
> To do that same thyng, or do it noght,
> Though God forwoot it er that I was wroght;
> Or if his wityng streyneth never a deel
> But by necessitee condicioneel.   (VII. 3234–50)

In this passage, Chaucer shows more detailed knowledge about academic issues than anywhere else in his work. He had heard of arguments about the consistency or inconsistency between God's foreknowledge or providence and human free will, and even about 'conditional necessity'. Of course, Chaucer is citing Bradwardine as a theologian and not as a participant in the exercises of the Oxford Calculators, but the exercises of the Calculators were not entirely irrelevant to these abstruse theological arguments.

In the conception of science shared by the *moderni*, where each scientific discipline has principles on the basis of which it proves conclusions, one might assert that a conclusion is necessary *if* the principles of the science are true. This might be one kind of 'conditional necessity'. With respect to future contingents, one might say that *if* God knows that something will happen, then it will happen. This might be thought of as another kind of conditional necessity, except that God, in the medieval conception, is not in time.

Even for humans there could be multiple levels of knowledge and doubt. One might know something, and yet not know that one knows it. Consider Gaetano of Thiene's commentary on Heytesbury's 'To know and to doubt' (*De scire et dubitare*), one of the sections of Heytesbury's *Rules for Solving Sophismata*. The preceding discussion has concerned whether you could doubt the proposition 'Socrates is running' when you see in front of you Socrates running. Perhaps you believe the person you see running is Plato rather than Socrates, and so forth.

Gaetano then turns to an example from Aristotle's *Posterior Analytics*, Book One. The question is whether it is possible for someone to doubt whether he knows that such and such is the case. For the affirmative he argues, on the authority of Aristotle, that it is possible that the first person who demonstrated that an eclipse of the moon is caused by the interposition of the earth between the sun and the moon could doubt whether his proof was sufficient, and therefore he could doubt whether he knows how to demonstrate that the moon is eclipsed.[41] So here Gaetano is considering not knowledge that something is the case based on observation or intuitive cognition, but knowledge that something is the case because it follows from having a scientific demonstration that it is the case.

Do Chaucer's works reflect such a propensity to use demonstrative reasoning? Beyond Bradwardine's name, what jumps out from Chaucer's work that might link it to Oxford Calculators? Most obvious is what is said to the Clerk in the prologue to his tale, 'I trowe ye studie aboute som sophyme' (IV. 5). This clearly refers to the type of sophisms disputed by Oxford students. The remark is matter-of-fact and without any obvious satire. A more important trace of the Oxford Calculators occurs in the Reeve's Tale, where the miller within the tale connects Cambridge students (but there is nothing to indicate that they would differ from Oxford students) to disputations concerning quantity. When the students seek to spend the night at the miller's house, the miller says something that presumably reflects what a miller might associate with students:

> The millere seyde agayn, 'If ther be eny,
> Swich as it is, yet shal ye have youre part.
> Myn hous is streit, but ye han lerned art;
> Ye konne by argumentes make a place
> A myle brood of twenty foot of space.
> Lat se now if this place may suffise,
> Or make it rowm with spech, as is youre gise'.   (I. 4120–6)

William Woods connected this text to a passage in which Albert of Saxony discusses what God could put inside the smallest empty space.[42] But the text cited by Woods does not involve 'mak[ing] room with speech', as the miller says. It is much more likely that the miller has in mind the sorts of cases that students proposed when arguing about sophismata.

In his questions on Aristotle's *De generatione et corruptione*, for instance, Richard Kilvington asks whether a continuum is divisible *in infinitum*.[43] If it were, he says, then a column or cylinder could be divided into proportional parts and a line could be wound around it one whole turn for each proportional part. It follows that the line will be infinite.[44] In this way, with words, Kilvington has imagined an infinite line within a finite space, as the miller says the students have been taught how to do with words. Many other similar examples can be found in the works of the Calculators. The linking of students to having learned an art by which they might make room with speech is clearer evidence that Chaucer knew the sorts of things that the Oxford Calculators did than the simple use of the word 'sophism' or related words.

The longest passage in the *Canterbury Tales* that has been described as reflecting the ideas of the Oxford Calculators occurs at the end of the Summoner's Tale. Glending Olson has argued in detail that what happens there reflects the measure languages of the Oxford Calculators. The resolution of the friar's complaint that he has been made to promise that he will divide equally what has been given him—which turns out to be a fart—does indeed use language 'loaded with academic, particularly logical/mathematical meaning.'[45] The squire, standing nearby carving the meat, suggests that the fart can be divided equally with the aid of a cartwheel, putting a friar at the end of each spoke. And he says that he has a demonstrative proof ('By preeve which that is demonstratif' [III. 2272]) that the sound and the smell of the fart will be equally divided. The lord, the lady, and everyone but the friar say that the squire has spoken as well as Euclid or Ptolemy, and that Thomas, the man who set the conditions for the friar, spoke subtly and with high wit (2243–92).

The division of a quantity into equal or unequal parts (often proportional parts) was indeed a problem that occurred in the work of the Oxford Calculators. Does the reference at the end to Euclid and Ptolemy indicate a university context? Also typical of the scholastic context (and of the Oxford Calculators in particular) is the claim to solve a problem by laying out a technical approach through which the solution emerges. In the context of the Summoner's Tale, however, the person offering a solution is not a cleric, but the lord's squire. Moreover, the problem is not really that the friar and the others at the meal could not think of a way of dividing the fart equally, but that the friar has been insulted by having been encouraged to put his hand down the backside of Thomas, where he was led to believe that he would find something valuable. Not only is the friar made fun of by this supposed solution to his problem of dividing the fart equally, but he is further ridiculed by saying that he should be at the centre of the wheel and receive more of the fart because he is more worthy than the other monks in his convent. The main point of the story is not that it is possible to divide a fart equally, but that, thanks to Thomas, the friar has gotten his just comeuppance for his greed, venality, and hypocrisy—though the lord and the others at his table do not seem to come to this conclusion. In this sense, the story reflects far more Wyclif's critique of the friars' materialism and accumulation of wealth, than it does the academic exercises common to the arts faculties of universities in general or of the Oxford Calculators in particular.[46]

As compared to Boethius, to the *antiqui*, and to John Wyclif, the Oxford Calculators are much more to be associated with technical language and methods such as the analytical languages found in Heytesbury's *Rules for Solving Sophisms*.[47] It is not surprising, then, that it is easier to see traces of their work in the *Canterbury Tales*, where such academic methods can be associated with someone who is supposed to have studied at a university. But even in a work like the *Canterbury Tales*, the technical work of the Oxford Calculators did not translate easily into the vernacular: one does not find that Chaucer is familiar with the analytical languages. In particular, the term '*latitudo*', perhaps the technical term most specific to the Calculators, is not found in the concordance to Chaucer either as a cognate or translated into an English word such as 'breadth'. Like his probable teacher Ravenstone, Chaucer does not seem particularly interested in technical and logical disputations. In sum, I do not believe that Chaucer even in the *Canterbury Tales* reveals much knowledge of or interest in the details of the most distinctive methods and doctrines of the Oxford Calculators, that is in the analytical languages, the sophisticated use of the *logica moderna*, and the combination of mathematical with logical techniques.

All the less would one expect to find traces of the Oxford Calculators in Chaucer's dream visions, but I think one finds there the sunnier and more optimistic attitude toward the possibility of science that one finds in the Oxford Calculators, as compared to the later, more pessimistic view of John Wyclif. Passages in the *House of Fame* that might be thought to reflect calculatory ideas in fact reflect earlier texts. The Goddess Fame is supposed to change her shape, sometimes appearing smaller and sometimes larger (1364–76). But this idea of varying size and shape is already found in *The Consolation of Philosophy* in the description of Lady Philosophy.[48] Elsewhere in the *House of Fame* there are passages that echo either the standard Aristotelianism of Boethius or Aristotelianism of the twelfth or thirteenth centuries. How little human fame or fortune counts is emphasized in the *Consolation of Philosophy* by considering how small the earth is in relation to the spheres of the stars and planets.[49] As he is carried up into the atmosphere, the dreamer in the *House of Fame* says that the whole world appears no more than a point (HF 904–7). This brings to mind a passage in Boethius (1972–8). Interestingly, if Chaucer had known as much about astronomy as John North says he knew at the end of his life, he might have known that in astronomical terms, the earth is not a point in relation to the moon (more exactly, the moon shows parallax when seen from different parts of the earth, so that distances on the earth cannot be ignored in locating the moon).

The location of Fame's dwelling-place, 'Ryght even in myddes of the weye / Betwixen hevene and erthe and see' (HF 714–15), which derives from Chaucer's source in Ovid, *Metamorphoses* Book Twelve, does not make sense in terms of the Aristotelian cosmos. If one tries to match 'in the middle between heaven and earth and sea' to the Aristotelian cosmos, one obtains not a specific location, but the whole sphere of air (or of air and fire), with the sphere of the moon (or the spheres of fire and of the moon) over it ('heaven') and the earth and sea alternating below. This is hardly the sort of place to which the eagle carries the dreamer.

How is it that what is said on earth would naturally move to the House of Fame? In a sort of nominalistic twist, the oral reports that move naturally to the place of the House of Fame are said to be nothing but broken air (765–70). This might be thought to represent the kind of ontological parsimony associated with William of Ockham and adopted by most of the Oxford Calculators—there is no particular form associated with sound, but only air in a certain configuration and motion—except that it can be found commonly in earlier grammar books.[50] Moreover, if sound is nothing but broken air, then, like all other air, it will move upwards. Chaucer explains how this will happen by using the standard Aristotelian concept of natural place, but then too by analogy to waves on the surface of water (706–8; 725–46; 757–60). The two explanations, the one using the natural motion of the air upwards, and the other using waves in a medium, are not consistent with each other. This is much more likely to be meant 'in game' than taken 'in ernest'. Even harder to take seriously is the sudden claim that once the sound reaches the House of Fame it will somehow arrange itself into the shape of the person who spoke (1068–84). The sorts of resources that the eagle draws on here are not particularly those of the Oxford Calculators—nor, on the other hand, those of Wyclif—but rather typical naturalistic explanations of scholastic Aristotelians.

Oddly, these supposedly scientific explanations are used in a jumbled and inaccurate way, but what is more noteworthy from my point of view is that the university-like explanations, albeit in the mouth of an eagle, are presented as attractive speculations. Chaucer seems to have had an amateur interest in natural science—and, eventually, if we can believe John North, he had considerable expertise in astronomy. Thus, what the philosophical visions do seem to have in common with the Oxford Calculators are the features of their thought that they share with the other fourteenth-century *moderni*, in particular an optimistic view of the possibilities of natural science.

Although all of Chaucer's texts could be said to represent a time when already Wyclif was active and already the Great Schism of the Papacy had begun, I take the *House of Fame* to reflect an earlier, more optimistic time, while the Summoner's Tale reflects a later time when there was a greater sense that something was wrong in Christendom. Might the difference in tone between the *House of Fame* and the *Canterbury Tales* be used as evidence of changes in the intellectual climate in England and at Oxford in particular during the later decades of the fourteenth century? Does the evidence of anticlericalism, and in particular of animus against the friars, in the works of Chaucer increase over time? With regard to my subject matter, I seem to see more influence of Wyclif in passages from the *Canterbury Tales* than in the dream visions or other earlier works, but this mainly consists in expressed anticlericalism, particularly with regard to the mendicants and to their greed and failure to live up to Christian ideals. Whereas the dream visions may spoof or parody academic learning, as for instance by putting it in the mouth of an eagle in the *House of Fame*, they do so in a context generally of beauty and pleasure. On the other hand, the parody of clerical learning in the Summoner's Tale occurs in a context emphasizing the greed and hypocrisy of the friar. Whether this anticlericalism reflects the program of Wyclif at Oxford or whether both Chaucer and Wyclif are reflecting wider changes in British and European society cannot be answered by me here.

Notes

1. A good place to start is J. A. W. Bennett, *Chaucer at Oxford and Cambridge* (Oxford: Oxford University Press, 1974). More recently, the work of Kathryn Lynch is notable; see Kathryn L. Lynch, 'The "Parliament of Fowls" and Late Medieval Voluntarism', *The Chaucer Review* Part I, 25, no. 1 (1990), 1–16; Part II, 25, no. 2 (1990), 85–95. See also Chapters 22 and 26 in this volume.

2. Edith Sylla, 'The Oxford Calculators', in *The Cambridge History of Later Medieval Philosophy*, eds. Norman Kretzmann, Anthony Kenny, and Jan Pinborg (Cambridge: Cambridge University Press, 1982), 540–63.

3. For the *logica moderna*, see Norman Kretzmann, 'Syncategoremata, Exponibilia, Sophismata', in Kretzmann et al., *Cambridge History of Later Medieval Philosophy*, 211–45; for Bradwardine, see H. Lamar Crosby, Jr, *Thomas Bradwardine: His Tractatus de Proportionibus: Its Significance for the Development of Mathematical Physics* (Madison, WI: University of Wisconsin Press, 1955).

4. E.g., Glending Olson, 'Measuring the Immeasurable: Farting, Geometry, and Theology in the Summoner's Tale', *The Chaucer Review* 43, no. 4 (2009), 414–27; see Carolyn Collette and Nancy Mason Bradbury, 'Time, Measure, and Value in Chaucer's Art and Chaucer's World', *The Chaucer Review* 43, no. 4 (2009), 347–50; Suzanne Conklin Akbari, *Seeing Through the Veil: Optical Theory and Medieval Allegory* (Toronto: University of Toronto Press, 2004), 199–201, where Akbari suggests that in his descriptions of indecision and decision-making, Chaucer may reflect the sorts of things that John Dumbleton wrote about the latitudes of certainty and doubt. For nominalism, see Richard J. Utz, 'Negotiating the Paradigm: Literary Nominalism and the Theory and Practice of Reading Late Medieval Texts', in *Literary Nominalism and the Theory of Rereading Late Medieval Texts: a New Research Paradigm* ed. R. J. Utz (Lewiston, ID: Edwin Mellen Press, 1995).

5. See Neal Ward Gilbert, 'Ockham, Wyclif, and the "Via Moderna"', *Miscellanea Mediaevalia*, Bd. 9, *Antiqui und Moderni* (Berlin and New York: Walter de Gruyter, 1974), 85–123; Maarten J. F. M. Hoenen, '*Via Antiqua* and *Via Moderna* in the Fifteenth Century: Doctrinal, Institutional, and Church Political Factors in the *Wegestreit*', in *The Medieval Heritage in Early Modern Metaphysics and Modal theory, 1400–1700*, eds. Russell L. Friedman and Lauge O. Nielsen (Dordrecht, 2003), 3–36.

6. Richard Utz, 'Negotiating the Paradigm', 3n6. William Courtenay thinks that the influence of the nominalists at Oxford, if it ever was strong, began to weaken by 1350, if not earlier. See William Courtenay, *Schools and Scholars in Fourteenth-Century England* (Princeton, NJ: Princeton University Press, 1987), 356–7.

7. See the articles collected in *Ockham and Ockhamism. Studies in the Dissemination and Impact of His Thought*, ed. William J. Courtenay (Leiden and Boston, MA: Brill, 2008).

8. See Morton Bloomfield, 'Fourteenth-Century England: Realism and Rationalism in Wyclif and Chaucer', *English Studies in Africa* 16, no. 2 (1973), 59–70.

9. Edith Sylla, 'John Buridan and Critical Realism', *Early Science and Medicine* 14 (2009), 211–47; *eadem*, 'The Oxford Calculators' Middle Degree Theorem in Context', *Early Science and Medicine* 15 (2010), 338–70.

10. See David Steinmetz, 'Late Medieval Nominalism and the "Clerk's Tale"', *The Chaucer Review* 12 (1977), 38–54, at 39–41 and 52 n. 8. Steinmetz rejects the equation of nominalism and skepticism, as well as the image of Ockham's voluntarism (under the label 'nominalism') presented by Robert Stepsis, '*Potentia Absoluta* and the *Clerk's Tale*', *Chaucer Review* 10 (1975–6), 129–46.

11. Norman Kretzmann and Barbara Ensign Kretzmann, *The Sophismata of Richard Kilvington*; text edition (Oxford: Oxford University Press for the British Academy, 1990); introduction, translation and commentary (Cambridge: Cambridge University Press, 1990).

12. John Murdoch, 'Philosophy and the Enterprise of Science in the Later Middle Ages', in *The Interaction between Science and Philosophy*, ed. Y. Elkana (Atlantic Highlands: Humanities Press, 1974) and John Murdoch, 'From Social into Intellectual Factors: An Aspect of the

Unitary Character of Late Medieval Learning', in *The Cultural Context of Medieval Learning*, eds. John E. Murdoch and Edith Dudley Sylla (Boston, MA: Reidel, 1975), 271–348.

13. Curtis Wilson, *William Heytesbury. Medieval Logic and the Rise of Mathematical Physics* (Madison, WI: University of Wisconsin Press, 1960), 8–18.

14. Norman Kretzmann, 'Incipit/Desinit', in *Motion and Time, Space and Matter*, eds. Peter K. Machamer and Robert G. Turnbull (Cleveland, OH: Ohio State University Press, 1976), 101–36.

15. See John Murdoch, 'Infinity and Continuity', in Kretzmann et al., *Cambridge History of Later Medieval Philosophy*, 584 and n. 56.

16. See Edith Sylla, 'Medieval Concepts of the Latitude of Forms: The Oxford Calculators', *Archives d'Histoire Doctrinale et Littéraire du Moyen Age* 40 (1973), 223–83.

17. See Simo Knuuttila and Anja Inkeri Lehtinen, 'Change and Contradiction: A Fourteenth-Century Controversy', *Synthese* 40 (1979), 189–207, at 194.

18. Edith Sylla, 'Swester Katrei and Gregory of Rimini. Angels, God, and Mathematics in the Fourteenth Century', in *Mathematics and the Divine*, eds. Teun Koetsier and Luc Bergmans (Amsterdam: Elsevier, 2005), 249–71.

19. See Edith Sylla, 'The Transmission of the New Physics of the Fourteenth Century from England to the Continent', in *La Nouvelle Physique du XIVe Siecle*, eds. Stefano Caroti and Pierre Souffrin (Florence: Casa Editrice L. S. Olschki, 1997), 65–110.

20. Neal Ward Gilbert, 'Richard de Bury and the "Quires of Yesterday's Sophisms"', in *Philosophy and Humanism. Renaissance Essays in Honor of Paul Oskar Kristeller*, ed. Edward P. Mahoney (New York: Columbia University Press, 1976), 229–57.

21. Although two of the four appearances of this word in Larry D. Benson, *A Glossarial Concordance to the Riverside Chaucer* (New York: Garland Publishing, 1993) occur in Chaucer's translation of Boethius.

22. Bloomfield, 'Fourteenth-Century England', 67, argues that 'Chaucer is a rational poet who will go with reason as far as it will go'.

23. Collette and Bradbury, 'Time, Measure, and Value', 347, quoting John Murdoch, 'From Social into Intellectual Factors', 287.

24. J. D. North, *Chaucer's Universe* (Oxford: Clarendon Press, 1988), viii.

25. See North, *Chaucer's Universe*, 427–36. For Dorigen's belief that it is impossible to remove the rocks, see the Franklin's Tale, V.1001 ('For wel I woot that it shal never bityde') and V. 1333–4, and 1341–5, ('"Allas!" quod she, "that evere this sholde happe! / For wende I nevere by possibilitee / That swich a monstre or merveille myghte be! It is agayns the proces of nature"'). For Ockham's use of the proposition 'from the impossible anything follows', see Eleonore Stump, 'Obligations: A. From the Beginning to the Early Fourteenth Century', in Kretzmann et al, *Cambridge History of Later Medieval Philosophy*, 332–4; Gilbert, 'Richard de Bury', 244n38. Of course, the logicians would distinguish between logical impossibility and natural impossibility.

26. Kathryn L. Lynch, *Chaucer's Philosophical Visions* (Cambridge: D. S. Brewer, 2000), 18–21, considers the possibility that Chaucer was a university-trained man.

27. Donald R. Howard, *Chaucer: His Life, His Works, His World* (New York: E. P. Dutton, 1987), 25.

28. This is what emerges from Howard, *Chaucer*, 26, but Courtenay, *Schools and Scholars*, 102, says that Ravenstone's books include some on logic.

29. Howard, *Chaucer*, 74–8.

30. For a brief notice on Strode, see Kimberly Georgedes, 'Ralph Strode', in *A Companion to Philosophy in the Middle Ages*, eds. Jorge J. E. Gracia and Timothy B. Noone (Oxford:

Blackwell Publishing, 2003), 552. See also Rodney Delasanta, 'Chaucer and Strode', *The Chaucer Review* 26, no. 2 (1991), 203–218. Compare with Utz, 'Negotiating the Paradigm', 10–13. For the suggestion that Chaucer might have learned about Oxford thought from Strode, see Akbari, *Seeing through the Veil* (note 4), 199–200.

31. A. B. Emden, *Biographical Register of the University of Oxford to a.d.1500*, 3 vols. (Oxford: Clarendon Press, 1957), 1807–8.

32. Delasanta, 'Chaucer and Strode', 205. Compare with Utz, 'Negotiating the Paradigm', 10–13.

33. Paul Spade, *The Mediaeval Liar: A Catalogue of the Insolubilia-Literature* (Toronto: The Pontifical Institute of Mediaeval Studies, 1975), 87–91; Alfonso Maierù, 'Le ms. Oxford, Canonici misc. 219 et la *Logica* de Strode', in *English Logic in Italy in the 14th and 15th Centuries*, ed. A. Maierù (Naples: Bibliopolis, 1982), 87–110; J. M. Fletcher, 'Developments in the Faculty of Arts 1370–1520', in *The History of the University of Oxford Volume 2, Late Medieval Oxford*, eds. J. I. Catto and Ralph Evans (Oxford: Clarendon Press, 1992), 338, lists Strode along with Heytesbury, Dumbleton, and Bradwardine, among Oxford logicians influential on the Continent in this period. In the Renaissance, the humanist Angelo Poliziano criticized the *barbari moderni*, naming Burley, Herveus, Ockham, Heytesbury, and Strode, quoted by Lisa Jardine, 'Humanist Logic', in *The Cambridge History of Renaissance Philosophy*, eds. Charles Schmitt, Quentin Skinner, and Eckhard Kessler, et al. (Cambridge: Cambridge University Press, 1988), 194.

34. *Johannis Wyclif Opera minora*, ed. Johann Loserth (London: Wyclif Society by C. K. Paul & Co., 1913; HathiTrust Digital Library), 175. Wyclif also (176) raises the issue of how the word 'time' in the Bible should be understood, as opposed to the way it might be understood in contemporary logical analysis of texts.

35. See Emily Michael, 'John Wyclif's Atomism', in *Atomism in Late Medieval Philosophy and Theology,* eds. Christophe Grellard and Aurélian Robert (Leiden and Boston, MA: Brill, 2009), 183–220. Norman Kretzmann, 'Continua, Indivisibles, and Change in Wyclif's Logic of Scripture', in *Wyclif in his Times,* ed. Anthony Kenny (Oxford: Clarendon Press, 1986), 31–65.

36. J. I. Catto, 'Wyclif and Wycliffism at Oxford 1356–1430', in Catto and Evans, *Late Medieval Oxford*, 175–261.

37. We do know that in the early sixteenth century, many of the techniques of the Oxford Calculators were still part of the Oxford curriculum, albeit in simplified form. See E. J. Ashworth, 'The "Libelli Sophistarum" and the Use of Medieval Logic Texts at Oxford and Cambridge in the Early Sixteenth Century', *Vivarium* 17 (1979), 134–58.

38. Emden, *Biographical Register of the University of Oxford*, 927–8.

39. See, for example, Alessandro Conti, 'Paul of Venice', in Stanford Encyclopedia of Philosophy, http://plato.stanford.edu/entries/paul-venice.

40. Alfred Crosby, *The Measure of Reality: Quantification and Western Society, 1250–1600* (Cambridge: Cambridge University Press, 1987).

41. *Tractatus Hentisberi de scire et dubitare per famossissimum doctorem Gaetanum compilata.* Printed with William Heytesbury, *Regule solvendi sophismata.* (Venice 1494), 17ra.

42. See William F. Woods, 'Symkyn's Place in the "Reeve's Tale"', *Chaucer Review* 39 (2004), 17–40, at 17.

43. Elzbieta Jung and Robert Podkonski, 'Richard Kilvington on Continuity', in *Atomism in Late Medieval Philosophy and Theology*, eds. Christoph Grellard and Aurélien Robert (Leiden: Brill, 2009), 65–84, at 65.

44. Jung and Podkonski, 79n37, from Erfurt SB Ampl. O 74, f. 39rb-va, 'Quod probo sic: quia capio aliquam lineam gyrativam ductam super primam partem proportionalem ipsius A, quae sit B; B ergo est quantitas continua cuius convenit addere maiorem partem in infinitum quarum nulla est pars alterius nec econverso, igitur convenit devenire ad aliquam lineam infinitam actu…'.

45. Olson, 'Measuring the Immeasurable', (note 4), 414.

46. See Fiona Somerset, '"As just as is a squyre": The Politics of "Lewed Translacion" in Chaucer's *Summoner's Tale*', *Studies in the Age of Chaucer* 21 (1999), 187–207.

47. See Neal Ward Gilbert, 'Ockham, Wyclif, and the "Via Moderna"', (note 5) and 'Richard de Bury and the "Quires of Yesterday's Sophisms"', (note 19).

48. Boethius, *The Consolation of Philosophy*, ed. Douglas C. Langston (New York: W. W. Norton, 2010), 1.pr1; in this edition, pages 3–4. Compare with Chaucer, 1.pr1.12–19.

49. Boethius, *Consolation of Philosophy*, 2.pr7; in Langston's edition, pages 21–49.

50. See Martin Irvine, 'Medieval Grammatical Theory and Chaucer's *House of Fame*', *Speculum* 60 (1985), 856.

BIBLIOGRAPHY

Catto, J. I. and Ralph Evans, eds., *The History of the University of Oxford, Volume II, Late Medieval Oxford* (Oxford: Clarendon Press, 1992). See especially the chapters by Ashworth and Spade, Courtenay, Catto, Fletcher, and North.

Gilbert, Neal Ward, 'Richard de Bury and the 'Quires of Yesterday's Sophisms', in *Philosophy and Humanism. Renaissance Essays in Honor of Paul Oskar Kristeller*, ed. Edward P. Mahoney (New York: Columbia University Press, 1976), 229–57.

Hudson, Anne and Michael Wilks, *From Ockham to Wyclif* (Oxford: Basil Blackwell for the Ecclesiastical History Society, 1987).

Kenny, Anthony, *Wyclif in his Times* (Oxford: Clarendon Press, 1986). See, esp., Norman Kretzmann, 'Continua, Indivisibles, and Change in Wyclif's Logic of Scripture', 31–65.

Kretzmann, Norman and Barbara Ensign Kretzmann, *The Sophismata of Richard Kilvington*; text edition (Oxford: Oxford University Press for the British Academy, 1990); introduction, translation and commentary (Cambridge: Cambridge University Press, 1990).

Michael, Emily, 'John Wyclif's Atomism', in *Atomism in Late Medieval Philosophy and Theology*, eds. Christophe Grellard and Aurélian Robert (Leiden: Brill, 2009), 183–220.

Murdoch, John E., 'From Social into Intellectual Factors: An Aspect of the Unitary Character of Late Medieval Learning', in *The Cultural Context of Medieval Learning*, eds. John E. Murdoch and Edith Dudley Sylla (Dordrecht: Reidel, 1975), 271–348.

Somerset, Fiona, '"As just as is a squyre": The Politics of "Lewed Translacion" in Chaucer's *Summoner's Tale*', *Studies in the Age of Chaucer* 21 (1999), 187–207.

Sylla, Edith, 'The Oxford Calculators', in *The Cambridge History of Later Medieval Philosophy*, eds. Norman Kretzmann, Anthony Kenny, and Jan Pinborg (Cambridge: Cambridge University Press, 1982), 540–63.

Wilson, Curtis and William Heytesbury, *Medieval Logic and the Rise of Mathematical Physics* (Madison, WI: University of Wisconsin Press, 1960).

PART V

CHRISTIAN DOCTRINE AND RELIGIOUS HETERODOXY

CHAPTER 26

··

WYCLIFFISM AND
ITS AFTER-EFFECTS

··

STEPHEN E. LAHEY

IT was difficult to be indifferent to John Wyclif during the last decades of the fourteenth century. The Oxford theologian had made a name for himself in the 1370s by emerging from the halls of the university to craft arguments against bishops on behalf of John of Gaunt, Duke of Lancaster. Soon, relations between the duke and the church had become so acrimonious as to render the polemics of the caustic don a politically disastrous affair. Wyclif had concluded publicly that transubstantiation was metaphysically impossible, and was expelled from Oxford in the same summer that London erupted in violent rebellion. Had he not been in the employ of the duke, he would certainly have been compelled to explain himself at Avignon; instead, he was exiled to Lutterworth in Leicestershire, where he was free to revise, rewrite, and edit his writings amidst the cows and the incurious peasants. He lived for three more years, dying on 31 December 1384. During that period, he compiled a unique body of written work in Latin and English, a collection of formal philosophy and theology, political and ecclesiological treatises, and treatises, sermons, and commentaries on scripture and moral theology that would have a powerful effect in England and Bohemia well into the fifteenth century.[1]

Wyclif's confrontations with the church were frequent and very public during the last years of his life.[2] His assertion that the king ought to take control of the church of the realm, divesting it of all material holdings and winnowing miscreants from ranks of the clergy, infuriated the Bishop of London and the Archbishop of Canterbury. He was ordered to explain himself in a formal trial at Lambeth in 1377; he appeared with the duke, who quickly got into a shouting match with William Courtenay, Bishop of London. The trial ended in chaos. Three months later, Pope Gregory XI weighed in with a list of nineteen errors associated with Wyclif's thought, hoping that Edward III would do something. Edward was suffering from dementia, though, and died before the bulls reached England. Bishop Courtenay made another attempt at a trial in February 1378, scotched at the last minute by Joan of Kent, widow of the Black Prince. Courtenay already had more than enough reason to despise Wyclif. The year before, two of the duke's men had broken into Westminster Abbey in pursuit of a fugitive who had sought sanctuary there, and murdered both the fugitive and a nearby priest. Wyclif had appeared with the duke and presented a defence so offensive as to cause even the duke to blanch. Over the next two years, as his radical ideas became more well-known, Wyclif publicly asserted that transubstantiation was impossible. By the time of the Peasant's Revolt in the summer of 1381, when havoc played throughout London's streets and the duke had concerns that made protecting a heretical Oxford professor impossible, the English church had had enough. Bishop Courtenay—now Archbishop of Canterbury— intended to silence Wyclif. One of the leaders of the Peasant's Revolt, the renegade priest John Ball, whose couplet 'Whanne Adam delved and Eve span, who was thann a gentil man'? defined the spirit of the Revolt, was asserted to have been a disciple of Wyclif.[3] This was the same leader rumoured to have been instrumental in the murder of the previous Archbishop, Simon Sudbury. Wyclif was no longer merely an embarrassing problem. As far as the church was concerned, he was a threat to the realm. Courtenay called for a synod at Blackfriars to deal with the threat in May 1382. On the second day of the council, London experienced a minor earthquake, providing a name: the Earthquake Council. Wyclif had been in Lutterworth for a year at this point, but his ideas remained popular in Oxford. Courtenay forced Robert Rigg, the chancellor of the university, to direct an official repudiation of Wycliffism there, leading to the excommunication of several of Wyclif's acolytes.[4] In the meantime, Wyclif had been actively engaged in organizing a band of university-trained preachers, some of whom he had likely supervised in the translation of the first vernacular English Bible. These 'poor preachers' were commissioned to wander through the countryside and villages, evangelizing as the first disciples had done, free from the control of bishop or fraternal order.

Wycliffism is a very broad label, applicable to a number of separable subjects.[5] It could describe the species of realist ontology he formulated in response to Ockhamist conceptualism and the associated 'propositional realism' underlying his logical and semantic system.[6] Again, it could refer to the species of spatiotemporal atomism he developed in his philosophical analysis of Aristotle's physics. Or it could be used to refer to the remarkable hermeneutics of scripture he taught, an approach to the Bible that comes very close to the Muslim veneration of Qur'an as a divine incarnation. Again, it could refer to the theory of dominion he articulated in his treatises on just earthly governance and legislation. While each of these has a bearing on the body of thought that would be associated with his name in the last part of the fourteenth and the fifteenth century in England and Bohemia, they were of interest to a very small number of highly educated people. When an English bishop or a Czech noble asked someone whether they were a 'Wycliffite', they were not interested in discussing ontology or theoretical physics, and only very rarely willing to enter into a discussion of the metaphysics of scriptural or royal authority. Instead, the term 'Wycliffism' referred to the ideas directly relevant to the popular movements threatening ecclesiastical authority. The best-known issues can be listed:

1. The church has over-emphasized sacramental theology and neglected preaching the word of God.
2. Confession and absolution have been given undue pride of place in the practice of the church, providing unscrupulous ecclesiastics an excellent opportunity to oppress the laity.
3. Images and pilgrimages do more to hinder the salvation of the faithful than they do to aid it.
4. Praying to saints means that the one praying would elevate a dead man or woman to the place of mediator: an office that is Christ's alone.
5. The church is the body of the elect, whom God foreknows from eternity to be favoured by grace for salvation.
6. The papacy and the church hierarchy are a Caesarian institution given a poisonous hold on Christendom by the Donation of Constantine.
7. The church ought to be wholly divested of all temporal holdings.
8. The fraternal orders, indeed, all orders, are 'private religions' and should be abolished as schismatic.
9. Clergy who shirk their offices are not true priests or bishops; true clergy may be recognized by holiness of life and a hunger to preach the gospels.
10. Private property is a consequence of the Fall and, in an ideal state, would be inimical to the Christian life.

These ten are the best-known critiques of the ecclesiastical status quo associated with Wycliffism, and versions of each can be associated with both Lollard and Hussite ideology.[7] Likewise, the genesis of each can be found in Wyclif's writings in some form or other. Numbers 2, 3, and 4 appear only briefly in Wyclif's works, but entire treatises are devoted to the others.[8]

This list is generally well known and, until recently, has been taken to define Lollardy and the Hussite ideology.[9] The question naturally arises, though: are these criticisms worth risking excommunication and a horrible death outside the faith? To modern eyes, the righteous anger of the clear-eyed rebel towards an unjust institution is a worthy cause for martyrdom. The popular understanding of Che Guevara, William Wilberforce, or Dietrich Bonhoeffer, among many others, comes to mind. But an ideology that offers nothing but a laundry list of complaints about the injustices and inadequacies of the institution that defines society would not strike the late medieval mind as worth risking one's salvation to defend. There is always more to heresy than criticism of the status quo; the Waldensians, the Cathars, and the Beguines all had positive, definite ideas about how to live the Christian life. Wycliffism also had a distinct and recognizable moral theology, one that captivated people, convincing them that the movement had captured the essence of Christ's teachings in a way that had been lost by the institutional church. Very few Wycliffites, whether Lollard or Hussite, advocated the abolition of the catholic ideal.[10] Instead, the movement appears to have taken hold in England and in Bohemia as an ideology of positive reform, an engine for the rejuvenation and revitalization of the church and society.

To assume that Wycliffism was simply a critical reaction to social, political, and ecclesiastical reality is to side with its many enemies, from Thomas Walsingham, Thomas Netter, Jean Gerson, and Pierre d'Ailly in the fifteenth century to Eamon Duffy and Richard Rex in the twenty-first, all of whom could see nothing but the negative in Wycliffism. Duffy and Rex have dismissed Wycliffism as the creation of nervous chroniclers and gullible scholars.[11] Given the widespread depiction of the movement as being defined by what its leaders oppose, this is understandable. But without a careful analysis of the moral theology that undergirds the movement, it would be premature to dismiss Wycliffism as theologically sterile, 'a critique of religion rather than an alternative religion'.[12]

THE STRUCTURE AND CONTEXT
OF WYCLIFFISM

The reforms of the fourth Lateran council of 1215–16 included particular emphasis on preaching and teaching the laity the elements of the faith, and English implementation of this was defined by Archbishop John Pecham's Lambeth Constitutions of 1281. One result of this was a vast catalogue of literature defining the principles of pastoral theory and practice; students of late medieval English pastoral theology have a wide variety of theorists available, each with a confident understanding of what a priest's business entailed and how it should be carried out.[13] There was also a wealth of homiletic handbooks designed to instruct preachers in the proper construction of homilies and sermons and filled with useful examples, illustrations, and ways of explicating the virtues, vices, and moral teaching of the Old and New Testaments.[14]

In discussing Wyclif's thoughts on this subject, two figures stand out. The first is Robert Grosseteste, Bishop of Lincoln (1235–59), whom many fourteenth-century ecclesiastics regarded as the ideal English bishop and theologian. Even before Pecham's Lambeth Constitutions, Grosseteste had been active in delineating the business of parish priests: 'The work of pastoral care consists not only in administering the sacraments, saying the canonical hours, and celebrating Mass . . . but in truly teaching the life of truth, in condemning vices by instilling fear in correcting vices severely and with firm command where necessary and rigidly chastising them . . .'.[15]

The second is Robert Holkot, OP (d.1349), a leading figure among the 'classicizing friars'. Readers of Dante's *Purgatorio* marvel at the skill with which Dante weaves examples from the Bible and classical pagan literature into his insightful and theologically sensitive depiction of the relation of the capital sins to the theological and cardinal virtues, but the use of rich and creative depictions within moral instruction was not the province of poets alone. Beryl Smalley has identified a group of English friars active in the early decades of the fourteenth century who developed the use of 'word pictures': sophisticated exemplary devices designed to captivate and draw the audience into their sermons.[16] Of these, Holkot stands out. He was a skilled philosopher whose commentary on the

Sentences was influential throughout the rest of the century at Oxford. A daring advocate of Ockhamist conceptualism, Holkot was likely one of the 'Pelagians' targeted by Thomas Bradwardine.[17] He was also a skilled and inventive exegetical writer; his *Commentary on the Book of Wisdom* was very popular with preachers in England and on the Continent well into the sixteenth century.[18]

The warmth of Wyclif's admiration for Grosseteste is in dramatic opposition to the icy disdain he held for Holkot. His embrace of the teachings of the Bishop of Lincoln is obvious to any of his readers. In contrast to other schoolmen, Wyclif cited relatively few contemporary figures as authoritative; with the exception of occasional references to Thomas Aquinas, Grosseteste stands out as chief among scholastic theologians in Wyclif's pastoral writings. One of the most important of Wyclif's pastoral treatises is *De mandatis divinis*, which appears to have begun as a commentary on the Decalogue patterned on Grosseteste's own *De decem mandatis*.[19]

Wyclif's attitude towards Holkot is not as easily recognizable. As was customary, Wyclif rarely made direct reference to his opponents in his philosophical works. Indeed, readers of fourteenth-century Oxford commentaries on the *Sentences* are frequently stymied by the frequent use of '*quidam*' to refer to the author of a given position or argument. In this case, careful analysis of the possible contenders for many of Wyclif's sharpest attacks on *quidam* reveals Holkot as a likely target with some regularity.[20] Wyclif's homiletic method, which appears explicitly in his *De officio pastoralis* and implicitly in *De mandatis, Opus evangelicum,* and the *Sermones*, is determinedly opposed to the classicizing of the friars, which he regards as little better than blasphemous. Particularly odious, he notes, is the habit of introducing distracting little stories as a way of entertaining the audience.[21] Nothing should vie with scripture for the attention of the faithful. In this, Wyclif follows directly in Pecham's footsteps, who argued that 'parade of learning, sensational and amusing anecdotes, and prolixity should be avoided, for the first two distract the attention of the listeners, and the last causes boredom and a scanty audience'.[22]

Wyclif's pastoral works, which should be understood to include his sermons as well as his extended commentary on the gospels, have received relatively little scholarly attention. Yet these are the works with which he was most closely identified in the decades immediately following his death. The evidence for this lies in several alphabetized theological commonplace books of varying length, apparently compiled by university-trained students of Wyclif. The longest, with 509 entries, is entitled *Floretum*; the mid-sized version is called *Rosarium sive floretus minor*; and the smallest, containing 303 entries, is entitled *Rosarium*. There are numerous copies of these works throughout England and Bohemia. The entries include biblical figures, virtues, vices, and issues concerned with ecclesiastical theory and practice. Each entry includes references to—and often quotations from—scripture, patristic writers, canon law, and most importantly for our purposes, to various treatises by Wyclif.[23] Of these, the most frequently cited are the *Sermones, Trialogus, Opus evangelicum,*and *De mandatis divinis*. Hudson dates these to no later than 1396, and while it is impossible to establish Wyclif's hand in these commonplace books, it is reasonable to examine his own treatises for evidence of connections holding between them.

Wyclif's intention seems to have been to create an order of preachers whose purpose was to spread his vision of a Bible-based Christian life to the faithful.[24] He makes reference to educating and inspiring 'simple priests' in several of his works, including *Dyalogus*, Sermon I.16, and *Epistola missa ad simplices sacerdotes*.[25] On the assumption that Wyclif had in mind the creation of a kind of anti-fraternal order the purpose of which was to 'fight fire with fire', it is reasonable to look for evidence that these texts are organized to be used as guidebooks for these poor preachers. The evidence, in fact, is plain.

The guide many medieval theologians used to describe the organization of the Christian life, whether regular or secular, lay or ordained, was Augustine's *Enchiridion*. Augustine's structure is simple: the Christian life should be organized around the three theological virtues, which both the Creed and the Lord's Prayer teach. He aligns Faith with the substance of what a Christian is to believe, including all that would become the basis for the medieval catechism, Hope as the basis for understanding prayer, specifically the Lord's Prayer, and Love as the basis for describing the commandments and laws that describe the Christian life. Thomas Aquinas famously made use of this model in his *Compendium theologiae*, a guide for the Christian life that was unfinished at the time of Thomas's death. In it he describes the articles of the faith on the model of the Nicene Creed and describes Hope using the Lord's Prayer. His introduction assigns Love to the elements of the law, following upon Romans 13:10; had he lived to begin this, it is likely that he would have begun with the Decalogue and moved into Christ's teachings on the moral life.[26]

Using this pattern, it is relatively easy to organize Wyclif's four works. The element concerned with explicating the substance of the faith is effectively covered by *Trialogus*. This treatise is patterned on Peter Lombard's *Sentences*, with consideration of God in Book One, creation in Book Two, morality and the Incarnation in Book Three, and sacraments in Book Four. Unlike the Lombard's work, which was the basis for medieval academic theology, Wyclif presents the material in the form of a three-way dialogue between Alithia, the knowing student, Pseustis, the lying friar, and Phronesis, the voice of wisdom (Wyclif himself). This work stands out from all other treatises composed by Wyclif as being obviously written for non-theologians. It is in Latin, and contains references to material from a Bachelor of Arts curriculum, but its lively tone and brisk pace indicate that Wyclif meant it for a less rigorously educated readership.[27] Wyclif has no other explicit analysis of the Creed, aside from two sermons.[28] He wrote four distinct commentaries on the Lord's Prayer though—more than most other theologians of the period. The first, a distinct treatise entitled *De Virtute Orandi* inserted into *De mandatis divinis*, is likely the earliest of these. The second is his *De oracione dominica*, a much later work designed more to attack the friars. Wyclif composed a sermon that serves as an analysis of the prayer's logic, and finally, he devotes a portion of the second book of *Opus evangelicum* to the prayer.[29] Wyclif's theological interest lies in the third connection, between love and the law. The structure of *De mandatis* suggests a considerable evolution in its development. The first several chapters serve as a theologically dense analysis of justice, the right, and law, but at chapters Six and Seven, the focus of the work shifts to the nature of divine law, and the relation of the Old Law to the New Law. Chapter Ten begins with discussion of the fact that fear and love are the two principles that compel observation of God's laws, and after a brief discussion of fear, Wyclif develops a complex account of how our love for God is defined and guided by God's laws. Because we are commanded to love God and love our neighbours, he argues, it is possible to divide the Decalogue into the commands that bind us in love to God, and those that bind us in love to our neighbours. Scattered amidst the next twenty chapters are brief treatises, like the one on the Lord's Prayer, and extended digressions on the relation of the duty to honour one's parents to that of honouring one's spiritual superiors. It is easy to interpret the 'catch-all' nature of *De mandatis* as at once a disquisition on the relation of the Old Law to love and as a homiletic manual. While Williel Thomson dates the treatise to the mid-1370s, it seems likely that Wyclif engaged in considerable editing and redacting of its contents during his final years at Lutterworth. Its correlate is the *Opus evangelicum*, Wyclif's extended exegetical analysis of Matthew 5–7, 23–5, and the priestly sermon in John 13. The first two books address the Sermon on the Mount, emphasizing the applicability of the Beatitudes and the teachings that follow to the Christian life. Many of the sermons, too, have the moral doctrine of the gospels and the epistles as their subject matter.

This structure relates the four works to one another according to a respected pattern for organizing the Christian moral life, but it remains hypothetical. This is not a unique problem for Wyclif's works. Scholars have come to accept two other collections of Wyclif's works as canonical. The first is his *Summa de ente*, containing six treatises on God and the divine attributes, and seven on creation. The second is his *Summa theologie*, containing ten treatises on the relation of God's law to scripture, and to human justice in church and state. To a lesser extent, a third collection, *De logica,* unites several distinct— and not obviously connected—treatises on semantics and spatiotemporal atomism, and has been taken to predate these two *Summas*. Anne Hudson has argued convincingly that the organization of the treatises into what we know as the *Summa theologie* may be the product of hands other than Wyclif's, based on the great difficulty of dating the treatises with certainty. Further, Ivan Mueller has thrown the certainty with which scholars have regarded the organization of the treatises of the *Summa de ente* into some doubt.[30] Hudson's general admonition is to avoid conclusively dating any of the works normally assigned to the period before Lutterworth, because of the strong likelihood that Wyclif revised and restructured them during the final years of his life. Two of the major works discussed here, *Trialogus* and *Opus evangelicum*, can be dated to these final years, and the majority of the sermons date to this period as well.[31] Given the likelihood that *De mandatis* was extensively revised, based on analysis of its contents, the *Enchiridion* organization is tenable and reasonable, if not certain.

WYCLIFFISM AS A MORAL THEOLOGY

There are two main themes running through these later works: first, the many problems of the contemporary church and second, the way to live a biblically based Christian life. The first theme includes the threat that transubstantiation poses to Christian doctrine, the damage the friars do to the church and her members, and the corruption of the 'Caesarean clergy' (namely, the bishops) and the poison with which it infects the church. Because of the great controversy these works caused, this is the best known element of Wyclif's works. The second theme includes a strong emphasis on the primacy of scripture in defining orthopraxy and orthodoxy, and the fundamental elements of the Christian life that Wyclif believed should be preached to the laity. The basis for both of these lies in Wyclif's belief that the divine ideas have such importance for theology, both theoretical and practical, that all Christian attempts to understand reality must begin in them, and in particular in their most available manifestation: Holy Scripture. The source of all contemporary errors lies in the attempt to put the products of our reasoning before sacred writ.

The reason why scripture exceeds virtue morality, or any other moral theory coming from human reason, is connected to Wyclif's ontology. On reading Wyclif's philosophical treatises, one would think that he was the sole advocate of a traditional Christian Neo-Platonism in a university filled with Ockhamists. Indeed, he went so far as to exclaim that all that was wrong with the world could be traced back to the denial of universals by the 'modern' doctors.[32]

In fact, Wyclif's metaphysics was an articulation of the realism of Henry of Ghent (d.1293), which had more recently been championed by Walter Burley (c.1344). In this ontology there is a strong connection between universals and particulars, each of which has a dependence on the contents of God's knowledge, or the divine ideas. While Ockhamists tended to dismiss the divine ideas in their explication of how reality is ordered, Henry, and now Wyclif, placed great emphasis on their importance. Henry was willing to countenance divine ideas for possibilities that were not actualized in creation, but for Wyclif, there are no divine ideas of counterfactuals. God knows every created reality as a distinct idea, which ideas are naturally arranged by genera and species. That is, God knows every human soul through a divine idea for it, which idea itself is ordered within God's understanding of humanity, which itself is something distinct from individual human beings.

Leaving aside the complex issues this poses regarding determinism, which Wyclif pursues with relish in the *Summa de ente*, the result of this position is that Wyclif reads the reference to the book of life in Revelations 20:12 as of critical importance to his moral theory.[33] He understands this to refer both to the divine ideas, considered in their entirety, and to the divine idea of Holy Scripture in particular.[34] The result of this double reference is that Wyclif believes the Bible to be the arbiter of all created truth whatsoever; our attempts to create moral systems that are not grounded in divine law as described by scripture must fail. Hence the Christian life depends upon an understanding of the Bible.[35] Any departure from its teaching, and any case of giving some other teaching pride of place, must result in grievous error.

Wyclif's denial of transubstantiation was certainly the most dramatic of his life, and the one for which he has been best known, at least in Roman Catholic literature. His sacramental theology is grounded in the traditional scholastic understanding of a sacrament as a sign, and in approach is in the tradition of Peter Lombard's *Sentences*.[36] The fourth book of *Trialogus*, entitled *De signis*, surveys the seven sacraments, explores the proper understanding of how each is a sign of the grace for which it is a vehicle, and explains how to avoid confusing the sign for the gift it signifies. His later works are filled with attacks on those who worship the sign rather than the signified, confusing the vehicle for its contents. In the beginning of *Trialogus IV*, he has his interlocutor pose this question:

> It appears first, that a sign and the signified are convertible with being. For every creature is a sign of the Creator, just as smoke naturally signifies fire. God is the sign of anything that can be signified, since He is the Book of Life in which anything that can be signified is inscribed; and through the same it follows, that anything would be a sign. So if by definition a sacrament is the sign of a sacred thing, it appears that everything that can be signified is indeed a sacrament, because every creature signifies its creation, and indeed, its Creator, and thus signifies a sacred thing, and God signifies with many sacred creatures, and Himself as well.[37]

Wyclif's answer is that the number of sacraments is the result of man's agency, but pulls back from the possibility that anything whatever is a sacrament because it signifies God. This allows him to explain how the sacraments function within the church, but it also gives him leeway to argue in *De officio pastoralis* that preaching is even more important than administering the sacraments: 'Preaching the gospel exceeds prayer and administration of the sacraments to an infinite degree.'[38] Wyclif never denied the efficacy of the Eucharist as a sacrament and insisted upon the real presence of Christ in the consecrated elements throughout his life. The problem rested in following Innocent III's assertion that the consecrated elements change from bread and wine into the real body and blood of Christ. Wyclif's arguments regarding what occurs when the priest consecrates the elements are grounded in his understanding of how change occurs in time and space and the impossibility of God annihilating any part of creation.[39] His interest during his later years was not to continue to argue about the nature of Eucharistic change, but to attack those who encouraged veneration of the sacrament for idolatry.

His other criticism of sacramental practice was the emphasis on auricular confession. The standard practice was to define penance as having three parts, 'like a harp', namely: 'the contrition of the heart, the confession of the mouth, and the works of satisfaction...'.[40] Wyclif rejected this tendency to anatomize the sacrament to define it. The essence of penance is within the penitent mind, an act of confession to God. No one, whatever his status or office, is capable of assessing the contrition of another in this act:

> From this it is clear, further, that it would be a Lucifer-like presumption for men baselessly to cook up the idea that this or that imposition of hands upon the head absolves one from sin. What, I ask, does this perceptible sign – a bull with its seal, or a monetary gift – do to contrition in the soul of the sinner? Truly, it does no more to the destruction of a sin than it does to the sanctification of the sinner. So these confessors commonly deceive both themselves and those they shrive with these lies. It is clear that a viator can take it that his sin is destroyed or that he is contrite in his soul only through hope in the mercy of Jesus Christ, a marked sorrow, and a holy life.[41]

These are the bases for Wyclif's arguments against the abuse of sacraments in his later works, and for the subsequent development of Lollard and Hussite critiques of sacramental theology.

The conflict with the friars is also a complex issue. On the face of it, the friars would seem to be the logical allies of Wyclif. Both Wyclif and the Franciscans were dedicated to a radical conception of poverty, a recreation of the life of Christ and the apostles in a world that seemed not to have changed very much in the past fourteen centuries. Wyclif held a passion for preaching scripture in common with all four orders of friars and for teaching the morality of Christ to the people without concern for episcopal authority. Wyclif could rival the Dominicans in his rage against the misuse of philosophical innovation to make the faith fit into an Aristotelian mould. Finally, Wyclif actually initiated an order of poor preachers, itinerant teachers of Christ's law meant to refresh and rejuvenate a faltering Christianity just as Francis and Dominic had done. Was the basis of his antagonism for the friars simply envy? If so, it would have been a soul-defining envy, for Wyclif's later writings against the friars are voluminous. The short pieces he wrote against them fill over 500 pages in the Wyclif Society edition of his *Polemical Works*, and his vituperations boil over in prolonged arguments in the *De dotatione ecclesie* (also known as the *Supplementum trialogi*) and in sections of *De apostasia* and *De blasphemia*. A more theologically feasible explanation for his attacks on the friars lies in his understanding of threat of division within the body of Christ.

According to Wyclif, the moral truth necessary for salvation is contained wholly and perfectly in scripture. Any situation the wayfarer might face in this pilgrimage on earth has its model or its ethical maxim in the Bible. The eternal arbiter of divine justice became one of us, and founded a new religion that did not supersede Judaism but instead folded its wisdom and law traditions into the complete perfection of the law of Christ. The perfect life of Christ serves as an exemplar for all human action, and we are meant to pay as close attention to His actions as described in the gospels as to His words. The unity and interconnected reality of the human species has Christ as its centre point in the divine understanding. In other words the sect Christ founded, the Christian religion, is the means through which every member of the species can understand what is right and just.

We are to note very carefully that Christ's teachings do not cease with the ascension; while each epistle may have come from the hand of an apostle, every word in them is more than divinely inspired: every word is eternal, universal truth. So the fact that the threat of pseudo-apostles crops up in the letters of Paul, of Peter, and of James is important. Even more important is the fact that none of these men attempted to start their own version of Christianity. Their patron and the author of their rule of life was Christ, and none of the apostles presumed to add upon His words with their own innovations or ideas. They recognized the divine authority with which Christ guided the formation and the continuation of the Christian life and submitted themselves to it as every Christian is meant to do. As Christ is the exemplar for human perfection, the lives of the apostles are exempla for lives devoted to the service of Christ. So when a saintly person, who lives by the rule of Christ, guides other Christians, it is always on the understanding that the saintly person has absolutely nothing to add to the eternal truth of Christ's law. But when such a person strays into the place of patron or legislator, the spectre of blasphemy threatens the religion: 'Whether Benedict, or Dominic, or Francis, or anyone else gathers together a new sect, he ought not be praised, nor ought he be followed; this is even more the truth for a sect imagining itself to have another patron or some worthless history behind it, as is true of the Augustinians or the Carmelites.'[42]

Wyclif is not simply anti-fraternal. He is anti-sectarian, rejecting the legitimacy of rules for monks, nuns, and anchorites as well as the friars. In other pieces Wyclif even warns that the possessioners, the cloistered monks and nuns living in rich and long-established houses, are as much a danger to Christianity as are the friars.[43] The friars' special problem is that when they are preaching about Christ's law, they are actively engaged in preaching a moral code they do not actually practice. Their arguments that Francis or Dominic only augment the perfection of Christ's law with a means by which His faithful servants might more effectively teach it are wholly illogical. Had Jesus been but a man, it would be sensible and logical that another man might come along to make it easier to teach the thoughts of Jesus; people do that with Aristotle's ethics all the time. But we are not 'Jesusans'—followers of Jesus the man—we are Christians, followers of the divine legislator, whose laws need no augmentation, even for those who would teach the law.[44] The fact that Wyclif gathered together disciples and sent them out into England to preach and live a life of apostolic exemplary purity sounds very much like the founding of another order of preaching friars. This is why he works so hard to denounce them. Each of the friars' patrons was so close to the apostolic ideal, but erred so seriously in creating a rule with which to gild the lily of Christ's perfect law.

Polemics against the abuses of the clergy were hardly in short supply in late medieval England. Wyclif's were not in themselves unusual; while he hints at a universal priest-hood in De civili dominio, in no way did he reject the need for a special class of Christians endowed with preaching and pastoral responsibilities.[45] The difficulties arose with his expectations of the moral lives of those ordained for these offices. He states the matter simply: in addition to having the responsibility of pruning the false shoots of heresy from the church, the chief responsibility of a priest is to 'dispose its branches that they may better bear fruit for the blessing of the Church'. Two things qualify an individual for these duties: 'the holiness of the pastor', and 'the wholesomeness of his teaching'.[46] Throughout his later writings, Wyclif fulminated against clergy who indulge in the pomp and luxury of secular lords, calling them 'satraps' for their love of fine vestments, ornate churches, and sumptuous meals. Christ's example of apostolic purity, he argued, was ideally meant for all Christians, but especially for the 'evangelical lords' dedicated to serving the needs of the church. The words that fall from the mouths of preachers who embody Herod rather than Christ can hardly be taken as suitable guidance for the Christian life.[47]

Accusations of Donatism have been made against Wyclif from his own day to the present, not least because of his stipulation that the church consists of the body of the Elect. While this has always been a part of Augustinian Christianity, Wyclif's emphasis on the predestined grace of the true members of the church, particularly in De ecclesia, and the consequent falsity of the mundane church's claims to moral authority, lead to a clear argument. If the true church, including the churches militant, dormant, and triumphant, includes only the Elect, and if Christ intended for his ministers to live in apostolic poverty as He did, then any clergy who does otherwise must not be like Christ, and so is not among the Elect. Obeying such priests and bishops was certainly questionable; the secular lords were required to punish them, and the secular commons were invited to question their authority. Donatists, of course, actually murdered priests who did not measure up to their standards, as the mob did with Archbishop Sudbury in 1381. This Wyclif could not countenance, but his critics then and now have been energetic in pointing out the inconsistency in his reasoning. Donatists argued that the sacraments of a flawed priest were invalid, though, which Wyclif never suggested, at least as far as the standard seven sacraments were concerned. However, his claims for the primacy of preaching and his emphasis on the need for moral purity in the preachers' lives certainly encouraged his contemporary critics, particularly the Carmelite Thomas Netter.[48] It also led both his English and his Bohemian followers to uncritical acceptance of the Donatist attitude.[49]

THE CHRISTIAN LIFE

It is much more difficult to identify a positive moral theology within Wyclif's writings, perhaps because his tendency to criticize and complain about how his contemporaries have corrupted the institutionalized practices of Christianity is so often in the way.[50] Among his criticisms was his frustration with preaching the fundamental elements of Christian behaviour through the virtues. From the time of Augustine, framing morality in terms of virtues, as the ancients had done, was problematic. If what motivates a virtuous action is anything other than love for God, could the action be considered virtuous?[51] Christian morality, as a result, began to develop away from the classical model of the virtues and towards a more collectively based understanding in which divine commands and the examples provided by biblical lives of piety and purity were idealized. This was generally true, at any rate, until the emphasis on auricular confession at the Fourth Lateran Council in 1215.[52] The need for regularized moral teaching and direction led to a more legalistic framework in instructing the moral life, and a systematized virtue ethic became useful for preaching and shriving. Aquinas's virtue ethics is generally thought to be the ideal for later medieval understanding of the practical aspects of Christian life. But Aquinas had applied his formidable philosophical abilities to the relation of the Aristotelian virtues to Augustinian theology because of the popularity of a much simpler and easily taught explanation of the relation of virtue to vice made popular by William Peraldus, OP (d. 1271). Peraldus's compendious *Summa de virtutibus et vitiis, or Summa aurea,* served as an encyclopaedia for clergy — particularly for the friars—well into early modernity. And while Aquinas's philosophical account was widely respected, Peraldus's work was foremost in an entire genre of moral handbooks for clergy. The important development, for Wyclif, was Ockham's assertion that one

could have one moral virtue without having any of the others. This was a major departure from standard virtue ethics, and for Wyclif, it appeared to open the door to teaching
virtues as the pagans had done, without concern for coherence between theology and
moral philosophy.

Wyclif's response was to argue vigorously in *Trialogus* for the interconnected nature
of the virtues. Further, he believed that the standard method of teaching the virtues, in
which one describes the dangers of a vice and juxtaposes it with the beneficial aspects of
an opposing virtue, tended to draw unsuspecting Christians away from the truth about
morality: that love of God is what lies at the base of any morally good act. His description of the virtues and vices in *Trialogus* appears to adopt the standard vice-virtue juxtaposition, but is based on the idea that any given virtue is opposed by all the vices, and
that while a given vice, say Pride, is best opposed by Humility, yet any of the other
virtues work together in allowing Humility the capacity to overcome Pride.[53] But Wyclif's
heart is not in the virtues and vices as the main themes in preaching the Christian life, as
can be seen by comparing his descriptions with Peraldus; in many cases, he lifts his summaries directly from the *Summa aurea*.[54] For him, the heart of moral teaching lies in the
divine law of scripture. Christ Himself provides the right way to order the many moral
injunctions and commands of scripture. The summary of the Law that Christ provides
in Matthew 22:37, Mark 12:30, and Luke 10:27 (citing Deuteronomy 6:5), in which one is
to love God and love one's neighbours, provides the basis. He explores the right relation
to God in his analysis of the first four commandments in *De mandatis* chapters Fifteen
to Twenty-One, and the right relation to one's neighbours in the 'second table' of the
Decalogue in chapters Twenty-Two to Thirty. In these analyses, virtue plays very little
part. Instead, the exempla provided by biblical figures and the inherent logic of its moral
commands provide the substance of his description of how the Christian ought to live.

The New Law of the Gospel was generally recognized to be epitomized in the Sermon
on the Mount in Matthew 5–7, and also by the Priestly Sermon in John 13–17. Wyclif's
reliance on Augustine's *De sermone domini in monte* is paramount in this description of
the reasons why the Beatitudes should be foremost in every Christian's mind in their
daily actions. Also prominent in this work is the *Opus imperfectum* then attributed to
John Chrysostom, a mainstay in medieval moral theology. Grosseteste and Jerome also
figure as guides to preaching the Christian life, but aside from two brief references to
Aquinas, Wyclif's faith is in the moral theology of the Fathers.

If all Wyclif had left to his followers were these two generally academic commentaries
on the Decalogue and some sections of Matthew and John, it would be difficult to make
the case that his understanding of the Christian life had an impact on the preaching of the
Lollards and the Hussites. The connecting element is the two collections of Wyclif's Latin
sermons. The first collection is quite large, including 120 sermons on the Gospels and
fifty-eight on epistolary readings, and Wyclif likely organized them to be a homiletic
guide for preachers during his final years in Lutterworth. The second collection is a miscellany of forty sermons dating to Wyclif's years in Oxford in the 1370s. We find neither
the dyspeptic choler of Wyclif's polemics, nor the arid intellectualism of his theological
treatises in these sermons; instead, they stand as fourteenth-century exempla of a serious,
generally conservative, biblically-oriented preaching style, without allegorical exegesis,

diverting stories, or references to popular culture. If we divide late medieval English preaching into two camps, in which the classicizing friars and educated seculars represent the style of 'Alexandrine' preaching that emphasizes virtues and vices; and if the staid exegesis and biblicism of Fitzralph and Bradwardine represent the 'Antiochene' response to modern innovation, then Wyclif's sermons fit effectively into the latter group.

This is not to say that Wyclif's sermons are unremarkable. In fact, they articulate the biblically grounded, law-based depiction of Christian morality of the *De mandatis* and *Opus evangelicum* very effectively.

An instance of Wyclif's style in preaching will illustrate this. He appears to have written a short treatise entitled *The Six Yokes* as an aid to extemporaneous preaching, which he then divided up and wove into five of the sermons from the larger collection. The point of the image of the yoke is to underscore the way we are united to one another in God's service, and Wyclif crafted the metaphor to allow preachers to begin on any of a number of subjects, lead back to one of the six yokes, and from there to the other five. *The Six Yokes* begins in a sermon surveying the Beatitudes, which leads to the certainty that Christ's blessings upon those who are persecuted will lead to their heavenly joy. And as an example of Christ's ties to all the faithful, Wyclif continues, it will be useful to think about what ties us to one another in general.

> So that the simple priests may have matter for preaching, there are six secular yokes that effectively bear the vehicle of Christ. The first is between Christ and the simple faithful, the second is between spouses joined together by the law of the Lord, the third is between the parent and the natural child, the fourth is between the master of the house and his bondsmen and servants, the fifth is between the secular lord and his subjects or tenants, and the sixth is generally between those who are neighbours.[55]

The yoke binding Christ to the faithful is their observance of his commandments as are evident to all who search the Gospels for them. The next sermon in the list is on Matthew 4:18, about Christ calling simple men to preach the gospel, and their obedience to Him. This leads to the next two yokes, which are based in the mutual respect that comes from submitting oneself to another person, whether as a wife does to a husband, or as a child to a parent. The next two sermons are less applicable to the next two yokes, which are more directly applicable to Sermon 31, on Matthew 10:16, on being sent like sheep in the midst of wolves. Any Christian needs prudence and patience in a church so beset with wolfish clergy and friars and can expect to be persecuted by such as the apostles were. The friars and Caesarian clergy provide exempla of evil mastery, while the fourth yoke binding men to one another, that of master and servant, can best be described as ties in which faith, hope, and love are mutually exchanged in God's service. The fifth yoke, between lord and subject (certainly a favourite topic for Wyclif), has been spliced into a sermon on Luke 10:1 that describes Christ's designation of seventy-two lesser disciples. This is more of a forced tie between gospel subject and yoke, but once on the subject of the right relation of lord to subject Wyclif provides an effective summary of his theory of reciprocity between the two. The final yoke is described in the next sermon on

John 12:24–5, usually understood as enjoining martyrdom. Just as martyrdom is the supreme act of giving to the church, so we ought take the *caritas* behind it to each of our relations to every one of our neighbours, which provides Wyclif the opportunity to describe the sixteen conditions of *caritas* and its centrality to the Christian life.

Contained within *The Six Yokes* are references to obedience to the law of Christ, the three theological virtues, the necessity of mutual respect and reciprocity in any just dominative relation, and the emphasis on *caritas* or love that pervades Wyclif's moral theology. It is not difficult to imagine a minimally educated preacher memorizing the contents of this treatise and using it for any occasion in which ties between people matter, whether in the context of a biblical reading, a time of joining or loosing—such as a wedding or a funeral—or as the basis for stirring up trouble with church authorities.

CONCLUSION

This chapter can only point to the complexity of Wyclif's understanding of how the Christian moral life should be understood and taught, and how he illustrates it with brief examples. This moral theology is not likely to have caught the interest of officials hunting Lollards or Hussites, but it is notable for its departure from the more popular preaching style of the friars. For Wyclif, preaching the gospel by dwelling on the virtues was tantamount to elevating a human creation over the divine creation of scripture. His antipathy for the friars is therefore of a piece with his reactionary emphasis on the importance of preaching about divine commands instead of juxtaposing virtues and vices.

Wyclif, or one of his copyists, placed this phrase at the beginning of his great treatise *De civili dominio*: 'Civil law presupposes divine law; civil lordship presupposes natural lordship'. Wycliffism can be described similarly: the Christian life presupposes the law of Christ; Christian lordship presupposes the imitation of Christ. All of its criticisms of the fourteenth-century church spring from Wyclif's conviction that the church had departed from scripture's guidance, and all of its injunctions for the Christian life begin with Wyclif's belief that scripture is the perfect vehicle for teaching and living the perfect life. Lollardy and the Hussite movement may have come to different, if equally disappointing ends in the fifteenth century, but as Tudor Puritanism and twentieth-century Protestant evangelicalism would show, Wycliffism was anything but sterile.

NOTES

1. The most complete bibliography of Wyclif and related studies can be found at lollardsociety. org.
2. Joseph Dahmus, *The Prosecution of John Wyclyf* (New Haven, CT: Yale University Press, 1952). The standard biography remains Herbert Workman, *John Wyclif: A Study of the English Medieval Church*, 2 vols. (Oxford: Clarendon Press, 1926). More recently see G. R. Evans, *John Wyclif: Myth and Reality* (Oxford: Lion, 2005).

3. Thomas Walsingham, *Chronicon Angliae, ab anno domini 1328 usque ad annum 1388*, ed. E. M. Thompson, Rolls Series, 64 (1874), 321; see Andrew Prescott, 'John Ball', *Oxford Dictionary of National Biography* (Oxford: Oxford University Press, 2004).

4. J. I. Catto and Ralph Evans, eds., *The History of the University of Oxford Volume 2: Late Medieval Oxford* (Oxford: Oxford University Press, 1992).

5. Scholars continue to dispute the proper use of 'Wycliffite' as regards its synonymy with 'Lollard'. In this discussion, I will refer to 'Wycliffism' as what Wyclif thought and wrote in his Latin works. I will refer to his English and his Bohemian followers, many of whom happily thought of themselves as 'Wycliffite', as 'Lollards' or 'Hussites' simply to distinguish between what Wyclif said, and what those who read or heard of his thoughts said and did. I leave to other, better-qualified scholars the question of how much of Wyclif's thought is reproduced in the bodies of literature associated with these movements. For recent discussion, see Fiona Somerset, *Clerical Discourse and Lay Audience in Late Medieval England* (Cambridge: Cambridge University Press, 1998), and Andrew Cole, *Literature and Heresy in the Age of Chaucer* (Cambridge: Cambridge University Press, 2008).

6. For Wyclif's philosophical system, see Alessandro Conti, 'Wyclif's Logic and Metaphysics', in *A Handbook to John Wyclif, Late Medieval Theologian*, ed. Ian C. Levy (Leiden: Brill, 2002), 67–126. For Wyclif's propositional realism, see Laurent Cesali, *Le réalisme propositionnel: Sémantique et ontology des propositions chez Jean Duns Scot, Gauthier Burley, Richard Brinkley, et Jean Wyclif* (Paris: Vrin, 2007). For Wyclif as commentator on Aristotle's physics, see Emily Michael, 'John Wyclif's Spatiotemporal Atomism', in *Atomism in Late Medieval Philosophy and Theology*, eds. Christophe Grellard and Aurelien Robert (Leiden: Brill, 2009). For Wyclif's ontology and hermeneutics of scripture, see Ian C. Levy, *John Wyclif: Scriptural Logic, Real Presence, and the Parameters of Orthodoxy* (Marquette, WI: Marquette University Press, 2003). For a survey of these topics, see Lahey, *John Wyclif* (Oxford: Oxford University Press, 2009).

7. This list is culled from Anne Hudson's survey of Wycliffism in *The Premature Reformation* (Oxford: Oxford University Press, 1988).

8. The criticisms can be aligned with the treatises in this way: 1. *De officio pastoralis*; 5. *De ecclesia*; 6. *De potestate pape*; 7. *De civili dominio*; 8. *De quattuor sectis novelis* and *De nova prevaricancia mandatorum*, among others 9. *De symonia, De apostasia, De blasfemia*; 10. *De civili dominio*. This list is by no means definitive; the criticisms can be found throughout Wyclif's Latin works.

9. See Gordon Leff, *Heresy in the Later Middle Ages: the Relation of Heterodoxy to Dissent c.1250–c.1450* (Manchester: Manchester University Press, 1967); Malcolm Lambert, *Medieval Heresy* (Oxford: Oxford University Press, 2002); Richard Rex, *The Lollards* (New York: Palgrave Macmillan, 2002). For a less hostile account, see Hudson, *Premature Reformation*.

10. Of particular interest is Howard Kaminsky, 'Wycliffism as Ideology for Revolution', *Church History* 32 (1963), 57–74. See also his *A History of the Hussite Revolution* (Berkeley, CA: University of California Press, 1967; repr. Wipf & Stock, 2002) for a fuller analysis of the Hussite ideology as more than simply reaction against extant abuses.

11. See Eamon Duffy, *The Stripping of the Altars*, 2nd ed. (New Haven, CT: Yale University Press, 2005), and Richard Rex, *The Lollards* (New York: Palgrave, 2002).

12. See Duffy, *Stripping of the Altars*, xxvii. Duffy's assessment of the theology of Lollardy as the 'chilling and depressing body of material all to obviously infected by the dyspepsia of the movement's founder' may be accurate, but this does not mean that such puritanical strains did not find approving ears. After all, this apparently cold and sterile biblicism

would find a ready audience in Tudor England, and another version of it continues to find one in some strains of contemporary American Protestantism.

13. Examples of the best known of these include John Mirk's *Instructions for Parish Priests* (c. 1400), ed. Gillis Kristensson (Lund: C. W. K. Gleerup, 1974); William Pagula's *Ocula sacerdotal* (c.1320s); Ranulf Higden's *Speculum curatorum* (1340); Archbishop Thoresby's *Lay Folks' Catechism* (1350s), eds. T. F. Simmons and H. E. Nolloth, EETS o.s. 118 (London: K. Paul, Trench, Trübner, 1901; repr. Woodbridge: Boydell & Brewer, 2006) See W. A. Pantin, *The English Church in the Fourteenth Century* (Cambridge: Cambridge University Press, 1955), 189–219. See also Joseph Goering, *William de Montibus (c.1140–1213): The Schools and the Literature of Pastoral Care* (Toronto: Pontifical Institute of Mediaeval Studies, 1992).

14. Siegfried Wenzel, *Latin Sermon Collections from Later Medieval England* (Cambridge: Cambridge University Press, 2005), 229–52.

15. Robert Grosseteste, Sermon 14, printed in E. Brown, *Fasciculus rerum expetendarum ac fugiendarum, prout ab O.[rtwinus] G.[ratius] editus est Coloniae, A.D. 1535 Reformationis urgent,* 2 vols. (London: R. Chiswell, 1690); translated in Wenzel, *Latin Sermon Collections,* 234.

16. Beryl Smalley, *English Friars and Antiquity in the Early Fourteenth Century* (Oxford: Blackwell, 1960).

17. Bradwardine, author of *De causa Dei,* was likely a personal associate of Holkot; both were members of the highly educated circle of Richard de Bury, Bishop of Durham.

18. Robert Holkot, *Super libros sapientiae* (Hagenau, 1494; repr. Frankfurt: Minerva G. M. B. H., 1974); see also Beryl Smalley, 'Robert Holcot, OP', *Archivum Fratrum Praedicatorum* 26 (1956), 5–97. For Holkot as philosopher, see Hester Gelber, 'Robert Holkot', *Stanford Encyclopedia of Philosophy,* http://plato.stanford.edu/entries/holkot/#Bib.

19. See R. W. Southern, *Robert Grosseteste: The Growth of an English Mind in Medieval Europe* (Oxford: Oxford University Press, 1992), 289–307.

20. See Stephen E. Lahey, *John Wyclif* (Oxford: Oxford University Press, 2009), 48–9.

21. John Wyclif, *De ordinatione fratrum, Polemical Works,* ed. R. Buddensieg, vol.1 (London: Wyclif Society), 96.15–20.

22. Decima Douie, *Archbishop Pecham* (Oxford: Oxford University Press, 1952), 42.

23. See Anne Hudson, 'A Lollard Compilation and the Dissemination of Wycliffite Thought', *Journal of Theological Studies* 23 (1972), 65–81; see also her *Premature Reformation*), 106–110; and her 'A Lollard Compilation in England and Bohemia', *Journal of Theological Studies* 25 (1974), 129–140.

24. Gordon Leff has argued against this in *Heresy in the Later Middle Ages,* 524, n.5, as has K. B. McFarlane, in *John Wycliffe and the Beginnings of English Nonconformity* (London: English Universities Press, 1953), 100. Michael Wilks met the challenges of these in his 'Royal Priesthood: The Origins of Lollardy', in *The Church in a Changing Society: CIHEC Conference in Uppsala 1977* (Uppsala: Almqvist & Wisell, 1978), 63–70, but shifted to conceiving of Wyclif's aim as being a top-down reformatory movement. See also Lahey, *John Wyclif,* 166–7.

25. *Dyalogus sive speculum ecclesie militantis,* ed. A. W. Pollard (London: Wyclif Society, 1886); *Sermones,* ed. J. Loserth, vol. 1 (London: Wyclif Society, 1886); *Epistola missa ad simplices sacerdo* in *Opera Minora,* ed. J. Loserth (London: Wyclif Society, 1913), 7–8.

26. See Jean-Pierre Torrell, OP, *Thomas Aquinas. Vol.1: The Person and His Work* (Washington: Catholic University of America, 1996), 164–6; and *Vol.2: Spiritual Master* (Washington: Catholic University of America, 2003), 323.

27. See John Wyclif, *Trialogus cum Supplemento Trialogi*, ed. G. Lechler (Oxford: Clarendon Press, 1869); also my translation, *John Wyclif's Trialogus* (Cambridge: Cambridge University Press, 2013).

28. See Sermon I.44, in *Sermones*, vol.1 (London, Wyclif Society 1886), 291–7; Sermon IV.34, in *Sermones*, vol.4 (London: Wyclif Society 1889), 290–6.

29. See *De mandatis divinis*, eds. J. Loserth and F. D. Matthew (London: Wyclif Society, 1922), ch. 19–20; *De oracione dominica* in *Opera minora*, ed. J. Loserth (London: Wyclif Society, 1913), 383–92; Sermon I.29 in *Sermones* vol.1, 197–9; *Opus evangelicum*, vol. 1, ed. J. Loserth (London: Wyclif Society, 1895), 256–311.

30. See Anne Hudson, 'The Development of Wyclif's *Summa Theologie*' in *John Wyclif: Logica, politica, teologia,* eds. M. T. Fumagalli, Beonio Brocchieri, S. Simonetta (Florence: Sismel, 2003), 57–70; also Ivan Mueller, 'A "Lost" *Summa* of John Wyclif', *From Ockham to Wyclif Studies in Church History, Subsidia* 5 (1987), 179–83.

31. For the dating of the sermons, see Anne Hudson, 'Wyclif's Latin Sermons: Questions of Form, Date and Audience', *Archives d'histoire doctrinale et littéraire du moyen âge* 68 (2001), 223–48.

32. *De universalibus* ch. 3, l.162–165 In Ivan J. Mueller, ed., *John Wyclif, Tractatus de universalibus* (Oxford, 1985).

33. On Wyclif's determinism, see Ian Levy, 'Grace and Freedom in the Soteriology of John Wyclif', *Traditio* 60 (2005), 279–337; Lahey, *John Wyclif*, 169–98.

34. Wyclif, *De veritate sacrae scripturae* I.vi, in *John Wyclif: On the Truth of Holy Scripture*, trans. Ian Levy (Kalamazoo, MI: TEAMS, 2001), 97; Wyclif, *De Ideis*, eds. V. Herold and I. Mueller (Leiden: Brill), forthcoming.

35. Wyclif describes the tie between the divine ideas and scripture in *Trialogus* I.8–9 and III.31, and makes reference to this argument in *De mandatis,* ch.12, 111.

36. See Stephen Penn, 'Wyclif and the Sacraments' in *A Companion to John Wyclif: Late Medieval Theologian*, ed. Ian Christopher Levy (Leiden: Brill, 2006), 241–91.

37. Wyclif, *Trialogus* IV.1.

38. Wyclif, *De officio pastorali*, II.1, ed. Lechler (Leipzig: A. Edelmannum, 1863), 32; translated by Ford Lewis Battles, in *Advocates of Reform*, ed. Matthew Spinka (Philadelphia, PA: Westminster Press, 1953), 49.

39. See Ian C. Levy, *John Wyclif: Scriptural Logic*; Lahey, *John Wyclif*, 102–34.

40. Wyclif, *Trialogus* IV.23.

41. Wyclif, *Trialogus* IV.24.

42. Wyclif, *De fundatione sectarum, Polemical Works*, 24.20–5.

43. See Wyclif, *De religionibus vanis monacharum* in *Polemical Works*, vol.2, 435–40, and Wyclif, *De nova praevaricantia mandatorum* in *Polemical Worksi*, vol.1, chapter 5, 131–5.

44. Wyclif, *De civili dominio* III.2, 15.5–23. In J. Loserth, ed. *De civili domino*, vols. II–IV (London: Wyclif Society, 1885).

45. Wyclif, *De civili dominio* I.11,73.20–74.12. Wyclif, *De officio regis*, ed. A. W. Pollard (London: Wyclif Society, 1887), chapter 6, 147.5ff. For discussion of the tension within Wyclif's thought on the need, or lack thereof, for a class of ordained Christians, see David Aers, 'John Wyclif's Understanding of Christian Discipleship', in *Faith, Ethics and Church: Writing in England, 1366-1409,* ed. David Aers (Cambridge: D. S. Brewer, 2000), 119–149.

46. Wyclif, *De officio pastoralis*, I.1, trans. in Spinka, *Advocates of Reform*, 32.

47. Wyclif, *De Civili Dominio* III.5, 65.22–77.13.

48. Wyclif, *Doctrinale*, V.1 (ii.44).

49. For Donatism in Lollardy, see Hudson, *The Premature Reformation*, 316–318; in Hussite theology, see Howard Kaminsky, *A History of the Hussite Revolution* (Berkeley, CA: University of California Press, 1967), 98–204. For a full analysis of Wyclif's donatism, see Ian Levy, 'Was John Wyclif's Theology of the Eucharist Donatistic?', *Scottish Journal of Theology* 53 (2000), 137–53.

50. See Ian Levy, 'Wyclif and the Christian Life', in *A Companion to John Wyclif: Late Medieval Theologian*, ed. Ian Christopher Levy (Leiden: Brill, 2006), 293–364.

51. Augustine, *De civitate Dei*, 19.26.

52. In this very general description I follow John Mahoney, *The Making of Moral Theology* (Oxford: Clarendon, 1987).

53. See Wyclif, *Trialogus* III.10–11.

54. See Johann Loserth, *Johann von Wiclif und Guilelmus Peraldus* (Wien: In Kommission bei Alfred Hölder, 1916).

55. From *Sermones* II.27 (Matthew 5:1), ed. Johann Loserth (London: Wyclif Society, 1887), 202.

BIBLIOGRAPHY

Hornbeck, Patrick, Fiona Somerset, and Stephen Lahey, eds. and trans., *Wycliffite Spirituality* (New York: Paulist Press, 2014).

Hudson, Anne, *The Premature Reformation: Wycliffite Texts and Lollard History* (Oxford: Oxford University Press, 1988).

Kaminsky, Howard, *A History of the Hussite Revolution* (Berkeley, CA: University of California Press, 1967).

Kaminsky, Howard, 'Wycliffism as Ideology of Revolution', *Church History* 32 (1963), 57–74.

Lahey, Stephen, *John Wyclif* (Oxford: Oxford University Press, 2009).

Lahey, Stephen, trans., *John Wyclif: Trialogus* (Cambridge: Cambridge University Press, 2013).

Levy, Ian C., ed., *A Companion to John Wyclif: Late Medieval Theologian* (Leiden: Brill, 2006; repr. 2011).

Levy, Ian C., *John Wyclif's Theology of the Eucharist in Its Medieval Context: Revised and Expanded Edition of: Scriptural Logic, Real Presence, and the Parameters of Orthodoxy* (Milwaukee, WI: Marquette, 2014).

CHAPTER 27

'ANTICLERICALISM', INTER-CLERICAL POLEMIC AND THEOLOGICAL VERNACULARS

KATHRYN KERBY-FULTON, MELISSA MAYUS, AND KATIE ANN-MARIE BUGYIS

THE BACKGROUND (KATHRYN KERBY-FULTON)

> Ac me thynketh loth, thogh Y Latyn knowe, to lacken eny secte,
> For alle be we brethrene thogh we be diuerse clothed.[1]

CHAUCER'S slightly older contemporary and fellow London poet, William Langland, intruded these surprisingly candid lines into the thick of one of the most fiercely anti-mendicant episodes of *Piers Plowman* (the Feast of Patience). Though he knows Latin himself, the poet says, he is reluctant to blame any religious order ('secte'), because 'alle be we brethrene', even if diversely robed.[2] This candid little 'aside' from Chaucer's fellow poet shatters many comfortable modern assumptions about the twin topics assigned to us here: (1) 'anticlericalism', which in Chaucer, as in Langland, is more often staged as a form of *inter-clerical polemic*; and (2) 'vernacular theology', recently re-conceptualized as the 'theological vernacular', and more recently expanded to include even Latin itself. As we will argue here, 'anticlericalism' is a concept useful only within very real limits when one is faced with the complexities of contemporary religious polemic, since many of these supposedly 'anti-clerical' texts were *clerically*-authored and employed in debates *between clerics*—which is just how Chaucer, too, portrays them. And the second half of our assignment, 'vernacular theology', has become similarly complex: reconceptualized by Ian Johnson in 2011 as the 'theological vernacular' (a shift discussed by Katie Bugyis below), even more recent studies of medieval language acquisition and multilingualism have now given us a further complication: 'vernacular Latin' (in Christopher Cannon's phrase).[3] With these changes scholarly focus has shifted from emphasis on traditional ideas of Latin as a formal, rhetorical language with classical roots and a learned literary theory,[4] to keener awareness of Latin as also a vast, flexible and ubiquitous 'service' language, more often heavily vernacularized in word order and syntax, a working language productive of multiple medieval genres used by clergy, clerical proletariat, and literate laity alike.

Langland tips us off in the lines quoted above to exactly why these complexities matter: even as a 'man of the cloth', he wrote critiques of his fellow clergy, and despite confessing to such moments of regret, he never stopped. But it would be a gross error therefore to call Langland an 'anticlerical' writer: rather, informed critique of the clergy is what responsible, literate, indeed *clerical* people traditionally did, and inter-clerical polemic was centuries old by Langland's time.[5] Nor, despite Lady Holy Church's initial patronizing commission to Will (I.135–6), was the poet writing simply for the laity: not only is his text littered with untranslated Latin, but he indicates in the quote above that his Latinate 'bretherne' are in his audience, too (the apology makes no sense if they are not). Since it was Langland who set the biggest English poetic precedent for Chaucer in London's nascent English-reading community, these issues are crucial for Chaucerians, too. Chaucer himself rarely deviates from this tradition of staging all such rivalries as *between clerics*—with, as we will see, some characteristically cautious twists.

Much of what Middle English scholars call 'anticlericalism' today, whether delivered in the vernacular or not, is actually '*inter*-clerical polemic' (writing in which orders ['sectes'] rebuke *each other*); or in certain cases, '*intra*-clerical polemic' (criticism arising *within* factions of a single order).[6] Together, these account for the lion's share of negative comment against religious figures in the Middle Ages. Such critique spilled over into vernacular texts in spades, creatively deployed by their authors—but it did *not* originate with them. What we call antimendicantism, for instance, as my co-author Melissa Mayus explains in relation to William of St Amour below, is actually a highly technical Latin polemic derived from (and masquerading as) biblical exegesis.[7] It originated in the mid-thirteenth century among the University of Paris's secular clergy, and was later heavily propagated in Latin by the friars' many clerical rivals throughout the later Middle Ages, including the monastic orders. Chaucer's antimendicantism is drawn directly and indirectly (e.g. via French poets) from this inter-clerical Latinate debate, as source studies show.[8] But less noticed has been Chaucer's keen awareness of fraternal *intra*-clerical polemic as well, both controversies among the orders of friars, and those within the Franciscan order itself. So, for instance, the Falstaffian Friar John in the Summoner's Tale brags of his order's asceticism by invoking Elijah (III.1890), an allusion that would not be lost on those who knew intra-fraternal polemic: the Carmelite order claimed to go back to the time of Elijah (!) so as to 'out-originate' even St. Francis and St. Dominic.[9]

And battles *within* Franciscan ranks themselves over issues of strict adherence to the Rule of St Francis, also, as John Fleming noted some years ago, show up 'in negative refraction in the character of Friar John in Chaucer's Summoner's Tale'.[10] Langland, Richard FitzRalph, John Wyclif, and many of Chaucer's reform-minded clerical contemporaries of all stripes were alert to this polemic, but Chaucer is not often credited with such deep appreciation of its minutiae, and he should be.

Although Chaucer's command of antimendicant literature was sophisticated, a chunk of what we see in his writing was a re-appropriation of a Latin tradition first borrowed for literary purposes by great French vernacular poets like Rutebeuf and Jean de Meun. Chaucer, however, was not quite as daring as Jean (a Paris-trained clerk himself apparently), so he mitigated some of what he found in the *Romance of the Rose* for English consumption by shoving the worst traits further down the clerical hierarchy to embellish his Pardoner rather than his Friar.[11] Melissa Mayus will discuss this issue in more detail below, but here I allude to it to underline one of the key points traditionally tying 'anticlericalism' and 'vernacular theology' together in the minds of modern scholars. As Nicholas Watson wrote in a 2006 essay: 'writing about religion in the vernacular is a *political* act … and, because this is so, all vernacular writing about religion is connected, part of a single field or arena of discourse'.[12] Watson rightly points to the political as significant in many cases, and Chaucer's vernacularization of antimendicant thought (both from French and Latin) certainly did involve 'political' strategy, as his strategic displacements down the clerical ladder indicate.

But are *all* decisions to write theology in the vernacular 'political'? Some choices would have been simply necessary and pragmatic, for instance, as the author gauged the target audience's educational abilities. Other decisions to write in English were imitative of earlier, established English genres, and often uncontroversial: take, for instance, the hundreds of Middle English religious lyrics, often ignored by literary scholars.[13] Still other poets opted for English because it can often do more specific poetic or cultural work (the alliterative tradition springs to mind), as Marjorie Harrington has recently shown of the English religious poem *Erþ* when set against the disappointing poetry of its adjacent Latin translation in Harley 913.[14] Here the Latin is the pragmatic choice, allowing the gist of the text to go viral among clergy internationally, but the poetic technique and richness in the English one is superior, and, I would add, perhaps closer to the creative ideals of 'vernacular theology' as originally conceptualized by Nicholas Watson. By contrast, the Prologue to Chaucer's Prioress's Tale, which heavily paraphrases texts from the Little Office of the Virgin, the Mass of the Holy Innocents, and snippets of Dante, is so rhetorically Latinate that a medieval reader could virtually hear the liturgical performance behind it. Even the Dantean passages are barely 'vernacular': lines VIII.469–72, for instance, are so difficult and subjunctive-laden that modern editors are forced to construe them in the notes.[15] And Chaucer never once translates the oft-repeated Latin name of the antiphon the tale's clergeoun sings, *Alma redemptoris*. In genres where poetic tradition mattered then, either language might automatically trump the other. In some cases, one just *had* to have English or Latin (or French) for poetic or canonical effect. This is what more recent scholarship now understands as cultural *multilingualism*, in which languages operate at parity. Emphasizing instead, as Christopher Baswell says, 'the improbability and illogic of a single, authoritative tongue',[16] for such scholars, English is not the perpetual 'underdog' or the 'political' choice. So we now have many approaches to vernacularity, but the same caveat, I believe, applies to all: any one of them can quickly become reductive or essentializing.

Until fairly recently, the study of 'vernacular theology' has been approached from the political perspective, most marked in the many 'after Arundel' discussions of the 1990s and early 2000s.[17] But with the development of the sociolinguistic concepts of multilingualism, and the near simultaneous return of interest in poetics and literary language for its own sake ('formalism'), several newer ways of studying vernacularity have now destabilized the universality of a political approach. First, one has to account for the great diversity of intellectual and linguistic demands English works make on readers, even among manuscripts of Chaucer's own works. As Tim Machan has noted, English was too unstable and various in dialect to be a *lingua franca*.[18] Most importantly, current work on grammatical manuscripts has shown that English is not in fact *any* medieval *reader's* mother tongue—extant primers and grammars indicate that reading was apparently always taught beginning with Latin. And it was most certainly not any fourteenth-century writer's *written* mother tongue: in Chaucer's time, all writing was initially taught in Latin.[19] And as Jocelyn Wogan-Browne explains, even French, another language often treated as a vernacular, was always, in late medieval England, in fact a language normally acquired later in the literacy process.[20] Even in many 'blue collar' jobs, including those of reeves (like Chaucer's Reeve) stewarding estates, accounts were kept in their own workmanlike Latin.[21] This does not mean that there was no concept of English as a 'single arena' but such an arena would contain challenging dialect obstacles and transmission issues for any aspiring vernacular theologian. More promising, I would suggest, is the sense of a nascent or evolving identity for English *literary* texts noted by palaeographers: increasingly in Chaucer's lifetime even scribes fluent in the newer Secretary hands switched back to the older *Anglicana formata* hands to copy English poetry.[22] Stable Secretary hands arrive late to the copying of literature in English, and one can observe something of a conscious vernacular script choice for many poetic texts: this is indeed an *idea* of the vernacular,[23] and even something approaching a sense of 'single arena', but it is not universal for English language texts, and not notably related to the theological.

Studying the manuscripts written for Chaucer's earliest audiences gives us evidence for this type of awareness, and for the striking dependency on Latin that several glossators (at least one of which was likely Chaucer himself) and annotators of the *Canterbury Tales* exhibit. In narrative sections of tales there is often less marginal glossing: for instance, after the Prologue is concluded, glossing in the Prioress's Tale drops off; similarly, the Wife's Prologue, with all its exegetical polemic in her monologue is heavily glossed in Latin in all our best early witnesses, including Ellesmere, but her Tale is only lightly glossed.[24] Moreover, these glosses even include some lexical or syntax aids in Latin for audiences not used to reading in Middle English: in other words, Latin is the crutch used to help early readers of Chaucer read English.[25] Modern scholars forget that reading in Middle English was not easy in the late fourteenth century: not only did it present formidable dialect and spelling challenges, but it changed rapidly, making older manuscripts hard to read. The idea that translation into English 'universalizes' reading experience is therefore problematic, less so the oral one, and so perhaps Johnson's more neutral 'theological vernacular' helps us negotiate these rocky shoals for a different reason: because it emphasizes, as Katie Bugyis shows below, performativity.

Chaucer's fascination with clerical critique encompasses not only friars, but elements from the inter-clerical polemic of the secular clergy, sometimes where we least expect it. Take Chaucer's clerical dandy and sore loser at love, Absoloun, the parish clerk (I.3347) from the Miller's Tale, surely an uncomplicated anticlerical portrait? Not so fast. Again, an example from Chaucer's most famous predecessor is helpful in understanding just what is and what isn't 'anticlerical' in this satirical portrait: in *Piers Plowman*, Langland represented a particular type of dandified lax priest as a 'proud priest' in the vanguard of Antichrist.[26] In a picture worth a thousand words, the scribe-illustrator of the Douce 104 *Piers Plowman* recognized the type and drew the 'Proud Priest' (see Figure 27.1), shown with his index finger pointing to his identity in the verses of the text. Visually unrecognizable as a priest apart from his tonsure, he wears tight, stylish clothing and a large sword dangles obscenely between his legs. The tendency for modern readers is to instantly assume that both Langland and the Douce illustrator are indulging in the 'anti-clerical' here.[27] But one finds these injunctions against dandified clothing and pointed shoes issued all over Latin literature *written by clerics for clerics*.[28] In fact, this Douce 104 iconography, like so much else that appears 'anticlerical' at first blush, comes also from Latin treatises written by clerics—in this particular case, from a pastoral manual such as William of Pagula's *Oculus sacerdotis* (see Figure 27.2 where the shocking scene is portrayed in full) or James le Palmer's *Omne bonum* (Figure 27.3). Both are works aimed at a Latin-literate clerical audience. Even contemporary episcopal records furnish historical examples, e.g. visitation records of the York vicars choral contain several complaints against clerics out on the town, 'turbulent vicars...sometimes dressed as laymen and with knives and daggers hanging between their legs'. These are not, then, 'anticlerical' but *inter-clerical* products. Does the simple fact of translation into English make something anticlerical? Hardly, when the poet himself, as we saw earlier, self-identifies as clerical; moreover, in the process of 'vernacularization' Langland even *softened* the critique of the pastoral manuals: his corrupt priests, he tells us,[29] come from Ireland, a place remote enough and wild enough in the English imagination to make anything possible. Not so William's and James's corrupt priests, nor the York vicars choral of episcopal records. The Douce 104 scribe, working in English not Latin, also pulled his punches: he was actually copying in Ireland, so he made Langland's priests hail from *Wales* (see Figure 1). Chaucer's Absoloun is even safer than any of these, portrayed as still in minor orders (a member of the clerical proletariat), so not bound by vows of chastity. Whatever else we might call these moments of vernacularization, especially Chaucer's, we couldn't call them daring.

'Political' then, I would add, can mean *self*-censoring in the vernacularization process. If modern scholars are looking for the *avant garde* or the shocking, they are often going

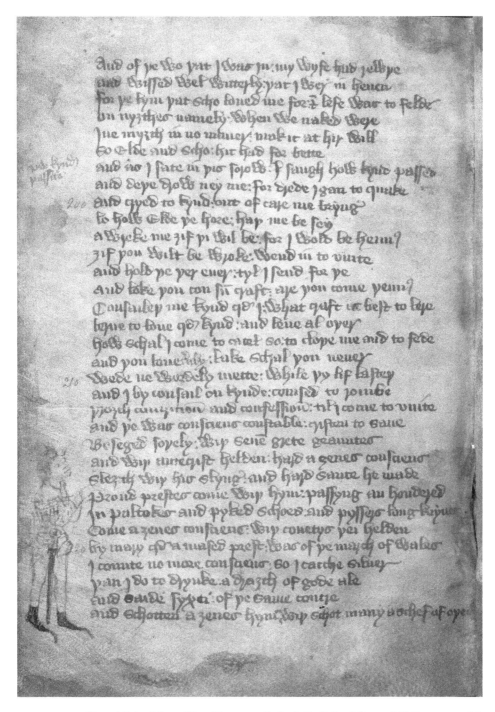

FIGURE 27.1 'Proud Priest' from *Piers Plowman*, Oxford, Bodleian Library, MS Douce 104, fol. 109v, showing him in the vanguard of Antichrist, with tonsure visible despite fashionable, secular clothing and dangling sword. Dated 1427 by its Middle-Hiberno English scribe-illustrator, written in a government hand.

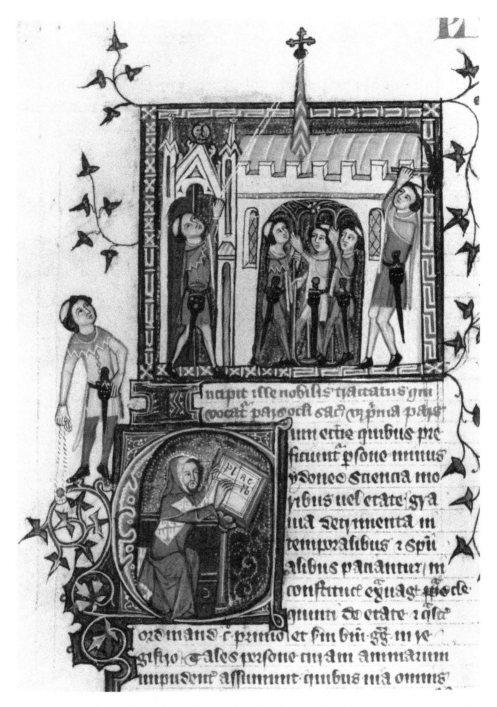

FIGURE 27.2 Clerics destroying a church, from William of Pagula's pastoral manual, *Oculus sacerdotis*, Hatfield House, Herts, Marquess of Salisbury, MS Cecil Papers 290, fol 13. English, second half of the 14th c.

FIGURE 27.3 'De habitu clericorum' from *Omne bonum*, showing correctly dressed priests confronting fashionably secular priests, tonsured but with dangling swords; ©The British Library Board from London, British Library; MS Royal 6.E.VI, fol. 197. English, 1360₇₅.

to be disappointed in vernacular texts, even in vernacular Wycliffite texts (authors of the latter, for instance, visibly softened strident critiques of the clergy borrowed from the twelfth-century abbess, Hildegard of Bingen, one of the more passionate advocates of the twelfth-century Gregorian reform movement later admired by Wycliffites).[30] So these issues of daring and of originality in texts are far from uniform across the Middle English works engaging theology. An excellent essay by Vincent Gillespie addresses this issue, offering a succinct history of 'Vernacular Theology': the label was first used by Ian Doyle in 1953 who asserted that 'there was little or no original thought in the vernacular'; then by Bernard McGinn, who in 1994 took a pan-European view and concluded that the vernacular 'not only created distinctive theological models, it also produced new, sometimes challenging insights into the mysteries of the faith'. An important instance of this originality for McGinn was Meister Eckhart's use of German vocabulary that would be untranslatable in Latin. Nicholas Watson then in 1995 used the concept in his influential

Speculum essay in 'an attempt to distance scholarship from its habitual adherence to a clerical, Latinate perspective'.[31]

Looking at the problem two decades later, one can't help but observe that in English departments at least, 'habitual adherence to a clerical, Latinate perspective' was already as scarce as hen's teeth even in 1995, and has since become even scarcer. If anything, some rebalancing is in order now: part of what we wish to do here is to gently remind readers of how heavily indebted our English writers often were to Latin sources, even for *satire against clergy*, and, of course, to French ones—French repeatedly complicates this picture because it, too, was increasingly the language of certain elites in Chaucer's time. While no one would wish to return to Doyle's 1953 assessment (nor did Doyle himself), Latin sources cannot be wholly ignored. In the little instance regarding the 'proud priests' above, Langland's reshaping of this pastoral trope for poetic purposes is brilliant: in effect he dropped it into his own multi-level allegory of just the kind of eschatological exegesis William of St Amour had levelled against the friars, but now spreading the blame among clergy more generally. William of Pagula and James le Palmer will never be considered a match for Langland's literary genius because literature in any language can often go places theology cannot (what, indeed, Barbara Newman called 'imaginative theology'). But it is Langland's deftness, not his vernacularity, that creates theological genius. Scholars of antimendicantism have already realized that they are often dealing more with an imaginative construct than with real history, and it is important that scholars of 'anticlericalism' realize some of the same issues, especially for those of us who deal in literary texts.[32]

As Jill Mann established long ago about Chaucer's General Prologue portraits of ecclesiastical figures,[33] it is largely Latin sources that underlie his satire, even—indeed, especially—those that ridicule clergy. Latin Goliardic poetry in particular nourished Chaucer: he must have been steeped in that sophisticated Latin poetic tradition that poked fun far more outrageously at the sacred than Chaucer dared in English. First developed among clerks in the fledging universities of the Middle Ages, by Chaucer's time Goliardic poetry was widely collected in clerical compilations, especially—and counterintuitively for us—in Latin monastic and fraternal anthologies as well.[34] Again, one does not know how to use the term 'anticlerical' in such circumstances. In fact, one shouldn't. What should be recognized in Chaucer, however, is his crackerjack ability to soften or nuance an often vicious Latin tradition: for example, in one of many such instances, Jill Mann notes that the 'siren songs' attributed acerbically to nuns become, in Chaucer's hands, the Prioress's sweet singing (just slightly nasal, which was in fact a real-life professional technique to mitigate long hours in choir).[35] When Chaucer pulls his punches, he can do so with great delicacy. However, sometimes he comes out swinging: as Derek Pearsall writes of the Latin misogynist theology out of which the Wife of Bath's Prologue is constructed, it 'must have been one of the more sterile legacies of his traditional reading'.[36] By the time Chaucer was done with it, not only had he 'humanized, domesticated and anglicized the rampant shrew...of European satire', but he had also managed to pose a serious challenge to Patristic and monastic misogyny. As if that weren't dazzling enough, he also, in the Wife's Prologue, gently satirized both overly literal biblical interpretations, *and* critiques of them.[37] This kind of displacement was one of the key weapons in Chaucer's theological vernacular. Another brilliant use of displacement appears in the *House of Fame*, which satirizes nominalist or Ockhamesque theology of salvational 'just desserts' under the guise of a whimsical exploration of who deserves fame.[38] When we speak of Chaucer, genius, it seems, transcends linguistic boundaries and political strategies, and 'vernacularity'. Thus, Vincent Gillespie's description of Julian of Norwich's 'skilful use of different linguistic codes, registers, narrative voices, and rhetorical levels of style'[39] would describe Chaucer's methods as well.

What does this leave us in the literary realm that could be called genuine 'anticlericalism'? In fact, not so much as we once thought. Certain populist genres seem a safe bet: Chaucer's fabliaux, for instance, have genuine anticlerical elements that don't appear to derive from inter- or intra-clerical polemic. The lecherous Daun John of the Shipman's Tale, for example, is a generically named monk, but Latin estates satire cannot wholly account for his role in the tale ('closer to the pure fabliau type' than any of Chaucer's tales).[40] Chaucer did not try for a shred of religious sentiment here, suggesting perhaps Continental fabliau sources, different from even the genuinely anticlerical treatment of monks in home-grown tales like the Robin Hood ballads (first alluded to in English in *Piers Plowman*). For instance, in a text like 'Robin Hood and the Monk', Little John seems to think nothing of summarily dispatching a fat monk to meet his Maker, yet the entire plot turns on Robin Hood's yearning to go to church and pray to Mary. This mix of genuine anticlericalism (which I would define as *lay resentment of clerical privilege*) and simultaneous devotion to a higher religious power may get us closer to English lay-based anticlericalism and its complexity. Perhaps Chaucer's unsentimental Daun John explains why the spurious 'Gamelyn' travels incognito with the *Tales*, though violently anticlerical in spots, violence that arises in a romance context unconnected with any obvious inter-clerical polemic. 'Gamelyn' appears early and repeatedly, and ever only in the *Tales* manuscript tradition, where it is used as a substitute for the unfinished Cook's Tale—for instance in the early Corpus Christi College MS of the *Tales* copied by Scribe D, a man just recently identified as a possible associate of Ralph Strode (one of the two dedicatees of the *Troilus*).[41] One could also examine aspects of the 'town vs. gown' conflicts of the Miller's and Reeve's Tales as a genre of anticlericalism, though a very specialized one emerging in college towns (we have already seen Absoloun's debt to Latin pastoral polemic).

These, then, are some of the places where we might find genuine or 'spontaneous' anticlericalism in literary sources, uninfluenced by inter-clerical polemic, or even Latin estates satire. Genuine anticlericalism, like genuine 'vernacular theology', is harder to find than we have thought. Theology in the vernacular may often make 'political' choices (whether daring or cautious); and at times, as McGinn noted of Meister Eckhart's indispensable German terminology, offer some unique untranslatable elements. Though no longer viewable as a 'single field or arena', as Chris Cannon says, it has been 'an immensely valuable category'.[42] In the hands of a genius, such as Julian or Langland, it sings. And Chaucer, though not one of our most creative theological vernacularizers, wielded nuance with the best.

CHAUCER AND INTER-CLERICAL
POLEMIC (MELISSA MAYUS)

A number of 'anticlerical' strains of satire and criticism were in heavy circulation by the time Chaucer began writing the *Canterbury Tales*. The most prevalent such strain was likely the 'antimendicant' tradition, which had its main sources in the thirteenth-century writings of William of St Amour and the fourteenth-century writings of Richard FitzRalph. William of St Amour was a master of theology and an active leader of the secular clergy at the University of Paris; his objections to the fraternal orders were cast as eschatology and conditioned by his biblical exegesis.[43] William's most influential antimendicant work is *De periculis novissimorum temporum*, an exegetical commentary on 2 Timothy 3 which does not actually mention any of the fraternal orders; instead, it warns against scriptural figures, false apostles, 'penetrantes domos, pseudopraedicatores' [forerunners of the Antichrist], and other figures which William argued heralded the end of the world. Despite the fact that William did not call the friars by name, he and others clearly equated them with the apocalyptic figures of his treatise. The way in which William employed indirect confrontation can be seen early in *De periculis* when he states: 'We declare at the outset that what follows is said for the admonition and instruction of the entire church, and is not proclaimed against any person or against any status approved by the church. Rather, we speak against the sins of evil men and the dangers to the church at large.'[44] Richard FitzRalph picked up William of St Amour's antifraternal fight a century later in England, but his approach was much more ecclesiastical than St Amour's, which is obvious in the very title of his major antifraternal work, *Defensio curatorum*.[45] FitzRalph argued that the mendicant orders were liable to offer easy penances in exchange for monetary donations, thus depriving parish priests of part of their income as well as part of their communication with their parishioners; he also complained that friars were quick to usurp the place of secular clergy in burying the wealthy dead and in collecting donations that would otherwise go to the secular clergy. Examples of this type of argument abound in *Defensio curatorum*, such as when FitzRalph lists as a particular evil the 'wiþholdinge of offryngis þat men þat beþ y-schryue vseþ for to paye hem þat heriþ her schrifte; and freres appropreþ siche offryngis to her owne vse; & by þe lawe siche offryngis beþ dewe to parische chirches'.[46] In short, FitzRalph's major accusation levelled against the friars was that they disrupted the hierarchy of the church by usurping the most lucrative roles of the secular clergy.[47]

The difference between William of St Amour's eschatological approach to antimendicantism and Richard FitzRalph's ecclesiastical approach has been well documented, and previous scholars have also noted where the antimendicant claims of William of St Amour, FitzRalph, and others have appeared in the *Canterbury Tales*, sometimes arguing that Chaucer was promoting a point of view that was pro-secular clergy and antimendicant.[48] However, although the antimendicant claims he uses carry theological and polemical weight, Chaucer was a poet rather than a theologian, and his approach to and use of antifraternal/anticlerical sources is much more literary rather than theological or polemical.[49] In order to get some picture of the literary as opposed to the theological or polemical aspects of 'anticlericalism' in the *Canterbury Tales*, we must take into consideration the tales and prologues of the Summoner, Pardoner, and Friar, as well as their portraits and the portrait of the Monk in the General Prologue and how the anticlericalism of all of these—both tales and portraits—work alone and in comparison with each other. The combined picture that emerges when we take all of these tales and portraits into account is that Chaucer was not pursuing a simple antimendicant agenda. This does not mean that the *Canterbury Tales* can be said to be pro-mendicant or even decidedly neutral on the question either, rather that the picture is too complex to be called decidedly anything. Chaucer uses 'anticlerical' language in the *Canterbury Tales* in a way that is far too slippery and sophisticated to be pinned down to a single theological or polemical agenda.[50] For example, echoes of standard antimendicant claims are woven through the pilgrims' portraits and the Summoner's Tale, but it's the Pardoner who mimics the friar-figure Faus Semblant from Jean de Meun's *Romance of the Rose*, and it's the Summoner in the Friar's Tale who overuses the words 'brother' and 'brethern'. By spreading the 'antimendicant' rhetoric amongst both fraternal and non-fraternal characters, and by making it difficult to form a moral judgment upon his clerical characters, Chaucer uses familiar antimendicant language and claims not to make a simple antimendicant argument, but rather to highlight the inter-clerical debates playing out among his pilgrims.

Before we venture into examples from the *Canterbury Tales*, some clarification of terms is necessary. One of the basic issues any discussion of 'anticlericalism' must address is exactly what 'anticlericalism' means and how it relates to other terms such as 'antifraternal' and 'antimendicant'. 'Anticlerical' alone perhaps makes most sense when referring to lay critique of clergy, which appears very clearly in the Shipman's Tale, as discussed by Kathryn Kerby-Fulton above. 'Antifraternal' or 'antimendicant' refers to the language and the accusations commonly levelled at the fraternal orders; connected to these terms are the terms 'inter-mendicant', and 'intra-mendicant', which best refer to 'antimendicant' language and claims when they are used between friars of the same order or of different orders. It is easy to use 'anticlericalism' as a blanket term to refer to all of these categories, but as it appears in Chaucer 'anticlericalism' is not just derived from rhetoric directed against the mendicant orders or even clerics in general, rather it is a complicated debate about what each clerical/fraternal role *should* be, what the author or his characters thinks it *currently* is, and how well each clerical role is being fulfilled by its current occupants. Perhaps a better way to think of the issues at play here is to consider them as part of 'inter-clerical' or 'intra-clerical' debate. Thus, since so many of the 'antifraternal' and 'anticleri-cal' elements in the *Canterbury Tales* are used by clerical rather than lay figures, these elements actually paint a picture of 'intra-clerical' polemic.

The language and claims of intra-clerical polemic begin in the portraits of the General Prologue. For example, the portrait of Friar Huberd draws on multiple antimendicant ideas which were long familiar staples of antimendicant literature by Chaucer's time. Echoing the kinds of antimendicant claims made by William of St Amour and FitzRalph, Friar Huberd is a suspiciously accomplished beggar. He specifically claims the power of confession, which would be an annoyance to members of the secular clergy. The papacy had indeed granted friars the right to take confessions, but the secular clergy would have preferred to retain that task solely for themselves in order to gather more donations and keep in closer touch with their parishioners. Likewise, Friar Huberd advocates giving gentle penances that make him yet more popular and further erode the secular clergy:

> For he hadde power of confessioun,
> As seyde hymself, moore than a curat,
> For of his ordre he was licenciat.
> Ful swetely herde he confessioun,
> And plesaunt was his absolucioun.   (I.218–22)

The narrator goes out of his way to say that the Friar was 'licenciat', meaning that he had an official ecclesiastical license to preach or hear confessions. This is a technical term which shows that the Friar was operating within legal limits and possibly hints at the justification the Friar himself would give for his actions, especially as the previous line contains the phrase 'As seyde himself'. Thus with one line Chaucer is able to clarify both the Friar's legitimate legal standing and hint that the Friar was prepared to defend his claim against the secular clergy. In addition to the insinuations that he is using the power of confession in a way that undermines the secular clergy, the portrait of the Friar also appears to be influenced by other standard antimendicant claims in that the Friar is a particularly persuasive speaker, and 'In alle the ordres foure is noon that kan / So muchel of daliaunce and fair langage' (I.210–11), at once implies that the Friar's eloquence is not to be trusted and that he represents all four fraternal orders.[51] It is also telling that while 'daliaunce' could simply mean 'polite conversation', by the 1390s it could also mean '[a]morous talk or to-do; flirting, coquetry; sexual union',[52] and thus Chaucer adds yet another layer of ambiguity to the Friar's portrait. Finally, Friar Hubert prefers to dress as a 'maister' (261) rather than as a 'povre scoler' (260), shuns the company of the poor in order to court the powerful, and has ambiguous dealings with young women. All in all, the Friar's portrait shows Chaucer making good use of antimendicant rhetoric in order to portray a mendicant figure, yet at the same time he weaves enough ambiguity into the portrait to leave some doubt as to whether or not we can call the portrait itself 'antimendicant'.[53]

The portrait of the Monk, while not influenced by antimendicant claims, does hint at some anticlerical influence and inter-clerical conflict. In this portrait we get the Monk's own understanding of his ordained place in life and how well he believes he fills that place, which is to say that he sees no reason to live strictly within the rules of his order and he refuses to engage in either scholarly or physical labour (I.173–88).[54] Yet, even given these clear echoes of anticlerical tradition, Chaucer still manages to give the character some appealing characteristics, and he avoids making the outright accusations that mark more strident satire. When considering the question of the anticlerical tradition as it is embodied in these two portraits, Jill Mann argues that 'We find that we cannot pinpoint with exactness the target of Chaucer's satire. Previous tradition raises the expectation that we shall be called on to make a moral judgment on the holder of, or aspirant to monastic office, but we are not, in this case, given enough information to do so'.[55] The Monk is surely not an ideal cleric and he reflects estate satire on monks in general by being inordinately fond of eating, by preferring hunting to praying, and by dressing too well.[56] Yet he does not have any of the unpleasant characteristics which afflict the Pardoner and Summoner, and there is enough ambiguity in his general liveliness and in lines such as 'Now certeinly he was a fair prelaat' (204) to prevent us from calling the portrait purely anticlerical.

The Pardoner's portrait provides us with the first example of how Chaucer also complicates the reader's ability to make a neat moral judgment by applying elements of traditional satire in unexpected places. Specifically, he applies traditional antimendicant complaints to a non-fraternal character. The Friar is not the only character in the Prologue said to have a particular gift for winning gains with deceptive speech; the Pardoner is also described as gifted in this regard:

> Wel koude he rede a lessoun or a storie,
> But alderbest he song an offertorie;
> For wel he wiste, whan that song was songe,
> He moste preche and wel affile his tonge
> To wynne silver, as he ful wel koude;
> Therefore he song the murierly and loude.   (I.709–14)

Thus even when a traditionally antifraternal trait is given to the Friar in the *Tales*, that same trait is also given to the Pardoner, and we see the specifically antifraternal effect of that trait dissipated.[57] The Pardoner's portrait also places the Pardoner in direct conflict with the secular clergy, another detail that we might expect to hear about a friar rather than a pardoner. Lines 701 to 706 relate how the Pardoner was able to use his false relics to fool a 'povre person' and all of that parson's flock, managing to collect more money from them in one day than the parson could collect in two months. Later in her book Mann discusses the Pardoner as well, noting that despite the physical and moral disgust raised by the Pardoner, amusement at the end of his portrait allows the claim that 'in more ways than his skill in selling absolution, the Pardoner has resemblances with the "merye" Friar'.[58]

The dispersal of traditional 'antimendicant' traits and complaints gets even wider when we move from the portraits of the General Prologue into the tales. Interestingly, it is the clerical characters that are most prone to weaving 'anticlerical' and 'antimendicant' elements into their stories, thus giving us reason to see these elements as part of an ongoing interclerical debate among the pilgrims. The most obvious place to begin an examination of antimendicantism in the *Tales* is with the Summoner's Tale. The friar of this tale gets straight to the heart of the antimendicant issue by abusing his position in order to beg immoderately. He also exhibits many of the other defects that were commonly attributed to friars. He receives much more than the bare minimum of what he needs to live, and even has a servant with him to carry a bag for the extras. He recalls William of St Amour's warnings against the 'penetrantes domos' by poking through the village 'hous by hous' until he finds and enters the house where he sees the best chance of profit (III.1765–77). He is overly familiar with the wife in the house and he claims willingness to accept any food she might deign to offer while simultaneously ordering a huge meal. He accepts the title of master from her, and he preaches eloquently to Thomas on the subject of avoiding wrath and then succumbs to it himself. Finally, the matter of his title returns when he runs to see the lord in the village and manages to disclaim any desire to be called 'maister' while still reminding his listeners that he 'had in scole that honour' (2184–8).[59] Thus in at least one tale we have antimendicant complaints appearing attached to a friar, but as we shall see, non-fraternal characters are also subject to these same complaints.

This application of antimendicant rhetoric and claims in places where we would not necessarily expect them in more traditional satire is particularly striking in the Pardoner's Prologue and Tale, where Chaucer draws definite parallels between his Pardoner and the friar character Faus Semblant from the *Romance of the Rose*.[60] For instance, the Pardoner loudly declares that no local clergy can hinder him in his scheming—just as Faus Semblant does in lines 6361 to 6369 of the *Romance of the Rose*—when he tells the other pilgrims that:

> First I pronounce whennes that I come,
> And thanne my bulles shewe I, alle and some.
> Oure lige lordes seel on my patente,
> That shewe I first, my body to warente,
> That no man be so boold, ne preest ne clerk,
> Me to destourbe of Cristes hooly werk.   (VI.335–340)

Another quotation from the Pardoner's Prologue that is of particular interest occurs at lines 447 to 448 when the Pardoner proclaims, 'I wol noon of the apostles countrefete; / I wol have moneie, wolle, chese, and whete', when it was often the friars in particular who were supposed to be following the example of the apostles in voluntary poverty, rather than pardoners. Thus the Pardoner takes on many of the stereotypical faults of friars, but his fraternal parallels are not limited to faults; lines 412 to 420 of the Pardoner's Prologue also make conspicuous use of the word 'brethren', another potential example of (anti) fraternal language appearing where it is not expected.[61]

Finally we get to the Friar's Tale, and again find antimendicant material applied to an unexpected character. As noted earlier, a common complaint against friars was that they would hear confessions only for money, rather than through any desire to do people good. Yet, in Chaucer's hands this complaint is laid on a summoner, not a friar; Friar Huberd accuses the summoner in his tale of blackmail and of profiting by using personal information about people to extort money from them:

> This false theef, this somonour, quod the Frere,
> Hadde alwey bawdes redy to his hond,
> As any hauk to lure in Engelond,
> That tolde hym al the secree that they knewe,

> For hire acqueyntance was nat come of newe.
> They weren his approwours prively.
> He took hymself a greet profit therby.   (III.1338–44)

Granted, the summoner in this tale is using spies to suss out questionable behaviour in other people and is not hearing confessions or trying to give absolution, but he is profiting directly from privately hearing the wrongdoings of the people in a parish. Also, just like the Pardoner, the summoner of the Friar's Tale makes conspicuous use of the words 'brother' and 'brethren'. He and his demonic companion swear 'For to be sworne bretheren til they deye' (III.1405) and then proceed to refer to each other as 'brother' throughout the rest of the tale.

Previous scholars have been correct to identify antimendicant and anticlerical elements in the *Canterbury Tales*; however, Chaucer leaves enough ambiguity in his 'anticlerical' material—such as the portrait of the Monk—to prevent his audience from forming an immediate moral (anticlerical) judgment. He also builds confusion into his presentation of 'antimendicant' material by diffusing traditional antimendicant claims among the pilgrims—regardless of their specific clerical roles—thus making it impossible to label him as an antifraternalist, or even to say that the *Canterbury Tales* have an antimendicant bent. Instead of thinking of Chaucer as an antimendicant or anticlerical writer, it perhaps makes more sense to think of him as a writer who observed and made use of antimendicant and anticlerical elements in order to create a picture of inter-clerical and intra-clerical infighting woven throughout the *Canterbury Tales*. Such a cagey position would be very useful for Chaucer. A definite polemical stance would invite the reader to make an immediate judgment, while the presentation of an inter-clerical debate makes snap judgments difficult and instead invites the reader to consider a more nuanced view. There are also purely practical reasons to consider. William of St Amour's *De periculis* was, after all, condemned, and FitzRalph had died before a verdict could be reached on the various ecclesiastical suits which he and the friars were pursuing against each other. In more recent times, the anticlerical controversy in general and the antimendicant controversy in particular had become somewhat entangled with the Wycliffite movement.[62] Taking a definite stand on anticlerical issues would have been a risky undertaking, but submerging these issues into an ongoing inter-clerical debate among his pilgrims gave Chaucer a way to invite reflection on them without also inviting retribution on himself.

THEOLOGICAL TRANSLATIONS: A CASE STUDY OF CHAUCER, THE SECOND NUN, AND ST CECILIA (KATIE ANN-MARIE BUGYIS)

Scholars increasingly argue, and others are willing to concede, that Chaucer was, on occasion, a 'religious' poet,[63] even 'a writer capable of sophisticated theological thought'.[64] Very few claim that he 'did' theology,[65] certainly not in the 'speculative', 'mystical', or 'prophetic' modes that have been prized most in works of 'vernacular theology'.[66] Moreover, Chaucer's recourse to and promotion of the vernacular, though perhaps informed by Wycliffite models for English translation in the later decades of his career,[67] do not clearly evince any 'daring', 'political', or 'ideological' motivation, nor did he signal, in word or deed, any decisive break from 'orthodox', 'Latinate', 'clerical' culture.[68] As Melissa Mayus has shown here, Chaucer was often in dialogue with this culture, some-times even as a virtual member under various clerical guises, and in his writings, especially his translations, he expresses nothing but the complex interrelation, not the impassable division or hierarchical arrangement, between Latin and other vernaculars.[69] He understood well that all languages are equally contingent and, therefore, (in)capable of translating the 'sentence' of different 'tonges' (Tr 1393–8; see also Tales VII.961–4). This apparent equality shared among all languages led him to conclude: 'diverse pathes / leden diverse folk the righte way to Rome' (Astr 39–40).

The heuristic usefulness of the term 'vernacular theology' itself, irrespective of its application to Chaucer's writings, also has come under greater scrutiny. Critics of the term have questioned its politicization of the act of writing theology in the vernacular, and its creation of 'a single field or arena of discourse' that elides the differences, linguistic or otherwise, among Middle English texts included in the canon of 'vernacular theology'. Other scholars have worried that the term forces Latin and English (along with other European vernaculars) into an inflexible binary, that it over privileges the vernacular, that it fails to capture the *mouvance* of texts, their reinscriptions and reconfigurations through processes of transmission and reception.[70]

Few critics of 'vernacular theology' have offered an alternative heuristic; most prefer to insist instead that '[w]e need more, not fewer, terms for exploring this rich, understudied field [of medieval religious studies]'.[71] Ian Johnson has proposed a constructive alterna-tive, suggesting the replacement of the 'noun-based term' with 'the more adjectival and conditional collocation "theological vernacular" '.[72] For Johnson, this term communi-cates not 'the existence of a discrete phenomenon, an integral "thing" or corpus', but 'a more contingent, discontinuous, and dispersible coming into being'.[73] Most attractive among the features of the 'theological vernacular' that Johnson articulates are its dynamic, performative quality, its ongoingness, incompleteness, even, as he admits, '(in)competence'—all essential features, it would seem, to any theological utterance, whether oral or textual, which cannot, nor should, assert total comprehension of the truths to which it refers. Every utterance must be *in via*, open to begetting 'a range of further read-erly performances and further textual adaptations'.[74] It also focuses attention on vernacu-larity, without making it the 'single most important feature or *raison d'etre*' of medieval vernacular texts.[75] Arguably, it even raises the possibility of considering Latin as 'the great medieval European vernacular', as Alastair Minnis has suggested.[76] Certainly, according to Johnson's account, the relationship between Latin and other vernaculars need not be viewed as necessarily agonistic or hierarchical, but as interdependent and often collaborative. Finally, the 'theological vernacular' has the capacity to include, and be interested in, texts that have too often been deemed insufficiently 'exotic' to merit consideration as works of 'vernacular theology'.[77] Through analysing Chaucer's *Boece*,

Johnson effectively demonstrates that the 'theological vernacular' is not the preserve of 'original' works of theology; translations, even of 'not-primarily-pious text[s]', by writers not readily identified as 'theological' or 'religious', can exhibit sophisticated 'theological vernacularizing'.[78]

The criteria for judging whether a vernacular utterance is 'theological' are left undetermined by Johnson, perhaps intentionally so, lest some utterance fail to be considered as 'theological' because it was not spoken or written in a particular form, with particular content, to a particular audience, by a particular author with a particular intent. Insistence on certain particulars would surely risk excluding many writings from consideration as performances of the 'theological vernacular', and Johnson is clearly, and I think rightly, interested in minimizing this risk. Most, if not all, of Chaucer's writings would be discounted immediately if the 'theological' of the 'theological vernacular' were to be overdetermined, as they have tended to be in discussions of 'vernacular theology'. Johnson's analysis of Chaucer's *Boece*, however, encourages further reading in the poet's *oeuvre* to see if other instances of 'theological vernacularizing' can be detected.

Chaucer's Boethian lyrics, *Troilus and Criseyde*, and the *Knight's Tale* may prove particularly fruitful sites for such investigation, as all these texts owe their geneses to the 'discursive mastery' that the poet achieved through the *exercitatio* of translating the *Boece*.[79] More promising still are the tales told on the pilgrims' way to Canterbury that scholars have been more inclined to identify as 'religious'—the tales of the Prioress, the Second Nun, the Man of Law, and even the Clerk—or the performances of pilgrims who seem to possess a clear flair for or vested interest in the 'theological', like the Wife of Bath, the Pardoner, and the Parson, to name but the three most obvious candidates. The space that remains in this chapter does not permit the investigation of the 'theological vernacular' in all these sites, but hopefully the close study of one site—the Second Nun and her tale, the legend of St Cecilia—will motivate pursuits of the other leads.

The Second Nun and her tale may seem to be a rather safe or banal choice. The source-texts of her tale, unlike the *Boece*'s, are clearly devotional, if not theological. Chaucer also introduced very few changes to the content of these sources and even preserved much of the order and syntax of the original Latin. The conservative nature of Chaucer's translation may suggest that his retelling of the legend of St Cecilia was not designed to be 'essentially religious and didactic', because if it had been, he would have done more 'to correct its doctrinal teaching, heighten its appeals to emotion, adapt certain details to the experience and expectations of a contemporary audience, or simply improve the coherence of the narrative', as Sherry Reames has concluded.[80] Yet such an assessment of the *Second Nun's Tale* seems to depend on a narrow definition of translation as *only* the transfer of text from one language to another and, thus, fails to consider all the changes and crossings that constitute Chaucer's performance as translator. Considered in their totality, Chaucer's *translations* are anything but conservative; they are utterly transformative. Latin becomes English (and, in places, Latin again through the glosses supplied to the tale);[81] prose becomes verse; two versions of St Cecilia's life become a single, nearly seamless legend; an independent saint's life becomes one among many pilgrims' tales (and, in some manuscripts, an independent saint's life again);[82] text becomes (mostly) speech; and a male author (almost) becomes a female preacher, as both a nun and martyr. Whether any of these translational transformations were designed to be 'didactic' is difficult, if not impossible, to determine, as several would have gone undetected by most members of Chaucer's (and the Second Nun's) audience, both imagined and actual. However, they all merit consideration as potential acts of the poet's 'theological vernacularizing'.

Chaucer did not originally retell the life of St Cecilia as a tale for the *Canterbury Tales*, but as an independent saint's legend. If Mary Giffin was correct in her dating of the legend's composition and her claims to the historical circumstances that motivated its writing, Chaucer may have first translated the legend as early as 23 June 1383, as a gift to be given by Richard II (1367–1400) to Norwich Cathedral Priory on the occasion of the elevation of one of its own community members, Adam Easton (c.1330–97), to Cardinal Priest of S. Cecilia in Trastevere.[83] Certainly Chaucer had finished his first translation attempt by the time that he had composed the *Legend of Good Women*, where he, the dreamer-poet, confesses to the god of Love that he had 'maad the lyf also of Seynt Cecile' (LGW F 426; G 416); Chaucer's confession helps to set the *terminus ante quem* of his 'lyf' to roughly the mid 1380s. Beyond Adam Easton's elevation, other contemporary events may have occasioned Chaucer's translation, such as the schism in the church (1378–1417) and the increasingly apparent corruption of the papacy.[84] Whatever the initial (and subsequent) precipitating cause(s) was, it seems likely that Chaucer's retelling of the legend was to serve as a more general critique of overweening, morally compromised secular and religious powers and as a vision of reform guided by the 'history' of the church's exemplary beginnings, given his choice and manipulation of source-texts.[85]

Chaucer seems to have based his original translation of the life of St Cecilia only on the *Legenda aurea* of the Dominican friar Jacobus de Voragine (c.1230–98).[86] Yet the translation of the life that was included in the *Canterbury Tales* and voiced by the Second Nun was not based on the *Legenda aurea* alone, as Sherry Reames was the first to discover. Midway through this version of the translation, Chaucer decided to change source-texts. From roughly line 342 on, his translation depends primarily on an anonymous series of Matins lessons for St Cecilia's feast day that is not found in any extant office book of Sarum or other British rites. Rather, it is only found in breviaries and lectionaries copied for the Vatican, the Franciscans, and other religious communities that followed the 'use of the Roman curia' (henceforth the 'Franciscan abridgment').[87] Significantly, not only does Chaucer's source-text change at this point in the translation, but his versification and style do too; they exhibit 'a sudden leap in mastery of the stanza form', a transformation that suggests to Sherry Reames that 'the second half of the tale must have been written a good deal later than the first half'.[88] Chaucer may not have completed the version of the life of St Cecilia that appears in the *Canterbury Tales* until the late 1380s.[89]

If indeed Chaucer (and not an earlier editor or scribe of his exemplar) was responsible for switching, but not completely replacing, his source-text, his reasons for doing so are not entirely clear. He does not even admit that he is translating more than one source, but insists instead that he (or the Second Nun) is following 'the wordes and sentence' of only one author, 'hym that at the seintes reverence / The storie wroot' (VIII.81-3), who is identified as 'Iacobus Ianuensis' in the gloss near line 85 of the *Second Nun's Prologue* in most all the extant manuscript copies of the *Canterbury Tales*.[90] Tacitly combining multiple sources for a translation certainly accords well with Chaucer's authorial practices as a *compilator*, as Tim Machan has noted,[91] but such an explanation still leaves unanswered the question of why Chaucer chose the particular sources that he did. Reames argues that desire for a more succinct account of Cecilia's life may explain Chaucer's partial substitution of the *Legenda aurea*. She also posits that interest in adding a source that concentrated on Cecilia as a preacher may have motivated his choice of the Franciscan abridgment over Matins lessons found in English office books. Those Matins lessons were more readily available to the poet, but would have 'produce[d] a tamed, domesticated, decorous version of the female hero'.[92] By translating the Franciscan abridgment, Chaucer was able to recount more briefly the evangelical efforts of Cecilia's male converts and focus primarily on her preaching activities, especially during her trial before the Roman prefect Almachius, a scene either dramatically compressed in or completely omitted from English breviaries.[93] The Franciscan abridgment even recalls that the consecration of Cecilia's house as a church was an act that she first performed— 'consecrarem'—and then Pope Urban reiterated—'consecravit'.[94] Though Chaucer deflects the force of Cecilia's agency in this scene by expressing her desire for the consecration of her house within a prayer said just before death—'I myghte do werche / Heere of myn hous perpetuelly a cherche' (VIII.545–6)[95]—he bolsters her identity as a preacher in the final lines of the preceding stanza by slightly altering the original Latin: rather than 'non cessavit omnes quos nutrierat perdocere et in fide dominica confortare' [Cecilia did not cease to teach and comfort in the Lord's faith all those whom she nurtured],[96] she 'nevere cessed hem the feith to teche / That she hadde fostred; hem she gan to preche' (VIII.538–9). So emended, Cecilia 'emerges as the tale's true preacher', as Lynn Staley has underscored.[97]

Joining the Franciscan abridgment to the Dominican *Legenda aurea* also enhances the reading of the tale's ultimate teller, the Second Nun, as a preacher. She bases her tale on a combination of Dominican and Franciscan sources instead of on a breviary of English Benedictine use, which would have provided the lessons that she may have occasionally been charged with reading to her fellow sisters at the hour of Matins on the feast of St Cecilia in her capacity as the 'chapeleyne' (I.164) of her community.[98] Though the Second Nun's readership would have been able to detect only her use of the *Legenda aurea* as a source behind her translation, this recognition would have still shaped how they viewed her, because she was translating and publicly telling a tale from a source expressly designed for clerics to deliver on the feast days of particular saints, perhaps supplemented with lessons of their own devising to address the current needs of their audiences.[99] Thus, by telling a tale based on the *Legenda aurea*, the Second Nun appears to preach a *de sanctis* type of sermon to a congregation of pilgrims.[100]

The Second Nun captures her audience's attention and motivates the telling of her tale with an opening lesson against 'Ydelnesse' (VIII.2). She reminds them that the only way to keep 'The ministre and the norice unto vices' at bay is to ever be engaged in 'leveful bisynesse' (VIII.1, 5). '[T]o putte us fro swich ydelnesse' the Second Nun does her 'feithful bisynesse' by setting herself to the task of translating the legend of St Cecilia, the 'bisy bee' (VIII.23, 24, 195).[101] According to the Second Nun, the activity of 'translacioun' offers the most effective antidote to idleness, both for herself and for her audience, when it is undertaken 'After the legende ... right of [the] glorious lif and passioun' of the saint, whose very name means 'lastynge bisynesse' (VIII.25–6, 98). Performed as an act of 'imitation and ethical repetition', translation is sure to engender moral transformation, thus serving as the best activity that a preacher can undertake; it allows her not only to practice what she preaches, but also to become it.[102] So transformed, the Second Nun acts as an authorized preacher, another Cecilia, telling 'hir wise loore' (VIII.414).

The reasons behind Chaucer's decision to include his translation of the legend of Cecilia in the *Canterbury Tales*, and to have this tale told by a nun, are also not completely apparent. The telling of a saint's life to a group of pilgrims en route to Canterbury, to venerate the famed English saint Thomas Becket at his shrine, seems to befit the occasion well. In addition, as Katherine Lewis has noted, assigning the tale to the Second Nun is 'significant and makes sense in contemporary terms because of the observable connection between hagiography (especially the lives of female saints) and women readers, both lay and religious'.[103] The transference of the tale from Chaucer's own hand to the Second Nun's may also have provided the poet just the 'guise' he needed to level criticisms at unjust secular and ecclesiastical powers without taking full responsibility for their circulation, as Lynn Staley has considered likely.[104] Whatever the reasons behind these translations were, Chaucer seems to have performed them hastily, maybe even left them unfinished.

Much of the original textuality of Chaucer's original 'lyf of Seynt Cecile' still appears in the tale, especially in the prologue, where the Second Nun mentions the 'storie' she plans 'to endite'/'write', which, she hopes, others will 'reden' (VIII.32, 78, 80). She also highlights the writtenness of the authorities on which her tale depends, encouraging others to 'reden' or 'see' what she 'writen fynde' (VIII.30, 35, 83, 86, 94, 113, 120, 124, 271). Yet narratorial interjections, such as 'to tellen short and pleyn' and 'that I yow devyse', found later in the tale, mostly in the part based on the Franciscan abridgment, seem to complicate any strict reading of the Second Nun's performance as merely textual, especially when it is viewed within the tale-telling contest set by the Canterbury frame (VIII.119, 360, 367, 391, 394). Her words can be read or heard, as both oral and textual, or neither, occupying a liminal space where it is safe for a woman to preach, protected against accusations of unrightfully assuming the priestly office of preacher.[105]

Chaucer's translation of his Latin prose sources into Middle English verse also seems to still be *in via*. As mentioned earlier, there is a noticeable seam where Chaucer stitched his translations of the *Legenda aurea* and the Franciscan abridgment together. Comparison of Chaucer's facility in rhyme royal on either side of the seam helps to chart his maturation as a poet, but it also raises vexing questions about his decision to unite two translations that, at least to the mind of the present-day critic, differ markedly in versification and style and, thus, potentially reveal the varying degrees of his (in)competence as a poet.[106] Perhaps, as Reames speculates, Chaucer had left the original version of his 'lyf of Seynt Cecile' unfinished and only completed it when he wanted to incorporate it into the *Canterbury Tales*. Or else Chaucer had finished the original version but decided to revise the second half completely on the basis of a new source in order to make it sound more like a tale that the Second Nun would tell.[107] Either way, Chaucer did not dramatically alter the first half of the original 'lyf'; thus, whether by accident or design, the tale reads like a work in progress.

More curiously, Chaucer himself still peeks through, under the Second Nun's veil, as the tale's original translator, when s/he refers to her/himself as an 'unworthy sone of Eve' (VIII.62).[108] So self-identified, the Second Nun seems to be the more appropriate addressee of the question posed by Almachius to Cecilia during her trial: 'What maner woman artow?' (VIII.424). Though this identification should serve as an important reminder to readers that in every pilgrim's performance in the *Canterbury Tales*, 'Chaucer is engaged in an element of ventriloquism', as Carol Meale has cautioned,[109] the Second Nun's apparent claim to manliness would not have been unusual, or necessarily unsuitable, for a woman religious to make. By word and deed, a select few of the Second Nun's forebears had merited the title of *virago* through assuming 'the properties of virtuous masculinity'.[110] By identifying herself as 'an unworthy sone of Eve', the Second Nun also creates a neat juxtaposition with the Virgin Mary, 'dogter dere of Anne' (VIII.70), and echoes the paradoxical epithets that Mary garners in the *invocacio*: 'Thow Mayde and Mooder, doghter of thy Sone ... Thow humble, and heigh over every creature' (VIII.36, 39).

Judging the suitability of the Second Nun's claim to manliness is rendered nearly impossible given her shadowy, indistinct presence in the *Canterbury Tales*. Unlike most all the other pilgrims whose appearances and personalities are given flesh in the General Prologue's portraits and in many of the prologues and endlinks to tales, the Second Nun is defined only by her monastic office and her immediate travel companions, her prioress and three priests (I.164–5). Little more detail is given to her appearance in the miniature supplied for her in the Ellesmere Chaucer.[111] Many of her facial features—red mouth, rosy complexion, and high forehead—seem to be borrowed from the General Prologue's portrait of the Prioress. But unlike the Prioress, whose artist clearly painted her in a Benedictine habit, the Second Nun, in her simple brown habit, does not belong to any readily identifiable order.[112] Her artist evidently knew how to paint a Benedictine habit, as his miniature of the Monk demonstrates, but apparently he did not follow, or his supervisor did not direct him to follow, the precedent set by his fellow artist's miniature of the Prioress and depict her consoror as a Benedictine too. Of course, according to the General Prologue's portrait of the Prioress, it is not entirely clear that she and the Second Nun are indeed Benedictines, for the Prioress is only said to have spoken French 'After the scole of Stratford atte Bowe' (I.125), thus suggesting, but not confirming, that she is the superior of the Benedictine priory of St. Leonard's.[113]

The Second Nun's ambiguous embodiment—neither present nor absent, neither male nor female, neither Benedictine nor of any other order—may, like her textual orality (or oral textuality), free her to perform activities otherwise denied to women and laymen, like preaching.[114] Yet as a no-body, the Second Nun is also able to take on any body—Cecilia's or Chaucer's—and her hearers/readers, in turn, are able to take on hers, to carry on her 'bisynesse', to 'amende' the 'werk' (VIII.84) that she has begun, but not yet completed. For the Second Nun and, I daresay, for Chaucer, the work of translation is never finished, especially when it is performed theologically. It is always, necessarily ongoing, because the 'theological', whatever tongue it is vernacularized in, must admit that the total comprehension and expression of Truth is an eschatological hope, not a present possibility, certainly not for one translator. The work of translation is capable of pursuing Truth, but it must ever be undertaken in community, open to further transformations through corrections and adaptations by future translators, scribes and readers—imitators and critics alike.

Though never a self-professed theologian, or, arguably, a 'religious' poet, Chaucer ably demonstrated his fluency in 'theological vernacularizing' through many of his poetic creations. And though he rarely took up this task in his own voice, he did express a variety of theological 'mateere' by sounding through his wide cast of characters, from his gods to his pilgrims, and even to his own constructed narratorial self. Quite deftly, and likely sensibly given the changing ecclesiastical climate of late fourteenth-century England, Chaucer *qua* Chaucer eschewed the role of the theologian, but under the veil of his many fictive guises, he readily and often daringly did become a theological vernacularizer. Certain guises proved more habitable for this role than others, but even the seeming failure of some did not render them any less instructive; they still revealed something of what the *habitus* of the theological vernacularizer should be. But in donning the habit of the Second Nun Chaucer unveiled something fundamental about the nature of the theological task itself: it is always essentially an act of translation.

Notes

1. William Langland, *Piers Plowman*, C.15.78–9.
2. Editors usually offer these lines as part of parenthetic comment by Langland, but if Will is seen as part of the 'clerical proletariat', the voicing becomes more complicated. See Derek Pearsall's note to line 76, where he follows the practice of previous editors. All quotations are from his *Piers Plowman: A New Annotated Edition of the C-Text* (Exeter: Exeter University Press, 2008); Kerby-Fulton, 'The Clerical Proletariat: the Underemployed Scribe and Vocational Crisis', for *Journal of the Early Book Society* 17 (2014), 1–34.
3. See Christopher Cannon, 'Vernacular Latin', *Speculum* 90(3) (2015), 641–53, on vernacular theology, 648.
4. Nicholas Watson, 'The Idea of Latinity', *The Oxford Handbook of Medieval Latin Literature*, ed. David Townsend and Ralph Hexter (Oxford: Oxford University Press, 2012), 124–128, helpfully summarizes these perspectives.
5. Wendy Scase, *Piers Plowman and the New Anticlericalism* (Cambridge: Cambridge University Press, 1989), in recognition of this centuries-old critique among clergy, added the adjective 'new' to 'anticlerical'. But her study never accounts for the fact that the poet regarded *himself* as a member of the clergy, and would not have seen his work as anticlerical. See the review of Scase's book by Robert Worth Frank, *SAC* 13 (1991), 232–235.
6. This terminology is used in several types of studies, e.g. Kathryn Kerby-Fulton, *Books under Suspicion: Censorship and Tolerance of Revelatory Writing in Late Medieval England*

(Notre Dame, IN: University of Notre Dame Press, 2006); Fiona Somerset's Introduction, on the "inter-clerical controversies in Oxford" (20), *Clerical Discourse and Lay Audience in Late Medieval England* (Cambridge: Cambridge University Press, 1998, 2005); Geoffey Dipple, *Antifraternalism and Anticlericalism in the German Reformation* (London: Routledge, 1996); Catherine Saucier, *A Paradise of Priests: Singing the Civic and Episcopal Hagiography of Medieval Liège* (Rochester, NY: University of Rochester Press, 2014), 139.

7. Penn R. Szittya, *The Antifraternal Tradition in Medieval Literature* (Princeton, NJ: Princeton University Press, 1986); Kathryn Kerby-Fulton, *Reformist Apocalypticism and Piers Plowman* (Cambridge: Cambridge University Press, 1990), 133– 153; Guy Geltner, ed., *William of St. Amour: De periculis novissimorum temporum* (Paris: Peeters, 2008); and most recently, Magda Hayton, 'Pierre d'Ailly's *De falsis prophetis II* and the *Collectiones* of William of Saint-Amour', *Viator* 44, no. 2 (2013), 243–66.

8. Robert Correale and Mary Hamel, *Sources and Analogues of the Canterbury Tales*, I and II (Woodbridge: Boydell and Brewer, 2002–5).

9. Not noted in the *Riverside Chaucer's* Explanatory Notes. On the 'mythic history' of the Carmelites, John Fleming, *An Introduction to Franciscan Literature in the Middle Ages* (Chicago, IL: Franciscan Herald Press, 1977), 251.

10. Fleming, *Introduction to Franciscan Literature*, 95. For Langland, see Kerby-Fulton, *Reformist Apocalypticism*, esp. 133–161; for Wyclif see Michael Wilks, *Wyclif: Political Ideas and Practice*, edited posthumously by Anne Hudson (Oxford: Oxbow, 2000).

11. Kathryn Kerby-Fulton, *Books under Suspicion*, 145–55; and for a recent detailed comparison with the French, see Yiren Shen, 'The voice lurking behind: Chaucer's use of Faus-Semblant in *The Canterbury Tales*', https://blogs.nd.edu/manuscript-studies/files/2015/04/ShenThesis150430.pdf

12. Nicholas Watson, 'Cultural Changes', *English Language Notes* 44 (2006), 130. See also his 'Censorship and Cultural Change in Late Medieval England: Vernacular Theology, the Oxford Translation Debate and Arundel's *Constitutions* of 1409', *Speculum* 70 (1995), 822 –64.

13. See Marjorie Harrington, 'Bilingual Form: Paired Latin and Vernacular Translations in Trilingual English Miscellanies, c.1250–c.1350', University of Notre Dame Ph.D. diss., 2017. See also Ingrid Nelson's *Lyric Tactics: Poetry, Genre, and Practice in Later Medieval England* (Philadelphia, PA: University of Pennsylvania State Press, 2017), and her final chapter on Chaucer's use of both French poetic forms and earlier English lyric traditions.

14. Marjorie Harrington, 'Of Earth You Were Made: Constructing the Bilingual Poem "Erþ" in BL MS Harley 913.' *Florilegium* 31 (2014): 105–137; for the English and Latin versions in MS Harley 913 itself, see fol. 62r.

15. See Larry D. Benson, ed., *The Riverside Chaucer* (Boston, MA: Houghton Mifflin Company, 1987), note to 469.

16. For a succinct account see 'General Introduction', Jocelyn Wogan-Browne et al., *Vernacular Literary Theory from the French of England: Texts and Translations, c. 1120–c. 1450* (Woodbridge: D. S. Brewer, 2016) 1–6, citing Baswell, 1.

17. See Vincent Gillespie and Kantik Ghosh, *After Arundel: Religious Writing in Fifteenth-Century England* (Turnhout: Brepols, 2011), and Katie Bugyis's section below.

18. T. W. Machan, 'French, English, and the Late Medieval Linguistic Repertoire', in *Language and Culture in Medieval Britain: The French of England c. 1100–c. 1500*, ed. Jocelyn Wogan-Browne (York: York Medieval Press, 2009), 363–72.

19. Christopher Cannon, *From Literacy to Literature: England, 1300–1400* (Oxford: Oxford University Press, 2016). For Alastair Minnis's parallel thoughts on Latin as a vernacular, see Katie Bugyis's discussion below.

20. See Cannon, 'Vernacular Latin'; Jocelyn Wogan-Browne, 'Invisible Archives? Later Medieval French in England', *Speculum* 90(3) (2015), 653–73. On both French and Latin as office vernaculars, see Kerby-Fulton, 'Competing Archives, Competing Languages: Office Vernaculars, Civil Servant Raconteurs, and the Porous Nature of French', *Speculum* 90(3) (2015), 674–700.

21. See Eileen A. Gooder, *Latin for Local History: An Introduction,* 2nd ed. (London: Longman, 1987), 84ff; Jeremy Catto, 'Practical Latin and Formal English in the 14th–15th Centuries', guest lecture, University of Notre Dame, 2014; and see his 'Written English: The Making of the Language 1370–1400', *Past and Present* 179(1) (2003), 24–59.

22. Theresa O'Byrne, 'Manuscript Production in Dublin: The Scribe of Bodleian e. Museo MS 232 and Longleat MS 29', *New Directions in Medieval Manuscript Studies and Reading Practices,* eds. Kathryn Kerby-Fulton, John J. Thompson and Sarah Baechle (Notre Dame, IN: University of Notre Dame Press, 2014), 271–91. See also Kerby-Fulton, 'Social History of the Book and Beyond: *Originalia,* Medieval Literary Theory and the Aesthetics of Paleography', the afterword to *The Medieval Manuscript Book: Cultural Approaches,* eds. Michael Johnston and Michael Van Dussen (Cambridge: Cambridge University Press, 2015), 243–54, citing Malcolm Parkes' and Ian Doyle's discussions of this.

23. My wording alludes to the title of the superb *Idea of the Vernacular: An Anthology of Middle English Literary Theory, 1280–1520,* eds. Jocelyn Wogan-Browne, Nicholas Watson, Andrew Taylor and Ruth Evans (Exeter: University of Exeter Press, 1999), which has a marvelous glossary of Middle English literary theoretical terms.

24. Stephen Partridge, 'Glosses in the Manuscripts of Chaucer's *Canterbury Tales*: An Edition and Commentary' (PhD diss., Harvard University, 1992).

25. See Kathryn Kerby-Fulton, Maidie Hilmo, and Linda Olson, *Opening Up Middle English Manuscripts* (Ithaca, NY: Cornell University Press, 2012), 211, and 214–21.

26. Langland, *Piers Plowman,* C.22.218–27.

27. Scase, *Piers Plowman and the New Anticlericalism,* in which such instances abound.

28. See Barry Dobson', The English Vicars Choral: an Introduction', *Vicars Choral at English Cathedrals,* eds. Richard Hall and David Stocker (Oxford: Oxbow Books, 2005), 8.

29. Langland, *Piers Plowman,* C.22.221.

30. Examples are discussed in Kerby-Fulton, *Books under Suspicion,* chapter 4: e.g., the case of William Taylor, 201–3.

31. Cited from Vincent Gillespie, 'Vernacular Theology', in *Oxford Twenty-First Century Approaches to Literature: Middle English,* ed. Paul Strohm (Oxford: Oxford University Press, 2007). See 401–2 for Doyle and McGinn; 405 for Watson, citing his 'Censorship and Cultural Change'.

32. Barbara Newman, *God and the Goddesses* (Philadelphia, PA: University of Pennsylvania Press, 2008); and on the literary dimensions of antimendicant polemic, see Penn R. Szittya's, *The Antifraternal Tradition.* For a broader attempt to deal with the rich relations of literature and theology in Middle English, see Jim Rhodes, *Poetry Does Theology: Chaucer, Grosseteste, and the* Pearl-*Poet* (Notre Dame, IN: University of Notre Dame Press, 2001).

33. Jill Mann, *Chaucer and the Medieval Estates Satire* (Cambridge: Cambridge University Press, 1973).

34. Harley 913, mentioned above, is a good example of a satirical collection made by a friar, and MS Bodley 851, the manuscript containing the Z text of *Piers Plowman* is a good example of a Benedictine collection, one among many monastic miscellanies that contain Goliardic poetry alongside other works ridiculing monks and clergy generally. See A. G. Rigg, 'Satire',

in *Medieval Latin: An Introduction and Bibliographical Guide,* eds. F. C. Mantello and A. G. Rigg (Washington: Catholic University Press of America, 1996), 562–8.

35. Mann, *Medieval Estates Satire,* 130.

36. Derek Pearsall, *The Canterbury Tales* (London: Routledge, 1985), 71–3.

37. Ralph Hanna and Traugott Lawler, 'The Wife of Bath's Prologue', *Sources,* ed. Correale and Hamel, II, 351–5.

38. Kerby-Fulton, *Books under Suspicion,* chapter 9, esp. 345ff.

39. Gillespie, 'Vernacular Theology', 402–3; see also '"[S]he do the police in different voices": Pastiche, Ventriloquism and Parody in Julian of Norwich', in *A Companion to Julian of Norwich,* ed. Liz Herbert McAvoy (Cambridge: Cambridge University Press, 2008), 192–207.

40. Derek Brewer, quoted in John Scattergood, 'The Shipman's Tale', *Sources,* Correale and Hamel, II, 566.

41. Estelle Stubbs and Linne Mooney have identified him as John Marchaunt, and made the connection with Ralph Strode. See their *Scribes and the City: London Guildhall Clerks and the Dissemination of Middle English Literature, 1375–1425* (York: York Medieval Press, 2013).

42. 'Vernacular Latin', 648.

43. The standard study of the development of antifraternal sentiments and their movement from Paris to London and England is Szittya's previously mentioned, *Antifraternal Tradition in Medieval Literature.* Szittya's book provides background information on the beginning of the mendicant controversy and carefully dissects both William of St Amour's eschatological approach to the antimendicant movement and FitzRalph's ecclesiastical approach before moving on to examine how both writers affected the English poetic tradition.

44. Geltner, *William of St. Amour,* 45. The Latin reads 'Protestamur autem ab initio, quod omnia que hic ad cautelam et instructionem ecclesie universe, non contra personam aliquam, nec contra statum aliquem ab ecclesia approbatum; sed contra peccata malorum et pericula ecclesie generalis dicturi sumus', Geltner, *William of St. Amour,* 44.

45. Several studies have expounded the dispute between FitzRalph and the friars. Among them are Szittya's *Antifraternal Tradition in Medieval Literature,* as well as Katherine Walsh, *A Fourteenth-century Scholar and Primate: Richard FitzRalph in Oxford, Avignon, and Armagh* (Oxford: Clarendon Press, 1981), T. P. Dolan, 'Richard FitzRalph's *Defensio Curatorum* in Transmission', in *Ireland, England and the Continent in the Middle Ages and Beyond,* eds. Howard B. Clarke and J. R. S. Phillips (Dublin: University College Dublin Press, 2006), 177–94, and Michael Haren, 'Diocesan Dimensions of a Die-hard Dispute', in *Ireland, England and the Continent in the Middle Ages and Beyond,* 164–76.

46. This quotation comes from John Trevisa's fourteenth-century Middle English translation, which can be found in Aaron Jenkins Perry, ed., *Dialogus inter militem et clericum, Richard FitzRalph's sermon: 'Defensio curatorum' and Methodius: 'the bygynnyng of the world and the ende of worldes'* (London: EETS Oxford University Press, 1925), 54; for the Latin edition see Edwardi Brown, *Fasciculus rerum expetendarum* (London: Richardi Chiswell, 1690), II. 466–86.

47. The root of the problem for both William and FitzRalph can be traced to the friars' mendicancy. The friars were theoretically supposed to be without property and accept only what they needed to survive on a day-to-day basis (a rule which caused much dissension within the mendicant orders, particularly among the Franciscans), however, the friars' perceived abuses of the right to beg for their sustenance—whether actual or symbolic—caused

problems for both writers. For a discussion of FitzRalph's involvement with the controversy surrounding mendicant poverty, see James Doyne Dawson, 'Richard FitzRalph and the Fourteenth-Century Poverty Controversies', *Journal of Ecclesiastical History* 34, no. 3 (1983), 315–44.

48. Szittya writes that 'Chaucer, Langland, Gower, Dunbar, Henryson all wrote against the friars, mainly in longer poems that depict, sometimes comically, sometimes somberly, the decay of human society near the end of an era' (*Antifraternal Tradition*, 183).

49. Earlier in this chapter Kathryn Kerby-Fulton includes a list of scholars who have used this terminology to discuss disputes that arose both between and within different orders. Some other critics have also gestured toward the idea of intra-clerical polemic in the *Canterbury Tales*. Charles R. Dahlberg, 'Chaucer's Cock and the Fox', *Journal of English and Germanic Philology* 53 (1954), 277–90, interprets the Nun's Priest's Tale as a reflection of the controversy between the friars and the secular clergy. See also Nicholas Havely, 'Chaucer, Boccaccio, and the Friars', in *Chaucer and the Italian Trecento*, ed. Piero Boitani (Cambridge: Cambridge University Press, 1983), 249–68, which notes that antimendicant criticism actually originated within the fraternal orders and lists antifraternalism as a single branch of the larger body of anticlericalism. Finally, G. Geltner's '"Faux Semblants": Antifraternalism Reconsidered in Jean de Meun and Chaucer', *Studies in Philology* 101, no. 4 (2004), 357–80, argues convincingly that Chaucer's use of antifraternalism actually reveals 'his refusal to commit to any particular point of view' (359).

50. G. Geltner makes a similar point about Chaucer's use of antifraternal language specifically in Friar Huberd's portrait in the 'General Prologue'. See G. Geltner, 'The Friar', in *Historians on Chaucer: The 'General Prologue' to the Canterbury Tales*, ed. Stephen H. Rigby and Alastair J. Minnis (Oxford: Oxford University Press, 2014), 156–69. Geltner argues that instead of using antifraternal language to attack friars in general, 'Chaucer's appropriation of anti-mendicant tropes attest his subtlety as a social satirist and master of ambiguity' (156).

51. Various antimendicant claims, including accusations that the friars misused the gift of eloquent speech, were over-fond of being called 'maister' and wearing impressive clothing, and that they abused their offices for financial gain and were untrustworthy around women, appear in a multitude of other sources besides William of St Amour and FitzRalph. For specific examples, see Robert P. Miller, ed., *Chaucer: Sources and Backgrounds* (New York: Oxford University Press, 1977), especially pages 235–68, and Muriel Bowden, *A Commentary on the General Prologue to the Canterbury Tales* (New York: Macmillan, 1959), especially pages 119–45. For an argument that Chaucer made use of specific antimendicant sources besides William of St Amour and FitzRalph, see Laurel Braswell, 'Chaucer and the Legendaries: New Sources for Anti-Mendicant Satire', *English Studies in Canada* 2 (1976), 373–81.

52. MED, s.v. 'daliaunce'.

53. The antimendicant rhetoric of the Friar's portrait is further complicated by the fact that he follows in the literary footsteps of the friar Faus Semblant from the *Roman de la rose*. See Larry D. Benson, ed., *The Riverside Chaucer* (Boston, MA: Houghton Mifflin Company, 1987), 808.

54. Jill Mann notes that 'The characteristics suggested by these lines—contempt for monastic authorities and for the cloistered life, physical laziness, neglect of study, dislike of the old strict rules—were traditionally associated with monks' (*Medieval Estates Satire*, 28). Mann goes on to give examples from other works that make use of this stereotype, including Gower's *Vox clamantis* and *Mirour de l'omme* as well as the *Carmina burana*, among others.

Many of the possible sources she notes for the Monk's portrait are Latin, aligning the portrait more closely with inter-clerical polemic than lay anticlericism.

55. Mann, *Medieval Estates Satire*, 33.

56. Ibid., 18–25.

57. Like the Friar, the Pardoner also follows in the literary footsteps of the friar Faus Semblant in the *Roman de la rose*. For a list of passages from the *Roman de la rose* that likely provided a model for the Pardoner's 'literary confession' see Larry D. Benson, ed., *The Riverside Chaucer* (Boston, MA: Houghton Mifflin Company, 1987), 905.

58. Mann, *Medieval Estates Satire*, 152.

59. The subject of antimendicantism in the Summoner's Tale has been thoroughly covered by earlier scholars, some of them mentioned in previous footnotes. Of particular interest here is John V. Fleming, 'Anticlerical Satire as Theological Essay: Chaucer's *Summoner's Tale*', *Thalia* 6, no. 1 (1983), 5–22, which argues that in the Summoner's Tale 'Chaucer uses anticlerical polemic as a means of advancing a deep religious argument grounded in conservative belief' (5). While Fleming's article makes several good and well-supported points, it seems to conflate anticlericalism with antimendicantism, and I would argue that by differentiating the two we can reach a much more nuanced understanding of how Chaucer is using them.

60. Geltner's 'Antifraternalism Reconsidered' is very useful here, yet Geltner focuses on the Summoner's Tale as the centre of anti-fraternalism in the *Canterbury Tales* and also as the place where Faus Semblant is reworked into the *Tales*. He argues that it was mostly just the form of Faus Semblant's speech that carried over into the rest of the tales by noting previous arguments and stating that, 'in the Pardoner's Prologue and in the Wife of Bath's Prologue he [Chaucer] drew on the confessional form and ironic tone of Faus Semblant's confession', and, 'In the Pardoner's Prologue and the Wife of Bath's Prologue he retained the superb form of ambiguous confession that characterizes Faus Semblant's original speech' (374–5). Yet, while I do not want to argue that Faus Semblant had no impact on the friar of the Summoner's Tale, it is the Pardoner who is most like the *Romance's* friar, Faus Semblant. For examples in addition to the lines quoted above in the text, compare lines 412–20 of the Pardoner's Prologue with the *Romance's* lines 6923–44 and the Pardoner's Prologue lines 439–46 with the *Romance's* lines 6781–96. See also Helen Cooper, *The Canterbury Tales* (Oxford: Oxford University Press, 1996), 261; and Kerby-Fulton, *Books Under Suspicion*, 152.

61. *The Riverside Chaucer* actually mentions this use of the word 'brethren' as evidence that the Pardoner may be identifying himself as a friar (824).

62. For information on the relationship between anticlericalism/antimendicantism and the Wycliffite movement, see Anne Hudson, *The Premature Reformation* (Oxford: Clarendon Press, 1988), especially pages 347–51.

63. See especially the essays contributed to *Chaucer's Religious Tales*, ed. C. David Benson and Elizabeth Robertson (Woodbridge: D. S. Brewer, 1990). According to Nicholas Watson, the increased interest in Middle English religious writings generated in the mid 1990s made it 'at once more urgent and less difficult to think of Chaucer as a religious poet'. Watson cites 'the failure of the hermeneutic revolution proposed in D. W. Robertson's *Preface to Chaucer* (1962)' as one of the chief obstacles to making 'any constructive critical use of the truism that Chaucer was a Christian'; 'Chaucer's Public Christianity', *Religion & Literature* 37 (2005), 99–114, esp. 99. See, by way of comparison, D. W. Robertson, *A Preface to Chaucer: Studies in Medieval Perspective* (Princeton, NJ: Princeton University

Press, 1962); David Lyle Jeffrey, ed., *Chaucer and Scriptural Tradition* (Ottawa: University of Ottawa Press, 1984). It is important to note that many scholars who do characterize some of Chaucer's poetry as 'religious' still want to distinguish his religious poetry from that produced by his contemporaries, namely the *Pearl*-Poet, Langland, and Gower, because, to these scholars' minds, 'Chaucer was above all a poet of this world, not the next'. Helen Cooper, 'Introduction', in *Chaucer and Religion*, ed. Helen Phillips (Woodbridge: D. S. Brewer, 2010), xi–xix, xvii. Such insistence upon casting Chaucer as a 'secular' poet may implicitly seek to disavow any affiliation with 'Robertsonianism'.

64. Laurel Broughton, 'Chaucer and the Saints: Miracles and Voices of Faith', in Phillips, *Chaucer and Religion*, 111–31, 131. Nicholas Watson and Ian Johnson also have characterized some of Chaucer's writings as 'theological': see Watson, 'Chaucer's Public Christianity', 112, 109; Johnson, 'The Ascending Soul and the Virtue of Hope: The Spiritual Temper of Chaucer's *Boece* and *Retracciouns*', *English Studies: A Journal of English Language and Literature* 88 (2007), 245–61; Johnson, 'Vernacular Theology / Theological Vernacular: A Game of Two Halves?', in Gillespie and Ghosh, *After Arundel*, 73–88. Alastair Minnis has noted the 'impressive' level of 'proficiency in theology' that Chaucer achieved as a layman in *Translations of Authority in Medieval English Literature: Valuing the Vernacular* (Cambridge: Cambridge University Press, 2009), 63.

65. Jim Rhodes is one of the few scholars to categorize and analyse some of Chaucer's writings as works of theology in *Poetry Does Theology*.

66. In his account of Chaucer's Christian 'ideology', Nicholas Watson has argued that the poet's 'whole mind was not swept up in the grand considerations of the faith in the manner of Langland, and he left no signs of ever having an original or speculative theological thought'; 'Christian Ideologies', in *A Companion to Chaucer*, ed. Peter Brown (Oxford: Blackwell, 2000), 75–89, 87. Moreover, according to Watson, Chaucer, unlike Langland, evaded 'the poet's prophetic role' throughout his life ('Chaucer's Public Christianity', 101). In his highly influential article on 'vernacular theology', Watson made the further claim that '*The Canterbury Tales* is not theologically daring in any explicit way' ('Censorship and Cultural Change', 858).

67. See Stephen Lahey, 'Wycliffism and its After-Effects', in Chapter 26 of this volume, and the bibliography cited therein.

68. For the application of such descriptors to 'vernacular theology', see Watson, 'Censorship and Cultural Change'.

69. Tim Machan, 'Chaucer as Translator', in Roger Ellis, *The Medieval Translator: The Theory and Practice of Translation in the Middle Ages* (Cambridge: D. S. Brewer, 1989), 56–67; Machan, *Techniques of Translation: Chaucer's Boece* (Norman, OK: Pilgrim Books, 1985).

70. A special issue of *English Language Notes* in 2006 was devoted to assessing the term 'vernacular theology' as a scholarly category or hermeneutic in medieval studies. Ian Johnson's, Stephen Kelly and Ryan Perry's, and Michael Sargent's essays in *After Arundel: Religious Writing in Fifteenth-Century England* raise many of the concerns listed above. See also Johnson, *The Middle English Life of Christ: Academic Discourse, Translation, and Vernacular Theology* (Turnhout: Brepols, 2013), esp. ch. 1; Perry, ' "Thynk on God, as we doon, men that swynke": The Cultural Locations of *Meditations on the Supper of Our Lord* and the Middle English Pseudo-Bonaventuran Tradition', *Speculum* 86 (2011), 419–54; Michael G. Sargent, 'The *Mirror* and Vernacular Theology in Fifteenth-Century England', in Nicholas Love, *The Mirror of the Blessed Life of Jesus Christ: A Full Critical Edition, Based on Cambridge University Library Additional MSS 6578 and 6686*, ed. Michael G. Sargent (Exeter: University

of Exeter Press, 2005), 75–97. I rehearse and add to their criticisms of 'vernacular theology' in 'Through the Looking Glass: Reflections of Christ's "trewe lovers" in Nicholas Love's *Mirror of the Blessed Life of Jesus Christ*', in *Devotional Culture in Late Medieval England: Diverse Imaginations of Christ's Life*, eds. Stephen Kelly and Ryan Perry, (Turnhout: Brepols, 2015), 461–85, esp. 461–3.

71. Linda Georgianna, 'Vernacular Theologies', *English Language Notes* 44, no. 1 (2006), 87–94, 92.

72. Johnson, 'Vernacular Theology / Theological Vernacular', 77.

73. Ibid.

74. Ibid.

75. Johnson, *Middle English Life of Christ*, 29.

76. Minnis, *Translations of Authority*, 11.

77. Johnson, 'Vernacular Theology / Theological Vernacular', 76.

78. Ibid., 80.

79. Rita Copeland, 'Rhetoric and Vernacular Translation in the Middle Ages', *Studies in the Age of Chaucer* 9 (1987), 41–75, 57–62.

80. S. L. Reames, 'Artistry, Decorum, and Purpose in Three Middle English Retellings of the Cecilia Legend', in *The Endless Knot: Essays on Old and Middle English in Honor of Marie Borroff*, eds. M. Teresa Tavormina and R. F. Yeager (Cambridge: D. S. Brewer, 1995), 177–99, esp. 191. Reames cites Robert W. Frank, Jr, who claims that the *Second Nun's Tale* is 'essentially untouched by pathos'; 'Pathos in Chaucer's Religious Tales', in Benson and Robertson, *Chaucer's Religious Tales*, 39–52, 43.

81. The glosses added to the *Second Nun's Prologue* and *Tale*, though relatively few when compared to those supplied to other tales and prologues, still merit greater consideration than they have hitherto received. Most of the glosses are in Latin to mark off sections in the narrative, to note certain passages, to (re)identify an authority or source, to disambiguate homographs, to clarify the referents of equivocal pronouns, and to translate certain, perhaps difficult, English words into Latin. In a few of the early manuscripts, a lengthy gloss from Gregory the Great's *Register* was marginally supplied beside the transition between the Second Nun's tale and prologue; this gloss relates a passage from one of Gregory's letters to Eulogius, which discourages translating only according to 'verborum proprietatem', and not 'sensum de sensu' (Partridge, *Glosses in the Manuscripts*, VIII–2). Norman Blake discussed the potential significance of this gloss: 'This title and note also indicate the learned and didactic nature of the tale, and they indicate to the reader in what way they should approach it'; 'Literary and Other Languages in Middle English', in *Genres, Themes, and Images in English Literature: From the Fourteenth to the Fifteenth Century: The J. A. W. Bennett Memorial Lectures, Perugia, 1986* (Tübingen, 1988), 166–85, 179.

82. The *Second Nun's Tale* was copied in two fifteenth-century manuscripts, separate from the *Canterbury Tales* frame: British Library, MS Harley 2382 (s. xv $^{3/4}$., Norfolk) and Manchester, Chetham's Library, MS 6709 (1485–90, Dunstable). In the Harley MS, the *Second Nun's Tale* appears under the heading 'Vita Sancte Cecilie'. Both manuscripts also contain copies of the *Prioress's Tale*. Carol Meale has remarked that the independent manuscript transmission of both tales testifies to their 'place within the tradition of popular piety'; 'Women's Piety and Women's Power: Chaucer's Prioress Reconsidered', in *Essays on Ricardian Literature: In Honour of J. A. Burrow*, ed. Alastair Minnis, Charlotte Morse, and Thorlac Turville-Petre (Oxford, 1997), 39–60, 58. See also Eileen Jankowski, 'Reception of Chaucer's Second Nun's Tale: Osbern Bokenham's Lyf of S. Cycyle', *The Chaucer Review* 30 (1996),

306–18; A. S. G. Edwards, 'Fifteenth-Century English Collections of Saints' Lives', *The Yearbook of English Studies* 33 (2003), 131–41, 141.

83. Mary Giffin, *Studies on Chaucer and his Audience* (Hull, 1956), 29–48; Broughton, 'Chaucer and the Saints', 131.

84. John Hirsch, 'The Politics of Spirituality: The Second Nun and the Manciple', *The Chaucer Review* 12 (1977), 121–46; Joseph Grossi, 'The Unhidden Piety of Chaucer's "Seint Cecile"', *The Chaucer Review* 36 (2002), 298–309.

85. Lynn Staley, 'Chaucer's Tale of the Second Nun and the Strategies of Dissent', *Studies in Philology* 89 (1992), 314–33; eadem, 'Chaucer and the Postures of Sanctity', 198–217; Reames, 'Artistry, Decorum, and Purpose', 198–9.

86. The *Legenda aurea* was a veritable medieval bestseller; it survives in over 500 manuscript copies and was translated into English as the *Gilte Legende* in 1438, possibly by a monk from St. Albans, and then again in 1483 by William Caxton (1415x24–1492). Paul Clogan, 'The Figural Style and Meaning of the *Second Nun's Prologue* and *Tale*', *Medievalia et Humanistica*, n.s., 3 (1972), 213–40; Oliver Pickering, 'Saints' Lives', in *A Companion to Middle English Prose*, ed. A. S. G. Edwards (Cambridge, 2004), 249–70; Mary Beth Long, 'Corpora and Manuscripts, Authors and Audiences', in *A Companion to Middle English Hagiography*, ed. Sarah Salih (Cambridge, 2006), 47–69. For the most thorough studies of the sources behind Chaucer's legend of St Cecilia, see Sherry Reames, 'The Sources of Chaucer's "Second Nun's Tale"', *Modern Philology* 76 (1978–9), 111–35; eadem, 'A Recent Discovery concerning the Sources of Chaucer's "Second Nun's Tale"', *Modern Philology* 87 (1989–90), 337–61; eadem, 'The Second Nun's Prologue and Tale', in *Sources*, ed. Correale and Hamel, I. 491–527.

87. Reames, 'The Second Nun's Prologue and Tale', 494–5.

88. Ibid., 496.

89. Reames, 'Mary, Sanctity and Prayers to Saints: Chaucer and Late-Medieval Piety', in *Chaucer and Religion*, 81–96, 95.

90. Partridge, *Glosses in the Manuscripts*, VIII–1.

91. Machan, 'Chaucer as Translator', 57–8.

92. Reames, 'Mouvance and Interpretation in Late-Medieval Latin: The Legend of St. Cecilia in British Breviaries', in *Medieval Literature: Texts and Interpretation*, ed. Tim Machan (Binghamton, 1991), 159–89, 188.

93. Reames, 'Artistry, Decorum, and Purpose', 181; eadem, 'Mary, Sanctity and Prayers to Saints', 94, n. 39.

94. See Reames's edition of the Franciscan Abridgment in 'The Second Nun's Prologue and Tale', 527.

95. Alastair Minnis, *Fallible Authors: Chaucer's Pardoner and Wife of Bath* (Philadelphia, PA: University of Pennsylvania Press, 2008), 335.

96. Reames, 'The Second Nun's Prologue and Tale', 527.

97. Staley, 'Chaucer and the Postures of Sanctity', 205. See also Laurel Broughton, 'Chaucer and the Saints', 116.

98. Identifying the Second Nun as a Benedictine is, of course, open to debate. The controversy surrounding this identification will be discussed near the end of this chapter. For the liturgical practices of women religious in late medieval England, see Anne Bagnall Yardley, *Performing Piety: Musical Culture in Medieval English Nunneries* (New York, 2006).

99. Sherry Reames, *The Legenda aurea: A Reexamination of its Paradoxical History* (Madison, 1985); Barbara Morenzoni, *De la sainteté a l'hagiographie: genèse et usage de la Légende dorée* (Geneva, 2001); Jacques Le Goff, *In Search of Sacred Time: Jacobus de Voragine and the Golden Legend*, trans. Lydia Cochrane (Princeton: Princeton University Press, 2014).

100. Claude Jones, 'The "Second Nun's Tale", a Mediaeval Sermon', *The Modern Language Review* 32 (1937), 283.

101. For the significance of Cecilia's (and the Second Nun's) bee-like identity, see Bugyis, 'Apian Transformations and the Paradoxes of Women's Authorial *Personae* in Late Medieval England', in *Desire, Faith, and the Darkness of God*, ed. Eric Bugyis and David Newheiser (Notre Dame IN: Notre Dame University Press, 2015), 129–152, 132–139.

102. Catherine Sanok has analyzed the Second Nun's 'rhetoric of imitation and ethical repetition' in both 'Performing Feminine Sanctity in Late Medieval England: Parish Guilds, Saints' Plays, and the *Second Nun's Tale*', *Journal of Medieval and Early Modern Studies* 32 (2002), 269–303, 290; and *Her Life Historical: Exemplarity and Female Saints' Lives in Late Medieval England* (Philadelphia, PA: University of Pennsylvania Press, 2007), 169–70.

103. Lewis, 'The Prioress and Second Nun', in *Historians on Chaucer: The 'General Prologue' to the Canterbury Tales*, 94–113, 111.

104. Staley, 'Chaucer and the Postures of Sanctity', 182, 202.

105. Sanok, 'Performing Feminine Sanctity', 289–90; Minnis, *Fallible Authors*, 336. See also Alcuin Blamires and C. W. Marx, 'Women Not to Preach: A Disputation in British Library MS Harley 31', *Journal of Medieval Latin* 3 (1993), 34–63; and the exchange between Fiona Somerset and Kathryn Kerby-Fulton in *Voices in Dialogue: Reading Women in the Middle Ages*, ed. Linda Olson and Kathryn Kerby-Fulton (Notre Dame, IN: Notre Dame University Press, 2005).

106. The significance of Chaucer's use of rhyme royal in the *Second Nun's Tale* and the 'religious' tales told by the Prioress, the Man of Law, and the Clerk has been much discussed. See Derek Pearsall, *The Canterbury Tales* (New York: Routledge, 1985), 259; Saul Nathaniel Brody, 'Chaucer's Rhyme Royal Tales and the Secularization of the Saint', *The Chaucer Review* 20 (1985), 113–21; Laurel Braswell, 'Chaucer and the Art of Hagiography', in *Chaucer and the Eighties*, ed. Julian Wasserman and Robert Blanch (Syracuse, NY: Syracuse University Press, 1986), 209–21, 218–19; Barbara Nolan, 'Chaucer's Tales of Transcendence', in Benson and Robertson, *Chaucer's Religious Tales*, 21–37, at 23; Gail Berkeley Sherman, 'Saints, Nuns, and Speech in the *Canterbury Tales*', in *Images of Sainthood in Medieval Europe*, eds. Renate Blumenfeld-Kosinski and Timea Szell (Ithaca, NY: Cornell University Press, 1991), 136–60, at 137.

107. Reames, 'The Second Nun's Prologue and Tale', 496.

108. The noun 'sone' appears in nearly all the eighty-four manuscript copies of the *Canterbury Tales* consulted by Manly and Rickert in which the *Second Nun's Prologue* and *Tale* appear, save two: London, British Library, MSS Lansdowne 851 and Sloane 1686, in which 'douhter' was written instead; *The Text of the Canterbury Tales: Studied on the Basis of All Known Manuscripts*, vol. 8 (Chicago, IL: Chicago University Press, 1940), 9.

109. Meale, 'Women's Piety', 40.

110. Lewis, 'The Prioress and Second Nun', 113. The application of the title *virago* to a few English Benedictine women religious, mainly abbesses and prioresses, during the central Middle Ages is discussed in Bugyis, *The Care of Nuns: Benedictine Women's Ministries in England during the Central Middle Ages* (Oxford: Oxford University Press, 2019), chapter two.

111. San Marino, Huntington Library, MS EL 26 C9, fol. 187r.

112. The miniatures of the pilgrims in the Ellesmere Chaucer were painted by three different artists. The miniature of the Prioress was painted by Artist 1, and the Second Nun's was painted by Artist 3, an artist, perhaps the apprentice of Artist 2, who possessed less skill than the other two. Edwin Piper, 'The Miniatures of the Ellesmere Chaucer', *Philological*

Quarterly 3 (1924), 241–56, 249; Richard Emerson, 'Text and Image in the Ellesmere Portraits of the Tale-Tellers', in *The Ellesmere Chaucer: Essays in Interpretation*, eds. Daniel Woodward and Martin Stevens (San Marino, 1995), 143–70, 146, 149, 163; Samantha Mullaney, 'The Language of Costume in the Ellesmere Portraits', in C. W. Marx, *Sources, Exemplars, and Copy-Texts: Influence and Transmission, Essays from the Lampeter Conference of the Early Book Society, 1997, Trivium* 31 (1999), 33–67, 39, 42; Laura Hodges, *Chaucer and Clothing: Clerical and Academic Costume in the General Prologue to the Canterbury Tales* (Cambridge: D. S. Brewer, 2005), 79; Maidie Hilmo, 'Iconic Representations of Chaucer's Two Nuns and their Tales from Manuscript to Print', in *Women and the Divine in Literature before 1700: Essays in Memory of Margot Louis*, ed. Kathryn Kerby-Fulton (Victoria: ELS Editions, 2009), 107–35, 131.

113. Of course, Chaucer's close connections with St. Leonard's, as well as with Barking Abbey, may bolster readings of the Prioress's and the Second Nun's Benedictine affiliations (Meale, 'Women's Piety', 45–6).

114. Sanok, 'Performing Feminine Sanctity', 289–90; Minnis, *Fallible Authors*, 336.

BIBLIOGRAPHY

Cannon, Christopher, 'Vernacular Latin', *Speculum* 90(3) (2015), 641–53.

Geltner, G., 'The Friar', in *Historians on Chaucer: The 'General Prologue' to the Canterbury Tales*, eds. Stephen H. Rigby and Alastair J. Minnis (Oxford: Oxford University Press, 2014), 156–69.

Gillespie Vincent, and Kantik Ghosh, eds., *After Arundel: Religious Writing in Fifteenth-Century England* (Turnhout: Brepols, 2011).

Johnson, Ian, 'Vernacular Theology / Theological Vernacular: A Game of Two Halves?', in *After Arundel: Religious Writing in Fifteenth-Century England*, eds. Vincent Gillespie and Kantik Ghosh (Turnhout: Brepols, 2011), 73–88.

Minnis, Alastair, *Fallible Authors: Chaucer's Pardoner and Wife of Bath* (Philadelphia, PA: University of Pennsylvania Press, 2008).

Reames, S. L., 'Artistry, Decorum, and Purpose in Three Middle English Retellings of the Cecilia Legend', in *The Endless Knot: Essays on Old and Middle English in Honor of Marie Borroff*, eds. M. Teresa Tavormina and R. F. Yeager (Cambridge: D. S. Brewer, 1995), 177–99.

Scase, Wendy, *Piers Plowman and the New Anticlericalism* (Cambridge: Cambridge University Press, 1990).

Szittya, Penn R., *The Antifraternal Tradition in Medieval Literature* (Princeton, NJ: Princeton University Press, 1986).

Wogan-Browne, Jocelyn, Nicolas Watson, Andrew Taylor, and Ruth Evans, eds., *The Idea of the Vernacular: An Anthology of Middle English Literary Theory, 1280–1520* (Exeter: University of Exeter Press, 1999).

CHAPTER 28

CHAUCER AS IMAGE-MAKER

DENISE DESPRES

LIKE any stonemason, carver of wooden or alabaster statues of saints for the parish, manuscript illuminator or glassworker, Chaucer was an artisan for whom the term 'image' held a multiplicity of meanings, inclusive of the creation of material images, the composition of poetry, and the process of recollection with the mind's eye. The medieval imaginative text, a construct of the *vis imaginativa*, was first and foremost 'an image, "seen in the mind' ".[1] The recollection of memorial images for meditation was a necessary tool in medieval culture for spiritual consolation and aesthetic pleasure. The vernacular text, whether Chaucer's Second Nun's Tale or The Miller's Tale, was the product of artistic ingenuity stimulated by a vast body of culturally meaningful images, whose reception, much like a layperson's response to a holy image, could not be strictly controlled. Nicolette Zeeman translates this dilemma into the hermeneutics of anxiety we are all familiar with in Chaucer's poetry: 'the idol is…the underside of the notion that the imaginative text is like an image. For a number of late-medieval writers, including Chaucer, the figure of the idol is a means of focusing on problematic aspects of imaginative textuality and its contents'.[2]

Zeeman focuses on the proliferation of idols in Chaucer's texts that signal poetic self-reflection upon and anxiety about the materiality of his classical, and thus textual or archival, inheritance. The painted chambers, temples, fountains, and libidinous statues of courtly poetry familiar to Chaucer's readers link body and *eros* to the dangerously ambiguous and malleable idolatrous past, signalling the openness of a seductive textuality uninformed by a Christian hermeneutic. But such anxieties or ambiguities about poetic 'making' and idolatrous reception are equally present in Chaucer's works employing religious images, and this is not surprising.

The fertile devotional culture of late medieval England that Chaucer carefully recreates in the expansive material world of the *Canterbury Tales* represents the full spectrum of attitudes toward religious images and its rhetorical counterpart framed by the fiction of pilgrimage, from the Prioress's luminous Marian images to the Parson's eschewal of rhetorical ornamentation and religious representation. If Chaucer, unlike his contemporaries Langland and Gower, overtly avoided such politically vexed subjects as Wycliffite *iconomachia* (a hostility to the veneration of religious images), he does nevertheless stimulate reader and listener to an awareness of the current arguments about artistic and imaginative making in a devotional and liturgical context from which no act of imaginative creation could be divorced.[3] Simply by offering a variety of religious tales in the context of pilgrimage, Chaucer acknowledges a complex code of image creation, ritual staging, and reception that informed contemporary debates about the nature and proper use of religious images, whether pictures, statues, relics in ornamental reliquaries, or manuscript illuminations.[4] Chaucer's engagement with the legitimacy of religious representation would have been of interest to *any* lay vernacular poet writing in an age of increasing suspicion of and anxiety about image. Both orthodox reformists and Lollard *iconomachs* rejected the image-saturated culture of contemporary devotionalism, arguing that its excessive and unrestrained materialism was a form of idolatry. Some Lollards extended this argument to a rejection of fiction and rhetorical ornamentation altogether.[5]

Chaucer, however, chose to explore the power of images in the contested framework of medieval pilgrimage; acknowledging the variety and multiplicity of holy objects and images at the centre of pilgrimage controversy, he deliberately entered a debate that ranged from approval of images as books for the laity to the necessary destruction of idols. His dramatic representation of religious images as objects of devotion as well as their problematic reception is informed by a traditional code of image response learned early in life in the parish, extending to both private devotions and public pilgrimage.[6] Thus, Chaucer's culturally self-reflective exploration of how religious images work goes well beyond the theologically interesting but practically reductive definitions of *dulia*, *hyperdulia*, and *latria*—terms never translated into the vernacular.[7] By representing image creation, devotion, and reception within the context of individual tales, Chaucer demonstrates that devotional images, like any other image, are inherently polymorphous and regenerative, as essential to cultic religion as to poetry in stimulating the power of imagination and memorial recollection; whether the feelings of devotion they stimulate are holy, however, is an issue he leaves for his reader to contemplate. Although Chaucer surely pondered such issues within a different conceptual framework than I offer here, he raises them—with his usual pragmatism—for his audience's consideration.

A LEARNED CODE OF RESPONSE

In *The Canterbury Tales* Chaucer depends upon his audience's familiarity with a complex religious visual hermeneutic rooted in material experience. Thomas Lentes's recent study of the devotional process of the holy gaze suggests we are only beginning to understand this conventional code of religious response to sacred images.[8] The relationship between what we have perceived as privileged mystical metaphors describing heightened spiritual experience, such as somatic responses to holy images or the Eucharist, and the everyday devotion of the laity, may turn out to surprise us. Like Margery Kempe's neighbours, we may have to adjust our reading of religious behaviours, reassessing how the textual and visual evidence points to somatic response as normative. At the root of his mapping of religious synesthetic experience is Lentes's claim that material evidence suggests that *many* medieval people—and by no means only the spiritually illuminated—experienced the literal presence of the saints and a tangible connection to the dead for whom they prayed through cult, whether they responded to holy images in the parish church; in the devotional books they carried to Mass; on portable objects such as reliquaries; or even on religious jewellery, such as the fifteenth-century Middleham Jewel or the fourteenth-century reliquary ring discovered in the Thames Hoard.[9] Ordinary vision made it 'possible for the pious to come into contact with the people from the hereafter in pictures, a contact that we can hardly imagine realistically'.[10] Gazing, which could trigger a host of physical responses from sweet tastes to sounds (as is evidenced frequently in medieval mystical writing, both male and female), was 'automatism of salvation', bringing the devout into 'contact with holy material' and in direct communication with the sacred.[11]

While Lollard reformers objected to the demonstrative and idolatrous response to images of the devout in public (of which Margery Kempe is, of course, an extreme example), 'movements of the entire body were a factor in the repertoire of gestures' that constituted a visible code of response to holy objects.[12] Neighbours within the parish, such as Margery's, seem to have been deeply aware of how members of the community responded to the ritual staging strategies incorporating images, statues, and holy objects essential to cultic devotion. Signs in themselves, the dramatic covering or uncovering of sacred images before the viewer was itself part of a liturgical language evoking emotional response and self-reflection.[13] Similarly, adorning and unadorning a statue of the Virgin elicited a bodily response, such as kneeling, prayer, or prostration as an acknowledgment of the essential and shared story of salvation. Just as guild ordinances set forth public actions from their members as evidence of charity and community, such as procession, the lighting of candles, prayer for the dead, and generous feasting to support the poor of the parish or the burial of the indigent (fining recalcitrant members), so there were expectations of bodily response to the salvific gaze in public processions that most likely influenced private responses. Rather than differentiating public and private responses to image, the kneeling, prostration, and kissing that indicated excessive or false emotionalism—or idolatry—to reformers were liturgical gestures that were replicated in private piety, reinforcing the ties between response to the liturgy and private image cult.[14] The public penances requiring image devotion that communities demanded as a sign of reintegration involved precisely the performance of oblations and bodily movements that acknowledged membership in a community defined by shared 'material artefacts, rituals, and beliefs'.[15] While Chaucer's pilgrims are no doubt realistic in their diverse needs and intentions in undertaking pilgrimage, their shared destination to the relics of St Thomas of Canterbury and responses to religious images in tales like the Prioress's deliberately heightens the tensions essential to the confessional drama of the framing device. As critics have pointed out for many years, a pilgrim's response to devotional images is a key indicator of his or her authentic place in this corporate community, and pilgrims like the Pardoner or the Parson, who reject or falsify holy matter and image, are problematic or ambivalent figures, particularly within the framework of pilgrimage. In exploiting or rejecting altogether this visual hermeneutic and code of response, such characters challenge the corporate nature of medieval religious identity.

This sometimes subtle line between orthodox image response and idolatry troubled not only Lollard critics, but equally contemporary orthodox writers such as the Augustinian canon Walter Hilton (who responded to Lollard *iconomachia* in a treatise on images in the late 1380s or early 90s) and Dominican theologian Roger Dymmock, regent of the London house after 1396.[16] Both sympathized with the Lollard rejection of the fine distinctions among *latria, hyperdulia*, and *dulia* in worship of the saints, voicing a shared concern that such subtleties—and thus awareness of one's own disposition in both public and private veneration of images—eluded ordinary folk.[17] Common people, they averred, did sometimes fail to distinguish between prototype and image, falling prey to material beauty and aesthetic appeal when they wept, knelt before and stroked these dead statues or bones in ornate reliquaries, or meditated upon them in private oratories and Books of Hours. Hilton and Dymmock were just two of the orthodox writers in the 1390s who addressed the subject of idolatry in Latin. Vernacular treatises, such as the *Bonus tractatis De decem mandatis*, reveal that other clergy felt compelled to instruct laypeople to distinguish proper veneration from idolatry.[18] The Decalogue had set forth undisputable law forbidding idolatry, and whether common folk honoured the myriad statues within the parish, or made pilgrimage to miracle producing shrines, the gifts they offered of jewellery, land, and even clothing in support of these objects or as votive offerings diminished Christ's social Gospel, encouraging a deadly literalism and materialism that, in their turn, orthodox Christians attributed to heretics and Jews both. The multiplication of images the industry of pilgrimage encouraged, through votive offerings, badges, and the foundation of new shrines pointed explicitly to the human dimension of profit that itself was a form of idolatry and the inescapable consequence of even well-intentioned image veneration. The difference between act and intention in such worship was a central issue; Hilton, in contrast to Dymmock, insisted upon the innocent intentions of ignorant worshipers who erred through ignorance and out of love.

FROM PARISH TO SHRINE: THE BUSINESS OF PILGRIMAGE

In every case, the main focus is the shrine…We travel to the painting or sculpture; we stop at them on the way; we erect new ones; and we take copies and souvenirs away with us. These images work miracles and record them; they mediate between ourselves and the supernatural; and they fix in our minds the recollection of experience.

> At every stage the image is indispensable, in all its variety... Along the way are simpler images, attached to poles and trees; then come the votive images by which thanks are registered; and finally the souvenirs we buy and take away with us.[19]

David Freedberg's description of the way in which pilgrimage replicates and circulates images, both now and in fourteenth-century England, suggests the limitations of employing 'iconography' and 'iconoclasm' as organizing concepts in an exploration of the veneration or rejection of late medieval religious images. Like Latin itself, the visual language of sacred symbols had developed into a fluid vernacular informed by evolving devotional practices, with an emphasis on pilgrimage.[20] The ever-present threat of idolatry—the worship of material images instead of God—did not restrain a sacramental culture that acknowledged the benefit of multiple religious objects and actions in a dynamic personal and communal search for holy encounter. Pilgrimage best exemplifies this search and was thus inextricably linked to liturgical practice and parish ritual, reinforcing a dominant reverence for holy material, for commemoration through object, and a potential overlapping of what theologians understood as the *cultus absolutus* (reverence to God through the saints) and the *cultus relativus* (honour paid to things related to holy persons).[21]

When Chaucer chose to link a series of tales through the framing device of pilgrimage, he undoubtedly recognized that this framework was a contested subject in the late 1380s and 90s, specifically in relation to the production and function of religious images and objects.[22] The sacramental aesthetic that informs much late medieval poetry was necessarily part of this larger discussion about the role of images in mediating divine truth, as well as the human creation, interpretation, and misinterpretation of images or objects bearing images (such as reliquaries).[23] Recent scholarship has focused on a wide range of orthodox and Lollard positions on images, as well as more localized cultic practice, altering our sense of Chaucer's material religious landscape with necessary consequences for rethinking his poetic hermeneutic, particularly in the *Canterbury Tales*, which coincides with dramatic spectacles of English heresy and iconoclasm.[24] The rapid proliferation of new cult images in the fourteenth and fifteenth centuries, as well as easily and inexpensively reproduced devotional images, such as the Veronica, the Man of Sorrows, and the *Arma Christi*, reveal that the Church could not maintain a 'hegemony over the production and patronage of images' or control lay patronage and virtually independent artists.[25] Through such proliferation, an either idolatrous (depending on one's sensibilities) or creative and fluid market in religious images was made possible by the economic and material realities of late medieval life.[26] These realities no doubt altered or influenced the conventions that established orthodox image usage and performance. The recombinative nature (the cross-pollination of devotional images, such as the *Arma Christi* and the Man of Sorrows) of medieval devotionalism, in addition to a multiplicity of images, made ripe the occasion for hermeneutical crisis.[27]

Controversies over pilgrimage, relics, statues, and increasingly the images that dominated the late medieval devotional scene resulted from disagreement or scepticism about these semiotic strategies and resultant practices. Eamon Duffy argues that the fraudulent statues and shrines that succeeded could only do so by '*imitating* [emphasis mine] the conventions of the cult of saints, conventions which informed *a code* immediately understood by "simple people"'.[28] Yet the orthodox debates about intentionality and acts in veneration suggest a more complicated reality. Chaucer's religious tales acknowledge this tension between a vibrant, evolving religious culture of image in which vernacular poets and artists participated and a fixed code of veneration so explicit that it could be imitated for fraudulent ends. In both the Pardoner's Prologue and the Prioress's Tale Chaucer dramatically acknowledges the untidy reality of cultic veneration and the linked issue of 'entente' (VI.403). Further, the very pilgrimage framework that provided Chaucer with a dramatic opportunity for competing religious tales implies multiplicity in religious representation, for pilgrimage depends upon images that mediate the sacred in both subjective and objective ways: communally *and* individually through ritual performance and personal meditation. Thus competing religious tales engage the hermeneutical issues central to Chaucer's game or play in a particularly sensitive way; it is our assumption, our hermeneutic, that anachronistically postulates an unrefined or binary opposition between the sacred and profane, iconography and iconoclasm, and proper or idolatrous intentions. As James Simpson argues in his compelling 'historiography of culture', no diachronic reading of 'medieval' as synonymous with the uncontained imagination and 'Reformist' (or 'Reformation') as wholly aniconic can truthfully reflect their shared anxieties about the uncontrollable and 'mesmeric power of the image'.[29]

David Freedberg's description of pilgrimage at the beginning of this section points to the nuanced issues that troubled both Lollard iconomachs and orthodox reformers, such as the replication of crude secondary images that are both commemorative and holy by virtue of proximity to the original (such as badges); the gaudy dressing up and ornamentation of crude wooden statues to stage the feast days of the liturgical year; and especially the reproduction of mementos that distinguish, for example, the Virgin of Boulton from Our Lady of Walsingham or Ipswich, raising doubt about identical but troublingly localized prototypes. Similarly distasteful to reformers was the money spent on the abundant votive offerings of thanks that lent the already image-saturated holy space a pervasive and pagan corporeality. The wax votive offerings at medieval shrines, sometimes even of silver and gold, of a foot, a breast, an eye, a hand, were meant to invite reflection on bodily restoration and resurrection rather than fragmentation, to witness, express gratitude, and visually compel pilgrims to greater devotion.[30] But because votive offerings testify to the 'specificity of event and the perpetual assertion of the heavenly operative as distinctive and peculiar to the place', in their multiplicity they raise questions about the efficacy and agency of the discrete shrine's prototype: Why do some shrines diminish in their healing powers? And why are some saints more efficacious in some places than others (a question the hagiographers themselves entertain)?[31]

In Chaucer's England, proper disposition towards objects, images, relics, and statues was made even more complex by their equally fluid identity as material and person. Relics dominated the devotional scene of early medieval religion; in their perceived connection to *persons*, relics defy purely material categorization, belonging 'like slaves... to that category unusual in Western society, of objects that are both persons and things'.[32] The prevalence of devotional images and statues in late medieval England—some alleged to weep or exude oil, to bleed or bear other corporeal characteristics—underscores the fluid boundaries between the early medieval cult of relics and the late-medieval cult of holy images. It is true that images and statues did not always 'contain matter and spirit in a miraculous fusion that exemplifies the resurrection of the body', yet they functioned like relics in their manifestation of the immediate and tangible influence of holy people; this is why 'the spectral lives of images in the popular imagination suggest that images crossed the line between matter and spirit or the living and the dead'.[33] As both 'persons and things', Patrick Geary explains, relics signified to believers a living relationship of sacred transaction.[34] This sacred transaction, in turn, helps us understand why the proper response to a healing relic, statue, or image is a corresponding gift of a personal item, such as a necklace, ring, or a cast of the body part the saint restored to health (an especially appropriate gift in the case of a relic, reproducing a fragment as sign of the resurrected body). By the fourteenth century, not only relics, but also images and statues were perceived as 'security deposits left by the saints . . . as guarantees of their continuing interest in the earthly community'; consequently, such objects cannot be fully comprehended outside of personal and communal medieval relationships.[35] The complexity of this communal reality—for such it was for the majority of medieval people—places modern readers, like Lollard iconoclasts, in a difficult position. The corporeality and personhood of images, relics, and statues as they figured in medieval devotional culture contradicted the notion of holy object as a sign of an immaterial idea. The evidence of medieval religious material culture, whether a relic in a reliquary shaped like a hand, a statue that emits a healing oil, an image of a bleeding Host in a Book of Hours, or a pax of carved bone depicting the Lamb of God, all challenge this reductive hermeneutic.

IMAGE-BEARING PILGRIMS

Far from ignoring such thorny issues, Chaucer incorporates multiplicity and dramatizes the ambiguities between licit and illicit images from the outset of the General Prologue. The selectively descriptive portraits in Chaucer's General Prologue do not merely set forth an estates satire reflective of the competing professions and orders that comprise Middle English society. The pilgrim portraits also provide us with a sense of the wider community comprising the living and dead—the community of saints who were patrons, advocates, and friends to their clients in a tangible and reciprocal relationship of giving. The saints themselves belonged to various estates in Heaven, with Mary as co-redemptrix and thus reverenced with *hyperdulia*; while universal saints (the apostles and martyrs) and local saints, subject to the changing fashions of time and regional influence, merited *dulia*. All serve as advocates or intercessors for the living and the dead in Purgatory (the vast majority of the departed faithful). Chaucer's General Prologue acknowledges this extended community made visible through the materials of devotion as a fact of everyday life. The General Prologue opens with testimony to the universal efficacy of Saint Thomas Becket's intercession on behalf of the sick. Pilgrims come 'from every shires ende / of Engelond' seeking his help (I.15–16). But these pilgrims acknowledge the saintly patronage of others as well. The Yeoman bears a silver Christopher on his breast. The Prioress has received more than her share of attention for *not* bearing the expected and appropriate religious image and, instead, sporting the fashionable gold rosary with its ambiguous pendant inscription (Chaucer's wickedly explicit and self-conscious acknowledgment of the difficulties of reading images!). The Franklin imitates his patron Saint Julian in his hospitality, and The Wife of Bath's indiscriminate appetites, sexual and devotional alike, direct her from vigils, processions, and miracle plays to the epicentre of the *mappa mundi*, underscoring her reductive corporeal hermeneutic rooted in feminine carnality. While the Pardoner profits from the fraudulent trade in relics with his 'glas' of 'pigges bones' (700), he also sews a 'vernycle' (685) on his cap, the popular replica of the cloth with which Saint Veronica wiped Christ's face and which subsequently bore its imprint. All serve to punctuate the evolving and much scrutinized image practices that were challenged not only by Lollard reformers but equally by orthodox spiritual directors and reformers such as Dymmok and Hilton, who lamented the inherent ambiguities attending such devotional conventions.[36] What such visible signs meant to the pilgrims, to Chaucer's audience, and to us is worth consideration. To reduce the problem of images in Chaucer's work to the influence of Lollard *iconomachy* is to ignore the equally stringent concerns of orthodox reformist writers in response to this proliferation of images that increasingly made artists—such as the makers of the ubiquitous wooden and alabaster statues in parish Churches, or poets like Chaucer—commercial agents in late medieval lay devotionalism and failed to make transparent the spiritual motives of patrons as various as the Prioress and the Pardoner. Why does the Pardoner, rather than the Prioress or Wife of Bath, wear the faddish 'vernycle'? Chaucer acknowledges his own participation and implication in this growing economy of sacred images, not so much to affirm a doctrine of proper conduct in relation to relics, pilgrimage, statues, and images of saints, I suspect, but to dramatize the regenerative power of images and explore 'what makes images work' in the sphere of contemporary lay piety and, in turn, poetic making.[37] After all, his framework is not merely pilgrimage, but a storytelling competition that takes place during a pilgrimage.[38]

Chaucer's pilgrimage framework—like actual pilgrimage—admits the power and multiplicity of images, enabling the poet to spatialize, localize, and temporalize devotional imagery in his exploration of religious narrative. The journey to Canterbury allows for tales that span the hagiocentric cult of the saint's relic to the christocentric cult of the Eucharist, from the largely shared, communal devotion of a saint to the personal relationship of saint and client. The *Canterbury Tales* are stories whose origins and thus religious inflections mark different cultic moments in an evolving religious trajectory that informed medieval devotional and liturgical practice.

Nonetheless, Chaucer's selection of religious tales is both highly conventional and selective, illustrating contemporary devotional tastes in its historical coverage, cultic practice, and generic diversity. As we might expect, his selection appeals to the material religious experience of fourteenth-century English readers. The medieval English laity, for example, had a profound reverence for early female virgin martyrs like Cecilia and Katherine, whose lives were the subject of many retellings and whose statues were ubiquitous in parish Churches due to their special intimacy with their bridegroom, Christ.[39] Local church authorities clearly approved such desire for physical proximity to the sacred made accessible through images, for even small parishes were saturated with vividly coloured statues of saints in carved niches, on wall murals, chantry altars, in carved alabasters, stained glass, altar clothes, and misericords.[40] Each church—however small—like each extant medieval manuscript, reflects a discrete history of patrons, owners, users, and a religious community comprising individuals and groups with specific needs, tasks, and multifaceted identities connected to their use of images and holy objects. Similarly, the Marian iconography that informs the tales of calumniated wives and the Prioress's Tale has its counterpart in Middle English devotional habit. Marian miracles feature widely in English Books of Hours, linking private reading and prayer to parish cults of the Virgin that supported sometimes within one parish, as Faversham in Chaucer's Kent, four and perhaps more images of the Virgin, some with their own chapels and altars.[41] Sentimental religious romances featuring virtuous wives also reflect the increasing number of married-women saints who appear in fourteenth-century England, most prominently the Lancastrian prophet and patron, Saint Brigit of Sweden.[42] These stories have visual counterparts in contemporary parish churches and provide Chaucer's tales with a devotional and liturgical context that is current, its appeal both individual and communal. All of these stories reflect upon the diversity and individual *charism* within the community of saints, a point Chaucer foregrounds in underscoring both personal choice of tale and reception. Such contestation embraced rather than discouraged religious tastes and preferences and realistically reflects the strong bonds among saints, specific clients, and the wider community in fourteenth-century English parishes. Critics of pilgrimage attacked idolatry, luxury, and hypocrisy or outward show of devotion, but especially the multiplicity of shrines that invited the layperson or guild to favour a saint, perceive one relic or statue as more efficacious than another, and put trust in the healing power of a particular saint located erroneously in a specific, inanimate 'stoke' or 'stone' rather than in God.

RELICS IN MOTION: THE PARDONER'S PROLOGUE

The Pardoner's success in shearing simple parishioners depends precisely upon the hermeneutical crisis of image proliferation and a paraliturgical code of image veneration I have outlined in my chapter. The Pardoner mimics ritual gestures in ritual space with ritual language.[43] He understands acutely how the holy gaze works; his rags and animal bones ensconced in the glass and crystal cases are typical of late medieval reliquaries that increasingly called the devotee's attention to rather than distracted the gaze from the materiality of the fragment.[44] The Pardoner recognizes that relics in their gilded, ornamental receptacles—like the pendant, relic-bearing amulets we now see in museum collections—have a powerfully synesthetic effect: they 'stire hem to devocioun' (VI.346). They also tempt the simple, simultaneously, to mistake spiritual for material gain. His relics, which are openly—and admittedly—bits of sheep bone, animal parts that co-inhabit the realm of flesh and decay (unlike the Virgin's milk, clothing, or other objects that had proximity to the body of Christ—they signify personhood, as odd as that may seem to us), are compelling even though they cannot serve an authentically integrative function. They are the conceptual opposite of votive offerings, saints' images, or genuine relics that—enhancing the reality of the mystical body in the Eucharist itself—are visible signs of the wholeness of person in anticipation of bodily resurrection.[45] Idolatry in the reformist sense of the word places at the centre of human engagement 'the dead-matter, that is, non-procreative' materialism that begins and ends with itself.[46] The sensory feeling of salvation the Pardoner mocks as separate from genuine spiritual awareness of Christ's saving mercy supports the objections of critics like the Parson that all such stuff is illusion. Yet, despite the Pardoner's insistence that he tempts simple folk with promise of gain, he cannot ascertain the 'entente' of these poor folk any more than the pilgrims can understand his own during the telling of his tale. Thus the arguments of Hilton and Dymmock over innocence and intentionality inform the Pardoner's Prologue as deeply as do Lollard anxieties about idolatry.

THE HERMENEUTICS OF IMAGE
VENERATION RESTORED

The Prioress challenges any reductive sense of image veneration as 'idolatry' by restoring both image (figured as the typically lifelike and approachable statue of the Virgin) and relic (the body of the little chorister) to an authenticating narrative and geography in a regenerative context: from image veneration sacred boundaries are remapped, culminating in the establishment of a shrine. Through the sacred language of liturgical devotion, she attempts to dismantle any lingering doubts about the authenticity of genuine images and remaps all space for orthodox worship. In doing so, she reflects the ordinary practices of medieval parishioners whose spiritual geography linked the sacred space of the parish to the web of outlying fields donated by guilds to support votive lights of patron saints.[47] Kathleen Kamerick explains that 'this ligature between holy images and plots of earth in the parish marked spatial distinctions outside the church walls, as the guild lights in front of images did within the church. Holy images in this way took part in the spiritual mapping of a community's territory…they were bound not only to private devotions and communal rituals but to the land itself.'[48]

This re-appropriation of the sacred is linguistic as well as geographical. The Prioress begins her Marian miracle in prayer punctuated with the luxurious mystical images from the service for Matins in the Little Office of the Blessed Virgin.[49] The Matins image in most Books of Hours was the Annunciation, an image evoked specifically in her Prologue by lines in the third stanza of rhyme royal. Her story, too, argues for the miraculous sacralisation of the flesh in a world imperilled by precisely the Pardoner's sort of deathly carnality, the essential theme of meditation on the Incarnation at Matins. Her story simultaneously argues for the intercessory power of the Virgin and, by the tale's end, the sanctity of the relics of the little clergeon and martyr.[50] However, the power she lauds cannot be manipulated, feigned, or destroyed, but takes effect only through carefully prescribed ritual, whose attendant visual code the Prioress carefully reconstructs as a corrective to the Pardoner's kind of ventriloquism. Her tale affirms precisely those orthodox ritual behaviours in the context of consecrated images that reformers rejected for their externality. When the little clergeon sees 'th'ymage / of Cristes mooder, hadde he in usage, / As hym was taught, to knele adoun and seye / His *Ave Marie*, as he goth by the weye' (VII. 505–8). The material images of the Virgin and the little clergeon in the Prioress's Tale are enveloped in liturgical echoes of the Little Office, as well as from the feast days of the Holy Innocents, Saint Nicholas, and Saint Thomas Becket, invoking linked images of martyrdom and innocence that give a historical and devotional context to her tale. They are imbued with power not because they hold some promise of material comfort or worldly security for the devout; rather, the power of such images is made operative by the rote prayers of the smallest of believers who need not even comprehend them literally.

The Prioress's Prologue and Tale draws these verbal and physical images from their places in the liturgy, the parish Church, and the pilgrimage shrine, gathering the Christian folk within the tale—Chaucer's pilgrims and the book's reader—as witnesses to a narrative dramatizing the sanctity and power of religious images. She responds explicitly to the Pardoner's mockery of lay gullibility in her argument for the accessibility of the holy to common folk, as infants and children are precisely those whose dominant sensory responses direct their yet-undeveloped faculty of reason. Her tale suggests that images are not mere books for the illiterate laity, but that they are receptacles of divine power for those like the clergeon and his friend, who 'kan but small grammeere' (VII. 536). In contrast to what the Pardoner implies, rote learning can be meaningful in the absence of literal comprehension *if* it is rooted in a loving will and proper intention, as the clergeon demonstrates. Like the Pardoner, the Prioress attends to an 'entente' critical for comprehending the clergeon's response to the statue of Mary as something other than idolatry: that is, the faith that makes possible his martyrdom. His innocent 'automatism' or holy gaze upon and verbal response to the statue of Mary illustrates orthodox behaviour whether or not the clergeon knows the difference between *latria* and *hyperdulia* or *dulia*. The Prioress's Tale thus instructs visual devotional literacy in the fashion of the Book of Hours, whose images historically served as an aid in teaching children to read. The image of Mary that the Prioress evokes in her Prologue, and that the clergeon routinely venerates on his way to and from school, is not a 'sign' of an abstract or theological idea, but a tangible figuration of Mary's literal omnipresence as exemplar and helper, co-redemptrix and specialist saint.

Her tale, however, goes further than asserting the efficacy of those lifelike statues especially condemned by iconoclasts by offering a meditation on the 'making' or authentication of holy images and relics from the sacred bodies of martyrs. Chaucer deliberately invokes the liturgical language from the Mass for the Feast of the Holy Innocents (closely linked in the Christmas season with Thomas Becket's martyrdom) to elevate even further the ritual sequence at the conclusion of the tale. The laity within the tale model proscribed ritual action when they process with the clergeon on his bier to the spiritual centre of the town, the high altar within the abbey church. What follows is a ritual consecration, enacted after the Mass but prior to the martyr's entombment, through the sprinkling of holy water on the body: 'And after that, the abbot with his covent / Han sped for to burien hym ful faste; / And whan they hooly water on hym caste, / Yet spak this child, whan spreynd was hooly water, / And song O Alma redemptoris mater!' (VII.637–41).

In exploring what makes images work in a wide range of religious cultures, David Freedberg concludes:

> Consecration is never an empty ceremony. It involves at least one process—like washing, anointing, crowning or blessing—that brings about an intended change in the sacred status of an image. By its very nature consecration is a ritual act, and not merely a ceremonial one, even when it seems to be the simplest of performances. It is usually explicitly physical, but it can also be entirely verbal. The verbal and liturgical elements are never wholly absent, and they are often operative.[51]

The Prioress's synthesis of Marian miracle and saint's translation restores the mechanisms that authenticate holy material. Mary's miraculous intercession and the removal of the grain evoke from the monks within the tale and model for the pilgrims the devotional response appropriate for all believers: weeping, prostration upon the ground, and praise of the Blessed Virgin. The culmination of the tale is the production of the relic, the enclosing of his body 'in a tombe of marbul stones cleere' (VII.681).[52] The audience thus also witnesses how the smallest of children, unlettered and impoverished, can become a saint, like Saint Hugh of Lincoln.[53] Entombed and visible in a reliquary, empowered by both consecration and an oral or written tradition for communal memory, the clergeon is literally more alive in death than in life; in death alone can he assume his rightful place, moving from the periphery of the community where he is neglected, endangered, and sacrificed, to the centre, where he ascends to his own role of patron and protector in imitation of the Blessed Virgin.[54]

In the Canterbury Tales, Chaucer employs the conventions of religious images in multiple rhetorical and material contexts, imbuing them with the same creative self-reflection with which we see him engage the potentially idolatrous images from the cult of courtly love. I have argued for a reading of Chaucer's religious texts that is historically sensitive to the limitations of our critical vocabulary—a vocabulary permeated with aesthetic and ontological assumptions that are historically insensitive to Chaucer's text and which therefore diminish his representation of the material practices of medieval religion that, while far from static, functioned according to physical and visual conventions of space, ritual, and reception. Recovering the visual codes that both informed medieval image makers and reader reception demands further cross-disciplinary excavation informed by a willingness to struggle with hermeneutic assumptions that are counterintuitive, even morally repulsive, to most contemporary readers. Chaucer yoked literalism and a deathly materialism in his figuration of carnal and spiritually fractured storytellers and characters within the tales themselves: women, heretics, Jews and all nonreproductive and hence 'queer' figures who challenge a Christian sacramental ontology fall into the category of the abject.[55] Wholeness depends upon an individual bodily impermeability replicated in a bodily politic that expels contaminants, a process as natural in his medieval anthropology as bleeding to restore the balance of the humours. How this sacramental ontology informs and defines the complex communities he represents is promising territory for new scholarly investigation. In the end, in interpreting Chaucer's poetry, we must imagine his world as richly and sympathetically as we can with everything we have left at our disposal.

NOTES

1. Nicolette Zeeman, 'The Idol of the Text', in *Images, Idolatry and Iconoclasm in Late Medieval England*, eds. Jeremy Dimmick, James Simpson, and Nicolette Zeeman (Oxford: Oxford University Press, 2002), 43–62.
2. Zeeman, 'Idol of the Text', 44.
3. This is the subject of Sarah Stanbury's evocative study in *The Visual Object of Desire in Late Medieval England* (Philadelphia, PA: University of Pennsylvania Press, 2008); although I do not agree with many of her conclusions, I am deeply indebted to her book's rich arguments about the potency and ambiguity of fourteenth-century material religious culture.
4. Derek Pearsall, *The Life of Geoffrey Chaucer* (Oxford: Blackwell, 1992), 240.
5. Maidie Hilmo, *Medieval Images, Icons, and Illustrated English Literary Texts, From the Ruthwell Cross to the Ellesmere Chaucer* (Aldershot: Ashgate, 2004).
6. Eamon Duffy, *The Stripping of the Altars, Traditional Religion in England 1400–1580* (New Haven, CT: Yale University Press, 1992), 197.
7. The distinction between *latria*, worship appropriate to God alone; *hyperdulia*, reverence to the Virgin Mary; and *dulia*, reverence to the saints, was problematic. Margaret Aston notes that 'the mere fact that the Greek terms *latria*, *dulia*, and *hyperdulia* never acquired clear vernacular equivalents (or even Latin ones) reveals the remoteness of this theology from everyday realities'. See *England's Iconoclasts, Volume I. Laws against Images* (Oxford: Oxford Clarendon Press, 1988), 28. For discussions of the Parson's *iconomachia*, see Karen Winstead, 'Chaucer's Parson's Tale and the Contours of Orthodoxy', *The Chaucer Review* 43 (2009), 239–59; and Michaela Paasche Grudin, 'Credulity and the Rhetoric of Heterodoxy: From Averroes to Chaucer', *The Chaucer Review* 35 (2000), 204–22.
8. Thomas Lentes, '"As Far as the Eye Can See"': Rituals of Gazing in the Late Middle Age', in *The Mind's Eye, Art and Theological Argument in the Middle Ages*, eds. Jeffrey F. Hamburger and Anne-Marie Bouche (Princeton, NJ: Princeton University Press, 2006).

9. Marta Bagnoli, Holger A. Klein, C. Griffith Mann, and James Robinson, eds., *Treasures of Heaven, Saints, Relics, and Devotion in Medieval Europe* (New Haven, CT: Yale University Press, 2010), 115. See Alfred Gell, *Art and Agency, An Anthropological Theory* (Oxford: Oxford Clarendon Press, 1998), 96–153.

10. Lentes, ' "As Far as the Eye Can See" ', 360. See also Margaret Aston, *England's Iconoclasts*: 'Participation in the sacraments was relatively rare; communion with the saints through their representations a common, if not daily, experience. It was also a living relationship. Those who served the saints and acted as votaries before their images anticipated and often obtained a response' (20).

11. Lentes, ' "As Far as the Eye Can See" ', 361.

12. Ibid., 362.

13. Ibid., 363.

14. Ibid., 366–7.

15. Kathleen Kamerick, *Popular Piety and Art in the Late Middle Ages, Image Worship and Idolatry in England 1350–1500* (New York: Palgrave, 2002), 128.

16. Kamerick, *Popular Piety*, 27–42; Nicholas Watson, ' "Et Que Est Huius Ydoli Materia? Tuipse": Idols and Images in Walter Hilton,' in *Images, Idolatry, and Iconoclasm in Late Medieval England*, eds. Jeremy Dimmick, James Simpson, and Nicolette Zeeman (Oxford: Oxford University Press, 2002), 95–111.

17. See Margaret Aston, *Lollards and Reformers, Images and Literacy in Late Medieval Religion* (London: Hambledon Press, 1984), 177–92; Kamerick, *Popular Piety*, 43–68; Duffy, *Stripping of the Altars*, 155–205; James Simpson, 'The Rule of Medieval Imagination', in Dimmick et al. *Images, Idolatry, and Iconoclasm*, 4–24; and Watson, 'Et Que Est Huius Ydoli Materia? Tuipse', 95–111.

18. Kamerick, *Popular Piety*, 38–42.

19. David Freedberg, *The Power of Images, Studies in the History and Theory of Response* (Chicago, IL: University of Chicago Press, 1989), 100.

20. See Mary Carruthers, *The Book of Memory* (Cambridge: Cambridge University Press, 1990), 256: 'Iconography, in art as well as literary criticism, treats images as direct signs of something, as having an inherent meaning that will be universal for all readers.'

21. Richard P. McBrien, ed., *The HarperCollins Encyclopedia of Catholicism* (San Francisco, CA: Harper Collins, 1995), 1096. The articles in this volume concerning idolatry, iconoclasm, relics, sacraments and sacramentals specify important shifts and developments in Catholic Canon Law. For example, Catholic sacramentals (as opposed to the seven Sacraments) are now viewed as 'dynamic signs used in celebration' similar to and in support of the seven sacraments, as opposed strictly to the traditional clerical and lay use of rosaries, medals, holy water, sacred images, votive candles and so forth (McBrien, *Encyclopedia of Catholicism*, 1148–9).

22. See Andrew F. Larson, 'Are All Lollards Lollards'? in *Lollards and Their Influence in Late Medieval England*, eds. Fiona Somerset, Jill C. Havens, and Derrick G. Pitard (Woodbridge: The Boydell Press, 2003), 59–72; Andrew Cole, 'William Langland and the Invention of Lollardy', in Somerset et al., *Lollards and Their Influence*, 37–58; Aston, *England's Iconoclasts*, 96–143.

23. See McBrien, *Encyclopedia of Catholicism*, 1148. 'The sacramental aesthetic is the principle that informs embodiment or representation in medieval religious culture. The orthodox Roman Catholic position has consistently defined the principle of sacramentality as 'the notion that all reality, both animate and inanimate, is potentially or in fact the bearer of

God's presence and the instrument of God's saving activity on humanity's behalf...the principle of sacramentality constitutes one of the central theological characteristics of Catholicism'.

24. See Aston, *Lollards and Reformers*, 1–47. Also see Sarah Stanbury, *The Visual Object of Desire in Late Medieval England* (Philadelphia, PA: University of Pennsylvania Press, 2008), 38. Henry Knighton's notorious description of William Smith and Richard Waytestathe's burning of a wooden statue of Saint Katherine as fuel for cooking cabbage stew in his *Chronicle* dates the event to 1382, although Stanbury places the event 'as late as 1389 when Archbishop Courtenay gave Smith the penance of walking barefoot and bareheaded in a Leicester procession, carrying an image of St. Katherine in his right hand',24. Lay devotion to saints' images was merely one strain of late-medieval piety among a plethora of practices verging on the idolatrous to reformist-minded Christians.

25. Michael Camille, *The Gothic Idol, Ideology and Image-Making in Medieval Art* (Cambridge: Cambridge University Press, 1989), 211–12.

26. Camille, *Gothic Idol*, 219. In a lucid exploration of cult image, popular reception, and materialism, Sarah Stanbury ('The Vivacity of Images: St. Katherine, Knighton's Lollards, and the Breaking of Idols', in Dimmick et al. *Images, Idolatry and Iconoclasm in Late Medieval England*, 150) argues of the widely popular fifteenth-century Saint Katherine: 'saints' images in late medieval England bespeak a highly materialist promise of life, the powers of the body to resist not only pain, but death, and to do so through transactions that are often remarkably commercial. The ties to capital that circulate around the narratives and cult images of Katherine are dramatized most strikingly in her own *passio*; and even as she forgoes the world and denounced idols as dead substances, Katherine herself becomes a far more dynamic form of currency'.

27. For an example, see Caroline Walker Bynum, *Wonderful Blood* (Philadelphia, PA: University of Pennsylvania Press, 2007), plate 25, which reproduces a wall painting (c. 1400) of the Mass of Saint Gregory, the saints, and the *Arma Christi*. Also see 'Instruments of the Passion', British Library Royal MS 6.E.vi f. 15r, reproduced in Anthony Bale, *The Jew in the Medieval Book, English Antisemitisms, 1350–1500* (Cambridge: Cambridge University Press, 2006), 148.

28. Duffy, *Stripping of the Altars*, 197.

29. Simpson, 'Rule of Medieval Imagination', 18.

30. The photograph is, of course, the modern votive image, but it has not replaced wax body parts as images of thanks. See Freedberg, *Power of Images*, 151, plate 86.

31. Freedberg, *Power of Images*, 155.

32. Patrick J. Geary, *Living with the Dead in the Middle Ages* (Ithaca, NY: Cornell University Press, 1994), 196.

33. Stanbury, *Visual Object of Desire*, 117; 8.

34. See Gell, *Art and Agency*, 96. Gell radically challenges the theoretical underpinnings of most medieval scholarship on iconoclasm and iconography; he argues 'that works of art, images, icons, and the like have to be treated in the context of an anthropological theory, as person-like; that is, sources of, and targets for, social agency. In this context, image-worship has a central place, since nowhere are images more obviously treated as human persons than in the context of worship and ceremonies...Idolatry...emanates, not from stupidity or superstition, but from the same fund of sympathy which allows us to understand the human, non-artefactual, "other" as a copresent being, endowed with awareness, intentions, and passions akin to our own.'

35. Geary, *Living with the Dead*, 202.

36. See Watson, 'Et Que Est Huius Ydoli Materia? Tuipse'; Aston, *England's Iconoclasts*, 96–146; Kamerick, *Popular Piety*, 13–42; Anne Hudson, *The Premature Reformation: Wycliffite Texts and Lollard History* (Oxford: Clarendon Press, 1988).

37. I am borrowing Freedberg's term (*Power of Images*, 82–98).

38. Karen Winstead cautions in her discussion of Chaucer's Parson: 'Identifying the views of any of the Canterbury pilgrims with Chaucer's own is of course dangerous; Chaucer surely valued such ambiguity' and contributed 'in English an orthodox discourse that was at once more traditional and more flexible than that which the Arundelians sought to impose' ('Chaucer's Parson's Tale', 254–5).

39. See Duffy, *Stripping of the Altars*, 170; Stanbury, *Visual Object of Desire*, 33–75; Winstead, *Virgin Martyrs: Legends of Sainthood in Late Medieval England* (Ithaca, NY: Cornell University Press, 1997); and Sheila Delany, *A Legend of Holy Women, A Translation of Osbern Bokenham's Legends of Holy Women* (Notre Dame, IN: University of Notre Dame Press, 1992), ix–xxxiii.

40. Stanbury, *Visual Object of Desire*, 2–7, 69–105; Camille, *Gothic Idol*, 197–241.

41. Duffy, *Stripping of the Altars*, 155.

42. Stanbury, *Visual Object of Desire*, 122–52.

43. The most pointed example, of course, of the Pardoner's blasphemy is his inference to Transubstantiation as 'cooking'; see Paul Strohm, 'Chaucer's Lollard Joke: History and the Textual Unconscious', *Studies in the Age of Chaucer* 17 (1995), 23–42. Strohm notes, 'In the heated controversial climate surrounding Chaucer's retelling, this same joke could not help but be perceived as Eucharistic. Because of the wide use of its terms to discover and harass Lollards, its inherent multiplicity could hardly resist some degree of stabilization within a Lollard frame of reference' (28).

44. See Bynum, *Fragmentation and Redemption, Essays on Gender and the Human Body in Medieval Religion* (New York: Zone, 1991), 171. Bynum notes that 'even artists fragmented the body. Liturgical and artistic treatment of relics came increasingly to underline the fact that they are body parts … By the fourteenth century, however, holy bones were owned and worn by the pious as private devotional objects; they were often exhibited in reliquaries that mimicked their shape (for example, head, arm, or bust reliquaries) or in crystal containers that clearly revealed they were bits of bodies.'

45. See Stanbury, *Visual Object of Desire*, 117. Stanbury notes of the Pardoner's fetishes: 'These falsified objects are relics, of course, and not devotional images. As relics, their materiality is crucial to their efficacy, for the relic, unlike the image, contains matter and spirit in a miraculous fusion that exemplified the resurrection of the body'. Nonetheless, statues and images also participated in this corporeality, exuding holy oil, milk, blood, and tears, thereby linking images and statues to relics in a sacred economy.

46. Zeeman, 'Idol of the Text', 60.

47. Kamerick, *Popular Piety*, 112–88.

48. Ibid., 117.

49. Benson notes that Chaucer may also be drawing from the introit of the Mass of the Holy Innocents. See Larry D. Benson, gen. ed., *The Riverside Chaucer*, 2nd ed. (Boston, MA: Houghton Mifflin, 1987), 914 n. 453–9.

50. See Kamerick: 'Medieval people perceived in or through holy images the same supernatural presence that they believed was embodied in the host … traditionally, holy images have been linked to relics and reliquaries' (*Popular Piety*, 9). See also Stanbury, *Visual*

Object of Desire, 171. Stanbury acknowledges that the Prioress's Tale 'explicitly describes the making of a shrine', yet claims that 'Chaucer suggests that liturgical spectacle opposes, rather than expresses, vernacular piety. The performance of liturgical and Eucharistic ritual opposes the living articulation of sanctity through language.' I argue here that precisely the opposite is true of the Prioress's Tale, and we cannot know Chaucer's intent in restoring image veneration through explicit historical reference to the shrine of Hugh of Lincoln. However, Chaucer's close Lancastrian ties with the Fraternity of Lincoln Cathedral make Stanbury's argument implausible. See Roger Dahood, 'The Punishment of the Jews, Hugh of Lincoln, and the Question of Satire in Chaucer's Prioress's Tale', *Viator* 36 (2005), 465–91.

51. Freedberg, *Power of Images,* 83.
52. See Denise L. Despres, 'Cultic Anti-Judaism and Chaucer's Litel Clergeon', *Modern Philology* 91 (1994), 413–27.
53. See Gavin I. Langmuir, 'The Knight's Tale of Young Hugh of Lincoln' in *Toward a Definition of Antisemitism* (Berkeley, CA: University of California Press, 1990), 237–62.
54. Geary, *Furta Sacra, Thefts of Relics in the Central Middle Ages* (Princeton, NJ: Princeton University Press, 1978), 127–8. Roger Dahood argues convincingly for the genealogy of the Prioress's Tale in a subgroup of tales that assimilated 'The Chorister' to historical English narratives of Jews crucifying Christian boys, and specifically to Hugh of Lincoln. The Prioress's Tale is rooted in a source—a saint's translation narrative—that clearly distinguishes itself from 'play' or fiction, commemorating the movement of the saint from liminality between life and death, from the cesspit to the high altar, to rest entombed (or take up permanent residence to be accurate) at the heart of the religious community. Translation narrations, as Geary outlines, feature a number of literary characteristics that Chaucer is careful to incorporate from his protoype, including liturgical readings, a greater emphasis on the physical remains than on the saint's virtues (appropriate to a *passio* or *vitae*), a close connection with a specific Church or monastery's dedication, 'and other forms of liturgical and secular procession'. The *translatio*'s focus on the liminal period of a saint's miraculous transformation between life and death undercuts any literal distinction between inert dead matter and spiritual potency after death. See Dahood, 'English Historical Narratives of Jewish Child-Murder, Chaucer's *Prioress's Tale* and the Date of Chaucer's Unknown Source', *Studies in the Age of Chaucer* 31 (2009), 125–40.
55. See, for example, Chapter 27 of this volume.

BIBLIOGRAPHY

Aston, Margaret, *Lollards and Reformers, Images and Literacy in Late Medieval Religion* (London: Hambledon Press, 1984).

Bagnoli, Marta, Holger A. Klein, C. Griffith Mann, and James Robinson, eds., *Treasures of Heaven, Saints, Relics, and Devotion in Medieval Europe* (New Haven, CT: Yale University Press, 2010).

Camille, Michael, *The Gothic Idol, Ideology and Image-Making in Medieval Art* (Cambridge: Cambridge University Press, 1989).

Dimmick, Jeremy, James Simpson, and Nicolette Zeeman, eds., *Images, Idolatry, and Iconoclasm in Late Medieval England* (Oxford: Oxford University Press, 2002).

Duffy, Eamon, *The Stripping of the Altars, Traditional Religion in England 1400–1580* (New Haven, CT: Yale University Press, 1992).

Hamburger, Jeffrey F. and Anne-Marie Bouche, eds., *The Mind's Eye, Art and Theological Argument in the Middle Ages* (Princeton, NJ: Princeton University Press, 2006).

Hilmo, Maidie, *Medieval Images, Icons, and Illustrated English Literary Texts, From the Ruthwell Cross to the Ellesmere Chaucer* (Aldershot: Ashgate, 2004).

Kamerick, Kathleen, *Popular Piety and Art in the Late Middle Ages, Image Worship and Idolatry in England 1350–1500* (New York: Palgrave, 2002).

Simpson, James, 'The Rule of Medieval Imagination,' in Dimmick et al., *Images, Idolatry, and Iconoclasm in Late Medieval England* (Oxford: Oxford University Press, 2002), 4–24.

Stanbury, Sarah, *The Visual Object of Desire in Late Medieval England* (Philadelphia, PA: University of Pennsylvania Press, 2008).

PART VI

....

THE
CHAUCERIAN
AFTERLIFE

....

CHAPTER 29

GEOGRAPHESIS, OR THE AFTERLIFE OF BRITAIN IN CHAUCER

JEFFREY JEROME COHEN

ITS duration stretching far beyond the span of human life, stone abides within an alien temporality, one in which mere years yield to slow centuries. For its material offer of endurance beyond mortal frame, stone has become for us synonymous with lasting memory and long history. Yet even if it does not share our rapid tempo, rock is not immune to human impress: 'Men may so longe graven in a stoon', declares the narrator of Chaucer's Franklin's Tale, 'Til som figure therinne emprented be' (V.830–1). The mason who incises letters or art into rock figures the diligent work of friends upon grieving Dorigen, the heroine of the Franklin's story. When her husband pursues knightly adventure across the sea, Dorigen is held by long sorrow at his absence. Her moment of becoming-stone, of being incised as if she were marble, unfolds after her companions so long 'conforted hire' that she received 'the emprentyng of hire consolacioun' (834). Chaucer's metaphor works by activating the unhurried temporality which stone inhabits. It posits that Dorigen in her lingering sorrow travels at a lithic pace, and insists as well that even within this slow velocity mutual human and rocky motion is constant, taking the form of an 'emprentyng', a transformative and enduring inscription, a lingering touch between the human and the inorganic. The figurative emprentyng of comfort upon Dorigen is borne of human hands, and therefore short-lived. Yet this inscription opens her immediately to a second and more enduring impress, this time by 'grisly rokkes blake' (859) that crowd her horizon and fill her with fears of death and oblivion.

John Friedman has connected lithic imprinting in the Franklin's Tale to the 'enigmatic and pagan symbols which dot the coastal areas of southern Brittany', signs etched into the prehistoric menhirs for which the region is still famous.[1] Such standing stones and dolmens dot Ireland and the British archipelago as well, most famously as part of Stonehenge. In this chapter I will trace the ways in which stone—in the form of Neolithic mounds marking the entrance to the Otherworld in Welsh and Irish narratives, and the menhirs of Stonehenge—leave a discernible 'emprentyng' upon Chaucer's work. These rocky narratives surface from time to time to inscribe in his text a history of the island that challenges the contemporary conflation of the kingdom of England with the island of Britain. Through *geographesis* (a writing of and a writing by stone) British history impresses Chaucerian narrative, making visible an insular capaciousness seldom glimpsed in his works.

When in the Man of Law's Tale King Alla of Northumbria travels 'Scotlond-ward, his foomen for to seke' (II.718), his anachronistic crossing of the Scottish border is the sole visit to that country recorded in the Chaucerian corpus. Alla's proto-English kingdom also contains a remnant of the 'olde Britons dwellynge in this ile', men and women who have not yet fled with their compatriots 'to Walys' (II.545, 544). *Yet* is the operative word here: these furtive Britons endure long enough to provide the king the Bible necessary for truthful oaths (II.666), but Northumbria's Christian future is also an explicitly non-Celtic one, orienting the nation towards distant Italy, not the remainder of the Christian island from which it has been carved. The Britons living in circumspect 'privitee' among the pagans will vanish from the text once Alla christens and thereby realigns his kingdom. The Man of Law's Tale concludes, naturally, in Rome.

The absence of Britain from Chaucer's vision of England is surprising, considering what we can reconstruct of his biography. As a youth he served a royal household that counted Ulster among its dominions. Prince Lionel presided over an important parliament in Kilkenny, and the subjugation of Ireland was a ceaseless English project. In 1378 Chaucer was involved in legal transactions concerning estates and castles in Pembrokeshire, offering a critically underexamined connection to Wales.[2] John of Gaunt, the powerful duke to whom Chaucer's *Book of the Duchess* is addressed, was deeply entangled in Scottish affairs. Yet despite dwelling on an archipelago shared with non-Anglophone peoples, despite being connected to their geographies through histories both national and potentially personal, Chaucer never mentions the Irish. He relegates the Scots and the Welsh to Britain's 'olde' history. The island's contemporary vitality unfolds within a circumscribed domain, often not too far from Chaucer's London (a 'mede' of 'floures white and rede' in the *Legend of Good Women* [F 41–2]; the urban workplace and household of a bookish writer glanced upon in the *House of Fame*) or, most famously, along the road connecting that city to Canterbury. The General Prologue seemingly unites all of England through the movements of its pilgrims, but no matter where the palmers originate they talk as if they were native Londoners. Drawing the kingdom so tightly together also implicitly excludes those nations with which England shared its island. No Welsh, for example, embark on the pilgrimage, nor are readers ever invited to suppose that non-English Britons might have wanted to make the journey.

Chaucer is an author at once internationally minded and resolutely metropolitan. He suffers a Londoner's myopia, through which Lombardy often seems closer than Monmouthshire.[3] Transmarinal geographies abound. Oxford, Cambridge, Southwark, and Bath appear alongside unlocatable but comfortably English farmyards, taverns, domestic interiors. A few glimpses of the culturally complex, polyglot archipelago Chaucer inhabited do surface, as when the General Prologue obliquely acknowledges the Norman Conquest (the Man of Law has memorized all the judgments 'from the tyme of kyng William' [I.324]), or during the barnyard ruckus of the Nun's Priest's Tale, compared to the noise of Jack Straw and his retinue 'whan that they wolden any Flemyng kille' (VII.3396). As this comparison of xenophobic violence to animal cacophony makes clear, such surfacings tend to trivialize their material, or to immure a potentially discomfiting present within the island's distant past.

Chaucer's relation to Britain can be discerned in a throwaway line from the Franklin's Tale. The knight Arveragus departs his native Brittany to tournament 'in Engelond, that cleped was eek Briteyne' (V.810). The easy equivalence of a part (the kingdom of 'Engelond') for the whole (the island of 'Briteyne') is also a substitution of an Anglophone and London-centric fragment for a multilingual and multiply centered entirety. England becomes the newer name for Britain; Britain is thereby relegated to history ('cleped was': Britain's temporality is entirely past tense). Geographically, culturally, and temporally reductive, the line nonetheless hints at Chaucer's obscured relationship to England's British past, and to the texts instrumental in making that long insular history known to the English. The Franklin's Tale is a self-declared Breton *lai*, a narrative poem associated with the magical but superseded history of the island: 'Thise olde gentil Britouns in hir dayes/Of diverse aventures maden layes' (V.709–10). Such narrative poems were composed primarily in England, first in French (Marie de France perhaps originated the type) and later in English.[4] The *lais* stage a postcolonial encounter between a parvenu culture and an aboriginal one, working through in aesthetically pleasing ways complicated issues of heritage, belatedness, cultural influence, and hybridity.

Like romance, Breton *lais* owe an evident debt to Geoffrey of Monmouth's *History of the Kings of Britain* (c.1136).[5] This Latin chronicle of the island's early days is told from a British point of view, and was quickly translated into French, English, and Welsh. Though not without its critics, Geoffrey's text became the dominating narrative of the pre-English past, tracing insular history from the arrival of the Trojan refugee Brutus to the eventual fall of the Britons under the Saxons (that is, the English). The story's pinnacle is a lengthy account of Arthur's reign. Through Geoffrey's *History* England received its indelible British inheritance. Through this matter of Britain, in turn, Arthurian romance (the Wife of Bath's Tale) and the Breton *lai* (the Franklin's Tale) became possible. These textual traditions together ensured that England possessed a sense of history deeper than that narrated by its native historians, men who generally ignored the Britons in favor of the English, or those destined to become that people (Bede, William of Malmesbury, Henry of Huntingdon, Matthew Paris).

London-born Geoffrey Chaucer knew very well of this anterior Geoffrey, a writer from the borderland where England and Wales interpenetrate. Yet he only once mentions his literary forebear's name, preceding that reference with the wrong national designator: Geoffrey of Monmouth is 'Englyssh Gaufride' (HF 1470). Through a similar process of anglicization Arthur himself had been transformed from a British monarch to an English king. Aside from this lone mention of 'Gaufride'. Chaucer leaves the English debt to Geoffrey of Monmouth's British history unspoken. Like the black rocks off the coast of Brittany that figure so prominently in the Franklin's Tale, however, that which is submerged inevitably resurfaces, bringing into sight other ways of narrating the insular past.

ISLANDS AND REMEMBRANCE

An island distant in time and space from Britain sheds some light on the fraught relations between these two Geoffreys. The anthropologist Richard Price has movingly examined how a contemporary way of life can be petrified into a dead past, even as those who continue to reside within a domain now designated 'history' endure.[6] Through processes Price calls postcarding, museumfication, patrimonialization, and folklorization, Martinique's 'traditional culture' was frozen into revered objects and texts, thereby estranging a mode of life from those who lived it. Price creates a visual-textual *métissage* of a book that surfaces a 'subterranean vein' of collective memories submerged beneath the monolith of official versions of the past.[7] Authorized visions of the island's history overwrote ongoing colonial conflict, thereby stilling continuing struggle into the vague and homogenous 'long ago' of museum displays and superseded narratives. This relegation denies the possibility of coevalness and perdurance to those whose history is being scripted for them.

Price focuses upon Médard Aribot, an artist who participated in collective resistance against French imperialism and was exiled to Devil's Island. The child of an African father, Aribot grew up on an island where the slavery reinstituted by Napoleon was 'a living and vivid memory'.[8] After his return to Martinique, he built a colorful house where he dwelled for some time, but which fell eventually into ruin. Fifty years later, the power of Aribot's story 'seemed tangible to rural Martiniquans' since the world they inhabited was still 'hemmed in by sufficiently palpable (post)colonial structures' for his struggle to remain their own.[9] Passing the site of the crumbled dwelling reminded locals of an important moment of resistance, especially because France was then transforming the island into the engine of a transatlantic tourism machine. In 1987 the home was renovated to render its freshly painted walls and newly paved walkways a picturesque roadside attraction. Dubbed 'The House of the Convict', no special history was attached to the rebuilt structure beyond its status as an object incarnating an earlier, more pastoral way of life, a vague emblem of lost days. Postcards with the seabound boulder known as Diamond Rock looming behind the empty dwelling began to circulate. The house became, like the dark monolith in blue water with which it was paired, an image floating free of a particular and grounding history.

Price explores what happens to people who find themselves deprived through such aestheticization of their own past, especially when a difficult history is obliterated by dreamy 'official folklore'.[10] What present is left open to the Martiniquans who find their lives estranged from contemporaneity? What is lost to the demand to assimilate culturally, linguistically, cognitively to the nation of France? What happens when local history is absorbed into an 'amorphous, atemporal period of "before"'[11] in order to allow this transformation to proceed unquestioned? What future remains after a people's lived time is materialized as artifacts or as an archive that can be consumed by others rather than 'actively produced' within an *ongoing* present, when 'everyday lives are turned into folklore before their very eyes'?[12] How might 'subterranean' narratives that challenge dominating histories be brought to the surface, reinvigorated, brought out of stillness into life? Visually anchored to a black rock supposed to drain the gingerbread house of its disruptive narrative, supposed to aestheticize in order to dehistoricize, can Aribot's challenge be recovered? Can Diamond Rock looming at the sea edge offer remembrance of a particular human story rather than lithic oblivion?

Price's anthropological inquiry details how coevality might be strategically denied a subaltern population, stilling its vivacity into petrified history. His work is directly relevant to the Britain within England, especially as the former stands in postcolonial relation to the latter. Though they called themselves *Cymru, Brytaniaid, Prydein*, the aboriginal Britons had been dubbed by the English *Welsh* (Old English *wealh*, 'foreigner, slave'). These Britons continued to share an island with the English. They shared a long past while coinhabiting the present. Yet as in Price's narrative of converting that which is contemporaneous into remote history, the Britons were doomed by English writers to inhabit a sometimes picturesque (in romance), sometimes feral (in historiography), and always distant temporality. Those Welsh who had endured into the present were barbarians, the degenerate remnant of a people whose insular hegemony had long ago come to its end. William of Newburgh, writing at the close of the twelfth century, can stand in for any number of similarly disdainful English historians: 'The Britons were gradually crushed by [the English], as the invaders penned the wretched remnants (*miseras eorum reliquias*), now called the Welsh, in trackless mountains and forests.'[13] These roadless, wooded hills can be the setting for enchanting romances like *Sir Gawain and the Green Knight* and Chrétien de Troyes's *Le conte du graal*, stories to be delectated at a great distance in time and space from their setting.[14] The modernity of these 'mountains and forests', however, is all Welsh barbarism.

Geoffrey of Monmouth may have composed his *History* to boost the reputation of the Welsh at a time when they were potential allies in an English civil war.[15] Even if confederates were not inspired by this vision, the Welsh themselves were justifiably enamored. The glories of Arthur and his court became important to national pride. Without Geoffrey of Monmouth, there would likely have been no King Arthur, at least not as the flawed but luminous, empire-building regent we now possess. Geoffrey fashioned a Briton warlord of provincial repute into a charismatic, Norman-style monarch of world fame. Arthur's court in the *History of the Kings of Britain* contains an inbuilt call to imitation, to endurance and expansion through mimesis: 'All the noblest were stirred to count themselves as worthless if they were not dressed or armed in the manner of Arthur's knights' ('*ad modum militum Arturii*').[16] In part through this invitation to performance, in part through its author's creation of a world that could transcend its own historical context, Geoffrey's text also offered the portal through which history was transubstantiated into romance.

The very moment of genre innovation can even be located, perhaps, during a compellingly strange episode in the *History*. The treacherous British king Vortigern, having disastrously allied himself with the Saxons, is betrayed by his confederates and faces the extinction of his realm. He retreats into Wales, 'unsure what to do'.[17] Geoffrey's next line is extraordinary, for it comes from nowhere and immediately transports the surrounded, confined history to an unanticipated space: '*Vocatis denique magis suis, consuluit illos iussitque dicere quid faceret*' ('Then he called forth his magicians, consulted them and commanded them to tell him what to do').[18] Despite having recounted 1700 years of action since Troy's fall, the *History of the Kings of Britain* has until this moment never indicated that its world might be inhabited by 'magi'. Laconic wonders have appeared from time to time (a rain of blood, a sea monster, a streaking comet), but these phenomena seem inhuman, even when they gloss unfolding human actions. Nor do these sudden magicians prove sufficiently enchanting as guides to the otherworld that Geoffrey is opening. Their dramatic entrance is a mere prelude for the introduction of Merlinus Ambrosius, enigmatic progeny of an incubus and a nun.[19] Geoffrey calls Merlin '*vates*', a Latin noun that can mean prophet, oracle, or teacher. *Vates* is also the ancient noun revived by Virgil to designate *poet*.

An extraordinary and inscrutable young man, Merlin possesses not magic so much as '*ingenium*',[20] an author's genius for creating unexpected stories from what appears to be the inert matter of the world. Vortigern has been attempting to build a tower to immure himself from his Saxon foes. The stones daily set upon each other are swallowed each evening by the earth. Merlin orders the worksite excavated and the pool beneath drained.[21] He announces that two hollow rocks ('*duos concauos lapidos*') will be discovered, each concealing a dormant dragon. After emerging from the sleepy captivity of their lithic prisons, these monsters grapple ferociously. Merlin interprets this draconic battle allegorically, as the plot of Geoffrey's *History of the Kings of Britain* itself: the red dragon of Britain will be overcome by its white nemesis, incarnating the Saxons, at least until the advent of a mysterious 'boar of Cornwall'.

This vague prophecy gave at least some Welsh readers of Geoffrey's work hope that British glory might possess a future as well as an antiquity. The English historians William of Malmesbury and William of Newburgh, for example, mocked the native Britons for expecting the return of their fabled king. Geoffrey never mentions Arthur's messianic reappearance. He leaves Arthur paradoxically to be healed of mortal wounds on the island of Avalon.[22] The Merlin sections of the *History* nonetheless teem with futurity. Arthur and Merlin never meet in Geoffrey's text: Merlin vanishes from the narrative after engineering the king's birth, in circumstances that eerily reproduce those of his own. Yet the saturation of Merlin with an uncanny glimmer of things to come cannot help but to affix itself to Arthur as well. Geoffrey reproduces a book of Merlin's ambivalent and therefore never-settled prophecies, capable of startling to amazement those who hear them.[23] Merlin plots the birth of Arthur through anachronism, through 'strange arts, unheard of in your time' ('*nouis artibus et tempore tuo inauditis*')[24] arts that transform Uther Pendragon bodily into another man. When Uther's brother Aurelius desires to commemorate those who perished in a Saxon massacre, Merlin creates an everlasting architecture for the British dead by transporting Stonehenge from Ireland to Britain, as 'a new structure to stand forever as a memorial to such heroes'.[25] As the *History* comes to its close, an angelic voice asserts that the British will not hold the island again 'until the time came which Merlin foretold to Arthur',[26] even though Merlin and Arthur never meet in the text. Merlin, in other words, enters the narrative to ensure that Britain perdures.

Or not. From an English point of view granting the Britons an era of past distinction was perversely a means of asserting that this history had come to its termination. As Price demonstrated on Martinique, as the British Empire well knew as it annexed India, or as the United States found as it expanded Pacificward into American Indian lands, the renown of an anterior culture is useful to praise so long as its nobility is thereby locked deep in history. Transformed into a controlled mythology, coveted aesthetic objects, and a deadened body of knowledge, a monumentalized antecedent culture can pave the way for a new power's arrival, for a natural and desirable *translatio imperii*. So long as the kings of Britain could be absorbed into a culminating English story, their rebuke to English self-assurance could be contained. Merlin himself perhaps provides the model for this kind of supersessionary translation. The '*mistici lapides*' ('occult stones') that form the '*chorea gigantum*' ('Giant's Ring', Geoffrey's designation for Stonehenge) were brought from Africa to Ireland by ancient giants. Though their lithic enchantment persists into the present ('There is not a stone among them that does not carry some medicinal power'),[27] Merlin robs them of their particular history when he transports the monoliths across the sea to Salisbury. The Giant's Ring becomes a memorial to British history, submerging its African and Irish origins.

A challenge to imperial smugness always remains implicit in such hijacking and willed forgetting of 'native' history. Likewise, the incarceration of a living culture by projection backwards in time must be ongoing, never complete. Still, English writers did not agonize over their relations to their Welsh, Scottish, or Irish neighbors. As in the Franklin's Tale's blithe subsumption of Britain into England, writers like Chaucer were content to employ 'England' as a synonym for 'Britain', a *pars pro toto* that, whether propelled by colonialist strategy or cheerful obliviousness, functioned the same. This substitutionary practice had good precedent. About twenty years after the completion of the *History of the Kings of Britain*, the poet Wace transformed Geoffrey of Monmouth's laconic Latin prose into lively French verse. In the process he converted Geoffrey's 'regum Britanniae' [kings of Britain] into regents 'ki Engleterre primes tindrent' [who were the first rulers of England].[28] Henry of Huntingdon, writing slightly earlier in the same century, spoke in his *Historia Anglorum* (*History of the English*) of 'the most celebrated of islands, formerly called Albion, later Britain, now England', invoking another 'lost' insular name to stress the land's changing linguistic fortunes. The supersessionary timeline Henry establishes runs from Albion (prehistory) to Britain (early history) to England (modernity), with each designation an equivalent to and wholesale replacement of the preceding name. Chaucer inherited a historiographic tradition in which the Britons may have had their Arthurian flourishing, especially as depicted by the romances spawned by Geoffrey of Monmouth's *History*, but that moment of vitality had long passed. Contemporaneity, like the naming of the island, belonged to the English.

OLDE DAYES AND FAIRY MOUNDS

Chaucer inhabited a linguistically diverse, culturally restless archipelago. Yet the geography from which he wrote appears in his work as a diminished space, its heterogeneity a historic feature. The Wife of Bath's Tale is set in 'th'olde dayes of the Kyng Arthour' (III.857), and therefore unfolds within the Arthurian antiquity bequeathed to England by the *History of the Kings of Britain*. Chaucer, however, has little interest in the monarch. Invoking Arthur provides the narrative its *mise-en-scène*. The king appears briefly, as a judge who grants the ladies of his court a measure of 'sovereynetee' in deciding the fate of a rapist knight. In some ways Chaucer is simply continuing a long tradition in which Arthur's dominating presence in Geoffrey of Monmouth is eclipsed by attention to the knights of his court and the adventures they pursue. Thus Chrétien de Troyes, composing the first Arthurian romances, wrote of Yvain, Erec, Lancelot, Perceval. Arthur figures as a relatively weak character, a ruler not completely in control of his court. In *Sir Gawain and the Green Knight*, a Middle English romance roughly contemporary with the Wife of Bath's Tale, Arthur appears in the inaugurating and concluding scenes. The narrative reserves its energy for Gawain and his quest to accept a return axe stroke. Still, in most Arthurian narratives the king and his court of Logres or Camelot are the pivot upon which the action turns, permeating the story even during episodes of errantry and absence. To return to *Sir Gawain and the Green Knight*: Gawain departs from king and companions in the search to fulfill his vow. After long wandering he arrives at a remote architecture hewn of ancient stone. Perhaps a Neolithic tomb, the Green Chapel seems to inhabit an utterly alien geography, to stand at the doorway to another world. Yet there the Green Knight is revealed as ordinary Bertilak, sent on his mission to terrorize Guenevere by the king's own sister, Morgan le Fey. Gawain discovers as the poem nears its bitter conclusion that he has been a secondary character in a narrative centered upon the intrigues of court all along, that even when farthest from the Round Table, Arthur dominates the story all the same.

In the Wife of Bath's Tale, by contrast, King Arthur is no more necessary to the narrative's unfolding than the 'elf-queene, with hir joly compaignye' (860), glimpsed dancing in a field. Elves and king are decorative, a romantic patina for a story little invested in its location within British time and space. Arthur is quickly displaced by the 'olde wyf' (1000) and the 'lusty bacheler' (883) who learns to love her; the story ends not with the Arthurian court, but the private space of a post-nuptial bedroom. The plot belongs to the Loathly Lady and the nameless knight who grants her 'maistrie' (1236)—or, more properly, belongs to the Wife of Bath and the pilgrimage exchange of stories, to the road connecting London to Canterbury rather than to the world containing Arthur and Britain. In *Sir Gawain and the Green Knight* Morgan is described as 'le Fey' ('the Fairy', glossed also as 'goddess') to indicate that she is a potentially dangerous magician, a female Merlin. No comparable figure haunts the Wife of Bath's Tale. Here the fairies are deracinated, voided of danger, creatures of a vague enchanted past.[29] 'Fulfild of fayerye' seems to mean filled with jollity, charm, allure:

> In th'olde dayes of the Kyng Arthour,
> Of which that Britons speken greet honour,
> Al was this land fulfild of fayerye.
> The elf-queene, with hir joly compaignye,
> Daunced ful ofte in many a grene mede.
> This was the olde opinion, as I rede;
> I speke of manye hundred yeres ago.   (III.857–63)

The Britons who speak with such reverence of Arthur are by implication a living remnant of that dead past (the 'olde dayes' of the island are accessible now only through books and book-learning ['as I rede']).[30] Yet from Arthur we move quickly to frolicking elves and green fields, with emphasis upon historical remoteness ('olde opinion', 'manye hundred yeres'), on the gap between history and present day. As the Wife of Bath begins her tale, little trace surfaces of the vigorous, beguiling, and contradictory Arthur envisioned by Geoffrey of Monmouth, a figure who remained central to contemporary Welsh nationalism.[31]

Irish and Welsh narratives depict the denizens of the Otherworld as mysterious, sometimes menacing. They admix danger with wonder. Their world touches the quotidian one, and can be glimpsed in liminal spaces like the roiled ocean or accessed through portals like ancient burial mounds. As Alf Siewers has shown, the Otherworld offers glimpses of nonhuman temporalities, doorways to times and spaces that challenge the self-assuredness of those entranced by their allure.[32] The Wife of Bath's Tale does include Otherworldly inhabitants, but its potential peril is immediately superseded by that of a more modern instantiation. Abduction by elves is invoked as the tale begins only to become friars 'thikke as motes' in a sunbeam, providing the blessings that have driven these creatures away (868).[33] 'Ther is noon oother incubus but he' (880) says the Wife of the contemporary 'lymytour', (874) and the lascivious cleric takes the place of the *incubus daemonium* (incubus of the demons) who in Geoffrey of Monmouth engendered Merlin upon an unsuspecting nun: 'Between the moon and the earth there live spirits whom we call incubi. They are part human, part angel, and take on human form at will and sleep with women'.[34] The sublunary Wife of Bath's Tale does not offer any medial space between the earth and the empyrean: its fairies, elves, and incubi have become wanton friars wandering the English countryside. The story glosses knightly rape as a prelude to love and finds its enduring magic in domestic relations.

And so those dangerous mounds that in Irish and Welsh narratives offer conveyance to another realm are flattened into a 'grene mede' upon which the queen of the elves and her merry retinue dance. The whole story is pushed into distant, vanished history: 'I speke of manye hundred yeres ago', the Wife of Bath observes, 'But now kan no man se none elves mo' (III.863–4). Fairies, elves, and Britons constitute a lost insular epoch. British history may be preserved in Arthurian stories, but across the contemporary landscape move only bodies that are London-looking and English. Modernity in the *Canterbury Tales* belongs to wool dealers, reeves, bakers, parsons, franklins, millers, merchants. No wonder the Squire's Tale declares that 'Gawayn, with his olde curteisye' now dwells in the lost realm of 'Fairye' (V.95–6). Geoffrey of Monmouth's Arthur becomes, like the 'fayerye' amongst whom he finds himself immured, folklore rather than history. In the plot of the Wife of Bath's Tale, Arthur and his retinue become no more substantial than capering elves.

ROCKS THAT DO NOT VANISH

The Franklin's Tale has typically been understood through reference to a story-within-a-story in Boccaccio's *Filocolo,* specifically Menedon's Tale (Book Four, adapted later for the *Decameron*).[35] Much of Chaucer's plot patently derives from this narrative, in which a woman, happily married to a knight, makes a rash promise to a would-be lover, placing herself in unwanted and perilous straits. Yet the Franklin's Tale announces itself not as a version of an Italian story but as a work that 'olde gentil Britouns…rymeyed in hir firste Briton tonge' (V.709, 711). 'Britoun' here can mean 'Breton' or 'Briton' (geographies intimately connected linguistically and culturally; Geoffrey of Monmouth makes much of their co-extensiveness in the *History of the Kings of Britain*). Whether the lay comes from Wales or Brittany, however, it is, like the Wife of Bath's Tale, a narrative of the ancient past, one that is kept 'in remembraunce', rather than a story with any connection to Chaucer's English modernity. Though not Arthurian, the names of the main characters (Aurelius, Arveragus, and perhaps Dorigen) are lifted from the pages of Geoffrey of Monmouth's *History*.[36] Breton *lais* as a genre are not all that Britannic or Bretonic, representing an English attempt at what Richard Price called museumfication and folklorizing, playing up the magic of an anterior culture in order to immure an unwanted presence in a superseded past. Such retrogressive enchantment tinges this world with nostalgia, renders its expanses charming and beautiful and dangerously alluring, even as it utterly estranges that world, rendering it resolutely premodern. Its time becomes that of the undifferentiated, amorphous, non-historical past, a period that can now be enjoyed only as 'remembraunce'. The Franklin worries that he cannot add the expected 'colour' (rhetorical ornamentation [723]) to the Britoun narrative that lives in his memory. The story he tells, however, is worse than 'bare and pleyn' (720): not just sparse but subtractive, transporting Geoffrey of Monmouth's characters out of their British narrative completely and fitting them into a Mediterranean story not their own. Yet in a way Geoffrey's *History* resurfaces, a persisting 'subterranean memory' that rises to limn the edges of its world, like the 'grisly rokkes blake' (859) that figure so prominently in the tale.

Rocks persist. Thus the lithic is integral to dreaming the afterlife: because bodies do not endure, they are sealed within or buried beneath lapidary weight. Since narrative is ephemeral, we imitate God on Sinai and carve what we want to preserve in stone. We know that rock is not nearly as permanent as we desire: Moses smashed the first set of commandments when he espied the Golden Calf. Theseus in the Knight's Tale speaks of how 'harde stoon…wasteth' under the treading of 'oure feet', at the incessant passing that is time (I.3021–3). Sometimes this lapse yields only erosion, wear, obliteration. Yet slow, concerted effort is also the means by which stone accepts human signification, so that it might carry forward the tales we incise. This process is described in the Franklin's Tale as that by which 'Men may so longe graven in a stoon/Til som figure therinne emprented be' (V.830–1)—the process through which Dorigen, rock-like, is opened up to dangerous transformation. At the same time, Chaucer's text is being impressed by rock, by stone that arrives from another place (Ireland by way of Africa), from a text that lithically inscribes a history not his own.

Rock is the best material humans possess for materializing their hopes for endurance. Wished-for commemoration spurs the erection of a memorial, as when Geoffrey of Monmouth's Aurelius honors the British dead by commanding 'carpenters and stone masons from all districts…to employ their skills to build a new structure to stand forever as a memorial' to the British dead.[37] Aurelius fears that the corpses of those slain by the Saxons will be forgotten, that interred beneath the sod their story will wane. Thus the desire of Aurelius for *lapides*, stone, as the material of remembrance, resulting in Merlin's transporting the Giant's Ring from Ireland to Salisbury. Writing of the incessant sonority of visual art, Gilles Deleuze and Félix Guattari observe: 'A monument does not commemorate or celebrate something that happened but confides to the ear of the future the persistent sensations that embody the event.'[38] But what happens when that sensation, that affective history persisting like stone is not especially desired, what happens when rock brings into present memory stories thought to be safely consigned to the receding past?

Stone can be reassuring in its indifference to human time. Stone's perdurance can also convey a challenge, even a menace. In the picture postcards from Martinique described by Price, Médard's house (colonial history transported, decontextualized, and reinvented as a colorful remnant of forgotten past) is haunted in its background by the looming form of vast, dark Diamond Rock. Likewise the Franklin's Breton *lai* (Geoffrey of Monmouth transported, decontextualized, and reinvented to yield a patina of enchanted history while denying the 'olde gentil Britouns' vitality, contemporary meaning) is haunted by vast and looming lithic forms. In Menedon's Tale from the *Filocolo*, Dorigen's counterpart promises to grant an undesired suitor her love if he can create a garden in winter's chill. The would-be lover locates an elderly herbalist who accomplishes the impossible task, creating a May of blossoms in barren January. The erotic symbolism is difficult to miss. Plants and flowers are so integral to medieval expressions of sexuality that it is exaggerating only slightly to say that human sexuality is a kind of vegetal sexuality. Chaucer makes an unprecedented and, to interpreters, baffling switch in his version of the story, substituting baleful rocks at the sea edge for blossoms and an enclosed garden. What could be colder, less sexual, more inhuman than rocks? Their ominous presence dominates the tale, a seeming distraction from the conversation on love, generosity, and gentility that it has inherited from Boccaccio—a conversation better had within and about a 'gardyn ful of leves and floures' (V.908) than before disconcerting 'grisly rokkes blak' (859).

Dorigen's wish is that these stones impinging upon her with anxious reminders of violence and death would sink below her field of vision, could be forgotten. The rocks that take the place of Boccaccio's winter flowers surface in Chaucer's text saturated not just with personal anxiety about a husband's safe return from 'Briteyne' but with history, with a narrative of some other powerful rocks and of another sea. Dorigen stands in relation to these rocks much as modern and perhaps medieval observers find themselves in relation to Neolithic structures: pondering who built them, what purpose they serve, marveling at their beauty and perhaps shivering at their portentousness. Thus Dorigen wonders how a providential God could allow the coming into being of 'grisly feendly rokkes blake' (868), a 'foul confusion / Of werk' and 'werk unresonable' rather than a 'fair creacion' (869–72). She labels the black rocks 'werk' four times in ten lines, emphasizing the stones as fabrications rather than as natural or unintended worldly elements. These *werks* menace, annoy (875, 884), even destroy and slay (876), leaving 'an hundred thousand bodyes of mankynde' (877). Yes, these 'rokkes' are works of nature or God, not man. And yet their presence in a Breton lai that plunders names from the *werk* of Geoffrey of Monmouth cannot help but to evoke some other stones that are themselves a dangerous kind of *werk*, especially as they are launched into the English future as a mobile, lithic British memorialization device.

The unwanted suitor in the Franklin's Tale is named, of all things, Aurelius. He himself, like Dorigen, believes the task of swallowing the black rocks into the oblivious sea an impossible undertaking. His namesake in Geoffrey of Monmouth's *History* holds a similar belief about stone's immobility. Merlin informs him 'If you wish to mark their graves with a lasting monument [*perpetuo opere*, literally "everlasting work"—or, as Chaucer would say, "werk"], send for the Giants' Ring, which is on Mount Killaraus in Ireland'.[39] Merlin's breezy suggestion that 'huge rocks' (*grandes lapides*), 'beyond the strength of any man', could be relocated to Salisbury is met by Aurelius's incredulous laughter.[40] Stone is, for the uninspired king, immobile. Yet Merlin teaches Aurelius that the world's materiality is vibrant, vivacious, that one who possesses sufficient *ingenium* can make an unmoving and unyielding lithic circle whirl. Geoffrey of Monmouth's *Chorea Gigantum* is typically translated 'Giants' Circle', but the words also mean Giants' Song and—more than anything—Giants' Dance.[41] Merlin activates the kinetic power of stone, its ability to move and to thereby incarnate multiple histories. Stone is a song that history cannot silence, a whirl it cannot deaden.

Whereas the Aurelius of Geoffrey's *History* reacts to the suggestion of vital stone with laughter, the Aurelius of the Franklin's Tale responds to the same seeming impossibility with copious tears. He languishes in bed for 'two yeer and moore' (V.1102), until his brother locates a Merlin-like figure in Orleans whose 'magyk natureel' (1125) can open the world to potentialities so far unrealized. This clerk specializes in a book-derived magic, the possibilities of which erupt within a manuscript-lined study that suggests perhaps Chaucer's own place of writing.[42] The clerk's demonstration of his powers to Aurelius seems a recipe for composing romances and *lais*:

> He shewed hym, er he wente to sopeer,
> Forestes, parkes ful of wilde deer...
> Tho saugh he knyghtes justyng in a playn;
> And after this he dide hym swich plesaunce
> That he hym shewed his lady on a daunce.   (V.1189–90, 1198–1200)

A spellbinding easily disenchanted: the scene ends abruptly when the clerk claps his hands to dismiss the 'revel', (1204) revealing that they have never departed the house and its 'studie' full of 'bookes' (1214). The enchantment can be quickly dissolved for more mundane concerns; the world in motion that it brings to visibility can be quickly swapped for the sedentary space of the clerk's dinner table ('Is redy oure soper?' [1210]). The Franklin himself will reject this restless magic as a 'supersticious cursednesse' of the old days (1272), even as he is fascinated by its vibrancy. In its application to the 'grisly rokkes blake' (859), this bookish magic may in fact involve nothing more than consulting a table of tides ('tables Tolletanes...ful wel corrected' [1273–4]). The rocks were either 'sonken under grounde' (1269) or 'were aweye' (1268)—that is, had been moved. No matter what the mechanism ('illusiouns and swiche meschaunces/As hethen folk useden in thilke dayes' [1292–3]), the outcome is the same: Chaucer repeats that to all concerned it seemed like the rocks had been transported ('all the rokkes were aweye' [1296]) by difficult to comprehend means ('a monstre or merveille' [1344]).

The rocks that with the magician of Orleans's help 'were aweye' from Dorigen's sight bring to the surface of the text more than is evident at a quick glance, a history that the clerk's clapping of hands and shelving of books cannot dismiss. The magician's namesake Aurelius is, after all, a British king intimately connected to the transporting of huge rocks, stones that form a lasting memorial to British history.[43] Merlin explains the necessity of transporting the particular rocks of the *Chorea Gigantum* because each one radiates curative powers. Like Dorigen, Merlin drenches every rock in meaning, so that they grow to dominate the text as well as his desires. These rocks do not destroy life like the black stones of Brittany's coast. They give to those who have perished in battle an enduring and *living* memory. They materialize in the present an anticolonial history, while bringing into that moment other stories (tales of giants and Africa and Ireland) that no matter how overwritten remain legible. Geoffrey's *Chorea Gigantum*, Stonehenge, transformed into 'grisly rokkes blake' (859) limning the coast of Brittany, menaces the romantic dreams of a Chaucerian heroine, a perturbing eruption of a forgotten but strangely itinerant, enduringly vivacious British history into his English tale.

As Aurelius languishes in unreturned ardor for Dorigen, he wishes for a world in which the unremitting motion of the heavenly spheres might yield to human desires. He begs Apollo (the sun) and Diana (the moon) to space themselves so evenly in their rotations that two years of flooding sea-surge will drown the rocks (1031–64). His prayer assumes that water will still itself at its highpoint, and that rock will remain immobile. Yet as the encyclopedist Isidore of Seville wrote:

> Mundus est is qui constat ex caelo, [et] terra et mare cunctisque sideribus. Qui ideo mundus est appellatus, quia semper in motu est; nulla enim requies eius elementis concessa est.[44]

> [The universe consists of the heavens and the earth, the sea and all the stars. It is called the universe (*mundus*) because it is always in motion (*motu*) for no rest is given to its elements.]

No element in the perpetual motion machine that was for medieval writers the physical universe can remain immobile. Rocks will move. Sometimes this motion is discernible from coastlines. At other times it is a migration from the ancient British expanses of one text into the English domain of another. Britain and insular history might be difficult to discern in Chaucer's work, but they are there, a subterranean memory that surfaces, a history inscribed in stone.

NOTES

1. John Friedman, 'Dorigen's "Grisly Rokkes Blake" Again', *Chaucer Review* 31(2) (1996), 140.
2. Simon Meecham-Jones, "'Englyssh Gaufride' and British Chaucer? Chaucerian Allusions to the Condition of Wales in the *House of Fame*', *Chaucer Review* 44 (2009), 3. See also Meecham-Jones, 'Where Was Wales? The Erasure of Wales in Medieval English Culture', in *Authority and Subjugation in Writing of Medieval Wales*, eds. Ruth Kennedy and Simon Meecham-Jones (New York: Palgrave Macmillan, 2008), 27–55; and Jeffrey J. Cohen, 'Postcolonialism', in *Chaucer: An Oxford Guide*, ed. Steve Ellis (Oxford: Oxford University Press, 2005), 448–62.
3. On Chaucer's orientation, see James Simpson, 'Chaucer as a European Writer', in *The Yale Companion to Chaucer*, ed. Seth Lerer (New Haven, CT: Yale University Press, 2006), 60; John Bowers, 'Chaucer after Smithfield', in *The Postcolonial Middle Ages*, ed. Jeffrey Jerome Cohen (New York: Palgrave, 2000), 53–66; and David Wallace, *Chaucerian Polity: Absolutist Lineages and Associational Forms in England and Italy* (Stanford, CA: Stanford University Press, 1997), 156–81. For a penetrating analysis of what orientation in its relation to race and violence means for Geoffrey Chaucer, Geoffrey and Monmouth and medieval romance writ large, see Geraldine Heng, *Empire of Magic: Medieval Romance and the Politics of Cultural Fantasy* (New York: Columbia, 2004).
4. The Britishness of the *lais* is well argued by Emily K. Yoder, 'Chaucer and the "Breton" Lay', *Chaucer Review* 12(1) (1977), 74–7. The medieval French and English words for Briton and Breton were the same; the cultures of Brittany and Wales were continuous. Breton *lais* could, that is, be as accurately called Briton *lais*.
5. Geoffrey of Monmouth, *The History of the Kings of Britain: An Edition and Translation of De gestis Britonum (Historia regum Britanniae)*, ed. Michael D. Reeve, trans. Neil Wright (Woodbridge: Boydell Press, 2007).
6. Richard Price, *The Convict and the Colonel: A Story of Colonialism and Resistance in the Caribbean,* 2nd ed. (Durham, NC: Duke University Press, 2006).
7. Ibid., 60.
8. Ibid., 61.
9. Ibid., 172.
10. Ibid., 173.
11. Ibid., xi.
12. Ibid., 183, 186.
13. P. G. Walsh and M. J. Kennedy, *The History of English Affairs* (Warminster: Aris and Phillips, 1988), 1:30–1.
14. For a sensitive reading of the complexities of the English delectation of British loss, see Patricia Clare Ingham, *Sovereign Fantasies: Arthurian Romance and the Making of Britain* (Philadelphia, PA: University of Pennsylvania Press, 2001), 77–106.

15. See John Gillingham, *The English in the Twelfth Century: Imperialism, National Identity and Political Values* (Woodbridge: Boydell Press, 2000), 19–39. On Geoffrey's inherent ambivalence, see Michelle Warren, *History on the Edge: Excalibur and the Borders of Britain, 1100–1300* (Minneapolis, MN: University of Minnesota Press, 2000), 25–30.

16. Geoffrey, *History of the Kings of Britain*, 9.154.

17. Ibid., 6.105.

18. Ibid., 6.106.

19. At least that is the story told by an otherwise unknown man at Vortigern's court, Maugantius (Geoffrey, *History*, 6.107). Stephen Knight has recently argued that Merlin's father may be an angel, or be unknown, like that of other Welsh saints born to nuns, but an incubus-father is not so rare as Knight implies: *Merlin: Knowledge and Power Through the Ages* (Ithaca, NY: Cornell University Press, 2009), 25.

20. Geoffrey, *History of the Kings of Britain*, 8.128.

21. Ibid., 6.108.

22. 'Sed et inclitus ille rex Arturus letaliter uulneratus est; qui illinc ad sananda uulnera sua in insulam Auallonis euectus' (Ibid., 11.178).

23. Ibid., 8.118.

24. Ibid., 8.137.

25. Ibid., 8.128.

26. Ibid., 9.205.

27. Ibid., 8.129.

28. Wace, *Wace's Roman de Brut: A History of the British Roman de Brut*, ed. and trans. Judith Weiss (Exeter: University of Exeter Press, 2002), 4.

29. An extreme example of this kind of combinatory approach to the past is the Breton *lai Sir Orfeo*, which admixes classical mythology (the story of Orpheus), the fairy Otherworld (Eurydice does not die, but is abducted by a fairy lover), and English history (the modern name for Thrace becomes Winchester).

30. Though I do not possess the space to explore the issue here, the superseded past which the Britons inhabit render them uncannily similar to the figure of the Jew in the medieval Christian imagination.

31. On Arthur, Welsh nationalism, and the complexities of postcolonial identities, see Patricia Clare Ingham, *Sovereign Fantasies* and Michelle R. Warren, *History on the Edge*. Ingham powerfully reads the Wife of Bath's Tale as creating a pastoral space in which the present struggles of the Welsh are made invisible by an idealized, lost history: 'Pastoral Histories: Utopia, Conquest, and the Wife of Bath's Tale', *Texas Studies in Literature and Language* 44 (2002), 35–46.

32. Alfred K. Siewers, *Strange Beauty: Ecocritical Approaches to Early Medieval Landscape* (New York: Palgrave Macmillan, 2009).

33. Susan Crane writes of these friars, metaphorized as dust floating through a ray of sun, that they 'oddly weightless…their sexual aggressiveness is a vestige of wilder spirits…The friar follows in the footstep of the elf who persists in the Christian image of the incubus'; *Gender and Romance in Chaucer's* Canterbury Tales (Princeton, NJ: Princeton University Press, 1994), 163–64. Crane also sees continuity among the elf queen, the loathly lady, and the Wife of Bath.

34. Geoffrey, *History of the Kings of Britain*, 6.107.

35. For an overview of Chaucer's relation to his source see Dominique Battles, 'Chaucer's "Franklin's Tale" and Boccaccio's "Filocolo" Reconsidered', *Chaucer Review* 34.1 (1999), 38–59.

36. Kathryn L. Lynch explores the connection between the names in the two narratives in 'East Meets West in Chaucer's Squire's and Franklin's Tales', in *Chaucer's Cultural Geographies*, ed. Kathryn L. Lynch (New York: Routledge, 2002), 89.
37. Geoffrey, *History of the Kings of Britain*, 8.127.
38. Gilles Deleuze and Félix Guattari, *What is Philosophy?*, trans. Hugh Tomlinson and Graham Burchell (New York: Columbia University Press, 1994), 176.
39. Geoffrey, *History of the Kings of Britain*, 8.128.
40. Ibid., 8.129.
41. John B. Friedman notes that a tenth-century collection of *mirabilia* (MS Bodley 614) contains 'an illustration showing a ring of stones and a group of distraught-looking women'. According to the text they are seven sisters who danced on a feast day and were cursed to dance eternally: petrification as eternal punishment, as well as 'a medieval description of a Breton megalithic circle containing a number of menhirs' ('Dorigen's "Grisly Rokkes Blake" Again', 139).
42. Though as Susan Crane points out, the exact type of magic practised is left ambiguous (*Gender and Romance in Chaucer's* Canterbury Tales, 136–43).
43. So far as I know the first to suggest a connection between the rocks in the Franklin's Tale and the *History of the Kings of Britain* was William H. Schofield, 'Chaucer's *Franklin's Tale*', *PMLA* 16 (1931), 417–18.
44. Isidore of Seville, *Etymologiae*, ed. W. M. Lindsay, 2 vols. (Oxford, 1911), Book 3, 29. Robert Bartlett cites the passage to illustrate the medieval idea that the four constituent elements of the cosmos (earth, air, fire, water) are always in motion, a restless *machina mundi*. See *The Natural and the Supernatural in the Middle Ages* (Cambridge: Cambridge University Press, 2008), 38.

BIBLIOGRAPHY

Bowers, John, 'Chaucer after Smithfield', in *The Postcolonial Middle Ages*, ed. Jeffrey Jerome Cohen (New York: Palgrave, 2000), 53–66.

Cohen, Jeffrey J., 'Postcolonialism', in *Chaucer: An Oxford Guide*, ed. Steve Ellis (Oxford: Oxford University Press, 2005), 448–62.

Crane, Susan, *Gender and Romance in Chaucer's* Canterbury Tales (Princeton, NJ: Princeton University Press, 1994).

Heng, Geraldine. *Empire of Magic: Medieval Romance and the Politics of Cultural Fantasy* (New York: Columbia University Press, 2004).

Ingham, Patricia Clare, *Sovereign Fantasies: Arthurian Romance and the Making of Britain* (Philadelphia, PA: University of Pennsylvania Press, 2001).

Lerer, Seth, ed., *The Yale Companion to Chaucer* (New Haven, CT: Yale University Press, 2006).

Meecham-Jones, Simon, 'Where Was Wales? The Erasure of Wales in Medieval English Culture', in *Authority and Subjugation in Writing of Medieval Wales*, eds. Ruth Kennedy and Simon Meecham-Jones (New York: Palgrave Macmillan, 2008), 27–55.

Simpson, James, 'Chaucer as a European Writer', in Seth Lerer, *The Yale Companion to Chaucer* (New Haven, CT: Yale University Press, 2006), 55–86.

Smith, D. Vance, 'Chaucer as an English Writer', in Seth Lerer, *The Yale Companion to Chaucer* (New Haven, CT: Yale University Press, 2006), 87–121.

Wallace, David, *Chaucerian Polity: Absolutist Lineages and Associational Forms in England and Italy* (Stanford, CA: Stanford University Press, 1997).

Warren, Michelle, *History on the Edge: Excalibur and the Borders of Britain, 1100–1300* (Minneapolis, MN: University of Minnesota Press, 2000).

CHAPTER 30

VERNACULAR AUTHORSHIP AND PUBLIC POETRY

John Gower

T. MATTHEW N. McCABE

INSPIRED by a range of continental models, both medieval and classical, Chaucer's ideas about poetic authority have a fascinating counterpart in the writings of his greatest English rival, John Gower. Like Chaucer, but unlike virtually every other contemporary or earlier writer of English letters, Gower presents himself as an elite literary author in the tradition of the classical *auctores*, above all Ovid.[1] It is no coincidence that two of Chaucer's most striking claims to author status—the 'Go litel bok' envoy to *Troilus and Criseyde* (5.1786–1860), and the 'Chaucer' signature in the Man of Law's Introduction, whose significance for the development of Chaucer's self-conscious authorial position Sheila Delany has stressed (II.77–89)[2]—both contain clear references to Gower.[3]

The ending of the *Confessio amantis* suggests that Gower, in turn, could not reflect on his position as an English poet without thinking of Chaucer. After Venus addresses Amans as 'John Gower'[4]—thus allowing Gower to 'sign' his name in the poem for the first and last time—Venus, in the poem's 'first recension', bids him farewell with the words, 'Gret wel Chaucer whan ye mete,/As mi disciple and mi poete', and charges him to convey to Chaucer her commandment 'to sette an ende of alle his werk' and 'make his testament of love'.[5] Gower thus returns the favour, signalling his admiration for Chaucer's stature as a nationally significant author in Venus's statement: 'Of Ditees and of songes glade,/The whiche he for mi sake made,/The lond fulfild is overal'.[6] These lines may recall Chaucer's reference to 'Petrark, the lauriat poete' whose rhetoric 'Enlumyned al Ytaille of poetrie' (Tales IV.31–3). But the passage also highlights differences between Gower's and Chaucer's paths to becoming national authors, as Gower shows impatience with his friend's refusal to leave his 'songs and ditties' of Venus for a worthier cause.[7] If Chaucer's and Gower's bids for a quasi-Petrarchan position as national author are mutually dependent, they are also contestative, as each writer attempts to define this role to the exclusion of the other.

Whereas previous discussions of Gower's emergent sense of poetic authority have tended to focus on Gower's relationship to aristocratic French literature or on his indebtedness to classical texts and their attendant scholastic commentaries,[8] the present chapter seeks to recall attention to the very novelty of Gower's claim to be a nationally significant, elite, literary author by examining specific articulations of this claim and investigating what was at stake in such pretensions. Classical and French models notwithstanding, it is easy to forget how few works composed in English by 1390, ostensibly the year of the *Confessio*'s completion,[9] had asserted their connectedness to a European, elite poetic tradition. It is just as easy to forget that virtually all post-Conquest writers who used English did so in ways that are self-consciously parochial, if not deliberately self-marginalizing.[10] Yet somehow, by 1390 or 1393, Gower was capable of some quite astonishing claims to literary authority, as we shall see.

In what follows I argue that, taken together, the various authorial signatures found in the manuscripts—including the poems 'Quam cinxere', 'Explicit iste liber', and 'Eneiodos bucolis' and the corpus-sealing colophon 'Quia vnusquisque'—suggest that it is Gower's self-positioning with respect to an English public, at least as much as his engagements with individual patrons, that provides the main platform for his self-presentation as an elite author. Positing that the idea of an English literary public was in large part the recent invention of Chaucer—though perhaps twelve years younger than Gower, Chaucer was already prolific in English poetry by the time Gower seems to have begun the *Confessio amantis* in the mid-1380s, and Gower's most significant claims to authorship all postdate, and are in large part predicated upon, that poem—this chapter concludes with preliminary reflections on what significance Gower's attempted revision of Chaucerian notions of authorship and publicity might hold for this crucial period in the formation of an English poetic tradition.

AUTHORSHIP, PUBLIC AND DIDACTIC

In the 'standard' form of the *Confessio* manuscripts which he appears to have closely managed the exemplars of,[11] Gower concludes the work with a sequence of two Latin poems and one Latin prose colophon that, as Derek Pearsall notes, together 'represent the English poet in an extraordinary light, not merely kissing the steps on which the classical poets stand, which is what Chaucer modestly advises his book of *Troilus* to do, but clambering up them'.[12] Chaucer's gesture in the *Troilus* envoy echoes an audacious self-authorizing move of Boccaccio,[13] an author Gower seems to have had no more direct knowledge of than he had of Dante or Petrarch. But Pearsall's implied comparison of Gower to Boccaccio is nonetheless revealing. Indeed, without positing an indirect influence of Italian ideas of authorship via Chaucer,[14] Gower's self-conception as a poet of national significance would be exceedingly difficult to account for—for all intents impossible—so remarkable are Gower's aspirations.

Modest only insofar as Gower restricts his field of literary conquest to England, the series begins in 'Explicit iste liber' with the prayer that his book may 'go its way' and 'flourish', before specifying the desired destination in national terms: 'Qui sedet in scannis celi det vt ista Iohannis/Perpetuis annis stet pagina grata Britannis' [May He who sits in the throne of heaven grant that John's writings may remain for all time pleasing to the Britons].[15] The second poem, 'Quam cinxere freta', declares that Gower's works have already become the property of the nation:

> Quam cinxere freta, Gower, tua carmina leta
> Per loca discreta canit Anglia laude repleta.
> Carminis Athleta, satirus, tibi, siue Poeta,
> Sit laus completa quo gloria stat sine meta.[16]

[In diverse regions, O Gower, England, which the waters girdle round, full of praises sings your happy songs. Champion of song, satirist, or poet – may your praise be full where glory stands without limit.][17]

The notion that Gower's songs are 'happy' to be sung 'in diverse regions' makes explicit Gower's claim to have gained a Chaucer-like national stature as an author. More specifically, the poem's reference to England's being 'filled' with praise (*laude repleta*) recalls Gower's own appraisal of Chaucer's quasi-Petrarchan 'filling' of the land with 'Ditees and songes'.

But if Gower's ambitions might thus far seem to resemble Chaucer's, the next piece, the four-paragraph prose summary of Gower's career 'Quia vnusquisque' locates these ambitions on grounds that would seem very un-Chaucerian. Speaking about Gower in the third person, the piece describes his literary career in terms of spiritual bookkeeping:

> Quia vnusquisque, prout a deo accepit, aliis impartiri tenetur, Iohannes Gower super hiis que deus sibi sensualiter donauit villicacionis sue racionem, dum tempus instat, secundum aliquid alleuiare cupiens, inter labores et ocia ad aliorum noticiam tres libros doctrine causa forma subsequenti composuit.[18]
>
> [Because each man is bound to impart to others just as he has received from God, John Gower, wishing while time remains to alleviate somewhat the account of his stewardship for the things with which God plainly has endowed him, composed, between labour and rest, for the instruction (trans. Galloway: 'for the notice') of others, three books of doctrine in the following form.]

The synopses of the *Mirour de l'omme*, *Vox clamantis*, and *Confessio amantis* that follow have been criticized for misrepresenting the content of these works.[19] Nevertheless, given its position in the *Confessio* manuscripts, 'Quia vnusquisque' is remarkable for raising the seemingly quotidian matter of Gower's didactic mission immediately following the assertions of literary celebrity in 'Explicit iste liber' and 'Quam cinxere'.

Alternatively, it would be accurate to say that 'Quia vnusquisque' makes didactic mission the very grounds of Gower's claim to literary celebrity. On the latter reading, *ad aliorum noticiam* might be seen to signify not only others' 'notice' of moral doctrine but also their 'notice' of Gower.

Didacticism unmistakeably plays a central role in Gower's self-promotion as an author, as becomes even clearer in the poem 'Eneidos bucolis'. Included in four of the five earliest copies of the *Vox* and also in Bodleian Library MS Fairfax 3, the poem purports to have been written by a 'certain philosopher' but is attributed by its most recent editor to Gower himself.[20] The poem is of interest here because it not only locates the basis of Gower's literary celebrity in the poet's didactic mission, but reveals something of the reasoning behind this.

Like 'Quia vnusquisque' and reminiscent also of Gower's tomb in Southwark Cathedral, where the recumbant figure of the poet rests his head on three books,[21] 'Eneidos bucolis' promotes the *Mirour*, *Vox*, and *Confessio* as a trilogy. The poem compares Gower's tripartite oeuvre to Virgil's, but, far from making Gower a minor Virgil in a bid to rechannel the cultural capital of *Romanitas*, it asserts the English poet's superiority by means of an argument that, rather interestingly, works to decentre the very idea of a culturally translatable *imperium*. While the poem initially depicts Virgil as supreme among poets in absolute terms—'metra perhennis/Virgilio laudis serta dedere scolis' [The meters...woven together/By Virgil, have given matter of perpetual praise to the schools][22]—this Virgil soon gives way to a merely national, Italic Virgil: 'Illeque Latinis tantum sua metra loquelis/Scripsit, ut Italicis sint recolenda notis' [He wrote his poems only in the Latin tongue,/So that they might be appreciated by the famous Italian worthies].[23] But surprisingly, what follows is not a conventional narrative of *translatio studii et imperii* to Gower's Britain, for the poem's next move effectively circumvents the secular institutions on which such translations normally depend. Having begun by locating Virgil's power in the 'schools' (*scolis*),[24] the poem now transposes *scola* into a new, public register: 'Te tua set trinis tria scribere carmina linguis/Constat, ut inde viris sit scola lata magis' [But it is clear that you wrote your three poems in three languages,/So that broader schooling might be given to men].[25] The speaker's interest in *scola lata magis* centres on two elements: Christianity and accessibility. Gower's poetry is lauded for treating themes more serious (compare with *seris*)[26] than the 'vanities' indulged by Virgil. In the last lines, this seriousness becomes equated with Christian religion:

> Ille quidem vanis Romanas obstupet aures,
>   Ludit et in studiis musa pagana suis;
> Set tua Cristicolis fulget scriptura renatis,
>   Quo tibi celicolis laus sit habenda locis.[27]
>
> [He indeed astounded the ears of the Romans with vanities,
> And the pagan Muse played in his studies.
> But your writing glows for reborn Christians,
> Whereby praise will be given you in heavenly places.]

Contrasting Gower's religious correctness with Virgil's 'pagan Muse', the speaker bases his preference for Gower's writings partly on their Christianity. But the appraisal also invokes criteria of openness and accessibility. Whereas Virgil 'astounded' Roman ears—*obstupet* might be read in various ways, all of which evoke miscomprehension in some form—Gower's trilingual *scola lata magis*, significantly, called *scriptura*, is essentially illuminative (*fulget*). English plays no small part in this poetics of accessibility. The account of Gower's trilingualism privileges *lingua Anglica*, if not explicitly as the most intimate, accessible language of 'Anglia', at least as Gower's own maternal tongue: 'Gallica lingua prius, Latina secunda, set ortus/Lingua tui pocius Anglica complet opus' [First the French tongue, Latin second, then at last English,/The speech of your birth, completes a more potent work].[28] English is privileged as the tongue of origin and consummation alike, even if, in a strategy reminiscent of Dante's *De Vulgari Eloquentia*, the argument is promulgated in the traditional language of intellectual authority, Latin.

Thus lauding him for giving English audiences a new degree of access to Christian truth, 'Eneidos bucolis' presents Gower as powerfully self-sufficient, as a poet virtually free of the need to catch the reflected glory of *Romanitas* or any other source of cultural capital, secularly understood. Rather, Gower's claim to 'newness' hinges on Gowerian poetry's embodiment of a species of vernacular theology, if this term is understood in its broadest sense.[29]

To be sure, there are problems with the picture given here. 'Eneidos bucolis' seems to elide Gower's dependence on secular patrons, though, as I will argue in the next section, it is possible to overstate the importance that patronage held for Gower. More seriously, perhaps, one might wonder if 'Eneidos bucolis' overstates the importance of spiritual concerns in the *Confessio*, for example, and exaggerates the consistency of Gower's commitment to public accessiblity in works such as the *Vox*. But even if one understood the metatextual packaging constituted by 'Eneidos bucolis' and the other pieces we have examined as grossly misrepresentative of the content and motivation of Gower's *oeuvre*, this packaging would remain highly significant if only on the level of promotional strategy. The enthusiasm shown in 'Eneidos bucolis' for the public dissemination of theological and other forms of knowledge would still have important implications for Gower's audience's taste, at least insofar as that taste was anticipated and cultivated by Gower and the collaborators and scribes responsible for promoting his works.

But in fact the 'Quia vnusquisque', 'Eneidos bucolis', and related pieces have a significance greater than even this, because they are, to a considerable degree, accurate. The four pieces we have surveyed represent Gower's *oeuvre* accurately at least insofar as concerns both the *scale* of Gower's life's work, and the preoccupation of Gower's *oeuvre* with didactic and public concerns. Putting aside theology for the time being, the didactic and public interests foregrounded in the colophon sequence already pervade Gower's works themselves, the totality of which exudes an 'almost obsessive' sense of 'poetic mission'.[30] More importantly still, Gower's sense of mission was inextricably connected to his thinking about poetic authority and the posthumous reception of his works. In all extant versions of the *Confessio* he clearly sought 'the worldes eere/In tyme comende after this'[31] as he did also in both major versions of the *Vox*.[32] In this respect, as in others,[33] his literary *oeuvre* seems to align well with the principle of public didacticism foregrounded retrospectively, not only in the *Confessio* colophons but also in those manuscripts of the *Vox* which include 'Quia vnusquisque' and in 'Eneidos bucolis', and in the *Vox* and *Confessio* themselves.

GOWER'S *VOX POPULI:* LAY IDENTITY
AND AGENCY

Gower's practice of writing almost exclusively in some manner of public, reformist, functional vein and his habit of clothing his author status in piety and zeal for the common good invite his comparison to Langland. Langlandian influence is most evident when, as often, Gower rests his authority on—in effect occults himself within—the 'common voice'.[34] One crucial aspect of Gower's authorial position, then, is its participation in the mode of writing that Anne Middleton termed 'public poetry': like Langland, Usk, Clanvowe, and others, Gower writes 'as if' to a common audience that seems fully to emerge as a discursive possibility only in the last quarter of the fourteenth century.[35] But such affinities offer little help in explaining the scale of Gower's ambitions, for apart from Gower himself, none of these writers present themselves as nationally significant authors. Notwithstanding his riddling signature, 'Long Will', Langland seems to have carefully contrived to make a name only for 'his elusive hero Piers Plowman', and his alliterative imitators in the '*Piers Plowman* tradition' presented their work anonymously.[36] Gower, by contrast, proudly signed his work and regarded authorship as a potential source of personal glory, even as he ostentatiously renounces this.[37] The question arises, why should Gower's role as an instructor of the public embolden him to claim the status of an author?

As far as authorial self-promotion is concerned, a considerable advantage that Gower seems to have held over Langland and the writers in the *Piers Plowman* tradition was his position relative to elite cultures, both secular and ecclesiastical. Clearly Gower's dedications of his various works provide important evidence of his intended audience, but it would be a mistake to assume that Gower restricted his intended audience to the recipients of presentation copies. The versatility of Gower's thinking about audience finds a fitting emblem in Gower's famous revision of the *Confessio*'s dedication—'And for that fewe men endite/In oure Englissh, I thenke make/A bok for king Richardes sake'[38]— whereby the last line became 'A bok for Engelondes sake'.[39] At the same time, the continued presence of the original Ricardian dedication and the thirty-seven-line account of the poem's genesis, in Gower's encounter with King Richard while boating on the Thames, in copies made after Gower's revision of the preface indicate that a royal dedication posed no threat to his work's early popularity—far from it.[40] The dedications of the *Confessio* and *Vox* to Richard II, Henry Bolingbroke, and Thomas Arundel exist alongside the passages, discussed at the end of the last section, in which Gower reflects on the possibility of a much more general readership extending into posterity. Far from existing in tension, particular address and public address appear mutually reaffirming in Gower's thinking about audience, as is attested by the *Confessio* colophon, 'Explicit iste liber', which amidst more general reflections on the national reception of Gower's writings interjects a brief prayer that Gower' writings may 'rest' in the safe keeping of Henry Bolingbroke 'Count of Derby'.[41]

One reason why Gower could find so great a convergence between his twin goals of securing patrons and securing a public was presumably that he located his public within a social elite for whom such signs of aristocratic patronage were likely to command respect and elicit desire. Although by the late fourteenth century the potential readership of secular literature comprised non-gentles from the middle strata of society, a large part of the appeal of this literature for such groups seems to have resided in the access to courtliness that it was perceived to offer.[42] In any case, it is clear that the public which Gower seems to have felt most naturally inclined toward is an elite public, one of gentle affiliation if not precisely identifiable with a particular gentle social sector. Gower's adaptation in the *Confessio* of the psychological machinery of the still-fashionable *Roman de la Rose* suggests the gentle affiliation of Gower's public in that work. He used a similar device already in the *Mirour*,[43] and though this work, which is extant in only one manuscript, has not usually been seen as publicly oriented, the comprehensiveness of the poem's social vision, as well its opening—'Escoulte cea, chascun amant,/Qui tant perestes desirant/Du pecché, dont l'amour est fals' [Listen to this, every lover who seems so desirous of sin, whose love is false][44]—may show Gower experimenting with public orientation already in this work. Gower actually addresses 'gentile Engleterre' in the envoy to the *Cinkante Balades*,[45] and he appears to have targeted a very similar public— again, alongside whatever specific recipient he may have had in mind[46]—in the more widely disseminated *Traitié*,[47] which is extant in thirteen manuscripts and a fifteenth-century English version.

As various commentators have noted, Gower's self-identification with the social elite sits oddly with the invocations of *vox populi* that are so prominent a feature of his rhetorical self-positioning.[48] So loudly and persistently does Gower claim throughout his early estates satires that the opinions he records represent the *vox populi* that he seems to have felt obliged to soften this aspect of the *Vox* after the 1381 uprising, when he added, somewhat self-contradictorily, an unequivocal condemnation of the animalistic speech of the miscreant *vulgus* in the 'visio' which became *Vox* I.[49] In the version presumed to have existed before this change, his invocations of the *vox populi* would have been prominently visible as bookends around the estates satire that, after the short, proemial book that is now Book II, made up the body of the work.[50] The prominence this arrangement affords such gestures illustrates the fundamental importance that *vox populi* held for Gower's authorial self-positioning.

For critics such as David Aers, the most interesting aspect of Gower's rhetorical position is the strength of its resolution in defending the interests of 'the dominant classes': the account of the Rising of 1381 that makes up *Vox* I 'dehumanize[s] the rebels' and particularly their jackdaw spokesman, who is 'the people's orator, the rival to the *"vox populi*" of Gower's poem'.[51] While Aers's analysis is accurate so far as it goes, it misses a subversive quality inherent in Gower's rhetorical position. Gower's *vox populi* stance shares with the rhetorical stances of more radical writers—Langland, Rolle, and Julian of Norwich, for example—an interest in the opportunities created as the laity rose in profile in the religious discourses of the fourteenth century.

Gower's *vox populi* topos has an anticlerical cast that is insufficiently appreciated, for example, in Fisher's account of how Gower's role stands 'opposite' the 'demagogues' Langland and the Lollards.[52] Although he deploys the *vox populi* topos occasionally against secular lords[53] and against lawyers[54] (and if these last were his professional colleagues, the example becomes a special case), most instances where Gower uses the trope to dissociate himself from criticisms directed against a particular estate, and all the earliest instances, target church officials or monks: three in the *Mirour*[55] and three in the *Vox*.[56] Popular denunciations of the clergy legitimate Gower's writing; he writes only when the natural shepherds of the people have egregiously failed.

It is possible to read Gower, as Sheila Lindebaum does, as 'trying to enforce a workable poetic alternative until political and religious institutions repair themselves'.[57] But especially when we consider that the figure of the satirist was not traditionally a lay figure, on closer inspection, Gower's rhetorical position takes on a greater significance. By investing the voice of the laity with a degree of value thitherto unprecedented, Gower's *vox populi* rhetoric creates new possibilities for a critique based not on status but on reason,[58] a critique that if anything is further authorized by its location outside the ecclesiastical establishment. Gower represents common speech as a source of learning alternative, and in opposition to, clergial discourse: 'Vox populi cum voce dei concordat, vt ipsa/In rebus dubiis sit metuenda magis:/Hec ego que dicam dictum commune docebat,/Nec mea verba sibi quid nouitatis habent' ['The voice of the people agrees with the voice of God, so that in doubtful matters it ought to be held in greater awe. Common talk has taught me what I shall say, and my words contain nothing new'].[59] In context, 'doubtful matters' (*rebus dubiis*) denotes the crisis of truth that exists when, with Pharisees in Moses' seat,[60] the church is systemically corrupt; thankfully, in such a crisis, the laity themselves become capable of imparting knowledge (*docebat*). Gower closes the chapter with a prayer that not only fosters solidarity among those victimized by corrupt clerks—the laity *en masse*—but even raises the remarkable possibility of extraclergial access to *stabilem fidem*, if not explicitly to God himself: 'Et licet instabilis vanus sit et actus eorum,/Da populo stabilem semper habere fidem' [And even if their (i.e. the canonically elected Church officials) conduct is false and un-steadfast, grant that Thy people always retain their firm faith'].[61]

In a related passage in the *Mirour*, Gower adopts a still more markedly lay position and evokes a sense of lay solidarity when he complains that ecclesiastics have failed 'us'. Again he raises the possibility, however doubtfully, of extraclergial mediation:

> Mais qant les clercs nous sont failly,
> Ne say desore avant par qui
> Porrons du nostre creatour

> Avoir reless de sa mercy,
> Ainz que nous soions malbailly;
> Et c'est le pis de ma dolour.[62]

[But since the clerics have failed us, I do not know by whom in the future we can have forgiveness through the pardon of our Creator before we are in trouble; and that is the greatest of my sorrows.]

Certainly, Gower does not appear confident that a mediator of divine grace alternative to the *clercs* will present itself. Yet it is notable that his next move, taking this thought further, involves his most explicit self-description in the entire extant *Mirour*. Gower is no ecclesiastic; his self-description seems to place him in the legal profession.[63] He claims that his non-clerkly status makes him vulnerable to the charge of 'ill will' against the clergy:

> Mais s'aucun m'en soit au travers,
> Et la sentence de mes vers
> Voldra blamer de malvuillance,
> Pour ce que je ne suy pas clers,
> Vestu de sanguin ne de pers,
> Ainz ai vestu la raye mance...[64]

[But if someone should have an opinion on the subject opposite to mine and should want to blame the charges of my verses on ill-will, because I am not a cleric clothed in scarlet and blue, rather I have worn only striped sleeves...]

While it makes sense for Gower to concede the point that he is not a *clerc* before proceeding to make his real defense—that he merely reports 'the consensus of the people'— Gower's disavowal of learning would seem excessive:

> Poy sai latin, poy sai romance,
> Mais la commune tesmoignance
> Du poeple m'ad fait tout apers
> A dire, que du fole errance
> Les clercs dont vous ay fait parlance
> Encore sont ils plus divers.[65]

[I know little Latin and little French. But it is the consensus of people that has determined me to say quite openly that there is still greater diversity of foolish error among the clerics.]

Gower's protracted self-disparagement, and his emphatic denunciation of clergial folly in lines 21,778–90, are easily explained, however, if here, as in the *Vox* passage, Gower shows himself sensitive to a rhetorical climate in which traditional marks of authority— in this case a knowledge of French and Latin literature—were, at least in some contexts, potentially a liability.

To appreciate what is at stake in Gower's extraclergial position it is useful to consider one further item in the metatextual packaging of Gower's writing, the 'Gower the

Archer' portrait found in several early manuscripts of the *Vox*.[66] The portrait shows Gower as an archer taking aim at a *mappa mundi*-like disc, above which are the verses,

> Ad mundum mitto mea iacula, dumque sagitto;
> At vbi iustus erit, nulla sagitta ferit.
> Sed male viuentes hos vulnero transgredientes;
> Conscius ergo sibi se speculetur ibi.

[I send my darts at the world…wherever there is a just man, no one will receive arrows. I badly wound those living in transgression, however. Therefore, let the thoughtful man look out for himself.][67]

The admonishment 'let the thoughtful man look out for himself' takes on greater significance in light of the general estates satire in the body of the *Vox* which follows. Gower's catalogue of transgressors includes literally all ranks of society, and the epigram thus seems to make the flattering suggestion to every potential reader that he might possess the necessary resources to perform a needed spiritual self-examination. A similar symbolic inclusion of all ranks occurs within the body of the work (though, to be sure, this sense of inclusivity became weakened after the addition of the Book I 'visio'). Making allowances for those members of the body politic whom Gower considered reprobate as individuals,[68] the *Vox* grants all estates access to the redemptive purpose that informs Gower's general address, admitting all, at least symbolically, into the poem's readership. Importantly, the process by which the 'thoughtful man look[s] out for himself' is wholly independent of the priesthood.

Gower's symbolic inclusion in his readership—perhaps most vivid in the *Vox* and *Confessio*, but discernible also in the *Mirour*—of groups whose social and economic position would have excluded them in fact is important because it argues *a fortiori* for the significance of the openness of his invitation to those audiences—the plurality is crucial—who did enjoy access to books in one or more of the languages in which Gower wrote. Gower's rhetorical position is also remarkable for investing the authority of judgment in a private lay person. Gower claims this authority for himself, but, as we have seen, the manner in which he does so presupposes a considerable degree of lay solidarity and in turn effects a quite substantial extension of agency to the laity.

POETRY 'IN OURE ENGLISSH': WHAT IS IT?

One of the most remarkable features of Gower's writings, then, is their invitation of readers to practise public criticism and their equipping such readers for this practice. While such tendencies, in Gower and other writers, have not passed wholly unrecognized since Anne Middleton's seminal essay of 1978, scholars invested in proving the existence of a Ricardian 'public sphere'[69] have not sufficiently attended the extent of such public criticism's theological interests. Gower's deployment of theological doctrine as a strategy by which to authorize public critique is particularly striking in the case of the *Vox*. Though rarely discussed, *Vox* II systematically treats such topics as the Trinity, Creation, Incarnation, Fall, Restoration, faith, icons, and idols within an extended meditation on sin.[70] Given that this book functions as a preface to the five books of estates satire that follow, the arrangement suggests that theology and social criticism were more closely related in Gower's mind than we might think; while Gower's theology elsewhere takes other forms, generally locating itself even from scholastic sources, similar meditations on sin and redemption occur alongside political discussion in the short poems 'Rex celi deus' and *In Praise of Peace*, and, in a Marian vein, in the *Mirour*.[71] Thus, while Gower's moral vision is indeed notable for its 'secularity'[72] if the term denotes an orientation to this world and an elevation of lay interests and lay perspectives, it is nonetheless clear that this 'secularity' (or layness or worldliness) has a more significant religious dimension than some accounts suggest.

When one recalls that 'Eneidos buccolis' valorizes not only public access but, specifically, the access to truth which the mother tongue grants to English Christians, it is the less surprising that the *Confessio amantis*, Gower's 'bok for Engelondes sake', yields a particularly rich return when read in light of this religious dimension. Writing on religious topics in English at a time when 'Anticristes Lollardie' was prominent enough to warrant Gower's stern denunciation[73] necessarily brought with it opportunities as well as risks, if only because new conditions of expression enables old doctrines to find new meanings. While this is not the place to examine either work in detail, both the *Confessio* and *In Praise of Peace* adopt in their handling of religious material strategies not seen in his Latin writing. English emerges as a tongue whose chief resources for expressing theological truth reside not in technical precision—even less so than in Gower's poetically self-aware Latin, however fraught with linguistic angst though it may be[74]—but in intimacy, polyseymy, and affect—for example when Gower juxtaposes natural human 'pite' and divine 'grace' in ways that frequently assign the natural passion a salvific function.[75] Given Genius's double identity as both an out-of-bounds priest and a surrogate of Nature,[76] it is perhaps unsurprising that many similar moves can be adduced, and that Genius's priesthood, notwithstanding the real limitations of that office, extends a *kinde* of grace—a nature that Gower characteristically represents as already infused with grace—to vernacular readers broadly: *scola lata magis* indeed.[77]

Gower's practices in English are not diametrically opposed to his practices in French and Latin. As we have seen, Gower's *Vox* and *Mirour* adopt an extraclergial stance and present extraclergial wisdom in an accessible style, and it would be easy to demonstrate elements of a poetic similar to that of 'Eneidos bucolis' in the lay theology of either, as indeed of other writings by Gower. But the *Confessio*, aided no doubt by Chaucer's example as well as by Gower's own growing sense of achievement, marks the culmination of these processes. Relatively free from the clergial associations that for him still mark Latin, English appears to have given Gower the liberty to cultivate poetic resources that may, like such treatises as *The Prickynge of Love* and *Pore Caitif*, witness a robust doctrine of the Incarnation underwriting a high view of lay and vernacular spirituality.[78]

Gower's ability to push the boundaries of vernacular cultural mediation even as he reshapes the resources of an elite European poetry gave his poetry a quality not found in contemporary writings, and this distinction may explain the success of his poetry during his lifetime,[79] as well as why, by 1390, he should have felt justified in claiming to have achieved the standing of a nationally significant author.

When we consider how ostentatious piety underwrites Gower's claim to national author status, it is tempting to find an analogue in Chaucer's Retraction, appended to the *Canterbury Tales*. There, the movement of Chaucer's thought 'from hennes forth unto my lyves ende' and the general movement from 'woldly vanitees' to God's eternity *per omnia secula* give the passage a strong future orientation (X.1085–92), but the Retraction remains a literary testament, deeply invested in the fate of Chaucer's works in this world. Significantly, then, it is precisely when Chaucer reflects abstractly on the unknown readers who will make up his works' general public in the future ('hem alle that herkne this litel tretys or rede') that he most strongly affirms the excellence of 'doctrine' ('For oure book seith, "Al that is writen is writen for oure doctrine," and that is myn entente'), though he of course regrets that lack of 'konnynge' has hindered his ability to focus on 'Boece…and othere bookes of legendes of seintes, and omelies, and moralitee, and devocioun' as consistently as he might have liked (X.1081–3, 1087).

It is reasonable to read the Retraction as a record of Chaucer's struggle with two related problems that also exercised Gower: where might be found a basis for an elite English poetry of lasting, national significance? And what should the resulting national poetry be? If we take the further step of viewing the Retraction as, at least in part, a public relations device attesting what strategy Chaucer thought the best means by which to consolidate his reputation, such a reading would suggest that Gower's solution to these problems—his combining of an earnest, Christian public address with the poetic resources of elite European culture as the twin bases of the new edifice, English poetry— may have exerted a significant influence on the Chaucerian tradition not only via the early Chaucerians Hoccleve and Lydgate[80] but also on Chaucer himself. Even if it is deemed not to bear the trace of Gower's influence, the Retraction, insofar as it intentionally refashions Chaucer's reputation as a national poet, attests that the Gowerian synthesis of literary authority with an invocation of a broad Christian public possessed a compelling internal logic around 1400 that may still, with effort, be discerned by modern readers. The recurring, heady mixture of ideas of lay access, on the one hand, and Christian doctrine and piety, on the other, may play a more central role in ideas of English literary authority, as these emerged during the late fourteenth and early fifteenth centuries, than has commonly been thought.

NOTES

1. For the importance of Ovid to Chaucer's and Gower's self-positionings as authors, see, respectively, James Simpson, 'Chaucer as a European Writer', in *The Yale Companion to Chaucer,* ed. Seth Lerer (New Haven, CT: Yale University Press, 2006), 55–86; and James

Simpson, *Sciences and the Self in Medieval Poetry: Alan of Lille's* Anticlaudianus *and John Gower's* Confessio Amantis (Cambridge: Cambridge University Press, 1995), 134–66, 284–9.

2. Sheila Delany, *The Naked Text: Chaucer's* Legend of Good Women (Berkeley, CA: University of California Press, 1994), 14, 33.

3. For the Gowerian allusions of the Man of Law's Introduction, see *Canterbury Tales* II.77–89 and note; and Peter Nicholson, 'The *Man of Law's Tale*: What Chaucer Really Owed to Gower', *Chaucer Review* 26 (1991), 153–74.

4. John Gower, *Confessio amantis*, VIII.2908. Unless otherwise noted, henceforward all references to Gower's works are to G. C. Macaulay, ed., *The Complete Works of John Gower*, 4 vols. (Oxford: Oxford University Press, 1899–1902).

5. Gower, *Confessio*, VIII.2941*–57*. In quotations from the *Confessio*, I follow Macaulay's practice of indicating with an asterisk lines not found in his base manuscript, Bodleian Library MS Fairfax 3. Translations of the *Mirour* and *Vox* are based on *The Mirour de l'omme (The Mirror of Mankind)*, trans. William Burton Wilson and revised by Nancy Wilson Van Baak (East Lansing, MI: Colleagues, 1992) and *The Major Latin Works of John Gower*, trans. Eric W. Stockton (Seattle, WA: University of Washington Press, 1962). In both cases, occasionally I modify the translation without further notice.

6. Gower, *Confessio*, VIII.2945*–7*.

7. Wim Lindeboom, *Venus' Owne Clerk: Chaucer's Debt to the* Confessio amantis (Amsterdam: Rodopi, 2007), 51. See also John H. Fisher, *John Gower: Moral Philosopher and Friend of Chaucer* (New York: New York University Press, 1964), 207, 208, 215.

8. See respectively Ardis Butterfield, '*Confessio amantis* and the French Tradition', in *A Companion to Gower*, ed. Siân Echard (Cambridge: D. S. Brewer, 2004), 165–80; and both Alastair Minnis, *Medieval Theory of Authorship: Scholastic Literary Attitudes in the Later Middle Ages*, 2nd ed. (Philadelphia, PA: University of Pennsylvannia Press, 1988), 160–210, and Derek Pearsall, 'Gower's Latin in the *Confessio amantis*', in *Latin and Vernacular: Studies in Late-Medieval Texts and Manuscripts*, ed. A. J. Minnis (D.S. Brewer: Cambridge, 1989), 13–25.

9. For the most part, scholars have accepted the internal dating of several manuscripts 'in anno quartodecimo Regis Ricardi', i.e. 1390, as a reliable indicator of when the first version of the poem was completed; see R. F. Yeager, 'Gower's Lancastrian Affinity: The Iberian Connection', *Viator* 35 (2004), 483–515 at 496 ff. and Fisher, *John Gower*, 116–27.

10. For discussion of how Chaucer positions his English writing as 'subsidiary and belated' to the European tradition, see especially Simpson, 'Chaucer as a European Writer'. Similar effects are found also in Gower's poetry; see T. Matthew N. McCabe, *Gower's Vulgar Tongue: Ovid, Lay Religion, and English Poetry in the* Confessio amantis (Cambridge: D. S. Brewer, 2011).

11. Derek Pearsall, 'The Manuscripts and Illustrations of Gower's Works', in Echard, *Companion to Gower* (Cambridge: D.S. Brewer, 2004), 73–97, at 80.

12. Pearsall, 'Gower's Latin', 24.

13. See Giovanni Boccaccio, *Il Filocolo*, 2.376–8.

14. On the revolutionary character of Italian *Trecento* ideas of authorship, see Alison Cornish, *Vernacular Translation in Dante's Italy: Illiterate Literature* (Cambridge: Cambridge University Press, 2011), 10, 11. On the significance of such ideas for late fourteenth-century English ideas of authorship, see Jocelyn Wogan-Browne et al., *The Idea of the Vernacular: An Anthology of Middle English Literary Theory, 1280–1520* (University Park, PA: Penn State University Press, 1999), 12.

15. Macaulay, *Complete Works*, 3:478; trans. Andrew Galloway in John Gower, *Confessio amantis*, ed. Russell A. Peck (Kalamazoo, MI: Medieval Institute, 2000–2005), 1:277 (slightly modified).

16. Gower, 'Quam cinxere freta', 3:479.

17. Macaulay, *Complete Works*, 3:479; trans. Galloway, *Confessio*, 278 (slightly modified).

18. Macaulay, *Complete Works*, 3:479. Text of Bodleian Library MS 3883 (Fairfax 3), quoted from Macaulay, *Complete Works*, 3:479.

19. See for example Pearsall, 'Gower's Latin', 24–5.

20. R. F. Yeager, 'John Gower's French and his Readers', in *Language and Culture in Medieval Britain: The French of England c.1100–c.1500*, eds. Jocelyn Wogan-Browne et al. (York: York Medieval Press, 2009), 135–45, at 135. See R. F. Yeager, ed. and trans., *John Gower: The Minor Latin Works with In Praise of Peace* (Kalamazoo, MI: Medieval Institute, 2005), 83–6, at 83; henceforward, all citations are taken from this edition and translation, though with occasional alterations of the translation. The *Vox clamantis* manuscripts in question are Glasgow, Hunterian MS T.2.17, British Library, MSS Cotton Tiberius A.iv and Harley 6291, and Oxford, All Souls MS 98, but not Huntington Library, MS HM 150.

21. For an illustration and discussion of Gower's tomb, see John Hines *et al.*, 'Iohannes Gower, Armiger, Poeta: Records and Memorials of his Life and Death', in Echard, *Companion to Gower*, 23–41, at 36–41.

22. Gower, 'Eneidos bucolics', 1–2.

23. Ibid., 7–8.

24. Ibid., 2.

25. Ibid., 9–10.

26. Ibid., 6.

27. Ibid., 13–16.

28. Ibid., 11–12.

29. For discussion of this term and the broadening of 'theologies' it implies, see especially Nicholas Watson, 'Cultural Changes', *English Language Notes* 44 (2006), 127–37, at 132. I am not equating 'vernacular' with 'English'. For Latin as a medieval vernacular, see Alastair Minnis, *Translations of Authority in Medieval English Literature: Valuing the Vernacular* (Cambridge: Cambridge University Press, 2009), 11.

30. Siân Echard, 'Gower's "bokes of Latin": Language, Politics, and Poetry', *Studies in the Age of Chaucer* 25 (2003), 123–56, at 154; See R. F. Yeager, *John Gower's Poetic: The Search for a New Arion* (Cambridge: D. S. Brewer, 1990), 66; Russell Peck, *Kingship and Common Profit in Gower's* Confessio amantis (Carbondale, IL: Southern Illinois University Press, 1978), 4, 63.

31. Gower, *Confessio*, prol., 10–11; see I, ii, 5–8.

32. See Gower, *Vox*, I, prol., 1–2, 31–2; II, prol., 1–2.

33. For assessments of the unity of Gower's literary careers, see, in addition to the references in the previous note, also Fisher, *John Gower*, 135–6.

34. Anne Middleton, 'The Idea of Public Poetry in the Reign of Richard II', *Speculum* 53 (1978), 94–114, at 98–102); examples are discussed below.

35. For more recent appraisals of this phenomenon, see Emily Steiner, *Documentary Culture and the Making of Medieval English Literature* (Cambridge: Cambridge University Press), 143–90; and Claire Sponsler, 'Lydgate and London's Public Culture', in *Lydgate Matters: Poetry and Material Culture in the Fifteenth Century*, eds. Lisa H. Cooper and Andrea Denny-Brown (New York: Palgrave Macmillan, 2008), 13–33, at 14–15, 22–3.

36. Anne Middleton, 'William Langland's "Kynde Name": Authorial Signature and Social Identity in Late Fourteenth-Century England', in *Literary Practice and Social Change in Britain,* ed. Lee Patterson (Berkeley, CA: University of California Press, 1990), 15–82, at 17.

37. See Gower, *Vox* I, prol., 19–30.

38. Gower, *Confessio,* prol., 22–3, 24*.

39. Ibid., 24.

40. The thirty-one manuscripts classified by Macaulay as 'first recension', the largest group, as well as some of the 'second recension' manuscripts, contain the Ricardian dedication. See Macaulay, *Complete Works,* 2:cxxviii; See Pearsall, 'Manuscripts and Illustrations', 74–5.

41. Gower, 'Explicit iste liber', 5–6.

42. See Emma Lipton, *Affections of the Mind: The Politics of Sacramental Marriage in Late Medieval English Literature* (Notre Dame, IN: University of Notre Dame Press, 2007), 8–12.

43. Winthrop Wetherbee, 'John Gower', *The Cambridge History of Medieval English Literature,* ed. David Wallace (Cambridge: Cambridge University Press, 1999), 593.

44. Gower, *Mirour de l'omme,* 1–3.

45. Gower, *Cinkante balades,* LI.25.

46. For speculation about the poem's intended recipient, see Cathy Hume, 'Why did Gower Write the *Traitié?',* in *John Gower: Trilingual Poet: Language, Translation and Tradition,* ed. Elisabeth Dutton (Cambridge: D. S. Brewer, 2010), 263–75.

47. See Gower, *Traitié,* XVIII.22–3.

48. For instance, Gower, *Mirour* 21,776–77; Gower, *Vox,* III.11–12; VI.15–16; VII.1467–70; 'O Deus Immense', 61–4; Gower, *Confessio,* prol., 119–24. For a recent discussion of this theme with relevance to the question of literary authorship, see Lynn Arner, *Chaucer, Gower, and the Vernacular Rising: Poetry and the Problem of the Populace after 1381* (University Park, PA: University of Pennsylvania Press, 2012).

49. For discussion of the *vox populi* trope in the *Vox clamantis,* see Maria Wickert, *Studies in John Gower,* trans. Robert J. Meindl (Washington: University Press of America, 1981), 75–83; and Steven Justice, *Writing and Rebellion: England in 1381* (Berkeley, CA: University of California Press, 1994), 209–13.

50. Gower, *Vox,* III, prol., 11–14; VII.1468–72. See Fisher, *John Gower,* 102–9.

51. David Aers, '*Vox populi* and the Literature of 1381', in Wallace, *Cambridge History of Medieval English Literature,* 441–2. See also Steven Justice, *Writing and Rebellion: England in 1381,* (Berkeley, CA: University of California Press, 1994), 211.

52. Justice, *Writing and* Rebellion, 105. See Mishtooni Bose, 'Writing, Heresy, and the Anticlerical Muse', in *The Oxford Handbook of Medieval Literature in English,* eds. Elaine Treharne and Greg Walker (Oxford: Oxford University Press, 2010), 291–2.

53. Gower, *Confessio,* prol., 119–24; 'O Deus Immense', 61.

54. Gower, *Vox,* VI, prol., 15–18.

55. Gower, *Mirour,* 18,445–56, 19,057–68, 21,776–7.

56. Gower, *Vox,* III. prol., 11–14; III.1267–70; IV.19–20.

57. Sheila Lindenbaum, 'London Texts and Literate Practice', ed. Wallace, 292.

58. On the characterization of the classical public sphere, see Craig Calhoun, 'Introduction: Habermas and the Public Sphere', in *Habermas and the Public Sphere* (Cambridge: MIT Press, 1992), 1. The alleged Ricardian sphere is discussed below.

59. Gower, *Vox,* III.1267–70.

60. Gower, *Vox,* III.1271, 1265–6 (at 1271).

61. Gower, *Vox*, III.1305–6, 2139–42.

62. Gower, *Mirour*, 21,763–8.

63. See Hines et al., 'Iohannes Gower, Armiger, Poeta', in Echard, *Companion to Gower*, 23–41 (at 25); and Conrad Van Dijk, *John Gower and the Limits of the Law* (Cambridge: D. S. Brewer, 2013), 3–7.

64. Gower, *Mirour*, 21,769–74.

65. Gower, *Mirour*, 21,775–80.

66. For discussion and a reproduction of the illustration from London, BL MS Cotton Tiberius A.iv, see Pearsall, 'Manuscripts and Illustrations', 84–85. In addition to those manuscripts cited by Pearsall, Macaulay suggests that Oxford, All Souls, MS 98 likely had the illustration on a leaf now missing; see idemCE: Please replace this abbreviation with a consistent short title., *Works*, 4: lx–lxi.

67. Yeager, *John Gower: The Minor Latin Works*.

68. See, for example, Gower, *Vox*, VI.405–16, 617–28.

69. See variously Joyce Coleman, *Public Reading and the Reading Public in Late Medieval England and France* (Cambridge: Cambridge University Press, 1996), 93–7, 133–4; C. David Benson, *Public Piers Plowman: Modern Scholarship and Late Medieval English Culture* (University Park, PA: Penn State University Press, 2004), xvi, xvii, 115, 158, 216; and Maura Nolan, *John Lydgate and the Making of Public Culture* (Cambridge: Cambridge University Press, 2005), 5–6, 15–17. David Lawton first introduced the term to Middle English studies in a discussion of the following century in 'Dullness and the Fifteenth Century', *English Literary History* 54 (1987), 761–99, at 791–4.

70. Gower, *Vox*, II.349–630.

71. Gower, *Mirour*, 26,605–29,945.

72. See especially Middleton, 'Idea of Public Poetry', 100, 105; Simpson, *Sciences and the Self*, e.g. 196n; Larry Scanlon, *Narrative, Power, and Authority: The Medieval Exemplum and the Chaucerian Tradition* (Cambridge: Cambridge University Press, 1994), 245–97.

73. See Gower, *Confessio*, prol., 349; V.1807–12.

74. See especially Echard, 'Gower's "Bokes of Latin"', 125. For the *Vox* in Anglo-Latin context, see David R. Carlson, 'The Invention of the Anglo-Latin Public Poetry (circa 1367–1402) and its Prosody, Especially in John Gower', *Mittellateinisches Jahrbuch* 39 (2004), 389–406.

75. See Gower, *In Praise of Peace*, 337–57; Gower, *Confessio*, II.3187–497.

76. See George Economou, 'The Character Genius in Alan de Lille, Jean de Meun, and John Gower', *Chaucer Review* 4 (1970), 203–10. For an account that emphasizes the darker tones of Gower's genius, see Hugh White, *Nature, Sex, and Goodness in a Medieval Literary Tradition* (Oxford: Oxford University Press, 2000), 174–219.

77. See further McCabe, *Gower's Vulgar Tongue*.

78. See Nicholas Watson, 'Conceptions of the Word: The Mother Tongue and the Incarnation of God', *New Medieval Literatures* 1 (1997), 85–124.

79. See Derek Pearsall, 'The Gower Tradition', in *Gower's* Confessio Amantis: *Responses and Reassessments*, ed. A. J. Minnis (Cambridge: D. S. Brewer, 1983), 179–97, at 184–85.

80. Considerable evidence for the influence of Gower's earnest counsellor pose and public orientation on Hoccleve and Lydgate, though less of the evidence pertaining to the religiosity of the texts in question, is discussed by Diane Watt, 'John Gower', in *Cambridge Companion to Middle English Literature*, ed. Larry Scanlon (Cambridge: Cambridge University Press, 2009), 153–64, 159–63.

BIBLIOGRAPHY

Amer, Lynn, *Chaucer, Gower, and the Vernacular Rising: Poetry and the Problem of the Populace after 1381* (University Park, PA: University of Pennsylvania Press, 2012).

Carlson, David, *John Gower, Poetry and Propaganda in Fourteenth-Century England* (Cambridge: D. S. Brewer, 2012).

Echard, Siân, ed., *A Companion to Gower* (Cambridge: D. S. Brewer, 2004).

Fisher, John, *John Gower: Moral Philosopher and Friend of Chaucer* (New York: New York University Press, 1964).

Middleton, Anne, 'The Idea of Public Poetry in the Reign of Richard II', *Speculum* 53 (1978), 94–114.

Minnis, A. J., ed., *Gower's* Confessio amantis: *Responses and Reassessments* (Cambridge: D. S. Brewer, 1983).

Nicholson, Peter, *Love and Ethics in Gower's* Confessio amantis (Ann Arbor, MI: University of Michigan Press, 2005).

Saez-Hidalgo, Ana, Brian Gastle, and R. F. Yeager, *The Routledge Research Companion to John Gower* (New York: Routledge, 2017).

Yeager, R. F., ed., *Chaucer and Gower: Difference, Mutuality, and Exchange* (Victoria: University of Victoria Press, 1991).

CHAPTER 31

....

LYDGATE'S CHAUCER

....

ANTHONY BALE

IT is not an overstatement to say that much of what we think about Chaucer, and indeed much of what we know about Chaucer, is mediated by the fifteenth-century generation which received and remade Chaucer's poetry in the decades after his death. The elementary question of Chaucer's physical appearance starts not with Chaucer but with his fifteenth-century literary heirs, Thomas Hoccleve (c.1368–1426) and John Lydgate (c.1370–1451), for it is in manuscripts of *their* works that Chaucer's portrait frequently appears: as character in, cause of, and inspiration for their works. The fifteenth-century panel portrait of Chaucer against a black background in London's National Portrait Gallery looks like a stand-alone portrait of a distinguished gentleman, apparently speaking or lecturing, with just an armorial badge for recognition; but, in fact, this portrait, like most of the fifteenth-century representations of the poet, derives from an illustration in a manuscript of Hoccleve's *De regimine principum*.[1] Another frequently reproduced image of Chaucer (which, for many years, was the cover illustration of the ubiquitous *Riverside Chaucer* paperback) shows 'Chaucer' the poet-pilgrim leading a band of pilgrims. Many readers would be forgiven for believing that this image comes from a manuscript of Chaucer's *Canterbury Tales*; however, it is a picture of Chaucer from a manuscript of a fifteenth-century poem, and continuation of *The Canterbury Tales*, *The Siege of Thebes* by the prolific English poet and monk John Lydgate. Lydgate's *Siege of Thebes* is one of several fifteenth-century continuations to *The Canterbury Tales*, such as *The Pilgrim's Tale*, *The Plowman's Tale* and the prologue to *The Tale of Beryn*.[2] Lydgate was instrumental in establishing Chaucer as the father-figure of English poetry, in founding an English poetic idiom based on Chaucer's works, in integrating Chaucerian language and narratives into religious and didactic poetry, and more generally establishing an English culture of laureateship and poetic patronage in which Chaucerian vernacular poetry was amongst the most highly prized forms of composition.

In this chapter I will neither survey Lydgate's debts to Chaucer nor give a full account of Lydgate's career. Instead, I will explore some of the ways in which Lydgate received and (re)constructed Chaucer's poetry, taking as my focus the richly ambivalent relationship between Lydgate and his 'master' Chaucer. My chapter alights on three specific kinds of relationship between Lydgate and Chaucer: first, the texture of Lydgate's allusions to Chaucer's poetry, in a 'minor' dramatic poem, *The Mumming at Bishopswood*. Second, I explore the relationship between, and the fault-lines of, Chaucerian and Lydgatean 'poetic' imaginations in Lydgate's *Siege of Thebes*. Finally, I explore the relationship of patronage between Lydgate and the Chaucer family: Chaucer's son Thomas and granddaughter Alice. The emphasis throughout this chapter is on the specifics, the syntactic warp and weft, of Chaucerian emulation: rather than seeing Lydgate simply in a servile role, and his poetry a corrupt copy of Chaucer's, this chapter takes as its starting point that formal emulation does not equate to interpretative reproduction. In other words, Lydgate's use of Chaucer finds new meanings for Chaucer's poetry.

CHAUCER AS *AUCTOR*: THE CONTOURS OF LYDGATEAN HOMAGE

Critics have often judged Lydgate's mode of Chaucerian emulation rather harshly, discerning in Lydgate's poetry a brash, pedantic mode of prolix imitation and aureate plagiarism: in the words of Derek Pearsall, one of the most influential critics of Lydgate, 'like the scratching of an old gramophone record—and it is difficult even to tell when the needle has stuck'.[3] However, sixteenth-century readers of Chaucer and Lydgate were often content to elide the two poets. For example, William Thynne's 1532 Chaucer incorporated 'non-Chaucerian' elements into a text with Chaucer's name on it;[4] likewise John Stow's 1561 edition of Chaucer's works presented Lydgate's *Siege of Thebes* as a Canterbury tale, as did later sixteenth-century editions of Chaucer.[5] The attribution to Chaucer of Lydgate's poem might be read as an effacement of Lydgate's historical moment.[6] Alternatively, this elision could reveal the reception of Lydgate as an eloquently-Chaucerian poet: part of the Chaucer canon, not an unsightly ganglion at its edge.[7] For, as John Bowers has lucidly described, when we read 'Chaucer's' *Canterbury Tales* today we are reading a 'fabrication', which unites texts around the principle of Chaucer-the-author according to our own concerns of Chaucerian genius, and not the more open concerns such as rearrangement, miscellaneity and continuation which animated fifteenth-century readers.[8]

John Lydgate was born in Suffolk, in the village of Lidgate, around 1370, and was educated at Oxford, probably at the Benedictines' Gloucester College;[9] from an early age he came under the ambit of, and eventually into the membership of, the wealthy, influential and highly literate Benedictine monastery of St Edmund at Bury St Edmunds (Suffolk). Later, he seems to have spent some time outside religious institutions, travelling to Paris around 1426 and was, between 1423 and 1432, prior of Hatfield Broad Oak (Essex). Superficially at least, Lydgate's background was quite different from Chaucer's: provincial rather than metropolitan; resolutely monastic rather than secular; educated at the university and suffused with a pious Latinity rather than the new French and Italian literatures which had such an influence on Chaucer.

As Douglas Gray notes, Lydgate never claims to have met Chaucer;[10] the scant biographical information available suggests that, during the late 1380s and 1390s (the period both of Lydgate's young adulthood and of Chaucer's intense productivity as a mature poet), Lydgate focused on ecclesiastical, rather than poetic, development (becoming deacon in 1393 and priest in 1397).[11] Yet within about twenty years of Chaucer's death, Lydgate had become celebrated for a distinctive poetic idiom in which Chaucer was evoked in terms previously applied to classical or Christian *auctores*. Throughout his writing Lydgate identifies Chaucer as an authorial entity in relation to English writing: as Lydgate's 'father',[12] as 'founder' of English/British letters, as 'inventor' of remarkable figures ('Floure of Poetes'), and as Lydgate's *causa materialis*—the material out of which Lydgatean poetry is crafted—through emulation and citation of Chaucer's 'making'. Lydgate repeatedly refers to Chaucer as 'my maister Chaucer', putting himself in a position of crafting materials handed down by a master to whom he is apprenticed.[13]

The Mumming at Bishopswood provides a good example of Lydgate's reworking of Chaucerian material. This mumming is one of several innovative dramatic poems composed by Lydgate and has been dated to the late 1420s; it was performed at Bishopswood, part of the medieval park of the Bishop of London on the hilly ridge north of London.[14] It was performed for members of London's government, who would have been able to see the cities of London and Westminster and the town of Southwark beneath them. This May Day playlet, described in a fifteenth-century rubric as an 'honurable dyner', comprised a dumb show and ceremonial meal in which allegorical figures of Flora, Veer (Spring) and May were introduced by a herald, and it is replete with allusions to Chaucer's *Canterbury Tales*. An examination of the first three stanzas of the prologue alone provides a clear example of Lydgate not mining Chaucer's poetry, but reshaping it.

> Mighty Flourra, goddes of fresshe floures,
>   Whiche clothed hast the soyle in lousty grene,
> Made buddes springe with hir swote showres
>   By influence of the sonne so sheene;
>   To do plesaunce of entent ful clene
> Unto th'estates wheoche that nowe sitte here,
> Hathe Veere doune sent hir owen doughter dere,
> Making the vertue that dured in the roote,
>   Called of clerkes the vertue vegytable,
> For to trascende, moste holsome and moste swoote,
>   Into the crope, this saysoun so greable.
>   The bawmy lykour is so comendable
> That it rejoythe with the fresshe moysture
> Man, beeste, and foole, and every creature
> Whiche hathe repressed, swaged, and bore doune
>   The grevous constreinte of þe frostes hoore;
> And caused foolis, for joye of this saysoune,
>   To cheese theire makes thane by natures loore,
>   With al gladnesse theire courage to restore,
> Sitting on bowes fresshly nowe to synge
> Veere for to salue at hir home comynge.[15]

Lydgate's 'source' here is, clearly, the famous opening-lines of the General Prologue to *The Canterbury Tales*: Chaucer's 'shoures soote' (I.1) are Lydgate's 'swote showres'; Chaucer's 'yonge sonne' (7) is Lydgate's 'sonne so sheene'; Chaucer's 'droghte of March...perced to the roote' (2) and 'vertu engendred' (4) is Lydgate's 'vertue that dured in the roote'; Chaucer's 'tendre croppes' (7) become Lydgate's 'crope'; Chaucer's 'licour' (3) is Lydgate's 'bawmy lykour'; Chaucer's 'corages' of his 'smale foweles' (11, 9) become the 'courage' of Lydgate's 'foolis', and so on. This prologue also resonates with the description of Flora in Chaucer's *Book of the Duchess* (402–15), with its invocation of the 'floures' which grow after the 'colde morwes' of 'wynter', and the similar description of Flora's 'swoote breth' in *The Legend of Good Women* (F 171–82), the 'goddesse of the floury mede'. Likewise, the mating rituals of birds described by Chaucer in *The Parliament of Fowls* are echoed in the spring 'saysoune', in Lydgate's poem, in which birds 'cheese þeire makes...by natures loore'.[16] So, at the level of diction and rhetoric, Lydgate was clearly working closely with Chaucer's poetry, and felt that the description of spring in Chaucer's General Prologue provided a fitting set of terms through which to describe a London springtime of the late 1420s.[17]

However, Lydgate's lexical borrowings from Chaucer by no means represent a borrowing of meaning; imitation is not the same as repetition. In Chaucer's General Prologue the fecund optimism and assertions of 'felawshipe' of the first lines gives way first to *curiositas* (as people 'longen...to goon on pilgrimages,/And palmeres for to seken straunge strondes' (I.12–13)) and then to ironic and satiric accounts of each pilgrim's 'condicioun' and 'degree' (38, 40) and then to the competitive, hierarchical divisiveness of the tale-telling contest. Conversely, in the prologue to the *Mumming at Bishopswood*, spring heralds optimism and perfect rule, an assertion of prosperity and good natural and social order:

> Buddes shal blosme of trouthe and unytee,
>   Pleinly for to exyle duplicytee,
> Lordes to regne in theire noble puissance,
> The people obeye with feythful obeyssaunce.[18]

This is not simply a replacement of cynical Chaucer by naive Lydgate; rather, it is a wholesale rewriting of Chaucerian estates' satire. Lydgate makes this clear as the prologue goes on to say that, under the ideal government, 'Of alle estates there shal beo oone ymage', in an accommodating state of orderly hierarchy, which, as Clare Sponsler observes, seeks to embrace the lowliest as part of the 'truwe comunes':[19]

> Thus as þe people, of prudent pollycye,
>   Pryncis of the right shal governe,
> The Chirche preye, the juges justefye,
>   And knighthode manly and prudently discerne,
>   Til light of trouthe so clerely the lanterne:
> That rightwysnesse thorughe this regyoune
> Represse the derknesse of al extorcyoune.[20]

As he does throughout his poetry, Lydgate finds a 'real world', regiminal application for Chaucerian rhetoric, a public sphere mediated through Chaucer's poetry. But, in constructing this, Chaucerian matter shifts from the estates satire of *The Canterbury Tales* to a bold assertion of estates harmony. In fact, the *Mumming at Bishopswood* becomes a piece of princely counsel, an assertion of the benefits of right rule along with a warning of the dangers of bad rule, echoing other Lydgatean texts such as *The Fall of Princes* and *The Serpent of Division*, as the monkish counselor Lydgate adapts—and then transforms—the Chaucerian precedent to his own moment. In his writing, Lydgate returns repeatedly to ideas and ideals of 'common profit', but this is no naïve idealization: the 'derknesse' of 'extorcyoune' is everywhere, Lydgate's poetry anxiously beseeching spiritual and secular authorities to unite against it.

CHAUCERIAN OCCASION AND NON-EVENT: LYDGATE'S *SIEGE OF THEBES*

Two of the most useful recent major studies of Lydgate, by Maura Nolan and Robert Meyer-Lee, have focussed attention on the public and political relationships negotiated through the patronage networks of Lydgate's poetry.[21] One of the most arresting features of Lydgate's poetry is its extravagant apostrophes to patrons, from his Henry V (in the *Troy Book*) to his abbot at Bury, William Curteys (in the *Lives of Ss Edmund & Fremund*). Much painstaking work has been done to show how varied and dynamic the patronage contexts of Lydgate's poetry were. However, it is easy to forget that not all Lydgate's poetry has a discernible patronage context or occasion.

Critics have long described one of Lydgate's earlier poems, *The Siege of Thebes*, as such a work. *The Siege of Thebes* occupies a space in Lydgate's canon between Henry Noble McCracken's definitions of 'minor' poetry—namely shorter works, mostly read by non-royal or indeterminate audiences—and the larger-scale 'laureate' texts, especially the *Troy Book* (to which, to some extent, *The Siege of Thebes* can be seen as a counterpart, continuation or addendum). The poem, comprising over 4700 lines, is best known for its short (176-line) prologue in which Lydgate imagines himself as part of Chaucer's pilgrimage band from *The Canterbury Tales*. The remainder of the poem, an account of three generations of disastrous Theban rulers, is taken from a French source with cross-references to Boccaccio's *De casibus virorum illustrium* and framed by a closing-reference to Chaucer's Knight's Tale. The *Siege* was almost certainly written in the early 1420s, as suggested by a complicated internal reference to its own date, and certainly before the death of Henry V in 1422, as shown by the Henrician encomium in the closing lines (discussed further below).

It has become accepted wisdom that *The Siege of Thebes* has no patron.[22] Axel Erdmann and Eilert Ekwall, early editors of the *Siege*, note, 'the *Siege of Thebes* was not, like the *Troy Book* and the *Fall of Princes*, made to order, for the pleasure of some noble patron.'[23] Joyce Coleman writes that '[i]n the *Siege* we see Lydgate writing to his own sense of how literature functions'.[24] The poem's recent editor, John Bowers, argues that, in lacking a noble patron, the *Siege* is a 'poet's poem'.[25] These critics are correct: neither is there a precise historical occasion pertaining to the poem nor does the poem have clear patrons behind it.[26]

Does the lack of a 'noble patron'—or, at least, a clearly discernible or identifiable one—necessarily mean that Lydgate was somehow liberated and thereby better able to set his own literary agenda? On the contrary: in short, Lydgate's poems 'imagine' or make space for an occasion and a patron, what Seth Lerer has called an 'allegory of commission', whether they actually had a patron or not.[27] The imaginative 'causes' and fictive occasions voiced in *The Siege of Thebes* are particularly useful for discerning the ways Lydgate uses Chaucer's poetry as fictive occasion. For, even without a precise patron-as-cause, the *Siege* takes as its stimulus an imaginative conceit of 'Chaucer-as-occasion' (and implicitly therefore Chaucer as a kind of patron).[28] At the same time Lydgate directs this poem away from the 'patron-plus-poet' relationship seen elsewhere, finding instead an imaginary 'cause' which is part of a sustained and sophisticated poetics of authority, imagination and Chaucerian reproduction.[29] Daniel Kline has written of *The Siege of Thebes* that it 'struggles' with an 'Oedipal' relationship to Chaucer's poetry, 'aggressively' attempting to establish its own subjective and poetic arena; Kline states that '[t]hrough the mechanism of the *Siege*, Chaucer "writes" Lydgate into existence, simultaneously positioning Lydgate as loyal son and Chaucer as regal founder'.[30] Kline identifies a 'circuit of repression and deference' and 'tactical "misreading"' in which Lydgate struggles to 'overthrow Chaucer's paternal presence'.[31] Kline's suppositions about Lydgate's psychology provide an engaging way of reading Lydgate's knotted relationship with Chaucer, but one might identify more *literary*, rather than psychological, traces in the *Siege* of a characteristically Lydgatean entanglement with authority—both literary and political—which never fully or convincingly resolves itself.

In *The Siege of Thebes* Lydgate plays with a range of conceits of occasion. It is a poem profoundly concerned with the causes of poetry, imaginary poetic occasion and the modes of poetic utterance, in particular the possibility of writing poetry in the shadow of Chaucer. The poem's prologue commences with an ostentatious proclamation of its own temporal occasion, marking its moment through astrological references to a specific date: 27–28 April in the year 1421:[32]

> Whan brighte Phebus passed was the Ram
> Myd of Aprille and into Bole cam,
> And Satourn old with his frosty face
> In Virgyne taken had his place,
> Malencolik and slowgh of mocioun,
> And was also in th'oposicioun
> Of Lucina the mone moyst and pale,
> That many shour fro hevene made avale;
> Whan Aurora was in the morowe red,
> And Jubiter in the Crabbes hed...[33]

The precision, and prolixity, with which Lydgate sets up the date of his composition might lead us, using the historicist or materialist methodologies prevalent in Lydgate criticism, to seek an equally precise historical stimulus for the poem, some actual event in April 1421 which makes a 'real' sense of Lydgate's Theban story. Attempts to find such a date, however, emphatically draw a blank.[34] Henry V probably visited Bury, during April, on a fund-raising trip from Lincoln to London via the shrine of Our Lady of Walsingham in Norfolk.[35] This is not, however, a convincing or precise 'occasion', particularly given the poem's valorisation of peace and corresponding critique of martial royal judgement. Likewise, if we look closely for a specific temporal occasion the poem may appear to be deeply inappropriate: for around this time Henry's brother, the Duke of Clarence, was buried at Canterbury Cathedral (where his alabaster effigy can still be seen), and the levity with which Lydgate treats the return journey from Canterbury suggests that such events were not foremost in his mind!

Alternatively, the April dating might simply refer to a point at which Lydgate was writing (or commenced or completed) the poem, or it connects Lydgate's work with Chaucer's *Canterbury Tales,* which takes place in April. Rather than fulfilling a propagandistic role, celebrating some specific Lancastrian moment, the opening of *The Siege* blurs and merges Lydgate's Lancastrian present with the Ricardian past of Chaucer's General Prologue. The General Prologue is set around 17 April and so *The Siege* pretends, or half-pretends, to continue Chaucer's work, an imaginary ten days later.[36] The poem 'half-pretends' because the anachronistic, or diachronic, muddle of Lydgate's prologue ruptures at the outset the conceit of the poem as a seamless continuation of Chaucer's text. 'Lydgate', aged 'nygh fyfty yere of age'[37] and setting his poem in the early 1420s, happens upon Chaucer's fourteenth-century Canterbury pilgrims on their return journey from Canterbury. Axel Erdmann approached Lydgate's conceit with a mixture of humour, earnestness and perplexity:

> The palpable anachronism involved in this idea did not deter [Lydgate], and it would not, I suppose, much strike the general reader, nor does it, indeed, essentially diminish the quaint interest of his conceit. But it is obvious that Lydgate, who about thirty at the time of Chaucer's death, could not at 'ny3 fyfty 3ere of age' have found still remaining at Canterbury the same company of pilgrims with which Chaucer had come there.[38]

Erdmann's co-editor, Eilert Ekwall points out Lydgate's 'confused and faulty remembrance'.[39] John Bowers suggests that '...the *Prologue* presents itself as a network of verbal borrowings rather than a coherent fiction—as an artefact made from a Chaucerian artefact, not from real life'.[40] As Bowers argues, we will inevitably become frustrated should we try to justify poetry to 'real life'; *The Siege* is a fiction, and part of its imaginative nature is that it resists the neat containment of time and occasion. Indeed, towards the end of the poem a similar device occurs: at Deptford, on the way out from Southwark 'Lydgate' of the Knight's Tale says 'if ye remembre ye han herde it to forn',[41] pretending that the oral recital of the story is part of the actuality of the pilgrimage. A few lines later, however, the source as 'text' returns: 'The *Knyghtys Tale* reherseth every del/Fro poynt to poynt, yif ye looke wel...',[42] putting the text back into another category, of exemplary reading to be looked up 'wel', existing as something separate from the pilgrimage fiction. Notably, Chaucer's flawed character of the Monk, in particular the Monk's interaction with the Host, is a template for Lydgate's own 'Lydgate' persona. 'Lydgate' is asked if his name is 'Daun Pers ,/Daun Domynyk, Dan Godfrey, or Clement',[43] echoing Chaucer's Host's question to the Monk if he is called 'John', 'Thomas', or 'Albon' (VII.1929–30). The Host tells 'Lydgate' that he looks 'so pale al devoyde of blood',[44] like Chaucer's Monk to whom Harry Bailley says 'thou hast a ful fair skyn' (1932). The Host's command to 'Lydgate'—'What? Look up, monk! For by kokkis blood,/Thow shalt be mery...'[45]— likewise seems to be based on Chaucer's Host's (more courteous, or more teasing) injunction: ' "My lord, the Monk", quod he, "be myrie of cheere" ...' (1924).[46] As Scott-Morgan Straker has observed, many of these parallels with Chaucer's Monk are ironic inversions: the Monk's 'horse in greet estaat' becomes 'Lydgate's "palfrey slender", Chaucer's Monk wears luxurious clothing, 'the finest in the lond', whereas 'Lydgate' wears a 'thred-bar hood', and so on.[47] Straker convincingly argues that these references allow Lydgate to speak from a pious, monastic identity so he can resist the Host's demand for a merry tale or unholy 'jape' and thus, subtly, 'improves'—at least religiously—on Chaucer's text, and Chaucer's Monk, in what Straker calls 'an act of calculated self-authorization'.

There are other careful, if sardonic, references in diction to *The Canterbury Tales* in the Prologue to *The Siege of Thebes*: Lydgate's covenant-like 'newe lawe' reverberates with the Man of Law's 'newe lawe' (II.337); the Host's exhortation to 'Lydgate' to 'preche not of non holynesse!' echoes Chaucer's Host's injunction to the Clerk, 'precheth nat, as freres doon in Lente...' (IV.12); Lydgate's Host swears 'a twenty deuelway!' identical to Chaucer's Canon's Yeoman (VIII.782); the Host is addressed in both texts as 'gouernor' (I.813); Lydgate's empty purse, his 'voide male', reverses Chaucer's Host's unbuckled 'male' (I.3115).[48] Moreover, James Simpson has argued that Lydgate's main narrative of the destruction of Thebes 'enlists the energies of Chaucer's Theban narrative, the Knight's Tale, to shape a powerful, prudential admonition concerning the treacherousness of history'.[49] In this light, Lydgate was far from careless and slipshod in his allusions to Chaucer; such references rather suggest a sustained and subtle attempt to echo the tone, texture and details of Chaucer's poetry, with Lydgate writing with a intimate and profound knowledge of Chaucer's diction inflecting his poetry.

Lydgate draws the reader's attention both to the absence and fame of his source-poet; as Bowers says, this 'intrusion has the unsettling effect of reminding us that we are reading an account altered by the absence of its original pilgrim-narrator'.[50] Moreover, Lydgate famously conflates (rather than 'confuses') Chaucer's characters of the Summoner, the Pardoner (both as described in the General Prologue) and Simpkin from the Reeve's Tale; Lydgate writes,

> ...in her teermes rude,
> And ek also with his pylled nolle
> The Pardowner beerdlees al his chyn

> Glasy-eyed and face of cherubyn,
> Tellyng a tale to angre with the frere,
> As opynly, the storie kan yow lere...[51]

Bowers and Straker have traced these references, which take from Chaucer the Pardoner's boozy glassy-eyes and beardlessness (I.684–90), the cherubic Summoner's friar-baiting (I.624–7, III.1665) and the 'piled' hair of both Simpkin (I.3915) and the Summoner (I.630) to create what Straker calls 'an emblem of Chaucer's degenerate clerics'.[52]

Lydgate's description of the Pardoner is so detailed, so precisely muddled, that it creates incoherence in the Chaucerian exemplar. This is entirely commensurate with the more general interrogation of the nature of the poetic authority articulated by Lydgate in his prologue. As Joyce Coleman has observed, Lydgate here freely mixes *topoi* and conventions of speaking, reading and hearing literature, putting the text in an active relationship with its mediation and reception:[53] the 'Canterbury talys/Complet and told', Chaucer's Pardoner 'Tellyng a tale to angre with the frere,/As opynly the storie kan yow lere', the tales by Chaucer 'Echon ywrite/and put in remembraunce/By hym that was, yif I shal not feyne,/Floure of poetes throughout al Breteyne':[54] poetry is at once for telling, writing, remembering, learning, even for vexing friars. We are invited to 'Rede [Chaucer's] making' to find 'trouthe', that famously nebulous Chaucerian concept. Chaucer's is a poetry 'Which never shal appallen in ["Lydgate"s] mynde'.[55] Chaucer is praised as he

> To whom be gove pris, honure, and gloyré
> Of wel seyinge first in oure language,
> Chief registrer of this pilgrimage,
> Al that was tolde forgeting noght at al,
> Feyned talis nor thing historial,
> With many proverbe divers and unkouth,
> Be rehersaile of his sugrid mouth,
> Of eche thyng keping in substaunce
> The sentence hool withoute variance,
> Voyding the chaf sothly for to seyn...[56]

These are very rich and ambivalent lines indeed. Chaucer is at once the best rhetorician and the most accurate and complete 'registrer' of the Canterbury pilgrimage. A multiplicity of tidings appear, not unlike the babble of the *Parliament of Fowls* and the *House of Fame*, of 'making', memory, 'seyinge', 'forgeting', 'feyned talis', 'thing historial', 'proverbe', 'rehersaile', the 'sugrid mouth', 'sentence', 'trouthe'. Chaucer's poetry is praised, surely disingenuously, for containing neither 'Feyned talis nor thing historial': peculiar praise for a text known to Lydgate as 'Canterbury talys'[57] and cited within Lydgate's quasi-historical Theban poem of pagan antiquity. Moreover, Lydgate's praise of Chaucer's ability to avoid the 'chaf', itself echoing the closing injunctions of The Nun's Priest's Tale (VII.3443), is at odds with Lydgate's notion that Chaucer's poem contains absolutely everything, 'Al that was tolde forgeting noght at al'. Likewise, the very idea of *The Canterbury Tales* as *compilatio*, and with it the purpose of laureate vernacular poetry, oscillates in these lines between moral edification, skill in rhetoric, and a kind of mnemonic accuracy. As Straker comments, Lydgate's aim seems to have been both to extol Chaucer as foundation of English poetry, but also to probe the unstable nature of this foundation.[58] So entangled in the causes and uses of poetry does Lydgate's prologue become that, having set up lavish if ambiguous praise of Chaucer, the narrative defers the stimulus of poetry from cause to chance:

> And this whil that the pilgrymes leye
> At Canterbury wel logged on and all,
> I not in soth what I may it call –
> Hap or fortune in conclusioun –
> That me byfil to entren into toun.[59]

So having described a range of imaginative stimuli and invoked several kinds of occasion—of 27–28 April, of spring, of pilgrimage, of Chaucer and his poetry—Lydgate here retreats, ironically at the point at which he starts to describe his narratorial alter-ego 'Lydgate' in terms culled from Chaucer's Monk's sequence! In thus describing the approach to writing as 'hap or fortune' Lydgate claims to defer his own authorial status (as 'efficient' or executive cause of the text) to that of Chaucer, but does so only after he has questioned the foundations of both *The Canterbury Tales* and of vernacular poetry. Thus the prologue, an intertext of uncertain allusions, closes not with references to source, occasion or patron, but with an emphasis on the first-person 'Lydgate':

> whan I saugh it wolde be no bette,
> I obeyde unto his biddynge,
> So as the lawe me bonde in al thinge;
> And as I coude with a pale cheere,
> My tale I gan anon as ye shal here.[60]

The repeated 'I' reveals the turning of our attention to the poet, combined here with hesitation *topoi* (and, incidentally, a possible allusion in Lydgate's 'pale cheere' to the 'sory chere' (1.14) of Chaucer's narrator in *Troilus and Criseyde* or the 'face pale' 'with sorweful cheere' of Chaucer's Dorigen [V.1353]). Thus the prologue to *The Siege of Thebes* is an incoherent fiction, a fiction that pretends to a range of occasions whilst embracing none wholeheartedly, with an equally inchoate sense of its own formal status. The same is true of the rest of the poem.

Lydgate uses Chaucerian authorial interjections—'quod I', 'I shal yow platly lere', 'I rede'—throughout the poem.[61] This is no more or less complicated than it is in Chaucer's work, pointing, as in *The Canterbury Tales* and *Troilus*, to the rhetorically-constructed and sometimes partial nature of poetry. Lydgate's favoured techniques seem here to be drawn from Chaucer's *Troilus* and its playful attitude towards writerly experience and its limitations: Lydgate's poem abounds with phrases pointing out the narrative's lacunae, 'I can not seyn nor mor therof devise', 'For therupon, yif I shulde dwelle,/A long space it wolde occupie', '...I ha leyser non nor space/To reherce and put in rembraunce/Hooly the maner of her daliaunce...', 'This dirke dreme; this was hid and cloos'.[62] Such devices are conventional, but further compel an acknowledgement of the 'written-ness' or 'constructed-ness' of Lydgate's account and its partial relationship to its ostensible Chaucerian occasion.

More forcefully, Lydgate's poem moves through several implied audiences, each suggesting a different imagined context for the poem's iteration. The prologue and the first sequence of the poem proper (the *'prima pars'* dealing with King Amphion) bear out Bowers's description of the work as a 'poet's poem': not only is Chaucer praised fulsomely along with Boccaccio,[63] but versifying is seen to be a force, and *causa efficiens*, in itself: Amphion raises the Theban walls through 'his swete song' and 'werbles sharpe' of his harp, thanks to his excellence in the 'craft of rethorik'.[64] Amphion is described as 'Chief cause first of his fundacioun',[65] an Aristotelian (or Scholastic) description of efficient or executive cause.[66] Lydgate here imagines versifying without external patronage and with divine and civic occasion; it is a 'derke poysye' which, 'thorgh glade aspectes' and 'wordes swete', achieves a mysterious socio-political harmony: 'ther was noon/ Disobeysaunt with the kyng to goon'.[67] Concord is achieved here not just *through* the poet, but *in* the poet.

> And thus the wallis made of lym and stoon,
> Were reysed first be syngyng of this kyng,
> Lich as poetys feyne in her writyng,
> Passyng rich and royal of entaille.[68]

As several critics have noted, Amphion provides a powerful precedent—from a time long before Chaucer—for the efficacy of rhetoric.[69] However, Lydgate's diction is richly ambivalent: that which poets 'feyne' in their writing could refer to creating, composing, disguising, adulterating, or dissembling.[70]

The poem soon moves into another of its dominant modes, and one quite distant from the Chaucerian prototype, that of regiminal advice writing. The later parts of the poem appear to be addressed, albeit implicitly, to a prince, and the marginal gloss in the manuscript (London, British Library Arundel MS 119) which once belonged to the Count and Countess of Suffolk, picks up on this: 'Nota. What the goodlihede of a prince avaylleth to wynne the hertes of his puple'.[71] The poem's implied audiences continue to mutate: addressed to 'every man', 'prynce, lorde, or kyng', 'man and child':[72] implied audiences—one noble and princely, one domestic and infantile—which do not reflect the Chaucerian constitution of the band of Canterbury pilgrims—which features neither princes nor children. 'Lydgate' is, however, cast in his now-familiar role as advisor, the voice of wise monition. The implied audiences of *The Siege* change again, several times. At several points we, the audience, are addressed as readers or students: 'As Marcian ynamed de Capelle/In his book of weddyng can you telle';[73] 'As in story ye may rede her toforn'; 'As bookes olde wel reherce konne'; 'as bookes specifye'.[74] In each case it is suggested that we might look outside or around the text to continue our reading, to supplement Lydgate's account. Towards the close of the poem, as Lydgate increases the frequency of his allusions to the Knight's Tale, we are referred back to *The Canterbury Tales* if we wish to know what happened to Theseus: 'The *Knyghtys Tale* reherseth every del/fro poynt to point, yif ye looke wel...'.[75] Again, *The Canterbury Tales* is seen as external to and separate from Lydgate's text, even as Lydgate continues the conceit of 'telling' a Canterbury tale.

The Siege of Thebes poses difficult questions about the kinds of evidence—allusions implicit and explicit, audiences real, implied and imagined—that we consider in determining a poem's passage into the world. At the poem's close, Lydgate's references to the Knight's Tale merge with diction taken from the Treaty of Troyes of May 1420: the treaty's 'ut Concordia, Pax, & Tranquillitas inter praedicta Franciae & Angliae Regna perpetuo futuris temporibus observentur' appears to be echoed in Lydgate's 'Pees and quyet, concord and unyte'.[76] The parallel in diction is convincing, but smacks of a somewhat fleeting glance at contemporary events, rather than an occasion for the poem itself. Indeed, the poem's admonitory take on kingship, as well as its incestuous and tyrannical kings, sit uncomfortably with the royal concord expounded at its close. Emphatically, we cannot see Henry V as the poem's patron, even if we can pick out his shadow in the poem's closing lines. If we accept this allusion to the Treaty of Troyes we can, as historicist critics, locate the poem in place and time, but we are not necessarily, as literary critics of imaginative poetry, much the wiser about the poem's meanings or its tricks of authorial voice. As Alexandra Gillespie has commented, 'Lydgate...places no more trust in the author as a stabilizing force in fiction than his "master" Chaucer does, and he utilizes Chaucer's disruptive fictions accordingly'.[77] The *Siege* might, more productively, be seen as a key moment in Lydgate's passage into the ambivalent terrain of laureateship, both in its incipient attempts at styling Chaucer as the occasion of poetry and Lydgate's attempts to redefine and assume the Chaucerian garland.

LYDGATE AND THE CHAUCERIAN INHERITANCE

As well as negotiating his imagined position as Chaucer's literary heir, Lydgate engaged directly with Chaucer's actual heirs: Chaucer's son, Thomas (c.1367–1434), and granddaughter, Alice (c.1404–75). A brief discussion of Lydgate's poetic engagement with these figures is therefore necessary here, in as much as they were complicit with Lydgate in the poetic construction of Chaucer's literary memorialization.

Thomas Chaucer, politician, diplomat and administrator, was fêted in one or two poems by Lydgate. Again, there is little hard evidence that Lydgate knew Thomas Chaucer personally, although their shared proximity to Henry V (whom Lydgate had known when they were students at Oxford) would make this more than plausible.[78] The intimate tone of one of Lydgate's poems, the *Ballade on the Departing of Thomas Chaucer*, written to mark Thomas Chaucer's departure on an embassy to France, suggests Lydgate's involvement with the powerful and elegant coterie at Chaucer's house at Ewelme (Oxfordshire);[79] as well as being Chaucerian in subject-matter, the poem was clearly written to make careful use of Chaucerian diction. As Derek Pearsall has observed, the *Ballade of Thomas Chaucer* includes a prayer to Lucina and Neptune for calm seas, a prayer which mirrors that of Aurelius in the Franklin's Tale: Chaucer's Franklin's address to 'Lucina the sheene', who 'of the see is chief goddesse and queene' and Neptunus, the holder of 'deitee in the see' (V.1045–9) is mirrored closely in Lydgate's 'Lucyna, qwene and empyresse/Of waters alle' whilst Neptune is requested 'Hym [i.e. Thomas Chaucer] to fauour whane he is on þe see'.[80] So, on a superficial level, we can say that Geoffrey Chaucer's poetic imagining of a nobleman's sea-journey in the Franklin's Tale appealed to Lydgate as a way of styling Thomas Chaucer's embarking on a sea-journey 'in real life'.

The allusive homage in Lydgate's *Ballade to Thomas Chaucer* is more complex and multifaceted than this. The whole of Lydgate's poem is informed by Chaucer's Franklin, a character described by Geoffrey Chaucer as 'Epicurus owene sone' (I.336), 'to lyven in delit was evere his wone' (335) and, crucially, 'an housholdere, and that a greet, was he' ([339], echoed in the *Ballade to Thomas Chaucer*, invoking 'þ'agreable sonne/Of housholding').[81] Geoffrey Chaucer describes the Franklin as 'Seint Julian . . . in his contree' (340), the patron saint of hospitality, and likewise Thomas Chaucer's wife is advised by Lydgate to retain the following mnemonic to bring her husband home safely:

> Saynt Iulyan, oure ioye and al oure gloyre,
> Come hoome ageyne, lyche as we desyre,
> To suppowaylen al þe hole shyre.[82]

The praise of Thomas Chaucer *as* Franklin is, characteristically, ambiguous: the Franklin is a self-described 'burel man' (V.716), an unlettered yokel, who 'lerned nevere rethorik, certeyn' (718); nonetheless, this ignorant franklin goes on to invoke Parnassus and Tully and gives, of course, a brilliant rhetorical performance in his romance of Dorigen's Armorica. Likewise, to style Thomas Chaucer's wife as a type of Dorigen is a dubious exemplar, at least in terms of flattery. It would be easy to over-read Lydgate's Chaucerianism here: the point is, perhaps, lexical more than strictly thematic, although the Franklin's description of love and departure obviously suggested the tone of Lydgate's poem. Chaucer's poetry gave a form for the expression, in English, of concepts and fashions previously given in French, but Lydgate's *version* of Chaucer is charged with internal contradictions and ambivalent praise.

Meanwhile, Thomas Chaucer's only child, Alice, is known to have been an enthusiastic reader of Lydgate's poetry, and was probably the patron of at least two of his works, *The Interpretation and Virtues of the Mass* and, with her third husband William de la Pole, Earl of Suffolk (1396–1450), *The Miracle of St Edmund, 1441*. Carol Meale has also suggested Alice Chaucer as a possible patron of *The Siege of Thebes*, a manuscript of which (British Library MS Arundel 119) she owned, and Alice's first husband, Thomas

Montacute, earl of Salisbury (1388–1428), was the patron of Lydgate's translation of Guillaume de Deguileville's *Pelerinage de la Vie Humaine* (1426–7).[83]

The patronage of the *Virtues of the Mass* has been ascribed to Alice Chaucer on the basis of a manuscript inscription (in Oxford, St John's College MS 56), and her patronage is certainly plausible based on the kinds of literary culture in which gentlewomen of Alice Chaucer's kind were involved in the mid-fifteenth century.[84] The *Virtues of the Mass* is a sophisticated extended paraphrase of a gradual prayer and, as with the 'Lydgate' persona in *The Siege of Thebes*, sees Lydgate adopting and adapting Chaucerian diction within a devotional frame or, in the words of one recent critic, 'squeezing spiritual metaphor from an amazingly wide range of secular realities'.[85] The Chaucerian echoes in *The Virtues of the Mass* are too many to list, and appear at the level of echo rather than allusion. For example, the first stanza exhorts the reader to construct an image 'As in a myrrour presentyng in fygure/The morall menyng of that gostly armure',[86] which neatly reverses Troilus's idealization-cum-deification of Criseyde in Chaucer's *Troilus and Criseyde*:[87] 'Thus gan he make a mirour of his mynde,/In which he saugh al holly hire figure' (1.365–6). More generally, and characteristically of Lydgate, *The Virtues of the Mass* uses aureate diction—'deuocion', 'contemplacion', 'affecioun', 'restauracioun'—a high-register Latinate English, only made possible by Chaucer's lexical inventiveness, rendered innovatively by Lydgate in a devotional rather than romance medium.

More directly, we can discern the influence of Alice Chaucer behind Lydgate's writing of a miracle poem in late 1441, by which time Lydgate was an old man. This poem, which describes St Edmund's miraculous saving of a little boy who fell in the River Thames from London Bridge, was, it seems, a kind of 'thank-you present' from Lydgate to Alice, then countess of Suffolk, and her husband. But, again, the contemporary Lydgatean event was suffused with Chaucerian diction, this time from the Prioress's Prologue and Tale from *The Canterbury Tales*. At least eight times in the short miracle, Lydgate alludes to the Prioress's sequence, particularly at moments involving childhood imperilled and maternal woe: the subject-matter shared by Chaucer's and Lydgate's poems. A comparison of the first lines shows how Lydgate worked closely with Chaucer's material; Lydgate's tale of a little boy imperilled by urban hazards opens thus:

> Laude of our lord vp to the hevene is reysed
> Above the sonne and bryght sterrys cleere,
> And in his seyntes our lord Jhesu is preysed,
> As offte is seyn by ther devout prayeere.[88]

Lydgate has used Chaucer as his source here, not only in the appropriateness of the boy-hero's miraculous revival, but also in the performative terms of Marian praise articulated by Chaucer's Prioress:

> O Lord, oure Lord, thy name how merveillous
> Is in this large world ysprad, – quod she –
> For noght oonly thy laude precious

> Parfourned is by men of dignitee
> But by the mouth of children thy bountee
> Parfourned is...'   (VII.453–8)

The correspondence is indirect but suggestive; more direct borrowings occur when Lydgate uses the rhetorical topos of doubt, 'as I best kan or may', identical to that used by Chaucer's Prioress (VII.460), when Lydgate describes the 'bussh vnbrennt', identical to the Prioress's description of the burning bush (468), or the 'smal konnyng' mentioned by Lydgate, akin to the 'wayk' 'konnynyg' of the Prioress or the 'smal grammeere' of her boy-hero (481, 536).[89]

On the very day on which the miracle Lydgate's poem describes took place—20 November 1441, which was also the Feast of St. Edmund—we know that Lydgate was in London with Alice Chaucer's husband, Suffolk, and Adam Moleyns (d. 1450), a close friend of Thomas Chaucer and referred to affectionately by Lydgate in the *Departing*. At the time Moleyns was clerk of the royal council. On this day, Suffolk and Moleyns sponsored Lydgate's petition for a new annuity; on the day after, 21 November, the annuity was granted, at Westminster. Such were the miraculous interconnected workings of patronage, piety, and poetry! Alice Chaucer was almost certainly present, not least because the site of Lydgate's miracle poem—on Lower Thames Street, by London Bridge—is just yards from her house, the Manor of the Rose on Suffolk Lane.[90] In Lydgate's little miracle poem, the Chaucers—Geoffrey, Thomas, Alice—were all, in their different ways, *causes* of Lydgate's poetry.

Lydgate's mediation of Chaucer was by no means a dead end. In fact, it established the template for prestigious poetry for the later Middle Ages: Lydgate's extravagant, aureate yet princely and pious version of Chaucer is echoed in the works of similar East Anglian cleric-poets—Osbern Bokenham (c. 1392–c. 1464), John Capgrave (1393–1464), John Metham (fl. 1449)—as well as fifteenth-century *belletrists* like Charles d'Orleans (1394–1465) and John Skelton (1460–1529), and the Scots Chaucerians, especially Robert Henryson (d. c.1490), William Dunbar (c.1460–c.1515) and Gavin Douglas (c.1476–1522). This chapter has only scratched the surface of Lydgate's incredibly varied career and his profound relationship to the idea of Chaucer and his poetry. Fifteenth-century sources suggest that Lydgate was understood not as a pale imitation of Chaucer, but as his heir; a fifteenth-century poem connected with the Duke of Suffolk describes Lydgate as coming 'after Chaucer to occupye his place'.[91] It is clear that, within his own lifetime, Lydgate established himself as a poetic 'brand', to use Robert Meyer-Lee's apt term.[92] Lydgate was a commodity, celebrity and authoritative voice: that is, something like a laureate poet, whose writing offers an early example of each generation remaking Chaucer's poetry according to its own concerns.

Notes

1. See Michael Seymour, 'Manuscript Portraits of Chaucer and Hoccleve', *Burlington Magazine* 124 (1982), 618–23; David R. Carlson, 'Thomas Hoccleve and the Chaucer Portrait', *Huntington Library Quarterly* 54 (1991), 283–300.

2. For the primary texts, see John M. Bowers, ed., *The Canterbury Tales: Fifteenth-Century Continuations and Additions* (Kalamazoo, MI: Medieval Institute Publications, 1992). Critical perspectives are given in John Bowers, 'The *Tale of Beryn* and the *Siege of Thebes*: Alternative Ideas of the *Canterbury Tales*', *Studies in the Age of Chaucer* 7 (1985), 23–50; Kathleen Forni, *The Chaucerian Apocrypha: A Counterfeit Canon* (Gainesville, FL: University Press of Florida, 2001); A. C. Spearing, 'Lydgate's *Canterbury Tale: The Siege of Thebes* and Fifteenth-Century Chaucerianism', in *Fifteenth-Century Studies: Recent Essays*, ed. Robert F. Yeager (Hamden: Archon Books, 1984), 333–64.

3. Derek Pearsall, *John Lydgate* (London: Routledge, 1970), 165.

4. Alexandra Gillespie, *Print Culture and the Medieval Author: Chaucer, Lydgate and their Books 1473–1557* (Oxford: Oxford University Press, 2006), 202.

5. See Robert R. Edwards, 'Translating Thebes: Lydgate's *Siege of Thebes* and Stow's Chaucer', *English Literary History* 70 (2003), 319–41.

6. Likewise, other poems now ascribed to Lydgate were, in the sixteenth and seventeenth centuries attributed to Chaucer—e.g. *The Complaint of the Black Knight*, called the 'maying or disport of chaucer' in early editions, is almost certainly by Lydgate. See Derek Pearsall, 'Lydgate as Innovator', *Modern Language Quarterly* 53 (1992), 5–22.

7. On the more general issues involved in the reception of Chaucer in the fifteenth century see Gillespie, *Print Culture*; Thomas Prendergast, *Chaucer's Dead Body: From Corpse to Corpus* (New York: Routledge, 2004); Seth Lerer, *Chaucer and his Readers: Imagining the Author in Late Medieval England* (Princeton, NJ: Princeton University Press, 1993); Stephanie Trigg, *Congenial Souls: Reading Chaucer from Medieval to Postmodern* (Minneapolis, MN: University of Minnesota Press, 2002).

8. See Bowers, 'Tale of Beryn'.

9. Most of what we know of Lydgate's biography is from his own poetry; the evidence is summarized by Douglas Gray in his life of Lydgate in the *Oxford Dictionary of National Biography* at odnb.com.

10. See Gray's life of Lydgate in the *Oxford Dictionary of National Biography*.

11. Prendergast, *Chaucer's Dead Body* discusses the context in which Lydgate 'imagined' Chaucer's death as a 'personal loss' and the consequent ways in which 'Lydgate is so insistent on Chaucer's loss that he symbolically does away with Chaucer in order to lay claim to his poetic mantle' (12).

12. See Lerer, *Chaucer and his Readers*, 85–91.

13. Ibid., 48–9.

14. The approximate location, between the villages of Hampstead and Highgate, is remembered in Bishopswood Road in Highgate; a map, showing Bishopswood at the edge of Hornsey Great Park, can be found in *VCH Middlesex* 6:104. Ralph Flenley, 'London and Foreign Merchants in the Reign of Henry VI', *English Historical Review* 25 (1910), 644–55, at 653. Flenley notes how, later in Henry VI's reign, Londoners massed at Bishopswood to attack Lombards in London, and that it was clearly a known public space: Edward IV and Henry VII were both greeted here in preparation for their entrance to London. Two bishops of London of the time were very close to the Lancastrian court: John Kemp (bishop 1421–6), who was prominent in the English council during Henry VI's minority, and Robert Fitzhugh (bishop 1431–5), Henry VI's proctor and ambassador and noted anti-Lollard preacher. Both Kemp and Fitzhugh are plausible figures uniting Lancastrian politics and London religious culture.

15. The mumming has been edited recently by Clare Sponsler in John Lydgate, *Mumming and Entertainments* (Kalamazoo, MI: Medieval Institute Publications, 2010), from which these references are taken, 1–20.

16. John Lydgate, *The Mumming at Bishopswood*, 18.

17. For a similar reading, emphasizing Lydgate's indebtedness to French literary culture in the mumming, see Claire Sponsler, *The Queen's Dumbshows: John Lydgate and the Making of Early Theater* (Philadelphia, PA: University of Pennsylvania Press, 2014), 56–9.

18. Lydgate, *Mumming at Bishopswood*, 46–9.

19. Ibid., 50, 55.

20. Ibid., 64–70.

21. Maura Nolan, *John Lydgate and the Making of Public Culture* (Cambridge: Cambridge University Press, 2005); Robert Meyer-Lee, *Poets and Power from Chaucer to Wyatt* (Cambridge: Cambridge University Press, 2007).

22. Alain Renoir, *The Poetry of John Lydgate* (Cambridge, MA: Harvard University Press,1967), 111; Pearsall, *John Lydgate*, 151; Paul Strohm, *England's Empty Throne: Usurpation and the Language of Legitimation, 1399-1422* (New Haven, CT: Yale University Press, 1998), 187; Daniel Kline, 'Father Chaucer and *The Siege of Thebes*: Literary Paternity, Aggressive Deference, and the Prologue to Lydgate's Oedipal Canterbury Tale', *Chaucer Review* 34 (2000), 218.

23. Axel Erdmann and Eilert Ekwall, eds. *Lydgate's Siege of Thebes*, EETS e.s. 108, 125, vol 1. (London, 1911–30), xiv.

24. Joyce Coleman, *Public Reading and the Reading Public in Late Medieval England and France* (Cambridge: Cambridge University Press, 1996), 200.

25. Bowers, 'Tale of Beryn', 42.

26. James Simpson has suggested that the poem's occasion can be traced to the period after the death of Henry V, when friction between brothers and the threat of civil war loomed large; see James Simpson, '"Dysemol daies and fatal houres": Lydgate's *Destruction of Thebes* and Chaucer's *Knight's Tale*', in *The Long Fifteenth Century: Essays for Douglas Gray*, eds. Helen Cooper and Sally Mapstone (Oxford: Clarendon Press, 1997), 15–33, at 15–21.

27. Lerer usefully describes 'an exploration of relationships of power and powerlessness that define the quality of patronized literature', *Chaucer and his Readers*, 31.

28. This point is suggested by Pearsall who writes that 'The association [in *The Siege of Thebes*] was also convenient in that it provided a literary "occasion" for the poem. All Lydgate's poems, as I have said, are in a sense occasional poems, for he was not the kind of poet who writes from the pressures of his own creative imagination'. Pearsall, *John Lydgate*, 153.

29. This is also true of Lydgate's *Temple of Glas*, which is based on Chaucer's *House of Fame*). On *The Temple of Glas*, see Lerer, *Readers*, 63–72. J. Allen Mitchell has suggested that Katherine of Valois may be the elusive dedicatee of the poem, in 'Queen Katherine and the Secret of Lydgate's *Temple of Glas*', *Medium Aevum* 77 (2008), 54–76. Mary Flannery has likewise argued that 'Lydgate's view of his role as a poet is far more ambitious — and less anxious — than previously thought', a position supported by her detailed readings of *The Fall of Princes* and *Troy Book*; see Mary C. Flannery, *John Lydgate and the Poetics of Fame* (Cambridge, D. S. Brewer, 2012), 9.

30. Kline, 'Father Chaucer', 217. Similarly, see Nicholas Watson, 'Outdoing Chaucer: Lydgate's *Troy Book* and Henryson's *Testament of Crisseid* as Competitive Imitation of Chaucer', in *Shifts and Transpositions in Medieval Narrative*, ed. Karen Pratt (Cambridge: D. S. Brewer, 1994), 89–108.

31. Kline, 'Father Chaucer', 217.

32. The date is established by Johnstone Parr, 'Astronomical Dating for Some of Lydgate's Poems', *PMLA* 67 (1952), 253–6.

33. References are from Robert R. Edwards, ed., *John Lydgate: The Siege of Thebes* (Kalamazoo, MI: Medieval Institute Publications, 2001), 1–10.

34. In terms of political history, the date is not particularly auspicious, coming just a few weeks after the routing of English by the Franco-Scottish army at Baugé; this defeat significantly shook English authority in France and at Baugé several key Lancastrians were killed, including Henry's brother and heir, Thomas, Duke of Clarence (1387–1421). See Desmond Seward, *Henry V as Warlord* (Harmondsworth: Sidgwick & Jackson, 1987), 173–6.

35. Frank Taylor, ed., 'The Chronicle of John Strecche for the Reign of Henry V (1414–1422)', *Bulletin of the John Rylands Library* 16 (1932), 51. Strecche, a Rutland Augustinian, mentions a range of East Anglian towns visited by the king and queen, but not Bury.

36. See 'Explanatory Notes: Fragment I: General Prologue', in *The Riverside Chaucer*, 799 (nn.7–8).

37. John Lydgate, *The Siege of Thebes*, 93.

38. Erdmann and Ekwell, *Lydgate's Siege of Thebes*, vol. 1: vi.

39. Ibid., vol. 2: 96.

40. Bowers, 'Tale of Beryn', 41–2.

41. Lydgate, *Siege of Thebes*, 4522.

42. Ibid., 4531–2.

43. Ibid., 82–3.

44. Ibid., 89.

45. Ibid., 126–7.

46. See too Lydgate's thoughts on 'game' and 'play' (159–61) which echo those of the Monk's sequence (VII.1963–4).

47. Scott-Morgan Straker, 'Deference and Difference: Lydgate, Chaucer and *The Siege of Thebes*', *Review of English Studies* 52 (2001), 1–21; see 6–7 on Chaucer's Monk.

48. Lydgate, *Siege of Thebes*, 130, 167, 162, 181, 76.

49. Simpson, 'Dysemol daies', 15.

50. Bowers, 'Tale of Beryn', 41.

51. Lydgate, *Siege of Thebes*, 33–6.

52. Straker, 'Deference and Difference', 3. Lydgate's Host's talk of farting ('Yif nede be, spare not to blowe!' [112]) may also glance at the farting of the Miller's Tale and the Summoner's Tale, although the Host's dietary advice, to settle digestion, seems to be taken from canonical medical reference works. The Host, accurately and conventionally, recommends 'some fenel Rede,/Annys Comyn or coriandre sede' for indigestion (113–120). According to standard reference guide *De proprietatibus rerum*, Bartholomeus Anglicus (d. 1272) fennel (*feniculo*) root 'purgeþ þe reynes, and helpiþ dropesye...' (2:960), aniseed (*anisio*) can be used 'to...destroye ventosite' (2:909), cumin (*cimino*) likewise can be used 'to abate þikkenes of fumosite, and to comforte dygestioun, and to abate ventosite...' (2:932) and coriander (*coriandro*) 'brediþ slepe' (2:933). Quoting John Trevisa, *On the Properties of Things: John Trevisa's Translation of Bartholomaeus Anglicus, de Proprietatibus Rerum: A Critical Text*, eds. M. C. Seymour et al., 3 vols. (Oxford: Clarendon Press, 1975–88).

53. Coleman, *Public Reading*, 200–2.

54. Lydgate, *Siege of Thebes*, 18–19, 35–6, 38–40.

55. Ibid., 43, 44.

56. Ibid., 46–55.

57. Ibid., 19.

58. Straker, 'Deference and Difference', 5.

59. Lydgate, *Siege of Thebes*, 66–70.

60. Ibid., 172–6.

61. Ibid., 176, 196, 802.

62. Ibid., 817, 992–3, 1476–7, 1525.

63. Ibid., 199, 213.

64. Ibid., 194–222.

65. Ibid., 190.

66. See A. J. Minnis, *Medieval Theory of Authorship: Scholastic Literary Attitudes in the Later Middle Ages* (London: Scholar Press, 1984), 28. In keeping with the Scholastic theory of cause, which held that authors were an efficient (first) cause directed by the divine *auctor*, Lydgate describes how Amphion is the 'chief cause first' of poetry and thereby of Thebes itself, authorized by 'Mercurye god of Eloquence' (215).

67. Lydgate, *Siege of Thebes*, 214, 218, 229, 231–2.

68. Ibid., 240–4.

69. See J. Marotta, 'Amphion: The Hero as Rhetorician', *Centrepoint* 2 (1977), 63–71; Straker, 'Deference and Difference', 10, on how Amphion show how the 'clerical and poetic vocations' are interdependent; Simpson, 'Dysemol daies', 18–20.

70. See the materials given in the *Medieval English Dictionary*, s.v. 'feinen' (v.).

71. MS, f. 5v; the manuscript's glosses are printed in Lydgate, *Siege*, ed. Erdmann with Ekwall, 1:14.

72. Lydgate, *Siege of Thebes*, 802, 802, 1019.

73. Lydgate is referring here to Martianus Capella's *De nuptiis Philologiae et Mercurii*, an allegory of the marriage of Philology and Mercury. It is referred to in Chaucer's Merchant's Tale (IV.1732–41).

74. Lydgate, *Siege of Thebes*, 837–8; 1015; 2561; 2809.

75. Ibid., 4531–2.

76. Ibid., 4703; this is pointed out in Derek Pearsall, *John Lydgate 1371–1449: A Bio-Bibliography* (Victoria, BC: University of Victoria, 1997), 22; Edwards's note to this line usefully notes that 'Lydgate echoes the terms of the Treaty of Troyes, reached in 1420. At the end of Troy Book, he refers to the same "convencioun" (5:3398) and sees in Henry V's marriage to Katherine of Valois the promise of 'Pes and quiete' (5:3435); the most compelling 'political' reading of the poem is given by Edwards, 'Translating Thebes'.

77. Gillespie, *Print Culture*, 21; see also Amanda Leff, 'Lydgate Rewrites Chaucer: the General Prologue Revisited', *Chaucer Review* 46 (2012), 472–9.

78. See Pearsall, *Lydgate: A Bio-Bibliography*, 18; Seth Lerer, 'Chaucer's Sons', *University of Toronto Quarterly* 73 (2004), 906–15, which engagingly places Thomas Chaucer in relationship to Lewis Chaucer, the putative other Chaucer boy; see also Mary-Jo Arn, 'Thomas Chaucer and William Paston Take Care of Business: HLS Deeds 349', *Studies in the Age of Chaucer* 24 (2002), 237–67, with a salient biography of Thomas Chaucer (238–9) and a useful discussion of Thomas Chaucer's styling of himself in relation to his Chaucer forebears (254–62).

79. A further Lydgate poem, *My Lady Dere*, has sometimes been associated with Thomas Chaucer, although this is possibly a mis-attribution by John Shirley. See Pearsall, *Lydgate: A Bio-Bibliography*, 20–1.

80. Lydgate, *Siege of Thebes*, 1–2, 13–14.

81. Ibid., 23.

82. Ibid., 68–70.

83. Carol Meale, 'Reading Women's Culture in Fifteenth-Century England: The Case of Alice Chaucer', in *Mediaevalitas: Reading the Middle Ages*, eds. Piero Boitani and Anna Torti (Cambridge: D. S. Brewer, 1996), 92–9. Meale ('Reading Women's Culture', 83–4) also offers a useful discussion of Alice Chaucer's book collection, recorded in the Ewelme Muniments.

84. See Carol M. Meale and Julia Boffey, 'Gentlewomen's Reading', in *The Cambridge History of the Book in Britain, Vol. III: 1400–1557*, eds. Lotte Hellinga and J. B. Trapp (Cambridge: Cambridge University Press, 1999), 526–40, at 527.

85. Lisa H. Cooper and Andrea Denny-Brown, 'Lydgate Matters', in *Lydgate Matters: Poetry and Material Culture in the Fifteenth Century*, eds. Lisa H. Cooper and Andrea Denny-Brown (Basingstoke: Palgrave Macmillan, 2008), 7.

86. Lydgate, *Siege of Thebes*, 4–5.

87. As Gillespie, *Print Culture*, 106, comments, Criseyde was, in the fifteenth and early sixteenth centuries, '[t]he consummate Chaucerian image for the generation and the reception of texts'.

88. Quoting from Anthony Bale and A. S. G. Edwards, eds., *John Lydgate's Lives of Ss Edmund and Fremund and the Extra Miracles of St Edmund* (Heidelberg, Winter 2009), 1–4.

89. Bale and Edwards, *John Lydgate's Lives*, 123, 172, 220.

90. This occasion is described and analyzed in more detail in Anthony Bale, 'St Edmund in Fifteenth-Century London: The Lydgatian *Miracles of St Edmund*', in *St Edmund King and Martyr: Changing Images of a Medieval Saint*, ed. Anthony Bale (Woodbridge: York Medieval Press, 2009), 145–62.

91. See Pearsall, *John Lydgate*, 163.

92. Meyer-Lee, *Poets and Power*, 52, 183.

BIBLIOGRAPHY

Bale, Anthony, 'A Norfolk gentlewoman and Lydgatian patronage: Lady Sibylle Boys and her cultural environment', *Medium Aevum* 78 (2009), 261–80.

Bower, John, 'The Tale of Beryn and the Siege of Thebes: Alternative Ideas of the Canterbury Tales', *Studies in the Age of Chaucer* 7 (1985), 23–50.

Edwards, Robert R., 'Translating Thebes: Lydgate's *Siege of Thebes* and Stow's Chaucer', *English Literary History* 70 (2003), 319–41.

Forni, Kathleen, *The Chaucerian Apocrypha: A Counterfeit Canon* (Gainesville, FL: University Press of Florida, 2001).

Kline, Daniel, 'Father Chaucer and *The Siege of Thebes*: Literary Paternity, Aggressive Deference, and the Prologue to Lydgate's Oedipal Canterbury Tale', *Chaucer Review* 34 (2000), 217–35.

Lerer, Seth, 'Chaucer's Sons', *University of Toronto Quarterly* 73 (2004), 906–15.

Meyer-Lee, Robert, *Poets and Power from Chaucer to Wyatt* (Cambridge: Cambridge University Press, 2007).

Pearsall, Derek, 'Lydgate as Innovator', *Modern Language Quarterly* 53 (1992), 5–22.

Perry, R. D., 'Lydgate's Virtual Coteries: Chaucer's Family and Gower's Pacifism in the Fifteenth Century', *Speculum* 93 (2018), 669–698.

Prendergast, Thomas, *Chaucer's Dead Body: From Corpse to Corpus* (New York: Routledge, 2004).

Simpson, James, '"Dysemol daies and fatal houres": Lydgate's *Destruction of Thebes* and Chaucer's *Knight's Tale*', in *The Long Fifteenth Century: Essays for Douglas Gray*, eds. Helen Cooper and Sally Mapstone (Oxford: Oxford University Press, 1997), 15–34.

Spearing, A. C., 'Lydgate's *Canterbury Tale*: The *Siege of Thebes* and Fifteenth-Century Chaucerianism', in *Fifteenth-Century Studies: Recent Essays*, ed. Robert F. Yeager (Hamden: Archon Books, 1984), 333–64.

Watson, Nicholas, 'Outdoing Chaucer: Lydgate's *Troy Book* and Henryson's *Testament of Crisseid* as Competitive Imitation of Chaucer', in *Shifts and Transpositions in Medieval Narrative*, ed. Karen Pratt (Cambridge: Cambridge University Press, 1994), 89–108.

CHAPTER 32

DIALOGISM
IN HOCCLEVE

JONATHAN M. NEWMAN

THOMAS Hoccleve was one of the most widely read poets of the fifteenth century *in* the fifteenth century. A younger contemporary of Chaucer's, he wrote a number of Middle English poems on religious and secular themes, from short lyrics to a 5000-line poem of political advice, to 'a mirror for princes' in his poem *The Regiment of Princes*. Hoccleve's Victorian editor F. J. Furnivall wrote that the 'chief merit of Hoccleve is that he was the honourer and pupil of Chaucer.'[1] Hoccleve portrays his experience of contemporary London by writing conversations between himself and others that he meets as a mid-level clerk in a royal administration of ever-increasing size and complexity in a similar manner to Chaucer's reproduction of the experience of pilgrimage by depicting conversations among pilgrims in the *Canterbury Tales*. Hoccleve's portrayal is by turns funny and poignant, satiric and sentimental. It remains difficult to deny the greater amplitude of Chaucer's imaginative range and technical skill as a storyteller and versifier; nevertheless, the growth in critical interest in Hoccleve in the last few decades comes in part because Hoccleve's poetry seems to offer more direct access to something that Chaucer, with his preference for ancient and legendary subject matter, frequently conceals—the embeddedness of his writing within contemporary social and material practices.

Using the textual decorum of poetic address to reproduce sometimes indecorous social encounters, Hoccleve's poetry tests the conditions and possibilities of communication through dialogue: this examination is Hoccleve's distinct achievement as a poet. Hoccleve frames his texts as dialogues between himself and others in such a way that he evokes a sense of lived experience. Dialogism in Hoccleve's poetry is an ethical as well as rhetorical, poetic, or narrative technique; it makes moral reflection and self-correction part of the basis of his self-narration.

Hoccleve's poetry attempts dialogue on both an intra-textual and the extra-textual levels. On the intra-textual level, he stages conversations between his own vividly drawn persona and a fictive interlocutor: for example, the allegorical god 'Health' (*La male regle*), the old beadsman (*Regiment of Princes*), and a 'Friend' (*The Series*). On the extra-textual level, *La male regle, The Regiment of Princes*, and *The Series* all entertain the hope of being read by powerful contemporaries of Hoccleve, including Thomas Neville, Prince Henry, the Countess of Westmoreland, and Humphrey of Gloucester. Whether these powerful men and women actually read or responded to Hoccleve's poems, their names have prompted scholars to read Hoccleve's poetry in a political register. These names, like Hoccleve's own, make permeable the boundary between intra- and extra-textual dialogues; his poems index textual personae to historical persons and invite his readers to identify with the attitudes and knowledge of his textual addressees. Situating his narratorial self in a representation of his daily life, his poetry demands an equally concrete intra-textual addressee to give motive and shape to his discourse. But the moral and pragmatic aim of his texts is also shaped by the extra-textual addressee, or 'superaddressee' (in Bakhtin's terminology), an external authority 'whose sanction is decisive for the acceptance or non-acceptance of the text's words as legitimately expressing the world'.[2]

The much-remarked sense of anxiety and instability one senses in Hoccleve's poetic persona comes, I will argue, from a certain pessimism about whether this extra-textual authority is even listening. Medieval texts frequently identify their authors and intended readers by name; Hoccleve not only casts his text as interaction according to received conventions, but calls attention to the fact that he is doing so in a distinctly self-conscious way—not just use, but mention. In this way, he draws attention to the fact that a persona is a mask with a function and thus foregrounds the basic problem of communication through the sensible sign: namely, 'its potential to falsify or "counterfete" inner meaning'.[3] Another (and equally important) frustration that Hoccleve expresses about his efforts to communicate is not falseness but simple indifference, a lack of charity about extending a speaker the courtesy of trying to understand him.

CAREER AND WORKS

One external authority with which Hoccleve's work converses (its 'superaddressee') is Chaucer. Chaucer canonizes himself in the envoi of his *Troilus and Criseyde* when he enjoins his poem to '...kis the steppes where as thow seest pace/Virgile, Ovide, Omer, Lucan, and Stace' (5.1791–2). Hoccleve ratifies this canonization, naming Chaucer 'the firstë fyndere of our faire langáge'.[4] It has been argued that Hoccleve sought his own place in literary history by affiliating himself to his 'fadir' and 'maistir deere'.[5] As his own scribe, Hoccleve places Chaucer's portrait in the margin of one autograph copy of *The Regiment of Princes*, next to the reverential passage just quoted. By means of this gesture, Hoccleve attaches himself to Chaucer's prestigious literary authority; he would also ally himself to political authority by dedicating his holograph of the *Series* to Joan Neville, the Countess of Westmoreland, 'mother-in-law to Mowbray the Earl Marshal, sister-in-law to Lord Furnival, aunt to both Duke Humphrey and Henry V—and incidentally niece of Geoffrey Chaucer'.[6] These efforts were a reach for Hoccleve, who was not brought up or appointed to high office and exalted circles.[7]

Our records of Hoccleve's life outside of his poetry centre on his employment as a clerk of the Privy Seal beginning at the age of twenty in 1387. As Privy Seal clerk, a mid-level administrator in the royal government, Hoccleve survived on an annuity granted by the king.[8] This annuity was suspended more than once by a parliament asserting its authority over England's fiscal management, and these interruptions in Hoccleve's liveli-hood provided the occasion for two of his more well-known poems, *Lamale regle* and *The Regiment of Princes*. In *La male regle* (1405), he humorously confesses his former profligate lifestyle while petitioning the Chancellor of the Exchequer for payment.[9] *The Regiment of Princes*, a mirror for princes written for Prince Henry around 1411, features a conversation between him and an old beadsman (a beggar that prays for almsgivers), who consoles the anxious poet during another suspension of pay. In each case, the life records suggest Hoccleve regained his annuity, but then, according to events described in *The Series*, his careers as Privy Seal clerk, poet, and social climber were interrupted by a 'wylde infirmitee', a five-year episode of mental or neurological illness.[10]

Beginning with 'My Complaint' and 'the Dialogue', *The Series* (c.1419) is a miscellany of secular and religious poems that also find the poet rehearsing anxieties to a specific addressee, but instead of money, the poet is now anxious about the lingering stigma he suffers after his mental infirmity abates. Hoccleve avoids describing the experience of madness itself except to say that it 'caste and threew' him out of himself.[11] Instead, he relates the feeling of social alienation he experienced after returning to public work at Westminster's Privy Seal office around 1416. He worked almost his whole lifetime in the King's Office of the Privy Seal, producing official documents such as warrants, writs, grants, and pardons until his retirement in 1425.[12] Late in his career, he devised a formu-lary of document templates for successors to use.[13]

By the time of Hoccleve's death in 1426, John Lydgate was eclipsing him as the most prominent and widely read of Chaucer's successors.[14] After the fifteenth century, Hoccleve was all but lost in obscurity until the nineteenth century when he came to be valued as an inferior imitator of Chaucer by philologists and as a witness to the contem-porary life of London and Westminster by administrative historians such as T. F. Tout. To Furnivall, Hoccleve's inferiority to Chaucer was both moral and artistic; with his 'weakness, his folly, and his cowardice . . . we wish he had been a better poet and a man-lier fellow'.[15] Ironically, this estimation of Hoccleve's inferiority derives from no other source than the anxious and self-abjecting poetic persona found in *La male regle*, the Prologue to the *Regiment of Princes*, and *The Series*. Furnivall's contempt is the calculated effect of Hoccleve's art, an art tutored by Chaucer's work if not the man himself as once supposed.[16]

Notwithstanding Hoccleve's formal imitation of Chaucer, their poetic personae differ significantly. Chaucer's authorial persona, his textual representation of his extra-textual self, appears only diffidently in his poems. Hoccleve, to the contrary, talks as himself, about himself, and to himself with an obsessive consistency recalling middle-period Woody Allen films. Critical studies of Hoccleve's poetry have debated the autobiograph-ical factuality and political and artistic purposes of this self-representation. Furnivall supposed that Hoccleve attended Chaucer's deathbed and executed his literary affairs.[17]

In contrast, Greetham argues that Hoccleve's 'dialogue form, interludic disposition, and contemplative, ironic, tone' comprise a fictional persona, a narratorial self that is no more than a textual effect.[18]

Although particular dialogues in Hoccleve's poems may be fictions, their cumulative effect is to portray an author with workaday fears and joys. Whether his addressees are personifications like *La male regle*'s Health and Reason, or flesh-and-blood people like the *Regiment*'s Old Man and the Dialogue's Friend, they do more than provide an occasion for conventional self-dramatization in these poems. The precarity of two people trying to understand each other is a fundamental concern for Hoccleve. If he inverts the *Canterbury Tales* to place the frame—the situation for storytelling—at the centre, he does so to examine how situation changes storytelling from monologue to dialogue and, more broadly, how acts of communication relate to 'whatever wordless intentions and assumptions might lie behind them, that is, to their performative field'.[19] In Hoccleve's poetry, as in Chaucer's, stories are tokens of exchange like words, money, gestures of deference or domination, or articles of clothing; Hoccleve's fascination with the way communication is mediated by these tokens, especially dialogical speech, is the common thread that connects his several major works with one another and with the legacy of Chaucer's writing. To see how, we must first define dialogue and its medieval varieties more closely.

Modes of dialogue:
Genre and situation

In its most elementary sense, dialogue means two people talking to one another. This situation can assume an extraordinary diversity of forms enacted for a range of equally diverse purposes. In varying proportions, Hoccleve's dialogues combine different kinds of discourse that have both a literary or fictive mode and an extra-textual or 'real-life' mode, including especially discourses of petition, confession, complaint, and consolation. As 'speech genres', these foundational medieval discourse types shape utterances comprising face-to-face interactions, institutional diplomacy, and literary traditions.[20] In each of these cases, speech genres correspond to 'typical situations of speech communication, typical themes, and consequently, also to particular *contacts* between the *meanings* and actual concrete reality under certain typical circumstances'.[21] Speech genres also entail specific roles that confer privileges and duties on speaker and addressee for the duration of the exchange.[22] Petitionary and confessional situations, for example, are speech genres belonging to the religious and political spheres of live social interaction. Petition was foundational to religion, as in the Lord's Prayer, and confession itself was continuous with the petition to God for forgiveness. Petition and confession were also instrumental to the practice of government and law; the parliamentary bill of the Middle Ages was not a drafted law, but a petition to the king to redress some grievance, to which a law might be decreed in response. Confession, complaint, and consolation are common medieval literary forms and petition has a long history in medieval poetry, from love lyrics to penitential prayers to begging poems.[23]

Hoccleve's uses of the literary genres of complaint, confession, consolation, and petition each owe something to Chaucer, Gower, and Langland. What distinguishes Hoccleve is the freewheeling way in which he combines these genres in seemingly naturalistic settings by casting them in the form of dialogues featuring his own authorial person; this pattern opens his dialogical poetics to the discursive flavour of spoken interaction grounded in the working life of a late medieval urban royal bureaucrat. Combining the various discourse types in both their 'everyday' and literary realizations in *La male regle*, *The Regiment of Princes*, and *The Series*, Hoccleve's dialogism works against its Chaucerian background to comment explicitly about the stakes of dialogue and about the difficulties and possibilities of verbal communication itself.

La male regle mock-confesses a misspent youth to a mock-allegorical confessor, the personified deity 'Health', and despite a superficially repentant tone, the poet's recollections of good times with the tavern's easy company smacks of nostalgia. Describing himself as older, poorer, and sicker, Hoccleve recalls his former lifestyle as a fashionable young London clerk about London whose free-spending ways buy the affection and attention of 'venus femel lusty children deere', 'tauerneres', 'Cookes', and 'bootmen', each night until 'Hete & vnlust and superfluitee' drive him home to bed.[24] Strohm and others have pointed out a political valence to this seemingly personal confession: the attention which workmen and servants pay to Hoccleve in the *male regle* travesties the flatteries of a magnate's well-heeled entourage.[25] Flattery is an obsessive concern in medieval literary discourse about politics and government; like other poets who would offer political and moral advice, Hoccleve is concerned to distinguish himself from flatterers.[26] Yet his problem with flattery extends beyond self-interest, as flattery universally corrupts the possibility of communication in good faith:

> Men setten nat by trouthe now adayes.
> Men loue it nat. Men wole it nat cherice.
> And yit is trouthe best at all assayes.
> When þat fals fauel, soustenour of vice,
> Nat wite shal how hire to cheuyce,
> Ful boldely shal trouthe hir heed vp bere.[27]

This is one of several passages in which Hoccleve uses the term 'cheuyce' in the sense of justifying or fending for oneself.[28] The word also meant to obtain or offer security on a loan—falsehood will finally obtain no credit from truth, so to speak. The two meanings of this word speak to the transactional nature of discourse, and this particular transaction is directed to Henry IV's chancellor of the exchequer, Thomas Neville (called in the poem by his title of Lord Furnivall), whom Hoccleve playfully deifies as Wealth, a real-life counterpart to the allegorical god Health addressed elsewhere in the poem.[29] The transactions undertaken in this poem are multiple; he couches a plea for financial assistance in a mock confession that asks its audience not so much to absolve him as to examine its own habits of waste at the levels of self-government and government of the wider realm. For Lee Patterson, such characteristic moments of provocation in Hoccleve's poetry reveal a compulsive tactlessness, yet the aim of this tactlessness is not self-sabotage but the enactment of a dialogical poetics that compels a moral response, not abstractly, but in the context of a lived relationship.[30]

Hoccleve combines self-critique and effrontery again in his longest and most popular work, *The Regiment of Princes*. In its prologue, a sleepless Hoccleve, worried about finances, encounters an Old Man on the edge of town who seeks to console him in his poverty and then encourages him to write a poem to the prince in hope of favour and remuneration. The poem's second part—its ostensible body—is a mirror for princes offering didactic stories about political leadership. Strohm and others are correct in seeing the juxtaposition of begging and advice in the two sections as reflecting on new conditions of literary production under Lancastrian rule.[31] Hoccleve's poem, however, looks beyond its historical situation. Like other moral-didactic story collections of the later Middle Ages (for example, the *Roman de la rose* and the *Confessio amantis*), *The Regiment of Princes* is partly derived from didactic moral and philosophical dialogues in the Boethian tradition. The dynamic of complaint and consolation between a hapless narrator and a wise respondent in the *Regiment*'s prologue is particularly dependent on *The Consolation of Philosophy*.[32] *The Consolation of Philosophy*'s insistence on the therapeutic qualities of conversation informs the *Regiment*'s dialogue with the Old Man.[33] Both consolation and confession are specifically therapeutic modes of speech:

> Ryght so, if þe liste have a remedye
> Of þyn annoy that prikkeþ þe so smerte,
> The verray cause of þin hyd maladye
> Þow most discouer & telle out al thyn herte.[34]

Hoccleve's poem, however, represents these discourse types as more treatment than cure, needing continuous reapplication to keep his heart's sickness at bay. This model of therapeutic speech differs from the Old Man's prescription: rather than seeing communication as a means to reach mutual understanding and peace, the very act of communing confers a provisional peace.

Communication in *The Regiment of Princes* does not follow a script predetermined by a single genre; instead, Hoccleve shuttles between at least the two modes of confession and consolation. The result is as messy and polyphonic as the lived encounters that make up social experience, but it is much preferable to isolation and silence, as the Prologue's Old Man suggests when he describes the silence of the religious dissident John Badby when facing execution by burning. Badby's silence refuses Prince Henry's dialogue;[35] in contrast, Hoccleve sustains and profits from his dialogue with the Old Man. The Prologue, in fact, offers this dialogue as a model of productive exchange that anticipates Hoccleve's own advice to his prince in the *Regiment*'s body, the mirror for princes that is ostensibly the point of the text. As a mirror for princes in the tradition of the *Secretum secretorum*, the *Regiment* echoes that text's dialogical encounter between Aristotle and Alexander.[36] Thus Hoccleve's own encounter with Prince Henry, mediated by and enacted through the text of the *Regiment* itself, is reflected in two encounters. One is a kind of parody or burlesque of the prince-advisor relation—the encounter between Hoccleve and the Old Man—while the other is a valorization of that same relation as Aristotle and Alexander. Hoccleve's transaction with Prince Henry is reflected in the funhouse mirror of superimposed literary genres, and again, the cumulative effect of these supcrimposed genres is to draw a multi-dimensional narrator, since Hoccleve's humanistic mode of writing associates genres with specific kinds of selves.

Besides the Boethian, confessional, and regimental discourses that provide the literary material of Hoccleve's writing, his representation of contemporary social, economic, and political experiences sometimes recalls another literary source, namely, the period's flourishing tradition of alliterative complaint.[37] Like Langland or the author of *Mum and the Sothsegger*, Hoccleve could unleash torrents of invective against social abuses, corruption, and ostentatious waste; in the *Regiment*, the Old Man resembles the bee-keeper in *Mum and the Sothsegger* in this regard.[38] But although he can veer toward the Langlandian, Hoccleve rejects the alliterative long line with its stable of archaic synonyms in favour of Chaucer's pentameter line and urbane diction and, as discussed above, these formal features are not the only aspects of the *Regiment's* that fix it in the tradition of vernacular courtly didacticism. The idiosyncratic authorial persona that emerges as a common feature of Hoccleve's poetry draws from these sources, genres, and traditions to convey the experience of a sensitive individual in an ill-defined social role as a lay bureaucratic clerk.

POETIC PERSONA

Critics of *The Regiment of Princes* have often examined Hoccleve's authorial persona as a vehicle for speaking about matters of public or political interest, either on his own behalf or as the agent of political superiors.[39] In doing so, Hoccleve's persona differs both from the Langlandian voice in the wilderness and from the smiling courtly maker. Yet Hoccleve's self-representation derives certain characteristics from both of these conventional poses. Despite his social criticism, his relentless focus on his personal fears of poverty, old age, sickness, obscurity, and isolation distinguish him from the comprehensive visionary engagement of *Piers Plowman's* Will. His bookish self-deprecation, as Greetham and others have pointed out, owes something to the Chaucerian narrator in the *Book of the Duchess*, the *Legend of Good Women*, the *House of Fame*, and the *Canterbury Tales*. Hoccleve's obsessive narration of private difficulties also distinguishes his textual persona from the diffident Chaucerian persona.[40] Chaucer, inviting readers to eavesdrop with him at the periphery of others' conversations, does not disclose any unconventional or distinctive concerns. While Hoccleve's insomnia in the *Regiment* is caused by financial anxiety, Chaucer's sleeplessness in the *House of Fame* merely offers an occasion for literary and philosophical rumination. Chaucer's internal debate no more than rehearses a disputation of authorities on the nature of dreams, a debate to which he finally remains neutral. And Chaucer's humility, as Lee Patterson argues of his exchange with Harry Bailey, is a sometimes less-than-subtle assertion of mastery; there is a kind of condescension in Chaucer's self-humiliation before Harry Bailey.[41]

The personas of Chaucer and Hoccleve also differ strikingly in the degree to which they refer to the contemporary world beyond the text; Chaucer's persona is borne above contemporary events, as it were, by a giant eagle, as in the *House of Fame*, or separated from them by the carnivalesque game-time of a story contest. Hoccleve's persona, speaking about financial worries and the experiential geography of London and Westminster, engages real-life events and persons in a more direct and obvious manner. The several discourse types from which Hoccleve draws—among them complaint, counsel, consolation, and petition—are available to him as shaped by Chaucer, but in Hoccleve's own persona they intersect to fashion a representation of subjectivity enriched by multiple perspectives and motivations.

Hoccleve's persona, even when not talking to anybody else in particular, is never monological. The multiple types of discourse allow Hoccleve to create the sense of what Bryan calls a 'live authorial presence' while avoiding perfect alignment between author and authorial persona.[42] The Hoccleve we encounter in his texts is never simply a beggar, disconsolate dreamer, frustrated office-seeker, wry penitent, or sententious counsellor; he is often all at once, and though each role has a strictly literary genealogy, his amalgamation of these roles resembles the complex, saturated social determination that characterizes the daily experience of social interaction. From this multi-dimensional persona the impression emerges of what we might call a personality, but even the provisional unity in the speaking subject provided by a singular event of interaction is compromised by the multiple social roles and multiple discourse types (or 'speech genres') that inform that event. Socially and literarily over-determined, Hoccleve cannot talk as himself, and cannot make himself present to himself by talking to another.

This foundational instability in his social role contributes to his poetry's prevailing emotional tone of anxiety, especially since he represents himself not as curious observer but as a worried petitioner. In his most well-known original works, he invariably represents himself as seeking some concrete favour or benefit. He depicts courtly life from its periphery, and his identification with the Lancastrian affinity is attenuated by the distance which his relatively humble position as a clerk of the Privy Seal places between him and the royal household.[43] As he enjoyed what prosperity he did on the basis of the king's preferment, he may have imagined himself as a courtier; that may have been the only governmental vocabulary available for Hoccleve and his contemporaries to conceive his role.[44] But when we glimpse his everyday life as he describes it—devising formulas and documents for official complaints and petitions, huddled over his desk in silence with his fellow clerks at the Office of the Privy Seal—Hoccleve seems more civil servant than courtly accessory.[45] This experience of isolation, combined with his professional role as a communicator and mediator, may have prompted Hoccleve's analytical attention to the conditions, properties, promise, and failure of communication, of the ways in which different situations and motivations for communication affect its outcomes.

'COMMUNYNGE': THERAPEUTIC
DIALOGUE

In the Boethian dialogue of Hoccleve's narrator with the Old Man in the *Regiment*, the latter's efforts to win Hoccleve's trust and reciprocity invites the reader's active engagement and moral self-scrutiny. The text presumes to open dialogue with its intended reader, Prince Henry. As in *La male regle*, Hoccleve here travesties the relation between lord and subject, deprecating himself by implicitly identifying himself with the 'poore olde horë man' in the Prologue, a self-styled plain-speaker.[46] Initially, Hoccleve rejects the value of such conversation—the counsellor's 'art will end in his speech'. It also calls into question the relationship between being and seeming, a persistent concern to Hoccleve.[47] This problem is of special concern to Hoccleve because it impairs the possibility of communication. How can dialogue built from infinitely falsifiable language possibly do any good?

Addressing this problem, the Old Man advises Hoccleve not to judge the worth of counsel from the appearance and status of the counsellor, but neither does he suggest that his advice's value is self-evident or self-authorizing. Instead, he builds a relationship between himself and Hoccleve through his persistent efforts at communicating; it is this relationship which finally valorizes the content of his advice. Hoccleve's resistance finally gives way, and he becomes an active participant in the therapeutic Boethian dialogue:

> Graunt mercy, derë fadir, of youre speche;
> Ye han ryght wel me comforted & esyd;
> And hertily I praye yowe, and byseche,
> What I first to yow spak be nat displesyd. [48]

He acknowledges the power of communication to work internal change and console him: 'Youre confort deepe in-to myn hertë synketh.'[49] The Old Man now anatomizes the cause of Hoccleve's initial resistance through an impersonated articulation of Hoccleve's inward reaction:

> I wote wel, sone, of me þus would þou þinke:–
> Þis oldë dotyd Grisel holte him wyse,
> He weneþ maken in myn heed to synke
> His lewed clap, of which set I no pryse;
> He is a nobil prechour at deuyse;
>   Gret noyse haþ þorgh hys chynnëd lippës drye
>   Þis day out past, þe deuel in his eye.[50]

Offered in jest, this stanza has serious implications for the possibilities and purpose of communication; to contemplate one's own external appearance through the eyes of another is partially to contemplate that other person's interiority.

Shared literacy offers a broader avenue for communication. Anticipating *The Series*, the *Regiment of Princes* connects education with a capability for ethical discernment and reflection. The Old Man tells Hoccleve that

> Lettered folk han gretter discrecioun,
> And bet conceyuë konne a mannes sawe,
> And raþer wole applië to resoun,
> And from folyë soner hem with-draw,
> Þan he þat noþer reson can, ne law,
> Ne lerned haþ no maner of letterure.[51]

In this situation, Hoccleve and the Old Man can communicate with each other on the basis of shared *letterure*, advanced clerical literacy. Chaucer's Miller remarks that 'every clerk anon right heeld with oother' (Tales I.3847), that literacy creates solidarity among the literate. But literacy is more than an in-group marker; it provides its in-group with a shared set of procedural tools for communication and persuasion. In discussing heresy, Hoccleve and the Old Man establish their shared faith in orthodox doctrine and commitment to learned methods of reasoning. The Old Man's confessional interrogation emphasizes the importance of both these common faiths by means of a confessional line of questioning that hovers between accusation and concern:

> 'Sone, if god wolë, þou art non of þo
> Þat wrapped ben in þis dampnacïoun,?'
> 'I? criste forbede it, sire!' seyde I þo.[52]

The Prologue's dialogue thus affords Hoccleve a chance to affirm his faith in 'þe sacrament/ of the auter',[53] a prudent manoeuvre for those writing in English after Arundel's Constitutions.[54]

This exchange also implies the frightening possibility that a true expression could be received as false, the orthodox believer taken for a heretic. The consequences of miscommunication could be as high as excommunication and burning, as with the Prologue's account of the trial of John Badby, the first layman executed under anti-Lollard legislation.[55] Prince Henry apparently offered amnesty, even a pension, if Badby would recant his denial of transubstantiation, but Badby would not:

> He heeld forþ his oppynyoun dampnáble,
> And cast oure holy cristen feiþ a-syde,
> As he þat was to þe fende acceptáble.
> By any outward tokyn resonáble,
>> If he inward hadde any repentaunce,
>> Þat wote he, þat of no þing haþ doutaunce.[56]

The face reveals the inner self through a conscious sign, a 'tokyn resonable'. Thus, the 'discrecioun' enjoyed by 'lettered men' operates in a community of faith, but faith is a spiritual and mental disposition that can only be communicated through signs, and can therefore be dissimulated. Secret heresy poses a grave threat to communication. For this reason, Bryan, among others, has viewed the passage about Badby as articulating Hoccleve's own frustration and anxiety about being ultimately unable to communicate.[57] Yet the Old Man and Hoccleve share a faith in both orthodox doctrine and the intellectual procedures of clerical literacy, and this shared faith makes community and thus communication possible between them. In turn, this possibility allows Hoccleve to escape despair and to ask Prince Henry for his annuity and advise him in the form of translated conciliar literature. Working through the sources of mistrust that impeded communication, the Old Man thus models the mental labour necessary for dialogue. And this work is not accomplished through abstract debate but through reference to Hoccleve's own life and the lives of those he has seen and known.

This kind of a layered, self-conscious way of relating to others can assist a hospitable orientation toward the other, yet it still holds danger that Hoccleve will describe more fully in *The Series*—a paralyzing anxiety conditioned by an over-acute awareness of how others perceive and respond to him. *The Series* opens with 'My Complaint', which foregrounds Hoccleve's frequent theme of the failure of communication and isolation of the speaker, and then tests the possibility of communication with a Friend whose interruption of his solitude begins the Dialogue. It connects this danger again to the disparity between interior disposition and social performance. In this case, the problem crystallizes not around the inability to perceive the true self of another through his face (as with Badby), but in Hoccleve's own inability to represent his true self to others through his appearance. This inability is the cause of the stigma that he suffers on account of the mental illness he experienced toward the second half of the 1410s:

> Vpon a look / is hard men hem to grownde
> What a man is / therby the soothe is hid;
> Whethir his wittes / seeke been or sownde
> By contenance / is it nat wist ne kid.[58]

Hoccleve cannot be heard or understood: nothing he can do is considered anything but a manifestation of madness. His social persona, to his understanding, is irrevocably tainted.

In this way, Hoccleve's authorial persona resembles Chaucer's Pardoner. Lee Patterson describes the Pardoner as attempting mock-confession to secure solidarity, connection, understanding, or at least regard for his abilities from his fellow pilgrims, but the Pardoner undermines himself by trying to make the other pilgrims his victims after he has already let them in on his confidence game: 'defiant and self-hating', writes Patterson, 'the Pardoner yearns towards the release of confession but is unable to bring himself to it'.[59] This release is not simply a matter of being heard by others, but of honouring their capacity to understand; in this sense, release is not a moment of gratification, but an escape from the prison of isolation. Hoccleve better understands this; the self-knowledge in communion that he seeks requires full understanding and not just superficial ratification from others. In 'My Complaint', he writes:

> The greef aboute myn herte / so swal
> And bolned euere / to and to so sore
> *Þat needes oute* / I muste therwithal.
> I thoghte I nolde / keepe it cloos no more
> Ne lette it in me / for to eelde and hore;
> And for to preeue I cam of a womman
> I brast out / on the morwe / and thus began.[60]

Release, for Hoccleve, is release of the grief 'that needs oute'—*oute* is a form of the word 'utter', referring to the therapeutic discourse of confession. As we saw in the Prologue to *The Regiment of Princes*, the Old Man characterizes confession as therapeutic. In that instance, as in *La male regle*, confession culminates in a petition for a suspended annuity that will provide not only money to live on, but also an acknowledgment of his service and ratification of his social role. In 'My Complaint', Hoccleve casts around for a remedy to his ill-feeling. His real motivation seems to be to claim others' respect and attention and recognition of him as somebody like them—'to preeve I cam of a womman', a phrase suggesting no more than his common humanity in the face of social alienation.

As in the *Regiment*, the problem for communication here lies in Hoccleve's own inability to represent his true self to others through his appearance, now reinforced by the stigma he suffers on account of his mental illness:

> Vpon a look / is hard men hem to grownde
> What a man is / therby the soothe is hid;
> Whethir his wittes / seeke been or sownde
> By contenance / is it nat wist ne kid.[61]

Hoccleve cannot be heard or understood because everything he does or says can be interpreted as manifesting madness, and he is thus trapped in his isolation. He cannot attain trustworthy communication such as that established with the Old Man in the *Regiment*. Jennifer Bryan sees Hoccleve's isolation as self-imposed by his persistence in talking to himself about himself, yet he invites his reader into his inner world as he utters his self-doubts in the form of a dialogue with himself.[62] This dialogue treats some traditional concerns of consolation and Boethian dialogue: the unreliability of fortune, fame, and wealth, and the paltriness of personal desire compared to the magnificence of providential mercy.

'My Complaint' has no actual dialogue as commonly understood; its dialogical framework is structured by the narrator's exchange with himself and with a book in his study. The self-encounter it depicts is most vividly realized in a scene in which Hoccleve contemplates the division between inner and outer self as he stares at a mirror, wondering how to look convincingly sane. This mirror resembles devotional literature's mirrors of self-scrutiny, which provide Hoccleve with psychological or spiritual categories to anatomize the disposition of his soul.[63] Devotional literature models confessional speech as interaction between speaking subjects; it thus provides a discourse of inwardness predicated on outwardness. In the same way, grasping for an understanding of his own fractured self, Hoccleve addresses himself as something other. One crucial feature of the 'mirror scene' is the way it doubles Hoccleve and gives external visual form to his introspection. The image of his person reified in the mirror as a thing unresponsive to his will illustrates the dynamic of his self-alienation:

> And in my chambre at hoom / whan þat I was
> Myself allone / I in this wyse wroghte:
> I streighte vnto my mirour / and my glas
> To looke how þat me / of my cheere thoghte,
> If any othir were it / than it oghte;
> For fayn wolde I / if it had nat been right,
> Amendid it / to my konnynge and might.[64]

Identifying himself with the image in the mirror, he searches it for signs of the way it can represent him to others. He tries to adopt the point of view of other people who daily scrutinize his face for signs of continued madness, dramatizing the continual pull on identity exerted by a social interaction couched in visual rather than verbal exchange.

Thus, through the poetic utterance of 'My Complaint', Hoccleve does what he cannot do in face-to-face interaction. He makes himself known as healed, confessed, and justified:

> See how the curteys leche / souerain
> Vnto the seeke / yeueth medecyne
> In neede / and him releeueth / of his pyne.[65]

He has confessed to and been made right by God, the ultimate 'superaddressee' or sanctioning external authority; on this basis, his complaint, rather than penitential self-disclosure, is a petition for recognition and understanding. But unlike Chaucer's Pardoner, whose self-disclosure repels his fellow pilgrims, Hoccleve cannot find anybody willing to listen at all. His 'communyng' fails to reach others, and the consolation he finds is in a book which advises him to 'repente' and 'mercy crye' to God.[66] Hoccleve's response to this is surprising; he acknowledges the need for auricular confession, but transfers it from author to the reader, switching out of confessional self-narration in order to proclaim his newly attained Boethian indifference to worldly reputation:

> For euere sythen / set haue I the lesse
> By the peples / ymaginacioun,
> Talkynge this and þat / of my seeknesse,
> Which cam / of Goddes visitacioun.[67]

Hoccleve's declared purpose is now to bear witness to the operation of divine grace in him, to show himself as exemplary. The attitude is quite different here from that of penitential lyrics; the authorial persona in 'My Complaint' takes as given the poet's reconciliation with God through a prior act of confession. On that basis, Hoccleve declares his indifference to worldly opinion and freedom from worry about how others perceive him. And yet in the very situation that frames this utterance is an irony that undercuts this tranquil stance, as Hoccleve articulates his indifference to reputation in a poem expressly written to repair his public reputation.

His effort to repair his reputation does, nevertheless, proceed on a more secure footing—not as a madman whose symptoms have subsided, but as a reformed penitent whose mind was broken and then restored by 'Goddes visitacioun'. At the beginning of the 'Dialogue' he shares this ambition with the Friend, who does not think this is a good idea and urges Hoccleve away from self-disclosure:

> Reherce thow it nat / ne it awake;
> Keepe al þat cloos / for thyn honoures sake.
> How it stood with thee / leid is al asleepe,
> Men han foryete it / it is out of mynde.[68]

For the Friend, the sanctioning external authority is public reputation, but this is precisely what Hoccleve has rejected; he holds it no 'repreef or shame'[69] to speak of his chastisement by God. We may doubt the Friend's sincerity, however, since he later reveals that Hoccleve's mental illness has really not been forgotten. The Friend suggests that Hoccleve's persistence in his poetic labours is potentially dangerous to Hoccleve since his 'brain' is perhaps not 'right wel stablisshid'.[70] Thus, even a friend who presents himself as Hoccleve's ally sees the poet through the lens of a stigma that undermines his credibility and compromises his efforts to communicate. For several hundred lines, Hoccleve and his Friend debate the advisability of Hoccleve's continuing his poetic efforts, with the Friend warning about the potential for relapse induced by strenuous mental labour. While the Old Man in the *Regiment* advises Hoccleve to speak out to find relief, the Dialogue's Friend, to the contrary, silences Hoccleve in the supposed interest of his well-being. Hoccleve's response to the Friend again reflects upon the unknowability of the relation between inner and outer; the private nature of individual experience constrains the degree to which communication is possible: '[H]e lyueth nat þat can/Knowe how it standith with anothir wight/So wel as himself'.[71] Hoccleve nevertheless suggests the possibility of 'communyng' if people were to listen in charity and suspend their judgment: 'Beforn the doom, good were avisament'.[72] The word 'avisament' suggests a kind of discourse like advice or counsel, but the word also entails perception, reflection, and deliberation; the word thus suggests the possibility for discourse to bring about communication—communing—that bridges isolated interiorities. If Hoccleve is petitioning for money in his earlier poems, here he petitions for understanding, and this appeal would seem to prevail with his Friend:

> 'Had I nat taastid thee / as þat I now
> Doon haue / it had been hard, maad me to trowe
> The good plyt / which I feele wel þat thow
> Art in / I woot wel thow art wel ynow,
> Whatso men of thee ymagyne or clappe'.[73]

Unfortunately, winning this Friend's understanding does not provide Hoccleve's self-narration with a happy ending, as the Friend goes on to urge Hoccleve to re-win the favour of ladies lost when he wrote the 'Letter of Cupid'. This returns Hoccleve to his anxiety about being misconstrued, his constant sense of embattledness and injured right, and his awareness of his social reputation. This time, however, the anxiety has been transmogrified by a Chaucerian literary artifice: Hoccleve finds himself in the position of the Chaucerian narrator in the *Legend of Good Women*, and must make amends to women.

In this way, as a *poet*, Hoccleve can turn outwards toward the world again, and we would leave Hoccleve in this optimistic stance at the conclusion of the 'Dialogue', but for two problems. First, the communicative discourse sought and nearly achieved by Hoccleve is recuperated into the dominating discourse of an external authority. According to Sebastian Langdell, the Dialogue is Hoccleve's muted, typically anxious articulation of his frustration at writing for a political and literary culture unwilling to extend his work a nuanced and thoughtful reading; rather, the Friend epitomizes the totalitarian orthodox cultural pressures of Lancastrian court culture by putting a monological orthodox gloss on Hoccleve's complex rendering of the tale of Jereslaus's wife.[74] Dialogue, shoaled on a reef of authorized monological glossing, does not connect people.

Second, literary texts can fail as dialogue because they are, after all, a single utterance. Their intra-textual dialogues are reported speech, and fail to breach their textual limits if they are not read as such. As an utterance, a text belongs to the poet alone. Dialogue is represented by letters on a page that only speak to the eyes of the reader that meets them. As Sarah Tolmie says of *The Regiment of Princes*, in a text of advice, the prince cannot respond.[75] Any represented response is rigged by the author. In this scenario, Hoccleve inverts the hierarchy of clerk and prince in a textual realm where poetic authority is paramount, but this escapist fantasy is flimsy.

And yet, by creating a countervailing authority, by reporting the process by which a monological voice is imposed on a dialogical one, Hoccleve's relentless self-narration never forecloses the possibility of dialogue. By depicting dialogues that mix genres, situations, and motivations, Hoccleve demands unclear and conflicting responses; but this lack of clarity allows a space for revision, renegotiation, and understanding. As a principle of openness, modifiability, response to and responsibility for the other, dialogue offers Hoccleve a way to mention—as well as use—the inscription of power into interaction.

NOTES

1. Frederick J. Furnivall, 'Forewords', in *Hoccleve's Works: The Minor Poems*, eds. F. J. Furnivall and I. Gollancz (Oxford: Oxford University Press for Early English Text Society, February 1970), xxx.
2. M. M. Bakhtin, *Problems of Dostoevsky's Poetics*, ed. and trans. Caryl Emerson (Minneapolis, MN: University of Minnesota Press, 1984), 183; Jacob Mey, *When Voices Clash: A Study in Literary Pragmatics* (New York: de Gruyter, 1998), 283.

3. Paul Strohm, 'Hoccleve, Lydgate and the Lancastrian Court', in *The Cambridge History of Medieval English Literature*, ed. David Wallace (Cambridge: Cambridge University Press, 1999), 647; on the distinction between *use* and *mention*, see John R. Searle, *Speech Acts: An Essay in the Philosophy of Language* (Cambridge: Cambridge University Press, January, 1970), 73–7.

4. Thomas Hoccleve, *Hoccleve's Works III. The Regement of Princes*, ed. Frederick J. Furnivall (London: Kegan Paul, Trench, Trübner & Co. for EETS, 1897), 4978.

5. Hoccleve, *Regement of Princes*, ed. Furnivall, 1961; Jerome Mitchell, 'Hoccleve's Supposed Friendship with Chaucer', *English Language Notes* 4 (1966), 9–12; Albrecht Classen, 'Hoccleve's Independence from Chaucer: A Study of Poetic Emancipation', *Fifteenth-Century Studies* (1990), 59–81; John Bowers, 'Thomas Hoccleve and the Politics of Tradition', *Chaucer Review* 36 (2002), 352; Nicholas Perkins, 'Haunted Hoccleve?' *Chaucer Review* 43 (2008), 103–39.

6. J. A. Burrow, *Thomas Hoccleve* (Brookfield: Variorum-Ashgate, 1994), 28.

7. Burrow, *Thomas Hoccleve* 1–3.

8. Gerald Harriss, *Shaping the Nation* (Oxford: Clarendon Press, 2005), 44.

9. Thomas Hoccleve, *La male regle*, in *Hoccleve's Works: The Minor Poems*, eds. Frederick J. Furnivall and I. Gollancz (Oxford: Oxford University Press for Early English Text Society, 1970), 25–39.

10. Burrow, *Thomas Hoccleve*, 40–2.

11. Ibid., 40–2.

12. Hoccleve, *Complaint*, 3.

13. Ethan Knapp, *The Bureaucratic Muse: Thomas Hoccleve and the Literature of Late Medieval England* (University Park, PA: Penn State University Press, 2001), 1–13.

14. Robert J. Meyer-Lee, *Poets and Power from Chaucer to Wyatt*, ed. A. J. Minnis (Cambridge: Cambridge University Press, 2007).

15. Furnivall, *Hoccleve's Works III: The Regement of Princes*, xxxviii.

16. Jerome Mitchell, 'Hoccleve's Supposed Friendship with Chaucer', *English Language Notes* 4 (1966).

17. Furnivall, *Hoccleve's Works: The Minor Poems*, xxxi.

18. D. C. Greetham, 'Self-Referential Artifacts', *Modern Philology* 86 (1989), 248.

19. Sarah Tolmie, 'The *Prive Scilence* of Thomas Hoccleve', *Studies in the Age of Chaucer* 22 (2000), 281–309.

20. M. M. Bakhtin, 'The Problem of Speech Genres', in *Speech Genres and Other Late Essays*, ed. Michael Holmquist (Austin, TX: University of Texas Press, 1986), 61–102.

21. Ibid., 87.

22. Norman Fairclough, *Language and Power* (New York: Longman, 1989), 19.

23. J. A. Burrow, 'The Poet as Petitioner', in *Essays on Medieval Literature* (Oxford: Clarendon Press, 1984), 161–76.

24. Hoccleve, *male regle*, 138, 179, 180, 195, 189.

25. Strohm, 'Hoccleve, Lydgate, and the Lancastrian Court' 640–61; J. A. Burrow, 'Autobiographical Poetry in the Middle Ages: The Case of Thomas Hoccleve', in *Middle English Literature: British Academy Gollancz Lectures*, ed. J. A. Burrow (Oxford: Oxford University Press, 1989), 7.

26. Amanda Walling, 'Friar Flatterer', *Yearbook of Langland Studies* 21 (2007), 57–76.

27. Hoccleve, *male regle*, 281–8.

28. 'O woman! how shalt thow thy self chevice'? Hoccleve, 'The Letter of Cupid', in Furnivall, *The Minor Poems*, 325; also Hoccleve, *Male regle* 1402; MED, s.v. 'chevishen'.

29. Eva M. Thornley, 'The Middle English Penitential Lyric and Hoccleve's Autobiographical Poetry', *Neuphilologische Mitteilungen* 68 (1967), 295–321; Ethan Knapp, 'Bureaucratic Identity and the Construction of the Self in Hoccleve's *Formulary* and *La male regle*', *Speculum* 74. 2 (1999), 371.

30. Lee Patterson, ' "What is Me?" ': Self and Society in the Poetry of Thomas Hoccleve', *Studies in the Age of Chaucer* 23 (2001), 437–70.

31. Strohm, 'Lancastrian Court', 644.

32. Greetham, 'Self-Referential Artifacts', 242–51.

33. Nicholas Perkins, *Hoccleve's Regiment of Princes: Counsel and Constraint* (Cambridge: D. S. Brewer, 2001), 111.

34. Hoccleve, *Regiment of Princes*, 260–3.

35. Ibid., 281–322.

36. Judith Ferster, *Fictions of Advice: The Literature and Politics of Counsel in Late Medieval England* (Philadelphia, PA: University of Pennsylvania Press, 1996).

37. Helen Barr, *Signes and sothe: Language in the* Piers Plowman *Tradition* (Cambridge: D. S. Brewer, 1994).

38. Thomas Hoccleve, *Mum and the Sothsegger*, 1111ff, in *Richard the Redeless and Mum and the Sothsegger*, ed. James M. Dean (Kalamazoo, MI: Medieval Institute Publications Western Michigan University, 2000); Sarah Tolmie, 'Prive Silence', 281–309.

39. Larry Scanlon, *Narrative, Authority, and Power: The Medieval Exemplum and the Chaucerian Tradition* (Cambridge: Cambridge University Press, 1994); Robert J. Meyer-Lee, *Poets and Power from Chaucer to Wyatt*; Paul Strohm, *England's Empty Throne* (New Haven, CT: Yale University Press, 1998); Bowers 'Thomas Hoccleve and the Politics of Tradition', 364–5; Derek Pearsall, 'Hoccleve's *Regement of Princes*: The Poetics of Royal Self-Representation', *Speculum* 69 (1994), 386–410; Kathleen E. Kennedy, 'Hoccleve's Dangerous Game of Draughts', *Notes and Queries* 5(4) (2006), 410–14.

40. Greetham, 'Self-Referential Artifacts', 242.

41. Lee Patterson, '"What Man Artow?": Authorial Self-Definition in The Tale of Sir Thopas and The Tale of Melibee', *Studies in the Age of Chaucer* 11 (1989), 117–75.

42. Jennifer Bryan, *Looking Inward: Devotional Reading and the Private Self in Late Medieval England* (Philadelphia, PA: University of Pennsylvania Press, 2008), 176, 203; Bakhtin, 'Speech Genres', 324.

43. Knapp, *Bureaucratic Muse*, 20–9.

44. Burrow, 'Hoccleve and the "Court"', 70–80.

45. Hoccleve, *Regiment of Princes*, 988–94.

46. Ibid., 122.

47. Strohm, 'Lancastrian Court', 647.

48. Hoccleve, *Regiment of Princes*, 750–4.

49. Ibid., 777.

50. Ibid., 400–6.

51. Ibid., 155–60.

52. Ibid., 372–4.

53. Ibid., 380–1.

54. Pearsall, 'Poetics of Royal Self-Representation', 403–6.

55. Peter McNivel, s.v. 'John Badby', *Oxford Dictionary of National Biography*, at odnb.com.

56. Hoccleve, *Regiment*, 317–22.

57. Bryan, *Looking Inward*, 197–8.

58. Thomas Hoccleve, *Thomas Hoccleve's Complaint and Dialogue*, ed. J. A. Burrow (Oxford: Oxford University Press, 1999), 211–14.

59. Lee Patterson, 'Chaucerian Confession: Penitential Literature and the Pardoner', *Medievalia at Humanistica* 7 (1976), 168.

60. Hoccleve, 'My Complaint', 29–35 (emphasis mine).

61. Ibid., 211–14.

62. Bryan, *Looking Inward*, 180–1.

63. Ibid., 177.

64. Hoccleve, 'My Complaint', 155–61.

65. Ibid., 236–8.

66. Ibid., 365–71.

67. Ibid., 379–82.

68. Hoccleve, 'Dialogue', 27–30.

69. Ibid., 55.

70. Ibid., 307.

71. Ibid., 477–9.

72. Ibid., 483.

73. Ibid., 485–9.

74. Sebastian Langdell, '"What world is this? How vnderstande am I?": A Reappraisal of Poetic Authority in Thomas Hoccleve's *Series*', *Medium Aevum* 78 (2009), 288.

75. Tolmie, 'Prive Silence', 284–5.

BIBLIOGRAPHY

Bertolet, Craig E., 'Social Corrections: Hoccleve's *La Male Regle* and Textual Identity', *Papers on Language and Literature* 51(3) (2015), 269–98.

Bowers, John, 'Thomas Hoccleve and the Politics of Tradition', *Chaucer Review* 36(4) (2002), 352–69.

Burrow, J. A., *Thomas Hoccleve* (Brookfield: Variorum-Ashgate, 1994).

Knapp, Ethan, *The Bureaucratic Muse: Thomas Hoccleve and the Literature of Late Medieval England* (University Park, PA: Penn State University Press, 2001).

Lawton, David, 'Dullness and the Fifteenth Century', *English Language History* 54(4) (1987), 761–99.

Malo, Robyn, 'Penitential Discourse in Thomas Hoccleve's *Series*.' *Studies in the Age of Chaucer* 34 (2012), 277–305.

Meyer-Lee, Robert J., *Poets and Power from Chaucer to Wyatt* (Cambridge: Cambridge University Press, 2007).

Mitchell, Jerome, 'Hoccleve's Supposed Friendship with Chaucer', *ELN* 4 (1966), 9–12.

Patterson, Lee, ' "What is Me?": Self and Society in the Poetry of Thomas Hoccleve', *Studies in the Age of Chaucer* 23 (2001), 437–70.

Pearsall, Derek, 'Hoccleve's *Regement of Princes*: The Poetics of Royal Self-Representation', *Speculum* 69 (1994), 386–410.

Perkins, Nicholas, *Hoccleve's Regiment of Princes: Counsel and Constraint* (Cambridge: D. S. Brewer, 2001).

Simpson, James, "Nobody's Man: Thomas Hoccleve's *Regement of Princes*," in *London and Europe*, eds. Julia Boffey and Pamela King (London: Westfield Publications in Medieval Studies, 1995), 150–80.

Spearing, A. C., 'Hoccleve and the "Prologue" and "Hoccleve's Series." ' In *Medieval Autographies: The 'I' of the Text.* Conway Lectures in Medieval Studies (Notre Dame, IN: University of Notre Dame Press, 2012), 129–208.

Strohm, Paul, 'Hoccleve, Lydgate and the Lancastrian Court,' in *The Cambridge History of Medieval English Literature*, ed. David Wallace (Cambridge: Cambridge University Press, 1999), 640–61.

Tolmie, Sarah, 'The *Prive Scilence* of Thomas Hoccleve', *Studies in the Age of Chaucer* 22 (2000), 281–309.

CHAPTER 33

OLD BOOKS AND NEW BEGINNINGS NORTH OF CHAUCER

Revisionary Reframings in The Kingis Quair and The Testament of Cresseid

IAIN MACLEOD HIGGINS

LONG SHADOW, BRIGHT SHADE, AND RICHLY INSTRUCTIVE CORPUS

ALTHOUGH we have no way of knowing when Chaucer composed it, the final fragment of the *Canterbury Tales* presents itself as a conclusion to his life's work. It is therefore fitting that the *chronographia*, or rhetorical time-telling set piece with which this closing fragment opens, shows him indirectly taking his artistic measure. Here, late in the literary day, under the judicial sign of Libra, the 'I' whom Harry Bailey had earlier jestingly called a 'popet' (VII.701), reveals himself as cutting quite an imposing figure: 'For ellevene foot, or litel moore or lesse,/[His] shadwe was at thilke tyme' (X.6–7). This summative Chaucerian shadow, depicted with subtly ironic indecision about its precise measure, was certainly long enough to leave those of his fifteenth- and early sixteenth-century successors who worked in it feeling downright dull.[1] Paradoxically, however, these successors also saw the overshadowing Chaucer as a bright shade whose instructive glow lit their way to a new view of their shared sources, offering luminous models of the revisionary, re-combinative work that turned a vernacular maker into a literary authority. Indeed, although many readers since the eighteenth century have judged the post-Chaucerian poets to have sung derivatively 'with vois memorial' in the shadow of a 'laure[ate]...that may not fade' (Anel 18–19), these 'dull' writers sometimes caught genuine literary fire from Chaucer's 'enlumynyng' example, starting with his language. What better guide after all than the poet who left exemplary 'bookes of his ornat endytyng/... to al this land enlumynyng'?[2] To invoke his shade was to share in his afterglow, and sometimes even to suggest that one was magnifying it. Thus when William Dunbar claims in *The Goldyn Targe* that Chaucer's 'fresch anamalit termes celicall/This mater coud illumynit haue full brycht', he does so in one of his gaudiest poems, summoning the long shadow yet showing off his own stylish refraction of the maker who once '[w]as ... of oure Inglisch all the lycht'.[3]

As both long shadow and bright shade, Chaucer was clearly a standard against whom fifteenth- and sixteenth-century poets in England and Scotland could take linguistic measure of themselves, testing the refractive power of their instruments in the full-spectrum light of his legacy. As they did so, however, they faced a challenge unknown to him. In a way impossible to Virgil, Ovid, Machaut, Dante, or Boccaccio, he haunted their language as no English predecessor had haunted his, turning up in echoes of diction, tricks of syntax, and turns of verse.[4] Chaucer's was thus the face whose traces they saw in the literary mirror, the body whose lineaments ghosted their textual forms.[5]

Of course, Chaucer was more than a literary patriarch whose linguistic and metrical DNA were everywhere. 'Both one and many', like the 'familiar compound ghost' of T. S. Eliot's 'Little Gidding',[6] he was a shifting, enchanting, and enabling practitioner of almost every medieval genre, a 'grant translateur'[7] who, through his deep engagement with the literary modes and *materia poetica* that he helped bring from France and Italy, left an especially instructive literary corpus. Continental and classical poets continued to be influential, to be sure, but they could now be re-read through Chaucer's prismatic shade; and the two English poets often invoked with him, Gower and Lydgate, continued to provide alternatives to his precedents, but neither quite offered the shimmering body of his stylistic, tonal, and generic range, the richness of his (habitually Boethian) interest in history, dreams, desire, freedom, and necessity, or his subtle explorations of the inter-play of the literary, the ideological, the personal, and the social. Even when elaborating the commonest *materia*, Chaucer can almost always be seen taking distinctive mediating measures. To those who could make something of it, Chaucer's profoundest legacy was his dynamic, dialogic handling of form in the broadest sense. More than inert structural props or common-place-holders, his frames do significant work, and they do so above all by calling attention to their mediating role, often through a medium so pervasive, persuasive, and distinctive that most readers experience it as a 'character': the disarming, charmingly intimate, yet canny textual effect known as Chaucer's narrator. But even where his narrator's voice is not predominant, Chaucer presses against inherited forms, stretching them, so as to shape both his matter and potential responses to it, setting his making into dialogue not only with its sources and intertexts, but also with itself and the reader.

A fine example of Chaucer's sense of significant form, and one relevant to the ensuing discussion of two quite different Scottish responses to him, can be found in the text invoked above: the Parson's Prologue. Linking the final fragment to its predecessor while both contextualizing it in relation to the *Canterbury Tales* as a whole and occa-sioning its particular challenges to the work's conceptions of literary value and temporal horizons, this text does what such framing and transitional passages typically do in Chaucer: it uses individualized, localized speech acts to raise and keep in play important literary and extra-literary questions that resonate intra- as well as inter-textually. Some of the internal resonances reach back to the first fragment, linking ends to openings and raising complex questions of literary place and temporality, both inside and outside the text. The '[d]egreës nyne and twenty' (X.4) marking the sun's descent at the close of the pilgrims' time-passing game, for example, recall the '[w]el nyne and twenty' 'sondry folk' whose arrival '[a]t nyght' (I.23–5) helps open the collection. Similarly, the Parson's testy exchange with the Host over the way to 'knytte[n] up wel [their] greet mateere' (X.28) recalls the first link and Harry's request to the Monk for '[s]omwhat to quite with the Knyghtes tale' (I.3119) only to be interrupted by the upstart drunken Miller—a moment that acts as a starting over, revising the inaugural decorum whereby, '[w]ere it by aventure, or sort, or cas' (I.844), the highest-ranking male pilgrim opened the game. Connecting the two moments is not only the Host's phrase 'unbokel[ing]' the 'male' (I.3115; X.26)—a punning reminder of the contest's transformation into a clash amongst men—but also the outcome of such unbuckling: consequential interplay between the expected and the unexpected.

Every 'unbokeling', clearly, is also a 'quitting': a leave-taking setting out, a relinquishing of silence for dialogism, a gesture of (self-)exculpation or revenge, and a discharging of both debts and verbal weapons in a patriarchal literary system. As the above examples show, the poetics of literary framing—both of overture and closure *and* of continuation—involves dialogic, even agonistic, spatio-temporal relations. Composing and comprehending occur backwards and forwards, within and across works, such that parts and wholes shadow one another and shade into each other in various and complex ways.

Such Chaucerian alertness to far-reaching literary questions and a way with significant form can be seen in the two Scottish works that respond most fully to his corpus: *The Kingis Quair* and Robert Henryson's *The Testament of Cresseid*. Other Scottish works, including some by Dunbar, Gavin Douglas, and David Lindsay, also drew creatively on Chaucer together with native and Continental traditions,[8] but *The Kingis Quair* and *The Testament of Cresseid* represent the most sustained engagements with his literary modes. The focus here will be on their revisionary reframing of Chaucerian mediation to shape new beginnings and altered endings. As Helen Phillips noted: 'It always repays the reader to scrutinize the choice, ordering, and handling of frames: one of the many respects in which we must learn to *read* the conventions of Chaucerian verse, not merely note them.'[9]

RECYCLING 'NORTH NORTHWARD' ON FORTUNYS QUHELE: CHAUCERIAN REFRAMINGS IN *THE KINGIS QUAIR*

The Kingis Quair, a courtly poem in 'both English and Scots',[10] is the first sustained Scottish engagement with Chaucer. Attributed in its only extant copy to James I (1394–1437),[11] it might have been made in England near the end of his imprisonment there (1406–23/24), since its ostensibly autobiographical account of the narrator's liberation through reciprocated love reads like an allegory of James's life before age thirty.[12] The notable fact here, however, is its presence in an anthology of English and Scottish Chauceriana, some of it known to the *Quair* poet. The 'Scotticized' English intertexts include genuine Chaucerian works (*Troilus and Criseyde*, the *Parliament of Fowls*) and misattributions (Lydgate's *Complaint of the Black Knight*).[13] Formally, *The Kingis Quair* most resembles the *Parliament*, being a lyrico-narrative variation on the visionary fictions inspired by the *Roman de la rose* and Boethius's *De consolatione philosophiae*. Boethius himself is initially invoked not just as the philosopher of fortune but also as its *poet*, as if to signal the work's *poetic* intertextuality. Likewise invoked, but not until the last of the 197 stanzas 'in lynis sevin' (rhyme royal), are the poet's 'maisteris', Gower and Chaucer,[14] while unnamed intertexts include Lydgate and perhaps Hoccleve and the *dit amoureux*.[15] Such multiple intertextual relations, characteristic of Boethian courtly works,[16] are important to a full understanding of the poem, but the Chaucerian engagements are the most extensive and hence the focus here. Certainly, the *Quair* poet's mention of the seven-line stanza in dedicating his book to two English 'poetis laureate'[17] points to Chaucer as the vernacular master against whom he would be measured.[18] Particularly significant are the reworkings of passages from *Troilus* and the Knight's Tale[19] and the adaptations of framing modes from *Troilus*, the *Book of the Duchess*, the *Parliament*, and even the *Canterbury Tales*. These latter revisions—the subject of the rest of this chapter—are worth scrutinizing because they are effective whether or not one recognizes their intertexts or those of the reworked passages for which they establish the immediate context of understanding.

Besides drawing attention to the work's artful structure and to the narrator as an intermediary with a personal stake in the story (his 'auenture'),[20] the poem's elaborate framing establishes microcosmic-macrocosmic relations between the narrator (as reader, writer, prisoner, and lover) and both the all-encompassing cosmos and the memory-containing book. As well, the framing highlights the poem's internal and external spatio-temporal representations and links its ending to its beginning, showing that each is implicated in the other and that understanding the whole work requires rereading. The repetition of the poem's first line, 'Heigh in the hevynnis figure circulere', at the end of the penultimate stanza is only the most obvious sign thereof. It is presumably significant, moreover, that the poem does *not* finish with this closing of the overtly thematized circle (as *Pearl* does), but moves in its final stanza to name Gower and Chaucer. In so doing, it steps outside itself to place its maker alongside his recent English contemporaries who, like him, have circled back to Boethius and his legacy as a starting point. The poem's last two stanzas, then, ask that the work be read *both* intra- and inter-textually, with particular attention also to the ways into and out of the text.

Inspired perhaps by the *Parliament*'s layered opening and *Troilus*'s recursive closing, the *Quair* poet gives his work at least three beginnings and an even more elaborately layered close. The work begins in stanza 1, again in 14, and yet again in 20, and perhaps also in 30 (where the core narrative starts); and it ends in some five layers between stanzas 181 and 197. Even the core narrative is layered, in that the central dream vision (stanzas 74–172) occurs only after some forty stanzas of scene-setting (30–73) and receives a confirmatory dénouement (173–80) that blurs the boundary between the dream and the waking world. Such intricate layering also involves the poem's polysemic time-frame: Beginning 1, for example, occurs at midnight in winter (January–February) and lasts till matins, while Beginning 3 occurs at midday in spring (March) some eighteen years earlier and ends on the opening winter morning. Clearly, such a structure insists that the poem be read as product and process at once, as both a recounting of experience and a reading thereof: specific circumstances are fitted into a received frames of reference, but the frames are also reshaped to fit the circumstances.

What this layered framing does first is to thwart conventional expectations and delay forward movement even as it works inward to the narrator's crisis and then back out again to a resolution. Indeed, the expected dream, which occupies half of the entire text, does not begin until more than one third of the way through. Thus anyone who reads this leisurely account of 'so litill' undergoes an experience like that of the narrator, who not only requires the help of Gude Hope and Patience in his passage from Venus to Minerva, but also has to step willingly onto Fortune's wheel to achieve his goal of reciprocated, virtuous heterosexual love.[21] In conflating the narrator's and the reader's experiences like this, the poem not only teaches that a proper relation to desire takes time, it also *enacts* that teaching. Time is of the essence, clearly, as a single chance event (falling in love) is shown to be deeply transformative through the long reflection enacted in beginning with a post-visionary act of reading Boethius, delaying the vision, and retracing the extensive visionary journey towards understanding. Most of the poem's internal action takes place within a day, within one turn of the heavens, but that action is framed by some twenty hard years in the narrator's life, seasonal cycles, and the long tradition of Boethian poetic reflection. The poem's time, moreover, is spatially marked and experienced, such that the structural turns and returns do thematic as well as formal work, subsuming 'in the hevynnis figure circulere' differently temporal enclosures from the smaller to the larger: book, body, bed, chamber, garden, the 'lusty plane' where Fortune dwells with her wheel.[22]

Although key moments in these places recur with variations emphasizing the trope of (en)circling, they do not, as already noted, quite lead in expected directions, thereby enacting the counter-trope of 'toltering' or 'weltering'.[23] This habit of turning unexpectedly is established at the outset, playing a variation on the opening of the *Book of the Duchess*. Here sleeplessness does not lead through reading an old book to dreaming; instead, mere waking leads through reading both to sore eyes and to a more focused mental state, which then leads to reflection on the personal implications of that reading and finally to writing 'Sum new[e] thing'.[24] The act of writing is prompted by the matins bell,[25] a symbol not only of the outside world impinging on the narrator's self-absorption and thus metaphorically *reawakening* him, but also of a culturally-specific world in which one's time must be redeemed. This bell echoes the one heard at the end of the *Duchess*, but the latter is a 'castell' (or courtly) bell and it 'smyte[s] houres twelve' (1322–3), not a canonical hour (a temporal echo of the cosmic cycle evoked in the opening stanza).

Thus whereas the (midnight?) castle bell that wakes Chaucer's narrator, book still in hand and now deciding to write his dream, signals formal closure, the morning prayer bell that metaphorically *reawakens* the *Quair*'s narrator signals a new beginning. Having already closed the *Consolation* and laid it at his head,[26] a gesture that at once displaces Boethius and keeps him in mind, the narrator now picks up a pen and begins his own 'buke' (the one we are reading) by making a '✠',[27] another richly significant gesture. The '✠' of course signals that this account will unfold under Christ, one of many such textual signs, and it is also the initial sign in a children's horn-book, thus suggesting the poem's basic didactic nature; but it is first of all an inky icon whose physicality emphasizes the reality of the narrator's experience recalled and renewed by its writing.

It is as if the surrounding frame of the *Duchess* had been detached, compressed, and placed at the start of *The Kingis Quair*, a revision that besides placing ends into beginnings distances reading from dreaming. Whereas Chaucer's Ovidian reading (like the Tullian reading in the *Parliament*) is prospective and therefore implicated in the immediately-following dream, the *Quair* poet's Boethian reading is retrospective and therefore partly in contrast to, partly interpretative of the delayed dream. The narrator's experience and his interpretation of it could not be more different from Chaucer's or Boethius's, despite the superficial similarities between their situations as nighttime readers or prisoners of fortune, a difference gaudily confirmed in the core narrative's dénouement. There, in a waking episode that seems to be still in the dream and that fuses natural, courtly, and Christian symbolism, the narrator, uncertain as to the truth of his vision, receives a visit from 'a turtur quhite as calk' carrying a 'fair[e] branche, quhare writtin was with gold' divine confirmation of his 'confort'.[28] After immediately reading 'this/First takyn...of all [his] help and blisse', he 'pyn[s it] vp' 'at [his] beddis hed':[29] the very spot where earlier in the poem but later in life he set down his Boethius. This textualized return can be read as setting *The Kingis Quair* dialogically vis-à-vis Boethius's work (and Chaucer's). In some books at least, as in some lives and in some 'auentures', nature, courtly custom, and the Christian cosmos can all come harmoniously together with Fortune, as they do here at the core narrative's end (which is not the work's close).

Narrating this embedded 'auenture', then, is a figure familiar from the *Duchess* and the *Parliament*, and partly adapted from *Troilus and Criseyde*. Unlike these narrators, however, this reader, writer, and onlooker also becomes a prisoner and a lover, fusing the roles of bookish mediator and worldly actor. Reading the poem as James I's, and contrasting his social position with Chaucer's, A. C. Spearing suggests that the poet's 'kingly rank entitles him to be a lover'.[30] This is a persuasive but not a necessary claim, since it is not textually motivated and the *Roman de la rose* offers a precedent for a literate narrator as lover—a work to which the *Quair* poet alludes when he prays for 'all the hertis dull' that have no 'curage at the rose to pull'.[31] Whatever its inspiration, this transformation of onlooker into lover is a significant (re)innovation, since it complements the layered framing by refracting through a single, but temporally changing consciousness the various experiences in the text and thus partly blurs the outsider/insider dialectic of Chaucer's dream poems.

Besides this perspective-altering expansion of the narrator's role, the *Quair* poet significantly changes the Chaucerian way of having the narrator appear. In the *Duchess*, the *Parliament*, and *Troilus*, the narrator makes his presence felt immediately and his initial self-characterization helps call the text into being. *The Kingis Quair*, in contrast, opens with a stanza-long *chronographia* and the narrator first appears in the second stanza. Separated formally, setting and narrator are nevertheless linked not only by their juxtaposition, but also by an ambiguous syntax. Since these opening lines can be parsed in several ways, I quote here from a transcription of the unpunctuated manuscript text:[32]

> Heigh In the hevynnis figure circulere
> The rody sterres twynklyng as the fyre
> And In Aquary Citherea the clere
> Rynsid hir tressis like the goldin wyre
> That late tofore in fair and fresche atyre
> Through capricorn heved hir hornis bright
> North northward approchit the myd nyght
>
> Quhen as I lay In bed allone waking
> New partit out of slepe a lyte tofore
> Fell me to mynd of many diverse thing
> Off this and that...[33]

At first glance, especially given the verbal echoes, this opening resembles not so much Chaucer as another Chaucerian revision: Lydgate's *Temple of Glas*. Lydgate remains closer to Chaucer than does the *Quair* poet, however, since he too introduces the narrator immediately, mixing his self-presentation with his *chronographia*, whereas the *Quair* poet keeps the two formally distinct, if not necessarily syntactically separate. Cosmos and narrator are thus joined and distinguished in the very same opening, and this double movement recalls an altogether different Chaucerian model: the start of the *Canterbury Tales*. There, after establishing the natural, cyclical 'long[ing]' of 'folk to goon on pilgrimages' (I.12), Chaucer cuts straight to his narrator: 'Bifil that in that seson on a day,/In Southwerk at the Tabard as I lay/Redy to wenden on my pilgrymage/To Caunterbury.../At nyght' (19–23). In both cases, then, the narrator's about-to-be-interrupted repose is placed first in seasonal, then in human time.

What distinguishes the two openings, however, is the at once broader and narrower reach of the movement in *The Kingis Quair*. Chaucer's opening acknowledges the cosmic context, but is firmly set on earth and his narrator emerges as someone involved in a 'social practice'. Fittingly, it is the arrival of other pilgrims that ends his repose, taking the work in a social direction. In contrast, *The Kingis Quair* opens high in the cosmos, whose capacious circles and orderly movement are then set against the bed with its lone inhabitant, newly awake and mentally unfocussed because of a never-explained interruption that takes the work in an intellectual and psychological direction. Unlike the disturbed insomniac of the *Duchess* or the questing narrators of the *Parliament* and the *Canterbury Tales* (or even of *Troilus*), this narrator simply 'can...noght say quharfore' he has awakened and found his mind wandering.[34] Offering neither crisis nor quest, the work opens without narrative urgency, but rather with a kind of unhurried description found throughout the work. The Boethian book that the narrator happens to pick up is thus implicitly presented as a lucky find, a fortunate omen that unexpectedly keeps the narrator interested instead of putting him to sleep (not until the eleventh stanza, with its tolling matins bell, does a note of urgency enter the poem, and it does so paradoxically because the narrator has laid the book aside to think in a more orderly way, reflecting on his past). Much as the Host's lottery to choose the first tale-teller 'happily' ratifies the social order, the choice of book here just happens to concern an isolated individual, the cosmos, and the workings of fortune. Cosmos and book contain both each other, then, along with the intermediary narrator whose emergence links them.

The other important 'container' here is of course the bed, which (like the narrator's bed in the *Duchess*) has only a single occupant. Given that this poem (in contrast to the mournful *Duchess*) celebrates virtuous heterosexual love, which paradoxically can only be achieved through both patience and grasping Fortune's wheel, it is fitting that the opening turn of the cosmic wheel can be read as bringing either Venus or the Moon into prominence, thus placing the work under the signs of eros *and* mutability, two of its central concerns, both of which impinge on the narrator and his half-full bed. This ambivalent reading is possible because although 'Citherea' refers to Venus, 'hir hornis bright' evoke the Moon (some editors thus consider 'Citherea' a mistake for 'Cinthia').[35] The bright horns, however, can also be understood as representing a popular aristocratic hairdo,[36] and early readers could plausibly have had both images in mind on reading this passage. In any case, the formally inaugural but chronologically later planetary influence (whether Venus or the Moon) seems to be moving 'north northward':[37] the same direction as the Scottish king is about to travel, if James I is the author.[38] This phrase might allude to the *Parliament* narrator's seeing Venus 'north-north-west'. (PF 117). If so, it strengthens one's impression that *The Kingis Quair* is not only its Scottish author's gift to the absent woman at the poem's heart, but also his homage to 'maister' Chaucer, the poet whose bright shade, brilliantly refracted and reframed, he means to carry home as royal tribute.

'THE NORTHIN WIND HA[S] PURIFYIT THE AIR': REOPENING CLOSURE IN *THE TESTAMENT OF CRESSEID*

Unlike *The Kingis Quair*, which signals its multiple Chaucerian revisions only allusively and is openly framed as Chaucerian only in its sole surviving copy, Robert Henryson's *The Testament of Cresseid* presents itself as an avowedly partial lyrico-narrative response to one work, *Troilus and Criseyde*. Like the *Quair*, however, it too was later reframed, if ambiguously enough that for centuries it was sometimes read as Chaucer's.[39]

No freestanding copy survives before 1593, the date of the first Scottish witness,[40] and there is sufficient uncertainty about both Henryson's dates and the order of his works that its composition can be located only in the mid- to late- fifteenth century.[41] There is no uncertainty, however, as to how the *Testament* positions itself against *Troilus*, although as with the *Quair* critics disagree in their reading of the Chaucerian revisions. Like its 'Anglo-Scots' precursor, the *Testament* brings beginnings and ends together with revisionary aims mostly by elaborating the opening frame, the closing frame being much compressed. The imbalance, seemingly uncharacteristic of a poet as alert to form and decorum as Henryson, is undoubtedly deliberate and presumably explained by the fact that his poem brings beginnings and ends together by inserting itself into a narrative gap in the final book of *Troilus*, thus also audaciously framing itself 'within' and prying open a prior work.

In response to Chaucer's 'tragedye' (Tr 5.1786), Henryson offers what he calls 'ane cairfull dyte', 'this tragedie', 'narratioun', and 'ballet schort', opening the question of the generic dominant.[42] It is also an open question whether the titular designation 'testament' is authorial.[43] Clearly, Henryson is drawing attention to generic difference even as he signals his poem's kinship with Chaucer's through the rhyme royal stanza.[44] In fact, by making his narrator a reader and incorporating into his relatively short poem (616 lines) several smaller genres (Cresseid's dream, the pageant of the gods, Cresseid's complaint in the *Anelida* stanza, her testament, and Troilus's epitaph for her), he also signals his work's affinities with lyrico-narratives like *The Kingis Quair*. If Henryson knew the *Quair* (a plausible conjecture), his bleak depiction of the ends of heterosexual desire can also be read as critiquing its optimistic revision of Chaucer's Boethian tragedies.[45] Chaucer's *Troilus*, too, of course, has a narrator like those in dream poems plus inset texts, but they make up a small part of his much larger work. Consequently, and even more than in the *Quair*, the complexifying effects of the reading narrator and the mixed genres are magnified in Henryson's poem.

These effects are created by the lopsided frame, which takes ninety-one lines to re-open Chaucer's poem, and fourteen to fashion its own close. Fully one sixth of the work, then, is devoted to shaping the reader's response, and to doing so mostly before the story begins. Within the reframing, Henryson's most significant strategic moves are as follows. He allusively links his opening not only to that of *Troilus*, but also to its ending and that of his own work, setting up a complex reflection on both writing and reading. Mediation and its limits are thematized here, but also enacted, as Henryson transforms Chaucer's remaking narrator who 'Ne dar to Love, for [his] unliklynesse' (1.16) into a spatially confined reader who can no longer make love. Besides signalling stylistic, tonal, and formal differences that have more than literary consequences, his opening revises the cosmology of Chaucer's ending, raising questions of perspective, temporality, and justice. Perhaps paradoxically, but certainly to enable a freer exploration of these questions, the opening also insists on the fictionality of a story that Chaucer historicizes, bringing questions of decorum and exemplarity to the fore as well. By the time Henryson's poem turns to Cresseid, then, she has been thoroughly framed, and no less so than in Chaucer's opening where one first meets her by learning that 'that she forsook [Troilus] er she deyde' (1.56). Clearly, the *Quair* poet's lady-love was lucky to be such a distant object of desire that she barely figured in the text.

'Ane doolie sessoun to ane cairfull dyte/Suld correspond and be equiualent:/Richt sa it wes quhen I began to wryte/This tragedie,'[46] the *Testament* begins, quietly asserting a principle of balance, of natural decorum. This understated start contrasts sharply with the opening of *Troilus*, whose emotionally involved narrator, with his ornate style, invoking the muses' aid for his important historical love story, announces a very different principle of psychological decorum: 'to a sorwful tale, a sory chere' (1.14). Reading these openings retrospectively, one can see already the ends of their means, the literary reasons (at least) why the stories treat their heroine so differently.[47] Henryson's opening also enacts his poem's most crucial formal difference from Chaucer's: compression, a change whose effects are intensified by the tight spaces in which everyone moves, including the narrator. Indeed, even the later pageant of the planetary gods, the poem's most expansive moment, depicts them as if descending on Cresseid[48] to deform her body with their cosmic weight, a radical revision of the *Troilus's* most expansive moment, where the hero's 'goost ful blisfully' (5.1808) rises through the spheres to transcend the pains of fleshly love. No wonder the opening stanza forces a pause on 'this tragedie': an allusion to Chaucer's ending that ties the new poem's principles of natural decorum and compression to its concern with fitting closure.

Rather than leaping to the relentlessly prefigured 'tragic' conclusion, however, one should pause on the strategic and ideological view of decorum. So famous are Henryson's opening lines, so counterpointed against Chaucer's, and so syntactically subtle that one hardly notices how the correspondence between work and world is set the wrong way around: the season should fit the genre, the distich declares, which can only happen by chance or by literary design. Given that this declaration is followed by an impossible 'oppositioun'[49] of Venus and the setting sun, it is hard not to read the *chronographia* as a signal of the work's fictive status. Another signal, if it is not a happy accident, is the acrostic 'O FICTIO'[50] formed in the very stanza in which the narrator puts Chaucer's book down and picks up 'ane vther quair' that just happens to recount 'the fatall destenie/Of fair Cresseid, that endit wretchitlie.'[51] Whether or not the acrostic was intended hardly matters, though, since the next stanza, which begins 'Quha wait gif all that Chauceir wrait was trew?',[52] openly raises the question of fiction, truth, and authority. Henryson knew that the poem which Chaucer calls 'a *tragedye* because he thought of it as dealing with history'[53] was deeply concerned with 'trouthe', but his narrator seems to shrug the question off. Not only does he leave it unanswered, he seems untroubled by the question that follows from it: whether the other quair's story was 'authoreist, or fenȝeit of the new/Be sum poeit throw his inuentioun.'[54] Much as the departure from Chaucer draws attention to the paradox of Henryson's dependent independence, so the apparent unconcern with truth and fiction paradoxically makes them a central concern.

The crucial difference with Chaucer, I would argue, is the substitution of moral for historical truth. For Henryson, fictional freedom entails moralizing, as the opening of the *Morall Fabillis* makes clear: 'feinȝeit fabils of ald poetre' might not be 'al grounded vpon truth', but their original purpose, and their justification, is 'to repreif thee of thi misleving,/O man, be figure of ane vther thing'.[55] Here that figure is the Cresseid who, first called 'fair', is called 'lustie' in the stanza raising the question of truth.[56] The new adjective can be a poetic synonym of 'fair' and is not always pejorative, but the next three stanzas ensure that the pejorative sense overwhelms the positive. Abandoned by Diomeid after he 'had all his appetyte,/And mair, fulfillit of this fair ladie',[57] then 'excuse[d]' by the narrator, 'als far furth as [he] may', 'fair Cresseid' is here reduced between the two men to a mere moral figure and crushed, in the central line of the middle stanza, to a textual trace of 'fleschelie lust sa maculait'.[58] In fact, she is literally 'effed' by the narrator, who utters his disgust with some paradoxically delicate 'rum, ram, ruffing' in stanzaic verse:

> O *fair* Creisseid, the *flour* and A per se
> Of Troy and Grece, how was thow *fortunait*
> To change in *filth* all thy *feminitie*,
> And be with *fleschelie* lust sa maculait,
> And go amang the Greikis air and lait,
> Sa giglotlike takand thy *foull* plesance!
> I haue pietie thow suld *fall* sic mischance![59]

This brutal moment looks ahead to, and is quietly echoed in, Troilus's closing alliterative reduction of Cresseid to an exemplary epitaph[60]—whose 'goldin letteris' in 'merbell gray' bleakly mirror those 'writtin…with gold' on a 'fair[e] branche' of 'red iorofflis with thair stalkis grene' brought to the lover at the end of *The Kingis Quair* to confirm his virtuous, heaven-blessed, soon-to-be reciprocated desire.[61] At the same time, however, this brutal effacing of the 'A per se' (foreshadowing her leprous defacing) follows from the revisionary cosmology of the poem's opening—much as the 'newis glad' (or gospel) of love promulgated in the *Quair* follows from its initial sketch of the sky.[62]

Unexpectedly, given the narrator's claim that seasons should mirror genres, 'this tragedie'[63] opens in Aries, the sign of spring and the sun's heat returning northward. Conventionally, Aries should stir or revive love, as it does in the *Quair*,[64] but here it does contrary (if in the event decorous) work, provoking a southern counter-movement of northern air that soon drives the narrator all the way to *Troilus*. 'Schouris of haill' that Aries stirs 'fra the north' bring such cold that he is forced at sunset from his 'oratur' to his 'chalmer'[65]—constrained like Cresseid by space and time on 'this litel spot of erthe' (Tr 5.1815). Unable therefore to pray to Venus to 'mak grene' his 'faidit hart', this quondam lover resorts for 'curage' to 'the fyre', for 'comfort' to 'ane drink', and for 'sport' to 'ane quair…/Written be worthie Chaucer', but his mix of natural and cultural aphrodisiacs leads only to venereal dis-ease:[66] the bleakly ironic return and fall of Cresseid,[67] who in Chaucer's story had failed to make her promised return in Aries (Tr 4.1592, 5.1190). The dominant force in Henryson's spring opening is thus not the (disappearing) sun, but 'the northin wind' whose 'blastis bitterly/Fra Pole Artick come quhisling loud and schill', and this wind does more than drive the narrator from his 'oratur': it 'purifyi[s] the air'.[68] Real enough in a Scottish spring, this cold counter-wind is also utterly literary, recalling the north's association with judgment: in *Piers Plowman*, for example, where during the Harrowing of Hell 'Rightwisnesse' comes 'Out of the nyppe of the north'.[69] Clearly, Henryson's poem can be seen here as poising itself to strike a hard, northern blow against Cresseid, indeed to strike her down. No wonder the narrator shrinks not only from the wind, but also from his own text, all but disappearing after he 'effs' Cresseid in claiming to excuse her.

Given the rich complexity, even the apparent contradictoriness, of the *Testament's* opening, it is also no wonder that critics disagree in their readings of the poem's treatment of Cresseid. Whether this was Henryson's aim is unknowable, although given his deliberately dialogic frame and his insistence in the *Morall Fabillis* that 'The nuttis schell thocht it be hard and teuch,/Haldis the kirnell sueit and delectabill',[70] it seems a reasonable inference that his poem *of* judgment is likewise *about* judgment: Henrysonian and Chaucerian at once, perhaps agonistically so.[71] In the spirit of the dialogic works discussed here and of their willingness to reopen closure, it might be fitting to conclude by suggesting two contradictory readings of the *Testament's* inaugural frame. A Langlandian reading, inspired by the possible allusion to 'Rightwisnesse' and moving the poem from its Chaucerian orbit into the larger medieval Christian universe, might insist on the poem's (knowing?) limitations, arguing that real (as opposed to fictional) justice belongs to a circle also joined by truth, peace, and mercy. A queered feminist reading, in contrast, might note not only the misogyny of a poem which perversely drops the expected dream vision on a dumped woman, or the boundary-blurring competition amongst men (Troilus, Diomeid, plus the two narrators) for female spoils, but also the potential homoeroticism here: in contrast to the *Quair* poet's royal (heterosexual) tribute, Henryson's vision of Cresseid's demise sticks it to Chaucer in the end.

NOTES

1. Seth Lerer, *Chaucer and his Readers: Imagining the Author in Late-Medieval England* (Princeton, NJ: Princeton University Press, 1993), 23. David Lawton, 'Dullness and the Fifteenth Century', *English Literacy History* 54(4) (1987), 761–99, argues persuasively against taking the poets at their word here.

2. Thomas Hoccleve, *The Regiment of Princes*, ed. Charles R. Blyth (Kalamazoo, MI: Medieval Institute Publications, 1999), 1973–4.

3. *The Poems of William Dunbar*, ed. Priscilla Bawcutt, 2 vols. (Glasgow: Association for Scottish Literary Studies, 1998), no. 59, ll. 257–58, 259; emphasis added. On 'enlumynyng' poets, see Lois A. Ebin, *Illuminator, Makar, Vates: Visions of Poetry in the Fifteenth Century* (Lincoln, NE: University of Nebraska Press, 1988), 19–48, 74–90. Gavin Douglas is the first Scottish poet to call his tongue Scots, distinguishing it from 'sudron' (*Eneados*, Prologue to Book 1, 105–24).

4. But see Martin J. Duffell and Dominique Billy, 'From Decasyllable to Pentameter: Gower's Contribution to English Metrics', *Chaucer Review* 38(4) (2004), 383–400.

5. Alliterative poets are a significant exception. See Ralph Hanna, 'Alliterative Poetry', in *The Cambridge History of Medieval English Literature,* ed. David Wallace (Cambridge: Cambridge University Press, 1999), 488–512; and Felicity Riddy, 'The Alliterative Revival', in

The History of Scottish Literature. Vol. 1: Origins to 1660 (Mediaeval and Renaissance), ed. R. D. S. Jack (Aberdeen: Aberdeen University Press, 1988), 39–52.

6. T. S. Eliot, *Four Quartets* (1944; repr. London: Faber, 1959), 44.

7. Eustache Deschamps, Balade 285 (*'O Socrates plains de philosophie'*).

8. Helpful studies of Chaucerian modes in Scotland include Ebin, *Illuminator*, 49–131; Louise O. Fradenburg, 'The Scottish Chaucer', in *Writing After Chaucer: Essential Readings in Chaucer and the Fifteenth Century*, ed. Daniel J. Pinti (New York: Garland, 1998), 167–76; Carolyn Ives and David Parkinson, 'Scottish Chaucer, Misogynist Chaucer', in *Rewriting Chaucer: Culture, Authority, and the Idea of the Authentic Text, 1400–1602*, eds. Thomas A. Prendergast and Barbara Kline (Columbus, OH: Ohio State University Press, 1999), 186–202; Gregory Kratzmann, *Anglo-Scottish Literary Relations 1430–1550* (Cambridge: Cambridge University Press, 1980); plus the relevant essays in Julia Boffey and Janet Cowen, eds., *Chaucer and Fifteenth-Century Poetry* (London: King's College London, Centre for Late Antique and Medieval Studies, 1991); and Ruth Morse and Barry Windeatt, eds., *Chaucer Traditions: Studies in Honour of Derek Brewer* (Cambridge: Cambridge University Press, 1990).

9. Helen Phillips, 'Frames and Narrators in Chaucerian Poetry', in *The Long Fifteenth Century: Essays for Douglas Gray*, eds. Helen Cooper and Sally Mapstone (Oxford: Clarendon Press, 1997), 71–97 (at 81; emphasis in original). See also Judith M. Davidoff, *Beginning Well: Framing Fictions in Late Middle English Poetry* (London: Associated University Presses, 1988).

10. C. D. Jeffery, 'Anglo-Scots Poetry and *The Kingis Quair*', in *Actes du 2e colloque de langue et de littérature écossaises*, eds. Jean-Jacques Blanchot and Claude Graf (Moyen Age et Renaissance; Strasbourg: Université de Strasbourg, 1979), 207–21, at 217.

11. The two scribal notes (fols. 191v, 211r) are quoted by Julia Boffey, '*The Kingis Quair* and the Poems of Bodleian Library MS Arch. Selden. B. 24', in *A Companion to Early Scottish Poetry*, eds. Priscilla Bawcutt and Janet Hadley Williams (Woodbridge: Boydell and Brewer, 2006), 62–74, at 67.

12. See Sally Mapstone, 'Kingship and the *Kingis Quair*', in *The Long Fifteenth Century*, eds. Cooper and Mapstone, 52–69; and Joanna Martin, *Kingship and Love in Scottish Poetry, 1424–1540* (Aldershot: Ashgate, 2008), 19–29.

13. Boffey and A. S. G. Edwards, 'Bodleian MS Arch. Selden. B. 24 and the "Scotticization" of Middle English Verse', in *Rewriting Chaucer*, eds. Prendergast and Kline, 166–85.

14. John Norton-Smith, ed., *James I of Scotland: The Kingis Quair* (Oxford: Clarendon Press, 1971; repr. Leiden: Brill, 1981), 1373.

15. On the sources, see Alessandra Petrina, *The Kingis Quair of James I of Scotland* (Padua: Unipress, 1997), 87–115. Norton-Smith's notes signal Lydgatean echoes. On Gower and Hoccleve as intertexts, see Joanna Martin, 'The Translations of Fortune: James I's *Kingis Quair* and the Rereading of Lancastrian Poetry', in *Langage Cleir Illumynate: Scottish Poetry from Barbour to Drummond, 1375–1630*, ed. Nicola Royan (Amsterdam: Rodopi, 2007), 43–60. On the *dit*, see William Calin, 'The *dit amoureux* and the Makars: An Essay on *The Kingis Quair* and *The Testament of Cresseid*', *Florilegium* 25 (2008), 217–50.

16. On literary Boethian traditions, see Michael D. Cherniss, *Boethian Apocalypse: Studies in Middle English Vision Poetry* (Norman, OK: Pilgrim Books, 1987) and Winthrop Wetherbee, 'The *Consolation* and Medieval Literature', in *The Cambridge Companion to Boethius*, ed. John Marenbon (Cambridge: Cambridge University Press, 2009), 279–302.

17. James I, *Quair*, 1376.

18. The poet might also be drawing attention to an un-Chaucerian numerological structure: see Alice Miskimin, 'Patterns in *The Kingis Quair* and the *Temple of Glass*', *Papers on Language and Literature* 13 (1977), 339–61.

19. See Boffey, 'Chaucerian Prisoners: The Context of *The Kingis Quair*', in *Chaucer and Fifteenth-Century Poetry*, eds. Boffey and Cowen, 84–102; A. Ebin, 'Boethius, Chaucer, and the *Kingis Quair*', *Philological Quarterly* 53 (1974), 321–41; and Walter Scheps, 'Chaucerian Synthesis: The Art of *The Kingis Quair*', *Studies in Scottish Literature* 8 (1971), 143–65.

20. See James I, *Kingis Quair*, 68, 154, 182, 698, 702, 736, 1250, 1349.

21. Ibid., 1269; 736–40, 870.

22. Ibid., 1, 1372, 1058.

23. See ibid., 57, 162, 696, 1135, 1145.

24. Ibid., 51, see 10–11 with 53–4, 89.

25. Ibid., 74–91.

26. Ibid., 52.

27. Ibid., 91. Only the editions by Alexander Lawson (1910), Jean Robert Simon (1967), and Walter W. Skeat (1911) actually print the symbol as in the manuscript.

28. Ibid., 1235, 1242, 1249.

29. Ibid., 1255–60.

30. A. C. Spearing, 'Dreams in *The Kingis Quair* and the *Duke's Book*', in *Charles d'Orléans in England (1415–1440)*, ed. Mary-Jo Arn (Cambridge: D. S. Brewer, 2000), 123–44, at 129.

31. James I, *Kingis Quair*, 1296–8.

32. Alexander Lawson, ed., *The Kingis Quair and the Quare of Jelusy* (London: Adam and Charles Black, 1910), 3.

33. James I, *Kingis Quair*, 1–11.

34. Ibid., 11.

35. Ibid., 3, 6.

36. Norton-Smith, ed., *James I*, 52.

37. James I, *Kingis Quair*, 7.

38. All editions but one make 'North northward approchit the myd nyght' (7) a distinct syntactic unit, separate from 'heved hir hornis bright' (6). The exception is Boffey, ed., *Fifteenth-Century English Dream Visions* (Oxford: Oxford University Press, 2003), whose text reads 'heved hir hornis bright/North northward; approchit the mydnyght,//Quhen as I lay'. I follow her reading here.

39. Kathleen Forni, *The Chaucerian Apocrypha: A Counterfeit Canon* (Gainesville, FL: University Press of Florida, 2001), 106–25.

40. Denton Fox, ed., *The Poems of Robert Henryson* (Oxford: Oxford University Press, 1981), xciv–v. All quotations from Henryson's poems are from this edition.

41. Ibid., xiii–xxii (esp. xx).

42. Ibid., 1, 4, 65, 610.

43. Fox thinks the title 'likely' authorial (Fox, *Poems of Robert Henryson*, civ). On Chaucer's poem's genre, see Lee Patterson, 'Genre and Source in *Troilus and Criseyde*', in *Acts of Recognition: Essays on Medieval Culture* (Notre Dame, IN: University of Notre Dame Press, 2010), 198–214.

44. On Henryson's innovative use of this stanza, see David Parkinson, ed., *The Complete Works*, (Kalamazoo, MI: Medieval Institute Publications, 2010), 23.

45. The Chaucerian intertext's dominance has been such that critics rarely read the *Testament* and the *Quair* together.

46. Henryson, *The Testament of Cresseid*, 1–2.
47. The most searching discussion of her fate is Gayle Margherita, 'Criseyde's Remains: Romance and the Question of Justice', *Exemplaria* 12(2) (2000), 257–92.
48. Jill Mann, 'The Planetary Gods in Chaucer and Henryson', in *Chaucer Traditions*, eds. Morse and Windeatt, 91–106, at 96.
49. Henryson, *Testament*, 13.
50. Ibid., 57–63.
51. Ibid., 61–3. William Stephenson, 'The Acrostic "Fictio" in Robert Henryson's *The Testament of Cresseid* (ll. 58–63)', *Chaucer Review* 29, no.2 (1994), 163–5. On the other 'source', see most recently Robert L. Kindrick, 'Henryson's "Uther Quair" Again: A Possible Candidate and the Nature of Tradition', *Chaucer Review* 33(2) (1998), 190–220.
52. Henryson, *Testament*, 64.
53. Patterson, 'Genre and Source in *Troilus and Criseyde*', 208–10 (quotation at 208).
54. Henryson, *Testament*, 66–7. John MacQueen, *Robert Henryson: A Study of the Major Narrative Poems* (Oxford: Clarendon Press, 1967), 55, notes that 'invention' is here first used in its modern sense and in 'a literary manifesto'. See also A. C. Spearing, *Textual Subjectivity: The Encoding of Subjectivity in Medieval Narratives and Lyrics* (Oxford: Oxford University Press, 2005), 22–3.
55. Henryson, *Testament*, 1–2, 6–7.
56. Ibid., 42, 63; 69.
57. Ibid., 71–2. Note how that strategically placed iambic foot 'and mair' bears reprovingly down on Cresseid.
58. Ibid., 87, 78, 81.
59. Ibid., 78–84.
60. Ibid., 607–9.
61. James I, *Kingis Quair*, 606, 604; 1241–2.
62. Ibid., 1248.
63. Henryson, *Testament*, 4.
64. James I, *Kingis Quair*, 134–43.
65. Henryson, *Testament*, 6, 8, 28.
66. Ibid., 24, 29–42.
67. Blasphemy is of course the named cause of Cresseid's divine punishment: ibid., 274–94.
68. Ibid., 14, 17, 19–20, 17.
69. *Piers Plowman*, B 18.163–4; C 20.167–8.
70. Henryson, *Morall Fabillis*, 15–16.
71. Nickolas A. Haydock, *Situational Poetics in Robert Henryson's* Testament of Cresseid (Amherst: Cambria Press, 2011) came to my attention after this chapter was written, but its account of how 'Henryson's text emerges from Chaucer's, but fouls its own nest' (244) complements the reading offered here.

BIBLIOGRAPHY

Boffey, Julia, 'Chaucerian Prisoners: The Context of *The Kingis Quair*', in *Chaucer and Fifteenth-Century Poetry*, eds. Julia Boffey and Janet Cowen. (London: King's College London, Centre for Late Antique and Medieval Studies, 1991), 84–102.
Boffey, Julia and A. S. G. Edwards. 'Bodleian MS Arch. Selden. B. 24 and the "Scotticization" of Middle English Verse', in *Rewriting Chaucer: Culture, Authority, and the Idea of the*

Authentic Text, 1400–1602, eds. Thomas A. Prendergast and Barbara Kline (Columbus, OH: Ohio State University Press, 1999), 166–85.

Cooper, Helen and Sally Mapstone, eds., *The Long Fifteenth Century: Essays for Douglas Gray* (Oxford: Clarendon Press, 1997).

Ebin, Lois A., *Illuminator, Makar, Vates: Visions of Poetry in the Fifteenth Century* (Lincoln, NE: University of Nebraska Press, 1988).

Ives, Carolyn and David Parkinson, 'Scottish Chaucer, Misogynist Chaucer', in *Rewriting Chaucer: Culture, Authority, and the Idea of the Authentic Text, 1400–1602,* eds. Thomas A. Prendergast and Barbara Kline (Columbus, OH: Ohio State University Press, 1999), 186–202.

Mapstone, Sally, 'Kingship and the *Kingis Quair*', in *The Long Fifteenth Century: Essays for Douglas Gray*, ed. Helen Cooper and Sally Mapstone (Oxford: Clarendon Press, 1997), 52–69.

Margherita, Gayle, 'Criseyde's Remains: Romance and the Question of Justice', *Exemplaria* 12(2) (2000), 257–92.

Martin, Joanna, 'The Translations of Fortune: James I's *Kingis Quair* and the Rereading of Lancastrian Poetry', in *Langage Cleir Illumynate: Scottish Poetry from Barbour to Drummond, 1375–1630*, ed. Nicola Royan (Amsterdam: Rodopi, 2007), 43–60.

Mooney, Linne R. and Mary-Jo Arn, eds., *The Kingis Quair and Other Prison Poems* (Kalamazoo, MI: Medieval Institute Publications, 2005).

Phillips, Helen, 'Frames and Narrators in Chaucerian Poetry', in *The Long Fifteenth Century: Essays for Douglas Gray* ed. Helen Cooper and Sally Mapstone (Oxford: Clarendon Press, 1997), 71–97.

Index